# PSYCHOLOGY
## Custom Edition for Texas Tech University

Saul Kassin

Taken from
*Psychology*, Fourth Edition
by Saul Kassin

Cover Art: *Untitled 12*, by Jan Lhormer.

Taken from:

*Psychology*, Fourth Edition
by Saul Kassin
Copyright © 2004 by Prentice-Hall, Inc.
A Pearson Education Company
Upper Saddle River, New Jersey 07458

10  9  8  7  6  5  4  3  2  1

ISBN 0-536-74984-1

BA 998239

BK

Please visit our web site at *www.pearsoncustom.com*

PEARSON CUSTOM PUBLISHING
75 Arlington Street, Suite 300, Boston, MA 02116
A Pearson Education Company

# Experimetrix

**Psychology Research Participation**

Momentum™ Experiment Scheduling System
Web based experiment scheduling and tracking.

Whether or not you choose to participate in research for part of your grade in this class, you will need to set up an account on a web-based system called Experimetrix. Even once you have created an account on Experimetrix, you are still free to choose the paper option or the participation option. Included on the following pages are detailed instructions about how to access and use the system. Below are some specific things you need to know about Experimetrix:

1. You must register in Experimetrix to sign-up for experiments and receive credit for your participation in the research.

2. You must log on to Experimetrix **within 72 hours** of registering on Experimetrix or your registration information will be lost and you will need to register again.

3. There is a computer in the Copy Room, Rm. 108 in the Psychology Building, that is dedicated to Experimetrix. Feel free to use this computer to sign-up for experiments and to check your experiment schedule. **This computer MAY NOT be used for any other purpose.** The Copy Room will be open 8:00 - 5:00, Monday through Friday, while classes are in session.

4. All the information you need about how to use Experimetrix should be in the following pages. If you have any additional questions, please ask your instructor.

If you do choose to participate in research, here are some additional points for you to know:

1. Do not expect to receive credit for participating in an experiment immediately following that experiment. Allow one week after your participation for your credit to appear in the system.

2. The last day to participate in an experiment is the last scheduled day of classes for the semester.

# STUDENT START PAGE

## Getting Started

1. Go to the TTU Experimetrix Sign-Up Home (http//:www.experimetrix.com/ttu) and select **"new user"**

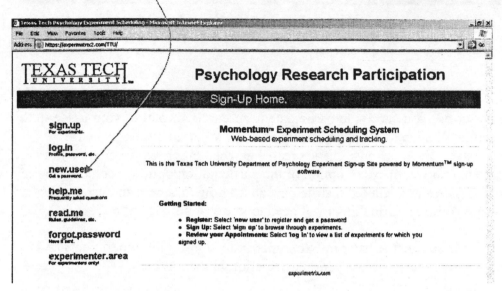

2. Fill in the appropriate information. **Use your most frequently used E-Mail Address.** When finished select **"Register"**.

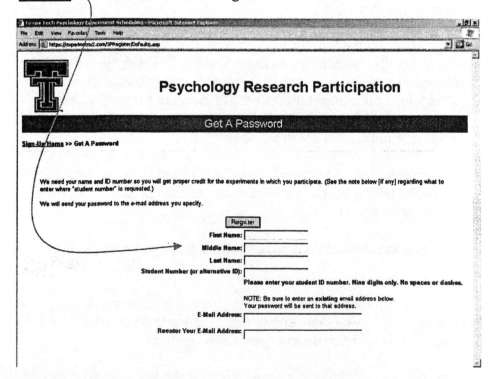

Your logon and password will be sent to your E-mail Address. **You must logon within 3 days or your information will be dropped from the system.**

## Selecting Course Credit

Before you can sign up for an experiment you must specify what section your credits go to. To do this,

1. Go to the TTU Experimetrix Sign-Up Home (http//:www.experimetrix.com/ttu) and select "**login**"

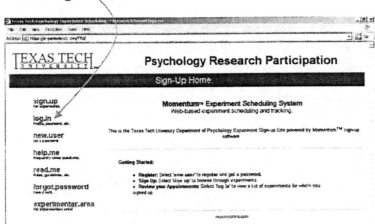

2. Put your **logon** and **password** in the appropriate boxes and select "**Logon**" To verify that you have logged in to the system, **PLEASE PRINT OUT A COPY OF THE SCREEN THAT APPEARS NEXT** (shown below) **AND GIVE IT TO YOUR INSTRUCTOR BY THE DATE SPECIFIED ON YOUR SYLLABUS.** (To print, select "**File**", then "**Print**" from the menu at the top of the screen.)

3. Select "**Edit Your Course Selection**"

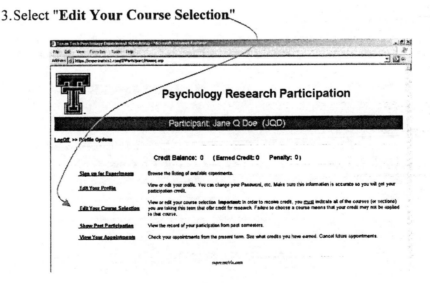

4. Place a **check** in the box next to the section you are in and select "**Apply Changes**"

## Signing up for Experiments

Note: Before you can sign up for an experiment, you must specify what section your credits go to. Follow the steps on the previous page to do so.

### *If you have just finished editing your course selection:*

1. Select "**Profile Options**" at the top of the page.

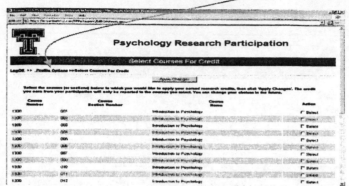

2. Then select **"Sign up for Experiments"**

3. Select "**View Schedule**" of the experiment you want to sign-up for.

4. Select "**Sign-Up**" by the time you want to sign up for.

5. Re-enter your **logon** and **password** in the appropriate boxes and select "**Sign-Up**". You are now signed up for that experiment. In order to sign up for more than one experiment you must go back to the **"Experiment List"**

6. Then, repeat steps 3 through 5.

### *If you have already selected your course and are logging in to a new session:*

1. Go to the **Sign Up Home** at  http://www.experimetrix.com/ttu  and select "**sign-up**"

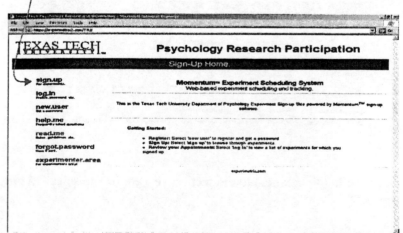

2. Put your **logon** and **password** in the appropriate boxes and select "**Logon**"

3. Now, follow steps 3 through 5 in the above description.

### Canceling Appointments

1. Unless otherwise noted in the contact information, appointments can be canceled up until 2 hours before the experiment.

2. Go to http://www.experimetrix.com/ttu and select "**login**"

3. Put your **logon** and **password** in the appropriate boxes and select "**Logon**"

4. Select "**Cancel**" on the line of the time you want to cancel.

5. You will be prompted about whether you want to cancel your time. Select "**ok**" if you want to cancel your time.

### How to View your Schedule and Credits

1. Go to the Sign-up Home at http://www.experimetrix.com/ttu

2. Select "**login**"

4. **Logon** and **password** in the appropriate boxes and select "**Logon**". Your schedule as well as the credits you have earned is at the bottom of the page.

# Specializations: Psychology at TTU

 **Human Factors**[1]

**What is human factors?** According to the Human Factors & Ergonomics Society, human factors is concerned with the application of what we know about people, their abilities, characteristics, and limitations, to the design of equipment they use, environments in which they function, and jobs they perform. Other terms that have been used to refer to human factors are ergonomics, applied experimental psychology, human factors engineering, and engineering psychology. The primary objective of human factors is to design a system so that people can use it safely and effectively. To achieve this aim, it is important to understand the strengths and weaknesses of people. Surely, it is easier to design equipment to accommodate the skills of a human being than it is to redesign the human being! It is best to incorporate the principles of human factors into the design before a system is constructed because it is costly to redesign a system after it has been built.

*Human factors is a multidisciplinary science.* Most design problems cannot be solved with mere common sense. Human factors specialists draw on various disciplines to develop solutions to design problems. These include specialties within psychology such as cognition, perception, and social psychology; and specialties outside of psychology such as computer science, engineering and mathematics.

*Human factors is a profession.* The Human Factors and Ergonomics Society is a nonprofit organization of human factors professionals (www.hfes.org). It has about 5000 members, sponsors an annual conference, and publishes research in the journal Human Factors. Human factors professionals are practitioners who help industry and government solve real-world problems, and educators who train students in human factors. Individuals can become "board-certified" by passing an examination. The certificate they receive provides evidence of their expertise in human factors. Similarly, programs can become accredited by submitting their curriculum to a committee for review. Accreditation is awarded when the curriculum meets the recommended standards for training.

**When did the field of human factors originate?** Many sources cite the 1940s as the origin of human factors. World War II has been credited largely for the development of human factors because psychological research was needed to solve applied problems. These included issues pertaining to personnel selection, use of equipment by soldiers, and training and operations.  Today, the field of human factors  is much broader  and addresses issues pertaining to medical devices, aerospace, manufacturing, cognitive engineering, computers, education, automation, consumer products, communications, environmental design, forensics, safety, training, agricultural equipment, and virtual environments.

**What is an example of human factors?** Consider a hypothetical situation in which the Department of Transportation wants to reduce the number of rear-end collisions, and you are hired to help. How would you tackle this problem? You might think about possible causes of rear-end collisions. You suspect that they occur when drivers fail to notice that the car in front of them has slowed down. To notice that the car has slowed down, drivers must detect the brake lights. You realize that this requires visual perception and you start reading about how drivers use their eyes while they drive and about the limits of vision. Drivers notice events that are located close to where they are looking; if a warning light occurred there, they would notice it. Where do drivers look most often? Although drivers scan traffic scenes they often look straight ahead, and they look through the windshields of the car in front of them so that they can see events farther ahead. You now realize that you can help the Department of Transportation. You recommend that another brake light should be placed in the rear windshield of all cars. The brake light will be located in the driver's line of vision and will be noticed better than the traditional brake lights. In fact, the center, high-mounted brake light has been mandated in cars since the 1980s. The discipline of human factors was instrumental in this design. By applying their knowledge about the limits and capabilities of the human performer, scientists and engineers improved the design of automobiles and reduced the incidence of rear-end collisions.

**Where do human factors professionals work?** Job opportunities for human factors specialists are diverse. They work in private industry, consulting organizations, government agencies, military research centers, and academic institutions.

**What do human factors professionals do?** Human factors specialists often work on a team with other professionals such as engineers, economists, and safety experts. As part of their duties they may conduct oral presentations, prepare written reports, apply human factors principles, analyze tasks, interview users, specify user requirements, design field or laboratory data collection procedures, perform statistical analyses, interpret results, and review and summarize literature.

**Are there many jobs in human factors?** Job opportunities in human factors have been plentiful and lucrative. As in all fields, opportunities are impacted by the economy. However, in the past decade, all of the graduates of Texas Tech University's doctoral program have secured employment. Recent graduates have reported starting annual salaries between 60K and 75K. Arguably, human factors is the most marketable and lucrative discipline within experimental psychology.

**Examples of employment secured by graduates of Texas Tech University:** At State Farm Insurance, human factors specialists have been hired to evaluate websites and other products to determine whether insurance agents can use them with ease and satisfaction. They also assess office equipment and workstations to ensure safety and comfort. Human factors specialists have been hired at NASA/Johnson Space Center to assist with the International Space Station. They identify potential problems that astronauts may encounter while performing various tasks. They also conduct research to improve habitability for astronauts who must live and work in small spaces for long periods of time. Other employers include Lucent Technologies, Federal Aviation Administration, General Electric, Hewlett-Packard, IBM, Lear Corporation, NIOSH, NOVA Research Co., Oakhill Technology, Roche Diagnostics, SBC Technology, US Army, and US Air Force.

**How do I become a human factors professional?** Students typically complete human factors training in departments of psychology or engineering. Human factors specialists must have solid training in research methods and design, statistics, knowledge of human behavior, and knowledge of human factors principles, methods, and literature. A variety of skills also is valuable such as oral and written communication skills, computer programming, and mathematics. There also are many opportunities for internships through which students get hands-on experience during graduate school.

**How much education is required?** Currently, there are job opportunities for individuals with the B.A., M.A., and Ph.D. The Psychology Department at Texas Tech University (www.psychology.ttu.edu) offers these degrees, including a five-year combined BA/MA degree in Experimental Psychology with a Specialization in Human Factors. The Human Factors Program at Texas Tech University is fully accredited by the Human Factors and Ergonomics Society.

**Why would I want to become a human factors professional?** Working in the field of human factors is exciting and rewarding. Human factors professionals help people and society by designing equipment, tasks, tools, environments, and systems that result in safer, more effective, and more satisfying use. They apply what they know about theories and basic facts of human behavior to solve real-world problems. They work with other professionals as a team toward a common goal. Work activities often permit a great deal of independence and involve a variety of tasks and skills (it is not boring!).

### Additional Readings

Proctor, R. W., & van Zandt, T. (1994). *Human Factors in Simple and Complex Systems*. Boston: Allyn and Bacon.

Sanders. M. S., & McCormick, E. J. (1993). *Human Factors in Engineering and Design* (7th Edition). New York: McGraw-Hill.

Wickens, C. D., Gordon, S. E., & Liu, Y. (1998) *An Introduction to Human Factors Engineering*. New York: Addison-Wesley.

Wickens, C. D., & Hollands, J. G. (2000). *Engineering Psychology and Human Performance* (3rd Edition). New Jersey: Prentice-Hall.

 **Applied Cognitive Psychology[2]**

**What is Applied Cognitive Psychology?** Applied cognitive psychology deals with applications of basic research on memory, thinking, problem solving, and language to real world situations and problems. There is some overlap between this area of psychology and Human Factors psychology. Applied cognitive psychology uses methods and theories from experimental psychology in an attempt to gain a scientific understanding of cognitive phenomena that occur in the real world of human experience and activity, and to solve the practical problems that arise in these everyday settings.

**How Does One Become an Applied Cognitive Psychologist?** Students in this discipline are trained in research design and statistical methods, and engage in laboratory research as well as research in real-world settings. Hands-on research experience is an essential part of training. Students are encouraged to apply their knowledge of cognitive psychology to areas including instructional technology, human-factors problems, and health-related applications. Combining coursework in psychology and other areas, along with research that originates in psychology and related departments, creates many possibilities for students to design credible and innovative courses of study leading to a Ph.D.

**Where do Applied Cognitive Psychologists Work?** Graduates from applied cognitive programs are employed in academia, where they teach and do research, and in industry, where they work in areas of research and development.

 # Personality / Social Psychology[3]

**What Is a Personality/Social Psychologist?:** A boy, barely a teenager, sprays his schoolyard with bullets. A black woman and white man become lifelong friends despite living in a town filled with racial conflict and strife. A group of top-level executives—the best and the brightest—blunder into an avoidable decision that bankrupts their company, all because they fail to share crucial information with one another.

What causes people to become murderously violent? Why do some people maintain their racial prejudices throughout their lives whereas others replace their hatreds with tolerance and respect? When do people work best as a group and when are they better off alone? If you find questions such as these intriguing, you should consider a career in personality and/or social psychology.

**What Is Personality/Social Psychology?** How do people come to be who they are? How do people think about, influence, and relate to one another? These are the broad questions that personality and social psychologists strive to answer. By exploring forces within the person (such as traits, attitudes, and goals) as well as forces within the situation (such as social norms and incentives), personality and social psychologists seek to unravel the mysteries of individual and social life in areas as wide-ranging as prejudice, romantic attraction, persuasion, friendship, helping, aggression, conformity, and group interaction. Although personality psychology has traditionally focused on aspects of the individual, and social psychology on aspects of the situation, the two perspectives are tightly interwoven in psychological explanations of human behavior.

**The Science of Personality/Social Psychology:** At some level, we are all personality and social psychologists, observing our social worlds and trying to understand why people behave, think, and feel as they do. In the aftermath of schoolyard shootings we can hardly help but hypothesize answers to the many questions that come to mind. We do the same when we encounter less dramatic events in our everyday lives: Why is that person smiling at me? Will my professor be a hard grader? How might I persuade my neighbor to keep his cats off my car? But personality and social psychologists go beyond pondering such questions and their possible answers. If the lives of individuals and social groups are full of mystery, then personality and social psychologists are the detectives investigating these mysteries. Systematically observing and describing people's actions, measuring or manipulating aspects of social situations, these sleuths use the methods of science to reveal the answers to the kinds of puzzling questions we each encounter every day.

**Basic and Applied Research:** Scientists in all fields distinguish between basic and applied research. Basic research in personality and social psychology tends to focus on fundamental questions about people and their thoughts, feelings, and behaviors. Where does an individual's personality come from? How stable is personality, and when and how does it change? What causes us to fall in love, hate our neighbor, or join with others to clean our neighborhoods. How are the psychologies of being male and female similar, how are they different, and why? How does culture shape who we become and how we interact with one another? Questions such as these aim at the very heart of human nature.

Applied research in personality and social psychology focuses on more narrow arenas of human life, such as health, business, and law. By employing the lessons learned from basic research, and by searching for insights specific to particular domains, applied research often seeks to enhance the quality of our everyday lives. Personality and social psychologists contribute to areas as diverse as health, business, law, the environment, education, and politics. For example, personality and social psychologists have designed, implemented, and evaluated programs to help employers hire and train better workers; to make it easier for people with cancer to cope successfully with their challenge; to increase the likelihood that people will reduce pollution by relying on public transportation; to reduce prejudices and intergroup conflict in the classroom and in international negotiations; to make computers and other technologies more user-friendly; and to make many other societal contributions as well.

Of course, the distinction between basic and applied research is often a fuzzy one. One can certainly perform basic research in applied domains, and the findings from each type of research enrich the other. Indeed, it would be fair to say that most personality and social psychologists have both basic and applied interests.

**Where Do Personality and Social Psychologists Work?** Because personality and social psychologists combine an understanding of human behavior with training in sophisticated research methods, they have many opportunities for employment. Many teach and do research in universities and colleges, housed mostly in departments of psychology but also in departments of business, education, political science, justice studies, law, health sciences, and medicine. The research of such individuals may be based in the laboratory, in the field, in the clinic, or in historical archives. Many personality and social psychologists are employed in the private sector as consultants, researchers, marketing directors, managers, political strategists, technology designers, and so on. Personality and social psychologists also work in government and nonprofit organizations, designing and evaluating policy and programs in education, conflict resolution, environmental protection, and the like.

**Becoming a Personality / Social Psychologist:** Although some personality and social psychologists go to graduate school to earn a terminal masters degree (M.S. or M.A.), most seek a doctoral degree (Ph.D.). For some careers, a master's degree may be sufficient. Generally, however, the doctorate is preferred by employers and is usually necessary for employment as a professor at a university or college.

Most Ph.D. programs in personality and social psychology require 4-5 years of training and study. The goal of most programs is similar: To prepare each student to become an independent, professional researcher. As a result, most programs teach the conceptual foundations and knowledge of the discipline, develop the student's ability to think theoretically, and train the student in research methodology, data analysis, and research writing and presentation. Programs differ, however, in the areas of research they focus on and in their emphasis on training students for academic versus nonacademic careers. Because graduate training revolves around research, it is important that students pay particular attention to the specific faculty members with whom they are likely to work. Prospective students should give full consideration not only to the perspectives and research activities of a potential graduate program on the whole, but also to those of their probable faculty mentors.

Admission to graduate programs in personality and social psychology is very competitive; there are far more applicants than openings (most programs enroll just a few new students each year). As a result, entry qualifications are rigorous: Most admitted students have earned high undergraduate grades and a bachelor's degree from an accredited university or college; many have been undergraduate psychology majors, although this isn't a requirement in many programs; most have had experience doing psychology research; most have demonstrated strong quantitative, verbal, and analytical abilities, as revealed in their scores on the Graduate Record Exam (GRE); and most have been evaluated by their undergraduate teachers in confidential letters of recommendation as being smart, talented, creative, hard-working, and conscientious. Of course, different programs have different standards and criteria for admission, and the prospective student should explore those articulated by programs of interest.

Most personality and social psychology programs provide financial assistance to their graduate students in the form of teaching or research assistantships, and many schools waive tuition and fees at the graduate level. This, too, varies from school to school.

**Examples of employment secured by graduates of Texas Tech University:** Recent graduates of TTU's doctoral program in social psychology are now working as postdoctoral research fellows, Senior Public Administration Analysts, professors, and instructors in Departments of Psychiatry and psychology at colleges and universities across the United States; as Research Psychologists with the U.S. Army; and as the Director of Outcomes Evaluation for a large health care consortium.

**For More Information:** Students seeking admission into graduate school have several useful sources of information available to them. The American Psychological Association publishes annually a list of graduate programs in Graduate Study in Psychology and Associated Fields. The Society of Personality and Social Psychology has a webpage (www.spsp.org) with information on how to become a student affiliate and links to a list of graduate programs with webpages. Each graduate program will mail program descriptions by request. By reading journals such as Journal of Personality and Social Psychology,

Personality and Social Psychology Bulletin, and Personality and Social Psychology Review, students can expose themselves to cutting-edge research in personality and social psychology. S imilar i nformation c an b e d iscovered by s earching r elevant c omputerized databases (e.g., PsycINFO). Finally, students can gain much useful information by consulting with the personality and social psychologists in the psychology departments at their home or nearby colleges and universities.

The fields of personality and social psychology are fascinating and increasingly important. We invite you to check them out!

 ## Counseling Psychology[*]

**What is Counseling Psychology?** Counseling psychology as a psychological specialty facilitates personal and interpersonal functioning across the life span with a focus on emotional, social, vocational, educational, health-related, developmental, and organizational concerns. Through the integration of theory, research, and practice, and with a sensitivity to multicultural issues, this specialty encompasses a broad range of practices that help people improve their well-being, alleviate distress and maladjustment, resolve crises, and increase their ability to live more highly functioning lives. Counseling psychology is unique in its attention both to normal developmental issues and to problems associated with physical, emotional, and mental disorders. Populations served by Counseling Psychologists include persons of all ages and cultural backgrounds. Examples of those populations would include late adolescents or adults with career/educational concerns and children or adults facing severe personal difficulties. Counseling Psychologists also consult with organizations seeking to enhance their effectiveness or the well-being of their members. Counseling Psychologists adhere to the standards and ethics established by the American Psychological Association.

**What Do Counseling Psychologists Do?** Counseling Psychologists participate in a range of activities including teaching, research, psychotherapeutic and counseling practice, career development, assessment, supervision, and consultation. They employ a variety of methods closely tied to theory and research to help individuals, groups, and organizations function optimally as well as to remediate dysfunction. Interventions may be either brief or long-term; they are often problem-specific and goal-directed. These activities are guided by a philosophy that values individual differences and diversity and a focus on prevention, development, and a djustment a cross t he l ife s pan w hich i ncludes v ocational concerns.

**Where Do Counseling Psychologist Work?** Counseling Psychologists are employed in a v ariety of settings depending on the services they provide and the client populations they serve. Some are employed in institutions of higher learning--including counseling centers--as teachers, supervisors, researchers, and service providers. Others are employed i n i ndependent p ractice p roviding c ounseling, p sychotherapy, a ssessment, a nd consultation services to individuals, families, groups, and organizations. Additional settings in which counseling psychologists practice include community mental health centers, Veterans Administration Medical Centers and other medical facilities, family services centers, health maintenance organizations, rehabilitation agencies, business and industrial organizations, and consulting firms.

**How Does One Become a Counseling Psychologist?** Most counseling psychology training programs are accredited by the American Psychological Association. The list of accredited programs appears each year in the journal, the American Psychologist. Both accredited and non-accredited training programs are listed in the book, Graduate Study in Psychology. The APA accords accreditation to doctoral programs in counseling psychology that meet certain criteria with respect to faculty, curriculum, facilities, and other considerations. Counseling psychology programs usually are housed in departments of psychology or educational psychology or in colleges of education. Counseling psychology doctoral programs usually require at least four to five years of graduate study, involving coursework and integrated training experiences in a variety of topical areas and professional skills. These include (a) instruction in the core areas of psychology (biological, cognitive/affective, and social bases of behavior; individual differences; history and systems of psychology); specialized instruction in theories of counseling and personality, vocational psychology, human life span development, psychological assessment and evaluation, psychopathology, measurement and statistics, research design, professional ethics, supervision, and consultation; (c) supervised practica focused o n t he d evelopment o f c ounseling, p sychotherapy, a ssessment, a nd c onsultation skills; (d) the equivalent of a one year full-time predoctoral internship in professional psychology; and (e) completion of an original psychologically-based dissertation. Entrance to doctoral programs in counseling psychology is competitive and selective; there are far more applicants to the programs than can be admitted. Factors important in the selection process include a bachelor's (and possibly master's) degree earned from an accredited college or university, consistently high college grades, and coursework and/or volunteer or work experience that match the orientation of the particular doctoral program to which one is applying. Scores on standardized scholastic aptitude tests such as the Graduate Record Exam (GRE) usually are considered as well.

**Would You Like to Learn More?** For more information on the training and professional activities of Counseling Psychologists, the following sources can be consulted: The Counseling Psychologist (the official journal of Division 17 [Counseling Psychology] of the American Psychological Association), Journal of Counseling Psychology, (published by the American Psychological Association), the American Psychological Association (Located in Washington, D.C.), and various textbooks on counseling psychology.

 **Clinical Psychology**[5]

**What is clinical psychology?** The field of Clinical Psychology integrates science, theory, and practice to understand, predict, and alleviate maladjustment, disability, and discomfort as well as to promote human adaptation, adjustment, and personal development. Clinical Psychology focuses on the intellectual, emotional, biological, psychological, social, and behavioral aspects of human functioning across the life span, in varying cultures, and at all socioeconomic levels.

**What do clinical psychologists do?** The Clinical Psychologist is educated and trained to generate and integrate scientific and professional knowledge and skills so as to further psychological science, the professional practice of psychology, and human welfare. Clinical Psychologists are involved in research, teaching and supervision, program development and evaluation, consultation, public policy, professional practice, and other activities that promote psychological health in individuals, families, groups, and organizations. Their work can range from prevention and early intervention of minor problems of adjustment to dealing with the adjustment and maladjustment of individuals whose disturbance requires them to be institutionalized.

Practitioners of Clinical Psychology work directly with individuals at all developmental levels (infants to older adults), as well as groups (families, patients of similar psychopathology, and organizations), using a wide range of assessment and intervention methods to promote mental health and to alleviate discomfort and maladjustment.

Researchers study the theory and practice of Clinical Psychology, and through their publications, document the empirical base of Clinical Psychology. Consultants, Teachers, and Clinical Supervisors share the Clinical Psychology knowledge base with students, other professionals, and non-professionals. Clinical Psychologists also engage in program development, evaluate Clinical Psychology service delivery systems, and analyze, develop, and implement public policy on all areas relevant to the field of Clinical Psychology. Many Clinical Psychologists combine these activities.

Assessment in Clinical Psychology involves determining the nature, causes, and potential effects of personal distress; of personal, social, and work dysfunctions; and the psychological factors associated with physical, behavioral, emotional, nervous, and mental disorders. Examples of assessment procedures are interviews, behavioral assessments, and the administration and interpretation of tests of intellectual abilities, aptitudes, personal characteristics, and other aspects of human experience and behavior relative to disturbance.

Interventions in Clinical Psychology are directed at preventing, treating, and correcting emotional conflicts, personality disturbances, psychopathology, and the skill deficits underlying human distress or dysfunction. Examples of intervention techniques include psychotherapy, psychoanalysis, behavior therapy, marital and family therapy, group therapy, biofeedback, cognitive retraining and rehabilitation, social learning approaches, and environmental consultation and design. The goal of intervention is to promote satisfaction, adaptation, social order, and health.

**Where do clinical psychologists work?** Clinical Psychologists work throughout the United States in a variety of settings including individual practice, mental health service units, managed healthcare organizations, hospitals, schools, universities, industries, legal systems, medical systems, counseling centers, governmental agencies, and military services.

**Qualifications to practice clinical psychology:** An earned doctorate from a Clinical Psychology program represents the basic entry level for the provision of Clinical Psychology services. Unique to Clinical Psychology training is the requirement of substantial course work in the areas of personality and psychopathology, resulting in comprehensive understanding of normal and abnormal adjustment and maladjustment across the life span.

The American Psychological Association sets the standards for Clinical Psychology graduate programs and recognizes programs meeting these standards through an accreditation process. All states require a license to practice Clinical Psychology.

**Examples of employment secured by graduates of Texas Tech University[6]:** Recent graduates work in a wide variety of education, agency, and private practice settings in both health and "mental health." Examples include private and public hospitals and outpatient services, public health, VA hospitals, prisons, university health science centers and university psychology departments, private practice, and university counseling centers

[1] Written by Patricia R. DeLucia, Ph.D., Texas Tech University (Final Version 5/28/03)

[2] Written by Roman Taraban, Ph.D., Texas Tech University (Final Version 5/20/03)

[3] Written by Steven Neuberg, Ph.D., Arizona State University and reproduced with permission from the Society for Personality and Social Psychology, Division 8 of the American Psychological Association, with the exception of the section titled, "Examples of employment secured by graduates of Texas Tech University," which was written by Richard McGlynn, Ph.D., and Erin E. Hardin, Ph.D., Texas Tech University.

[4] Reproduced with permission from the Society of Counseling Psychology, Division 17 of the American Psychological Association.

[5] Reproduced with permission from the Society of Clinical Psychology, Division 12 of the American Psychological Association.

[6] Written by Stephanie Harter, Ph.D., Texas Tech University (Final Version 5/21/03)

For more information about these specialties, the types of research being done in each of these specialties at Texas Tech, or general information about psychology at TTU, visit the department of psychology's web page at **http://www.psychology.ttu.edu**

# BRIEF CONTENTS

iii

# CONTENTS

# FEATURE BOXES

## Debunking the Myth

## Psychology and

## How To

## THE PROCESS OF DISCOVERY

Some of my best friends are psychologists. They all have different backgrounds and interests; some teach at colleges and universities, others work for government or private organizations; some do laboratory research, others write books, and still others help people with personal problems. Yet despite the differences, these friends are, to a person, excited about their work, the field, and the contributions being made by this intelligent and useful discipline.

I had three goals in writing this textbook. *First and foremost, I want to get students thinking like psychologists.* No author can invoke critical thinking in students the way a parent spoon feeds a baby. Critical thinking is a frame of mind, an attitude that forms naturally in response to information that is engaging and personally relevant—which leads me to the special features of this book. Determined to get the student reader to think like a psychologist, and to do so without gimmicks, I have created a number of innovative features for this textbook that are described below.

*My second goal is to teach students that psychology is not a mere laundry list of names, dates, and terms, but is a dynamic and evolving process of discovery.* Every psychology textbook presents the discipline as a science. Indeed, many authors devote a whole second chapter to research methods. I have taken a more integrated approach. Because research methods are central to psychology's identity and development, this topic is introduced fully and comprehensively in Chapter 1, along with the field itself. In learning about research methods, from the use of case studies to experiments and meta-analysis, students are shown that science is a process that is slow, cumulative, and dynamic.

*My third goal is to spark in students the hunger, passion, and excitement that psychologists have for their work.* Toward this end, I have tried to write a book that is not only readable, but also warm, personal, interactive, contemporary, relevant, and newsy. I have not ducked the hot and sticky issues. The ethics of animal research, the nature and nurture of homosexuality, and the recovery of repressed childhood memories are just a few of the current controversies that I have confronted head-on by reviewing available research. I have also made it a point to illustrate the principles of psychology with vivid events from the worlds of sports, entertainment, literature, politics, law, and world events. I never, ever, resort to "John and Mary in the dorm" hypotheticals to illustrate a point. The examples I use thus reflect my conviction that students, like the rest of us, have a deep and vested interest in a world that extends past the borders of the college campus.

## ORGANIZATION OF THIS BOOK

Take a peek at the Table of Contents, and you'll see that this textbook contains eighteen independent chapters, from the introduction to psychology and its methods through the various areas of neuroscience, cognitive, developmental, social, and clinical psychology to an integrative capstone chapter on health and well-being.

Like its predecessors, this edition offers a broad, balanced, and mainstream look at psychology today. Thus, I have filled the pages with detailed descriptions of classic studies from psychology's historical warehouse and with new research findings, some hot off the presses, that address current issues. There are four aspects of this book's organizational structure that I want to spotlight for instructors.

## COVERAGE OF RESEARCH METHODS

Many introductory textbooks separate the introduction of psychology from its methods of inquiry, often presented in a parenthetical second chapter. I have taken a more integrated approach that presents psychology's research methods as part and parcel of its history, development, and current identity as a science.

All the material you'd expect to find in a chapter on research methods appears in Chapter 1—including discussions of where psychologists do their research, how they measure psychological variables, and the inferences that we can and cannot draw from descriptive research, correlational studies, and experiments. Noting that the base of scientific knowledge builds slowly, one step at a time, this coverage includes a section on literature reviews and meta-analysis. It also contains a section on ethical dilemmas that confront both the animal and human research communities.

The central focus on research methods is reinforced in each and every chapter, which opens with *What's Your Prediction?*—an activity that carefully describes the procedures of an actual published study and calls on students to predict the results. The actual results are then revealed, followed by a discussion of what they mean. This activity, more than any other I've tried in the classroom, gets students, like psychologists, to think critically about research methods. Look at these chapter opening activities, and you'll see that many involve laboratory or field experiments; others involve correlational studies; three describe self-report surveys, one a neuropsychological case study, and one an archival study that tracked intelligence test scores over time. In some cases, students are asked to imagine being a subject; in others, they are cast into the role of the researcher or an observer.

To further reinforce this type of focus on research methods, I have added a new feature, *What's Your Prediction?* exercises, throughout the text. Within the margin of each and every chapter, students are presented with a brief description of a new, high-interest study. In light of the chapter material they've read, they are asked again to predict the results, which then are revealed.

## A NEW CHAPTER ON NATURE AND NURTURE

The nature–nurture debate is a classic in all areas of psychology and always the subject of intense debate. At one end, the strict biological position states that we share a common evolutionary heritage that makes us all similar—and that we are predisposed by genetics to exhibit differences in the way we think, feel, and behave. At the other end, a strict environmental position says that our fate is shaped by learning, culture, nutrition, family background, peer groups, and critical life events.

Drawing on a current renaissance in evolutionary theory, the discoveries of the Human Genome Project, and recent developments in behavioral genetics, I have created a new chapter entitled "Nature and Nurture." The purpose of this new chapter is to educate psychology students about basic genetics, natural selection, and the emerging field of evolutionary psychology, and to introduce the nature–nurture debates, heritability studies, and recent work on the interaction of biology and environment. This chapter concludes with discussions of the nature and nurture of gender and sexual orientation.

## A Chapter on Social and Cultural Groups

Psychologists have always been fascinated by differences among cultures—and among racial and ethnic groups within cultures. In the wake of September 11, 2001, the twenty-first century has thus far been plagued with unspeakable acts of hatred, conflict, and violence among religious and ethnic groups all over the world. The topic is thus generating a great deal of scientific interest and controversy. Diversity issues are addressed throughout this text. Similarities and differences are noted, for example, in perception, emotion, reasoning, intelligence, child and adult development, social behavior, the structure of personality, and psychopathology.

To bring together this most important new work in the area of human diversity, I have also dedicated an entire chapter to this subject. Chapter 14, entitled "Social and Cultural Groups," examines such topics as individualism, collectivism, and the cultural differences between East and West; acculturation and ethnic identity among immigrants; cognitive and motivational roots of stereotyping, prejudice, and inter-group conflict; and racism in America. As this chapter reveals, "No two people are alike, yet everyone is basically the same."

## A Capstone Chapter on Health and Well-Being

All introductory psychology texts that I've seen come to an end on whatever happens to be the final word of the last substantive chapter. Typically, no effort is made to integrate the material or to provide students with a sense of closure. A feature unique to this text is a closing capstone chapter that brings together all areas of psychology on a hot topic that is dear to everyone: health and well-being. Following an initial discussion of "mind over matter," Chapter 18 presents some of the latest research on the self, the health implications of self-awareness, stress and coping, and the exciting new work in the area of psychoneuroimmunology. As noted in this final chapter, "The mind is a powerful tool. The more we know about how to use it, the better off we'll be."

## SPECIAL FEATURES

### New "Process of Discovery" Interviews

I am particularly excited about a new feature that I have called "The Process of Discovery," or POD. Building on my desire to get students to think like psychologists, the purpose of POD interviews is to give students a first-hand glimpse into eminent psychologists and their stories, *in their own words*, of how they came upon their major contributions. Across chapters, psychology's leaders answer four questions: (1) How did you first become interested in psychology? (2) How did you come up with your important discovery? (3) How has the field you inspired developed over the years? (4) What's your prediction on where the field is heading?

For me, reading the process of discovery stories told by psychologists who have shaped the field was a labor of love. Through it, I learned how Michael Gazzaniga came to test his first split-brain patient, how Robert Sternberg became interested in intelligence, how Hazel Markus came to realize that Western conceptions of the self made no sense in Japan, how a psychoanalyst by the name of Aaron Beck came to formulate cognitive therapy, and how Eleanor Gibson's inspiration for the visual cliff came from a family vacation to the Grand Canyon—and her concern for her young daughter who "danced on the rim." Shortly after Daniel Kahneman described how he became interested in cognitive illusions, he won a Nobel Prize.

Needless to say, I think that this feature will serve as a valuable learning tool, a source of inspiration, and an archival resource for both students and teachers of psychology.

## "WHAT'S YOUR PREDICTION?" STUDIES

To orient students to the material in each chapter—and to get them thinking in operational terms—I open each chapter with a detailed account of an actual study. Some are classics in the field; others are new. Some are laboratory experiments; others are field studies, archival studies, or self-report surveys. In some, students are asked to imagine being a subject in an experiment. In others, they are cast into the role of the researcher or an observer. In all cases, I set the stage with a vivid account of the procedures used. After students have read about the situation and have imagined being part of it, they are asked to predict the results. The actual findings are then revealed, followed by a discussion of what it all means.

I have used this technique in the classroom for many years and have found that it works like a charm. After students become personally committed to a prediction, they sit at the edge of their seats, eager to know what happened. Then when the results are revealed, they think long and hard about the study and its methods—particularly when the results contradict their predictions. Now *that's* critical thinking. This activity is so effective that all chapters now contain additional *What's Your Prediction?* exercises in the margin that feature new, high-interest studies that extend the material presented in the body of the text.

**Feature Boxes**   In every chapter, you will find one or two special, high-interest boxes designed to get students thinking like psychologists. Toward this end, I have written three types of boxes: "Psychology and . . . ," "How To," and "Debunking the Myth."

**"Psychology and . . ."**   These days, some of the most exciting work in all areas of psychology connects basic theories and research, on the one hand, to various real-world applications, on the other. Psychologists are animated by many fertile domains of application. To represent some of these areas, "Psychology and . . ." boxes describe applied research in such areas as health, education, law, sports, and current events. Beginning with a new box entitled *"Psychology and World Events: Psychological Consequences of Terrorism,"* this feature will enable students to see psychology from an enticing other perspective—"out there," in action, and in the public forum.

**"How To"**   As all instructors know, students often ask how psychology relates to their own well-being. "How To" boxes are designed to answer this question by describing some of the ways that students can use psychology to improve aspects of their own lives. Practical advice is thus presented on a whole range of matters—such as how to improve your memory, how to overcome insomnia, and how to avoid social blunders when traveling in foreign cultures.

*"Debunking the Myth"*   These boxes present popular conceptions about people, the mind, and behavior, or conclusions prematurely drawn from early research for which there is no empirical support. It's my hope that "Debunking the Myth" boxes will encourage students to reflect on—and reevaluate—their own intuitive theories, beliefs, and commonsense conceptions on a whole range of psychological matters.

## NEW CONTENT IN THE FOURTH EDITION

From one area to the next, this book is remarkably up to date. I have taken a fresh look at the latest theoretical and research developments within each and every chapter. In doing so, I have tried to strike a balance between "classics" from psychology's historical warehouse and new studies hot off the presses. But my main goal is to describe the state of psychology *today*—and to do so in a way that is responsible. As in any text, the scholarship must be accurate and current. Therefore, the more than two hundred new references rely most heavily on research appearing in high-quality journals. In particular, I'd like to draw your attention to the following topics, which are either new to this edition or have received expanded coverage:

- Psychological consequences of terrorism (Chapter 1)
- Neurogenesis (Chapter 2)
- Influence without awareness (Chapter 4)
- Corporal punishment (Chapter 5)
- Transmission of animal "cultures" by imitation (Chapter 5)
- Change blindness (Chapter 6)
- Creation of false memories (Chapter 6)
- Animal cognition (Chapter 7)
- The Human Genome Project (8)
- Processes of natural selection (Chapter 8)
- Evolutionary roots of aggression and altruism (Chapter 8)
- Sibling effects on child development (Chapter 8)
- Infants as minimathematicians (Chapter 9)
- Early puberty onset trends (Chapter 9)
- Developmental trajectories of self-esteem (Chapter 9)
- How environments multiply the influence of genes on IQ (Chapter 10)
- Stereotype threat effects on performance (Chapter 10)
- The global obesity epidemic (Chapter 11)
- Animal emotions (Chapter 12)
- Affective forecasting (Chapter 12)
- Automatic and unconscious social influences (Chapter 13)
- Attributions as social constructions (Chapter 13)
- Implicit stereotyping (Chapter 14)
- Andreasen's "synthetic model" of mental illness (Chapter 16)
- Trend toward the "manualization" of psychological treatments (Chapter 17)
- How new drugs are brought to market (Chapter 17)
- Gender differences in reactions to stress (Chapter 18)

## STATISTICAL APPENDIX

For those who wish to analyze research results using descriptive and inferential statistics, this appendix leads students, step by step, through methods of describing data, measures of central tendency and variability, the normal distribution, correlations, *t* tests, and the analysis of variance.

## INSTRUCTOR AND STUDENT SUPPLEMENTS TO ACCOMPANY *PSYCHOLOGY, FOURTH EDITION*

The Fourth Edition's supplements package has gone through extensive revision and refinement to provide you and your students with the best teaching and learning materials, both in print and media formats.

### PRINT AND MEDIA SUPPLEMENTS FOR THE INSTRUCTOR

*NEW* Instructor's Resource Binder   This binder includes an exhaustive collection of teaching resources for both new and experienced instructors alike. Organized by chapter, this binder includes the Instructor's Resource Manual, the Test Item File, Prentice Hall's Introductory Psychology Transparencies, 2004, the Instructor's Resource CD-ROM, and the TestGen Computerized Testing Software. All of these supplements are described below.

Instructor's Resource Manual   Created by Alan Swinkles of St. Edward's University, each chapter in the manual includes the following resources, organized in an easy-to-reference Chapter Outline: Introducing the Chapter; Learning Objectives; Lecture Suggestions and Discussion Topics; Classroom Activities, Demonstrations, and Exercises; Out-of-Class Assignments and Projects; Multimedia Resources; Video Resources; Transparencies Masters; and Handouts. Designed to make your lectures more effective and to save you preparation time, this extensive resource gathers together the most effective activities and strategies for teaching your Introductory Psychology course.

Test Item File   Created by John Caruso of University of Massachusetts, Dartmouth, this test bank contains over 4,500 multiple choice, true/false, and short answer essay questions. Each question references the section and page number in the text; provides an easy, moderate, or difficult key for level of difficulty; and lists the question type of factual, conceptual, or applied.

*NEW* Prentice Hall's TestGen   Available on one dual-platform CD-ROM, this test generator program provides instructors "best in class" features in an easy-to-use program. Create tests using the TestGen Wizard and easily select questions with drag-and-drop or point-and-click functionality. Add or modify test questions using the built-in Question Editor and print tests in a variety of formats. The program comes with full technical support and telephone "Request a Test" service.

*NEW* Instructor's Resource CD-ROM   Included with the Instructor's Resource Binder, this valuable, time-saving supplement provides you with an electronic version of a variety of teaching resources all in one place so that you may customize your lecture notes and media presentations. This CD-ROM includes PowerPoint slides customized to the Fourth Edition, electronic versions of the artwork in the text chapters, electronic versions of the Overhead Transparencies, electronic files for the Instructor Resource Manual and the Test Item File as well as clips from Prentice Hall's *Video Classics in Psychology* CD-ROM formatted for in-class presentation.

**PowerPoint Slides for *Psychology, Fourth Edition*** Created by Christopher Robinson of University of Alabama, Birmingham, each chapter's presentations highlight the key points covered in the text. Provided in two versions—one with the Chapter Graphics and one without—to give you flexibility in preparing your lectures. Available on the Instructor's Resource CD-ROM or on Prentice Hall's *Psychology Central* Web site described below.

***NEW* Prentice Hall's Introductory Psychology Transparencies, 2004** Designed to be used in large lecture settings, this set of over 130 full-color transparencies includes illustrations from the text as well as images from a variety of other sources. Available in acetate form, online at *Psychology Central* or on the Instructor's Resource CD-ROM.

***NEW Psychology Central* Web Site at www.prenhall.com/psychology** Password protected for instructor's use only, this site allows you online access to all Prentice Hall's Psychology supplements. You'll find a multitude of resources for teaching introductory Psychology. From this site you can download any of the key supplements available for *Psychology, Fourth Edition* including the following: Instructor's Resource Manual, Test Item File, PowerPoint Slides, Chapter Graphics, and electronic versions of the Introductory Psychology Transparencies, 2004. Contact your Prentice Hall representative for the User ID and Password to access this site.

**Online Course Management with *WebCT, BlackBoard,* or CourseCompass *FREE*** upon adoption of the text, instructors interested in using online course management have their choice of options. Each course comes preloaded with text specific quizzing and testing material and can be fully customized for your course. Contact your Prentice Hall representative or visit www.prenhall.com/demo for more information.

## VIDEO RESOURCES FOR INSTRUCTORS

***NEW* Prentice Hall Lecture Launcher Video for Introductory Psychology** Adopters can receive this new videotape that includes short clips covering all major topics in introductory psychology. The videos have been carefully selected from the *Films for Humanities and Sciences* library and edited to provide brief and compelling video content for enhancing your lectures. Contact your local representative for a full list of video clips on this tape.

***The Brain* Video Series** Qualified adopters can select videos from this series of eight, one-hour programs that blend interviews with world-famous brain scientists and dramatic reenactments of landmark cases in medical history. Programs include The Enlightened Machine, The Two Brains, Vision and Movement, Madness, Rhythms and Drives, States of Mind, Stress and Emotion, and Learning and Memory. Contact your local representative for more details.

**The *Discovering Psychology* Video Series** Qualified adopters can select videos from this series produced in association with the American Psychological Association. The series includes thirteen tapes, each containing two half-hour segments. Contact your local sales representative for a list of videos.

**ABC News Videos for Introductory Psychology, Series III** Qualified adopters can obtain this series consisting of segments from the *ABC Nightly News with Peter Jennings, Nightline, 20/20, Prime Time Live,* and *The Health Show.*

*Films for Humanities and Sciences* Video Library   Qualified adopters can select videos on various topics in psychology from the extensive library of *Films for the Humanities and Sciences*. Contact your local sales representative for a list of videos.

## PRINT AND MEDIA SUPPLEMENTS FOR THE STUDENT

**Study Guide**   Written by Pamela Regan, California State University, Los Angeles, this student study guide helps students master the core concepts presented in each chapter. Each chapter includes learning objectives, a brief chapter Summary, a Preview Outline of the text chapter, and three different practice tests.

**Companion Web Site at www.prenhall.com/kassin**   Authored by Kathy Demitrakis, Alberquerque Technical Vocational Institute and Christopher Robinson, University of Alabama, Birmingham, this online study guide allows students to review each chapter's material, take practice tests, research topics for course projects and more! The *Psychology, Fourth Edition* Companion Web site includes the following resources for each chapter: Chapter Objectives, Interactive Lectures, five different types of quizzes that provide immediate, text-specific feedback and coaching comments, WebEssays, WebDestinations, NetSearch, *NEW* FlashCards, and *NEW Live!Psych* Activities (described below). Access to the *Psychology, Fourth Edition* Web site is free and unrestricted to all students.

*NEW Live!Psych* Activities   This series of thirty-three highly interactive media simulations, animations, and activities was developed to teach the key concepts—and often the concepts students find most challenging—crucial to understanding Psychology. Designed to get students to interact with the material and to appeal to different learning styles, these *Live!Psych* Media Labs were created in consultation with psychology instructors and carefully reviewed by a board of experts to ensure accuracy and pedagogical effectiveness. Each *Live!Psych* Media Lab is integrated into the presentation of the text material through the use of the *Live!Psych* Icon. Chapter specific *Live!Psych* activities can be found on the Companion Web site at www.prenhall.com/kassin. A special thank you goes to Lynne Blesz-Vestal, the content author, and to the members of our *Live!Psych* review board: Kim Ainsworth-Darnell (Georgia State University); Eric J. Chudler (University of Washington); Margaret Gatz (University of Southern California); Karen Hoblit (Victoria Community College); Gail Knapp (Mott Community College); John Krantz (Hanover College); Nancy Simpson (Trident Technical College); and Chuck Slem (California Polytechnic, San Luis Obispo).

*Video Classics in Psychology* CD-ROM   Using the power of video to clarify key concepts presented in the text, this CD-ROM offers original footage of some of the best-known classic experiments in psychology, including Milgram's obedience study, Watson's Little Albert, Bandura's BoBo doll, Pavlov's dog, Harlow's monkey, and others. In addition, students can see interviews with renowned contributors to the field such as B. F. Skinner, Carl Rogers, Erik Erickson, Carl Jung, and others. Each video is preceded by background information on the importance of that experiment or researcher to the field and is followed by questions that connect the video to concepts presented in the text. The *Video Classics in Psychology* CD-ROM can be packaged free with *Psychology, Fourth Edition*. Contact your local sales representative for the value pack ISBN.

*NEW The Prentice Hall Guide to Evaluating Online Resources with Research Navigator: Psychology, 2004*   This guide provides students with a hands-on introduction to the Internet, teaches students how to critically evaluate online resources, and guides students through the research process for three different types of research projects using *Research Navigator*. Access to *Research Navigator,* a customized research database for students of psychology described below, comes FREE with this guide!

*Research Navigator*™   *Research Navigator* features three exclusive databases full of source material, including:

- *EBSCO's ContentSelect Academic Journal Database,* organized by subject. Each subject contains 50 to 100 of the leading academic journals for that discipline. Instructors and students can search the online journals by keyword, topic, or multiple topics. Articles include abstract and citation information and can be cut, pasted, emailed, or saved for later use.

- *The New York Times Search-by-Subject One Year Archive,* organized by subject and searchable by keyword or multiple keywords. Instructors and students can view the full text of the article.

- *Link Library,* organized by subject, offers editorially selected "best of the Web" sites. Link Libraries are continually scanned and kept up to date providing the most relevant and accurate links for research assignments.

To see how this resource works, take a tour at www.researchnavigator. com, or ask your local Prentice Hall representative for more details.

*Mind Matters* CD-ROM   Free when packaged with a new text, *Mind Matters* features interactive learning modules on history, methods, biological psychology, learning, memory, sensation, and perception. Each module combines text, video, graphics, simulations, games, and assessment to reinforce key psychological concepts.

## SUPPLEMENTARY TEXTS

Contact your Prentice Hall representative to package any of these supplementary texts with *Psychology, Fourth Edition* at a reduced price:

*Psychobabble and Biobunk, Second Edition*   by Carol Tavris. This expanded and updated collection of opinion essays written for *The Los Angeles Times*, *The New York Times*, *Scientific American,* and other publications encourages debate in the classroom by applying psychological research and the principles of scientific and critical thinking to issues in the news.

*Forty Studies that Changed Psychology, Fourth Edition* by Roger Hock (Mendocino College). Presenting the seminal research studies that have shaped modern psychological study, this brief supplement provides an overview of the environment that gave rise to each study, its experimental design, its findings, and its impact on current thinking in the discipline.

*The Psychology Major: Careers and Strategies for Success*   by Eric Landrum (Idaho State University), Stephen Davis (Emporia State University), and Terri Landrum (Idaho State University). This 160-page paperback provides valuable information on career options available to psychology majors, tips for improving academic performance, and a guide to the APA style of research reporting.

*Experiencing Psychology*   by Gary Brannigan (State University of New York at Plattsburgh). This hands-on activity book contains thirty-nine active learning experiences corresponding to major topics in psychology to provide students with hands-on experience in "doing" psychology.

*How to Think Like a Psychologist: Critical Thinking in Psychology, Second Edition* by Donald McBurney (University of Pittsburgh). This unique supplementary text uses a question-answer format to explore some of the most common questions students ask about psychology.

## ACKNOWLEDGMENTS

This book is the product of a team effort—and the team was superb. I want to thank Susanna Lesan and Barbara Gerr, my developmental editors, for their tireless efforts, insights, and suggestions for improving this book. I cannot overstate my admiration for their work and the extent to which I have benefited from their experience and wisdom. Somehow, they managed to keep me and this project on track when our time was most pressured. I also want to thank Julie Tesser for her help in locating the often striking photographs that adorn the pages of this book. I am also grateful to the production staff at Prentice Hall for their commitment to excellence—especially Kathleen Sleys, this book's production editor, who worked long hours and weekends to pull the project together and get it out on time. Turn the pages, from cover to cover, and you'll see why I am indebted to those responsible for the design, artwork, and other aspects of production. Finally, I want to thank Jennifer Gilliland, Executive Editor of Psychology, who early on had a vision for this edition and a willingness to commit the resources needed to realize it.

I want to thank Pamela C. Regan for writing the excellent Study Guide that accompanies this book, Alan Swinkels for writing the Instructor's Manual, John Caruso for his work on the Test Item File, Kathy Demitrakis and Christopher Robinson for their work on the Companion Website and Lynne Blesz-Vestal for her work on the *Live!Psych* Activities.

Finally, I could never have written this textbook without the many thoughtful reviews provided by friends and colleagues at other institutions. Through the various stages of each edition, these teachers and scholars gave me invaluable insights, corrections, references, examples, and alternative points of view—all of which helped make me a better author and this a better book. For their expertise and generosity, I thank:

Eugene Abravanel, *George Washington University*
Lewis R. Aiken, *Pepperdine University*
Tony Albiniak, *University of South Carolina   Coastal Carolina College*
Larry M. Anderson, *Kwantlen College*
Virginia Andreoli Mathie, *James Madison University*
James R. Averill, *University of Massachusetts—Amherst*
Gregory F. Ball, *Johns Hopkins University*
Marie Banich, *University of Illinois at Urbana-Champaign*
Judith Barker, *Cuyahoga Community College*
Patricia Barker, *Schenectady Community College*
Carol M. Batt, *Sacred Heart University*
Joe S. Bean, *Shorter College*
Robert C. Beck, *Wake Forest University*
Charles Blaich, *Wabash College*
Marc Bornstein, *National Institute of Child Health and Human Development*
John J. Boswell, *University of Missouri—St. Louis*
Francis X. Brennan, *Wilkes University*
Jack H. Brennecke, *Mt. San Antonia College*
Robert C. Brown, *Georgia State University*
Danuta Bukatko, *College of the Holy Cross*
David W. Carroll, *University of Wisconsin—Superior*
John L. Caruso, *University of Massachusetts—Dartmouth*

John C. Cavanaugh, *University of Delaware*
John S. Childers, *East Carolina University*
Larry Christensen, *Texas A&M University*
Charles E. Collyer, *University of Rhode Island*
John Colombo, *University of Kansas*
Marla Colvin, *Cuyahoga Community College Metro*
Maureen Conrad, *Sacred Heart University*
Joseph G. Cunningham, *Brandeis University*
John P. Davis, *University of Washington*
Robin DiMatteo, *University of California—Riverside*
V. Mark Durand, *State University of New York—Albany*
Robert A. Emmons, *University of California—Davis*
Martha Ewing, *Collin County Community College*
Morton P. Friedman, *University of California—Los Angeles*
Margaret Friend, *San Diego State University*
Mauricio Gaborit, *Saint Louis University*
William Peter Gaeddert, *State University of New York—Plattsburgh*
Grace Galliano, *Kennesaw State College*
Rod Gillis, *University of Miami*
David Goldstein, *Duke University*
Mary Alice Gordon, *Southern Methodist University*
Robert L. Gossette, *Hofstra University*
Peter Gram, *Pensacola Junior College*

Richard A. Griggs, *University of Florida*
Douglas L. Grimsley, *University of North Carolina*
Jim Hail, *McLennan Community College*
Lynn Halpern, *Brandeis University*
Elaine Hatfield, *University of Hawaii—Honolulu*
Holly Hillary, *Nassau Community College*
Michael P. Hoff, *Dalton State College*
Cynthia Holland, *Cuyahoga Community College West*
Allen Huffcutt, *Bradley University*
John C. Jahnke, *Miami University*
Patricia A. Jarvis, *Illinois State University*
Timothy Jay, *Massachusetts College of Liberal Arts*
John Jonides, *University of Michigan—Ann Arbor*
Cindy Kennedy, *Sinclair Community College*
Frederick L. Kitterle, *Stephen F. Austin State University*
Stephen B. Klein, *Mississippi State University*
Mike Knight, *University of Central Oklahoma*
Richard S. Lehman, *Franklin & Marshall College*
Paul E. Levy, *University of Akron*
Robert M. Levy, *Indiana State University*
Richard Lewis, *Pomona College*
Dan Lipscomb, *Collin County Community College*
Charles A. Lowe, *University of Connecticut*
Mark Marschark, *University of North Carolina—Greensboro*
Melanie Martin Arpaio, *Baruch College of CUNY*
Louis D. Matzel, *State University of New Jersey—Rutgers*
Joan K. McDermott, *Towson State University*
David McDonald, *University of Missouri—Columbia*
Susanne W. McKenzie, *Dawson College*
Steven E. Meier, *University of Idaho*
Rick Mitchell, *Hartford Community College*
Steven O. Moldin, *Washington University School of Medicine*
Timothy H. Monk, *University of Pittsburgh School of Medicine*
Douglas Moore, *Temple University*
Joel Morgovsky, *Brookdale Community College*
James H. Nelson, *Parkland College*
Todd D. Nelson, *California State University*
Michael Numan, *Boston College*
Richard Panman, *State University of New York—New Paltz*

Fred Patrizi, *East Central University*
David G. Payne, *State University of New York—Binghamton*
Roger D. Phillips, *Lehigh University*
Michelle Pilati, *Hondo College*
Gordon Pitz, *Southern Illinois University*
Cornelius P. Rea, *Douglas College*
Arthur S. Reber, *Brooklyn College*
Gretchen Reevy, *California State University—Hayward*
Peter A. Reich, *University of Toronto*
Ed Reid, *Shelby State Community College*
Judith C. Reiff, *University of Georgia*
Sean P. Reilley, *Morehead State University*
Daniel Rosenbaum, *Detroit College of Business*
Laurie Rotando, *Westchester Community College*
Timothy A. Salthouse, *Georgia Institute of Technology*
Connie Schick, *Bloomsburg University*
David A. Schroeder, *University of Arkansas*
Edwin A. Schwartz, *College of San Mateo*
Barry D. Smith, *University of Maryland—College Park*
William P. Smotherman, *State University of New York—Binghamton*
Thomas Spencer, *San Francisco State University*
Patricia N. Taylor, *Sumter Area Technical College*
David G. Thomas, *Oklahoma State University*
Elayne M. Thompson, *William Rainey Harper College*
Arthur Tomie, *State University of New Jersey—Rutgers*
Robin R. Vallacher, *Florida Atlantic University*
Lori R. Van Wallendael, *University of North Carolina—Charlotte*
Scott R. Vrana, *Purdue University—West Lafayette*
Paul J. Wellman, *Texas A&M University*
Bernard E. Whitley, Jr., *Ball State University*
Paul Whitney, *Washington State University*
Gordon Whitman, *Sandhills Community College*
Gail M. Williamson, *University of Georgia*
Robert Winningham, *Western Oregon University*
William Youngblood, *Metropolitan State University*
Georgann Zachary, *Arkansas Tech University*
Sharon B. Zeitlin, *University of Toronto—Scarborough*
Betty Zimmerberg, *Williams College*

*Saul Kassin*

Saul Kassin is Professor of Psychology at Williams College in Williamstown, Massachusetts. Born and raised in New York City, he graduated with a B.S. from Brooklyn College in 1974. He received his Ph.D. in personality and social psychology from the University of Connecticut in 1978. He then spent one year at the University of Kansas and two at Purdue University. He was awarded a prestigious U.S. Supreme Court Judicial Fellowship in Washington, D.C., and then worked as a postdoctoral fellow in the Psychology and Law Program at Stanford University.

Kassin is coauthor of *Social Psychology* (now in its fifth edition). He also has authored or edited many other books and has written numerous articles on the topics of social and cognitive development, and on the psychology of jury decision-making, eyewitness testimony, police interrogations and confessions, and other aspects of law. He has served on the editorial boards of several major journals. Away from work, Kassin has an insatiable appetite for sports, politics, rock music, travel, and ethnic food.

# Introducing Psychology and Its Methods

## THINKING LIKE A PSYCHOLOGIST

### THE SITUATION

When you first signed up to take Introductory Psychology, you weren't really sure what you were in for. You may have read about Sigmund Freud or B. F. Skinner, you may have seen a child psychologist on a TV talk show, or you may have heard a therapist giving personal advice on the radio. You may even have taken a psychology course in high school, had exposure to psychology in other classes, or done some reading on your own. Whatever your background may be, it's important to realize that you come into this course with many intuitive or commonsense theories about people. Everyone does. What are some of *your* theories? And are they correct in light of what psychologists know on the basis of scientific research?

### MAKE A PREDICTION

Let's stop and evaluate some of your intuitive beliefs about people. The ten statements below concern topics in psychology that you will find in this book (the chapters in which they appear are shown in parentheses). Read each statement carefully and write down whether you think it is generally TRUE or FALSE. When you've finished, try to estimate the number of answers you got correct.

_____ 1. Although 90 percent of Americans are right-handed, left-handedness is common in many nonindustrialized cultures. (2)

_____ 2. Some people dream; others do not. (4)

_____ 3. Behaviorists often use punishment to eliminate unwanted behaviors. (5)

_____ 4. Human memory capacity is limited and cannot truly be increased through the use of memory "tricks." (6)

_____ 5. Contrary to popular belief, the ability to memorize new material does *not* decline in old age. (9)

_____ 6. Children's IQ scores are *not* predictive of their grades in school. (10)

_____ 7. A smile has different meanings in different cultures. (12)

_____ 8. If you're assaulted on the street, you are more likely to get help if there are three onlookers than if there's only one. (13)

_____ 9. A schizophrenic is someone with a multiple or split personality. (16)

_____ 10. People who think about themselves a lot are healthier and happier than those who do not. (18)

## THE RESULTS

Now that you have completed the commonsense psychology quiz, you are ready to read this section on how to score it. In fact, the scoring is easy: All ten statements are false. So how well did you do? This is a true-false quiz, so you could expect to get about five answers right just by guessing or flipping a coin. Did you do any better than that? Did you do worse?

## WHAT DOES IT ALL MEAN?

Look back at the statements in this quiz and you'll notice that they cover a broad spectrum of topics, including sleep and dreams, intelligence and education, memory, aging, helping in emergencies, and mental health. These topics represent psychology today—a remarkably diverse discipline with many areas of specialization.

If you did not get a perfect score on the test, you'll also have noticed that at least some of the answers are not obvious as a matter of common sense. For example, later in this book we'll see that right-handedness predominates in all human cultures and across all generations. We'll also see that everyone dreams, that behaviorists advise against the use of punishment, that a smile has the same meaning all over the world, that there are ways to powerfully boost memory, and that people are less likely to help in an emergency when others are present—contrary to the belief that there is safety in numbers. And there's a lot more. But for now, let's step back and define what psychology is and look at its history and its methods.

As you prepare for the challenges of life in the twenty-first century, there are many directions you can take. In the future, as in the past, it will be essential to be equipped with the most basic tools of literacy: reading, writing, arithmetic, an awareness of geography, a sense of history, and some knowledge of general science. Knowing a second or third language will be helpful, too. You may be especially intrigued by business or the world of high technology.

But tomorrow, like yesterday and today, the key to success in life will be understanding people—including yourself. How do we make important life decisions? Can people accurately bring back memories repressed from childhood? What motivates us to work hard or slack off, or to pursue one career instead of another? Why are some men and women homosexual and others heterosexual? Why do some teenagers get so depressed that they commit suicide, and what can be done to prevent it? What is intelligence, and how can it be measured? Why do some athletes choke under pressure? What causes prejudice, religious intolerance, and terrorism, and why are these problems so widespread? If you find these questions interesting and important, and if you think the answers should be sought in a serious manner, then the study of psychology should be part of your future.

## WHAT IS PSYCHOLOGY?

- *How would you define psychology?*
- *Is psychology the study of the human mind, or does it focus on behavior?*
- *How has the field changed over the years?*
- *What do you see as important issues and areas of specialization?*

**Psychology** is the scientific study of behavior and the mind. If you dissect this definition, you'll see that it contains three elements. First, psychology is a *scientific* enterprise. At an intuitive level, everyone is a psychologist—you, me, the bartender who listens to one drunken sob story after another, and the novelist who paints exquisite verbal portraits of fictional characters. Unlike those who rely on their personal experience, however, psychologists employ systematic, objective methods of observation.

The second key element in the definition of psychology is that it is the study of behavior. The term *behavior* refers to any activity that can be observed, recorded, and measured. It may be as simple as the blink of an eye or as complex as making the decision to get married.

Third, psychology is the study of the *mind*. For many years, researchers flinched at the mere use of the term. It was like talking about spirits or souls or ghosts in the human machine. Today, the term *mind* is used to refer to all conscious and unconscious mental states. These states cannot actually be seen, but psychologists try to infer them from observable behavior.

## HISTORICAL ROOTS

Having its origins in philosophy, psychology is said to have a long past but a short history. There is truth in this statement. The Greek philosopher Socrates (470–399 BCE) and his followers Plato and Aristotle wrote extensively about human nature. They wrote about pleasure and pain, the senses, imagination, desire, and other aspects of the "psyche." They also speculated about whether human beings were innately good or evil, rational or irrational, and capable of free will or controlled by outside forces. At about the same time, Hippocrates (460–377 BCE), the "father of modern medicine," referred to the human brain as an "interpreter of consciousness." He also tried to differentiate for the first time among different psychological disorders. Years later, Roman physician Galen (130–200 CE) theorized that every individual is born with one of four personality types or "temperaments."

Many other men and women have planted more recent seeds. French mathematician and philosopher René Descartes (1596–1650) theorized that the body is a physical structure, that the mind is a spiritual entity, and that the two interact only through a tiny structure in the brain. This position, known as **dualism**, implied that although the body could be studied scientifically, the mind—as the product of a willful "soul"—could not. Thomas Hobbes (1588–1679) disagreed. He and other English philosophers argued that the entire human experience, including our conscious thoughts and feelings, are physical processes emanating from the brain—and therefore are subject to study. In this view, which later became known as monism, the mind and body are one and the same.

Psychology also has its origins in physiology (a branch of biology that deals with living organisms) and medicine. In the nineteenth century, physiologists began studying the brain and nervous system. For example, German scientist Hermann von Helmholtz (1821–1894) studied sensory receptors in the eye and ear and investigated such topics as the speed of neural impulses, color vision, and space perception. Gustav Fechner (1801–1887), another German scientist, founded psychophysics, the study of the relationship between physical stimuli and our subjective sensations of those stimuli.

Within the medical community, there were two particularly notable developments. In an influential textbook, German psychiatrist Emil Kraepelin (1856–1926) likened mental disorders to physical illness and devised the first comprehensive system for classifying the various disorders. In Paris, neurologist Jean Charcot (1825–1893) discovered that patients suffering from nervous disorders could

**psychology**   The scientific study of behavior and the mind.

**dualism**   The assumption that the body and mind are separate, though perhaps interacting, entities.

**introspection** Wundt's method of having trained observers report on their conscious, moment-to-moment reactions.

*Wilhelm Wundt*

*William James*

sometimes be cured through hypnosis, a psychological form of intervention. From philosophy, physiology, and medicine, then, psychology is deeply rooted in the past (Hilgard, 1987; Watson & Evans, 1991).

**Pioneers in the Study of the Mind** The history of modern psychology is a history of both great thinkers and the social, cultural, and political climates in which they lived. Dean Keith Simonton (2002) thus said of psychology's history that it springs from a combination of individual genius and *zeitgeist*, which is German for "spirit of the times."

Modern experimental psychology was born in 1879, in Germany, at the University of Leipzig. It was there that physiologist Wilhelm Wundt (1832–1920) founded the first laboratory dedicated to the scientific study of the mind. At the time, no courses in psychology were being taught because the discipline did not exist on its own. Yet many students from Europe and the United States were drawn to Wundt's laboratory, comprising the first generation of scholars to call themselves psychologists. This distinguished group included G. Stanley Hall (who in 1891 founded the American Psychological Association [APA], with twenty-six members), James McKeen Cattell (the first to study individual differences), and Hugo Münsterberg (among the first to apply psychology to industry and the law). Overall, 186 students were awarded doctoral degrees under Wundt's supervision, including 33 from the United States (Benjamin et al., 1992). Over the course of his career, Wundt published 53,735 pages of material, edited psychology's first journal, and wrote its first book. His goal, as stated in the book's preface, was ambitious: "to mark out a new domain of science."

Wundt's approach to the study of the mind was a far cry from the "armchair speculation" of the philosophers of his time. Among the methods he developed was intensive **introspection,** in which trained observers reported on their moment-to-moment reactions to tones, visual displays, and other stimuli presented to them. In this way, Wundt studied such topics as attention span, reaction time, color vision, and time perception. In one study, for example, he had an observer look at a block of twelve letters for a fraction of a second, then immediately report as many as he could remember. Six letters seemed to be his limit. What would happen if the number of letters in the array were varied? How would others do if given the same task? By recruiting people to serve as participants, varying stimulus conditions, and demanding that all observations be repeated, Wundt was laying the foundation for today's psychology experiment.

In the United States, this budding new field was hearing a second voice. That voice belonged to William James (1842–1910)—a medical school graduate who went on to become a professor at Harvard University. In 1875, James (whose brother Henry was the famous novelist) offered his first course in psychology. He was very different from Wundt, but he too was influential. While Wundt was establishing psychology as a rigorous new laboratory science, James was arousing interest in the subject matter through rich ideas and eloquent prose. Those who studied with James described him as an "artist" (Leary, 1992). This group included G. Stanley Hall (who had also worked with Wundt), Mary Whiton Calkins (a memory researcher who conducted one of the first studies of dreams and in 1905 became the first female president of the American Psychological Association), and Edward Thorndike (known for his work on animal learning and for the first textbook on educational psychology).

In 1890, James published a brilliant two-volume text entitled *Principles of Psychology*, and in 1892 he followed it with a condensed version. In twenty-eight chapters, James wrote about habit formation, the stream of consciousness, individuality, the link between mind and body, emotions, the self, and other deep and challenging topics. The original text was referred to as "James"; the brief version was nicknamed

"Jimmy." For American psychology students of many generations, at least one of these books was required reading. Now, more than a hundred years later, psychologists continue to cite these classics. The brief version can still be found in the paperback section of many bookstores.

A third prominent leader of the new psychology was Sigmund Freud (1856–1939), a neurologist from Vienna. Quite far removed from the laboratory, Freud was developing a very different approach to psychology through clinical practice. After graduating from medical school, he saw patients who seemed to be suffering from ailments that had no physical basis. These patients were not consciously faking, and they could often be "cured" under hypnosis. Based on his observations, Freud formulated **psychoanalysis**—a theory of personality, a form of psychotherapy, and one of the most influential schools of thought in modern history. Freud and his many followers (most notably, Carl Jung, Alfred Adler, and Karen Horney) left a permanent mark on psychology.

Freud (1900) introduced his theory in *The Interpretation of Dreams*, the first of twenty-four books he would write. In sharp contrast to Wundt and James, who defined psychology as the study of conscious experience, Freud argued that people are driven largely by *un*conscious forces. Indeed, he likened the human mind to an iceberg: The small tip above the water is the conscious part, and the vast region submerged beneath the surface is the unconscious. Working from this assumption, Freud and his followers developed personality tests and therapy techniques designed to penetrate this hidden but important part of the human mind (see Chapters 15 and 17).

Despite the differences in their approaches, Wundt, James, and Freud were the pioneers of modern psychology. Indeed, they were ranked by twenty-nine prominent historians as the first, second, and third most important psychologists of all time (Korn et al., 1991). Many others also helped shape this new discipline (see Table 1.1). In 1885, German philosopher Hermann Ebbinghaus published the results of classic experiments on memory and forgetting, using himself as a subject. In 1886, American Lightner Witmer opened the first psychological clinic. He later established the first journal and training program in a new helping profession that he would call "clinical psychology" (McReynolds, 1997). In 1905, French psychologist Alfred Binet devised the first major intelligence test in order to assess the academic potential of schoolchildren in Paris. And in 1912, Max Wertheimer discovered that people see two stationary lights flashing in succession as a single light moving back and forth. This illusion paved the way for Gestalt psychology, a school of

**psychoanalysis**   Freud's theory of personality and method of psychotherapy, both of which assume that our motives are largely unconscious.

*Sigmund Freud*

| TABLE 1.1 | PIONEERS OF MODERN PSYCHOLOGY |
|---|---|
| **Wilhelm Wundt** | At the University of Leipzig, Germany, established the first psychology laboratory (1879). |
| **Hermann Ebbinghaus** | In Germany, conducted classic experiments on memory and forgetting (1885). |
| **Lightner Witmer** | In the United States, established first psychological clinic (1886). |
| **William James** | At Harvard University, published *The Principles of Psychology* (1890). |
| **G. Stanley Hall** | Founded the American Psychological Association (1892). |
| **Margaret Floy Washburn** | First woman to receive a Ph.D. in psychology (1894). |
| **Edward Thorndike** | In the United States, reported on the first experiments on animal learning (1898). |
| **Sigmund Freud** | In Vienna, introduced psychoanalysis in *The Interpretation of Dreams* (1900). |
| **Alfred Binet** | In Paris, developed the first modern intelligence test for assessing schoolchildren (1905). |
| **Mary Whiton Calkins** | Became the first female president of the American Psychological Association (1905). |
| **Ivan Pavlov** | In Leningrad, discovered classical conditioning in research with dogs (1906). |
| **Max Wertheimer** | In Germany, discovered the illusion of apparent movement, which launched Gestalt psychology (1912). |
| **John Watson** | Defined psychology as the study of behavior, sparking behaviorism in the United States (1913). |

thought based on the idea that what people perceive is different from the sum of isolated sensations. In the emergence of psychology as the study of mental processes, there were many, many heroes.

**The Behaviorist Alternative**   The first generation of psychologists was just beginning to explore conscious and unconscious mental processes when they were struck by controversy about the direction they were taking: Can a science really be based on introspective reports of subjective experience or on mental processes that supposedly reside in the unconscious? Should understanding how the mind works be the goal of this new science? There were those who did not think so.

In 1898, Edward Thorndike ran a series of novel experiments on "animal intelligence." In one study, he put cats into a cage, put food outside a door, and timed how long it took for them to learn how to escape. After several trials, Thorndike found that the cats, by repeating behaviors that "worked," became quicker with practice. Then in 1906, Russian physiologist Ivan Pavlov made another key discovery. Pavlov was studying the digestive system in dogs by putting food in their mouths and measuring the flow of saliva. After repeated testing, he found that the dogs would salivate in anticipation, before the food was in the mouth. At first, Pavlov saw this "psychic secretion" as a nuisance. But soon he realized what it revealed: that a very basic form of learning had taken place.

Interesting. But what do puzzle-solving cats and salivating lab dogs have to do with psychology? Indeed, what's the relevance to people of *any* animal research? To answer these questions, John Watson—an American psychologist who experimented with dogs, cats, fish, rats, monkeys, frogs, and chickens—redefined psychology as the study of observable behavior, not of the invisible and elusive mind. Said Watson, "Psychology as the behaviorist views it is a purely objective experimental branch of natural science. Its theoretical goal is the prediction and control of behavior" (1913, p. 158). Sensations, thoughts, feelings, and motivations may fuel speculation for the curious philosopher, but if something can't be seen, then it has no place in psychology. Psychoanalysis, barked Watson, is "voodooism" (1927, p. 502). As for using animals, Watson—like others who were influenced by Darwin's theory of evolution—saw no reason to believe that the principles of behavior would differ from one species to the next.

American psychologists were immediately drawn to the hard-boiled approach of **behaviorism**. The behaviorist's research goals were clear: Vary a *stimulus* in the environment and observe the organism's *response*. There were no fuzzy ideas about mental processes inside the head, just stimulus–response connections. It was all neat, clean, and objective. Watson himself was forced out of academic psychology in 1920 when it became public that he had an extramarital affair with his research assistant. He divorced his wife, married the assistant whom he loved, and left psychology as a result of this incident. (Watson then went into advertising, where he applied the principles of conditioning and became a leader in the industry.) But behaviorism was alive and well. Psychology was defined as the scientific study of behavior, and animal laboratories were springing up all over North America.

Behaviorism had many proponents and was popular for many years. After Watson, another leader emerged: B. F. Skinner, the psychologist who coined the term *reinforcement,* invented an apparatus for use in testing animals, and demonstrated in numerous experiments with rats and pigeons that behavior is controlled by reward contingencies in the environment. Skinner first reported on his experiments in 1938. Later, he and others used his findings to modify behavior in the workplace, the classroom, the clinic, and other settings. To the day he died, Skinner (1990) maintained that psychology could never be a science of mind.

**behaviorism**   A school of thought that defines psychology as the scientific study of observable behavior.

**The "Cognitive Revolution"**   Behaviorism dominated psychology in the United States and Canada from the 1920s through the 1960s. Ultimately, however, psychologists were unwilling to limit their scope to the study of observable behavior. There was too much happening inside the human organism that was interesting and hard to ignore. Physiologists were locating new pathways in the brain that regulate thoughts, feelings, and behavior. Animal researchers were finding that inborn biological instincts often interfere with learning. Child development researchers were noticing that children pass through a series of cognitive stages in the way they think about the world. Those interested in social relations were finding that our interactions with other people are influenced by the way we perceive and interpret their actions. Those studying psychoanalysis were increasingly coming to appreciate the powerful influences of unconscious motivation. And psychologists who called themselves humanists argued that people strive not only for reward but also to achieve "self-actualization," a higher state of fulfillment. There were many, many voices in the wilderness waiting to be heard.

The most dramatic change that took place in psychology was (and still is) the "cognitive revolution." The term **cognition** refers to the mental processes that intervene between a stimulus and response—including images, memories, expectations, and abstract concepts. At least in the United States, the cognitive psychologies of Wundt and James were swept under the proverbial rug for years during the rise of behaviorism. The subject matter was considered too "soft" and nonscientific. In the 1960s, however, the pendulum swung back and cognitive psychology reemerged, stronger than ever, in a trend that has continued to this day (Robins et al., 1999).

What rekindled this interest in mental processes? One source of inspiration was the invention of the computer. Built for information-processing purposes, computers provided a new and intriguing model of the human mind. The computer receives input in the form of symbols, converts the symbols into a special code, stores the information, and retrieves it from memory when directed to do so. Computer hardware was likened to the brain, and computer programs provided a step-by-step flowchart model of how information about a stimulus is processed to produce a response. Computers were at the cutting edge of science, so the metaphor was readily accepted (Neisser, 1967; Newell et al., 1958).

A second source of inspiration came from Swiss psychologist Jean Piaget. Beginning in the 1920s, Piaget studied the way children think. He developed various tasks that revealed how children of various ages reason about people, objects, time, nature, morality, and other aspects of the world. From dozens of studies described in his more than forty books and 62,935 pages of writing, Piaget theorized that from infancy to adolescence, all children advance through a series of cognitive stages. Despite the dominance of behaviorism in the United States, Piaget had a large following in Europe, and his writings—which were translated into English in the 1950s and 1960s—were ultimately deemed too important to ignore.

The cognitive revolution was also fueled by developments in the study of language. B. F. Skinner (1957) had argued that the laws of learning control the acquisition of language in much the same way that they control the way a laboratory rat learns to press a metal bar to get food. However, linguist Noam Chomsky (1959) charged that such an account was naive. Chomsky noted that children all over the world start to speak at roughly the same age and proceed at approximately the same rate without explicit training or reinforcement. He argued convincingly that our capacity for language is innate and that specialized cognitive structures are "hard-wired" into the human brain as a product of evolution. Chomsky's theory dealt a serious blow to behaviorism and sparked a great deal of interest in psycholinguistics—a topic that has played a key role in the cognitive revolution.

**cognition**   A general term that refers to mental processes such as thinking, knowing, and remembering.

**basic research** "Pure science" research that tests theories and builds a foundation of knowledge.

**applied research** Research that aims to solve practical human problems.

Today, very few psychologists identify themselves as strict behaviorists. Free to probe beneath the surface, researchers have thus made some fascinating discoveries. For example, psychologists now know that people all over the world smile when they're happy; that memories of the past can be altered by misinformation; that our views of one another are biased by first impressions; that personality traits are partly inherited; and that drugs can be used to treat certain psychological disorders. Behaviorism has had a profound, lasting, and positive impact, but psychology's horizons have expanded beyond it in exciting ways.

## EXPANSION OF PSYCHOLOGY'S HORIZONS

Just over one hundred years ago, psychology was in its infancy. Since that time, it has grown larger and stronger (see Figure 1.1). Psychology has developed in four important ways. First, there are many more areas of basic research today than in the past. The goals of **basic research** are to test theories, study processes, discover general principles, and build a factual foundation of knowledge for the field. Psychology now has many subfields, and each focuses on mind and behavior from a somewhat different perspective.

Second, psychology has expanded in the area of **applied research.** Although some psychologists believe that the discipline should remain a pure and basic laboratory science, others want to study people in real-world settings, using the results to solve practical human problems. Some specific areas of applied research include health, education, business, law, religion, politics, engineering, behavior in the military, and sports.

Third, psychology has become more open and inclusive as a profession and contains within its ranks a more diverse group of people than in the past. When psychology was forming as a new discipline, virtually all psychologists were white, male, and from North America or Europe. This has changed dramatically over time, particularly in recent years—a change that has both elevated the pool of talent within the field and brought in important new perspectives on the human condition. Today, there are more female and minority psychologists than ever before, as well as more psychologists from other parts of the world.

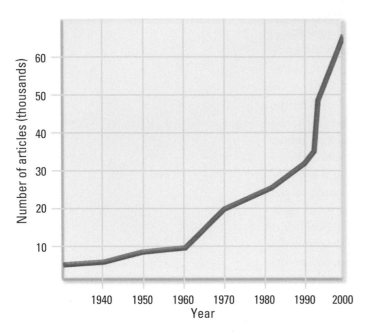

**FIGURE 1.1   Growth of psychology**
As measured by the number of articles published, psychology has flourished over the years and is currently in the midst of an enormous growth spurt.

*Psychology is a diverse discipline. Its interests include the social behavior of large crowds (left) and the study of animal conditioning (right).*

Fourth, psychology has strengthened over the years by refining its research methods. Human beings are complex and difficult to study. As individuals, we differ in our biological makeup, age, experience, and cultural background. The way we behave in one setting may differ from the way we behave in another. The inner workings of the mind can never actually be "seen." In fact, we often lack insight even into ourselves. To meet these challenges, researchers use various tests, mazes, inkblots, shock-generating devices, computerized perception tasks, brain scans, and sophisticated instruments that record physiological states. Most important, as we'll soon see, psychology stands high on the shoulders of the scientific method.

**Psychology as a Basic Science**   Psychology is now a highly specialized discipline in which researchers examine people from a number of different perspectives. The product of evolution, human beings are, first and foremost, biological animals, genetically predisposed to behave in some ways rather than others. Many psychologists focus on these biological aspects of human nature. For some, this means studying the neuroscience of the human body, brain, and nervous system—and their influence on our behavior. Others recently have found that trauma, good friends, and other "psychological" variables affect the body's immune system—and our physical health. Still others bring biological perspectives into psychology through the study of animal behavior, the evolutionary origins of human behavior, behavioral genetics, and the influences of hormones and drugs.

Also important in psychology today is a focus on internal psychological processes and what goes on "inside the head." With the computer serving as a model of the human mind, cognitive psychologists study the ways in which people are competent, rational, and objective in the way they process information about the world. They study such topics as sensation and perception, consciousness, learning, memory and forgetting, thought, and language. Also focused on inner processes, many researchers study the ways in which we warm-blooded humans are driven by motivations and emotions.

Another major perspective is provided by developmental psychologists, who focus on the ways in which people develop over the lifespan. In this perspective, an important issue is the "nature–nurture" debate concerning evolutionary, genetic, and biological influences on us—and the ways in which these influences are tempered by environmental factors from parents, siblings, peers, and culture as a whole. Some developmental psychologists study prenatal development; some study infants, children, or adolescents; others specialize in various aspects of adulthood and old age. Still others are interested in intelligence, testing, and the psychology of education.

Human beings are gregarious animals, not isolated hermits, so a social psychological perspective is also necessary to fully understand the human experience. Drawn together by the belief that social situations sometimes cause us to behave in ways that are "out of character," social psychologists focus on the influences of other people on the individual. By observing people in carefully staged social settings, researchers in this area study a range of behaviors—including attraction, conformity, persuasion, aggression, altruism, and group dynamics. They also study cultural influences and the intergroup problems of stereotyping, prejudice, and discrimination.

Clinical psychology is the largest and most visible branch of the discipline (see Figure 1.6). In contrast to those who strive to understand what's "normal," clinical psychologists study people who are "abnormal" in their perceptions, thoughts, feelings, and behavior.

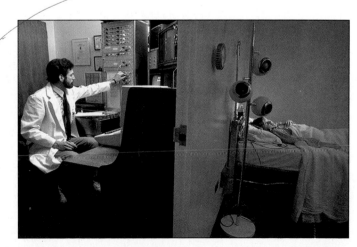

*In a laboratory study, behavior is observed in a controlled environment—such as a sleep laboratory.*

*Psychology and World Events*

# PSYCHOLOGICAL CONSEQUENCES OF TERRORISM

The terrorist assault on the World Trade Center and the Pentagon on September 11, 2001, was a trauma like no other. In New York City, the morning was sunny, bright, and clear until 8:46 A.M., when a Boeing 767, hijacked by Middle Eastern terrorists, crashed into the north tower of the World Trade Center. Eighteen minutes later, a second jet stabbed the south tower. Nobody knew it at the time, but both towers would soon collapse, a third hijacked jet would slam into the Pentagon outside of Washington, D.C., and a fourth, possibly headed for the White House, would dive into the woods of Pennsylvania. In all, more than three thousand sons and daughters, mothers and fathers, brothers and sisters, friends, coworkers, classmates, and rescue workers would be killed.

For many years to come, historians will write about the events of 9/11. In some respects, however, psychological perspectives are needed to shed light not only on what caused a group of human beings to kill themselves and others, but also on the psychological consequences for the rest of us. Whether they were present or not, Americans all over the world were affected. The theories and studies described in this book will offer some important insights in this regard. You'll read, for example, about how each of us will likely form and retain a vivid "flashbulb memory" of where we were, who we were with, and what we were doing the moment we heard about the attacks. And you'll read about how, as a result of this horrific, high-profile event, people now overestimate the risk of flying, even though driving is statistically more dangerous. For now, let's consider two predictable effects of terrorism—on our mental health and well-being, and on the way we view ourselves and the social groups around us.

## MENTAL HEALTH AND WELL-BEING

Surveys consistently show that most people are happy most of the time. In any given one-year period, however, an esti-

mated 28 percent of American adults suffer from anxiety, depression, or some other form of psychological distress (Kessler et al., 1994). Some mental-health problems are rooted in biological vulnerabilities; others spring from bad life experiences such as war, poverty, neglect, or physical and sexual abuse.

At times, a single trauma can trigger what is known as *posttraumatic stress disorder,* or *PTSD*. In a nationwide telephone survey conducted the week of 9/11, 90 percent of Americans who were not themselves present during the attack said they were stressed by it—and 44 percent reported "substantial" symptoms such as recurring thoughts and memories, difficulty falling or staying asleep, difficulty concentrating, crying, irritability, and unprovoked outbursts of anger (Schuster et al., 2001). These problems were far more common among New Yorkers than among people living in other cities and towns, including Washington, D.C. (Schlenger et al., 2002). Even within Manhattan, researchers compared local residents who lived varying distances from ground zero and found that the closer they lived, the more traumatized and depressed they were from the experience (Galea et al., 2002). For those directly touched, one wonders how long the effects will last. In some cases, loved ones will need to be patient. Time has the power to heal. In people diagnosed with PTSD, however, the symptoms may persist for several months or years.

## PERCEPTIONS OF "US" AND "THEM"

Do you ever think about death, or your own mortality? As with other living creatures, we humans are biologically programmed for self-preservation. Unique among species, however, we are conscious of—and terrified by—the inevitability of our own demise. How do we cope with the threat of death that privately haunts us? In recent years,

Based on the study of human personality and the belief that people have a capacity for change and renewal, clinical psychologists—and other mental-health workers—routinely seek to diagnose and treat psychological disorders such as anxiety, depression, and schizophrenia. In a related pursuit, counseling psychologists provide marriage, family, career, and guidance counseling to people with less severe problems.

Jeff Greenberg, Sheldon Solomon, and Thomas Pyszczynski (1997) have proposed and tested "Terror Management Theory" to explain how people cope with the fear of their own mortality. According to the theory, all human cultures construct—and individuals accept—worldviews about how, why, and by whom the earth was created; the purpose of our existence; a sense of history, complete with heroes, villains, momentous events, and traditions. These worldviews provide meaning and purpose—and a buffer against people's anxiety about death.

How will people be affected in the long term by the World Trade Center attack and the ever-present threat of terrorist annihilation, which serve to remind us of how vulnerable we are? In their book, *In the Wake of 9/11*, Pyszczynski and his colleagues (2002) predict that a fear of terrorism will motivate people to validate their own cultural worldviews and lash out at those who challenge and threaten those same views. These are normal human tendencies, they note, that become exaggerated when people are confronted by thoughts of death. In a series of clever experiments, these investigators found that after research subjects were prompted to imagine their own death, they became friendlier to others who are similar and supportive of cherished cultural values and more hostile to those who are different, foreign, or not supportive of those values. These studies correctly suggested that as Americans recover from the trauma of 9/11, and try to protect themselves from the terror that it triggered, they would exhibit a surge of national pride and patriotism—and some measure of intolerance for difference and dissent. What about the future? As world leaders seek to prevent additional acts of terrorism using political, economic, and military muscles, psychologists will try to understand the impacts of this violence on us all.

*As predicted by Terror Management Theory, many Americans after 9/11 exhibited a surge of patriotism, flying flags from their homes, cars, and businesses.*

**Psychology as a Responsive Science**   Psychology is—and always has been—a science that is *responsive* to current events. From the beginning, psychologists from all basic areas of specialization have sought to apply what they have learned to the solution of important human problems. Early in the twentieth century, French psychologist Alfred Binet developed the first modern intelligence test

*"There are no such things as applied sciences, only applications of science."*

—LOUIS PASTEUR

to help schools identify children needing special attention. After the Nazi horrors of World War II, psychologists began intensively to study obedience to authority, propaganda, prejudice, and aggression. Today, researchers study traumatic stress and other psychological consequences of terrorism. (See *Psychology and World Events*.)

Psychology today has a number of important domains of application. Health psychologists, many of whom work in medical schools, study a range of problems, such as how stress affects the heart and the immune system, what coping mechanisms are most adaptive, and why people live longer if they have friends and other social connections than if they are alone. Educational psychologists study such topics as intelligence and testing, classroom management, and academic motivation. Industrial/organizational (I/O) psychologists focus on human behavior in the workplace, as they study personnel selection, leadership in management, motivation, and worker productivity. Consumer psychologists focus on advertising and other aspects of behavior in the marketplace. Environmental psychologists study the relations between people and their physical surroundings—including the effects of street noise, heat, and population density. Many psychologists also work in the legal system, consulting with attorneys and judges, testifying in court, teaching in law schools, and researching such issues as jury selection and decision making, eyewitness identifications, lie-detector tests, prison reform, and the insanity defense (see *The Process of Discovery*). Still others work as psychologists in sports, politics, and other exciting areas. As with all other basic sciences, psychology has strayed from the laboratories of the ivory tower into the real world. The secret is out.

**Values, Ethics, and Social Responsibility**   The application of psychology—or any other science, for that matter—raises hard and sometimes tricky questions about values, professional ethics, and social responsibility (Koocher & Keith-Spiegel, 1998). For example, should research be suppressed if it yields socially sensitive results? It's easy in the abstract for psychologists to assert that they must seek the truth regardless of where it may lead, but what about the policy implications? Should IQ-test scores of different racial and ethnic groups be compared? And if some groups score lower than others, should the disparity be reported? What about studies suggesting that the testimony of young children, often essential to the prosecution of sex abusers, cannot be trusted?

These kinds of questions recently erupted in an intense, divisive, and public controversy within psychology. In 1998, Bruce Rind and his colleagues published in a prestigious journal a quantitative review of fifty-nine studies, suggesting, contrary to popular belief, that victims of child sexual abuse are *not* inevitably impaired later in life—that "child sexual abuse does not cause intense harm on a pervasive basis regardless of gender in the college population" (p. 46). You might think of this as welcome news. But through a convoluted chain of events in which the article was condemned by radio personality Dr. Laura Schlessinger, the national news media, and even the U.S. Congress, the American Psychological Association (APA)—which publishes the journal in which the article appeared—was accused of promoting pedophilia. The APA responded with conciliatory gestures that some psychologists saw as appropriate but that others saw as unsupportive of academic and scientific freedom. This storm came to a head when the editor of another APA journal overturned an earlier decision to publish a critique of how APA handled the matter (Lilienfeld, 2002). This entire episode was chronicled in a special 2002 issue of the *American Psychologist* on "interactions among scientists and policymakers."

Additional questions confront those who apply psychology. Is it ethical to dispense mental-health advice on TV or radio? Should psychologists use their scientific

## THE PROCESS OF DISCOVERY

# GARY L. WELLS
*How to Improve Eyewitness Identifications*

**Q: How did you first become interested in psychology?**

**A:** When I took my first psychology course, I noticed something different between it and the other courses I was taking. Whereas most people who made the great discoveries in math, chemistry, and other disciplines were dead, almost everyone in my psychology textbook were still alive; many were young. That meant that psychology was in its early stages and that I had a chance to contribute something important. This is still true today. Psychology is a young discipline and many of our best discoveries will come from students sitting in our classrooms today.

**Q: How did you come up with your important discovery?**

**A:** My discoveries about eyewitnesses came about the way that I think most discoveries happen: through an attitude of skepticism and a belief in the power of scientific proof. When I was in graduate school, I was shocked to learn that the legal system had never collected data on the accuracy of eyewitnesses even though it relied heavily on their identifications.

Psychology's methods were perfectly suited for testing eyewitness performance. We stage crimes for unsuspecting bystanders and then show them a lineup, so we know for sure whether they identified the actual culprit or an innocent person. One of the most striking findings was that eyewitnesses often make mistakes even if they are positive they are right. In fact, observers, like judges and juries, cannot tell if these identifications are accurate or mistaken. Clearly, we had to find ways to prevent mistaken identifications from occurring in the first place.

**Q: How has the field you inspired developed over the years?**

**A:** Amazing things have happened. First, many researchers joined in the effort to improve how police conduct lineups. Then in the 1990s, cases surfaced in which DNA tests freed innocent people convicted of crimes they did not commit. It turns out that over three-fourths of these people were in prison primarily because of mistaken identifications.

Our studies are now having an impact on how police conduct lineups. Recently, former U.S. Attorney General Janet Reno took note of the problems and directed the National Institute of Justice to develop guidelines for police on how to collect good eyewitness evidence. Along with four other psychologists, I became a part of a group that included police, prosecutors, and defense attorneys from across the country. In 1999, we published the first ever set of guidelines, all based on psychology research. Police departments soon began using techniques we had recommended. In 2001, for example, the state of New Jersey adopted our call for *double-blind lineups*—that those who test eyewitnesses not know which lineup member is the suspect, thereby preventing them from consciously or unconsciously influencing the witness's decision. Progressive police departments are looking toward scientific psychology to help them solve crimes with fewer mistakes.

**Q: What is your prediction for where the field is heading?**

**A:** I think we are heading into a new era in which psychology is used more heavily by the justice system. I even envision a time in the not too distant future in which research psychologists are routinely involved in major criminal investigations and in the training of detectives.

---

*Gary L. Wells is Distinguished Professor of Liberal Arts and Sciences and Professor of Psychology at Iowa State University.*

---

credentials to promote drug company products or to lobby for gay rights, abortion rights, handgun control, profiling at airports, and other political causes? Should psychologists testify as experts in trials involving questions of competence or insanity? Working in a discipline that addresses many delicate topics, psychologists routinely must face these important questions. To illustrate some of these fascinating links between basic and applied psychology, every chapter of this text contains one or more special boxes designed to highlight relevant research in an important and interesting domain of application. Whether the topic is health and medicine, education, business, law, sports, politics, world news, or the environment, these applications boxes will help to animate all aspects of the field.

Archives of the History of American Psychology—The University of Akron.

*In 1894, Margaret Floy Washburn (left, 1871–1939) became the first woman to receive a Ph.D. in psychology. She spent most of her career at Vassar College for women. In 1908, she wrote* The Animal Mind, *a book that was important to the emerging study of animal behavior. (Archives of the History of American Psychology—The University of Akron.) Mary Whiton Calkins (right, 1863–1930) studied at Harvard University with William James and went on to have a distinguished career. She was never granted her Ph.D., however, because she was a woman. In 1905, Calkins was elected the first female president of the American Psychological Association.*

## A DIVERSITY OF PERSPECTIVES

When Wundt, James, Freud, and others were defining this new discipline in the late nineteenth and early twentieth centuries, virtually all psychologists were white, male, and from North America or Europe. In part, this situation existed because of discrimination and other societal barriers that made it difficult for women and minorities to enter the professional ranks. Consider the distinguished career of Mary Whiton Calkins. In the 1890s, Calkins successfully completed graduate coursework at Harvard to the acclaim of William James and her other professors there. She went on to write two textbooks and a number of important research articles, she founded one of the first psychology laboratories in the United States at Wellesley College, and in 1905 she was elected first female president of the American Psychological Association. Yet at the time, Harvard University would not grant her a Ph.D. because she was a woman. The pages of psychology's history are filled with other important women who faced institutional obstacles (O'Connell & Russo, 1990). Today, a majority of psychologists entering practice in North America are women (Denmark, 1998).

Minorities were also highly underrepresented in the early years of psychology. In 1920, Francis Sumner, who studied at Clark University with G. Stanley Hall, became the first African American to earn a Ph.D. in psychology. He went on to publish two articles about the higher education of African American youths (Sawyer, 2000). Since that time, others of Asian, African, and Hispanic descent have joined the ranks—and many have made significant contributions. Consider the landmark case of *Brown v. Board of Education of Topeka* (1954), in which the United States Supreme Court ruled for the first time that racially separate schools were unequal and had to be integrated. In support of its opinion, the Court cited studies by Kenneth B. Clark, an African American psychologist whose research suggested that racial segregation makes black school children feel inferior. Behind the scenes, Clark played a pivotal role in the application of psychology to the civil rights movement. This was also the first time that the U.S. Supreme Court had cited psychology research in an opinion.

The demographic face of psychology today is different, as it includes more women, minorities, and others from the international community. Clearly, the more

In 1920, Francis Sumner became the first black person to earn a Ph.D. in psychology. Today, there are several hundred African American psychologists.

Kenneth B. Clark is an African American psychologist whose research was cited by the United States Supreme Court in Brown v. Board of Education (1954), a landmark ruling that outlawed the racial segregation of public schools.

perspectives brought to bear on the study of mind and behavior, the better. In the past, researchers typically observed the behavior of predominantly male college students on the assumption that the results would apply generally to men and women all over the world. This assumption was largely unchallenged for many years until finally, in the 1960s and 1970s, a new generation of researchers, many of whom were female, identified important similarities and differences between men and women. As we'll see in later chapters, the study of sex and gender is now basic to all areas of psychology. Also, researchers of varying nationalities are now testing psychology's theories in different parts of the world. These studies enable us to determine the extent to which certain patterns of human behavior are "universal" or found only in certain populations. As we'll see throughout this text, "Everyone is basically the same, yet no two people are alike."

Diversity considerations within the profession are also important in the mental-health area. In countries with heterogeneous populations, such as the United States and Canada, many racial and ethnic minority groups have their own unique languages, worldviews, lifestyles, experiences, and problems. Some researchers now specialize in diagnosing and treating Asian American groups (Kurasaki et al., 2002). Others focus on mental health in Latino American populations (Lopez & Carrillo, 2001). To be most helpful in treating individuals from diverse populations, psychotherapists need to understand the ways in which their clients are "culturally different" (Cuellar & Paniagua, 2000; Sue & Sue, 2002).

## REVIEW QUESTIONS

- *What is psychology?*

- *Describe the different ways in which Wundt, James, and Freud helped to define the field of psychology.*

- *What is behaviorism? How is it different from the approaches used by Wundt, James, and Freud?*

- *Identify three important intellectual advances that contributed to the "cognitive revolution" in psychology. In what way(s) does the cognitive perspective differ from earlier approaches?*

- *Distinguish between basic and applied research. Describe the basic areas of specialization within psychology. In what areas has psychology been applied?*

## SCIENTIFIC METHODS

- *What are scientific methods, and why are they important?*
- *Is it better to study people in a laboratory or in natural settings?*
- *Why do psychologists devise subtle measures of behavior when they can just ask people about themselves?*
- *What ethical concerns have been raised about using human participants in research?*
- *What about the use of animals?*

*"At the heart of science is an essential tension between two seemingly contradictory attitudes— an openness to new ideas, no matter how bizarre or counterintuitive they may be, and the most ruthless skeptical scrutiny of all ideas, old and new."*

—CARL SAGAN

It happens all the time. I'll see a report on the evening news, a magazine story, or an ad for a new product, and I'll react with a mixture of curiosity and skepticism. For example, I've heard that students can raise SAT scores 150 points by taking a test-preparation course, that a full moon triggers bizarre behavior, that workaholics drive themselves to an early grave, that pornography incites rape, that cell phones increase the risk of car accidents, and that girls start talking before boys do. Some of these claims are true; others are not. My reaction is always the same: "Hmm. Interesting," I'll say to myself. "But prove it!"

Many of us are drawn to psychology because people are fascinating and the subject matter is important. What unifies the entire discipline, however, is its commitment to scientific methods. A basic goal in science is one that should be modeled by everyone: **critical thinking.** Critical thinking is a skill, and it's also an attitude. Psychologists are trained to practice critical thinking. This means that we challenge blind assumptions, distrust our intuition in favor of systematic observation, maintain a healthy air of skepticism, revise our theories in the light of evidence, scrutinize carefully the methods used to derive that evidence, and search for alternative explanations. (See *How to Think Critically about "Experts."*)

The objective of scientific inquiry is to generate creative ideas and entertain these ideas with an open mind—but, at the same time, to be cautious, to demand that all claims be tested, and then to scrutinize the results. The "art" in science is to achieve a balance between these competing objectives. It's good to be creative but not intellectually sloppy. Similarly, it's good to be critical, even skeptical, but not closed-minded. The key to thinking like a psychologist is learning how to walk these fine lines. And that means knowing something about psychology's methods of research.

## THE RESEARCH PROCESS

1.1

The research process involves coming up with ideas and questions, and then proceeding through a series of steps designed to answer the questions in a systematic manner. The first step is to come up with a theory, or at least a loose set of ideas. As discussed earlier, you already have many intuitive theories on psychological issues. Everyone does. When I was choosing a graduate school to attend, I had to decide whether or not to leave my hometown to go to the best possible program— which meant leaving behind a girlfriend. What should I do? What effect would distance have on our relationship? One friend was certain he knew the answer: "Absence makes the heart grow fonder." Those words of encouragement made sense to me until a second friend said with equal certainty, "Out of sight, out of mind." Just what I needed. Two contradictory assumptions, both derived from common sense.

Psychological theories are more formal than the hunches we come up with in everyday conversation. A **theory** is an organized set of principles that describes, predicts, and explains a phenomenon. We can derive a theory from logic, a world event, a personal experience or an observation, another theory, a research finding, or an accidental discovery. Some theories are broad and encompassing; others account for only a thin slice of behavior. Some are simple; others contain a large number of interrelated propositions.

The second step in the research process is to formulate from one's theory specific testable predictions, or **hypotheses**, about the relationship between two or more

**critical thinking**   The process of solving problems and making decisions through a careful evaluation of evidence.

**theory**   An organized set of principles that describes, predicts, and explains some phenomenon.

**hypothesis**   A specific testable prediction, often derived from a theory.

## *How To*

# THINK CRITICALLY ABOUT "EXPERTS"

It's easy to find instant psychological analysis on just about any topic. Bookstore shelves are lined with self-help paperbacks. On cable and radio talk shows, Laura Schlessinger, Joy Brown, and other psychologists freely dispense advice on topics ranging from potty training to gambling and sex. As with other psychology professors, I often get phone calls from newspaper reporters looking for quotable answers to questions like, "What do New Year's resolutions mean?"

Are psychologists suited in these ways to counsel people about their personal problems? In the realm of psychological therapy and counseling, the answer is an emphatic yes. We'll see in Chapter 17, on the treatment of psychological disorders, that when it comes to helping people make positive changes in their mental health, psychotherapy is effective. Part of what makes therapists useful in this way is that they come to know, understand, support, and form personal relationships with their clients. But are psychologists similarly effective at dispensing advice to virtual strangers?

In a book entitled *Escaping the Advice Trap,* Wendy Williams and Stephen Ceci (1998) gathered fifty-nine real-life relationship problems from their own families and friends, and then sought solutions for each problem from two to five experts selected from a pool of a hundred eminent psychologists and psychiatrists. When they compared the solutions proposed by the different experts, they found that there was remarkably little agreement. In one case, for example, a young wife complained that her husband spends too much money on her and the children even as they are saving for a house. One psychologist suggested that she controls her husband's impulsive buying, another told her to loosen up and join in his spending, and a third advised her to seek a compromise of their values. "Just

because a person is an expert," note Williams and Ceci, "doesn't mean that his or her advice is right for you, or that a second expert wouldn't give you the opposite opinion."

Reflecting on their observations, Williams and Ceci (1998) urge people to be critical consumers of advice from psychological experts who are not intimately familiar with who they are and the situation they are in. Williams and Ceci go on to propose twelve "golden rules" of personal decision-making, including the following:

- There are two or more sides to every story.
- Always seek a second (or third) opinion.
- The truth usually rests somewhere in the middle.
- When in doubt, sleep on it.
- If you're too close to a problem, it can be difficult to see a solution.
- Keep it simple, stupid (KISS).
- You are the one and only expert on your own life.

"We're planning on sending him away to be reared by experts."

---

variables. Researchers can then test these hypotheses to evaluate the theory as a whole. In a typical study, psychologists would test one or more specific hypotheses derived from the theory. If the results support the hypotheses, confidence in the theory is increased. If the results fail to support the hypotheses, the theory as a whole is revised, qualified, or discarded. To formulate a testable hypothesis, researchers must provide **operational definitions** that specify, in concrete "how-to" terms, the

**operational definition**   A concrete definition of a research variable in terms of the procedures needed to control and measure it.

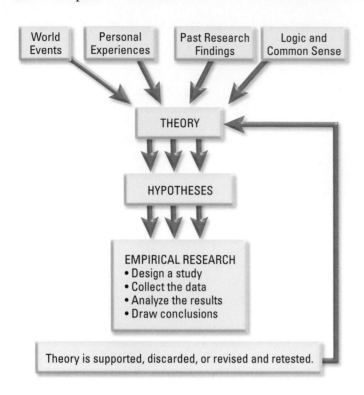

FIGURE 1.2 **The research process**

procedures needed to control and measure the variables in the hypothesis. Over the years, for example, psychologists have tried to determine what causes aggression. To do so, they gave research subjects an opportunity to administer painful electric shocks to another subject and they operationally defined aggression as the number and intensity of shocks administered.

Once researchers have a theory, hypothesis, and operational definition in place, they are ready for the next and remaining steps—to design the study, collect data from human or animal participants, analyze the results, and draw a conclusion (see Figure 1.2). There is no magic formula for determining how to test a hypothesis. In fact, as we'll see, studies vary along at least three dimensions: (1) the setting in which observations are made, (2) the ways in which psychological variables are measured, and (3) the types of conclusions that can be drawn. Let's separately examine each of these dimensions.

## RESEARCH SETTINGS

There are two types of settings in which people can be studied. Sometimes, data are collected in a laboratory, usually located at a university, so that the environment can be regulated and the subject carefully observed. **Laboratory research** offers control, precision, and an opportunity to keep conditions uniform for different participants. For example, bringing volunteers into a sleep lab enables the psychologist to monitor their eye movements and brain waves, record the exact time they fall asleep, and get dream reports the moment they awaken. Likewise, bringing a parent and child into a special playroom equipped with hand-picked toys, two-way mirrors, a hidden camera, and a microphone enables the psychologist to record every word uttered and analyze every nuance of their interaction. To study the way juries make decisions, I recruit people to serve on mock juries so that I can videotape and analyze their deliberations.

Laboratory research is common in science. NASA physicists construct special chambers to simulate weightlessness in space; chemists spark chemical reactions in the test tube; botanists study plant growth in the greenhouse; and meteorologists use wind tunnels to mimic atmospheric conditions. Similarly, psychologists often find it necessary to simulate events in a laboratory. There is, however, a drawback. Can someone sleep normally in a strange bed with metal electrodes pasted to the scalp? Will a parent and child interact in the playroom the way they do at home? Do mock juries reach verdicts the same way real juries do? Being an artificially constructed world, the laboratory may at times elicit atypical behavior.

The alternative is **field research** conducted in real-world locations. The psychologist interested in sleep and dreams may have participants report back periodically on their experiences. The parent and child could be visited in their own home. And jurors could be questioned about their decision-making process after a trial is over. The setting chosen depends on the behavior to be measured. Indeed, psychologists have observed people in city streets, classrooms, factories, offices, singles bars, subways, dormitories, elevators, and even public restrooms. To understand behavior in real-world settings, there is no substitute for field research. Unfortunately, the psychologist "out there" cannot control what happens to his or her participants or measure with precision all aspects of their experiences. That's why the most fruitful approach is to use both laboratory and field settings.

**laboratory research** Research conducted in an environment that can be regulated and in which participants can be carefully observed.

**field research** Research that is conducted in real-world locations.

| TABLE 1.2 | THREE WAYS TO "OBSERVE" PEOPLE | | |
|---|---|---|---|
| **Method** | **Description** | **Advantages** | **Disadvantages** |
| **Self-reports** | Ask people to report on themselves in interviews, surveys, or questionnaires. | People often reveal inner states that cannot be "seen" by others. | People distort self-reports to present themselves in a favorable light. |
| | | | People are not always aware of their own inner states. |
| **Behavioral observations** | Observe behavior firsthand, openly or covertly, sometimes using special tasks or instruments. | Behavior can be measured objectively. | Inner states can only be inferred from behavior, not actually seen. |
| | | | People may behave differently if they know they are being observed. |
| **Archival records** | Observe behavior secondhand, using available records of past activities. | The behavior occurs without the biasing presence of an observer. | Records of past activities are not always complete or accurate. |

## PSYCHOLOGICAL MEASUREMENTS

Regardless of where observations are made, many different types of measurements can be taken. These types fall into three categories: self-reports, behavioral observations, and archival records. These three types of observations, and the advantages and disadvantages of each, are summarized in Table 1.2.

**Self-Reports**   One way to assess a person's thoughts, feelings, or behavior is to go right to the source and ask. This is the method of **self-report.** Through interviews, questionnaires, or diaries, people are asked to report on their behavior, perceptions, beliefs, attitudes, and emotions. Self-reports are quick and easy to get. The information, however, can be inaccurate and misleading.

There are two problems with self-reports. First, people sometimes distort their responses in order to present themselves in a favorable light. It's hard to get anyone to admit to failures, mistakes, and shortcomings. Studies show, for example, that people overestimate their own contributions to a joint effort (Ross & Sicoly, 1979), report after the occurrence of an event that they knew all along it would happen (Hawkins & Hastie, 1990), hide their feelings of prejudice (Crosby et al., 1980), and overestimate the accuracy of their own predictions (Dunning et al., 1990). When James Shepperd (1993) asked college students about their SAT scores and then checked their academic records, he discovered that they overestimated their actual scores by an average of seventeen points.

A second problem with self-report data is that even when respondents try to be accurate, they are often limited in their ability to do so. Long ago, Freud noted that people block certain thoughts and wishes from awareness. And studies show that people often lack insight into the causes of their own behavior (Nisbett & Wilson, 1977). In a surprising illustration of the limits of self-reports, Stanley Coren (1993), an expert on handedness, notes that when he asks people whether they're right- or left-handed, 7 percent answer incorrectly. "One man who confidently reported that he was a right-hander, when tested to see which hand he used to throw a ball, aim a dart, cut with scissors, and the like, performed every single action with his left hand. His only detectable right-handed activity was writing" (p. 34).

**self-report**   A method of observation that involves asking people to describe their own thoughts, feelings, or behavior.

**behavioral observation** A form of research that is based on the firsthand observation of a subject's behavior.

**archival research** A form of research that relies on existing records of past behavior.

1.2

*Behavioral observation is critical to psychology. In this study, a four-month-old baby is tested to see whether she knows that an object in motion will not stop in midair.*

Self-report measures are common in psychology, sometimes even essential. As you read through this book, however, you'll see that researchers often go out of their way to collect data in more subtle, indirect ways. Now you know the reason: The source is not always the best source.

**Behavioral Observations** It is said that actions speak louder than words—and many researchers would agree. Many years ago, the Nielsen ratings of TV shows (which determine the cost of advertising and success of programs) were derived from the results of surveys and diary forms mailed to viewers. Realizing that these self-reports are flawed, however, Nielsen Media Research later installed "People Meters" in thousands of sample households across the country to electronically record what viewers are watching, when, and for how long. Similarly today, Internet marketing companies measure the value of specific Web sites by monitoring the number of users who enter the site, the amount of time spent there, and the frequency with which users click on the advertising banners.

In psychology as well, the major alternative to self-reports is firsthand **behavioral observation.** To animal researchers, the pressing of a metal bar, the running of a maze, and the consumption of food pellets are important behaviors. Sucking, smiling, crying, moving the eyes, and turning the head are significant sources of information for those who study infants. As for those who study adults, psychologically relevant behaviors range from the blink of an eye to the choice of a marital partner or career. Even changes in internal states (such as respiration, heart rate, eye movements, brain waves, hormone levels, muscle contractions, and white blood-cell activity) can be monitored with the use of special instruments.

Behavioral observation plays a particularly important role in the study of subjective experience. One cannot crawl under a subject's skin and see what's on his or her mind. But researchers can try to infer various internal states from behavior. It is usually (though not always) safe to assume, for example, that recognition reveals the presence of a memory, that solving difficult problems reveals intelligence, and that the person who breaks into a cold sweat and runs at the sight of a snake has a fear of snakes.

**Archival Records** A third way to collect information about people is to conduct **archival research** that involves examining records of past activities instead of ongoing behavior. Archival measures used in psychology include medical records, birthrates, literacy rates, newspaper stories, sports statistics, photographs, absenteeism rates at work, personal ads, marriages, and divorce. A major advantage of these kinds of measures is that by observing behavior secondhand, researchers can be sure that they did not influence the participants by their presence. An obvious limitation is that existing and available records of human activity are not always complete or detailed enough to be useful.

Archival measures are particularly valuable for examining cultural or historical trends. For example, Coren (1993) wanted to know if right-handedness was always dominant among humans (today, roughly 90 percent of the population is right-handed). So he went through a collection of art books and analyzed 1,180 drawings, paintings, and engravings that depicted an individual using a tool or a weapon. The drawings ranged from Stone Age sketches dated 15,000 BCE to paintings from the year 1950 CE. Yet Coren found that 90 percent of all characters were portrayed as right-handers—and that this percentage was the same thousands of years ago as in the twentieth century.

## RESEARCH DESIGNS

Regardless of how and where the information is obtained, researchers use **statistics** to summarize and then analyze the results. In some cases, statistical tests are used simply to describe what happened in terms of averages, percentages, frequencies, and other quantitative measures. In other cases, analyses are used to test inferences about people in general and their behavior. More about the use of statistics in psychological research is available in the Appendix of this book. For now, it is important to note that the types of conclusions that are drawn are limited by the way a study is designed. In particular, three types of research are used: descriptive studies, correlational studies, and experiments.

**Descriptive Research**   The first purpose of research is simply to describe a person, a group, or a psychological phenomenon through systematic observation. This goal can be achieved through case studies, surveys, and naturalistic observations.

*Have human beings always been predominantly right-handed? This Greek vase from 500 BCE depicts running warriors. As with 90 percent of all people depicted in ancient artwork, these warriors brandished their spears in their right hands.*

**Case Studies**   Sometimes it is useful to study one or more individuals in great detail. Information about a person can be obtained through tests, interviews, firsthand observation, and biographical material such as diaries and letters written. **Case studies** are conducted in the hope that an in-depth look at one individual will reveal something important about people in general. The problem with case studies is that they are time consuming and often are limited in their generality. To the extent that a subject is atypical, the results may say little about the rest of us.

Nevertheless, case studies have played an influential role in psychology. Sigmund Freud based his theory of personality on a handful of patients. Behaviorist John Watson used a case study involving an infant to try to debunk psychoanalysis. Swiss psychologist Jean Piaget formulated a theory of intellectual development by questioning his own children. Neuroscientists gain insights into the workings of the brain by observing and testing patients who have suffered brain damage. Cognitive psychologists learn about memory from rare individuals who can retain enormous amounts of information. Psycholinguists study language development by recording the speech utterances of their own children over time. Intelligence researchers learn about human intellectual powers by studying child prodigies, chess masters, and other gifted individuals. Social psychologists pick up clues about leadership by analyzing biographies of great leaders. And clinical psychologists refine the techniques of psychotherapy through their shared experiences with patients. When an individual comes along who is exceptional in some way or when a psychological hypothesis can be answered only through systematic, long-term observation, the case study provides a valuable starting point.

**Surveys**   In contrast to the in-depth study of one individual, **surveys** describe an entire population by looking at many cases. In a survey—which can be conducted in person, over the phone, through the mail, or over the Internet—people can be asked various questions about themselves. Surveys have become very popular in recent years and tell us, for example, that 95 percent of American men and women have sexual fantasies (Laumann & Michael, 2001), that 96 percent believe in God

**statistics**   A branch of mathematics that is used for analyzing research data.

**case studies**   A type of research that involves making in-depth observations of individual persons.

**survey**   A research method that involves interviewing or giving questionnaires to a large number of people.

**epidemiology**   The study of the distribution of illnesses in a population.

**random sample**   A method of selection in which everyone in a population has an equal chance of being chosen.

1.3

(Golay & Rollyson, 1996), that 49 percent daydream about being rich (Roper Reports, 1989), that 80 percent are happy (Diener, 2000), and that 60 percent would like to lose weight (Harris Poll, 2002). In case you've been wondering, 37 percent of women and 18 percent of men squeeze the toothpaste tube from the bottom (Weiss, 1991).

Surveys are sometimes necessary to describe psychological states that are difficult to observe directly. For example, this method is a vital tool in **epidemiology**—the study of the distribution of illnesses in a population. How many children are awakened by nightmares? What percentage of college students are struck by test anxiety? How common are depression, drug use, and suicide? These kinds of questions are vital for determining the extent of a problem and knowing how to allocate healthcare resources. Surveys are also useful for describing sexual practices. With AIDS spreading at an alarming rate, it's important to know how sexually active people are, whether they use condoms, and whether some segments of the population are more at risk than others. Today, surveys are so common, and the results have such significant implications, that the methods (which, after all, rely on self-report) should be carefully scrutinized. Two factors are particularly important in this regard: who the respondents are and how the questions are asked (Krosnick, 1999; Tourangeau et al., 2000).

To describe a group, any group—males, females, college students, redheads, Americans, or all registered voters—researchers select a subset of individuals. The entire group is called the *population;* the subset of those questioned constitutes a *sample.* For a survey to be accurate, the sample must be similar to or representative of the population on key characteristics such as sex, race, age, region, income, education, and cultural background. Short of questioning everyone in the population, the best way to ensure representativeness is to use a **random sample,** a method of selection in which everyone has an equal chance of being chosen.

Survey researchers usually pick names arbitrarily from a phone book or some other list. This seems like a reasonable strategy (and the larger the sample, the smaller the margin of error), but no sample is perfect. Not everyone has a telephone, some people have unlisted numbers, and some people who are called may not be home or may refuse to participate. Prior to the 1936 presidential election, pollsters for the magazine *Literary Digest* mailed postcards to more than ten million people selected from telephone directories and automobile registration lists. The cards asked the respondents to indicate for whom they intended to vote. Based on the more than two million cards that were returned, the *Literary Digest* predicted that Republican Alfred Landon would defeat Democrat Franklin D. Roosevelt in a landslide. In fact, the opposite occurred. The problem: At the time, more Republicans than Democrats owned telephones and automobiles, which skewed the poll results. For a sample to accurately reflect its parent population, it must be selected in a manner that is random, not biased.

A second factor to consider is the way in which survey questions are asked. Studies show that the answers people give are influenced by the wording of the questions, the context in which they are asked, and other extraneous factors (Schwarz, 1999). The following examples illustrate the point.

- When survey respondents were asked about "assisting the poor," only 23 percent said that too much money was being spent. Yet among those asked about "welfare," 53 percent gave this negative response (*Time,* 1994).
- College students tried to estimate the distance from New York City to San Francisco (3,200 miles). Among those first asked if the distance is more or less than 1,500 miles, the average estimate was 2,600. Yet among those first asked

if the distance was more or less than 6,000 miles, the average estimate was 4,000 (Jacowitz & Kahneman, 1995).

■ Unhappily married men and women were asked to rate how satisfied they were with their lives. Those who were first asked a set-up question about marriage reported being much less satisfied with life in general than those who were not first asked about marriage. Among happily married men and women, the set-up question increased their ratings of satisfaction (Schwarz, 1999).

■ Eighty-eight percent of participants thought condoms were effective in stopping AIDS when condoms were said to have a "95 percent success rate." However, when condoms were said to have a "5 percent failure rate," only 42 percent of the participants were similarly optimistic (Linville et al., 1992).

**Naturalistic Observations**   A third descriptive approach is to observe behavior as it occurs in the real world. **Naturalistic observations** are common in sociology and anthropology, where field-workers seek to describe a group, organization, or culture by "living" in it for long periods of time. Psychologists use this method as well to study parents and their children, corporate executives, factory workers, nursing-home residents, and others.

Naturalistic observation is particularly common among ethologists, who study the behavior of animals in their natural habitats. For example, Jane Goodall (1986, 2000) has spent more than forty years watching chimpanzees in African jungles. She has observed their social structure, courting rituals, struggles for dominance, and child-rearing practices. She observed cannibalism and a war between chimpanzee troops. She also saw the chimps strip leaves from twigs and use the twigs to fish termites out of nests—a finding that disproved the widely held assumption that only humans are capable of making tools. In another program of research, Dorothy Cheney and Robert Seyfarth (1990) observed vervet monkeys in Kenya and discovered that these monkeys behave as if they know the kinship bonds within the group, use deception to outsmart rivals, and use vocal calls in ways that are more sophisticated than anyone before had expected. To truly understand primates, and perhaps their similarities to humans, one has to observe their behavior in the wild—not captive in a zoo or laboratory.

**naturalistic observation**   The observation of behavior as it occurs naturally in real-world settings.

**correlation**   A statistical measure of the extent to which two variables are associated.

*Naturalistic observation is a common form of descriptive research. For many years, Jane Goodall has observed chimpanzees in the wild.*

**Correlational Studies**   Description is a nice first step, but science demands much more. A second goal is to find connections, or correlations, between variables so that one factor can be used to predict another. Correlational research is reported in psychology—and in the news—with remarkable frequency. Consider a few examples: The more violence children watch on TV, the more aggressive they are. College graduates earn more money than nongraduates. The more optimistic people are, the less often they get sick. Adults who exercise regularly live longer than those who do not. People who are shy have fewer friends than those who are outgoing. So what do these statements of correlation *really* prove? And what do they not prove?

A **correlation** is a statistical measure of the extent to which two factors are associated. Expressed in numerical terms, *correlation coefficients* range from −1 to +1. A positive correlation exists when the two variables increase or decrease together, in the same direction. The link between TV violence and aggression is positive—more of one means more of the other; so are the correlations between education and income and between exercise and longevity. In contrast, a negative correlation exists when an increase in one variable is accompanied by a decrease in the other, and vice

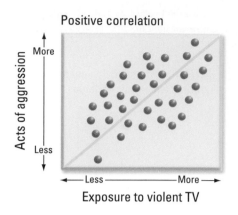

Positive correlation

Acts of aggression (More / Less)

Exposure to violent TV (Less — More)

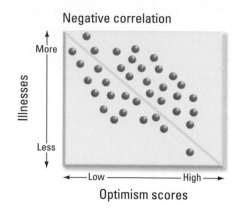

Negative correlation

Illnesses (More / Less)

Optimism scores (Low — High)

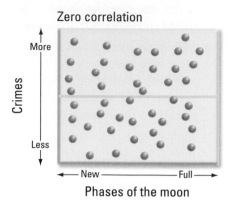

Zero correlation

Crimes (More / Less)

Phases of the moon (New — Full)

**FIGURE 1.3  Visualizing correlations**
Scatterplots provide a graphic representation of the observed relationship between two variables. The graphs above illustrate a positive correlation (left), a negative correlation (center), and a zero correlation (right). Each point locates the position of a single subject on the two variables. The solid straight lines show what the correlations would look like if they were perfect.

1.4

versa. The link between optimism and illness is in a negative direction, as is the one between shyness and friendships.

Correlation coefficients vary not only in direction but also in strength. The higher a correlation is, regardless of whether it is positive or negative, the stronger the link is between variables. Correlations that are very low, near zero, indicate that two variables are independent. Contrary to popular opinion, for example, research shows, that there is no correlation between phases of the moon and criminal activity or between intelligence-test scores in infancy and adulthood. In short, full moons and infant test scores cannot be used to predict crime or adult IQ. As shown in Figure 1.3, the direction and strength of a correlation can be represented in a **scatterplot**.

Correlational studies serve an important function: Based on existing associations, researchers can use one variable (or more) to make *predictions* about another variable. Before interpreting correlations, however, two important limitations guide the cautious scientist. First, correlations between psychological variables are seldom perfect. Human beings are complex creatures and their behavior is multidetermined. If you know a boy who spends twenty hours a week watching professional wrestling, or playing violent video games such as Mortal Kombat, you might predict that he gets into fights at school. But the positive correlation between media violence exposure and aggressiveness is far from perfect, and you may well be wrong. Similarly, not every optimist is healthy and not every college graduate brings home a hefty paycheck. Unless a correlation is close to 1, it can be used only to make general statements of probability, not predictions about specific individuals.

**Correlation and Causation**  The types of conclusions that can be drawn from correlational evidence are limitless. It's tempting to assume that because one variable predicts another, the first must have caused the second. Not true. This interpretation is an error often committed by lay people, college students, the news media, and sometimes even researchers themselves. Think about the correlations described earlier. Now, admit it: Didn't you assume that exposure to TV violence *causes* aggression, that a college diploma brings financial reward, that optimism fosters health, that exercise prolongs life, and that shyness inhibits friendships? Regardless of how intuitive or accurate these conclusions may be, the cardinal rule of statistics is: *Correlation does not prove causation.*

**scatterplot**  A graph in which paired scores (*X, Y*) for many participants are plotted as single points to reveal the direction and strength of their correlation.

It's important to know and understand this rule. It does not mean that correlated variables are never causally related, only that *the link may or may not be causal*. Think again about our examples, and you'll see there are other ways to interpret these correlations. Sure, it's possible that media violence (X) triggers aggression (Y). But based solely on the observation that these two variables go hand in hand, it's also possible that the causal arrow points in the opposite direction—that children who are aggressive (Y) are naturally drawn to violent TV shows (X). Or perhaps both variables—watching violent shows and aggressive behavior—are caused by a third factor (Z), such as the absence of involved parents at home.

Reconsider our other examples and you'll further appreciate the point. Perhaps people become optimistic because they are healthy or are shy because they lack friends. As for the fact that college graduates earn more money than high-school graduates, being smart or coming from an upper-middle-class family (Z) may both propel a student through college (X) and lead to their financial success (Y). In a similar vein, maybe adults who exercise live longer because they also tend to smoke less, drink less, and eat healthier foods (see Figure 1.4).

### Experiments

Correlation allows prediction, but to *explain* a relationship between variables, we need a more exacting method of research: the scientific experiment. In an **experiment**, the psychologist seeks to establish causal connections by actively controlling the variables in a situation and measuring the subject's behavior. The factor an experimenter manipulates (the proposed cause) is called the **independent variable**, so named because it can be varied on its own, "independent" of any other factors. The behavior that is being measured (the proposed effect) is known as the **dependent variable** because it is said to "depend" on the experimental situation. If you were to test the hypothesis that exposure to TV violence causes aggression, TV violence would be the independent variable, and aggression would be the dependent variable.

The purpose of an experiment is to focus on a causal hypothesis by manipulating the independent variable, keeping other aspects of the situation constant, and observing behavior. A true experiment contains two essential sets of ingredients. The first is control over the independent variable and use of a comparison group. Second is the random assignment of participants to conditions. By means of these ingredients, any differences in behavior can logically be traced back to the independent variable (see Figure 1.5).

**Control and Comparison**   I heard a report on the radio recently that half of all couples who live together before marriage later get divorced. "Wow, that's high," I said to a friend. "I wonder why." Then it hit me. "Wait a second. Isn't there a 50 percent divorce rate in the United States?"

To evaluate the significance of any number, you have to ask the question "Compared to what?" In its most basic form, a typical experiment compares research participants who are exposed to the independent variable with others, similarly treated, who are not. Those who receive the treatment make up the **experimental group**; the others constitute the **control group**. To the extent that the two groups differ in behavior, the difference can then be attributed, with varying degrees of certainty, to the independent variable. The key is to *vary one factor, keep other aspects of the*

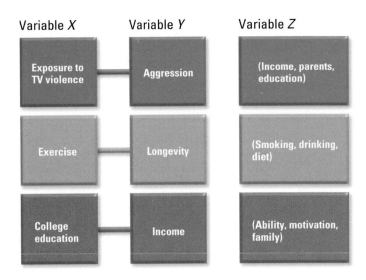

| Variable X | Variable Y | Variable Z |
|---|---|---|
| Exposure to TV violence | Aggression | (Income, parents, education) |
| Exercise | Longevity | (Smoking, drinking, diet) |
| College education | Income | (Ability, motivation, family) |

**FIGURE 1.4   Explaining correlations**
There are three possible ways to explain the association between two variables, X and Y. Look at the examples above and consider possible alternatives (Z refers to extraneous variables). In 1998, the magazine *American Demographics* reported on a survey of ten thousand American adults which showed that the more educated people are, the less frequently they have sex. That same year, researchers surveyed adults in Norway and Sweden and found that the more time people spend on cell phones, the more headaches they suffer. Does a college degree dampen the sex life, and do cell phones cause headaches? Can you come up with other possible interpretations of these correlations?

*"No amount of experimentation can ever prove me right; a single experiment can prove me wrong."*

—ALBERT EINSTEIN

**experiment**   A type of research in which the investigator varies some factors, keeps others constant, and measures the effects on randomly assigned participants.

**independent variable**   Any variable that the researcher manipulates in an experiment (the proposed cause).

**dependent variable**   A variable that is being measured in an experiment (the proposed effect).

**experimental group**   Any condition of an experiment in which participants are exposed to an independent variable.

**control group**   The condition of an experiment in which participants are not exposed to the independent variable.

FIGURE 1.5 **Basic model of an experiment**
To test the hypothesis that TV violence triggers aggression, researchers select a subset of the population, randomly assign these participants to an experimental (exposure) or control (no-exposure) group, and measure subsequent behavior.

"One group gets tiny copies of the
'*Times,*' the other gets tiny copies of
the '*Post.*'"

*Live!*
**psych**

1.5

*situation constant, and measure the effect.* To test the hypothesis that media violence triggers aggression, for example, researchers bring children, adolescents, or adults into the laboratory, show rock'em-sock'em films or video games to half of them (the others would watch nonviolent films and games or else nothing at all), and measure subsequent aggression in a laboratory or field setting (Anderson & Bushman, 2001; Wood et al., 1991).

The comparison between an experimental and a control group provides the building blocks for more complex experiments. This basic two-group design can be expanded upon in three ways. The first is to create more than two levels of the independent variable. Instead of comparing the presence and absence of TV violence, for example, one might form three groups by varying the amount, or "dosage," of exposure (high, medium, low). Second, researchers can manipulate more than one independent variable in the same experiment. For example, they might vary not only the amount of exposure but also the context in which the violence is portrayed (cartoons, films, sports, or video games). The separate and joint effects of these variables can then be evaluated. The third way to increase the complexity of an experiment is to use more than one dependent variable, or to measure the dependent variable on more than one occasion. In our example, aggression could be measured both before and after the exposure to violence.

**Random Assignment** The second essential ingredient of an experiment is that participants be assigned to conditions in an arbitrary manner. **Random assignment** ensures that everyone in a study has an equal chance of being put into an experimental or control group. If I were to show *Psycho* to children in one school and *Mary Poppins* to those in another school, it would later be impossible to know if observed differences in aggression were produced by this exposure or whether they reflect preexisting differences between the schools. Similarly, if I were to let the children pick their own condition ("Which show would you rather see?"), observed differences might mean that those who chose the violent show were more aggressive to begin with.

By flipping a coin to determine which children in a sample are in the experimental and control groups, a researcher can neutralize individual differences. Assuming that enough participants are recruited, the two conditions would contain roughly equal numbers of male and female children as well as rich and poor, active and passive, and bright and dull. Similarly, to evaluate the health benefits of exercise, we might recruit volunteers and assign half of them randomly to take part in an experimental aerobics program. Chances are that both the exercise and the no-exercise groups would then have an equal mixture of men, women, smokers, health-food

**random assignment** The procedure of assigning participants to conditions of an experiment in an arbitrary manner.

eaters, couch potatoes, and so on. Then if exercisers turn out to be healthier, the reason would be clear.

**Literature Reviews**   Seeking to describe, predict, and explain psychological phenomena, researchers use a diverse assortment of investigative tools—including single case studies, large-scale surveys, naturalistic observations, correlational studies, and experiments in laboratory and field settings. Yet regardless of the method used, there is a humbling lesson in this scientific enterprise. It is that knowledge accumulates slowly, in increments, one small step at a time. There are no "critical" experiments, and no single study can literally "prove" a hypothesis.

There *are* exciting new discoveries destined to become research classics. But each raises questions, the most important being: Will a finding replicate? **Replication** is an essential property of science. It refers to the process of conducting a second, nearly identical study to see if the initial findings can be repeated. If the result does not replicate, the cautious scientist concludes that the findings may not be reliable enough to pursue further. If the result does replicate—in other words, if the result is consistent enough to stand the test of time—then attention shifts to a second important question, that of **generalizability:** Is a finding limited to a narrow set of conditions, or does it apply across a broad range of circumstances? Just how generalizable is the result? Suppose you found that media violence causes aggression. Would the result be the same if the study were conducted in another culture or if children of a different age group were used? What if participants were shown different materials or if aggression were measured in a different way? Once replication is achieved, the next step is to establish the boundaries of the phenomenon. As with some fine wines, good science takes time.

Science demands replication and generalizability, but it is often difficult to make sense of the growing bodies of evidence. One study may show that exposure to media violence causes aggression in children, but another study may produce contradictory or ambiguous results. Why the disparity? Sometimes many studies are needed before clear patterns begin to emerge. There are two ways to discern these patterns. One is to conduct a review of the research literature, noting the strengths or weaknesses of various studies, making comparisons, and arguing for certain conclusions. In contrast to the interpretive, somewhat subjective style of a review, the second method is to use a recently developed quantitative technique known as **meta-analysis.** Meta-analysis is a set of statistical procedures that is used to review a body of evidence by combining the data and results from multiple studies (Cook et al., 2001; Hunt, 1997; Rosenthal & DiMatteo, 2001). By "meta-analyzing" a sample of *studies* the way researchers "analyze" individual *participants,* reviewers can draw precise conclusions concerning the strength and breadth of support for a hypothesis. Many of the conclusions drawn in this textbook were informed by the reviews and meta-analyses published by others.

To summarize, advances in psychological knowledge are made through primary research in the form of descriptive studies, correlational studies, and experiments. As the data from these efforts accumulate in the published literature, patterns begin to emerge. These patterns become revealed in reviews and statistical meta-analyses. The various tools of discovery discussed here are summarized in Table 1.3.

# ETHICAL CONSIDERATIONS

All professions wrestle with ethical questions, and psychology is no exception. Regardless of whether a psychologist teaches for a living, administers tests, offers counseling and psychotherapy, conducts research, writes books, consults with the news media or experts in other areas, or testifies in the courts, ethical dilemmas

**replication**   The process of repeating a study to see if the results are reliable enough to be duplicated.

**generalizability**   The extent to which a finding applies to a broad range of subject populations and circumstances.

**meta-analysis**   A set of statistical procedures used to review a body of evidence by combining the results of individual studies.

| TABLE 1.3 | THE TOOLS OF DISCOVERY |
|---|---|
| **Method** | **Purpose** |
| **Descriptive research** | To *describe* the thoughts, feelings, and behaviors of an individual or group using case studies, surveys, and naturalistic observations |
| **Correlational studies** | To uncover links, or "correlations," between variables so that one factor can be used to *predict* another |
| **Experiments** | To test hypotheses about cause and effect in order to establish that one factor can *cause* another |
| **Literature reviews** | To *summarize* an existing body of research in a narrative review or in a statistical meta-analysis of studies previously conducted |

abound (Koocher & Keith-Spiegel, 1998). For the scientists of psychology, questions arise most often concerning the use and treatment of research participants.

**Ethics Considerations in Human Research**  When I took introductory psychology in my first year of college, I signed up for all sorts of experiments. In one, other students and I were preparing to fill out questionnaires when our experimenter—a young female graduate student—was mugged by an intruder, right there in front of us, in the classroom! Soon after the commotion subsided, a security officer walked in and asked us to describe what happened and to pick the culprit from a set of photographs. In fact, the "crime" had been staged, and we were unsuspecting participants in a study of eyewitness memory. Years later, I came to realize that this experiment was a classic. It was an awesome experience.

That same semester, I spent an hour trying to memorize one hundred strings of letters (I still see them in my dreams: PTVPS, PVV, TSSSXS), only to be tested afterward for whether I had discerned the rules that were used to generate these items (I didn't even know there were rules). The session was harmless but boring. Then three years later, I heard more about the research (the task was designed to simulate the way people learn grammar, by mere exposure) and was so intrigued by it (people seem to "learn" the grammar without even realizing there is one) that I seized upon an opportunity to get involved by serving as an experimenter. That experience was my *real* introduction to psychology.

I was also in a third experiment I'll never forget. I was given an IQ test containing SAT-like analogies and math questions and was told afterward that my score was very low, in the 25th percentile. I don't remember exactly how bad I felt, but after I left and walked down the hall, I was approached by a student conducting a survey. Would I answer some questions? Not being in the mood, I said no. Suddenly my experimenter reappeared to tell me that there was no survey and that the feedback I was given earlier was false. The purpose was to see if having a positive or negative experience in one situation (some participants were told they scored high on the IQ test) influences whether people are then willing to help someone in an unrelated situation (the student with the survey).

My encounters as a psychology subject were, I think, quite typical. In most experiments, participants fill out questionnaires; work on learning, problem-solving, perception, or memory tasks; or interact socially with other people. Physiological functions may be recorded, responses may be made on a computer keyboard, or behavior may be videotaped. Some experiments are interesting and fun; others are tedious and relatively boring. Most of them are inoffensive. But sometimes participants are asked personal questions or are stressed, saddened, or put into a bad mood—or are deceived about the true purposes of the experiment. Witnessing a crime and being told I had failed an IQ test were temporarily upsetting experiences. Trying to memorize letter strings was not. In all cases, I was misled about what was being tested.

What ethical issues are raised by research involving human subjects, and how are these issues resolved? There are three specific concerns: the participant's right to privacy, the possible harm or discomfort caused by experimental procedures, and the use of **deception.** In response to these concerns, researchers must follow guidelines established by professional organizations, university ethics committees, and government granting agencies. For example, the American Psychological Association (1992) urges its members to (1) tell prospective participants what they will encounter so they can give their **informed consent,** (2) instruct participants that they're free to withdraw from the experiment at any time, (3) minimize all harm and discomfort, (4) keep the data obtained from participants confidential, and (5) if deception is necessary, "debrief" participants afterward by fully explaining the purposes and proce dures of the study.

The principles contained in these guidelines are important, and all investigators are responsible for the well-being of those who take part in their research. Some psychologists argue that these rules should be followed without exception. Others point out that many important issues could not then be investigated. In practice, ethical decisions are seldom clear-cut. For example, informed consent is necessary, and everyone agrees that deception is undesirable, but it's often impossible to test a hypothesis on a fully informed participant. Think about my own experiences. Had I known in advance that I would witness a staged crime, had I known that I was supposed to look for patterns while memorizing letters, and had I known that the IQ test I took was phony, I would have behaved in ways that were not natural and spontaneous. As a matter of compromise, therefore, many researchers describe to participants the procedures that they may encounter but withhold complete disclosure of the key variables and hypothesis until later, when participants are debriefed.

Other types of judgment calls also must be made from time to time. For example, is it ethical to put participants under stress—perhaps by presenting impossible problems to solve, showing a pornographic film, sharing the negative results of a test they took, or leading them to think temporarily that they inflicted harm on another person? Is it ethical to study pain tolerance or to ask participants to recount a traumatic episode? When the polio vaccine was tested in 1954, two million children were selected for study, but many received a placebo (a dummy medication that contains no active ingredients) instead of the real vaccine. More recently, in the 1990s, AIDS researchers in a number of developing countries administered placebos to hundreds of HIV-infected pregnant women instead of AZT—an expensive drug that would have prevented these women from passing on the virus to their babies. Were these studies ethical? Similarly, is it ethical for psychologists testing a new remedy for anxiety or depression to randomly assign half the participants to a no-treatment control group? In making these kinds of decisions, researchers weigh the costs to the individual participants against the benefits to science and humanity. In weighing these outcomes, however, there is widespread disagreement among psychologists of differing values (Kimmel, 1991; Rosnow et al., 1993).

**Ethics Considerations in Animal Research**  When Charles Darwin (1859) introduced his theory of evolution in *The Origin of Species*, he not only revolutionized conceptions of human history but also set the stage for the use of animals in research. Human beings, said Darwin, are biologically related to other creatures on the planet. Hence, the study of animals has relevance for understanding

**deception**  A research procedure used to mislead participants about the true purposes of a study.

**informed consent**  The ethical requirement that prospective participants receive enough information to permit them to decide freely whether to participate in a study.

*Animal researcher Jessica Szymczyk (top) writes: "I've been a vegetarian since I was 13 years old. . . . I don't buy or wear fur. I refuse to wear or use leather if at all possible. . . . So why am I working in a biomedical research lab that uses animals in its experiments? . . . The work we do is crucial. My love for animals matches anyone's, but there's no question . . . as to who would come first." Animal-rights activists protest the use of animals for research purposes (bottom).*

people. Does it ever. Over the years, psychology has made great strides using animals to study the brain and nervous system, vision and other senses, learning, reasoning, social behavior, anxiety, stress, and other psychological disorders, aggression, addiction, spinal cord injury, the workings of the immune system, and the impact of various drugs. Mice, rats, rabbits, cats, dogs, apes, monkeys, and even birds, fish, insects, and sea slugs have all proved valuable in this endeavor.

There are three reasons for using animals in research: to learn more about certain kinds of animals, to evaluate the cross-species generality of the principles of behavior, and to examine variables that cannot ethically be imposed on human participants. Many years ago, for example, medical researchers noted a correlation between cigarette smoking and lung cancer, but they could not determine if there was a causal link by forcing randomly selected people to smoke. Similarly, psychologists cannot inject humans with steroids to test the hypothesis that testosterone fuels aggression. For questions like these, animal research is the only alternative.

Is it ethical to experiment on animals? Many animal-rights activists say no—and are quite vocal in their opposition (Langley, 1989). A number of years ago, at a psychology convention in Washington, D.C., a hundred or so demonstrators waved posters with pictures of mutilated dogs and cats. Their claim was that research animals are routinely shocked senseless, starved to death, locked in isolation chambers, and injected with painful mind-altering drugs. Animals are entitled to the same rights as humans, they said. On a few rare occasions, militants broke into research laboratories, vandalized the equipment and records, and even stole experimental animals. In one incident, the words *ANIMAL KILLER* were spray-painted in black across the garage door of a National Institutes of Health researcher.

To understand how psychologists respond to these charges, it helps to know what both sides stand for. Everyone, including those in the research community, consider themselves to be advocates for animal *welfare* and support the establishment of shelters for lost pets, inoculation programs, the prevention of cruelty to animals, and the protection of endangered species (Johnson, 1990). Indeed, researchers argue that although food deprivation, mild shock, drugs, and surgery are sometimes performed, allegations of mistreatment are exaggerated. Caroline Coile and Neil Miller (1984) analyzed 608 animal-based research articles published in the preceding five years and found that the charges were not supported in a single instance.

As formalized in the American Psychological Association's Code of Ethics (1992), researchers have a moral obligation to treat animals humanely and minimize their pain and suffering. However, many researchers and activists part company over the issue of animal *rights*. In the eyes of some activists, it is wrong to kill chickens for food, cows for leather, insects to save crops, or rats for research purposes because humans and other living beings should be treated equally. A poster held up at an animal-rights march scorned the Amish use of horses to plow cornfields as a form of animal exploitation. In a 1996 survey of more than three hundred activists, most said they were strict vegetarians and did not use leather products. Ninety percent said they would eliminate all animal research and 55 percent favored laboratory break-ins to achieve that goal (Plous, 1998). As expressed by PETA (People for the Ethical Treatment of Animals), "Animals are not ours to eat, wear, experiment on, or use for entertainment" (http://www.peta-online.org).

Psychologists and medical researchers defend their practices by pointing to the many ways in which their work has helped to improve the quality of human life and arguing that it would be immoral *not* to use animals for our most serious problems (Miller, 1985). Animal studies were instrumental in the development of a rabies vaccine, in organ transplants, and in understanding diseases such as cancer and diabetes. Animal studies have contributed to the treatment of anxiety, depression, and other mental disorders, and they have shed light on what is currently known about neuromuscular disorders, Alzheimer's disease, alcoholism, aggression, ulcers, and obesity. Indeed, recent animal research has played a pivotal role in helping us to understand the links between psychology and the immune system (Carroll & Overmier, 2001).

Should animals be sacrificed to spare, prolong, or enhance the quality of human life? Should scientists seeking a cure for AIDS, cancer, or Alzheimer's disease, or a biochemical treatment for schizophrenia use mice to test new drugs? Most animal activists say no; most researchers say yes. What do *you* think? In general, do you support or oppose the use of animals in psychological research? Scott Plous (1996) posed this question to more than a thousand psychology majors at forty two colleges and universities. The result: 72 percent supported, 18 percent opposed, and 10 percent were not sure. This generally positive response paralleled the results of a national survey of professional psychologists—and is interesting in light of the fact that the contributions of animal research are often *not* explicitly noted in introductory psychology textbooks (Domjan & Purdy, 1995).

## PSYCHOLOGY TODAY

- *In what ways is psychology strongly influenced by biological perspectives?*
- *Why do researchers study people from different cultures and ethnic groups?*

Before psychology became established in science, it was popularly associated with astrology, numerology, handwriting analysis, and psychic powers. To this day, the phenomena of "parapsychology" continue to fascinate people. Yet you are in no way influenced by the movements of planets and stars (I'm a Taurus and, yes, often I'm stubborn, but who isn't?); your personality cannot be judged by the size of your nose, the bumps on your head, or the way you curve your *S* when you write; and nobody can predict the future by analyzing your dreams or reading your palm. The problem with these claims is that despite their widespread appeal (according to Gallup polls, more Americans believe in ESP than in evolution) and despite thousands of experiments, there is no convincing empirical support for these various claims (Marks, 1986).

Grounded in the older disciplines of philosophy, biology, and medicine, and firmly rooted in the conviction that mind and behavior can be studied only by using scientific methods, psychology has made enormous progress as a field of study. From the first subject to be tested in Wundt's original Leipzig laboratory, to the first patient to lie on Freud's couch, to the first psychologist hired to work in an applied setting, to the barrage of new discoveries concerning the links among mind, body, and health, psychology has come a long, long way.

Although psychologists study basic processes, psychology is also a responsive science, leading researchers to touch on some of the most important and socially sensitive topics of our generation. The similarities and differences between men and women; racial and ethnic diversity; sexuality; AIDS; abortion; adoption; terrorism; IQ testing; obesity and dieting; and the effects of Ritalin, Prozac, Viagra, and other drugs are among the topics now being addressed. If you're interested in the possibility of a future career in psychology, refer to the list of major subfields (what psychologists do) and employment settings (where they do it) presented in Figure 1.6. To see where today's newly graduated psychologists work, refer to the chart in Figure 1.7 (Smith, 2002).

## REVIEW QUESTIONS

- *Distinguish between lab and field research. What are the advantages and disadvantages associated with each research setting?*

- *What are the three different methods by which psychologists measure variables? What are the potential limitations of each type of measurement?*

- *Compare and contrast the three kinds of research designs used by psychologists.*

- *What are the primary ethical concerns when dealing with human participants? How do psychologists attempt to address these concerns?*

**Fields of specialization**

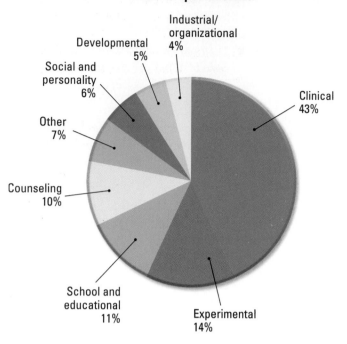

**Employment settings**

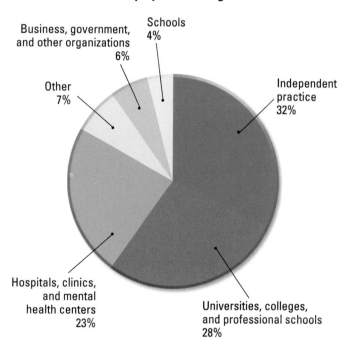

**Figure 1.6   Psychology as a profession**
The American Psychological Association has more than 155,000 members. Based on data reported in 1997, this graphic shows what these members do for a living (their fields of specialization, top) and where they do it (employment settings, bottom).

In recent years, psychology has grown by leaps and bounds. At the college level, psychology's popularity is unprecedented. According to the U.S. Department of Education, it is currently the second largest college major, behind only business administration. There are more women in the field than ever before, more minorities, more articles being published, and more topics being studied. The American Psychological Association now has as members more than 155,000 researchers, educators, clinicians, consultants, and students—and contains fifty-three divisions, each dedicated to a particular area of specialization. Across the northern border, the Canadian Psychological Association was founded in 1939. In addition, a group of scientifically oriented psychologists recently established an organization dedicated solely to basic and applied *research* (APA and CPA also address the concerns of practicing clinical and counseling psychologists). This new organization, which was founded in 1988, is called the American Psychological Society, or APS. It has twelve thousand members. APA, CPA, and APS have Internet Web sites, where you can check for news updates on the latest advances in psychology.

## BIOLOGICAL PERSPECTIVES

Increasingly, all branches of psychology are being influenced by two broad perspectives: biological and sociocultural. At the heart of a biological perspective is the notion that humans, like other species, have an evolutionary history that predisposes us to behave in certain adaptive ways to survive and reproduce. We'll see in discussions of thought and language, intelligence, sexual attraction, adolescence, aggression, altruism, and various psychological disorders, that **evolutionary psychology** is a growing force and has a great deal to say about the possible innate and universal tendencies in human mind and behavior (Plotkin, 1998; Buss, 1999).

Related to this interest in evolution is an increasing interest in the study of **behavioral genetics**—a subfield that examines the effects of genes on behavior. Nobody disputes the claim that there is a genetic basis for height, weight, skin color, and other physical attributes. But can the same be said of our psychological makeup? Is musical talent an inherited trait? What about athletic ability, shyness, happiness, or the tendency to commit suicide? We'll see in Chapter 8 that researchers try to estimate the contribution of genetic factors by looking at the similarities between pairs of individuals who vary in their genetic relatedness. In other chapters, we'll also see that this method has been used to estimate the genetic bases of sexual orientation, infant temperament, intelligence, personality, and psychological disorders such as schizophrenia (Plomin et al., 2000; Carson et al., 1999).

A third important biological perspective is provided by a large and growing body of research in **behavioral neuroscience**, the study of the links between the brain and behavior. Triggered by recent breakthroughs in biomedical technology, which enable researchers to observe the living brain in action, this area is generating a great deal of excitement. Two related areas are also making important contributions. One is *clinical neuroscience*, which

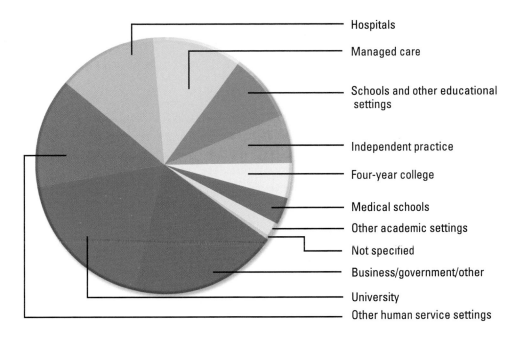

- Hospitals
- Managed care
- Schools and other educational settings
- Independent practice
- Four-year college
- Medical schools
- Other academic settings
- Not specified
- Business/government/other
- University
- Other human service settings

**FIGURE 1.7   Where new psychologists are getting jobs**
According to the American Psychological Association, newly graduated Ph.D. psychologists continue to find employment in a wide range of settings. As shown, the most common are in business and government, universities, human services, and hospitals.

For information on psychology in education, as a profession, and in the news, you can visit the Web sites of the American Psychological Association (http://www.apa.org) and the American Psychological Society (http://www.psychologicalscience.org).

**evolutionary psychology**   A subfield that uses the principles of evolution to understand human social behavior.

**behavioral genetics**   A subfield that examines the role of genetic factors on behavior.

**behavioral neuroscience**   A subfield that studies the links among the brain, nervous system, and behavior.

focuses on how abnormalities in the brain and nervous system can alter perceptions, thoughts, language, memory, emotions, and motivations and can trigger the onset of various psychological disorders (Yudofsky & Hales, 2002). The other related area is *cognitive neuroscience,* in which researchers record physical activity in different parts of the brain as a subject reads, speaks, looks at pictures, listens to music, or solves math problems. In this way, researchers are able to pinpoint regions and activities in the brain that correspond to different operations of the mind (Gazzaniga et al., 2002).

## SOCIOCULTURAL PERSPECTIVES

Just as evolutionary and biological perspectives are prominent today, so are sociocultural perspectives. Now that we have entered the twenty-first century, communication satellites, cell phones, and the Internet bring together people from vastly different cultures—and raise questions about the ways that we are all similar and different. Are there, psychologists ask, "universals" in human nature, ways in which everyone is fundamentally the same? In what ways are people from different parts of the world distinct from one another because of the regions and cultures in which they live?

Over the years, psychologists have tried to identify lawful patterns of behavior that are universally applicable to all members of the human species. People in general, we have been told, see better in daylight than in darkness, prefer reward to punishment, remember landmark events better than trivial ones, undergo an identity crisis in adolescence, strive to boost self-esteem, lash out at others when frustrated, and suffer depression after the loss of a loved one. Are these universal tendencies? Until recently, psychologists had

*This market in Mali is bustling with activity. In what ways are the people depicted in this scene similar to you and everyone else on the planet? In what ways are they different? Sociocultural perspectives focus on how people are influenced by culture, language, the region they live in, and other aspects of their surrounding environment.*

**cross-cultural research** A body of studies designed to compare and contrast people of different cultures.

**multicultural research** A body of studies designed to compare and contrast racial and ethnic minority groups within cultures.

| TABLE 1.4 CULTURAL SIMILARITIES AND DIFFERENCES: PUTTING YOUR COMMON SENSE TO THE TEST |
|---|
| Roughly 90 percent of North Americans are right-handed. Are there human cultures in which this preference is not shown? (2) |
| Do people in all regions of the world use "beds" for sleeping in a horizontal position? (4) |
| Do people interpret experiences differently as a result of the language they speak? (7) |
| Do babies all over the world start to walk and talk at the same age, or are these timetables culturally determined? (9) |
| Do adolescents all over the world reach puberty at the same age, or are there marked differences? (9) |
| Are eating disorders such as anorexia found among women in all cultures, or are they a uniquely Western affliction? (11) |
| Is smiling a universal expression of joy, or are there cultures in which people do not smile when they are happy? (12) |
| Do people in different cultures agree about what constitutes an attractive face, or is beauty culturally defined? (13) |
| Do people all over the world suffer from depression, or are there cultures in which this problem is not found? (16) |

studied only a small segment of the human population. All that has changed. Today, more and more psychologists do **cross-cultural research**, by which they compare people from different regions of the world who have lived very different lives (Berry et al., 2002). Cross-cultural similarities and differences are discussed throughout the text and are highlighted in Chapter 14, "Social and Cultural Groups." In Table 1.4, you'll see a preview of the kinds of questions that psychologists ask and the chapters in which these questions are addressed.

In addition to comparing people from different parts of the world, psychologists also conduct **multicultural research**, the study of racial and ethnic groups within cultures. As in most countries, the populations of North America are heterogeneous and diverse—and are becoming more so with time. This diversity is an important fact of social life in all open societies, and it raises profound questions for psychologists in all areas of the discipline. Are there racial and ethnic differences in intelligence-test scores? If so, what do these differences mean? How do immigrants torn between two cultures form a new identity, and what special problems do they face? Why are racism and other forms of prejudice so pervasive and what can be done about them? What special problems do gays and lesbians face as a result of their minority status? These topics are discussed throughout the text, particularly in Chapter 14.

## REVIEW QUESTIONS

- *In what ways has the biological perspective influenced the field of psychology?*

- *In what ways has the sociocultural perspective influenced the field of psychology?*

## THINKING LIKE A PSYCHOLOGIST ABOUT PSYCHOLOGY AND ITS METHODS

Psychology is a *broad* discipline that examines the biological roots of experience, internal cognitive and affective processes, the nature and nurture of human development, social and cultural influences, and the diagnosis and treatment of clinical disorders. Psychology is also a *dynamic* discipline. New theories are always being proposed, and old ones supported, revised, and discarded; new research methods are developed, and old ones are refined. On an ongoing basis, psychology is also a *responsive* discipline that tackles problems posed by world events and in such areas as health, education, race relations, and law. Finally, despite all the diversity and specialization, psychologists throughout the discipline value critical thinking and a commitment to *scientific* research methods as a mean of gaining knowledge about human behavior.

There are so many new developments, so many emerging areas of specialization, so many practical applications, and so many refinements in scientific methods, that it is impossible to cover the entire field in a single textbook. Also, because psychology is so dynamic, its knowledge evolves somewhat

"In this field, Dudley, you miss a few hours and you're no longer on the cutting edge."

over time. To be sure, some of the conclusions drawn in this book may differ from those appearing in textbooks of the 1990s—and some may require further revision in the years to come. To the extent possible, I have presented in this book the state of psychology *today.* Drawing on all of the areas, we will close with a "capstone" chapter on some of the fascinating new discoveries in health and well-being. As you'll see, the theme of this final chapter, and of the book as a whole, is: "The mind is a powerful tool. The more we know about how to use it, the better off we'll be."

## SUMMARY

In tomorrow's world, the key to success in life will be the same as it is today: understanding people. Psychology is a serious means of pursuing this understanding.

### WHAT IS PSYCHOLOGY?

**Psychology** can be defined as the scientific study of behavior and the mind.

### HISTORICAL ROOTS

Psychology's origins can be traced to ancient Greek philosophers and physicians. During the Renaissance, Descartes developed **dualism,** a theory that the mind is spiritual and the body physical. This theory implied that the mind could not be studied scientifically. Thomas Hobbes and others disagreed, arguing that thoughts and feelings are physical processes.

Modern experimental psychology began in 1879 when Wilhelm Wundt established his laboratory in Germany. Wundt used a method of **introspection,** in which trained observers described their reactions to stimuli. In the United States, William James wrote his classic *Principles of Psychology;* and in Vienna, Sigmund Freud developed **psychoanalysis** to examine the unconscious mind.

The emerging discipline faced a major controversy: Should psychologists speculate about the invisible mind, as Freud and Wundt did, or should they confine themselves to observable behavior? **Behaviorism,** as defined by John Watson, held that psychology should concentrate on what can be seen and measured. Studying the way organisms respond to stimuli, behaviorists such as B. F. Skinner refused to speculate about mental processes.

Behaviorism dominated American psychology from the 1920s through the 1960s. Then the focus shifted to **cognition,** the mental processes that intervene between a stimulus and response. The computer, which offers a model of the human mind, helped inspire this "cognitive revolution." So did the child development theories of Jean Piaget and the linguistic theories of Noam Chomsky.

### EXPANSION OF PSYCHOLOGY'S HORIZONS

Since its early days, psychology has expanded considerably. It now includes specialized areas of both **basic research** and **applied research,** it is more diversely represented, and it relies on sophisticated research methods.

The chapters of this textbook cover several broad areas of basic research. The biological perspective focuses on the links between the mind and body. The cognitive perspective considers whether human beings are generally competent in the way they learn, think, remember, and process information. The study of human development addresses changes from infancy through old age and tackles the nature–nurture debate. Social psychology considers the extent to which social situations overpower individuals. And clinical psychology deals with personality, disorders, treatment, and the question of whether people have the capacity for change.

Psychology is also a responsive science that has expanded in terms of its applications. Today, psychologists work in applied settings and use their theories and research to better understand such areas as health and medicine, education, business, law, sports, and current events.

### A DIVERSITY OF PERSPECTIVES

Today there are more female, minority, and non-Western psychologists than in the past. This increased diversity within the professional ranks has strengthened psychology by providing new perspectives.

### SCIENTIFIC METHODS

Connecting all strands of psychology is an emphasis on **critical thinking** and scientific methods.

## The Research Process

Research is a multistep process that begins with a **theory**, an organized set of principles that describes, predicts, and explains an aspect of human behavior, and provides testable propositions known as **hypotheses** and **operational definitions** of key variables. Investigators must then plan the study, collect data, analyze the results, and draw a conclusion. Psychological studies vary in their settings, their ways of measuring variables, and the types of conclusions the research is designed to reach.

## Research Settings

There are two types of research settings: **laboratory research**, valuable for its control and precision; and **field research**, conducted in real-world environments.

## Psychological Measurements

**Self-reports** are interviews or questionnaires in which people report on their own thoughts, feelings, or behavior. These are easy to administer but are sometimes misleading. The alternatives are direct **behavioral observation** and the **archival research** that uses records of past behavior such as medical files and public documents.

## Research Designs

No matter how the information is collected, researchers use **statistics** to analyze it and draw conclusions. The types of conclusions they reach depend on the research design.

There are three types of descriptive studies designed simply to describe a person, group, or phenomenon. **Case studies** collect detailed information about a particular person. **Surveys** use interviews or questionnaires to draw conclusions about an entire population. To make a survey as accurate as possible, researchers study a **random sample**, so that each individual in the group has an equal chance of being chosen. **Epidemiology**, the study of the distribution of illnesses in a population, is a particularly important form of survey research. The third type of descriptive study, **naturalistic observation**, involves the measurement of behavior in natural settings.

When description is not enough, researchers often employ correlational studies. A **correlation** is a statistical measure of the extent to which two factors are associated. In numerical terms, correlation coefficients range from $+1$ to $-1$ and can be shown on a **scatterplot**. Researchers use correlational studies to make predictions about one variable based on what they know about another variable. Correlation, however, does not prove causation.

To study causal links, researchers turn to the **experiment**, where the investigator manipulates an **independent variable** (the proposed cause) and measures a **dependent variable** (the proposed effect). Then the researcher compares the **experimental group** of participants to a **control group** that was not exposed to the independent variable. An effective experiment requires **random assignment** of participants, so that each participant has an equal chance of being in either group.

Finally, psychological research often includes reviews of the existing evidence. By summarizing the current state of knowledge, research reviews can help resolve the questions of **replication** (Would a new study produce the same results?) and **generalizability** (Is the finding applicable under other sets of conditions?). Various studies can be summarized through literature reviews and through **meta-analysis**, a set of statistical procedures for combining the results of individual studies.

## Ethical Considerations

Like other professions, psychology faces ethical issues—questions, for example, about the use and treatment of research participants. For human participants, concerns include the subject's right to privacy, the harm or discomfort that may be caused, and the use of **deception**. Research guidelines stress the need to obtain **informed consent** from participants, to let them know they can withdraw at any time, to minimize discomfort, to keep data confidential, and to debrief participants afterward. When the experimental participants are animals, researchers must treat them humanely and minimize their suffering.

# PSYCHOLOGY TODAY

Because of the richness of psychological research and its many applications, there are more people in psychology today than ever before, and their work touches on many vital public policy topics.

## Biological Perspectives

Triggered by advances in biomedical technology, biological perspectives are prominent. **Evolutionary psychology** considers possible ways in which evolutionary forces predispose us to behave in certain ways. **Behavioral genetics** examines the effects of genes on psychological makeup and behavior. **Behavioral neuroscience** examines the links between neural activity in the brain and behavior. Clinical neuroscience focuses on how abnormalities in the brain and nervous system can cause psychological disorders. And cognitive neuroscience examines the links between the brain and normal mental activities.

## Sociocultural Perspectives

Increasingly, psychologists are testing the universality of their principles in **cross-cultural research** all over the world. With increasing diversity in the populations in many countries, there is also an increase in **multicultural research**, studies of racial and ethnic groups within cultures.

## KEY TERMS

psychology (**p. 5**)

dualism (**p. 5**)

introspection (**p. 6**)

psychoanalysis (**p. 7**)

behaviorism (**p. 8**)

cognition (**p. 9**)

basic research (**p. 10**)

applied research (**p. 10**)

critical thinking (**p. 18**)

theory (**p. 18**)

hypotheses (**p. 18**)

operational definitions (**p. 19**)

laboratory research (**p. 20**)

field research (**p. 20**)

self-report (**p. 21**)

behavioral observation (**p. 22**)

archival research (**p. 22**)

statistics (**p. 23**)

case studies (**p. 23**)

surveys (**p. 23**)

epidemiology (**p. 24**)

random sample (**p. 24**)

naturalistic observations (**p. 25**)

correlation (**p. 25**)

scatterplot (**p. 26**)

experiment (**p. 27**)

independent variable (**p. 27**)

dependent variable (**p. 27**)

experimental group (**p. 27**)

control group (**p. 27**)

random assignment (**p. 28**)

replication (**p. 29**)

generalizability (**p. 29**)

meta-analysis (**p. 29**)

deception (**p. 31**)

informed consent (**p. 31**)

evolutionary psychology (**p. 35**)

behavioral genetics (**p. 35**)

behavioral neuroscience (**p. 35**)

cross-cultural research (**p. 36**)

multicultural research (**p. 36**)

## THINKING CRITICALLY ABOUT PSYCHOLOGY AND ITS METHODS

1. Historically, psychologists have been white males of North American or European descent. How might this fact have influenced the questions psychologists asked and/or the theories they developed?

2. Most psychologists, at one time or another, have had to defend the notion that psychology is a science. Why do you think it is important for psychologists to view psychology as a scientific enterprise? Do you agree that psychology is the *scientific* study of behavior and the mind? Why or why not?

3. In the past several years, we have seen a dramatic increase in violence in schools, including adolescents shooting teachers and classmates. How might the different theoretical approaches discussed in this chapter (e.g., the behaviorist, cognitive, biological, etc., perspectives) attempt to explain such behavior?

4. Suppose you wanted to study school violence. Design three separate studies—one descriptive, one correlational, and one experimental—that would allow you to examine this issue. Would you use a case study, survey, or naturalistic observation for your descriptive study? What variables would you measure in your correlational study? What would be the independent and dependent variables in your experiment? What type of measurements would you collect in your studies? What sorts of conclusions about school violence would each study allow you to make?

5. Do you personally believe that research should utilize animal participants? What are the arguments for and against using animals as research participants?

# Behavioral Neuroscience

# ONE BRAIN OR TWO?

## THE SITUATION

You've seen pictures of the human brain, so you have a fairly good sense of what it looks like. You know that the whole brain works together, but you've also read that the right and left sides (or "hemispheres") have different strengths—that the left side handles reading and other verbal processes, whereas the right side is involved more in visual and spatial tasks. And you've read that each hemisphere controls the opposite side of the body.

You're only mildly interested. But wait. What if the two halves of a person's brain were to become physically separated from each other? Would each side compensate for the loss and function on its own, or would the person flounder? This sounds like one of those hypothetical problems that philosophers like to ponder, but it's real. On rare occasions, people who suffer life-threatening seizures undergo a radical form of surgery in which the cable of nerves that connect the brain's right and left hemispheres is completely severed. In these "split-brain" patients, the two sides of the brain can no longer communicate. The question is: What is the effect?

Now imagine the following situation. The year is 1961 and a split-brain patient by the name of W.J. agrees to take part in a psychological experiment in which you are assisting. After introductions, you show W.J. a series of cards, each containing a red-and-white geometrical pattern, and a set of cubes—each containing two red sides, two white sides, and two mixed sides divided along the diagonal. His task is to arrange the blocks in squares that match the patterns on the cards (see Figure 2.1). Oh, there's one hitch. You tell W.J. that he can use only one hand to assemble the blocks. On some cards, you tell him to use his right hand and keep the left one tucked under the table. On other cards, you tell him to use only his left hand. Can W.J. match the patterns? Does it matter which hand he uses?

## MAKE A PREDICTION

Reread the situation and examine the clues given earlier about the human brain, the type of surgery that W.J. had, and the nature of the task he is being asked to complete. Also keep in mind that W.J. is a normal and intelligent man—at least he was before the surgery. Putting all these pieces together, do you think he is able to complete the task with his right hand? What about with his left hand? Make two predictions, one for each hand.

|                    | yes        | no         |
|--------------------|------------|------------|
| Left-hand success  | _____   | _____   |
| Right-hand success | _____   | _____   |

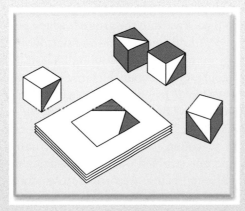

FIGURE 2.1    The block-design task given to W.J.

## THE RESULTS

Before W.J. was tested, researchers Michael Gazzaniga and Roger Sperry were not sure what to expect. W.J. seemed normal in conversation, but perhaps both sides of an integrated brain are needed for complex mental activities. Or perhaps one side is sufficient if it's the one that specializes in the task at hand. The result was dramatic: W.J. could assemble the block patterns with his left hand, but not with his right hand. In fact, as his right hand struggled, the left hand occasionally sneaked up from under the table to help out!

## WHAT DOES IT ALL MEAN?

W.J. was the first split-brain patient ever tested, but others later confirmed the basic result: The left hand succeeded at the spatial block-design task because the left hand is controlled by the "spatial" right hemisphere. Yet his right hand—because it is controlled by the left hemisphere and was unable, after the surgery, to receive signals from the right side—was clueless. This case study involving W.J. shows that the brain's two hemispheres specialize in different types of mental activities—something we normally don't notice because the hemispheres are connected and both sides are involved in everything we do. More important, this study shows that when the two halves are disconnected, they act as two separate brains. Reflecting on the implications, Gazzaniga (1992) notes that "each half brain seemed to work and function outside of the conscious realm of the other" (p. 122).

Case studies such as this one have played a major role in our understanding of the human brain and its links to the body and the mind. The brain is a complex anatomical structure, and researchers today have many tools at their disposal to study how it works. In this chapter, we'll examine the human brain, how it's built, its place in the nervous system, and the psychological functions that it serves.

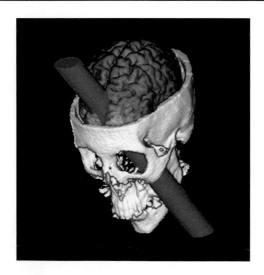

**FIGURE 2.2    Phineas Gage's skull**
Using photographs and measurements of Gage's skull, and computerized images of normal brains, Hanna Damasio and her colleagues (1994) plotted the possible paths of the tamping iron and produced this computerized reconstruction of the damage to the prefrontal cortex of Gage's skull. Gage's skull and tamping iron are now on display on the fifth floor of the Harvard Medical School Library.

At twenty-five years of age, Phineas Gage was a supervisor for the Rutland & Burlington Railroad in Vermont. He was bright, well liked, and energetic. On the afternoon of September 13, 1848, Gage and his coworkers were in Vermont blasting rock to pave the way for new railroad tracks. To do this, they drilled holes in the rock and packed the holes with gunpowder and sand, using a three-foot-long rod called a tamping iron. All of a sudden, a spark ignited the powder, causing an explosion that propelled the rod upward like a missile. As shown in Figure 2.2, the rod (which was an inch and a quarter in diameter at one end but comes to a sharp point at the other end) pierced Gage's left cheek behind the eye, exited the front-top part of his skull, flew fifty feet into the air, and landed in a pile of dirt, covered with blood and brain matter.

Gage was catapulted backward to the ground, where he began to shake. To everyone's amazement, he was still alive. Minutes later, with blood pouring down his face, Gage was sitting up, moving about, and talking to those around him. Doctors soon stopped the bleeding, cleaned out the loose bits of bone and brain tissue, and packed the wound. Within a few months, Gage was back at work. He showed no loss of intellectual ability. But the front part of his brain, the area known as the frontal lobes, was badly damaged. As a result, this normally soft-spoken, controlled, and considerate young man had become irritable, demanding, unable to plan for the future, and unrestrained—at times engaging in gross profanity. In many ways, Gage was not a social being. According to his doctor, the change in his personality was so profound that he was "no longer Gage." To complete the sad story: Gage lost his job, traveled with P.T. Barnum's circus, and exhibited his skull and

*This is a three-dimensional plaster life mask of Phineas Gage. Recognizing the historic value of his case, doctors in Boston made it, one year after the accident, by having Phineas close his eyes and inserting straws into his nose so he could breath while liquid plaster was poured over his face. You can see the large scar on his forehead.*

*In 1998, the small town of Cavendish, Vermont (72 miles north of my home in Williamstown, Massachusetts), memorialized Phineas Gage by dedicating a plaque in his honor. The plaque tells the story of what happened and its significance for the study of behavioral neuroscience.*

tamping iron all over the country. Twelve years after the accident, at thirty-seven, Gage died. To this day, however, his case remains important in the history of brain science (Damasio, 1994; Fleischman, 2002; Harlow, 1868; Macmillan, 2000).

Psychologists now know that the frontal lobes are involved in thinking, planning, setting goals, and inhibiting impulses. But the case of Phineas Gage told us much more. It told us that the human brain and nervous system are not a single or simple entity but rather an integrated "system" consisting of different specialized parts. And it told us that the links among the brain, the mind, and behavior can be revealed by the effects of damage to specific structures. These points set the stage as we begin to explore the biological roots of the human experience. As we'll see, all aspects of our existence—every sight, sound, taste, and smell, every twitch, every movement, every feeling of pleasure or pain, all our dreams, learned associations, memories, thoughts, emotions, and even our personalities and social interactions—are biological events. Behavioral neuroscience is the subfield of psychology that focuses on these links (Kandel et al., 2000).

## THE BODY'S COMMUNICATION NETWORKS

- *How do the sensory organs, muscles, and other parts of the body prepare for action?*
- *What are the body's communication networks, and how does the brain act as a central command center?*

The human brain weighs only about three pounds. With its gnarled mass of cells, it feels like a lump of jelly and looks like an oversized, wrinkled gray walnut. The brain is an extraordinary organ—capable of great feats and more complex than any

The world's heaviest known brain weighed 5 lb. 1 oz. The lightest healthy brain weighed 1 lb. 8 oz. (*1999 Guinness Book of Records*)

**central nervous system (CNS)** The network of nerves contained within the brain and spinal cord.

**peripheral nervous system (PNS)** The network of nerves that radiate from the central nervous system to the rest of the body. The PNS comprises the somatic and autonomic nervous systems.

**somatic nervous system** The branch of the peripheral nervous system that transmits signals from the sensory organs to the CNS, and from the CNS to the skeletal muscles.

**autonomic nervous system** The branch of the peripheral nervous system that connects the CNS to the internal muscles, organs, and glands.

computer. It is one of those "miracles" of life that inspire philosophers and scientists alike.

## THE NERVOUS SYSTEM

The brain is the centerpiece of the body's nervous system, an elaborate electrochemical communication network that connects the brain and spinal cord to all sensory organs, muscles, and glands. The nervous system is divided into two major parts: central and peripheral. The **central nervous system (CNS)** consists of the brain and the spinal cord. The spinal cord is a long tubular column of neural tissue surrounded by a ring of bone that runs from the lower back up to the base of the skull. Basically, it is a transmission cable filled with nerve fibers and pathways—and it serves as an "information superhighway." Later in this chapter, we'll see that the spinal cord transmits signals from sense organs and muscles below the head up to the brain and funnels signals from the brain to the rest of the body. Injury to the spinal cord can cause partial or complete paralysis.

The **peripheral nervous system** (PNS) consists of all the nerves that radiate from the CNS to the rest of the body—from the top of the head out to the fingers, toes, and skin. The peripheral nervous system is divided into two components: somatic and autonomic. The nerves of the **somatic nervous system** transmit signals (such as sights, sounds, tastes, smells, and pain) from the sensory organs and skin to the CNS. They also relay motor commands from the CNS to the skeletal

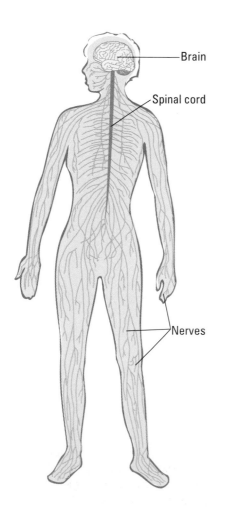

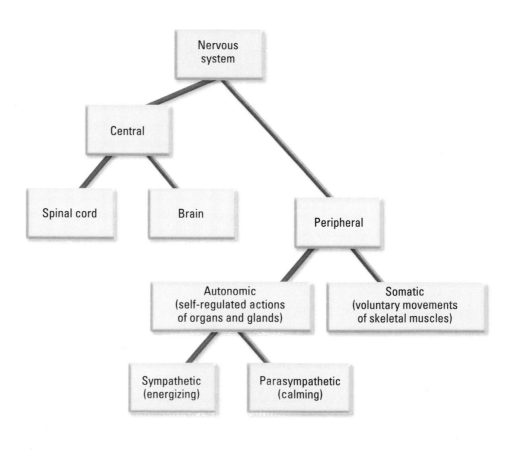

FIGURE 2.3　**Divisions of the nervous system**

muscles of the arms, legs, torso, and head, thus directing the body's voluntary movements. The nerves in the **autonomic nervous system** connect the CNS to all of the smooth *in*voluntary muscles and organs (such as the heart, stomach, and liver) and to the body's many glands, which secrete hormones (see below). As the term *autonomic* implies, this system automatically regulates internal states such as heartbeat, blood pressure, body temperature, digestion, hormone levels, and glucose levels in the blood. As we'll see later in this book, people can learn to use biofeedback, yoga, and other techniques to exert some control over these bodily functions.

The autonomic nervous system itself has two parts: sympathetic and parasympathetic. In light of the functions served by these subsystems, they may be thought of as the body's "departments of war and peace." The **sympathetic** division energizes the body for action. In times of stress, it directs the adrenal glands, which rest atop the kidneys, to secrete more of the hormones epinephrine and norepinephrine (also known as *adrenaline* and *noradrenaline*)—thereby increasing the heart rate and heightening physiological arousal. The pupils dilate to let in more light, breathing speeds up to bring in more oxygen, and perspiration increases to cool down the body. When action is no longer necessary, as when the stress subsides, the **parasympathetic** division takes over and restores the body to its pre-energized state. The heart stops racing, the pupils contract, breathing slows down, and energy is conserved. The blood levels of epinephrine and norepinephrine slowly diminish, and the body relaxes, cools down, and returns to normal. As we'll see in Chapter 12, these systems play a vital role in the experience of emotion.

To summarize, the nervous system is divided into two parts, central and peripheral. The CNS contains the brain and spinal cord. The PNS is further subdivided into the somatic and autonomic systems. In turn, the autonomic system contains both sympathetic (arousing) and parasympathetic (calming) divisions. This overview of the nervous system is presented in Figure 2.3.

## THE ENDOCRINE SYSTEM

Closely linked to the nervous system is the body's second communication system. The **endocrine system** is a collection of ductless glands that regulate growth, sexual development, reproduction, metabolism, mood, and certain aspects of behavior by secreting chemical messengers called **hormones** (the word *hormone* means to "set in motion"). Hormones are produced in tissue and secreted into the bloodstream, which then carries them to "target organs" throughout the body. Compared to the speedy transmission of impulses through the nervous system, hormonal messages may take several seconds, hours, or even days to take effect. Once they do, however, the impact is often long lasting. Dozens of hormones are produced by the body. Some of the major glands, along with their locations and their functions, are illustrated in Figure 2.4.

As we'll see later, a small but important structure in the brain called the hypothalamus controls the endocrine system through the **pituitary gland,** a pea-size gland that sits at the base of the brain. The pituitary can be thought of as the master gland of the endocrine system. Upon command from the control center in the brain, the pituitary releases a hormone that stimulates the production of

**sympathetic nervous system**   The division of the autonomic nervous system that heightens arousal and energizes the body for action.

**parasympathetic nervous system**   The division of the autonomic nervous system that reduces arousal and restores the body to its pre-energized state.

**endocrine system**   A collection of ductless glands that regulate aspects of growth, reproduction, metabolism, and behavior by secreting hormones.

**hormones**   Chemical messengers secreted from endocrine glands, into the bloodstream, to various organs throughout the body.

**pituitary gland**   A tiny gland in the brain that regulates growth and stimulates hormones in other endocrine glands at the command of the hypothalamus.

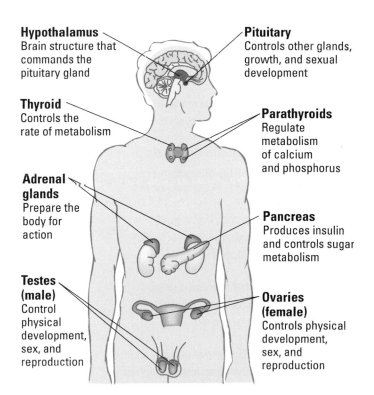

**Hypothalamus**
Brain structure that commands the pituitary gland

**Pituitary**
Controls other glands, growth, and sexual development

**Thyroid**
Controls the rate of metabolism

**Parathyroids**
Regulate metabolism of calcium and phosphorus

**Adrenal glands**
Prepare the body for action

**Pancreas**
Produces insulin and controls sugar metabolism

**Testes (male)**
Control physical development, sex, and reproduction

**Ovaries (female)**
Controls physical development, sex, and reproduction

FIGURE 2.4   **Major endocrine glands**
Taking commands from the hypothalamus, the glands of the endocrine system regulate growth, reproduction, metabolism, and behavior by secreting hormones into the bloodstream. These hormones are carried to certain "target organs" throughout the body.

## REVIEW QUESTIONS

- *Distinguish between the central and peripheral nervous systems. What additional distinctions can be made within the peripheral nervous system? What functions are controlled by each of these systems?*

- *What is the endocrine system? What processes are controlled by this system?*

- *How do the nervous and endocrine systems communicate with one another?*

2.1 *Live!* psych

**neurons** Nerve cells that serve as the building blocks of the nervous system.

**sensory neurons** Neurons that send signals from the senses, skin, muscles, and internal organs to the central nervous system.

**motor neurons** Neurons that transmit commands from the central nervous system to the muscles, glands, and organs.

**interneurons** Central nervous system neurons that connect sensory inputs and motor outputs.

**neural networks** Clusters of densely interconnected neurons that form and strengthen as a result of experience.

*"Living threads more numerous than stars frame the universe of my mind."*

—DANIEL P. KIMBLE

hormones in other endocrine glands. In turn, many hormones flow from the bloodstream back to the brain—which sends a signal to the hypothalamus that more or less additional secretion is needed. The importance of hormone regulation for the maintenance of the body is apparent when an endocrine gland malfunctions in some way. For example, when a thyroid gland produces too little hormone, people become easily tired and sensitive to cold. When the thyroid produces too much of the hormone, people tend to get nervous and irritable and lose weight.

Notice that there is a constant flow of communication between the nervous system and the endocrine system. Indeed, the brain regulates the release of hormones the same way that a thermostat maintains the temperature of a room. If you set a thermostat at 70 degrees and the temperature dips below that level, the heat comes on until the room tops 70, at which point it shuts itself off. Similarly, if a hormone drops below a certain level, the hypothalamus signals the pituitary and other glands that more is needed. Then once the hormone levels are sufficient, the hypothalamus signals the pituitary gland to stop the additional release of hormones. With the brain in command, the nervous system and endocrine system work together.

## THE NEURON

- *What are neurons and how are they constructed?*
- *How do neurons transmit information throughout the body?*
- *What are neurotransmitters, and what do they contribute to the process?*

From a broad overview of the nervous system, we turn to its specific parts. We begin with the tiny but numerous building blocks and the electrical and chemical impulses that fire throughout the body. In humans and other animals, the nervous system consists of two main types of cells: nerve cells and glial cells.

Playing the lead role in this system are the nerve cells, known as **neurons.** Neurons send and receive information throughout the body in the form of electrochemical signals. There are three types of neurons. **Sensory neurons** send signals from the senses, skin, muscles, and internal organs to the CNS. When you see an awesome sunset, scrape your knee, or enjoy the flavor of a terrific meal, messages fire from your eyes, knee, and taste buds. These messages are then relayed up to the brain. **Motor** (motion-producing) **neurons** transmit commands the other way around—from the CNS to the muscles, glands, and organs. Once the sunset, injured knee, and delicious food "register," you and your body react. Finally, **interneurons** serve as neural connectors within the central nervous system. Among their functions is to link input signals from the sensory neurons to output signals from the motor neurons.

No one knows for sure how many neurons there are in the human brain, but researchers estimate that the number is between 100 and 200 billion—as many as the number of stars in our galaxy. If you were to count one neuron every second, you would need six thousand years to count them all. Even more mind-boggling is the fact that each neuron is linked to more than a thousand other neurons, thus providing each of us with literally trillions of connections among the neurons in the brain. It's important to realize that individual neurons are not distributed evenly or haphazardly throughout the body. Rather, they cluster into interconnected working groups known as **neural networks.** Much like habits, neural cell connections are strengthened by usage and experience, allowing for fast and efficient communication within networks.

The nervous system also has a supporting cast of smaller cells that are called **glial cells,** or neuroglia. The word *neuroglia* is derived from the Latin and Greek words meaning "nerve glue." These cells are so named because they provide structural support, insulation, and nutrients to the neurons, thereby "gluing" the system together. They also play a role in the development and repair of neurons and the speed of the neural signals throughout the system. Glial cells are much smaller than the neurons they support. But because they outnumber neurons ten to one, they constitute about half of the brain's total mass (Travis, 1994; Kandel et al., 2000).

To appreciate how various neurons work together within the nervous system, let's trace the neural pathway of a simple **reflex,** defined as an automatic response to external sensory stimulation. You are probably familiar with the "knee jerk" reflex elicited during a medical checkup. Using a rubber mallet, the doctor taps your patellar tendon, located just below the knee, causing your leg to kick forward. You don't have to think about it; the reaction is immediate and automatic. How? As shown in Figure 2.5, the knee stretches your thigh muscle, which sends a sensory signal to the spinal cord, which sends a motor signal right back to the thigh muscle. Tap, kick! This two-step chain of events takes only fifty milliseconds because it does not involve higher mental processes in the brain.

**glial cells**   Nervous system cells, also called neuroglia, that provide structural support, insulation, and nutrients to the neurons.

**reflex**   An inborn automatic response to a sensory stimulus.

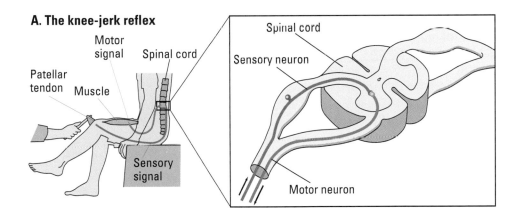

**A. The knee-jerk reflex**

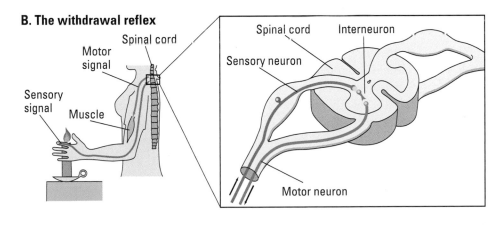

**B. The withdrawal reflex**

FIGURE 2.5

**A. The knee-jerk reflex**
A tap on the knee sends a sensory signal to the spinal cord, which sends a motor signal back to the muscle. Tap, kick!

**B. The withdrawal reflex**
Touch a hot object, and your hand will immediately pull away. In this case, sensory and motor neurons are linked by an interneuron.

**soma** The cell body of a neuron.

**dendrites** Extensions from the cell body of a neuron that receive incoming impulses.

**axon** Extension of the cell body of a neuron that sends impulses to other neurons.

**myelin sheath** A layer of fatty cells that is tightly wrapped around the axon to insulate it and speed the movement of electrical impulses.

*wt matter!*
*grey matter!*

Reflexive behaviors can be very adaptive. When your hand touches a hot iron or the thorn of a rose bush, a sensory neuron sends a quick message to the spinal cord and connects to an interneuron, which activates a motor neuron, causing your hand to pull away. The entire reaction takes place in the spinal cord—before you and your brain feel the pain and before too much damage is done.

In the case of more complex forms of behavior—say, driving a car, working on a math problem, playing a musical instrument, talking to a friend, or reading this fascinating sentence—more extensive activity is needed than is possible within the spinal cord. Sensory inputs travel toward the spinal cord (via the somatic nervous system), but they are then forwarded up to the brain and "processed" before a behavioral "decision" is reached. This decision is sent back down through the spinal cord and out to the muscles, which results in behavior. Most of the behaviors that interest psychologists are of this sort.

## STRUCTURE OF THE NEURON

The neuron is a lot like other cells in the body. It is surrounded by a membrane and has a nucleus that contains genetic material. What makes the neuron so special is its ability to communicate. Everything that we do and all that we know depend on the transfer of signals from one neuron to another.

It's hard to describe the dimensions of a "typical" neuron because these cells come in hundreds of different shapes and sizes, depending on their specific function. But the various neurons do have certain structural features in common. As illustrated in Figure 2.6, every neuron has a roundish **soma,** or cell body, which stores the nucleus of the cell and maintains a chemical balance. Connected to the cell body are two types of branched fibers, or tentacles. The **dendrites** (derived from the Greek word for "tree") *receive* impulses from sensory organs or other neurons. The more dendrites there are, the more information can be received. The **axon** (so named because of its axlelike shape) *sends* the impulse from the neuron to other neurons. Some axons are short and stubby; others are several feet long and slender (some run from the spine down to the muscles of your big toe). At the end of each axon are branches with knoblike tips called axon terminals. As we'll see, these tips contain vital chemical substances to be released onto other cells. Many axons are also covered with the **myelin sheath,** a shiny white layer of fatty cells. Produced by the glial cells, the myelin sheath is tightly wrapped around the axon to insulate it. This insulation helps to speed up the movement of electrical impulses by preventing leakage. The importance of this insulation can be seen in multiple sclerosis, a disease in which the myelin sheath degenerates, slowing signals to the muscles and resulting in the eventual loss of muscle control. To summarize, neural signals travel from the dendrites, through the (cell body) soma, down the axon, and into the axon terminals.

## THE NEURON IN ACTION

To understand how messages are transmitted from the axon of one neuron to the dendrites of another, you need to know that these messages occur in the form of electrical impulses. Here is a brief lesson in the electricity of the nervous system.

Every neuron is covered by a membrane, a semipermeable skin that permits some chemicals to pass through more easily than others. Dissolved in fluid on both sides of the membrane are electrically

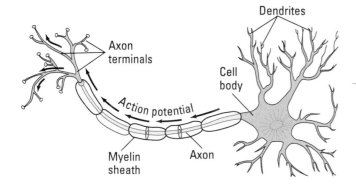

**FIGURE 2.6 Structure of the neuron**
Every neuron consists of a soma, or cell body, and two types of branched fibers. Dendrites receive electrical impulses from sensory organs or other neurons and the axon relays these impulses to other neurons or muscles. As shown, many axons are insulated with the myelin sheath, a fatty layer that speeds the movement of the impulses.

charged particles called *ions*. Three kinds of ions are most important: sodium (positively charged ions that do not pass easily through the membrane, so remain concentrated outside the cell), potassium (positively charged ions that cross easily and are concentrated inside the cell), and negatively charged ions that are trapped permanently inside the cell. When a neuron is at rest, the inside of the cell has a negative charge relative to the outside, making it a store of potential energy—much like a tiny battery.

When the dendrites of a neuron are stimulated, usually by other neurons, this delicate balance is suddenly altered. The semipermeable membrane breaks down, permitting the positively charged sodium ions outside the cell to rush in. For an instant, the charge inside the cell becomes less negative and, as a result, may trigger an **action potential**—a quick burst of electrical energy that surges through the axon like a spark along a trail of gunpowder. Depending on the neuron, most impulses travel at speeds ranging from two miles an hour up to two hundred miles an hour, which is faster than a car but three million times slower than the speed of electric current passing through a wire. At top speed, then, it takes an action potential one-hundredth of a second to run along an axon from the spinal cord to a muscle in the finger or toe. Then after an impulse has passed, the positive ions inside the cell are pumped back to the outside of the membrane. The neuron returns to its resting state and is once again ready for action.

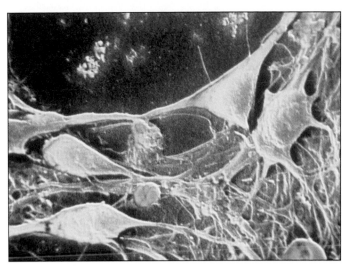

*As shown, neurons transmit electrochemical signals throughout the body.*

The stimulation of a neuron does not always trigger the firing of an electrical impulse. At any given moment, a neuron may be receiving signals on its dendrites from very few or from hundreds, even thousands, of other neurons. Whether the neuron fires depends on the sum total of signals impinging upon it. Only if the combined signals exceed a certain minimum intensity, or **threshold,** does the neuron's membrane break down and begin to transmit an electrical impulse. If it does not, no impulse is created. In other words, the action potential is an *all-or-none response.* Either it fires or it does not. This effect is like firing a gun. If you squeeze the trigger past a certain point (the threshold), bang! The bullet is launched. If not, nothing happens. You can't half-shoot, and you can't vary the intensity of the shot.

The firing of an electrical impulse is as quick as the blink of an eye, but it has profound significance. Information in the nervous system is made up of action potentials. Every thought, dream, or emotion you have, every action you take, and every decision you make is coded in the form of action potentials. For neuroscientists, cracking the action potential code is a key to understanding the language of the nervous system and unlocking new discoveries about the biology of our minds and behavior.

## HOW NEURONS COMMUNICATE

A neural impulse races from the receiving dendrites (the starting line), through the cell body, and down the axon. What happens when the signal reaches the axon terminals? And how does it then get to the dendrites of the next neuron? The transmission of messages in the nervous system is like a relay race. When the impulse reaches the end of one cell, it passes the electrochemical baton to the next cell or to a muscle or gland. How is this accomplished? Scientists used to think that the branching axons and dendrites of adjacent neurons always touched, thus enabling impulses to travel seamlessly, the way an electrical current crosses two extension cords that are plugged together. We now know that this is not the main way it

**action potential**   An electrical impulse that surges along an axon, caused by an influx of positive ions in the neuron.

**threshold**   The level of stimulation needed to trigger a neural impulse.

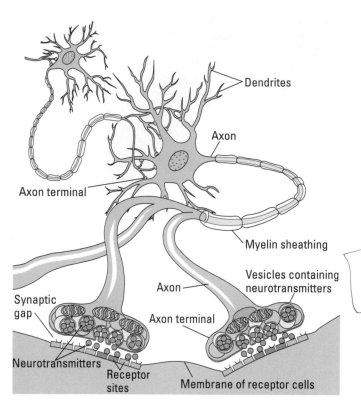

**FIGURE 2.7   How neurons communicate**
When an impulse reaches the axon terminal, it forces the release of neurotransmitters, which are stored in tiny vesicles. These chemicals squirt across the synaptic gap and bind to receptors on the receiving neuron. There are different neurotransmitters. Each fits only certain receptors, the way a key fits only one lock.

works. Rather, there is a narrow gap between neurons that is roughly one-millionth of an inch wide. This gap is called a **synapse**, from a Greek word meaning "point of contact." The question is: How does the impulse cross this synaptic gap to the next neuron?

The answer has to do with the action of **neurotransmitters**. When an electrical impulse reaches the knoblike axon terminal, it forces the release of chemical messengers called neurotransmitters—so named because they aid in the *transmission* of information from one *neuron* to another. These chemical substances are manufactured by the neuron and stored in tiny round packets called synaptic vesicles. Upon release, the neurotransmitters literally squirt across the synaptic gap and bind to specialized **receptors** on the dendrites of the receiving neuron or on muscles or glands.

There are different types of neurotransmitters. Some will excite (fire) an action potential in the next neuron, whereas others will inhibit (restrain the firing of) the next action potential. It's a truly remarkable process. There are many different neurotransmitters and many different types of receptors, and each with its own shape. This fact is significant because a neurotransmitter binds snugly only to certain receptors, the way a key fits only one lock. The entire electrochemical process is illustrated in Figure 2.7.

## NEUROTRANSMITTERS

Anxiety, feelings of calm, sadness and depression, pain, relief, memory disorders, drowsiness, hallucinations, paralysis, tremors, and seizures all have something in common: a link to the activity of neurotransmitters. The human nervous system is a prolific chemical factory. To date, researchers have identified approximately seventy-five neurotransmitters and have further suggested the possibility of many more (Webster et al., 2001).

The activities of certain neurotransmitters—where in the body they're produced, their effects on mind and behavior, and their responsiveness to drugs—are well understood. (See Table 2.1, which describes some of the more important neurotransmitters and the chapters in which they are discussed.)

**synapse**   The junction between the axon terminal of one neuron and the dendrites of another.

**neurotransmitters**   Chemical messengers in the nervous system that transmit information by crossing the synapse from one neuron to another.

**receptors**   Specialized neural cells that receive neurotransmitters.

| TABLE 2.1 | MAJOR NEUROTRANSMITTERS | |
|---|---|---|
| **Neurotransmitter** | **Function** | **Chapter** |
| **Acetylcholine (ACh)** | Links motor neurons and muscles. Also facilitates learning and memory. Alzheimer's patients have an undersupply of ACh. | 9 |
| **Dopamine** | Concentrated in the brain, it is linked to muscle activity. A shortage can cause Parkinson's disease; an excess of dopamine receptors is linked to symptoms of schizophrenia. | 16,17 |
| **Endorphins** | Distributed throughout the CNS, these natural opiates relieve pain. | 3 |
| **Norepinephrine** | Widely distributed in the CNS, it increases arousal. Too much may produce a manic state; too little may lead to depression. | 12, 16, 17 |
| **Serotonin** | Produced in the brain, it lowers activity level and causes sleep. Too little is linked to depression. | 4, 16, 17 |
| **GABA (gamma aminobutyric acid)** | Produced in the brain, it lowers arousal and reduces anxiety. It is the main inhibitory neurotransmitter in the nervous system. | 17 |

The first substance identified as a neurotransmitter was **acetylcholine (ACh)**, which is found throughout the nervous system and is most concentrated in the parts of the brain that control motor behavior. Using powerful electron microscopes, researchers can see the sacs that store and release ACh molecules and have found that ACh is the chemical key that links the motor neurons and muscles. Thus, whenever you walk, talk, ride a bike, dance, throw a ball, or take a breath, ACh is released. What would happen if you somehow blocked the release of all ACh in the system? Think about the link that would be severed, and you'll have the answer. Curare, a poison that some South American Indians put on the tips of their hunting arrows, blocks the ACh receptors, causing complete paralysis of the skeletal muscles. Consider the opposite condition. What would happen if you were to flood the synapses between motor neurons and muscles with ACh? The toxic bite of a black widow spider does just that, resulting in violent muscle contractions, sometimes even death. ACh may also play a role in the formation of new memories. As we will see in Chapter 9, people with Alzheimer's disease, a degenerative brain disorder that destroys memory, have abnormally low levels of ACh.

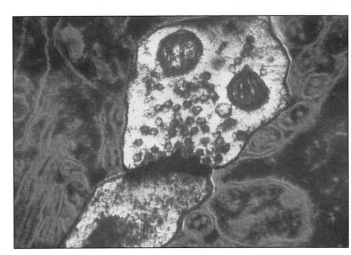

*Micrograph of neurotransmitters in synaptic vesicles (top) squirting across the synaptic gap (center) to a receiving neuron (bottom).*

Another neurotransmitter, **dopamine**, is also involved in the regulation of movement. Parkinson's disease, a motor disorder that is characterized by hand tremors, stooped posture, slowness, and a loss of control over one's voluntary movements, is caused by the death of neurons that produce dopamine. For people with this disease, the symptoms can often be eased with L-dopa, a chemical substance that the neurons convert into dopamine, which replenishes the supply. We'll see later in this chapter that a promising new approach is to implant healthy tissue containing dopamine into the brains of Parkinson's patients. We'll also see in Chapters 16 and 17 that many schizophrenia sufferers have an oversupply of dopamine receptors in the brain. Their symptoms can often be treated with drugs that block the activity of dopamine.

 2.2

Another exciting discovery is that the brain produces its own morphine, a painkiller. As part of a research study, Candace Pert and Solomon Snyder (1973) injected laboratory animals with morphine, a powerful and addictive painkilling drug derived from opium. To their surprise, they found that the morphine bound to certain receptors in the brain the way neurotransmitters do. This discovery is only mildly interesting, you may think. But wait. Why would the brain have receptors for a chemical produced outside the body? Doesn't a special receptor for morphine mean that the brain produces its own morphinelike substance? The answer is yes, and the neurotransmitter is called an **endorphin** (from the words *endogenous*, which means "internal," and *morphine*). Since this discovery, researchers have found that endorphins and their receptors, and other similar substances, are distributed throughout the central nervous system (Cooper et al., 2002).

What triggers the release of endorphins? Sensations of pain and discomfort—as triggered by physical injury, or by the labor pains that precede childbirth (Akil, 1982). In fact, research has shown that women with higher endorphin levels in the bloodstream are less sensitive to pain and less likely to experience premenstrual mood problems such as tension, irritability, and depression (Straneva et al., 2002). Over the years, some researchers have speculated that the exhilarating and intense "runner's high" described by many long-distance runners and bicyclists might result from the release of endorphins (Farrell et al., 1982). Yet others note that while exercise seems to be addictive for some people, there is no evidence for an

**acetylcholine (ACh)** A neurotransmitter found throughout the nervous system that links the motor neurons and muscles.

**dopamine** A neurotransmitter that functions as an inhibitor and is involved in the control of voluntary movements.

**endorphin** A morphinelike neurotransmitter that is produced in the brain and is linked to pain control and pleasure.

## REVIEW QUESTIONS

- *What are the three types of neurons and what function does each serve?*

- *Draw a neuron and label the major parts. What role does each part play in the transmission of information?*

- *How do neurons communicate with one another? What role do neurotransmitters play in this process?*

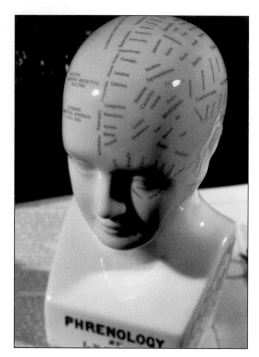

*In 1873, Mark Twain visited Lorenzo Fowler, a phrenologist. "I found Fowler on duty," Twain wrote, "amidst the impressive symbols of his trade . . . marble white busts, hairless, every inch of the skull occupied by a shallow bump, and every bump labeled in black letters." Fowler sold hundreds of busts like these. The one shown here can be seen at the Smithsonian Institution in Washington, DC.*

**phrenology**  The pseudoscientific theory that psychological characteristics are revealed by bumps on the skull.

endorphin-triggered runner's high—that the whole notion is the scientific version of an urban legend (Kolata, 2002). For now, the causes and effects of endorphins are not clearly understood. It is clear, however, that the human body comes equipped with a natural, built-in pharmacy for pain relief.

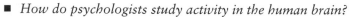

# THE BRAIN

- *How do psychologists study activity in the human brain?*
- *Do different parts specialize in certain functions or operate as an integrated system?*
- *Does each side of the brain have its own "mind"?*
- *How could this hypothesis be tested, and what do you think would be the result?*

Encased in a hard protective skull, the brain is the crown jewel of the nervous system. It weighs only about three pounds and constitutes only 1/45th of the human body's average weight. But, as we saw earlier, it contains billions of neurons and trillions of synaptic connections. For those who are interested only in anatomy, it was easy to determine the physical *structure* of the brain by dissecting brains removed from dead animals and from humans who had donated their bodies to science. For behavioral and cognitive neuroscientists, however, the task is more challenging: to determine the *functions* of the living brain and to understand its influences on the way we think, feel, and behave.

## TOOLS OF BEHAVIORAL NEUROSCIENCE

Before the term *neuroscience* had ever been uttered, Viennese physician Franz Joseph Gall (1758–1828) founded **phrenology,** the pseudoscientific theory that psychological characteristics are revealed by bumps on the skull. Apparently, as a young boy, Gall "noticed" that his friends who had the best memories also had prominent eyes and large foreheads. From this he speculated that the brain structure involved in verbal memory must lie behind the eyes. Similarly, Gall believed that speech, math ability, aggression, and other traits are "localized" in certain regions of the brain. In believing that there were many parts to the brain and that the parts were involved in different mental functions, Gall was on the right track. In using bumps on the skull to find these links, however, he was very much on the wrong track (Damasio, 1994; Zola-Morgan, 1995).

To fully understand and evaluate what researchers currently know about the human brain, it helps to be aware of *how* they arrive at that knowledge—the methods they use and why they use them. Thanks in part to advances in medical and computer technology, today's behavioral neuroscientists are like explorers on a new frontier. As we'll see, four types of research methods are commonly used: clinical case studies, experimental interventions, electrical recordings, and imaging techniques.

**Clinical Case Studies**  One approach to studying the brain is the clinical case study, in which researchers observe people with brain damage resulting from tumors, diseases, head injuries, or exposure to toxic substances. In the case of Phineas Gage, discussed earlier, massive damage to the frontal lobes was followed by changes in his personality (specifically, an inability to control impulses), yet his intellectual abilities remained unchanged. Thus, the case showed that the frontal lobes are involved in the control of behavior. Other case studies have also proved invaluable. Neurologist Oliver Sacks tells colorful and provocative stories about brain-damaged patients who exhibited specific deficits in speech, memory, motor behavior, sleep, and even their self-concept. In *An Anthropologist from Mars* (1995), for example, Sacks described an artist who suffered brain damage from a car accident. He lost all color vision but eventually gained more sensitivity to forms, textures, and patterns. As a result, he became a more productive painter than ever—in black and white.

Clinical evidence is tantalizing and often enlightening, but it cannot provide the sole basis for behavioral neuroscience. One drawback is that when one part of the brain is damaged, nearby neurons sometimes sprout new branches, and other structures sometimes take over the function. These forms of compensation are wonderfully adaptive, but they mask the effects of damage. Another drawback is that natural injuries are seldom localized, so the resulting deficit may not really be traceable to a single structure. In the Phineas Gage situation, for example, the skull was pierced by a long rod that was over an inch in diameter—hardly a surgical incision.

A third drawback of case studies in brain and behavior is that they often cannot be used to establish cause and effect. In a fascinating use of the case study method, neuroscientist Sandra Witelson gained access to the brain of physicist Albert Einstein, one of the greatest geniuses of modern history. When Einstein died in 1955, the pathologist who did the autopsy removed the brain and preserved it in a jar. More than forty years later, Witelson and her colleagues (1999) compared Einstein's brain tissues with those of other men who had died at a similar age. They found that the overall size of Einstein's brain was about average, but a region used in visuospatial and mathematical thinking was 15 percent wider than the others tested. It may be tempting to conclude from this result that Einstein was born with a brain uniquely gifted for physics, but the researchers were quick to suggest another possibility—perhaps this region of Einstein's brain grew *because* he used it so often. Clinical evidence alone cannot solve the puzzle.

*"By the deficits we may know the talents, by the exceptions we may know the rules, by studying pathology we may construct a model of health."*
—LAURENCE MILLER

**Experimental Interventions**   A second method of brain research is to "invade" the brain through an experimental intervention and then measure the effects on behavior. One invasive technique, often used by animal researchers, is to purposely disable, or "lesion," a part of the brain by surgically destroying it. Often this is done by anesthetizing an animal, implanting an electrode into a specific site in the brain, and passing a high-voltage current through it to burn the tissue.

Another technique is to administer drugs that are suspected of affecting neurotransmitters and other activity in the brain. Over the years, the effects of many substances on the brain and behavior have been tested in this manner—substances such as alcohol, caffeine, adrenaline, nicotine, and the sex hormones testosterone and androgen.

Yet another form of intervention is through the use of electrical brain stimulation. In these studies, a microelectrode is inserted in the brain and a mild electrical current is used to "activate" the neurons in a particular site. Most of these experiments are conducted with animals, but on occasion clues are derived from human brain-surgery patients. How does this occur? Since no two brains are exactly alike, brain surgeons often must "map" a patient's brain so they don't accidentally destroy key functions. Toward this end, the patient is given a local anesthetic and kept awake for the procedure. While treating epilepsy patients, for example, neurosurgeon Wilder Penfield stimulated different brain areas along the surface and found that, depending on the region he stimulated, the patients would report visual images, tingling sensations, muscular twitches, and other reactions (Penfield & Roberts, 1959).

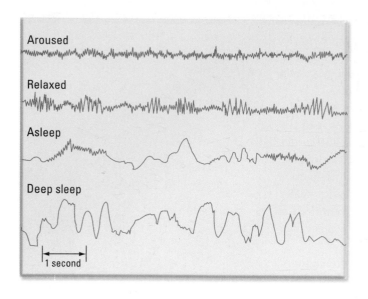

**FIGURE 2.8** **The EEG**
Through electrodes on a subject's scalp, the electroencephalograph records electrical activity in the brain and displays the output in line tracings called brain waves. Varying in their frequency (cycles per second) and amplitude (voltage), EEG patterns differ according to a person's mental state.

**electroencephalograph (EEG)** An instrument used to measure electrical activity in the brain through electrodes placed on the scalp.

**CT (computerized tomography) scan** A series of X rays taken from different angles and converted by computer into an image that depicts a horizontal slice of brain.

**PET (positron emission tomography) scan** A visual display of brain activity, as measured by the amount of glucose being used.

**magnetic resonance imaging (MRI)** A brain-scanning technique that uses magnetic fields and radio waves to produce clear, three-dimensional images.

**Electrical Recordings** The most exciting advances in behavioral neuroscience arise from techniques that are not invasive to the human subject. In 1929, German psychiatrist Hans Burger invented a machine that could detect, amplify, and record waves of electrical activity in the brain using metal disc electrodes pasted to the surface of the scalp. The instrument is called an **electroencephalograph (EEG)**, and the information it provides is in the form of line tracings called *brain waves* (see Figure 2.8).

As we'll see in later chapters, researchers using the EEG have found that brain waves differ depending on whether a person is excited, relaxed, pensive, drowsy, or asleep. It can also be used for diagnosing brain damage from tumors, strokes, infections, and various neurological disorders. For example, people with epilepsy have seizures because a certain portion of the brain is overexcitable and prone to fire in a wild manner, setting off electrical spikes, or "explosions." The EEG may even be useful for diagnosing *psycho*pathological conditions such as attention deficit disorder, schizophrenia, and depression (Niedermeyer & Da Silva, 1999; Nunez, 2003).

There are limits, however, to what EEG recordings can tell us. The problem is that the EEG merely summarizes all the electrical activity of billions of neurons firing along the brain's surface. Thus, as one group of researchers put it, "we are like blind men trying to understand the workings of a factory by listening outside the walls" (quoted by Hassett, 1978). For greater precision, some animal researchers use microelectrodes, wires with tips so tiny that they can stimulate or record the activity of a single cell.

**Brain-Imaging Techniques** When people think about the wonders of high technology, what comes to mind is global communication satellites and giant-size telescopes that can spy on the distant galaxies of the universe. But recent advances in technology have also enabled us to turn the scientific eye on ourselves, to inner recesses of the human brain never previously seen. Designed to provide visual images of the live human brain, without our ever having to lift a scalpel, this new technology uses computers to combine thousands of still "snapshots" into models of the brain in action. As described in *Images of Mind* (Posner & Raichle, 1994), there are several basic types of imaging techniques. Three of the most common, all popularly known by their initials, are CT, PET, and MRI.

First introduced to medicine in the 1970s, the **computerized tomography (CT) scan** is a computer-enhanced X-ray of the brain. In this technique, X-ray beams are passed through the head at 1-degree intervals over a 180-degree arc, and a computer is used to convert this information into an image that depicts a horizontal slice of the brain. This technique takes advantage of the fact that when a highly focused beam of X rays is passed through the body, the beam is affected by the relative density of the tissue through which it passes. CT scans are invaluable for diagnosing tumors and strokes and for identifying brain abnormalities in people who suffer from schizophrenia and other psychological disorders.

A second revolutionary imaging technique, one that can be used to map activity of the brain over time, is the **positron emission tomography (PET) scan**. Because glucose supplies the brain with energy, the level of activity in a given region of the brain can be measured by the amount of glucose it burns. After a tiny amount of radioactive glucose is injected into the brain, the scanner measures the amount of it consumed in different regions. The results are then fed to a computer, which produces an enhanced color picture (Martin et al., 1991). Can the PET scan actually spy on our thought processes? In a way, yes. Look at Figure 2.9, and you'll see the PET scans of a person with his eyes and ears open or closed. (In these scans, "hot" colors such as red, orange, and yellow indicate more activity, whereas cool colors such as violet, blue, and green mean less activity.)

Using the PET scan, psychologists have made some interesting discoveries. One is that it may be possible to distinguish among different types of psychological disorders by measuring brain activity (Andreasen, 1988; Resnick, 1992). For example, researchers had schizophrenia patients relax with their eyes closed and press a button whenever they started to hear imaginary voices and when they stopped hearing these voices. The result: On PET scans, hallucinating lit up certain areas of the brain more than others (Silbersweig et al., 1995).

Another interesting discovery is that certain regions of the brain become active when people think about the self. To demonstrate, researchers had subjects make different types of judgments about personality-trait words such as gentle, stubborn, and friendly. On some trials, subjects were asked to judge whether each word described them; on other trials they judged how desirable each trait was, how many syllables the word had, or whether it accurately described some other person. The results revealed that part of the right frontal lobe lit up when subjects made judgments about the self, but not when they made other types of judgments. As seen in PET scans, self-reflection is, in some ways, a unique mental state (Craik et al., 1999).

A "new and improved" technique is **magnetic resonance imaging (MRI)**. MRI is similar to a CT scan, but instead of using an X-ray it passes the subject's head through a strong but harmless magnetic field to align the brain's atoms. A quick pulse of radio waves is then used to disorient the atoms, which give off detectable signals as they return to normal. As shown in Figure 2.10, the MRI can produce clear and detailed pictures of the brain's soft tissues (Atlas, 2002). Particularly important today is a high-speed version of MRI known as *functional MRI* (fMRI), used to take moving pictures of the brain in action. The method is noninvasive and does not involve the use of radioactive materials, so researchers can do hundreds of scans on the same person to get detailed information about a particular brain's activity.

Still other techniques are being developed as you read this book. As shown in Figure 2.11, one new method combines EEG and MRI. In this method, the researcher simultaneously records electrical signals from up to 125 points on the scalp. He or she takes a new reading every few milliseconds as the subject receives some stimulus or engages in a specific task. A computer then analyzes changes across the different locations and creates an ongoing videolike record of electrical activity at the surface of a three-dimensional MR map of the brain (Gevins et al., 1995).

This new technology is generating tremendous excitement among psychologists who are interested in attention, perception, memory, and other cognitive processes (D'Esposito, 2002). Researchers are now saying, "This is the wonder technique

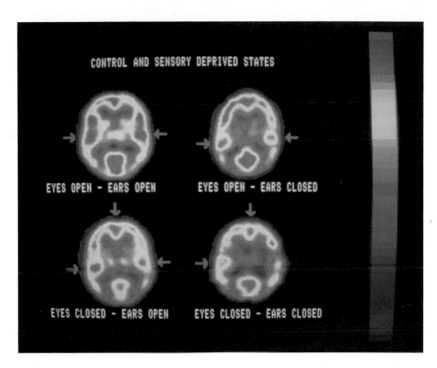

**FIGURE 2.9   PET scans**
After radioactive glucose has been injected into the brain, a scanner measures how much glucose is consumed in different regions. The results are displayed in a computer-enhanced picture in which hotter colors (red, orange, yellow) indicate more activity. In these images, visual areas of the brain "lit up" when the subject's eyes were open, as did auditory areas when the subject's ears were stimulated with sound.

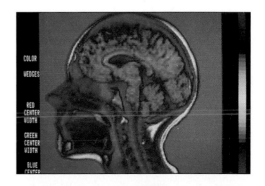

**FIGURE 2.10   The MRI**
Magnetic resonance imaging yields the best resolution for visualizing brain structures.

*In this fMRI study of face recognition, conducted at the National Institute of Mental Health, the participant from inside the magnet must match the face at the top of the display with one of those at the bottom. The result is a vivid picture of the brain's activity during the process of face recognition.*
(© 1994 Ray Chernush)

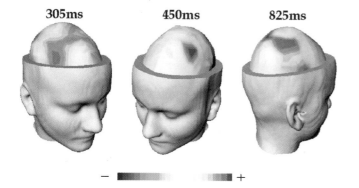

FIGURE 2.11 **Recording activity in a three-dimensional brain**
Using 124 electrodes attached to a soft helmet, electrical signals are recorded all over the scalp, measuring changes per milliseconds. Also using a computer to create ongoing MR images, researchers can generate a videolike record of activity in a three-dimensional model of the brain.

we've all been waiting for," and calling it "the most exciting thing to happen in the realm of cognitive neuroscience in my lifetime" (Blakeslee, 1993).

Does the brain respond differently to music than to words, or to rhythm than to melody? Is the brain of an artist different from that of a physicist? Some psychologists worry that these techniques will invite researchers to assume mistakenly that certain complex mental functions occur exclusively in local regions of the brain (Sarter et al., 1996; Uttal, 2001). Others are eager to use fMRI and other imaging technologies to explore these new frontiers (Cabeza & Nyberg, 2000; Raichle, 1994). Using fMRI, for example, researchers have found that certain parts of the human brain "light up" as uniquely activated when people work on arithmetic calculations than on other types of cognitive tasks (Rickard et al., 2000), form mental images of human faces as opposed to places (O'Craven & Kanwisher, 2000), and judge a person's emotions rather than physical characteristics (Gur et al., 2002).

## REGIONS OF THE BRAIN

The human brain is a unique product of evolution. In some ways it is similar to the brains of "lower" animals; in other ways it is quite different. Salmon, caribou, and migrating birds have navigational abilities unparalleled in our own species. Dogs, cats, and certain other mammals have senses of hearing and smell that are downright superhuman. Yet no other animal on the planet can solve problems, think about itself and the future, or communicate as we do. As we'll see, these relative strengths and weaknesses can be traced to the unique structure of the human brain.

Although the brain is a single organ containing interconnected pathways of nerve fibers, neuroscientists have found that there are really three mini-brains rolled into one. The *brainstem* is the old "inner core" that rests atop the spinal cord and helps to regulate primitive life-support functions such as breathing, heartbeat, and muscle movements. Surrounding the brainstem, the *limbic system* provides an increased capacity for motivation, emotional responses, and basic forms of learning and memory. And in the *cerebral cortex,* the wrinkled outer layer of the brain, "higher" mental processes enable more complex forms of learning, memory, thought, and language. The cerebral cortex is the last part to develop in the life of an individual. It also developed last in the species as a whole (see Figure 2.12).

**The Brainstem** As the spinal cord enters the skull, it enlarges into the **brainstem**, the primitive inner core. As illustrated in Figure 2.13, the brainstem contains three key structures: the medulla, the pons, and the reticular formation. Located just above the spinal cord, the **medulla** controls some of our most vital, involuntary functions—swallowing, breathing, and heart rate—and contributes to muscle control. As we'll soon see, it's also a "crossover" point where nerves from one side of the brain connect to the opposite side of the body. There's nothing particularly exotic about the medulla, but if it were severed, blood pressure would drop to zero, breathing would stop, and death would soon follow. Just above the medulla is a

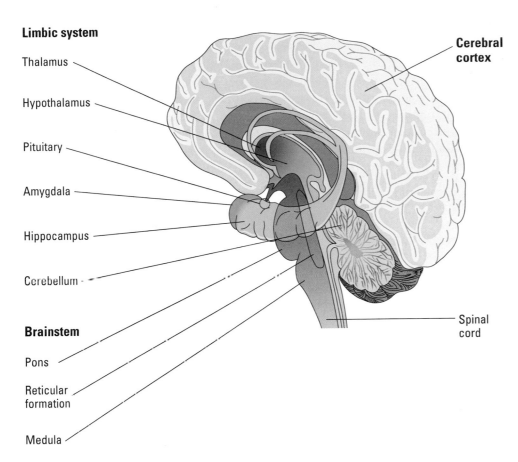

**Limbic system**

Thalamus

Hypothalamus

Pituitary

Amygdala

Hippocampus

Cerebellum

**Brainstem**

Pons

Reticular formation

Medula

Cerebral cortex

Spinal cord

**brainstem**    The inner core of the brain that connects to the spinal cord and contains the medulla, pons, and reticular formation. *Life support*

**medulla**    A brainstem structure that controls vital involuntary functions. *crossover point/lateral*

**pons**    A portion of the brainstem that plays a role in sleep and arousal.

**reticular formation**    A group of nerve cells in the brainstem that helps to control sleep, arousal, and attention.

**cerebellum**    A primitive brainstem structure that controls balance and coordinates complex voluntary movements.

FIGURE 2.12    **The human brain**
There are three main regions of the human brain. The brainstem is the old "inner core" that controls life support functions. The limbic system regulates motivation, emotion, and basic forms of learning and memory. The cerebral cortex, which features the wrinkled outer layer of the brain, controls "higher" mental processes that enhance learning, memory, thought, and language.

bulbous structure called the **pons** (meaning "bridge"), which helps to connect the lower and higher regions of the brain. The pons also has neurons that play a role in sleep and arousal. Damage to this area can put a person into a coma. Finally, the **reticular formation** is a netlike group of nerve cells and axons that project throughout the brain and help to control sleep, arousal, and attention. It is here that sensory information is filtered in or out of our consciousness.

Also attached to the back of the brainstem is the **cerebellum**, a peach-sized structure that means "little brain." Look again at Figure 2.13, and you'll see that the cerebellum resembles a miniature brain attached to the brain, wrinkles and all. This structure is one of the oldest in the nervous system and is highly developed in fish, birds, and lower mammals. It plays a role in learning and memory, but its primary functions (like that of certain other structures distributed throughout the brain) is balance and the coordination of muscle movements. In this regard, the cerebellum is like a sophisticated computer. It receives and integrates information from all the senses, takes into account the positions of the limbs, and makes rapid-fire calculations as to which muscle groups must be activated in order to run, jump, dance, break a fall, or throw

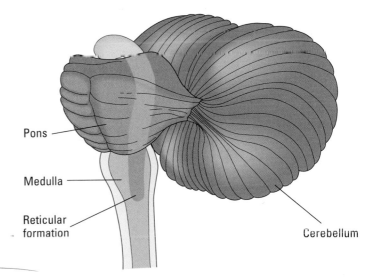

Pons

Medulla

Reticular formation

Cerebellum

FIGURE 2.13    **The brainstem**
The brainstem is the most primitive structure of the brain. Resting atop the spinal cord, it contains the medulla, pons, and reticular formation and is attached to the cerebellum.

**basal ganglia** Masses of gray matter in the brain that help to initiate and coordinate deliberate movements.

**limbic system** A set of loosely connected structures in the brain that help to regulate motivation, emotion, and memory.

**thalamus** A limbic structure that relays neural messages between the senses and areas of the cerebral cortex.

**amygdala** A limbic structure that controls fear, anger, and aggression.

a ball (Houk et al., 1996). The cerebellum is also activated by certain aspects of music. In a study of eight conductors listening to Bach, PET scans revealed that when the expected rhythm was altered, blood flow to parts of the cerebellum increased, even though the conductors had not moved a muscle (Parsons & Fox, 1998). Even among ordinary research participants, those trained to learn complex rhythms—compared to those exposed to random sequences—exhibit more activity in parts of the cerebellum (Ramnani & Passingham, 2001).

Alongside the cerebellum are the **basal ganglia,** large masses of gray matter that are involved in the coordination of slower, more deliberate movements such as turning the head or reaching for an object. Damage to the cerebellum and basal ganglia can make it difficult to coordinate various motor behaviors. The reason drunken drivers can't pass the roadside test given by the police ("Close your eyes, put out your arms, and touch your nose with the index finger") is that alcohol affects these areas.

**The Limbic System** Continuing up from the brainstem is a ring of loosely connected structures collectively known as the **limbic system.** Just above the inner core, yet surrounded by the cerebral cortex, the limbic system contains several structures that play a role in the regulation of motivation, emotion, and memory. Brain researchers disagree as to which structures actually qualify as "limbic" and whether they really form a unified "system." Still, the key structures here include the thalamus, the amygdala, the hippocampus, and the hypothalamus (see Figure 2.14).

**The Thalamus** Directly atop the brainstem, and buried like the pit inside a peach, is the **thalamus** ("inner chamber"). The thalamus is a sensory relay station that directs neural traffic between the senses and the cerebral cortex. All input from what you see, hear, taste, and touch is received in the thalamus and then sent for processing to the appropriate region of the cortex. For example, there's a special nucleus located in the thalamus that receives visual input from the optic nerve behind the eye and sends the information to the visual cortex. It's interesting that the sense of smell completely bypasses the thalamus because it has its own private relay station that directs input from the nose to the olfactory bulb, which sits near areas that control emotion. This may explain why perfume, cookies baking in the oven, freshly cut grass, and other scents often arouse powerful emotions in us.

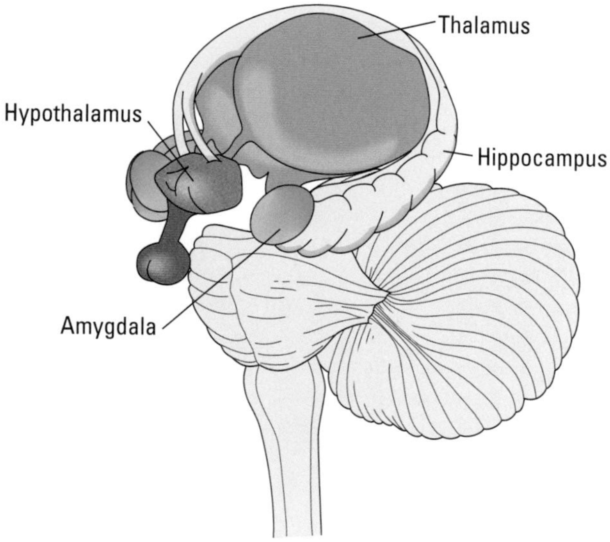

**FIGURE 2.14 The limbic system**
Just above the inner core, yet surrounded by the cerebral cortex, the limbic system plays a role in motivation, emotion, and memory. As shown, this system is composed of many structures, including the thalamus, amygdala, hippocampus, and hypothalamus.

**The Amygdala** The **amygdala** is an almond-shape bulge that has at times been called an "aggression center." This phrase oversimplifies both the behavioral functions of the amygdala and the biological roots of aggression. But there is a link, and experiments have shown that stimulation of the amygdala can produce anger and violence, as well as fear and anxiety (Davis, 1992). In fact, experiments suggest that the amygdala plays a more general role in learning, memory, and the experience of both positive and negative emotions (Aggleton, 2001; Rolls, 1999).

In 1937, psychologists Heinrich Kluver and neurosurgeon Paul Bucy found that lesions of the temporal lobe, including the amygdala, calmed ferocious rhesus monkeys. Later experiments on other wild animals revealed the same mellowing effect. Can amygdala lesions be used to treat people who are uncontrollably violent? In one case, Julia, a twenty-one-year-old woman, had suffered from epilepsy since childhood. Every now and then, she would have seizures that were accompanied by fits of rage, temper tantrums, and violent outbursts. Julia was dangerous to herself and others. Four times she tried to commit suicide. In one incident, she plunged a dinner knife into the chest of a woman who had accidentally bumped into her. Eventually Julia's father called neurosurgeon Vernon Mark for help. Mark implanted electrodes in Julia's brain to record electrical activity, and he detected abnormal discharges in the amygdala. Next he tried electrical stimulation. In most sites, nothing happened. But activating the amygdala triggered explosive attacks. At one point, Mark stimulated the amygdala while Julia was playing the guitar. Suddenly she stopped, stared into space, and smashed the guitar against the wall, just missing the doctor's head. Mark treated Julia by destroying part of her amygdala, and her fits of rage eventually, over time, subsided (Mark & Ervin, 1970).

Apparently, there is a link between the amygdala and aggression. We'll see in Chapter 17, however, that the use of psychosurgery—operating on the brain as a way to alter behavior—raises profound ethical questions (Valenstein, 1986; Pressman, 1998).

**The Hippocampus**   The largest structure in the limbic system is the **hippocampus**, which is Greek for "seahorse," whose shape it roughly resembles. Research reveals that the hippocampus plays a key role in the formation of new memories. In rats, monkeys, and many other animals, hippocampal lesions cause deficits in memory. In fact, when the structure is removed from black-capped chickadees—food-storing birds whose brains have an unusually large hippocampus compared to nonstoring birds—they lose the natural ability to recover food they had previously stored (Hampton & Shettleworth, 1996). In humans, brain scans reveal that the hippocampal area is shrunken in people with severe memory loss, even while surrounding areas of the brain are intact (Squire, 1992). As we'll see in Chapter 6, long-term memories are not necessarily stored in the hippocampus, but they may well be formed there (Gluck & Myers, 2000).

**The Hypothalamus**   At the base of the brain, there is a tiny yet extraordinary limbic structure called the **hypothalamus** (which means "below the thalamus"). The hypothalamus is the size of a kidney bean, weighs only about half an ounce, and constitutes less than 1 percent of the brain's total volume. Yet it regulates the body's temperature and the activities of the autonomic nervous system, controls the endocrine system by triggering the release of hormones into the bloodstream, helps regulate basic emotions such as fear and rage, and is involved in basic drives such as hunger, thirst, sleep, and sex. The hypothalamus is also home to one of the brain's true "pleasure centers," an area associated with strong feelings of pleasure when it is stimulated (Wise, 1996; Rolls, 1999). If you had to sacrifice an ounce of brain tissue, you wouldn't want to take it from the hypothalamus.

**The Cerebral Cortex**   The **cerebral cortex** is the outermost covering of the brain. Its name is derived from the words *cerebrum* (which is Latin for "brain") and *cortex* (which means "bark"). It is the newest product of evolution, overlaid on the older structures. If you were to examine the cerebral cortex of various species, you would see that the more complex the animal, the bigger the cerebral cortex is relative to the rest of the brain. You would also notice that in complex animals, the cortex is wrinkled, or folded in on itself, rather than smooth, and is lined with ridges and valleys. This wrinkling allows for more tissue to fit compactly inside the skull (just as crumpling up a piece of paper allows one to squeeze it into a small space).

As shown in Figure 2.15, the cerebral cortex is virtually absent in all fish, reptiles, and birds. But it is present in mammals (particularly in primates, dolphins, and whales) and is the most highly developed in humans. In volume, it constitutes 80 percent of the human brain (Kolb & Whishaw, 1990). Whenever you read, write, count, speak, reflect on the past, think about the future, or daydream about being rich and famous, billions of neurons are firing in the cerebral cortex.

 2.3

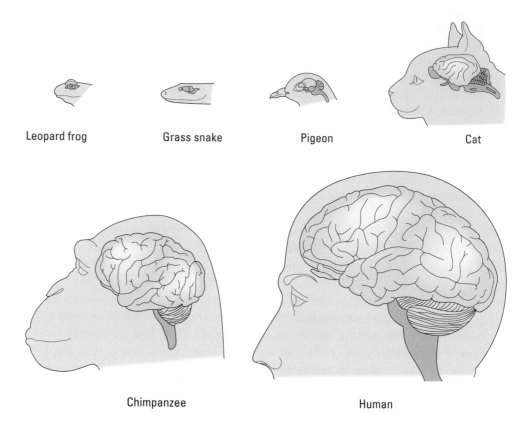

Leopard frog  Grass snake  Pigeon  Cat

Chimpanzee  Human

**FIGURE 2.15** **The cerebral cortex in animals**
From fish and birds to mammals, primates, and humans, there is an increase in the relative size and wrinkling of the cerebral cortex.

The cortex is divided into left and right hemispheres, and each hemisphere is further divided along deep grooves, called fissures, into four sections called lobes. These are the *frontal lobes* (in front, just behind the forehead), the *temporal lobes* (at the temples, above the ears), the *parietal lobes* (in the back, at the top of the skull), and the *occipital lobes* (in the back, at the base of the skull). Although these regions describe the anatomy of the cerebral cortex, most psychologists prefer to divide the areas of the brain according to the functions they serve. As shown in Figure 2.16, the functional regions include the sensory areas of the cortex, the motor cortex, the association cortex, and two special areas where language is processed and produced.

**Sensory and Motor Areas**   While operating on his hundreds of epilepsy patients, Wilder Penfield, in 1947, stimulated exposed parts of the cortex with a tiny electric probe and thereby "mapped" the human cortex. One of Penfield's great discoveries was that certain areas of the brain specialize in receiving sensory information. When he touched the occipital lobe in the back of the brain, patients "saw" flickering lights, colors, stars, spots, wheels, and other visual displays. This area is the primary visual cortex—and damage to it can leave a person blind. Or damage to a specific part of it may result in a more specific visual deficit. For example, in *The Man Who Mistook His Wife for a Hat* (1985), Oliver Sacks (1985) tells a story about a patient who suffered occipital lobe damage. As this patient looked for his hat while preparing to leave Sacks's office, he grabbed his wife's head and tried to lift it. Suffering from visual agnosia—an inability to recognize familiar objects—this patient had apparently mistaken his wife for a hat.

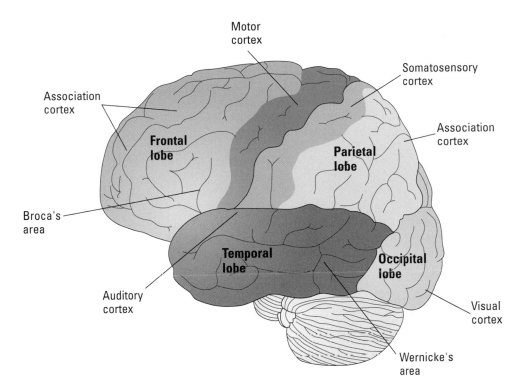

**FIGURE 2.16   The cerebral cortex**
The cortex is divided along deep grooves, or fissures, into four lobes. Within these lobes, areas are further distinguished by their functions. These include the sensory areas (visual, auditory, and somatosensory), the motor area, the association areas, and two special areas found in the left hemisphere—Broca's area and Wernicke's area—where language is processed are produced.

Penfield discovered other sensory areas in the cortex as well. When he stimulated a small area of the temporal lobe, called the auditory cortex, the patients "heard" doorbells, engines, and other sounds. Indeed, damage in this area can cause deafness. And when he stimulated a narrow strip in the parietal lobe, the **somatosensory cortex,** patients "felt" a tingling of the leg, hand, cheek, or other part of the body. In general, Figure 2.17 shows that the more sensitive to touch a body part is, the larger is the cortical area devoted to it. Today, researchers continue to study this system in an effort to uncover "the brain's own body image" (Nelson, 2001).

Mirroring the somatosensory cortex is another narrow strip that specializes in the control of motor functions. Once again, much of what we know came from Penfield's work. Stimulating different parts of this strip triggers movement in different parts of the body. Stimulate the top, and a leg twitches; stimulate the bottom, and the tongue or jaw moves. All six hundred muscles of the human body are represented in this area, called the **motor cortex.** As in the somatosensory cortex, the greater the need for precise control over a body part, the larger is its area in this strip. Thus, Figure 2.17 shows more surface area devoted to the face, hands, and fingers than to the arms and legs.

**Association Areas**   The cerebral cortex does more than just process sensory information and direct motor responses. There are also vast areas that collectively make up the **association cortex.** These areas communicate with both the sensory and motor areas and house the brain's higher mental processes. Electrical stimulation of these sites does not elicit specific sensations or motor twitches in specific parts of the body, so it's hard to pin these areas down. But damage to the association cortex can have devastating results. In the frontal lobes, such damage can change someone's

**somatosensory cortex**   The area of the cortex that receives sensory information from the touch receptors in the skin.

**motor cortex**   The area of the cortex that sends impulses to voluntary muscles.

**association cortex**   Areas of the cortex that communicate with the sensory and motor areas and house the brain's higher mental processes.

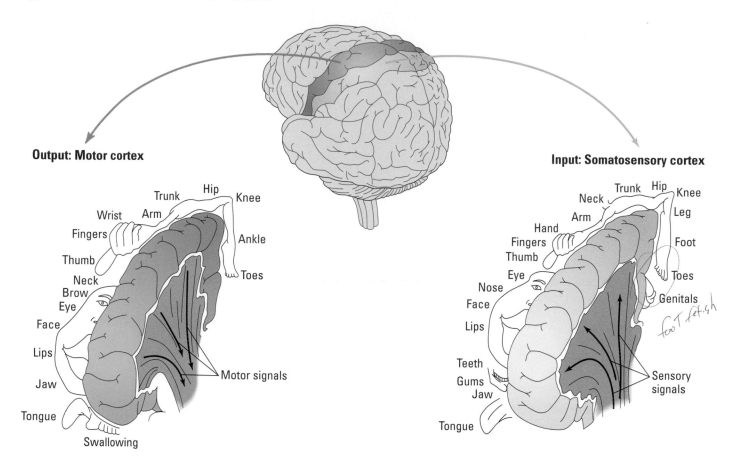

**FIGURE 2.17    The somatosensory and motor areas**
Each part of the body is represented in the somatosensory (right) and motor (left) cortex. Note that the amount of tissue devoted to a body part does not correspond to its actual size. Rather, more area is devoted to parts that are most sensitive to touch (such as the lips) and in need of fine motor control (such as the thumbs).

personality, as in the case of Phineas Gage. In other association areas, damage can impair specific kinds of memories, distort our spatial awareness, render us oblivious to emotions, or cause odd speech deficits (Saper et al., 2000).

**Language Areas**   For the most part, our ability to adapt to life's demands through learning, memory, and thought processes is spread throughout the regions of the cortex. But language—a complex activity for which humans, and in some ways only humans, are uniquely prepared—is different. Carved within the cortex are two special areas dedicated to language. One plays a role in the production of speech; the other, comprehension. In 1861, French physician Paul Broca observed that people who have suffered damage in part of the frontal lobe of the left hemisphere lose the ability to form words to *produce* fluent speech. The words sputter out slowly, and what is said is often not grammatical ("Buy milk store"). This region of the brain is called **Broca's area** (Schiller, 1992).

A few years later, German neurologist Carl Wernicke (1874) found that people with damage to part of the left temporal lobe (subsequently called **Wernicke's area**) lose their ability to comprehend speech. In short, people with language disorders, or aphasias, demonstrate that there are at least two distinct cortical centers for language. People with Broca's aphasia can comprehend speech but have trouble producing it. Those with Wernicke's aphasia can speak, but their comprehension is

**Broca's area**   A region in the left hemisphere of the brain that directs the muscle movements in the production of speech.

**Wernicke's area**   A region in the left hemisphere of the brain that is involved in the comprehension of language.

impaired. Interestingly, these two areas are connected by a neural pathway, thus forming part of a language circuit within the brain (Geschwind, 1979; Brown & Hagoort, 1999).

**The Integrated Brain** Even though Penfield was able to pinpoint or "map" various locations in the cortex that house sensory and motor functions, we mustn't overstate the case for localization. Although different cortical regions *specialize* in certain functions, the healthy human brain operates as an *integrated* system. This point is illustrated by the role of the brain in language, whereby different cortical areas are activated depending on whether a word is read, spoken, written, or presented in music—or even whether it is a verb or a noun (Caramazza & Hillis, 1991). Consider what it takes simply to repeat the written word *ball*. From the eyes, the stimulus must travel for processing to the visual cortex. The input must then pass through the angular gyrus to be recorded, to Wernicke's area to be understood, and then to Broca's area, where signals are sent to the motor cortex, which drives the muscles of your lips, tongue, and larynx so that you can repeat the word (see Figure 2.18).

It's also important to note that this model may not accurately describe the ways in which different brain regions interact to produce language. Figure 2.18 seems to suggest that the neural events related to language occur in serial fashion, one step at a time. In fact, evidence suggests that language and other complex mental processes may be more accurately represented by *parallel* models in which neural signals move along several routes at once and are processed simultaneously (Peterson et al., 1989). As in an orchestra, it takes the coordinated work of many instruments, often playing together, to make music.

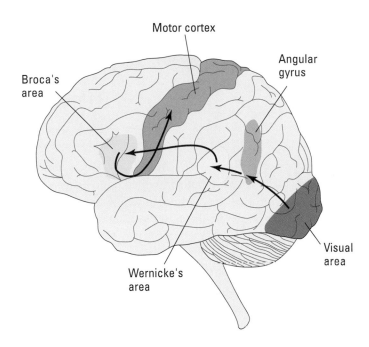

**FIGURE 2.18  Language processing**
Although different regions specialize in certain functions, the brain operates as an integrated system. The "simple" act of speaking a written word, for example, requires a coordinated effort of the eyes, the visual cortex, and angular gyrus, Wernicke's area, Broca's area, and the motor cortex.

# THE SPLIT BRAIN

Before the first known psychology laboratory was founded, in 1879, scientists interested in the nervous system and intrigued by the relationship between the body and the mind debated an old question concerning the brain. The "traditional" view was that the left and right hemispheres were symmetrical, mirror images of each other. Just as the body has two eyes, two ears, two legs, and two hands, the brain has two identical hemispheres. The symmetry argument seemed self-evident: The brain looks like the two identical halves of a walnut packed together inside a shell.

Others argued that things are not always as they seem. Portrait artists know fully well that the human face is not perfectly symmetrical; one eye may be larger than the other, or one cheek may have a dimple that the other does not. The same asymmetry is true of the brain. As we saw, Broca (1861) and Wernicke (1874) both found key language centers only in the left hemisphere. From the start, this finding gave rise to the notion that the left hemisphere is "dominant" (Jackson, 1958)—a notion also used to explain why most people in the world are right-handed (see *Psychology and Health*). Indeed, nearly all right-handers and a majority of left-handers process language mainly in the left hemisphere. This finding also suggested that the two hemispheres are specialized for different functions. Carrying this idea a giant step further, German physicist Gustav Fechner (1860) proposed that each side of the brain has its own mind. If your brain

*Something I owe to the soil that grew—*
*More to the life that fed—*
*But most to Allah who gave me two*
*Separate sides of my head.*
*I would go without shirt or shoes,*
*Friends, tobacco, or bread*
*Sooner than for an instant lose*
*Either side of my head.*

—RUDYARD KIPLING (*KIM*, 1901)

# BEING LEFT-HANDED IN A RIGHT-HANDED WORLD

With which hand do you write? Which hand do you use to throw a ball? In which hand do you hold your toothbrush or a knife? In which hand do you hold a match to strike it? In short, are you mostly right-handed or left-handed?

Roughly 90 percent of people are right-handed, a percentage that is remarkably consistent over time and place. Compelling archeological evidence suggests that this preference is prehistoric. Fossils show that Paleolithic stone tools and weapons were made for the right hand. Most hand tracings believed to have been made by Cro-Magnon people were of the left hand—which means they were drawn with the right hand. And sketches of men and women found on cave walls and inside Egyptian tombs typically depict the subjects using the right hand. This asymmetry is not the likely product of culture but, rather, of a human genetic predisposition toward right-handedness (Annett, 2002; Corballis, 1997).

Modern studies, too, show that right-hand predominance is universal; even most thumb-sucking fetuses suck the right thumb rather than the left (Hepper et al., 1990). This bias is not found in cats, rats, or monkeys.

Chimpanzees, our closest relatives, do tend to use the right hand for pointing, begging for food, and otherwise communicating—but this bias is not very pronounced (Hopkins & Leavens, 1998; Hopkins & Pearson, 2000). It's interesting that whereas nine out of ten humans are right-handed, only eight out of ten exhibit a preference for the right foot, seven out of ten for the right eye, and six out of ten for the right ear (Coren, 1993). Yet some situations do appear to favor left-handedness. For example, since the start of major-league baseball more than a hundred years ago, the number of left-handed batters and pitchers—who enjoy a competitive advantage—steadily increased before stabilizing at about 30 percent (Goldstein & Young, 1996).

Does "handedness" really matter? Perhaps. Research shows that left-handers are more likely to emerge as gifted athletes, mathematicians, and artists. But they are also more likely to have allergies, reading disabilities, and certain other disorders. Investigating the links between cerebral lateralization and behavior, Clare Porac and Stanley Coren (1981) surveyed 5,147 men and women of all ages in North America. To their surprise, the percentage of

*Famous lefties—Barry Bonds, Paul McCartney and Julia Roberts*

left-handers in the population steadily declined over the life span. As shown in Figure 2.19, 15 percent of the ten-year-olds were left-handed, compared to only 5 percent of fifty-year-olds and less than 1 percent of eighty-year-olds. At the age of 85, right-handers outnumbered left-handers by a margin of 200 to 1. Some researchers have since replicated this puzzling finding (Halpern & Coren, 1993).

For the psychologist detective the question is, why is there an age-related drop in the number of left-handers in the population? There are two possible explanations. One is the *longevity hypothesis,* which states that left-handers simply have a shorter life span. In support of this view, Coren and Halpern (1991) examined 987 death certificates and found that the average age of death was higher for right-handers than for left-handers. Yet other researchers have found that the differences in longevity are small (Harris, 1993). In one study, investigators surveyed six thousand people, fifteen to seventy years old, about their hand preferences. Nine years later, 387 of these respondents had died—and none of the deaths were related to handedness (Ellis et al., 1998). A second possible explanation is the *modification hypothesis:* The number of left-handers

diminishes with age because many natural lefties switch to the right hand because of pressures from parents, teachers, or an environment that is far better suited to right-handedness. Modification may be the more plausible explanation. Indeed, the decline in left-handedness is matched by an increased number of right-handers who say they had switched when younger (Hugdahl et al., 1993).

Psychologists may disagree about why there are relatively few left-handers in the elderly population, but all agree that the physical environment is designed more for the comfort and safety of right-handers. Scissors and pruning shears have handles shaped so that one hole is angled correctly for the right thumb and the other hole is for the other fingers of the right hand. In schools, spiral notebooks, chairs with built-in desktops on the right, and even rulers are designed for the right hand. In the workplace, portable power saws, computer keyboards, and certain types of heavy machinery create problems as well. For example, on-off and safety switches are almost always on the right side for quick use in an emergency. It's no wonder, says Coren (1993), that lefties are so often stereotyped as clumsy and awkward.

These inconveniences may be like booby traps hazardous to the health of left-handers. Coren asked nearly two thousand college students to report on accidents they had experienced in the past two years. Responses showed that left-handers were 89 percent more likely to have accident-related injuries requiring medical attention in sports, at work, at home, and, most of all, driving a car. Why are cars a risk? Coren notes that driving on the right side of the road puts the steering wheel on the left and the gear shifting on the right—a design that favors right-handedness. Can anything be done to improve matters? Yes. The physical environment can be made more "user friendly" for left-handers. Tool grips can be designed for lefties at no extra cost, on-off and safety switches can be placed on both sides of a machine, and left-handed kitchen utensils, power tools, school supplies, and office equipment can be made available. Many ambidextrous items can also be manufactured—such as soup ladles with two pouring lips, knives with serrated edges on both sides of the blade, tools with finger grooves that can accommodate either hand, and instrument panels with controls that are centered. Solutions would not be difficult to implement.

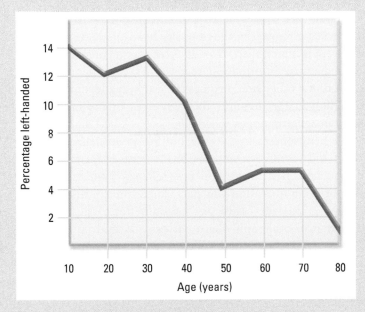

**FIGURE 2.19   Left-handedness across the life span**
In a study of 5,147 individuals, the percentage of left-handers in the sample declined with age (Coren, 1993).

**corpus callosum** A bundle of nerve fibers that connects the left and right hemispheres.

**split brain** A surgically produced condition in which the corpus callosum is severed, thus cutting the link between the left and right hemispheres of the brain.

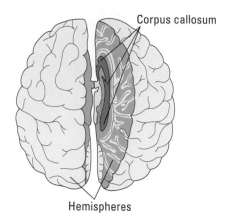

FIGURE 2.20 **The corpus callosum**
Containing millions of nerve fibers, the corpus callosum joins the left and right hemispheres.

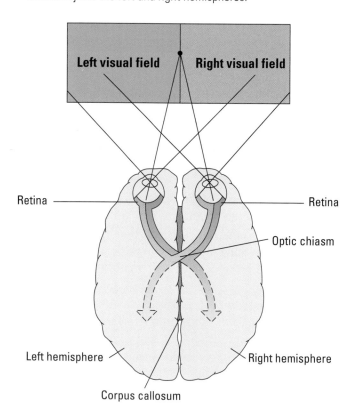

FIGURE 2.21 **Visual processing**
Both eyes send information to both hemispheres, but images in the right half of the visual field are sent to the left hemisphere, and images in the left half of the visual field are sent to the right hemisphere. Each image is instantly sent to the other side through the corpus callosum.

could be divided in half, he speculated, you would have two separate streams of consciousness. What a fascinating concept for an experiment! At the time, Fechner had no idea that such an experiment would one day come to pass.

## Split–Brain Studies

For people with severe epilepsy, seizures are the brain's equivalent of thunder-and-lightning storms. A seizure usually starts in one small area, but it quickly spreads across the brain from one side to the other. The experience can be terrifying, and at times life-threatening. In the past, neurosurgeons tried to control the problem by removing the overactive area, but these operations had only limited success. To prevent the seizures from spreading, a more radical approach was needed. The goal was to separate the two hemispheres. The method was to cut the **corpus callosum,** a four-inch-long, quarter-inch-thick bundle consisting of millions of white nerve fibers that join the two hemispheres (see Figure 2.20). This **split-brain** surgery often eliminates epileptic seizures, as hoped. But are there psychological side effects? Was Fechner right in proposing that a split brain, in which the link between the two hemispheres is severed, contains two separate minds?

Before we examine the effects of split-brain surgery, let's consider the divisions of labor within the brain. Recall that the left hemisphere receives sensory input from, and sends motor commands to, the right side of the body (hands, legs, arms, and so on), whereas the right hemisphere communicates with the left side of the body. Processing visual and auditory input is somewhat more complex. Both eyes send information to both hemispheres, but images in the right half of the visual field are sent to the left hemisphere, and images in the left half of the visual field are sent to the right hemisphere. In other words, if you're looking straight ahead at someone, images on the left are sent by both eyes to the right hemisphere, and images on the right are sent by both eyes to the left hemisphere (see Figure 2.21). Auditory inputs are also sent to both hemispheres, but sounds received in one ear register in the opposite hemisphere first.

If your brain is intact, then this odd crossover arrangement poses no problem because information received by each hemisphere is quickly sent to the other side through the corpus callosum. By sharing information in this manner, the two sides of the brain work as a team. But what happens when the neuron-filled highway that connects the hemispheres is severed? In 1963, two neurosurgeons, Philip Vogel and Joseph Bogen, described the case of a forty-eight-year-old man who had severe epileptic seizures following a head injury. A split-brain operation was performed (the corpus callosum was cut), and it was successful. As for side effects, the man's behavior, like that of other split-brain patients, seemed normal (tests generally show that perceptual abilities, intelligence, memory, and personality are unaffected). But when researchers probe beneath surface appearances, some unusual effects are revealed (Iaccino, 1993; Gazzaniga, 1998; Springer & Deutsch, 1998).

Roger Sperry (who was awarded a Nobel prize in 1981 and died in 1994), Michael Gazzaniga (his student), and others have helped bring this picture into focus through an ingenious series of studies, such as the one cited at the beginning of this chapter. Involving split-brain patients, the basic procedure was to present information to one hemisphere or the other, and then to measure what the subject "knew" by testing each hemisphere separately.

In one study, Sperry (1968) asked a female patient, identified as N.G., to stare at a black dot in the center of a screen. Then, for only a fraction of a second, he flashed a picture of a spoon either to the right or left of the dot and asked, "What do you see?" The result was fascinating. When the image was shown in the right visual field, and thus sent to the left hemisphere, N.G. was quick to reply that she saw a spoon. But when the image was presented on the left side and sent to the right hemisphere, she could not say what she saw. Why not? As noted earlier, speech is controlled by the left hemisphere. If an image in the right side of the brain cannot cross over to the left side, then the person cannot transform what is seen into words. But wait. How do we know that N.G. actually saw the spoon? Maybe the right hemisphere is just stupid. To probe further, Sperry asked N.G. to reach behind a screen and feel an assortment of objects, such as a pencil, an eraser, a key, and a piece of paper. "Which of these did you see before?" Easy. Touching the objects with her left hand (which sent the sensations to the right hemisphere), she selected the spoon. The right side knew all along it had seen a spoon, but only the left side could say so (see Figure 2.22).

In a second, similar study, Gazzaniga (1967) had split-brain patients stare at a black dot and flashed the word *teacup* on the screen. The letters *tea* were presented to the left visual field (the right hemisphere), and *cup* was presented to the right visual field (the left hemisphere). If you were the subject—and if your corpus callosum was intact—you would see the full word, *teacup*. But the split-brain patients reported seeing only *cup*, the portion of the word that was flashed to the left hemisphere. Again, how do we know they actually saw the second part of the word? When told to choose between the two parts by pointing with the left hand, they pointed to *tea*, the letters sent to the right hemisphere. As in the spoon study, each hemisphere was in touch with only half of the total input. Under normal circumstances, stimuli reaching both hemispheres are blended to form a unified experience. Disconnected, each hemisphere has a mind of its own.

In a third study, Jerre Levy and others (1972) took pictures of faces, cut them vertically in half, and pasted different right and left halves together. These composite photographs were then presented rapidly on slides. As in other studies, subjects stared at a center dot so that half of the image fell on either side. Look at the stimulus presented in Figure 2.23. When asked what they saw, subjects said it was a child. Because they were forced to respond in words, the left hemisphere dominated, causing them to name the image in the right visual field. But when subjects were told to point to the face with the left hand, they pointed to the woman wearing glasses, whose image was projected on the left side. Remarkably, split-brain patients did not seem to know that the composite face was unusual.

### How Split-Brain Patients Adapt

Split-brain patients exhibit so much "disconnection" in laboratory tests that one wonders how they manage to get along in their everyday affairs. To be sure, some instances of bizarre behavior have been observed. One patient had trouble dressing because he would pull his pants up with one hand and pull them down with the other. Another couldn't decide what to wear one morning because she would pick one item of clothing from the closet with her right hand and a different item with her left hand. In instances like these, one hand literally does not know what the other hand is doing.

Although there are stories like these to be told, severe disconnection experiences are not all that common. Why not? One possibility is that some input reaches both hemispheres through "subcortical" (below the cortex) structures that remain connected after the corpus callosum is cut. Justine Sergent (1990) explored this issue in a split-brain study in which she flashed pictures of celebrities to the left or right

**FIGURE 2.22    Sperry's split-brain experiment**
When the image of a spoon was projected to the right hemisphere, the split-brain patient could not say what she saw. Yet when she felt various objects with her left hand, she selected the spoon. The right side knew all along that it saw the spoon, but only the left side could say so (Sperry, 1968).

2.4

## THE PROCESS OF DISCOVERY

# MICHAEL S. GAZZANIGA
### Splitting the brain . . . and the mind

**Q: How did you first become interested in psychology?**

**A:** I think it is virtually impossible to not be interested in psychology. For me it started in college, at Dartmouth, when I took a course on emotions, then migrated into studying visual perception. This all came while I was majoring in zoology, which is where I learned about Roger Sperry's work on how neurons grew back in a specific manner. Sperry wrote with such compelling clarity I was immediately drawn to his work. He was at Caltech and my home was nearby, so I wrote him to ask for a summer job. He was able to provide one and that summer changed my life. Sperry was doing split-brain work on animals. I was intrigued and became interested in psychological aspects of brain function.

**Q: How did you come up with your important discovery?**

**A:** When I returned to Dartmouth, I thought it would be a great idea to test patients that had been operated upon to cure their epilepsy at the University of Rochester. These tests would indicate if information presented to one side of the brain would be known to the other side of the brain. I wrote to Sperry with my ideas and he supported my effort. Those studies didn't get done. I, however, was bitten by the intellectual questions, so I applied to graduate school, abandoned medical school plans, and started my work with Sperry. I was there for only moments when Sperry, knowing of my interest in human testing, told me to prepare for a possible patient.

I built a tachistoscope, devised test stimuli, and all the rest. One summer day the first split-brain patient came for preoperative testing. I ran my tests and because his brain was intact, he behaved completely normally, being able to name stimuli presented to either half

brain. He was then taken home to await surgery. Dr. Peter Vogel and Joseph Bogen soon operated, and after a recovery period he returned to Caltech for postoperative testing. That is a day I will never forget. The patient was in a wheel chair, and I rolled him into the testing room I had devised. I first showed him a picture in his right visual field and he easily named it. I then showed a picture to his left hemisphere. He said nothing had been presented! The human split-brain research story was born.

**Q: How has the field you inspired developed over the years?**

**A:** There are many things that have happened, including the naming of the field, cognitive neuroscience. With the advent of brain imaging, electrical recordings, animal models, and gene expression work, the field has rocketed to a complexity and activity level that is staggering in its importance and yield.

**Q: What's your prediction on where the field is heading?**

**A:** It is a risky enterprise to attempt to predict the future. Charles Townes, the Nobel Laureate who invented the laser once remarked, "The beautiful thing about a new idea is that you don't know about it yet." New ideas will come along as they are needed. In this field, my guess is that computational ideas will come to the front and instruct us on how the nervous system computes and therein generates our psychological lives bounded by reason, perception, language, and emotions.

---

*Michael S. Gazzaniga is Director of the Center of Cognitive Neuroscience at Dartmouth College.*

hemisphere and asked a series of probing questions. At one point, she presented a picture of Robert Redford to the patient's right hemisphere and asked, "Is this a man or a woman?" The patient responded, "I am not sure . . . a man." Below is part of the interview:

Q: Does this man look familiar to you?
A: I think so.
Q: Where have you seen him?
A: I don't know.
Q: What does he do for a living?
A: Is he a movie actor? . . . Yes, an actor.

A

B
"Whom did you see?"

"It was the child."

C
"Point to the person you saw."

FIGURE 2.23    **Levy's split-brain experiment**
Split-brain subjects stared at a dot and viewed a composite of two faces (A). When asked what they saw, subjects chose the child—the image sent to the verbal left hemisphere (B). But when subjects pointed to the face with the left hand, they chose the woman with glasses—whose image was received by the right hemisphere (C) (Levy et al., 1983).

Q: What kind of character does he play?
A: A playboy.
Q: What do you mean?
A: He is quite handsome, don't you think?
Q: How do you know he is handsome?
A: Well, I know.
Q: Can you picture him? Can you describe his face?
A: No, I can't say what he looks like but I think he's handsome.
Q: Can you recall some movies of his you saw?
A: I know I have seen him play, but I can't tell any movie.
Q: Do you know his name?
A: No.

Now notice what happened when the same picture was presented to the patient's left hemisphere.

Q: Did I show this face before?
A: No.
Q: Does he look like the one you just saw?
A: No. I don't know.
Q: Do you know who he is?
A: Yes. He is quite handsome too . . . Robert Redford.

These scripts are typical of the split-brain syndrome: The patient's right hemisphere could not identify or describe Robert Redford's picture when it was presented in the left visual field. And when it appeared in the right visual field, the patient did not know that she had seen it before. But notice that even though she could not identify the picture through the right hemisphere, somehow she knew that it depicted a handsome male actor. Sergent speculated that the disconnection in split-brain patients is only partial, not complete, and that at least some information may have slipped into the right hemisphere through subcortical structures (Hoptman &

**cerebral lateralization** The tendency for each hemisphere of the brain to specialize in different functions.

Davidson, 1994). Although it's not clear how much cross-talk occurs in these lesser structures, research suggests that our right and left hemispheres "cooperate" when we need to perform complex tasks (Banich, 1998; Weissman & Banich, 2000).

**Cerebral Lateralization** Split-brain research has generated tremendous excitement in behavioral neuroscience. When the corpus callosum is severed, most input to one hemisphere is trapped, unable to pass to the other side. As a result, neither hemisphere knows what the other is doing. But what about the day-to-day operations of a normal and healthy brain, corpus callosum and all? We know that speech is usually located in the left hemisphere, but are there other asymmetries in the human brain? Are other functions similarly **lateralized**? Does one side or the other control math, music, or the ability to recognize faces?

Several different methods are used to determine whether hemispheric differences exist in the "connected" brain. One method is to compare people with damage to the right or left hemisphere. A second method is to present various tasks and then measure activity in both sides of the brain using EEG recordings, measures of cerebral blood flow, or the imaging techniques described earlier. To the extent that a given task is processed in one hemisphere more than in the other, that hemisphere should be relatively more active. A third method is to present a stimulus to either the right or left hemisphere and measure the speed with which subjects act on the information. If the input has to be relayed through the corpus callosum to the other side, it will take a subject up to twenty milliseconds longer to make a response. A fourth method is to briefly sedate the right or left hemisphere and then test for disruptive effects.

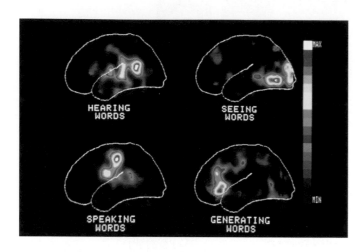

**FIGURE 2.24** **The talking left hemisphere**
PET scans show that a single word activated different left-hemisphere areas depending on whether it was heard, seen, spoken, or thought about. Notice that these "lit-up" areas are in the visual cortex, auditory cortex, Broca's area, and frontal lobes, respectively.

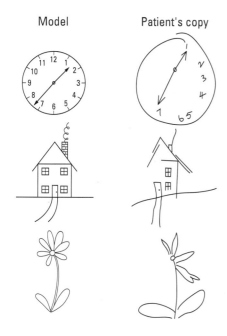

**FIGURE 2.25** **Neglect syndrome**
A patient with a stroke in the right hemisphere was asked to copy model pictures. Like many neglect syndrome patients, he almost completely overlooked the left side of each drawing.

Using an array of tools, researchers have uncovered many strands of evidence for hemispheric lateralization in the normal human brain (Davidson & Hugdahl, 1995; Hellige, 2000; Iaccino, 1993; Springer & Deutsch, 1998). As we saw, the left hemisphere largely controls verbal activities—including reading, writing, speaking, and other aspects of language. It has long been known that damage to Broca's and Wernicke's areas, which reside in the left hemisphere, produces various types of aphasias, or speech disorders. Studies also show that people recognize words, letters, and other verbal stimuli faster when these stimuli are sent directly to the left hemisphere. Deaf people also appear to rely on the left hemisphere more than the right for reading sign language (Corina et al., 1992). Finally, PET scans show that different regions of the left hemisphere (and some areas of the right hemisphere as well) "light up" depending on whether subjects are listening to words that are spoken (hearing), reading words on a screen (seeing), saying words aloud (speaking), or coming up with related words (thinking). A sample PET scan appears in Figure 2.24 (Peterson & Fiez, 1993).

Whereas the left hemisphere is a verbal specialist, there is now converging evidence that the right hemisphere plays a vital role in nonverbal activities such as visual-spatial tasks, music, and the recognition of other people's faces and emotional states. Laboratory studies show that people are usually faster at locating dots, drawing three-dimensional objects, and recognizing faces when the material is presented to the right hemisphere than to the left (Bradshaw & Nettleton, 1981). Clinical case studies also illustrate this point (Corballis et al., 2002). For example, Gazzaniga (1985) instructed a split-brain patient to draw a cube and found that he produced a better drawing with the left hand than with the right—even though he was right-handed. Right hemisphere damage may also cause people to lose their sense of direction while driving, have trouble locating items in a familiar supermarket, or even get lost in their own homes (Newcombe & Ratcliff, 1990).

In some cases, right hemisphere damage caused by a stroke or an accident triggers a disruption of spatial awareness called "neglect" (Vallar, 1998). People with neglect syndrome lose all awareness of the left side of space—including the left side of their own bodies. When asked to bisect a horizontal line, these patients draw the line to the right of center. In actual life tasks, they may comb their hair only on the right side of the head, shave only the right side of the face, or eat food only if it's on the right side of the plate (see Figure 2.25).

The evidence clearly suggests that there is specialization, with the left side more verbal and the right side more visual and spatial. But some researchers believe that the key difference between the two hemispheres is not in *what* kind of input is processed but in *how* that input is processed. In essence, research suggests that the left hemisphere processes information in analytical, piecemeal style—as used in word analogies, arithmetic, and logical problem solving—and that the right hemisphere processes information in a more global, holistic style—as used in music, art, and various forms of creative expression. In one study, for example, Gazzaniga tested a split-brain patient's perceptions of a painting that depicted a face made up of a pattern of small fruits. When the image was presented to the right hemisphere, the patient reported seeing the face, but when the same image was shown to the left hemisphere, he perceived only the fruits. The right side saw the whole; the left side saw the parts (see Reuter-Lorenz & Miller, 1998).

Regardless of how the differences between left and right hemispheres are characterized, it's important not to overstate the case for lateralization. Neither hemisphere has exclusive control over certain functions, and both sides can process different kinds of information (Efron, 1990). As we'll see in the coming pages, our brains are highly adaptive—and often capable of reorganization. If one side is damaged, the other often compensates for the lost functions. This reorganization is most likely to occur when damage is sustained early in life, before the brain has fully matured. In an interesting PET scan study, researchers observed normal adults and patients with left-hemisphere damage as they listened to and then repeated sentences. As you might expect, these verbal tasks activated primarily the left hemisphere in the normal subjects. Yet these same tasks activated both hemispheres about equally in subjects damaged late in life and primarily the right hemisphere in those who had suffered the damage in childhood. The more time the damaged left brain had to reorganize, the more verbal the right hemisphere became (Muller et al., 1999). It's no wonder that with old age, which brings about a decline in certain cognitive functions, people compensate by using both sides of the brain. As a result, older adults are more bilateral than younger adults—less likely to exhibit left-right differences in specialization (Cabeza, 2002; Reuter-Lorenz & Miller, 1998).

**One Mind or Two?**    Let us now step back for a moment and reflect on the big picture: Does bisecting the brain produce two separate minds, as Fechner had long ago proposed? From the start, Sperry (1966) argued that severing the corpus callosum leaves the split-brain patient with two minds and that "what is experienced in the right hemisphere seems to lie entirely outside the realm of experience of the left hemisphere." Sir John Eccles (1965), who had won a Nobel prize in physiology, disagreed. According to Eccles, the right hemisphere cannot think without the speech capabilities of the left side.

The research has clearly supported Sperry's claim. At one point, researchers encountered a split-brain patient, known as P.S., who had a unique ability to

## WHAT'S YOUR PREDICTION

Most people in the world are right-handed. Yet psychologist Lee Salk (1962) once noticed that mothers tend to hold their infants on the left side of their body. Is this true? Shouldn't most people, being right-handed, prefer the right arm for something as precious as a human baby? What about books, boxes, and other objects? Imagine you are holding a three-month-old baby in one arm. Are you using your right arm or left? Now imagine that you're holding an antique vase, or a shoebox. Which arm are you using now? Jason Almerigi and others (2002) tested three hundred college students. What percentage do you think saw themselves using the right arm for a baby—25, 50, 75, more? What about for inanimate objects? The result confirmed Salk's observation: Although 76 percent said they'd use the right arm to hold objects, 66 percent said they'd use the *left* arm for an infant. This result is found consistently—not just for imaginary tasks, but in actual practice (Harris, 2002). How can this be explained? Is it possible that people hold infants on the left arm in order to free up the right hand? The preference is clear, but at this point more research is needed to determine the reason for it.

## REVIEW QUESTIONS

- *Compare and contrast the four different methods used to study the brain.*

- *What structures comprise the brainstem? What functions does each structure serve?*

- *Identify the structures of the limbic system and describe the functions served by each structure.*

- *Describe the functional areas of the cortex.*

- *What have psychologists learned about cerebral lateralization from split-brain patients? What methods do psychologists use to study cerebral lateralization in intact brains?*

communicate with the right hemisphere by arranging Scrabble letters with the left hand in response to questions. To put the dual-mind hypothesis to the test, Joseph Ledoux and his colleagues (1977) questioned each hemisphere separately and found that the two sides often disagreed. For example, when P.S. was asked what job he would like, his left hemisphere said he wanted to be a "draftsman," but his right hemisphere spelled out "automobile racer."

Although split-brain patients seem to have two independent streams of consciousness, their behavior is reasonably well integrated. It's important to be cautious in generalizing to individuals whose brains are intact. The fact that our right and left hemispheres are specialized in no way implies that they function independently. Through the corpus callosum and other lesser structures, information between the hemispheres is exchanged with such speed that we enjoy a seamless, well-synchronized experience.

## PROSPECTS FOR THE FUTURE

- *Is the adult brain fixed in its structure, or does it have a capacity to change as a result of experience?*
- *Is it possible for people to recover functions lost to brain damage?*
- *Can healthy tissue be transplanted from one brain into another?*

## THE BRAIN'S CAPACITY FOR GROWTH AND REORGANIZATION

The human brain is an impressive organ. Encased in a hard protective skull, it is complex and has a great deal of **plasticity** (from the word *plastic*)—a capacity to change as a result of usage, practice, and experience (Huttonlocher, 2002; Nelson, 1999).

**The Benefit of Plasticity: Growth through Experience** Psychologists used to believe that the neural circuits of the adult brain and nervous system were fully developed and no longer subject to change. Then a series of provocative animal experiments showed that this is not so. Mark Rosenzweig (1984) built an "amusement park" for rats to examine the effects of an enriched environment on neural development. Some rats lived together in a cage filled with ladders, platforms, boxes, and other toys, whereas others lived in solitary confinement. The enriched rats developed heavier, thicker brains with more dendrites and synapses than those who were deprived. In fact, the growth can be quite specific. Rats flooded with visual stimulation formed 20 percent more synaptic connections per neuron in the visual cortex than those who were raised in darkness (Greenough et al., 1987). "Acrobatic" rats trained to run between pylons on elevated runways formed new synaptic connections in the cerebellum, the structure involved in balance and motor coordination (Greenough et al., 1990). And food-storing mountain chickadees allowed to store and recover seeds from various locations exhibited more growth in the hippocampus than birds deprived of this opportunity to "exercise" their spatial memory (Clayton, 2001). Similar results in birds, mice, squirrels, and monkeys of different ages have confirmed a basic point: Experiences spark the growth of new synaptic connections and mold the brain's neural architecture (Rosenzweig, 1996; Kolb & Whishaw, 1998).

**plasticity** A capacity to change as a result of experience.

Plasticity has profound practical implications for human development and adaptation. Earlier we saw that people who suffer severe damage to the verbal left hemisphere often recover language-related abilities because parts of the right hemisphere, over time, compensate for the loss of these functions (Muller et al., 1999). Reorganization within the brain can help people compensate for other types of loss as well. For example, brain-imaging studies have shown that in people who are blind, the visual cortex—which is deprived of visual input—is activated by other types of stimulation such as sound and touch (Sadato et al., 1999). Similarly, in people who are deaf, the auditory cortex becomes activated in response to touch (Levanen et al., 1998). Illustrating "cross-modal plasticity," these findings may help to explain in common observation, that when people lose their sight, or their hearing, other senses become sharpened as a result.

Neural plasticity has other implications, too. Avi Karni and Leslie Ungerleider (1996) tested the proposition that repeated stimulation of a body part would cause corresponding changes in the human brain. Every day these researchers had six men perform one of two finger-tapping sequences for ten to twenty minutes. After five weeks, they had the men tap out both the practiced and nonpracticed sequences. Using fMRI, they found that tapping the practiced sequence lit up a larger portion of the primary motor cortex.

If sheer usage can spark the buildup of new synaptic connections among neurons, then an individual's life experiences should leave a permanent mark on his or her brain. In an interesting test of this hypothesis, researchers autopsied a number of human brains and measured the degree of synaptic branching in Wernicke's area of the left hemisphere. Then they probed into the backgrounds of these deceased subjects and found that the more educated they were, the more branching there was in this language-rich part of the brain (Jacobs et al., 1993). Other researchers have similarly found that, when their often-used fingers are stimulated, blind Braille readers and string musicians exhibit more activity in the somatosensory cortex than the average person (Pascual-Leone et al., 1993; Elbert et al., 1995). Similarly, researchers played tones of varying frequencies of thirty-seven professional musicians and nonmusicians and found that the part of the auditory cortex that responds to sound was more active in the musician's brain—and it contained 130 percent more gray matter. Perhaps years of experience had stimulated the growth of extra neurons in this music-sensitive structure (Schneider et al., 2002).

The recent analysis of Albert Einstein's brain is a case in point. We noted earlier that whereas Einstein's brain was average-sized overall, a highly specific region that is active in visuospatial and mathematical thinking was 15 percent larger than normal. Einstein may well have been born with a brain uniquely gifted for physics. But it's possible, as the researchers were quick to point out, that this part of his brain bulked up in size as a result of constant usage (Witelson et al., 1999). "Practice may not always make perfect, but it is likely to make a lasting impression on your brain" (Azar, 1996).

**The Cost of Plasticity: The Case of the Phantom Limb**   Plasticity is an adaptive feature of the nervous system. However, recent studies indicate that the brain's plasticity can also be a burden, as in the case of amputation. Psychologists have long been puzzled by phantom pain—the fact that amputees often feel excruciating pain in the area of their lost limb, sensations that would often last for years. To lessen the pain, puzzled physicians and their patients have sometimes resorted to desperate measures such as shortening the stump or cutting sensory tracts in the spinal cord, typically without success. In the past, some interpreted the pain as a form of denial, or wishful thinking; others believed that frayed nerve endings in the stump were inflamed and irritated, thereby fooling the brain into thinking that the limb was still there. It now appears that neither of these explanations is correct and that the phantom pain results, ironically, from the brain's own capacity for reorganization and growth.

This possibility was first raised when Michael Merzenich and his colleagues (1983) severed the nerve of the middle finger in an adult monkey and found that the area of the somatosensory cortex dedicated to that finger did not wither away. Rather, nearby neurons activated by other fingers filled in the dormant region. The sensations produced by these neurons may thus fool the brain into thinking that the limb is still there. Consistent with this account, a study of human amputees revealed that the more cortical reorganization that had occurred, as detected in brain scans, the more pain the patients felt (Flor et al., 1995; Karl et al., 2001).

In *Phantoms in the Brain*, neuroscientist V.S. Ramachandran presents this perspective in a story about seventeen-year-old Tom Sorenson, who lost his left arm in an accident. Tom was driving home from soccer practice one day when an oncoming car swerved into his lane, forcing him to spin out of control and throwing him from the driver's seat. "As he was hurled through the air, Tom looked back and saw that his hand was still in the car gripping the seat cushion, severed from his body like a prop in a Freddy Krueger horror film" (Ramachandran & Blakeslee, 1998, p. 21). Over the next few weeks, Tom could feel the ghostly presence of his lost arm, as he "wiggled" his fingers and "reached" for objects. Armed with his theory about the cause of this pain, Ramachandran blindfolded Tom, stroked different areas of his body surface with a Q-tip, and asked him to report where he felt the sensations. When he touched the cheek, Tom said he felt it on his cheek—and also in his missing thumb. When he touched the lower jaw, Tom felt the sensation in his jaw—and also in his missing pinkie. Using this painstaking step-by-step method, Ramachandran eventually found a complete sensory "map" of Tom's missing hand on his face.

What had happened? After the accident, the patch of cortex that was connected to Tom's missing hand was now receiving sensory input from other parts of his body, including the face. The result: "Every time he smiles or experiences some spontaneous activity of facial nerves, the activity stimulates his 'hand area,' thereby fooling him into thinking that his hand is still there" (p. 40).

## REPAIRING THE DAMAGED BRAIN: NEW FRONTIERS

The brain has great capacity for enrichment, but alas, we are mortal and our bodies are fallible. Strokes, spinal cord injuries, diseases that strike at the core of the nervous system, exposure to toxic substances, and addictions to alcohol and other drugs are just some of the causes of brain damage. The possible effects include paralysis, motor disorders, thought and speech disorders, blunted emotion, changes in personality, and a loss of sensory capabilities, consciousness, and memory. (See *Psychology and Sports*.)

**Neurogenesis**   Scientists used to believe that adult brains do not produce new neurons—that the death of brain cells results in permanent loss. It now appears, however, that the production of new brain cells—a process called **neurogenesis**—continues well beyond infancy. The human brain may acquire billions of new cells between birth and age six, which are incorporated into existing neural circuits and help to construct new ones (Blakeslee, 2000). Neurogenesis may slow in adulthood, but it does not stop completely. The adult brain, too, has special cells that divide and produce new neurons. The discovery of neurogenesis in adults can be traced to the mid-1960s when researchers studying adult mice found new brain cells in the

**neurogenesis**   The production of new brain cells.

hippocampus, the structure involved in forming new memories. Within a few years, scientists observed this in the brains of other adult mammals, such as guinea pigs and rabbits, and in birds. For instance, new cells are created in the brains of adult canaries that learn new songs and in adult chickadees that store memories for where their winter seed stashes are hidden. Elizabeth Gould and her colleagues (1999) similarly discovered that they could increase the number of new neurons in the brains of adult monkeys.

Does all this mean that neurogenesis occurs in the brains of adult humans? Although more evidence is needed, the possibilities are exciting. If you get an ulcer, break a finger, or scrape your knee, new cells will be produced to heal the wound. Scientists of the past assumed that the brain did not have this same capacity to heal itself. Once a neuron is damaged, after all, it is forever disabled. Yet every now and then, we hear stories of "miraculous" recoveries from brain damage. What makes this possible is the adaptive capacity to compensate for loss by strengthening old synaptic connections and by sprouting new axons and dendrites to form new connections. Earlier we saw that healthy brain tissue will sometimes pick up lost functions—which is why children with substantial damage to the left hemisphere learn to speak, and many adults who suffer strokes later recover their speech and motor abilities. Neurogenesis may also occur in the brains of adult humans, putting us on the verge of exciting new treatments for brain disorders.

**Neural Transplantation**   Is it possible to more effectively restore the brain through medical intervention? For the millions of people each year who are struck by Parkinson's disease, Alzheimer's disease, and other degenerative nerve disorders, can the damaged brain and nervous system be repaired? *Superman* actor Christopher Reeve, who compressed his spinal cord in a horseback-riding accident, is now paralyzed from the neck down. Reeve has said that his goal is to some day stand up. Will this be possible? As unlikely as these ideas seemed just a few years ago, progress is being made on a number of fronts (Fawcett et al., 2001; McDonald, 1999). In September 2002, just before Reeve's fiftieth birthday, his doctors reported that after years of physical therapy, Reeve can now feel human touch, experience pain, and move his fingers (McDonald et al., 2002).

One exciting development is that researchers have been busy trying to transplant healthy tissue from the central nervous system of one animal into that of another animal in a surgical procedure known as a **neural graft.** In amphibians and fish, researchers long ago demonstrated that it was possible to transplant neurons in cold-blooded animals. In classic experiments from the 1940s, Sperry transplanted eyeballs in frogs and found that these grafts formed new pathways to the brain and restored vision. Would neural grafting work as well in warm-blooded mammals? To find out, a team of researchers destroyed a dopamine-producing area of the brainstem (called the *substantia nigra*) in laboratory rats. As they had anticipated, the lack of dopamine caused severe tremors and other symptoms that mimicked Parkinson's disease. Next, they implanted healthy tissue from brains taken from rat fetuses and observed, after four weeks, a 70 percent decline in symptoms (Perlow et al., 1979). In later experiments with rats, mice, and primates, researchers also used neural grafting in other regions of the brain to reverse cognitive learning deficits, spatial deficits, and alcohol-induced memory loss (Brasted et al., 2000; Kimble, 1990; Sinden et al., 1995).

News from animal laboratories is encouraging. But can brain grafts help people suffering from degenerative nerve disorders? In March 1982, a male Parkinson's patient in Stockholm, Sweden, agreed to serve as a human guinea pig. Barely able to move without medication, he underwent an experimental operation. The

*Superman actor Christopher Reeve was paralyzed from the neck down in a horseback-riding accident in which his spinal cord was compressed. Remarkably, as a result of intensive physical therapy, Reeve has regained sensation and some movement—which, according to his doctors, is the first case of partial reversal after years of paralysis.*

*In 1998, actor Michael J. Fox disclosed for the first time that he has Parkinson's disease. Here, he testifies before a U.S. Senate committee on the funding of research on neurological disorders.*

**neural graft**   A technique of transplanting healthy tissue from the nervous system of one animal into that of another.

# HEAD INJURY IN CONTACT SPORTS

How often have you seen an athlete take a crushing blow to the head, go down, lie still for a few moments, and then stumble off the field looking dazed? Elite NFL quarterbacks Bret Favre, Kurt Warner, and Drew Bledsoe have all suffered from concussions. So do thousands of other athletes every year, professionals and amateurs, who play soccer, hockey, and other contact sports. What happens in a concussion, what are its effects, and can they be prevented?

A **concussion** is an alteration in a person's mental state caused by trauma to the head. From a neurological perspective, a concussion occurs when a jarring blow causes axons to become stretched, twisted, or sheared, interrupting signals between neurons (see Figure 2.26). The most common changes in mental state following a concussion are temporary confusion and amnesia, and these symptoms may occur right after the trauma or up to fifteen minutes later.

Concussions vary a great deal in their severity. Mild "Grade 1" concussions tend to cause headaches, dizziness, disorientation, blurred speech, and a ringing in the ears. In sports, this type of concussion is difficult to diagnose and is commonly referred to as a "dinger" (athletes like to describe the state as "having their bell rung"). At the other extreme are severe "Grade 3" concussions, which are easy to spot because they cause unconsciousness for a brief or prolonged time. This type of injury can damage the brainstem and disrupt such autonomic functions as heart rate and breathing. Over time, it may also result in such symptoms as persistent headaches, vision problems, memory loss, sleep loss, an inability to concentrate, a lack of tolerance for loud noises and bright lights, fatigue, and anxiety

or depressed mood. How can a coach or athletic trainer know that an athlete has just suffered a concussion? Here are some common symptoms (American Academy of Neurology, 1997; Bailes et al., 1998):

- Stares vacantly into space or looks confused
- Is slow to answer questions
- Is easily distracted and unable to follow instructions
- Slurs speech or talks in gibberish
- Stumbles and cannot walk a straight line
- Is disoriented, often walking in the wrong direction

**FIGURE 2.26** **Anatomy of a concussion**
How often have you seen an athlete take a crushing blow to the head, go down, and leave the game? Featured NFL quarterbacks suffer repeated concussions. So do thousands of other athletes each year. But with what effect?

**concussion** An alteration in a person's mental state caused by trauma to the head.

neurosurgeons removed part of his adrenal gland, which produces dopamine, and injected the tissue directly into his brain (Parkinson's disease results from a shortage of dopamine). But the result was disappointing. The patient showed some minor improvement during the first couple of weeks, but he soon reverted to his presurgery state (Backlund et al., 1985). Undiscouraged, others pursued the use of brain grafts in Parkinson's patients with varying degrees of success. In 1987, Mexican researchers stirred up a good deal of excitement when they reported that transplanted dopamine-producing tissue produced marked improvement in two patients (Madrazo et al., 1987). More clinical studies were then conducted. The

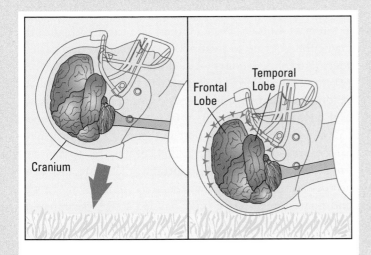

Cranium

Frontal Lobe

Temporal Lobe

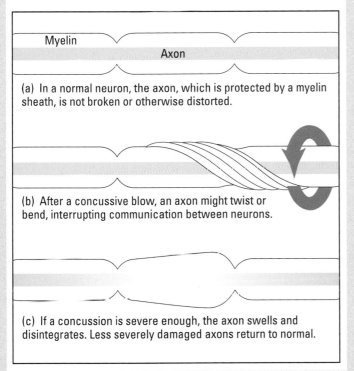

Myelin

Axon

(a) In a normal neuron, the axon, which is protected by a myelin sheath, is not broken or otherwise distorted.

(b) After a concussive blow, an axon might twist or bend, interrupting communication between neurons.

(c) If a concussion is severe enough, the axon swells and disintegrates. Less severely damaged axons return to normal.

- Doesn't know the current time, day, or place
- Repeatedly asks the same question and forgets the answer
- Becomes highly emotional, crying for no apparent reason

Doctors fear that people who suffer repeated concussions may face lasting cognitive declines. So what can be done to minimize the damage to athletes? There are two steps to be taken. The first is to require the use of safety equipment that would lessen the risk of getting a concussion. In the National Football League, the standard helmet contains an inflatable sack to cushion the blow, but most players don't inflate it because it makes the helmet too tight. There is also ProCap, a helmet that contains a shock-absorbing polyurethane cushion attached to the exterior, but players complain that this device is bulky. Perhaps one or the other of these extra-protective helmets should be required. A second precautionary step appropriate to all sports is to ensure that any player who takes a blow to the head be sidelined immediately and carefully examined for symptoms. For this purpose, standardized brief examination methods are being developed (McCrea et al., 1997).

Today, neurologists are wondering if the newest roller coasters can cause brain trauma by jostling the brain's soft tissue, causing it to press up against the skull. A few years ago, no roller coaster surpassed 200 feet in height; today, "hypercoasters" reach up to 400 feet. A few years ago, roller coasters gained speed by gravity; today, many are catapulted by motors designed to launch rockets. As thrilling as the rides can be (I love roller coasters), they subject riders to powerful physical forces—such as gravity, or G-force, jerk, roll, pitch, and yaw. Research is currently underway to examine the effects on the brain (Gilbert, 2002).

results were not as dramatic, but they too revealed at least modest improvement in many patients (Gage, 1993). Particularly encouraging news came from Sweden, where researchers implanted brain tissue from immature human fetuses and found that the patients exhibited improvement (Lindvall et al., 1992).

As we navigate the twenty-first century, neuroscientists are poised at the edge of an interesting new frontier: using fetal tissue to repair the damaged brain. As with many scientific discoveries, however, controversy surrounds progress. Is it ethical to use medical procedures that generate a need for fetal tissue? Few people would object to using miscarried fetuses to save lives, but what about the use of aborted fetuses? Would such use encourage women to conceive children and have abortions in order to help ailing family members, or to make a profit? As neural grafting becomes more effective, this debate is sure to heat up. Another question concerns whether the procedure is ready to be used on human beings. Some researchers "call for patience rather than patients" (Sladek & Shoulson, 1988) and warn of the medical risks of the procedure (Stein & Glasier, 1995). Others are eager to realize the clinical possibilities of using neural grafting to treat people who suffer from various cognitive and motor disorders (Barker & Dunnett, 1999; Freed, 1999).

Recent studies offer an exciting direction for future efforts to repair the damaged brain. Neuroscientists have long held that new nerve cells cannot be produced in the adult brain. New axons and dendrites may sprout, forming new synaptic connections, but the growth of new neurons was considered impossible. Neurogenesis researchers have recently discovered that the adult human brain does spawn new nerve cells in the hippocampus, a structure that is important in learning and memory. This discovery, and the possibility that neuroscientists may some day find a way to stimulate the growth and migration of nerve cells, has led some researchers to speculate that the human brain harbors great potential for its own repair (Fawcett et al., 2001; Kempermann & Gage, 1999).

## REVIEW QUESTIONS

- *What is meant by neural plasticity? Describe some of the evidence demonstrating the plasticity of the brain.*

- *In what ways are researchers attempting to repair damage to the brain?*

# THINKING LIKE A PSYCHOLOGIST ABOUT BEHAVIORAL NEUROSCIENCE

The study of the split-brain patient described at the outset of this chapter gave us a glimpse into the fascinating and developing world of behavioral neuroscience. This research illustrates why it is valuable to observe individuals who are exceptional in some way and tells us that each region of the brain is involved in different psychological processes. But as we have seen elsewhere in this chapter, researchers use other methods as well, including powerful brain scans, to discover linkages among the brain, the mind, and behavior. And although different areas of the brain act as "specialists," the healthy human brain operates as an integrated system—and has the capacity to change as a result of usage, practice, and experience.

To this day, the human brain and nervous system remain one of the great frontiers in science. From the trillions of tiny building blocks, consisting of axons, dendrites, synapses, and neurotransmitters, to the structures of the brainstem, limbic system, and cerebral cortex, there is a solid biological foundation for the study of mind and behavior. The goal, as we'll see in later chapters, is to understand the links between the human body and psychological processes that range from visual perception to moral development, social aggression, and the health benefits of psychotherapy.

# SUMMARY

Phineas Gage's dramatic brain injury showed that the human brain and nervous system form an integrated system of specialized parts—the concern of *behavioral neuroscience.*

## THE BODY'S COMMUNICATION NETWORKS

The body has two communication networks: the nervous system and the endocrine system.

## THE NERVOUS SYSTEM

The human nervous system has two basic parts. The **central nervous system (CNS)** includes the brain and the spinal cord. The **peripheral nervous system (PNS)** consists of the nerves that radiate from the CNS to the rest of the body.

The PNS is further divided into two components. The **somatic nervous system** transmits signals from the sensory organs and skin to the CNS. It also relays motor commands from the CNS to the skeletal muscles. The **autonomic nervous system** connects the CNS to the involuntary muscles, organs, and glands, thus regulating such functions as heartbeat and temperature. The autonomic nervous system has two parts: the **sympathetic nervous system**, which energizes the body for action, and the **parasympathetic nervous system,** which returns the body to its normal state.

## THE ENDOCRINE SYSTEM

The **endocrine system** is a collection of ductless glands that regulate growth, metabolism, and other functions by secreting **hormones** into the bloodstream. These secretions are controlled in the brain by the hypothalamus, which signals the **pituitary gland.**

# THE NEURON

**Neurons,** or nerve cells, transmit and receive information throughout the nervous system. **Sensory neurons** transmit information from the senses, skin, muscles, and internal organs to the CNS. **Motor neurons** send commands from the CNS to the muscles, glands, and organs. **Interneurons** serve as connectors within the CNS. Neurons cluster into interconnected working groups called **neural networks. Glial cells** help support, insulate, and nourish the neurons. A simple **reflex** like the knee jerk illustrates the speed of neural signals.

## STRUCTURE OF THE NEURON

Each neuron has a rounded body, called the **soma,** and two types of branched fibers: **dendrites,** which receive impulses, and an **axon,** which sends impulses through its terminals. Many axons are covered with **myelin sheath,** a fatty insulating layer that speeds impulses.

## THE NEURON IN ACTION

A neuron transmits messages by means of an electrical process. When dendrites receive signals of sufficient strength, the cell's membrane breaks down. Positively charged sodium ions rush in, altering the charge inside in such a way that a burst of electrical energy known as an **action potential** surges through the axon as soon as a certain necessary level of stimulation, or **threshold,** is reached.

## HOW NEURONS COMMUNICATE

To transmit a signal across the **synapse,** the tiny gap between two neurons, the sending neuron releases chemical **neurotransmitters** from vesicles in its axon terminals. These chemicals bind to **receptors** on the dendrites of a receiving neuron. There are many neurotransmitters in the body, and each fits only certain receptors.

## NEUROTRANSMITTERS

**Acetylcholine (ACh)** is a neurotransmitter that links motor neurons and muscles. ACh has an excitatory effect on muscles. **Dopamine,** in contrast, inhibits muscles and helps control voluntary movements. Alzheimer's disease, Parkinson's disease, and schizophrenia have all been linked to problems with these chemical messengers. Other neurotransmitters called **endorphins** serve as the body's own pain relievers.

# THE BRAIN

The basic anatomy of the brain has long been known, but behavioral neuroscientists face the more difficult task of understanding how it functions.

## TOOLS OF BEHAVIORAL NEUROSCIENCE

Although **phrenology** was misguided in linking mental characteristics to bumps on the skull, it correctly supposed that functions are localized in particular parts of the brain.

Today, neuroscientists use four methods to study brain functions: (1) clinical case studies of people with brain damage; (2) invasion of the brain through surgery, drugs, or electrical stimulation; (3) electrical recordings of activity using the **electroencephalograph (EEG)**; and (4) brain-imaging techniques, such as **computerized tomography (CT), positron emission tomography (PET),** and **magnetic resonance imaging (MRI).**

## REGIONS OF THE BRAIN

The brain consists of three main parts: the brainstem, the limbic system, and the cerebral cortex. Each of these comprises several important structures.

The **brainstem** is the inner core. It contains the **medulla,** which controls vital involuntary functions such as breathing; the **pons,** involved in sleep and arousal; and the **reticular formation,** a netlike group of cells that filter sensory information and help control sleep, arousal, and attention. Nearby are the **cerebellum** and **basal ganglia,** which play an important role in balance and coordination.

Above the brainstem is the **limbic system,** which helps govern motivation, emotion, and memory. It includes the **thalamus,** a relay station for sensory information; the **amygdala,** linked to fear, anger, and aggression; the **hippocampus,** which performs a key function in memory formation; and the **hypothalamus,** which helps regulate the autonomic nervous system, emotions, and basic drives.

The outermost 80 percent of the brain, the wrinkled **cerebral cortex,** controls higher-order mental processes. Anatomically, it consists of two hemispheres and four lobes. It can also be divided into areas based on function: (1) Sensory areas specialize in receiving sensory information. For example, the **somatosensory cortex** receives information from the touch receptors in the skin. (2) The **motor cortex** controls the voluntary muscles. (3) The **association cortex** areas communicate with the sensory and motor areas and house higher mental processes. Within the association cortex, two areas specialize in language. **Broca's area** directs the production of speech, and **Wernicke's area** is involved in language comprehension.

## THE SPLIT BRAIN

Researchers have investigated Fechner's idea that each side of the brain has its own mind. The studies rely on the fact that the left hemisphere communicates with the right side of the body, and the right hemisphere with the left side. The hemispheres are connected by, and share information through, the **corpus callosum**. Experiments with **split-brain** patients, in whom the corpus callosum has been severed, show that each hemisphere has a somewhat different version of experience.

Other research has tried to determine which functions are **lateralized**, or controlled by a single side of the brain. The key language centers are in the left hemisphere. The right hemisphere plays a crucial role in nonverbal functions. But the most important distinction may be the style of processing. The left hemisphere seems to rely on analytical processing, whereas the right hemisphere is more holistic.

Research supports the notion that the two hemispheres, when their links are cut, produce separate streams of consciousness. But in the healthy brain, they exchange information so quickly that our mental experience is a seamless whole.

## PROSPECTS FOR THE FUTURE

Recent advances in the study of the brain have addressed two questions: Does the adult brain have a capacity to change and adapt as a result of experience, and is it possible to repair a damaged brain?

### THE BRAIN'S CAPACITY FOR GROWTH AND REORGANIZATION

Research shows that the brain has **plasticity**, a capacity to change. Specifically, certain experiences can spark the branching of new dendrites and the growth of new synaptic connections. This enables the brain to compensate for damage. But it also causes people with amputated limbs to experience phantom pain.

### REPAIRING THE DAMAGED BRAIN: NEW FRONTIERS

Advances in understanding the brain have shown that *neurogenesis* continues past infancy and have led to attempts at brain repair. With the **neural graft** procedure, researchers have transplanted brain tissue from one animal to another in an effort to reduce deficits in brain function. Among human beings, the greatest hope may involve the transplantation of fetal tissue, a highly controversial procedure. Contrary to what has been believed, recent studies show that new nerve cells can be produced in the mature brain.

## KEY TERMS

central nervous system (p. 44)

peripheral nervous system (p. 44)

somatic nervous system (p. 44)

autonomic nervous system (p. 44)

sympathetic nervous system (p. 45)

parasympathetic nervous system (p. 45)

endocrine system (p. 45)

hormones (p. 45)

pituitary gland (p. 45)

neurons (p. 46)

sensory neurons (p. 46)

motor neurons (p. 46)

interneurons (p. 46)

neural networks (p. 46)

glial cells (p. 47)

reflex (p. 47)

soma (p. 48)

dendrites (p. 48)

axon (p. 48)

myelin sheath (p. 48)

action potential (p. 49)

threshold (p. 49)

synapse (p. 50)

neurotransmitters (p. 50)

receptors (p. 50)

acetylcholine (ACh) (p. 51)

dopamine (p. 51)

endorphin (p. 51)

phrenology (p. 52)

electroencephalograph (EEG) (p. 54)

computerized tomography (CT) scan (p. 54)

positron emission tomography (PET) scan (p. 54)

magnetic resonance imaging (MRI) (p. 54)

brainstem (p. 57)

medulla (p. 57)

pons (p. 57)

reticular formation (p. 57)

cerebellum (p. 57)

basal ganglia (p. 58)

limbic system (p. 58)

thalamus (p. 58)

amygdala (p. 58)

hippocampus (p. 59)

hypothalamus (p. 59)

cerebral cortex (p. 59)

somatosensory cortex (p. 61)

motor cortex (p. 61)

association cortex (p. 61)

Broca's area (p. 62)

Wernicke's area (p. 62)

corpus callosum (p. 66)

split brain (p. 66)

lateralized (p. 70)

plasticity (p. 72)

neurogenesis (p. 74)

neural graft (p. 75)

concussion (p. 76)

## THINKING CRITICALLY ABOUT BEHAVIORAL NEUROSCIENCE

1. What is the difference between the "mind" and the "brain"?

2. Advances in brain-imaging technology allow us to see the human brain at work. What kinds of questions do you think we might be able to answer with these sophisticated techniques?

3. What is your opinion of the right-brain education debate? What is the evidence for and against right- versus left-brain learning? In what ways might lateralized functions and integrated functioning each contribute to the learning process?

4. Research investigating neural plasticity suggests that life experiences can alter the neural circuitry of the brain. What are the advantages and disadvantages of this phenomenon? What are some of the real-world implications of this research (e.g., for child rearing, the treatment of stroke victims, etc.)? Is this notion of plasticity consistent with the evolutionary perspective discussed in the previous chapter? Why or why not?

# Sensation and Perception

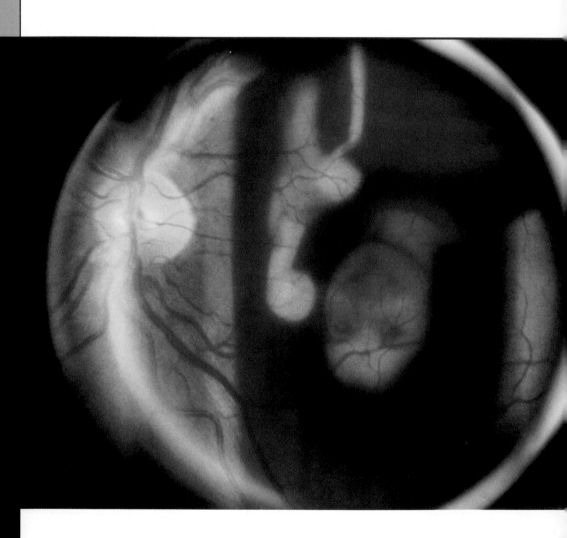

# DOES CULTURE INFLUENCE DEPTH PERCEPTION?

## THE SITUATION

You have always assumed that when it comes to vision, hearing, and other biological senses, all people are basically the same. But you also suspect that the way each of us perceives the world is influenced by our life experiences and cultural backgrounds. So which is it? Thinking about the problem, you realize that one possible way to tease apart biological and cultural influences is to select an important aspect of perception, create a task to measure it, and then compare people from different parts of the world.

In reading up on the visual system, you learn that images projected on the eye's retina are flat and two dimensional. So, you wonder, how do people judge depth and distance? How do people know that one object in the visual field is closer than another? Is depth perception innate among humans, or are certain types of life experience necessary? To examine these questions, you create the drawings shown in Figure 3.1 and ask the following question: Which animal is nearer the hunter: the antelope or the elephant? The task seems easy. To you, the elephant looks farther away because its image is so small and because it stands either on a hill that is partly blocked (*top*) or at the top of a road with converging lines that form an upside-down V (*bottom*).

## MAKE A PREDICTION

Determined to test people from very different backgrounds and cultural experiences, you show the drawings to English-speaking men and women. Then you travel to southern Africa and present the same pictures to both illiterate and educated Bantus living in a rural area. What will you find? Will everyone, as you do, see the pictures in three-dimensional terms and see the antelope as nearer than the elephant? Using the table below, put a check mark next to the group(s) in which you think most participants will see the antelope as closer than the elephant:

Educated Westerners    _____
Educated Bantus        _____
Illiterate Bantus      _____

FIGURE 3.1    **Which animal is closer to the hunter?**

## THE RESULTS

This study, conducted by W. Hudson (1960), was one of the first to examine perception from a cross-cultural perspective. Using drawings like those shown on the previous page, Hudson found that compared to Western adults, illiterate Bantu participants saw the pictures as flat and the elephant as closer to the hunter. And what about the school-educated Bantus? It's interesting that in this group, most participants saw the antelope as closer. Apparently, seeing three-dimensional depth in two-dimensional displays is a skill that people develop—probably from exposure to books, photographs, artwork, and other flat visual representations of reality.

## WHAT DOES IT ALL MEAN?

Among researchers who study vision and other senses, certain aspects of perception—such as our ability to perceive depth and distance—seem biologically "hard-wired" and universal. From the two eyes to the neural pathways that carry visual signals to the brain, most humans are similarly equipped. Yet other researchers, such as those who study people from different cultures, have come to realize that in some ways our perceptions are influenced by our experiences. It's interesting, for example, that people living in urban environments that contain many edges and right angles are more susceptible than those living in open spaces to certain line-based optical illusions (Deregowski, 1989). So are the processes of perception biologically based or learned? As we'll see in this chapter, both views are correct.

---

Before you were born, you spent nine months floating in a warm, wet, mostly dark sac of fluid. You swished around a bit from the movement, and you could hear the drumlike beat of your mother's heart. But none of this quite prepared you for the sensations that later make life so worth living. The thunderous noise of ocean waves crashing into the shore, the haunting vision of a bright full moon against the black night sky, the colors of a rainbow splashed over a canvas, the rich sweet flavor of chocolate ice cream sliding down a cold throat, and the warm tingly feeling inside that comes with a lover's embrace—the world out there has lots to offer, and our sensory systems bring some of it into the brain with radarlike sensitivity.

In this chapter, we will examine the psychology of sensation and perception. These terms are used to describe different stages in the process by which we acquire information about the world. In **sensation,** our eyes, ears, and other sensory receptors absorb raw physical energy. Through the process of **transduction,** this raw energy is converted into neural signals that are sent to the brain. In **perception,** these signals are then selected, organized, and interpreted (see Figure 3.2).

Psychologists used to treat sensation and perception as separate. Sensation was considered a strictly *physiological* process involving the various sense organs, receptors, neural pathways, and regions of the brain. Perception was considered a purely *psychological* process by which we derive meaning from these sensations. In this view, the body supplied the raw material and the mind made sense of that material. We now know, however, that in this continuous stream of events, there is no bright line dividing sensation and perception. As we'll see, the interaction between body and mind is seamless, but because different processes are at work, psychologists still find it useful to make the distinction.

*"How sense-luscious the world is."*

—DIANE ACKERMAN

**sensation**   The processes by which our sense organs receive information from the environment.

**transduction**   The process by which physical energy is converted into sensory neural impulses.

**perception**   The processes by which people select, organize, and interpret sensations.

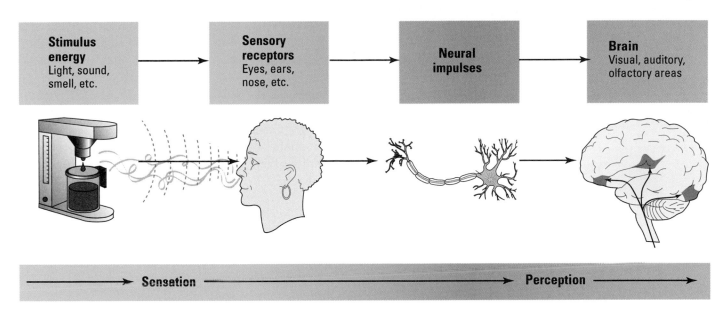

| Stimulus energy<br>Light, sound, smell, etc. | → | Sensory receptors<br>Eyes, ears, nose, etc. | → | Neural impulses | → | Brain<br>Visual, auditory, olfactory areas |
|---|---|---|---|---|---|---|

Sensation ⟶ Perception ⟶

**FIGURE 3.2   Processes of sensation and perception**

This distinction comes to life in a poignant true story told by neurologist Oliver Sacks (1995). Virgil, a fifty-year-old Oklahoma man, had been blind since the age of six. Because Virgil could see light and faint shadows, a local ophthalmologist suggested that it might be possible to restore his eyesight through surgery. Starting with the right eye, the doctor removed a thick cataract that blanketed the retina, inserted a new lens implant, and bandaged the eye for twenty-four hours. The next day, the bandage was removed. It was the moment of truth. But Virgil did not cry out with joy or react in any other way. Instead, he stared blankly at the surgeon, silent and bewildered. As Sacks put it, "The dramatic moment stayed vacant, grew longer, sagged." Was the operation a success? Could Virgil see? In a manner of speaking, yes. He said he could detect light, forms, movement, and color, all mixed up in a confusing and cluttered blur. But only when the doctor started to speak did Virgil realize that he was staring at a face. His retina was alive and well, but his brain could not make sense of the information. There was sensation, but no perception.

Even as the weeks passed, Virgil remained disoriented. In the supermarket, he was overwhelmed, even stressed, by all the visual stimulation—the bright lights, the shelves lined with cans and jars, the fruits and vegetables, and the people wheeling carts up and down the aisles. "Everything ran together," he said. Virgil could not identify by sight common objects such as chairs and tables that he recognized easily by touching. He also lacked the ability to perceive depth. He was confused by shadows, often stopping to step over one. Yet he saw a staircase as a flat surface of parallel and crossing lines rather than as a three-dimensional solid object. Movement posed additional problems. He would recognize his dog one moment, but then wonder if it was the same animal when he saw it from a different angle.

For reasons that are unclear, Virgil suddenly became ill, collapsed, and almost died. He had a respiratory illness and needed a constant supply of oxygen. By the time he returned home from the hospital, he had to carry an oxygen tank wherever he went. Unable to work, Virgil lost his job, his house, and, once again, his eyesight. Extensive tests found no response to light whatsoever—and no electrical activity in the visual cortex. He was totally blind. But all was not lost. As Sacks (1995) put it,

**psychophysics** The study of the relationship between physical stimulation and subjective sensations.

**absolute threshold** The smallest amount of stimulation that can be detected.

"Now, at last, Virgil is allowed to not see, allowed to escape from the glaring, confusing world of sight and space, and to return to his own true being, the intimate, concentrated world of the other senses that had been his home for almost fifty years" (p. 152).

This chapter will begin with the study of sensation, the raw material that transforms the brain into a mind. We will examine the physiology of vision, hearing, smell, taste, touch, and other sensory systems. Then we will examine the psychological processes of perception that enable us to comprehend and interpret this raw material. As we'll see, the world "out there" comes to us through an interaction of physical energy, the body, and the mind.

## MEASURING THE SENSORY EXPERIENCE

- *How does physical energy become a psychological experience?*
- *What's the minimum amount of stimulation needed to register on our senses, and how can this be measured?*
- *What is the smallest change in stimulation that people can detect, and how can this be measured?*

Light, vibration, odor-filled molecules, cold winds, warm breezes, and the collision of bodies. The first generation of psychologists, including Wilhelm Wundt, raised the most basic of questions: Whatever the stimulus, how does physical energy become a psychological experience? How much light is necessary to see? How can you hear a pin drop or detect minute variations in pitch well enough to tune a musical instrument? How different must two wines be for a wine taster to tell them apart? Inspired by the work of Gustav Fechner (1860), questions of this nature gave birth to psychology's first subfield, **psychophysics**: the study of the relationship between physical stimuli and subjective sensations. The key to psychophysics is measurement. Because sensation is subjective, it cannot be measured using objective instruments the way you assess height, weight, or time. There are no yardsticks, or scales, or stopwatches—only the subject and his or her self-report. New procedures thus had to be devised to maximize the accuracy of these reports (Gescheider, 1997). Much of the material discussed in this chapter was derived from these psychophysical procedures.

### ABSOLUTE THRESHOLDS

What is the minimum amount of light that we can see, the weakest vibration that we can hear, or the faintest odor that we can smell? How much sugar needs to be added to a food for us to taste more sweetness? What is the slightest amount of skin pressure, as in a tickle, that we can feel? Just how sensitive are our sensory systems? Researchers interested in a sensation begin by trying to determine an **absolute threshold**, the minimum level of stimulation that an organism can detect.

Absolute threshold can be derived in different ways. One method is simply to ask a subject to adjust the intensity of a stimulus until it is barely detectable. A second method is to gradually increase the intensity level and ask the subject from one trial to the next if he or she detects the stimulus. A third method is to vary the stimulus presentation randomly, again checking with the subject on each trial. Over the years, research has shown that absolute thresholds are not "absolute." There is no single point on the intensity scale at which people suddenly detect a stimulus.

| TABLE 3.1 | SOME ABSOLUTE THRESHOLDS |
|---|---|
| **Sensory System** | **Absolute Threshold** |
| Vision | A lit candle thirty miles away on a dark, clear night |
| Hearing | The tick of a watch twenty feet away in total quiet |
| Smell | One drop of perfume dispersed throughout a six-room apartment |
| Taste | One teaspoon of sugar in two gallons of water |
| Touch | The wing of a bee falling on your cheek from a height of one centimeter |

**signal-detection theory**   The theory that detecting a stimulus is jointly determined by the signal and the subject's response criterion.

Rather, detection rates increase gradually. Psychophysics researchers thus define absolute threshold as the point at which a stimulus can be detected 50 percent of the time. Defined in this way, some of our absolute thresholds are highly impressive (see Table 3.1).

## SIGNAL-DETECTION THEORY

Imagine you're a subject in a classical psychophysics experiment. You're sitting in a darkened room staring at a blank wall, and the experimenter presents a series of flashes varying in brightness. Did you see it? What about the next one, and the one after that? On some trials, the flashes are clear, well above threshold, so you say *yes*. But on other trials, you're just not sure. With the experimenter waiting for a response, what do you say? Confronted with this dilemma, some subjects prefer to say *yes* (when in doubt, go for it). Others, more cautious, say *no* (unless it's clear, don't go out on a limb). These tendencies to respond *yes* and *no* in uncertain situations are individual response biases—and they have little to do with sensation. The problem for the researcher, then, is that a subject's responses are influenced not only by the strength of the signal but also by background factors such as his or her personality, motivation, and expectations.

Enter signal-detection theory. Based on the assumption that performance is jointly determined by the strength of a signal and the subject's response criterion (his or her willingness to say *yes* rather than *no*), **signal-detection theory** gave rise to a more sophisticated method. On some trials, a weak stimulus is presented. On others, no stimulus is presented. By comparing a subject's "hit" versus "miss" rate on stimulus trials to his or her tendency to commit "false alarms" by saying *yes* in blank trials, a researcher can mathematically separate the subject's detection performance from the response bias (Green & Swets, 1966; Wickens, 2001). The method of establishing absolute thresholds was based on the assumption that a threshold is determined solely by the stimulus. But signal-detection theory recognizes that response biases are also at work. This approach provides the psychologist with a valuable tool for analyzing why air-traffic controllers are so quick to detect danger signals on the radar screen, why overeager witnesses identify innocent suspects in police lineups, or why doctors tend to overdiagnose certain diseases from available test results (Swets, 1996). Signal-detection theory has also been used to evaluate how clinical psychologists make the prediction that someone will suffer from mental illness, commit suicide, or erupt in violence (McFall & Treat, 1999).

## DIFFERENCE THRESHOLDS

Sensory capacities are measured not only by our ability to detect low levels of stimulation but also by the extent to which we can detect subtle differences. This ability is determined by asking subjects to compare the brightness of two light bulbs, the

*Tuning a piano requires a heightened ability to detect subtle differences among tones.*

---

## REVIEW QUESTIONS

- *What is an absolute threshold and how is it measured?*

- *In what way is signal-detection theory a more sophisticated method of measurement than absolute thresholds?*

- *What is a just noticeable difference? How is it measured?*

- *What is Weber's law? How does it help us measure sensory experience?*

---

loudness of two tones, the weight of two blocks, and so on. Given one stimulus, the subject is asked to adjust the level of another stimulus so that the two are the same. Or subjects are given the two stimuli and asked to report whether they are the same or different. Either way, it is possible to pinpoint the smallest change in stimulation that subjects can detect 50 percent of the time. This point is called the difference threshold, or **just noticeable difference (JND)**.

While measuring difference thresholds, Ernst Weber (1834) quickly noticed that JNDs increase with the size or intensity of the stimulus—and that the magnitude of a JND is a constant *proportion* of the original stimulus. In other words, as the stimulus increases in magnitude, a greater change is needed before it can be detected. This general principle is known as **Weber's law.** To illustrate, the JND for weight is 1/50, or 2 percent. In other words, if you lift a 50-ounce object, and then a 51-ounce object, you will probably notice that the second one is heavier than the first. However, you would not feel a difference between one object that weighs 50 pounds and another that weighs 50 pounds, 1 ounce. Again, there is an absolute difference of 1 ounce; but a JND of 2 percent means that if your reference point is a 50-pound object, you'd not detect a difference unless the second object is equal to or greater than 51 pounds. Except at the extremes, Weber's law provides a good estimate of our difference thresholds. It can also be applied to other senses—though each has a different threshold. For example, the JND is 2 percent for brightness, 10 percent for loudness, and 20 percent for the taste of salt.

**just noticeable difference (JND)**  The smallest amount of change in a stimulus that can be detected.

**Weber's law**  The principle that the just noticeable difference of a stimulus is a constant proportion despite variations in intensity.

---

## SENSATION

- *How does the human visual system convert light into meaningful color images?*
- *How does the auditory system convert vibrating air molecules into meaningful sounds?*
- *What about the chemical senses of smell and taste, or the ability to feel pressure, warmth, cold, pain, and balance?*

Back in school, I was taught that there are five senses: vision, hearing, taste, smell, and touch. This simple notion can be traced to the writings of Aristotle (384–322 BCE). Even today, people who believe in "extrasensory" perception, or ESP, call it the "sixth sense." In fact, we have more than five sensory modalities. Vision has two subsystems, one for daylight and one for nighttime conditions. The chemical senses of taste and smell are easily distinguished, but touch is really a mixture of several skin senses—including pressure, pain, warmth, and cold. We also have a keen sense of balance and of the position and movement of our body parts. Combined, these various systems bring in a steady stream of information from the world around us.

*"From a swirling sea of energies, each sense selects its own."*

—DANIEL P. KIMBLE

## VISION

You and I are visual creatures. How many times have you said, "Show me." "I'll believe it when I see it." "I saw it with my own eyes." "Out of sight, out of mind." "See?" "My eyes are playing tricks on me." Like other aspects of human anatomy, our visual system is a highly adapted product of evolution. The earliest forms of life could "see" in the sea through faint patches of membrane that were sensitive to light. They could tell brightness from dark and even turn toward the light source. In contrast, other features—such as shapes, textures, motion, and color—could be detected later, only by more advanced forms of life (Land & Fernald, 1992).

**Light**  For every sensory system, physical energy is the source of stimulation. The stimulus input for vision is light—a form of energy known as electromagnetic radiation that travels through empty space in oscillating waves. As illustrated in Figure 3.3, what we see as light comes from a narrow band in the spectrum of electromagnetic radiation. All matter gives off electromagnetic radiation of different wavelengths (a wavelength is measured by the distance between waves). The sun and other stars give off radiation that includes light. So do fires and electric lamps. Visible wavelengths range from about 380 to 760 nanometers (a nanometer is one billionth of a meter). Thus, some waves (such as X rays, ultraviolet rays, and gamma rays) are too short for us to see and fall below our visible range. Others (such as infrared rays, TV signals, radio waves, and radar) are too long for us to see, so they exceed our visible range. Other organisms have sensory capabilities that are different from ours. For example, most insects can see shorter wavelengths in the ultraviolet spectrum, and most fish and reptiles can see longer wavelengths in the infrared spectrum.

The *length* of a light wave determines its hue, or perceived *color*. To the human eye, white light is made up of all visible wavelengths combined. Short wavelengths look bluish, medium wavelengths look greenish, and long wavelengths look reddish. The picturesque colors of the visible spectrum can be seen in a rainbow or in the spectrum of colors produced when white light passes through a glass prism. A second property of light is its intensity, or *amplitude,* as measured by the height of the peaks in the wave. As wavelength determines color, amplitude determines *brightness.* The higher the amplitude, the brighter the light appears to be. A third physical property of light is its *purity,* as measured by the number of wavelengths that make up the light. Purity influences the *saturation,* or richness, of colors. The fewer wavelengths there are in a light (the purer it is), the richer or more saturated is the color.

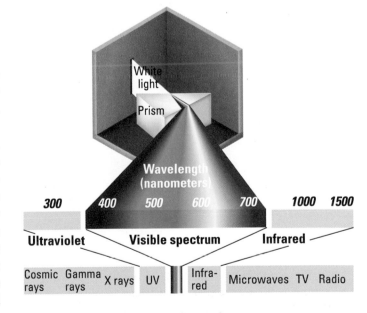

**FIGURE 3.3**  **The electromagnetic spectrum**
The human eye is sensitive to only a narrow band of electromagnetic radiation. As shown, visible wavelengths range from 380 to 760 nanometers.

The peregrine falcon has the sharpest eyesight of any animal. Under ideal conditions, it can spot a pigeon more than five miles away.

**cornea**    The clear outer membrane that bends light so that it is sharply focused in the eye.

**iris**    The ring of muscle tissue that gives eyes their color and controls the size of the pupil.

**pupil**    The small round hole in the iris of the eye through which light passes.

**lens**    A transparent structure in the eye that focuses light on the retina.

**accommodation**    The visual process by which lenses become rounded for viewing nearby objects and flatter for viewing remote objects.

3.1    *Live!* psych

A pure red light made up of only a narrow band of wavelengths would give off a rich fire-engine or tomato-like color. In contrast, white light—which contains all visible wavelengths—is completely unsaturated and lacking in color.

**The Visual System**    Light waves provide the stimulus input for vision, but what is actually seen depends on the capabilities of the visual system that's in place. Accordingly, different species see the world in different ways. Eagles can spot a tiny field mouse moving in the grass a mile away. Owls can see at night, in low levels of illumination. Cows and sheep have their eyes on the sides of the head, enabling them to spot predators sneaking up from behind. And bees can judge the angle at which light strikes the eye, so they know the sun's position in the sky—even on a gray, overcast day. Each species has evolved visual systems uniquely suited to its way of life (Archer et al., 1999).

**The Eye**    The fantastic journey of neural impulses through the human visual system begins with the eye—an extension of the brain and the most exposed part of the central nervous system. Lying in a protective bony socket within the skull, the eye converts, or transduces, light waves into electrochemical neural impulses. The major structures of the human eye are presented in Figure 3.4.

Light rays from the outside world first pass through the **cornea**, a clear, curved membrane, or "window." The cornea bends light so that it is sharply focused within the eye. Abnormalities in the shape of the cornea cause astigmatism, usually experienced as a selective blurring of parts of the image at a particular orientation, such as horizontal. Next comes the ring-shaped **iris**, which gives the eye its color. The iris is a muscle that is controlled by the autonomic nervous system. Its function is to regulate the size of the **pupil**—the small, round hole in the iris through which light passes. The iris causes the pupil to dilate (enlarge) under dim viewing conditions to let in more light and to contract (shrink) under brightness to let in less light.

Behind the pupil, light continues through the **lens**, another transparent structure whose function is to fine-tune the focusing of the light. The lens brings an image into focus by changing its shape, in a process called **accommodation**. Specifically, the lens becomes more rounded for focusing on nearby objects and flatter for more distant objects (the cornea, which has a fixed shape, cannot make these adjustments

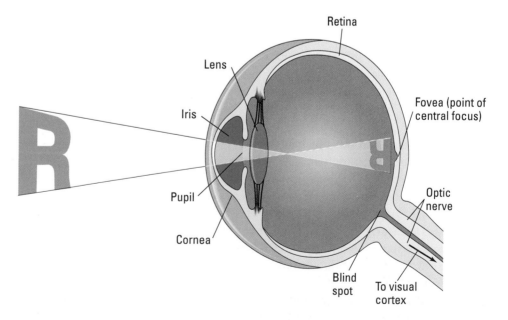

FIGURE 3.4    **Structures of the human eye**

for different distances). With age, the lens loses much of its elasticity and keeps the flatter shape appropriate for viewing at a distance. As a result, many middle-aged people start to need glasses for reading or bifocals with a near-vision portion in the lower part of the glass.

Filling the central part of the eyeball is a clear jellylike substance called the vitreous humor. Light passes through this fluid before it reaches the retina. The **retina** is a multilayered screen of cells that lines the back inside surface of the eyeball. It is one of the most fascinating tissues in the body—both because of its function, which is to transform patterns of light into images that the brain can use, and because of its structure, which illustrates many basic principles of neural organization (see Figure 3.5). In an odd twist of nature, the image projected on the retina is upside down. That is, light from the top part of the visual field stimulates photoreceptor cells in the bottom part of the retina, and vice versa.

The retina has aptly been called an extension of the brain (Gregory, 1998). It has several relatively transparent layers and contains 130 million photoreceptor cells that convert light energy into neural activity. The layer closest to the back of the eyeball is lined with two specialized types of nerve cells called rods and cones (again, see Figure 3.5). **Rods** are long, thin, cylindrical cells that are highly sensitive to light. They are concentrated in the sides of the retina and are active for black-and-white vision in dim light. Under impossibly ideal conditions, rods have the capacity to detect the light produced by one ten-billionth of a watt. On a perfectly

**retina**   The rear, multilayered part of the eye where rods and cones convert light into neural impulses.

**rods**   Rod-shaped photoreceptor cells in the retina that are highly sensitive to light.

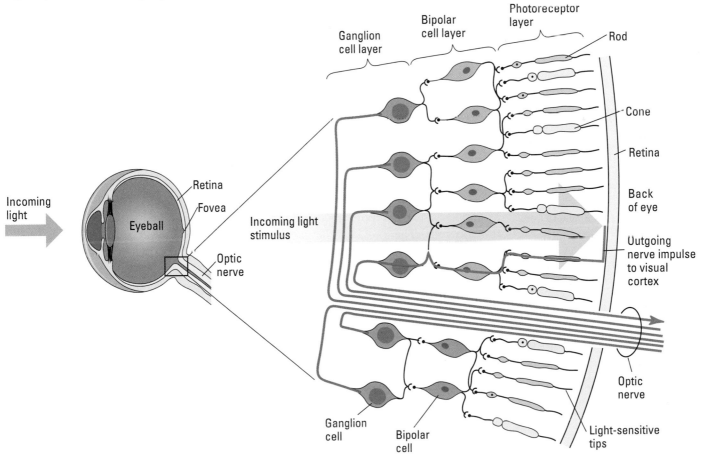

**FIGURE 3.5   The retina**
The back wall of the retina has three major layers containing 130 million photoreceptor cells. Light-sensitive rods are concentrated in the sides of the retina, and color-sensitive cones are clustered in the center.

*This photo shows how rods and cones, magnified approximately 14,000 times, line the back wall of the retina.*

clear, pitch-dark night, that's like seeing the light of a match struck thirty miles away. **Cones** are shorter, thicker, more tapered cells that are sensitive to color under high levels of illumination. Cones are densely clustered in the center of the **fovea**, the pinhead-size center of the retina. Unlike the rest of the retina, the fovea contains only cones, and the ratio of rods to cones increases in the outer edges of the retina.

In owls and other nocturnal (active only at night) animals, the retina contains only rods. Thus, they can see at night but their vision is in black and white. In chipmunks, pigeons, and other diurnal (active only during the day) animals, the retina contains only cones. Thus, they are virtually blind at night. In animals that are active both day and night, the retina has a mixture of rods and cones. For example, the human retina has about 120 million rods and 7 million cones, enabling us to see colors under normal lighting and to make out forms under low levels of illumination. Individuals whose retinas contain no rods suffer from night blindness; those without cones lack all color vision.

Often, we need to adjust to radical changes in illumination. It's happened to me, and I'm sure it has happened to you, too. You step inside a darkened movie theater on a sunny day. As you start walking down the aisle, however, you have to put your arms out and inch slowly forward, stumbling around as if you were blind. After a few minutes, you can see again. This experience illustrates **dark adaptation**, the process by which eyes become more sensitive to light in a dark environment. It takes about thirty minutes for you to fully adapt to the dark—at which point the eyes become ten thousand times more sensitive. It also takes time to adjust to bright light. That's why, when you leave a movie theater during the day, everything seems so "washed out" that you have to squint at first to keep out the glare. This is an instance of **light adaptation**, the process by which our eyes become less sensitive to light under high levels of illumination.

When light strikes the rods and cones, it sparks a chain of events within a network of interconnected neurons that results in vision. Rods and cones contain photopigments, chemicals that break down in response to light, thus triggering neural impulses. These impulses activate bipolar cells, which, in turn, activate nearby ganglion cells. The axons of the ganglion cells form the **optic nerve**, a pathway that carries visual information from each eyeball to the brain. The area where the optic nerve enters the eye has no rods or cones, only axons. So each eye has a **blind spot.** You don't normally notice it because your eyes are always moving, but you can find your blind spot through a simple exercise (see Figure 3.6).

Psychologists used to think that electrical impulses were delivered from the retina to the brain, as on an assembly line. It was as if there was a simple division of labor, whereby the retinal neurons "received" sensory information and passed it along on a conveyer belt to the visual cortex for perceptual "processing." We now know that the mechanisms of vision are more complex. Ultimately, signals from 130 million rods and cones are funneled through a mere 1 million axons in the optic nerve. Think for a moment about these numbers, and you'll realize what they mean: that the bipolar and ganglion cells must be integrating and compressing signals from multiple receptors. The retina is a "smart" optical instrument. Not only does it receive light, but it also processes visual information (Casanova & Ptito, 2001; Hoffman, 1998; Palmer, 1999).

Any ganglion cell that represents a cluster of neighboring rods and cones receives input from a sizable portion of the retina. This region is called a **receptive field.** By

**cones**   Cone-shaped photoreceptor cells in the retina that are sensitive to color.

**fovea**   The center of the retina, where cones are clustered.

**dark adaptation**   A process of adjustment by which the eyes become more sensitive to light in a dark environment.

**light adaptation**   The process of adjustment by which the eyes become less sensitive to light in a bright environment.

**optic nerve**   The pathway that carries visual information from the eyeball to the brain.

**blind spot**   A part of the retina through which the optic nerve passes. Lacking rods and cones, this spot is not responsive to light.

**receptive field**   An area of the retina in which stimulation triggers a response in a cell within the visual system.

**FIGURE 3.6   The blind spot**
Look at the illustration of two playing cards. Cover your right eye and look at the eight of spades card. When the eight of spades is about sixteen inches from your eye, the king of spades on the left will vanish. You do not see a space because your brain closes the gap [Adapted from Rodgers (1998) *Incredible Optical Illusions,* p. 119].

**visual cortex**   Located in the back of the brain, it is the main information-processing center for visual information.

**feature detectors**   Neurons in the visual cortex that respond to specific aspects of a visual stimulus (such as lines or angles).

recording the activity of individual ganglion cells, researchers have found many different types of receptive fields (Kuffler, 1953). The most common are circular "center-surround" fields in which light falling in the center has the opposite effect of light in the surrounding area. Some cells are activated by light in the center and inhibited by light in the surrounding area (center-on cells), whereas others work the opposite way, inhibited by light in the center and activated by light in the surrounding area (center-off cells). This arrangement makes the human eye particularly attuned to brightness-and-darkness contrasts in the visual field—contrasts that indicate corners, borders, and edges. There's an old joke about an art dealer who tries to sell a blank canvas. "What is it?" asks the prospective buyer. "A white cow in a snowstorm," says the dealer. Funny or not, this joke underestimates our visual acuity. A white cow would differ in brightness from white snow, and its body would differ in texture, thus forming a subtle but discernible outline against the background.

**Visual Pathways**   Axon fibers of ganglion cells form the optic nerve, which is the first part of the visual pathway that links each eyeball to the brain. The two optic nerves meet at the optic chiasm, where axons from the inside half of each eye cross over to the opposite half of the brain. This arrangement means that the left visual field of both eyes is projected to the right side of the brain, and the right visual field of both eyes is projected to the left side of the brain. After reaching the optic chiasm, the nerve fibers travel along two tracts, through the thalamus, the relay station where sensory signals are directed to appropriate areas of the **visual cortex.** Located in the back of the brain, the visual cortex is the main information-processing center for visual information (see Figure 3.7).

**The Visual Cortex**   Once information from the ganglion cells reaches the visual cortex, it is processed by **feature detectors**—neurons that are sensitive only to certain aspects of a visual image, such as lines or angles. This aspect of vision was first revealed by David Hubel and Torsten Wiesel (1962), who implanted microelectrodes in the visual cortexes of cats (and later monkeys) projected different types of visual stimuli on a screen, and measured the electrical activity of single cells. Do

*In 1666, Sir Isaac Newton intercepted a beam of sunlight with a prism and found that white light contained all visible colors of the spectrum. Shown above are his handwritten notes about this discovery: "I procured me a triangle glass prisme, to try therewith the celebrated phanemena of colours."*

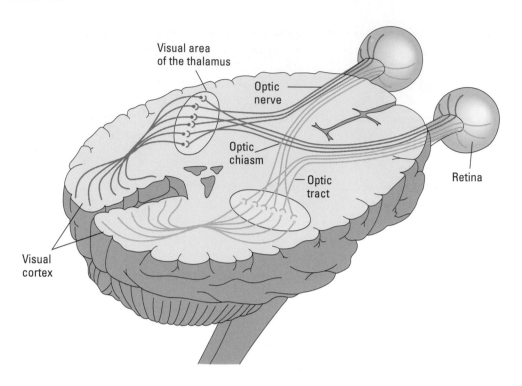

FIGURE 3.7    **Visual pathways**
From both eyes, the optic nerves meet at the optic chiasm, where the signals cross to the opposite half of the brain. The nerve fibers travel in two tracks through the thalamus, where they are directed to the visual cortex.

different neurons specialize in certain types of information? If so, the goal was to map or "decode" the visual cortex (see Figure 3.8).

In a painstaking series of studies, Hubel and Wiesel (1979) discovered that three types of neurons service the visual cortex and that each type has its own specialists at work. *Simple cells* are activated by highly particular images. For example, some simple cells fire in response to a vertical line in the middle of the screen but not to a line that is off-center or tilted at a different angle. Other simple cells fire in response to horizontal lines, wider lines, or lines tilted at a forty-five-degree angle. The stimulus–response connection is that specific. *Complex cells* receive input from many simple cells. Although complex cells specialize in certain types of images, they react to those images anywhere in the visual receptive field—center, bottom, side, and so on. Finally, *hypercomplex cells* receive input from complex cells and respond to stimulus patterns. If one simple cell is activated by /, a second by \, and a third by -, the

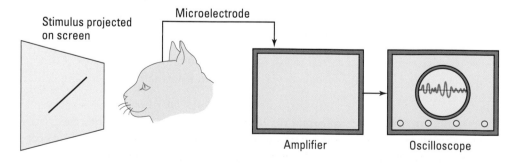

FIGURE 3.8    **Hubel and Wiesel's apparatus**
Hubel and Wiesel implanted microelectrodes in a cat's visual cortex, projected visual stimuli, and measured single-cell activity. These signals were amplified and displayed on an oscilloscope.

hypercomplex cell might react to a combination of these features, as in the letter *A*. When you consider the complexity of words, faces, landscapes, three-dimensional objects, skylines, and other images that enrich our lives, it's no wonder that the visual cortex is tightly packed with more than one hundred million neurons.

In 1981, Hubel and Wiesel were awarded a Nobel prize for their work. In the years since their discovery of feature detectors in the visual cortex, others have identified neurons that fire primarily in response to highly specific features such as color, form, movement, and the depth of a visual stimulus (Livingstone & Hubel, 1988; Hubel, 1996). Certain areas of the visual cortex also specialize in complex patterns, or configurations. For example, experiments with monkeys indicate that some cells are activated by the image of a hand (Gross et al., 1972), whereas others fire in response to faces (Bayliss et al., 1985) and upward or downward movements (Logothetis & Schall, 1989). Some neurons are most responsive to bull's-eyes, concentric circles, and spiral patterns (Gallant et al., 1993); others are responsive to starlike shapes (Sary et al., 1993), depth-related cues (Cumming & DeAngelis, 2001), and certain wavelengths and colors (Moutoussis & Zeki, 2002). It seems that the visual system is uniquely prepared to detect biologically adaptive types of visual stimulation. Indeed, damage to certain areas of the visual cortex produces very specific deficits—such as a complete or partial loss of color vision, face recognition, or an ability to see stationary or moving objects (Zeki, 1992).

**Color Vision**   Ruby-red apples. Yellow taxi cabs. Lush green grass. Although some animals see the world in pale shades (including the bull, which is supposedly enraged by the sight of a matador's bright-red cape), all mammals have some form of color vision (Jacobs, 1993). For us humans, color is a particularly vital part of the visual experience. It is also linked in interesting ways to emotion. Thus, sadness feels blue, anger makes us see red, death is mourned in black, and jealousy brings a visit from the green-eyed monster.

People think that color is an objective property of objects. In fact, it is a property of organisms. When sunlight shines on a red rose, only the long red rays in the spectrum are reflected into our eyes. All other wavelengths are absorbed in the flower's surface. (If no wavelengths were absorbed, then the rose would appear white.) Ironically, then, the rose holds everything but red. Most people can discriminate among two hundred different colors and thousands of different shades. How do we do it? There are two major theories of color vision: the trichromatic theory and the opponent-process theory (Kaiser & Boynton, 1996; Lennie, 2000).

Early in the nineteenth century, physiologists Thomas Young (1802) and Hermann von Helmholtz (1852) argued that the human eye is receptive to three primary colors—red, blue, and green—and that all other colors are derived from combinations of these primaries. By recording the neural responses of individual cones to different wavelengths of light, twentieth-century researchers later confirmed the Young-Helmholtz **trichromatic theory** (Schnapf et al., 1987; Wald, 1964). Specifically, there are three types of cones, each having a different photochemical that produces a particular response to light. One type fires most when struck by short wavelengths, so it picks up the color blue. The second type is most sensitive to the middle wavelengths, for the color green. The third type is most sensitive to long wavelengths, for the color red. In short, blue cones, green cones, and red cones serve as the building blocks for color vision. The different combinations of cones produce other colors in the eye's "palette." Activate both red and green cones, for example, and you will see the color yellow. Activate all three types of cones, and white is produced (see Figure 3.9). This, by the way, is what happens on a color TV screen, where pictures are formed from tiny red, green, and blue dots.

**trichromatic theory**   A theory of color vision stating that the retina contains three types of color receptors—for red, blue, and green—and that these combine to produce all other colors.

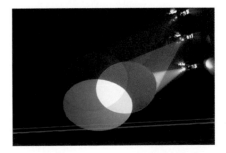

**FIGURE 3.9   Trichromatic theory**
As shown, any color can be produced by mixing blue, green, and red light waves. When all three colors are combined, white is produced.

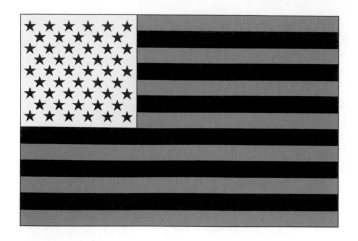

**FIGURE 3.10** **Afterimages**
Stare at this flag for sixty seconds, then look at a white sheet of paper. According to the opponent-process theory, you should see a negative afterimage that converts green to red, yellow to blue, and black to white. If you don't see an afterimage right away, blink and look again.

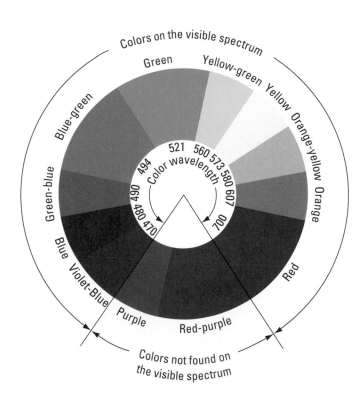

**FIGURE 3.11** **The color wheel**
As shown, opponent colors are directly across from each other in the circle (red is across from green, blue is across from yellow). The numbers on the spokes are wavelengths, expressed in nanometers.

**afterimage** A visual sensation that persists after prolonged exposure to and removal of a stimulus.

German physiologist Ewald Hering (1878) was not completely satisfied with the trichromatic theory. As he saw it, yellow was a primary color, not a derivative of red and green. He also noticed that certain color combinations just don't seem to exist. A mix of red and blue gives rise to varying shades of purple, but what is reddish green? Another puzzling phenomenon that didn't fit was the occurrence of negative **afterimages.** An afterimage is a sensation that persists after prolonged exposure to a stimulus. Stare at the image presented in Figure 3.10 for sixty seconds and in good lighting. Then look at a blank white sheet of paper. What do you see? In situations such as this one, staring at a green image leaves a red afterimage, yellow leaves a trace of blue, and black leaves white.

Putting the pieces together, Hering proposed the **opponent-process theory** of color vision. According to this theory, there are three types of visual receptors, and each is sensitive to a pair of complementary or "opponent" colors. One type reacts to the colors blue and yellow, a second type detects red and green, and a third type detects variations in brightness ranging from black to white. The color wheel in Figure 3.11 illustrates how these primary colors and their "companions" line up on nearly opposite sides of the circle. Within each pair of red-green, blue-yellow, and black-white receptors, some parts fire more to one color whereas other parts react to its opposite. That's why we never see bluish yellow or reddish green, but we might see bluish green and reddish yellow. While seeing one color at a specific spot on the retina, you cannot also see its opposite on the same spot (Conway, 2002).

The opponent-process theory can explain two aspects of color vision that its predecessor theory could not. First, it explains afterimages. Staring at the green stripes in Figure 3.10 causes the green-seeing cells to fire. Then, when the green color is removed from view, these parts of the cells become temporarily fatigued, leaving only the red parts to fire normally (Vimal et al., 1987). This process tips the neural balance to red, which produces a brief "rebound" effect (staring at yellow and black triggers a similar rebounding of blue and white).

Second, opponent-process theory can explain color blindness, usually a genetic disorder. In actuality, only about one in 100 thousands people are color "blind," seeing the world in only black, white, and shades of gray (Nathans, 1989). Rather, color-deficient people tend to confuse certain colors. The most common problem, particularly among men, is red-green color blindness, which is an inability to distinguish between red and green because both appear gray (how ironic that these are the universal traffic colors for stop and go!) See Figure 3.12. Though very rare, a second form of color blindness is the inability to distinguish between—you guessed it— blue and yellow.

For many years, researchers debated the relative merits of the trichromatic and opponent-process theories of color vision. As often happens in either-or debates, it now appears that both theories are correct—and that the way people sense color is a two-step process. According to this view, the human retina contains red, blue, and green cones, as suggested by the trichromatic theory. But in the thalamus—where these signals are sent en route to the

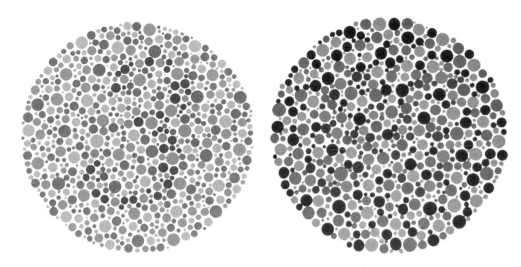

**opponent-process theory**   The theory that color vision is derived from three pairs of opposing receptors. The opponent colors are blue and yellow, red and green, and black and white.

**audition**   The sense of hearing.

**FIGURE 3.12   Test of color deficiency**
In items like these, people with red-green color blindness have difficulty seeing the numbers embedded in the pattern. The inability to distinguish between red and green, as in these patterns or in traffic signals, caused a 1996 train crash near Hoboken, New Jersey. According to the National Transportation Safety Board, the engineer, who had failed a color-vision test, failed to detect the red signal. New Jersey Transit now requires all of its engineers to pass a color-vision test consisting of fourteen circular plates of polka dots in which numbers are formed by slightly contrasting colors.

visual cortex—single-cell recordings reveal that the neurons operate in accordance with the opponent-process theory. That is, some cells are excited by red and inhibited by green, and vice versa. Other cells react to blue and yellow. Color vision is complex and still not fully understood (Abramov & Gordon, 1994; Gegenfurtner & Sharpe, 2000).

# HEARING

 3.2

If you had to suffer one fate—to be blind or to be deaf—which would you choose? It's a morbid question, I know. Ask around, however, and you'll find that most people would rather lose their hearing than their eyesight. Yet Helen Keller, like many others who are both blind and deaf, wrote that deafness was by far the greater handicap.

It's easy to take the sounds of everyday life for granted—and, indeed, we often say that "silence is golden." But auditory sensations surround us and inform us. The chatter of voices, the clanging of dinner dishes, music throbbing from stereo speakers, a creaking old floor breaking the silence of night, the trickling of water over pebbles, the whisper of a secret, the crunching of potato chips, a figure skater's blade scraping the ice, the hum of a fluorescent lamp, the crack of a wooden bat against a baseball, the clinking of champagne glasses on New Year's Eve, the screeching of a train roaring into the station, and the one I've become the most accustomed to—the woodpecker-like tapping of fingers on a computer keyboard. These are just some of the familiar sounds of life. But what is sound, and how do we hear it?

**Sound Waves**   Every sensation is born of energy. For vision, or seeing, the stimulus is light. For **audition,** or hearing, the stimulus is sound. As in light, sound travels in waves. Physically, sound is *vibration,* a pattern of rapid wavelike movement of air molecules. First, something has to move—an engine, vocal cords, violin strings, or clapping hands. The movement jolts the surrounding molecules of air, and these collide with other air molecules. Like the ocean, sound ripples in waves that ebb and flow in all directions. It loses energy from one ripple to the next, however, which is the

**white noise** A hissing sound that results from a combination of all frequencies of the sound spectrum.

| TABLE 3.2 PHYSICAL AND SENSORY DIMENSIONS OF SOUND | |
|---|---|
| **Physical Dimension** | **Sensory Dimension** |
| Frequency | Pitch |
| Amplitude | Loudness |
| Complexity | Timbre |

reason sound fades at a distance. Sound travels through air at 750 miles per hour—much slower than the speed of light, which is 186,000 miles per second. That's why, in thunderstorms, you see lightning before you hear the accompanying thunder.

Like light, sound waves can be distinguished by three major properties (see Table 3.2). The first is wavelength, or *frequency*. As molecules of air push outward from a source, they expand and compress in cycles. Frequency, measured by the number of cycles completed per second, is expressed as hertz (Hz). One cycle per second equals one Hz. Subjectively, the frequency of a sound wave determines its *pitch* (the highness or lowness of a sound). The higher the frequency, the higher the pitch. Humans can hear frequencies ranging from about 20 Hz to 20,000 Hz—in music, the equivalent of almost ten octaves. Homing pigeons and elephants can hear lower frequencies. Bats, dogs, and dolphins hear at higher frequencies (dogs can hear at 50,000 Hz, which is why a "silent" dog whistle is not silent to a dog). Most of the sounds we need to hear, and certainly those we enjoy hearing, are well within this range. The lowest note on a piano is 27.5 Hz, the highest note is 4,180 Hz, and the voices of conversation range from 200 to 800 Hz. When all frequencies of the sound spectrum are combined, they produce a hissing sound. This hissing is called **white noise**—named by analogy to the white light that results from the combination of all wavelengths in the visible light spectrum.

The second property of sound is *amplitude*. Amplitude refers to the intensity, or height, of each sound wave. In physical terms, the amplitude of a wave determines its *loudness*. The greater the amplitude, the louder the sound. We may not be able to hear a pin drop, but our ears are responsive to a remarkably wide range of amplitudes. Indeed, the loudest sound we can tolerate without pain is billions of times greater in amplitude than the softest sound we can hear. For variations within this range, amplitude is measured in decibels (dB). The box on page 101 provides examples of the loudness of various sounds at different dB levels. You'll see that dB levels over 120 are painful and can cause permanent damage to the ears (Kryter, 1994).

A third property of sound is purity, or *complexity*. Strike a tuning fork, and you'll produce something rare: a pure tone consisting of a single frequency of vibration. In reality, most sounds are complex mixtures of waves of different frequencies. Speech, music, a ringing bell, and a breaking window are familiar examples (Bregman, 1990; Krumhansl, 1991). The complexity of a sound determines its *timbre*, or tonal quality. Play the same note at the same loudness on a piano, trumpet, saxophone, tuba, and violin, and what you'll hear are differences in timbre.

**The Auditory System** Philosophers like to ponder the age-old question, "If a tree falls in a forest, but no one is around to hear it, does it make a sound?" This really is a profound question. We know that the fall of a tree sends waves of molecules blasting through the air, but we also know that without an auditory system to catch these molecules—well, you make the call. As in vision, hearing requires that energy be detected, converted into neural impulses, and relayed to the brain. As shown in Figure 3.13, this complex process begins in the three-part (outer, middle, and inner) structure of the human ear.

Sound waves are collected in the *outer ear*, beginning with the fleshy pinna. Some animals, such as dogs, cats, and deer, can wiggle this structure like a radar dish to

According to the *Guinness Book of Records*, the loudest noise ever documented was in 1883, when the Indonesian island volcano Krakatoa erupted.

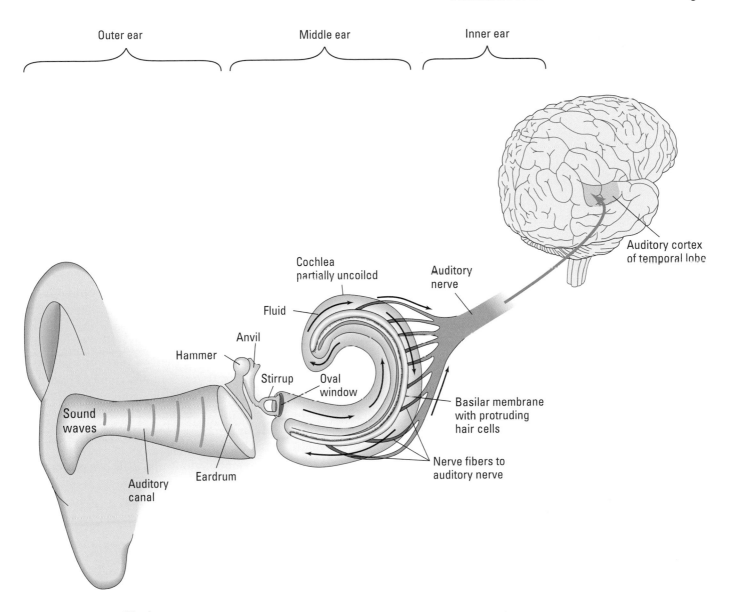

Outer ear    Middle ear    Inner ear

Cochlea partially uncoiled

Fluid

Anvil

Hammer

Stirrup    Oval window

Sound waves

Auditory canal    Eardrum

Auditory nerve

Auditory cortex of temporal lobe

Basilar membrane with protruding hair cells

Nerve fibers to auditory nerve

**FIGURE 3.13   The human ear**
As shown, the process of hearing begins in the three-part (outer, middle, and inner) structure of the ear. From the auditory nerve, signals are relayed to the auditory cortex.

maximize the reception of sound (humans cannot). Research shows that the folds of the pinna enable people to pinpoint the location of sounds—for example, whether they come from above us or below, in front or behind. The sound waves are then funneled through the auditory canal to the eardrum, a tightly stretched membrane that separates the outer and middle portions of the ear. The eardrum vibrates back and forth to the waves, thereby setting into motion a series of tiny connecting bones in the *middle ear*—the hammer, the anvil, and the stirrup (for you trivia buffs, these are the three smallest bones in the body). This middle-ear activity amplifies sound by a factor of thirty. The last of these bones, the stirrup, then vibrates against a soft *inner-ear* membrane called the oval window. This vibration is transmitted to the fluid that fills the canals of the cochlea, a snail-shape tube—and the resulting motion presses up against the basilar membrane, which brushes up against an array of sixteen thousand sensitive hair cells. These hair cells bend, exciting fibers in the auditory nerve—a bundle of axons that link to auditory centers of the brain. Also in

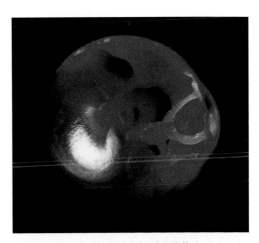

*In this photograph of the middle ear, you can see the eardrum (left), hammer (top), anvil (center), and stirrup (right).*

**auditory localization** The ability to judge the direction a sound is coming from.

the inner ear are semicircular canals, which, as we'll see later, play a critical role in balance (Hudspeth, 2000).

To summarize, the "plumbing" and "wiring" that turn sound waves into meaningful input are fairly intricate. Sound waves collected in the outer ear are transmitted into a salt-watery fluid and then transformed into electrical impulses in the inner ear. From the auditory nerve, signals then cross to the other side of the brain. Next, they get routed to the thalamus, where they're relayed to areas of the auditory cortex. Once there, the signals are processed by cells that specialize in high, middle, or low frequencies of sound (Hirsh & Watson, 1996; Yost, 2000).

**Hearing Abilities** Hearing is not one sensory ability but many. People can detect sound, understand spoken language, and appreciate the acoustical qualities of music. Everyone with normal hearing can distinguish between sounds that are loud and soft or between those produced by horns and those produced by stringed instruments. Although only one in ten thousand people have "absolute pitch" (an ability to identify a musical note as middle C, F-sharp, or B-flat), we can all make judgments of "relative pitch"—enabling us to know, for example, that a child's voice is higher than a man's (Takeuchi & Hulse, 1993). In many ways, our auditory competence is impressive.

One particularly adaptive aspect of normal hearing that we take for granted is **auditory localization**—the ability to tell the *direction* a sound is coming from. Localization is needed to determine if the blaring siren you hear is coming from behind you on the road, or if the approaching footsteps are coming from your left or your right. This skill was vital to the survival of our primitive ancestors and is a matter of life and death to all animals of prey.

Unless you're being fooled by the visual manipulations of a skilled ventriloquist, it's usually easy to tell if a sound is coming from your left or your right, and we have this ability even as infants. In fact, if you stand to the left or right of an infant and shake a rattle, the baby will often turn its head in your direction, as if locating the source (see Chapter 10).

What makes auditory localization possible is that we hear in stereo, using two ears spaced about six inches apart. If you're at a noisy gathering and someone on your left calls your name, your left ear receives the signal before the right ear does (it's closer to the source) and more intensely (your head is a barrier to the more distant ear). The six inches of brain tissue and skull that separate your ears may seem too little to matter, but our auditory system is sensitive. Unless a sound is directly above, below, in front of, or behind us, the brain can detect small differences in timing and intensity between the ears—and use these differences to locate the source. This process is shown in Figure 3.14 (Middlebrooks & Green, 1991; Konishi, 1993). Researchers are now trying to determine the extent to which people can identify not only the direction of a sound but also its distance from them (Zahorik, 2002).

Auditory localization is not always so easy. If you're at the same noisy gathering and someone directly behind you calls your name, both ears will receive the input at the same time and at the same intensity. What then? Lacking physical cues to locate the source, you will turn your head as if it were a radar dish in an effort to produce controlled differences in the timing and intensity of the signals to the two ears. The objective in such circumstances is to "fine-tune" the reception of information. It's interesting in this regard that people who have been blind from an early age localize sounds better than sighted people do. Having to adjust to life without visual cues, blind people compensate for their deficiency by becoming more sophisticated in the use of auditory information (Lessard et al., 1998).

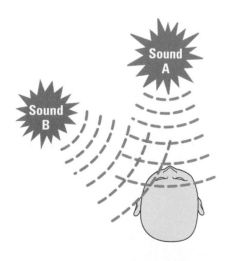

**FIGURE 3.14 Auditory localization**
The brain is able to detect small differences in the timing and intensity of sound between the two ears—and can use these differences to localize the source.

## Psychology and Health

# WHEN IS LOUD TOO LOUD?

When I was a teenager, my parents would warn me that the constant blaring of my stereo and the Grateful Dead marathons I went to would hurt my ears. "Parents," I muttered to myself, "what do they know?" Sure, my ears would be ringing after a rock concert, and sure, voices would seem muffled for a while, but my ears were back to normal the next day. Or were they?

*Consumer Reports* (1999) estimates that twenty-eight million Americans—more than 10 percent of the population—have suffered from full or partial hearing loss, often because of noise. Research indicates that exposure to intense noise can cause such violent vibrations in the inner-ear that it can damage hair cells and permanently impair hearing. When does "sound" become "noise"? When does "loud" become "too loud"? The amplitude of a sound, which determines its loudness to the human ear, is measured in terms of decibels (dB). To understand this scale, it's important to know that loudness increases in orders of magnitude (a 20 dB sound is ten times as intense as a 10 dB sound, a 40 dB sound is one hundred times as intense as a 20 dB sound, and so on). Constant daily exposure to sounds of over 85 dB (heavy street traffic, subways, jackhammers, snowmobiles, lawnmowers, and vacuum cleaners) can flatten the inner-ear hair cells over time and cause a gradual loss of hearing. Even a brief assault by an ear-shattering sound that exceeds 140 dB (a gunshot, explosion, or rocket launch) can tear the delicate inner-ear tissues and cause permanent hearing loss. Look at Figure 3.15, and you'll see that danger to the ear is all around us.

Most current research on sound exposure focuses on the occupational hazards of noise in factories, airports, construction sites, and other work settings (Kryter, 1994). But there's also a lot of concern about exposures to amplified music vibrating from huge speakers. Spend two hours at a rock concert or turn the stereo volume up to full blast, and you may be putting your ears at risk (West & Evans, 1990). Many experts claim that if your Walkman can be heard by someone near you, then you're damaging your ears. And the loss can be irreversible. In 1986, the Who entered the *Guinness Book of World Records* for the loudest rock concert ever when they blasted sounds that measured 120 dB at a distance of 164 feet from the speakers. Unless their ears were protected, everyone within a 164-foot radius probably suffered irreversible hearing loss. The Who's Peter Townshend (and other rock musicians) is now

partially deaf. He also complains of a constant hissing and ringing in his ears. According to audiologist Dean Garstecki, director of a hearing impairment program, "We've got 21-year-olds walking around with hearing loss patterns of people 40 years their senior" (Toufexis, 1991).

Much of the noise that surrounds us is unavoidable. But too often people don't realize how harmful it is. Baggage handlers and others who work on airport runways wear ear protectors, which can muffle noise by about 35 dB. If necessary, you too can do this by purchasing quieter power tools, home appliances, and other products and by wearing inexpensive soft foam earplugs or acoustic earmuffs (Prasher & Luxon, 1998). Just as you wouldn't stare at the sun's penetrating rays, you shouldn't expose the delicate structures of your ears to piercing, high-volume sound waves. As my parents used to say, "Can't you just turn the volume down a little?"

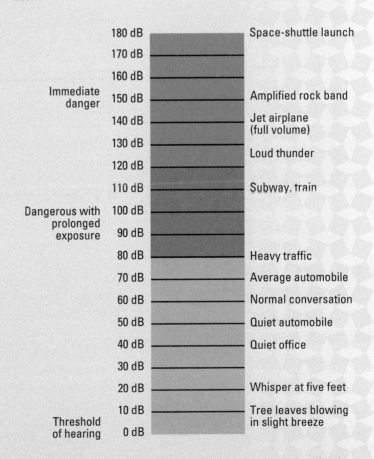

| | |
|---|---|
| | 180 dB — Space-shuttle launch |
| | 170 dB |
| | 160 dB |
| Immediate danger | 150 dB — Amplified rock band |
| | 140 dB — Jet airplane (full volume) |
| | 130 dB — Loud thunder |
| | 120 dB |
| | 110 dB — Subway, train |
| Dangerous with prolonged exposure | 100 dB |
| | 90 dB |
| | 80 dB — Heavy traffic |
| | 70 dB — Average automobile |
| | 60 dB — Normal conversation |
| | 50 dB — Quiet automobile |
| | 40 dB — Quiet office |
| | 30 dB |
| | 20 dB — Whisper at five feet |
| | 10 dB — Tree leaves blowing in slight breeze |
| Threshold of hearing | 0 dB |

**FIGURE 3.15   Common sounds and the amounts of noise they produce, in decibels**

**conduction hearing loss** Hearing loss caused by damage to the eardrum or bones in the middle ear.

**sensorineural hearing loss** Hearing loss caused by damage to the structures of the inner ear.

**olfactory system** The structures responsible for the sense of smell.

**Hearing Disabilities** It's natural to take your sensory competence for granted—until you don't have it. Today, millions of people have hearing impairments that range from a partial loss to profound deafness. There are two kinds of hearing impairment. The symptoms are the same, but the causes and treatment are very different. One type is **conduction hearing loss,** in which damage to the eardrum or to the bones in the middle ear diminishes their ability to conduct sound waves. Fortunately, hearing can be partially restored through surgery or by means of a hearing aid that amplifies sound waves—provided that the inner-ear structures are intact. A far more serious problem is **sensorineural hearing loss,** caused by inner-ear damage to the cochlea, hair cells, or auditory nerve. Sensorineural hearing loss can be caused by certain diseases, by biological changes due to old age, or by exposure to intensely loud noises. (See *Psychology and Health.*) Researchers have long believed that once neural tissue is destroyed, it cannot be repaired or replaced. Recent studies have shown, however, that hair cells taken from guinea pigs, rats, and humans can be regenerated (Lefebvre et al., 1993; Warchol et al., 1993). What remains to be seen is whether these regenerated hair cells can be rendered functional, bringing sound back to people who are deaf (Shinohara et al., 2002).

Although it is not currently possible to regenerate working auditory hair cells in humans and although conventional hearing aids do not restore hearing in sensorineural hearing loss, researchers have developed and tested artificial cochlea implants, or "bionic ears." Intended for people with damaged hair cells, this device has a tiny microphone in the outer ear that sends sound to a miniature electrode implanted in the cochlea. This electrode stimulates the auditory nerve—and an impulse is fired to the brain. Cochlea implants may enable many people who are profoundly deaf to detect the presence of sound, perhaps for the first time in their lives. The sensations produced by these devices seem to vary from one user to another. Some wearers derive little benefit from the implants. However, others are able to understand speech. They cannot make out distinct words, but they can detect clear changes in volume and pitch—and can even recognize simple melodies and vowel sounds, all of which makes lipreading easier (Pijl & Schwarz, 1995; Fu & Shannon, 1999; Tyler et al., 1995). Deaf children who wear cochlea implants get higher scores on language achievement tests than those who do not (Tomblin et al., 1999). Clearly, this approach is a promising one.

## OTHER SENSES

Psychologists know more about seeing and hearing than about other sensory systems, but these other systems are also essential to the adaptive human package. You can't see or hear the heat of a fire, the sting of a bee, the stench of a gas leak, or the bitter taste of a poisonous plant. Nor can you see or hear the sensuous pleasures of a scent-filled rose, creamy chocolate, or a soothing massage. Human beings have developed the ability to detect, process, and integrate information from many sources.

**Smell** Dogs are known for their ability to sniff out faint scents and to track down animals, criminals, and illegal drugs over time and long distances. That is why the U.S. government uses trained dogs in airports to help detect terrorist explosives (Buckley, 1996) and, more recently, to assist in the detection of the biological weapon anthrax (Miller & Klaidman, 2002).

In a contest of smelling ability, we humans would have little to brag about compared to our canine buddies—who may well have the keenest noses in the animal kingdom (Marshall & Moulton, 1981). But our own sense of smell, the product of the body's **olfactory system,** is more sensitive than you may realize—and potentially more important. In the past, for example, medical doctors used the smell of sweat,

*Shing Ling has been trained to detect early cancer in humans. Apparently, cancer patients have a subtle odor on their breath compared to healthy people. You and I cannot smell it, but researcher Michael McCulloch is training dogs to detect tumors from breath samples before the most sophisticated technology can. More research is needed, but initial results are encouraging.*

breath, urine, and other body odors to diagnose illness. Today, "aromatherapy" is based on the controversial notion that inhaled odors and oils absorbed through the skin can help ward off illness (Vroon et al., 1997).

All smells have a chemical origin (Buck, 2000). Depending on their molecular structure, substances emit odor-causing molecules into the air. Some objects, such as glass and metal, have no smell (any scent these objects may emit comes from impurities on the surface). Other objects, like the musk oil extracted from animal sweat glands, produce overpowering odors. By breathing through the nose and mouth, we inhale these airborne odorant molecules—which dissolve and become trapped by *olfactory receptors* in the moist yellow lining of the upper nasal passages just above the roof of the mouth. There are about ten million of these hairlike receptors in the human nose (the average dog has two hundred million). Certain molecules seem to fit certain types of receptors the way a key fits a lock. Once activated, they trigger an action potential in the *olfactory nerve.* This nerve connects the nose to the *olfactory bulb,* a bean-size organ that distributes information throughout the cortex and to the nearby limbic-system structures that control memory and emotion. It's interesting that smell is the only sensation that is not routed to the cortex through the thalamus. As shown in Figure 3.16, the olfactory bulb is its own private relay station (Doty, 2001).

Unlike other animals, humans do not need a sense of smell to mark territory, track prey, signal danger, establish dominance hierarchies, or attract a mate. Also, language does not provide an adequate supply of olfaction words, which makes it hard for people to describe smells (Richardson & Zucco, 1989). Yet the millions of olfactory receptors in the nose enable us to distinguish among ten thousand different odor molecules—including the proposed "primary" odors of vinegar, roses,

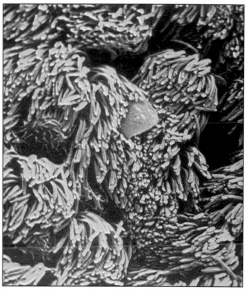

*When airborne odor molecules dissolve in the nose, they are trapped by the hairlike olfactory receptors shown in this picture.*

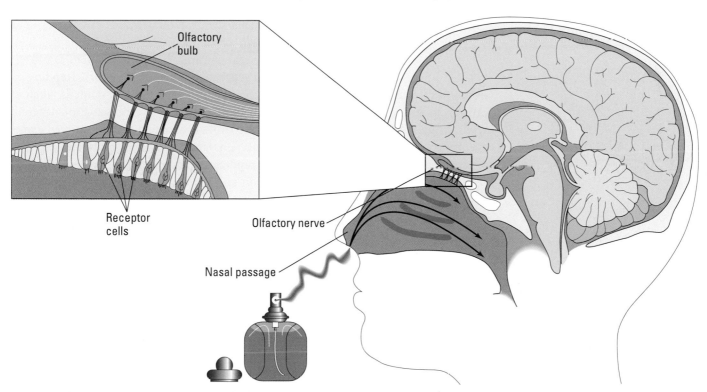

**FIGURE 3.16   The olfactory system**
Once in the nose, odorant molecules are trapped by olfactory receptors. These receptors send signals through the olfactory nerve to the olfactory bulb, which communicates with various parts of the brain.

Perfumers say they can distinguish as many as five thousand different types of odors.

mint, rotten egg, mothballs, dry-cleaning fluid, and musk (Amoore et al., 1964). Using high-resolution brain-imaging technology, Benjamin Rubin and Lawrence Katz (1999) exposed laboratory rats to chemicals that smelled like bananas, caraway, peanut butter, and spearmint and found that each odor sparked a unique pattern of receptor activity in the olfactory bulb.

Some smells have powerful effects on people—which is, perhaps, why so much money is spent on mint-flavored mouthwashes, deodorants, pine- and lemon-scented air fresheners, herbal shampoos, and perfumes. The olfactory bulbs extend some of their axons directly into the brain's limbic system, so it's not surprising that certain familiar smells—such as a whiff of cologne, a musty attic, or biscuits cooking in the oven—often bring on a rush of memories and emotions (Engen, 1982).

Our sense of smell is influenced by many factors. To begin with, individuals differ in their sensitivity. Helen Keller, who was blind and deaf from infancy, called smell "the fallen angel of the senses." She had a prodigious olfactory sense and wrote that she could often smell storms brewing. You might think that professional perfumers and whiskey blenders could also distinguish odors better than the average person, though there is no evidence for this claim. At the other end of the spectrum are people with *anosmia,* or odor blindness, that can be caused by serious head injury, viral infection, or toxic exposure. It's ironic that Ben Cohen, the co-founder of Ben & Jerry's Ice Cream, is anosmic—which is why, he says, his ice cream is rich and smooth in its texture.

People from different cultures have the same olfactory capacity—and similar likes and dislikes when it comes to the smell of plants, fruits, spices, and body odors. Universally, people are drawn to flowers and other perfume-like fragrances and disgusted by foul and sulfurous odors (Miller, 1997). At the same time, people from different parts of the world are uniquely and adaptively attuned to the smells that surround them. In *Aroma: The Cultural History of Smell,* Constance Classen and others (1994) illustrate the point in several cultures. In an Amazonian rainforest in Colombia, the Desana separate the musky smell of "deep forest" animals (such as the jaguar), and the sweet smell of "open field" animals (such as various rodents). They also say they can detect by nose the presence of different neighboring tribes—based on whether those tribes eat a steady diet of hunted game, fish, or roots and vegetables. In Ethiopia, Dassanetch farmers and cattle herders mark the passage of calendar time by a predictable alternation of smells, from the burning and decay odors of the dry season and the new plant growth scents of the rainy season.

*"Each of us has an 'olfactory passport'—a personal aroma, in the form of body and breath odors."*
—PIET VROON

For reasons unknown, however, women outperform men at identifying different smells (Doty et al., 1985)—a difference that can be seen in fMRI brain scans showing that odors trigger more olfactory activation in women than in men (Yousem et al., 1999). Odor sensitivity also changes with age. Young babies cannot talk, but they do respond nonverbally to odor. Put a swab of honey under a baby's nose, and you may well see a smile. Put a swab of rotten egg under the nose, and the baby will grimace (Steiner, 1979). Even at the tender age of two weeks, nursing infants prefer their own mothers' body odor to that of other women (Cernoch & Porter, 1985). Among adults, olfactory sensitivity peaks in middle age and declines as people reach their seventies and eighties. This age trend was revealed in a *National Geographic* survey of 1.42 million subscribers who responded to a scratch-and-sniff odor recognition test (Gilbert & Wysocki, 1987).

Smell is a primitive sense—yet so successful, suggests Diane Ackerman (1990), "that in time the small lump of olfactory tissue atop the nerve cord grew into a brain" (p. 20). Given this view, it's hardly surprising that researchers have tried to identify pheromones in human beings. **Pheromones** are chemicals secreted by animals that transmit signals to others, usually of the same species. Ants, bees, termites, and other insects secrete chemicals that attract mates and "release" other behaviors. Equipped with sensitive chemoreceptors on his antennae, for example, the male emperor moth can detect the scent of a virgin female more than six miles away. Many mammals are also sexually excited by scent, which is why female dogs in heat send neighboring male dogs into a state of frenzy. Are humans similarly aroused? If so, could the scent be bottled and manufactured? For perfumers, the potential is easy to imagine.

Studies show that people can recognize others by their body odor. In this research, various subjects would shower using the same soap and then wear a T-shirt for at least twenty-four hours. After the shirts were collected, subjects would sniff them and try to identify the wearer. The result: College students can usually recognize their own shirts, mothers can pick out the shirts worn by their own children, and people in general can discriminate by odor between the shirts worn by men and women (Russell, 1976). There is even evidence to suggest that the menstrual cycles of women living together—such as mothers and daughters, sisters, and roommates— become synchronized through smell (Stern & McClintock, 1998).

Is there any evidence for the existence of human pheromones that serve as sexual attractants, or "love scents" (Kodis et al., 1998)? Some perfumes and colognes currently found in stores contain *alpha androstenol,* a sexual pheromone secreted by male pigs (it is also found in human underarm secretions). To date, there's no evidence to suggest that this chemical has the desired effect on behavior. However, it is possible that certain scents put people into a romantic mood. In *Scentsational Sex: The Secret to Using Aroma for Arousal,* psychiatrist Alan Hirsch (1998) reported the results of studies showing that people are powerfully influenced not by manly, sweet, or earthy colognes, but by odd mixtures of everyday odors—such as pumpkin pie and lavender (for men), or licorice candy mixed with cucumber (for women). So what are we to conclude? At this point, the research evidence is scant. It is clear, however, that human sexuality is far too complex to be chemically "controlled" by scent.

**Taste**    Taste is a product of the body's **gustatory system** (Doty, 1995). Like smell, taste is a chemical sensation. Put a morsel of food or a squirt of drink in the mouth, and it will come into contact with clusters of hairlike receptor cells called **taste buds.** There are about ten thousand taste buds in the mouth. Some cling to the roof and back of the throat, but most line the trenches and bumps on the surface of the tongue. Taste buds are most densely packed on the tip of the tongue but are virtually absent from the center of the tongue. Within each taste bud, between 50 and 150 receptor cells absorb the chemical molecules of food and drink—and trigger neural impulses that are routed to the thalamus and cortex. These cells are replaced every ten days, so if you burn your tongue on hot soup, the damage to your receptors will be repaired (see Figure 3.17).

There are four primary tastes: sweet, salty, sour, and bitter. However, the *flavor* of a food is determined not only by taste but by other factors as well. You may have noticed that after you've brushed your teeth in the morning, orange juice tastes bitter. After you've eaten artichokes, water tastes sweet. Chemical residues from the substance already eaten mix with what you're currently eating to produce a new taste sensation. Temperature, texture, and appearance are also important factors, which is why no one likes warm

**pheromones**    Chemicals secreted by animals that transmit signals—usually to other animals of the same species.

**gustatory system**    The structures responsible for the sense of taste.

**taste buds**    Nets of taste-receptor cells.

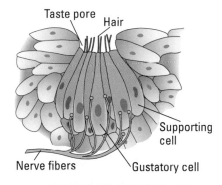

Taste pore    Hair

Supporting cell

Nerve fibers    Gustatory cell

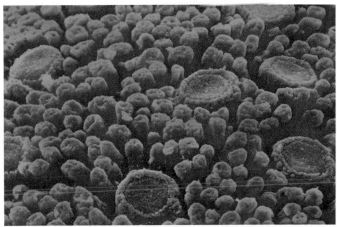

**FIGURE 3.17    Taste buds**
This photograph is of the surface of a human tongue, magnified seventy-five times. As shown in the sketch, the taste buds are located in the large round areas called papillae.

It seems hard to believe, but if you slice an apple and an onion into small cubes, hold your nose, and conduct a blind taste test, you'll have trouble telling the two foods apart.

soda or soggy potato chips and why the great chefs prepare dishes for the eye as well as for the palate. By far the most important determinant of flavor is odor. When I have a cold and my nose is all stuffed up, I lose my appetite. For me, there is no joy to chewing on food without flavor. Indeed, research shows that people lose their ability to identify common flavors—such as chocolate, vanilla, coffee, wine, and even onion and garlic—when they're prevented from smelling the food (Mozell et al., 1969).

The more taste buds that dot your tongue, the more sensitive you're likely to be to various tastes. Children have more taste buds than adults do, for example, which may explain why they are often so picky about eating "grown-up" foods. Even among adults, individuals differ in the number of taste buds they have—and in their sensitivity to taste. Indeed, recent studies have shown that people can be divided into three groups: nontasters, medium tasters, and supertasters. At one extreme, nontasters (25 percent of the population) are unable to detect certain sweet and bitter compounds and are less sensitive in general to taste. At the other extreme, supertasters (also about 25 percent of the population) react strongly to certain sweet and bitter compounds. Compared to most, supertasters use only half as much sugar or saccharin in their coffee or tea. They also suffer more oral burn from the active ingredient in chili peppers. These differences in taste sensitivity correspond nicely to our physiological makeup. Using videomicroscopy to count the number of taste buds on the tongue, researchers have found that nontasters have an average of 96 taste buds per square centimeter, medium tasters have 184, and supertasters have 425. Put differently, the number of taste buds on the human tongue can range from a low of 500 to a high of 10,000 (Bartoshuk & Beauchamp, 1994; Miller & Reedy, 1990).

**Touch** Every organism has a sense of touch. Sea snails withdraw their gills at the slightest pressure. Sponges sense an intruder by feeling the water around them quiver. As for us humans, often feeling is believing. Put up a "wet paint" sign, and you'll find, paradoxically, that it seems to invite touching rather than inhibit it. Tactile sensations are unique in many ways. To begin with, touch is the only sensation with receptors that are not localized in a single region of the body. We need eyes to see, ears to hear, a nose to smell, and a tongue to taste. But the organ of touch, and the site of its sensory receptors, is *skin*.

Skin is by far the largest organ of the body. It covers two square yards and weighs six to ten pounds. It is multilayered, waterproof, elastic, and filled with hair follicles, sweat-gland ducts, and nerve endings that connect to the central nervous system. When you consider all the sensations that emanate from your skin—feeling hot, cold, wet, dry, sore, itchy, scratchy, sticky, gooey, greasy, tingly, numb, and hurt—you can see that touch involves not one sensory system but many (Heller & Schiff, 1991; Craig & Rollman, 1999).

The sensations of touch are vital for survival. Without it, you would not know that you're in danger of becoming frostbitten or burned; you would not know if you've been stung by a bee; you would be unable to swallow food. When other sensory systems fail, touch takes on even more importance. All of us can feel the differences among leather, sandpaper, brick, cork, velvet, and other textures (Hollins et al., 1993). Indeed, most of us react with disgust to substances that are scabby, slimy, gooey, oily, clammy, and sticky (Miller, 1997). But for Virgil, the blind man whose eyesight was temporarily restored, shapes and textures are particularly important for recognizing objects. When passed a bowl of fruit, he could easily distinguish among a slick plum, a soft fuzzy peach, a smooth nectarine, and a rough, dimpled orange. He was even able to "see" through the disguise of an artificial wax pear that had fooled everyone else. "It's a candle," he said, "shaped like a bell or a pear" (Sacks, 1995, p. 149).

It's important to distinguish between passive and active touch. In passive touch, a person's skin is contacted by another object, as when a cat rubs up against your leg. In active touch, it is the person who initiates the contact, as when you pet your cat. Psychologically, the effects are different. James Gibson (1962) tested subjects' ability to identify cookie cutters shaped like stars, triangles, circles, and so on. When the objects were pressed lightly onto the hand (passive), they were identified correctly 29 percent of the time. When subjects actively explored the shapes with their fingers, the accuracy rate increased to 95 percent. Other research, too, shows that people can make fine discriminations among common objects when they explore by grasping, lifting, holding, squeezing, rubbing, and tracing the edges. For example, merely touching an object reveals temperature, rubbing a finger across it reveals texture, and molding the hand around it reveals its shape and volume (Klatsky & Lederman, 1992).

Active touch is what allows Virgil to feel the differences among plums, peaches, oranges, and nectarines. It's also the key to *Braille*, the alphanumeric system that allows many blind people to read. Braille letters and numbers consist of coded patterns of raised dots on a page that readers scan with their fingertips. Some Braille readers achieve a reading rate as high as 200 words per minute—which is remarkable considering that the average rate among sighted readers is 250 words per minute (Foulke, 1991). In one experiment, blind people using their Braille-reading fingers outperformed blindfolded sighted adults by 20 percent in their ability to discriminate different shapes by touch (Stevens et al., 1996).

Most psychologists agree that the sense of touch consists of four basic types of sensations: pressure, warmth, cold, and pain. Researchers initially thought that there was a separate receptor in the skin for each of these four sensations, but it now appears that only *pressure* sensations have unique and specialized nerve endings dispersed throughout the body. One of the most striking aspects of touch is that sensitivity to pressure or vibration is different from one part of the body to another. To determine the thresholds for touch (how much force it takes before a subject reports a feeling), researchers would apply a thin rod or wire to different areas of skin and vary the pressure (Weinstein, 1968). Figure 3.18 shows that the hands, fingers, and face are the most sensitive areas; the calves, thighs, and arms are the least sensitive. In all cases, pressure causes nerve endings to fire messages through the spinal cord, brainstem, and thalamus en route to the somatosensory cortex (Burton & Sinclair, 1996; Greenspan & Bolanowski, 1996).

**Temperature**   Normal human body temperature is 98.6 degrees Fahrenheit, or 37 degrees Celsius (temperatures at the surface of the skin are slightly lower). There are two striking facts about the sensation of temperature. First is that it is, to a large extent, *relative* to your current state. To demonstrate, fill three buckets with tap water—one cold, one hot, and one at room temperature. Place your right hand into the cold water and your left hand into the hot water, and leave them there for a minute. Then place both hands together into the third bucket. You can probably predict the amusing result: Both hands are now in the same water, yet your right hand feels warm and your left hand feels cool. If you ever plunged into a cold pool or eased yourself into a hot tub, you know that the sensations are triggered by temperatures that are well above or below your own current "adaptation level" (Hensel, 1981).

The second fact about temperature is that there are two separate sensory systems—one for signaling warmth, the other for signaling cold. Early studies showed that some spots on the skin respond more to warming and others more to cooling (Dallenbach, 1927). "Hot" is a particularly intriguing sensation in that it is triggered when these warm and cold spots are simultaneously stimulated. Thus, when people grasp two braided pipes—one with cold water running through it, the other

*Using Braille, blind people learn to read by running their fingers over coded patterns of raised dots.*

**WHAT'S YOUR PREDICTION**

People can distinguish objects by touch. Can we also identify live human faces in this way? If so, do we rely on "geometric" cues (like nose size and cheekbone structure) or "material" cues (like skin texture and temperature)? Andrea Kilgour and Susan Lederman (2002) had college students manually explore an unfamiliar live face up to the hairline. All the students wore blindfolds, headphones, and nasal ointment to ensure that they relied only on a sense of touch. Afterward, they tried to identify that face by hand from a group of three faces. Keeping in mind that they could guess correctly 33 percent of the time, how accurate do you predict the students were—33, 50, 75, 90, or 100 percent? What if they felt plaster masks of the same faces, which preserved geometric information but not material cues, would that make them more accurate or less? The results were interesting. Students who felt live faces were accurate 79 percent of the time; those who felt masks were accurate in 59 percent of their identifications. Apparently, we *can* recognize faces by hand, as blind people do, by using both geometric and material cues.

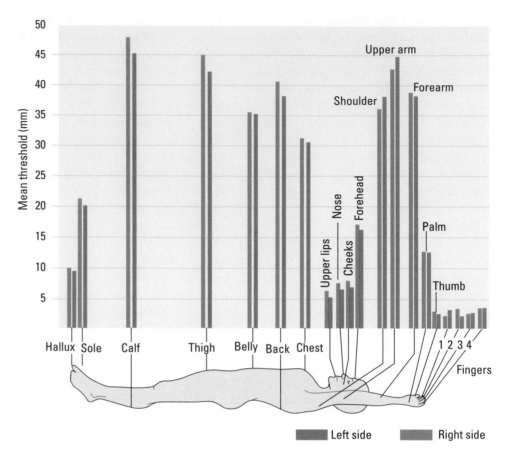

**FIGURE 3.18    Sensitivity to touch**
Thresholds for touch are estimated by applying varying degrees of pressure to the skin (a lower threshold means greater sensitivity). Shown are the average thresholds for male subjects (the relative values for females are similar but slightly lower overall). The genital areas, which are likely to contain the lowest thresholds, were not tested.

**FIGURE 3.19    The thermal grill**
When people grasp two braided pipes—one with cold water running through it, the other with warm water—the sensation is "very hot" and painful.

with warm water—they will pull away, complaining that the device is literally too hot to handle (see Figure 3.19). This effect of the "thermal grill" is found not only among humans but also in other animals. Apparently, the brain interprets the dual firing of both types of temperature receptors as being caused by a burning hot stimulus. Is the sensation a mere illusion? No. PET and other imaging studies show that gripping the entire grill (but not the warm or cold bars alone) activates regions of the brain that are responsive to pain (Craig et al., 1996; Casey & Bushnell, 2000; Hofbauer et al., 2001).

**Pain**    Pain is a dentist's drill boring through a tooth. Pain is stepping on a thumbtack. Pain is a pulled muscle, a splitting headache, a backache, sunburn blisters, and stomach cramps. Ouch! Whatever the source, people are understandably motivated to avoid and escape from pain. Yet pain is crucial to survival because it serves as a red flag, a warning system that signals danger and the risk of tissue damage. Life without pain may sound great, but it would be a life that is not likely to last very long. The case of a seven-year-old girl named Sarah illustrates the point. Born with a congenital indifference to pain, she often injures herself without realizing it. As a result, her body is scarred by burns, cuts, scrapes, and bruises (Restak, 1988).

Pain is a subjective, emotionally charged sensation. No single stimulus triggers pain the way that light does vision, no nerve endings in the skin are specially dedicated to pain over other sensations, and people with similar injuries often experience different degrees of pain. Clearly, the conditions that lead us to report pain include not only the threat of bodily harm but also culture, religion, personality, expectations, and other factors. Even gender plays a role, as male research subjects tend to have a greater tolerance for painful stimulation than do female subjects (Berkley, 1997; Keogh & Herdenfeldt, 2002). Theories of pain must take all of these factors into account (Kruger, 1996; Gatchel & Turk, 1999).

**Gate-Control Theory**  If you have a sore leg muscle or if you scrape your knee, nerve endings in the skin send messages to the spinal cord through one of two types of nerve fibers. Dull, chronic aches and pains—as in a sore muscle—are carried to the spinal cord by "slow," thin nerve fibers that also respond to nonpainful touch. Sharp, acute, piercing sensations—as when you scrape your knee—are relayed through "fast" myelinated fibers. In short, an express lane to the spinal cord is reserved for acute, emergency-like sensations. But how are these signals then sent from the spinal cord to the brain? And can they be blocked when the pain is too intense to bear?

In answer to these questions, Ronald Melzack and Patrick Wall (1965) proposed the **gate-control theory** of pain. According to this theory, the nervous system can process only a limited number of sensory signals at once. When the system is full, a neural "gate" in the spinal cord either blocks or allows the upward passage of additional signals to the brain (the gate is not an actual structure but a pattern of inhibitory neural activity). Research shows that although Melzack and Wall were wrong about the physiological details of their theory, they were generally right about the key point: that pain signals to the brain can be blocked (Humphries et al., 1996; Jessell & Kelly, 1991; Melzack & Wall, 2001).

*When asked by his dentist, "Where does it hurt?" philosopher Bertrand Russell replied: "In my mind, of course."*

This theory has a valuable practical implication: that you can partially shut the gate on pain by creating competing sensations. If you fall and hurt your knee, rubbing it hard will send new impulses into the spinal cord—and inhibit other pain signals. That's one reason it often helps to put ice on a bruise or to scratch the skin near a mosquito bite. For chronic pain, such interventions as deep massage, electrical stimulation, and acupuncture may provide temporary relief in the same way. It seems paradoxical, but as the theory correctly suggests, you can ease the pain by causing additional pain.

What's nice about gate-control theory is the idea that our sensory system enables us to partially regulate how much pain we have to endure. To further help matters, our bodies send in reinforcements in the form of *endorphins*, neurotransmitters that are distributed throughout the central nervous system and are released in response to pain or discomfort (see Chapter 2). Studies show that endorphin-rich areas are also involved in the "gating" of pain signals—and that pain can be reduced by electrically stimulating these areas (Watkins & Mayer, 1982; Barbaro, 1988).

**Psychological Control**  One psychological approach people often use is to block the pain from awareness. Just try not to think about it, okay? This advice sounds great, but beware: The strategy can backfire. Research shows that the more we try to suppress a particular thought, the more readily that thought pops to mind. Try not to think about the itch you're not supposed to scratch, and the harder you try, the less likely you are to succeed (Wegner, 1989). For adaptive reasons, pain sensations may be particularly hard to suppress. Almost regardless of where we are, whom we're with, and what we're doing, pain has a way of stealing the spotlight of our attention (Eccleston & Crombez, 1999).

Fortunately, there's a solution: distraction. In studies of pain tolerance, researchers have found that people can best manage the effects of intense physical discomfort—and exhibit less activation in pain-responsive areas of the brain—by

**gate-control theory**  The theory that the spinal cord contains a neurological "gate" that blocks pain signals from the brain when flooded by competing signals.

**kinesthetic system** The structures distributed throughout the body that give us a sense of position and movement of body parts.

**vestibular system** The inner ear and brain structures that give us a sense of equilibrium.

**synesthesia** A rare condition in which stimulation in one sensory modality triggers sensations in another sensory modality.

focusing their attention on something else, preferably something pleasant like a picture, music, film, or odor, or even just a mental image of a familiar place (Villemure & Bushnell, 2002). That is why expectant mothers in prepared-childbirth classes are taught to cope with labor pains by staring at a "focal point" (a key chain, a wall hanging, a doorknob, or anything else) and concentrating on special breathing techniques. As we'll see in Chapter 4, hypnosis can also be used to combat pain, in part through a refocusing of attention. Mind over sensation.

**Coordination** The five traditional senses and their subdivisions are vital adaptive mechanisms, but by themselves they do not enable us to regulate sensory input through movement. To bend, lean, stretch, climb, turn the head, maintain an upright posture, and run from danger, we need to sense the parts of our bodies as well as our orientation in space. The **kinesthetic system** monitors the positions of various body parts in relation to each other. Just as vision comes to us through sensory receptors in the eye, coordination of movement is provided by receptors in the joints, tendons, and muscles. These receptors are linked to motor areas of the brain. Without this system, an acrobat could not turn somersaults and cartwheels. Nor could gymnasts, dancers, and athletes perform their feats of bodily magic. Nor, for that matter, could you and I walk upright, deliver a firm handshake, aim food into our mouths, or touch our noses with the tip of the index finger.

*From riposte to parry, skillful fencers, so precise and fluid in their movements, exhibit a remarkable sense of coordination.*

A related sensory mechanism is provided by the **vestibular system,** which monitors head tilt and location in space. Situated in the inner ear, this system has two parts: (1) the *semicircular canals,* three fluid-filled tubes that are set at right angles to one another, and (2) two *vestibular sacs,* which are also filled with fluid. Whenever you move about, the movement rotates and tilts your head, causing the fluid to slosh back and forth, which pushes tiny hair cells. In turn, these hair cells send impulses to the cerebellum, which signals from moment to moment whether you are sitting, lying down, or standing on your head. The vestibular system provides us with the sense of equilibrium, or balance. But sometimes this delicate sense is disrupted by an excess of fluid or by certain types of motion. The result may be car sickness, sea sickness, or the dizzying aftereffects of twirling in circles (Howard, 1986).

## KEEPING THE SIGNALS STRAIGHT

In a world filled with lights and colors, voices and musical tones, smells and tastes, and feelings of cold, warmth, pressure, pain, and other sensations, our sensory ability seems marvelously adaptive. How do we bring in so much information without becoming overwhelmed? With neural impulses flooding the brain from different receptors throughout the body, it's amazing that we don't get our signals crossed. Why is it that we see light and hear sound rather than the other way around?

There are, however, interesting exceptions. Exhibiting a very rare condition known as **synesthesia** ("joining the senses"), some individuals report that they actually experience sensory "crossovers"—that bright lights are loud, that the sound of a jazz trumpet is hot, that colors can be felt through touch, or that they can "enjoy the sweet smell of purple" or "taste the sound of raindrops" (Stein & Meredith, 1993). As described in Richard Cytowic's (1993) *The Man Who Tasted Shapes,* a number of fascinating cases have been reported over the years. Recent studies indicate that the condition is found in only one out of two thousand people—and that most are women (Cytowic, 2002; Harrison, 2001).

Can the self-reports of those claiming to have synesthesia be trusted? Although there is reason to be skeptical, recent studies provide intriguing evidence. In one study, nine women with word-color synesthesia and nine controls were asked to report on the color sensations triggered by 130 letters, words, and phrases. When retested a year later, without warning, the synesthetic women reported the identical sensations 92 percent of the time—compared to only 38 percent in the control group. In a second study, six synesthetic women and six controls listened to words while blindfolded. PET scans revealed that this auditory stimulation activated the language areas of the brain in both groups. Among the synesthetic women, it also activated certain areas of the *visual* cortex (Paulesu et al., 1995). Other studies, too, have provided independent evidence of this rare condition (Martino & Marks, 2001; Smilek et al., 2002).

Although there are exceptions, our sensory systems generally do not cross. The reason is that different receptors are sensitive only to certain types of energy and stimulate only certain nerve pathways to the brain. Rods respond to light, not to sound, and they transmit impulses through the optic nerve, not the auditory nerve. There may be "normal" exceptions—as when pressing on a closed eyelid stimulates the optic nerve and causes you to "see" a flash of light—but each sensory system operates independent of the others (Gardner & Martin, 2000).

Two other aspects of sensation enable us to respond to volumes of information without confusion. First, all of our sensory systems are designed to detect novelty, contrast, and change—not sameness. After constant exposure to a stimulus, sensation fades. This decline in sensitivity is known as **sensory adaptation.** We saw earlier that the eyes gradually adapt to bright light and darkness. The same is true of the other senses. After a while, you simply get used to the new contact lenses in your eyes, the new watchband on your wrist, the noise level at work, or the coldness of winter. To those sensitive to smells that often pervade the hallways of apartment buildings (or dormitories), it is comforting to know that people also adjust to chronic odors (Dalton & Wysocki, 1996). By adapting to repeated stimulation, you are free to detect important changes in the environment.

A second adaptive mechanism is selective attention. As we will discover in Chapter 4, people can choose to focus on some sensory input and block out the rest. This selective attention enables us to pick out a face or a voice in a crowded room or to find distractions from pain and discomfort. Parents thus can hear their baby cry over the sounds of a TV, traders on the floor of the stock exchange can hear orders to buy and sell amid all the noise, and commuters in a city can spot yellow cabs in the street through all the commotion of rush-hour traffic. People are not passive sensation-recording devices. We have a way of "zooming in" on sensations—such as pain—that are personally important.

# PERCEPTION

- *In what ways is perception an active mental process?*
- *How do we manage to identify objects despite apparent changes in their size, shape, and other features?*
- *How do we perceive depth in three-dimensional space?*
- *Are perceptual skills inborn or learned from experience?*
- *Why, with all our impressive abilities, do we fall prey to perceptual illusions?*

Our sensory systems convert physical energy from a multitude of sources into neural signals that are transmitted to the brain. But we do not see inverted retinal

## REVIEW QUESTIONS

- *What are the physical properties of light waves and how do they correspond to our sensory experiences?*

- *How does the eye translate light waves into neural impulses and what happens to them in the visual cortex?*

- *According to the trichromatic theory, how do we see color? According to the opponent-process theory, how do we see color?*

- *What are the physical properties of sound waves and how do they correspond to our sensory experiences?*

- *How does the auditory system translate sound waves into meaningful sounds?*

- *How does the olfactory system produce the sense of smell? In what way is this process different from our other senses?*

- *What are the four basic tastes and what factors contribute to their perception?*

- *In what way is the sense of touch different from our other senses?*

- *What two systems contribute to our sense of coordination?*

**sensory adaptation** A decline in sensitivity to a stimulus as a result of constant exposure.

**FIGURE 3.20** **Reversible figures**
What do you see—a young woman or an older woman? Visual input can be perceived in different ways (Archives of the History of American Psychology).

**FIGURE 3.21**
"It may take a magician to pull a rabbit out of a hat, but we all possess sufficient magic to pull a duck out of a rabbit" (Shepard, 1990).

**reversible figure** A drawing that one can perceive in different ways by reversing figure and ground.

**Gestalt psychology** A school of thought rooted in the idea that the whole (perception) is different from the sum of its parts (sensation).

images, hear the bending and swaying of hair cells in the cochlea, or smell the absorption of odorant molecules in the nose. These and other sensations must be further processed to make sense. Perception is not a mere "copying" process, and the brain does more than just serve as a sensory Xerox machine. As perceivers, we must select, organize, and interpret input from the world in ways that are adaptive. Putting the sensory pieces together is a "constructive" mental process (Hoffman, 1998; Palmer, 1999).

To illustrate this point, look at the picture in Figure 3.20. What do you see? When I first saw it, I didn't hesitate to say it was an elegant young woman looking over her right shoulder. Then I read the caption, which revealed that the picture is a **reversible figure** that could also be seen as an "old hag." Huh? I stared and stared, but I just could not see it. All of a sudden, I did a double take. There it was! The lines and shading had not changed, yet now I saw the woman's chin as a nose. I took another look a few minutes later, and once again all I could see was a young woman. The point is, visual input can often be processed in different ways. The sensation may be the same, but the perception can vary from one person and moment to the next (see also Figure 3.21).

When Virgil's eyesight was restored at the age of fifty, he was able to detect lights, shadows, colors, shapes, and textures, but he could not separate one figure from another or identify common objects just by looking at them. In busy settings such as a supermarket, he was so overwhelmed by sensory information that "everything ran together." In this section, we examine the ways in which the brain organizes and interprets sensory input. As in much of the research, we will focus on visual perception.

## PERCEPTUAL ORGANIZATION

In 1912, Max Wertheimer discovered that people perceive two stationary lights flashing in rapid succession as a single light moving back and forth. This illusion of apparent motion explains why we see flashing neon signs as a continuous stream rather than as a series of separate lights. At the time, this illusion also paved the way for **Gestalt psychology**—a school of thought arising in Germany that was founded on the premise that the whole (perception) is different from the sum of its parts (sensations). The word *gestalt* is German for "pattern" or "whole," and Gestalt psychologists believed that humans have an inborn tendency to construct meaningful perceptions from fragments of sensory input. A classic example is the way we listen to music. A melody has a form that is different from the individual notes that make it up. So if the melody is transposed to another key, even if that means changing every note, listeners would still recognize the music because its form would be the same. The perception of music is based on a gestalt, not on a particular set of notes (Koffka, 1935; Kohler, 1947; Rock & Palmer, 1990). The same is true of the way people view and extract meaning from works of art and complex visual scenes (Albright & Stoner, 2002; Livingstone, 2002).

**Figure and Ground** The first gestalt principle of perceptual organization is that people automatically focus on some objects in the perceptual field to the exclusion of others. What we focus on is called the *figure*. Everything else fades into the *ground*. A teacher standing in front of a blackboard, the printed black words on this page, the lights on the car ahead of us on a dark highway, a scream in the night, and the lead singer's voice in a rock band—all are common figures and grounds. Gestalt psychologists were quick to point out that these perceptions are in the eyes (or ears) of the beholder—but also that we are prone to "figurize" objects that are close to us, novel, intense, loud, and moving rather than still. As in the reversible figure shown earlier, however, the image in Figure 3.22 shows that you can mentally flip-flop the figure and ground from one moment to the next. It's as if each of us is shining a spotlight on a portion of the sensory field—and can move that spotlight if necessary.

**Gestalt Laws of Grouping**   Another principle of perceptual organization is that we tend to group collections of shapes, sizes, colors, and other features into perceptual wholes. The natural grouping tendencies are not arbitrary; rather, they follow simple rules like those shown in Figure 3.23. The Gestalt psychologists argued that these tendencies are inborn, and they may have been right. Research shows that even young infants "group" stimulus objects in the predicted ways (Quinn et al., 1993; Van Giffen & Haith, 1984). Some of these laws of grouping are:

- **Proximity.**   The closer objects are to one another, the more likely they are to be perceived as a unit. The lines in Figure 3.23(A) are thus seen as rows rather than as columns because they are nearer to one another horizontally than vertically.

- **Similarity.**   Objects that are similar in shape, size, color, or any other feature tend to be grouped together. The dots in Figure 3.23(B) form perceptual columns rather than rows because of similarities in color.

- **Continuity.**   People perceive the contours of straight and curved lines as continuous flowing patterns. In Figure 3.23(C), we see points 1 and 2 as belonging to one line, and points 3 and 4 as belonging to another. The same pattern could be seen as two V shapes, but instead we perceive two smooth lines that form a cross in the center.

- **Closure.**   When there are gaps in a pattern that resembles a familiar form, as in Figure 3.23(D), people mentally "close" the gaps and perceive the object as a whole. This tendency enables us to recognize imperfect representations in hand drawings, written material, and so on.

- **Common fate.**   Extending upon the static grouping principles of proximity and similarity, we find that objects moving together in the same direction, or sharing a "common fate," are perceived as belonging to a single group. Examples include marching bands, schools of fish, flocks of birds, and sports fans sending the "wave" around a stadium.

The principles of Gestalt psychology describe how people transform raw visual input—lights, shadows, lines, points, shapes, and colors—into meaningful displays. More recent research has focused as well on the question of how our brains combine these simple features into larger units, enabling us to identify common objects such as chairs, airplanes, bottles, and so on. According to Irving Biederman (1987), people can recognize common objects from a quick glance, based on exposure times as brief as one tenth of a second. The reason, he says, is that we perceive objects by breaking them down into simple, three-dimensional component shapes called *geons* ("geometric ions") and then matching the unique pattern of shapes to "sketches" stored in memory. Biederman has identified thirty-six geons that, when combined, enable us to identify the essential contours of all objects—the way that an alphabet of twenty-six letters can be used to form thousands of words (see Figure 3.24).

**FIGURE 3.22**   **Figure and ground** Depending on whether you see the white or black areas as figural, this drawing may be perceived as a vase or as two people facing each other.

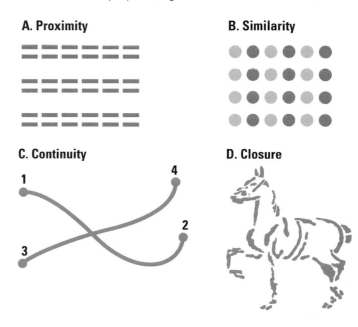

**A. Proximity**

**B. Similarity**

**C. Continuity**

**D. Closure**

**FIGURE 3.23**   **Gestalt laws of grouping**

*When surfing the internet, I encountered an odd survey question: Is a zebra a white horse with black stripes or a black horse with white stripes? What would you say? neither color is figural in Gestalt terms, and survey responses were split.*

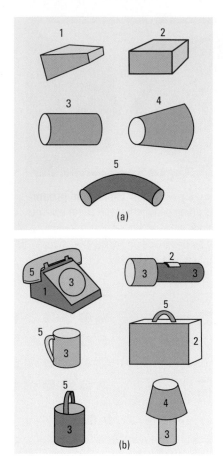

**FIGURE 3.24** **Identifying objects**
According to Biederman, people perceive objects by breaking them down into simple, three-dimensional component shapes called geons (a). Just as letters of an alphabet can be combined to produce a large number of words, combinations of geons create thousands of different objects (b).

3.3

**size constancy** The tendency to view an object as constant in size despite changes in the size of the retinal image.

**shape constancy** The tendency to see an object as retaining its form despite changes in orientation.

Theories of how people organize visual information and identify common objects help to explain the effortless nature of perception—and the confusion that results when figures are concealed from view through camouflage. But what happens to our perception of an object when its retinal image changes from one moment to the next? How do we know that objects have depth when the images projected on the retina are flat and two-dimensional? How are interpretations of input influenced by characteristics of the perceiver? As we'll see, people are highly adept, yet often fooled, by disparities between sensation and perception.

## PERCEPTUAL CONSTANCIES

Unlike a camera or microphone stationed on a tripod, the human perceiver is active and mobile. And unlike the portrait or landscape hanging on a wall, many of the objects of our perception are likewise active and mobile. As the perceiver and perceived move about, the image projected on the retina may change in size, shape, brightness, color, and other properties. But this is not a problem. Thanks to perceptual constancies, perceptions remain stable despite radical changes in sensory input (Rock, 1997).

**Size Constancy** Size constancy is the tendency to view an object as constant despite changes in the size of its image on the retina. You've noticed this phenomenon countless times. You'll be watching from the ground as an airplane pokes its nose through a cloud to descend for a landing. Or a friend will walk away and eventually fade into the distance. Visualize these moving pictures. As the plane approaches, its image looms larger and larger. And as your friend walks away, the image gets smaller. If you didn't know better, the changing sensations might lead you to think that the airplane was growing and that your friend was shrinking right before your eyes.

But we do know better—for two reasons. One has to do with experience and familiarity. You know that airplanes are bigger than people and that people are bigger than insects, so your perceptions remain stable despite variations in retinal image size. Distance cues provide a second source of information. As objects move around in space, we perceive the change in distance and adjust our size perceptions accordingly. In other words, we know that the closer an object is, the larger the image it casts on the retina, so we make the adjustment.

This skill is so basic that it can be observed in infants, shortly after birth. Alan Slater and his colleagues (1990) showed newborns in a maternity ward a large or small black-and-white block. After they became familiarized to it, they were shown either the same block at a different distance or a different-sized (larger or smaller) block. Did the babies recognize the familiar block when distance was varied? Infants are visually attracted to novel objects, so the researchers recorded their eye movements as the blocks were shown. The result: They spent more time looking at a new block than at an old block presented at a different distance. Through size constancy, they "recognized" the original blocks despite the change in distance.

The capacity for size constancy may be present in infancy, but cultural and environmental experiences also play a role. In 1961, anthropologist Colin Turnbull studied Pygmies who lived in a densely wooded central African forest. At one point, he took a native named Kenge for a Jeep ride out of the forest. It was Kenge's first trip away from home—and he was disoriented. Standing on a mountain overlooking miles of open plain, Kenge saw buffaloes and thought they were insects. Then he saw a fishing boat in the middle of a lake and thought it was a floating piece of wood. The problem? Turnbull came to realize that "in the forest the range of vision is so limited that there is no great need to make an automatic allowance for distance

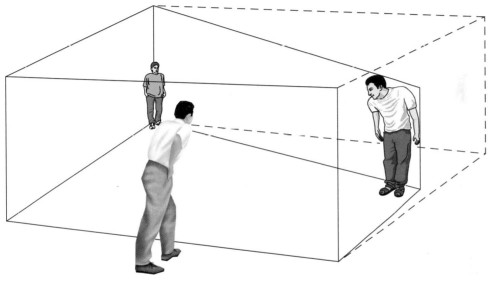

**FIGURE 3.25**   **The Ames room**
Adelbert Ames designed this room to distort perceptions of size. The room seems rectangular, which makes the two figures look equally distant. But the right corner is closer to the peephole (and has a lower ceiling) than the left. The person on the right is thus perceived as bigger because distance cues are masked.

when judging size" (1961, p. 252). As for the rest of us, the perceived link between size and distance makes us vulnerable to some striking illusions (see Figure 3.25).

**Shape Constancy**   Also important is **shape constancy**, the tendency to see an object as retaining its form despite changes in orientation. Take a coin, hold it up at eye level so that the "head" side faces you, and it will reveal a circular appearance. Rotate it 45 degrees, and it casts an elliptical, egg-shape image on the retina. Turn it another 45 degrees, and it looks like a straight line. The changes in orientation are dramatic, yet you still see the coin as a flat, circular object (see Figure 3.26). As with size, shape constancy is inborn. But it may also require visual experience. Indeed, you may recall that Virgil found it difficult to recognize moving objects—including his own pet dog—when he saw them from another angle of view (Sacks, 1995).

**FIGURE 3.26**   **Shape constancy**
People see objects as retaining their form despite changes in their orientation.

*Note how these Buddhist monks in Thailand appear to be the same size even though the images they project on your retina shrink with distance.*

# DEPTH AND DIMENSION

Perceptual constancies enable us to identify objects despite changes in sensory input. But there's another problem: How do we know that objects in three-dimensional space have depth, and how do we perceive distance when images projected on each retina are flat and only two-dimensional? Two types of information are used in **depth perception**: binocular cues and monocular cues.

**Binocular Depth Cues** With eyes on the sides of their heads, deer, sheep, and other prey can use peripheral vision to see predators sneaking up from behind. By contrast, the eyes of lions, owls, and other predators are squarely at the front of the head, an arrangement that maximizes depth perception and enables them to track their prey. Look into the mirror, and you'll see that human eyes are the eyes of a predator. Our binocular (two-eyed) vision, in turn, allows us to use two binocular depth cues: convergence and binocular disparity.

**Convergence** refers to the fact that the eyes turn in toward the nose or "converge" as an object gets closer, and move outward or "diverge" to focus on objects farther away. Hold your finger up at arm's length and slowly move it toward your nose. As you refocus, you can actually feel your eye muscles contracting. This signals the brain about the object's distance from the eyes.

The second cue is **binocular disparity.** With our eyes set about 2.5 inches apart on the face, each retina receives a slightly different image of the world. To demonstrate, hold your finger about 4 inches from your nose and shut your right eye. Then shut only your left eye and look at the finger. Right. Left. As you switch back and forth, you'll see that each eye picks up the image from a slightly different vantage point. Now hold up your finger farther away, say at arm's length, and repeat the routine. This time you'll see less image shifting. The reason: Binocular disparity decreases with distance. Special neurons located in the visual cortex use this retinal information to "calculate" depth, distance, and dimensionality (Cumming & DeAngelis, 2001).

If two eyes combine to give us a three-dimensional look at the world, can flat pictures do the same? In the nineteenth century, British physicist Charles Wheatstone invented the first stereoscope—an optical instrument that brought two-dimensional pictures to life. To create the illusion, Wheatstone photographed a scene twice, using two cameras spaced inches apart. He then mounted both pictures side by side on the device, using mirrors to overlap the images. This technique underlies the View-Master—a toy that shows three-dimensional scenes in double-view cardboard slides. It is also being used in the development of virtual reality (VR) systems in which simulated environments are projected on a screen mounted inside a helmet. A head tracker on the top of the helmet and computerized gloves sense head and body movements and signal the computer generating the image to change the scene according to the viewer's changing position. The U.S. military uses VR to train fighter pilots and ground troops. Of relevance to depth perception, it appears that the experience feels most realistic at short distances when the VR displays stereoscopic images—that is, separate but overlapping images to each eye.

**depth perception** The use of visual cues to estimate the depth and distance of objects.

**convergence** A binocular cue for depth perception involving the turning inward of the eyes as an object gets closer.

**binocular disparity** A binocular cue for depth perception whereby the closer an object is to a perceiver, the more different the image is in each retina.

**Monocular Depth Cues**   Binocular depth cues are useful at short distances. But for objects that are farther away, convergence and binocular disparity are uninformative. At such times, we can utilize **monocular depth cues,** which enable us to perceive depth, quite literally with one eye closed. These are cues that many artists use to bring a flat canvas to life. What are they? Look at the pictures accompanying each description, and see for yourself.

- **Relative image size.**   We saw earlier that as the distance of an object increases, the size of its retinal image shrinks—and vice versa. Object size can thus be used to judge depth.

- **Texture gradient.**   As a collection of objects recedes into the horizon, they appear to be spaced more closely together, which makes the surface texture appear to become denser.

- **Linear perspective.**   With distance, the parallel contours of highways, rivers, railroad tracks, and other rowlike structures perceptually converge—and eventually reach a vanishing point. The more the lines converge, the greater the perceived distance.

- **Interposition.**   As most objects are not transparent, those nearer to us will partly or completely block our view of more distant objects. This overlap provides a quick and easy way to judge relative distances.

- **Atmospheric perspective.**   The air contains a haze of dust particles and moisture that blurs images at a distance. This blurring, or atmospheric perspective, makes duller and less detailed objects appear farther away.

- **Relative elevation.**   Below the horizon line, objects that are lower in our field of vision are seen as nearer than those that are higher. Above the horizon line, however, objects that are lower are perceived as farther away.

- **Familiarity.**   Experience provides familiar reference points for judging distance. We know the approximate size of houses, people, cars, and other objects, and this knowledge helps us judge their distance. In fact, the presence of a familiar object in a scene helps us judge the sizes and distances of everything around it.

*"Virtual reality is only possible because we, the customers, construct what we perceive."*

—DONALD HOFFMAN

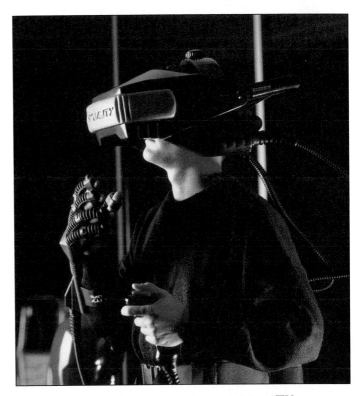

*Virtual reality headsets contain two miniature TV screens for stereo vision. To simulate reality, they are most realistic at short distances when they display separate but overlapping images to each eye.*

   **3.4**

**Origins of Depth Perception**   With normal vision, interpreting the layout of objects in an environment is easy and requires no conscious thought or effort. Why is depth perception so easy? Clearly, a rich array of depth cues is available to one or both eyes—especially when we're moving about (Gibson, 1979). But how do we know how to interpret these cues? Assuming you're not a visual artist or mathematician, how do you effortlessly interpret angles of convergence, linear perspective, texture gradients, relative elevations, and other "geometric" types of information? How do you know that railroad tracks are parallel even though they seem to converge? You may think this is an odd question because, well, "you just know." But were you born with these skills, or did you learn them from experience?

**Perceptual Experience**   The average person has an enormous amount of experience with depth perception. Is this experience necessary? Case studies of blind people who had their eyesight surgically restored during adulthood suggest that experience is critical to depth perception. Sacks (1995) observed that Virgil

**monocular depth cues**   Distance cues, such as linear perspective, that enable us to perceive depth with one eye.

*Texture gradient.*

*Linear perspective.*

*Interposition.*

*Atmospheric perspective.*

**visual cliff** An apparatus used to test depth perception in infants and animals.

**perceptual set** The effects of prior experience and expectations on interpretations of sensory input.

sometimes stepped over shadows so he would not trip or failed to step up on a staircase that, for all he knew, was a flat surface consisting of parallel and crossing lines. Richard Gregory (1998) studied a similar patient by the name of S.B. and described his perception of depth as "peculiar." At one point, S.B. thought he could touch the ground below his hospital window with his feet—even though his window was on the fourth floor. The importance of perceptual learning and experience is also evident in cross-cultural studies. We saw earlier that when a Pygmy named Kenge was taken from his dense forest home to the open plain, he saw distant buffaloes as insects and a large boat as a floating log. As described at the start of this chapter, research also shows that people who lack exposure to three-dimensional representations in artwork find it difficult to judge relative distance from pictures (Deregowski, 1989).

**Depth Perception As Inborn** Experience may seem necessary, but studies of infants suggest otherwise. Infants cannot tell us what they see, so Eleanor Gibson and Richard Walk (1960) devised the **visual cliff**, a clever nonverbal test of depth perception. As shown in Figure 3.27, the apparatus consists of a glass-covered table top, with a shallow one-inch drop on one end and a steep "cliff" on the other end. Infants six to fourteen months of age were placed in the middle of the table, and their mothers tried to lure them into crawling to one side or the other. The entire surface was covered by sturdy transparent glass, so there was no real danger. The result: Six-month-old babies would crawl to their mothers at the shallow end. But despite all the calling, clapping, waving, and encouragement, most did not crawl out over the cliff. Clearly, they had perceived the steepness of the drop.

Does the visual cliff experiment prove that depth perception is innate? Not necessarily, argued critics. Perceptual learning begins at birth, so by the tender age of six months an infant has already experienced over a thousand waking hours—and has had lots of perceptual practice. What about younger babies? They may not be able to crawl, but their bodies can communicate to an astute researcher. Accordingly, Joseph Campos and his colleagues (1970) moved two-month-old infants from one side of the glass top to the other and found that the infants exhibited a change in heart rate when placed over the deep side but not over the shallow side. These infants were too young to fear the situation as you and I would, but they "noticed" the difference. Additional studies have shown that most newborn lambs, chicks, ducklings, pigs, cats, rats, and other animals that can walk the day they're born also avoid the deep end of the visual cliff (Walk, 1981).

Is depth perception innate or is it the product of visual experience? As the pieces of the puzzle have come together, it seems that both factors are at work. Using binocular cues—and, later, monocular cues—infants are capable of perceiving depth and dimension. But early experience is necessary for this skill to emerge. Thus, newborn rats and cats that are initially reared in a dark laboratory step over the visual cliff when first tested, and formerly blind humans have trouble making judgments of depth when their eyesight is surgically restored. As the saying goes, you have to "use it or lose it."

## THE PROCESS OF DISCOVERY

# ELEANOR J. GIBSON
### *The Visual Cliff*

**Q: How did I first become interested in psychology?**

**A:** At Smith College, I took my first course out of sheer curiosity and also because it fulfilled a laboratory requirement, allowing me presumably to skip something harder, such as physics (I had to take physics eventually, since I chose to major in psychology and needed it). My first class led me on to a course in comparative psychology, and I was hooked. The course was titled "Animal Psychology" and it *was* about animals. I loved it.

As a senior I took "Advanced Experimental Psychology," taught by Professor James Gibson. Only six students took the course because it was very demanding. We did several experiments each term, setting them up ourselves and getting our own subjects. I did my senior thesis with Professor Gibson and then a master's degree. In 1932, a year after graduation, we were married; it was all a great beginning to an eminently satisfying career. I went on to get my Ph.D. in 1938 from Yale University.

**Q: How did you come up with your important discovery?**

**A:** James Gibson and I had two children, raised in their early years during World War II while he did visual perception research in the Air Force. After the war, as the family drove home across the continent, picnicking daily on the way, we spent one lunch time at the Grand Canyon. Jean, three years old, danced about on the rim of the canyon, making her mother very nervous. As I clung to her clothing, James said, "Don't worry, she can see the depth as well as you can." Yes, but would she avoid it?

Some years later, I decided to find out. While at Cornell University, I set up a mock cliff, with sturdy glass over what appeared to be a sheer drop. My subjects included various animal species, but babies were of greatest interest. On the whole, the babies avoided the cliff. But they were all very interested in looking at it!

**Q: How has the field you inspired developed over the years?**

**A:** How has the field developed over the years? Well, lots of people have made lots of cliffs, with varied surfaces under them, at various depths, and comparing many subjects. It's a nice experiment to run with a course in comparative psychology since it is easy to construct a cliff and students can try a variety of subjects if they are so inclined—kittens, for example.

**Q: What's your prediction on where the field is heading?**

**A:** I'm not sure where this field is at this moment. The cliff doesn't provide a very sensitive measure of depth perception, so there is no development going on in that respect. What it does do, its major and perhaps only claim for surviving, is present a real, natural situation for investigating an interesting developmental question. The cliff may be artificial, but it approximates a real and important kind of event.

*Eleanor J. Gibson, awarded a National Medal of Science in 1992, is Professor of Psychology Emeritus at Cornell University.*

## PERCEPTUAL SET

At any given moment, your interpretation of sensory input can be influenced by prior experiences and expectations, which create a **perceptual set.** To illustrate, look at Figure 3.28. The middle drawings in this series are ambiguous: They can be seen as either a man's face or the figure of a kneeling young woman. Which do you see? It turns out that interpretations are biased by prior experience. Subjects who were first shown the drawing on the far left saw the middle pictures as a man's face, whereas those who were first shown the drawing on the far right saw the same pictures as a kneeling woman (Fisher, 1968). This finding highlights an important point about perception: At times, we see what we expect to see.

**FIGURE 3.27   The visual cliff**
This apparatus is used to test depth perception in infants and animals.

**perceptual illusions** Patterns of sensory input that give rise to misperceptions.

To experience some interactive perceptual illusions online, visit *Grand Illusions* at www.grand-illusions.com.

**FIGURE 3.28** **Perceptual set**
What you see in the middle drawings depends on the order in which you look at the pictures. Subjects who start at the far left see the drawings in the middle as a man's face; those who start at the far right see a woman's figure.

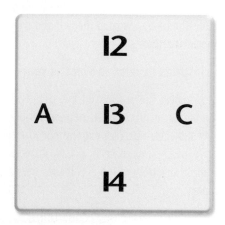

**FIGURE 3.29** **Context effects**
Indicating the effects of context on perception, people see the middle item as B or 13 depending on whether it is surrounded by letters or numbers.

Perceptual sets are established not only by past experience but also by the context in which a stimulus is perceived. In Figure 3.29, for example, the same physical pattern of black and white is used for the letter *B* as for the number *13*. Look closely and you'll see that the *B* and *13* are physically identical. Which of the two you "see" depends on whether the surrounding context consists of letters or numbers. The same phenomenon can influence our perceptions of color. Look at the "color shuffle" presented in Figure 3.30. On the left you'll see an array of colored squares arranged so that you can see a smooth transition of colors. On the right, you'll see the same colored squares randomly ordered. Notice how different the two sets of identical colors appear to be (for example, the two squares marked "1" are printed in the same color, as are the two squares marked "2"). The colors we see depend in part on the broader context in which they appear (Hoffman, 1998).

By leading us to see what we expect to see, perceptual sets can lead us astray. Imagine that you're looking at a slide that is completely out of focus. Gradually, it is focused so that the image becomes less blurry. At each step, you're asked, "Can you recognize the picture?" The response you're likely to make is interesting. Subjects have more trouble identifying the picture if they watch the gradual focusing procedure than if they simply view the final image. In trying to interpret the initially blurry image, subjects exposed to gradual focusing formed perceptual sets that later interfered with their ability to "see straight" once presented with improved evidence (Bruner & Potter, 1964).

## THE WORLD OF ILLUSIONS

The brain's capacity to transform sensations into accurate perceptions of reality is impressive. Without conscious thought, effort, or instruction, we often manage to perceive size, shape, depth, and other properties in an accurate manner. But the mind also plays tricks on us. Magicians, ventriloquists, and artists count on it. So do perception psychologists. Over the years, researchers have learned a great deal about how people perceive the world by probing the systematic ways in which we also *mis*perceive the world. **Perceptual illusions** are all around us (Wade, 1990; Rodgers, 1998). A few examples illustrate the point.

■ A puddle glistens on the asphalt highway in front of you. It seems about a mile away. But as you drive, the road stays dry and the wet spot remains out of reach. There is no puddle, of course, just a "mirage"—an illusion caused by a layer of hot air sitting below cooler air and casting a mirror-like reflection from the sky onto the road.

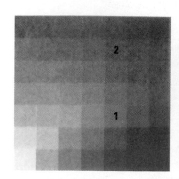 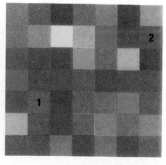

**FIGURE 3.30** **The color shuffle**
(Hoffman, 1998).

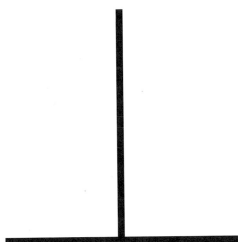

**FIGURE 3.31    The horizontal-vertical illusion**
The horizontal-vertical illusion can be seen in the St. Louis Gateway Arch and in the perpendicular lines drawn to the right.

■ Baseball players claim that some pitchers can throw a "rising fastball." The laws of physics state that this is impossible. So why do players insist that the fastball rises? Apparently, it's an illusion that occurs when the batter underestimates the speed of a fast pitch (Bahill & Karnavas, 1993).

■ If you've ever driven through St. Louis, then you've seen the towering Gateway Arch. Look at Figure 3.31. Is the arch taller than it is wide? Most people say *yes*—and this illustrates the common "horizontal-vertical illusion." In fact, the height and width of the Gateway Arch are both 630 feet.

What's interesting about perceptual illusions is that they often stem from the overapplication of rules that normally serve us well. Look at the two vertical lines with the arrowed tips in Figure 3.32. Which is longer? Most people see the line on the right as slightly longer than the one on the left. Measure them, however, and you'll see that they are the same length. Now compare the two sides of the horizontal line. Again, which is longer? Most people see these lines as equal. Wrong. In this case, the line on the left is longer than the one on the right. As devised by Franz Müller-Lyer, in 1889, these comparisons illustrate the classic and pervasive **Müller-Lyer illusion.**

Why is the Müller-Lyer illusion so compelling? There are several possible explanations (Nijhawan, 1991). One is that the arrowed tips trick us into overapplying the linear-perspective depth cues and the principle of size constancy. As also shown in Figure 3.32, the vertical configuration on the left side resembles the near outside corner of a room or building, whereas that on the right resembles a far inside corner. Because both lines cast equal-size retinal images, we assume that the farther one must be larger. Part of the problem, then, is that people mistakenly apply a rational rule of three-dimensional depth perception—that distance decreases image size—to a flat two-dimensional figure (Gregory, 1998). Interestingly, however, the illusion is not purely visual. It is also found in blindfolded people who make the line judgments

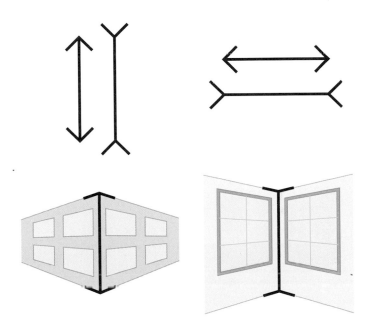

**FIGURE 3.32    The Müller-Lyer illusion**

**Müller-Lyer illusion**    An illusion in which the perceived length of a line is altered by the position of other lines that enclose it.

**Ponzo illusion** An illusion in which the perceived length of a line is affected by linear perspective cues.

FIGURE 3.33 **The Ponzo illusion**

3.5

by running their fingers along raised plastic lines with arrowed tips (Millar & Al-Attar, 2002).

Look at the horizontal lines in Figure 3.33, and you'll see a second illusion. The tendency to view the horizontal line on top as longer than the one on the bottom is called the **Ponzo illusion.** Can you see why this misperception is common? Think again about depth perception, and you may notice that the linear perspective that provides the context for these lines makes the top one seem farther away. As in the Müller-Lyer illusion, the two lines cast the same-size retinal image, so the one that seems more distant is perceived to be larger. In fact, the more depth-perception cues there are in the background, the stronger is the illusion (Leibowitz et al., 1969). Consistent with this explanation is the fact that people from certain African cultures that live in rural "noncarpentered" environments—without right angles, corners,

*The Moon illusion. Viewed low over the San Francisco skyline (right), the moon seems larger than when it is seen higher in the sky (left).*

squares, and hard edges—are less likely to be fooled by the Müller-Lyer and Ponzo illusions (Deregowski, 1989; Segall et al., 1966).

A third illusion that seems to stem from depth-related cues is the most spectacular but also the most puzzling. Have you ever noticed how a full moon looks larger when it's low on the horizon than when it's high in the sky? The moon is the moon, of course. It does not change in size or in its distance from the earth. So, what causes this **moon illusion?**

Throughout history, scholars have tried to understand this phenomenon. Then in 1962, Lloyd Kaufman and Irvin Rock brought it to the attention of perception psychologists, which stimulated many theories and explanations. Some psychologists claimed that the increased perceived size is caused by buildings, trees, and other earth-bound depth cues that make the moon seem farther away and thus trick us into "seeing" a larger object. Indeed, if you peer at the low moon through a tube, apart from surrounding cues, it will appear smaller. But others have found that people sometimes perceive the horizon moon as closer, not more distant (Coren & Aks, 1990), that the illusion does not occur when the target object is a star instead of the moon (Reed & Krupinski, 1992), that the illusion persists even when the moon is projected at different angles without depth cues, as in the total darkness of a planetarium (Suzuki, 1991), and that the illusion can also be created indoors by projecting a point of light straight ahead, horizontally, or elevated at an upward angle (Suzuki, 1998). To this day, the moon illusion remains something of a perceptual mystery (Hershenson, 1989).

## REVIEW QUESTIONS

- *Identify the various Gestalt laws of grouping.*

- *What are size constancy and shape constancy? Why are they important to perception?*

- *Describe the cues used to perceive depth. When are monocular cues more informative than binocular ones?*

- *What is the evidence that depth perception is inborn? What is the evidence for the role of experience?*

- *How do expectations and prior experiences influence perception?*

- *What are some common perceptual illusions and why do they occur?*

# EXTRASENSORY PERCEPTION

- *Is it possible to perceive something in the absence of a physical stimulus?*
- *What is ESP, and what types of extrasensory powers do psychics claim to have?*
- *What is the evidence for and against these claims?*
- *Where do you stand: Are you a believer or a skeptic?*

Every New Year's Eve, "psychics" make predictions for the year to come. From political fortunes to natural disasters, the soothsayers claim they can see the future the way you and I see the sun rise and set. Can they really? With varying degrees of accuracy, scientists make predictions all the time. Astronomers tell us when we'll see the next solar eclipse, economists forecast economic growth rates, and meteorologists warn us about upcoming storms. But there's a difference between these forms of prediction and psychic fortune-telling. Scientists base their predictions on sensory input, whereas psychics claim to have **extrasensory perception,** or ESP—an ability to perceive in the absence of ordinary sensory information.

Psychologists as a group have long been skeptical, if not downright cynical, about these claims. Indeed, this entire chapter is dedicated to the proposition that perception is the product of *physical* energy received by *sensory* receptors and interpreted by the *brain.* Yet pollsters have consistently found that more than half of all Americans believe in ESP—57 percent, to be precise, in a recent poll conducted by CBS News (2002). So what is the basis for this belief? Are there people who can read minds, levitate or move objects without contact, have "out of body" experiences, communicate with ghosts, see the future in dreams, or identify serial killers for the police? To evaluate the evidence, we must first make some distinctions.

*Is this a UFO? Many people are quick to believe what they see with their own eyes. Look at the full picture on the next page, however, and you'll appreciate that things are not always as they seem.*

**moon illusion**   The tendency for people to see the moon as larger when it's low on the horizon than when it's overhead.

**extrasensory perception (ESP)**   The alleged ability to perceive something without ordinary sensory information.

**parapsychology** The study of ESP and other claims that cannot be explained by existing principles of science.

## THE CASE FOR ESP

The claims vary widely, but **parapsychologists**—who study psychic phenomena through case studies and experiments—distinguish among three types of extrasensory power (Broughton, 1991). The first is *telepathy,* or mind-to-mind communication, an ability to receive thoughts transmitted by another person without the usual sensory contact. The second type is *clairvoyance,* the ability to perceive remote events via "extra" sensory channels or contact with another person. The third type is *precognition,* the ability to see future events, also without direct contact with another person. Whatever the details, these phenomena are all thought to involve perception without sensation (some psychics also claim to have telekinesis, the ability to move objects or influence events without material contact).

These are the claims. Why are there so many believers? And what's the evidence? According to Thomas Gilovich (1991), the reason so many people believe in ESP is that the evidence "seems" overwhelming. Stage magicians, TV psychics, paperbacks that make millions of dollars from tales of the occult, coincidences that seem to defy explanation, and the friend who has a premonition come true—all conspire to leave an impression that where there's smoke, there must be fire. So, where's the fire?

In the 1930s, Duke University professor J. B. Rhine sought for the first time to document ESP through rigorous laboratory experiments. Considered the founder of parapsychology, Rhine devised a special set of ESP cards, each designated by a distinct, easy-to-recall symbol on one side (see Figure 3.34). Subjects were asked to guess the symbol on each card, and the number of their "hits" was compared to chance performance (for 25 cards, subjects can be expected by guesswork to make 5 correct responses). This procedure was used to test for telepathy (a "sender" looked at the cards and the subject tried to read his or her mind), clairvoyance (the cards were placed face down), and precognition (the subject predicted the sequence of cards before the deck was shuffled). In many hours of painstaking research, Rhine obtained close to 100,000 responses from various subjects. Then in 1934, he reported the results: using a 25-card deck, his subjects averaged 7.1 correct identifications—a statistically significant and large improvement over pure chance performance. The skeptics were baffled. Had they been too close-minded, like those who laughed at Galileo, Edison, and the Wright brothers, or like those who once used the term *impossible* to describe space travel and the splitting of the atom?

## THE CASE AGAINST ESP

In a way, Rhine's (1934) studies were like much of parapsychology's history—promising high points, inevitably followed by disappointment. Researchers scrutinized Rhine's methods and found that many subjects had been allowed to handle

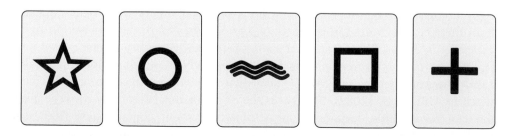

FIGURE 3.34 **ESP cards**
As devised by Rhine (1934), these five arbitrary symbols have been used in many hundreds of ESP experiments.

the cards, which made it possible to cheat; that the cards could be identified by warped edges, spots, and other physical marks; and that faint images of the symbols could be seen when held up to light. Worst of all, Rhine's most impressive subject could not replicate his performance for outside experimenters.

Over the years, hundreds more experiments were performed. Some gave what seemed to be clear and compelling "evidence" of psychic powers. But typically the findings obtained in one laboratory could not be reproduced in another. And often hoaxes were exposed. A live stage psychic has associates who circulate through a crowd before the show and spy on conversations, picking up personal information that can later be used (Wiseman, 1997; Polidoro, 1999).

It's important to realize that many parapsychologists are exacting in their methods and honorably motivated to seek the truth. But it's also important to realize that many so-called psychics are frauds. In 1974, physician Andrew Weil investigated an Israeli psychic named Uri Geller, who claimed that he could bend metal without touching it, start broken watches, and guess the contents of sealed envelopes. Apparently true to his word, Geller performed these remarkable feats and convinced Weil of his psychic powers. Then Weil met James Randi, a famous magician. Amazingly, Randi duplicated many of Geller's feats—through trickery. Illustrating the power of perceptual sets, Weil marveled at how the mind (in this case, his own) "sees what it expects to see." For his part, Randi (1980) offered $10,000 to anyone who could perform a single paranormal feat in his presence. Today, the James Randi Educational Foundation offers one million dollars "to anyone who can show, under proper observing conditions, evidence of any paranormal, supernatural, or occult power or event." To date, no one has claimed the prize.

*These objects may look like spaceships, but they are actually lenticular (lens-shape) clouds. This picture was taken in Santos, Brazil.*

## THE CONTINUING CONTROVERSY

What are we to conclude about extrasensory perception? Some forms of ESP, such as the ability to "will" the movement of objects, openly defy the laws of physics. But parapsychologists argue for the possibility that people can receive messages from others through a sensory medium that simply has yet to be identified—and they point to new studies as evidence of this phenomenon (Broughton, 1991). For example, Daryl Bem and Charles Honorton (1994) used the *ganzfeld procedure* in which a "receiver" sits in a reclining chair in a soundproof chamber. A red floodlight is shined at the eyes, which are covered by Ping Pong ball halves. Headphones placed over the ears play continuous white noise. In a separate room, a "sender" spends thirty minutes concentrating on a visual stimulus—a drawing, picture, or film. The receivers talk aloud about what they are thinking. Afterward, they are given four stimuli and asked to rate the extent to which each one matches their earlier thoughts. Despite the lack of access to sensory information, the receivers in these studies are said to have achieved a 32 percent "hit" rate—which is statistically higher than the 25 percent expected by chance.

Do these new studies prove that ESP exists? It depends on whom you ask. Some critics point out that the research methods are still flawed in important ways, so they take a skeptical wait-and-see attitude (Hyman, 1994). They note that the history of ESP research is filled with initial demonstrations that later failed to replicate. Indeed, despite thousands of studies, there is no sound empirical support, nor is there a single individual who can demonstrate psychic powers to independent

*You can visit the James Randi Educational Foundation and read about its million-dollar paranormal challenge at www.randi.org/.*

investigators (Marks, 1986). Chairing a committee that spent two years studying ESP for the U.S. Army, John Swets concluded, "The committee finds no scientific justification from research conducted over a period of 130 years for the existence of parapsychological phenomena" (Swets & Bjork, 1990). This conclusion thus far remains correct. In recent years, several research teams have tried to replicate Bem and Honorton's *ganzfield test* results—and researchers continue to disagree over whether the results are reliable (Milton & Wiseman, 1999; Storm & Ertel, 2001). At this point, there is no good evidence for the phenomenon. Yet the one safe prediction I can make is that we have not heard the last of this perennial debate.

# THINKING LIKE A PSYCHOLOGIST ABOUT SENSATION AND PERCEPTION

Sensation and perception are processes by which we make sense of the world around us. The process begins with the raw stimuli that impinge on various sensory receptors, sending signals through neural pathways to specialized regions of the brain. In this way, light is converted to vision, vibration to sound, odorant molecules into smell, and so on. That's the physiological part. But the human mind is active, and people do not perceive stimuli the way a photocopy machine reproduces an image. As perceivers, people select, organize, and interpret input from the world in ways that are sensible and adaptive. Thus, perception is an active and constructive mental process.

Human beings are sometimes remarkable in their ability to convert raw sensations into an accurate representation of reality. Without conscious thought, effort, or instruction, we can perceive sizes, shapes, depths, distances, colors, the location of sounds, subtle odors, tastes, touches to the skin, and other properties of our surrounding environment. Yet at times the mind plays tricks on us, fooling us into misperceiving reality, sometimes in predictable ways—as shown in the many demonstrations of perceptual illusions. This dual portrait of human beings is evident in other chapters too. In many ways, we are supremely competent on the one hand and yet subject to bias and distortion on the other.

# SUMMARY

Through **sensation** we absorb raw energy with our sense organs. **Transduction** converts this energy into neural signals to the brain, and then we select, organize, and interpret the signals through **perception**. Sensation and perception are interconnected. But as the story of Virgil demonstrates, they involve different processes.

## MEASURING THE SENSORY EXPERIENCE

**Psychophysics** uses special measuring procedures to study the link between physical stimuli and the sensations they arouse.

## ABSOLUTE THRESHOLDS

The **absolute threshold** is defined as the smallest amount of stimulation an organism can detect 50 percent of the time.

## SIGNAL-DETECTION THEORY

The original work on absolute thresholds assumed that the stimulus alone determined the threshold. But **signal-detection theory** takes the subject's response bias into account as well.

## DIFFERENCE THRESHOLDS

Researchers also measure the ability to detect differences between two levels of a stimulus. The smallest detectable change is called the difference threshold, or **just noticeable difference (JND)**. According to **Weber's law,** the JND is a constant proportion of the stimulus, so it increases as the stimulus increases.

## SENSATION

Humans have several distinct sensory modalities—more than the so-called five senses.

### VISION

The light we see is only a small band in the spectrum of electromagnetic radiation. The physical properties of light waves—length, amplitude, and purity—correspond, respectively, to our sensations of color, brightness, and saturation.

The human eye translates light waves into neural impulses. Light passes through the **cornea,** which bends the light to focus it. Behind the cornea, the ring-shape **iris** controls the size of the **pupil,** the hole through which light enters the eye. The **lens** continues the task of focusing the light, becoming rounder for nearby objects and flatter for remote ones—a process called **accommodation.** After passing through the vitreous humor, the light hits the **retina,** a multilayer screen of photoreceptor cells. The **rods** in the retina are responsible for black-and-white vision in dim surroundings. The **cones,** which provide for color vision, are concentrated in the **fovea,** the center of the retina. With millions of photoreceptors, the eye can adjust to lighting changes through **dark adaptation** and **light adaptation.**

The rods and cones stimulate bipolar and ganglion cells that integrate the information they receive and pass it on to the **optic nerve,** composed of the axon fibers of the ganglion cells. Because the area where the optic nerve enters the eye has no rods or cones, each eye has a **blind spot.**

The two optic nerves meet at the optic chiasm, where the axons split up so that fibers from inside half of each eye cross to the opposite side of the brain. The fibers travel through the thalamus to the **visual cortex.** There the image is processed by specialized neurons called **feature detectors.**

There are two theories of color vision. According to the **trichromatic theory,** the human eye has three types of cones, sensitive to red, green, and blue. However, this theory cannot explain **afterimages,** the visual sensations that linger after prolonged exposure to a stimulus. The **opponent-process theory** also assumes that there are three types of photoreceptors, but it contends that each kind responds to a pair of "opponent" colors. Both theories are correct. The retina contains the types of cones described by the trichromatic theory, but neurons in the thalamus operate in accordance with the opponent-process theory.

### HEARING

The stimulus for **audition,** or hearing, is sound—vibrations in air molecules caused by movement of an object. Our sensations of pitch, loudness, and timbre derive from the frequency, amplitude, and complexity of sound waves. **White noise** is the hissing sound we hear when all frequencies of the sound spectrum are combined.

Collected by the outer ear, sound waves travel through the auditory canal to vibrate the eardrum. The vibration continues through the bones in the middle ear, the oval window of the inner ear, the fluid of the cochlea, and the membrane that excites hair cells, which activate the auditory nerve. Like visual impulses, auditory signals cross to the opposite side of the brain and pass through the thalamus before reaching the auditory cortex.

The remarkable faculties of human hearing include **auditory localization,** our ability to judge a sound's direction. There are two types of hearing impairment: **conduction hearing loss** (caused by damage to the eardrum or middle-ear bones) and **sensorineural hearing loss** (resulting from damage to the inner ear).

### OTHER SENSES

Our sense of smell derives from the **olfactory system.** Odor-causing molecules dissolve and become trapped by receptors in the upper nasal passages, triggering the olfactory nerve. Instead of passing through the thalamus like other sensory information, the impulse goes straight to the olfactory bulb, which distributes the information to the cerebral cortex and to limbic structures. Researchers are investigating whether humans secrete **pheromones,** chemicals that transmit signals to other humans.

Like smell, taste is a chemical sensation. The **gustatory system** begins with **taste buds** in the mouth, which absorb molecules in food or drink and trigger neural impulses to the thalamus and cortex. There are four primary tastes: sweet, salty, sour, and bitter. The flavor of food depends in part on the number of taste buds that dot the tongue and in part on other factors such as odor.

Touch is based in the skin, the body's largest organ. Touch involves many sensory systems and the sensations of pressure, warmth, cold, and pain. Active touch, as used by Braille readers, provides much more information than passive touch.

Temperature is a sensation with two unusual aspects: It is generally relative to a person's current state, and it entails two separate sensory systems—one for signaling warmth and the other for signaling cold.

Pain is a subjective sensation with no single stimulus. The **gate-control theory** suggests that pain signals to the brain can be blocked when they become too intense. This theory explains why pain can often be eased by a competing sensation. Endorphins, the body's natural pain relievers, can also help control pain, as does the psychological technique of distraction.

Our sense of coordination derives from the **kinesthetic system.** Receptors in the joints, tendons, and muscles, linked to motor areas of the brain, help us register the body's position and movements. The related **vestibular system** includes structures in the inner ear that monitor the head's tilt and location in space, giving us our sense of equilibrium.

## KEEPING THE SIGNALS STRAIGHT

In the welter of sensations that confront us, three factors help us keep our signals straight. First, the different senses have different receptors—though some people have **synesthesia,** a very rare condition in which one sensory modality triggers sensations in another sensory modality. Second, our senses are built to detect novelty rather than sameness. As a result of **sensory adaptation,** our sensitivity to a stimulus declines as a result of constant exposure. Third, selective attention allows us to focus on one input and to block out the rest.

## PERCEPTION

Perception is an active, "constructive" process. As simple **reversible figures** demonstrate, perception involves selecting, organizing, and interpreting sensory information.

### PERCEPTUAL ORGANIZATION

Based on the idea that the whole (perception) is different from the sum of its parts (sensation), **Gestalt psychology** studies the way we construct meaningful perceptions. In any perceptual field, we focus on the figure rather than the background. We also group features into perceptual wholes according to the rules of proximity, similarity, continuity, closure, and common fate.

### PERCEPTUAL CONSTANCIES

Although sensory inputs are always changing, perceptual constancies keep our perceptions stable. Because of **size constancy,** we see an object as retaining its size even when its retinal image grows or diminishes. Because of **shape constancy,** we see an object's form as remaining the same when its orientation varies.

### DEPTH AND DIMENSION

Through **depth perception,** flat images on the retina are used to perceive distances in three-dimensional space. One binocular depth cue is **convergence,** the turning inward of the eyes when objects get closer. Another cue is **binocular disparity,** the difference in retinal image between the two eyes. The closer the object is, the greater the disparity. There are also **monocular depth cues** that permit depth perception, including relative image size, linear perspective, interposition, and atmospheric perspective.

Experiments with the **visual cliff** indicate that the capacity for depth perception may be inborn. But case studies of blind people whose eyesight was restored and cross-cultural evidence suggest as well that experience is needed to interpret depth cues correctly.

## PERCEPTUAL SET

Our prior experience and expectations often create a **perceptual set** that leads us to see what we expect to see.

## THE WORLD OF ILLUSIONS

Despite the brain's astonishing feats of perception, it falls prey to various **perceptual illusions.** In the **Müller-Lyer illusion,** the perceived length of a line is changed by the position of other lines that enclose it. The **Ponzo illusion** makes the length of two equal lines seem different if they appear to be at different distances. And in the **moon illusion,** the full moon looks larger when it's close to the horizon than when it's high in the sky.

## EXTRASENSORY PERCEPTION

More than half of all Americans believe in **extrasensory perception (ESP).** But is it possible to perceive something in the absence of sensory input?

### THE CASE FOR ESP

**Parapsychologists** distinguish three types of extrasensory power: telepathy, clairvoyance, and precognition. Rhine's studies suggested that all three types exist.

### THE CASE AGAINST ESP

Critics pointed out flaws in Rhine's methods, and similar problems were revealed by later experiments. Findings could not be reproduced, and many hoaxes have been exposed.

### THE CONTINUING CONTROVERSY

The debate continues. There appears to be new, more rigorous evidence for ESP, but skeptics are still critical of the methods. As yet, there is no sound empirical support for the existence of ESP.

## KEY TERMS

sensation (**p. 84**)

transduction (**p. 84**)

perception (**p. 84**)

psychophysics (**p. 86**)

absolute threshold (**p. 86**)

signal-detection theory (**p. 87**)

just noticeable difference (JND)
(**p. 88**)

Weber's law (**p. 88**)

cornea (**p. 90**)

iris (**p. 90**)

pupil (**p. 90**)

lens (**p. 90**)

accommodation (**p. 90**)

retina (**p. 91**)

rods (**p. 91**)

cones (**p. 92**)

fovea (**p. 92**)

dark adaptation (**p. 92**)

light adaptation (**p. 92**)

optic nerve (**p. 92**)

blind spot (**p. 92**)

receptive field (**p. 92**)

visual cortex (**p. 93**)

feature detectors (**p. 93**)

trichromatic theory (**p. 95**)

afterimage (**p. 96**)

opponent-process theory (**p. 97**)

audition (**p. 97**)

white noise (**p. 98**)

auditory localization (**p. 100**)

conduction hearing loss (**p. 102**)

sensorineural hearing loss
(**p. 102**)

olfactory system (**p. 102**)

pheromones (**p. 105**)

gustatory system (**p. 105**)

taste buds (**p. 105**)

gate-control theory (**p. 109**)

kinesthetic system (**p. 110**)

vestibular system (**p. 110**)

synesthesia (**p. 110**)

sensory adaptation (**p. 111**)

reversible figure (**p. 112**)

Gestalt psychology (**p. 112**)

size constancy (**p. 114**)

shape constancy (**p. 114**)

depth perception (**p. 116**)

convergence (**p. 116**)

binocular disparity (**p. 116**)

monocular depth cues
(**p. 117**)

visual cliff (**p. 118**)

perceptual set (**p. 118**)

perceptual illusions (**p. 120**)

Müller-Lyer illusion (**p. 121**)

Ponzo illusion (**p. 122**)

moon illusion (**p. 123**)

extrasensory perception (**p. 123**)

parapsychology (**p. 124**)

## THINKING CRITICALLY ABOUT SENSATION AND PERCEPTION

1. Distinguish sensation and perception. Can we have sensation without perception? How about perception without sensation?

2. Gestalt psychologists assume that the whole is greater than the sum of its parts. What exactly does this mean and what does it have to do with perception?

3. Children have more taste buds than adults, and we all have more taste buds at the tip of our tongues than at the center. From an evolutionary perspective, how might these differences be adaptive?

4. Suppose a friend wants to get a tattoo, but is worried about the pain involved. Your friend decides to deal with the pain by trying to ignore it. Is this a good strategy for managing pain? What other strategies would you advise?

# CHAPTER 4

# Consciousness

# DO SUBLIMINAL SELF-HELP TAPES WORK?

## THE SITUATION

You saw a newspaper ad seeking volunteers for a study of subliminal tapes, and you could not resist. No money is offered for participating, but you've heard about the power of subliminal (outside of conscious awareness) messages, so you sign up. During your first session, an experimenter hands you a cassette tape made by a company that specializes in subliminal materials. He asks you to listen to the tape once a day, every day, for five weeks. But first, you fill out some questionnaires, including some self-esteem scales and memory tests. When you've finished, you are handed a cassette tape labeled either "Subliminal Building Self-Esteem" or "Subliminal Memory Improvement."

With tape in hand, you go home and try it. All you can hear is classical music, but you know that the tape contains faint messages you cannot consciously detect, such as "I have high self-worth" or "My ability to remember is increasing daily." The tape is now part of your daily routine, and after five weeks, you return to the lab for testing. As before, you fill out some self-esteem scales and memory tests. Then depending on the group you're in, the experimenter asks, "Do you feel that the tape has improved your self-esteem (memory)?"

The procedure in this study is simple. Participants are exposed to positive subliminal messages concerning their self-esteem or memory. After five weeks, the experimenter measures both actual improvement on objective tests and self-rated improvement. There's just one hitch. Although half the participants receive tapes that are correctly labeled, the other half have tapes with the labels reversed (the self-esteem tapes have the memory label, and vice versa).

## WHAT'S YOUR PREDICTION?

So what do you think happens? Let's focus on the potential for improvement in memory. To some extent, objective-test scores should increase across the board simply because participants had practice taking such tests in the first session. But what about the added benefit to those who listened to the tape? In the first row of the table below, put an X in those conditions in which you think the tape produced an actual increase in memory-test scores. Then in the second row, put an X where you think the participants perceived an improvement in their memory.

| | MEMORY TAPE | | SELF-ESTEEM TAPE | |
| | M Label | SE Label | M Label | SE Label |
|---|---|---|---|---|
| ACTUAL | _____ | _____ | _____ | _____ |
| PERCEIVED | _____ | _____ | _____ | _____ |

## THE RESULTS

When Anthony Greenwald and his colleagues (1991) conducted this study, they asked two questions: (1) Did the memory tapes actually work, and (2) Did participants perceive that they worked? The key results are presented in the table below. First, scores on the objective memory test were no higher for those who listened to the subliminal memory tape than for those given the self-esteem tape. Second, participants perceived that their memory had improved—but that perception was based on which label was on the tape, not on which message the tape actually contained. People may believe in the power of the hidden message, but the tapes themselves had no real effect. Other research has shown that subliminal weight-loss tapes too are ineffective (Merikle & Skanes, 1992).

|  | MEMORY TAPE | | SELF-ESTEEM TAPE | |
|---|---|---|---|---|
|  | M Label | SE Label | M Label | SE Label |
| ACTUAL | _____ | _____ | _____ | _____ |
| PERCEIVED | X | _____ | X | _____ |

## WHAT DOES IT ALL MEAN?

Ever since psychology was born as a discipline, questions have been raised about consciousness and the extent to which we are influenced by information that is not in awareness. If you predicted that the subjects in this study did not benefit from subliminal self-help messages, you were right. (You were also right if you predicted that they believed the tapes to be effective, illustrating the power of suggestion.) If you think, however, that people are not in other ways subject to influence without awareness, stay tuned to the rest of this chapter. To fully understand the human organism, we must account for both what we attend to in our normal waking lives and the effects of sleep, dreams, hypnosis, and other less conscious processes.

Have you ever been offered "a penny for your thoughts"? As strange as it sounds, it's not always that easy to respond. From one moment to the next, there is an endless stream of new sights and sounds to absorb, new odors, internal sensations pressing for attention, thoughts, daydreams, and memories that pop to mind, problems that need to be solved, and other intrusions on what we call consciousness.

When psychology was born as a discipline, it was defined primarily as the study of consciousness. Wilhelm Wundt trained subjects to report on their own rapidly changing reactions to tones, visual displays, and other stimulus cues. William James wrote extensively about the functions and contents of "normal waking consciousness," and Sigmund Freud argued that people are driven by *un*conscious forces that stir beneath the surface. Despite this initial interest, however, the rise of behaviorism led many researchers to focus on observable behavior, not on the mind. It wasn't until the decline of behaviorism that interest in conscious and unconscious processes returned. Equipped with electrical recording devices, brain-imaging techniques, computers, and perceptual and cognitive tests, researchers made important new discoveries. In this chapter, we'll see that human consciousness ranges on a continuum from an alert waking state of attention to varying depths of sleep, dreams, hypnosis, and the "altered" states produced by psychoactive drugs. We'll also see that the more we know about consciousness, the more able we will be to regulate our own states of mind.

## ATTENTIONAL PROCESSES

- *In what ways is consciousness like a spotlight?*
- *Can people attend selectively to one stimulus among many? Do the stimuli we try to block out still register on the mind?*
- *How do people divide their attention in a way that permits them to engage simultaneously in more than one activity?*
- *Are we influenced by stimuli that never register in our awareness?*

The word **consciousness** has many different meanings, but psychologists tend to define it in terms of **attention**—a state of awareness that consists of the sensations, thoughts, and feelings that a person is focused on at a given moment. As implied by this definition, consciousness has a limited capacity. Whether you are mentally focused on a memory, a conversation, a foul odor, this sentence, or your growling stomach, consciousness is like a spotlight. It can shift rapidly from one stimulus to another, but it can shine on only one stimulus at a time. Try free associating into a tape recorder some time, and you'll find yourself mentally straying in what William James (1890) called the stream of consciousness.

Consciousness may be limited and the mind may wander, but three important and adaptive processes are at work. First, attention is selective—so, to some extent, people can control consciousness the way they control the channels of a television set. Second, for tasks that require little conscious effort, people can divide their attention and simultaneously engage in more than one activity. Third, even when people are conscious of one stimulus, they are also capable of reacting to other stimuli in the environment, which suggests that we can process information outside of awareness. As we'll see, these features enable us to widen, narrow, and move the spotlight of consciousness as needed (Pashler, 1998).

### SELECTIVE ATTENTION

Picture this scene. You're standing at a cocktail party with a drink in one hand and a spring roll in the other. In the background, there's music playing, as well as the chatter of voices. You're in the middle of a conversation with a friend when suddenly you overhear two other people talking about someone you know. Can you tune into the gossip and still carry on a conversation? How easy is it to attend selectively to one stimulus among many?

In a classic test of this **cocktail party phenomenon,** Colin Cherry (1953) presented subjects wearing headphones with two different messages, played simultaneously, one to each ear. In this dichotic listening task, subjects were told to "shadow"—that is, follow and repeat aloud, word for word—only one of the two messages. Were they able to do it? Yes, especially when the competing messages were different, as when one featured the voice of a man and the other the voice of a woman. But what happened to the message that subjects had filtered out and ignored? Later, subjects could not recall any of it. Even when they were stopped in the middle of the presentation and asked to repeat the unattended message, their ability to do so was limited. Through a process of **selective attention,** people can zoom in on a single auditory stimulus, but then they lose track of competing auditory stimuli.

To examine selective attention in another sensory modality, Ulric Neisser and Robert Becklen (1975) devised a visual analog of the dichotic listening task. They simultaneously showed subjects two videotapes, one superimposed over the other. One tape showed three people passing a basketball, and the other showed two people playing a hand-slapping game (see Figure 4.1). The task was to keep track of

**consciousness** An awareness of the sensations, thoughts, and feelings that one is attending to at a given moment.

**attention** A state of awareness consisting of the sensations, thoughts, and feelings that one is focused on at a given moment.

**cocktail party phenomenon** The ability to attend selectively to one person's speech in the midst of competing conversations.

**selective attention** The ability to focus awareness on a single stimulus to the exclusion of other stimuli, as in the cocktail party phenomenon.

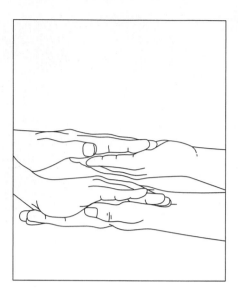  

FIGURE 4.1  **Selective attention**
Shown here are drawings of the two videotapes (left and center) and the resulting superimposed image (right). Subjects who were focused on the basketball players did not see the hand slappers, and vice versa (Neisser & Becklen, 1975).

one game or the other. As in the shadowing study, subjects could attend to only one stimulus at a time. In fact, the filtering process was so complete that out of twenty-four subjects who were focused on the basketball players, all but one failed to notice that the hand slappers had stopped their game at one point to shake hands. When the researcher later replayed this segment, these subjects were shocked at what they had missed. This result illustrates that information may be included or excluded from consciousness through a process of selective attention. To test your own ability at visual shadowing, see Figure 4.2.

## DIVIDED ATTENTION

Our consciousness may be limited, but the filtering process does not immediately or completely block out all of the extraneous information. In dichotic listening experiments, for example, most subjects do manage to hear the mention of their own names (Moray, 1959). They also manage to hear sexually explicit words, and words they had learned to associate with electric shock—even when these are irrelevant

> In performing an experiment like this one on man attention car it house is boy critically hat important shoe that candy the old material horse that tree is pen being phone read cow by book the hot subject tape for pin the stand relevant view task sky be red cohesive man and car grammatically house complete boy but hat without shoe either candy being horse so tree easy pen that phone full cow attention book is hot not tape required pin in stand order view to sky read red it nor too difficult

FIGURE 4.2  **Visual shadowing**
The passage above contains two messages—one in red ink, the other in blue. Read only the red-ink message aloud as quickly as possible. Now, without looking back, write down all the blue-ink words you can remember. The result? As in the dichotic listening studies, you probably did not recall many unshadowed words—even though the same words appeared over and over again.

stimuli spoken in the unattended ear. Many subjects in this situation could tell that something odd had occurred in the unattended ear when the speech in that ear was switched from ordinary English to English played backward (Wood & Cowan, 1995). Recent studies also show that people make rapid eye movements to examine the world around them, and that our eyes are naturally drawn to objects that are novel, bright, colorful, moving, and abrupt in their appearance—even, at times, when these stimuli intrude upon another task in which we are engaged (Pashler et al., 2001). As Jan Theeuwes and others (1998) put it, "Our eyes do not always go where we want them to go" (p. 379).

Is it possible, despite our selective tendencies, to divide attention among competing stimuli? Can you simultaneously watch TV and read a book, or drive a car, listen to the radio, and carry on a conversation? It depends on how much conscious effort is needed for the various tasks. Consider driving. When first learning to drive, you have to concentrate on how to operate the steering wheel, gas pedal, and brake, and on how to monitor traffic and watch for pedestrians, signs, and lights. At that point, driving is so *effortful* an activity that even the radio is distracting. As you gain more experience behind the wheel, however, driving then becomes an *automatic* process that does not require high levels of effort or awareness or your undivided attention. Once that happens, you can drive, listen, and talk all at the same time (Schneider & Shiffrin, 1977; Treisman et al., 1992).

The distinction between effortful and automatic processing explains how people are able to exhibit **divided attention** when at least one competing task is "on automatic." It's easy to walk, talk, and chew gum simultaneously, but for most of us it is difficult to play chess while watching TV. Consider the attention required to perform the complex motor behaviors needed in sports. When you first learn a sport—like golf, tennis, skiing, or skating—you tend to monitor every move you make. Then as you get better and more experienced, your movements become so automatic that you don't have to think about timing, breathing, head position, follow-through, and other mechanics. Experienced athletes should thus be able to divide their attention while performing in a way that novices cannot. To test this hypothesis, Sian Beilock and others (2002) observed experienced and novice golfers putting on an indoor green, then experienced and novice soccer players dribbling through cones in a slalom course. In both studies, the experienced athletes were better able to maintain their performance while attending to a competing auditory task.

To demonstrate the automatic nature of highly practiced activities, look at the patches of color in Figure 4.3. Beginning in the top left-hand column, try to name

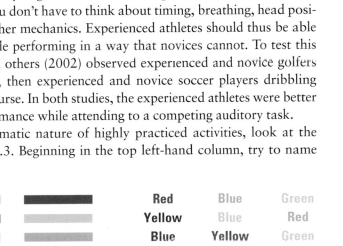

*Is it safe to talk on the phone while driving? Researchers examined the phone records of 699 motorists who were in accidents and who had cellular telephones. The accident rate was four times higher when drivers were on the phone than when not—even with hands-free headsets (Redelmeier & Tibshirani, 1997). A more recent British study using a driving simulator showed that subjects on the phone were slower to react and more dangerous behind the wheel than others who were legally drunk (Chynoweth, 2002). Driving may be a largely automatic process, but people need to stay alert to traffic and other changing conditions—which is why many states now prohibit motorists from talking on the phone while driving.*

| | | | Red | Blue | Green |
|---|---|---|---|---|---|
| | | | Yellow | Blue | Red |
| | | | Blue | Yellow | Green |
| | | | Green | Blue | Yellow |
| | | | Blue | Yellow | Red |
| | | | Red | Red | Green |

**FIGURE 4.3   The Stroop test**
In the left-hand task, name each color as fast as you can. In the right-hand task, name the color of ink in which each word is printed as fast as you can.

**divided attention**   The ability to distribute one's attention and simultaneously engage in two or more activities.

*Despite the jokes often made about us humans, it is easy to engage in two—or more—automatic activities at once.*

**Stroop test** A color-naming task that demonstrates the automatic nature of highly practiced activities such as reading.

**subliminal message** A stimulus that is presented below the threshold for awareness.

all the colors as fast as you can—and time yourself. Ready, set, go! That was easy, right? Now look at the list of color-printed words, and this time ignore the word and name the colors of the ink in which each word is printed. Again, do it as fast as you can and time yourself. If you followed these instructions, then you have just taken the **Stroop test,** which was devised in 1935 by John Stroop. As for the result, you probably found that the second task was far more difficult than the first and took about twice as long. When Stroop first presented his subjects with 100 items, he found that the first task took an average of 63 seconds, whereas the second took 110 seconds—a 74 percent slowdown in performance time. I took this test as an undergraduate and thought it would be easy. But I repeatedly paused, stammered, and got all tongue-tied, and I had to admit that the words, which contradicted the colors, kept getting in the way.

Researchers have used the Stroop test in hundreds of experiments, and they continue to debate the reasons for the effect (MacLeod, 1991). Still, one conclusion is clear: Experienced readers process word meanings automatically, without effort or awareness. It just happens. And because the test words contradict the colors (when they don't, performance is quicker), reading interferes with the color-naming task (Brown et al., 2002). Recent experiments also show that personally relevant and emotionally provocative words interfere with color naming more than neutral words do. Thus, people diagnosed as having a fear of spiders are highly disrupted by words such as *crawl* and *hairy,* while those overly concerned about their health are disrupted more by *cancer* and *blood* (Williams et al., 1996). In a study of people who had been physically injured in a serious automobile accident, those who were traumatized by the experience were slowed more than those who were not by such words as *wreck, crashed,* and *totaled* (Beck et al., 2001).

## INFLUENCE WITHOUT AWARENESS

Whereas Wundt and James pioneered the study of conscious processes, Sigmund Freud theorized that people are driven more by *un*conscious forces. Freud argued that there are three levels of awareness in the human mind: (1) *conscious* sensations, thoughts, and feelings that are currently in the spotlight of attention; (2) *preconscious* material that is temporarily out of awareness but is easy to bring to mind; and (3) an *unconscious* reservoir of material that is suppressed, banned from awareness. According to Freud, people are influenced by material that resides outside of awareness. Was he right?

For years, many researchers were skeptical of this claim. But then an outpouring of new studies brought unconscious processes to the forefront of modern psychology. These studies suggest that people can be influenced in subtle ways by **subliminal messages**—information that is presented so faintly or so rapidly that it is perceived "below" our threshold of awareness (Bornstein & Pittman, 1992; Merikle et al., 2001). Let's consider some examples that illustrate the point.

**Mere Exposure** In Chapter 13 we'll learn about a powerful principle of attraction called the mere exposure effect: The more often you see a stimulus—whether it's a word, an object, a melody, or a face—the more you come to like it (Zajonc, 1968). But must you be aware of the prior exposures for this effect to occur? Not necessarily. In a typical study, subjects are shown pictures of geometrical objects, each for only one to five milliseconds, which is too quick to register in awareness—and too quick for anyone to realize that some objects appear more often than others. After the presentation, subjects are shown each of the objects and asked two questions: Do you like it? Have you ever seen it before? Perhaps you can predict the result. The more frequently presented the object, the more subjects like it. And when asked if they've ever seen the liked objects before, they say *no.* This pattern of results demonstrates the mere exposure effect, a form of influence without awareness (Kuntz-Wilson & Zajonc, 1980; Bornstein, 1992; Zajonc, 2001).

**Priming**   Have you ever noticed that whenever a novel word slips into conversation, it suddenly gets repeated over and over again? If so, then you have observed **priming,** the tendency for a recently presented concept to "prime" responses to a subsequent "target" question. Thus, when subjects are asked to decide if the letters *D-O-C-T-O-R* form a word, they are quicker to say *yes* if the previous item was *N-U-R-S-E* than if it was *A-P-P-L-E* (Meyer & Schvaneveldt, 1971). What if the prime word is presented subliminally, below our threshold of awareness? When that is done, the result is the same—even when the prime word is presented so quickly that subjects could only recall seeing a flash of light (Marcel, 1983). In fact, subliminal presentations of drawn objects, such as hammers, chairs, and dogs, can be used to prime the identification of similar objects that are shown up to 15 minutes later (Bar & Biederman, 1998).

In a series of provocative experiments, John Bargh and Tanya Chartrand (1999) found that motivations and emotions are also subject to automatic influence without awareness. In one study, subjects took part in a "word search" puzzle that contained either neutral words or words associated with achievement motivation (*strive, win, compete, succeed, master*). Afterward, they were left alone and given three minutes to write down as many words as they could generate from a set of Scrabble letter tiles. When the three-minute limit was up, subjects were signaled over an intercom to stop. Did subjects, driven to obtain a high score, stop on cue or continue to write? Through the use of hidden cameras, the experimenters observed that 57 percent of the subjects primed with achievement-related words continued to write after the stop signal—compared to only 22 percent in the control group.

In a second study by Bargh and Chartrand (1999), subjects took part in a "reaction-time" task in which they were subliminally exposed to words that evoked strongly positive emotional reactions (*music, friends*), strongly negative reactions (*cancer, cockroach*), or more neutral—only mildly positive and negative—reactions. Afterward, they described their current mood state as part of what was supposed to be an unrelated experiment. Subjects were not aware of the words they had "seen" in the first task. Yet compared to those in the neutral-word groups, those previously exposed to positive words were in a happier mood, and those exposed to negative words were in a sadder mood (see Figure 4.4).

**Prosopagnosia**   Influence without awareness can also be seen in people with **prosopagnosia**—a rare condition, often resulting from damage to the temporal lobes, which impairs the ability to recognize family members, friends, celebrities, and other familiar faces, including one's own. Or does it? Although

**priming**  The tendency for a recently presented word or concept to facilitate, or "prime," responses in a subsequent situation.

**prosopagnosia**   A condition stemming from damage to the temporal lobes that disrupts the ability to recognize familiar faces.

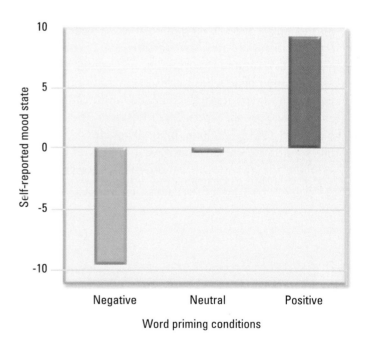

**FIGURE 4.4   Influenced mood without awareness**
As part of a reaction-time task, subjects were subliminally exposed to words that evoked positive, negative, or neutral reactions. They were not aware of the words they "saw." Yet when later asked to describe their mood states, subjects exposed to positive words were happier and those exposed to negative words were sadder. This effect indicates that our moods can be influenced without our awareness (Chartrand & Bargh, 1999).

## *Debunking the Myth*

# OF SUBLIMINAL ADVERTISING MANIPULATION

In 1957, Vance Packard published *The Hidden Persuaders,* an exposé of Madison Avenue. The book climbed the best-seller list and awakened in the public a fear of being manipulated by forces that they could not see or hear. What had Packard uncovered? In the 1950s, amid growing fears of communism and the birth of rock and roll, a group of advertisers reported that they had used *subliminal advertising*—the presentation of commercial messages below the level of conscious awareness. It started in a drive-in movie theater in New Jersey, where the words *Drink Coca-Cola* and *Eat Popcorn* were supposedly flashed on the screen during the film for a third of a millisecond. Although the audience never noticed the messages, Coke sales were said to have increased 18 percent and popcorn sales 58 percent over a six-week period of intermissions (Brean, 1958).

This incident was followed by many others. A Seattle radio station presented subaudible antitelevision messages during its programs ("TV is a bore"); department stores played music tapes over public-address systems that contained subaudible antitheft statements ("If you steal, you'll get caught"); and in what has become a multimillion-dollar industry, companies offer consumers audiotapes with subliminal self-help messages embedded in the music. In books entitled *Subliminal Seduction* (1973) and *The Age of Manipulation* (1989), William Bryan Key charged that advertisers routinely sneak faint sexual images in visual ads to heighten the appeal of their products. Concerns have also

been raised about rock music. In one case, the families of two young men who had committed suicide blamed the British rock band Judas Priest for subliminal lyrics on their *Stained Glass* album ("do it") that promoted satanism and suicide (*National Law Journal,* 1990). Clearly, many people believe in the power of hidden persuaders.

At the time of the New Jersey movie-theater scandal, controlled research on the topic was so sketchy, and the public was so outraged by the sinister implications, that the matter was quickly dropped. But today there is renewed interest and continued controversy. Can subliminal messages really induce us, without our awareness, to drink Coke, eat popcorn, or purchase a particular product? In 1982, Timothy Moore reviewed all the existing research and concluded that "what you see is what you get"—nothing, "complete scams." Moore may have been right. The original Coke-and-popcorn study was never published. It was later exposed as a publicity stunt, a hoax (Pratkanis, 1992). Indeed, there is no solid evidence of this covert form of influence. Like the study described at the start of this chapter, controlled experiments continue to show that although consumers may believe in the power of hidden messages, subliminal self-help tapes that promise to raise your self-esteem or to help you stop smoking, lose weight, and improve your sex life do not work (Pratkanis et al., 1994).

So why, you may be wondering, is there such strong evidence for perception without awareness in studies of mere

prosopagnosics cannot identify known faces, research shows that they exhibit unique patterns of eye movements, electrical activity in the brain, and increased autonomic arousal when presented with faces that are familiar rather than unfamiliar (Renault et al., 1989; Tranel & Damasio, 1985). And when asked to determine if two faces are the same or different, they make the judgments more quickly when one of the faces is familiar (Young & DeHaan, 1992). In short, it appears that prosopagnosics exhibit glimmers of "recognition"—they just don't realize it. We will revisit this phenomenon and others like it in Chapter 6, on memory.

**Blindsight**   Another rare condition is **blindsight,** a form of "vision" without awareness. When people suffer damage that is limited to the primary visual cortex, optic nerve fibers from the eyes may still be connected to other regions of the brain that process visual information. In such cases, the patient is consciously blind yet is able to locate and reach for objects, identify colors in flashing lights, track moving objects, and report "nonvisual feelings" during the presentation of visual stimuli

**blindsight**   A condition caused by damage to the visual cortex in which a person encodes visual information without awareness.

exposure, priming, prosopagnosia, and blindsight, but not in studies of subliminal persuasion? There seems to be a contradiction here. But if you think about it, the two sets of claims are so different that the contradiction may be more apparent than real. In laboratory settings, subliminal exposures have a short-term effect on simple judgments and actions. But in claims of subliminal persuasion, the exposure is presumed to have long-term effects on consumer purchases, on health, and even on the most profound of violent acts, suicide. Psychologists agree that we can process a great deal of information at an unconscious level, but they're also quick to point out that this processing is "analytically limited" (Greenwald, 1992).

Erin Strahan and others (2002) suggest that although people *perceive* subliminal cues, those cues will not *persuade* them to take action unless they are already motivated to do so. To test this hypothesis, they brought thirsty college students into the lab for a marketing study and provided drinking water to some but not others. Then, as part of a test administered by computer, they subliminally exposed these students to neutral words (*pirate, won*) or thirst-related words (*thirst, dry*). Did the subliminal "thirsty" message later lead the students, like automatons, to drink more in a taste test of Kool-Aid beverages? Yes and no. Figure 4.5 shows that the subliminal thirst primes had little impact on students whose thirst had just been quenched, but they clearly increased consumption among those who were water-deprived—and thirsty. For a subliminal message to influence behavior, it has to strike "while the iron is hot."

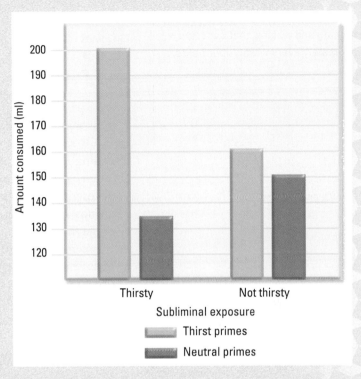

**FIGURE 4.5**
In this study, thirsty and nonthirsty subjects were subliminally exposed to neutral or thirst-related words. Afterward they participated in a beverage taste test in which the amount they drank was measured. Note that the subliminal thirst cues had little impact on nonthirsty subjects but increased consumption among those who were thirsty. Apparently, subliminal cues can influence our behavior, but only when we are otherwise predisposed (Strahan et al. 2002).

(Cowey & Stoerig, 1991; Wust et al., 2002). Thus, the person can react to certain visual cues without awareness. As noted, people may be conscious of one stimulus yet also react to other stimuli—and process information outside their awareness.

Although consciousness is limited by selective attention, people can perform certain tasks automatically and react to stimuli that are not "in the spotlight." This capacity of ours to simultaneously process information from many sources—and to do so outside of awareness—is highly adaptive. But can it be used against us? Are there limits to influence without awareness, or are we at the mercy of subliminal messages designed to shape our tastes, attitudes, and behavior? Can consumers be lured into purchasing certain products by subliminal messages embedded in advertisements? Can teenagers be provoked into violence by subliminal rap or rock music lyrics? Some people believe that subliminal stimuli are more powerful than ordinary "supraliminal" (above-threshold) stimuli because they bypass our conscious defenses. But is this fear well founded? The answer is provided by research on these so-called hidden persuaders (see Debunking the Myth).

## REVIEW QUESTIONS

- *What is the evidence that attention is selective?*

- *What is the Stroop effect and what does it tell us about automatic and effortful processing?*

- *Describe four examples of influence without awareness.*

**biological rhythm** Any periodic, more or less regular fluctuation in a biological organism.

**circadian rhythm** A biological cycle, such as sleeping and waking, that occurs approximately every twenty-four hours.

# SLEEP AND DREAMS

- *Are people, like animals, influenced by biological rhythms, or are we flexible in our sleeping schedules?*
- *How do researchers study sleep in the laboratory?*
- *What is REM sleep, and what makes it so special?*
- *What are dreams, why do we have them, and what do they mean?*
- *What are some ways in which sleeping can become impaired and then repaired?*

It may start with a deep yawn. Then the eyelids begin to fall. Then your head drops and you get that drowsy sense of calm before nodding off, tuning out, and calling it a day. For most people, falling asleep is a pleasurable experience. Why? What is sleep? Why do we need to have it? And what about dreams—what purposes do they serve and what, if anything, do they mean? The average person spends about eight hours a day sleeping and ninety minutes dreaming. Given an average life expectancy of seventy-five years, that amounts to about twenty-five years of sleep and five years of dreaming in a lifetime. Yet until recently, we knew very little about this important aspect of our lives. Shakespeare once referred to sleep as "the death of each day's life." Others, too, think of sleep as a state of complete dormancy. They are wrong. As we'll see, the sleeping brain is humming with activity (Carskadon, 1993; Dement & Vaughan, 1999; Pace-Schott et al., 2002).

## THE SLEEP-WAKE CYCLE

Many birds migrate south for the winter. Bears and raccoons hibernate. Certain plants open their leaves during the day and close them at night—even if kept in a dark closet. As biological organisms, humans are also sensitive to seasonal changes, the twenty-eight-day lunar cycle, the twenty-four-hour day, and the ninety-minute activity-rest cycle that is linked to variations in alertness and daydreaming. These and other regular fluctuations are forms of **biological rhythms.**

From a psychological standpoint, one internal clock is particularly important: Every twenty-four hours, we undergo a single sleep-wake cycle. This cycle and others that take roughly a day to complete are referred to as a **circadian rhythm.** Humans tend to be most active and alert during the middle of the day, when body temperature peaks, and least active and alert at night, when body temperature drops to its low point. The human circadian rhythm is also evident in fluctuations in blood pressure, pulse rate, blood-sugar level, potassium level, growth-hormone secretions, cell growth, and other physiological functions (Lavie, 2001).

Everyone is influenced by circadian rhythms, but everyone's inner clock is set somewhat differently. Think about yourself. Are you a morning person or a night person, a lark or an owl? If you had a choice, would you rather wake up at 6, 8, or 10 o'clock in the morning? How easy is it for you to work late into the night? During what time of day are you most productive? These kinds of questions can be used to determine your circadian rhythm (Smith et al., 1989). Although morning types fall asleep eighty-eight minutes earlier at night and awaken seventy-two minutes earlier in the morning (Kerkhof, 1985), few people are extreme in their preference. Most fall somewhere in the middle and adapt as needed to the schedules they must keep. Still, it helps to know when you're likely to be at your best. When subjects were tested for memory at 9 AM, 2 PM, and 8 PM, the larks performed worse as the day wore on, whereas owls performed better (Anderson et al., 1991). Among college students,

*"Larks see owls as lazy; owls see larks as party poopers."*

—RICHARD M. COLEMAN

larks are more likely than owls to take early morning classes—and they earn higher grades in those classes (Guthrie et al., 1995). Among older people, who tend to prefer early morning hours, performance on learning and memory tasks declines when they're tested late in the day (Intons-Peterson et al., 1999). Across a whole range of cognitive activities that require vigilance, research shows that people perform better during their "preferred" time of day (May & Hasher, 1998).

Is the circadian rhythm endogenous (set by an inner clock), or is the human body responsive to outside patterns of lightness and darkness? Ask Stefania Follini, an Italian interior designer. In January 1989, she descended into a Plexiglas bunker buried in a cave in New Mexico. Sealed off from sunlight, outside noises, changes in temperature, schedules, and clocks, she lived alone in this underground home for 131 days—a "free-running" period of time that allowed her body to establish its own rhythm. Her only link to the world was a personal computer. When Follini emerged from her isolation in May, she thought it was only March. Her "day" had extended to twenty-five hours, then to forty-eight. As time went on, she slept and woke up later and later. She stopped menstruating, ate fewer meals, and lost seventeen pounds.

Other volunteers were similarly isolated for extended periods of time. Some naturally settled into a "short" day, but most free-ran on a longer cycle that averaged twenty-five hours. With each successive cycle, these subjects tended to go to sleep a little later and to wake up a little later (see Figure 4.6). Body temperature and hormone levels tended to follow the same rhythm. Like Follini, these subjects drifted toward a longer day—then underestimated the amount of time they had been isolated. When reexposed to sunlight, the subjects readjusted their biological clocks.

Where is this timing device? Animal experiments have shown that the circadian rhythm is controlled in the brain's hypothalamus, just above the optic nerves, by two pinhead-size clusters of neurons called the suprachiasmatic nuclei, or SCN. How do the SCN function? You may recall from Chapter 3 that light passing through the eye is converted to neural signals and sent to the cortex through the optic nerve. Apparently, some of these optic nerve axons—and the information they convey about light—are diverted to the SCN. Nestled in the center of the brain, the pea-shape pineal gland also plays an important role. As darkness falls, the pineal gland produces melatonin—a hormone that facilitates sleep by letting the body know that it's dark outside. When light strikes the retina, melatonin secretion is slowed down. Spurred by books with titles like *The Melatonin Miracle, Melatonin: Nature's Sleeping Pill,* and *Boost Your Vitality with Melatonin,* melatonin has been in the news. As we'll see later, it is often used to treat people with chronic insomnia.

The circadian rhythm is synchronized like a fine watch by an interplay between the brain and environmental cues. But what happens when your rhythm is disrupted? One common source of disruption is air travel—specifically, flying across time zones, which throws your body out of sync with the new time of day and causes you to sleep at the wrong time. If you've ever flown from one coast to the other or overseas, then you may have suffered jet lag, a condition that makes you feel tired, sluggish, and grumpy. Most people find it easier to fly west, which lengthens the day, than to fly east, which shortens it. Because the body naturally drifts to a

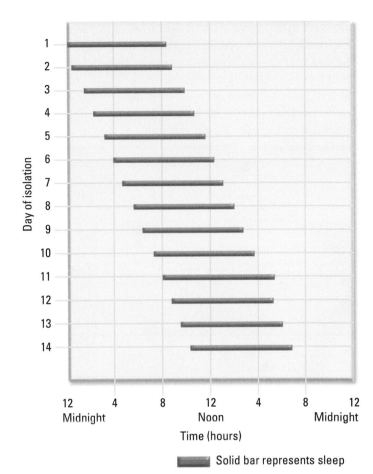

**FIGURE 4.6   The inner clock**
When people are placed in a "free-running" environment, isolated from all day and night cues, they typically drift toward a twenty-five-hour day. With each cycle, subjects go to sleep and wake up a little later.

As measured by the amount of time it takes to fall asleep, research shows that people are the sleepiest between 1 and 4 AM—and then again, twelve hours later, between 1 and 4 PM. If you find yourself getting drowsy in mid afternoon, you're not alone. This circadian low point—not daytime heat or a full lunch—may be the reason why people in many countries take a siesta, or afternoon nap.

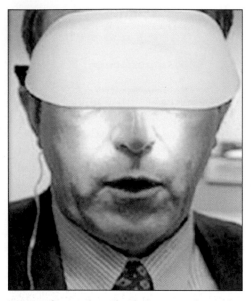

*To combat jet lag, this light visor, devised by Dr. Martin Moore-Ede, helps to adjust the body clock to a new time zone through controlled exposure to bright light. The visor is lightweight, battery-powered, and portable, and allows for a range of activities such as reading or watching TV.*

"Damn! I keep waking up in the middle of the day."

longer day, this makes sense. Flying westward goes "with the flow" rather than against it. Consistent with this analysis, research shows that long-distance travel within a time zone does not cause jet lag (Coleman, 1986).

In recent years, researchers have tested various strategies that long-distance travelers can use to combat jet lag. In *How to Beat Jet Lag*, Dan Oren and others (1995) offer a number of behavioral tips for the weary long-distance traveler (the book comes plastic-wrapped with an eye mask and dark glasses). Always get a full night's sleep before a long trip. Anticipate your new time zone. Drink lots of liquids to avoid dehydration, but avoid alcohol, which disrupts later sleep. If you plan to travel east—say, from Los Angeles to New York—you can facilitate the adjustment process by sleeping earlier than normal before you leave so that you more closely "fit" the light-dark cycle of the new time zone. As soon as you board the plane, set your watch to your destination's time zone and eat and sleep accordingly. Because of studies that indicate that bright-light exposure at night speeds the resetting of the inner clock, researchers also advise that, upon arrival, you spend the first day outdoors.

Can anything more be done to prevent jet lag from gripping us as we cross time zones in flight? In 1998, Scott Campbell and Patricia Murphy published an article in *Science* on a new technique for combating jet lag by resetting our internal clock. They reported that by shining a light on the backs of people's knees, they were able to shift the clock that regulates the sleep-wake cycle. Because the backs of the knees contain blood vessels just under the skin, they reasoned, it was possible to send a chemical timing signal through blood circulating through the body, not just through the eyes. More recent research, however, casts doubt on the claim. In a study also published in *Science*, Kenneth Wright and Charles Czeisler (2002) measured changes in the levels of melatonin in twenty-two subjects over a ten-day period. Some subjects were exposed to bright light behind the knee but not in the eye; others were exposed to light in the eye but not behind the knee; still others received no light. The result: the circadian clock was shifted by light to the eyes—but not by light to the back of the knee.

## NIGHT WORK, SLEEPING, AND HEALTH

We humans are diurnal creatures—active during the day and asleep at night. Thus, we like to work from 9 to 5 and then play, sleep, and awaken to the light of a new day. Yet an estimated 25 percent of all Americans—including emergency-room doctors and nurses, police officers, telephone operators, security guards, factory workers, and truckers—are often forced to work late-night shifts. The question is, what is the effect? Do people adapt over time to shift work and other late-night activity, or does it compromise their health and safety?

Both biological and social clocks set the body for activity during the daytime and sleep at night, so it's no surprise that many shift workers struggle to stay alert. People who choose night work fare better than those assigned on a rotating-shift basis (Barton, 1994). Still, shift workers in general get fewer hours of sleep than day workers, complain that their sleep is disrupted, and report being drowsy on the job. Often they blame their lack of sleep on ringing phones, crying babies, traffic, and other daytime noises. Part of the problem too is that the body's internal alarm clock tries to awaken the day sleeper. Either way, the adverse effects can be seen at work—where night-time energy levels are low, reaction times are slow, and productivity is diminished. In a survey of one thousand locomotive engineers, 59 percent admitted to having dozed off at the controls on several night trips (Akerstedt, 1988).

Can anything be done to lessen the dangers posed by shift work? Richard Coleman (1986) recommends that when rotating shifts are necessary, employers should maximize the number of days between shift *changes* (adjustment is easier in three-week cycles than in one-week cycles) and assign workers to successively later shifts rather than earlier shifts (a person who is rotated from the 4 PM shift to the midnight shift will adjust more quickly than one who is rotated in the opposite direction). In addition, it seems to take two days of rest, not one, for workers to fully recover from their nocturnal routine (Totterdell et al., 1995). Charles Czeisler and others (1990) found that the realignment of the circadian rhythm can also be speeded up by exposing shift workers to bright levels of light in the workplace and to eight hours of total darkness at home during the day. Within a week, the body's biological clock can be reset and the health risks of night work reduced. It takes only four hours of bright-light exposure one night to improve performance the next night (Thessing et al., 1994).

The National Highway Transportation Safety Administration estimates that up to 200,000 traffic accidents a year are sleep related—and that 20 percent of all drivers have dozed off at least once while behind the wheel. Overall, 1 to 3 percent of highway crashes in the United States are caused by driver sleepiness—a problem that most plagues young drivers, shift workers, drivers who use alcohol and other drugs, drivers with sleep disorders, and commercial truck drivers (Lyznicki et al., 1998). Drivers are five to ten times more likely to have an accident late at night than during the daytime hours. The reason is easy to find. Monitoring of EEG activity shows that those who drive in the middle of the night often take quick, two- to three-second **microsleeps,** which elevates the risk of accident (Kecklund & Akerstedt, 1993). A study of eighty long-haul truck drivers revealed that 56 percent had at least one episode of drowsiness and two drifted briefly into a light stage of sleep (Mitler et al., 1997). A study of thirty-five people in a driving simulator revealed a slowed heart rate and brain-wave patterns indicative of drowsiness. Over time, many subjects yawned, blinked quickly, closed their eyes, nodded off, drifted lanes, and made driving errors resulting in collisions (Lal & Craig, 2002). There are times when a person just can't avoid the situation. Often when I'm out of town and have to return for an early-morning class, I'll find myself driving late at night and fighting to keep my eyes open. Is there a way to counteract this tendency?

*To avoid traffic, many truckers drive at night. Due to drowsiness, however, they are more likely to have an accident during these hours than in the daytime.*

**microsleep** A brief episode of sleep that occurs in the midst of a wakeful activity.

In a controlled study, James Horne and L. Reyner (1996) evaluated the possible benefits of two coping strategies: a brief nap and a cup of coffee. Ten subjects, tested in the afternoon, were restricted to five hours of sleep the nights before the study and then placed into a simulated car. On the windshield was an interactive computer-generated screen that projected a four-lane highway, with a shoulder to the side and two audible "rumble strips" between lanes. The route itself was monotonous, but subjects had to steer along gentle curves and at times pass a slow-moving car. To measure driving performance, a computer kept track of the number of incidents in which they drifted from their lane or went off the side of the road. On three separate occasions, subjects drove for an hour, took a thirty-minute break, and then drove for another hour. Would subjects become sleepy—and sloppy—during the second hour? It depended on whether they were assigned, during the

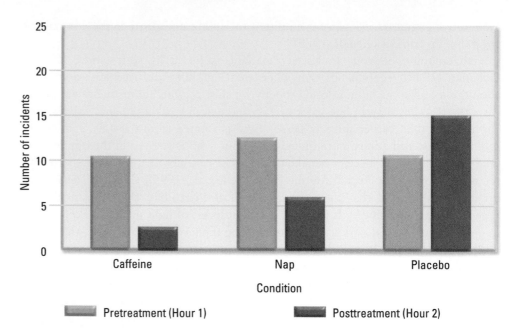

FIGURE 4.7 **How to keep from falling asleep at the wheel**
Subjects drove for two hours in a simulated car, with a break during which they drank a regular cup of coffee or a placebo cup of decaffeinated coffee, or took a fifteen-minute nap. As measured by the number of traffic incidents they had in the second hour compared to the first, the incident rate increased in the placebo group but was reduced in the coffee and nap conditions (Horne & Reyner, 1996).

break, to drink a cup of coffee, to drink a placebo (decaffeinated) cup of coffee, or to take a fifteen-minute nap. Look at the results in Figure 4.7, and you'll see that although the incident rate rose in the placebo group, it dropped in the coffee and nap conditions. Horne and Reyner concluded that "many vehicle accidents due to the driver falling asleep at the wheel could be avoided if the driver recognized the dangers beforehand and used the countermeasures investigated here" (p. 309).

## THE STAGES OF SLEEP

Just as activity levels follow a rhythm, so too does sleep. Every night, humans cycle through five distinct stages of sleep. Much of what is known about these stages first came to light in the 1950s, thanks to the pioneering collaborative work of Nathaniel Kleitman, Eugene Aserinksy, and William Dement. The scientific study of sleep is now highly active (Dement & Vaughan, 1999; Hobson, 2003; Pace-Schott et al., 2002).

To appreciate how these discoveries were made, imagine that you're a subject in a sleep study. As you enter the sleep lab, you meet an experimenter, who gives you some questionnaires to fill out, prepares you for the experience, and takes you to a carpeted, tastefully decorated, soundproof "bedroom." Electrodes are then taped to your scalp to record brain-wave activity, near your eyes to measure eye movements, and under your neck and chin to record muscle tension (see Figure 4.8). Other devices may also be used to measure your breathing, heart rate, and even genital arousal. The pillow is fluffy, the bed is okay, and the blanket is warm. But you know you're being watched, and you can feel the electrodes and wires on your skin, so you wonder how you'll ever manage to fall asleep. The experimenter reassures you that it may take a couple of nights to adapt to the situation.

4.1  *Live!* psych

To assess your own sleep behavior and learn more about sleep disorders, visit sleepnet.com at http://www.sleepnet.com.

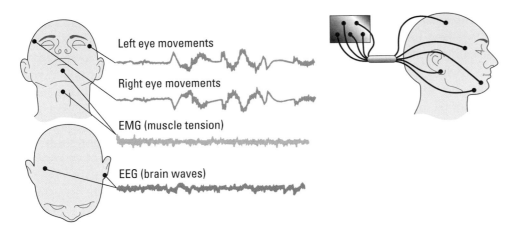

**FIGURE 4.8   Measuring sleep**
In sleep laboratories, researchers record brain-wave activity, eye movements, and muscle tension by taping electrodes to the scalp, near the eyes, and elsewhere on the face (Dement, 1978).

**Presleep**   The experimenter departs, shuts off the lights, and leaves you alone. As you try to settle down, EEG recordings reveal that all is well (see Figure 4.9). Typical of a person who is awake and alert, your EEG shows short, quick *beta waves*. This pattern indicates that different parts of your brain are producing small bursts of electrical activity at different times—a sure sign of mental activity. Your eyes move rapidly up and down and from side to side, and many of your muscles are tensed.

**Stages 1 to 4**   You start to become drowsy. Your breathing slows down, your mind stops racing, your muscles relax, your eyes move less, and EEG recordings show a slower, larger, and somewhat more regular pattern of *alpha waves* (alpha waves appear to occur when people are relaxed but not focused on something specific). For a minute or two, you drift into a "hypnogogic state" in which you may imagine seeing flashes of color or light, and perhaps you jerk your leg abruptly as you sense yourself falling. You are entering stage 1 sleep. Electrical activity in the brain slows down some more, in a pattern of *theta waves*. Your breathing becomes more regular, your heart rate slows, and your blood pressure drops. This is a period of very light sleep. No one makes a sound or calls your name, however, so you don't wake up.

After about ten minutes in stage 1 sleep, your EEG pattern shows waves that are even slower and larger. As you slip into stage 2 sleep, you become progressively more relaxed, the rolling eye movements stop, and you become less easily disturbed. On the EEG, stage 2 is marked by periodic short bursts of activity called sleep spindles. If the experimenter in the next room makes a noise, your brain will register a response—but you probably will not wake up. In the laboratory, subjects detect a change in a tone 95 percent of the time while awake, 47 percent of the time in stage 1 sleep, and only 3 percent of the time in stage 2 sleep (Cote et al., 2002).

After about twenty minutes in stage 2, you fall into the deepest stages of sleep. Stages 3 and 4 are hard to distinguish because they differ only in degree. Both are marked by the onset of very slow waves with large peaks, called *delta waves*, which last for about thirty minutes (delta waves seem to indicate that increasing numbers

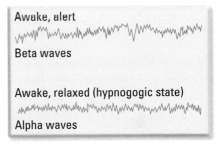

**Presleep**

Awake, alert

Beta waves

Awake, relaxed (hypnogogic state)

Alpha waves

**Non-REM**

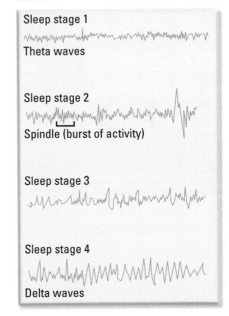

Sleep stage 1

Theta waves

Sleep stage 2

Spindle (burst of activity)

Sleep stage 3

Sleep stage 4

Delta waves

**REM**

REM stage

**FIGURE 4.9   The stages of sleep**
As recorded by the EEG, brain waves get larger and slower as sleep deepens from stages 1 to 4. You can see that REM sleep waves closely resemble those of the presleep state.

**REM sleep** The rapid-eye-movement stage of sleep associated with dreaming.

**NREM sleep** The stages of sleep not accompanied by rapid eye movements.

of neurons are firing together, in synchrony). At this point, you are "out like a light" or "sleeping like a rock." If the phone rings, you may not hear it. If you do answer the call, you'll sound dazed and confused. It is during the very deep sleep of stages 3 and 4 when young children may wet the bed or when you may walk or talk in your sleep. It's this stage that Mark Twain had in mind when he said, "There ain't no way to find out why a snorer can't hear himself snore." Yet in keeping with the adaptive and very selective nature of attention, certain noises will penetrate consciousness. New parents may be oblivious to the sounds of traffic outside, for example, but they're quick to hear the baby cry.

**REM Sleep** After an hour of deepening sleep, something odd happens— something first discovered in Kleitman's lab (Aserinksy & Kleitman, 1953; Dement & Kleitman, 1957; Kleitman, 1963). Rather than maintain your deep sleep, you begin to cycle backward to stage 3, then to stage 2. But then instead of returning to stage 1, you enter a new, fifth stage, marked by two dramatic types of changes. On the one hand, the EEG reveals a surge of short, high-frequency beta waves like those found when you were awake. Also indicating an increased level of activity, blood flow to the brain increases, your breathing and pulse rates speed up, and your genitals become aroused—even without sexual thoughts or dreams. On the other hand, you have lost skeletal muscle tone throughout the body. In fact, your arms, legs, and trunk are so totally relaxed that, except for an occasional twitch, you are completely paralyzed. You're also hard to awaken at this stage. This odd combination— of being internally active but externally immobile—has led some researchers to refer to this stage of sleep as paradoxical.

The most prominent change occurs in the eyes. The eyelids are shut, but underneath, your eyeballs are darting frantically back and forth as if you were watching a world-class Ping-Pong match. These *rapid eye movements* are so pronounced that this stage has been named **REM sleep**—and it is contrasted with stages 1 through 4, which are lumped together as non-REM, or **NREM, sleep.** What makes rapid eye movements so special is what they betray about the state of your mind. When sleeping subjects are awakened during non-REM stages, they report on dreams about 50 percent of the time. Yet when subjects are awakened during REM, they report on dreams about 80 percent of the time—and that includes subjects who came into the lab saying they don't ever dream (Foulkes, 1962). Clearly, everyone dreams throughout the night, during both REM and NREM sleep (Squier & Domhoff, 1998). But compared to the fleeting thoughts and images reported during stages 1 through 4, REM dreams are more visual, vivid, detailed, and storylike. In the mind's late-night theater, the production of dreams can be seen in the resurgence of activity within the eyes and brain.

From the time you fall asleep, it takes about ninety minutes to complete one cycle. The contrasts within this cycle are striking. Coleman (1986) describes NREM sleep as "an idling brain in a moveable body" and REM as "an active brain in a paralyzed body." In a full night's sleep, you are likely to recycle through the stages four to six times. The first time through the cycle, you spend only about ten minutes in REM sleep. As the night wears on, however, you spend less time in the deeper NREM periods and more time in REM sleep. During the last hour before you awaken in the morning, the REM period is thirty to sixty minutes long. This explains why people are so often in the middle of a dream when the mechanical tyrant we call an alarm clock rings. The sleep cycles and the progression of stages within each cycle are illustrated in Figure 4.10.

In all cultures of the world, beds are designed for sleep in a horizontal position. This universal behavior is highly adaptive. EEG recordings show that when people sleep in an upright position (even in a comfortable chair), they get little of the slow-wave sleep needed to feel refreshed.

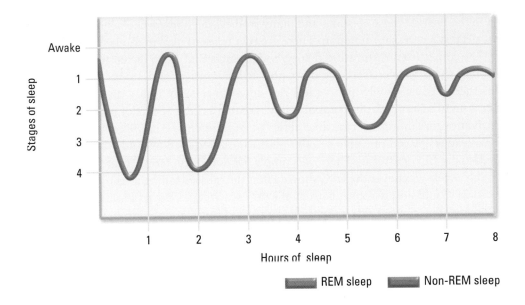

FIGURE 4.10   **A typical night's sleep**
People pass through four to six ninety-minute sleep cycles per night. As shown, progressively more time is spent in REM sleep and progressively less is spent in the deeper stages.

## WHY DO WE SLEEP?

Because humans spend a third of their lives in this state, it's natural to wonder: Why do we sleep? When we are tired, the urge to doze is overwhelming and very hard to fight, regardless of what we're doing or where we are. And if we are still tired when the alarm clock rings, we might shut it off, clutch our pillows to our ears, or just pretend we didn't hear it—even if we have a schedule to keep. Our need for sleep is powerful and irresistible. But why?

One way to investigate this question is to deprive people of sleep and see what happens. I pulled a few "all-nighters" when I was younger and "burned the midnight oil." You may have done so too, but probably not for periods of time that are long enough to push the limits. A unique opportunity to observe the effects of sleep deprivation presented itself in New York City in 1959. As part of a fund-raising drive, disc jockey Peter Tripp forced himself to stay awake and on the air for 200 hours. By the fifth day, Tripp's speech was slurred, and he was hallucinating and showing signs of paranoia (he believed that "enemies" were trying to drug his coffee). It seemed that sleep was essential to his mental health. But after sleeping for thirteen hours, Tripp had completely recovered.

A second highly publicized case came about in 1964, when seventeen-year-old Randy Gardner sought fame in the *Guinness Book of World Records*. As part of a high-school science project, and with the help of two friends, Gardner stayed awake for 264 hours—that's eleven straight days, a world record (which was later broken). When it was over, he held a news conference, during which he said, "It's just mind over matter." He went to sleep for fifteen hours, woke up feeling fine, and resumed his normal schedule. Follow-up tests confirmed that Gardner suffered no long-term ill effects. For many years, the Gardner story was surrounded by the myth that he suffered no ill effects during the episode. But daily tests administered to Gardner showed that his thinking was fragmented, his speech was slurred, he couldn't concentrate, he had memory lapses, and toward the end, he was hallucinating (Coren, 1996).

How much sleep do we need to function during the day and stay healthy? Clearly, people differ. Thomas Edison, inventor of the modern light bulb, required only about four hours a night. This fact is interesting given that Edison's 1913 light bulb precipitated a decline in the amount of sleep people get—from nine hours a night, measured in 1910, to . . . well, you make the call. As part of its "Sleep in America" poll, the National Sleep Foundation (2002) asked a random sample of a thousand adults to estimate the number of hours of sleep they get on weekdays and on weekends. What are your predictions? Look at Figure 4.12, and you'll see that Americans sleep an average of 6.9 hours on weekdays and 7.5 hours on weekends. Is this enough? How much sleep do *you* need? Do you sometimes sleep through your alarm or doze off in class? Sleep expert William Dement believes that Americans suffer from a "national sleep deficit" (Dement & Vaughan, 1999).

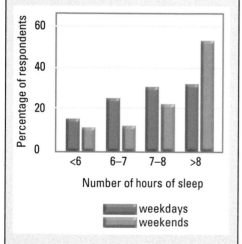

**FIGURE 4.12**
In its 2002 "Sleep in America" poll, the National Sleep Foundation surveyed a thousand adults about their sleeping habits. The resulting distribution shows that Americans average 6.9 hours of sleep on weekdays and 7.5 hours on weekends—and that individuals differ in the amount of sleep they normally get.

On the basis of these episodes and many studies, sleep researchers have concluded that sleep is a necessary function. There are two types of explanations for why this is so. One comes from restoration theory, which states that sleep recharges the battery, enabling us to recover from the day's physical, cognitive, and emotional demands. This theory explains why people feel run-down as the day wears on and refreshed after a night's sleep. It's also supported by research on the effects of prolonged sleep deprivation in laboratory rats. In a series of experiments, Allan Rechtschaffen and his colleagues placed rats on a circular platform surrounded by cold water and monitored their EEG patterns. There was ample food and the temperature was set at a suitable level. Whenever the EEG showed that the rat was falling asleep, however, the platform would slowly rotate, causing the rat to move in order to avoid being pushed into the water (control rats were similarly treated but were permitted to sleep). The results were striking. After twenty-four hours of sleep deprivation, the rats fell into unusually long periods of slow-wave deep sleep, suggesting that their brains were compensating for the prior loss. Two to three weeks of sleep deprivation resulted in a lowered body temperature, increased food intake, increased metabolism, weight loss, and a breakdown of the immune system, inevitably followed by death (Everson, 1995; Rechtschaffen & Bergmann, 1995; Rechtschaffen et al., 1999).

A second type of explanation for why we sleep comes from the circadian theory, which focuses on the evolutionary significance of sleep. All animals sleep or undergo regular intervals of inactivity. According to this view, sleep is a neural mechanism that has evolved over time so that animals can conserve energy and minimize their exposure to predators when they are not foraging for food or seeking a mate. Circadian theory correctly predicts that there are species-specific differences in sleep patterns. As shown in Figure 4.11, animals that sleep the longest find food easily and are well hidden from predators while sleeping. In contrast, animals that sleep the shortest amount of time spend more hours foraging and can defend themselves only by running away. Seen from this perspective, we humans sleep at night because we're not very well adapted to searching for food in the dark or protecting ourselves from nocturnal predators (Allison & Cicchetti, 1976; Horne, 1988).

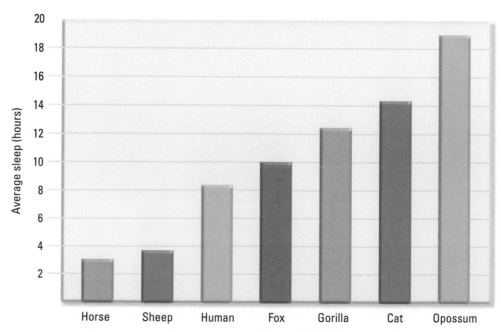

**FIGURE 4.11** **Daily hours of sleep: cross-species comparisons**

The question of why humans sleep is still something of an unsolved mystery. Restoration and circadian theories do not contradict one another, and many researchers believe that both mechanisms are at work (Borbely, 1986; Rechtschaffen & Siegel, 2000; Webb, 1992).

# DREAMS

Between the ages of twelve and eighteen, I had a strange recurring dream. At eye level, I would be looking across a straight, smooth, waxed-wood surface. Then from a distance, a silver ball would start to roll toward me. It started slowly at first but picked up speed as it came closer. As the ball rolled toward my nose, a voice inside it would repeat my name—and get louder as the ball got closer. I could never understand why the ball rolled, because, as the dreamer, I "knew" that the surface was perfectly horizontal. But roll it did, and I would always wake up just as the ball was about to hit my nose. Though not a scary dream, it had a haunting quality. Like most people, I wondered, "What does it mean?" So what are dreams, why do we have them, and what, if anything, do they mean?

*"Dreaming permits each and every one of us to be quietly and safely insane every night of our lives."*
—CHARLES FISHER

### The Nature of Dreams
Dreams are less puzzling now than they were before the 1953 discovery of REM sleep. Psychologists used to think that the mind was idling in sleep and that dreaming was a rare, and therefore significant, event. But then EEG recordings revealed that the sleeping human brain is active and that everyone dreams, without exception, several times a night. We now know that dreams are electrochemical events involving the brainstem and areas of the cortex and that the eyes flutter back and forth. What more is known about this mysterious state of consciousness, a state in which the mind is active but the sleeper is immobilized and hard to awaken?

Researchers now believe that REM sleep and the dreaming that often accompanies it are biologically adaptive. This belief arises from three sources of evidence. The first is that all mammals have REM sleep (most birds do too, but reptiles, amphibians, and fish do not)—from a high of 57 percent of all sleep time in the platypus to a low of 2 percent in the dolphin (Siegel, 2001). Second, the amount of REM sleep is greatest early in life, while the brain is developing—and there is evidence to suggest that REM sleep is necessary for brain maturation (Marks et al., 1995). Among premature infants, 60 to 80 percent of all sleep time is spent in the REM stage. That number drops to 50 percent in full-term newborns, 30 percent at six months, 25 percent at two years, and 20 percent in early childhood, before diminishing later in life. Third, when subjects are deprived of REM sleep one night, they exhibit a "rebound effect" by taking extra REM time the next night (Brunner et al., 1990).

*"From the conservative assumptions of three REM periods per night and two dream stories within each period, there is a resultant 150,000 dreams per person over a life span of 70 years."*
—WILSE B. WEBB

Is there a linkage between a sleeper's eye movements and dreams? This is a tricky question. Research shows that the longer a REM episode is, the more words an awakened subject uses to describe the dream—and the more elaborate the story. Similarly, the more active the brain is during REM, the more eventful are the dreams that are later reported. But patterns of eye movements do not seem to correspond to the images and actions of a dream—as when we follow characters in a film (Chase & Morales, 1983).

### What Do People Dream About?
What do people dream about? What do you dream about? Over the years, analyses of dream content have shown that certain themes seem to arise with remarkable frequency. Can you guess the three

To learn more about dreams, visit
http://www.dreamresearch.net.

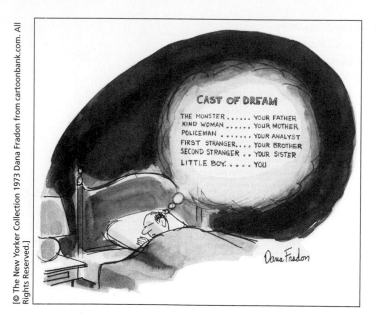

most commonly reported dreams? The first is of falling. The second is of being chased or attacked. The third is of repeatedly trying but failing to do something. Also common are dreams of flying, being unprepared or late for a big event, being rejected, and appearing naked in public (Stark, 1984).

Cataloging more than ten thousand dream reports, Calvin Hall and Robert Van de Castle (1966) found that 64 percent were associated with sadness, fear, or anger (falling dreams, which are reported by 80 percent of college students, usually cause people to awaken abruptly before crashing to the ground), and only 18 percent were happy or exciting (flying dreams, which are reported by one third of people, are almost always seen as fun and exhilarating). Dreamed acts of aggression outnumbered acts of friendship by more than 2 to 1. And 29 percent of all dreams were in color. Women are more likely than men to have dreams that take place indoors, often at home, and often with others who are familiar to them. Men are more likely to dream about having sex and about physical activities outside the home, often with strangers in unfamiliar surroundings. About 30 percent of the dreams reported by young children contain wild animals, but only 8 percent of adult dreams include animals—and these are mostly of dogs, horses, and other domesticated species (Domhoff, 1996; Van de Castle, 1994).

What influences the contents of our dreams? There are two documented sources. One is the concerns of everyday life. If you're struggling financially, if you've had a death in the family, or if you're studying for an important exam or are involved in an exciting new relationship, these issues may well slip into your dreams (Nikles et al., 1998). External stimuli are a second source of influence. Have you ever heard the radio alarm go off but slept through the music and dreamed you were at a concert? Dement (1992) sprayed water on subjects' hands during REM sleep, awakened them a short time later, and found that 42 percent—far more than normal—reported dreaming of rainfalls, leaking roofs, swimming pools, and the like. Similarly, 56 percent incorporated into their dreams the taped sounds of dogs, trains, bells, and other stimuli.

For some dreamers, there is a third source of influence that, in some ways, is the most interesting: themselves. As a general rule, people are not aware that they are dreaming *while* they are dreaming. But have you ever had the odd sensation of dreaming—and knowing that you were in a dream? This "half in-half out" state of consciousness is called **lucid dreaming.** Most people have experienced this state on only an occasional basis—as when a dream takes on such a bizarre quality that they know it cannot be real. But some people are frequent lucid dreamers, and it appears to be a skill that can be developed. In some studies, lucid dreamers were trained to signal the onset of a dream to an experimenter by moving their eyes and clenching their fists. Some lucid dreamers say that at times they can actually control the contents—and outcomes—of their own dreams. If true, then perhaps lucid dreaming can be used to resolve personal conflicts and tame the monsters in our nightmares (Gackenbach & Bosveld, 1989; LaBerge, 1992).

**Cultural Influences on Dream Reports**   In *Our Dreaming Mind,* Robert Van de Castle (1994) noted that dreams have always fascinated people. Almost three thousand years ago, the Assyrians believed that dreams were messages sent from evil spirits. Later, Egyptians believed they were messages sent by the gods. The Inuit of Hudson Bay and the Pantani of Malaysia believe that one's soul leaves the body during sleep and enters another world. Among the Kurds and Zulus,

**lucid dreaming**   A semiconscious dream state in which a sleeper is aware that he or she is dreaming.

dreaming of an adulterous affair is considered an offense, and if you dream of receiving a gift, you must compensate the gift giver in waking life. In Western cultures, people assume that dreams, if properly analyzed, tell us something about the dreamer's past, present, or future. To some extent, then, dreams reflect a culture's beliefs, values, and concerns (Shulman & Stroumsa, 1999).

Over the years, psychologists and anthropologists have looked for common themes in what people from different cultures tend to dream about. Summarizing this research, G. William Domhoff (1996) notes that certain aspects of the dreams found in Western cultures are found elsewhere as well. For example, it appears that people everywhere dream more often about acts of aggression than about friendship and kindness, and in these dreams, we are more likely to dream of being the victims of aggression than the perpetrators. Certain gender differences in dream content also seem to be universal. For example, men dream more about aggression, whereas women dream more about acquaintances, friends, and family members.

Although there are cultural similarities in dream reports, Domhoff (1996) notes that there are also some striking differences that uniquely reflect each culture's beliefs, values, and social structures. In India, devout Hindus who live gender-segregated lives report having precious few opposite sex characters in their dreams. In Japan, a "collectivist" society that places family and group interests ahead of those of the individual, people's dreams contain more human characters than are found in American dreams—and these characters are more likely to be familiar. Among the Yir Yoront hunters of Australia, men dream often of killing animals—and of sharing meat with familiar female characters and others. What we dream about is shaped by our waking lives—which, in turn, is shaped by the invisible hand of culture (see Schneider & Domhoff, 2002).

Our dreams may be influenced by inner concerns and external stimuli, by culture, and even by our own will. And most dreams are fairly mundane (Cipolli et al., 1993). But sometimes our dreams have a bizarre, magical quality—whereby time seems to stand still or speed forward, shadowy figures appear and vanish on cue, or we fall into bottomless pits, soar like Superman, and float in utter defiance of gravity. How can these qualities be explained? And what do they tell us about why we dream? No one really knows for sure, but there are two major theories.

**Freud's Interpretation** In 1900, Sigmund Freud published a classic book entitled *The Interpretation of Dreams*. According to Freud, all people are unconsciously motivated to satisfy sexual and aggressive urges. These ideas are too threatening to express or even to recognize, so we keep them from awareness through the use of psychological defense mechanisms. So far, so good. During sleep, however, our defensive guard is down, and pent-up drives can no longer be suppressed. It would be psychologically shattering to come face to face with our deepest, darkest urges. Such realizations would also disrupt our sleep. The solution: We construct dreams that express the fulfillment of these drives—but in ways that are too indirect and confusing to recognize. In short, the dream we remember in the morning is a disguised, scrambled expression of unconscious wishes. The drive is fulfilled, but in such a way that the psyche—and our sleep—are protected.

With his theory of psychoanalysis to guide him (see Chapter 15), Freud saw dreams as a "royal road" to the unconscious. He called the dream we remember in the morning the **manifest content**. The underlying thoughts, urges, conflicts, and needs that give rise to that dream constitute its **latent content**. According to Freud, the only way to uncover this unconscious latent material (which, after all, is the "true meaning") is to decode the dream and the symbols that disguise it. In the language of dreams, he said, kings and queens symbolize parents; small animals

*Can you become a lucid dreamer? Stephen LaBerge has invented some facilitating instruments, including* DreamLight, *a mask that picks up eye movements with an infrared detection device and transmits the data to an attached minicomputer. When the computer counts enough eye movements to determine that a REM period is underway, red lights flash inside the mask, signaling the sleeper, who can use the information to achieve lucidity. LaBerge tried using the tape-recorded phrase "This is a dream!" But he found that sounds tend to wake people up.*

**manifest content** According to Freud, the conscious dream content that is remembered in the morning.

**latent content** According to Freud, the unconscious, censored meaning of a dream.

## THE PROCESS OF DISCOVERY

# ALLAN HOBSON
### *Activation Synthesis Theory of Dreams*

**Q: How did you first become interested in psychology?**

**A:** I first became interested in psychology in my teenage years. One night, when I was about 15, I had a typical adolescent aha! experience. I recognized that my awareness of the wonders of the universe took place entirely within my own head! At that time I worked for an educational psychologist who told me that if I wanted to understand the mind I should go to Medical School and learn about the brain.

I did my college honors thesis on how Sigmund Freud borrowed his ideas about the unconscious mind from writers like Fyodor Dostoyevsky. My skepticism about the scientific validity of Freud's theories deepened in medical school when I saw how little solid evidence supported them. I specialized in psychiatry. Shocked by the realization that psychoanalysis was weaker than I had previously thought, I left my psychiatric residency after one year and went to the National Institutes of Health to learn how to do brain science.

**Q: How did you come up with your important discovery?**

**A:** At the NIH, I met Fred Snyder and Ed Evarts, who were studying sleep. When I first saw the brain activation of REM I realized that the physiological basis of dreaming could be determined. While training with Michel Jouvet, in France, I decided to use Evarts' single cell recording method to find out how Jouvet's REM sleep control system in the pontine brainstem worked. At the time, I didn't realize that solving that problem would lead to a new dream theory. But it did.

It turned out that nerve cells of the pons that manufactured brain chemicals needed to support waking were selectively inhibited in REM. This meant that a change in brain chemistry might cause the changes in consciousness seen in dreaming—such as the spontaneous visual imagery, defective thinking, loosening of associations, and memory loss. It was readily apparent that this new dream theory, which linked psychological changes in conscious experience to brain physiology, had far-reaching implications.

**Q: How has the field you inspired developed over the years?**

**A:** Recently sleep and dream research has received a tremendous boost from brain-imaging technology. Sleep-imaging findings have reinforced the brain-based theory of dreaming and added important details regarding the specific brain regions that turn on and off in waking and sleep. Genetics is also coming to play an important role in sleep science as it does in clinical biological psychiatry.

**Q: What's your prediction on where the field is heading?**

**A:** Freud is dead. Long live Freud! Why? Because he predicted the biological revolution that has occurred after his death. And because now we need a new dynamic psychology that fits with what we know about the brain. What is now within reach is a set of sciences reaching all the way up to the mind: from the gene to the nerve cell and their chemical signals; to networks and brain regions; and finally to behavioral and mental states.

*Allan Hobson is Professor of Psychiatry at Harvard Medical School, in Boston.*

---

**activation-synthesis theory** The theory that dreams result from the brain's attempt to make sense of random neural signals that fire during sleep.

If you worry that you talk in your sleep and might reveal something embarrassing, relax. Sleep talkers seldom reply to questions, and they tend to mumble only senseless words and phrases.

symbolize children; a house symbolizes the human body; and flying is the mental equivalent of having sex.

**Activation–Synthesis Theory**   Freud's theory is hard to prove or disprove, and many psychologists worry that it leads us to "overinterpret" dreams. Recent theories take a more neuropsychological approach. The most influential is the **activation-synthesis theory** of J. Allan Hobson and Robert McCarley (1977), which was later revised by Hobson (1988). According to this two-process theory, random neural signals firing in the brainstem spread up to the cortex (activation). Drawing on past experiences stored in memory, the brain then creates images and stories in an effort to make sense out of these random signals (synthesis). According to this account, the brightness, color, and clarity of dream images are triggered by random bursts of sensory neurons during REM sleep (Antrobus, 1991). Similarly, the physical-motion dreams that Freud described as typical (flying, climbing, falling) are triggered by the activity of motor neurons during REM sleep (Porte & Hobson, 1996).

**Comparing Perspectives**   Both Freud's account and activation-synthesis theory agree that the dream's manifest content is not meaningful. But they differ in two respects. The first concerns the interpretation of the manifest content. For Freud, the mind constructs bizarre dreams to disguise their true meaning from the dreamer. For Hobson, the brain constructs bizarre dreams because it has only limited information and operates on short notice. Thus, "the manifest content is the dream. There is no other dream" (Hobson, 1988, p. 258). The second key difference concerns the significance attached to the so-called latent content. Freud believed that dreams spring from deep unconscious wishes. Hobson and McCarley argued that dreams are the incidental by-product of neural overactivity.

Research continues to enlighten these dual perspectives on dreaming. For example, Allen Braun and others (1998) used PET scans on sleeping subjects and found that the limbic regions of the brain—areas that control our motivations and emotions—were highly active during REM sleep. In contrast, the frontal lobes—involved in the processes of attention, planning, logical thinking, and short-term memory—were inactive. These results may help to explain why dreams often seem bizarre and illogical. They're also consistent with Freud's contention that dreams reflect deep-seated motivations and emotions—something of a "wishing system," in the words of neuropsychologist Mark Solms (Carpenter, 1999). At this point, there is not enough research to declare a winner between these theoretical approaches. In fact, new theories are still being proposed. Building on the work of Solms (1997) and Foulkes (1999), G. William Domhoff (2001) has proposed that dreaming is a cognitive activity involving a special neural network in the forebrain, that it develops through childhood, and that the contents of our dreams are not that different from our waking thoughts, concerns, and feelings. At this point, all that is clear is that through a complex interplay of physiological and psychological processes, the mind is remarkably active during sleep.

## SLEEP DISTURBANCES

At some point in life, nearly everyone suffers from a sleep-related problem. You lie in bed, tossing and turning, brooding over something that happened or worrying about something that might. Or you keep nodding off in class or at work or in other embarrassing situations. Or you leap up in a cold sweat, with your heart pounding, from a realistic and terrifying nightmare. In general, there are three types of disturbances: sleeping too little (insomnia), sleeping too much (hypersomnia), and having disturbed or troubled sleep (parasomnia).

**Insomnia**   The sleep disturbance known as **insomnia** is characterized by a recurring inability to fall asleep, stay asleep, or get the amount of sleep needed to function during the day. Very few of us adhere to the daily "ideal" of eight hours for work, eight for play, and eight for sleep. On the contrary, people differ in the amount of sleep they want. Some are at their most alert after six hours a night, whereas others need nine or ten hours to get along. How much time is sufficient depends on who you are.

About 30 percent of the population complains of insomnia—and roughly half of these people consider the problem to be serious (American Psychiatric Association, 1994; Espie, 2002). It's not easy to know when someone has insomnia based on self-report, however. In a study that illustrates the point, Mary Carskadon brought 122 insomniacs into the laboratory and compared their self-perceptions to EEG

**insomnia**   An inability to fall asleep, stay asleep, or get the amount of sleep needed to function during the day.

## *How To*

# OVERCOME INSOMNIA

Is it a struggle for you to get up in the morning? Do you need to nap during the day? Do you often fall asleep while reading or watching TV? Do you sometimes feel drowsy while driving, or find it hard to stay awake in class? According to James Maas, author of *Power Sleep* (1998), if you answer *yes* to these kinds of questions you're probably sleep-deprived. Clearly, some of us get less sleep than we need because we're busy, rising early for work and partying by night. But others toss and turn long after their head hits the pillow, a symptom of insomnia. So, how long does it take you to fall asleep?

Without an EEG, it's hard to answer this question with any precision. People can recall lying in bed but cannot then pinpoint the "moment of sleep." If you're curious, try this exercise: Lie comfortably in bed, in a darkened room, and close your eyes. Drape your hand over the edge of the bed and lightly grip a metal spoon suspended over a plate on the floor. Write down the time, then relax and allow yourself to drift off. As you do, your muscles will relax, causing the spoon to slip from your hand and clang as it strikes the plate. The rattling noise will awaken you, at which point you can recheck the clock and calculate your "sleep latency"—the amount of time it took you to fall asleep (Dement & Vaughan, 1999).

At times, everyone has trouble falling asleep. But what should you do if the problem persists? Research shows that many people can help themselves simply by altering their own sleep-related behavior (Lichstein & Morin, 2000; Maas, 1998). Here are some useful tips:

- Record how much sleep you get in a night, and set that total as a goal. If you sleep four or five hours, aim for a four-hour schedule.
- Do not take naps during the day.
- Avoid all alcohol, caffeine, and cigarettes within five hours of bedtime; avoid exercise within two hours of bedtime; relax.
- Make sure the bedroom is dark, quiet, and comfortable when you go to bed. When you awaken, turn on the lights and lift the shades.
- Keep a rigid schedule. Get into bed at 1 AM, not earlier. Set the alarm for 5 AM—and get out of bed no matter what.
- If you're awake but relaxed, stay in bed.
- If you're awake and anxious, get out of bed and return when you are sleepy. Keep the alarm set, and get up when it rings.

*"The only thing wrong with insomniacs is that they don't get enough sleep."*

—W. C. FIELDS

measures of sleep. The next morning, the subjects estimated that it took them an hour to fall asleep and that they slept for 4 1/2 hours. But EEG tracings revealed that it took them only 15 minutes to fall asleep, which is average, and that they slept for 6 1/2 hours. More than 10 percent of all complaints are from "pseudoinsomniacs" who sleep normally but don't realize it. Part of the problem is that people with insomnia worry so much about getting to sleep, and then getting enough sleep, that they monitor themselves closely and overestimate the extent of the problem (Harvey, 2002).

Among people who do have trouble falling or staying asleep, insomnia is not a disease but a symptom with many causes. On average, psychiatric patients get less sleep than do people without mental disorders (Benca et al., 1992). Medical ailments, pain, stress, depression, jet lag, night work, shifting work schedules, old age, and alcohol and drug abuse are also linked to insomnia. In some cases, the only "problem" is that people who think they should sleep eight hours a night go to bed before they're really tired. The use of medications may also pose an ironic danger. Certain over-the-counter sleeping pills are not effective. Some prescription drugs will, at first, put the insomniac to sleep and prevent rude awakenings during the night. But sedatives may also inhibit certain stages of sleep and cause restlessness after the drug is terminated.

**narcolepsy** A sleep disorder characterized by irresistible and sudden attacks of REM sleep during the day.

- If you stick to this schedule, you should see results. If you want, you can then add thirty to sixty minutes to your schedule.
- Rest assured that you can get by on less sleep than you want and that a temporary loss of sleep will cause you no harm.

Can this advice get you to sleep better on your own, without the help of a professional? To answer this question, Veronique Mimeault and Charles Morin (1999) recruited fifty-eight people complaining of insomnia. For a six-week period, one-third was given a take-home course consisting of treatment booklets on sleep, insomnia, and the management of sleep problems. For a second group, the program included weekly phone calls from a therapist. In a third, no-treatment control group, subjects spent the time waiting for the program to begin. Before and after the treatment period, subjects recorded how long it took them to fall asleep each night as well as the total amount of time they slept. Did the self-help program work? Look at Figure 4.13, and you'll see that it did. Compared to subjects in the no-treatment control group, those who took part in the treatment program—regardless of whether or not they talked with a therapist—took less time to get to sleep and spent more time sleeping after the program than before.

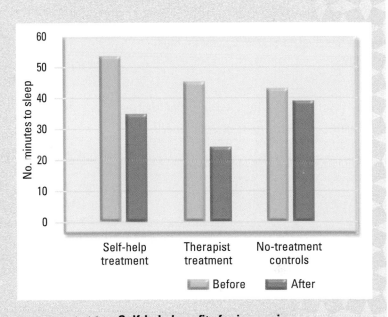

**FIGURE 4.13** **Self-help benefits for insomnia**
In this study, fifty-eight people with insomnia received a self-help program, additional care from a therapist, or no treatment. As shown, all treatment subjects—whether or not they had a therapist—took less time to fall asleep after the program than before it. With guidance, people can help themselves to overcome insomnia (Mimeault & Morin, 1999).

Numerous studies have shown that most people can successfully overcome insomnia by altering their behavior—but that the benefits are smaller for those who take sleeping pills (Lichstein & Morin, 2000; Morin et al., 1999; Murtagh & Greenwood, 1995). Some helpful tips are presented in the *How to Overcome Insomnia* box.

**Hypersomnia** Studies conducted in different countries show that about 5 percent of people complain of hypersomnia—being sleepy during the day and sleeping too much at night (Guilleminault & Roth, 1993). The most profound and most dangerous problem of this type is **narcolepsy,** which means "sleep seizure," an uncommon disorder that is characterized by sudden, irresistible attacks of drowsiness and REM sleep during the day (American Psychiatric Association, 1994).

A narcolepsy attack may strike without warning at any time—while playing basketball, eating a meal, having a conversation, working in an office, or having sex. The attack lasts from five to thirty minutes and plunges its victim into REM sleep. The narcoleptic's jaw will sag, the head will fall forward, the arms will drop, and the knees will buckle. This collapse is sometimes accompanied by the hypnogogic hallucinations that usher in the onset of sleep. As you might imagine, people with narcolepsy have problems at work and in their social lives. For example, they are often unfairly perceived to be lazy and uninterested (Douglas, 1998). Narcolepsy

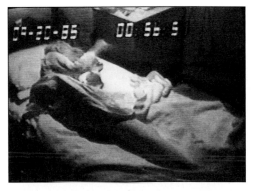

*Taken in a sleep lab, this photograph shows a man with REM sleep behavior disorder. While dreaming, he throws a punch at the bed—one of twelve punches he throws in this particular sequence. Fortunately, at this time, he is sleeping alone.*

**sleep apnea**   A disorder in which a person repeatedly stops breathing during sleep and awakens gasping for air.

**REM sleep behavior disorder (RBD)**   A condition in which the skeletal muscles are not paralyzed during REM sleep, enabling a sleeper to act on his or her nightmares, often violently.

*There is an old saying, "Laugh and the world laughs with you, snore and you sleep alone!"*

---

### REVIEW QUESTIONS

- *Distinguish biological and circadian rhythms. How do environmental cues of light and dark influence circadian rhythms?*

- *What are some of the problems experienced by shift workers? Why do these problems occur and what are some potential solutions?*

- *Identify the five stages of sleep.*

- *Why do we sleep?*

- *What is the evidence that REM sleep is biologically adaptive?*

- *What factors influence the content of our dreams?*

- *According to Freudian theory, why do we dream? According to activation-synthesis theory, why do we dream?*

can be life threatening. In one study, 40 percent of the narcoleptics who were questioned admitted they had fallen asleep while driving (Siegel et al., 1991). Although there is no cure, daytime sleep attacks can be minimized by taking regularly scheduled naps (Mullington & Broughton, 1993) and stimulant drugs (Fry, 1998).

**Parasomnias**   For some people, falling asleep at night and staying awake during the day are not a problem—but too often their sleep is disturbed. There are several specific disorders of this type. One particularly troublesome disturbance is **sleep apnea** (*apnea* means "to stop breathing"), which afflicts between 1 and 4 percent of Americans—mostly obese men. A person with sleep apnea will fall asleep normally but then stop breathing and awaken snorting like a buzz saw, choking, and gasping for air. Sleep-laboratory studies show that a person with sleep apnea will fall asleep again right away, but these partial awakenings can recur four hundred times during the night, thus preventing slow-wave sleep and making the person excessively tired and irritable during the day (Langevin et al., 1992). With some success, the problem can be treated surgically, or with continuous positive airways pressure (CPAP)—a plastic mask that gently pumps air into the nose. The air holds the person's throat open and prevents snoring (Piccirillo et al., 2000; Sullivan et al., 1981; Wittig, 1993). Of course, many people without apnea also snore while they sleep—much to the discomfort of roommates and bed partners.

*Nightmares* are vivid, anxiety-provoking dreams that sometimes haunt us during REM sleep—and awaken us. They are common, particularly among children, and should not be a source of concern unless they persist for long periods of time. About four out of five college students report having had at least one nightmare over the past year (Belicki, 1985). In daily dream logs collected from college students in Montreal, the average was about eleven nightmares per year (Zadra & Donderi, 2000).

Nightmares are not dangerous, except for people with **REM sleep behavior disorder (RBD)**—a very rare condition in which the skeletal muscles do not become paralyzed, as they should, during REM sleep. People with RBD have mobility to act on their nightmares and often do so in violent ways. As a result, 85 percent of sufferers have injured themselves and 44 percent have hurt their bed partners, sometimes seriously (Mahowald & Schenck, 1989; Schenck, 1993).

There are also NREM sleep disruptions. In *night terrors,* the person jolts abruptly from a deep sleep, in a state of panic, and gives off a loud, bloodcurdling scream. As with nightmares, this problem is more common among children than among adults. It's also more frightening, particularly for others in the household. Because it occurs during NREM sleep, however, the night-terror victim will usually not recall a dream and by morning will have forgotten the whole episode.

Another NREM experience is *sleepwalking,* in which a sleeper quietly sits up, climbs out of bed, and walks about with eyes open and a blank expression. Sleepwalkers may start slowly, but soon they're going to the bathroom, dressing, eating, and opening doors. They are prone to accidents such as falling down stairs, so it is safer to gently awaken a sleepwalker than to allow the person to wander about. People used to think that sleepwalkers were acting out dreams. But that's not the case. These episodes occur early in the night, during the deep, slow-wave stages of sleep. Sometimes sleepwalkers will wake up and be disoriented, but most often they just go back to bed. Like night-terror victims, sleepwalkers seldom recall their travels in the morning. In a rare and particularly curious variant of the problem, some individuals are said to have engaged in "sleepsex"—sexual acts performed while asleep (Rosenfeld & Elhajjar, 1998). Cleary, the brain is active even during sleep—and, clearly, consciousness is complex and multilayered.

# HYPNOSIS

- *What is hypnosis, and why has it always been controversial?*
- *Are some individuals more susceptible than others to hypnosis?*
- *Can people be hypnotized against their will and coerced to behave in certain ways?*
- *Is hypnosis useful in therapy?*
- *Is hypnosis an "altered" state of mind?*

About twenty-five years ago, Ernest Hilgard was demonstrating hypnosis in his psychology class. The student who volunteered to serve as a subject happened to be blind, so Hilgard hypnotized him and said that on the count of three he would become deaf—and would stay that way until touched on the right shoulder. One, two, three! Hilgard then banged blocks together and fired a starter's pistol that made everyone else leap from their seats. But the subject did not respond. His classmates shouted questions and taunted him, but still he did not respond. Then a hand went up. A student wanted to know if any part of the subject knew what was happening, because, after all, there was nothing really wrong with his ears.

It was a fascinating question. Hilgard said to the subject, "Perhaps there is some part of your mind that is hearing my voice and processing the information. If there is, I should like the index finger of your right hand to rise as a sign that this is the case." To everyone's surprise, even Hilgard's, the young man raised his finger and said, "Please restore my hearing so that you can tell me what you did." Hilgard then put his hand on the subject's shoulder and asked, "Can you hear me now?" The subject did. "I remember you telling me that I would be deaf at the count of three and have my hearing restored when you placed your hand on my shoulder. Then everything was quiet for a while. It was a little boring just sitting here so I busied myself with a statistical problem that I had been working on. I was still doing that when I felt my finger lift; that is what I want you to explain to me."

Next, Hilgard asked to speak with "that part of your mind that listened to me before, while you were hypnotically deaf." "Do you remember what happened?" The subject remembered it all—the count to three, the banging blocks, the starter pistol, and the questions from the class to which he did not respond. "Then one of them asked if I might really be hearing, and you told me to raise my finger if I did. This part of me responded by raising my finger, so it's all clear now." Hilgard lifted his hand from the subject's arm to restore the hypnotic state and said, "Please tell me what happened in the last few minutes." The subject replied, "You said . . . some part of me would talk to you. Did I talk?" The young man was assured that he would later recall everything, and the session was terminated (Hilgard, 1992). Hilgard called the aware part of this subject's mind a "hidden observer." This concept is controversial—and, as we'll see, it has profound implications for the study of consciousness. But first things first. What is hypnosis, how is it induced, and what are its effects?

## THE SEEDS OF CONTROVERSY

**Hypnosis** is a set of attention-focusing procedures in which changes in a person's behavior or state of mind are suggested. In one form or another, hypnosis has been around for centuries. But the earliest known reference to it is traced to Franz Anton Mesmer (1734–1815), a Viennese physician. Mesmer believed that illness was caused by an imbalance of magnetic fluids in the body—and could be cured by restoring the proper balance. Working in Paris, he would pass his hands across the

**hypnosis** Attention-focusing procedures in which changes in a person's behavior or mental state are suggested.

*Hypnosis is important in the history of psychology. This 1780 engraving depicts treatment by animal magnetism as practiced by Franz Mesmer. "Mesmerism" is today considered a form of hypnosis.*

patient's body and wave a magnetic wand over the infected area. Many patients would descend into a trance and then awaken feeling better. The medical community, however, viewed this treatment with skepticism, and in 1784 a French commission chaired by Benjamin Franklin found that there was no scientific basis for the "animal magnetism" theory, only "mere imagination." Mesmer was called a quack and run out of town. When he died, he was penniless. Yet to this day, we acknowledge his work whenever we describe ourselves as being mesmerized.

In the nineteenth century, the trancelike state Mesmer had created was called hypnotism, from the Greek word for "sleep." From that point on, hypnosis has had a rocky relationship with science (Forrest, 2001). On the one hand, stage hypnotists who swing pocket watches back and forth and try to make audience members cluck like chickens lead people to associate hypnosis with parlor games, carnivals, and magic shows. On the other hand, psychoanalysis originated with Freud's use of hypnosis to treat patients with various nervous disorders. Today, many health-care specialists use hypnosis with reasonable success to control pain and help patients break bad habits (Rhue et al., 1993; Kirsch et al., 1999). For researchers of consciousness, hypnosis is a useful and provocative phenomenon—though one that is not completely understood (Kirsch & Lynn, 1998; Kihlstrom, 1998; Woody & Sadler, 1998).

## THE HYPNOTIC INDUCTION

Hypnosis consists of two stages: an *induction,* which guides the subject into a pliable, suggestible frame of mind; then a specific *suggestion.* The induction process is not like casting a spell. There are no magical words or incantations to be uttered, and there is no single technique. But there is one essential ingredient: a focusing of attention.

Speaking in a slow, soft, monotonous tone of voice, the hypnotist asks the subject to concentrate on something. It could be anything. Hypnotists used to have subjects stare at a flame, a shiny object, or a swinging pendulum, but a spot on the wall will work just as well. So will the subject's imagination. "Imagine that you're lying on a quiet beach. You are so warm and relaxed on the soft white sand, under the sun. You're very tired, and your eyes are closed. You can hear the ocean waves crashing on the shore and the gulls flying overhead. And you can smell the warm, salt air. It's so sunny. Your skin is so warm. And you're so relaxed. Your eyes are growing tired. Very tired. Your eyelids are getting heavy. Heavy. They're starting to close." Whatever technique is used, the purpose is to help the subject filter out all distractions and focus his or her mental spotlight.

Once the subject is in a state of "relaxed alertness," he or she is ripe for stage 2, the suggestion. The hypnotist may begin with a quick test by suggesting that "your eyes are closed and your eyelids are shut so tight that you cannot open them no matter how hard you try." Sure enough, the subject's eyes remain closed. At that point, the subject is ready for more. The hypnotist may note that the subject's arm is filling with air like a balloon and that it's feeling lighter and lighter—and is rising in the air. The subject does not know why, but the arm rises, as if being pulled up on a string. The hypnotist may even invite the subject to enjoy the scent of "perfume"—and watch as he or she inhales the fumes from a jar of ammonia. Assuming the subject "passes" these preliminary tests, additional suggestions depend on the reasons for the hypnosis. Thus, a subject may be encouraged to block out pain, recall a traumatic past event, forget a past event, or break a bad habit when the session is over.

## HYPNOTIC RESPONSIVENESS

Contrary to popular belief, you cannot be hypnotized against your will. Nobody can. People also differ. Several years ago, Hilgard (1965) developed the Stanford Hypnotic Susceptibility Scale (SHSS), a twelve-item behavioral test that measures one's **hypnotic susceptibility,** or responsiveness to hypnosis. In this test, a brief induction is followed by suggestions for the subject to close his or her eyes, sway back and forth, stiffen an arm, lower a hand, see an imaginary person, and so on. Over the years, Hilgard has found that some people are highly susceptible to hypnosis and that others are invulnerable to hypnosis but that most fall somewhere between these extremes (Hilgard, 1982). In short, some types of people are more susceptible, and others are less susceptible, to hypnosis.

What accounts for these individual differences? Research has shown that college students who scored high or low in the early 1960s scored similarly when retested twenty-five years later (Piccione et al., 1989). This result tells us that there are stable personality differences between the highs and lows. But how are these differences to be interpreted? It's interesting to me that in discussions of hypnosis, students often seem eager if not proud to proclaim that they are too "independent" or too "strong-willed" to be hypnotized. But hypnotic responsiveness is not a sign of weakness. High scorers are not generally weaker or more conforming, compliant, or obedient. But they are more open to experience, have more vivid imaginations, and have an ability to become deeply absorbed in books, movies, and other activities (J. Hilgard, 1979; Nadon et al., 1991). High scorers also have a more sustained attention span and a greater ability to filter out distractions (Crawford et al., 1993). In one study, individuals highly responsive to hypnosis—often referred to as "virtuosos"—were actually led under hypnosis to experience themselves as members of the opposite sex (Noble & McConkey, 1995).

**hypnotic susceptibility**   The extent to which an individual is characteristically responsive to hypnosis.

# THE MYTHS AND REALITIES

Can a stage hypnotist make you strip naked in front of an audience, clap your hands together, and bark like a seal? Popular portrayals of hypnosis are sometimes accurate, but often they are not. Based on the results of controlled research, let us examine the effects of hypnosis and try to separate the myths from the realities.

**Coercion**  As noted earlier, people cannot be hypnotized against their will. But can subjects, once under hypnosis, be coerced into acts that violate the conscience? Are they completely at the mercy of a skilled hypnotist? For the sake of those who may benefit from the therapeutic uses of hypnosis, one would hope not. In response to the notion that the subject is under the hypnotist's control, Karen Olness (1993), a pediatrician and hypnotherapist, says, "Nonsense. All hypnosis is self-hypnosis" (p. 280). Most psychologists similarly reject the view that hypnosis renders us helpless. And as a general rule, hypnotized subjects reject immoral commands, knowing fully well that they are in control.

But there is evidence to suggest that hypnotic coercion can lead people to shed inhibitions and perform hurtful or antisocial acts—such as stealing, picking up a dangerous snake, selling an illicit drug, and mutilating the Bible. In one experiment, Martin Orne and Frederick Evans (1965) convinced hypnotized subjects to throw what they thought to be nitric acid into a research assistant's face. To see if this result proved that hypnosis can overpower the will, Orne and Evans told a second group of subjects only to pretend they were hypnotized, issued the same command, and found that they too threw the "acid." Additional studies as well suggest that subjects in hypnosis experiments are aware of what they are doing—and are confident that they would not be asked to harm themselves or someone else (Gibson, 1991). As we'll see later, these results may say more about obedience to authority than about hypnosis.

**Pain Relief**  "On the operating table, I put myself into a deeply relaxed state. I then concentrated on a favorite memory: living on a farm as a child. In my mind, I felt what it was like to lie on the grass, gaze up at the heavens, and see a bit of the barn out of the corner of my eye. As the surgeon cut into the base of my thumb, I reassured him that I felt no pain. . . . Although I was perfectly aware that I was undergoing surgery, I just wasn't very interested in it." This story, as described by Olness (1993, p. 277), embodies a real benefit of hypnosis: to serve as a psychological anesthetic.

In the classic test of this hypothesis, Hilgard and his colleagues (1975) instructed two groups of subjects to immerse one hand in a tank of ice water for almost a minute. Every ten seconds, they rated how much pain they felt on a 10-point scale. In one group, subjects were hypnotized and given the suggestion that they would feel no pain. In the second group, there was no hypnosis and no suggestion. The result was that the hypnotized subjects reported less pain than did the controls. We'll return to this study shortly to see what it implies about consciousness. What it implies about pain, however, is clear. Today, studies show that for people high in hypnotic responsiveness, hypnosis can be used to reduce pain—and that this effect can be achieved with or without the use of counter-pain images, such as suggestions that the hand is made of wood or is encased in a heavy protective glove (Hargadon et al., 1995). Not everyone can be hypnotized, and not all who are hypnotized will gain relief from pain. But for some, hypnosis can help in coping with dental work, childbirth, and the chronic pain of headaches, backaches, and arthritis (Montgomery et al., 2000).

**Posthypnotic Suggestion**  In the situations described thus far, the subject acts on the hypnotist's suggestions during the session. In a procedure known as

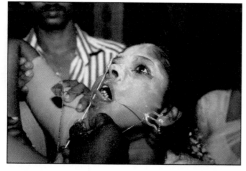

*Many claims about the power of hypnosis are controversial, but research shows that it does enable some people to tolerate pain. At Thaipusam, a Hindu Festival that honors the god of power and virtue, devotees enter an hypnotic trance during which time they endure painful types of mutilation—like long silver needles that pierce the tongue, cheeks, and other body parts.*

**posthypnotic suggestion,** the subject carries out the hypnotist's suggestion *after* the session is terminated. You've probably seen this procedure depicted on TV shows. With a snap of the finger, the subject would emerge from his or her "trance" and reflexively do something odd in response to a preset cue. But does it really work? It can, but only with some individuals. To demonstrate the point, Amanda Barnier and Kevin McConkey (1998) gave 120 prepaid postcards to subjects who were high in hypnotic susceptibility and instructed them, during hypnosis, to mail one post-card every day for four months. Afterward, they counted the number of cards re-ceived and found that more than half of all the postcards were sent in accordance with the hypnotic suggestion.

In reality, posthypnotic suggestion lacks dramatic flair. But when it is coupled with psychological therapy, it has been used effectively to help people with insom-nia, obesity, high blood pressure, and other behavior-related problems (Kirsch et al., 1995). It can also help speed the healing of warts and other skin conditions, and help in the medical treatment of asthma, nausea, and certain other conditions that have a psychological component (Pinnell & Covino, 2000).

**Memory Enhancement**   As in Hilgard's classroom demonstration, hypno-sis subjects often exhibit **posthypnotic amnesia,** an inability to recall events that occurred during the session. However, these memories have not been permanently erased. In response to a prearranged signal ("When I snap my fingers you'll recall everything that took place"), subjects can usually retrieve the lost events. Still, research suggests that hypnosis subjects do often exhibit temporary amnesia—and do so without effort or intention (Bowers & Woody, 1996).

At the other end of the hypnosis-memory spectrum, many hypnotists claim that the highly focused and relaxed state of mind produced by hypnosis enhances memory, a phenomenon known as **hypermnesia.** This claim has its roots in psychoanalysis—from Freud's reports that hypnotized patients sometimes relived repressed traumas from childhood—and has resurfaced in a rash of 1990s cases in which hypnosis was used to dredge up "memories" of child sex abuse.

In Chapter 6 on memory, we'll see that people cannot remember events from the first and second years of life. Yet research shows that people can be induced to report early childhood memories in hypnosis-like conditions. In one study, subjects asked for their earliest memories recounted events that occurred at about three and four years old. But after being induced to shut their eyes, visualize, and focus on the deep past, 78 percent "recalled" events that occurred before their second birthday and 33 percent even produced events from before their first birthday (Malinoski & Lynn, 1999). In a second study, 40 percent of those who were hypnotized and led to believe that hypnosis improves memory recounted events that took place before their first birthday (Green, 1999). In recent years, the use of hypnosis as a memory aid has come under particularly close scrutiny within the legal system. (See *Psychology and Law* on whether hypnosis can improve eyewitness testimony.)

## IS HYPNOSIS AN "ALTERED" STATE?

Since the time Mesmer first used hypnotism to treat medical ailments, there has been widespread interest in the phenomenon. Freud used hypnosis to unlock the un-conscious. Others have used it to relieve pain, to treat psychological problems, to uncover repressed memories, and to entertain audiences around the world. Using hypnosis is easy. The tougher question is: What is it? Does hypnosis produce an out-of-the-ordinary, trancelike, "altered" state of consciousness?

Psychologists are not in agreement on this question. Some say yes, others say no. As a general rule, *special-process* theorists maintain that hypnosis induces a unique

**posthypnotic suggestion**   A suggestion made to a subject in hypnosis to be carried out after the induction session is over.

**posthypnotic amnesia**   A reported tendency for hypnosis subjects to forget events that occurred during the induction.

**hypermnesia**   A term referring to the unsub-stantiated claim that hypnosis can be used to facilitate the retrieval of past memories.

## *Psychology and Law*

# DOES HYPNOSIS ENHANCE EYEWITNESS TESTIMONY?

It was an extraordinary case: A busload of California schoolchildren and their driver were abducted at gunpoint by three masked kidnappers and held for ransom in an underground tomb. Somehow, they managed to escape. The driver had tried to memorize the license plate number of the van the kidnappers used, but he could not later recall the number. He was then hypnotized by the police and was mentally transported back to the crime scene. All of a sudden, he blurted out all but one digit of the license plate—which led to the arrest and conviction of the abductors (Smith, 1983).

This story and others like it raise an intriguing question: Can hypnosis be used to refresh a witness's memory? Many police officers seem to think so and use hypnosis to help eyewitnesses recall details of violent crimes they seem to have forgotten. In one popular technique, devised by Martin Reiser (1980), subjects under hypnosis are asked to imagine that they are calmly watching a TV documentary about the event to be recalled and that they can rewind it, stop it, play it back, slow it down, speed it up, zoom in for close ups, and turn the sound volume up or down to improve hearing. Using this technique, police investigators have made some impressive claims about the memory-enhancing power of hypnosis (Hibbard & Worring, 1996).

The success stories are fascinating, but serious questions remain. When a hypnotized witness reports a memory, how do we know that the report is accurate? And if the recollection is later corroborated, how do we know that it was retrieved because of the hypnosis? To answer these questions, some researchers have studied actual cases. Others have conducted experiments in which subjects witness a staged event, report their memory, and then try to recall additional details—either under hypnosis or in a normal waking state. Consistently, the research has shown that although people report more information with repeated testing, they also inadvertently produce more distorted and false "memories" (Dinges et al., 1992; McConkey & Sheehan, 1995).

Another disturbing outcome of hypnosis is that it places witnesses in a state of heightened suggestibility. For example, Peter Sheehan and others (1991) showed 168 subjects a videotape of a staged bank robbery. In it, a man entered a bank, waved a pistol, warned the tellers not to press an alarm, ordered them to put the money on the counter, put

---

state of consciousness and that people are more responsive to suggestion while under hypnosis than in other states (Hilgard, 1986; Bowers, 1992). In contrast, a growing number of *social-cognitive* theorists maintain that hypnosis is not a distinct physiological state and that the same phenomena can sometimes be produced through relaxation, role playing, positive expectations, or mere suggestion—without hypnotic induction (Barber, 1969; Lynn et al., 1990; Spanos, 1986; Wagstaff, 1981).

**Special-Process Theories** According to Ernest Hilgard (1986), hypnosis can induce a state of **dissociation**—a division of consciousness into two or more parts that operate independently and are separated by an "amnesic barrier." In some ways, dissociation is a common experience—as when you drive somewhere, only to realize afterward that you "spaced out" and can't recall the route you took or the traffic signals you obeyed. One part of you drove, while another part of you daydreamed. In many people, says Hilgard, hypnosis produces a similar split in which one part of the mind goes along with hypnotic suggestions, while another part—a "hidden observer"—knows what's happening but does not participate.

**dissociation** A division of consciousness that permits one part of the mind to operate independently of another part.

To illustrate this concept, let's return to the pain-tolerance experiment described earlier, where subjects immersed a hand in ice water and periodically rated how much pain they were in (Hilgard et al., 1975). Look at Figure 4.15, and you'll see

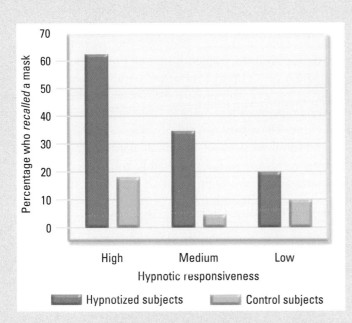

**FIGURE 4.14   Hypnosis and the suggestible eyewitness**
After seeing a staged crime, subjects were questioned in a hypnotized or waking state by an examiner who suggested that the culprit had worn a mask. Under hypnosis, many subjects—particularly those high in responsiveness—later incorporated this false suggestion into memory.

the money in a bag, and ran out. Subjects were immediately questioned about the incident. Half were then hypnotized; the others were not. Moments later, everyone was questioned by an examiner who "suggested" that the robber wore a mask over his face, which he did not. All the hypnotized subjects were then dehypnotized, and everyone was questioned again, this time by a new examiner.

Did anyone "recall" the robber wearing a mask? If so, how often did this occur? As illustrated in Figure 4.14, the results were quite striking—and sobering. Subjects were more likely to incorporate the false suggestion into memory when they were under hypnosis, and this was particularly true of those who had high or medium scores on a test of hypnotic susceptibility. Among the most vulnerable subjects—those who were both highly susceptible and were exposed to a hypnotic suggestion—false memories were created 63 percent of the time. Other researchers have confirmed this finding, leading us to conclude that hypnosis adds to the risk that witnesses will make memory errors and be influenced by misleading questions (Scoboria et al., 2002).

that subjects reported far less pain when they were hypnotized to "feel no pain" than when they were not. Compared to control subjects, who reached a pain level of 10 within twenty-five seconds, the average pain rating of hypnotized subjects never exceeded a 2 on the scale. In a fascinating variation on this study, hypnotized subjects were told to press a key with their free hand if "some part" of them was in pain. Look again at Figure 4.15, and you'll see what happened. Even though the hypnotized subjects reported low pain levels, their hidden observer was passively aware of the pain. Because these subjects reported two very different experiences at once, reasoned Hilgard, the hypnosis must have induced a state of dissociation. Well, perhaps.

**Social-Cognitive Theories**   The skeptics differ in their emphases, but all agree that the impressive effects of hypnosis stem from the power of social influence, not from any special process or trancelike state of altered consciousness. Perhaps highly responsive subjects are motivated to comply. Or perhaps they simply become so absorbed by the situation that they get caught up in their role the way dramatic actors often do. In support of this view, research shows that control subjects in the waking state often exhibit the same remarkable behaviors—when they are sufficiently motivated and believe they can succeed. Thus, pain tolerance

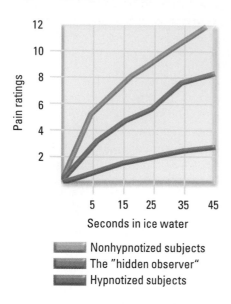

**FIGURE 4.15 Hypnosis, pain, and the "hidden observer"**
Subjects immersed a hand in ice water and rated the pain they felt. Those under hypnosis reported less pain than did controls. But by pressing a key, they also indicated that a part of them—a "hidden observer"—was aware of the pain (Hilgard et al., 1975).

## REVIEW QUESTIONS

- *What are the two stages of hypnosis?*

- *What characteristics are associated with susceptibility to hypnosis?*

- *Can hypnosis help control pain?*

- *Can hypnosis enhance memory?*

**4.2** Live! psych

in the ice-water test can be increased without a hypnotic induction (Spanos & Katsanis, 1989).

Although there are exceptions, most social-cognitive theorists do not believe that hypnosis subjects consciously fake their compliance with the hypnotist's suggestions (Kirsch & Lynn, 1995). Is it possible to test this hypothesis? Yes. If subjects are merely playing along, they might respond to suggestions in the hypnotist's presence—but certainly not in his or her absence. In fact, however, the hypnotic effects carry over. Eve Marie Perugini and others (1998) hypnotized highly responsive subjects but instructed low-responsive subjects to simulate the hypnosis. The hypnotic test was twice administered over a tape recorder—once in front of the examiner and once when the subject was left alone. The results were clear: In front of the examiner, both the hypnotized subjects and simulators complied equally with suggestions. But in the alone condition, a hidden camera revealed that highly responsive hypnosis subjects continued to pet imaginary cats, nod their heads to imaginary music, and respond to other suggestions even while the simulators did not. Additional studies too have shown that hypnotized subjects are not just deceiving the experimenter (Kinnunen et al., 1994; Reed et al., 1996). Hypnosis may not trigger a "special" process, but the behavior it produces reflects more than mere compliance.

At this point, hypnosis can be viewed in many ways. For example, highly responsive individuals in hypnosis may become so highly focused in their attention and so absorbed that the process feels "special." When college students were interviewed about their behavior in a campuswide hypnotism show, 28 percent of those who took part thought the hypnotist had complete control over their actions and that they could not resist the suggestions (Crawford et al., 1992). In addition, EEG recordings show that alpha-wave activity—which typically accompanies a drowsy, presleep state—increases during hypnosis, particularly among subjects high in hypnotic responsiveness (Graffin et al., 1995). PET scan studies also reveal that hypnosis activates certain areas of the cerebral cortex (Maquet et al., 1999; Rainville et al., 1999). On the other hand, some people succumb to hypnosis and comply with suggestions through normal channels of social influence, without a change in the state of their consciousness—which explains why our expectations, motivations, and rapport with the hypnotist play an important role (Sarbin, 1992; Kirsch & Lynn, 1999). In short, there may be two roads, both leading to the same state.

# CONSCIOUSNESS-ALTERING DRUGS

- *What drugs are considered "psychoactive," and why?*
- *When is a drug considered addictive?*
- *What are the effects on consciousness of alcohol and tobacco?*
- *What are the long-term health effects of illicit drugs such as marijuana, cocaine, and LSD?*

Throughout history, people all over the world have sought new ways to achieve altered states of consciousness. Dancing, chanting, twirling in circles, repetitive prayer, yoga, ritualized fasting, meditation, sensory isolation, and intoxicants such as opium, alcohol, marijuana, and cocaine are a few examples. The historical and cross-cultural consistency of these behaviors is so compelling that some researchers believe that humans have an inborn need to experience altered states of mind (Siegel, 1989; Weil & Rosen, 1993; Rudgley, 1999).

Alcohol, probably the first "mind-altering" substance used by humans, goes back about ten thousand years. According to Bert Vallee (1998), alcoholic beverages

*People all over the world behave in ways that alter states of consciousness. As shown, Chinese girls sip wine through bamboo straws, a woman on a beach sits in a lotus position while doing yoga, and Haitian men and women dance in a ritual voodoo ceremony.*

were the mother's milk of Western civilization before clean, pure water became available. He notes, for example, that the Bible contains many references to wine but little mention of water as a beverage. Other mind-altering drugs also have a long history, as opium was used six thousand years ago and hallucinogenic mushrooms and weeds go back about four thousand years (Palfai & Jankiewicz, 1991). More recently, Native Americans smoked tobacco as a goodwill offering. South Pacific islanders drink kava, a calming drink that is made from dried roots. Europeans celebrate special occasions with wine and champagne. Instances of drug use have even been observed in animals. Baboons eat tobacco, rabbits eat intoxicating mushrooms, and elephants seek out fermented fruit.

A quick but often dangerous way to alter consciousness is to use a **psychoactive drug**, a chemical that influences perceptions, moods, thoughts, or behavior. Depending on where in the world you are, a psychoactive substance may be legal or illegal. In most countries, caffeine, tobacco, alcohol, tranquilizers, and sleeping pills are legal. Marijuana, cocaine, crack, heroin, and LSD are illegal and are referred to as illicit drugs. As in our ancient past, humans are also in hot pursuit of the perfect aphrodisiac—a drug that is supposed to enhance sexual desire, pleasure, and performance (Rosen & Ashton, 1993).

Psychoactive drugs can become physically or psychologically addictive. **Physical dependence** is a physiological state in which continued drug use is needed to satisfy an intense craving and to prevent the dreaded onset of *withdrawal* symptoms such as shaking, sweating, and vomiting. Continued use of psychoactive drugs also produces *tolerance*, a condition in which larger and larger doses are needed to induce the same effect. Even without a physical addiction, people can also develop a **psychological dependence**, in which continued drug use is needed to maintain a sense of well-being.

As described in the coming pages and as summarized in Table 4.1, there are four major classes of psychoactive drugs: sedatives, stimulants, hallucinogens, and opiates. Drug use is a problem in general but is of greatest concern among youths. The drugs most commonly used by high-school seniors in the United States are presented in Figure 4.16. The trends in drug use from 1975 through 2001 are presented in Figure 4.17.

*People have used psychoactive drugs throughout history. In this Egyptian painting, dated 1350 BCE, the man on the left is sipping beer through a cane.*

**psychoactive drug**   A chemical that alters perceptions, thoughts, moods, or behavior.

**physical dependence**   A physiological addiction in which a drug is needed to prevent symptoms of withdrawal.

**psychological dependence**   A condition in which drugs are needed to maintain a sense of well-being or relief from negative emotions.

**sedatives** A class of depressant drugs that slow down activity in the central nervous system.

| TABLE 4.1 | CONSCIOUSNESS-ALTERING DRUGS | |
|-----------|------------------------------|---|
| **Type** | **Substance** | **Range of Effects** |
| Sedatives | Alcohol, barbiturates, benzodiazepines | Slowdown of body functions, relaxation, drowsiness, possibly depression and loss of consciousness |
| Stimulants | Caffeine, nicotine, amphetamines, cocaine | Speed up of body functions, alertness, energy, elation, jitteriness, loss of appetite |
| Hallucinogens | LSD, marijuana | Heightened sensory awareness, distorted perceptions of time and space, hallucinations |
| Opiates | Heroin, morphine, codeine | Suppressed pain, depressed neural activity, relaxation, drowsiness, euphoria |

For comprehensive information and up-to-date statistics on drug use, visit the National Institute on Drug Abuse at http://www.nida.nih.gov.

## SEDATIVES

**Sedatives,** or depressants, slow down activity in the central nervous system and produce calmness, drowsiness, and, in large doses, a loss of consciousness. The most commonly used sedatives are barbiturates, benzodiazepines, and, of course, alcohol. The first two are used for anesthetic purposes and in the treatment of anxiety and insomnia. As a rule, these drugs are highly addictive (Snyder, 1996).

Barbiturates are sedatives that have been used in the treatment of epilepsy, anxiety, and insomnia (Lickey & Gordon, 1991). The behavioral effects of barbiturates are similar to those of alcohol—such as drowsiness, slowness, and decreased performance on perceptual and cognitive tasks. In large doses, barbiturates also serve as an anesthetic, providing significant relief from pain. However, they tend to cause hangovers after the effects wear off. Barbiturates are among the most abused of all drugs.

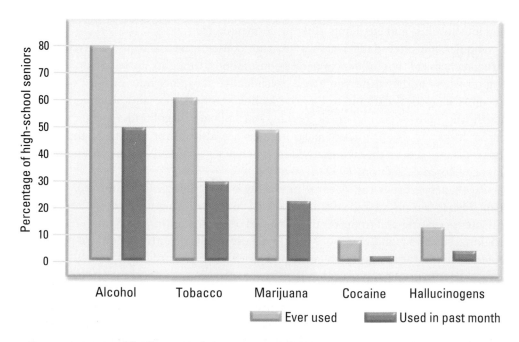

FIGURE 4.16 **The five most commonly used drugs**
Shown here are the percentages of American high school seniors in the class of 2001 who tried and regularly used various drugs—not for medical purposes (National Institute on Drug Abuse, 2002).

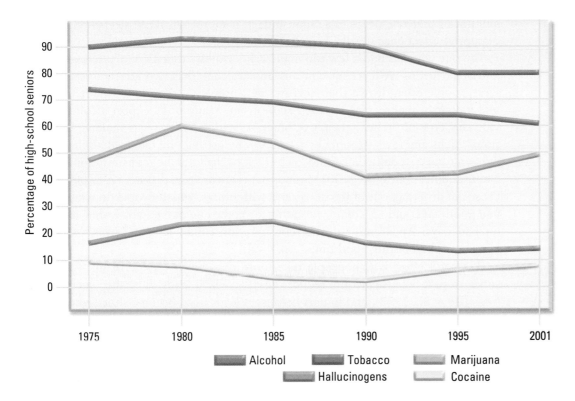

**FIGURE 4.17   Changing patterns of drug use, 1975–2001**
The U.S. government has been tracking the use of various drugs by high-school seniors since 1975. You can see that although lifetime usage rates dropped during the 1980s, the trend stabilized into the twenty-first century. Other, less common, drugs now being tracked include crack cocaine (3.7%), steroids (3.7%), and heroin (1.8%). Where will these numbers be in the years to come? (National Institute on Drug Abuse, 2002).

They are also addictive. Tolerance to barbiturates develops rapidly, and withdrawal symptoms are unpleasant. Mixing alcohol with barbiturates is especially dangerous.

Benzodiazepines, or minor tranquilizers, are another class of drugs often used in the treatment of anxiety and insomnia. Valium, Librium, and, more recently, Xanax are the most common "downers." Taken in pill form, they have a calming and relaxing effect and put people to sleep—usually for the entire night. Benzodiazepines are safer than barbiturates—except when mixed with alcohol. They have become the sedatives of choice for many people, though they can be quite addictive with prolonged use (see Chapter 17).

**Alcohol**   Alcohol is one of the most widely used drugs in the world. In 2002, on the basis of seventy thousand interviews, the National Household Survey on Drug Abuse revealed that 48 percent of Americans age twelve and older use alcohol on an occasional basis, that 20 percent sometimes engage in binge drinking (five or more drinks in one sitting), and that 6 percent are regular heavy drinkers. The question is, what are the effects?

*"First you take a drink, then the drink takes a drink, then the drink takes you."*

—F. SCOTT FITZGERALD

Regardless of whether it comes from a six-pack, a bottle of wine, or a glass of whiskey, gin, or vodka, alcohol is something of a paradox. It's known as a party drug that lifts spirits and lowers inhibitions, yet it has a sedative, depressant effect on the body. The symptoms include decreased visual acuity; diminished attention; lowered sensitivity to taste, smell, and pain; slowed reaction times; a loss of balance; slurred speech; and lowered performance on intelligence tests. Alcohol hastens the onset of sleep (as do most depressants) but does not increase the overall amount of time one sleeps in a night. In fact, it suppresses REM sleep—which has a disruptive effect once the alcohol wears off.

Anyone who has had a few too many drinks knows that alcohol alters awareness and behavior. As we'll see later in this book, alcohol has two effects in this regard. First, people often drown their sorrows in a bottle in order to escape from failure and its harsh implications for their self-esteem. Many of us expect alcohol to provide this type of "relief" (Leigh & Stacy, 1993) and to help us manage our emotional highs and lows (Cooper et al., 1995). By getting one hundred adult men and women to keep a daily diary, and keep track of their alcohol consumption, Cynthia Mohr and her colleagues (2001) found that there are two distinct types of drinking: (1) *social* drinking, out of the house and with others, which people do when they've had good days, and (2) *solitary* drinking, at home and alone, which they tend to do on bad days. Apparently, alcohol consumption comes in two forms: "Crying in your beer and toasting good times" (p. 489).

A second effect is that people take more risks when they're drunk than when sober, in part because alcohol reduces anxiety, which leads us to shed social inhibitions (Ito et al., 1996), and in part because it leads us to become shortsighted about the consequences of our actions, evoking a state of "drunken excess" (Steele & Josephs, 1990). In studies of college-aged men, Tara MacDonald and others (2000) fed alcoholic beverages to an "intoxicated" group of subjects, nonalcoholic beverages to a second "placebo" group, and nothing to a third "sober" group. The men then watched a videotaped scene involving a heterosexual couple engaged in sexual play when they realize they do not have a condom. The couple wonders what to do when the scene is paused, and subjects were asked whether they would proceed to have unprotected sex in that situation. The result: Those who felt sexually aroused by the scene and had consumed alcohol were more likely than all others to indicate a willingness to take the risk.

*"Drunkenness reveals what soberness conceals."*
—ENGLISH PROVERB

Put all these pieces together, and it's hardly surprising that drinking is statistically linked to highway fatalities, murders, assaults, child abuse, and other acts of recklessness and violence. Even in laboratory experiments, subjects are more aggressive after they're given alcohol to drink than when given a nonalcoholic beverage (Bushman & Cooper, 1990).

## STIMULANTS

**Stimulants** excite the central nervous system and stimulate behavior. Caffeine and nicotine are common mild stimulants. Amphetamines and cocaine have much stronger effects. These drugs speed up bodily functions (that's why amphetamines are known as speed or uppers), increase breathing and heart rates, heighten alertness, suppress appetite, and produce feelings of excitement, self-confidence, and even elation. For these reasons, people use stimulants to stay awake, lose weight, and elevate mood. In large amounts, they can make a person anxious, jittery, and hyperalert. As is often the case with psychoactive drugs, the user may come down from the high in a "crash" and feel tired, downbeat, and irritable. Like the sedatives, stimulants, including coffee, can be addictive (Silverman et al., 1992).

Amphetamines are synthetic drugs, often taken in pill form, for the treatment of asthma, narcolepsy, depression, and obesity. In low doses, amphetamines increase alertness and arousal, boost energy, relieve fatigue, and suppress appetite. In higher doses, these drugs can cause confusion, manic behavior, and aggression. Chronic amphetamine use can even trigger schizophrenia-like symptoms. Recently, amphetamine modifications have been synthesized in the pharmaceutical laboratory. One of these

**stimulants** A class of drugs that excite the central nervous system and energize behavior.

"designer drugs" is MDMA, or Ecstasy. In addition to its stimulant properties, MDMA is said to evoke a sense of well-being, particularly in relation to others (Shulgin, 1986). One powerful methamphetamine commonly known as "speed" comes in a smokable form ("ice") that is highly addictive and can be fatal.

Cocaine ("coke") is a natural drug derived from the leaves of the coca plant, a shrub native to South America. Its use as a stimulant was discovered hundreds of years ago by Peruvian Indians, who chewed coca leaves to overcome fatigue and increase stamina. Taken in this manner, small amounts of cocaine gradually enter the bloodstream. Today, cocaine in white powder form is usually inhaled through the nose ("snorted"), resulting in a quick and intense rush of euphoria. Its consciousness-altering effects, which last up to thirty minutes, are predictably followed by a crash caused by a temporary depletion in the supplies of dopamine and norepinephrine. A highly potent form of cocaine known as "crack" is smoked in a pipe or injected directly into the bloodstream. Crack gives a higher high but is followed by a lower low—and a craving for another "hit." It is dangerous and highly addictive (Platt, 2000).

## HALLUCINOGENS

**Hallucinogens** are the psychoactive drugs that cause the most dramatic alterations in consciousness. These drugs (which are also called psychedelics, from the Greek words meaning "mind expanding") distort perceptions of time and space and cause hallucinations—sensations without sensory input. The best-known hallucinogens are LSD and PCP. The latter (also called "angel dust") is a potent but dangerous painkiller. Marijuana, which has mixed sedative and stimulant effects, also acts as a mild hallucinogen.

LSD (lysergic acid diethylamide) is a synthetic drug that was first discovered in 1938 by Albert Hofmann, a Swiss chemist. At one point, Hofmann experimented on himself. He took what he thought to be a small dose of LSD and found himself for fourteen hours in a world he would never forget: "Everything in my field of vision was distorted as if seen in a curved mirror. . . . Familiar objects and furniture assumed grotesque, threatening forms . . . opening and closing themselves in circles and spirals, exploding in colored fountains" (Hofmann, 1980). Drug companies, researchers, and intelligence agencies in search of a truth serum soon went on to experiment with LSD. Even when they take small doses, acid "trippers" report that objects shimmer, colors become more vivid, their perception of time is slowed, old memories surface, and emotions range from euphoria to panic. Often, too, there is an eerie feeling of separation from one's own body, panic, and suicidal thoughts and actions (Miller & Gold, 1994). Many researchers believe that LSD and the other hallucinogens produce these effects by blocking activity of the neurotransmitter serotonin.

Marijuana is a milder and less potent hallucinogen. Derived from the leaves and flowering tops of the hemp plant, *Cannabis sativa,* marijuana has been cultivated for five thousand years in many parts of the world. Its major active ingredient is THC (delta-9-tetrahydrocannabinol), but it contains other chemicals that also have psychoactive effects. Marijuana is most often smoked in hand-rolled "joints" or pipes, but it may also be mixed into foods such as brownies. At low doses, marijuana may act like a sedative, producing a relaxed state and possibly a mild euphoria. It may also heighten awareness of colors, sounds, tastes, smells, and other sensations. At higher doses, it may distort perceptions of time and space. An estimated twelve million Americans use marijuana at least on occasion, making it the most commonly used illicit drug in the United States. Most alarming, according to the National

*In 1886, pharmacist John Pemberton created Coca-Cola and sold it, at first, as a headache remedy and stimulant. The drink contained cocaine, which was later replaced by caffeine. This 1914 ad highlights Coca-Cola's stimulating effects.*

**hallucinogens**   Psychedelic drugs that distort perceptions and cause hallucinations.

**opiates** A class of highly addictive drugs that depress neural activity and provide temporary relief from pain and anxiety.

Survey on Drug Use and Health, is that the rate of its usage is on the rise among youths twelve to seventeen years old (http://www.drugabusestatistics.samhsa.gov/).

Over the years, marijuana has been a subject of raging controversy, particularly in states that have legalized its use for medical purposes. Proponents claim that marijuana has medical benefits, but opponents argue that it poses serious health risks. So what is the evidence? On the positive side, marijuana may have certain clinical uses. Research shows that it helps combat nausea and weight loss in people with cancer and AIDS and helps to reduce pressure in the eyes of glaucoma patients. Several years ago, in a nationwide survey of cancer specialists, 48 percent said they would prescribe marijuana if it were legal, and 44 percent admitted that they had already recommended marijuana to at least one patient—even though it's illegal (Doblin & Kleiman, 1991). On the negative side, smoking marijuana, like smoking tobacco, can cause lung damage. It also slows reaction time and impairs motor coordination—hence the danger of driving or operating machinery while "stoned." Depending on the person and situation, it may also magnify feelings of anxiety, paranoia, or depression. Marijuana can also interfere with learning and the ability to form new memories. Unlike alcohol, which the body eliminates within hours, THC and its by-products linger in the body for a month or more (Iverson, 2000; Mack & Joy, 2001).

## OPIATES

**Opiates** are a class of drugs that are related to opium (an extract of the poppy plant), and they include morphine, codeine, and heroin. Their most prominent effect is to produce euphoria and analgesia (they also cause constipation). Because opiates depress neural activity, they are widely prescribed for the alleviation of pain—and have been used for this medical purpose for thousands of years. The user becomes drowsy and lethargic, yet happy and euphoric. Changes in consciousness are not particularly striking. These drugs are highly addictive, as the user quickly develops an insatiable need for more and larger doses. Heroin can be injected, smoked, or inhaled. Heroin users risk death through overdose, contaminated drugs, and AIDS contracted by sharing drug-injection needles.

People all over the world have sought to alter their states of consciousness, often by the consumption of psychoactive substances. Whatever the reasons for this desire, it is clear that drug use often turns to abuse and that social factors—like poverty, peer pressure, work stress, and a lack of personal fulfillment—play a role. In the United States, the number of people who use psychoactive drugs, which had declined over the past few years, is now on the rise for the first time in well over a decade. It is not clear, as a matter of public policy, how the problem can be solved. Thus, as policy makers debate the perennial question of whether to legalize the illicit drugs, many psychologists concede that they cannot confidently predict the impact of such a policy (MacCoun, 1993).

## REVIEW QUESTIONS

- *Identify the four classes of psycho-active drugs.*

- *What is the difference between physical dependence and psychological dependence?*

- *What are the physiological and psychological effects of sedatives, stimulants, hallucinogens, and opiates?*

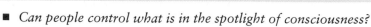

## CONSCIOUSNESS AND CONTROL

- *Can people control what is in the spotlight of consciousness?*
- *Why are we sometimes haunted by unwanted thoughts we try to suppress?*

Our ability to exert control over the contents of awareness is, at times, impressive. We saw earlier, for example, that lucid dreamers can sometimes control their dreams—and that almost anyone who is motivated can be trained to become a lucid dreamer. And we saw that although some of us can be hypnotized easily (a trait that requires the ability to focus attention and become absorbed), people cannot be hypnotized against their will—and those who are normally low in hypnotic susceptibility can learn to become more responsive to induction. Of course, when it comes to drug-induced altered states of consciousness, the choice is yours.

One particularly important way to control consciousness—meditation—first attracted great interest in the West in the 1950s when "beat generation" heroes like Jack Kerouac and Allen Ginsberg embraced Zen Buddhism. The interest broadened in the 1960s when the Beatles went to India to learn to meditate. In the 1990s, the number of people turning to meditation grew so dramatically that some meditation centers had to establish lotteries as a way to accommodate the applicants for retreats. Many are drawn by the promise of stress reduction, calm, equanimity, and even euphoria. But for experienced meditators, while they acknowledge these "side effects," the rewards are based on the analogy—more than three thousand years old—that disciplining the mind is like taming an elephant to make it useful. For them, the value of meditation lies not in some kind of bliss trip but rather in the heightened awareness of their everyday lives.

Despite these impressive abilities, there are times when the control of consciousness seems out of reach. The mind may wander, you may slip into a daydream, and you may become distracted despite your efforts at concentration. People who become dependent on a psychoactive drug may lose the ability to control their states of consciousness. And those who suffer from various anxiety-related disorders may become literally obsessed with certain thoughts (see Chapter 16).

Studying what he calls "ironic processes" in mental control, Daniel Wegner (1994) has found that, at times, the harder you try to control your own thoughts, the less likely you are to succeed. Try not to think about a white bear for the next thirty seconds, and chances are that very image will intrude upon your consciousness with remarkable frequency. Tell a jury to disregard an item of inadmissible testimony, and that censored material is sure to pop to mind as they deliberate on a verdict. Try not to worry about how long it's taking to fall asleep, and you'll stay awake. Try not to laugh in class or to think about the chocolate cake in the fridge or the itch on your nose—well, you get the idea.

According to Wegner, every conscious effort at control is met by a concern about failing to do so. This concern automatically triggers an "ironic operating process" as the person, trying *not* to fail, searches his or her mind for the unwanted thought. The ironic process will not necessarily prevail, says Wegner. Sometimes we can put the imaginary white bear out of mind. But if we're busy, distracted, tired, hurried, or under stress, then the ironic process, because it "just happens," will prevail over the intentional process—which requires conscious attention and effort. So, Wegner (1997) notes, "any attempt at mental control contains the seeds of its own undoing" (p. 148).

Ironic processes have been observed in a wide range of behaviors. In an intriguing study of this effect on the control of motor behavior, Wegner and others (1998) had subjects hold a pendulum (a crystalline pendant suspended from a nylon fishing line) over the center of two intersecting axes on a glass grid, which formed a "+". Some subjects were instructed simply to keep the pendulum steady, while others were more specifically told not to allow it to swing back and forth along the horizontal axis. Try this yourself and you'll see that it's not easy to prevent at least some movement. In this experiment, however, the pendulum swung horizontally more when this direction was specifically forbidden. To further examine the role of mental distraction, some subjects were also required to count backward from a thousand by sevens while controlling the pendulum. In this situation, the ironic

*Illustrating Wegner's proposition that "any attempt at mental control contains the seeds of its own undoing," research shows that people are most likely to overshoot a golf putt when they are specifically trying not to overshoot but are distracted while putting.*

"Believe me, you're just thinking about it too much."

effect was even greater. Among subjects who specifically tried to prevent horizontal movement but could not concentrate fully on the task, the pendulum swayed freely back and forth—in the forbidden direction. Using a similar method, these researchers found that people were most likely to overshoot a golf putt when they specifically tried not to overshoot but were distracted while putting. It may seem both comic and tragic, but at times our efforts at self-control backfire, thwarting even our best intentions. For psychologists, and everyone else for that matter, the key is to learn how to minimize these ironic effects.

## THINKING LIKE A PSYCHOLOGIST ABOUT CONSCIOUSNESS

"A penny for your thoughts?" Over the years, psychologists have equated consciousness with attention and have examined varying states of awareness, ranging from sleep and dreams to hypnosis and the effects of mind-altering drugs. We have seen in this chapter that people can sometimes control the contents of consciousness. Research on selective attention shows that as we focus the spotlight of awareness on one stimulus, we can screen out irrelevant competing information. At times, we can divide our attention, simultaneously engage in two or more activities, and process information without awareness. Yet there are also times when we cannot control what we think about—and that trying to do so can backfire.

## SUMMARY

### ATTENTIONAL PROCESSES

Psychologists generally define **consciousness** in terms of **attention**—an awareness of the sensations, thoughts, and feelings that one is attending to at a given moment.

### SELECTIVE ATTENTION

Studies of the **cocktail party phenomenon** demonstrate that people can use **selective attention** to focus on one stimulus and virtually exclude other stimuli from consciousness. Many of these studies use a dichotic listening task in which subjects hear competing messages over headphones and must follow what is said in one ear while ignoring the other.

### DIVIDED ATTENTION

Other listening experiments show that **divided attention** is possible: Some stimuli penetrate consciousness even when we are focused on something else. Moreover, if we are so experienced at a particular process that it becomes automatic, we can do other things at the same time. The **Stroop test** demonstrates that experienced readers process word meanings automatically, without effort or awareness.

### INFLUENCE WITHOUT AWARENESS

Research shows that people can be influenced by **subliminal messages**—information that is presented "below" our threshold of awareness. Mere exposure to a stimulus increases liking, even when the exposure is subliminal. This is shown in studies on **priming,** where subliminally presented concepts appear to facilitate, or "prime," responses in a subsequent situation. People with **prosopagnosia,** who cannot recognize familiar faces, show glimmers of recognition without knowing they are doing so. And people with **blindsight** react to certain visual cues without awareness. There is no strong evidence, however, that subliminal persuasion can change our long-term behavior.

### SLEEP AND DREAMS

Until recently, there were many myths about sleep and dreams, but little was actually known about these processes.

### THE SLEEP-WAKE CYCLE

As biological organisms, humans experience regular fluctuations known as **biological rhythms.** Our daylong **circadian**

**rhythm,** such as the sleep-wake cycle, is controlled by the suprachiasmatic nucleus of the hypothalamus, which detects light via the retina. Cut off from sunlight, humans tend to drift toward longer daily cycles. When our rhythms are disrupted, we may experience reactions such as jet lag.

## NIGHT WORK, SLEEPING, AND HEALTH

Both biological and social clocks set the body for activity during the daytime and sleep at night, so shift workers struggle to stay alert and experience problems on the job. Many traffic accidents occur at night, as drivers sometimes take brief **microsleeps** while driving. A brief nap or a cup of coffee can help drivers stay awake.

## THE STAGES OF SLEEP

Sleep follows a cycle of distinct stages: presleep; stages 1 to 4 of deepening sleep, as the body relaxes and brain waves become larger and slower; and **REM sleep,** characterized by rapid eye movements, increased pulse rate, brain waves like those of presleep, and totally relaxed muscles. It is during REM sleep that vivid dreams occur. Each night, as we pass through several cycles, we gradually spend more time in REM sleep and less time in non-REM, or **NREM, sleep.**

## WHY DO WE SLEEP?

Sleep is so necessary that when people try to stay awake for long periods, they fall into short microsleeps, a few seconds at a time. According to restoration theory, sleep helps us recover from the day's demands. Circadian theory offers an evolutionary explanation: Sleep helps animals conserve energy and avoid predators when not searching for food or seeking a mate. Individuals differ in the amount of sleep they require.

## DREAMS

Dreams, too, serve an adaptive function. As shown by studies that measure REM sleep, people do most of their dreaming early in life when the brain is still developing. Common themes include falling and being chased or attacked. Both daily concerns and external stimuli also influence dream content. Some people experience **lucid dreaming,** a semiconscious state in which they are aware of—and can control—their own dreams.

Freud accounted for the bizarreness of dreams by theorizing that they are disguised expressions of unconscious wishes. To interpret dreams, he said, one has to go beyond the **manifest content** to uncover the unconscious meaning, or **latent content.** A more recent hypothesis, the **activation-synthesis theory,**

contends that dreams begin with random neural signals in the brainstem. These signals spread up to the cortex, and the brain tries to make sense of them by constructing images and stories.

## SLEEP DISTURBANCES

Sleep disturbances are common. **Insomnia**—the inability to fall asleep, stay asleep, or get enough sleep—has many causes and can be cured through behavioral means. Hypersomnia (sleeping too much) is less frequent but more dangerous, particularly among those with **narcolepsy,** a disorder that causes sudden attacks of REM sleep during the day. There are other serious sleep disturbances, or parasomnias. People with **sleep apnea** snore loudly and repeatedly stop breathing during sleep and awaken gasping for air. **REM sleep behavior disorder (RBD)** is a condition in which the skeletal muscles are not paralyzed during REM sleep, enabling sleepers to act upon their nightmares, often violently. Other problems include night terrors and sleepwalking.

## HYPNOSIS

### THE SEEDS OF CONTROVERSY

**Hypnosis** is a set of attention-focusing procedures in which changes in a subject's behavior or mental state are suggested. It has a long and controversial history in psychology.

### THE HYPNOTIC INDUCTION

In the first stage of hypnosis, induction, the subject's attention is focused. In the second stage, suggestion, the subject responds to the hypnotist's cues.

### HYPNOTIC RESPONSIVENESS

People differ in their degree of **hypnotic susceptibility,** or responsiveness. Those who are most responsive tend to have vivid imaginations and long attention spans.

### THE MYTHS AND REALITIES

Contrary to myth, people cannot be hypnotized against their will or be coerced into violating their consciences. Evidence suggests, however, that hypnotized subjects may shed their inhibitions. Hypnosis can reduce pain. Through **posthypnotic suggestion,** the hypnotist can influence a subject's behavior even after the session ends. **Posthypnotic amnesia** is also common, though not permanent. But **hypermnesia,** the supposed enhancement of a witness's memory by hypnosis, has not been confirmed in experiments. Rather, hypnosis makes witnesses more vulnerable to false memories.

## IS HYPNOSIS AN "ALTERED" STATE?

Special-process theories maintain that hypnosis induces a unique state of suggestibility. According to one theory, the hypnosis subject experiences **dissociation,** a division of consciousness in which one part of the mind operates independent of another. Social-psychological theories see hypnosis as an ordinary state in which changes are produced by conscious faking or by processes of social influence. To some extent, both theories may be true.

## CONSCIOUSNESS-ALTERING DRUGS

Throughout history, people have sought altered states of consciousness, often by using consciousness-altering **psychoactive drugs,** chemicals that change perceptions, moods, thoughts, or behavior. Such drugs are addictive, creating either **physical dependence** or **psychological dependence.**

### SEDATIVES

Among psychoactive drugs, **sedatives** such as alcohol, barbiturates, and benzodiazepines slow activity in the central nervous system. Alcohol was the first and is one of the most widely used drugs in the world.

### STIMULANTS

**Stimulants,** including caffeine, nicotine, amphetamines, and cocaine, excite the central nervous system and energize behavior. They can be addictive.

### HALLUCINOGENS

**Hallucinogens,** or psychedelic drugs, such as LSD and marijuana, distort perceptions and can cause hallucinations. There is now controversy over the possible medical uses of marijuana and the health risks that it poses.

### OPIATES

The highly addictive **opiates,** such as heroin, morphine, and codeine, depress neural activity, relieve pain, and produce euphoria.

## CONSCIOUSNESS AND CONTROL

As studies of attention and hypnosis illustrate, people have a great deal of command over their own consciousness. Yet there are times when our minds wander and we cannot control the distractions. Often we must contend with an irony: The harder we try to manage our thoughts, the less likely we are to succeed.

# KEY TERMS

consciousness (**p. 133**)

attention (**p. 133**)

cocktail party phenomenon (**p. 133**)

selective attention (**p. 133**)

divided attention (**p. 135**)

Stroop test (**p. 136**)

subliminal message (**p. 136**)

priming (**p. 137**)

prosopagnosia (**p. 137**)

blindsight (**p. 138**)

biological rhythms (**p. 140**)

circadian rhythm (**p. 140**)

microsleep (**p. 143**)

REM sleep (**p. 146**)

NREM sleep (**p. 146**)

lucid dreaming (**p. 150**)

manifest content (**p. 151**)

latent content (**p. 151**)

activation-synthesis theory (**p. 152**)

insomnia (**p. 153**)

narcolepsy (**p. 155**)

sleep apnea (**p. 156**)

REM sleep behavior disorder (RBD) (**p. 156**)

hypnosis (**p. 157**)

hypnotic susceptibility (**p. 159**)

posthypnotic suggestion (**p. 161**)

posthypnotic amnesia (**p. 161**)

hypermnesia (**p. 161**)

dissociation (**p. 162**)

psychoactive drug (**p. 165**)

physical dependence (**p. 165**)

psychological dependence (**p. 165**)

sedatives (**p. 166**)

stimulants (**p. 168**)

hallucinogens (**p. 169**)

opiates (**p. 170**)

## THINKING CRITICALLY ABOUT CONSCIOUSNESS

1. Is hypnosis an altered state of consciousness? Compare the special process and social psychological answers to this question. Which do you find more compelling?

2. In what ways are we influenced by subliminal stimuli (i.e., stimuli presented below the level of conscious awareness)? Why might people continue to believe in the power of subliminal advertising?

3. A recent search of amazon.com yielded approximately sixty books on the interpretation of dreams. What advice would you give to someone about purchasing such books?

4. How can we use the concept of lucid dreaming to help people effectively deal with nightmares?

# Learning

# CAN PEOPLE LEARN WITHOUT REALIZING IT?

## THE SITUATION

As you enter the laboratory reception area, you are met by an experimenter, taken to a small room, and told that you will be taking part in a study of human memory. Next you're told that you'll have seven minutes to examine the following strings of letters and that you should simply try to "learn and remember as much as you can." Ready, begin:

| | | | | |
|---|---|---|---|---|
| PVV | TSSSXXVV | TSXXTVPS | PVPXTVPS | TSSXXVV |
| TSXS | PTVPXVV | TXXTVPS | TXXTTTVV | PVPXXVV |
| TSSXXVPS | TXXVPXVV | PTVPS | PTTTVPS | PTVPXV |

You look at these meaningless items one by one, trying to memorize. *P-V-V. T-S-X-S.* You just keep repeating them under your breath. After seven minutes, the experimenter stops you. Time's up. You can't wait to write down what you remember before you lose it—but the experimenter has other plans. He or she now reveals that the items were formed according to a set of rules, an "artificial grammar" if you will, and that he or she is interested in whether you know what the rules are. As the experimenter explains the test you're about to take, you get a sinking feeling in the pit of your stomach. "Uh-oh. There were rules? I wasn't looking for rules!"

The test is straightforward. On slides, you'll see one hundred new items made up of the same letters as before, one item per slide. Half the items will be grammatical (according to the rules); half will not. For each one, you are to press a button marked *YES* if you think the item is grammatical or *NO* if you think it's not. You should also rate your confidence in each judgment on a scale marked from 1 to 5. Oh, one more thing: Your responses will be timed.

The slide projector is turned on, the overhead lights are shut off, and you've got your fingers on the buttons ready to fire. First item: *PTTTVPVS.* It looks okay, as it contains the usual letters, and all. But are these letters ordered in a way that fits the grammar? "If I don't know," you ask, "should I just guess?" Instructed to respond to every item, you press a button and state your confidence. The next one is *PVTW.* Same routine. *PVPS. SVPXTW. SXXVPS.* Sometimes you answer quickly; at other times, you stare at the screen for a while before making a response. By the hundredth slide, you're ready for a cool drink and a nap.

## MAKE A PREDICTION

How well do you think people fare in this task? Having been in this experiment myself, I can tell you that many subjects shrug their shoulders in confusion. Based on what you've read, what do you think is the average test score? If all you did was guess, you would get roughly a 50 percent accuracy rate. If you came up with rules that were wrong, your score could be lower. If you knew the right rules, you would do better. So, what is your estimate, 10 percent? 30? 55? 90? Circle your prediction:

0  5  10  15  20  25  30  35  40  45  50  55  60  65  70  75  80  85  90  95  100%

## THE RESULTS

For thirty years, cognitive psychologist Arthur Reber (1993) has used experiments like this one to study "implicit learning"—the tendency for people to acquire complex, abstract concepts without awareness or intention. Consistently, Reber has found that subjects cannot describe the grammar that they use to form the letter strings, nor can they explain the reasons for their *YES* and *NO* judgments. Yet in the study just described, subjects made the correct response 77 percent of the time—and usually did so quickly.

## WHAT DOES IT ALL MEAN?

Implicit learning, which occurs without our awareness, is a primitive but powerful form of adaptation. Indeed, people learn this grammar not by actively searching for rules or by receiving explicit instruction but simply through exposure to properly formed letter strings. Without really trying, subjects learn the grammar the way we learn to speak in our native tongue, figure out how to behave properly in a new setting, or "calculate" the trajectory of a ball in flight in order to make the catch. Implicit mental processes such as these are common (Stadler & Frensch, 1998). To learn from experience, as the subjects did in this study, people must be attuned to associations between stimuli in their environment and between behavior and its consequences. As we'll see in this chapter, association is the basic building block for all learning.

*Programmed by instinct, spiders weave webs.*

**ethologists**   Scientists who study the behavior of animals in their natural habitat.

**fixed action pattern**   A species-specific behavior that is built into an animal's nervous system and triggered by a specific stimulus.

Every spring, a tiny freshwater fish called the stickleback performs an intriguing reproductive ritual. As the male's belly turns from dull gray to a bright red, he builds a nest and does a zigzag courtship "dance" to attract a female stickleback, sometimes brushing her belly with his stickles. He then escorts her to the nest, prods her tail to induce spawning, fertilizes her eggs, aerates the eggs by fanning the water, and vigorously attacks all red-bellied male intruders. Once the eggs hatch a week later, he guards the young and keeps them close by until they are ready to leave the nest.

Many land animals also exhibit adaptive, complex forms of behavior. When the herring-gull mother returns to the nest with food, newly hatched chicks peck at her bright yellow bill, causing her to regurgitate the food for their consumption. The honeybee uses a wax it secretes to build hives in which each comb consists of hexagonal cells that form a mathematically efficient, perfect design. The indigo bunting, a small bird, navigates south every winter, using as a guide the bright North Star, the only star in the Northern Hemisphere that maintains a fixed compass position through the night. Similarly prepared by instinct, the canary sings, the spider weaves its web, the beaver builds dams, and the newly hatched duckling follows the first moving object it sees, usually its mother. How do the stickleback and others know what to do? Simple. In many animal species, certain behaviors are programmed by instinct.

Inspired by Darwin's theory of evolution and led by Nobel Prize winners Konrad Lorenz and Nikolaas Tinbergen, **ethologists** study the behavior of animals in their natural habitat (Alcock, 1997; Eibl-Eibesfeldt, 1989). Based on their observations, these researchers refer to the instinctual behaviors as **fixed action patterns.** A fixed action pattern is a species-wide sequence of movements that is built into the nervous system and triggered or "released" by a specific stimulus. The response to the

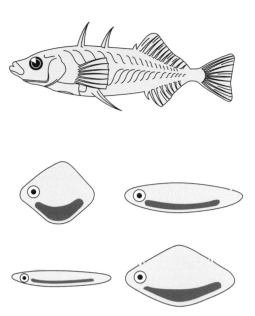

stimulus is automatic, like a reflex—no ifs, ands, or buts. Thus, the stickleback male attacks all red-bellied forms, even those that do not resemble a fish (see Figure 5.1). Similarly, the herring-gull chick pecks at all moving red dots, even if they do not resemble another bird (see Figure 5.2).

Do people exhibit fixed action patterns? Are we instinctual creatures? We'll see later that human newborns are equipped with adaptive, instinct-like behaviors in the form of reflexes. Upon birth, an infant will clutch anything that touches the palm of the hand, turn with an open mouth toward any object that grazes the cheek, start sucking when the lips are touched, and swallow when the back of the mouth is stimulated. These reflexes are not within the infant's control, and some disappear within a few months, never to return. Why are we humans less equipped with inborn, reflex-like rituals than the stickleback? Because we adapt to life's demands not by instinct but through learning.

When psychologists talk about **learning**, they are referring to a relatively permanent change in knowledge or behavior that comes about as a result of *experience*. Experience is necessary for us to speak, read, write, add and subtract, ride a bicycle, swim, play a saxophone or trumpet, or know how to charm a romantic partner. The topic of learning is near and dear to the heart of all psychologists—regardless of whether they study biological, cognitive, developmental, social, or clinical processes. Often what we learn makes us happier, healthier, and more successful; sometimes it does not. The beauty of adaptation by learning is that it is flexible, not rigidly preset like a stickleback's dance-and-attack ritual. In principle, this means that each of us can learn to behave in ways that benefit rather than harm ourselves and others. The question is: How does this learning take place?

The simplest form of learning is **habituation**—a tendency to become familiar with a stimulus merely as a result of repeated exposure. The first time it happens, a sudden loud noise or a blast of cold air has a startling effect on us and triggers an "orienting reflex." Among humans, the eyes widen, the eyebrows rise, muscles tighten, the heart beats faster, skin resistance drops, and brain-wave patterns indicate a heightened level of physiological arousal (Sokolov, 1963). On the second and third exposures to the stimulus, the effect is weakened. Then as we become acclimated or "habituated" to the stimulus, the novelty wears off, the startle reaction disappears, and boredom sets in.

Habituation is a primitive form of learning and is found among mammals, birds, fish, insects, and all other organisms. For example, sea snails reflexively withdraw

**FIGURE 5.1  Stickleback models**
Research shows that various red-bellied objects trigger male attack, yet a replica of another male stickleback without a red belly does not. The red belly is the stimulus that releases this fixed action pattern (Tinbergen, 1951).

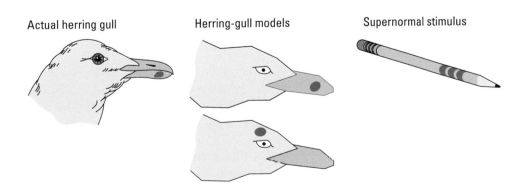

**FIGURE 5.2  Herring-gull models**
Research shows that pecking is released by the movement of any red dot—even on objects, such as a pencil, that do not resemble the gull's beak (Hailman, 1969).

**learning**  A relatively permanent change in knowledge or behavior that results from experience.

**habituation**  The tendency of an organism to become familiar with a stimulus as a result of repeated exposure.

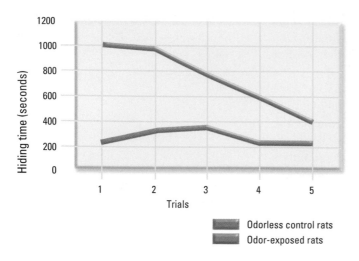

**FIGURE 5.3** **Habituation of fear**
Rats were exposed to a cat collar that contained or did not contain a cat's odor, causing them to run and hide. After several presentations, the odor-exposed rats hid for less and less time, eventually resembling the odorless control rats (Dielenberg & McGregor, 1999).

## REVIEW QUESTIONS

- *What is a fixed action pattern? Do people exhibit these patterns?*

- *How do psychologists define learning?*

- *What is habituation?*

their gills at the slightest touch. Then after repeated tactile stimulation, the response disappears (Kandel, 1979). Animals may also habituate to objects that naturally evoke fear after repeated and harmless exposure. When lab rats were presented with a cat collar smeared with a cat's odor, they ran from it and hid. Figure 5.3, however, shows that after several presentations the rats hid for decreasing amounts of time, eventually resembling control group rats exposed to an odorless collar (Dielenberg & McGregor, 1999).

Habituation also occurs in human infants. If a picture or sound is presented over and over again, an infant will eventually get bored, lose interest, look away, and exhibit a lower heart rate (Bornstein, 1989). Think about everyday life, and numerous examples of habituation will come to mind. People who move from a large city to the country or from a region of the world that is hot to one that is cold often need time to adjust to the sudden change in stimulation. Once they do, the new environment seems less noisy, quiet, hot, or cold. In a series of experiments, adults were subliminally exposed to words that arouse emotional reactions that are extremely positive (*free, beach, baby*) and negative (*cancer, war, hell*). Later, they rated these same words as less positive and negative than they did other, equally extreme, words that were not previously presented (Dijksterhuis & Smith, 2002). Habituation also has important implications for the power of rewards to motivate us. Regardless of whether the rewarding stimulus is food, water, or an opportunity to explore a new environment, it tends to lose impact, at least temporarily, with repeated use (McSweeney & Swindell, 1999).

In habituation, an organism learns from exposure that a certain stimulus is familiar. Over the years, however, psychologists have focused more on the ways in which we learn relationships between events. In this chapter, three such processes are discussed: classical conditioning, operant conditioning, and observational learning.

**5.1**

## CLASSICAL CONDITIONING

- *What did Pavlov learn from his experiments with salivating dogs?*
- *What is classical conditioning, and how is it relevant to human behavior?*
- *Is it possible to condition people to develop new fears or attitudes?*
- *Can bodily functions similarly be "trained"?*

I will always remember the summer of 1969 on the beach—the body surfing, bikinis, Frisbees, rock 'n' roll, the feel of hot sand between the toes, low-flying gulls, and warm air blowing the scent of salt water and coconut-oil suntan lotion. To this day, these memories flood my mind whenever I hear a song that was a radio hit at the time.

In stark contrast, I will never forget a cold, dark night in January 1976. I was in graduate school and had eaten dinner with a friend. Driving back to campus, I hit a patch of ice and skidded. Before I knew it, the car had scraped the wall of a brick building, turned on its side, and stalled. My friend and I were shaken but not hurt. Yet I vividly recall the red lights flashing on the dashboard, the smell of burned rubber, and the blast of cold air that hit my face when we climbed out through the door. I also recall the song that played on the radio as we tried to escape. For years, I would flinch whenever I heard it.

*Ivan Pavlov and some of the 200 other scientists who worked with him during his illustrious career.*

**classical conditioning**  A type of learning in which an organism comes to associate one stimulus with another (also called Pavlovian conditioning).

**unconditioned response (UR)**  An unlearned response (salivation) to an unconditioned stimulus (food).

**unconditioned stimulus (US)**  A stimulus (food) that triggers an unconditioned response (salivation).

Following Aristotle, modern philosophers and psychologists have long believed that the key to learning is *association,* a tendency to connect events that occur together in space or time. Can learning by association be studied in a scientific manner? Yes. In fact, many theories of associative learning have been proposed and tested over the years (Pearce & Bouton, 2001). With the arrival of the twentieth century, psychology was poised and ready for one of its most important discoveries.

## PAVLOV'S DISCOVERY

Enter Ivan Pavlov, a Russian physiologist. After receiving his medical degree in 1882, he spent twenty years studying the digestive system and won a Nobel Prize for that research in 1904. Pavlov was the complete dedicated scientist. Rumor has it that he once reprimanded a lab assistant who was ten minutes late for an experiment because of street riots stemming from the Russian Revolution: "Next time there's a revolution," he said, "get up earlier!" (Hothersall, 1990).

Ironically, Pavlov's most important contribution was the result of an incidental discovery. In studying the digestive system, he strapped dogs in a harness, placed different types of food in their mouths, and measured the flow of saliva through a tube surgically inserted in the cheek (see Figure 5.4). But there was a "problem": After repeated sessions, the dogs would begin to salivate *before* the food was actually put in their mouths. In fact, they would drool at the mere sight of food, the dish it was placed in, the assistant who brought it, or even the sound of the assistant's approaching footsteps. Pavlov saw these "psychic secretions" as a nuisance, so he tried to eliminate the problem by sneaking up on the dogs without warning. He soon realized, however, that he had stumbled on a very basic form of learning. This phenomenon was **classical conditioning**, and Pavlov devoted the rest of his life to studying it.

To examine the classical conditioning systematically, Pavlov needed to control the delivery of food, often a dry meat powder, as well as the events that preceded it. The animals did not have to be trained or "conditioned" to salivate. The salivary reflex is an innate **unconditioned response (UR)** that is naturally set off by food in the mouth, an **unconditioned stimulus (US)**. There are numerous unconditioned stimulus–response connections. Tap your knee with a rubber mallet and your leg

[Cartoon by John Chase]

**conditioned stimulus (CS)** A neutral stimulus (bell) that comes to evoke a classically conditioned response (salivation).

**conditioned response (CR)** A learned response (salivation) to a classically conditioned stimulus (bell).

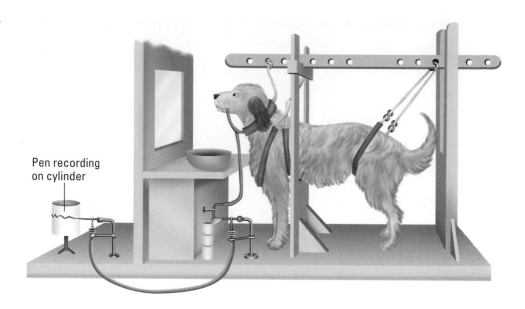

Pen recording on cylinder

**FIGURE 5.4  Pavlov's classical-conditioning apparatus**
Strapped into an apparatus like the one shown here, Pavlov's dogs were conditioned to salivate. Through a tube surgically inserted into each dog's cheek, saliva was recorded by a pen attached to a slowly rotating cylinder of paper.

**Before conditioning**

| Unconditioned stimulus (US, meat powder) | → | Unconditioned response (UR, salivation) |

| Neutral stimulus (bell) | → | No unconditioned response (no salivation) |

**During conditioning**

| Neutral stimulus (bell) + Unconditioned stimulus (US, meat powder) | → | Unconditioned response (UR, salivation) |

**After conditioning**

| Conditioned stimulus (CS, bell) | → | Conditioned response (CR, salivation) |

**FIGURE 5.5  Classical conditioning**
Note the sequence of events before, during, and after Pavlov's study. At first, only the US (meat) elicits a UR (salivation). After a neutral stimulus (bell) repeatedly precedes the US, however, it becomes a CS and can elicit a CR (salivation) on its own.

will jerk. Blow a puff of air into your eye and you'll blink. Turn the volume up on an alarm clock and, when it rings, your muscles will tighten. In each case, the stimulus automatically elicits the response. No experience is necessary.

Using the salivary reflex as a starting point, Pavlov (1927) sought to determine whether dogs could be trained by association to respond to a "neutral" stimulus—one that does not naturally elicit a response. To find out, he conducted an experiment in which he repeatedly rang a bell before placing food in the dog's mouth. Bell, food. Bell, food. After a series of these paired events, the dog started to salivate to the sound alone. Because the bell, which was initially a neutral stimulus, came to elicit the response through its association with food, it became a **conditioned stimulus (CS)**, and salivation, a **conditioned response (CR)**. With this experiment as a model, Pavlov and others trained dogs to salivate in response to buzzers, ticking metronomes, tuning forks, odors, lights, colored objects, and a touch on the leg.

Following the basic classical-conditioning procedure diagrammed in Figure 5.5, researchers have trained animals to react to a host of neutral stimuli that have been paired with an unpleasant or pleasant US. In one study, rats froze and did not move whenever they were put into a cage in which they had previously been exposed to high concentrations of carbon dioxide (Mongeluzi et al., 1996). In a second study, male quails became sexually aroused when they were placed into a chamber in which they had previously copulated with female birds (Domjan et al., 1998). In a third study, human subjects were conditioned to blink when given a whiff of a flowery odor that had earlier preceded puffs of air to the eye (Moore & Murphy, 1999).

As we'll see, classical conditioning affects us all in ways that we're often not aware of. We learn to salivate (CR) to lunch bells, menus, the smell of food cooking, and the sight of a refrigerator (CS) because these stimuli are often followed by eating (US). Similarly, we cringe when we hear the shrill sound of a dentist's drill because of past associations between that sound and pain. And we tremble at the sight of a flashing blue light in the rearview mirror because of its past association with speeding tickets. For me, the beach—which was the site of so many good times of the past—is a conditioned stimulus that fills me with peaceful, easy feelings.

**acquisition**  The formation of a learned response to a stimulus through the presentation of an unconditioned stimulus (classical conditioning) or reinforcement (operant conditioning).

## BASIC PRINCIPLES

Inspired by his initial discovery, Pavlov spent more than thirty years examining the factors that influence classical conditioning. Other researchers throughout the world also became involved. As a result, we now know that various species can be conditioned to blink when they hear a click that is paired with a puff of air to the eye, to fear colored lights that signal the onset of painful electric shocks, and to develop a dislike for foods they ate before becoming sick to the stomach (Ballard, 2002). We also know that there are four very basic principles of learning: acquisition, extinction, generalization, and discrimination.

**Acquisition**  Classical conditioning seldom springs full blown after a single pairing of the CS and US. Usually, it takes some number of paired trials for the initial learning, or **acquisition**, of a CR. In Pavlov's experiments, the dogs did not salivate the first time they heard the bell. As shown in the left panel of Figure 5.6, however, the CR increases rapidly over the next few pairings—until the "learning curve" peaks and levels off.

The acquisition of a classically conditioned response is influenced by various factors. The most critical are the order and timing of the presentation. In general, conditioning is quickest when the CS (the bell) precedes the onset of the US

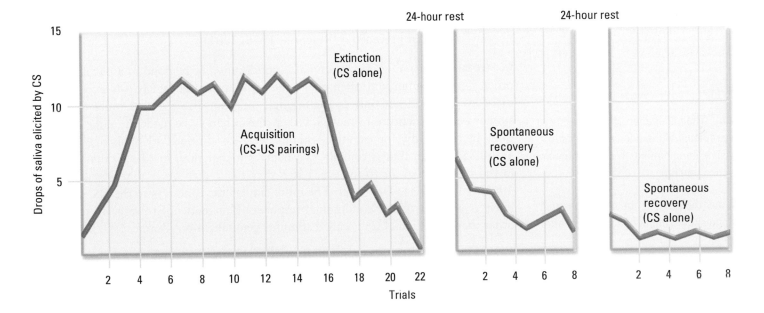

**FIGURE 5.6  The rise and fall of a conditioned response**
In classical conditioning, the CS does not evoke a CR on the first trial, but over time the CR increases rapidly until leveling off. During extinction, the CR gradually declines. After a brief delay, however, there is usually a spontaneous recovery, or "rebounding," of the CR—until it is completely extinguished.

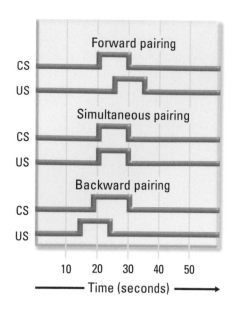

**FIGURE 5.7 Temporal relations in classical conditioning**
A key factor in classical conditioning is the timing of the CS and US. The three temporal patterns illustrated here are presented in order—from the most to least effective.

**extinction** The elimination of a learned response by removal of the unconditioned stimulus (classical conditioning) or reinforcement (operant conditioning).

**spontaneous recovery** The reemergence of an extinguished conditioned response after a rest period.

**stimulus generalization** The tendency to respond to a stimulus that is similar to the conditioned stimulus.

**discrimination** In classical and operant conditioning, the ability to distinguish between different stimuli.

(food)—a procedure called *forward* conditioning. Ideally, the CS should precede the US by about half a second and the two should overlap somewhat in time. When the onset of the US is delayed, conditioning takes longer and the conditioned response is weaker. When the CS and US are *simultaneous,* it takes even longer. And when the US is presented before the CS (a procedure referred to as *backward* conditioning), learning often does not occur at all (see Figure 5.7).

Once a buzzer, light, or other neutral stimulus gains the power to elicit a conditioned response, it becomes a CS—and can serve as though it were the US for yet another neutral stimulus. In one experiment, for example, Pavlov trained a dog to salivate to the sound of a bell, using meat powder as the US. After the CS–US link was established, he presented a second neutral stimulus, a black square, followed by the bell—but no food. The result: After repeated pairings, the black square on its own elicited small amounts of salivation. Through a process of "higher-order" conditioning, as shown in Figure 5.8, one CS was used to create another CS. In effect, the black square came to signal the bell, which, in turn, signaled the appearance of food (Rescorla, 1980).

**Extinction** In the acquisition phase of classical conditioning, a CR is elicited by a neutral stimulus that is paired with a US. But what happens to the CR when the US is removed? Would a dog continue to salivate to a bell if the bell is no longer followed by food? Would the screeching dentist's drill continue to send chills up the spine if it is no longer followed by pain? No. If the CS is presented often enough without the US, it eventually loses its response-eliciting power. This apparent reversal of learning is called **extinction** (look again at the middle panel of Figure 5.6).

Extinction is a gradual process. Pavlov found that when the same dog was returned for testing a day or two after extinction, it again salivated to the bell—a rebound effect known as **spontaneous recovery** (depicted in the right panel of Figure 5.6). Often the dogs were easily retrained after just one repairing of the CS and US. As confirmed in more recent research, extinction does not erase what was initially learned during acquisition—and retraining does not erase the effects of extinction. Rather, it appears that each learning experience suppresses, but does not destroy, those that preceded it (Rescorla, 1996, 2001).

**Generalization** After an animal is conditioned to respond to a particular CS, other similar stimuli will often evoke the same response. In Pavlov's experiments, the dogs salivated not only to the original tone but also to other tones that were similar but not identical to the CS. Other researchers have made the same observation. In one study, for example, rabbits were conditioned to blink to a tone of 1,200Hz (a pitch that is roughly two octaves higher than middle C) that was followed by a puff of air to the eye. Later, they blinked to other tones ranging from 400Hz to 2,000Hz. The result: The more similar the tone was to the CS, the more likely it was to evoke a conditioned response. This tendency to respond to stimuli other than the original CS is called **stimulus generalization** (Pearce, 1987).

**Discrimination** Stimulus generalization can be useful because it enables us to apply what we learn to new, similar situations. But there are drawbacks. As illustrated by the child who is terrified of all animals because of one bad encounter with a barking dog, or the racist who assumes that "they" are all alike, generalization is not always adaptive. Sometimes we need to distinguish between objects that are similar—a process of **discrimination**. Again, Pavlov was the first to demonstrate this process. He conditioned a dog to salivate in the presence of a black square (a CS) and then noticed that the response generalized to a gray-colored square. Next, he conducted a series of conditioning trials in which the black square was followed by food while the gray one was not. The result: The dog continued to salivate only to the original CS. In a similar manner, the dog eventually learned to discriminate between the color black and darker shades of gray.

## PAVLOV'S LEGACY

Classical conditioning is so powerful and so basic that it occurs in animals as primitive as the sea slug, the fruit fly, and even the flatworm (the body of the flatworm contracts in response to electric shock; if the shock is repeatedly paired with light, the flatworm's body eventually contracts to the light alone) and in animals as sophisticated as us humans (Turkkan, 1989; Krasne & Glanzman, 1995). Recently, psychologists have taken classical conditioning in two directions: Some want to better *understand* the phenomenon—how, when, and why it works—while others are eager to *apply* it to different aspects of the human experience.

**Theoretical Advances**   Inspired by their initial success and by the Darwinian assumption that all animals share a common evolutionary past, Pavlov and other early behaviorists made this bold claim: Any organism can be conditioned to any stimulus. It does not matter if the subject is a dog, cat, rat, pigeon, or person. Nor does it matter if the conditioned stimulus is a bell, light, buzzer, or odor. Whenever an initially neutral stimulus is paired with an unconditioned stimulus, the result is classical conditioning.

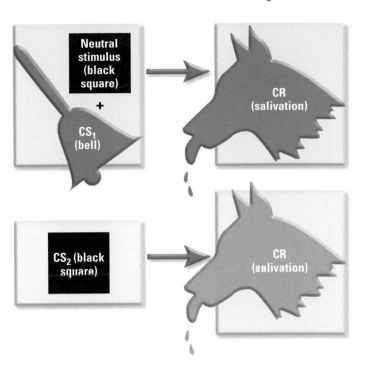

**FIGURE 5.8   Higher-order conditioning**
After Pavlov trained a dog to salivate (CR) to a bell (CS), he preceded the bell with another neutral stimulus, a black square. After repeated pairings, the dog would salivate to the square itself. In effect, one CS was used to create another CS.

The early behaviorists also insisted that a science of human behavior must focus only on external, objective, quantifiable events. A *stimulus* can be observed and measured. So can its effect on an overt *response*. Together, these form the basis for what is known as S–R psychology. As far as the organism itself is concerned—its instincts, drives, perceptions, thoughts, and feelings—the behaviorists would not speculate. In fact, Pavlov was said to have fined laboratory assistants who slipped into using "mentalistic" language. So where does the *organism* fit in? In recent years, researchers have come to appreciate some of the ways in which the "O" bridges the S and R—giving rise to a more flexible S-O-R brand of behaviorism. Two factors within the organism are particularly important: biological preparedness and cognitive representations.

**Biological Preparedness**   For survival purposes, all animals are biologically programmed by evolution to learn some associations more easily than others. This phenomenon was first discovered by John Garcia and Robert Koelling (1966). While studying the effects of radiation exposure on laboratory rats, they noticed that the animals would not drink from the plastic water bottles inside the radiation chambers. Since the radiation (US) was causing nausea (UR), they reasoned, perhaps the rats had acquired an aversion (CR) to the "plastic" taste of the water (CS).

To test this hypothesis, these investigators rigged an apparatus that worked as follows: When a rat licked a plastic drinking tube, it tasted sweetened water, saw a flash of light, and heard a loud clicking noise—all at the same time. The rats were then exposed to a high dose of X rays, which caused poisoning and nausea. The result: The rats later came to avoid the sweetened water after radiation poisoning, but they did not also learn to avoid the light or noise. The link between taste (CS) and poison (US) was so easily learned that it took only one pairing—even though the rats did not get sick until hours later (a far cry from the split-second CS–US interval that is usually necessary). Garcia and Koelling (1966) next found that when the US was a painful electric shock to the feet instead of X-ray poisoning, the rats continued to drink the water, but this time they avoided the audiovisual stimuli instead. In other words, although the rats were exposed to all stimuli, they proceeded to avoid only the flavored water after X-ray poisoning and only the light and noise after shock. Why was taste such a powerful CS when it was paired with poison but not with shock? And why were light and noise conditioned to shock but not to poison? Think about these associations for a moment, and one word will pop to mind: *adaptiveness*. In nature, food is more likely to produce stomach poisoning than a pain in the foot, and an external stimulus is more likely to cause a pain in the foot than stomach illness. If you get sick after eating in a new restaurant, you are likely to blame your illness on something you ate, not on the decor or the music that played. Clearly, we are "prepared" by nature to learn some CS–US associations more easily than others.

It is important to note that people acquire taste aversions, too—often with important practical implications. Consider, for example, an unfortunate side effect of chemotherapy treatments for cancer. These drugs tend to cause nausea and vomiting. As a result, patients often become conditioned to react with disgust and a loss of appetite to foods they had eaten hours before the treatment (Bovbjerg et al., 1992). Thankfully, the principles of classical conditioning offer a solution to this problem. When cancer patients are fed a distinctive maple-flavored ice cream before each treatment, they acquire a taste aversion to that ice cream—which becomes a "scapegoat" and protects the other foods in the patient's diet (Bernstein & Borson, 1986). Still, many cancer patients who had undergone chemotherapy and survived report that they continue to feel nauseous, and sometimes vomit, in response to the sights, smells, and tastes that remind them of treatment—as much as twenty years later (Cameron et al., 2001).

Research on the classical conditioning of fear reactions also illustrates the point that organisms are biologically predisposed to learn certain stimulus–response connections more than others. As we'll see in Chapter 16, people all over the world share many of the same fears. Particularly common are fears of darkness, height, snakes, and insects—relatively harmless objects, some of which we may never encounter. Yet very few of us are as terrified of automobiles, electrical outlets, appliances, and other objects that can be dangerous. Why? Martin Seligman (1971) speculated that the reason for this disparity is that humans are predisposed by evolution to be wary of stimuli and situations that posed a threat to our prehistoric ancestors.

Not everyone agrees with this evolutionary analysis (Davey, 1995). However, it is supported by various strands of research. When laboratory-raised rhesus monkeys saw a wild-reared monkey of the same species exhibit fear in the presence of a toy snake, they acquired an intense fear of snakes. But when they saw the other monkey show fear in the presence of a toy rabbit, they did not similarly acquire a fear of rabbits (Cook & Mineka, 1990; Mineka & Cook, 1993). Similar results are found in humans. When people are conditioned to fear an object that is paired with electric shock, their reaction—as measured by physiological arousal—is acquired faster and lasts longer when the object is a snake, a spider, or an angry face than when it is a "neutral" stimulus such as a flower, a house, or a happy face (McNally, 1987). This differential response to fear-relevant objects is so basic that it occurs even when the stimuli are presented subliminally, without awareness (Ohman & Soares, 1998).

After reviewing the research, Arne Ohman and Susan Mineka (2001) proposed that human beings are equipped by evolution with *fear modules* designed to help us defend against potentially life-threatening situations in the ecology of our distant ancestors. According to Oehman and Mineka, these fear modules have four characteristics: (1) they are highly selective, making us sensitive to some objects—such as heights, thunder, and snakes—but not others; (2) they elicit fear responses that are "automatic," requiring very little attention, thought, or effort; (3) the responses are hard to consciously control or avoid; and (4) the modules are controlled by neural circuits in the amygdala and hippocampus—primitive, subcortical limbic structures shared by all mammals (Maren, 2001).

**Cognitive Representations**   According to Pavlov, classical conditioning occurs whenever a neutral stimulus is paired with an unconditioned stimulus. With dogs salivating to bells, it all seemed rather passive, mindless, and automatic—a mechanical process in which the control of a reflex is simply passed from one stimulus to another. But is the process really that passive? Laboratory animals do not have to be geniuses to acquire a conditioned response, but they may be cognitively more active than Pavlov was willing to admit. Perhaps Pavlov's dogs salivated to his bells and tones because prior experience led them to *expect* food.

After years of research, Robert Rescorla (1988) concluded that classical conditioning is the process by which an organism learns that one event (CS) *predicts* another event (US). In other words, says Rescorla, a simple pairing of two stimuli is often not sufficient for conditioning to occur. Rather, the organism must also learn that one event signals the coming onset of another. To demonstrate, Rescorla (1968) exposed rats to an electric shock (US) that was always paired with a tone (CS). In one condition, every shock was accompanied by the tone—so the CS reliably predicted the US. In a second condition, the rat experienced the same tone–shock pairs but was occasionally shocked without the tone as well. In other words, although the two events were paired, the CS did not reliably predict the US (see Figure 5.9). As Rescorla expected, the rats acquired a fear of the tone in the first condition but not in the second. Apparently, classical conditioning requires more than a simple pairing of a CS and US. It requires that there be a reliable predictive relationship.

Rescorla's cognitive redefinition of the process of classical conditioning has lots of research support (Miller et al., 1995). This point of view is significant because it helps to explain various aspects of classical conditioning. For example, it explains why a conditioned response is hard to produce in a backward conditioning procedure in which the CS *follows* the US. The two stimuli co-occur, as in forward and simultaneous conditioning, but the CS cannot predict the US when it comes second in the sequence of events. Rescorla's model also explains why certain associations are learned more easily than others. You may recall that in the taste–aversion study described earlier, rats quickly learned to avoid food that was paired with stomach poisoning, and lights and noise that were paired with electric shock. But they did not similarly link food to external pain, or lights and noise to stomach poisoning. Why? As Rescorla (1988) put it, "Conditioning is not a stupid process by which an organism willy-nilly forms associations between any two stimuli that happen to co-occur. Rather the organism is better seen as an information seeker using logical and perceptual relations among events and its own preconceptions to form a sophisticated representation of its world" (p. 154).

**Practical Applications**   When Pavlov first found that he could train Russian dogs to drool to the sound of a dinner bell, nobody cared. In fact, E. B. Twitmyer, an American graduate student, had reported similar results at a psychology conference in 1904—the same year that Pavlov won the Nobel Prize. At the time, Twitmyer was studying the knee-jerk reflex in humans. Before each trial, he would ring a bell to warn subjects that a hammer was about to strike the knee. Like Pavlov, he found that the subject's leg would soon twitch in response to the bell—even before the

**Condition 1: Contiguity *with* predictive relationship**

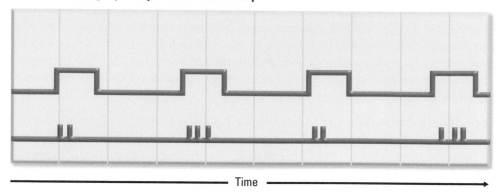

Time →

**Condition 2 : Contiguity *without* predictive relationship**

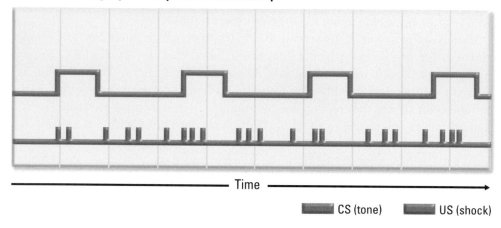

Time →

CS (tone)    US (shock)

FIGURE 5.9    **Classical conditioning: when the CS predicts the US**
Rescorla (1968) exposed rats to a shock (US) paired with a tone (CS). In one condition, every US was paired with the CS (top). In a second condition, shocks were sometimes administered without a tone—so the CS did not predict the US (bottom). Indicating that a predictive relationship is required, rats learned to fear the tone in the first condition but not in the second.

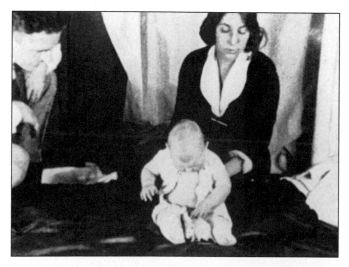

*Rosalie Rayner holds Little Albert as he plays with a white lab rat. Watson, left, observes the boy (Archives of the History of American Psychology—The University of Akron).*

knee was hit. Was this a profound development? You might think so, but Twitmyer's presentation attracted little interest.

**Conditioned Fears**    Psychologists finally took notice of classical conditioning in 1914, when behaviorist John Watson described Pavlov's work to a group of American psychologists. To demonstrate the relevance of the phenomenon to humans, Watson and his assistant Rosalie Rayner (1920) conditioned an eleven-month-old boy named Albert to fear a white laboratory rat. "Little Albert" was a normal, healthy, well-developed infant. Like others his age, he was scared by loud noises but enjoyed playing with furry little animals. Enter John Watson. Modeled after Pavlov's research, Watson presented Albert with a harmless white rat. Then just as the boy reached for the animal, Watson made a loud, crashing sound by banging a steel bar with a hammer, which caused the startled boy to jump and fall forward, burying his head in the mattress he was lying on. After seven repetitions of this event, the boy was terrified of the animal. What's worse, his fear generalized, leading him to burst into tears at the sight of a rabbit, a dog, a Santa Claus mask, and even a white fur coat (see Figure 5.10).

From an ethical standpoint, Watson and Rayner's study was shameful. They infected an innocent baby with a fear that seemed to spread like it was a contagious disease from one white and furry stimulus to the next—and they did not "decondition" him (in case you're wondering, ethics committees would not approve this study today). Watson said that the boy was taken away before he had a chance to do so, but others believe he may have known in advance that Albert's mother was going to remove her son from the research project (Harris, 1979). On the positive side, Little Albert's fear is a legend in the history of psychology because it established for the first time a link between Pavlov's dogs and an important aspect of the human experience. We now know that people can come to fear objects or places because they happened to be associated with aversive experiences. As we'll see in Chapter 17, classical conditioning spawned a revolutionary and effective method of treating these irrational fears and other anxiety-related disorders. In a development with particularly profound implications, researchers are also finding links between classical conditioning and the immune system. (See *Psychology and Health*.)

It is also important to note that babies can be conditioned to form positive *preferences* as well—for example, toward stimuli that are associated with maternal care. In one study, Regina Sullivan and her associates (1991) exposed newborns to a neutral odor. After each presentation, some were gently touched, an inherently pleasurable experience, while others were not. The next day, all the infants were returned to the lab and tested. As predicted, those for whom the odor was paired with the tactile stimulation were more likely to turn their heads toward that odor rather than away from it. This effect occurs not only in human infants but also in young rats, mice, hamsters, deer, guinea pigs, squirrel monkeys, and other species (Leon, 1992). Even human adults can be classically conditioned to form new preferences. For example, twenty heterosexual men were shown slides of moderately attractive, partially nude young women. For some of the men but not others, the slides were paired with clips from an X-rated erotic video. When the slides alone were later reshown, those in the paired condition became more sexually aroused—an instance of attraction by association (Lalumiere & Quinsey, 1998).

### Social Attitudes and Behavior

Not everyone was happy about the possible uses of classical conditioning. In *Brave New World*, novelist Aldous Huxley (1932) warned readers of a future in which diabolical world leaders use Pavlov's methods to control their followers. These concerns are unfounded. However, classical conditioning does affect our lives in many ways. Think about the classic movie *Jaws*. Early in the film, pulsating bass music is followed by the sight of a shark's fin and the bloody underwater mutilation of a young swimmer. Then it happens again and again. Before you know it, the music alone (CS)—even without the evil shark (US)—has the audience trembling and ducking for cover. Many other examples illustrate this point. Using powerful associations, American politicians wrap themselves in stars and stripes, the swastika strikes terror in the hearts of Jewish people, and the burning cross arouses fear among African Americans. In the words of Shelby Steele (1990), a black English professor, "there are objective correlatives everywhere that evoke a painful thicket of emotions . . . covering everything from Confederate flags and pickup trucks with gun racks to black lawn jockeys" (p. 154).

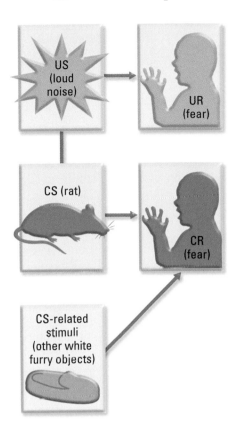

**FIGURE 5.10   The conditioning of Little Albert**
By linking a harmless white rat to an aversive loud noise, Watson conditioned a baby boy to react with terror to the rat. In fact, the fear spread, or "generalized," to other, superficially similar objects.

*Through classical conditioning, people often react with strong emotions to once neutral objects such as national flags and other symbols.*

## Psychology and Health

# CAN THE IMMUNE SYSTEM BE CLASSICALLY CONDITIONED?

Ever since the turn of the twentieth century, psychologists have known that reflexes and emotional reactions can be classically conditioned. But what about the human immune system—can it too be trained to respond to neutral stimuli? Thanks to recent research developments, we now know that it is also possible to train the body's immune system—and, as a result, certain aspects of our physical health and well-being (Ader & Cohen, 1993). Indeed, the pages of medical history are filled with stories that seem to indicate the effects of classical conditioning—as in the case of a hay fever patient whose allergy was so severe that just looking at a picture of a hay field would trigger an attack (Martin, 1998).

Consisting of more than a trillion white blood cells, the immune system guards our health by warding off bacteria, viruses, and other foreign substances that invade the body. When this system fails, as it does when it's ravaged by the AIDS virus, disease and death are the certain outcome (see Chapter 18). With that in mind, you can appreciate the following striking discovery. Psychologist Robert Ader had been using classical-conditioning procedures with rats in which he paired sweetened water with a drug that causes nausea—cyclophosphamide. Water, drug. Water, drug. As expected, the rats developed a taste aversion to the sweetened water. Unexpectedly,

however, many of the animals died because the drug Ader used weakened the immune system by destroying certain types of white blood cells. To further explore this phenomenon, Ader joined with immunologist Nicholas Cohen (1985) in a series of experiments. They repeatedly fed the rats sweetened water, which is harmless, followed by cyclophosphamide (US), which weakens the immune response (UR). The result: After several pairings, the sweetened water on its own (CS) caused a weakening of the immune response, followed by sickness and sometimes death (CR).

In light of this result, Dana Bovjberg and others (1990) wondered about cancer patients who take chemotherapy drugs. These drugs are designed to inhibit the growth of new cancer cells, but they also inhibit the growth of immune cells. With chemotherapy drugs always being given in the same room in the same hospital, is it possible, over time, that a patient's immune system is conditioned to react in advance to cues in the surrounding environment? Yes. In a study of women who had undergone several chemotherapy treatments for ovarian cancer, these researchers found that their immune systems were weakened as soon as they entered the hospital—before they were treated. Like Pavlov's bell, the hospital setting had become a conditioned stimulus, thus triggering a maladaptive change in cellular activity.

These discoveries raise an exciting question: If the immune system can be weakened by conditioning, can it similarly be strengthened, and activity levels increased? Research on this question is still in its early stages, but positive results in animals have shown that it can be done (MacQueen et al., 1989; Madden et al., 2001). In human studies, too, researchers have found that after repeatedly pairing sweet sherbet or other neutral stimuli with shots of adrenaline (which has the unconditioned effect of increasing activity in certain types of immune cells), the sherbet flavor alone later triggered an increase in the immune response (Buske-Kirschbaum et al., 1992, 1994). Might it one day be possible for medical doctors to use classical conditioning to help people fight AIDS and other immune-related diseases? Stay tuned. Pavlov's simple discovery may well prove useful in this battle (Ader & Cohen, 2001).

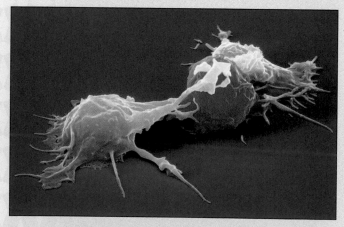

This color-enhanced microscopic image shows two "natural killer" immune cells (in yellow) engulfing and destroying a cancer cell (in red). The immune system contains more than a trillion specialized white blood cells.

These examples suggest that people form strong positive and negative *attitudes* toward neutral objects by virtue of their links to emotionally charged stimuli. In one study, college students were presented with a list of national names (German, Swedish, Dutch, Italian, French, and Greek), each repeatedly paired with words that had very pleasant (*happy, gift, sacred*) or unpleasant (*bitter, ugly, failure*) connotations. When the subjects later evaluated the nationalities by name, they were more positive in their ratings of those that had been paired with pleasant words than those with unpleasant words (Staats & Staats, 1958). In another study, subjects were exposed to a pleasant, neutral, or foul odor as they looked at pictures of people whom they did not know. Later, they were asked to rate the people in the pictures. Although no odors were pumped into the testing room during this second session, subjects showed a clear preference for faces earlier paired with the pleasant odor and an aversion to those paired with the foul odor (Todrank et al., 1995). Clearly, we can be classically conditioned to form likes and dislikes of neutral people, situations, and objects (De Houwer et al., 2001). That's why advertisers routinely try to link their products to sexy models, breathtaking scenery, upbeat music, beloved celebrities, nostalgic images, and other positive emotional symbols.

It's also possible to influence *social behavior* through classical conditioning. Consider the blue-and-yellow stripes on a VISA card, or the orange-and-yellow circles on a MasterCard. Through past associations, these logos may serve as visual cues that lead us to spend money. In one study, college students who were asked to estimate how much money they would be willing to spend on various consumer products gave higher estimates when there was a credit card lying on a table in the testing room than when there was not (Feinberg, 1986). In a second study, which was conducted in a restaurant, diners were randomly given tip trays for payment that were either blank or had a major credit card logo on it. With sixty-six cash-paying customers in the sample, the credit-card tray elicited an increase in tipping from 15.6 percent of the bill to 20.2 percent (McCall & Belmont, 1996).

## OPERANT CONDITIONING

- *What is operant conditioning and how does it differ from classical conditioning?*
- *What is reinforcement, and how does it differ from punishment?*
- *How do behaviorists explain the persistence of maladaptive behaviors like gambling?*
- *What are the biological and cognitive perspectives on operant conditioning?*

Classical conditioning may explain why people salivate at the smell of food, cringe at the sound of a dentist's drill, or tremble at the sight of a flashing blue light in the rearview mirror. But it cannot explain how animal trainers at Sea World teach killer whales to jump through hoops or dolphins to dance on water or sea lions to perform dazzling acrobatics—as when they play volleyball. Nor can it explain how we learn to solve equations, make people laugh, or behave in ways that earn love, praise, sympathy, or the respect of others. As we will see, the acquisition of voluntary, complex, and goal-directed behaviors involves a second form of learning.

### THE LAW OF EFFECT

Before Pavlov had begun his research, an American psychology student named Edward L. Thorndike (1898) was blazing another trail. Interested in animal intelligence, Thorndike built a "puzzle box" from wooden shipping crates so he could

**law of effect** A law stating that responses followed by positive outcomes are repeated, whereas those followed by negative outcomes are not.

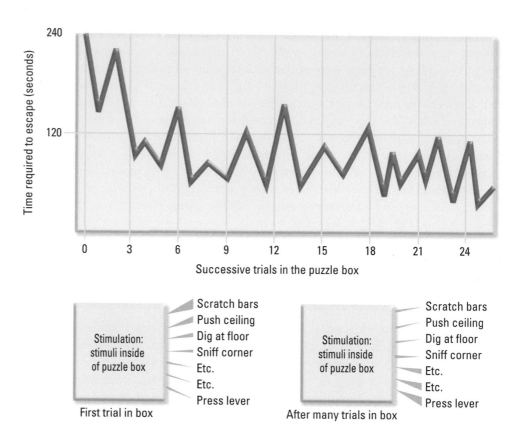

**FIGURE 5.11** **Thorndike's law of effect**
Thorndike's hungry cats initially engaged in various behaviors—sniffing, pawing, scratching the bars, pushing the ceiling, and pressing the lever that opened the escape hatch. Over a series of trials, the cats took less and less time to press the lever (*top*). Accordingly, Thorndike proposed that behaviors followed by a reward are "stamped in," whereas others fade away (*bottom*).

observe how different animals learn to solve problems. In one study, he put hungry cats into a cage, one at a time, with a door that could be lifted by stepping on a lever. He then placed a tantalizing chunk of raw fish outside the cage—and beyond reach. You can imagine what happened next. After sniffing around the box, the cat tried to escape by reaching with its paws, scratching the bars, and pushing at the ceiling. At one point, the cat accidentally banged on the lever. The door opened and the cat scampered out to devour the food. Thorndike repeated the procedure again. The cat went through its previous sequence of movements and eventually found the one that caused the latch to open. After a series of trials, Thorndike's cats became more efficient: They went straight to the latch, stepped on the lever, and ate the food (see Figure 5.11).

Based on studies like this one, Thorndike (1911) proposed the **law of effect:** Behaviors that are followed closely in time by a satisfying outcome are "stamped in" or repeated, whereas those followed by a negative outcome or none at all are extinguished. In the puzzle box, cats spent progressively more time stepping on the latch and less time poking at the bars and ceiling. In the case of humans, Thorndike's law of effect was used to describe the process of socialization. By using rewards and punishments, parents train their children to eat with a utensil and not to fling their mashed potatoes across the table. To the extent that we learn how to produce desirable outcomes, the process is adaptive.

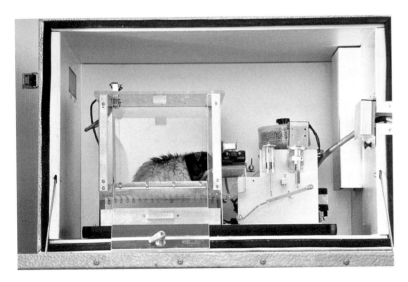

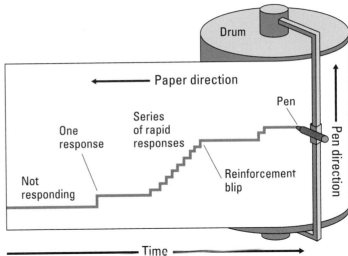

FIGURE 5.12   **The Skinner box**

## THE PRINCIPLES OF REINFORCEMENT

Following in Thorndike's footsteps, behaviorist B. F. Skinner transformed the landscape of modern psychology. But first things first. To study learning systematically, Skinner knew that he had to design an environment in which he controlled the organism's response-outcome contingencies. So as a graduate student in 1930, he used an old ice chest to build a soundproof chamber equipped with a stimulus light, a response bar (for rats) or pecking key (for pigeons), a device that dispenses dry food pellets or water, metal floor grids for the delivery of electric shock, and an instrument outside the chamber that automatically records and tabulates the responses. This apparatus came to be known as the **Skinner box** (see Figure 5.12).

Next, Skinner introduced a new vocabulary. To distinguish between the active type of learning that Thorndike had studied (whereby the organism operates on the environment) and Pavlov's classical conditioning (whereby the organism is a more passive respondent), Skinner coined the term *operant conditioning*. **Operant conditioning** is the process by which organisms learn to behave in ways that produce desirable outcomes. The behavior itself is called an "operant" because it is designed to operate on the environment. In other words, in contrast to classical conditioning—which involves the learning of associations between stimuli, resulting in a passive response—operant conditioning involves the learning of an association between a spontaneously emitted action and its consequences (Rescorla, 1987).

To avoid speculating about an organism's internal state, Skinner also used the term **reinforcement** instead of *reward* or *satisfaction*. Objectively defined, a reinforcer is any stimulus that increases the likelihood of a prior response. There are two types of reinforcers: positive and negative. A *positive reinforcer* strengthens a prior response through the presentation of a positive stimulus. In the Skinner box, the food that follows a bar press is a positive reinforcer. For humans, it's food, money, grades, hugs, kisses, and a pat on the back. Even mild electrical stimulation to certain "pleasure centers" of the brain, which releases the chemical neurotransmitter dopamine, has a satisfying effect and serves as a positive reinforcer (Olds & Milner, 1954; Wise, 1996; Rolls, 1999). In contrast, a *negative reinforcer* strengthens a response through the removal of an aversive stimulus. In a Skinner box, the termination of a painful electric shock is a negative reinforcer. Similarly, we learn to take aspirins to soften a

*Live* **psych**   5.2

"Boy, do we have this guy conditioned. Every time I press the bar down he drops a pellet in."

[Skinner (1956) American Psychologist, 11, 221–223/APA.]

**Skinner box**   An apparatus, invented by B. F. Skinner, used to study the effects of reinforcement on the behavior of laboratory animals.

**operant conditioning**   The process by which organisms learn to behave in ways that produce reinforcement.

**reinforcement**   In operant conditioning, any stimulus that increases the likelihood of a prior response.

*People are highly responsive to reinforcement, sometimes to their own detriment. In 1989, sixteen-year-old Kharey Wise confessed to police that he took part in a gang assault on a jogger in New York's Central Park. In December 2002, after Wise had spent twelve years in jail, his conviction was overturned. According to Wise, he had confessed to a crime he did not commit in order to escape a long and stressful interrogation—a form of negative reinforcement. (© 2002 ABC Photography Archives.)*

headache, fasten our seatbelts to turn off the seatbelt buzzer, and rock babies to sleep to stop them from crying.

It is important to keep straight the fact that positive and negative reinforcers both have the same effect: to strengthen a prior response. Skinner was quick to point out that punishment is not a form of negative reinforcement. Although the two are often confused, **punishment** has the opposite effect: It decreases, not increases, the likelihood of a prior response. There are two types of punishment. A *positive punisher* weakens a response through the presentation of an aversive stimulus. Shocking a lab rat for pressing the response lever, scolding a child, locking a criminal behind bars, and boycotting a product all illustrate this form of punishment designed to weaken specific behaviors. In contrast, a *negative punisher* weakens behavior through the removal of a stimulus typically characterized as positive. Taking food away from a hungry rat and grounding a teenager by suspending driving privileges are two examples.

To summarize, a reinforcement is a stimulus that strengthens a prior response through (1) the presentation of a positive stimulus, or (2) the removal of a negative stimulus. In contrast, punishment is a stimulus that weakens a response through (1) the presentation of a negative stimulus, or (2) the removal of a positive stimulus. The different types of reinforcement and punishment are summarized in Table 5.1.

**Shaping and Extinction** Modeled after the law of effect, Skinner's basic principle seemed straightforward. Responses that produce reinforcement are repeated. But wait. If organisms learn by the consequences of their behavior, where does the very first response come from? Before the first food pellet, how does the animal come to press the bar? As Thorndike had demonstrated, one possibility is that the response occurs naturally as the animal explores the cage. Skinner pointed to a second possibility: that the behavior is gradually **shaped**, or guided, by the reinforcement of responses that come closer and closer to the desired behavior.

Imagine that you are trying to get a hungry white rat to press the bar in a Skinner box. Where do you begin? The rat has never been in this situation before, so it sniffs around, pokes its nose through the air holes, grooms itself, rears on its hind legs, and so on. At this point, you can wait for the target behavior to appear on its own, or you can speed up the process. If the rat turns toward the bar, you drop a food pellet into the cage. Reinforcement. If it steps toward the bar, you deliver another pellet. Reinforcement. If the rat moves closer or touches the bar, you deliver yet another one. Once the rat is hovering near the bar and pawing at it, you withhold the next pellet until it presses down, which triggers the feeder. Before long, your subject

**punishment** In operant conditioning, any stimulus that decreases the likelihood of a prior response.

**shaping** A procedure in which reinforcements are used to gradually guide an animal or person toward a specific behavior.

| TABLE 5.1 | TYPES OF REINFORCEMENT AND PUNISHMENT | |
| --- | --- | --- |
| | **EFFECT ON BEHAVIOR** | |
| **Procedure** | **Increases** | **Decreases** |
| Presentation of stimulus | Positive reinforcement (feed the rat) | Positive punishment (shock the rat) |
| Removal of stimulus | Negative reinforcement (stop the shock) | Negative punishment (stop the food) |

*Using operant conditioning, Sea World animal trainers can get orca whales to jump on cue. To learn about animal training, you can visit Sea World, online, at* http://www.seaworld.org/infobooks/Training/home.html.

is pressing the bar at a rapid pace. By reinforcing "successive approximations" of the target response, you will have shaped a whole new behavior.

Shaping is the procedure that animal trainers use to get circus elephants to walk on their hind legs, bears to ride bicycles, chickens to play a piano, squirrels to water-ski, and dolphins to jump through hoops—which brings me back to Sea World. The dolphin trainer begins by throwing the dolphin a fish for turning toward a hoop, then for swimming toward it, swimming through it underwater, and finally jumping through a hoop that is held many feet up in the air. The process applies to people as well. Young children are toilet trained, socialized to behave properly, and taught to read through step-by-step reinforcement. Similarly, political candidates repeat statements that draw loud applause and abandon those that are met with silence—thereby creating messages that are shaped by what voters want to hear. Rumor has it that a group of college students once conspired to shape the behavior of their good-natured psychology professor. Using eye contact as a reinforcer, the students trained this professor to lecture from a certain corner of the room. Whenever he moved in that direction, they looked up at him; otherwise, they looked down. Before long, he was lecturing from the corner of the classroom, not quite realizing that he had been "shaped."

In classical conditioning, repeated presentation of the CS without the US causes the CR to gradually weaken and disappear. Extinction also occurs in operant conditioning. If you return your newly shaped rat to the Skinner box but disconnect the feeder from the response bar, you'll find that after the rat presses the bar some number of times without reinforcement, the behavior will fade and become extinguished. By the same token, people stop smiling at those who don't smile back, stop helping those who never reciprocate, and stop working when their efforts meet with continued failure.

**Schedules of Reinforcement**   Every now and then, scientists stumble into their greatest discoveries. Pavlov was a classic example. So was Skinner. Early in his research career, Skinner would reinforce his animals on a continuous basis: Every bar press produced a food pellet. Then something happened. At the time, Skinner had to make his own pellets by squeezing food paste through a pill machine and then waiting for them to dry. The process was time consuming. "One pleasant

Saturday afternoon," Skinner recalled, "I surveyed my supply of dry pellets and, appealing to certain elemental theorems in arithmetic, deduced that unless I spent the rest of the afternoon and evening at the pill machine, the supply would be exhausted by 10:30 Monday morning" (Koch, 1959, p. 368). Not wanting to spend the weekend in the lab, Skinner rationalized to himself that not *every* response had to be reinforced. He adjusted his apparatus so that the bar-press response would be reinforced on a partial basis—only once per minute. Upon his return the next week, however, he found rolls of graph paper with response patterns that were different from anything he had seen before. From this experience, Skinner came to appreciate the powerful effects of "partial reinforcement." Indeed, he and others went on to identify four schedules of reinforcement (see Figure 5.13), each having different effects on behavior (Ferster & Skinner, 1957).

**Fixed-Interval (FI) Schedule**   In the situation just described, reinforcement followed the first response made after a fixed interval of *time* had elapsed. In an FI-1 schedule, the response produces food after each new minute; or it may be made available only after every two (FI-2), ten (FI-10), or fifteen (FI-15) minutes. The schedule is fixed by time, and it tends to produce a slow, "scalloped" response pattern. After

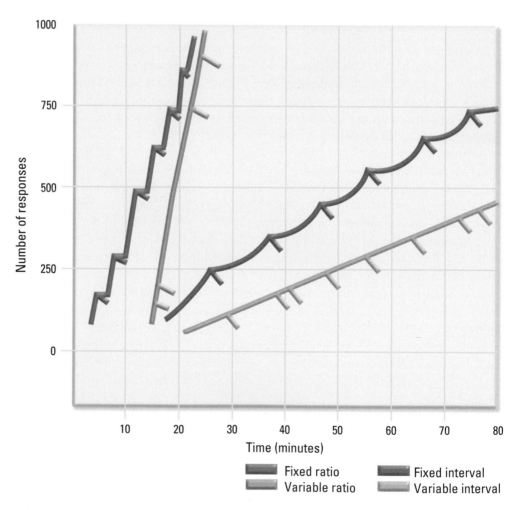

FIGURE 5.13   **Schedules of reinforcement**
These curves show the response patterns typically produced by different schedules of reinforcement. The steeper the curve, the higher the response rate (the slash marks on each curve indicate the delivery of a reinforcement). As you can see, the rate of responding is higher under ratio than interval schedules.

the animal learns that a certain amount of time must elapse, it pauses after each reinforcer and then responds at an accelerating rate until it nears the end of the cycle—which signals that the next reinforcement is available. The student whose rate of studying starts slow, increases before midterms, trails off after midterms, and picks up again before finals illustrates this reaction to an FI schedule.

**Variable-Interval (VI) Schedule**   Once animals learn what the fixed pattern is, they press the bar only as they near the end of each interval. To counter this lazy response pattern, Skinner tried varying the interval around an average. In other words, an interval may average one minute in length (a VI-1 schedule), but the actual timing of a reinforcement is unpredictable from one interval to the next—say, after fifty seconds, then two minutes, ten seconds, and one minute. The result is a slow but steady, not scalloped, pattern of responses. In effect, teachers who give pop quizzes are using a VI schedule to ensure that their students keep up with the reading rather than cram at the last minute.

**Fixed-Ratio (FR) Schedule**   In this situation, a reinforcer is administered after a fixed number of *responses*—say, every third response, or every fifth, tenth, or fiftieth. In an FR-10 schedule, it takes ten bar presses to get food. If thirty responses are needed, it is an FR-30 schedule. The response-to-reinforcement ratio thus remains constant. In a Skinner box, animals on an FR schedule exhibit a burst of bar presses until the food appears, pause briefly, then produce another burst. The result is a fast, steplike response pattern. Frequent-flier programs, where you can earn a free flight after 25,000 miles of air travel, CD clubs that offer a free CD after every fifth purchase, and the employer who pays workers after they produce a certain number of products, all operate on a fixed-ratio schedule.

**Variable-Ratio (VR) Schedule**   In this situation, the reinforcement appears after some average number of responses is made—a number that varies randomly from one reinforcement to the next. On a VR-15 schedule, a rat would have to press the bar an average of fifteen times, but the food may appear on the fifth response, then on the twentieth, fourteenth, twenty-first response, and so on. Unable to predict which response will produce a food pellet, animals on a VR schedule respond at a constant high rate. In one case, Skinner trained pigeons to peck a disk ten thousand times for a single food pellet! Slot machines and lotteries are rigged to pay off on a VR schedule, leading gamblers to deposit coins and purchase tickets at a furious, addictive pace. If you ever tried to call by phone or over the Internet for tickets to a hot concert or sports event only to receive a busy signal, chances are you too kept trying with dogged persistence. The reason: When it comes to getting through, our efforts are reinforced, as with slot machines, on a variable-ratio schedule.

Reinforcement schedules affect extinction rates as well as learning. Specifically, the operant response is more enduring and, later, more resistant to extinction when the organism is reinforced on a partial basis rather than on a continuous, 100 percent schedule. This phenomenon is called the **partial-reinforcement effect.** The rat that is fed after every bar press is quick to realize once the feeder is disconnected that the contingency has changed. But the rat that is fed on only an occasional basis persists more before realizing that reinforcement is no longer forthcoming. If you drop coins into a Coke machine and do not get the drink you ordered, you walk away. Because vending machines are supposed to operate on a continuous-reinforcement basis, it would be quickly apparent that this one is out of order. Deposit coins into a broken slot machine, however, and you may go on to lose hundreds more. After all, you expect slot machines to pay off on an irregular basis. The partial-reinforcement effect has some ironic implications. For example, parents who sometimes give in to a

*B. F. Skinner was born in 1904 and received his psychology degree from Harvard in 1931. He published his first paper in 1930, his last in 1990. He wrote nineteen books and hundreds of journal articles.*

*On August 10, 1990, B. F. Skinner made his final public appearance in Boston (as shown in this photograph)—at the APA's convention. He was there to receive an award for Outstanding Lifetime Contribution to Psychology. I was there—and so, it seemed, was everyone else I knew. Upon his introduction, Skinner was greeted with a thunderous standing ovation. Everyone in the audience knew they were watching a living legend. They also knew he was dying. The talk itself was vintage Skinner. For twenty minutes, he insisted, as always, that psychology could never be a science of the mind, only a science of behavior.*

*On August 17, 1990, one week after his Boston appearance, Skinner completed his last article, for the* American Psychologist. *He died the next day.*

**partial-reinforcement effect**   The tendency for a schedule of partial reinforcement to strengthen later resistance to extinction.

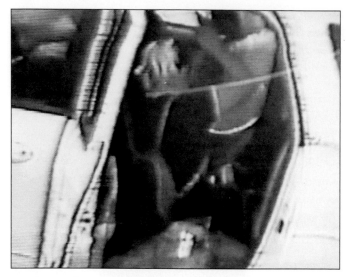

On September 13, 2002, Madeline Toogood was caught beating her misbehaving daughter by a parking lot security camera. Although some parents use corporal punishment to discipline their children, research suggests that it can have harmful long-term effects.

child's temper tantrums and at other times try to tough it out create "little monsters" with more tenacious, harder-to-eliminate outbursts than do parents who always (or never) give in.

**Punishment** In 1948, Skinner wrote *Walden Two*, a novel about a fictional society in which socially adaptive behaviors were maintained by various schedules of reinforcement. The book was a blueprint for the use of "behavioral engineering" to design a happy, healthy, and productive community. Skinner never hesitated to preach the use of reinforcement. Yet he just as adamantly opposed the use of punishment, even though it is a common form of behavior control. Think about it. Parents scold their children, police officers fine motorists for speeding, referees penalize athletes for committing fouls, and employers fire workers who are lazy. So what's the problem? Aren't these forms of punishment effective?

Research shows that punishment has mixed effects (Axelrod & Apsche, 1983). When it's strong, immediate, consistent, and inescapable, punishment does suppress unwanted behaviors. Shock a rat for pressing the response bar and it will quickly stop making the response. Yell, "No!" at the top of your lungs to a child playing with matches, and it is unlikely to happen again. Clearly, punishment can be an effective deterrent. In a research article entitled "Taking the sting out of the whip," Rebecca Bennett (1998) had 263 college students play the role of a corporate executive faced with an ethical dilemma. Those who selected an unethical path in order to maximize profits were then assessed a large or small fine and told that a competitor who had made the same choice was or was not similarly fined. Indicating the benefits of punishment, Bennett found that the large fine deterred subjects from later making another unethical choice. She also found that when the fine was even-handedly administered, the subjects did not become resentful, angry, or aggressive.

While potentially effective, punishment can have unwanted side effects. There are four specific problems in this regard. First, a behavior that is met with punishment may be temporarily inhibited or hidden from the punishing agent—but it is not necessarily extinguished. The child who lights matches and the teenager who smokes cigarettes may both continue to do so at school, at a friend's house, or at home when the parent is at work. Second, even when punishment does suppress an unwanted behavior, it does not always replace that behavior with one that is more adaptive. It's okay to lock up the convicted criminal, but to change his or her future behavior, some form of rehabilitation program is necessary. Third, punishment can sometimes backfire because a stimulus thought to be aversive may, in fact, prove rewarding. The neglected child who acts up and is scolded by busy parents may actually "enjoy" the attention and make trouble again in the future. Fourth, punishment can arouse fear, anger, frustration, and other negative emotions—leading the person to strike back, retaliate, tune out, or run away.

A particularly contentious debate concerns the use of *corporal punishment* by parents who use spanking to discipline their children. Defined as the use of reasonable physical force, which causes a child pain but not injury, corporal punishment is more common in some parts of the world than others. Some countries prohibit corporal punishment by law; yet most American parents support it. So, what are the effects? Elizabeth Gershoff (2002) meta-analyzed 88 studies spanning 62 years and involving 36,309 children whose parents varied in their use of corporal punishment. Overall, she found that children who were spanked were more likely to stop

"Your father and I have come to believe that incarceration is sometimes the only appropriate punishment."

misbehaving immediately afterward. However, they also had poorer relationships with their parents, were more aggressive and more antisocial, and were more likely as adults to have psychological problems and abuse their own spouses and children. These results echo what some psychologists have said for years about the role of spanking in the cycle of domestic violence (Straus & Donnelly, 2000). Still, critics of the study are quick to note that the correlations do not prove that spanking itself *causes* the negative effects, that spanking is too often accompanied by abusive parenting, and that the results do not speak to the effects of nonphysical forms of punishment (Baumrind et al., 2002).

Properly administered, punishment can be used to suppress unwanted behavior. Improperly administered, however, it can also create more problems than it solves. Thus, advised Skinner, it is better to use a combination of reinforcement (to bring out alternative desirable behaviors) and extinction (to extinguish the undesirable behaviors) in order to shape a new, more adaptive way of life.

**Stimulus Control**   In operant conditioning, organisms learn to respond in ways that are reinforced. But there is more to the story. A pigeon trained in a Skinner box learns to peck a key for food, but it may also learn that the response produces reinforcement only in the presence of certain cues. Because reinforcements are often available in some situations but not others, it is adaptive to learn not only *what* response to make but *when* to make it. If pecking a key produces food only when a green disk is lit, a pigeon may learn to discriminate and to respond on a selective basis. The green light is a **discriminative stimulus** that "sets the occasion" for the behavior to be reinforced (Ross & LoLordo, 1987).

When people learn to respond in some situations and not others, their behavior is said to be under "stimulus control." In human terms, this is often important for treating behavioral disorders. Consider the problem of insomnia. Studies show that insomniacs too often use the bed for nonsleeping activities such as watching TV, listening to the radio, reading magazines, and worrying about personal problems. In other words, the bed has become a discriminative stimulus for so many activities that it becomes a source of arousal, not relaxation. To counter this problem, insomniacs are advised, frequently with successful results, to lie in bed only for the purpose of sleeping (Morawetz, 1989).

An operant response may spread from one situation to another through the process of stimulus generalization. As in classical conditioning, the more similar a new stimulus is to the original discriminative stimulus, the more likely it is to trigger the response. In one study, pigeons were reinforced for pecking a key that was illuminated with yellow light. They were then tested with lights of different colors. The more similar the test lights were to the yellow discriminative stimulus—for example, green and orange as opposed to red and blue—the more likely the pigeons were to peck at it (Guttman & Kalish, 1956).

It now appears that even more subtle forms of discrimination are possible. In one clever study, eight pigeons were reinforced with birdseed to peck a key whenever a slide was projected into their cage. Half the pigeons were reinforced for the key press only in the presence of a painting by Monet, the French impressionist. The others were reinforced only in the presence of a painting by Picasso, the Spanish cubist. Showing an ability to both generalize and make fine discriminations, the pigeons in each condition later pecked when shown new paintings by the same artist (stimulus generalization) but not when shown new paintings by the other artist (discrimination). Remarkably, the pigeons even went on to generalize from Monet to other French impressionists, such as Renoir—and from Picasso to other cubists, such as Matisse (Watanabe et al., 1995).

**discriminative stimulus**   A stimulus that signals the availability of reinforcement.

Discrimination and generalization are important aspects of human operant conditioning. From experience, a child may learn that temper tantrums bring results from busy parents but not from teachers, that studying increases grades in social studies but not math, that lewd remarks elicit laughter in the locker room but not in the classroom, and that aggression wins praise on the football field but not in other settings. As adults, we routinely regulate our behavior according to situational cues.

**Self Control**   For many years, psychologists interested in operant behavior have studied the ways in which our life choices—for example, the economic decisions we make—are guided by our learned expectations for reinforcement (Mazur, 1998). In fact, the new and exciting area of *behavioral economics* has emerged in recent years, which brings together various aspects of psychology and economics (Brocas & Carrillo, 2003).

Some psychologists have theorized that people (and animals too, for that matter) make behavioral choices according to how reinforcing these choices have been. Simply put, the more reinforcement received for a particular type of response, relative to others that are possible, the more likely we are to make that response in a future situation (Herrnstein, 1970). This principle suggests that people tend to behave in ways that maximize the value of their own return. This makes sense, but wait. Are people always so rational? Don't we often behave in ways that detract from our own long-term interests—as when we smoke, gamble, drink too much, eat too much, blow the paycheck without saving for tomorrow, and engage in other bad habits? To reconcile the notion that people seek to maximize reinforcements in their lives with the fact that they often behave in ways that are not personally adaptive, researchers have studied self-control—the extent to which people pass up small but immediate rewards in exchange for more valuable future gains (Rachlin, 1995).

*"I am not trying to change people. All I want to do is change the world in which they live."*

—B. F. SKINNER

Research shows that we often do not exhibit self-control, and hence we do not maximize our own gains, because rewards seem less valuable to us when we have to wait to get them than when they are immediately available. What's more, the longer people have to wait for a given reward, the less valuable it seems (Kirby, 1997). Consider this choice: Would you rather have $5 today or $6 in a week? What about $50 today or $75 in six months? When presented with these types of choices, subjects often make the "myopic" (which means near-sighted) decision to select the smaller but immediate reward. As you might expect, some people are more impulsive, or more present-oriented, than others. For example, Kris Kirby and others (1999) presented a series of monetary choices to groups of heroin addicts and found that they discounted the value of the delayed-but-larger sum of money more than college students and others did. Similarly, Suzanne Mitchell (1999) found that smokers are more likely than nonsmokers to choose a smaller but more immediate sum of money.

## PRACTICAL APPLICATIONS OF OPERANT CONDITIONING

From the start, Skinner was interested in the practical, everyday applications of operant conditioning. In World War II, he worked for the U.S. government on a top-secret project in which he shaped pigeons to guide missiles toward enemy ships. Based on this work, the U.S. Navy recently trained dolphins and sea lions to locate explosive mines in the Persian Gulf and perform other dangerous underwater missions (Morrison, 1988). Similarly, the Coast Guard used pigeons to search for people lost at sea. The birds were strapped under the belly of a rescue helicopter and

*By electrically stimulating a pleasure center in the brain for reinforcement, researchers can shape rats to move in various directions. Perhaps some day, remote-controlled rodent will be trained to search through piles of rubble for disaster survivors.*

trained to spot floating orange objects (orange is the international color of life jackets). In response to this stimulus, the birds were conditioned to peck a key that buzzes the pilot (Simmons, 1981). In a provocative new form of operant conditioning, researchers fitted five rats with electrodes and battery-powered backpacks and delivered reinforcement in the form of mild electrical stimulation to a pleasure center in the brain. In this way, they shaped the rats to climb up, and move forward, left, and right. Some day, they speculated, we'll be able to navigate remote-controlled rodents through piles of rubble to search and rescue disaster survivors (Talwar et al., 2002).

Skinner was eager to use operant conditioning in other ways as well, but his efforts were sometimes misunderstood. In 1945, he constructed an "air crib" for his infant daughter, Deborah. This crib, which he called a "baby tender," was a temperature-controlled enclosed space equipped with an air filter, sound-absorbing walls, a stretched canvas floor, a safety glass window with a curtain, and a roll of diapers. The goal was to place the infant in an environment that was comfortable, safe, and stimulating. Skinner tried to market his new invention and wrote about it for *Ladies' Home Journal* in an article he titled "Baby Care Can Be Modernized." Unfortunately, the *Journal* editor changed the title to "Baby in a Box"—which led the public to think that he was experimenting on his daughter the way he did with rats and pigeons. Rumors later spread about his daughter's mental health. For years, many people believed that she had suffered a nervous breakdown and committed suicide. In fact, she is very much alive and well (Bjork, 1997).

*Skinner's daughter in the air crib he invented. Contrary to popular misconceptions, he did not put her in a Skinner box to shape her behavior.*

Over the years, Skinner advised parents to raise children with the use of reinforcement rather than punishment. He also invented a "teaching machine" that would enable students to learn at their own individualized pace by solving a graded series of problems and receiving immediate feedback on their answers. Today, computer-assisted instruction in schools is based on this early work (Benjamin, 1988). In fact, personal computers are now being used just as Skinner had envisioned to train students to type, play the piano, or practice their academic skills. Inspired by Skinner, other behaviorists have applied the principles of operant conditioning to get people to use safety belts, recycle wastes, conserve energy, or simply help themselves (Kazdin, 2001; Lattal & Perone, 1998; Martin & Pear, 1998). (See *How to Condition Yourself to Break a Bad Habit*.)

The use of operant conditioning is now commonplace in the health clinic, the workplace, the classroom, and other settings. For clinical purposes, it laid an important foundation for the techniques of behavior modification, in which reinforcement is used to change maladaptive thoughts, feelings, and behaviors (see Chapter 17). It also forms the basis for biofeedback—an operant procedure in which electronic instruments are used to provide people with continuous information, or "feedback," about their own physiological states. With the aid of electronic sensors to the body and an instrument that amplifies the signals, people can monitor—and then learn to regulate—their own heart rate, blood pressure, and muscular tension. Biofeedback can thus be used in the treatment of migraine headaches, chronic back pain, and other health problems (Schwartz et al., 1999).

Operant conditioning has also been extensively used in the workplace. In a study conducted within a large department store, Fred Luthans and others (1981) observed sales clerks from sixteen departments for a period of four weeks. The employees in half of these departments were then reinforced for productive performance with cash, time off, or a chance to win a company-paid vacation. The other half were not offered added incentives. As shown in Figure 5.14, the two groups were equivalent in their performance during the first phase of the study. In the second phase, however, the reinforced group improved dramatically, even after the

*How To*

# CONDITION YOURSELF TO BREAK A BAD HABIT

Do you need to diet or exercise in order to lose weight? Would you like to stop smoking? Do you have trouble falling asleep at night? Are you painfully shy in groups? Do you spend too much time watching TV? If you answered yes to any of these questions, then you can help yourself with an individualized program of operant conditioning, or "behavior modification." In a "how to" book on using operant conditioning for personal adjustment, David Watson and Roland Tharp (2001) describe series of steps that will help people reach their own behavioral goals:

1. *Identify the target behavior you want to change.* Make sure you define the problem in precise terms ("I eat too much junk" or "I don't exercise enough"), not in terms that are general and hard to pin down ("I am overweight").

2. *Record your baseline.* First, measure your current behavior level to get a baseline. If overeating is the problem, count the number of calories you consume in a seven-day period. If smoking is the problem, write down how many cigarettes you smoke each day. Keep careful written records so you can chart your progress, say on a graph. Also take note of the stimulus conditions in which the problem behavior occurs (where you are, what you're doing, and who you're with) and the effects it has (so you can see how it is being reinforced).

3. *Formulate your plan*
   ■ To increase the frequency of a wanted behavior, use positive reinforcement. The reinforcer can be anything: a day at the mall, a new CD, a long-distance calling card. Make the plan challenging but realistic—for example, "If I run three miles a day for ten days, I earn a trip to the mall." If you are not yet able to make the desired target response, shape your behavior using Skinner's method of successive approximations. If you cannot run a full three miles, for example, start by rewarding yourself for one mile a day for the first week, two miles a day for the next week, and so on, until you reach your goal.

   ■ To extinguish an unwanted behavior, you should either avoid the situations in which the behavior tends to occur or remove the reinforcements that sustain it. If, for example, you tend to overeat while talking on the kitchen telephone or watching TV, it would help to spend less time in these situations. To ensure that you follow through, the punishment should not be too severe.

4. *Implement the plan.* Once you start, keep a log of the frequency of the target behavior. If you see no improvement, reexamine the program (the reinforcer may be too weak, or you may have set goals that are too high or too easy to reach). If you need to boost your commitment, make a behavioral "contract" in front of friends.

5. *Maintain the change.* Once you reach your goal, the key is to stay there. It's better to phase the program out gradually rather than all at once. You can do this by lowering the reinforcement-to-behavior ratio until, eventually, the reinforcement is no longer necessary.

reinforcement period, but the control group did not. Similar effects have been produced in many other work settings.

Finally, operant conditioning is regularly used in the classroom. Skinner's teaching machine was one application, but there are others as well. For example, many teachers establish large-scale reinforcement programs in which children earn gold stars, ribbons, or "tokens" for engaging in desired behaviors—tokens that can be exchanged for toys, extra recess time, and other privileges. Skinner (1988) himself described how a sixth-grade teacher gave her students a card every time they handed in an assignment. The students put their cards into a jar and, at the end of the week, one card was randomly drawn, with the winner receiving a prize, like a portable radio. The result was a dramatic improvement in the number of assignments completed. Another use of operant techniques is "precision teaching." In this approach, the teacher, serving as a coach, organizes material for students and shows them how to measure and chart their progress to receive immediate feedback. Students are thus trained to teach themselves and each other (Lindsley, 1992).

## NEW DEVELOPMENTS IN OPERANT CONDITIONING

Believing that a science of behavior must restrict its focus to observable stimulus–response relationships, Pavlov did not account for aspects of the organism that influenced classical conditioning. In the realm of operant behavior, Skinner took the same narrow view, leaving others to study the impact of inborn biological predispositions and cognitive processes.

**Biological Constraints** Behaviorists used to think that animals and humans alike could be trained to emit any response that they were physically capable of making. We now realize, however, that there are biological limits to what an animal can learn. In 1947, Keller and Marian Breland, former students of Skinner, founded Animal Behavior Enterprises in Hot Springs, Arkansas. The Brelands were in the business of training animals to do tricks in county fairs, zoos, circuses, movies, and TV commercials. Indeed, they trained thousands of animals belonging to thirty-eight different species—including bears, whales, chickens, pigs, goats, and reindeer.

Despite their professional successes, the Brelands had to concede that biological predispositions often interfered with the shaping of a new behavior. At one point, for example, they tried to train a raccoon to pick up a wooden coin and deposit it into a piggy bank. But instead, the raccoon would clutch the coin or rub two coins together, dip them into the container, pull them out, and rub them again—rather than make the deposit that was reinforced with food. The Brelands also sought to train a pig in the same routine, but after a while the pig would drop the coin, push it with its snout, toss it in the air, and drop it again. What was the problem? In an article entitled "The Misbehavior of Organisms," Breland and Breland (1961) concluded that animals revert to species-specific behavior patterns, a powerful tendency they called *instinctive drift*. In the wild, raccoons manipulate food objects and dunk, or "wash," them, and pigs "root" for food in the ground—foraging instincts that inhibit the learning of new operant responses.

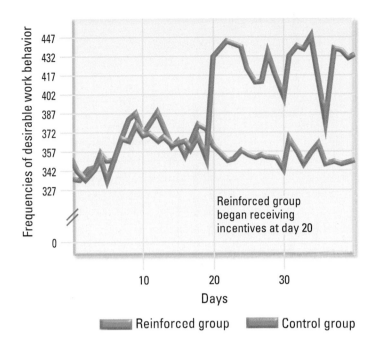

**FIGURE 5.14 Using reinforcement to boost job performance**
As observed in many studies, department-store salesclerks who were offered incentives improved their job performance, whereas those in the control group did not (Luthans et al., 1981).

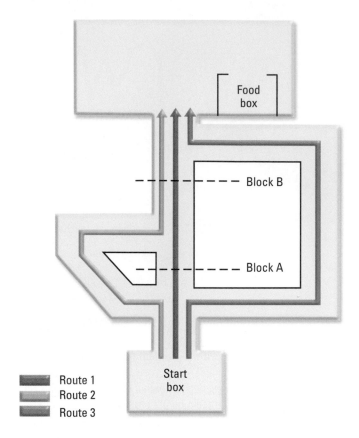

Route 1
Route 2
Route 3

**FIGURE 5.15** **Rats in a maze: evidence for a cognitive map**

Tolman trained rats to run a maze like the one shown here, but he then blocked the most direct routes to the goal box. Operating as if they had a cognitive map, the animals took the best available detours.

**latent learning** Learning that occurs but is not exhibited in performance until there is an incentive to do so.

Biological predispositions may also constrain an animal's ability to learn how to escape from danger. For example, rats are easily conditioned to freeze, run from one place to another, or attack another rat—if these responses are reinforced by the termination of a painful electric shock. Yet they are slow to learn to escape by pressing a lever, a response they easily learn to make for food and water. According to Robert Bolles (1970), an animal's innate defensive reactions compete with the learning of a new escape response. All this serves to remind us that behavior is guided not just by personal experience but also by an organism's evolutionary past. Like classical conditioning, in which some associations are more easily learned than others, operant learning is limited by an organism's own adaptive ways (Gould & Marler, 1987).

**Cognitive Perspectives** Up to the day he died, Skinner (1990) steadfastly refused to speculate about internal mental processes. Although this radical position still has its share of proponents (Poling et al., 1990), most psychologists now believe that it is important to understand internal cognitive processes—not only in humans but in animals as well (Bekoff et al., 2002; Boysen & Himes, 1999).

**Latent Learning** The first prominent theorist to adopt a cognitive position was Edward Tolman. According to Tolman (1948), animals in their natural habitat learn more than just a series of stimulus-and-response connections. They also acquire a "cognitive map," which is a mental spatial model of the layout—and they do so regardless of whether their explorations are reinforced. Thus, when Tolman trained rats to run a maze but then changed the starting place or blocked the most direct routes, the animals behaved as if they were using a street map of their surroundings: They took the best available detours (see Figure 5.15).

To examine whether spatial learning required that the rats be reinforced for their exploratory behavior, Tolman and Honzik (1930) conducted a classic experiment. Once a day for two weeks, they put three groups of rats into a complex maze and measured their speed in reaching the "goal box." One group was rewarded with food and improved considerably over time. A second group was not rewarded and did not improve much over time. From an operant standpoint, neither of these results is surprising. The third group, however, was the key to this experiment. In this group, the rats were not rewarded during the first ten days, but they received food beginning on the eleventh. The result: They showed immediate and dramatic improvement. On the eleventh day, before realizing that there was food in the goal box, they were just as slow as the no-reward group. But on the twelfth day, after one reinforcement, they were just as fast as the group that had been rewarded all along (see Figure 5.16).

This result was significant because it demonstrated what Tolman called **latent learning**, learning that lies dormant and is not exhibited in overt performance until there is an incentive to do so. By making this distinction between "learning" and "performance," Tolman was able to demonstrate that animals learn from experience—with or without reinforcement. More recent research provides additional support for this phenomenon (Keith & McVety, 1988).

**Locus of Control** Strict behaviorists claim that people are controlled by objective reinforcement contingencies. In contrast, a cognitive perspective holds that behavior is influenced more by our subjective interpretations of reinforcement. To illustrate the point, consider two incidents. The first was a demonstration by Skinner (1948) in which he dropped food pellets into a pigeon's cage on a random basis, leading the animal to repeat whatever it happened to be doing at the time. Soon this "superstitious" pigeon was busy turning, hopping on one leg, bowing, scraping, and raising its head. This pigeon—like most humans, says Skinner—was under the illusion that it had control, even though it did not. The second story concerns a young male psychotherapy patient named Karl S. who was depressed because he felt incompetent to find a job, friends, or a woman. E. Jerry Phares (1976), Karl's therapist, tried to raise his expectancy for success through a series of small achievements—applying for a job, striking up a conversation with a woman, and so on. Karl succeeded in these efforts but remained passive and pessimistic. The problem? He did not see the link between his actions and successful outcomes. In contrast to the superstitious pigeon, Karl had control but didn't realize it. So he didn't try.

According to Julian Rotter (1966), reinforcement influences behavior only if we perceive the two as causally connected. For students who believe that studying increases their grades, for workers who think that hard work will be rewarded, and for citizens who believe that they can influence government policy, reinforcement strengthens behavior. But for students who see grades as arbitrarily determined, for workers who think that getting ahead requires more luck than effort, and for citizens who feel that they're at the mercy of powerful leaders, reinforcement does not strengthen behavior. Research shows that people differ in their "generalized expectancies" for personal control and in their responsiveness to reinforcement. Those who have a relatively *internal* locus of control tend to believe that they determine their own destiny. Those with an *external* locus of control believe that luck, fate, and powerful others determine their reinforcements. Compared to externals, internals persist longer at laboratory tasks, get higher grades in school, and play a more active role in political and social affairs (Strickland, 1989; Rotter, 1990).

**Hidden Costs of Reward**    By focusing on how people interpret reinforcement, the cognitive perspective raises a second issue. After someone is rewarded for an enjoyable task, what happens to his or her interest and motivation once that reward is no longer available? Does reinforcement enhance motivation or detract from it? We'll address this issue in Chapter 11 when we discuss worker motivation. But for now, let's consider the implications for education, a topic close to Skinner's heart.

In a study conducted at a preschool, Mark Lepper and his colleagues (1973) gave children a chance to play with colorful felt-tipped markers—a chance most could not resist. By observing how much time the children spent on the activity, the researchers were able to measure their initial level of interest in it. Two weeks later, the children were randomly divided into three groups. In one, they were simply asked if they would draw some pictures with the markers. In the second, they were told that if they used the markers they would

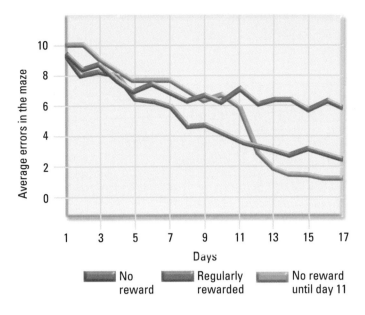

**FIGURE 5.16    Latent learning**
Tolman and Honzik (1930) put rats into a maze and measured how quickly they reached the goal box. Those rewarded with food improved; those without reward did not. A third group received no food until the eleventh day. Note that the rats in this last group showed a marked improvement from the eleventh day (before they knew there was food in the goal box) to the twelfth (after the first reward). These animals had exhibited latent learning, learning without reinforcement.

*"Behavioral psychology is the science of pulling habits out of rats."*

—DOUGLAS BUSCH

"It's over Clarissa. Our relationship Just had too many hidden costs."

## REVIEW QUESTIONS

- *How is operant conditioning different from classical conditioning?*

- *Distinguish between reinforcement and punishment. How do they influence conditioning?*

- *Describe the process of shaping.*

- *What are the four schedules of reinforcement proposed by Skinner? Why is a partial-reinforcement schedule more effective than a continuous schedule?*

- *Describe some practical applications of operant conditioning.*

- *How can biological influences limit the effectiveness of operant conditioning?*

- *What are some examples of the ways in which cognitive processes are important to operant conditioning?*

*"Children have never been very good at listening to their elders, but they have never failed to imitate them."*

—JAMES BALDWIN

receive a "Good Player Award," a certificate with a gold star and a red ribbon. In the third group, the children were not offered a reward for drawing pictures, but then—like those in the second group—they received a reward when they were finished.

About a week later, the teachers placed the markers and paper on a table in the classroom while the experimenters hid behind a one-way mirror. This time, without a hint of reward, the amount of free time the children spent playing with the markers was once again recorded. Children who had previously drawn pictures for the promise of a reward were now less interested in the markers. Yet children who were not rewarded or had received a surprise reward (so they did not feel as if they had played with the markers in order to get it) were not adversely affected. In follow-up research, Teresa Amabile (1996) found that people who are offered payment for drawing pictures, writing poems, making paper collages, and coming up with solutions to business problems also tend to produce less creative work.

This hidden cost of reward can have serious implications in the classroom. Take a child who loves to read and a teacher who awards gold stars for books completed. During the year, the child continues to read at a lively pace. But what will happen later on, when there are no gold stars? Will the child then begin to wonder if it is still worth the effort? And does this mean that reinforcement should never be used? No, not at all. If a child does not engage in the wanted behavior to start with, offering a reward can help. For the child who doesn't normally read, gold stars provide a necessary incentive in much the same way food pellets increase bar pressing in the Skinner box. Also, reward can be used to send different messages. When presented as a bonus (for superior performance) rather than as a bribe (for just doing it), reward will enhance rather than diminish a child's future motivation (Eisenberger & Cameron, 1996; Eisenberger & Rhoades, 2001). The same is true of praise, a form of verbal reinforcement. When people are praised for their work, and see that praise as sincere, they become increasingly motivated (Henderlong & Lepper, 2002).

To summarize, the lessons of a cognitive perspective are clear: People do not mindlessly repeat behaviors that happen to be followed by reinforcement but instead are influenced by their perceptions, beliefs, and expectations.

## OBSERVATIONAL LEARNING

- *Is learning by imitation a uniquely human form of learning?*
- *What kinds of behaviors are learned by observation, and what is the process like?*

Classical and operant conditioning are two ways in which organisms adapt and learn from experience. But something is missing. Forget the dogs, cats, rats, and pigeons that drool, press bars, peck keys, jump from shocks, and run mazes. What about the human learning of complex behavior? Don't we sometimes learn without direct experience? Think about the first time you danced, drove a car, or programmed a VCR. Now imagine how slow and inefficient you would have been if those skills had to be acquired from scratch—"shaped," as Skinner would say, through trial and error.

Complex new behaviors can also be learned by watching and imitating others. This form of learning occurs not only among humans but also in many types of animals (Heyes & Galef, 1996). In one experiment, for example, golden hamster pups were put in a cage with their mothers. Some of the mothers, but not others, had been specifically pretrained to use their teeth and front paws to get sunflower seeds that dangled from a chain. The question was whether the young hamster pups would learn to do the same just by watching—and the answer was *yes*. Although fewer than 20 percent were able to retrieve seeds in the presence of the untrained mother, that number was up to 73 percent in the trained-mother group (Previde & Poli, 1996). In a second experiment, naive pigeons watched through a window others of their species who were trained to get food from a feeder either by stepping on a bar or by pecking at it. When later given access to the same bar and feeder, the pigeons were more likely to use the technique they had previously seen used (Zentall et al., 1996). There is even evidence to suggest that "cultures" are transmitted through imitation in groups of whales and dolphins—as when humpback whales off the coast of Maine devised "lobtail feeding," a technique in which they slam their tail flukes onto the water, then dive and exhale, forming clouds of bubbles that envelope schools of prey fish. This behavior was first observed in 1981; by 1989 it was adopted by 50 percent of the whale population in that area (Rendell & Whitehead, 2001).

Human infants also exhibit rudimentary forms of imitation (Bremner, 2002). Research shows that they copy adults who stick out their tongues (Meltzoff & Moore, 1977; Anisfeld, 1991); use a certain hand to reach, point, wave, and make other gestures (Harkins & Uzgiris, 1991); or utter sounds such as *meh* and *bee* (Poulson et al., 1991). Similarly, toddlers imitate others of their own age grasping, pulling, pushing, and poking at various toys (Hanna & Meltzoff, 1993). It is clear that imitation is adaptive: By observing their peers and elders, young members of a species learn to interact and develop the skills of past generations.

## STUDIES OF MODELING

According to Albert Bandura (1986), people learn by watching others. These others are called models and the process is known as **observational learning**. In a classic experiment to demonstrate the point, nursery-school children were exposed to a live adult model who behaved aggressively (Bandura et al., 1961). In a typical session, the child would be sitting quietly, drawing a picture. From another part of the room, an adult approached a Bobo doll, an inflatable clownlike toy that is weighted on the bottom so that it pops back up whenever it is knocked down. For ten minutes, the adult repeatedly abused the doll—sitting on it, pounding it with a hammer, kicking it, throwing balls at it, and yelling, "Sock him in the nose! Kick him!"

After the outburst, the child was taken to a room filled with attractive toys but told that these toys were being saved "for the other children." Frustrated, the child was then taken to a third room containing additional toys, including—you guessed it—a Bobo doll. At that point, the child was left alone and observed through a one-way mirror. What happened? Compared to children exposed to a nonviolent model or to no model at all, those who had witnessed the aggressive display were far more likely to assault the doll. In fact, they often copied the model's attack, action for action, and repeated the same abusive remarks, word for word. The children had acquired a whole new repertoire of aggressive behavior. More recent research confirms the point: Among children and adolescents, exposure to aggressive models on TV and in the movies triggers aggression—not just in the laboratory but in the classroom, the playground, and other settings (Wood et al., 1991; Geen, 1998).

Observational learning can also have beneficial effects. In one study, snake phobics gained the courage to approach a live snake by first watching someone else do so—which is why models are often used in the treatment of phobias (Bandura et al., 1969). In a second study, bystanders were more likely to help a stranded

*Animals as well as humans learn by observation. In early morning, the English titmouse breaks into containers of milk delivered to the porches of many homes in England and skims the cream from the top. This clever behavior has been passed by observation from one generation to the next.*

 **5.3**

**observational learning**   Learning that takes place when one observes and models the behavior of others.

motorist or donate money to charity, two acts of generosity, if they had earlier observed someone else do the same (Bryan & Test, 1967). In a third study, young adolescents learned by watching others how to sharpen their argumentative writing skills—particularly when they observed models who were similarly strong or weak in their skill level (Braaksma et al., 2002).

## THE PROCESS OF MODELING

According to Bandura (1977, 1986), observational learning is not a simple, automatic, reflexlike reaction to models. Rather, it consists of two stages: acquisition and performance. You may recall that Edward Tolman had earlier made this distinction by noting that a newly acquired response often remains "latent" until the organism is motivated to perform it. Building on Tolman's work, Bandura described observational learning as a chain of events that involves four steps: attention, retention, reproduction, and motivation.

- **Attention.** To learn by observation, one must pay attention to the model's behavior and to the consequences of that behavior. Due to their ability to command our attention, parents, teachers, political leaders, and TV celebrities are potentially effective models.

- **Retention.** In order to model someone else's behavior minutes, days, weeks, months, or even years later, one must recall what was observed. Accordingly, modeling is likely to occur when the behavior is memorable or when the observer thinks about or rehearses the behavior.

- **Reproduction.** Attention and memory are necessary conditions, but observers must also have the motor ability to reproduce the modeled behavior. As closely as I watch, and as hard as I try, I will never be able to copy Michael Jordan's graceful flight to the basket.

- **Motivation.** People may pay attention to a model, recall the behavior, and have the ability to reproduce it—all laying a necessary foundation for modeling. Whether an observer takes action, however, is determined by his or her expectations for reinforcement—expectations that are based not only on personal experience but also on the experiences of others. This last point is important because it illustrates "vicarious" reinforcement: that people are more likely to imitate models who are rewarded for their behavior and less likely to imitate those who are punished. Apparently, learning can occur without direct, firsthand experience.

## REVIEW QUESTIONS

- *What is observational learning?*

- *Identify the two stages of observational learning proposed by Bandura.*

- *What four steps are involved in the process of observational learning?*

# THINKING LIKE A PSYCHOLOGIST ABOUT LEARNING

For about a century now, psychologists have studied with remarkable intensity the basic laws of classical conditioning, operant conditioning, and observational learning. To a large extent, the knowledge gained from this research has had far-reaching implications for a wide range of animal and human behaviors. Inspired by Pavlov and Skinner, the psychology of learning is grounded in hard-nosed S–R behaviorism. Today, however, a vast majority of researchers recognize that biological dispositions, cognitive processes, and other factors residing within the person play a critical role. Thus, we now know that all organisms are genetically prepared to learn some associations more easily than others, that beliefs about reinforcement can have a greater impact on behavior than the reinforcement itself, and that learning is also achieved by observing others.

In upcoming chapters, we'll see that many learning psychologists today are systematically exploring the inner workings of the human mind. Some are exploring the ways in which we can bolster our body's immune systems through classical-conditioning procedures (Ader et al., 1991). Others are newly focused on how learning experiences can alter the neural connections in the brain (Rosenzweig, 1996; Kolb & Whishaw, 1998). Clearly, there is great interest in the "O" part of S-O-R psychology. Learning theorists are also studying the acquisition of complex human skills—such as how we learn to read, speak, understand stories, solve math problems, recognize music, play chess, use computers, and drive cars (Holding, 1989). And they're interested in the way people learn complex material without really trying—through the kinds of unconscious or "implicit" processes described at the start of this chapter (Reber, 1993; Kirsner et al., 1998). Finally, as we'll see, there's great interest in applications of learning theory to child development, instructional issues, education, and the acquisition of knowledge (Glaser, 1990).

# SUMMARY

As in the case of the stickleback, ethologists have found that many aspects of animal behavior are programmed by inborn **fixed action patterns**. In contrast, human beings adapt primarily through **learning**, a relatively permanent change in knowledge or behavior that comes from experience. The simplest form of learning, found in lower organisms, is **habituation**, the tendency for an organism to become familiar with a stimulus as a result of repeated exposure.

## CLASSICAL CONDITIONING

The key to learning is association, a tendency to connect events that occur together in space or time.

### PAVLOV'S DISCOVERY

Studying the digestive system in dogs, Pavlov stumbled upon **classical conditioning**. In his experiments, the salivary reflex was the **unconditioned response (UR)**, and it was elicited by food, an **unconditioned stimulus (US)**. Through pairing of a bell with the food, the bell became a **conditioned stimulus (CS)** that on its own could elicit salivation, a **conditioned response (CR)**. This experiment serves as a model of classical conditioning in humans.

### BASIC PRINCIPLES

After Pavlov's initial experiment, he and others discovered four basic principles of learning: (1) the **acquisition** of a CR is influenced by the order and timing of the CS–US pairing; (2) in **extinction**, repeated presentation of the CS without the US causes the CR to lose its power, though there is an occasional rebound effect known as **spontaneous recovery**; (3) after an organism is conditioned to a CS, similar stimuli will often evoke the CR through **stimulus generalization**; and (4) **discrimination** is the opposite process, one of learning to distinguish between stimuli.

### PAVLOV'S LEGACY

As demonstrated by taste-aversion studies, research shows that animals are biologically prepared to learn some associations more easily than others. The process involves learning that one event (CS) predicts another event (US). There are many applications of classical conditioning. For example, people can be conditioned to develop fears or preferences and positive or negative social attitudes. Recent studies show that the body's immune cells can be classically conditioned as well.

## OPERANT CONDITIONING

The learning of voluntary, complex, goal-directed behaviors is achieved by a different form of learning, one that involves the link between an action and its consequences.

### THE LAW OF EFFECT

Using animals, Thorndike studied the **law of effect**: that actions followed by a positive outcome are repeated, whereas those followed by a negative outcome or no outcome are not.

### THE PRINCIPLES OF REINFORCEMENT

By testing animals in a controlled environment called a **Skinner box**, Skinner systematically examined **operant conditioning**, the process by which we learn to behave in ways that produce reinforcement. A **reinforcement** is any stimulus that strengthens a prior response. There are two types of reinforcers: positive (the presentation of a desirable stimulus) and negative (the withdrawal of an aversive stimulus). In contrast, **punishment** has the opposite effect of weakening, not strengthening, a prior response. Punishers may be positive (presentation of an aversive stimulus) or negative (withdrawal of a desirable stimulus).

Skinner found that complex new behaviors can be **shaped** through reinforcement of successive responses that come closer and closer to the target behavior. Skinner discovered the **partial-reinforcement effect,** that partial reinforcement increases resistance to extinction. He and others went on to identify four types of reinforcement schedules (fixed interval, variable interval, fixed ratio, variable ratio), each having different effects on learning and extinction. In addition, animals can be trained to respond only in the presence of a **discriminative stimulus** that signals the availability of reinforcement. Although punishment can often be used to suppress unwanted behavior, it has unwanted side effects and should be used cautiously. As in classical conditioning, generalization and discrimination are key aspects of operant learning. In addition, research shows that people tend to behave in ways that maximize their reinforcements—but they often prefer small immediate rewards over those that are larger but delayed, a problem of self-control.

## PRACTICAL APPLICATIONS OF OPERANT CONDITIONING

Skinner was interested in practical applications. Following in his footsteps, many behaviorists use the principles of operant conditioning to solve practical problems in clinical settings, the workplace, and the classroom.

## NEW DEVELOPMENTS IN OPERANT CONDITIONING

Although operant conditioning is broadly applicable, animal studies have shown that species-specific biological dispositions often interfere with the shaping of a new behavior. And although Skinner refused to speculate about mental processes, others have not. Thus, researchers have found that animals exhibit **latent learning** (learning without reinforcement), that people are more influenced by the perception of control over reinforcement than by objective contingencies, and that rewards sometimes undermine our intrinsic motivation.

## OBSERVATIONAL LEARNING

Complex new behaviors are often learned not through direct experience but through the observation and imitation of others.

## STUDIES OF MODELING

According to Bandura, we learn by watching others. These others are called models, and the process is called **observational learning.** Studies indicate that both desirable (helping) and undesirable (aggressive) behaviors may be learned in this manner.

## THE PROCESS OF MODELING

Observational learning involves not simple, reflexlike imitation but a four-step process that requires attention, retention, reproduction, and motivation. Through a process of vicarious reinforcement, people are most likely to imitate models who are rewarded for their behavior.

---

## KEY TERMS

| | | |
|---|---|---|
| ethologist (**p. 178**) | conditioned response (CR) (**p. 182**) | operant conditioning (**p. 193**) |
| fixed action patterns (**p. 178**) | acquisition (**p. 183**) | reinforcement (**p. 193**) |
| learning (**p. 179**) | extinction (**p. 184**) | punishment (**p. 194**) |
| habituation (**p. 179**) | spontaneous recovery (**p. 184**) | shaping (**p. 194**) |
| classical conditioning (**p. 181**) | stimulus generalization (**p. 184**) | partial-reinforcement effect (**p. 197**) |
| unconditioned response (UR) (**p. 181**) | discrimination (**p. 184**) | discriminative stimulus (**p. 199**) |
| unconditioned stimulus (US) (**p. 181**) | law of effect (**p. 192**) | latent learning (**p. 204**) |
| conditioned stimulus (CS) (**p. 182**) | Skinner box (**p. 193**) | observational learning (**p. 207**) |

# THINKING CRITICALLY ABOUT LEARNING

1. There has been some public discussion about lengthening jail sentences for certain types of criminal offenses. Given the evidence on the effectiveness of punishment as a means of behavior change, do you think this is a good idea? Why or why not? Can you offer any alternative strategies that would reduce criminal behavior?

2. In Anthony Burgess's novel, *A Clockwork Orange,* the main protagonist (Alex), a sadistic young man, was classically conditioned to become horribly ill at the sight of violence. During the conditioning sessions, a chemical substance that induced severe nausea was injected into his bloodstream as he was forced to view violent films. Identify the conditioned and unconditioned stimuli and responses involved in these conditioning sessions. Following the conditioning, Alex also became sick whenever he heard classical music, which had inadvertently accompanied the films. What learning principle can explain this outcome? Classical music had previously been Alex's favorite. If you wanted to restore his ability to enjoy his favorite music, how would you go about it?

3. A child has developed a fear of dogs. Suggest three different strategies—one based on classical conditioning, one based on operant conditioning, and one based on observational learning—that could help eliminate this fear. Which do you think would be most effective and long lasting? Why?

4. Research discussed in this chapter suggests that it is possible to classically condition immune system responses. What are the implications of this research for the treatment of disease? How might medical practitioners actually make use of this research in treating patients?

5. Would you expect there to be any cultural differences with respect to locus of control? If so, what factors might contribute to such differences?

6. I have often heard parents tell their children, "Do as I say, not as I do." How likely are children to heed such advice? Why?

# CAN A MEMORY BE CREATED?

## THE SITUATION

You sign up for a study of memory, and when you appear for the session, the experimenter says that you'll hear several lists of words over a tape recorder. Listen carefully. After each list, you will hear either a tone or a knocking sound to signal whether you should spend the next two minutes writing down the words in that list or working on some arithmetic problems. After the first list, you'll hear a second list, a third list, and so on, until you're finished. You have no questions, so the session begins.

The experimenter turns on the tape recorder and you hear a male voice reciting a word every 1.5 seconds. Try it: *bed, rest, awake, tired, dream, wake, night, blanket, doze, slumber, snore, pillow, peace, yawn, drowsy*. Got it? Now look away, take out a sheet of paper, and take two minutes to write down as many of these words as you can. Okay, time's up. Here's the next list: *note, sound, piano, sing, radio, band, melody, horn, concert, instrument, jazz, symphony, orchestra, art, rhythm*. Again, try to recall as many words as you can.

After completing all the lists, you are told that your ability to recognize the original words will now be tested. You'll receive a set of ninety-six words, some of which appeared earlier. For each word, you should indicate whether it is *new* (never presented before) or *old* (presented earlier on tape). Next, for each word you recognize as old, you're asked: Are you sure you vividly recall hearing the speaker say that word on tape? Try it. Cover the last paragraph and circle each of the following words that you recognize from before: *tooth, beach, sleep, art, traffic, pillow, kitten, music*.

As a participant in this experiment, you know that some of the test items are new, others old. What you don't know is that some of the new items were meaningfully related to words that did appear in the original lists. The experimenters referred to these as "lures." The question is, how easy was it to tell the difference?

## MAKE A PREDICTION

Think about the recognition test. Participants were reshown some of the same words they had seen just minutes earlier. So how well could they recognize these items? And will they ever "remember" hearing the lure words *not* on the list? To get you started, the percentage of old items correctly seen as old is presented below. As you can see, participants recognized 79 percent of these words—57 percent of which they were absolutely sure about. Using these numbers as a guideline and the table below, predict how often (0–100 percent) the participants falsely recognized and were sure about the lures that were never actually presented.

| RECOGNIZE? | OLD WORDS | NEW "LURES" |
|---|---|---|
| Yes | 79% | ____ % |
| Sure | 57% | ____ % |

## THE RESULTS

In this study, Henry Roediger and Kathleen McDermott (1995) were curious to see whether they could get people to create "false memories" of words not previously heard. So what did you predict? How often did participants "recognize" lure words compared to the percentage of old items correctly and confidently recognized? The results were striking. As shown below, participants could not tell the difference between words that were on the list and those that were not.

| RECOGNIZE? | OLD WORDS | NEW "LURES" |
|---|---|---|
| Yes | 79% | 81% |
| Sure | 57% | 58% |

## WHAT DOES IT ALL MEAN?

To appreciate what happened in this experiment, take another look at the test materials and your own responses. After hearing sleep-related words such as *bed* and *yawn* and music-related words such as *jazz* and *instrument,* didn't you think that you had also heard *sleep* and *music*—words that fit but were not actually on the list? Most people do. I was at a conference a few years ago where Henry Roediger, in a talk he titled "Creating False Memories in the Classroom," reproduced this result with an audience of psychology professors, including myself. Many other researchers have obtained this same result.

Psychologists liken human memory to a computer that faithfully records information for later use. This study reveals, however, that there is much more to the story. As we'll see in this chapter, remembering is an active process, and we sometimes *construct* memories in light of our own beliefs, wishes, needs, contextual factors, and information received from outside sources.

On November 22, 1963, thousands of Dallas residents watched one of the most tragic events in modern American history: the assassination of President John F. Kennedy. What happened? Some witnesses said they saw a lone gunman in the sixth-floor window of a nearby building. Others recalled the presence of two or three men in the same window. Still others insisted that they saw someone shooting from a grassy knoll. To add to the confusion, some witnesses recalled hearing three shots fired; others swore they heard five or six. To this day, no one is certain of what actually occurred.

The disputes over this historic trauma raise an important question: Can remembrances of the past be trusted? Human memory is often the subject of controversy. Sometimes we seem able to recall a face, a voice, the contents of a lecture, a foreign language, a news event, a first date, the birth of a child, or the death of a loved one with precision and certainty. Yet at other times, memory is limited, flawed, and biased—as when we forget a phone number we just looked up, the items on the grocery list we left at home, coursework from last semester, or the name of someone we recently met. How are experiences stored in the brain and then later retrieved? What causes us to preserve some events but not others? How accurate are our recollections of the past? To answer these questions, cognitive psychologists study **memory,** the process by which information is retained for later use (Baddeley, 1999; Schacter, 2001).

**memory**   The process by which information is retained for later use.

*After the 1963 assassination of John F. Kennedy, many eyewitnesses came forward. Some reported seeing one gunman in a sixth-floor window of a nearby building; others recalled two or three gunmen in the same building; still others thought the shots were fired from the ground. Such are the pitfalls of eyewitness memory.*

## AN INFORMATION-PROCESSING MODEL

 **6.1**

- *In what ways can human memory be likened to the working of a computer?*
- *What are the differences among sensory, short-term, and long-term memory?*

Aristotle and Plato likened memory to the stamping of an impression into a block of wax. Others, more recently, have compared memory to a switchboard, storage box, workbench, library, layered stack, and tape recorder. Today, cognitive psychologists like to compare the human mind to a computer and memory to an information-processing system. If you've worked on a computer, you will appreciate the analogy. Your PC *receives* input from a keyboard or mouse; it *converts* the symbols into a special numeric code; it *saves* the information on a hard drive, CD, or disk; it then *retrieves* the data from the disk to be displayed on a screen or sends it to a printer. If the computer crashes, if there's not enough space on the disk, if the file was deleted, or if you enter the wrong retrieval command, the information becomes inaccessible, or "forgotten."

Using the computer as a model, memory researchers seek to trace the flow of information as it is mentally processed. In this **information-processing model**, a stimulus that registers on our senses can be remembered only if it (1) *draws attention*, which brings it into consciousness; (2) *is encoded*, or transferred to *storage* sites in the brain; and (3) *is retrieved* for use at a later time (Atkinson & Shiffrin, 1968).

**information-processing model** A model of memory in which information must pass through discrete stages via the processes of attention, encoding, storage, and retrieval.

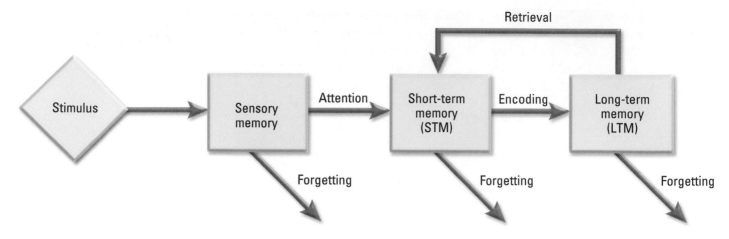

**FIGURE 6.1 An information-processing model of memory**
Many events register in sensory memory. Those that are noticed are briefly stored in short-term memory; those that are encoded are transferred to a more permanent facility. As shown, forgetting may be caused by failures of attention, encoding, or retrieval.

*In this collage, entitled* The Color of Memory, *artist Richard Schaffer portrays his view of using the computer (left) as a model of human memory (right). Interpreting this artwork, psychologist Daniel Schacter (1996) states: "Schaffer's piece suggests—and I strongly concur—that the computer is a retriever of information but not a rememberer of experiences" (p. 37). ("Color of Memory" watercolor collage by Richard E. Schaffer. Photo courtesy of Daniel L. Schacter collection.)*

**sensory memory** A memory storage system that records information from the senses for up to three seconds.

**short-term memory (STM)** A memory storage system that holds about seven items for up to twenty seconds before the material is transferred to long-term memory or is forgotten.

Within this information-processing approach, three types of memory have been distinguished: sensory, short-term, and long-term. **Sensory memory** stores all stimuli that register on the senses, holding literal copies for a brief moment ranging from a fraction of a second to three seconds. Sensations that do not draw attention tend to vanish, but those we "notice" are transferred to **short-term memory (STM)**, another temporary storage system that can hold seven or so items of information for about twenty seconds. Although STM fades quickly, information can be held for a longer period of time through repetition and rehearsal. When people talk about attention span, they are referring to short-term memory. Finally, **long-term memory (LTM)** is a somewhat permanent storage system that can hold vast quantities of information for many years. Science writer Isaac Asimov once estimated that LTM takes in a quadrillion separate bits of information in the course of a lifetime. Mathematician John Griffith estimated that, from birth to death, the average person stores five hundred times more information than the *Encyclopedia Britannica*. When people talk about memory, long-term memory is typically what they have in mind.

As depicted in the flowchart in Figure 6.1, this information-processing model is used to structure the present chapter. Note, however, that it is only a model and does *not* mean that the brain has three separate storage bins. This is only one view of how memory works. There is a radically different view. Most computers process instructions in fixed sequence, one linear step at a time. In contrast, the human brain performs multiple operations simultaneously, "in parallel." Thus, some cognitive psychologists have rejected the information-processing model in favor of parallel-processing models in which knowledge is represented in a weblike network of connections among thousands of interacting "processing units"—all active at once (Rumelhart et al., 1986).

As you read this chapter, you'll see that memory researchers ask two types of questions. First, how are memories stored? Is there a single unitary system, as some believe, or are there multiple memory systems, each uniquely dedicated to storing certain types of information? Second, to what extent are our memories of the past faithful to reality? We will see that researchers have exposed some serious flaws and biases in human memory—what Daniel Schacter (2001) has called the "sins" of memory. Thus, you'll notice this recurring theme: Human beings are both competent and incompetent, and both objective and subjective, in their processing of information.

## THE SENSORY REGISTER

- *Do fleeting traces of sensation linger in the mind even after a stimulus is removed?*
- *What is iconic memory, what is echoic memory, and how do they differ?*

Take a flashlight into a dark room, turn it on, shine it on a wall, and wave it quickly in a circular motion. What do you see? If you twirl it fast enough, the light will appear to leave a glowing trail, and you'll see a continuous circle. The reason: Even though the light illuminates only one point in the circle at a time, your visual system stores a "snapshot" of each point as you watch the next point. The visual image is called an icon, and the snapshot it stores is called **iconic memory** (Neisser, 1967).

### ICONIC MEMORY

People typically don't realize that a fleeting mental trace lingers after a stimulus is removed from view. Nor did cognitive psychologists realize it until George Sperling's (1960) ingenious series of experiments. Sperling instructed subjects to stare at the center of a blank screen. Then he flashed an array of letters for one-twentieth of a second and asked subjects to name as many of the letters as possible. Take a quick glance at Figure 6.2, and try it for yourself. You'll probably recall about a handful of letters. In fact, Sperling found that no matter how large the array was, subjects could name only four or five items. Why? One possibility is that people can register just so much visual input in a single glance—that twelve letters is too much to see in so little time. A second possibility is that all letters registered but the image faded before subjects could report them all. Indeed, many subjects insisted they were able to "see" the whole array but then forgot some of the letters before they could name them.

Did the information that was lost leave a momentary trace, as subjects had claimed, or did it never register in the first place? To test these alternative hypotheses, Sperling devised the "partial-report technique." Instead of asking subjects to list all the letters, he asked them to name only one row in each array—a row that was not determined until *after* the array was shown. In this procedure, each presentation was immediately followed by a tone signaling which letters to name: A high-pitched tone indicated the top line; a medium pitch, the middle line; a low pitch, the bottom line. If they saw the entire array, subjects should have been able to report all the letters in a prompted row correctly—regardless of which row was prompted. Sperling was right: subjects correctly recalled 3.3 letters per row. In other words, 10 letters (9.9), not 4 or 5, were instantly registered in consciousness before fading, held briefly in iconic memory. To determine how long this type of memory lasts, Sperling next varied the time between the letters and the tone that signaled the row to be recalled. As depicted in Figure 6.3, the visual image started to fade as the interval was increased to one-third of a second and had almost completely vanished two-thirds of a second later. Since this study, researchers have found when it comes to pictures of objects or scenes, words, sentences, and other visual stimuli briefly presented,

## REVIEW QUESTIONS

- *According to the information-processing model, what steps are involved in remembering?*

- *What are the roles of sensory memory, short-term memory, and long-term memory in the information-processing model?*

- *How do parallel-processing models of memory differ from the information-processing model?*

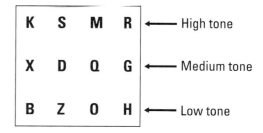

**FIGURE 6.2   Testing for iconic memory**
Here is an array of letters like that used by Sperling (1960). When subjects viewed this array for one-twentieth of a second and tried to name all the letters, they could recall only four or five. But when signaled after the items to recall only one row, they were able to recall three or four letters per line—for an average of ten letters.

**long-term memory (LTM)**   A relatively permanent memory storage system that can hold vast amounts of information for many years.

**iconic memory**   A fleeting sensory memory for visual images that lasts only a fraction of a second.

**chunking** The process of grouping distinct bits of information into larger wholes, or chunks, to increase short-term-memory capacity.

*In a neighborhood park in Geneva, Switzerland, residents socialize over a giant outdoor chessboard. Do you think chess masters could recall the configurations on this giant board as they can from their perspective on a table? This question has never been put to test.*

**WHAT'S YOUR PREDICTION**

If short-term memory is limited, then can people who steal the spotlight of our attention, like weapons, impair our memory for events around them? Or, do attention-getting people make us generally more alert, improving our memory? To find out, Stephen Schmidt (2002) showed people color pictures of male and female models engaged in different activities, like reading a book, pumping gas, picking apples, opening a gift, working on a computer, and drinking coffee. In one picture, half the models were clothed and the other half were completely naked. Think about the task and make two predictions: On a test of memory for the person (such as height, weight, race, hair length and color), did subjects remember more about the nude, or less? In their memory for other aspects of the scene (such as what objects were present), did they remember more or less? Showing that the spotlight of attention is limited, people exposed to a nude model remembered more about the person and less about background aspects of the scene.

According to Miller, STM can accommodate only seven items, and that number may be smaller, but there's a hitch: Although an item may consist of one letter or digit, these items can be grouped into chunks of words, sentences, and large numbers—thus enabling us to use our storage capacity more efficiently. To see the effects of chunking on short-term memory, read the following letters, pausing at each space; then look up and name as many of the letters as you can in correct order: *CN NIB MMT VU SA*. Since this list contains twelve discrete letters, you probably found the task quite frustrating. Now try this next list, again pausing between spaces: *CNN IBM MTV USA*. Better, right? This list contains the same twelve letters. But because the letters are "repackaged" into familiar groups, you had to store only four chunks, not twelve—well within our "magical" capacity (Bower, 1970).

**Chunking** enables us to improve our short-term-memory span by using our capacity more efficiently. You may be limited to seven or so chunks, but you can learn to increase the size of those chunks. To demonstrate, a group of researchers trained two male university students, both long-distance runners and of average intelligence, for several months. For an hour a day, three or four days a week, these students were asked to recall random strings of numbers. If they recalled a sequence correctly, another digit was added to the next sequence and the task was repeated. If they made a mistake, the number of digits in the next sequence was reduced by one. As shown in Figure 6.5, the improvement was astonishing. Before practicing, their memory span was four to seven digits. After six months, they were up to eighty items (Ericsson & Chase, 1982; Ericsson et al., 1980). In one session, for example, the experimenter read the following numbers in order:

89319443492502157841668506120948888856877273
1418610546297480129497496596228

After two minutes of concentration, the subject repeated all seventy-three digits, in groups of three and four. How did he do it? Given no special instruction, the subject developed his own elaborate strategy: He converted the random numbers into ages ("89.3 years, a very old person"), dates (1944 was "near the end of World War II"), and cross-country racing times for various distances (3492 was "3 minutes and 49.2 seconds, nearly a world's record for the mile").

The value of chunking is also evidenced by the way people retain information in their areas of expertise. Study the arrangement of pieces on the chessboard shown in Figure 6.6, and in five seconds memorize as much of it as you can. Chances are, you'll be able to reproduce approximately seven items. Yet after looking at the same arrangement for five seconds, chess masters can reproduce all the pieces and their row-and-column positions almost without error. It's not that chess masters are born with computerlike minds. When chess pieces are placed randomly on the board, they are no more proficient than the rest of us. But when the arrangement is taken from an actual game between good players, they naturally chunk the configurations of individual pieces into familiar patterns such as the "Romanian Pawn Defense" and "Casablanca Bishop's Gambit" (De Groot, 1965; Chase & Simon, 1973). Researchers estimate that chess masters can store up to fifty thousand such chunks in memory (Gobet & Simon, 1996). From years of experience, experts in all domains—including computer programmers, figure skaters, waiters and waitresses, bridge players, ballet dancers, and professional actors—exhibit these advantages in their short-term-memory performance (Vincente & Wang, 1998). In a test of memorization for street names presented in lists, taxi drivers outperformed others (Kalakoski & Saariluoma, 2001).

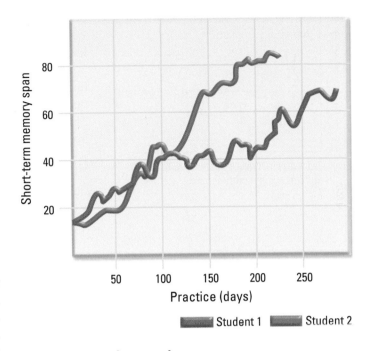

**FIGURE 6.5 Increased memory span**
Two students practiced memory-span tasks for an hour a day, three to four days a week, for six months. Remarkably, their short-term-memory span increased from seven digits to eighty (Ericsson & Chase 1982). One subject soon had a memory span that exceeded one hundred digits (Staszewski, 1988).

## DURATION

It has happened to me, and I'll bet it has happened to you, too. You look up a telephone number, repeat it to yourself, put away the directory, and start dialing. Then you stop. You hit the first three numbers without a hitch, but then you go blank, get confused (was that a 5 or a 9?), and hang up in frustration. After a few seconds, the phone number is gone, as if it evaporated, and is no longer in memory. Then there is the matter of names. I'll be at a social gathering and meet someone for the first time. We'll talk for a while, then I'll turn to introduce a colleague—only to realize with embarrassment that I already forgot the name of my new acquaintance.

These types of experiences are common because short-term memory is limited not only in the *amount* of information it can store but also in the length of *time* it can hold that information. What is the duration of short-term memory? That is, how long does a memory trace last if a person does not actively rehearse or repeat it? To measure how rapidly information is forgotten, Lloyd and Margaret Peterson (1959) asked subjects to recall a set of unrelated consonants such as MJK. So that subjects could not rehearse the material, they were given a number and instructed to count backward from that number by 3s: 564, 561, 558, 555, and so on. After varying lengths of time, subjects were cued to recall the consonants. After eighteen seconds, performance plummeted to below 10 percent (see Figure 6.7).

Knowing the fleeting nature of short-term memory, we can prevent forgetting by repeating information silently or aloud. That's why, if I do not have a pen and paper handy, I will repeat a phone number over and over again until I have dialed it. And

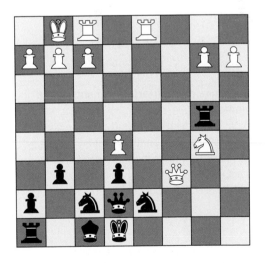

**FIGURE 6.6 The value of chunking**
Study this arrangement of chess pieces for five seconds. Then turn to the empty board on p. 226 and try to reproduce the arrangement as best you can. Unless you are a highly experienced chess player, the number of pieces you can place in the correct squares should approximate the magical number seven.

"Hi. I'm, I'm, I'm . . . You'll have to forgive me, I'm terrible with names."

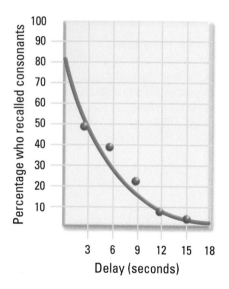

FIGURE 6.7 **Duration of short-term memory**

What is the duration of short-term memory? When subjects are kept from rehearsing material they are trying to recall, their short-term memory vanishes within twenty seconds (Peterson & Peterson, 1959).

**maintenance rehearsal** The use of sheer repetition to keep information in short-term memory.

**working memory** Term used to describe short-term memory as an active workspace where information is accessible for current use.

that's why I try to silently repeat a person's name while being introduced. Repetition extends the twenty-second duration of STM in the same way that chunking expands its four to seven item capacity.

The retention benefits of sheer repetition, also called **maintenance rehearsal,** were first demonstrated by Hermann Ebbinghaus (1885; reprinted in 1913), a German philosopher who was a pioneer in memory research. Using himself as a subject, Ebbinghaus created a list of all possible nonsense syllables consisting of a vowel inserted between two consonants. Syllables that formed words were then eliminated— which left a list of unfamiliar items (*RUX, VOM, QEL, MIF*), each written on a separate card. To study the effects of rehearsal, Ebbinghaus would turn over the cards, one at a time, and say each syllable aloud to the ticking rhythm of a metronome. Then, after reading the items once, he would start again and go through the cards in the same order. This procedure was repeated until he could anticipate each syllable before turning over the card. Ebbinghaus found that he could recall a list of seven syllables after a single reading (there's that magical number again) but that he needed more practice for longer lists. The more often he repeated the items, the more he could recall. Other studies have confirmed the point: "Rehearsal" can be used to "maintain" an item in short-term memory for an indefinite period of time.

## FUNCTIONS OF SHORT-TERM MEMORY

Short-term memory's limitations may seem to be a handicap, but in fact they are economic and adaptive. As with clearing outdated papers off a desk or purging old files from a computer disk, it helps to forget what is no longer useful. Otherwise, your mind would be cluttered with every sensation, every name, phone number, ZIP code, and morsel of trivia that ever entered the stream of your consciousness. If STM had unlimited capacity, you would constantly be distracted—possibly with devastating results. In Chapter 16, for example, we'll see that people who suffer from schizophrenia are often incoherent, jumping from one topic to the next as they speak, in part because they cannot filter out distractions.

**Working Memory** In the computer we call the human mind, STM is a mental workspace, like the screen. On a computer, material displayed on the monitor may be entered on a keyboard or retrieved from previously saved files. Similarly, STM contains both new sensory input and material that is pulled from long-term storage. All cognitive psychologists agree that people have fleeting memories that are limited in their capacity and duration (Coltheart, 1999; Gathercole, 2001). However, many researchers are critical of the traditional view that STM is a passive storage depot that merely holds information until it fades or is transferred to a permanent warehouse (Crowder, 1993).

To conceptualize STM as an active mental workspace where information is processed, Alan Baddeley (1992) and others prefer to use the term **working memory.** According to Baddeley, our working memory consists of a "central executive" processor and two specialized storage-and-rehearsal systems—one for auditory input, the other for visual and spatial images (see Figure 6.8). This working-memory system is critical for intelligent functioning. To interpret spoken or written language, for example, you have to remember the early part of a statement after it has receded into the past. Similarly, to solve an arithmetic problem, you have to keep track of the different steps you take—as in remembering to carry the 1 when adding 45 and 55 together. Research supports the notion that working memory contains separate systems for auditory and visual input—and that the system as a whole is highly adaptive (Andrade et al., 2002; Miyake & Shah, 1999).

**The Serial-Position Effect** Research also suggests that it may be useful to distinguish between short-term and long-term memory. Whenever people try to memorize a list, they inevitably recall items from the beginning and end of the list better than those sandwiched in the middle. The enhanced recall of early items in a sequence is called *primacy,* the advantage for the later items is called *recency,* and the combined pattern is known as the **serial-position curve.** This result was first discovered in the 1890s by Mary Whiton Calkins, the first female president of the American Psychological Association (Madigan & O'Hara, 1992). Since that time, researchers have consistently observed the same effect.

The serial-position curve is pervasive and is observed not only in human memory subjects but also in monkeys, pigeons, rabbits, and rats. In one study, for example, rats were put into different paths of a radial maze, one path at a time, where they were rewarded with food pellets. Later, the rats were given a series of choices between paths previously visited and new ones they had never seen before. As seen in their choices, the rats were more likely to "recognize" paths they had previously visited early and late in the sequence than those that were sandwiched in the middle. The rats recognized the middle paths only when they encountered a highly distinctive stimulus there (Reed & Richards, 1996).

What explains the serial-position effect? It appears that different factors are responsible for primacy and recency. Primacy is easy to understand. Imagine receiving a list of words and trying to recall them for a test: *chair, artichoke, bicycle, frame, teacher,* and so on. Chances are, you'll later recall the first word because you repeated it to yourself over and over again. You must divide your attention in half for the second word as you try to hold two in memory, divide your attention into thirds for the third item, and so on, through the list. In other words, primacy occurs because the first few words receive more attention and rehearsal than later ones—and are more likely to be transferred into long-term memory.

Explaining the recency effect is trickier. On the basis of the information-processing model described earlier, researchers argued that the last items in a list are recalled better because they are still fresh in short-term working memory when the test begins. Initially, studies supported this explanation. For example, Murray Glanzer and Anita Cunitz (1966) presented two groups of subjects with fifteen words to memorize. One group was tested right after the presentation; the second was distracted for thirty seconds and then tested. Look at Figure 6.9, and you'll see that subjects who were immediately tested exhibited the usual effect: The first items were recalled by rehearsal, the last ones had not yet faded, and those in the middle slipped through the cracks. But notice that there was no recency effect in the delayed-testing group—only primacy. After thirty seconds and no opportunity for rehearsal, the last few items vanished from working memory.

This explanation of the serial-position curve seems convincing, but there's a problem with it: Recency effects are often found in tasks that do not involve short-term memory. For example, take a blank piece of paper and write down as many U.S. presidents as you can name in the correct order. What do you come up with? Robert Crowder (1993) asked college students to complete this task, and he found primacy, recency, and the usual decline in the middle (see Figure 6.10). Let's see: Washington,

**Working memory**

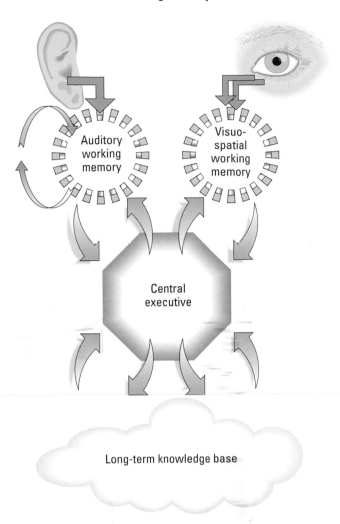

**FIGURE 6.8   Working memory**
According to Baddeley, STM is a "working memory" that contains a "central executive" processor and two specialized systems—one for auditory input, the other for visual and spatial input. Note that material can enter the conscious workspace from your senses or from your long-term store of knowledge. Also note that information can be held in this area through rehearsal—by saying it to yourself over and over or by visualizing it in a mental image.

**serial-position curve**   A U-shape pattern indicating the tendency to recall more items from the beginning and end of a list than from the middle.

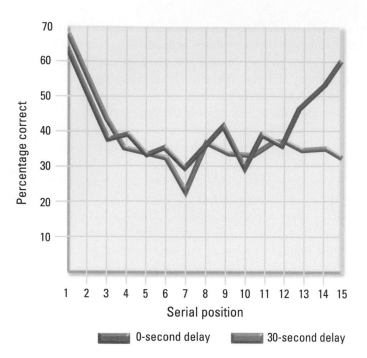

FIGURE 6.9 **The serial-position effect**
Subjects trying to memorize a list of words were tested immediately or after thirty seconds of distraction. In the first group, subjects recalled the first and last few items the best, yielding the U-shape serial-position curve. In the delay group, however, there was no recency effect. After thirty seconds without rehearsal, subjects forgot the later items (Glanzer & Cunitz, 1966).

---

## REVIEW QUESTIONS

- *What is the role of attention in memory?*

- *Distinguish among visual, acoustic, and semantic encoding.*

- *Discuss the capacity and duration limits of short-term memory. What strategies can be used to circumvent these limits?*

- *Why do some psychologists prefer the label "working memory" rather than short-term memory?*

- *What is the serial-position curve, and what does it tell us about short-term and long-term memory?*

---

Adams, Jefferson, . . . Lincoln, . . . Bush, Clinton, Bush. Notice that the one exception to the U-shape pattern is that Lincoln was recalled more frequently than would be expected from his middle position—a performance "spike" that is common when a distinctive item is embedded in an otherwise homogeneous list (Wallace, 1965; Schmidt, 1991).

At this point, it's clear that the serial-position curve is a pervasive phenomenon in memory. It's also clear, however, that other mechanisms are needed to explain it (Cowan et al., 1994; Thapar & Greene, 1993). For example, recent studies suggest the possibility that the first and last few items in a series are easier to recall because they stand out relative to the middle items (Neath & Crowder, 1996; Knoedler et al., 1999). We'll see later in this chapter that people tend to retain information that is distinctive, bizarre, emotional, or in other ways out of the ordinary.

## LONG-TERM MEMORY

- *What input is transferred from short-term memory into long-term memory?*
- *Where in the brain are these memories stored?*
- *How are memories retrieved, and why are they often forgotten?*
- *Who is H.M., and why is this amnesia patient so important?*
- *Why is it said that memory is reconstructive, and what are the implications?*

Do you remember your fourth birthday, the name of your first-grade teacher, or the smell of floor wax in the corridors of your elementary school? Can you describe

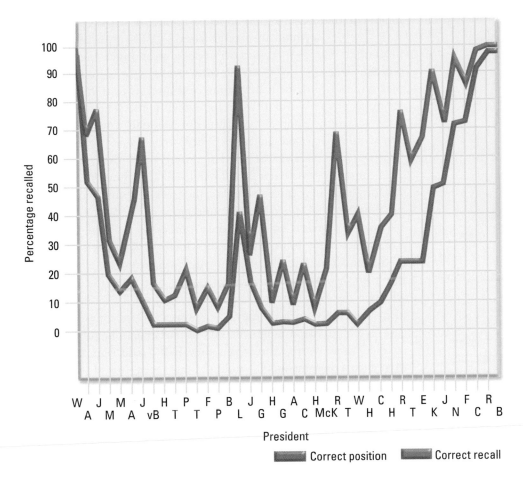

**FIGURE 6.10**   **The long-term serial-position effect**
When subjects tried to list U.S. presidents in correct order, the typical serial-position curve was found—except that Lincoln was often recalled. Note that although subjects performed better when they could recall the presidents in any order (the two Roosevelts and Kennedy were frequently recalled in this situation), primacy and recency effects were still evident (Crowder, 1993).

a dream you had last night or recite the words of the national anthem? To answer these questions, you would have to retrieve information from the mental warehouse of long-term memory. Like the hard drive on a computer, long-term memory is a relatively enduring storage system that has the capacity to retain vast amounts of information for long periods of time. This section examines long-term memories of the recent and remote past—how they are encoded, stored, retrieved, forgotten, and even reconstructed in the course of a lifetime.

## ENCODING

Information can be kept alive in short-term working memory by rote repetition, or maintenance rehearsal. But to transfer something into long-term memory, you would find it much more effective to use **elaborative rehearsal**—a strategy that involves thinking about the material in a more meaningful way and associating it with other knowledge that is already in long-term memory. The more deeply you process something, the more likely you are to recall it at a later time.

To demonstrate this process, Fergus Craik and Endel Tulving (1975) showed subjects a list of words, one at a time, and for each asked them for (1) a simple visual

**elaborative rehearsal**   A technique for transferring information into long-term memory by thinking about it in a deeper way.

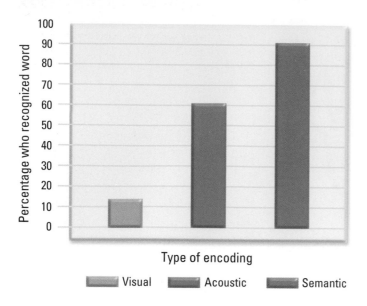

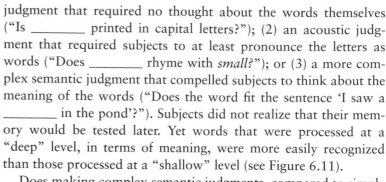

**FIGURE 6.11  Elaborative rehearsal**
Subjects read a long list of words and for each one judged how it was printed (visual), how it sounded (acoustic), or what it meant (semantic). The more thought required to process the words, the easier they were to recognize later (Craik & Tulving, 1975).

judgment that required no thought about the words themselves ("Is _____ printed in capital letters?"); (2) an acoustic judgment that required subjects to at least pronounce the letters as words ("Does _____ rhyme with *small*?"); or (3) a more complex semantic judgment that compelled subjects to think about the meaning of the words ("Does the word fit the sentence 'I saw a _____ in the pond'?"). Subjects did not realize that their memory would be tested later. Yet words that were processed at a "deep" level, in terms of meaning, were more easily recognized than those processed at a "shallow" level (see Figure 6.11).

Does making complex semantic judgments, compared to simple visual judgments, activate different regions of the brain? Is it possible to see physical traces of deep processing? Using functional MRI technology, John Gabrieli and others (1996) devised a study similar to Craik and Tulving's in which subjects were shown stimulus words on a computer and were instructed to determine whether the words were concrete or abstract (a semantic judgment) or simply whether they were printed in uppercase or lowercase letters (a visual judgment). As in past research, subjects later recalled more words for which they had made semantic rather than visual judgments. In addition, however, the brain-imaging measures showed that processing the words in semantic terms triggered more activity in a part of the frontal cortex of the language-dominant left hemisphere.

Perhaps the most effective form of elaborative rehearsal is the linking of new information to the self. In one study, subjects sat in front of a microcomputer and looked at forty trait words (for example, *shy, friendly, ambitious*). In some cases, they were told to judge whether the words were self-descriptive; in others, they judged the words' length, sound, or meaning. When asked to list as many of the words as they could, subjects remembered more after thinking about the words in reference to themselves than for other purposes (Rogers et al., 1977). Apparently, the self can be used as a memory aid: By viewing new information as relevant to ourselves, we consider that information more fully and organize it around common themes. The result is an improvement in recall (Symons & Johnson, 1997).

Memorizing—definitions, math formulas, poems, or historical dates—usually requires conscious effort. When I teach a large class, I pass out index cards on the first day and ask students to write down their names and a vivid personal detail that will help me remember who they are. Then I locate each student's photograph in the college "face book," match the face to the name, and run through the cards until I can identify each student. With tasks like this one, practice makes perfect. In 1885, Ebbinghaus read through a list of nonsense syllables 0, 8, 16, 24, 32, 42, 53, or 64 times and checked his memory for the items twenty-four hours later. As predicted, the more learning time he spent the first day, the better his memory was on the second day.

But there's more. Ebbinghaus and others found that retention is increased through "overlearning"—that is, continued rehearsal even after the material seems to have been mastered (Driskell et al., 1992; Semb et al., 1993). Long-term memory is also better when the practice is spread over a long period of time than when it is crammed in all at once, a phenomenon known as the "spacing effect" (Dempster, 1988). Harry Bahrick and Lynda Hall (1991) thus found that adults retained more of their high-school math skills when they had later practiced the math in college—and when that practice was extended over semesters rather than condensed into

a single year. When you think about it, this spacing effect makes adaptive sense. Names, faces, and events that recur over long intervals of time rather than in concentrated brief periods are probably, in real life, more important to remember (Anderson & Schooler, 1991).

Although the transfer of information to LTM often requires a great deal of thought and effort, certain types of information are encoded automatically and without conscious control. When I meet someone for the first time, I always have to work on recalling that person's name but I can easily and without rehearsal remember the face. It just happens. Similarly, people encode information about time, spatial locations, and event frequencies. In a study that provides evidence of this automatic processing, Lynn Hasher and Rose Zacks (1984) showed subjects a long list of words. Some subjects were warned in advance that they would be asked to recall how many times a certain word was presented. Yet others who were not similarly prepared were still just as accurate in their later estimates. Evidently, numerical frequencies are encoded without conscious effort.

## STORAGE

Whether the encoding process is effortful or automatic, cognitive psychologists have long been interested in the *format*, the *content*, and the *neural bases* of long-term memory as it is represented in the brain.

### Formats of Long-Term Memory
In long-term memory, information is stored in two forms or "codes": semantic and visual. Semantic coding is easy to demonstrate. When we process verbal information—such as a spoken phrase, a speech, a written sentence, or a story—what we store is the meaning of the information, not specific words. For example, Jacqueline Sachs (1967) had subjects listen to a tape-recorded passage. She then presented a series of sentences (for example, "He sent a letter about it to Galileo, the great Italian scientist") and asked if they were the same as or different from those of the original passage. Subjects correctly rejected sentences that changed the meaning ("Galileo, the great Italian scientist, sent him a letter about it"), but they did not reject sentences with the same meaning that were worded differently ("A letter about it was sent by him to Galileo, the great Italian scientist"). The reason: They had stored the semantic content of the passage—not an exact, word-for-word representation. In fact, people often read "between the lines" and recall hearing not just what was said but what was *implied*. For example, subjects who heard that a paratrooper "leaped out the door" often recalled later that he "jumped out of the plane." And mock jurors who heard a witness testify that "I ran up to the alarm" later assumed the witness had said, "I rang the alarm" (Harris & Monaco, 1978).

Although verbal information is stored in a semantic form, visual inputs and many long-term memories (including some of our most cherished childhood recollections) are stored as visual images. In visual coding, a mental picture is generated of an object or scene—a process that has implications for how people retrieve the information. To demonstrate, Stephen Kosslyn (1980) showed subjects drawings like the boat in Figure 6.12. Later, he asked the subjects to visualize each drawing, to focus on the right or left side of it, and then, as quickly as possible, to indicate whether a specific object was present by pressing a YES or NO button that stopped a clock. If the drawing is stored in a visual manner, reasoned Kosslyn, then it should take longer for subjects to "scan" their image for an answer

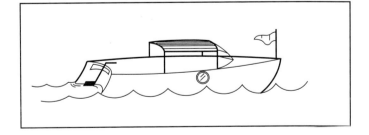

**FIGURE 6.12  Visual coding**
When subjects visualized the left rather than right side of this drawing, it took them longer to recall the flag. This result suggests that subjects "scanned" a mental image for the answer (Kosslyn, 1980).

**procedural memory** Stored long-term knowledge of learned habits and skills.

**declarative memory** Stored long-term knowledge of facts about ourselves and the world.

when the object is located away from the subject's focus of attention. That is exactly what happened. When subjects were mentally focused on the left rather than the right side of the drawing, for example, it took them longer to determine that a flag was present on the right side of the boat. In more recent experiments using PET scans, Kosslyn and others (1999) found that when subjects shut their eyes and tried to visualize patterns of stripes, parts of the visual cortex were activated—the same as when they actually viewed the stripes.

Mental images play an important role in long-term memory. Popular books on how to improve your memory advise people to use imagery, and research shows that this advice is well founded. As an illustration, try to memorize the following list of word pairs so that the first word triggers your memory of the second: *lawyer-chair, snowflake-mountain, shoes-milk, dog-bicycle, chef-pickle, student-sandwich, boy-flag*. You might try to master the list by silently repeating the items over and over. But now take a different approach: For each item, form an image in your "mind's eye" that contains the two words of each pair interacting in some way. For example, imagine a brown *dog* chasing a *bicycle* or a *student* eating a foot-long *sandwich*. This method should improve performance (Bower & Winzenz, 1970; Paivio, 1969).

Consistent with the notion that imagery facilitates memory, concrete words that are easy to visualize (*fire, tent, statue, zebra*) are more easily recalled than abstract words that are difficult to represent in a picture (*infinite, freedom, process, future*). To remember something, it's better to encode it in both semantic and visual forms than in either alone (Paivio, 1986).

**Contents of Long-Term Memory** Increasingly it seems that we have more than one type of long-term memory (Rolls, 2000). Following Endel Tulving (1985), researchers now commonly distinguish two types. One is **procedural memory**, a "know how" memory that consists of our stored knowledge of well-learned habits and skills—such as how to drive, swim, type, ride a bike, and tie shoelaces. The second type is **declarative memory**, which consists of both *semantic* memories for facts about the world—such as who Michael Jordan is, what a dollar is worth, what you need to access the World Wide Web, and what the word *gravity* means) and *episodic* memories that we have about ourselves—such as who our parents are, where we went to school, and what our favorite movie is (Tulving, 2002). This distinction is important, as we'll see later, because people with amnesia are

*There are two types of long-term memory. Procedural memory contains our knowledge of various skills—such as how to ride a bike. Declarative memory contains our knowledge of facts—for example, what a pyramid is or where it can be found.*

often unable to recall declarative memories of facts and events, yet they still retain many of the skills they had learned and committed to procedural memory.

With all that's stored in long-term memory—habits, skills, verbal information, and knowledge of words, names, dates, faces, pictures, personal experiences, and the like—it's amazing that anything can ever be retrieved from this vast warehouse. Surely our knowledge must be organized in memory, perhaps the way books are filed in a library. One popular view is that memories are stored in a complex web of associations, or **semantic networks.** According to proponents of this view, items in memory are linked together by semantic relationships (see Figure 6.13). When one item is brought to mind, the pathways leading to meaningfully related items are *primed*—thus increasing the likelihood that they too will be retrieved (Collins & Loftus, 1975; Anderson, 1983).

A good deal of research supports the notion that memories are stored in semantic networks. When subjects are given a list of sixty words that fall into four categories

**semantic network**    A complex web of semantic associations that link items in memory such that retrieving one item triggers the retrieval of others as well.

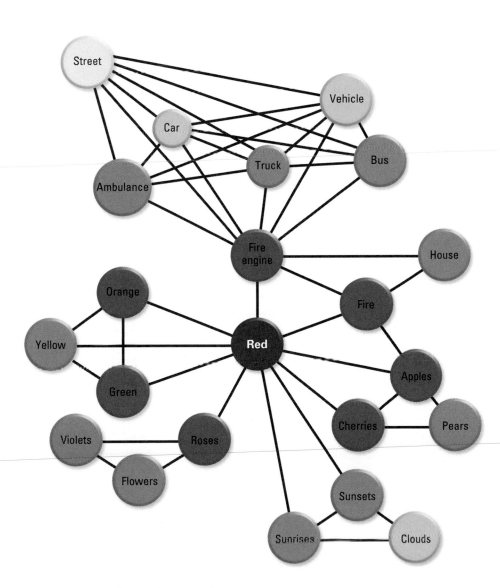

**FIGURE 6.13    Semantic networks**
According to semantic-network theories, memories are linked in a complex web of associations. The shorter the link between items, the more likely it is that the retrieval of one item will trigger that of the other (Collins & Loftus, 1975).

**lexical decision making** An experimental task that requires subjects to decide as quickly as possible whether a string of letters briefly presented is a word or nonword.

(animals, professions, names, fruits)—even if the words are presented in a mixed order—subjects later tend to recall them in clusters. In other words, retrieving *tiger* is more likely to trigger one's memory for *baboon* than for *dentist, Jason,* or *banana* (Bousfield, 1953; Romney et al., 1993).

Research on **lexical decision making** also illustrates the point. In these studies, people are given a string of letters (*nart, wire, bent, tise*) and must decide as quickly as possible if the letters form a word. Consistently, people make these decisions more quickly when the letter string comes after a semantically related word than after an unrelated word. Thus, subjects are quicker to decide on *fire* when the preceding word was *red* than when it was *clouds*. Subjects are even quicker in their decision making when given two target-related primes rather than only one (Balota & Paul, 1996). To sum up, researchers use lexical decision-making response times to map our underlying networks of associations—memory's filing system (McNamara, 1992).

**Neural Bases of Long-Term Memory** Is it possible to pinpoint a site in the brain that houses these associations? Do memories leave a physical trace that can actually be "seen"? Are there drugs that we can take to improve our memory? Although led astray, at times, by exciting developments, neuroscientists have long been intrigued by such possibilities (Squire & Schacter, 2002).

In 1959, James McConnell and his colleagues reported that they had chemically transferred the memory of one flatworm to another. In an ingenious study, they conditioned worms to contract when exposed to light, cut them in half, and found that the worms that regenerated from both the head and the tail ends were quicker to condition than new worms—suggesting that they had inherited a "memory." This result captured the public imagination, and indeed, McConnell himself speculated in a *Newsweek* article that "It may be that in the schools of the future students will facilitate the ability to retain information with chemical injections" (can you picture taking a memory pill to feed you a knowledge of this entire textbook?). But other researchers could not replicate the finding, and interest in memory transfer faded. In a sad postscript to the story, in 1985, James McConnell was the victim of an attempted assassination when he received a letter bomb sent by the then infamous Unabomber. Fortunately, McConnell survived (Rilling, 1996).

In another promising development, neurosurgeon Wilder Penfield reported that he had triggered long-forgotten memories in humans through brain stimulation. In the 1940s, Penfield was treating epileptic patients by removing portions of their brains. To locate the damage, he stimulated different cortical areas with a painless electrical current. Sometimes, his patients—who were awake during the procedure—would "relive" long-lost events from the past. For example, one woman said she heard a mother calling her child when a certain spot was stimulated. From reports like this, Penfield concluded that experience leaves a permanent "imprint" that can be played back years later as though there was a tape recorder in the brain (Penfield & Perot, 1963). This observation sparked a great deal of excitement until cognitive psychologists scrutinized the data and made two sobering discoveries. First, the phenomenon itself was very rare, reported by only a handful of Penfield's eleven hundred patients. Second, the "flashbacks" were probably dreamlike illusions, not actual memories (Loftus & Loftus, 1980; Neisser, 1967).

Despite these dead ends, today's researchers continue in hot pursuit of the *engram*—a term used to describe a physical memory trace. There are two objectives in this endeavor: (1) to locate the anatomical structures in the brain where memories are stored, and (2) to understand the neural and biochemical changes that accompany memories. Let us now examine some recent developments along these lines.

**Where Is the "Engram"?** Karl Lashley (1950) pioneered the search for memory traces in the brain. For thirty years, Lashley trained rats to run a maze, removed different structures from their brains, and then returned the rats to the maze to test their memory. No matter what structures he removed, however, the rats recalled at least some of what they had learned. Eventually, Lashley was forced to conclude that memories do not reside in any specific location.

Then along came H.M., a twenty-seven-year-old man who underwent brain surgery in 1953 for severe epileptic seizures. Two holes were drilled into the patient's skull above the eyes, and through a silver straw the surgeon removed parts of both temporal lobes and sucked out the entire **hippocampus**—a curved pinkish-gray structure in the limbic system (see Figure 6.14). The operation succeeded in controlling the man's seizures. But something was terribly wrong. What made H.M. one of the most famous neurology cases of all time is that the surgery had an unexpected side effect: It produced **anterograde amnesia,** an inability to form new long-term memories. (This should not be confused with **retrograde amnesia,** which is an inability to retrieve long-term memories from the past.)

H.M. still recalled the people, places, and events from before the surgery. He also performed as well as before on IQ tests and could still read, write, and solve problems so long as he stayed focused on the task. But he could not retain new information. He would meet someone new but then forget the person; or he would read an article without realizing that he had read it before; or he would not know what he ate for his last meal. One year after his family moved, H.M. still did not know their new address. It was as if new information "went in one ear, out the next" (Scoville & Milner, 1957; Milner et al., 1968). In his seventies, H.M. was the subject of *Memory's Ghost,* a book by Philip Hilts (1995). Hilts, who spent a great deal of time with H.M., tells of a remarkable experience. For H.M., he says, "Each moment is a surprise, a new puzzle to be worked out from a quick glance at the paltry evidence at hand as it comes rapidly upon him" (p. 139).

H.M.'s case is important for two reasons. First, he exhibited a very specific information-processing deficit. He could bring new material into short-term memory and he could retrieve long-term memories that were previously stored. But he could not form new long-term memories. For example, Bradley Postle and Suzanne Corkin (1998) tested H.M. to see if his performance in a verbal task was influenced, or "primed," by prior exposure to certain words. They found that he was influenced like anyone else by words that were common to the English language before his onset of amnesia—but that he was not influenced by words that became common after his amnesia—words such as *Afro, sushi, macho, nerd,* and *hacker.* Studying memory for places, Edmond Teng and Larry Squire (1999) tested another hippocampus-damaged patient and found that he could recall as well as anyone the spatial layout of the neighborhood he grew up in more than fifty years ago, but he could not recall his current neighborhood—the area he moved to after becoming amnesic.

The second reason H.M.'s case is important is that it was the first to prove what Lashley could not—that localized lesions in the brain have disruptive effects on memory. Specifically, H.M.'s case revealed that the hippocampus (and perhaps structures such as the amygdala and thalamus) plays a pivotal role. Recent studies in animals and humans have since confirmed the point: The hippocampus is essential for the explicit recollection of newly acquired information. Hippocampal lesions that mimic H.M.'s surgery produce a similar impairment in rats, monkeys, and other animals (Squire & Schacter, 2002).

The role played by the hippocampus is even evident in black-capped chickadees and other food-storing birds. In a remarkable feat of memory, they can locate up to six thousand caches, or storage sites, of food that they have buried weeks earlier in

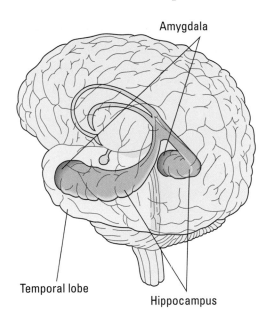

**FIGURE 6.14 The hippocampal region**
As shown here the hippocampus is located under the temporal lobe of the cerebral cortex. This structure is necessary for encoding and transferring new information into long-term memory.

**hippocampus** A portion of the brain in the limbic system that plays a key role in encoding and transferring new information into long-term memory.

**anterograde amnesia** A memory disorder characterized by an inability to store new information in long-term memory.

**retrograde amnesia** A memory disorder characterized by an inability to retrieve long-term memories from the past.

*This black-capped chickadee has a remarkable memory. During winter and early spring, this food-storing bird can locate many hundreds of caches of buried pine seeds.*

scattered locations—and they do not revisit old sites previously depleted. Studying California scrub jays, Nicola Clayton and Anthony Dickinson (1998) found that these birds can recall not only where they stockpiled their food but also what type of food they put at a particular site and when they put it there. Thus, these birds revisit old caches containing nonperishable peanuts and sunflower seeds, but they avoid older caches that contain worms, a favorite food that spoils over time. Anatomical studies have shown that food-storing birds have a larger hippocampus than do nonstoring birds—in part, because the process of recovering food from caches increases the density of neurons in the hippocampus (Clayton, 2001). These birds lose the ability to recover food when the hippocampus is removed (Sherry, 1992; Hampton & Shettleworth, 1996).

Is all of memory stored in the hippocampus? No. When this structure is surgically removed from monkeys, they lose most of their recall for events of the preceding month, but their more distant memories remain intact (Squire & Zola-Morgan, 1991). And among humans, older adults with a shrunken hippocampus are impaired in their ability to recall new words and pictures, but they can still revisit past events (Golomb et al., 1993). Together, the various strands of evidence point to the conclusion that the hippocampus plays a role in the initial encoding of information and serves as a way station from which information is sent for long-term storage to neural circuits in the cerebral cortex. The hippocampus is especially involved in our memories of places, providing us with something of a "cognitive map" (Best et al., 2001; Redish, 1999).

Clearly, not all aspects of memory require the hippocampus. As we'll see later, amnesics like H.M. do exhibit memory, but in indirect ways. They can be conditioned to blink to a tone that has been paired with a puff of air to the eye, and they can remember how to work a maze they have practiced—but they cannot recall the actual training sessions. Similarly, they form preferences for new music they hear but do not recognize the melodies in a test situation. And they retain their procedural memories of how to read, write, and use other previously learned skills. For these types of memory tasks, different structures are involved. For example, David McCormick and Richard Thompson (1984) located a microscopic spot in the *cerebellum* that controls the classical conditioning of the eyeblink reflex. Certain areas of the brain specialize in certain types of input, but for something as complex as memory, many areas are needed.

**The Biochemistry of Memory**   As some researchers try to locate where memories are stored, others seek to identify the accompanying biochemical changes that take place in the neural circuits. Most of these changes are likely to be found at the synapses, the tiny gaps between neurons that are linked together by the release of neurotransmitters.

One neurotransmitter that seems to play an important role in memory is *acetylcholine*. (See pp. 50–52 to review the functions of ACH.) Research shows that people with Alzheimer's disease—a degenerative brain disorder characterized by a striking loss of memory for new information (see Chapter 9)—have lowered levels of acetylcholine in the brain, a link supported by animal studies as well. This finding suggests the possibility that Alzheimer's patients can be treated with drugs that boost their levels of acetylcholine. The positive effects of this approach may be limited— partly because Alzheimer's disease, and human memory in general, involves more than one neurotransmitter (Thal, 1992). But these drugs may help to slow the rate of cognitive deterioration (Tune & Sunderland, 1998; Peskind, 1998).

Certain hormones are also involved in memory. In experiments with rats, James McGaugh (1990) has found that memory can be improved by moderate postlearning injections into the amygdala of *epinephrine*—a hormone that is naturally released during times of stress (McGaugh & Roozendaal, 2002). Thus, as he put it, "You get excited about something, you release a hormone, and the hormone has some actions that can strengthen memory" (Azar, 1999, p. 18).

Hormones do not enter the brain directly, so what explains their memory-enhancing effects? One possibility is that epinephrine triggers the release of the sugar glucose into the bloodstream. Once in the brain, glucose might then work directly or through its effects on neurotransmitters. So, can glucose treatments be used to enhance memory? Research suggests that it can. In one study, Paul Gold (1995) had twenty-two healthy senior citizens listen to a taped passage and then drink lemonade sweetened with glucose or saccharine, the sugar substitute. When tested the next day, those who had ingested the glucose recalled 53 percent more information from the passage. In another study, Claude Messier and others (1999) tested thirty-six healthy young adults and found that those with naturally low blood glucose levels performed 5 to 8 percent less well on a word memory task than others—except when fed a glucose-sweetened drink, which boosted their performance and eliminated the difference. Suggesting that it helps to eat a good breakfast the morning of an exam, other research has shown that glucose improves performance even when people ingest it after they've studied but before being tested (Manning et al., 1998).

Exploiting our desire to become cognitive super beings, some companies advertise over-the-counter treatments as memory enhancers. Do they work? The claims can only be tested through controlled research. For example, Paul Solomon and others (2002) tested the popular Ginkoba, which claims to enhance mental focus and improve memory. For six weeks, over two hundred healthy adults took the recommended dose of Ginkgo or a harmless gelatin placebo. Afterward, on standard tests of memory and other cognitive measures, the two groups did not differ. The investigators note that perhaps different doses, longer time frames, or more sensitive memory tests are needed for benefits to be observed. Clearly, more research of this sort is needed to critically evaluate all commercially motivated claims.

## RETRIEVAL

Once information is stored, how do you know it exists? Because people can openly report their recollections, this seems like a silly question. In fact, however, this is one of the thorniest questions confronting cognitive psychologists. Hermann Ebbinghaus (1885; reprinted in 1913) was not only the first person to study memory systematically but also the first to realize that a memory may exist without awareness. In his words, "These experiences remain concealed from consciousness and yet produce an effect which is significant and which authenticates their previous experience" (p. 2).

Memory without awareness illustrates how human beings can be both competent and incompetent at the same time, and it poses a profound challenge to the researcher: If people have memories they cannot report, how can we ever know these memories exist? To his credit, Ebbinghaus devised a simple but clever technique. He tested memory by its effect on performance. Acting as his own subject, he would learn a set of nonsense syllables and then count the number of trials it later took him to *relearn* the same list. If it took fewer trials the second time around than the first, then he must have retained some of the material—even if he could not consciously recite it.

In recent years, other techniques have been devised. Basically, there are two types of tests, and each assesses a different type of memory: one explicit, the other implicit. **Explicit memory** is a term used to describe the recollections of facts and events that people try to retrieve in response to *direct* questions. In contrast, **implicit memory** is

6.2

**explicit memory** The types of memory elicited through the conscious retrieval of recollections in response to direct questions.

**implicit memory** A nonconscious recollection of a prior experience that is revealed indirectly, by its effects on performance.

| TABLE 6.1 | DIFFERENCES BETWEEN EXPLICIT AND IMPLICIT MEMORY |
|---|---|
| **Explicit Memory** | **Implicit Memory** |
| Conscious retention | Nonconscious retention |
| Direct tests | Indirect tests |
| Disrupted by amnesia | Intact with amnesia |
| Encoded in the hippocampus | Encoded elsewhere |

a term used to describe the retention of information without awareness, as measured by its *indirect* effects on performance (Jacoby et al., 1993; Roediger, 1990; Schacter, 1992). Why is this distinction important? The reason, as we'll see, is that people often exhibit dissociations between the two types of tasks. That is, people will consciously forget (have no explicit memory of) an experience but at the same time show the effects (have an implicit memory) of that experience. There are different ways to interpret this pattern. Some psychologists believe that explicit and implicit memory are separate systems that are controlled by different parts of the brain, whereas others believe that the dissociations merely indicate differences in the way information is encoded and retrieved (Foster & Jelicic, 1999). Either way, it's useful to consider these two aspects of memory separately (see Table 6.1).

*Can you name the Seven Dwarfs? The answer appears on p. 235. (© Disney Enterprises, Inc.)*

**Explicit Memory**  Can you name all of Walt Disney's Seven Dwarfs? Try it. When I was put to the test, I could list only six. As hard as I tried, I could not come up with the seventh. This type of task, in which a person is asked to reproduce information without the benefit of external cues, is an example of a **free-recall** test of explicit memory. Other examples include taking an essay exam, describing a criminal's face to the police, and struggling to recall a childhood experience. Now try a different task. Consider the following names, and circle only those of the Seven Dwarfs: Grouchy, Gabby, Sleepy, Smiley, Happy, Jumpy, Droopy, Dopey, Sneezy, Goofy, Grumpy, Bashful, Cheerful, Wishful, Doc, and Pop. This task, which requires you to select a remembered item from a list of alternatives, is a **recognition** test. So are taking a multiple-choice exam and picking a criminal from a lineup, or identifying photographs from a family album.

Research shows that recall and recognition are both forms of explicit memory in that people are consciously trying to retrieve the information (Haist et al., 1992). There is, however, a key difference: People tend to perform better at recognition. The Seven Dwarfs task illustrates the point. When college students were asked to recall the characters on their own, they correctly produced an average of 69 percent of the names. Yet when they made selections from a list, the accuracy rate increased to 86 percent (Meyer & Hilterbrand, 1984). Even I was able to recognize the name that I could not recall (it was Bashful). Bahrick and others (1975) reported the same difference in a study of long-term memory. They showed people pictures of classmates taken from their high-school yearbooks. Seven years after graduating, subjects were able to correctly *recall* only 60 percent of the names belonging to each face. But those who only had to *recognize* the right names from a list of possible alternatives were 90 percent accurate—even when tested fourteen years after graduation.

The fact that recognition is easier than recall tells us that forgetting sometimes occurs not because memory has decayed but because the information is difficult to reclaim from storage. Retrieval failure is a common experience. Have you ever felt as

**free recall**  A type of explicit-memory task in which a person must reproduce information without the benefit of external cues (e.g., an essay exam).

**recognition**  A form of explicit-memory retrieval in which items are represented to a person who must determine if they were previously encountered.

though a word or a name you were trying to recall was just out of reach—on the tip of your tongue? In a classic study of the tip-of-the-tongue phenomenon, Roger Brown and David McNeill (1966) prompted this experience by giving students definitions of uncommon words and asking them to produce the words themselves. For example, what is "the green-colored matter found in plants"? And what is "the art of speaking in such a way that the voice seems to come from another place"? Most often, subjects either knew the word right away or were certain that they did not know it. But at times, subjects knew they knew the word but could not recall it—a frustrating state that Brown and McNeill likened to being on the brink of a sneeze.

The experience is an interesting one. When a word is on the tip of the tongue, subjects often come up with other words that are similar in sound or meaning. Groping for *chlorophyll,* subjects might say *chlorine* or *cholesterol.* For *ventriloquism,* they produce words such as *ventilate* and *vernacular.* In fact, a surprising number of people will guess the correct first letter, last letter, and number of syllables contained in the missing word. These cases reveal that the information is in memory but that people need "hints" to dislodge it (A. Brown, 1991). Thus, while people in their seventies and eighties have more tip-of-the-tongue experiences than do younger adults, they too can bring the words to mind when given the right prompting (Heine et al., 1999). The tip-of-the-tongue experience is common, frustrating, and effortful, and it tells us something about why stored memories are sometimes "lost" and how they can be retrieved (Schwartz, 2002).

Recognition is often easier than recall because recognition tasks contain retrieval cues, or reminders. A retrieval cue is a stimulus that helps us to access information in long-term memory. According to Tulving's (1983) principle of **encoding specificity,** any stimulus that is encoded along with an experience can later trigger one's memory of that experience. The retrieval cue may be a picture, a location, a word, a song, another person, or even a fragrance or the mood we're in.

**Context-Dependent Memory**    Tulving's principle gave rise to the interesting notion that memory is "context dependent"—that people find it easier to retrieve

**encoding specificity** The principle that any stimulus encoded along with an experience can later jog one's memory of that experience.

*From left to right, Snow White's Seven Dwarfs are Sneezy, Doc, Grumpy, Bashful, Happy* (front row), *and Sleepy and Dopey* (back row).

*With the names of American soldiers killed in action etched in black marble, the Vietnam Veterans Memorial in Washington, D.C., serves as a powerful retrieval cue for the veterans who survived and the loved ones of those who did not.*

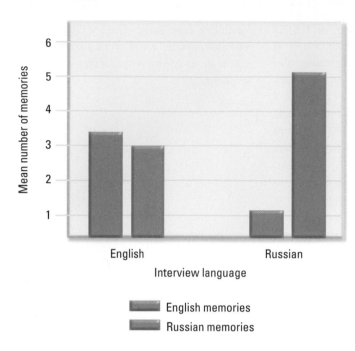

**FIGURE 6.15** **Memory as context dependent**
Russian-English bilinguals were prompted in English and in Russian to recall stories about certain types of events from their lives. Illustrating language-dependent memory, they recalled more Russian-experienced events when interviewed in Russian and more English-experienced events when interviewed in English (Marian & Neisser, 2000).

information from memory when they're in the same situation in which the information was obtained in the first place. In an unusual initial test of this hypothesis, researchers presented scuba divers with a list of words in one of two settings: fifteen feet underwater or on the beach. Then they tested the divers in the same setting or in the other setting. Illustrating context-dependent memory, the divers recalled 40 percent more words when the material was learned and retrieved in the same context (Godden & Baddeley, 1975).

More recent studies have reinforced the point. In one experiment, subjects reported on sixteen events from their own past while sitting indoors in a dimly lit cubicle or outdoors in a scenic garden. As in the scuba-diver study, those who were returned, two days later, to the same setting recalled more of the events from the previous session than those who were taken to the other setting (Eich, 1995). In a second study, subjects read an article while wearing headphones that played taped cafeteria noise or silence. They then took a memory test with the background noise playing or in silence. Sure enough, subjects recalled more facts from the article when the learning and test-taking situations were similarly noisy or silent than when they differed. This finding has an important practical implication: because classrooms are typically quiet during testing, it's best to study in a quiet setting (Grant et al., 1998). In a third study, Viorica Marian and Ulric Neisser (2000) interviewed Russian-English bilinguals both in English and in Russian, prompting them to retrieve stories of certain types of events from their own lives. Illustrating language-dependent memory, participants recalled more Russian-experienced events when interviewed in Russian and more English-experienced events when interviewed in English (see Figure 6.15).

With memory being somewhat context dependent, smells are especially potent reminders of the past (Schab & Crowder, 1995). A whiff of perfume, the top of a baby's head, freshly cut grass, the musty odor of a basement, a steamy locker room, the smell of mothballs in the attic, and the leathery scent of a new car—each may trigger what Diane Ackerman (1990) called "aromatic memories." Frank Schab (1990) tested this hypothesis in a series of experiments. In one, subjects were given a list of adjectives and instructed to write an antonym for each one. In half of the sessions, the sweet smell of chocolate was blown into the room. The next day, subjects were asked to list as many of the antonyms as they could—again, in the presence or absence of the chocolate aroma. The most words were recalled when the smell of chocolate was present at both the learning and the recall sessions. The aroma was encoded along with the words, so it later served as a retrieval cue.

Context seems to activate memory even in three-month-old infants. In a series of studies, Carolyn Rovee-Collier and her colleagues (1992) trained infants to shake an overhead mobile equipped with colorful blocks and bells by kicking a leg that was attached to the mobile by a ribbon. The infants were later more likely to recall what they learned—which they demonstrated by kicking—when tested in the same crib containing the same visual cues than when there were differences.

There's no doubt about it, we can often jog a memory by reinstating the initial context of an experience. This explains why I'll often march with determination into my secretary's office only to go blank, forget why I am there, return in defeat to my desk, look around, and ZAP! suddenly recall what it was I needed.

**State-Dependent Memory**   Internal cues that become associated with an event may also spark the retrieval of explicit memories. Illustrating the phenomenon of "state-dependent" memory, studies reveal that it is often easier to recall something when our state of mind is the same at testing as it was during encoding. If you have an experience when you are happy or sad, drunk or sober, calm or aroused, that experience—unless your emotional state is intensely distracting—is more likely to pop to mind or be free-recalled when your internal state later is the same than when it's different (Bower, 1981; Kenealy, 1997). Eric Eich (1995) has found that the reason it helps to be memory-tested in the same place where you learned the material is that the environment is likely to transport you back to the same mood state—and it's this mood state that serves as a retrieval cue.

When it comes to internal states and memory, there is a complicating factor: The mood we're in often leads us to evoke memories that are congruent with that mood. When people are happy, the good times are easiest to recall. But when people are sad, depressed, or anxious, their minds become flooded with negative events of the past. Currently depressed people thus report having more intrusive memories of death and other bad experiences compared to nondepressed controls (Brewin et al., 1999).

**Implicit Memory**   In 1911, physician Edouard Claparède described an encounter he had with a young woman who suffered from Korsakoff's syndrome—a brain disorder, common among chronic alcoholics, that impairs the transfer of information into long-term memory. When Claparède was introduced to the woman, he hid in his right palm a pin that pricked her painfully as the two shook hands. The next day, he returned to the hospital. Due to her memory disorder, the patient did not recognize the doctor and could not answer questions about their prior interaction. Yet when he reached out to shake her hand, she pulled back abruptly. Why did she refuse? After some confusion, all she could say was "Sometimes pins are hidden in people's hands" (Schwartz & Reisberg, 1991).

**Implicit Memory in Amnesia Patients**   Did Claparède's patient remember him or not? On the one hand, she knew enough to be afraid. On the other hand, she did not know why. It was as if she had a memory but didn't know it. As unusual as this story may seem, we now know that there are many others like it. As in the case of H.M., cognitive psychologists are keenly interested in people with amnesia. Earlier, researchers believed that amnesics lacked the ability to encode or store information in long-term memory. They could still perform "skills"—but could not keep new "information" in memory.

Or could they? In 1970, Elizabeth Warrington and Lawrence Weiskrantz published an article in *Nature* that challenged the prevailing view. These researchers gave a list of words to four amnesics and sixteen normal control subjects. Four memory tests were then administered. Two were standard measures of explicit memory—one a recall task, the second involving recognition. The other tests were indirect measures of implicit memory in which the subjects were asked merely to complete word fragments (such as k- - -ht, c-l- - -e, and t- - -v-s - on) and stems (for example, kni- - -, col- - - -, and tele- - - - - -) with the first "guess" that came to mind. The results are shown in Figure 6.16. As was expected, the control subjects scored higher than the amnesics on the

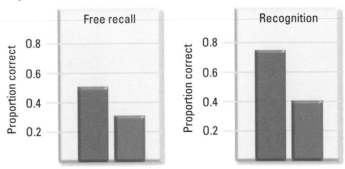

**Explicit tests**

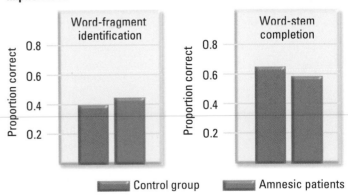

**Implicit tests**

■ Control group   ■ Amnesic patients

**FIGURE 6.16   Retention without awareness**
Amnesic patients and normal controls were tested for their memory of words previously learned. As you can see, the amnesics performed poorly on the measures of explicit memory (recall and recognition) but not on indirect measures of implicit memory (word-fragment and word-stem completion tasks). The amnesics retained the information but didn't know it (Warrington & Weiskrantz, 1970).

explicit-memory tests. But on the incomplete-word tasks, the amnesics were just as likely to form words that appeared on the original list. Like Claparède's Korsakoff's patient, they retained the information enough to use it. They just didn't realize it.

Today, many case studies indicate that amnesics know more than they realize. Consider H.M., the most celebrated amnesia patient of them all. At one point, *Memory's Ghost* author Philip Hilts (1995) visited H.M. in the hospital to interview him in the testing room, a place where as a patient he had spent many long hours. H.M. said he did not know where that room was—but then he stood up and reflexively turned his body in the right direction.

This dissociation—the tendency for amnesics to show signs of long-term retention of information without awareness—has now been amply observed in studies involving different types of amnesia and different implicit-memory tests. For example, researchers tried to classically condition an anterograde amnesia patient by pairing a harmless tone with electric shock. Although the patient could not later recall these sessions, he reacted with greater arousal whenever the tone was presented (Bechara et al., 1995). In another study, elderly patients with Alzheimer's disease, a progressive memory disorder, played a weather prediction game on a computer in which they had to guess *rain* or *shine* after learning, through trial and error, what clues signaled the correct prediction. Compared to healthy elderly controls, the Alzheimer's patients could not later recall the clues, the test, or the layout of the computer display. But they were accurate in their weather predictions—indicating that they had an implicit memory of what they had learned, a form of retention without awareness (Eldridge et al., 2002).

Finally, there's interesting research on what surgery patients can recall of events that took place in the operating room (Sebel et al., 1993). If you've had major surgery, you're probably scratching your head at this point. Yet in one study, twenty-five patients were read a list of word-pairs during their operations—after they were rendered "unconscious" by general anesthesia. Later on in the recovery room, and again after two weeks, these patients could not recall or recognize the items. But they frequently came up with the correct "guess" in response to the first word of each pair (Kihlstrom et al., 1990). In a second study, patients undergoing minor ear surgery were given a drug that makes them consciously sedated but then leaves them amnesic for the experience. While under this drug's influence, these patients were administered a mirror-reading task (try reading this sentence reflected in a mirror and you'll see it's not easy). The next day, they could not recall the task, yet they were quicker at reading words in a mirror when asked to do so. These patients had acquired the skill through practice even though they could not recall it (Thomas-Anterion et al., 1999).

These experiments can explain what happened to a woman who underwent a successful operation to remove a cyst but became deeply depressed afterward without knowing why. Weeks later, while in hypnosis, she recalled hearing the muffled voice of her surgeon during the operation utter the word *cancer,* and she was terrified. Although anesthetized, she had heard something that led her to become depressed even though she had no explicit memory of it (Coren, 1996).

**Implicit Memory in Everyday Life**   You don't have to suffer from brain damage or drug-induced amnesia to exhibit a dissociation between memory and awareness. Have you ever had the eerie feeling that you've been in a situation before, even though you had not? This is called *déjà vu,* and it is defined as the illusion that a new situation is familiar (the term is French for "already seen"). In a way, déjà vu is the opposite of amnesia. Whereas amnesics have memories without awareness or familiarity, the person with déjà vu has a sense of familiarity but no real memory. Estimates vary, but between 30 and 96 percent of people report having had such an episode (Sno & Linszen, 1990).

Déjà vu is not the only type of dissociation that is commonly experienced. Retention without awareness occurs in all of us—sometimes with interesting consequences. Let's now consider three consequences: false fame, eyewitness transference, and unintentional plagiarism.

1. *The false-fame effect.* Is Sebastian Weisdorf famous? He is not. But Larry Jacoby and others (1989) found a way to make him and other no-names famous overnight. They had subjects read aloud a long list of made-up names, supposedly to test the speed and accuracy of their pronunciation. Some of the names appeared repeatedly, but others were read only once. The next day, subjects received a new list of names—some famous, some nonfamous, and some from the first list that were nonfamous. Their task was to decide for each one whether it was the name of a famous person. This seems easy enough, and, for the most part, it was. Research participants easily distinguished between the names that were truly famous and those that were not, and they were sure that the names repeatedly presented the day before were not famous. But they misjudged as famous many of the names that were previously presented only once. Why? These names were familiar, but subjects did not know why. Not realizing that these names were from the first list, subjects made an assumption: If the name rings a bell, the person must be famous.

2. *Eyewitness transference.* False fame may seem amusing, but retention without awareness can also have serious consequences. Several years ago, psychologist Donald Thompson was falsely accused of rape on the basis of the victim's recollection. Luckily for Thompson, he was being interviewed live on television as the rape occurred—an interview, ironically, on the subject of human memory. Apparently, the victim was watching Thompson's show just before being attacked and then mistook him for the rapist. Was Thompson familiar to her? Yes, he was—but from the TV show, not from the crime scene. Thanks to his airtight alibi, Thompson was instantly vindicated. Perhaps others have not been so fortunate.

   The problem illustrated by this story is that sometimes witnesses remember a face but forget the circumstances in which they saw it. In one study, subjects witnessed a staged crime and then looked through mug shots (Brown et al., 1977). A few days later, they were asked to view a lineup. The result was startling: Subjects were as likely to identify an innocent person whose photograph was in the mug shots as they were to pick the actual criminal. This familiarity effect gives rise to the phenomenon of eyewitness transference, whereby a person seen in one situation is later confused in memory, or "transferred," to another situation—often with tragic consequences (Ross et al., 1994).

3. *Unintentional plagiarism.* False fame and unconscious transference occur when we are aware that something is familiar but we cannot pinpoint the correct source of that familiarity (Johnson et al., 1993; Mandler, 1980). In other words, the experience has an impact on behavior, but without our conscious awareness. There is another possible repercussion of implicit memory: unintentional plagiarism. In 2002, two popular historians and authors, the late Stephen Ambrose and Doris Kearns Goodwin were accused of lifting passages without quotation from other sources. Most of the sources were credited in footnotes, and both authors said the omission of quotation marks around the borrowed material was inadvertent, the unconscious result of careless recordkeeping.

   Have you ever had an insight you thought was original, only later to realize or be told that it was "borrowed" from another source? Are people who write, compose music, solve problems, tell jokes, or think up creative ideas vulnerable

*Doris Kearns Goodwin, a popular historian, was recently accused of lifting passages from other works without attribution. Had she fallen prey to unintentional plagiarism, a form of implicit memory?*

to unintentional plagiarism? Alan Brown and Dana Murphy (1989) had subjects in groups take turns generating items that fit a particular category (sports, four-legged animals, musical instruments, and clothing). After four rounds, they asked subjects individually to recall the items that they personally had generated and to come up with new ones from the same categories. As it turned out, 75 percent of the subjects took credit for at least one item of someone else's, and 71 percent came up with a "new" item that was given earlier. Some subjects inadvertently plagiarized their own ideas, but most often they "stole" from others in the group.

Additional research has shown that people are vulnerable to unintentional plagiarism in some situations more than others. Predictably, the problem is more likely to occur when the ideas taken are highly memorable, when the person who gave the original ideas has status, when the original ideas were shared in anonymous group situations, when subjects were distracted or in a hurry or not overly concerned about the origin of their ideas, and after a long period of time has elapsed (Marsh & Bower, 1993; Marsh et al., 1997; Tenpenny et al., 1998; Macrae et al., 1999). As in other research on implicit memory, these studies show that there is a bit of amnesia in us all. Commenting on the amount of unconscious plagiarism exhibited by research participants in his laboratory, Richard Marsh speculates that the problem is "a heck of a lot more common than anybody would realize" (Carpenter, 2002).

## FORGETTING

**6.3 Live! psych**

Before we celebrate the virtues of memory and outline the techniques we can use to improve it, let's stop and ponder the wisdom of William James (1890), who said, "If we remembered everything, we should on most occasions be as ill off as if we remembered nothing" (p. 680). James was right. Many years ago, Russian psychologist Alexander Luria (1968) described his observations of Solomon Shereshevskii, a man he called S., who had a truly exceptional memory. After one presentation, S. would remember lists containing dozens of items, recite them forward or backward, and still retain the information fifteen years later. But there was a drawback: No matter how hard S. tried, he could not forget. Images of letters, numbers, and other items of trivia were so distracting that he had to quit his job and support himself by entertaining audiences with his feats of memory. Sometimes it is better to forget—which is why some psychologists have suggested the paradoxical conclusion that forgetting is an adaptive, economical aspect of human memory (Anderson & Milson, 1989; Bjork & Bjork, 1996; Schacter, 1999).

*"Memory is the thing you forget with."*
—ALEXANDER CHASE

**The Forgetting Curve** Memory failure is a common experience in everyday life (see Table 6.2). I wish I had a dollar for every time I left something I needed at home, neglected to bring up a point in a conversation, or forgot the name of someone I met. To measure the rate at which information is forgotten, Ebbinghaus (1885; reprinted in 1913) tested his own memory for nonsense syllables after intervals ranging from twenty minutes to thirty-one days. As shown in the **forgetting curve** plotted in Figure 6.17, Ebbinghaus found that there was a steep loss of retention within the first hour, that he forgot more than 60 percent of the items within nine hours, and that the rate of forgetting leveled off after that. How quickly we forget.

The Ebbinghaus forgetting curve shows a rapid loss of memory for meaningless nonsense syllables. Does it apply to real-life memories as well? Bahrick (1984) tested nearly eight hundred English-speaking adults who took Spanish in high school. Depending on the subject, the interval between learning and being tested

**forgetting curve** A consistent pattern in which the rate of memory loss for input is steepest right after input is received and levels off over time.

## TABLE 6.2    FORGETTING IN EVERYDAY LIFE

How's your memory? Read the statements below and think about how often you've had each experience. The numbers in parentheses are the ratings given by the average person (Baddeley, 1990).

_____ 1. Forgetting where you have put something; losing things around the house (5)

_____ 2. Having to go back to check whether you have done something that you meant to do (4)

_____ 3. Failing to recognize, by sight, close relatives or friends that you meet frequently (1)

_____ 4. Telling friends a story or joke that you have told them once already (2)

_____ 5. Forgetting where things are normally kept, or looking for them in the wrong place (2)

_____ 6. Finding that a word is on the "tip of your tongue"; you know what it is but cannot quite find it (4)

_____ 7. Forgetting important details of what you did or what happened to you the day before (1)

_____ 8. Forgetting important details about yourself, such as your birthday or where you live (1)

_____ 9. Completely forgetting to take things with you, or leaving things behind and having to go back and fetch them (3)

_____10. Finding that the faces of famous people, seen on TV or in photographs, look unfamiliar (2)

Note: Subjects responded on the following scale: 1 = never in the last six months, 2 = once in six months, 4 = once a month, 5 = more than once a month, . . . 9 = more than once a day.

---

ranged from zero to fifty years. Compared to students who had just taken the course, those who were tested two to three years later had forgotten much of what they learned. After that, however, scores on vocabulary, grammar, and reading-comprehension tests stabilized—even among people who had not used Spanish for forty or fifty years (see Figure 6.18). A similar pattern was also found for the retention, for up to twelve years, of material learned in a college psychology course (Conway et al., 1991). In one study, Dutch researchers found that people remembered the street names from their elementary-school neighborhoods up to seventy-one years later (Schmidt et al., 2000). These kinds of impressive results have led Bahrick to argue that such knowledge may enter a *permastore*—a term he coined to describe permanent, very-long-term memory for well-learned material.

It's interesting that although this very-long-term curve is not identical to that reported by Ebbinghaus, there are similarities. Based on a summary analysis of 210 post-Ebbinghaus studies, David Rubin and Amy Wenzel (1996) concluded that his classic forgetting curve describes a consistent and lawful pattern of human retention and forgetting. They also raise the possibility that we may have several long-term memory stores corresponding to different periods of time (Rubin et al., 1999).

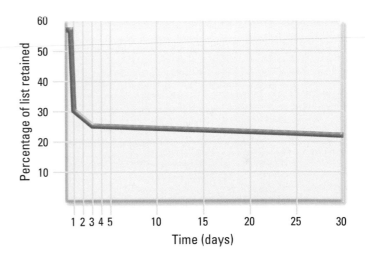

**FIGURE 6.17    The Ebbinghaus forgetting curve**
Ebbinghaus's forgetting curve indicates the rate at which nonsense syllables were forgotten. You can see that there was a steep decline in performance within the first day and that the rate of forgetting leveled off over time.

**Why Do People Forget?**   Knowing the rate at which information is lost is just the first step. The next important question is: Why? Do memory traces fade with time? Are they displaced by newer memories? Or do memories get buried, perhaps blocked by unconscious forces? As we'll see, forgetting can result from one of four processes: a lack of encoding, decay, interference, or repression. In the first two, the forgotten information is simply not in long-term-memory storage. In the second two, the memory may exist, but it is difficult, if not impossible, to retrieve.

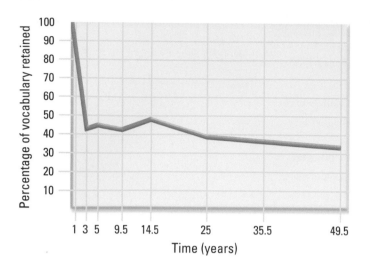

**FIGURE 6.18    Long-term forgetting curve**
This forgetting curve indicates the rate at which adults forgot the Spanish they took in high school. Compared to new graduates, those tested two to three years later forgot much of what they learned. After that, however, test scores stabilized (Bahrick, 1984).

**Lack of Encoding**    Do you know what an American penny looks like? Would you recognize one if you saw it? If you were born in the United States, you have looked at, held, and counted thousands of pennies in your life. Yet many people cannot accurately draw one from memory, name its features, or distinguish between a real penny and a fake. Look at the coins in Figure 6.19. Do you know which is the real one? Raymond Nickerson and Marilyn Adams (1979) presented this task to college students and found that 58 percent did *not* identify the right coin. The reason for this result is not that the subjects forgot what a penny looks like—it's that the features were never encoded into long-term memory in the first place. And why should they be? So long as you can tell the difference between pennies and other coins, there is no need to attend to the fine details. The penny is not the only common, everyday object whose features we fail to notice. People also have difficulty recalling the features of a dollar bill, computer keyboard, the front-page spread of their favorite newspaper, and even the layout of a telephone—objects we look at and use all the time (Rinck, 1999).

When it comes to encoding information, people can be so profoundly absent-minded that they exhibit "change blindness," a failure to detect changes that take place in their presence. In an astonishing demonstration of this phenomenon, Daniel Simons and Daniel Levin (1998) had a research assistant approach people on a college campus and ask for directions. While they were talking, two men walked between them holding a door that concealed a second assistant. With the subject screened from view, the two assistants switched places so that when the men carrying the door passed, subjects found themselves talking to a different person. Did subjects notice the switch? Would *you* have noticed it? Remarkably, out of fifteen subjects who were tested, only seven noticed the change. Other studies, too, have shown this type of visual forgetting from a lack of attention (Simons, 2000).

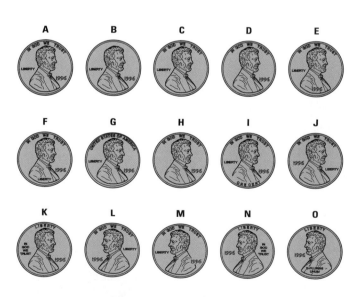

**FIGURE 6.19    Can you recognize a penny?**
Which of these pennies is the real thing? The answer appears on p. 243 (Nickerson & Adams, 1979).

**Decay**    The oldest theory of forgetting is that memory traces erode with the passage of time. But there are two problems with this simple explanation. One is that there is no physiological evidence of decay that corresponds to the fading of memory. The second is that time alone is not the most critical factor. As we saw earlier, memory for newly learned nonsense syllables fades in a matter of hours, but the foreign language learned in high school is retained for many years.

The key blow to the decay theory of forgetting was landed in 1924 by John Jenkins and Karl Dallenbach. Day after day, these researchers presented nonsense syllables to two subjects and then tested their memory after one, two, four, or eight hours. On some days, the subjects went to sleep between learning and testing; on other days, they stayed awake and kept busy. The subjects recalled more items after they had slept than when they were awake and involved in other activities. Jenkins and Dallenbach concluded that "forgetting is not so much a matter of the decay of old impressions and associations as it is a matter of interference, inhibition, or obliteration of the old by the new" (p. 612). To minimize forgetting, students may find it helpful to go to sleep shortly after studying, thus avoiding "new information" (Fowler et al., 1973). To learn more, see *How to: Improve Your Memory*.

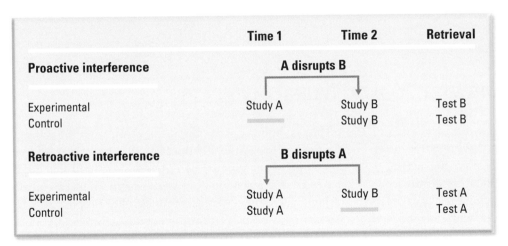

**FIGURE 6.20   Interference and forgetting**
As shown, proactive interference occurs when information acquired at Time 1 inhibits memory for material learned later. Retroactive interference occurs when information learned at Time 2 inhibits memory for material learned earlier. The more similar the two sets of items are, the greater is the interference.

**Interference**   By showing that memory loss may be caused by mental activity that takes place when we are awake, Jenkins and Dallenbach's study suggested a third explanation of forgetting—that something learned may be forgotten due to interference from other information. As summarized in Figure 6.20, there are two kinds of interference. In **proactive interference**, prior information inhibits our ability to recall something new. If you try to learn a set of names, formulas, phone numbers, or glossary terms, you will find it more difficult if you had earlier studied a similar set of items. Many years ago, Benton Underwood (1957) found that the more nonsense-syllable experiments subjects had taken part in, the more forgetting they exhibited in a brand-new study.

A related problem is **retroactive interference**, whereby new material disrupts memory for previously learned information. Thus, subjects in various experiments are at least temporarily less likely to recognize previously seen pictures of nature scenes, faces, and common objects if they are then exposed to similar photographs before being tested (Chandler, 1991; Wheeler, 1995; Windschitl, 1996). One learning experience can displace—or at least inhibit—the retrieval of another. That is why, when people go back and review a subset of to-be-remembered information, their memory for nonreviewed material suffers (Koutsaal et al., 1999).

**Repression**   More than a hundred years ago, Sigmund Freud, the founder of psychoanalysis, observed that his patients often could not recall unpleasant past events from their own lives. In fact, he observed, they would sometimes stop, pull back, and lose their train of thought just as they seemed on the brink of an insight. Freud called this repression, and he said it was an unconscious defense mechanism that keeps painful personal memories under lock and key—and out of awareness. We'll see in Chapter 16 that people who suffer childhood traumas such as war, abuse, and rape sometimes develop "dissociative disorders" characterized by apparent gaps in their explicit memory. Although repression has never been demonstrated in a laboratory setting, psychotherapy case studies suggest that memories can be repressed for long periods of time and recovered in therapy. As we'll see later in this chapter, however, it is difficult in actual cases to distinguish between dormant memories of actual past events and falsely constructed memories of experiences that never occurred (Loftus, 1993a; Read & Lindsay, 1997).

*The correctly drawn penny is shown in (A).*

I recently recovered a crucial repressed memory. But then I forgot it.

## *How To*

# IMPROVE YOUR MEMORY

Over the years, psychologists have stumbled on a few rare individuals who seemed equipped with extraordinary "hardware" for memory. But often the actors, waiters, and others who impress us with their extraordinary memories are ordinary people who use memory tricks called **mnemonics**—in other words, they tinker with memory's "software." Can you too boost your recall capacity and improve your study skills by using mnemonics? Let's consider the self-help implications of this chapter, many of which are described in paperbacks on how to improve your memory.

■ **PRACTICE TIME.** To learn names, dates, vocabulary words, or the concepts in a textbook, you'll find that practice makes perfect. In general, the more time spent studying, the better. Skimming or speed-reading will not promote long-term retention. In fact, it pays to *over*learn—that is, to review the material even after you think you have it mastered. It also helps to distribute your studying over time rather than cram all at once. You will retain more information from four two-hour sessions than from one eight-hour marathon.

■ **DEPTH OF PROCESSING.** The sheer amount of practice is important, but only if it's "quality time." Mindless drills may help maintain information in short-term memory, but long-term retention requires that you think actively and deeply about material—about what it means and how it is linked to what you already know. There are many ways to increase your depth of processing. Ask yourself critical questions about the material. Think about it in ways that relate to your own experiences. Talk about the material to a friend, thus forcing yourself to organize it in terms that can be understood.

■ **HIERARCHICAL ORGANIZATION.** Organize information hierarchically—as in an outline. Start with a few broad categories, then divide them into subcategories.

This is how experts chunk new information, and it works. When Andrea Halpern (1986) presented subjects with fifty-four popular song titles, she found that recall was greater when the titles were organized hierarchically than when they were scrambled. The implication for studying is clear: Organize your notes, preferably in the form of an outline—and be sure to review these notes later (Kiewra et al., 1991).

■ **VERBAL MNEMONICS.** Sometimes the easiest way to remember a list of items is to use verbal mnemonics, or "memory tricks." Chances are you have already used popular methods such as *rhymes* ("*I* before *E* except after *C*"; "Thirty days hath September, April, June, and November") and acronyms that reduce the amount of

*Every year, ordinary people trained in the use of common mnemonics compete in the Memory Olympics. Under pressure, these "mental athletes" try to memorize as fast as possible decks of playing cards (the world record is 34 seconds), lists of random words (the record is 174 words), pairs of names and faces (the record is 70), and so on. (© 2002 ABC Photography Archives.)*

## RECONSTRUCTION

Up to now, we have likened human memory to a computer that faithfully encodes, stores, and retrieves information from the recent and distant past. Clearly, however, there is more to the story. As we'll see, remembering is an active process in which we reconstruct memories according to our beliefs, wishes, needs, and information received from outside sources.

In 1932, Frederick Bartlett asked British college students to recall a story taken from the folklore of a Native American culture. He found that although they

**mnemonics** Memory aids designed to facilitate the recall of new information.

information to be stored (for example, ROY G BIV can be used to recall the colors of the light spectrum: *Red, Orange, Yellow, Green, Blue, Indigo,* and *Violet*).

■ METHOD OF LOCI.   Most books on improving memory recommend that verbal information be represented as visual images. One popular use of imagery is the method of loci, in which items to be recalled are mentally placed in familiar locations. It works like this: First you memorize a series of objects along a familiar route. For example, you might imagine your morning walk from the bedroom, to the bathroom, to the kitchen, and out the door. As you follow this path, visualize the objects you pass: your bed, then the bathroom door, shower, stairs, and so on. These places become pigeonholes for items to be recalled. To memorize a shopping list, for example, you could picture a dozen eggs lined up on the bed, a bag of red apples hanging on the bathroom door, and butter in the soap dish of the shower. When you take a mental stroll through the house, the items on the list should pop to mind. The trick is to link new items to others already in memory.

■ PEG-WORD METHOD.   Another powerful imagery mnemonic is the peg-word method, in which a list of words serves as memory "pegs" for the material to be recalled. The first step is to learn a list of peg words that correspond to numbers. For example: "one is a bun, two is a shoe, three is a tree," and so on. Next you hang each item to be recalled on each of the pegs by forming a mental image of the two interacting. As illustrated in Table 6.3, the images of a shoe kicking an apple, and a tree made from sticks of butter are easier to recall than words on a page. The more interactive the image, the better. Try it and you'll see how well it works. Most people are able to memorize ten new items in order with the peg-word mnemonic.

■ INTERFERENCE.   Because one learning experience can disrupt memory for another, you should guard against

| TABLE 6.3 | THE PEG-WORD MNEMONIC | |
|---|---|---|
| **Step 1** *Memorize these peg words in order.* | **Step 2** *Hang new items on the peg words.* | **Step 3** *Form a bizarre, interactive image.* |
| One is a bun | Bun—egg | |
| Two is a shoe | Shoe—apple | |
| Three is a tree | Tree—butter | |
| Four is a door | Door—cola | |
| Five is a hive | Hive—pasta | |
| Six is sticks | Sticks—tuna | |
| Seven is heaven | Heaven—steak | |
| Eight is a gate | Gate—sugar | |
| Nine is wine | Wine—chips | |
| Ten is a hen | Hen—lettuce | |

the effects of interference. This problem is common among students, as material learned in one course can make it harder to retain that learned in another. To minimize interference, follow two simple suggestions. First, study right before sleeping and review all the material right before the exam. Second, allocate an uninterrupted chunk of time to one course; then do the same for the others. If you study psychology, then move to biology, then go on to math and back to psychology, each course will disrupt your memory of the others—especially if the material is similar.

■ CONTEXT REINSTATEMENT.   Information is easier to recall when people are in the physical setting in which it was acquired—and in the same frame of mind. The setting and the mood it evokes serve as cues that trigger the retrieval of to-be-remembered information. That's why actors like to rehearse on the stage where they will later perform. So next time you have an important exam to take, try to study in the room where you'll take the test, ideally at the same time of day.

correctly recalled the gist of this story, they changed, exaggerated, added, and omitted certain details—resulting in a narrative that was more coherent to them. Without realizing it, subjects reconstructed the material to fit their own **schemas,** a term that Bartlett used to describe the preconceptions that people have about persons and situations. Other researchers have more recently replicated this result using the same Native American story (Bergman & Roediger, 1999).

It's now clear that schemas distort memory, often by leading us to fill in missing pieces. Research by Helene Intraub and others (1998) illustrates the point. In a series

*Live! psych* 6.4

**schemas**   Preconceptions about persons, objects, or events that bias the way new information is interpreted and recalled.

**FIGURE 6.21**

After subjects were shown close-up photographs of a scene like the one depicted on the left, they mentally extended the borders by reporting or drawing details that were not in the pictures but might plausibly exist outside the camera's field of view (*right*). According to Intraub and others (1998), scenes like this one activate perceptual schemas into which people fill in missing details.

of studies, they showed people close-up photographs of various scenes—such as a telephone booth on a street corner, a basketball on a gym floor, and a lawn chair on a grassy field. Consistently, subjects who were later asked to recall these scenes mentally extended the borders by reporting or drawing details that were not in the pictures but might plausibly have existed outside the camera's field of view (see Figure 6.21). Why? It appears that the scenes activated perceptual schemas that led subjects over time to insert new details into memory.

There are many other examples of how schemas influence memory. In one study, subjects were left waiting alone in a small cluttered room that the experimenter called an "office." (Before reading the next sentence, try the demonstration in Figure 6.22.) After thirty-five seconds, subjects were taken out and asked to recall what was in the room. What happened? Nearly everyone remembered the desk, chair, and shelves, objects typically found in an office. But many of the subjects also mistakenly recalled seeing books—items that fit the setting but were not actually present (Brewer & Treyens, 1981). Our schemas are sometimes so strong that an object that does not belong becomes particularly memorable. After spending time in an office, people are more likely to remember the presence of toy trucks, blocks, and finger paints than of textbooks, a typewriter, and an ashtray. But they are also more likely to imagine the existence of office objects that fit the setting but were not present (Pezdek et al., 1989; Lampinen et al., 2001).

**The Misinformation Effect** Memory is an active construction of the past—a construction that alters reality in ways that are consistent not only with prior expectations but also with postevent information. Consider the plight of those who witness street crimes. Afterward, they talk to each other, read about it in the newspapers, sometimes even watch coverage on television. By the time these witnesses are questioned by authorities, one wonders if their original memory is still "pure," uncontaminated by postevent information.

According to Elizabeth Loftus (1979), it probably is not. Using her studies of eyewitness testimony, Loftus proposed a theory of reconstructive

**FIGURE 6.22 "Office" schema**

Look at this picture of an office for thirty seconds. Then list all the objects you recall as being in the room.

*Subjects saw a slide show in which this car turns at a corner that has either a STOP sign (left) or a YIELD sign (right). Illustrating the misinformation effect, subjects who were later asked questions that implied the presence of the other sign were more likely to "recognize" the wrong slide (Loftus et al., 1978).*

memory. After people observe an event, she said, later information about the event—whether it's true or not—becomes integrated into the fabric of their memory.

A classic study by Loftus and her colleagues (1978) illustrates what has been called the **misinformation effect.** In that study, they presented subjects with a slide show in which a red car hits a pedestrian after turning at an intersection. Subjects saw either a STOP sign or a YIELD sign in the slides, but then embedded in a series of questions they were asked was one that implied the presence of the other sign ("Did another car pass the Datsun as it reached the _____ sign?"). The result: The number of subjects who later "recognized" the slide with the wrong traffic sign increased from 25 percent to 59 percent. Other studies soon confirmed the effect. Researchers thus misled subjects into recalling hammers as screwdrivers, Coke cans as cans of peanuts, breakfast cereal as eggs, green objects as yellow, a clean-shaven man as having a mustache, and a bare-handed man as wearing gloves. To make matters worse, these subjects are often quick to respond and confident in the accuracy of these false memories (Loftus et al., 1989).

This provocative theory has aroused controversy. Does misinformation permanently impair a witness's real memory, never to be retrieved again (Belli et al., 1994; Weingardt et al., 1995)? Or do subjects merely follow the experimenter's "suggestion," leaving a true memory intact for retrieval under other conditions (Dodson & Reisberg, 1991; McCloskey & Zaragoza, 1985)? Either way, an important practical lesson remains: Whether witnesses' memories are truly altered or not, their reports of what they remember are hopelessly biased by postevent information. And this misinformation effect is hard to erase (Johnson & Seifert, 1998). These findings have serious implications for our legal system. (See *Psychology and Law.*)

**The Creation of Illusory Memories** The misinformation effect led cognitive psychologists to discover that people sometimes create memories that are completely false. At the start of this chapter, we saw that people who heard a list of sleep-related words (*bed, yawn*) or music-related words (*jazz, instrument*) were often convinced just minutes later that they had also heard *sleep* and *music*—words that fit but were not actually on the list (Roediger & McDermott, 1995). This result is easy to find—even if the test is delayed twenty-four hours (Payne et al., 1996), even when subjects are forewarned about the false memory effect (Gallo et al., 1997), and even when the words are flashed so rapidly that subjects cannot recall

**misinformation effect**   The tendency to incorporate false postevent information into one's memory of the event itself.

## THE PROCESS OF DISCOVERY

# ELIZABETH F. LOFTUS
### *Memory as Reconstructive*

**Q: How did you first become interested in psychology?**

**A:** I was first introduced to psychological science as an undergraduate at UCLA. Although I was a math major, I took introductory psychology from Allen Parducci and got hooked. Nearly every elective I took was in psychology, so I had enough credits for a double major. Lucky for me (or perhaps wisdom) I continued on to graduate work in psychology at Stanford. I wanted to combine math and psychology, but I ended up becoming a cognitive psychologist with a strong interest in human memory.

**Q: How did you come up with your important discovery?**

**A:** After graduate school, I continued researching how information is stored and retrieved from long-term memory. But I felt an urge to do something that had social relevance. I had always been interested in law and came to appreciate that with this interest, and a background in memory, the perfect thing to study was the memory of witnesses—how accurate it is and how it can be distorted.

I designed some studies in which people were shown films of automobile accidents and questioned about them. We showed that a simple question like "How fast were the cars going when they *smashed* into each other?" led witnesses to estimate speeds greater than control witnesses asked "How fast were the cars going when they *hit* each other?" Those asked the leading "smashed" question were also more likely to claim to have seen broken glass, even though there was none. I went on to publish many studies showing this kind of malleability of memory.

**Q: How has the field you inspired developed over the years?**

**A:** Now there have been thousands of studies showing that memories can be shaped by suggestion. When the epidemic of repressed memory claims infected the mass media, I wanted to find a way to plant an entirely false memory into someone's mind to study how it might occur in real cases. Eventually I came up with the idea of planting a memory of being lost in a shopping mall at age 5, and eventually being rescued and reunited with the family. We found that about a quarter of people developed a false memory for being lost. Other researchers followed with more clever studies, planting false memories using false suggestions, guided imagination, dream interpretation, and other techniques. Even impossible or implausible memories, such as witnessing demonic possession, or kissing a frog, could be planted.

**Q: What's your prediction on where the field is heading?**

**A:** It's almost a guarantee that we will continue to study false memories. Here's a possible, albeit speculative, future scenario: We master the ability to create false memories and learn who is most susceptible, and who is resistant. We learn, through neuroimaging, what parts of the brain are similarly or differently activated when a person has a true memory versus a false one. We develop precise recipes for what works with what kinds of people. Perhaps the most potent recipes will involve the use of drugs. Already there are "date rape" drugs that can cause deep sedation, blackouts, and amnesia for what is experienced under its influence. Imagine the memory distortion potential of behavioral techniques with a pharmaceutical twist—and the critical questions we will face about how to prevent this technology from being used in nefarious ways. This will drive home an essential message: Memory, like liberty, is a fragile thing.

*Elizabeth F. Loftus is Distinguished Professor of Psychology and Social Behavior, and of Criminology, Law, and Society, at the University of California at Irvine.*

having seen them (Seamon et al., 1998). Some words and lists produce more false memories than others, but regardless of whether items pertain to the concepts *car, fruit, city,* or *sweet,* people falsely "recall" hearing related words that were not actually presented (Roediger et al., 2001; Stadler et al., 1999).

Other research highlights the danger as well. In one study, people "recalled" nonexistent common objects in a scene—like toasters, clocks, and shoes—when a co-witness, actually a plant working for the experimenter, had reported seeing these items (Roediger, Meade et al., 2001). In another study, college students were repeatedly asked about vivid childhood events. Some were true, according to their parents, but others were fabricated—like having a birthday party with pizza and a clown, spilling punch on the parents of the bride at a wedding, and evacuating a grocery store when its sprinklers went off. The students did not recall any of the fictitious events at first, but after a few interviews, 20 to 30 percent generated false recollections. Some described the memories as "clear" (Hyman et al., 1995; Hyman & Billings, 1998). In the laboratory, people were even led, through a process of imagination, to create false memories of having performed some bizarre behaviors two weeks earlier—like balancing a spoon on the nose, sitting on dice, and rubbing lotion on a chair (Thomas & Loftus, 2002).

In Chapter 17, we'll see that these studies are unsettling for what they imply about the memories of childhood abuse that adults sometimes "recover" while in therapy.

## AUTOBIOGRAPHICAL MEMORY

- *What autobiographical memories are people most likely to preserve?*
- *What makes some experiences particularly vivid and enduring?*
- *What is childhood amnesia, and why does it occur?*
- *How are our personal memories shaped by our sense of self?*

Suppose you were to sit down to write your autobiography. What would you say? What experiences stand out in your mind? Would your reports of the past be accurate or distorted in some way? To answer these kinds of questions, psychologist Marigold Linton (1982) kept an extensive diary and later used it to test her memory for the events of her life. Every day for six years, she wrote the date on one side of an index card and a description of something that happened to her. In all, the diary contained 5,000 entries—some important, others trivial. Once a month, Linton pulled 150 cards at random from her file and tried to recall the events and date them correctly. Like Ebbinghaus, she found that as time passed, her personal memories took longer to recall, were harder to date, and were less detailed—but that, right from the start, this fading occurred at a slower rate. More recently, two psychologists kept personal diaries for seven months and were then tested by colleagues who asked about events that were in the diaries and nonevents that seemed plausible but did not occur. The subjects knew in advance that items would be fabricated for the test, yet they still made several false recollections (Conway et al., 1996).

Many cognitive psychologists have recently traded in their nonsense syllables to study **autobiographical memory**—the recollections people have of the events and experiences that have touched their lives (Fivush et al., 2003; Rubin, 1996; Thompson et al., 1998). There are two key questions about these memories: (1) What aspects of our own past do we tend to preserve—and what are we likely to forget? (2) Are we generally accurate in our mental time travel, or does memory change as we get older?

### WHAT EVENTS DO PEOPLE REMEMBER?

When people are prompted to recall their own experiences, they typically report more events that are recent than are from the distant past. There are two consistent exceptions to this rule. The first is that older adults retrieve an unusually large number of personal memories from their adolescence and early adulthood years

## REVIEW QUESTIONS

- *What is elaborative rehearsal, and why is it important?*
- *Summarize the format, content, and neural bases of long-term-memory storage.*
- *Distinguish between context- and state-dependent memory. What is the evidence for each?*
- *Describe examples of implicit memory in everyday life.*
- *Describe four possible explanations for why people forget.*
- *How do schemas influence memory?*

*"The nice thing about having memories is that you can choose."*

—WILLIAM TREVOR

**autobiographical memory**   The recollections people have of their own personal experiences and observations.

## Psychology and Law

# EYEWITNESS IDENTIFICATION BIASES

"I'll never forget that face!" When these words are uttered, police officers, judges, and juries take notice. The problem is, witnesses make mistakes. In recent years, over one hundred convicted felons in prison, some on death row, were proved innocent by DNA tests not available at the time of their trials. More than 80 percent of these cases had contained one or more mistaken eyewitness identifications (http://www.innocenceproject.org/).

How can this happen? What factors compromise an eyewitness's memory? Common sense tells us that brief exposure, long distance, and dim lighting all limit our eye-witnessing abilities. This problem was evident in the rash of D.C. sniper shootings, in the fall of 2002, where witnesses to each shooting disagreed about who and what they saw—and whether the snipers drove a white van, which they did not (Barker & Kovaleski, 2002).

Researchers have uncovered other less obvious problems as well. We now know, for example, that people often have trouble recognizing members of a race other than their own, that the presence of a weapon draws attention and reduces a witness's ability to identify the criminal, and that witnesses who are highly aroused zoom in on central features of an event—say, the culprit or the victim—but then lose the ability to recall other details (Cutler & Penrod, 1995; Loftus, 1996; Thompson et al., 1998).

Sometimes additional problems arise from the way police officers gather evidence from eyewitnesses. One common technique is the live lineup, where the police present their suspect to the witness along with five or six "foils" who are similar in their appearance. Many structural and procedural aspects of the lineup situation can lead eyewitnesses to make false identifications (Buckhout, 1974; Wells,

Poole    Cotton

*Jennifer Thompson was traumatized twice: the first time when she was raped, the second when she learned that she had identified a man proved innocent by DNA tests ten years later. Here you can see Thompson talking to Ronald Cotton, the innocent man she picked from a lineup (left). Notice the resemblance between Cotton and Bobby Poole, her actual assailant (right). For more information about this case—which was featured on PBS Frontline's "What Jennifer Saw"—visit www.pbs.org/wgbh/pages/frontline/shows/dna/.*

(Fitzgerald, 1988; Jansari & Parkin, 1996). This "reminiscence peak" may occur because these early years are busy and formative in one's life. William Mackavey and others (1991) analyzed the autobiographies written by forty-nine eminent psychologists and found that their most important life experiences tended to be concentrated between the ages of eighteen and thirty-five.

1993). For example, research shows that anything that makes one lineup member more distinctive than the others increases his or her chance of being selected—which may explain the case of Steve Titus, a man falsely accused of rape when a victim picked his photograph from a set of six. The other men generally resembled Titus, but his picture was smaller and was the only one without a border. He was also the only man in the group who was smiling.

Instructions that police give to witnesses at a lineup are also critical. In an experiment by Roy Malpass and Patricia Devine (1981), students saw a staged vandalism and then attended a lineup. Half the students were led to believe that the culprit was in the lineup; the others were informed that he might or might not be present. The result: Subjects given the first, more suggestive instruction felt compelled to pick *someone*—so many identified an innocent person. Other studies have confirmed this basic finding: When witnesses are led to believe that the culprit is in the lineup, the risk of a false identification increases (Steblay, 1997).

Perhaps the most surprising aspect of eyewitness performance has to do with confidence. In a series of experiments, Gary Wells, Rod Lindsay, and others staged a crime in front of unwary subjects who underwent cross-examination after trying to pick the culprit from mug shots. Other subjects, acting as jurors, watched and rated these witnesses. Time and again, jurors overestimated eyewitness accuracy and could not tell the difference between those who were correct versus incorrect in their identifications (Lindsay et al., 1989; Wells et al., 1979). The problem: subjects are highly influenced by how confident witnesses are, a factor that does not reliably predict accuracy. This last statement is surprising, but studies have shown that the witness who declares, "I am absolutely certain," is only somewhat more likely to be right than the one who appears unsure (Wells & Murray, 1984; Penrod & Cutler, 1995; Sporer et al., 1995).

One reason that an eyewitness's confidence is not a reliable indicator of accuracy is that confidence can be raised and lowered by external factors. For example, Wells and Bradfield (1999) found that witnesses given confirming feedback about their false identifications ("Good, you identified the actual suspect") also went on to reinvent their memory of other aspects of the eyewitnessing experience. Compared to witnesses not given feedback, they reported that they had paid more attention to the event, had a better view of the culprit, and found the identification easier to make. These witnesses became more confident about the entire experience simply because of social feedback. The result may be that eyewitness confidence is even less predictive of accuracy (Bradfield et al., 2002).

The research on eyewitness memory has enabled psychologists to estimate eyewitness performance in different situations. But can anything be done to improve the system—to increase the eyewitness accuracy? In 1999, the U.S. Justice Department took a bold step: it assembled a group of psychologists, police, prosecutors, and defense lawyers to devise specific "how to" guidelines. Led by Gary Wells, this group went on to publish *Eyewitness Evidence: A Guide for Law Enforcement* (Wells et al., 2000). Among the recommendations offered are the following:

- When interviewing a witness, police should use open-ended questions ("Can you tell me about the car?"), followed if necessary by closed-ended questions ("What color was it?"). Leading questions ("Was the car red?") should be avoided.
- In composing a photographic or live lineup, police should present the witness with a suspect and at least five others who generally fit the witness's description of the culprit. The suspect should not stand out in any way.
- The witness should be told that it's as important to clear innocent persons from suspicion as to identify guilty parties. The witness should then be instructed that the criminal may or may not be in the lineup presented.

In the years to come, it will be interesting to see what impact these guidelines have on the way police conduct lineups, on the quality of eyewitness identifications, and on judges and juries who evaluate this evidence in the courtroom. For now, it's clear that psychologists who study human memory are playing a valuable, practical role in today's legal system.

A second exception to the recency rule is that people are quick to remember transitional "firsts." Think about your college career. What events immediately pop to mind—and when did these events occur? Did you come up with the day you arrived on campus or the first time you met your closest friend? What about notable classes, exams, parties, or sports events? When David Pillemer and his colleagues (1996)

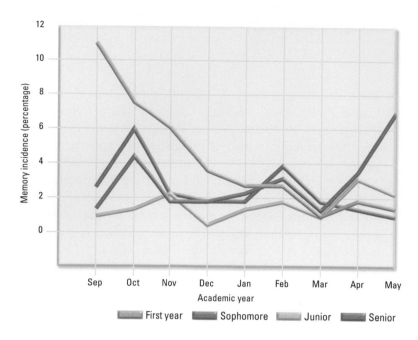

**FIGURE 6.23    Memorable transitions**
College graduates of varying ages were asked to recount their most memorable experiences while in college. You can see that among the memories that could be pinpointed in time, there was a large number from the first two months of their first year and a large number from the other major transitional period— the last month of their senior year.

**flashbulb memories**    Highly vivid and enduring memories, typically for events that are dramatic and emotional.

asked college juniors and seniors to recount the most memorable experiences of their first year, 32 percent of all recollections were from the transitional month of September. And when graduated college alumnae were given the same task, they too cited a disproportionate number of events from the opening two months of their first year—followed, interestingly, by the next major transitional period, the last month of their senior year (see Figure 6.23).

Obviously, not all experiences leave the same impression, and some dates are etched in memory for a lifetime. Marigold Linton (1982) found that unique events were easy to recall but that routines were quickly forgotten. More specifically, David Rubin and Marc Kozin (1986) had college students describe their clearest memories, and they found that births, deaths, weddings, accidents, injuries, sports events, romantic encounters, vacations, and graduations, were among the highlights that topped the list. Schrauf and Rubin (2001) had older Hispanic-American adults narrate their life stories and found that they produced the most recollections from the ages at which they left home and immigrated to the United States. Clearly, special events serve as autobiographical landmarks, reference points that we use to organize our personal memories (Shum, 1998).

Some events in our lives are so vivid that they seem to occupy a particularly special status in memory. Ask people who are old enough to remember November 22, 1963, and the chances are they can tell you exactly what was happening, where they were, and with whom the moment they heard the news that John F. Kennedy was shot. I, for one, will never forget that day—returning to my fifth-grade class after lunch, hearing the principal's voice crack over the loudspeaker, watching my teacher gasp, the silence of the bus ride home, the TV blaring as I walked through the door, and the tears streaming down my mother's reddened face.

Roger Brown and James Kulik (1977) questioned adults about that day and found that everyone had a memory that was as bold and vivid as a snapshot—not just of the assassination but of their own circumstances upon hearing the news. Brown and Kulik coined the term **flashbulb memories** to describe these very enduring, detailed, "high-resolution" recollections and speculated that humans are biologically equipped for survival purposes to "print" the most dramatic events in memory (as you may recall, physiological arousal releases hormones that can enhance memory). Research shows that flashbulb memories are triggered by events that are new to a person, important, surprising, and emotional (Conway, 1995).

Does this mean that information that is linked to emotional events is immune to forgetting? Not necessarily. Cognitive psychologist Ulric Neisser (1982) describes his vivid lifelong memory of the moment he heard that Pearl Harbor was bombed—how he was listening to a baseball game on the radio when the announcer broke in with the alarming news. Only years later did he realize that this so-called memory was impossible, that no baseball games were played on December 7, 1941. Research has confirmed Neisser's point that while some flashbulb memories are remarkably accurate, others are not (McCloskey et al., 1988). Either way, these recollections "feel" special and serve as prominent landmarks in the biographies we write about ourselves.

In contrast, there is a period of life that seems entirely lost to us. Think back to your earliest memory. It probably was not the sight of the doctor's hands in the delivery room, or the first time you waved, or even the first step you took as a toddler. An intriguing aspect of autobiographical memory is that most people generally cannot recall anything that happened before the age of three (Dudycha & Dudycha, 1941; Rubin, 1996). In one study, for example, Pillemer and others (1994) interviewed preadolescent children about a fire-drill evacuation they had experienced in preschool. Those who were four and five years old when the incident occurred were able to recall it seven years later; those who were three at the time could not. This memory gap, which is common, is known as **childhood amnesia**.

Why should this be? One possibility is that the forgetting is caused by the passage of time and by interference from later experiences. The problem with this explanation is that a college student may be unable to recall events from eighteen years ago, but a thirty-five-year-old can easily recall his or her college days after the same amount of time. Other explanations include the notion that young children lack the conceptual framework or self-concept for organizing information to be stored (Howe & Courage, 1993) and that the development of autobiographical memory is influenced by social factors—like the extent to which parents reminisce about the past with their young children (Harley & Reese, 1999).

Do early memories exist? It's hard to say. Some researchers have found that adults can recall certain critical events—moving, the birth of a sibling, being hospitalized, and the death of a family member—from the age of two, suggesting that there are exceptions to the rule (Usher & Neisser, 1993). Others caution that these reports may not be based on firsthand memories, but rather on stories told by parents, photographs, and other external sources (Loftus, 1993b; Eacott & Crawley, 1998). Still others maintain that people may have partial, implicit memories of the early years. Nora Newcombe and Nathan Fox (1994) found that ten-year-old children often reacted physiologically to slides of preschool classmates—even while failing to "recognize" those classmates. This finding is consistent with the fact that the hippocampus is not fully developed in the first few years of life and that infants and young children have memories that are *pre-explicit* (Nelson, 1995). It's also consistent with the fact that one- and two-year-olds can imitate people they see after long periods of time and show the long-term effects of other types of experience (Bauer, 1996). At some level, young children do remember the past. But these recollections are implicit—and not likely to become part of the autobiographical memories that form later in their childhood.

*Researchers are now testing the hypothesis that the terrorist attacks of September 11, 2001 will leave flashbulb memories in us all. Where were you, who were you with, and what were you doing the moment you heard the news? To me, it feels like yesterday that I heard the horrific news in a phone call just before my morning class. I promptly went to the lecture hall, told my students (many of whom had just crawled out of bed) what had happened, and cancelled class so we could watch the news on TV and call loved ones. I returned to my office just as the first of the twin towers had collapsed.*

## THE SELF AS PERSONAL HISTORIAN

By linking the present to the past and providing us with a sense of inner continuity, autobiographical memory is a vital part of our identity. Think about it. Who would you be if you could not remember your parents or childhood playmates, your successes and failures, the places you lived, the schools you attended, the books you read, and the experiences you had? It's clear that memories shape our self-concept. What's interesting is that the self-concept shapes our memory as well.

Forming an autobiography is also a social activity designed for and shaped by the people in our lives. In *Context Is Everything: The Nature of Memory*, Susan Engel

**childhood amnesia**   The inability of most people to recall events from before the age of three or four.

**hindsight bias** The tendency to think after an event that we knew in advance what was going to happen.

*"The unfolding drama of life is revealed more by the telling than by the actual events told."*

—DAN MCADAMS

## REVIEW QUESTIONS

- *In general, what types of events are people likely to recall?*

- *Why do researchers believe that most people exhibit childhood amnesia?*

- *Describe the two ways in which memory is influenced by the self-concept.*

(1999) notes that people relay stories about their past as a way of connecting with others and forming intimate relationships. These stories, in turn, become part of their identity. Says Engel, "Whatever germ of remembrance that begins as a totally internal and private moment is shaped and transformed by the social exchange through which it becomes materialized . . . it travels from the inner reaches of the mind out into the world and then is folded back again into one's identity" (pp. 80–81).

There are two ways that memory is shaped by the social self. First, people are motivated to distort the past in a manner that is self-inflated, or *egocentric*. Anthony Greenwald (1980) notes, "The past is remembered as if it were a drama in which the self was the leading player." To illustrate, let's turn the clock back to a momentous event in American history: the Watergate hearings of 1973. The witness was John Dean, former counsel to President Nixon. Dean had submitted a 245-page statement in which he recounted word for word details of conversations. Dean's memory seemed so flawless that he was dubbed "the human tape recorder." In an ironic twist of fate, it turned out that Nixon had actually taped the meetings Dean had recalled. Was Dean accurate? A comparison of his testimony with the tapes revealed that he correctly remembered the gist of his White House conversations, but he exaggerated his own role in these events—leading Neisser (1981), the cognitive psychologist who analyzed Dean's testimony, to wonder, "Are we all like this? Is everyone's memory constructed, staged, self-centered?" Research shows that the answer is *yes*—there is a bit of John Dean in all of us.

A second feature of autobiographical memory is the **hindsight bias,** the tendency to think after an event that we knew in advance what was going to happen. Historians are sometimes criticized for making the past seem inevitable in hindsight. We all do. After learning a new fact or an outcome—whether it's the result of a political election, an earthquake, the invasion of one country by another, or the winner of the last Super Bowl—people are quick to claim, "I knew it all along" (Fischhoff, 1975; Hawkins & Hastie, 1990).

When it comes to autobiographical memory, 20/20 hindsight leads people to revise their fading personal histories in ways that reflect favorably on the self. For example, George Goethals and Richard Reckman (1973) found that people whose attitudes on school busing were changed by a persuasive speaker later assumed that they had held their new attitude all along. Similarly, Michael Ross (1989) found that subjects, after they were persuaded by an expert that frequent tooth brushing was desirable, reported in the context of a subsequent experiment having brushed more often in the previous two weeks. Illustrating that memory can be biased rather than objective, the subjects "updated" the past in light of their new attitude. More recently, Bahrick and others (1996) had ninety-nine college students recall all of their high-school grades and then checked the accuracy of these reports against the actual transcripts. Overall, most grades were recalled correctly. But the errors made were typically grade *inflations*, especially when the actual grades were *low*. People sometimes revise their past to suit their image in the present.

Contemplating the social implications, Ross (1989) suggested that our revisionist tendencies may account for why all generations of parents seem to complain that today's children are not equal to those who grew up in the good old days. According to Ross, adults wrongly assume that they used to be as they are now—which makes the next generation seem deficient by comparison. From his studies of adult development, George Vaillant (1977) drew a similar conclusion: "It is common for caterpillars to become butterflies and then to maintain that in their youth they had been little butterflies. Maturation makes liars of us all" (p. 197).

# THINKING LIKE A PSYCHOLOGIST ABOUT MEMORY

Human memory is often a subject of controversy. In this chapter, we've seen that people can accurately recall faces, names, musical lyrics, skills such as riding a bike, high-impact world events, and personal experiences that stretch deep into their past. Cognitive psychologists have thus likened the human mind to a computer in which information is encoded, stored, and retrieved faithfully on demand. Within this model, researchers have sought to trace the flow of information as it is processed, and in doing so have distinguished between fleeting sensory memory, short-term working memory, and the somewhat permanent storage systems of long-term memory.

At the same time that cognitive psychologists marveled at our information-processing capacities, they also found that our memory is limited, flawed, and biased—as when we forget a phone number we just looked up or misidentify an innocent person as the criminal in a lineup. What's more, it's now clear that memory is an active and constructive process—and that we sometimes unwittingly develop "memories" that are completely false, often to feel better or boost our self-esteem. Commenting on this two-headed portrait of human memory as simultaneously competent and flawed, Schacter (1996) reminds us that, "the computer is a retriever of information but not a rememberer of experiences" (p. 37).

# SUMMARY

## AN INFORMATION-PROCESSING MODEL

Cognitive psychologists view **memory** as an **information-processing** system. **Sensory memory** stores sensations for a brief moment. Those that draw attention are transferred to **short-term memory (STM)**, and those that are further encoded are stored in **long-term memory (LTM)**.

## THE SENSORY REGISTER

The sensory register is the first step in the information-processing system.

### ICONIC MEMORY

The visual system stores images called icons in **iconic memory.** Using the partial-report technique, Sperling found that many items initially register in consciousness but that most last for only a fraction of a second before fading.

### ECHOIC MEMORY

The auditory system stores sounds in **echoic memory.** Echoic memory holds only a few items but lasts two or three seconds, sometimes longer.

## SHORT-TERM MEMORY

Sensations that do not capture attention fade quickly, but those we notice are encoded (in visual, acoustic, or semantic terms) and transferred to short-term memory. People usually encode information in acoustic terms.

### CAPACITY

Using a memory-span task, researchers found that short-term memory has a limited capacity. People can store seven items, plus or minus two. STM can be used more efficiently, however, if we group items into larger chunks, called **chunking.**

### DURATION

STM is also limited in the length of time it can hold information. Studies show that items are held in STM for up to twenty seconds. Through repetition or **maintenance rehearsal,** however, input can be held for an indefinite period of time.

### FUNCTIONS OF SHORT-TERM MEMORY

STM contains new sensory input and material from long-term memory. The limits of STM are adaptive, enabling us to discard information that is no longer useful. STM is not just a passive storage depot but an active workspace referred to as a **working memory.** When people memorize a list of items, they exhibit the **serial-position curve,** whereby items from the beginning and end are recalled better than those in the middle.

## LONG-TERM MEMORY

LTM is a relatively enduring storage system that can hold vast amounts of information for long periods of time.

### ENCODING

To transfer input to LTM, it is best to use **elaborative rehearsal**—specifically, engaging in "deep" processing and associating the input with information already in LTM. Retention is also increased through overlearning (continued rehearsal after the material is mastered) and through practice spaced over time rather than crammed in all at once.

## STORAGE

In LTM, information may be stored in semantic or visual form. In semantic coding, people store the meaning of verbal information, not just specific words. In fact, memories are stored in complex webs of association called **semantic networks.** In visual coding, people store input as mental pictures. Thus, the use of imagery, particularly when it is interactive and bizarre, improves memory.

There is more than one type of long-term memory. **Procedural memory** consists of learned habits and skills, whereas **declarative memory** consists of memories for facts about the world and about ourselves. Neuroscientists have sought to identify the physical traces of memory. In the case of H.M., the **hippocampus** was removed, producing **anterograde amnesia,** the inability to form new long-term memories (not **retrograde amnesia,** the inability to retrieve old memories from the past). Studies confirm that the hippocampus is involved in the encoding of information into long-term memory. Biochemically, the neurotransmitter acetylcholine plays a key role. So does the hormone epinephrine, which triggers the release of glucose.

## RETRIEVAL

There are two basic techniques by which retrieval can be tested, and each assesses a different aspect of memory: explicit and implicit. **Explicit memories** are the recollections consciously retrieved in response to direct questions. **Implicit memories** are nonconscious recollections that are indirectly measured by their effects on performance. This distinction is important because people may "forget" (have no explicit memory of) an experience and yet show the effects (have an implicit memory) of that experience.

In tests of explicit memory, people find it more difficult to produce a recollection in the form of **free recall** than **recognition.** Apparently, forgetting often occurs not because memory has faded but because the information is difficult to retrieve. Retrieval failure is indicated by the tip-of-the-tongue phenomenon and by the fact that memory is aided by retrieval cues. Research on **encoding specificity** indicates that any stimulus that is encoded along with an experience—including locations (which accounts for context-dependent memory) and internal states (which accounts for state-dependent memory)—can later jog memory of that experience.

Implicit tests uncover memories of which people are not aware by measuring their effects on performance. Many amnesia patients use material they cannot explicitly recall. As shown by the false-fame effect, the illusion of truth, unconscious transference in eyewitness testimony, and unconscious plagiarism, implicit memory is also common in everyday life.

## FORGETTING

Beginning with Ebbinghaus, researchers have found evidence for a specific **forgetting curve** in which there is an initial steep loss of retention, with the loss rate leveling off over time. Forgetting can result from a lack of encoding, physical decay, interference, or repression. There are two kinds of interference. In **proactive interference,** prior information inhibits one's ability to recall something new. In **retroactive interference,** new material disrupts memory for previously learned information. People can use various techniques, called **mnemonics,** to improve memorization ability.

## RECONSTRUCTION

Remembering is an active process in which people construct memories based on **schemas,** or preconceptions, and information from outside sources. Experiments by Loftus and others reveal that memory is also "reconstructive"—that after one observes an event, postevent input becomes integrated into the memory. When that information is false, the result is known as the **misinformation effect.** In other ways as well, false or illusory memories can be created.

# AUTOBIOGRAPHICAL MEMORY

**Autobiographical memory** consists of the recollections people have of their own personal experiences. What aspects of our own past do we preserve? Are these memories accurate?

## WHAT EVENTS DO PEOPLE REMEMBER?

People can best recall events from the recent rather than the distant past, though older adults report many memories from adolescence and early adulthood and people in general tend to recall transitional periods in their lives. For events that are particularly dramatic, people form **flashbulb memories** that are highly vivid and enduring—though not always accurate. Most people cannot recall events from before the age or three or four, a memory gap called **childhood amnesia.**

## THE SELF AS PERSONAL HISTORIAN

Autobiographical memory is vital to one's identity. Accordingly, our memories are shaped by our need for self-esteem. People thus distort the past in a manner that is egocentric and self-promoting, and they often think afterward that they knew all along what would happen, a phenomenon known as the **hindsight bias.**

| KEY TERMS |
| --- |

memory (p. 214)

information-processing model (p. 215)

sensory memory (p. 216)

short-term memory (STM) (p. 216)

long-term memory (LTM) (p. 217)

iconic memory (p. 217)

echoic memory (p. 218)

chunking (p. 220)

maintenance rehearsal (p. 222)

working memory (p. 222)

serial-position curve (p. 223)

elaborative rehearsal (p. 225)

procedural memory (p. 228)

declarative memory (p. 228)

semantic networks (p. 229)

lexical decision making (p. 230)

hippocampus (p. 231)

anterograde amnesia (p. 231)

retrograde amnesia (p. 231)

explicit memory (p. 233)

implicit memory (p. 233)

free recall (p. 234)

recognition (p. 234)

encoding specificity (p. 235)

forgetting curve (p. 240)

proactive interference (p. 243)

retroactive interference (p. 243)

mnemonics (p. 244)

schemas (p. 245)

misinformation effect (p. 247)

autobiographical memory (p. 249)

flashbulb memories (p. 252)

childhood amnesia (p. 253)

hindsight bias (p. 254)

## THINKING CRITICALLY ABOUT MEMORY

1. Given what you have learned about memory, what strategies would you use to help you remember the information from this chapter? Why would those strategies be effective?

2. What do psychologists mean when they say that memory is an active process?

3. Suppose you meet a person with damage to the hippocampus. What types of deficits, if any, would you expect this person to exhibit? Why?

4. Distinguish between explicit and implicit memory. How could one study implicit memory if people cannot report having such memories? Design a study that would allow you to assess implicit memory.

5. Speculate as to how you might determine the veracity of an allegedly "recovered" memory.

6. Hypothesize about the relative capacity and duration of tactile, olfactory, and gustatory memories. How could you go about testing these memory abilities?

# Thought and Language

# USING WORDS TO SHAPE THOUGHTS

## THE SITUATION

Along with other students who signed up for this laboratory experiment, you are told that you'll be seeing a series of films, each depicting a traffic accident. In fact, the segments you'll see were taken from driver-education films, and each will last five to thirty seconds. Pay close attention, you are told, because later you'll be asked specific questions about these events.

Over the next hour or so, you watch seven films. After each one, you are asked to write down what happened in your own words and then fill out a questionnaire containing specific questions, including the following question about speed: "About how fast were the cars going when they hit each other?" The experiment seems straightforward and to the point. The scenes are not that hard to watch, and the questions are relatively easy. What you don't know is that other students watching the same films are being asked a slightly different form of the speed question. For these other students, the verb *hit* has been replaced with the verbs *contacted* or *smashed*.

## MAKE A PREDICTION

Judging the speed of a moving object—like judging time and distance—is not as easy as it seems, which is why witnesses to automobile accidents often vary in their estimates. But consider this particular situation. The participants in this study knew they would be watching accident films, were focused on the films in a quiet and calm laboratory, and knew they would be questioned afterward. In the films that were shown, the collisions actually took place at 20, 30, and 40 mph. How were these events judged? When asked the basic *hit* question, the students estimated, on average, that the cars had been traveling at 34 mph. Do you think that estimates were higher, lower, or similar in response to the other forms of the question? On the mph scale below, circle your prediction of the speed estimates in the other conditions.

| | |
|---|---|
| HIT | 28 29 30 31 32 33 34 35 36 37 38 39 40 41 |
| CONTACTED | 28 29 30 31 32 33 34 35 36 37 38 39 40 41 |
| SMASHED | 28 29 30 31 32 33 34 35 36 37 38 39 40 41 |

## THE RESULTS

In this experiment, Elizabeth Loftus and John Palmer (1974) found that although everyone watched the same accident films, the wording of the speed question significantly affected how they saw these events. Compared to a mean of *34* mph in response to the *hit* question, the estimates were *32* mph in response to the *contacted* question and *41* mph in response to the *smashed* question. In fact, just the wording of the question completely altered the way students interpreted these events. When they were brought back one week later and asked if there was broken glass in the accident they had seen, one-third of those who initially were asked the *smashed* question said there was. In fact, there was not.

## WHAT DOES IT ALL MEAN?

More and more, psychologists who study the way people think and those interested in the way people communicate have come to realize that thought and language are seamlessly interconnected. In this chapter, we'll see that language is a tool we humans use for articulating concepts, solutions to problems, and other thoughts. But there's more to the story. As we'll see later in this chapter, the classic *hit-smash* study by Loftus and Palmer (1974) shows that the words we use to describe events can, to some extent, shape the way we think.

We humans are a funny species. As a civilization, we have invented the wheel, kept historical records to guide present and future generations, landed space ships on the moon, unlocked the atom, cracked the genetic code, and revolutionized the face of all we do with computers that bring us into the global Internet. When you stop to think about it, our list of triumphs is long and very impressive. Yet at the same time, we massacre each other in war, wreak havoc on the environment, discriminate against racial and ethnic groups different from our own, mistreat our partners in marriage, throw hard-earned money away in games of chance, take drugs that make us sick, and deceive ourselves into believing in alien abductions.

What is it about the way we humans think that leads us to be both rational and irrational? How do we solve difficult problems and then evaluate the solutions, and what kinds of errors are we prone to make along the way? Are we logical in our reasoning, or are the judgments and decisions we make infected with bias? And what role does language have to play in the way we think? What is language, and is it this capacity that most clearly separates humans from other animal species? In the coming pages, we will examine some of the basic processes of thought and language, then address the question of how they are related. But first, let's examine *concepts*—the basic building blocks of abstract thought and language.

## CONCEPTS

- *What are concepts, and how are they stored in memory?*
- *What is a prototype, and why is a robin considered "birdier" than a chicken?*

**concept** A mental grouping of persons, ideas, events, or objects that share common properties.

*Freedom. Sports. Cancer. Animals. Education. Furniture. Sex. War. Peace. Music. Heroes. Triangles. Happiness.* Each of these words represents a distinct **concept**—a mental grouping of persons, places, ideas, events, or objects that share common properties (Markman, 1999; Van Loocke, 1999). In Chapter 6, we saw that our long-term store of knowledge can be pictured as a complex but orderly network of semantic concepts. So when one concept in the network is activated, other closely related concepts pop to mind, or are *primed*. Look at the semantic network depicted in Figure 7.1. Note that a robin being a type of bird is illustrated by its linkage, and this linkage in itself is a concept that is stored in memory. What's interesting about semantic networks is that one concept can be used to bring others to mind. Thus, hearing the word *bird* makes it easier to pull *robin, chicken,* and *animal* from memory.

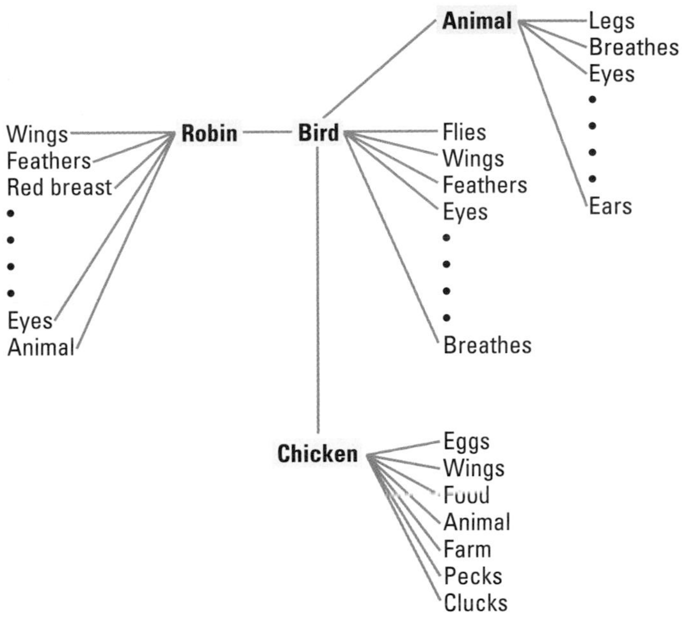


FIGURE 7.1 **A semantic network**
Long-term memory can be pictured as a complex web of concepts, some of which are cognitively closer than others. When one concept is "activated," others nearby in the network are primed.

To demonstrate priming of this sort, David Meyer and Roger Schvaneveldt (1971) presented subjects with pairs of letter strings and asked them to decide as quickly as possible if both letter strings formed words. On some trials, the two items in a pair were semantically related words (*nurse-doctor*). On other trials, the pairs included unrelated words (*bread-doctor*) or nonwords (*marb-doctor*). As it turned out, subjects were quickest to decide that the items were both words when they were related. Reading the first word of the pair primed semantically related words—thus giving the nurse-doctor subjects a "head start" on the second item and speeding up their decisions. Over the years, many researchers have replicated this result (McNamara, 1994).

Another important aspect of semantic networks is that some concepts are more closely related than others. As shown in Figure 7.1, *chicken* is farther from *bird* than *robin* is—even though both are members of the same category. Assuming it takes longer to reveal connections between concepts that are distant than between those that are closely related, researchers use reaction-time tasks to plot the psychological distances between concepts. If I were to time how long it takes you to verify that "a chicken is a bird" and then compare that to the amount of time it takes you to verify that "a robin is a bird," you would probably respond more quickly to the second statement (Collins & Loftus, 1975; McRae & Boisvert, 1998).

Some members of a category are perceived to be more typical than others. Thus, to most people, a robin is a "birdier" bird than a chicken, an ostrich, or a penguin—all of which have wings and feathers and hatch from eggs but do not fly. What makes a category member more or less typical? Look again at Figure 7.1 and notice the partial list of characteristics that are linked to the concepts *bird, robin,* and *chicken.* When people are asked to list properties of different concepts, the most typical members, called **prototypes**, have more of these properties (Smith et al., 1974; Rosch, 1975). Consider the categories listed in Table 7.1. The more prototypical an item is, the more easily we recognize it as a member of the group and use it to make judgments about the group as a whole (Whitney, 1986; Hampton, 1995).

**TABLE 7.1 TYPICALITY OF MEMBERS IN THREE CATEGORIES**

| | Typicality | | |
|---|---|---|---|
| **Category** | **High** | **Moderate** | **Low** |
| **Furniture** | Chair | Lamp | Vase |
| **Fruit** | Apple | Lemon | Coconut |
| **Vehicle** | Car | Boat | Blimp |

**prototype** A "typical" member of a category, one that has most of the defining features of that category.

*When you hear the word* pet, *what image comes to mind? For this particular concept, some animals (golden retrievers) are more prototypical of the category than others (rabbits or iguanas).*

The use of prototypes is illustrated in many studies. For example, Lance Rips (1975) had subjects read a story about an island that was inhabited by sparrows, robins, eagles, hawks, ducks, geese, and ostriches. Some subjects were informed that a disease had infected the robins, whereas others were told that the disease had infected the ducks. Subjects were then asked, "What other species would be infected?" Remembering what you just read about prototypes, can you anticipate the result? Subjects in the robin-infected group predicted that the disease would spread to all other bird species on the island. In contrast, the duck group predicted that only the geese, a "related" species, would be infected. Evidently, robins serve as a prototype for birds, but ducks do not. It's also interesting that the first words children use to describe objects within various categories usually pertain to prototypic members of those categories—apples rather than lemons, chairs rather than lamps, and so on (Poulin-DuBois, 1995).

Although many human concepts consist of taxonomies that are based on similarities among members such as dogs, foods, furniture, or rock bands, others bring items

| TABLE 7.2 | DO PEOPLE CATEGORIZE BY TAXONOMIC OR THEMATIC RELATEDNESS? | | |
|---|---|---|---|
| **Triad** | **Target Word** | **Taxonomic** | **Thematic** |
| 1 | French fries | baked potato | ketchup |
| 2 | camel | antelope | desert |
| 3 | Hawaii | Missouri | beach |
| 4 | beer | juice | party |
| 5 | movie theater | opera house | popcorn |
| 6 | pig | dog | barn |
| 7 | igloo | cabin | Eskimo |
| 8 | pepperoni | pork chops | pizza |
| 9 | saxophone | harp | jazz |
| 10 | diamond ring | bracelet | engagement |

together according to what we know about their "thematic relations." In other words, you might sort a list of foods into such taxonomic categories as meats, fruits, vegetables, and dairy products; or you might sort them according to how or when they are eaten—such as breakfast foods, main dishes, fast foods, and desserts. In a series of studies, Emilie Lin and Gregory Murphy (2001) presented people with triads of words. Each triad contained a target word and two related words—one taxonomically related, the other thematically related. The subject's task was to pick the related word that goes best with the target. Look at the ten triads in Table 7.2. How would you pair each one to form categories? What goes best with *French fries: baked potato* or *ketchup*? What about *movie theater: opera house* or *popcorn*? Across five studies, subjects selected the thematic choice 61 percent of the time. This result suggests that there is more than one way to conceptualize the world, and that people often construct categories according to thematic relations, not taxonomic similarity.

## SOLVING PROBLEMS

- *What are algorithms and heuristics? How are they more efficient as problem-solving methods than trial and error?*
- *What is an analogy, and what makes it a powerful tool?*
- *Why do some psychologists believe in problem solving by insight—and why do others think insight is just an illusion?*
- *What are some of the "blind spots" that impair our ability to solve problems?*

When you lock your keys in the car, play Scrabble, mediate a dispute between friends, or struggle to figure out a function on your computer, the solution you're looking for requires that you combine and manipulate concepts, often in new ways, to solve the problem or to make the necessary judgment. When a solution cannot simply be pulled from memory, it takes effort to obtain. As we'll see, it helps to view problem solving as a process that involves defining the problem, representing it in some way, then generating and evaluating possible solutions. These steps are not a fixed series of stages but rather are mental activities that we use in cycles. So if you're stuck on a problem and realize that you have not represented it correctly in the first place, you might start the process over again.

### REPRESENTING THE PROBLEM

Many problems we encounter come to us in the form of words and concepts activated from semantic networks. Playing the TV game *Jeopardy!*, trying to recite the lyrics of an old song, and working on a crossword puzzle are some examples. But there are other ways as well to depict problems.

**Mental Images**   Often people represent information through **images**, or mental pictures. To turn on the ignition of your car, do you turn the key to the right or to the left? What about the cold-water faucet in your kitchen sink? Which way do the hands of a clock move? (Yes, they move clockwise, but describe what that means.) What's the color of your psychology professor's eyes? And if you can picture a map of the world, which city is farther north, London or New York? To answer these questions, people generate visual images.

In the past, psychologists had to take people at their word when they said they had formed mental pictures. Today, there are more objective ways to study the "mind's eye"—and these methods have confirmed that imagery is a pervasive aspect of human thought. Consider some specific examples. In one study, Margaret

## REVIEW QUESTIONS

- *Define the term concept.*
- *Describe two consequences of storing concepts in semantic networks.*
- *What are prototypes, and how do they influence judgments?*

7.1

**image**   A mental representation of visual information.

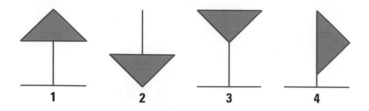

**FIGURE 7.2** **Mental-rotation tasks**
Imagine a capital letter *T*. Rotate it 90 degrees to the right. Put a triangle directly to the left of the figure so that it is pointing to the right. Now rotate the figure 90 degrees to the right. Got it? Now look at the images above and pick the correct one. You can check your answer by drawing the figure on paper or looking in the margin of page 266.

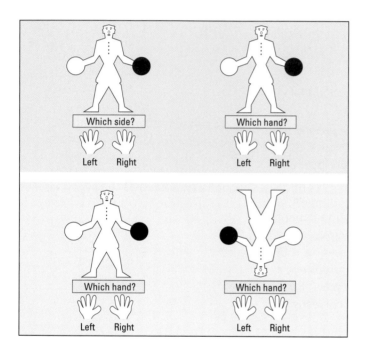

**FIGURE 7.3**
When shown the figures above, people were slower to determine if the black ball was in the figure's right or left hand than if it was on the right or left side of the screen (*top*). People were also slower to determine right and left when the figure appeared upside down as opposed to right side up (*bottom*). Making right-left judgments from another figure's perspective, particularly when it is upside down, requires mental rotation—which takes time (Zacks et al., 1999).

**mental models** Intuitive theories about the way things work.

**trial and error** A problem-solving strategy in which several solutions are attempted until one is found that works.

Intons-Peterson (1993) gave people verbal descriptions of simple line drawings, like the one in Figure 7.2, and found that the more rotations that were involved, the longer it took subjects to generate the image. This result suggests that people solve this problem by manipulating mental pictures of the described forms. Other research as well suggests that if mental rotation is needed to solve a spatial problem, people take longer to make the judgment (Shepard & Cooper, 1982). Still more evidence on the nature of imagery comes from brain-scanning studies, where researchers have found that when subjects engage in tasks requiring mental imagery, their brains become active in areas of the cortex normally involved in vision (Farah, 1989; Kosslyn et al., 1999).

In an interesting series of studies, Jeff Zacks and others (1999) showed subjects' drawings of human figures holding a white ball in one hand and a black ball in the other. For each drawing, subjects had to judge as quickly as possible whether the black ball was on the right side of the screen or the left, or whether the object was in the figure's right or left hand. It turns out that subjects were slower to make this second type of judgment because doing so meant they had to mentally rotate the figure in order to perceive right and left from that figure's perspective. Subjects were also slower to make right-left judgments when the figure was upside down as opposed to right side up, again because it required mental rotation. Using brain scans, these researchers also found that judgments requiring these mental transformations activated parts of the brain normally involved in processing visual-spatial information (see Figure 7.3). Additional studies have similarly identified the parts of the brain involved in making various mental transformations (Zacks et al., 2001).

To cognitive psychologists, it's clear that mental images play a role in human problem solving (Kosslyn, 1994). But is imagery a uniquely human thought process? Research in the developing area of animal cognition suggests not. In an intriguing experiment, depicted in Figure 7.4, Jacques Vauclair and others (1993) trained six wild baboons to move a cursor on a computer with the use of a joystick. In a series of trials, each subject then saw a sample stimulus flashed briefly on the screen (the letter *P* or *F*). This presentation was followed by two "comparison stimuli" that were rotated at varying degrees—one always matched the sample; the other was its mirror image. Using the joystick, the subjects had to select the comparison stimulus that matched the original sample. Each correct response was rewarded with food. Could the baboons perform the necessary mental rotation to achieve this task? Yes. In contrast to what many psychologists would have predicted, the accuracy rate was 70 percent. As in humans, their performance also varied according to the degree of rotation that was needed to make the comparison.

**Mental Models** Do you understand how a virus spreads from one computer to another? Can you describe how a car engine works? What about the economy: Do you know how the inflation and unemployment rates interact? At times, the problems that confront us can be best represented in the form of **mental models**, which are intuitive theories of the way things work. When accurate, these theories can be powerful tools for reasoning. By having specific mental models of how human beings, organizations, machines, and other things work, we can diagnose problems and adapt accordingly (Gentner & Stevens, 1983; Johnson-Laird, 1983, 2001).

Unfortunately, our mental models are often in error. Before reading on, try the problems in Figure 7.5. These problems are used to study *intuitive physics*—the mental models people have about the laws of motion. Research shows that people are poor intuitive physicists. Consider three common errors. First, many people wrongly believe in the "impetus principle" that an object set in motion acquires its own internal force, which keeps it in motion. So when asked to predict the path of a metal ball rolling through a spiral tube, a majority of subjects predicted that the ball would follow a curved path even after it exits the tube (McCloskey & Kuhl, 1983). A second error is the "straight-down belief" that something dropped from a moving object will fall in a straight vertical line. So when asked to predict the path of a ball dropped at shoulder height by a walking adult, most subjects wrongly assumed that the ball would fall straight down rather than in a forward trajectory (McCloskey et al., 1983). A third error is made in the "water-level task" shown in Figure 7.5. When shown a tilted glass or a container filled with liquid, some subjects—including many bartenders and waitresses—harbor the belief that the water surface tilts as well rather than remains parallel to the ground (Hecht & Proffitt, 1995).

It's interesting that physics students don't always perform better than others on these types of problems, which suggests that mental models can be difficult to change (Donley & Ashcraft, 1992; Kozhevnikov & Hegarty, 2001). It's also interesting that people can make these judgments more accurately by acting on physical objects—or just by imagining themselves doing so. For example, imagine two glasses of the same height, one wider than the other and both filled to the same level with water. If tilted, would the two glasses start pouring at the same angle? If not, which glass would pour first? Look at the problem as illustrated in Figure 7.6. It's tricky. But when people shut their eyes and tilt each glass until the imagined water reaches the rim, most correctly tilt the narrow glass farther than the wide one (Schwartz & Black, 1999).

## GENERATING SOLUTIONS

Once a problem is represented through words, static images, or mental models, we try out possible solutions and test to see if they work. If the problem is solved, life goes on. If not, we return to the proverbial drawing board to come up with new ideas. There are many different ways to find solutions, but there are four basic problem-solving processes: trial and error, algorithms, heuristics, and insight.

**Trial and Error**   **Trial and error** is the simplest problem-solving strategy there is, and it's often effective. You may recall from Chapter 5 that Edward Thorndike, in 1898, studied animal

**FIGURE 7.4**   **Can baboons mentally rotate objects?**
In this apparatus, six baboons were trained to use a joystick to move a cursor. The sample form on the left would be shown and then subjects would have to choose the rotated form on the right that matched the sample. As evident from a 70 percent accuracy rate, these baboons were able to mentally align objects to make these judgments (Vauclair et al., 1993).

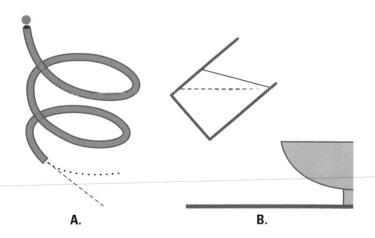

**A.**                     **B.**

**FIGURE 7.5**   **Intuitive physics**
A. Subjects were asked to draw the path that a marble would take as it exited this curved tube. Most subjects incorrectly drew a curved path (*dotted line*) rather than the correct straight path (*dashed line*). Our mental models of motion are often wrong.
B. In this task, subjects were asked to draw a line to illustrate the surface of water in the tilted container. Although the line should be depicted as perfectly horizontal to the ground, many people placed it at the tilted angle shown above.

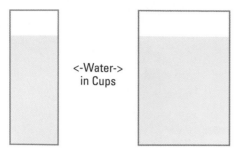

If tilted, would the two cups pour at the same angle or at different angles?

**FIGURE 7.6a**
Another intuitive physics problem.

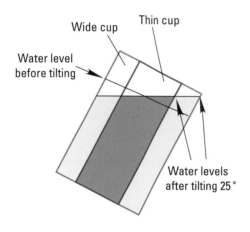

**FIGURE 7.6b**
As shown, the narrow glass must be tilted more than the wide one to pour.

*Solution to Figure 7.2: The answer is (3).*

**algorithm** A systematic, step-by-step problem-solving strategy that is guaranteed to produce a solution.

**heuristic** A rule of thumb that allows one to make judgments that are quick but often in error.

**means-end analysis** A problem-solving heuristic that involves breaking down a larger problem into a series of subgoals.

**analogy** A problem-solving heuristic that involves using an old solution as a model for a new, similar problem.

intelligence by putting cats in a "puzzle box," placing food outside a door, and timing how long it took for them to figure out how to escape. At first, the cats tried various ineffective behaviors. They tried reaching with their paws, but the food was too far away. They scratched at the bars, but that did not work. They pushed at the ceiling, but that did not work either. Then they would literally stumble upon the solution (which was to step on a lever that opened the door) and repeat that solution whenever they were in the box. The cats solved the problem by trial and error.

As you can imagine, this aimless, hit-or-miss approach is not the most efficient way to proceed. Yet I must confess that when I tinker with my computer and run into problems, I often start pecking furiously at the keyboard or probing and clicking with the mouse, hoping that something I do will effect a change. Sometimes this strategy proves enlightening. For example, Thomas Edison—the most prolific inventor in American history—tested thousands of light bulb filaments before stumbling on the one that worked. The problem is that this strategy often takes too long or fails completely. If possible, it's better to take a more systematic, planned approach.

**Algorithms and Heuristics** An **algorithm** is a step-by-step procedure that is guaranteed, eventually, to produce a solution. When you were taught in school how to solve two-digit addition problems or long division, you learned an algorithm. An alternative is to use **heuristics**, mental shortcuts, or rules of thumb, which may or may not lead to the correct solution. The "*I before E*" heuristic for spelling *I-E* words is a good example. To appreciate the difference between algorithms and heuristics, consider the following anagram problem: Unscramble the letters *L K C C O* to make a word. One strategy is to use an algorithm—to try all possible combinations by systematically varying the letters in each position. Eventually, you will form the correct word. An alternative is to use a heuristic. For example, you could try the most familiar letter combinations. A common ending for English words is *CK*, so you might start with this combination and arrive quickly at the solution: *CLOCK*.

If algorithms are guaranteed to produce solutions, why not use them all the time? The reason is that algorithms are not always available—and sometimes they take too much time to be practical. Thus, chess experts do not consider all the possible moves on the board, because there are simply too many of them. This strategy is fine for high-speed computers like "Deep Blue"—an IBM computerized chess master equipped with 512 processors acting in parallel to look ahead a certain number of steps and evaluate millions of positions and moves per second. But great players must rely instead on heuristics, such as "Get control of the center of the board."

Some heuristics are general, in that they can be used to solve a wide range of problems. One important general heuristic is the **means-end analysis** (Newell & Simon, 1972). This involves breaking a larger problem into a series of subgoals. For example, let's say you are starting a new job Monday and have to get to work on time. You could solve this problem by driving your car to work, but your car needs repair. So you set a subgoal of getting your car repaired. But this might require other subgoals, such as finding a mechanic. For some problems, the nested subgoals can get quite complex and involved. In fact, unless people carefully evaluate whether each step brings them closer to the endpoint, it is possible to lose track of what part of the problem is actually being solved (Simon, 1975). The benefits of formulating subgoals can be seen in the *Tower of Hanoi problem*, shown in Figure 7.7.

Another powerful problem-solving heuristic consists of the use of **analogies**. If you have previously solved some problem that seems similar to a new one, you can use the old solution as a model. The trick is to recognize that the second problem

*In February 2003, Garry Kasparov, the world chess champion from Azerbaijan, played IBM's chess master, Deep Junior to a draw. Like its computer predecessors, Deep Junior can analyze two hundred million positions per second (Kasparov can evaluate three positions per second). Unlike its predecessors, however, Deep Junior is programmed to play in a bold style that allows it to forfeit pieces to gain positional advantage.*

resembles the first. To illustrate, take some time to try to solve the following "tumor-and-radiation problem" (Gick & Holyoak, 1980):

> Suppose you are a doctor faced with a patient who has a malignant tumor in his stomach. To operate on the patient is impossible, but unless the tumor is destroyed the patient will die. A certain kind of ray, at a sufficiently high intensity, can be used to destroy the tumor. Unfortunately, at this intensity the healthy tissue that the rays pass through on the way to the tumor will also be destroyed. At lower intensities, the rays are harmless to healthy tissue, but they will not affect the tumor. What type of procedure might be used to destroy the tumor using the rays without injuring healthy tissue?

Do you have the answer? If not, read the following "general-and-fortress" story:

> A small country was ruled from a strong fortress by a dictator. The fortress was in the middle of the country, surrounded by farms and villages. Many roads led outward from the fortress like spokes in a wheel. A rebel general vowed to capture the fortress. The general knew that an attack by his entire army would capture the fortress. He gathered his troops at the head of one of the roads, ready to attack the fortress. However, the general learned that the dictator had planted mines on each of the roads. The mines were set so that small bodies of men could pass over them safely, but any large force would detonate the mines. This would not only blow up the road, but also destroy nearby villages. It seemed impossible to capture the fortress. But the general devised a plan. He divided his army up into small groups and dispatched each group to the head of a different road. When all were ready he gave the signal, and each group marched down a different road. Each group continued down its road to the fortress, so that the entire army finally arrived together at the same time. In this way, the general captured the fortress and overthrew the dictator.

Okay, now return to the radiation problem and try again. If you're still drawing a blank, here's a hint: Think of the general-and-fortress story as an analogy for the

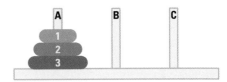

**FIGURE 7.7   Tower of Hanoi problem**
Your mission is to move three rings from peg A to peg C. You may move only the top ring on a peg and may not place a larger ring above a smaller one. See solution on page 268.

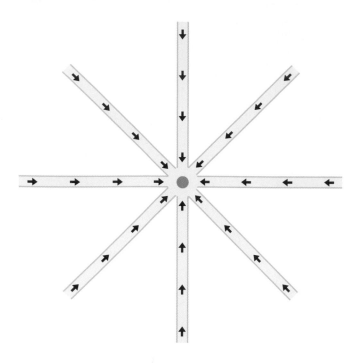

**FIGURE 7.8    The radiation analogy, animated**
The radiation problem illustrates the power of analogy in problem solving. In one study, researchers found that people are particularly likely to grasp the analogical link between problems when the radiation display was animated (Pedone et al., 2001).

*Solution to the Tower of Hanoi problem: To complete this mission, it helps to break the task into subgoals. The first is to get ring 3 to the bottom of peg C (move ring 1 to peg C, ring 2 to peg B, and ring 1 from peg C to peg B; then put ring 3 at the bottom of peg C). Your second subgoal is to get ring 2 to peg C (move ring 1 to peg A and ring 2 to C). The third subgoal is now easy: just move ring 1 over to peg C—and you're finished.*

**insight**    A form of problem solving in which the solution seems to pop to mind all of a sudden.

radiation-and-tumor problem. Look beneath the surface differences in the stories. Can you see the relevance of the general's strategy for the surgeon? The radiation solution is to use a low-intensity ray that can be aimed at the tumor from several directions. When all the rays reach the tumor, their effects will add up to that of a single high-intensity beam at the site of the tumor, and healthy tissue will not be destroyed. Demonstrating the usefulness of problem solving by analogy, Gick and Holyoak (1980) found that only 8 percent of naive subjects solved the radiation problem on their own, but among those who had first read the general-and-fortress story, the solution rate increased to 76 percent.

Analogical thinking plays a central role in science, where the heart has been likened to a pump, the brain to a computer, the eye to a camera, molecules to billiard balls, the telephone to an ear, and the spinning earth to a slowing toy top. Research shows that people are quicker to grasp and use new scientific concepts when these concepts are taught by analogy than when they are explained in literal terms (Donnelly & McDaniel, 1993)—and that the shorter the "mental leap" is between two problems, because they are similar in obvious ways, the more effective is the analogy (Holyoak & Thagard, 1997; Chen, 2002). Diagrams and animated displays may be particularly useful for getting people to notice the analogical link between problems. For solving the radiation problem, for example, subjects benefited a great deal from an animated version of Figure 7.8 (Pedone et al., 2001).

**Insight**    When people struggle with a problem, they usually try to monitor their progress to evaluate whether they're closing in on a solution (Kotovsky et al., 1985). But have you ever puzzled over something, felt as if you were stumped, and then come up with the answer abruptly, out of the blue, as if a light bulb flashed inside your head? Aha! If so, then you have experienced problem solving by **insight,** a process in which the solution pops to mind all of a sudden—and in which the problem solver doesn't realize the solution is coming and cannot describe what he or she was thinking at the time (Sternberg & Davidson, 1999).

Insight is an experience that seems to arise whenever people at an impasse relax the way they approach a problem, reframe it, switch from one strategy to another, remove a mental block, or identify an analogy from a prior experience (Simon, 1989; Knoblich & Ohlsson, 1999). Some researchers claim that these apparent flashes of insight actually result from a gradual, step-by-step process—but that sometimes we're just not aware of the progress we are making (Weisberg, 1992). Others find that certain types of tasks do seem to promote a special form of problem solving that has a sudden, all-or-none quality (Smith & Kounios, 1996). Is insight gradual but nonconscious, or is it truly sudden? It's hard to know for sure. Janet Metcalfe and David Wiebe (1987) had subjects work on different types of problems and periodically rate how "warm" they were getting on a seven-point scale. On multistep algebra problems, the ratings increased steadily as subjects neared a solution. On insight problems, however, the warmth ratings remained flat and low, then rose all at once, the moment subjects encountered a solution. It's interesting that when people working on insight problems are asked to describe their thinking along the way, which brings the process into consciousness, their performance deteriorates (Schooler et al., 1993).

People often report that they tried unsuccessfully for hours to solve a problem and then, after taking a break, came back and it "clicked": An insight quickly converted into a solution. The improved ability to solve a problem after taking a break from it is called the incubation effect. One puzzle that psychologists have used to investigate incubation effects in the laboratory is the "cheap-necklace problem," shown in Figure 7.9. Try it for five minutes before reading on. Using this problem, Silveira (1971) tested three groups of subjects. All groups worked on the same task for a total of thirty minutes. One group worked without a break. After fifteen minutes, however, the second group took a half-hour break and the third group took a four-hour break. During these rest periods, subjects were kept busy with other activities that prevented them from continuing to work on the necklace problem. The results provided strong evidence for incubation: Subjects who took a break were more likely to solve the problem than those who did not. In fact, the longer was the interlude, the better was the performance. The implication of this effect is clear. Sometimes it helps to take a break while trying to solve problems that require a critical insight—as in the cheap-necklace problem, where the key is to realize that you can't link all four chains (Anderson, 1990).

The history of science is filled with stories of discovery by flashes of insight. But is insight necessarily the product of a great mind? Many psychologists believe that other animals too are capable of insight, not just of trial-and-error problem solving. Many years ago, Wolfgang Köhler (1925) claimed that a chimpanzee named Sultan displayed insight in problem solving. Köhler put bananas and a long stick outside the chimp's cage, both out of reach, and put a short stick inside the cage. Sultan poked at the banana with the short stick, but it was too short to reach the fruit. After trying repeatedly, he gave up, dropped the stick, and walked away. Then all of a sudden, Sultan jumped up, picked up the short stick, and used it to get the longer stick—which he used to get the banana. Did this episode reveal insight? Many researchers are skeptical of such a claim and suggest that the apparent insight may be no more than an accumulation of learned behaviors (Epstein et al., 1984). Yet others agree with Köhler. Sociobiologist Edward O. Wilson tells a Sultan-like story of a chimp trying to reach some leaves: "He sat and looked at the tree for a long time, and went over to a log. He dragged it over to the tree, propped it against the trunk, then stood back and charged his ramp. It's extremely difficult to explain that, other than to say the chimp was consciously thinking" (Begley & Ramo, 1993).

This brings us back to questions about animal cognition and whether problem solving is uniquely human. Do other animals have insight or use heuristics? Are they capable of conscious thought? In *The Parrot's Lament,* Eugene Linden (1999) explored these questions by talking to animal researchers, zookeepers, and veterinarians, who tell stories about how their animals try to outsmart them, hide, plot to escape, manipulate, and wheel and deal for food—all signs of intelligence. Yet in *If a Lion Could Talk,* Stephen Budiansky (1998) warns against the tendency to conclude from such stories that horses, dogs, cats, and other animals have human traits, thoughts, and intentions. This debate is particularly intense within the scientific community, where some comparative psychologists (researchers who study and compare different species) believe that those who study people underestimate the cognitive capabilities of nonhuman animals (Balda et al., 1998; Bekoff et al., 2002; Vauclair, 1996). As we'll see later in this chapter, there is tantalizing evidence to suggest that chimpanzees and other apes can learn to solve problems that require the use of abstract symbols. We will take a closer look at this research when we discuss attempts to teach language to nonhuman primates.

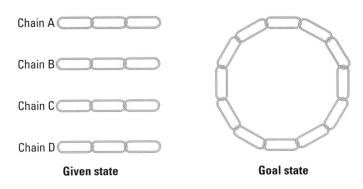

**Given state**                    **Goal state**

**FIGURE 7.9   The cheap-necklace problem**
Make a necklace out of the four separate chains. It costs two cents to open a link and three cents to close a link. You must make your necklace for fifteen cents or less. The solution can be found in Figure 7.13 on page 271.

"'Jeopardy!' is on."

**FIGURE 7.10 The nine-dot problem**
Connect all nine dots with four straight lines without lifting your pencil from the paper. The solution is revealed in Figure 7.15 (p. 273).

**FIGURE 7.11 Duncker's candle problem**
Using just the objects shown, how could you mount the candle on a wall? The solution appears in Figure 7.14 (p. 272).

**functional fixedness** The tendency to think of objects only in terms of their usual functions, a limitation that disrupts problem solving.

# "BLIND SPOTS" IN PROBLEM SOLVING

Using trial and error, algorithms, heuristics and insight, people often display a remarkable capacity to solve problems. As we have seen time and again, however, our competencies are often compromised by certain "blind spots." To appreciate some of these shortcomings, try the problems in Figures 7.10 and 7.11 before reading on. The solutions are revealed in the coming pages.

**Representation Failures** For many years, problem-solving researchers have used the "nine-dot problem" presented in Figure 7.10 (Burnham & Davis, 1969; MacGregor et al., 2001). This problem is notoriously difficult, and it seems to illustrate that failure often results from an incorrect problem representation. Even though the instructions say nothing about staying inside an imaginary square formed from the dots, almost everyone behaves as though the outside dots form a boundary that cannot be crossed (to see why, think back to the gestalt principles of perceptual grouping in Chapter 3). If you don't mentally handicap yourself in this way, the solution is simple. But people do, which is what makes the problem so difficult. Is this tendency to represent problems narrowly limited to clever laboratory puzzles and brainteasers? Sadly, no. As we'll see in Chapter 16, cognitively oriented clinical psychologists find that people often suffer needlessly because they conceptualize problems in ways that make them seem insurmountable.

**Functional Fixedness** The "candle problem" in Figure 7.11 illustrates a more specific type of representation failure. The difficulty in this case is one of **functional fixedness**, a tendency to think of objects only in terms of their usual functions. In the candle problem, for example, you'd struggle for as long as you see the matchbox as only a container, not as a possible shelf. A brick is a brick, but it can also be

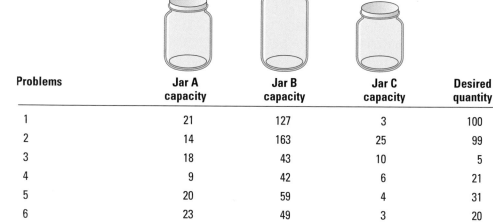

| Problems | Jar A capacity | Jar B capacity | Jar C capacity | Desired quantity |
|---|---|---|---|---|
| 1 | 21 | 127 | 3 | 100 |
| 2 | 14 | 163 | 25 | 99 |
| 3 | 18 | 43 | 10 | 5 |
| 4 | 9 | 42 | 6 | 21 |
| 5 | 20 | 59 | 4 | 31 |
| 6 | 23 | 49 | 3 | 20 |
| 7 | 15 | 39 | 3 | 18 |
| 8 | 28 | 76 | 3 | 25 |
| 9 | 18 | 48 | 4 | 14 |
| 10 | 14 | 36 | 8 | 6 |

**FIGURE 7.12 Luchin's water-jar problem**
Try to solve the following ten problems. In each case, use Jars A, B, and C, with the capacities indicated, to pour out the desired quantities of water (far-right column). For example, if Jar A has a capacity of 27 cups, B has 20 cups, and C has 4 cups, you could measure out 50 cups of water by using the formula 2A − C, or 54 − 4.

used as a paperweight. Finding creative new solutions to practical problems often requires that we think open-mindedly—or, as they say, "outside the box"—in order to see unusual uses for common objects (Sternberg & Lubart, 1991; Weisberg, 1986).

**Mental Sets**  The "water-jar problem" in Figure 7.12 illustrates another related blind spot, the inability due to past experience to view the problem from a new perspective. If you haven't tried this one yet, please do, then come back. How was it? Were you able to solve the first water-jar problem? If so, then you figured out the algorithm: B(127) − A(21) − 2C(6) = 100. Chances are that you also found problems 2 through 7 easy and whizzed through them with the same formula. But what about problems 8, 9, and 10, which required using a new formula? If you're like most students, you probably struggled on these—even though the solution (A − C) is simple. Why? The first few problems lead people to form a **mental set,** a tendency to use a strategy that has worked in the past. This reliance on prior strategies is also seen in mathematical thinking, where students trying to solve new arithmetic problems overapply rules that had worked for other familiar types of problems (Ben-Zeev, 1995).

As with the use of analogies to solve problems, mental sets are not all bad. After all, carrying over the B − A − 2C formula helped you with items 2 through 7. The drawback is that we often are slow to shed our mental sets when we need to. As I said, students tend to slow down on problems 8, 9, and 10—unless they work on these first, so that no mental set is formed. For an amusing look at mental sets in action, play hide-and-seek with young children, and you'll notice that they always go right back to the last place you hid.

**The Confirmation Bias**  The nine-dot, candle, and water-jar problems are tricky not because they are intellectually demanding but because people tend to be overly rigid in their thinking. But there's more. Once we think we have a solution, we fall prey to **confirmation bias,** a tendency to look only for evidence that will verify our beliefs—which can prevent us from realizing that we are in error. This bias is pervasive and has a negative influence on the way people approach the problems in their daily lives (Nickerson, 1998).

To demonstrate, Peter Wason (1960) gave students a three-number sequence, 2-4-6, and challenged them to figure out the rule he had used to generate this set. How should they proceed? By making up their own sequences and asking the experimenter to indicate whether or not they fit the rule. Subjects were told they could test as many sequences as they wanted and to state the rule only if they felt certain that they knew it. The task was straightforward and the rule behind 2-4-6 was easy: any three increasing numbers. Yet out of twenty-nine subjects, only six discovered the correct rule without first seizing upon one that was incorrect. What happened was this: Subjects would start with an initial hypothesis (adding by 2s, even numbers, skipping numbers) and then search only for confirming evidence. Thinking that the rule was "adding by 2s," a subject might test 6-8-10, 50-52-54, 21-23-25, and so on, yet never try disconfirming sets such as 6-8-4 or 3-2-1. When all the sequences fit, the subject would proudly and with confidence announce the wrong rule.

**Belief Perseverance**  As noted, people search for evidence that verifies their beliefs. But what happens when we confront information that plainly contradicts our beliefs? Do we revise our views, as logic would dictate? Not necessarily. In a

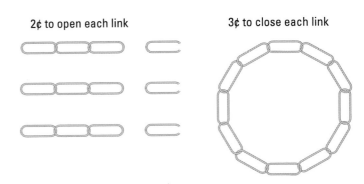

2¢ to open each link      3¢ to close each link

**FIGURE 7.13**  **Solution to the cheap-necklace problem**
The key is to realize that you can't link all four chains. To solve the problem, open every link on one chain (this costs six cents), then use these open links to join the three remaining chains (which costs nine cents).

**mental set**  The tendency to return to a problem-solving strategy that worked in the past.

**confirmation bias**  The inclination to search only for evidence that will verify one's beliefs.

## REVIEW QUESTIONS

- *Describe evidence that people sometimes use mental images to represent problems. What kinds of problems are likely to prompt the use of mental images?*

- *What are mental models? How do they help and/or hinder problem solving?*

- *Describe the four basic problem-solving strategies. What are the advantages and disadvantages of each?*

- *What "blind spots" interfere with effective problem solving?*

**FIGURE 7.14   Solution to Duncker's candle problem**
To solve this problem, you need to realize that the box can be used not only as a container but also as a shelf.

**belief perseverance**   The tendency to cling to beliefs even after they have been discredited.

**syllogism**   A logical problem in which the goal is to determine the validity of a conclusion given two or more premises.

series of studies, Craig Anderson and his colleagues (1980) found that our beliefs are often highly resistant to change. For example, subjects read case studies suggesting that the best firefighters are either risk takers or cautious types. Next, subjects were asked to come up with a theory for the suggested link. The possibilities are easy to imagine: "He who hesitates is lost" supports risk taking, and "You have to look before you leap" supports caution. Finally, when the experiment was supposedly over, subjects were told that the information they had received was totally false, manufactured for the sake of the experiment. Did this discrediting evidence erase subjects' newly formed beliefs? No, it was too late. Many subjects exhibited **belief perseverance**, clinging to their initial beliefs even after those beliefs had been discredited. Though hardly rational, it seems that our beliefs often outlive the evidence from which they sprung.

Many books on how to improve your problem-solving skills provide advice on how to eliminate blind spots (Nadler & Hibino, 1998). We now know that people have to learn to be more flexible in the way they represent problems, in the strategies they use, in the way they evaluate their initial beliefs, and in their responsiveness to discrediting information. At each stage, the key is to think flexibly and with an open mind.

## MAKING JUDGMENTS

- *What is syllogistic reasoning? What is conditional reasoning? How good are we at using these formal rules of logic?*
- *What are judgmental heuristics, and how do they illustrate that we often sacrifice accuracy in making speedy decisions?*
- *Why do so many people gamble against the odds, an irrational activity, and then persist in the face of defeat?*

People have to make decisions every day. Occasionally we are faced with choices that have a major impact on our lives and others. Where should I go to school? Should I get married? Should I take a less-than-ideal job while waiting for something better? Should I vote guilty or not guilty in the jury room? We all like to think of ourselves as thoughtful and logical decision makers who weigh costs and benefits, calculate the probabilities, and act accordingly. But are we that logical, really? Researchers study human decision making in tasks ranging from formal logic to everyday reasoning. The results have given rise to some rather surprising discoveries about *Homo sapiens,* the "rational animal" (Gilovich et al., 2002; Hastie & Dawes, 2001; Shafir & LeBoeuf, 2002).

## THE RULES OF FORMAL LOGIC

Throughout history, philosophers, psychologists, economists, and others have assumed that our natural way of thinking followed the laws of formal logic. To test this assumption, many psychologists have examined the ways in which people solve strictly logical problems.

**Syllogistic Reasoning**   One aspect of formal logic that has been studied extensively in psychology is syllogistic reasoning. A **syllogism** is a logical problem in which you are given premises that you must assume are true, then decide whether a certain conclusion can be drawn from these premises. For example, given the premises "All *A*s are *B*s" and "All *B*s are *C*s," is the conclusion "All *A*s are *C*s" a valid one? The answer is *yes*—given the premises, the conclusion must be true. Try

## TABLE 7.3   SYLLOGISM PROBLEMS

1. Some *A*s are *B*s.
   All *B*s are *C*s.
   Therefore, some *A*s are *C*s.

2. All *A*s are *B*s.
   Some *B*s are *C*s.
   Therefore, some *A*s are *C*s.

3. All robins are birds.
   All birds are animals.
   Therefore, all robins are animals.

4. All bananas are fruit.
   Some fruits are yellow.
   Therefore, some bananas are yellow.

Answers: (1) valid, (2) invalid, (3) valid, (4) invalid

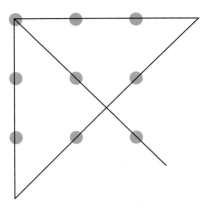

**FIGURE 7.15   Solution to the nine-dot problem**
To solve this problem, you need to realize that all four lines must extend beyond the square of dots.

the syllogisms in Table 7.3, and try to figure out why some seem so much harder to solve than others. For each set of premises, decide if the conclusion is valid. The answers appear at the bottom of the table.

As a general rule, we are not very good at syllogistic reasoning. Most people do find syllogisms easier, however, when they are stated concretely rather than in the abstract "All *A*s are *B*s" format. In fact, one strategy that people naturally use to solve abstract syllogisms is to rephrase them as concrete problems. The flaw in this strategy is that it can lead us to make mistakes when we fail to see that there can be more than one way to represent a given premise. Consider the proposition that "Some *A*s are *B*s." The diagrams in Figure 7.16 can be used to make this syllogism more concrete. But note that although the left diagram seems more natural, the right one is also a valid way to show the premise because whenever it's true that "All *A*s are *B*s," it's also true that "Some *A*s are *B*s." After drawing conclusions, people often don't double-check to see if their conclusions would be valid for *all* the different ways of representing the premises (Johnson-Laird, 1999).

A second disadvantage of making syllogisms more concrete is illustrated by the last item in Table 7.3. It's easy to make a logical mistake on this type of problem precisely because that specific conclusion is true based on general world knowledge. Yet the actual truth of the matter has nothing to do with whether the conclusion follows logically from the premises. To be sure, some bananas are yellow, as stated in the sample item, but that conclusion does not follow *logically* from the premises that are provided. When people believe that a conclusion is true or false, that belief tends to overwhelm their use of syllogistic logic (Oakhill et al., 1989; Klauer et al., 2000).

**Conditional Reasoning**   Another common type of problem derived from formal logic is that of *conditional reasoning*, which takes the form of "if-then" statements. To see what's involved in conditional reasoning, look at the problem shown in Figure 7.17. You're told that each of the four cards has a number on one side and a letter on the other. Your goal is to test the hypothesis that "if a card has a vowel on one side, then it has an even number on the other side." Using as few cards as necessary, which cards would you need to turn over in order to adequately test this hypothesis? Think about it. What's your answer?

Most people realize that the *E* has to be turned over. But another card is needed as well. Is it the one with the *4* showing? No, this card doesn't really help. If there's a vowel on the other side, the rule could still be invalidated by another card. If there's a consonant, the rule is not invalidated (the rule does not state that a card with a consonant cannot have an even number on the other side). The correct choices are *E* and *7*. A vowel on the other side of the *7* would invalidate the rule. In studies with college students, only 4 percent got the right answer. Most picked the *E* and the *4*, probing only for evidence that was consistent with their hypothesis (Wason, 1960). So if you missed it, you are not alone.

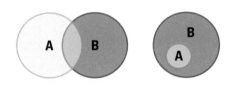

**FIGURE 7.16   Different representations of the same premise**
"Some *A*s are *B*s."

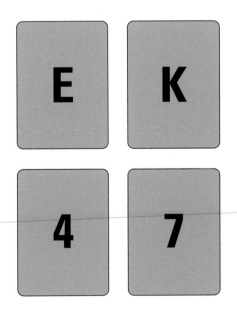

**FIGURE 7.17   A conditional-reasoning problem**
Each of the four cards has a number on one side and a letter on the other. Using as few cards as necessary, test the hypothesis that if a card has a vowel on one side, then it has an even number on the other side (Wason, 1960).

**FIGURE 7.18** **A conditional-reasoning problem with a familiar context**
Each of the four cards has an age on one side and a drink on the other. Using as few cards as necessary, test the hypothesis that if a person is drinking beer, then he or she must be over twenty-one.

This manifestation of the confirmation bias appears in a wide range of reasoning problems. For example, Deanna Kuhn (1991) interviewed people as to how they would evaluate their beliefs on important real issues (such as the causes of criminal behavior and school failure) and found that very few subjects realized that to truly evaluate their beliefs, they would need to consider disconfirming evidence. Everyone is vulnerable—and sometimes even motivated—to confirm their initial beliefs. For example, case studies in "pathological science" reveal that scientists have been known to test their pet theories in ways that do not allow for disconfirmation (Rousseau, 1992).

Is the confirmation bias an inevitable flaw in the way human beings reason? Patricia Cheng and others (1986) found that, compared to people with no formal training in logic, those who had completed a full-semester course in this discipline performed only 3 percent better. There is hope, however. Research shows that people perform well on conditional-reasoning tests using more familiar content. For instance, suppose you're trying to test this rule: "If a person is drinking beer, then he or she must be over twenty-one." In front of you are four cards, each with an age written on one side and what he or she is drinking written on the other. The four cards read *16, 25, cola,* and *beer.* Look at the problem presented in Figure 7.18. Now which cards would you turn over? In an actual experiment, 74 percent of the subjects chose *16* and *beer*—which is correct (Griggs & Cox, 1982). Why did they improve so much compared to the last experiment? It may be that because subjects are accustomed to thinking about drinking-age violations they were reminded in this case to search for disconfirming evidence.

What are the educational implications of this result? Is it possible to train people in the logic of conditional reasoning? To some extent, it is. But the key may be to teach this form of reasoning through the use of concrete problems, the way psychologists do—not through the presentation of abstract rules, as in philosophy. To test this hypothesis, Michael Morris and Richard Nisbett (1993) assessed the conditional-reasoning performance of first- and third-year graduate students enrolled in psychology or philosophy at Michigan, Chicago, and Brown universities. The results were striking: Philosophy students did not improve from the first year to the third, but the psychology students performed 33 percent better. After being trained to conduct experiments that test causal hypotheses, the psychology students had learned how to reason in "if-then" terms.

## BIASES IN JUDGMENT

Should I buy a sedan or a sports car, a desktop PC or a laptop? Should women over forty have routine mammograms? Should you pour money into stocks, bonds, or real estate? These are the kinds of decisions that people make every day—decisions that we base on intuitive judgments of probability, estimates we make about the likelihood of good and bad outcomes. How do we go about making these judgments? Do the decisions we make match those we *should* have made based on the objective probabilities? The pioneering work of Daniel Kahneman, Amos Tversky, and others has shown that people consistently use heuristics in making various judgments (Kahneman et al., 1982; Gilovich et al., 2002). Let's look at this research and what it tells us about ourselves.

**The Representativeness Heuristic** One rule of thumb that people use to make probability estimates is the **representativeness heuristic**—the tendency to judge the likelihood of an event's occurring by how typical it seems (Kahneman & Tversky, 1973). Like other heuristics, this one enables us to make quick judgments.

**representativeness heuristic** A tendency to estimate the likelihood of an event in terms of how typical it seems.

## THE PROCESS OF DISCOVERY

# DANIEL KAHNEMAN
## *Cognitive Heuristics*

**Q: How did you first become interested in psychology?**

**A:** I came to psychology in my late teens from an interest in philosophical questions, when I discovered that there was more hope of finding answers to such questions as "what are the causes of indignation?" or "why do people feel awe in cathedrals?" than to questions about the foundation of ethics or the existence of God.

**Q: How did you come up with your important discovery?**

**A:** After graduating in Psychology and Mathematics at the Hebrew University, in 1954, I served in the Israel Defense Forces. For part of my service I was a member of a team that selected candidates for officer training. There I made an observation that greatly affected my career. I noticed that my colleagues and I almost always felt great confidence in our assessments of the leadership potential of candidates we had interviewed or observed. What made that puzzling was that we were fully aware of research indicating that our ability to predict leadership effectiveness was actually negligible. I coined the term *illusion of validity* for that phenomenon.

The illusion of validity and the habit of looking for amusing errors in my own intuitions became central to my life fifteen years later, after obtaining my Ph.D. at the University of California, when the late Amos Tversky and I teamed up, first to study statistical intuitions, then to study decision making. Observations of persistent cognitive illusions in our own thoughts and preferences provided the starting point for most of our research.

We both did our best work in this collaboration, which endured for about fifteen years. The collaboration was productive because Tversky and I enjoyed our long and often funny conversations: he was a witty man as well as a deep thinker. The fun that we were having gave us the patience to produce some well-polished articles, the most important being a 1974 review of our studies of statistical intuitions and of judgments about uncertain events and a 1979 article introducing our "prospect theory" of decision making under risk. Both went through countless revisions as we slowly considered and tried to answer every possible objection. In part because of the care we had taken, and in part because we used simple and memorable examples, the work has had substantial influence on the study of human judgment and decision making.

**Q: How has the field you inspired developed over the years?**

**A:** This field of research is now thriving. It has attracted hundreds of talented investigators and is proving useful to many disciplines—including economics, management science, political science, law, and medical decision making. There has also been some interest in cognitive illusions among philosophers, which I find quite satisfying because of my childhood ambitions.

**Q: What's your prediction on where the field is heading?**

**A:** Opinions in the field are quite diverse. Many researchers share the vision that Tversky and I articulated, that the study of cognitive illusions is an important way to understand the mind. Others strongly disagree, and believe that a focus on errors yields a distorted portrayal of human abilities. The outcome of the debate is unpredictable. A review of the argument noted correctly that "there is no such thing as a last word" in the scientific conversation.

*Daniel Kahneman is Eugene Higgins Professor of Psychology, and Professor of Public Affairs, at Princeton University. In 2002, he was awarded a Nobel Prize for his research on decision making and economics.*

With speed, however, comes bias and a possible loss of accuracy. For example, which sequence of boys (B) and girls (G) would you say is more likely to occur in a family with six children: (1) B,G,B,G,B,G; (2) B,B,B,G,G,G; or (3) G,B,B,G,G,B? In actuality, these sequences are all equally likely. Yet most people say that the third is more likely than the others because it looks typical of a random sequence. As you'll see in *Debunking the Myth*, this use of the representativeness heuristic gives rise to a "gambler's fallacy" in games of chance.

## Debunking the Myths

# THAT CAUSE GAMBLERS TO LOSE MONEY

Anyone who has played poker for money, dropped coins into a slot machine, bet on a sports event, or bought lottery tickets knows how seductive gambling can be. Every year, people from all walks of life spend hard-earned money in casinos, racetracks, lotteries, and Internet gaming sites. Americans spend hundreds of billions of dollars a year in gambling activities, and they predictably lose 5 to 20 percent of that figure.

In *The New Gambler's Bible,* Arthur Reber (1996) notes that playing certain games, like blackjack and poker, and armed with a strategic understanding of probabilities, it is possible "to beat the casinos, the track, your bookie, and your buddies." As you might expect, however, most people are not adequately equipped to win. In fact, problem gamblers harbor more distorted beliefs than others do (Steenbergh et al., 2002).

Gambling is a puzzling phenomenon. Ordinarily, people avoid taking large financial risks. Offered a hypothetical choice between receiving a certain $1,000 or a 50:50 shot at $2,500, most people choose the smaller, guaranteed alternative (Kahneman & Tversky, 1984). So why do so many people gamble, and then persist in the face of defeat? There are different theories. From a cognitive perspective, there are three problems: (1) people harbor the illusion that they can control chance events, (2) they do not understand the laws of probability, and (3) they come up with biased explanations for their wins and losses.

In a series of experiments on the **illusion of control,** Ellen Langer (1975) found that people delude themselves into believing they can control the outcome in games of chance that mimic skill situations. When subjects cut cards against a competitor in a game of high card, they bet more money when their opponent seemed nervous rather than confident. When subjects played a lottery, they were more reluctant to sell their tickets after choosing a number themselves than after getting an assigned number. This hardly seems rational. But don't we all fall prey to these illusions? Watch people at slot machines and you'll see

*"I hope to break even today," said one gambler to another. "Why's that?" "I really need the money."*

that they try to control their luck by moving from one machine to another. Or watch players throwing dice in craps or backgammon, and you'll notice that they often roll hard for high numbers and soft for low numbers (Henslin, 1967).

The effects on gambling are clear. To exploit our tendency to infuse games of chance with an illusion of control, states infuse lotteries with "choice" by having players pick number combinations themselves. Go to the racetrack, and you will see bettors sizing up the horses and studying the racing forms. In casinos, the dealers are trained not to intimidate players by shuffling the cards in fancy ways. Why are people fooled? According to Langer, we need to feel that we can control the important events in our lives. In fact, the more people need to win, the more deluded they seem to become. In one study, for example, subjects took part in a random card drawing with a chance to win a McDonald's Big Mac hamburger. Those who were food-deprived and hungry at the time saw the task as more skill-based and were more confident of success than those who had just eaten (Biner et al., 1995).

Gambling also stems from common misguided notions about probability and prediction (Wagenaar, 1988). Suppose you flipped a coin six times. Which sequence of heads (H) and tails (T) would you be most likely to get: HHHTTT or HTTHTH? Most people pick the second alternative. Yet the two patterns are equally likely. Now suppose you could purchase a lottery ticket containing six numbers out of forty. Would you rather have the numbers 4-33-29-10-2-16, or 1-2-3-4-5-6? Given a choice, most people prefer the first ticket to the second (Holtgraves & Skeel, 1992). Yet out of 3,838,380 possible winning combinations, both are equally likely. In one daily number game, a number between 000 and 999 is randomly drawn every day, and the payoff is always 500 to 1—regardless of how many winners there are. It's not possible in this situation to strategically influence your chances. Yet a study of number selections showed

**illusion of control** The tendency for people to believe that they can control chance events that mimic skill situations.

that ticket purchasers shy away from numbers that had recently won (Halpern & Deveraux, 1989).

Why does this happen? Kahneman and Tversky (1972) find that the *representativeness heuristic* leads people to falsely assume that a sequence of events resulting from a truly random process should "look" random. Since a large number of coin flips will produce roughly a 50:50 split, people expect this ratio to emerge even in a small sample of flips. This assumption gives rise to the *gambler's fallacy*— the belief that random processes are self-correcting such that temporary deviations in one direction will be matched by later deviations in the opposite direction. That's why, after a string of heads, people tend to predict that the next coin will land on its tail or why, after a long run of red numbers on the roulette wheel, people rush to bet on black numbers. The gambler's fallacy is also the reason many slot-machine addicts believe that a machine is "hot" if it has not surrendered a jackpot for a long time.

Another problem with the way we judge probabilities stems from the *availability heuristic,* the tendency to overestimate the likelihood of dramatic, memorable events (Tversky & Kahneman, 1973). Think about it. One reason people buy lottery tickets despite the dreadfully low odds of winning is that they are influenced by the sight of multimillion-dollar winners on TV. The same is true of casinos. The last time I was in one, I had to fight the sense that everyone was winning. All around me, people were shrieking with joy, bells and sirens were blaring, lights were flashing, and coins were jingling into metal trays. What about all those who were losing? They were invisible—a silent majority, nowhere to be seen or heard. If I didn't know better, I would have thought that everyone was lucky except me. Winning was "available" and easy to overestimate.

The fact that we often bet money using defective prediction strategies explains part of the gambler's dilemma. But why do people persist after loss? One reason is that we selectively focus on evidence that fits our hypothesis. Bryan Gibson and others (1997) asked subjects to imagine how one of four playoff basketball teams would win the championship. Later, they found that subjects were most likely to bet money on the team whose winning they had earlier considered. Imagining a particular outcome makes it seem more likely to occur. A second reason is that we generate biased explanations for our wins and losses. In one study, subjects were questioned one week after betting on a series of pro football games. These explanations revealed that although they accepted winning without scrutiny, they often cited fluke events to explain away losses—a fumble on the goal line, a close call by the referee, or an injury to a key player—all to suggest that victory was otherwise close at hand (Gilovich, 1983). In another study, subjects who played a computerized three-wheel slot machine persisted and lost more money if they had experienced a "near miss," say by obtaining two cherries and a lemon where three cherries constitutes a jackpot (Kassinove & Schare, 2001).

These results bring to mind those regretful last words all of us have heard: "I was close; I could have won if . . . " Well, maybe next time.

*With the odds always favoring the house, casinos want to keep you gambling for long periods of time—and at a fast rate. Thus, the lighting is good, the air is cool, the stools have back supports, the drinks are free, beautiful women called "starters" are hired to attract the "high rollers," and blackjack dealers are required to deal 60 to 75 hands per hour.*

**availability heuristic** A tendency to estimate the likelihood of an event in terms of how easily instances of it can be recalled.

**anchoring effect** The tendency to use an initial value as an "anchor," or reference point, in making a new numerical estimate.

**framing effect** The biasing effects on decision making of the way in which a choice is worded, or "framed."

The problem with this heuristic is that it often leads us to ignore numerical probabilities, or "base rates." Suppose I tell you that there's a group of thirty engineers and seventy lawyers. In that group, I randomly select a conservative man named Jack, who enjoys mathematical puzzles and has no interest in social or political issues. Question: Is Jack a lawyer or an engineer? When Kahneman and Tversky (1973) presented this item to subjects, most guessed that Jack was an engineer (because he seemed to fit the stereotyped image of an engineer)—even though he came from a group containing a 70 percent majority of lawyers. In this instance, representativeness overwhelmed the more predictive base rate.

**The Availability Heuristic** A second mental shortcut that people use is the **availability heuristic,** the tendency to estimate the likelihood of an event based on how easily instances of that event come to mind. To demonstrate, Tversky and Kahneman (1973) asked subjects to judge whether there are more words in English that begin with the letter *K* or the letter *T*. To answer this question, subjects tried to think of words that started with each letter. More words came to mind that started with *T*, so most subjects correctly chose *T* as the answer. In this case, the availability heuristic was useful. It sure beat counting up all the relevant words in the dictionary.

As demonstrated, the availability heuristic enables us to make judgments that are quick and easy. But often, these judgments are in error. For example, Tversky and Kahneman asked some subjects the following question: Which is more common, words that start with the letter *K* or words that contain *K* as the third letter? In actuality, the English language contains many more words with *K* as the third letter than as the first. Yet out of 152 subjects, 105 guessed it to be the other way around. The reason for this disparity is that it's easier to bring to mind words that start with *K*, so these are judged more common.

The letter-estimation bias is harmless, but the availability heuristic can lead us astray in important ways—as when uncommon events pop easily to mind because they are very recent or highly emotional. One possible consequence concerns the perception of risk. Which is a more likely cause of death in the United States: being killed by falling airplane parts or being attacked by a shark? Shark attacks get more publicity, and most people say it is a more likely cause of death. Yet the odds of being struck by falling airplane parts are thirty times greater ("Death Odds," 1990). People who are asked to guess the major causes of death thus tend to overestimate the number of those who die in shootings, fires, floods, terrorist bombings, accidents, and other dramatic events—and to underestimate the number of deaths caused by heart attacks, diabetes, and other mundane and less memorable events (Slovic et al., 1982). Made relevant by current fears of terrorism, research shows that people's perceptions of risk are affected more by fear, anxiety, and other emotions than by cold probabilities (Loewenstein et al., 2001; Slovic, 2000).

Another consequence of the availability heuristic is that people are influenced more by a vivid life story than by hard statistical facts. Have you ever wondered why so many people buy lottery tickets despite the low odds, or why so many travelers are afraid to fly even though they're more likely to be injured or perish in a car accident? These behaviors are symptomatic of the fact that people are relatively insensitive to numerical probabilities and, instead, are overly influenced by graphic and memorable events—such as the sight of a million-dollar lottery winner rejoicing on TV or a photograph of bodies being pulled from the wreckage of a plane crash (Bar-Hillel, 1980). It may not be logical, but one memorable image is worth a thousand numbers.

**Anchoring Effects** Using the availability heuristic, people are influenced in their judgments by the facts that are most available in memory—and they fail to make adjustments to compensate for that bias. A related phenomenon is the

*Dramatic airline disasters are so memorable that people overestimate the risks of flying. In fact, mile for mile, travelers are far more likely to die in a car crash than on a commercial flight.*

**anchoring effect,** the tendency to use one stimulus as an "anchor," or reference point, in judging a second stimulus.

Imagine being asked, "What proportion of African nations are in the United Nations?" Think about it. What would be your estimate? Now suppose that before answering this question, the experimenter spun a roulette wheel marked with numbers from *1* to *100*. You think the outcome of the spin is random, but actually the wheel is rigged to stop either at *10* or at *65*. At that point, the experimenter asks, "Is the proportion of African nations in the United Nations above or below the wheel number? Then what, specifically, is your estimate?" As a result of this procedure, subjects vary their estimates according to the numerical reference point provided by the wheel number. Those for whom *10* was the initial anchor estimated that 25 percent of African nations were in the UN. Among those given *65* as an anchor, the estimate was 45 percent. Even though subjects assumed the wheel number to be arbitrary, it served as a starting point for their numerical estimates (Kahneman et al., 1982).

Additional studies have confirmed that anchoring effects are common and powerful. Thus, numerical reference points bias judgments of new events even among people who are offered prizes to be accurate and even among those who say afterward that they were not influenced by the anchor (Wilson et al., 1996).

Framing Effects    Overall, research shows that human beings have some powerful reasoning tools but that the reasoning process is flawed in serious ways. This theme repeats itself as we explore a topic that bridges thought and language. In a classic series of studies, Tversky and Kahneman (1981) found that decisions are shaped by the language used to describe a dilemma. This tendency to be influenced by the way an issue is worded, or "framed," is called the **framing effect.** To test for this effect, researchers present two versions of the same problem that are worded differently but are logically equivalent. According to reason, preferences should be unaffected by wording. But that's not what happens.

In one study, a vast majority of subjects thought condoms were effective in stopping AIDS when condoms were said to have a "95 percent success rate" but not when they were said to have a "5 percent failure rate" (Linville et al., 1992). In a second study, beach-goers read a brochure about sunscreen that was framed in terms of gains ("Using sunscreen increases your chances of maintaining healthy, young-looking skin") or losses ("Not using sunscreen decreases your chances of maintaining healthy, young-looking skin"). They were then given coupons that could be redeemed later in the day for a free sample-sized bottle of sunscreen. The result: 71 percent who read the gain-framed message redeemed the coupon, compared to only 53 percent who read the loss-framed message (Detweiler et al., 1999).

An important lesson can be drawn from framing effects. At the beginning of this chapter, we briefly considered the relationship between thought and language. In that context, framing effects suggest that thinking may be shaped by language. We'll take up this issue again shortly, when we discuss the nature of language.

Overconfidence    At times our judgments are correct; at times they are subject to bias. Nobody's perfect. But are we sufficiently aware of our own limitations? Some years ago, Baruch Fischhoff and his colleagues (1977) had people answer hundreds of general-knowledge questions and estimate the odds that each answer was correct. Consistently, the subjects were overconfident. Other studies soon revealed the same pattern. Regardless of whether people are asked factual questions ("Which river is longer, the Amazon or the Nile?"), to predict future world events ("Who will win the Super Bowl?"), or to evaluate their own ability to pick a criminal from a lineup, confidence exceeds performance (Kahneman & Tversky, 1996; Bornstein & Zickafoose, 1999).

**WHAT'S YOUR PREDICTION**

If anchoring leads us to set high or low reference points, what are the implications? Can trial lawyers raise or lower the amount of money that juries award by stating large or small amounts? Would juries see through the attempted influence, or see lawyers as greedy, and react against it? Or, are juries so focused on evidence that they disregard what lawyers ask for?

Mollie Marti and Roselle Wissler (2000) presented mock jurors with a case of a dock worker who fell and was badly injured, and who sued the trucking company responsible for the accident. There was no dispute that the company was at fault; jurors only had to decide on how much money to award the worker for pain and suffering. In one version of the case, the plaintiff's lawyer did not state a figure. In other versions, he asked for .75 million, 1.5 million, or 5 million dollars. Make a prediction: what effect do you think the requests had?

When no request was made, jurors gave an average of $680,000. Did the larger requests lead jurors to award more, less, or the same? Demonstrating an anchoring effect, Figure 7.19 shows that the more the lawyer asked for, the more he got. In fact, a follow-up study showed that jurors awarded even more when the lawyer sought $15 million. Thanks to anchoring effects, you can sometimes get what you ask for.

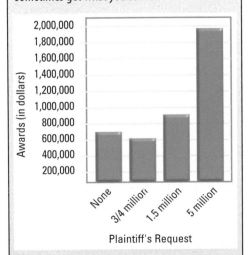

**FIGURE 7.19**
(Marti & Wissler, 2000)

In a study that illustrates this point, David Dunning and others (1990) asked students to make judgments of a more social nature—to predict how a target person would react in different situations. Some of the subjects made predictions about a fellow student whom they had just met and interviewed, and others made predictions about their roommates. In both cases, the subjects reported their confidence in each prediction, and accuracy was determined by the responses of the target persons themselves. The results were clear: Regardless of whether subjects judged a stranger or their roommate, they consistently overestimated the accuracy of their predictions. In fact, Kruger and Dunning (1999) found that people who scored low rather than high on tests of spelling, logic, grammar, and humor appreciation were the most likely to overestimate their own performance. Apparently, poor performers don't know what they don't know. In later chapters, we will see that as a general rule self-confidence is a virtue that promotes health, happiness, and success. The key is to avoid becoming so overconfident that we take foolish risks and make hasty decisions—as people often do when they place bets in the gambling casino.

## CAN HEURISTICS MAKE US SMART?

The research on heuristics portrays people as nonrational in the way they reason and as prone to error—which is why we often make poor decisions we later come to regret (Gilovich et al., 2002). But how can this bleak portrait of human beings be reconciled with the triumphs of civilization? Or, to put it another way, "If we're so dumb, how come we made it to the moon?" (Nisbett & Ross, 1980, p. 249).

To begin with, research shows that some individuals are more rational than others in the way they reason and make decisions (Stanovich & West, 1998). In fact, people can be taught in college and other educational settings to reason more logically (Kosonen & Winne, 1995; Lehman & Nisbett, 1990; Nisbett et al., 1987). But what's the goal? Often we don't have all the information we need or unlimited amounts of time to think, so instead we do the best we can by using heuristics. A number of years ago, Herbert Simon (1956) coined the term *satisficing* (by combining "satisfying" and "sufficing") to describe the way people make judgments that, while not logically perfect, are good enough. Today, many psychologists argue that people operate by a principle of "bounded rationality"—that we are rational *within bounds* depending on our abilities, motives, available time, and other factors.

In a book entitled *Simple Heuristics That Make Us Smart*, Gerd Gigerenzer and others (1999) noted that people seldom compute intricate probabilities to make decisions, but rather "reach into an adaptive toolbox filled with fast and frugal heuristics" (p. 5). They also noted that although not perfect, these heuristics serve us well, or at least, as Simon would say, well enough. Consider, for example, the recognition heuristic—that people, objects, or places we recognize have greater value than those we don't recognize (Goldstein & Gigerenzer, 2002). In a study of investment decision making in the stock market, Bernhard Borges and others (1999) asked people to indicate which publicly traded companies they had heard of—such as Kodak, Ford Motors, Coca Cola, Intel, and American Express. These researchers then created two stock portfolios, one containing high-recognition companies, the other low-recognition companies. After six months, the group of high-recognition stocks made more money than did the low-recognition stocks. In general, this group even outperformed the market. So, can a naive and ignorant investor pick winning stocks based on name recognition? The heuristic is not perfect, but it may be good enough. (For tips on becoming a more effective decision maker and problem solver, see *How to Improve Your Critical Thinking Skills*.)

## REVIEW QUESTIONS

- *Distinguish between syllogistic reasoning and conditional reasoning.*

- *What kinds of errors do people make when solving problems involving formal logic?*

- *Describe how the following bias judgments: the representativeness heuristic, the availability heuristic, the anchoring effect, and the framing effect.*

- *If heuristics produce biased judgments, why do we continue to rely on them?*

# How To

# IMPROVE YOUR CRITICAL THINKING SKILLS

The keys to improving your problem-solving and decision-making skills can be summarized by the term **critical thinking.** Critical thinking means solving problems and making decisions through a careful evaluation of evidence. When faced with important issues, forget old rules of thumb. Scrutinize what others say, consider their motives and emotions, probe beneath the surface of words, and consider the logic of the arguments. And if you can, don't rush to judgment; take your time. Thinking critically about arguments that others make, or that you make to yourself, can improve the quality of your decision making (Kuhn, 1991; Levy, 1997; Halpern, 2002). See Figure 7.20 for a summary of the steps involved in critical thinking.

The first step is to adopt an attitude of healthy skepticism. Most of us are not in the habit of probing for logical flaws in arguments, especially in the claims we make to ourselves, as shown by the research on the confirmation bias. So thinking critically requires conscious effort—and time. The next step is to identify the assumptions that are quietly hidden in an argument and consider whether they should be challenged. Sometimes a speaker's assumptions are clear from his or her use of facts. But people often present as "facts" beliefs that have not been verified. It's also important to avoid being too heavily influenced by smooth talking and jargon. A set of arguments may sound compelling and leave you nodding your head, but are they, really? Next, open your mind, step out of your "mental set," and try to imagine and evaluate alternative arguments. Better yet, fight the confirmation biases that haunt us all and search out contradictory evidence. Is it possible that there are other facts, and other perspectives, that are equally or more compelling? This step is especially hard when you're emotionally attached to an assertion, yet trying to imagine alternatives to it. Still, with practice you can do it. Finally, be prepared to tolerate uncertainty. You can never be sure what kind of person you would have become if raised by different parents, or how much of your childhood memories are real or imagined. Know what you don't know and guard against overconfidence—which breeds closed-mindedness.

Critical thinking is as much an attitude as it is a skill. As you learn new material in psychology and in other courses, stop to think about the invisible assumptions being made and evaluate the logic and plausibility of the material. Remember: You can't decide if you believe an argument until you understand it.

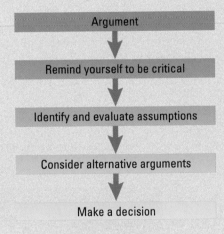

**FIGURE 7.20   Steps in critical thinking**

---

# LANGUAGE

- *With five thousand to six thousand languages spoken, why is it often said that all humans speak in the same tongue?*
- *What are the universal properties of all languages? Why don't even the most elaborate animal communication systems qualify?*
- *Can apes be taught language? Why is this notion so controversial?*

Language is a defining and adaptive milestone in human evolution. Linguist Noam Chomsky (1972) argued that the human brain is biologically hardwired for the acquisition of language. Thus, all cultures have language, all languages have

**critical thinking** The process of solving problems and making decisions through a careful evaluation of evidence.

*"Language is no more a cultural invention than is upright posture."*

—STEVEN PINKER

certain structural properties (such as nouns and verbs) in common, and children all over the world learn to fluently speak the language they hear, at about the same age, and without much effort or instruction. When it comes to language, it's clear that some form of learning occurs—but it's also clear that humans are born with a unique *sensitivity* to the sounds and structures of speech (MacWhinney, 1998). Terrence Deacon (1998) has argued that the human brain and language have co-evolved over millions of years. Steven Pinker (1994) sees the ability to learn, speak, and understand language as a powerful instinct, tightly woven into the human experience. "All over the world," he notes, "members of our species fashion their breath into hisses and hums and squeaks and pops and listen to others do the same. . . . We humans are fitted with a means of sharing our ideas, in all their unfathomable vastness" (Pinker, 1999, p. 1).

**Language** is a form of communication consisting of a system of sounds, words, meanings, and rules for their combination. In the coming pages, we will consider various forms of communication in the animal world, the unique properties of "language," the question of whether language can be learned by nonhuman animals, and finally, the relationship between thought and language.

## COMMUNICATION IN THE ANIMAL WORLD

Among humans, language is a primary means of communication. Other animal species have complex forms of communication as well. Ants send chemical signals secreted from glands in order to share information about food and enemies with other members of the colony. When honeybees discover a source of nectar, they return to the hive and communicate its location to the other worker bees through an intricate dance that signals both direction and distance. Male songbirds of various species sing in the spring to attract female mates and also to warn other males to stay away from their territory to avoid a fight. Dolphins talk to each other at great depths of the ocean by making a combination of clicking, whistling, and barking sounds. Vervet monkeys grunt quietly in relaxed social situations but give off loud

**language**  A form of communication consisting of sounds, words, meanings, and rules for their combination.

*The howling of the desert coyote and the spring song of the male bluebird are two of the many adaptive forms of communication found in the animal world.*

alarm calls that differ in sound according to whether the predator they see is a snake, eagle, or leopard.

There is no doubt that animals communicate in ways that benefit their survival. When the honeybee locates nectar and performs its dance, other bees leave the hive and buzz straight to the source—even if the one that discovered it is detained (von Frisch, 1974). And when a monkey produces an alarm call, other members of the group take action. Among East African vervets, a distinctive snake alarm leads others in the group to stand tall and peer into the grass, an eagle call leads them to look up and duck into bushes, and a leopard call leads them to run up a tree (Cheney & Seyfarth, 1992). Among chimpanzees, the ability to communicate gives rise to the development of distinct cultures. In a fascinating comparison of seven separate chimpanzee communities in Africa, a team of primate researchers identified thirty-nine behavior patterns that were present in some groups but absent in others—such as smashing open nuts with rocks, using leaves to fish for termites, or shaking branches to get attention. Like human groups, chimpanzee groups practice their own unique traditions, passed on from generation to generation (Whiten et al., 1999).

There are many other marvelous examples of adaptations that serve species well. So why do some scholars claim that "language" is a uniquely human capacity? To answer this question, we need to know more about what language is and the properties that are used to define it.

## CHARACTERISTICS OF HUMAN LANGUAGE

According to *World Almanac and Book of Facts 2003*, there are between five thousand and six thousand languages worldwide, to say nothing of the different dialects within each language. When all the dialects are taken into account, tens of thousands of variations can further be distinguished. It's amazing how different many languages seem on the surface. To appreciate this point, consider the principal languages, ranked in order of usage in the world's population: Mandarin Chinese, English, Hindi, Spanish, Russian, Arabic, Malay, Bengali, Portuguese, French, German,

*At a produce market in Beijing, this man and woman converse in Chinese—the most widely spoken language in the world.*

**semanticity** The property of language that accounts for the communication of meaning.

**phonemes** The basic, distinct sounds of a spoken language.

**morphemes** In language, the smallest units that carry meaning (e.g., prefixes, root words, suffixes).

**phrase** A group of words that act as a unit to convey meaning. Phrases are formed from combinations of morphemes.

**sentence** An organized sequence of words that expresses a thought, a statement of fact, a proposition, an intention, a request, or a question.

**generativity** The property of language that accounts for the capacity to use a limited number of words to produce an infinite variety of expressions.

Japanese, Urdu, and Javanese. Despite the differences, however, linguists are quick to note that from a Martian's perspective, all humans speak with a single tongue. The reason is that all languages share certain universal properties: semanticity, generativity, and displacement.

Semanticity **Semanticity** refers to the fact that there are separate units in a language and that these units have *meaning*.

The smallest units of speech are **phonemes,** the basic *sounds,* or building blocks, of all spoken languages. Each separate sound you hear when you pronounce the word unthinkable is one *phoneme*. English has twenty-six letters, but forty to forty-five phonemes. The word *tip* has three phonemes: *t, i,* and *p*. So do the words *ship* (*sh, i,* and *p*) and *chip* (*ch, i,* and *p*). Linguists estimate that human beings are physiologically capable of producing one hundred basic sounds. No one language uses all of them, however. Most contain between twenty and eighty phonemes. English speakers say *s* and *z* differently. In Spanish, they're one and the same. As a result of such differences in vocal experience, people sometimes struggle to pronounce the phonemes of other languages. For example, many Americans struggle to roll the German *r* or cough up the guttural *ch* sound of Arabic.

A string of randomly connected phonemes does not convey sound that is meaningful. The smallest unit that carries meaning is called a **morpheme.** Words, prefixes, and suffixes are all morphemes. Every word has one or more morphemes. Simple words like *dog, run,* and *think* contain one. The word *unthinkable* has three morphemes—the prefix *un-,* the root word *think,* and the suffix *-able*—and each adds to the total meaning of the word. The average American high-school graduate knows about forty-five thousand different words, and the average college graduate has a vocabulary that is nearly twice that size (Miller, 1991). It is quite remarkable that human beings are able to master a full language vocabulary so well, and so quickly, given that most word sounds are unrelated to meaning. There is no reason why a cat is called a *c-a-t* as opposed to a *d-o-g*. It just happens to be that way. There are exceptions to this rule, as some words do resemble the sounds they signify (such as *bang, crack,* and *oink*).

Combinations of morphemes become the building blocks for **phrases,** groups of words that act as a unit to convey meaning. One of my favorite quotes, by author Joseph Heller, is "When I grow up, I want to be a little boy." In this quote, the words "When I grow up" and "I want to be a little boy" are both phrases. Morphemes and phrases are then combined into larger units we call sentences. A **sentence** is an organized sequence of words that expresses a thought, a statement of fact, a proposition, an intention, a request, or a question.

Generativity A second property of language is **generativity,** the capacity it offers to use a finite number of words and rules for combining words to produce an infinite variety of novel expressions. Think about it. When I watched television coverage of the 2002 elections the night of November 5, I heard a news commentator say, "We won't be using exit polls tonight; instead we'll be calling these elections the old fashioned way, by counting votes." It was a pretty mundane sentence. But I doubt anyone in history had ever uttered it before.

Generativity gives language virtually unlimited flexibility as a system of communication. Two features of human language enable this flexibility. The first is that a phrase can always be added to the end of a sentence in order to form an entirely new sentence. Thus, you could go from the sentence "I like psychology" to "I like psychology this semester" to "I like psychology this semester, thanks to the professor," and so on. A second aspect of language that makes it flexible is that one expression can always be inserted inside another. This makes possible the construction of long, embedded sentences.

People usually understand these relatively complex sentences quite easily. But they can become mentally taxing. If you have ever sat on a jury, you know exactly what I mean. At the end of every trial, the judge instructs the jury on the law that should guide their decision making. Jurors are ordinary folks, not law-school graduates. Yet the instructions they receive are often so complex that they're practically impossible to understand. The following instruction on the term *negligence,* used by many judges, illustrates the point:

> One test that is helpful in determining whether or not a person was negligent is to ask and answer whether or not, if a person of ordinary prudence had been in the same situation and possessed the same knowledge, he would have foreseen or anticipated that someone might have been injured by or as a result of his action or inaction.

If language is so generative that we can produce limitless numbers of novel sentences, how are we able to comprehend each other as competently as we do? The key to managing generativity is **syntax**, rules of grammar that govern how words can be arranged in a sentence. Expressions are not random strings of unrelated sounds but rather words that are combined in familiar and orderly ways. Every language has its own unique syntax. For example, adjectives usually come *before* the noun in English (*white wine*) but *after* the noun in Spanish (*vino blanco*). We'll see in Chapter 10 that children learn most of the rules of their language by the age of five, and they do so without explicit instruction. Hardly anyone can explain the rules of grammar, yet most of us can instantly spot a statement that violates these rules. Which us brings another point to . . .

This brings us to another point about the generativity of language: Any one thought can be expressed in different ways. Regardless of whether I say, "The home team won the championship," "The championship was won by the home team," or "What the home team won was the championship," you grasp the meaning. As Chomsky (1965) explained, any underlying thought can be represented in more than one way. According to Chomsky, syntax provides us with a set of "transformational" rules for how to (1) put meaning into words when we speak and (2) derive meaning from words when we are spoken to.

Some transformations are easier to process than others. For example, Daniel Slobin (1966) asked people to read either active sentences ("The dog is chasing the cat") or passive sentences ("The cat is being chased by the dog") and to decide which of two pictures (a dog chasing a cat or a cat chasing a dog) depicted the sentence. He found that both children and adults were faster at choosing the correct picture when the sentence was active. Apparently, passively constructed sentences require more transformations, and therefore take more time, to get to the deep, underlying structure. The rules of transformation are not completely understood, and psychologists disagree over how such rules are implemented in the brain (Pinker, 1994; Rumelhart & McClelland, 1986). Still, the evidence suggests that we are on the right track in considering syntax to be separate from, but interacting with, meaning.

Displacement   A third property of language is displacement. **Displacement** refers to the fact that language can be used to communicate about things that are not in our immediate surroundings, matters that extend beyond the limits of the here-and-now. Thus, we reminisce about the good old days, we talk about our hopes and dreams for the future, we gossip about others behind their backs, and we discuss abstract ideas concerning God, politics, social justice, and love.

**syntax**   Rules of grammar that govern the arrangement of words in a sentence.

**displacement**   The property of language that accounts for the capacity to communicate about matters that are not in the here-and-now.

Most English sentences contain twenty words or fewer. According to the *Guinness Book of World Records,* however, the longest sentence ever printed contains 1,300 words.

As a means of communication, language is a highly social activity—and displacement enables us to tell others what we're thinking, how we're feeling, or what we plan to do next. These are complex messages, however, and social interaction is just that, a two-way interaction. To converse with others effectively, therefore, we need more tools than just an extensive vocabulary and an arcane knowledge of the rules of grammar. We must also have a sense of the *pragmatics,* or social context, of language and an understanding of how to use it (Hilton, 1995; Clark, 1996; Carston, 2002). In the words of Herbert Clark (1985), "Language is a social instrument. When we talk, we direct our words not to the air but to other people" (p. 179). Accordingly, says Clark, intricate rules guide the way speakers and listeners position themselves physically from each other, take turns in conversation, and communicate through the face, voice, body, and other nonverbal channels. We also tailor what we say to suit our audience and the situation we're in. People tend to take language pragmatics for granted. But tension frequently arises when these pragmatics break down—as when natives of very different cultures neglect to realize that the person they're trying to communicate with does not know their local expressions, jargon, and buzzwords (Axtell, 1993). In *You Just Don't Understand,* sociolinguist Deborah Tannen (1990) speculated that conflicts between men and women often arise because of gender differences in their communication style, or pragmatics.

At this point, let's stop for a moment and ponder some of the playful puzzles presented by the English language. In *Words and Rules: The Ingredients of Language,* Pinker (1999) notes that there are two basic building blocks in language: the *words* we learn, memorize, and store in a mental dictionary; and the *rules* we use to form complex words (such as plurals and past tense forms) and word combinations (such as phrases and sentences). Some rules are simple, as when we add *-ed* to a verb to create a past tense form of it. This rule for the thousands of regular verbs in the language is so predictable that English speakers automatically know how to convert new verbs into past tense forms. Without having to think about it, everyone knew that *fax* became *faxed,* that *spam* became *spammed,* and that *diss* became *dissed.* Tell a child that a man likes to *wug* (a made-up word) and that child will tell you that yesterday the man *wugged.* Yet English also contains about 180 irregular verbs that do not follow this simple rule, words with past tense forms that have to be memorized. Thus, the past tense of *spring* is *sprang,* but *cling* is *clung* and *bring* is not brang or brung but *brought.* Pinker describes other oddities for which the rules are less clear. For example, most of us know that the plural of *mother-in-law* is *mothers-in-law,* not *mother-in-laws.* But are people who pass by *passerbys* or *passersby?* Does Tiger Woods get two holes in one, or two hole in ones? And is the plural of a computer's pointing device called a *mouse,* or is it *mouses* or *mice?* For psycholinguists, the way people resolve these issues provides a glimpse into the mental rules that guide the language they use.

**Emergence of Language**   Paralleling the changes that take place in the way children think is their development of language (see Table 7.4). Between the ages of one and six, children acquire a vocabulary that consists of an estimated fourteen thousand words, an average of nine words per day. They also learn to combine words in ways that fit grammatical rules too complex for most of us to explain. What's amazing about these achievements is that boys and girls of all cultures absorb the words and grammar of language without formal instruction. It just happens. As in cognitive development, some children may speak sooner than others, but the sequence of achievements is the same for all (Brown, 1973; McNeil, 1970; Rice, 1989).

**Developmental Sequence**   Newborns communicate their needs by crying. In their second month, they also use the tongue to make more articulated *cooing*

---

For online dictionaries of many languages and specialized resources for medical, legal, financial, computing, and other terminologies, visit: http://www.yourdictionary.com.

## TABLE 7.4   MILESTONES IN THE EMERGENCE OF LANGUAGE

| Ages | Stages |
| --- | --- |
| 1–2 months | Cooing (oh, ah) |
| 4 months | Babbling (ah boo) |
| 8–16 months | First words |
| 24 months | Two- and three-word telegraphic speech |
| 2–3 years | Multiword sentences |
| 4 years | Adultlike, mostly grammatical speech |

sounds such as *oh* and *ah*. At about four months, babies begin playful **babbling,** vocalizing for the first time in ways that sound like human speech—*ah boo, da da,* and *ah gee.* As with crying and cooing, babbling is inborn. Regardless of whether the native language is English, French, Spanish, German, Hebrew, or Swahili, babies all over the world initially make the same sounds, including some they never hear at home (for example, the German *ch* and the rolled *r*). Even babies who are born deaf and cannot hear speech babble right on schedule.

Some time near the first birthday, give or take four months, babies utter their first real *words*. The sounds are brief and not clearly pronounced, but they communicate meaning in the native tongue—for example, *ba* for *bottle*. For the next few months, babies speak one-word utterances, and the number of words in their vocabulary increases sharply (Woodward et al., 1994)—from 4 or 5 at twelve months to 30 at eighteen months to 250 at two years. These utterances are not random. Babies tend to name objects and actions that they desire (a bottle, favorite toys, "more"), especially those that involve motion (cars, a pet dog)—just as Piaget would expect of a sensorimotor child (Nelson, 1973).

At about two years of age, there is a vocabulary explosion, as children accumulate hundreds of new words a year. At this point, children will pick up a new word they encounter in conversation—even when they hear it only once or twice. For building a vocabulary, it helps for young children to be spoken to. Observational research has shown that toddlers whose mothers were more talkative, compared to those whose mothers were less talkative, had 131 more words in their vocabularies at 20 months and 295 more words at two years (Huttenlocher et al., 1998).

Another important development in language occurs when children begin to form two- and three-word phrases. These early word combinations illustrate what is called **telegraphic speech** because—as in telegrams, kept short for cost reasons—they include only nouns, verbs, and some essential modifiers, yet make sense to the listener ("More juice" for "I want more juice," or "No sit chair" for "I don't want to sit in a chair"). It's interesting that these primitive sentence forms contain the seeds of grammar—"more juice" rather than "juice more," for example. It's also interesting that the statements are often *overextensions*. For example, until different animals can be distinguished, the two-year-old who uses the word *doggie* to call the family pet will use the same word about a cat, a horse, or a circus elephant. Language tells us a lot about a child's developing knowledge of the world.

By the age of three, four, or five, a child's mind contains a small dictionary of words ready to be used correctly. Although new words are learned without any explicit thought or instruction, an enriched linguistic environment can accelerate the process. For example, preschoolers who watch the educational TV show *Sesame Street* have larger vocabularies than those who do not (Rice et al., 1990). With increasing age, children construct longer and more complex sentences; learn to use plurals, pronouns, past tense, and other rules of grammar; and begin to appreciate puns and words with double meanings. At puberty, corresponding to the onset of

**babbling**   Spontaneous vocalizations of basic speech sounds, which infants begin at about four months of age.

**telegraphic speech**   Early short form of speech in which the child omits unnecessary words—as telegrams once did ("More milk").

Piaget's formal operational stage, children even come to appreciate abstract metaphors—"like two ships passing in the night."

**Developmental Theories** No one disputes the stages of language development in children or the sequence of those stages. But there are differences of opinion as to what it all means. Two issues in particular have been lively topics of controversy.

The first is our old friend, the nature–nurture debate. In 1957, behaviorist B. F. Skinner wrote a book entitled *Verbal Behavior,* in which he argued that children learn to speak the way animals learn to run mazes. They associate objects and words, imitate adults, and repeat phrases that are met by social reinforcement. Through trial and error, for example, a baby of English-speaking parents learns to repeat the babbling sounds that excite mom and dad but not foreign sounds that leave them cold. In response to Skinner, linguist Noam Chomsky (1959, 1972) argued forcefully that the human brain is specially hard-wired for the acquisition of language. Specifically, he argued that children are endowed from birth with a "universal grammar," core rules common to all human languages, and the ability to apply these rules to the language they hear spoken. The evidence in for this biological position is impressive: Language grows at a rate that exceeds all other kinds of learning, two-year-olds construct telegraphic statements they couldn't possibly have heard from adults, and children learn to speak properly even though nobody really stops to correct their grammar.

To some extent, it is clear that human beings are genetically prepared for language the way that computers are prewired for programming (Pinker, 1994). The environment we live in may provide the software that determines *what* language we learn to speak, but biology provides the hardware that controls when and *how* we learn it. It's also clear that in the acquisition of language, there is a critical, or at least sensitive, period during the first few years of life when humans are most receptive to language learning (Lenneberg, 1967). That is why adolescents and adults who learn a second language speak it with an accent, while children who acquire a new language before puberty speak it without an accent. The same pattern is true in the acquisition of grammar. In a study of Asian immigrants to the United States, the younger they were as children when they moved, the higher was their score on a test of grammar (Johnson & Newport, 1989).

The second debate concerns a chicken-and-egg problem: What comes first, thought or language? Piaget (1976) believed that children must understand a concept before they can use words to describe it. Thus, babies cannot say, "All gone," or "Bye-bye," or use other words that refer to the disappearance of objects until they understand the concept of object permanence. Yet other developmental psychologists believe that language shapes thought and that children develop concepts in order to understand the words they hear from others. Thus, the child who hears *dog* tries to understand the word by searching for objects that might fit (Bruner, 1983). It appears that both views are correct. Words and concepts emerge at roughly the same time—and the causal arrow points in both directions. Sometimes children use words to communicate what they already know, and sometimes they form concepts to fit the words they hear (Rice, 1989).

## CAN ANIMALS LEARN LANGUAGE?

Philosophers and scientists have long regarded the capacity for language and abstract thought as uniquely human—the dividing line between us and other animals. Is this still considered to be true, or has a new breed of comparative psychologists studying the once-taboo topic of animal thinking and awareness (Ristau, 1991; Balda et al., 1998; Bekoff et al., 2002; Boysen & Himes, 1999) discovered something new?

**The Talking Parrot**   At center stage in this emerging area are research projects aimed at teaching rudimentary language to nonhuman animals. In one such project, Irene Pepperberg (2000) and her colleagues spent more than twenty years teaching English to Alex, a one-pound African gray parrot. Everyone knows that these birds can "parrot" what people say, but do they understand the words that they use? Pepperberg makes a compelling case. She'll pick up an object from a crowded tray and ask, "What toy?" In response, Alex will name the object ("block") and respond at an 80 percent level of accuracy to questions about its color ("red"), shape ("square"), and substance ("wood"). Overall, Alex can use seventy-one words to name more than thirty objects, seven colors, five shapes, five numbers, actions, and materials. More often than not, he can also tell whether an object is the same as or different from, or bigger or smaller than, something else. He can even count how many items there are in a collection of items ranging from one to six.

To bring Alex to this level of competence, Pepperberg (2002) had two human trainers vocally and physically interact with the various objects. With Alex watching, one would point to an object and ask a question about it. The other, serving as a model, would give a programmed answer. If incorrect, the trainer would scold the model and remove the object from view. If the answer was correct, the model was praised and rewarded with the object. The learning process is thus a highly social experience that involves making eye contact with the parrot and pointing to the object while making reference to it. In training sessions with two new gray parrots, social interaction—specifically, eye contact—was necessary for learning.

*Alex, an African gray parrot, prepares to answer the question "What toy is blue and triangular?"*

**The Bottle-Nosed Dolphins**   In Hawaii, Louis Herman and others (1993) have been studying the language capabilities of two bottle-nosed dolphins, Phoenix and Akeakamai. In this project, researchers communicate with one dolphin through hand gestures and with the other dolphin through electronic whistlelike sounds transmitted through an underwater speaker system. In both cases, the distinct gestures or sounds refer to objects that are in the tank, the relationships between objects, actions to be taken, and location. The behavior of these sea mammals is astonishing in many ways. For example, when given commands consisting of two- to five-word sentences such as "Right water left Frisbee fetch"—which means "Take the Frisbee on your left to the stream of water on your right"—the dolphins perform to specification. They even respond to changes in syntax. The dolphins were trained in a system in which modifiers precede objects ("left Frisbee") and objects precede actions ("Frisbee fetch"). So when a command violates these rules of grammar, they do not obey.

Just how impressive are these dolphins? "If you accept that semantics and syntax are core attributes of human language," says Herman, "then we have shown that dolphins also account for these two features within the limits of this language" (Linden, 1993, p. 58). Perhaps this level of sophistication should not come as a surprise. Dolphins live in a complex social world in which communication among species members is vital to their survival (Herman & Uyeyama, 1999).

What do these projects tell us about the capacity of animals for language? Many animal cognition researchers believe that they are shattering old assumptions and breaking new ground. In contrast, skeptics make a convincing claim that these studies show little more than mimicry and rote learning—much like rats pressing a food bar in a Skinner box. Before addressing the controversy, however, let's first examine the most impressive evidence for the claim—evidence derived from our closest animal relatives, the great apes.

**The Great Apes**   By today's standards, the earliest attempts to teach language to apes were misguided. In 1933, psychologists Winthrop and Luella Kellogg raised a baby chimpanzee alongside their own son and tried to treat them in the same way.

"Although humans make sounds with their mouths and occasionally look at each other, there is no solid evidence that they actually communicate with each other."

[© 1997 By Sidney Harris]

Their son learned to coo, babble, and speak on schedule; the chimp did not. A similar attempt was later made by Cathy Hayes (1951), whose chimp could recognize pictures, categorize objects, and imitate behaviors, but not speak more than a few rudimentary words. After six years of intensive training, the only words the chimp could say were *cup, up, mama,* and *papa.* Conclusion: Apes do not have the cognitive capacity for language.

The problem with these studies is that chimps may not have the vocal musculature for uttering human phonemes, but is speech a necessary criterion for language? Of course not. What about the symbols on this page, the characters found in other alphabets, the printed characters in Braille that enable blind people to read, and the sign languages used by the deaf? To overcome the vocalization constraint, psychologists had to take creative new approaches, and they did. David Premack (1971) taught a chimp named Sarah to communicate by placing colored plastic chips, symbolizing words, on a magnetic board. Duane Rumbaugh (1977) then taught a chimp named Lana to communicate by pressing keys on a specially designed computer. Some of the more impressive projects involved the use of American Sign Language (ASL). Allen and Beatrice Gardner (1969) taught sign language to Washoe and four other chimps. Within four years, Washoe had a vocabulary of 132 words and the ability to combine signs to form simple sentences. In fact, Washoe and her friends communicated in sign language—and she even taught her adopted young son 68 different signs (Fouts et al., 1989). Also using sign language, Herbert Terrace (1986) trained a chimp he called Nim Chimpsky (after linguist Noam Chomsky), and Francine Patterson and Eugene Linden (1981) trained a gorilla named Koko, whose 600-word vocabulary is the largest recorded so far.

Combining the various techniques, Sue Savage-Rumbaugh and her colleagues (1998) taught a young pygmy chimp named Kanzi to talk by making hand signals, pointing to geometric symbols on a laminated board, and punching the symbols on a keyboard. Kanzi also understands spoken English. What sets this project apart from the others is that Kanzi learned the language the way human children do: not by explicit instruction but by mere exposure. The researchers had trained Kanzi's

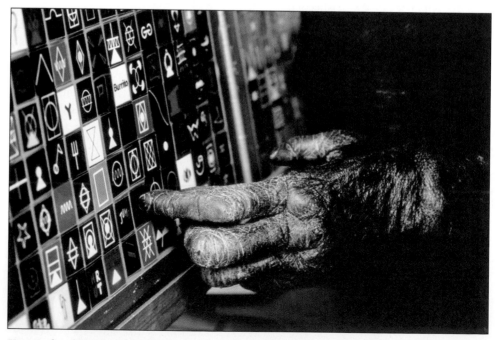

*Kanzi, the chimpanzee with the most advanced language skills, can "talk" by making hand signals and by pointing to symbols on a special board.*

mother, and he learned by watching. As Savage-Rumbaugh put it, "If Kanzi could learn without instruction, I wondered, why teach?"

**The Controversy**   The feats of Sarah, Lana, Washoe, Nim, Koko, Kanzi, and the others are impressive, even to the critics. Clearly, these are smart animals capable of learning. But is what they learned "language"? Some say yes; others say no. What do you think? To address this question, let's stop for a moment and focus on whether these evolutionary relatives of ours show the properties of semanticity, generativity, and displacement in their "language" behavior. These properties of language increase in complexity—from merely naming an object, to using that object label in an infinite number of sentence constructions, to talking about that object out of context. Thus, research with young children shows that they first use single words to communicate, then combine words into sentences, and finally talk about objects not in their immediate surroundings (Fenson et al., 1994).

**Semanticity**   Just about everyone agrees that the language apes satisfy this criterion. With vocabularies ranging from 130 to 600 words, these apes can produce words for concrete objects (*me, chair*), action verbs (*tickle, eat*), and even adjectives (*big, happy*). And they may know more than simple rote associations between signs or symbols and objects. Sherman, a chimp trained by Savage-Rumbaugh, pointed to the symbol "food" when shown a real banana or the symbol for banana. Koko the gorilla signed "finger bracelet" to describe a ring and "eye hat" to describe a mask (Patterson & Linden, 1981). And Kanzi, the chimpanzee with the most advanced skills, reacted appropriately to slightly different requests, such as "Show me the light," "Bring me the light," and "Turn the light on" (Savage-Rumbaugh et al., 1998).

**Generativity**   Can the apes combine words in lawful ways to produce novel expressions? Some researchers find that their apes do not distinguish—and perhaps cannot distinguish—between word combinations based on how they are ordered (Terrace, 1986). But others claim that their apes do use syntax to combine words they have never heard before. Syntax? Yes, that's the claim. When Washoe wanted to be tickled, she would sign "You tickle Washoe." When she wanted to do the tickling, it was "Washoe tickle you" (Gardner & Gardner, 1978). Kanzi may also understand sentences he never heard before. Once, with his back to the speaker, Kanzi heard "Jeanie hid the pine needles in her shirt." He then turned around, walked up to Jeanie, and searched her shirt (Savage-Rumbaugh et al., 1998).

**Displacement**   The most demanding criterion for language is displacement, the use of words to talk about matters not in the immediate surroundings. People do it all the time, but what about the language apes? Florence Patterson believes that Koko the gorilla used signs to make statements about past events and to express feelings—such as sadness over the death of her pet kitten (Patterson & Linden, 1981). Savage-Rumbaugh and her colleagues (1998) have reported that Kanzi also refers to past events. When a trainer asked Kanzi about a wound on his body, he replied, "Matata hurt"—presumably to say that Matata, his mother, had bitten him more than an hour earlier. These types of stories are not common, but they have captured the imagination.

**Conclusion**   The evidence has been tantalizing, but to this day skeptics insist that it's open to interpretation (Kako, 1999). Herbert Terrace (1985) argued that many "spontaneous" signs may simply be imitations or conditioned responses to subtle

"He says he wants a lawyer."

cues provided by the trainers. Further, he noted that researchers who work with the apes sometimes lose their objectivity and see in an animal's behavior what they are hoping to see—like children seeing pictures in the clouds.

Savage-Rumbaugh and her colleagues (1993) compared Kanzi's comprehension abilities to those of a two-year-old girl named Alia. In Chapter 10, we'll see that children all over the world develop quickly the ability to form sounds, words, phrases, and finally sentences. Clearly, no ape can *produce* language the way a normal human child can, but how much do they actually *know*? Research with toddlers reveals that they understand more than they're able to say, so this is an important distinction to make. In an extensive series of tests, which took nine months to complete, Kanzi and Alia were compared for their responses to 660 commands that were made in spoken English. The sentences were new to both subjects, they were structured in several different ways, and they often combined objects in ways that had never been encountered before ("Put the melon in the potty," "Go get the carrot in the microwave"). To ensure that the subjects could not pick up subtle clues from the experimenters' nonverbal behavior, the commands were given by one experimenter over an intercom, and each subject's behavior was recorded by a second experimenter from behind a one-way mirror. As it turned out, Kanzi responded correctly to 74 percent of the sentences, Alia to 65 percent. Both exhibited comprehension of spoken language, semantics, and syntax. It appears that Kanzi, and presumably other language apes as well, know far more than they can tell. Table 7.5 presents a sample of the 660 requests made to Kanzi. Words and syntax were varied, and comprehension was measured by the correctness of his behavioral response, where C = correct, PC = partially correct, and N = incorrect (Savage-Rumbaugh et al., 1993).

So what are we to conclude? It is clear that apes can be taught words and can understand sentences in which these words are combined according to rules of grammar. It is equally clear, however, that the apes have a small vocabulary and a simple syntax compared to that found in young children. There's also no hard evidence to suggest that they can talk about abstract matters, such as whether humans can master language.

A *New York Times* article on this debate reveals the extent of the disagreement (Johnson, 1995). As a result of the research, it's clear that many scientists believe that the line separating "us" and "them" is not as clear as was once thought. Thus, in response to those who maintained that Kanzi's feats do not meet the criteria for language, philosopher Stuart Shanker complained that "linguists keep moving the

| TABLE 7.5 | KANZI'S KNOWLEDGE OF ENGLISH | |
|---|---|---|
| **Sentence** | **Kanzi's Response** | **Scoring** |
| "Throw the orange to Rose." | Kanzi picks up the orange, turns, and hands it to Rose. | PC |
| "Make the snake bite the doggie." | He picks up the toy snake and puts it on top of the toy dog. | C |
| "Make the doggie bite the snake." | He picks up the toy dog and puts it on top of the snake. | C |
| "Can you pour the ice water in the potty?" | He picks up the bowl of ice water, heads to the potty, and carefully pours it in. | C |
| "Take the telephone to the colony room." | He goes to the colony room, but takes nothing with him. | PC |
| "Put the raisins in the yogurt." | He pours the yogurt on the raisins. | N |
| "Hide the toy gorilla, hide him." | He tries to push the toy gorilla under the fence. | C |

goal post." For other scientists, nothing has changed. Steven Pinker said, "In my mind this kind of research is more analogous to the bears in the Moscow circus who are trained to ride unicycles." Equally adamant, Chomsky likened the ape language experiments to trying to teach people to flap their arms and fly. "Humans can fly about 30 feet—that's what they do in the Olympics. Is that flying?" At this point, it is safest to conclude that what these apes have learned may have all the properties that linguists postulate as necessary features of language—but that the animals' language is cruder and more rudimentary than ours.

## THE RELATIONSHIP BETWEEN THOUGHT AND LANGUAGE

- *Do words we speak determine, constrain, or shape the way we conceptualize the world?*
- *What is the impact of using sexist language—and what about the use of euphemisms?*
- *What is "critical thinking," and how can it be put into action?*

This chapter has shown that thought and language are interrelated cognitive activities. Having now examined them separately, we are faced with the question "What is the nature of their interrelationship?"

### THE LINGUISTIC-RELATIVITY HYPOTHESIS

Common sense tells us that language is a useful tool for expressing thought, but that it is not necessary. Thus, child-development researchers have found that young children understand concepts before they have words to explain them (Flavell et al., 1993) and that they can assign objects to categories even when they do not have the relevant vocabulary (Gershkoff-Stowe et al., 1997).

In the fifth century BCE, Herodotus, a Greek historian, argued that the Greeks and Egyptians thought differently because the Greeks wrote from left to right and Egyptians from right to left. Many years later, inspired by anthropologist Edward Sapir, Benjamin Lee Whorf (1956) theorized that the language we speak—the words, rules, and so on—determines the way we conceptualize the world. This notion, that our thoughts are "relative" to our linguistic heritage, is called the **linguistic-relativity hypothesis.** This hypothesis gave rise to a profound prediction: that people of different cultures who speak different languages must think in different ways (Lucy, 1992; Gumperz & Levinson, 1996). As we'll see shortly, this hypothesis led researchers to span the globe in search of cross-cultural comparisons.

Does language have the power to shape the way people think? As a result of many years of research, nobody believes that language *determines* thought the way genes determine a person's height. But most psychologists do agree with a less radical claim: that language *influences* thinking (Bloom, 1981; Hardin & Banaji, 1993; Hunt & Agnoli, 1991; Lucy, 1992). The eyewitness study described at the start of this chapter—in which estimates of automobile speeds were influenced by the wording of the "how fast were they going?" question (Loftus & Palmer, 1974)—clearly illustrates this point. Many others do as well. In one study, researchers showed subjects line drawings and varied the label that accompanied each one (see Figure 7.21). Afterward, subjects redrew these figures from memory in ways that were distorted by the labels (Carmichael et al., 1932). In a second study, subjects were

## REVIEW QUESTIONS

- *What is language?*
- *Identify the three universal properties of language.*
- *What is syntax, and why is it important?*
- *Summarize the evidence suggesting that animals can acquire language.*

*"The mystery of language was revealed to me. . . . Everything had a name, and each name gave birth to a new thought."*

—HELEN KELLER

**linguistic-relativity hypothesis**   The hypothesis that language determines, or at least influences, the way we think.

| Original figures | Labels | Sample drawings |
|---|---|---|
| | Curtains in a window | |
| | Diamond in a rectangle | |
| | Crescent moon | |
| | Letter "C" | |
| | Eyeglasses | |
| | Dumbbell | |
| | Ship's wheel | |
| | Sun | |
| | Kidney bean | |
| | Canoe | |

**FIGURE 7.21  Words that distort memory for images**
Subjects who saw figures like those shown (*left*) later redrew these figures from memory in ways that fit the different labels they had been given (*right*).

*In an article entitled "Eskimo Words for Snow," anthropologist Laura Martin (1986) debunked the myth that the Eskimo people have four hundred words for snow. Where did this myth come from? In 1911, Franz Boas said there were four words. Whorf expanded the count to seven and implied there were more. His article was then cited in popular books, and in the same way that rumors spread, the number grew with each successive telling of the story. The result, said linguist Geoffrey Pullum (1991), was "The great Eskimo vocabulary hoax."*

presented with pictures of faces or color chips, and half were asked to describe them. Those who had put what they saw into words later had more difficulty recognizing the original faces and colors. Did language in this case disrupt thought? Yes, according to the investigators, "some things are better left unsaid" (Schooler & Engstler-Schooler, 1990).

If language can influence thought, then words are tools that can be used to socialize our children, sell products, mold public opinion, and stir the masses. People in power are aware of this connection and choose their words carefully. As colorfully documented by William Lutz (1996), the result is "doublespeak"—language that is designed to mislead, conceal, inflate, confuse, and distort meaning. Thus we are told that a new tax is a "user's fee," that companies that fire employees are merely "downsizing," that recession is "negative economic growth," that civilian war deaths are "collateral damage," and that plastic handbags are made of "genuine imitation leather." Even more common are the euphemisms we all use to talk about touchy subjects. Thus, we say that people who died "passed away," that pornographic movies are "adult films," and that we need to use the toilet in a "restroom" (Allan & Burridge, 1991; Holder, 2002).

## CULTURE, LANGUAGE, AND THE WAY WE THINK

According to Whorf's linguistic-relativity hypothesis, people who speak different languages think about the world in different ways. To illustrate, Whorf (1956) pointed to cultural variations in the use of words to represent reality. He noted, for example, the Hanunoo people of the Philippines have 92 names for rice—in contrast to the crude distinction North Americans make between "white rice" and "brown rice." Similarly, although English has only one word for snow, Eskimos have several words—which, he argued, enables them to make distinctions that others may miss between "falling snow, snow on the ground, snow packed hard like ice, slushy snow, wind-driven flying snow—whatever the situation may be" (p. 216). Even grammar shapes thought, claimed Whorf. For example, he compared English to the language of the Hopis. In English, you can use the same numerical modifier for units of time ("five days") as for concrete objects ("five pebbles"). In the Hopi language, by contrast, different numerical modifiers are used in each case. Whorf argued that this feature causes the speakers of each language to perceive time differently.

Evaluating the linguistic-relativity hypothesis is not easy because people who speak different languages differ in other ways as well. Many bilingual people say that Whorf is right, citing as personal evidence the odd sense that they think differently in each language—and sometimes get "lost in translation" (Hoffman, 1989). However, there are flaws in both the theory and the research. First, even if members of two cultures did think differently, who's to say that the difference in their language came first? Second, Eskimos may have several words for snow, but does that mean they think about snow differently? After all, people in other regions of North America distinguish between slush, fresh powder, packed powder, hail, wet snow, and the "loose granular" substance often found on ski slopes.

What about something as universal as color perception? Does the vocabulary of colors in a language influence the way its speakers think about color? Eleanor Rosch (1973) studied the Dani, an aboriginal people living in Papua, New Guinea. The English language contains eleven words to describe basic colors: red, yellow, blue, green, brown, orange, pink, purple, black, white, and gray. Yet the Dani language has only two color words: *mola* for light hues and *mili* for dark hues. So can Dani speakers make fine discriminations among colors? Yes. They see differences among colors of the same name the way non-Eskimos distinguish between types of snow. Rosch had presented Dani and English-speaking subjects with color chips, one by one, like those shown in Figure 7.22. Moments later, she asked them to select the same color from a large array of chips and found that although the English-speakers were somewhat more accurate overall, the Dani were most often able to select the right basic colors even though their language did not have names for them. Other cross-cultural researchers have also observed that people categorize colors similarly despite differences in their language of color (Davies et al., 1998).

Interested in whether language provides a lens through which we think about time, Lera Boroditsky (2001) compared Mandarin Chinese and English speakers. Apparently, languages differ in terms of the spatial metaphors used to describe time. In English, we talk horizontally about time, looking *forward* to a brighter future, completing projects *ahead* of schedule, putting the past *behind* us, or pushing *back* a deadline. In Mandarin, people speak vertically about time, with earlier events described as *shang*, or up, and later events as *xia*, or down. To see if differences in the way people talk about time shape the way they think about time, Boroditsky asked Mandarin and English speakers some initial questions that primed them to think in terms of either horizontal or vertical spatial relations (see Figure 7.23). Following these primes, all participants were asked to respond as quickly as possible to purely temporal true-false questions, such as "March comes earlier than April." Consistent with the differences in how the two languages describe time, English speakers were quicker to answer time questions after being primed to think in horizontal terms, whereas Mandarin speakers were quicker when primed to think in vertical terms. As shown in Figure 7.23, these results support the notion that experience with a language can shape the way one thinks.

*"It's good to be open-minded, but not so open that your brains fall out."*

—JACOB NEEDLEMAN

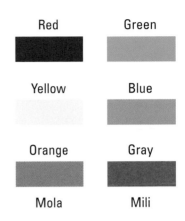

**FIGURE 7.22**
Among the Dani, all colors on the left are called *mola*, whereas all those on the right are called *mili*. Yet when asked to do so, the Dani are able to distinguish among the colors within each set.

## PSYCHOLOGICAL IMPACT OF SEXIST LANGUAGE

Over the past few years, some colleges and universities replaced the term *freshman* with *first-year student*. The reason: The existing term was considered sexist for using the generic masculine form. Sparking controversy among theologians are recent efforts to rewrite "God's words" of the Bible in more inclusive, gender-neutral terms.

Whatever the political and religious arguments may be, the psychological question is: "Does sexist language influence the way we think about men and women?" What do you think? Is the term *mail carrier* rather than *mailman* silly and awkward, or does the change help break down gender stereotypes? Is it harmless or sexist to talk about "the evolution of *man*," our "fore*fathers*," "*brother*hood," and the "chair*man* of the board"? And what about the generic use of the masculine pronoun *he* to refer to all human beings? Is it okay to say, "a doctor must be trained if *he* is to be competent?" Drawing on the linguistic-relativity hypothesis, many people feel strongly about this issue.

For psychologists, the task is to determine whether the use of generic masculine nouns and pronouns triggers images of men to the exclusion of women. The results

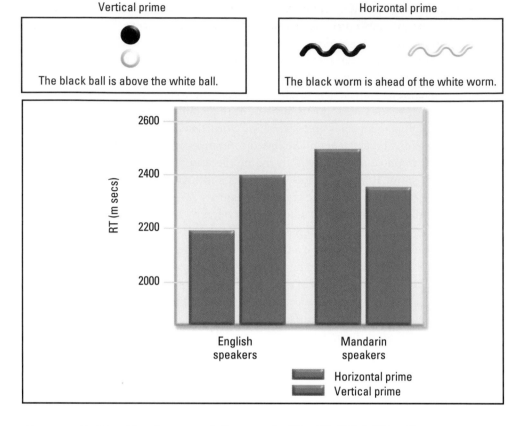

**FIGURE 7.23** **How Language Influences the Way We Think About Time**
In English, we speak horizontally about time; in Mandarin, people also speak vertically about time, Boroditsky (2001) primed native English and Mandarin speakers by initial questions to think in vertical or horizontal terms (top left, right). Afterward, when asked temporal true-false questions ("March comes earlier than April"), English speakers were quicker after horizontal primes (bottom, left) and Mandarin speakers were quicker after vertical primes (bottom, right).

of this research support the hypothesis that *man, he,* and other masculine words, even when used generically, lead people to think of men. In one study, for example, male and female college students were asked to make up stories based on a topic sentence: "In a large co-ed institution, the average student will feel isolated in ____ courses." Into the blank, the researchers inserted the pronoun *his, his* or *her,* or *their.* Did the pronoun in the topic sentence make a difference? Yes. When *his* rather than a neutral term was used, 65 percent of the stories written were about men (Moulton et al., 1978). Similar results have been found in studies of adults

| TABLE 7.6 | GUIDELINES FOR NONSEXIST LANGUAGE |
|---|---|
| **Common Sexist Terms** | **Nonsexist Alternatives** |
| Man, mankind | People, humanity, human beings |
| Manpower | Work force, personnel |
| Freshman | First-year student, frosh |
| Chairman | Head, chair, chairperson |
| Foreman | Supervisor |
| Policeman | Police officer |
| He, his, him | He or she, his or her, him or her, or they, their, them |
| Mothering | Parenting, nurturing, caregiving |
| Female doctor | Doctor |
| Male nurse | Nurse |

(McConnell & Fazio, 1996). These studies suggest that the use of generic masculine terms is seen as exclusive, not inclusive, of women. Some alternatives to common sexist terms are presented in Table 7.6. Reading time experiments also show that the generic plural pronoun *they* provides a cognitively efficient, gender-neutral alternative to *he* or *she* (Foertsch & Gernsbacher, 1997).

Whorf's original hypothesis—that we can think only in terms provided for in language—was undoubtedly overstated. But this should not blind us to the fact that language does make it easier to conceptualize the world in some ways rather than others. The use of sexist words is one practical implication of linguistic relativity, but there are other implications, too. In the global village, translating ideas from one language to another is tricky and sometimes results in misunderstanding. The people of the world do not just speak differently but also interpret events through different lenses. At this point, more research is needed to explore this link between language and thought and what it means for intercultural relations.

## REVIEW QUESTIONS

- *What is the linguistic-relativity hypothesis?*

- *How does sexist language influence the way we think?*

- *What is critical thinking? What steps are involved in thinking critically?*

## THINKING LIKE A PSYCHOLOGIST ABOUT THOUGHT AND LANGUAGE

Psychologists who study thought and language—like those who study learning and memory—have come to realize that people are complex, "two-headed" creatures, competent in some ways, flawed in others. Often we solve difficult problems through trial and error, algorithms, heuristics, and a great capacity for creative insight. Yet often we get stuck mentally and fail to find obvious solutions because of functional fixedness, mental sets, and confirmation biases that keep us from fully testing our ideas. The same dual portrait characterizes the way people make decisions. Sometimes, we're capable of performing feats of formal logic, as in problems involving syllogistic and conditional reasoning. Yet often we put our minds on "autopilot" and allow ourselves to be misled by availability, representativeness, anchoring effects, framing effects, and other heuristics.

Then there's language. Despite recent successes in teaching apes to communicate, it is clear that the human capacity for language—whether measured by semanticity, generativity, or displacement—is impressive and unmatched. Yet it is also clear that words can be used to shape, and sometimes distort, the way we think. People are complicated creatures, both competent and flawed at the same time.

The good news is that we have the capacity to improve on the way we think and, therefore, on our ability to adapt to changing circumstances. Earlier, we saw that even when we feel stumped on a problem, it is possible to find the insight we need by representing it in a different way, opening our minds to alternative approaches, or perhaps just taking a break. We also saw that people can be taught to reason in more logical ways. There are many ways for us to maximize the use of our cognitive abilities.

## SUMMARY

People are both rational and irrational at the same time. Why is this so?

## CONCEPTS

Research shows that when a **concept** is activated in a person's mind, other related concepts in the semantic network are primed and emerge more readily from memory. **Prototypes,** concepts that seem "typical" of a particular category because they have most of its defining properties, come most readily to mind and have the strongest influence on our judgments.

## SOLVING PROBLEMS

When we cannot find a solution by retrieving the answer from memory, we go through three steps: representing the problem, generating possible solutions, and evaluating those solutions.

### REPRESENTING THE PROBLEM

Representing the problem often involves activating concepts from our semantic memory. It can also involve mental **images** of visual information and intuitive **mental models** of how things work. Our mental models, though useful, are sometimes inaccurate.

## Generating Solutions

Once we have represented a problem, we generally choose from four basic problem-solving strategies: trial and error, algorithms, heuristics, and insight. **Trial and error** entails trying various solutions until one works. In contrast, an **algorithm** is a step-by-step procedure guaranteed to produce a solution eventually. **Heuristics** are rules of thumb that lead to quicker but not always accurate solutions. One general heuristic is **means-end analysis**, the breaking down of a problem into subgoals. Another is the use of **analogies**, which involve taking an old solution as a model for a new problem. Sometimes, in a flash of **insight**, a solution pops to mind. In long problem-solving sessions, people often exhibit the incubation effect, whereby sudden insight occurs after they take a break.

## "Blind Spots" in Problem Solving

Our "blind spots" in problem solving can result from a number of factors. A problem may be represented incorrectly. Or we may fall into **functional fixedness**, thinking of objects only in terms of their usual functions. A **mental set**, taking us back to a strategy that worked in the past, can also be a hindrance. **Confirmation biases** dispose us to look only for evidence that supports our initial beliefs. And **belief perseverance** leads us to stick to our beliefs even when they have been discredited.

## MAKING JUDGMENTS

Studies of decision making have brought further discoveries about the rationality of human beings.

## The Rules of Formal Logic

In solving logical **syllogisms**, people often restate the problem in concrete terms to make it easier, but doing so can cause mistakes. In conditional-reasoning problems, people often err because of the **confirmation bias.**

## Biases in Judgment

In making everyday decisions, we consistently rely on judgmental heuristics. The **representativeness heuristic** leads us to judge an event's likelihood by its apparent typicality, so that we ignore numerical probabilities. The **availability heuristic** is the tendency for estimates of event likelihood to be influenced by how easily instances come to mind. The **anchoring effect** is the tendency for an initial value to serve as a reference point in making a new judgment. And studies of the **framing effect** demonstrate that decisions can be biased by the way an issue is worded. Despite the various biases, people are consistently overconfident about their judgment abilities.

Gambling is an irrational but popular activity. There are many explanations for why people gamble, including the **illusion of control,** the tendency for people to believe that they can control chance situations that mimic skill situations, and various heuristics that produce misconceptions about the laws of probability. Through careful evaluation of evidence, **critical thinking** can help us improve our problem solving and decision making. Thinking critically involves having a skeptical attitude, probing underlying assumptions, and considering alternative arguments.

## LANGUAGE

**Language** is a form of communication consisting of a system of sounds, words, meanings, and rules for their combination. It is the adaptive product of evolution.

## Communication in the Animal World

Animals such as honeybees and dolphins communicate in ways that are crucial to their survival. Yet many researchers have maintained that "language" itself is uniquely human.

## Characteristics of Human Language

All languages share the properties of semanticity, generativity, and displacement. **Semanticity** refers to the fact that language has separate units of meaning. The smallest meaningful units are **morphemes.** In all spoken languages, morphemes are made up of basic sounds called **phonemes.** Combinations of morphemes become **phrases.** A **sentence** is an organized sequence of words.

Through the property of **generativity**, language can turn a finite number of words into an infinite variety of expressions using the processes. **Syntax,** the formal grammar, provides the rules for transforming the deep structure of a statement into various possible surface structures.

Finally, all languages are capable of **displacement,** or communication about things beyond the here-and-now. Such communication also involves pragmatics, our knowledge of the social context of language.

Language development proceeds in a regular sequence: from cooing to **babbling,** single words, **telegraphic speech,** and full sentences. Evidence supports the view that humans are specially "wired" for language, that there is a critical period, and that words and concepts develop jointly, each influencing the other.

## Can Animals Learn Language?

Animals as different as parrots, dolphins, and apes have been trained to exhibit some features of language. In experiments, apes have clearly met the semanticity criterion and they may at times exhibit generativity, but there is little hard evidence for displacement. Thus, there is controversy about whether the apes are producing language per se.

## THE RELATIONSHIP BETWEEN THOUGHT AND LANGUAGE

It is assumed that thought gives rise to language, but does language also shape thought? What is the relationship between these cognitive activities?

### THE LINGUISTIC-RELATIVITY HYPOTHESIS

Going beyond the traditional view that thought shapes language, Whorf's **linguistic-relativity hypothesis** predicts that language can shape the way we think.

## CULTURE, LANGUAGE, AND THE WAY WE THINK

Some research indicates that people from different cultures think differently, but investigators disagree about the interpretation. Today, research suggests that language influences but does not completely determine thought.

### PSYCHOLOGICAL IMPACT OF SEXIST LANGUAGE

Consistent with the linguistic-relativity hypothesis, research indicates that sexist language influences the way children and adults conceptualize the roles of men and women.

## KEY TERMS

concept (p. 260)

prototype (p. 261)

image (p. 263)

mental models (p. 264)

trial and error (p. 264)

algorithm (p. 266)

heuristic (p. 266)

means-end analysis (p. 266)

analogy (p. 266)

insight (p. 268)

functional fixedness (p. 270)

mental set (p. 270)

confirmation bias (p. 270)

belief perseverance (p. 272)

syllogism (p. 272)

representativeness heuristic (p. 274)

illusion of control (p. 276)

availability heuristic (p. 278)

anchoring effect (p. 278)

framing effect (p. 278)

critical thinking (p. 281)

language (p. 282)

semanticity (p. 284)

phonemes (p. 284)

morphemes (p. 284)

phrase (p. 284)

sentence (p. 284)

generativity (p. 284)

syntax (p. 285)

displacement (p. 285)

babbling (p. 287)

telegraphic speech (p. 287)

linguistic-relativity hypothesis (p. 293)

## THINKING CRITICALLY ABOUT THOUGHT AND LANGUAGE

1. Imagine that you are developing a workshop to teach people to become better problem solvers. What specific strategies would you include in your workshop? What suggestions would you give to promote the use of insight? What specific tactics would you recommend to eliminate the blind spots?

2. Suppose scientists invented a pill that would allow you to make all your decisions in a completely rational manner. Would you choose to take such a pill? Why or why not?

3. What psychological processes contribute to gambling? What advice would you give to help a person overcome a gambling addiction?

4. Discuss the debate over animal thought and language. Present the arguments both for and against the proposition that animals can think and learn language. What criteria do you think should be used to determine whether the animals presented in this chapter are displaying language? Are there any characteristics of human language that you think animals could never demonstrate?

5. Do computers think? Do they have language capability? Why or why not?

6. Discuss the practical implications of the research concerning the psychological impact of sexist language.

# Nature and Nurture

# NATURE OR NURTURE?

## THE SITUATION

You know from past research that about 15 to 20 percent of all healthy babies are inhibited, timid, and wary of strangers. You also know that 25 to 30 percent are outgoing, fearless, and eager to approach new people. These differences are apparent early in life and remain stable through childhood. But where does this trait come from? Are some infants just born that way, as parents often assume, or does temperament arise from early experiences?

To tease apart these dual effects, you decide to conduct a twin study. From monthly birth records, you contact all parents of recently born twins. Many agree to take part in your study, and you go on to recruit 178 pairs. About half are genetically identical, or monozygotic (MZ), twins; the other half are genetically nonidentical, fraternal, or dizygotic (DZ), twins. All sets of twins live together. You make appointments so that a mother and her children come to the laboratory when the twins are fourteen months old. Then they return for follow-up visits at twenty and twenty-four months old.

Along with two assistants, you meet the mother and her twins in a reception room. You explain the procedure and place a bib with an identifying letter on each child. One child is randomly selected to join the mother and a second assistant in a playroom, while the other stays in the reception area. Once the testing is complete, the children switch places.

The floor of the playroom is covered with toys. The mother sits on a sofa on the side and is asked not to pay attention to the child unless needed. At this point, the child is free to play. With the entire session being videotaped, two events are then staged to provide additional opportunities to observe the child's behavior. First, a new assistant, a stranger, enters the room holding a toy truck. Soon, she invites the child to play with her (if the child has not already done so). Next, the assistant who brought the mother and child into the playroom opens a cabinet and pulls out an unfamiliar object—a blue stuffed toy monster or a robot made of tin cans and colored lights. After two minutes, the child is encouraged to approach the object (if he or she has not already done so).

To determine each child's level of inhibition, you review the session tapes and record how long it took the child to approach the toys, the stranger, and the unfamiliar object. You also record the percentage of time spent near the mother during these phases. These standardized behavioral measures are then combined and the child is given an overall inhibition score.

Once all the sessions are scored, the data are ready to be analyzed. The question: What is the *correlation* between pairs of twins? If one twin is inhibited, what is the likelihood that the other is inhibited as well? If you paired unrelated children at random, the correlation would be 0 (remember, a correlation coefficient can range from 0 to +1 or −1). At the other extreme, the behaviors of the identical twin pairs—who have the same genes and live in the same home—should be highly correlated. But what about the comparison group of fraternal twins? If variations in temperament are genetically determined, their correlation should be much lower, even though they live in the same home. But if temperament stems from experience, the correlations should be about the same for the identical and the fraternal twins. It would also be interesting to know whether the correlations remain stable from the first time the children are tested, at fourteen months old, to the third time, after ten months of additional life experience.

## THE PROCESS OF DISCOVERY

# ROBERT PLOMIN
*The Nature of Nurture*

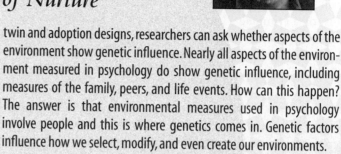

**Q: How did you first become interested in psychology?**

**A:** In college, at DePaul University, I began as a philosophy major. I didn't do well at it because I kept trying to re-phrase philosophical questions as testable psychological questions. I finally realized that anything that could be tested empirically was no longer considered philosophy. That realization made me switch. I went on to get my Ph.D. in psychology, in 1974, from the University of Texas.

**Q: How did you come up with your important discovery?**

**A:** The two discoveries in which I played a part came from thinking about what genetic research tells us about the environment. Genetic research, such as twin and adoption studies, asks whether genetic influences are important. However, such studies also tell us that the environment is important. Studies of identical twins provide the evidence for this conclusion. Although members of an identical twin pair are *genetically* identical, like clones, they are not identical *psychologically*. For example, if an identical twin is schizophrenic, the chances that the co-twin is schizophrenic is 50 percent, not 100 percent.

The first discovery is what we called the *nonshared environment*. Siblings growing up in the same family resemble each other psychologically, but the reason for this resemblance is genetics—siblings are 50 percent similar genetically. When siblings are not genetically related (such as two unrelated children adopted into the same family), they are not at all similar in personality or psychopathology. The environment is important, but environmental effects on psychological traits are not shared by two children growing up in the same family.

The second discovery has to do with what we called *the nature of nurture*. By measuring environmental factors in genetically sensitive twin and adoption designs, researchers can ask whether aspects of the environment show genetic influence. Nearly all aspects of the environment measured in psychology do show genetic influence, including measures of the family, peers, and life events. How can this happen? The answer is that environmental measures used in psychology involve people and this is where genetics comes in. Genetic factors influence how we select, modify, and even create our environments.

**Q: How has the field you inspired developed over the years?**

**A:** Research on both topics—the nonshared environment and the nature of nurture—have developed by incorporating measures of the environment into twin and adoption studies. The goal of research on nonshared environment has been to identify the environmental mechanisms that make two children growing up in the same family so different. But this has not been easy. Research on the nature of nurture has asked whether genetics also influences associations between environmental measures and psychological outcomes. They do.

**Q: What's your prediction on where the field is heading?**

**A:** I see two directions for future research. One is to bring together research on genetic and environmental factors. The other is in molecular genetics, as we try to identify the specific genes responsible for the widespread influence of genetics in psychology.

*Robert Plomin is MRC Research Professor and Deputy Director of the Social, Genetic and Developmental Psychiatry Research Centre at the Institute of Psychiatry, King's College University in London.*

different directions—both between families and within families as well (Dunn & Plomin, 1990; Hetherington et al., 1994).

What aspects of the nonshared environment make siblings so different from one another? Do siblings differ because they are treated differently by parents and others within the home, or do the differences stem more from the environment outside the home? In a book entitled *The Limits of Family Influence*, David Rowe (1994) reviewed the behavioral-genetic research and concluded that the effects of the home environment are short-lived and have surprisingly little impact on our adult personalities. Consistent with this proposition, Judith Harris (1995) concluded, "Whether a child resides at 42 Oak Street or at 56 Oak Street is a variable that has no long-term consequences" (p. 482). Rather, the most important aspects of the nonshared environment come from peer groups, friends, and others *outside* the home. Hillary Rodham Clinton once quoted an African saying that "It takes a village to raise a child." Apparently, that village has many people, including peers, who exert a strong and lasting influence on the development of children into adults.

This position has sparked a heated controversy about the importance of parents. In *The Nurture Assumption*, Harris (1998) argued that children turn out as they do not because of their mothers and fathers but because of their peers. Research confirms that peers exert influence, particularly among adolescents. Indeed, the best predictor of whether a teenager will become a smoker is whether his or her friends smoke. So does it *not* matter in the long run whether parents discipline their sons and daughters, hug them, read to them, teach them values, help them with homework, or take them places? Does this mean that new parents should worry less about parenting?

Some psychologists admit that there's a kernel of truth to Harris's argument and that it is ultimately adaptive for children to pay more attention to peers—their future mates, coworkers, and competitors. But other child development researchers charge that she overstates the case and neglects recent studies that contradict her argument (Collins et al., 2000). Still others note that parents substantially guide the all-important peer-selection process by the neighborhoods they live in, their family income and access to various resources, and the schools that they choose for their children—the work of invisible parental hands that Harris did not account for (Bradley & Corwyn, 2002; Leventhal & Brooks-Gunn, 2000; Linver et al., 2002; Vandell, 2000).

## THE INTERPLAY OF NATURE AND NURTURE

As researchers have struggled to disentangle the contributions of nature and nurture, they have come to realize that there is yet another complicating factor: *Genetic and environmental influences are not independent.* Studies have shown that identical twins receive more similar treatment from their parents than fraternal twins do. In fact, the more genetically similar any two siblings are, the more similar their experience is at home. To some extent, then, our genetic makeup influences the way others treat us, the kind of environment that we live in, and the way we perceive and recall the details of that environment (Scarr & McCartney, 1983; Plomin et al., 1994; Hur & Bouchard, 1995).

Urie Bronfenbrenner and Stephen Ceci (1994) suggested a "bioecological" model of development to account for the interaction of nature and nurture. According to this model, infants at birth are endowed with genetic predispositions, but these potentials will ultimately influence them as adults only to the extent that life experiences foster rather than inhibit their expression. There may be a genetic component to intelligence, but children raised in poverty and under stress may not realize their potential, whereas those who grow up in intellectually stimulating homes are more likely to achieve. Even with height, a highly heritable characteristic, children who are malnourished may not grow to be as tall as they could be.

William Dickens and James Flynn (2001) recently proposed a similar theory on the powers of nature and nurture to influence intelligence. According to their

**WHAT'S YOUR PREDICTION**

A critical aspect of childhood is gender role development, whereby children come to behave as boys and girls. How does this come about? Are we "hardwired" to become masculine or feminine? What role do parents and other family members play? John Rust and others (2000) theorized that older siblings play a role—that preschoolers with older brothers are more masculine in their behavior, whereas those with older sisters are more feminine. In their study, mothers of 5,542 three-year-olds rated their children's preferences for various masculine and feminine activities. They then compared the profiles of preschoolers who did not have an older sibling with those who did. Do you think it mattered? For solo children, on a scale from 24 (highly feminine) to 120 (highly masculine), boys averaged 63 and girls 37. Using these numbers as a reference point, try to predict the scores of boys and girls with older brothers and sisters. Now look at Figure 8.8, and you'll see that children with older brothers had higher scores (more masculine); those with older sisters had lower scores (more feminine). In other words, the results supported the nurture hypothesis that children's gender role development is influenced by older siblings, an aspect of their family environment.

|       | Solo | Brother | Sister |
|-------|------|---------|--------|
| Boys  | 63   | 65      | 59     |
| Girls | 37   | 40      | 35     |

**FIGURE 8.8**

## REVIEW QUESTIONS

■ *Describe two methods behavioral geneticists use to distinguish environmental influences from genetic ones.*

■ *Summarize the impact of studies of twins and adoptees on the nature-nurture debate.*

■ *If siblings are raised in the same home by the same parents, how can they experience nonshared environments?*

# SANDRA SCARR
## *The Nature and Nurture of Intelligence*

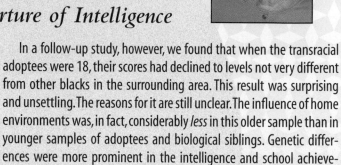

**Q: How did you first become interested in psychology?**

**A:** In 1954, I went to Vassar College with a strong interest in psychology, which meant "understanding people." Vassar's version of psychology was conditioned eye blinks and maze running rodents. Sociology and anthropology represented the human side of the social sciences, so I migrated to these majors.

**Q: How did you come up with your important discovery?**

**A:** After graduating, I worked as a research assistant at NIMH. From there I went to Harvard, where I received my Ph.D. and became interested in child development and genetics, a combination that continued throughout my career.

In 1967, I began a large twin study of black and white school children's achievement and IQ test scores. *Science* published two of my major articles. By comparing identical and fraternal twins' aptitude and school achievement, I showed that intellectual development was heavily influenced by genetic variability, but more so among advantaged than disadvantaged children.

When opportunities abound, genetic differences shine through. When opportunity is restricted, individuals do not have the chance to express their genetic individuality to the fullest extent, and individual differences are more influenced by the lack of environmental support. This was a revolutionary way to think about the impact of environments on genetic expression in human behavior.

In 1970, I began two major studies (and a thirty-year collaboration) with Richard Weinberg. Our *Minnesota Transracial Adoption Project* involved 101 white families who had adopted black children. We showed that these children, at the average age of 7 years, were performing far better on IQ tests than black children reared in black families in the same area, but that individual differences among them were due more to genetic variability than to environmental differences.

In a follow-up study, however, we found that when the transracial adoptees were 18, their scores had declined to levels not very different from other blacks in the surrounding area. This result was surprising and unsettling. The reasons for it are still unclear. The influence of home environments was, in fact, considerably *less* in this older sample than in younger samples of adoptees and biological siblings. Genetic differences were more prominent in the intelligence and school achievement scores of these late adolescents than among younger children.

**Q: How has the field you inspired developed over the years?**

**A:** The two adoption studies changed our whole way of thinking about how the environment works. Rather than the home environment having a cumulative impact over development, its influence *wanes* from early childhood to adolescence. We began to think of how older children and adolescents make their own environments to a greater extent than younger ones by choosing activities that interest them, by choosing friends, and by the influences they have on others in the community.

**Q: What's your prediction on where the field is heading?**

**A:** Recently, psychology has come to appreciate how genetic factors shape behavior and the choices people make in their lives. In the future, we will identify specific genes that contribute to individual differences in personality, talents, and interests. Genes do not determine behavior, but our unique combinations of genes influence how we perceive, feel about, and act upon the world. To a large extent, each person makes his or her own environment. Understanding that process will occupy psychology for many years to come.

*Sandra Scarr is Professor of Psychology* emeritus *at the University of Virginia.*

theory, children who are brighter than average at birth will have initial success in school, which will bring praise from parents and teachers, motivate them to work hard, draw them to peers who are studious, and encourage them to attend college—all of which breeds intellectual success. Yet those who are not as bright at birth will have less initial success, receive less praise, lose their motivation, befriend weaker students, and fail. In this way, genetic dispositions create environments that, in turn, multiply the influence of genes.

# THE NATURE AND NURTURE OF . . .

- *How are men and women similar? How are they different?*
- *Are the psychological differences between men and women primarily rooted in biological factors or social experiences?*
- *Why is the debate about the nature and nurture of homosexuality so heated?*
- *What evidence is there for a "gay gene"? What about a "gay environment"?*

If you were to search for books on the topic of "gender," how many do you think you'd find? In January 2003, I conducted an online search and uncovered 6,382 book entries in *Amazon.com* and 8,755 on *BarnesandNoble.com*. A search of "sex differences" yielded 1,036 and 1,698 entries.

Throughout human history, philosophers, scientists, and social scientists, have debated the influences of nature and nurture. Like Internet "popup ads" that invade your computer screen, these debates just keep on coming. In part, the issue is driven by sheer intellectual curiosity; in part, it is fueled by the potential for social and political implications. So, psychologists study the similarities and differences between men and women and among individuals from diverse social, cultural, and ethnic groups; they study the nature and nurture of language, emotion, intelligence, musical and artistic talent, sexual orientation, personality, health, happiness, and mental illness. Aspects of the nature–nurture debates can be found throughout this textbook. For now, let's focus on the nature and nurture of gender and of sexual orientation.

## GENDER: A GREAT DIVIDE?

Do you sleep in the nude? Some 19 percent of men say yes, compared to only 6 percent of women. How much of your TV-watching time do you spend in charge of the remote control? Men say 55 percent, women 34 percent. How many items of clothing do you buy in a year? Women estimate 52, men only 33. Did you cry at your own wedding? Among women, 45 percent say yes, compared to 25 percent of men. Are you more likely to refuse sex than your partner is? To this question, 43 percent of women say yes, compared to only 22 percent of men. In search of a gender gap, pollsters have uncovered differences along every imaginable dimension—and then some.

It is common for pollsters to find a "gender gap" in the ways that men and women describe their beliefs, attitudes, preferences, and behavior (Weiss, 1991). What do these results mean? Why are people so fascinated by even the silliest and most trivial of sex differences? And why, as Carol Jacklin (1989) put it, has the study of sex differences become a "national preoccupation"?

Browse the shelves of any bookstore and you'll see one paperback after another that addresses this topic. There are books for men and books for women, books that preach the masculine ideal and books that tell us how to be more feminine, books that portray men and women as similar and books that focus on presumed differences—like *Why Men Don't Listen and Women Can't Read Maps* (Pease & Pease, 2001). In *You Just Don't Understand*, sociolinguist Deborah Tannen (1990) argues that women and men have different conversational styles, which leads to misunderstanding. In *Men Are from Mars, Women Are from Venus*, John Gray (1997) argues that men and women don't just speak differently, but think, feel, and behave differently. In *Brain Sex*, Ann Moir and David Jessel (1989) cite research evidence to conclude that men and women behave differently "because their brains are different" (p. 5). In *Sex on the Brain*, Deborah Blum (1997) argues that the differences between men and women result from an interaction of biological and environmental factors. When it comes to the nature and nurture of gender, we ask: In what ways are men and women different, in what ways are they alike, and what causes these effects?

*Leta Hollingworth was a pioneer in the study of sex differences. At a time when many scientists were claiming that women were intellectually inferior to men, she published some of the earliest studies in the psychology of women. In 1914, she wrote a book titled* Functional Periodicity: An Experimental Study of the Mental Abilities of Women during Menstruation. *(Archives of the History of American Psychology; University of Akron.)*

*How* **Are Men and Women Different?**   To children, the notion that there are innate differences between the sexes is immortalized in a poem: "What are little boys made of? Frogs and snails and puppy dogs' tails. What are little girls made of? Sugar and spice and all that's nice." Ingredients aside, are males and females really that different?

Certain biological sex differences are a simple fact of life. At puberty, the onset of sexual maturation is brought on by rising hormone levels—estrogen and progesterone in females, and testosterone in males. Girls reach puberty at about the age of eleven, boys at thirteen. On average, adult men are five inches taller than women and twenty to thirty pounds heavier, have 40 percent more muscle and 12 percent less fat, and sweat more. The average woman can arm-curl 52 percent as much weight as the average male and bench-press 37 percent as much. The average man has a million more red blood cells in each drop of blood than the average woman, absorbs 30 percent less alcohol into his bloodstream (controlling for differences in body weight, this explains why men hold their liquor better than women), and has 10 percent more lung volume than women of the same size. Men are also more likely to be left-handed, snore in their sleep, become bald as they age, and have a deficiency in color vision. According to the National Center for Health Statistics (2003), the average American female, at birth, is expected to live for seventy-nine years and the average American male for seventy-four years.

Statistics such as these seem innocent enough—and are not a subject of debate. Biological approaches become politically charged, however, when psychological differences between men and women are found—and when the differences are attributed to sex hormones, brain anatomy, and other innate factors. The reason for the political heat is that our views on the nature of men and women inform important policy questions such as whether military women should be allowed into combat, or whether men should be given equal consideration in child-custody suits. What reliable sex differences are there in human behavior, and why? Some scientists claim that men and women are so inherently different that to suggest otherwise is "to build a society based on a biological and scientific lie" (Moir & Jessel, 1989, p. 5). In *The Mismeasure of Woman*, psychologist Carol Tavris (1992) argues just as forcefully that "there is nothing *essential*—that is, universal and unvarying—in the natures of women and men" (p. 21). Let's look at some of the evidence and consider the arguments on both sides.

**Sexuality**   One way in which men and women differ is in their sexual attitudes and behavior. Surveys conducted worldwide show that, from adolescence through adulthood, men on average are more sexually permissive and adventurous than women. They are also more likely to think about sex spontaneously, seek out erotic materials, and initiate sex without commitment. In general, men seem to view the world in more "sexualized" terms.

In one study, Antonia Abbey (1982) arranged for pairs of male and female college students to talk for five minutes, and for other students to observe these interactions. When she later questioned the actors and observers, Abbey found that the males were more sexually attracted to the females than vice versa—and that they rated the female actors as more promiscuous and seductive than the women had rated themselves. Other research confirms this point: Among men more than women, eye contact, a friendly remark, a brush against the arm, a compliment, and an innocent smile are often seen as sexual come-ons (Kowalski, 1993). These misperceptions occur not only in the laboratory but also between strangers, acquaintances, and casual friends who meet at parties, school, work, and other settings (Abbey, 1987; Saal et al., 1989). Reviewing all this research, Roy Baumeister and others (2001) conclude that "men desire sex more than women" (p. 270).

**Physical Aggression**   Most men are also more physically aggressive than most women. Think about it. Hunting, combat, rough-and-tumble play, and barroom brawls are all male-dominated activities. No matter when, where, or how you measure it, males on average exhibit more physical aggression than females. Worldwide, men commit more violent crimes than do women (according to FBI statistics, 89 percent of all people arrested for murder, assault, and rape are male). In laboratory experiments in which participants believe they are administering painful shocks to another person, men select higher voltage shocks (Bettencourt & Miller, 1996; Knight et al., 1996). School-age boys are also more likely than girls to play highly physical, competitive games (Maccoby, 1998). Even among children three to six years old, boys are more physically aggressive (Loeber & Hay, 1997). The only exception to the rule is that female children and adults show more verbal, or "relational" aggression than males do—by criticizing others, for example, or spreading hurtful gossip behind their back (Oesterman et al., 1998; Simmons, 2002).

**Cognitive Abilities**   Sex differences have also been found in cognitive abilities. In Chapter 10, we'll see that although boys and girls are equally skilled at arithmetic in elementary school, male students begin to surpass females in mathematical problem solving in junior high school—a difference that persists into adulthood (in 2002, for example, male high-school students outscored females by 34 points on the math portion of the SAT-I). Males also perform better on certain visual-spatial tasks—such as imagining how three-dimensional objects will appear when rotated, how flat objects appear when folded, or how solid objects appear when unfolded (Master, 1998; Levine et al., 1999).

Paralleling the apparent male advantage in math and spatial relations, women typically perform better at grammar, spelling, reading comprehension, and certain verbal-fluency tasks. In elementary school, boys are four times more likely than girls to stutter and five to ten times more likely to have a reading disorder (Halpern, 2000). And in high school, girls score higher on tests of reading comprehension and foreign languages (Hedges & Nowell, 1995; Stumpf & Stanley, 1998). Finally, there are small but consistent sex differences in "social sensitivity." Specifically, women are better at using facial expressions, tones of voice, and other nonverbal cues to determine how other people are feeling (Hall, 1984).

*Why* **Are Men and Women Different?**   Are male-female differences like the ones just described rooted in innate biological differences between the sexes? Or do these disparities stem from the different and sometimes unequal social experiences that affect men and women? Let's examine these two perspectives.

**Biological Perspectives**   Even before a baby is born, it has a full genetic heritage contained within its 23 pairs of chromosomes. The twenty-third pair controls our sex. Everyone receives an X chromosome from the mother, but there's an equal chance that the father will donate an X or a short and stumpy Y chromosome to the pair. If the chromosome is an X, the offspring will be female (XX); if it is Y, the offspring will be male (XY).

Six or so weeks after conception, male and female embryos look very much the same and are similarly equipped. In those that are genetically female, ovaries are formed. In those that are genetically male, undescended testes secrete the male hormone testosterone. The presence of *testosterone* sparks the growth of the male sex organs, whereas its absence results in the development of female sex organs. In other words, having an XY or XX genetic endowment does not itself guarantee male or female development. If testosterone is not secreted in an XY embryo, the

"Because my genetic programming prevents me from stopping to ask directions—that's why!"

genetically male baby will be born with a girl's genitals. If testosterone is injected into an XX embryo, the genetic female will form the genitals of a normal male. During this stage of fetal development, the ovaries secrete very little estrogen and so play a minimal role in this process (Wilson et al., 1981; Breedlove, 1994).

Research suggests that certain male-female differences may be linked to testosterone and estrogen (Dabbs, 2000; Kimura, 1999). These hormones are presumed to have two types of effects. First, during the prenatal life of an organism, they have long-term *organizational* effects on the developing nervous system—which may account for the existence of certain differences between adult male and female brains (remember, experience can help mold the plastic brain). Then later in life, beginning at puberty, fluctuating levels of the sex hormones have short-term *activational* effects on behavior.

It is widely believed that testosterone fuels male sexual behavior. That's why castration (the surgical removal of the testes, which lowers testosterone production) has been used over the years to prepare harem guards, ensure celibacy, and rehabilitate sex offenders. Research shows that castration has the intended effect. Testosterone is not essential for sexual performance, but men with lowered levels often have less sexual interest and desire—and "testosterone therapy" can be used to increase that desire (Rabkin et al., 2000). There appears to be a similar link between ovarian hormones and sexuality in women. Estrogen is not necessary for performance, but sexual appetites fluctuate across the menstrual cycle (Carter, 1991).

There's also a strong connection between testosterone and aggression. If immature male mice are injected with testosterone, they attack other males; if they're castrated, aggression levels subside. Similarly, castration transforms a wild stallion into a gentler horse and an aggressive dog into a domesticated pet. In rats, monkeys, and other animals, males become more aggressive at the onset of sexual maturation, when testosterone levels surge, and less aggressive as testosterone levels decline later in adulthood. In laboratory experiments with rats and other animals, injections of testosterone increase aggression, whereas castration, which lowers testosterone, has the opposite effect (Breuer et al., 2001). In humans, correlational studies show that men and women with high levels of testosterone tend to be bold, courageous, energetic, competitive, and yes—aggressive (Dabbs, 2000). Among teenagers and adults, the use of anabolic steroids is linked to unprovoked acts of violence, or as it is sometimes called, "roid rage" (Pope et al., 2000). Most interesting, perhaps, are studies of transsexuals who voluntarily altered their sex hormone levels through sex-change treatments. In this group, female-to-male transsexuals became more aggressive after treatment, and male-to-female transsexuals became less aggressive (van Goozen et al., 1995; Cohen-Ketteinis & van Goozen, 1997).

There is less evidence for the effects of testosterone on cognitive skills. According to Norman Geschwind and Peter Behan (1982), prenatal testosterone washes over the fetal brain. This slows the development of the left hemisphere, where language skills are housed, and permits enhanced growth of the right hemisphere, which is associated with spatial skills. Consistent with this hypothesis that the male brain is right-dominated is the fact that more males than females are left-handed (as you may recall, the right hemisphere controls the left half of the body and vice versa). This male right-dominance, speculated Geschwind and Behan, explains why most talented math students are male, why men perform better on visual-spatial tasks, and why women excel in various language-related tests. Is there a link between sex hormones and cognitive performance? It's too early to tell. There is some tantalizing evidence showing that on spatial tasks, males who reach puberty late due to unusually low testosterone levels perform worse than other males, whereas women with elevated testosterone levels outperform other women (Hausman et al., 2000;

Kimura, 1999). In other studies, however, the results are small and not that consistent (Collaer & Hines, 1995; Liben et al., 2002).

**Environmental Perspectives**   When a baby is born, the first question everyone asks is the same: "Is it a boy or a girl?" The newborn is then given a male or female name, dressed in blue or pink clothing, and showered with masculine or feminine gifts. Over the next few years, the typical boy receives toy trucks, baseball bats, building blocks, tools, guns, and chemistry sets, and his sister plays with dolls, stuffed animals, kitchen toys, sewing kits, and tea sets. In school, boys are guided into math and science, and girls are expected to seek out art, music, and literary activities. These distinctions persist in college, as male students are more likely to major in math, economics, and the hard sciences, whereas females predominate in education, the arts, and the humanities. At work, men become doctors, builders, airline pilots, engineers, and bankers; women become secretaries, teachers, nurses, flight attendants, and bank tellers. Men and women may love, work, play, and have families together, but in many ways, they are part of different social groups and live in different worlds. Over the years, psychologists have studied the impact of these worlds on men and women (Swann et al., 1999).

The fact that males and females have different life experiences may explain the sex differences that are often observed. If you grew up in the United States, for example, you were probably taught to believe that it's more important for boys than for girls to learn to compete, fight, and defend themselves. You may also think it's more appropriate for the man to ask the woman for a date as well as to pay, drive, and initiate a goodnight kiss. Experience promotes sex differences through a continuous process of social learning. Parents, teachers, and other socializing agents communicate **gender roles** to children at an early age, serve as same-sex role models, and use reward and punishment to shape behaviors that are gender-appropriate. The models that surround children are powerful sources of influence. For example, Gary Levy (1989) found that girls with mothers who worked outside the home were more flexible in their perceptions of male and female sex roles than were those whose mothers worked in the home.

What takes place in the home is only part of what influences gender roles. In 1991, Hugh Lytton and David Romney summarized the results of 172 studies and found that although parents tend to direct children to engage in sex-typed activities, in other ways they treat their sons and daughters in a similar manner. But the social learning of gender roles is supported by a host of other cultural institutions. Studies show that "Dick and Jane" readers, cartoons, TV shows, and magazines overportray male and female characters in traditional roles. Gone are the days when women were depicted only as homemakers who frantically shopped, cooked, cleaned, and ironed everything in sight. Still, some sex stereotyping remains—for example, in TV commercials, magazine advertisements, children's books, and MTV music videos. The result is that boys are taught to be masculine, and girls are taught to be feminine.

Experience shapes not only our behavior but also our beliefs. According to Sandra Bem (1981), experience leads people to form **gender schemas**—a network of beliefs about what it means to be male or female that influence the way we perceive ourselves and others. Research shows that children begin to identify themselves as boys or girls by the age of three—and then divide the world into masculine and feminine categories soon after that (Biernat, 1991;

**gender roles**   Sex-typed behaviors promoted by social learning.

**gender schemas**   A network of beliefs about men and women that influence the way we perceive ourselves and others.

"We've gathered enough. Let's hunt."

*Sex differences in occupations are sometimes so striking that we're quick to notice female construction workers and others who break the mold.*

Martin et al., 1990). By middle childhood, boys and girls have a stable, multidimensional concept of their own gender and how they feel about it (Egan & Perry, 2001). Even infants can tell the difference. In one study, nine-month-olds who were shown pictures of all-male or all-female faces spent less and less time looking—until a face of the opposite sex appeared. This result tells us what the infants themselves could not: that they can distinguish between men and women (Leinbach & Fagot, 1993).

In some cultures of the world, "sexist" traditions are quite strong. In Sudan, as currently ruled by Islamic fundamentalists, women must wear veils over the face and may not leave the country without permission from their fathers, husbands, or brothers. In Israel, where Jewish religious law prevails, a wife cannot get divorced without the consent of her husband—leaving thousands of women known as the Agunot ("the anchored") married against their will. In India, a Hindu system of dowries requires that the bride's family pay the groom cash and gifts equal to his social standing. As a result, girls are considered a burden on their parents. And in mainland China, where males are economically more valuable than females, and where the government controls population growth by limiting couples to one or two children, many female infants are aborted, abandoned, given up for adoption, or killed at birth.

Needless to say, prescribed sex roles vary widely from one culture to the next. Consider your reaction to statements such as "The first duty of a woman with young children is to home and family," "When a man and woman live together, she should do the housework and he should do the heavier chores," and "Most women interpret innocent remarks or acts as being sexist." Some sexist sentiments are benign, but others betray a degree of hostility. Either way, research shows that people in Nigeria, Pakistan, South Africa, and Cuba agree more with these kinds of statements than do people from Australia, the Netherlands, England, and the United States (Williams & Best, 1990; Glick et al., 2000).

Cultures vary in their sex-role traditions, but stereotypes about men and women seem to be universal. If you had to describe the typical man and woman, what would you say? In a large-scale study, 2,800 college students from thirty countries were asked to check off adjectives from a list that are believed to describe men or women. Consistently, men were said to be adventurous, strong, dominant, assertive, task-oriented, aggressive, and independent. As consistently, women were said to be sensitive, gentle, dependent, emotional, sentimental, weak, submissive, and people-oriented (Williams & Best, 1982). These stereotypes are also evident in children's descriptions of others (Best & Williams, 1993).

Male and female stereotypes are so deeply ingrained in us that they influence our behavior literally from the moment a baby is born. In a fascinating study, first-time parents of fifteen girls and fifteen boys were interviewed within twenty-four hours of the birth. There were no actual differences between the male and female newborns in height, weight, or superficial physical appearance. Yet the parents of the girls rated their babies as softer, smaller, and more finely featured, and the fathers of boys described their sons as stronger, larger, more alert, and better coordinated (Rubin et al., 1974). Parents are also gender-biased in their perceptions of motor development. In one study, Emily Mondschein and others (2000) asked twenty-three mothers to rate the crawling abilities of their eleven-month-old infants. Boys and girls tend to crawl at the same age. Yet relative to their performance on an adjustable sloping walkway, the mothers overestimated their boys and underestimated the girls. These gender-different expectations can have important child-rearing consequences. To demonstrate, Barbara Morrongiello and Tess Dawber (2000) showed mothers a videotape of a boy or girl (depending on whether their own child was male or female) climbing, sliding, and swinging on a playground. The mothers were asked to imagine that the child was theirs and to stop the tape and describe if they'd intervene. Mothers of daughters, compared to mothers of sons, intervened more quickly, saw the situations as more dangerous, and tolerated less risk-taking.

Gender stereotypes are so widespread that you may wonder if they are accurate and, if not, why they persist. Enlightened by years of research on sex differences, psychologists can now draw the following conclusion: Conventional wisdom contains a kernel of truth, but it may oversimplify and exaggerate that truth (Maccoby & Jacklin, 1974; Feingold, 1994; Swim, 1994). Yes, most men are more competitive, aggressive, and assertive than most women. And yes, most women are more socially sensitive, nurturing, and cooperative than most men. But the stereotype about these differences may be stronger and more numerous than the differences themselves.

A study by Carol Lynn Martin (1987) illustrates the point. She presented people with a list of thirty traits that were "masculine," "feminine," or neutral and asked them to circle those that were self-descriptive. A separate group of participants received the same list and estimated, for each trait, the percentage of men and women in general for whom it was an accurate description. By comparing the percentage of male and female participants who *actually* found the traits self-descriptive with the *estimated* percentages, Martin found that expectations outstripped reality. In actuality, the masculine traits were just slightly more self-descriptive of men and the feminine traits of women, but the estimated differences were more substantial. Like the cartoonist who draws caricatures, we seem to mentally stretch, expand, and enlarge the ways in which men and women differ.

Clearly, the behavior of men and women all over the world is scripted by the gender roles they're expected to play. To what extent are these differences and roles socially constructed? Is it possible, for example, that male sexuality, and aggression, and the male strengths in mathematical problem solving and spatial skills are all socially constructed? What about the verbal skills and interpersonal sensitivity of women?

Biologically oriented researchers offer convincing evidence that some of the differences in mathematics are so consistent over time and across cultures that they must be inborn. Socially oriented researchers, however, warn that these comparisons are misleading because boys and girls are often not raised on a level playing field. For example, boys receive more support in math from parents and teachers (Chipman et al., 1985; Jacobs, 1991). Studying the development of math skills in children from hundreds of families, Jacquelynne Eccles and others (1990) found that parents who believe that girls are generally weak at math see their daughters as less competent, set lower expectations for them, and guide them in other directions. Sure enough, these girls lose interest and confidence and avoid future math-related pursuits. This may be why many elementary school girls—even though they perform as well as or better than boys in math—see themselves as less competent (Eccles et al., 1993). In a longitudinal study of five hundred children from grades 1 through 12, Frederick and Eccles (2002) found that parents' math expectations early on predicted their children's sense of math competence as they got older—regardless of their initial aptitude.

The strongest evidence for a cognitive gender gap is found in performance on visual-spatial tasks—a difference that appears over time and across cultures (Halpern, 2000; Kimura, 1999). It's possible, however, that at least part of the male advantage in this domain stems from differences in experience. Research shows that boys are permitted to stray farther from home than girls and engage in more "scouting" activities. Boys are more likely to own building blocks, erector sets, and other spatial manipulation toys. They are also more likely to play billiards, basketball, and other sports that involve making judgments of moving objects. To some extent, the more spatial experience one has, the better is one's performance on visual-spatial tests. Thus, in one study, four-year-old boys *and* girls who were trained with wooden blocks, dominoes, Tinkertoys, and geometric shapes later scored higher on a spatial test than children who were not similarly trained (Baenninger & Newcombe, 1989). Other studies have shown that playing action video games improves spatial performance in both boys and girls (Okagaki & Frensch, 1994; Subrahmanyan & Greenfield, 1994).

Turning from the cognitive to the social domain, studies reveal that women are more sensitive than men to how others are feeling—a skill often referred to as "female intuition." Some researchers speculate that this advantage is rooted in the left-dominant female brain (Moir & Jessel, 1989). Others argue that women acquire interpersonal sensitivity out of social necessity. Sara Snodgrass (1985) speculated that women are better than men at reading other people for self-protective reasons—because they occupy subordinate roles in society. After all, isn't it more important for workers to know how the boss is feeling and for students to know how their professor is feeling than vice versa? To test this hypothesis, Snodgrass paired a man and a woman in each of several work teams and assigned one or the other to be the leader. In general, she found that the subordinate was more sensitive to the leader's nonverbal cues than the leader was to the subordinate's—regardless of gender. Thus, she suggested that "women's intuition" be called "subordinate's intuition" to reflect the fact that low status, not sex, is what motivates insight into others. She also found another reason why subordinates are good at reading their superiors: People in power are freer to express their positive and negative views, which makes them easier to read (Snodgrass et al., 1998).

**A Biosocial Theory of Sex Differences**   Men and women differ both in their biological makeup and in the ways they are treated, literally from the moment of birth. So, what is the origin of the differences that exist? And why do gender stereotypes exaggerate these differences? In answer to these questions, Alice Eagly and Wendy Wood have proposed and refined a "biosocial theory" of sex differences (Eagly & Wood, 1999; Wood & Eagly, 2002).

According to this theory, sex differences emerge from an interaction of nature and nurture. The nature part involves biological differences between men and women—with men built larger, stronger, and faster; and with women equipped for childbearing and nursing. Historically, across cultures, these physical attributes spawned a division of labor between the sexes both at home and in the work setting. In a study of 185 nonindustrial societies, Murdock and Provost (1973) found that the percentage of men versus women engaged in different productive activities varied a great deal, though some types were almost exclusively male, and others were predominantly female (see Table 8.3). This universal "alliance between men and women" seems designed both to enable mothers to have and care for

**TABLE 8.3    DIVISIONS OF LABOR IN NONINDUSTRIAL SOCIETIES**

The percentages of men who engaged in various work activities across 185 nonindustrial cultures show that some activities were predominantly male or female, whereas others were less rigidly gender-typed (Murdock & Provost, 1973).

| "Male" Activities | "Swing" Activities | "Female" Activities |
|---|---|---|
| Hunting large game (100) | Crop planting (54) | Pottery making (21) |
| Lumbering (99) | Harvesting (45) | Gathering of wild foods (20) |
| Mining (94) | Milking (44) | Spinning (14) |
| Butchering (92) | Basket making (43) | Doing laundry (13) |
| Clearing land (91) | Mat making (38) | Cooking (8) |
| Fishing (87) | Loom weaving (33) | Preparing vegetal food (6) |

babies and to exploit men's physical stature. According to U.S. Census Bureau statistics, some pronounced divisions of labor still exist today (see Table 8.4).

Although biology predisposes human societies to divide the labor out of necessity and convenience, traditional gender roles are flexible and influenced by social and environmental factors. That's why male and female work roles vary from culture to culture—and why such radical changes have taken place in recent years. In most industrialized countries today, unlike in the past, women can use contraception to control their reproductive fate, the birth rate is lower, and fewer jobs require physical size, strength, or speed. As a result of these social changes, note Wood and Eagly (2002), more women than ever work for pay outside the home, more women are becoming college educated, and men are sharing more in the responsibility for child care and other housework. These changes can be seen not only through birth, education, and employment statistics but also in people's attitudes and aspirations.

Recently, Alison Konrad and her colleagues (2000) meta-analyzed the "job attribute preferences" of some 650,000 American men and women surveyed between 1970 and 1998. On average, men cared more about salaries, promotions, freedom, power, challenge, and the opportunity for leadership; on average, women preferred work that offered good hours, an easy commute, and a chance to work with people and make friends. These differences are predictable by common stereotypes of men and women. Yet when these investigators separated the surveys according to the year they were conducted, they found that the gender differences were smaller in the 1990s than they had been just two decades earlier.

There is perhaps no domain of human activity that is more rigid about gender roles than war, a lethal form of intergroup violence. In a biosocial analysis of gender and war, international relations expert Joshua Goldstein (2001) analyzes wars throughout human history, in societies all over the world, and finds that it is dominated almost exclusively by men. Women have on occasion participated as combatants, and the historical record shows they performed well. Yet women are seldom mobilized, even when nations are under siege—and desperate. At present, roughly twenty-three million soldiers serve in the militaries of the world, and 97 percent are male. Among combat forces, 99.9 percent are male, with women serving in support roles, for example, as typists and nurses.

How has this "gendering of war" come about, and what sustains it? Consistent with Eagly and Wood's (2002) biosocial theory, Goldstein's historical and anthropological analysis leads him to conclude that both nature and nurture play essential roles. First, men innately are better suited for combat as a result of testosterone, size, strength, and brains adapted for long-distance mobility and aggression. Second, to motivate soldiers to overcome their natural reluctance to kill, gender roles are sharpened in all militaries, so as to equate "manhood" with toughness on the battlefield. This masculine mindset is weakened by the presence of women in the ranks—yet strengthened by women in feminine support roles such as mothers, wives, sweethearts, and nurses. In short, Goldstein concludes that the gendering of war stems from a combination of biological differences that favor men for combat and culturally constructed gender roles designed to mold these men into tough, brave, masculine soldiers.

**Putting Sex Differences in Perspective**   "Not including purely physical differences, do you think men and women are basically similar or basically different?" When this question was asked in a 1993 Gallup poll, 56 percent of the

| TABLE 8.4 | SEX DIFFERENCES IN OCCUPATION | |
|---|---|---|
| Occupation | % Men | % Women |
| Airline pilot | 96 | 04 |
| Auto mechanic | 99 | 01 |
| Bartender | 47 | 53 |
| Child-care worker | 03 | 97 |
| Computer programmer | 66 | 34 |
| Dentist | 90 | 10 |
| Dental assistant | 01 | 99 |
| Grade-school teacher | 14 | 86 |
| College instructor | 57 | 43 |
| Lawyer, judge | 77 | 23 |
| Physician | 78 | 22 |
| Registered nurse | 06 | 94 |
| Telephone repairer | 88 | 12 |
| Telephone operator | 13 | 87 |

*Source:* U.S. Bureau of the Census.

**sexual orientation** One's sexual preference for members of the same sex, opposite sex, or both sexes.

men surveyed and 73 percent of the women chose the "different" option. But think about some of the well-established principles of psychology, and you may come to realize that men and women are similar in many ways we take for granted. Differences make news; similarities do not.

Ponder the material presented elsewhere in this book and you'll see the point. Boys and girls alike crawl, walk, and smile at about the same age, and both become curious about sex in adolescence. Similarly, both men and women see better in daylight than in the dark, fall prey to optical illusions, sleep an average of six to eight hours a night, and behave in ways that bring reward. Both men and women can hold about seven items in short-term memory, use shorthand cognitive heuristics to make judgments, affiliate with others in times of stress, and suffer from a range of psychological disorders. In their social behavior, too, we'll see that both men and women are biased by first impressions, attracted to others who are similar, and more likely to help others when alone than in a group of bystanders. The list of similarities that escape our daily notice is long and impressive.

## SEXUAL ORIENTATION

The nature–nurture debates are often fueled by politics, ideology, and a struggle for power and resources. This sounds dramatic, I know, but it describes one of the most contentious questions in society today concerning the origins of **sexual orientation**—defined as one's sexual preference for members of the same sex (homosexuality), the opposite sex (heterosexuality), or both sexes (bisexuality). Let's see what's at stake and what the research shows.

**The Numbers Game** As national leaders, policy makers, and the public debate such issues as gay marriage and adoption rights, political and emotional rhetoric often substitutes for scientific information. How common is homosexuality, and where does it come from? Throughout human history, and in all cultures, a vast majority of people have been heterosexual in orientation. But just how vast is this majority? For many years, researchers have tried to determine the number of gay men and lesbians in the population, and for many years the surveys have produced a range of results—and a great deal of controversy. Debate over population statistics may not seem like an emotionally charged issue, but gay-rights activists and their opponents believe that the more homosexual men and women there are perceived to be, the more political clout they will have as a group (Rogers, 1993).

*Although researchers can only estimate the population prevalence of homosexuality, many men and women are openly gay. On July 1, 2000, Vermont became the first state to grant legal benefits for "civil unions" in same-sex couples. Here, Carolyn Conrad and Kathleen Peterson leave the Brattleboro, Vermont, Town Hall, after becoming the first couple to take advantage of that law.*

Seizing upon certain combinations of numbers in the early sex surveys conducted by Alfred Kinsey and his group (1948, 1953), the popular media sometimes claim that 10 percent of the population is homosexual. But more recent studies have consistently yielded lower estimates. A 1970 survey funded by the Kinsey Institute revealed that 3.3 percent of American men sampled said that they had frequent or occasional homosexual sex (Fay et al., 1989). Then between 1989 and 1992, the National Opinion Research Center reported that only 2.8 percent of American men and 2.5 percent of women had exclusive homosexual activity. Taken together, recent large-scale surveys conducted in the United States, Europe, Asia, and the Pacific suggest that the size of the exclusively homosexual population in the world is 3 or 4 percent among men and about half that number among women (Diamond, 1993).

Although an exclusive homosexual orientation is rare among humans and other animals, homosexual *behaviors* are not. In a book entitled *Biological Exuberance*, Bruce Bagemihl (1999) reports that sexual encounters among male-male and female-female pairs have been observed in more than 450 species—including giraffes, goats, birds, chimpanzees, and lizards. Among humans, the incidence of homosexual behavior varies from one generation and culture to the next, depending on prevailing attitudes. In *Same Sex, Different Cultures*, Gilbert Herdt (1998) notes that in part of the world, stretching from Sumatra to Melanesia, it's common for adolescent males to engage in homosexual activities before marriage—even though homosexuality as a permanent trait is virtually nonexistent. It's important, then, to realize that sexual orientation cannot be viewed in black-or-white terms but along a continuum. In the center of that continuum, 1 percent of people describe themselves as actively *bi*sexual.

The "numbers game" is a debate about broad averages, but the numbers vary according to demographics in the population. For example, 3 or 4 percent of American men see themselves as gay, but the male homosexual population ranges from only 1 percent in rural areas to 9 percent in some of the largest cities (Binson et al., 1995). Particularly interesting, though somewhat puzzling, is the *fraternal birth order effect*, the observation that having older brothers (but not sisters) increases the odds of male homosexuality. More precisely, the odds are 2 percent for men without an older brother, 3 percent with one older brother, 4 percent with two older brothers, and 8 to 9 percent with five or more older brothers (Blanchard, 1997). The reason for this effect is unclear. Ray Blanchard (2001) speculates that male pregnancies alter a mother's immune response to certain antigens in a way that influences development in subsequent male fetuses.

## Origins of Homosexuality

What are the roots of human homosexuality? As you might expect, both biological and environmental theories have been proposed. The Greek philosopher Aristotle believed that homosexuality was inborn but was strengthened by habit; psychoanalysts argue that it stems from family dynamics and the child's overattachment to a parent of the same or opposite sex; learning theorists point to reinforcing sexual experiences with same-sex peers in childhood. There is little evidence, however, to support these claims. In a comprehensive study, Alan Bell and others (1981) intensively interviewed fifteen hundred homosexual and heterosexual adults about their lives. There were no differences in their family backgrounds, absence of a male or female parent, relationship with parents, sexual abuse by someone of the same or opposite sex, age of onset of puberty, or high-school dating patterns. Except for the fact that homosexual adults described themselves as less conforming as children, the two groups could not be distinguished by past experiences. Both groups strongly felt that their sexual orientation was set long before it became "official."

Increasingly, researchers are finding some evidence of a biological disposition. In a highly publicized study, neurobiologist Simon LeVay (1991) autopsied the brains of nineteen homosexual men who had died of AIDS, sixteen heterosexual men (some of whom had died of AIDS), and six heterosexual women. LeVay examined a tiny nucleus in the hypothalamus known to be involved in regulating sexual behavior and known to be larger in heterosexual men than in women. The specimens were numerically coded, so LeVay did not know whether the donor he was examining was male or female, straight or gay. The result: In the male homosexual brains he studied, the nucleus was half the size as in male heterosexual brains and was comparable to those found in the female heterosexual brains. This research is fully described in LeVay's (1993) book *The Sexual Brain*.

Let's stop for a moment and ponder the implications. When LeVay's study was published in *Science*, a storm of controversy erupted. Emerging from the laboratory, LeVay soon found himself in the spotlight—on TV news shows, on talk shows, and in magazines. Within the gay community, reactions were polarized. At first, some worried that the findings would somehow be used to discriminate against gays, called LeVay homophobic, and referred to his work as antihomosexual. But wait. LeVay himself was openly gay. Still, "one critic said that I wanted to prove that it's

*Bruce Bagemihl (1999) reports that homosexual encounters can be found in certain species of animals. As shown, male giraffes often rub against each other and become sexually aroused while "necking."*

When it comes to beliefs about the nature and nurture of homosexuality, public-opinion polls show that straights and gays see it differently.

Homosexuality is something people are born with:

| | |
|---|---|
| Overall population | 33% |
| Gay respondents | 75% |

Gay men and lesbians can change their sexual orientation:

| | |
|---|---|
| Overall population | 56% |
| Gay respondents | 11% |

*Source: Newsweek (August 17, 1998)*

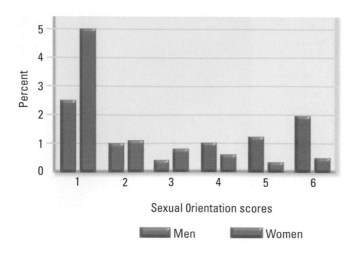

**FIGURE 8.9    Sex differences in sexual orientation scores**
In a study conducted in Australia, sexual orientation was measured on a seven-point scale that ranged from 0 (exclusively heterosexual) to 6 (exclusively homosexual). Among both men and women, 92 percent were exclusively heterosexual. As for the remaining 8 percent, more men were homosexual (5-6), while more women were bisexual (1-3). These differences suggest that the origins of sexual orientation may not be the same for men and women (Bailey et al., 2000).

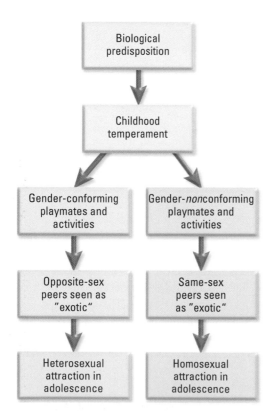

**FIGURE 8.10    Bem's developmental theory of homosexuality**
According to Bem, genes determine gender-relevant behaviors in childhood. Later, adolescents become attracted to the sex that is different. Thus, childhood "tomboys" and "sissies" are prone to seek members of the same sex.

not my fault I'm gay" (quoted in Nimmons, 1994, p. 68). The more common reaction was to embrace the notion that sexual orientation is a biological condition so that people would be tolerant rather than judgmental. Thus, LeVay reported that "many gay men sent my study to their parents . . . and parents, in turn, wrote to say the study helped them understand their kids." When it comes to what LeVay (1997) calls "Queer Science," research is frequently used and abused for social and political purposes.

It's important to recognize that LeVay's study revealed only a correlation between sexual orientation and the size of this hypothalamic nucleus and cannot be used to draw conclusions about cause and effect. LeVay himself notes that "I didn't show that gay men are born that way" and that "since I looked at adult brains, we don't know if the differences were there at birth or if they appeared later" (Nimmons, 1994, p. 66). In fact, researchers studying the effects of prenatal hormone levels had previously found that men whose mothers were under severe stress during pregnancy (stress lowers prenatal testosterone levels) were somewhat more likely to become gay (Ellis & Ames, 1987) and that women exposed to high levels of prenatal testosterone were more likely to become lesbians (Dittman et al., 1992).

Perhaps the most convincing support for the biological roots of sexual orientation comes from twin studies suggesting that there is a genetic predisposition. Michael Bailey and Richard Pillard (1991) surveyed 167 gay men and their twins and adopted brothers. Overall, 52 percent of the identical twins were gay, compared to only 22 percent of fraternal twins and 11 percent of adoptive brothers. Two years later, Bailey and others (1993) conducted a companion study of lesbians with similar results.

The origins of homosexuality are complex for two reasons. First, although there is strong evidence for a biological disposition, this does not necessarily mean that there's a "gay gene" (Hamer et al., 1999). Second, it's not clear that sexual orientation for men and women is similarly rooted. In a study conducted in Australia, Bailey and his colleagues (2000) had hundreds of pairs of twins rate their sexual orientations on a seven-point continuum that ranged from "exclusively heterosexual" to "exclusively homosexual." Look at Figure 8.9, and you'll notice a difference in the distributions of responses for men and women. In both cases, 92 percent classified themselves as exclusively heterosexual. Among the others, however, more women said that they had bisexual tendencies (sometimes referred to in personal ads as "bi-curious") and more men said that they were exclusively homosexual. This finding is consistent with Baumeister's (2000) conclusion from past research—that when it comes to sex, women are more flexible than men are, having, as he puts it, more *erotic plasticity*. Hence, women are more likely than men to change their sexual practices and preferences over the course of a lifetime.

Seeing sexual orientation as emerging from both nature and nurture, Daryl Bem (1996, 2000) believes that homosexuality is the product of a *psycho*biological—and developmental—process. According to Bem, genes determine an individual's temperament at birth, leading some infants and young children to be naturally more active, energetic, and aggressive than others. These differences in temperament will draw some children toward male playmates and "masculine" activities (rough-and-tumble play, contact sports) and others toward female playmates and more "feminine" activities (playing house, hopscotch). Bem refers to those children who prefer same-sex playmates as gender-conformists and to those who prefer opposite-sex playmates as gender-nonconformists ("sissies" and "tomboys").

Activity preferences in childhood may be biologically rooted, but what happens next is the psychological part. According to Bem, gender-conforming children come to see members of the opposite sex as different, unfamiliar, arousing, and as he puts it, "exotic." Gender-nonconforming children, in contrast, come to see their same-sex peers as different, unfamiliar, arousing, and exotic. Later, at puberty, as children become physically and sexually mature, they find that they are attracted to members of the same or opposite sex—depending on which is the more exotic. Bem describes his proposed chain of events as the "exotic becomes erotic" theory of sexual orientation (see Figure 8.10).

At present, there is only sketchy evidence to support this interesting theory. It's true that genetic makeup can influence temperament and predispose a child to favor certain kinds of activities over others (Kagan, 1994). It's also true that gay men are more likely to have been "sissies" and that lesbians are more likely to have been "tomboys" as children (Bell et al., 1981; Bailey & Zucker, 1995). It's even true that people are genetically predisposed to be sissies and tomboys as children (Bailey et al., 2000). But do peer preferences in childhood influence adult sexual orientation, as Bem suggests, because exotic becomes erotic? Or, is there a "gay gene" that fosters gender nonconformity in childhood as well as homosexuality later in adolescence and adulthood? And can a single theory explain homosexuality in both men and women, or are separate theories needed, as some have suggested (Peplau et al., 1998)?

More research is needed to answer these kinds of questions and tease apart the biological and social influences. Whatever the fine details turn out to be, however, one point looms large: People do not willfully choose their sexual orientation, nor can they, it appears, easily change it. Hence, setting aside the religious, moral, and politically explosive question of whether gay people *should* seek to change their sexual orientation, there's widespread disagreement about the effectiveness of sexual "reorientation" or "conversion" therapies (Haldeman, 2002; Shidlo & Schroeder, 2002; Throckmorton, 2002).

## REVIEW QUESTIONS

- *Describe some effects of testosterone on behavior.*

- *Cite some examples of male and female stereotypes. Where do such beliefs come from?*

- *What evidence exists of a biological basis to homosexuality?*

# THINKING LIKE A PSYCHOLOGIST ABOUT NATURE AND NURTURE

In the history of psychology, few broad questions spark livelier discussion, both within the field and outside it, than the debates about human nature and nurture. This issue cuts to the heart of questions about who we are, how we get that way, and the degree to which each of us is similar to all others, or unique.

The studies of genetics and evolution tell us that all people share a common, universal architecture—a biological basis for the proposition that everyone is basically the same. Within the nucleus of each cell of the body, twenty-three pairs of chromosomes are filled with DNA, which include genes, which help make proteins, the building blocks of life. Passed across the generations, from parents to offspring, genes provide the transport vehicle for heredity. The Human Genome Project tells us that 99.9 percent of the DNA sequences in the human genome are identical in all of us.

Then there's the evolutionary proposition that animals share a common ancestor but evolved over time through natural selection in order to adapt—physically and in behavior—to different and changing environments. Consistent with this notion is the recent finding that humans and mice share 99 percent of the same genes. In the grander biological scheme of life on our planet, you and I are practically identical twins.

Enter the nature–nurture debates. Sure, everyone is similar in ways we take for granted—like having two eyes, a nose, and ten fingers; like walking, talking, sleeping, squinting, living in social groups, and smiling when happy. No one in the debate disputes the obvious similarities. But within a population of people in a given place, to what extent are the differences rooted in genetic or environmental factors? Studying families—in particular, twins and adoptees—some researchers argue that people are predisposed by their genetic makeup to become shy, sociable, smart, athletic, artistic, cheerful, or depressed. Focused on the forces of nurture, others argue that people are shaped more by learning, culture, nutrition, families, peers, and other life experiences.

The question is not, "Which is more important, nature or nurture?" (that is like asking someone to choose between air and water). Clearly, the answer is that "both are essential." The real debate is over the amount of the variance in the population that is attributable to nature or nurture and, more importantly, how the influences of nature and nurture combine to make us who we are. Throughout the textbook, you will encounter variants of this debate. You may have encountered some already. You'll see that psychologists are trying to sort out the dynamic interplay of genes and environments in determining intelligence, happiness, temperament and personality, sexual orientation, as well as such problems as obesity, drug addictions, and various types of psychological disorders. Nature–nurture questions are classic to psychology—and here to stay.

## SUMMARY

What shapes who we are: nature or nurture?

### GENES

**Genetics** is the branch of biology that deals with heredity. Genes are the biological units of heredity.

### WHAT GENES ARE AND HOW THEY WORK

Each of the trillions of cells in your body contains in its nucleus twenty-three pairs of **chromosomes** consisting of strands of **DNA** made up of segments called **genes.** When an egg and a sperm cell unite to form a zygote, each passes along twenty-three chromosomes. The biochemical recipe they contain determines the unique characteristics of the offspring, including its sex. In 2001, scientists announced that they had completed sequencing the **human genome**—the genetic blueprint for making a human being.

### HOW GENES AFFECT BEHAVIOR

Scientists have pinpointed links between genes and specific physical traits. However, the relationship between **genotype,** the underlying DNA sequence that an individual inherits, and **phenotype,** an organism's observable properties, is more complex. Your personality is the product of a dynamic interaction between many genes and your environment.

### EVOLUTION

Scientists are finding new implications of Charles Darwin's theory of evolution for other disciplines, including psychology.

### NATURAL SELECTION

In 1859 Darwin introduced the principle of **natural selection,** the evolutionary process by which some genes in a population spread more than others, causing a species to change over time. This occurs because those organisms that are better suited to their environment pass **adaptations**—advantageous traits that address specific environmental challenges—to more offspring. When **mutations,** random errors in gene copying, result in new versions of genes, those that help an organism survive and reproduce increase from generation to generation. The purpose of any organism is to propagate its genes.

### EVOLUTIONARY PSYCHOLOGY

**Evolutionary psychology** applies the principles of evolution to human social behavior, suggesting that traits such as aggression may have adaptive value. **Inclusive fitness,** the idea that genes are preserved through the offspring of genetic relatives as well as one's own offspring, may explain why animals sometimes risk their lives to help relatives, a theory known as **kinship selection. Reciprocal altruism** proposes that the apparently selfless act of helping strangers may actually be adaptive over time because it increases the chances that others will return the favor. Because natural selection works at the pace of generations, current adaptations match the past environment, not the present.

### THE NATURE–NURTURE DEBATES

What makes us different from each other: our genes or our environment? This is the subject of the classic **nature–nurture debate** among psychologists.

### THE PURSUIT OF HERITABILITY

To measure the effect of genes on behavior, researchers conduct **family studies** to see how much blood relatives resemble each other in a particular trait. To distinguish genetic from environmental influences, they calculate **heritability**—a statistical estimate of the variability of a given trait within a group that is attributable to genetic factors. One useful way of testing nature and nurture is through the **twin-study method:** comparing the similarities between pairs of identical twins and same-sex fraternal twins. Another is **adoption studies,** in which twins and other siblings reared together are compared to those separated by adoption.

## GENETIC INFLUENCES

Studies of twins and adoptees have shown that there is a genetic component to intelligence, personality, and many psychological disorders. Still, human behavior is too complex to be merely the inevitable result of heredity.

## ENVIRONMENTAL INFLUENCES

Studies of twins and adoptees also show that environment plays a key role in shaping behavior. Even siblings reared in the same home experience nonshared environments, and peers and older siblings can be powerful influences as well as parents.

## THE INTERPLAY OF NATURE AND NURTURE

Genetic and environmental influences are not independent. Research shows that genetic dispositions create environments that multiply the influence of genes.

## THE NATURE AND NURTURE OF...

A key aspect of the nature–nurture debate is how much each influences gender and sexual orientation.

## GENDER: A GREAT DIVIDE?

How different are men and women? Studies show that men tend to be more interested in sex, more physically aggressive, and better at math and certain visual-spatial tasks than women, while women are typically more verbal and sensitive. Research suggests that some of these differences may be linked to the sex hormones testosterone and estrogen. Yet **gender roles** communicated to children through social learning teach boys to be masculine and girls to be feminine, and experience leads us to form **gender schemas**: networks of beliefs about what it means to be male or female. According to a recently proposed "biosocial theory," sex differences emerge from an interaction of nature and nurture. Still, many similarities between the sexes go largely unnoticed.

## SEXUAL ORIENTATION

One of the most contentious nature-nurture debates surrounds **sexual orientation.** Though numerical estimates of the exclusively homosexual population vary, the proportion is small—yet homosexual behavior is not uncommon among species and human cultures. Recent studies have found evidence that homosexuality may have biological roots, but more research is needed to tease apart its biological and social influences.

## KEY TERMS

genetics (**p. 303**)

chromosomes (**p. 303**)

deoxyribonucleic acid (DNA) (**p. 304**)

genes (**p. 304**)

human genome (**p. 305**)

genotype (**p. 307**)

phenotype (**p. 307**)

natural selection (**p. 308**)

adaptations (**p. 309**)

mutations (**p. 310**)

evolutionary psychology (**p. 311**)

inclusive fitness (**p. 312**)

kinship selection theory (**p. 312**)

reciprocal altruism (**p. 313**)

nature-nurture debate (**p. 314**)

family studies (**p. 314**)

heritablity (**p. 316**)

twin-study method (**p. 316**)

adoption studies (**p. 316**)

gender roles (**p. 327**)

gender schemas (**p. 327**)

sexual orientation (**p. 332**)

## THINKING CRITICALLY ABOUT NATURE AND NURTURE

1. What is heritability and how is it studied? Is it possible to separate the effects of genes and environment?

2. In what ways have your peers and your parents helped shape you?

3. Why do people often help non-related friends, acquaintances, and even strangers? Do animals do this too? How might this be adaptive in terms of evolution?

# Human Development

# HOW OLD DO PEOPLE FEEL?

## THE SITUATION

You know that people change as they get older, for better and for worse, and that development is a lifelong process. At the same time, you've heard it said that "age is a state of mind" and that "you're only as old as you feel." Hmm, you wonder. To what extent do people feel their chronological age? As children, did we tend to feel older than we were, or younger? How do we feel in relation to our age as adults?

Imagine that you are a developmental psychologist. To answer this question, you need to ask people to tell you how old they feel. So you devise a questionnaire in which you ask respondents to write down their actual age and then to specify how old they feel, how old they look, how old they behave, and so on. You realize that you need to survey people of different ages, so you recruit high-school and college students, faculty members from your university, adults taking part in an educational workshop, and local senior citizen centers. You send out 298 questionnaires, and 188 are completed and returned. Those who participate range in age from fourteen to eighty-three.

## MAKE A PREDICTION

By averaging each respondent's answers to various "how old do you feel" questions, you can calculate his or her "subjective-age identity." So what do you think you'd find? How old do *you* feel? Look at Figure 9.1. The diagonal line that you see illustrates the pattern you would have if subjective ages were identical to chronological ages—in other words, if people felt exactly as young or old as they truly were. If you think that this is what happened, then all you have to do is trace over that existing line. Otherwise, use it as a guide and (without looking at the figure below) put an X at the age felt by the average 15-year-old, then do the same for those at the ages of 25, 35, 45, 55, 65, 75, and 85. If you think that people in a particular age group feel younger than they are, place the X below the existing line. If you think they feel older, put the X above the line. Connect the Xs and you'll have your predicted subjective-age line.

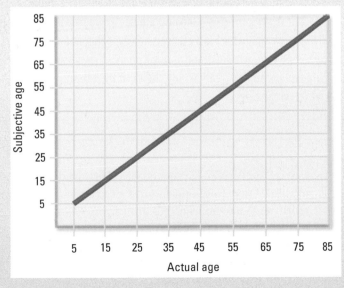

FIGURE 9.1

## THE RESULTS

Based on research suggesting that life satisfaction has more to do with our subjective age than with chronological age, Joann Montepare and Margie Lachman (1989) conducted the study just described. As you can see, the results are plotted alongside the comparison line in Figure 9.2. So how did you do? Look closely at the figure and you'll notice three interesting findings: (1) Teenagers in general feel older than they are; (2) adults feel younger; and (3) the tendency for adults to feel younger becomes more pronounced with advancing age.

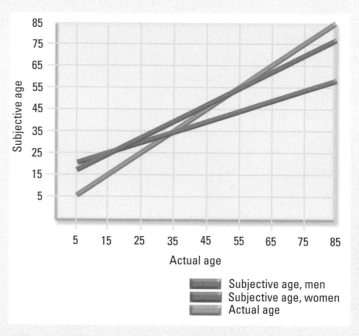

**FIGURE 9.2**

## WHAT DOES IT ALL MEAN?

One of the most important and recurring questions in developmental psychology concerns the extent to which people change over the course of a lifetime, particularly during the adult years. We'll see in this chapter that development is a lifelong process in which we change—physically, cognitively, and socially—as we get older. We'll also see, however, that in other respects each of us is the same person today as we were five years ago and will remain that person five years from now. In this context, Montepare and Lachman's (1989) study shows, at least to some extent, that we age less in our minds than we do on the clock.

---

Like most parents, I will never forget the birth of my daughter and then, three years later, my son. After nine long months of excitement and anticipation, the moment of truth had arrived. The "baby's room" was furnished and freshly painted, our work schedules were rearranged, anxious grandparents were called, the car was filled with gas, the hospital's birthing room was on reserve, and our obstetrician was ready for action. With these logistical pieces in place, every ounce of our attention turned to what was about to happen and what it would mean for our lives. My head spun with questions. How long will the birthing process take?

Will it go smoothly? Will the baby be okay? Will it be a boy or a girl? Will he or she grow up to be happy, loving, smart, and successful? What will the future hold?

# BASIC DEVELOPMENTAL QUESTIONS

- *What is the goal of developmental psychology?*
- *What strategies are used to measure the changes due to age?*

When it comes to understanding people, it often seems that playwrights, philosophers, poets, and artists are a step ahead of the rest of us. In the seventh century BCE, the Greek poet Solon described nine stages in human development, beginning in the cradle and ending in the grave. Then, in roughly 500 BCE, the Chinese philosopher Confucius described six life phases spanning the ages of fifteen to seventy. At the end of the sixteenth century, William Shakespeare immortalized his vision of seven life stages. And in Sweden, an unnamed artist depicted the ages of man and woman in ten-decade pyramids that peak at the age of fifty. In some cultures, the human life span is pictured as a straight line. In others, it is thought of as a circle, spiral, square, or change of seasons (Kotre & Hall, 1990).

Inheriting the wisdom of past generations, psychologists view human development as a lifelong process. The study of **developmental psychology** thus examines the kinds of questions that parents ask about their offspring and that all of us ask about ourselves: How do individuals *change* as they get older? Will an infant with a precocious smile become a sociable adult? Is the early-walking toddler a future athlete? Is the preschooler who clings to mom fated to become a dependent spouse? And is the overanxious college student doomed to a life of anxiety? Focusing on the extent to which development is characterized by stability or change, this chapter explores biological, cognitive, and social aspects of development across the life span, from conception through infancy, childhood, adolescence, adulthood, and old age.

First, let's step back and consider the major strategies used in developmental research. As illustrated in Figure 9.3, there are two basic approaches. In **cross-sectional studies**, people of different ages are examined at the same time and their responses are compared. For example, when intelligence researchers test people in their twenties through seventies, they typically find that older adults obtain lower scores than younger adults. This method of comparison is quick and is easy to implement, but the results should be interpreted with caution. In cross-sectional intelligence studies, for example, the pattern of decline apparently caused by age might instead result from a "cohort effect"—a difference between generations. Today's twenty-year-olds spend more years in school than did their grandparents, who grew up during World War II. Lower scores among the older adults may stem from a relative lack of educational opportunity, not from the effects of chronological age.

A second method is to conduct **longitudinal studies**, in which the same subjects are retested at different times in their lives in order to measure truly age-related changes. Using this method, researchers might observe people at one point in their lives, and then collect follow-up data from those same people days, weeks, months, or years later. In the research on age and intelligence, this

**developmental psychology**   The study of how people grow, mature, and change over the life span.

**cross-sectional study**   A method of developmental research in which people of different ages are tested and compared.

**longitudinal study**   A method of developmental research in which the same people are tested at different times to track changes related to age.

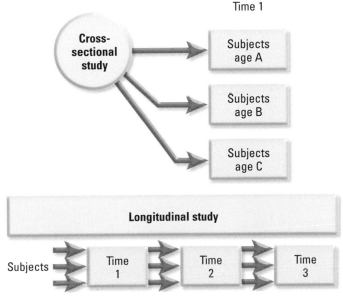

**FIGURE 9.3   Developmental research strategies**
In cross-sectional studies, subjects of different ages are examined at the same time and compared for differences. In longitudinal studies, the same subjects are tested at different times in order to measure change.

## REVIEW QUESTIONS

- *What is developmental psychology?*
- *Compare and contrast cross-sectional and longitudinal studies.*

strategy has revealed that there is less of a decline in performance when measured as the same people grow older. The cross-sectional study may reveal *differences* between groups, but only the longitudinal study measures *change* as a function of age. The main drawback of the longitudinal approach is logistical. These long-term studies take a great deal of time—and require patience from researchers and cooperation from their subjects.

# PRENATAL DEVELOPMENT

- *What are the three stages of prenatal development?*
- *How do alcohol, cigarettes, and cocaine affect the process?*
- *What is the womb like as a sensory environment?*
- *Can expectant parents "teach" the fetus by reading stories or playing music?*

Recognizing that the passage from the womb into the outside world is a profound one, Westerners celebrate the birthday as the starting point in a person's development. In fact, birth is not so much a beginning as it is a transition. The real beginning occurs nine months earlier, at the moment of conception. That is why the Chinese calculate age from that moment and consider the baby to be a one-year-old at birth.

## THE GROWING FETUS

Prenatal development during the nine months of pregnancy is divided into three stages: *germinal* (the first two weeks after conception), *embryonic* (third to ninth weeks), and *fetal* (ninth week to birth). From one stage to the next, dramatic biological and behavioral changes take place—and environmental influences are plentiful. These developments are illustrated in Figure 9.4.

First, there is the germinal stage. Thanks to conception, life begins with one remarkable new cell called a **zygote**—about the size of the period at the end of this sentence, yet fully equipped with a rich genetic heritage. Very quickly, a process of cell division takes place: The first cell splits into two, four, eight, and so on. After two and a half days, there are twelve to sixteen cells. By the fourth day, there are more than a hundred cells clustered together in a ball, traveling from the Fallopian tube into the uterus and increasing in both their number and their diversity. Some cells will form muscles and bone; others will form the stomach, liver, and so on. At two weeks, the ball of cells attaches to the uterine wall, braced and ready for eight and a half months in a new home. By the time this zygote is born, it will consist of hundreds of trillions of cells.

Once the zygote is firmly attached to the uterine wall, the germinal stage is over, and the zygote is called an **embryo.** It is at this point that all parts of the body begin to form—an oversize head with a primitive brain and central nervous system, eyes, ears, a nose, and a mouth with lips and teeth, a heart and circulatory system, arms, legs, fingers, toes, and a tail. During this stage, organs start to function, including a heart that pumps blood and beats, quickly, for the first time. Also during this stage, the male hormone testosterone is secreted in embryos that are genetically male, but not in those destined to become female. All the pieces of an individual are in place in an embryo, yet at eight weeks of age it is only an inch long and weighs a tenth of an ounce. You could hold one in the palm of your hand.

From the ninth week on, the embryo becomes a conspicuously human **fetus.** At first, the cartilage in the bones starts to harden and there is rapid growth of the brain, heart, lungs, genitals, and other internal organs and body parts. Depending

**zygote** A fertilized egg that undergoes a two-week period of rapid cell division and develops into an embryo.

**embryo** The developing human organism, from two weeks to two months after conception.

**fetus** The developing human organism, from nine weeks after conception to birth.

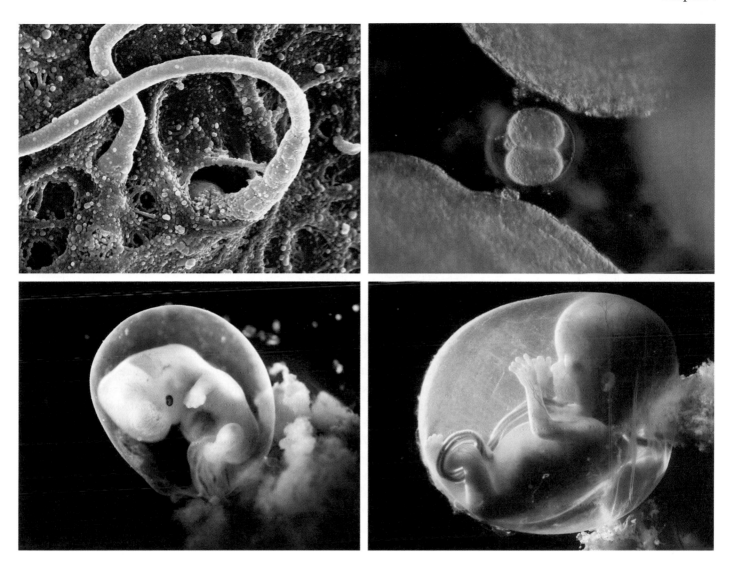

FIGURE 9.4    **Prenatal development**
Just prior to conception, a sperm penetrates the ovum wall (*top left*). After thirty hours, the
fertilized ovum divides for the first time and each cell contains genes from both the mother and the
father (*top right*). After six weeks, parts of the embryo's body have formed and the heart beats
(*bottom left*). At four months, the fetus is two to four inches long and has a conspicuously human
appearance (*bottom right*).

on its age, the fetus can squirm, open its eyes, suck its thumb, kick its legs, and turn
somersaults. By the seventh month, the key life-support systems are sufficiently developed so that the fetus can breathe, circulate blood, digest nutrients, and dispose
of wastes. At this point, the two-pound fetus has a fighting chance to survive if born
prematurely. If born on schedule, it will weigh an average of seven pounds.

Although fetal development follows a biological clock, it is also influenced by
external factors. Depending on the stage of development, exposure to harmful substances called **teratogens** (from the Greek *teras*, meaning "monster") can have devastating effects. Obstetricians warn expectant mothers that malnutrition, X rays,
AIDS, German measles and other viral infections, certain antibiotics, painkillers,
large doses of aspirin, heavy exposure to paint fumes, and a long list of drugs can
all prove dangerous (see Table 9.1). Some teratogens cannot be avoided—and some
problems will arise without exposure to toxic substances. There are no guarantees.

**teratogens** Toxic substances that can
harm the embryo or fetus during prenatal
development.

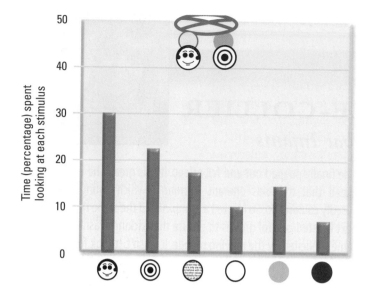

**FIGURE 9.5  Visual preferences in newborns**
Fantz (1961) recorded the amount of time newborns spent gazing at various disks. As shown, they looked more at the patterns than at solids, and they looked most of all at the human face.

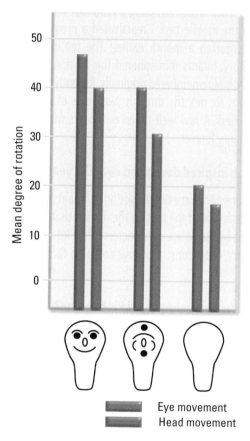

Eye movement
Head movement

**FIGURE 9.6  Newborn orientation toward the face**
In this study, a face, a scrambled pattern, or a blank form was moved slowly past each infant's field of view. As you can see, the infants tracked the face more than they did the other patterns (Johnson et al., 1991).

times closer—with the best distance being about eight inches (Banks & Salapatek, 1983). The problem is that the newborn's lenses do not focus on objects at a distance and cannot detect subtle differences in light, shading, or color. For that reason, soft pastel colors in the crib do not arouse as much interest as a newspaper with bold print or a checkerboard that has stark black-on-white contrast (Adams & Maurer, 1984). What would it be like to see through the eyes of a newborn baby? According to Daphne and Charles Maurer (1988), the world would look like "a badly focused snapshot that has been fading in the sun for so many years that you can barely identify the subject" (p. 127).

Newborns may be limited in their vision, but their sensory abilities develop quickly and they have marked preferences for certain kinds of stimulation. Just hours after birth, for example, infants distinguish between light and dark, stare at objects that show contrast, and can track slow movement with their eyes. In an especially intriguing study, Robert Fantz (1961) recorded the amount of time that two- to five-day-old infants spent gazing at each of the six disks illustrated in Figure 9.5—a human face, a bull's-eye, newsprint, and three solids colored red, white, and yellow. As shown, the infants preferred to look at the patterns over solids. Lo and behold, their favorite pattern was the human face. This finding raised an intriguing question: Do faces just happen to provide the right kind of visual stimulation, or is the human nervous system primed to pay special attention to social stimuli? Is the attraction a mere happy coincidence or the clever design of evolution?

Research supports the evolutionary interpretation. To be sure, newborns look at any object that has complexity, contrast, and a symmetrical pattern of eyelike dots in an outline—whether that object resembles a face or not (Kleiner, 1987). But infants tested within an hour or two of birth exhibit a unique level of interest in facelike stimuli. Mark Johnson and others (1991) presented newborns with head-shaped forms that depict a properly featured face, a scrambled face, or a blank, featureless face. The experimenter moved each pattern slowly across each infant's field of view and recorded the extent to which the infants rotated their heads and eyes to follow the visual stimulus. As shown in Figure 9.6, the infants tracked the facelike pattern more than they did the scrambled and blank patterns. It appears that humans are born with a special orientation toward the face (Morton & Johnson, 1991; Valenza et al., 1996; Mondloch et al., 1999). They can even distinguish between the faces of their own mothers and those of female strangers (Walton et al., 1992; Pascalis et al., 1995).

Other lines of research also indicate that newborns are "tuned in" to the face as a social object. Andrew Meltzoff and Keith Moore (1983) found that within seventy-two hours of birth, babies not only look at faces, but also often mimic gestures such as moving the head, pursing the lips, or sticking out the tongue (see Figure 9.7). This rudimentary form of imitation occurs even when the model is a stranger (Meltzoff & Moore, 1992). In another study, newborns were videotaped as they watched an adult wear a happy, sad, or surprised expression. Observers who later saw only the tape were able to guess the adult's expression from changes in the baby's face (Field et al., 1982). What do these findings mean? It's not clear that newborns are capable of deliberate and coordinated imitation. But they do react automatically to certain facial cues—almost as if babies were born with a "social reflex," to the delight of parents all over the world.

**Hearing and Auditory Preferences**   Slam the nursery door while a newborn is asleep, and it will open its eyes wide and fling out its arms. Clearly, the newborn can hear. But what does it hear, and how well? As with vision, the human auditory system is not completely developed at birth. The baby's outer ear is small, its eardrum does not vibrate effectively, and the auditory cortex is still immature. For the first week or so, the baby's ears are also clogged with amniotic fluid, which muffles sound. The result of all this is that the newborn baby is hard of hearing, compared to adults.

Though not in perfect form, the newborn reacts to life's sounds in consistent ways. If you stand on the baby's right or left side and shake a rattle, you'll notice that it slowly turns its head in your direction, as if trying to locate the source of the sound (see Chapter 3). Newborns cannot easily detect low-pitch sounds, but they are particularly sensitive to high-pitch sounds, melodies, and the human voice (Aslin, 1989). They can tell the difference between tones that are one note apart on the musical scale, between the mother's voice and that of another woman, and between speech sounds that are as similar as *pa* and *ba*. As measured by changes in sucking rate, newborn infants can distinguish among multisyllable words that vary in stress patterns or rhythm (Sansavini et al., 1997). By twenty weeks old, they're more likely to turn toward the sound of their own names than to similar other names (Mandel et al., 1995). They also seem to enjoy music. By recording the amount of time spent looking at stereo speakers as they deliver sound, researchers have found that infants show a measurable preference for Mozart and European folk songs over sounds that are "dissonant" or unpleasant to most adults (Trainor & Heinmiller, 1998; Zentner & Kagan, 1998).

In light of these various findings, it's interesting to consider the way adults talk to babies. In cultures all over the world, men, women, and children use baby talk, or "motherese"—a form of speech that is slow, clear, simple, high in pitch, rhythmic, songlike, and practically giddy, just the kinds of sounds that seize a newborn's attention. Infants like listening to higher-pitched voices (Trainor & Zacharias, 1998). They also prefer to hear baby talk than ordinary adult conversation. So when babies listen to tapes of women talking, they turn their head more toward the sound when the woman is talking to a baby than to another adult (Fernald, 1985; Fernald et al., 1989). Soon we'll see how marvelously adaptive this is for the development of language.

## SENSITIVITY TO NUMBER

Of all the recent discoveries about infants and what they know, perhaps the most startling come from experiments suggesting that babies are minimathematicians. In 1992, Karen Wynn showed five-month-old infants one or two Mickey Mouse dolls being put on a puppet stage and covered by a screen (see Figure 9.8). Next, they saw her add a doll to the one behind the screen (1 + 1) or take one away (2 − 1). The screen was then lowered so the babies could see how many dolls were now on stage. Sometimes the number was correct (2 in addition, 1 in subtraction); at other times, it was incorrect (1 in addition, 2 in subtraction). Can infants add and subtract? If they could, reasoned Wynn, they would "expect" correct outcomes and be surprised by incorrect outcomes. That is what happened. By recording their looking time, Wynn found that the babies looked longer at the incorrect—and apparently unexpected—outcomes. Using similar methods, Wynn and others have discovered that five-month-olds have a rudimentary ability not only to add and subtract but also to tell the difference between two objects or event sequences and three (Canfield & Smith, 1996; Wynn, 1996).

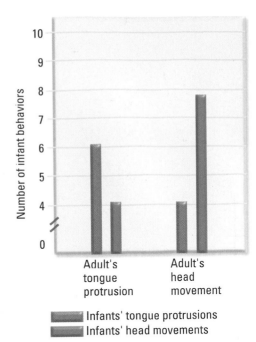

**FIGURE 9.7    Newborn imitation**
An adult experimenter either stuck out his tongue or moved his head in front of newborn babies. Videotaped records showed that the infants were more likely to respond by imitating the same gesture (Meltzoff & Moore, 1989).

**FIGURE 9.8    Can infants add and subtract?**
Five-month-olds saw a sequence of events that illustrated the addition (1 + 1 = 2) or subtraction (2 − 1 = 1) of Mickey Mouse dolls. In each case, a correct or incorrect outcome was revealed. The infants looked longer at outcomes that were incorrect and, apparently, unexpected (Wynn, 1992).

This research has sparked a controversy over whether infants are born with an innate sensitivity to numbers. Studies have shown that when infants are habituated to a certain number of objects, say two blocks or rubber ducks, they look longer at a new display containing one or three objects than another two-object display. In other words, they seem to notice the difference in number. Or do they? Melissa Clearfield and Kelly Mix (1999) argue that these infants may have responded to a change in the overall amount of material in the display, not in the discrete number of objects present. To test this hypothesis, they habituated infants, six to eight months old, to two black squares on a white board. Then they showed either three small squares that combined to produce the same amount of black space or two large squares that produced a larger combined black space. The result: The babies looked longer at the total change in space, or surface area (the two large squares) than at the change in number (the three small squares). Other studies have found similar results (Feigenson et al., 2002; Mix et al., 2002).

Yet in an experiment involving continuous motion, Sharon and Wynn (1998) tested six-month-old infants to see if they could distinguish the number of times a puppet jumped in the air—two versus three. They found that if the infants had been habituated to seeing three jumps rather than two, they looked longer when the puppet then jumped only twice. More recently, Wynn and others (2002) presented infants with collective entities—groups of dots that move together like a flock of birds or a school of fish. First they habituated the infants to four groups of three dots, or to three groups of four dots. Then they presented alternating displays of four groups of two and two groups of four and found that babies looked longer at the new display that had the number of collectives they had not seen before—regardless of the number of dots within them. Do infants have a rudimentary awareness of number? Stay tuned for future research developments.

The human newborn is not a miniature adult and is obviously too helpless to survive on its own. Thanks to recent research, however, we are in a better position to appreciate a newborn's capacities. From the moment of birth, babies are equipped with primitive but adaptive reflexes. They're also prepared to experience certain forms of stimulation, especially those provided by human contact—faces, voices, and mother's scent. And they are capable of rudimentary forms of learning and memory. In a particularly intriguing program of research, Carolyn Rovee-Collier (1988) hung a mobile over the crib of six-week-olds, attaching the mobile by a ribbon to one of their legs so they could move it. When these infants were brought back two weeks later, they remembered which leg to kick. Newborn capacities like these have existed for generations, but only now are we beginning to appreciate them.

## REVIEW QUESTIONS

- *What is habituation and how is it used in developmental research?*

- *What reflexes do newborns exhibit?*

- *What kinds of visual and auditory preferences do newborns demonstrate?*

- *Describe the evidence supporting and opposing the idea that newborns have an awareness of numbers.*

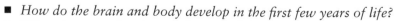

## THE INFANT AND GROWING CHILD

- *How do the brain and body develop in the first few years of life?*
- *What changes take place in the way children think, reason, and speak?*
- *Is an infant's first attachment to the mother critical? How is it affected by being in a day-care center?*
- *Why are childhood friendships considered "developmental advantages"?*

The newborn has come a long way—both in our minds and in its own short history of development. But there is much more to come. First, there is an *infant,* from the Latin word meaning "without language." The infant grows into a walking and talking toddler, who then graduates on the first day of school to the category of *child*. Puberty spurs the *adolescent*, though what it means to be an *adult* is anybody's guess. Throughout the rest of this chapter, we look at biological, cognitive, and social aspects of development and consider the interplay among them.

## BIOLOGICAL DEVELOPMENT

During the first year or so, babies grow at a pace never to be equaled again. On average, babies double their birth weight in five months and triple it by their first birthday. They grow ten inches in height during the first year, and another four to six inches the year after. To the distress of parents without hand-me-downs, a baby's clothing size changes almost every month. Though it is not always accurate, there's a general rule of thumb you might find remarkable: By the second birthday, most babies have reached half of their adult height.

**Physical Growth** Matching the observable changes in body size, other aspects of growth also proceed at a fast pace. Cartilage turns to bone, muscle fibers thicken, and teeth break through the gums. Most impressive are the changes that occur in the brain and nervous system—and what these changes mean for cognitive and social development. At birth, an infant's brain weighs close to a pound and is fully equipped with all of the 100 to 200 billion neurons it will have in its lifetime. But the brain and nervous system are immature, and relatively few synaptic connections have formed. Starting in the first year, the neural axons grow longer, the dendrites increase in number, and a surplus of new synaptic connections are carved into the brain—trillions, more than can possibly be used (see Figure 9.9). Then in childhood, the brain undergoes a pruning process in which often-used synaptic connections survive while unused connections are eliminated. The neurons also become more tightly wrapped in myelin sheath, the fatty substance that enhances the speed of neural transmission. This process of myelination continues to early adolescence.

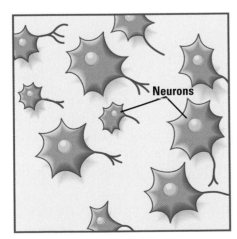

**1** At birth, the infant's brain has a complete set of neurons but not very many synaptic connections.

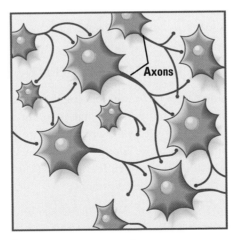

**2** During the first year, the axons grow longer, the dendrites increase in number, and a surplus of new connections is formed.

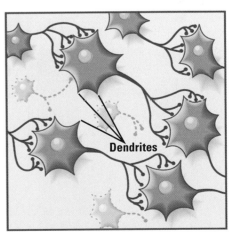

**3** Over the next few years, active connections are strengthened, while unused connections atrophy.

**FIGURE 9.9 The developing brain**
At birth, the infant's brain has a complete set of neurons but relatively few synaptic connections (1). During the first year, the axons grow longer, the dendrites increase in number, and many new connections are formed (2). Over the next few years, the active circuits are strengthened, while those that are unused atrophy (3).

For more information on Piaget and his work, you can visit the Jean Piaget Society at http://www.piaget.org/.

The brain's maturation is closely linked to psychological development. For example, natural increases in the number of synaptic connections, or "pathways," in the brain are often accompanied by advances in cognitive ability (Fischer, 1987; Goldman-Rakic, 1987; Epstein, 2001). The same is true of myelination. At birth, the brainstem and spinal cord—which govern simple reflexes—are well myelinated and in working order. The visual cortex is less developed, as is the newborn's vision. Those parts of the cortex that control attention and information processing are not fully myelinated until the ages of four to seven years, which is when children become capable of reading and simple arithmetic (Parmelee & Sigman, 1983). In short, growth spurts in the brain correspond nicely to developments of the mind.

**Motor Skills**  From infancy to childhood, physical growth—as measured by gains in height and weight—is the most predictable change that takes place. The second most predictable is the coordination of *motor skills*. On average, babies can lift their heads at 2 months, sit without support at 5.5 months, crawl at 10 months, and walk at 12 months. Children differ somewhat in their *rate* of motor development, but the *sequence* of events is usually the same: Lifting the head precedes sitting, which precedes crawling, standing, and walking. Infants differ in the way they learn to crawl and then walk. For example, some begin by inching along on their bellies before crawling on hands and knees; others do not (Adolph et al., 1998). More advanced activities like running, jumping, climbing stairs, and throwing a ball develop later and are less rigid in their sequence. So are fine motor skills like gripping a pencil, tying a shoelace, and using a fork (Wade & Whiting, 1986).

Cultural factors also play a role. For example, infants in parts of Africa sit at an earlier age than do their American peers because their parents use rolled-up blankets to prop them up into sitting positions in a hole in the ground. Yet these same precocious sitters are slower to crawl because their parents discourage it (Rogoff & Morelli, 1989). The physical environment also plays a role. An analysis of birth dates revealed that infants born in the summer and early fall crawl three weeks later than do those from the same area who are born in the winter and spring. By the time summer and fall babies are ready to move about, the day is shorter and the temperature is colder (Benson, 1993).

## COGNITIVE DEVELOPMENT

You don't have to be a psychologist to notice physical growth or the development of motor skills. The real challenge is to unravel the mystery of how children of different ages think—not just what they know but *how* they come to know it and the mistakes they make along the way (Siegler, 1998). To understand this aspect of development, we turn to Jean Piaget (1896–1980), the most influential figure in the study of cognitive development.

**Piaget's Theory**  Born in Switzerland, Piaget was a precocious boy interested in seashells, birds, and mechanics. He published his first article at the age of ten and was offered a curatorship at a natural history museum in Geneva while in high school. At twenty-one, Piaget earned a Ph.D. in biology, then studied psychology in Paris and took a job administering intelligence tests to schoolchildren. As luck would have it, this experience proved to be a turning point—for Piaget and for psychology.

While testing, Piaget became intrigued by the mistakes children made. Far from being random or idiosyncratic, he realized, these errors signaled that young children use a logic that is foreign to adults. To understand this logic, Piaget had children explain their answers, a simple but informative method. From these interviews, Piaget published a series of articles, and in 1921 he was named director of a child

*Jean Piaget.*

development institute in Geneva. The seed was planted. In the years that followed, Piaget studied thousands of children, including his own. By the time he died in 1980, he had written more than forty books on how children think about people, nature, time, morality, and other aspects of the world (Piaget & Inhelder, 1969; Ginsberg & Opper, 1988). Today, anyone interested in cognitive development—parents, educators, or philosophers—begins with Piaget.

Piaget's theory rests on the assumption that children are curious, active, and constructive thinkers who want to understand the world around them. According to Piaget, infants and children form **schemas,** or mental representations of the world, in order to make sense of it. Through a process of **assimilation,** he said, children try to fit new information into their existing schemas. Through the process of **accommodation,** they modify existing schemas to fit new information. Viewed in this way, development is not a process by which children merely "copy and paste" what they are told. Rather, the creation of knowledge occurs "through a complex interplay between preexisting knowledge and new information gathered through interaction with the external world" (Siegler & Ellis, 1996, p. 212).

In a study that illustrates how children form and revise their conceptions in light of new information, Stella Vosniadou and William Brewer (1992) asked children of varying ages about the shape of the earth. Seeing that the ground they walk on is flat, preschoolers believe the earth as a whole is flat—either rectangular or disk-shaped. What happens when they're told that the earth is spherical? Rather than shed their incorrect schemas for an accurate representation, they incorporate the sphere into their beliefs that the earth is flat by constructing the synthetic models shown in Figure 9.10. Many first-graders adopt the "dual earth" notion that the earth is round but that humans live on a flat surface. By the third grade, many children see the world as a "flattened sphere" or as a "hollow sphere"—like a fishbowl with people living on the bottom. By fifth grade, most have adopted the correct "sphere" model. Gradually, then, through a dynamic interplay of assimilation and accommodation, children form new and accurate conceptions of, quite literally, the world.

Another assumption made by Piaget is that as children get older, they advance through a series of chronological *cognitive stages,* each distinguished by a specific kind of thinking. For Piaget, cognitive development is like climbing a staircase, one step at a time. This view has two implications. First, even though some children advance more quickly than others, the sequence is universally the same: The first stage must precede the second, which must precede the third, and so on. In this way, each stage holds both the fruits of the past and the seeds of the future. Second, even though the cognitive stages build upon one another, the increments are seen as qualitative and abrupt, not quantitative and gradual—in other words, like climbing stairs, not a ramp. As shown in Figure 9.11, Piaget described four stages in cognitive development: (1) sensorimotor, (2) preoperational, (3) concrete operational, and (4) formal operational.

**Sensorimotor Stage**   Beginning at birth and lasting about two years, infants come to know the world by touching, grasping, smelling, sucking, chewing, poking, prodding, banging, shaking, and manipulating objects. Piaget called this the **sensorimotor stage** of development. As far as infants are concerned, an object exists only for the moment and only when it is in direct sensory contact. In fact, research shows that the way infants explore objects changes predictably with age. Beginning at one month old, they learn about the shape, texture, and substance of objects with the mouth (Gibson & Walker, 1984). At five months, they also acquire information with their hands (Streri & Pecheux, 1986) or by coordinating movement of the hands, eyes, and mouth together (Rochat, 1989). This sensorimotor mode can be

**schemas**   In Piaget's theory, mental representations of the world that guide the processes of assimilation and accommodation.

**assimilation**   In Piaget's theory, the process of incorporating and, if necessary, changing new information to fit existing cognitive structures.

**accommodation**   In Piaget's theory, the process of modifying existing cognitive structures in response to new information.

**sensorimotor stage**   Piaget's first stage of cognitive development, from birth to two years old, when infants come to know the world through their own actions.

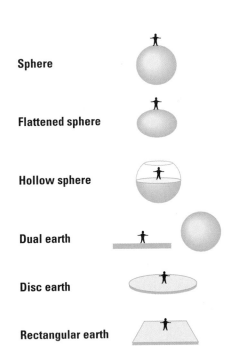

Sphere

Flattened sphere

Hollow sphere

Dual earth

Disc earth

Rectangular earth

**FIGURE 9.10   Changing schemas of the earth**
Compared to preschoolers, who think the world is flat, school-age children at first assimilate the spherical model into their schemas, then accommodate their schemas to form an accurate representation (Vosniadou & Brewer, 1992).

**object permanence** Developing at six to eight months, an awareness that objects continue to exist after they disappear from view.

**separation anxiety** Among infants with object permanence, a fear reaction to the absence of their primary caretaker.

*By uncovering the hidden toy, this baby is demonstrating object permanence.*

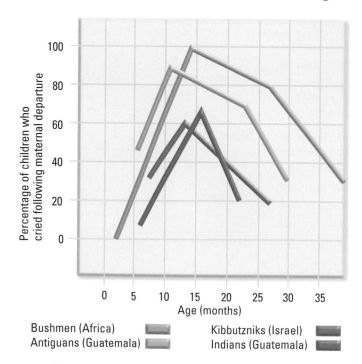

The adolescent can reason abstractly and think in hypothetical terms.

**Formal operational (12 years–adult)**

The child can think logically about concrete objects and can thus add and subtract. The child also understands conservation.

**Concrete operational (7–12 years)**

The child uses symbols (words and images) to represent objects but does not reason logically. The child also has the ability to pretend. During this stage, the child is egocentric.

**Preoperational (2–6 years)**

The infant explores the world through direct sensory and motor contact. Object permanence and separation anxiety develop during this stage.

**Sensorimotor (0–2 years)**

**FIGURE 9.11    Piaget's stages of cognitive development**
Piaget portrayed development as a staircase in which the different steps, or stages, are distinguished by specific kinds of thinking.

seen in the way young babies try to stuff crayons, toys, and limbs into the mouth—and in the way they pull, push, shake, squeeze, and bang everything they can get their fingers on.

According to Piaget, the crowning cognitive achievement of the sensorimotor stage is the development of **object permanence**, an awareness that objects continue to exist even after they disappear from view. This may not seem to be much of an accomplishment, but Piaget (1952) noticed that whenever he covered a toy with his beret or a handkerchief, babies younger than eight months old did not protest, made no effort to retrieve it, and were unaware of its absence—even when the toy made noise. Quite literally, out of sight means out of mind. Given this lack of object permanence, it is no wonder that until babies approach their first birthday, they never seem to tire of playing peek-a-boo, a game in which each round is met with a fresh look of surprise.

Object permanence may be linked to important aspects of social development. It is probably not a coincidence that just as babies become capable of recalling objects that are out of view, they also begin to experience **separation anxiety**, a fear reaction to the absence of their primary caretaker. The baby who is not aware of its mother when she isn't perceptible will not seem distressed by her absence. However, the baby who has achieved object permanence is capable of missing its mother and cries frantically the moment she slips out of sight. As with other aspects of sensorimotor development, this pattern—of object permanence accompanied by several months of separation anxiety—can be seen in cultures all over the world (Kagan, 1976; Whiting & Edwards, 1988). Figure 9.12 provides a clear illustration of this point. A longitudinal study of

Percentage of children who cried following maternal departure

Age (months)

Bushmen (Africa)
Antiguans (Guatemala)
Kibbutzniks (Israel)
Indians (Guatemala)

**FIGURE 9.12    Separation anxiety**
Cross-cultural researchers have found that the rise and fall of separation anxiety follow a similar pattern among infants in different parts of the world (Kagan, 1976).

babies during their first year showed that although they matured at different rates, their cognitive gains were associated with the amount of distress they felt when separated from their mothers (Lewis et al., 1997).

**Preoperational Stage**   Some time during the second year, developments in memory lend permanence to people no longer in view, and peek-a-boo games give way to hide-and-seek. At eight months old, a delay of two or three seconds is enough for babies to become distracted from the location of a hidden object. At ten months, they can wait eight seconds, and at sixteen months, twenty to thirty seconds (Kail, 1990). At twenty months old, babies who watched an adult hide a Big Bird doll in a desk drawer or behind a pillow were able to find the toy even on the next day (DeLoache & Brown, 1983). The second year is also a time when children become more verbal and more abstract in their thinking. For the first time, words and images are used to symbolize objects. And one object may be used as a symbol for another. Thus, children pretend that the spoon is an airplane and their mouth a runway, and they understand that when an adult pretends to pour tea over a toy monkey, the monkey becomes "wet" (Harris & Kavanaugh, 1993; Kavanaugh et al., 1997).

Despite enormous cognitive gains, the two-year-old does not think like an adult or even like a school-age child. According to Piaget, preschoolers are in a **preoperational stage,** during which they reason in an intuitive, prelogical manner, unable to perform mental operations. Preoperational thought has two key features. The first is that the child is **egocentric,** or self-centered—unable to adopt the perspective of another person. At this stage of development, children tend to assume that you can tell what they are thinking, that you know all the people in their lives, or that you can see a picture in a book they are reading. Play a hiding game with three-year-olds, and they'll stand in full view and cover their eyes—assuming that if they cannot see, then they cannot be seen. Or eavesdrop on a conversation between four-year-olds and you will hear each of them jabbering away and taking turns—oblivious to what the other is saying. These "collective monologues" are also evidence of egocentrism.

A second limitation at this stage is that the preoperational child does not understand **conservation,** the idea that physical properties of an object stay the same despite superficial changes in appearance. To illustrate, take a tall, thin eight-ounce glass of lemonade and pour it into an eight-ounce cup that is shorter and wider. You and I know that the quantity of liquid stays the same regardless of changes in shape, but to the preschooler the tall, thin glass holds more to drink. As illustrated in Figure 9.13, there are other examples as well. Flatten a ball of clay and the preoperational child will think there is less. Roll the clay into a long thin snake, and the child will think there is more. Or if you use a handful of pennies, the child will think there are more if you spread them out than if you push them close together. What these demonstrations show is that, until the age of seven, children can't seem to *center* on two object features at a time (height and width, for example) or mentally reverse such operations as pouring, rolling, flattening, or spreading. Very simply, "What you see is what you get."

**preoperational stage**   Piaget's second stage of cognitive development, when two- to six-year-olds become capable of reasoning in an intuitive, prelogical manner.

**egocentric**   Self-centered, unable to adopt the perspective of another person.

**conservation**   The concept that physical properties of an object remain the same despite superficial changes in appearance.

 9.3

**Conservation of liquid**

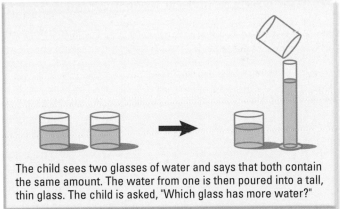

The child sees two glasses of water and says that both contain the same amount. The water from one is then poured into a tall, thin glass. The child is asked, "Which glass has more water?"

**Conservation of substance**

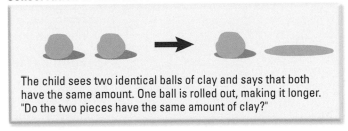

The child sees two identical balls of clay and says that both have the same amount. One ball is rolled out, making it longer. "Do the two pieces have the same amount of clay?"

**Conservation of number**

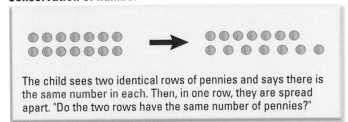

The child sees two identical rows of pennies and says there is the same number in each. Then, in one row, they are spread apart. "Do the two rows have the same number of pennies?"

FIGURE 9.13   **Tasks used to test conservation**
According to Piaget, the ability to conserve marks the transition from the preoperational to the concrete operational stages of cognitive development.

**concrete operational stage** Piaget's third stage of cognitive development, when children become capable of logical reasoning.

**formal operational stage** Piaget's fourth stage of cognitive development, when adolescents become capable of logic and abstract thought.

Egocentrism and failures at conservation both seem to have something in common: The preoperational child cannot think about objects or events in more than one way. Unable to see from another person's point of view or to take another perspective on the same object, toddlers often have trouble distinguishing reality (what they know) from appearance (what they see). John Flavell and others (1986), for example, let nursery-school children feel a soft sponge that looked like a rock. When asked (1) what the object *really is,* and (2) what the object *looks like right now,* a majority of children gave the same response to both questions. Those who knew it was a sponge by feeling it also said it *looked* like a sponge, and those who said it looked like a rock also thought it *was* a rock. Many years ago, on the eve of Halloween, I discovered this confusion the hard way. In front of my then four-year-old daughter, I put on a gorilla mask. She watched me put the mask on and knew it was me but then she burst into tears, making me feel awful. It was as if appearance had become reality.

**Concrete Operational Stage** At about the age of seven, children advance to what Piaget called the **concrete operational stage,** becoming capable of logical reasoning. As they enter school for the first time, children are able to take the perspective of another person and understand that various object properties can stay the same despite surface changes in their appearance. They can now group similar objects into categories, order the objects according to size or number, and appreciate the logic that if A is greater than B, and B is greater than C, then A is greater than C. Capable of performing concrete operations, the first-grader can also be taught to add and subtract without counting (Resnick, 1989).

Piaget believed that conservation marks the beginning of a major advance in cognitive development, one that lasts to the age of eleven or twelve. However, even though concrete operational children appear to reason like adults do in response to specific problems, they do not think on an abstract level. Children may know that 2 is an even number and that $2 + 1$ is an odd number, and they may well realize the same for $4 + 1$, $6 + 1$, and $100 + 1$—but they will not necessarily put the pieces together to form the more general principle that any even number plus one yields an odd number. The ability to use methods of logic—inductive reasoning, deductive reasoning, and systematic hypothesis testing—is the hallmark of Piaget's next stage, the formal operational stage of cognitive development.

**Formal Operational Stage** What distinguishes Piaget's third and fourth levels of development is the ability to formulate solutions in advance and to reason on a logical, hypothetical level. To illustrate, imagine how you might approach the following test. You have four beakers, each containing a colorless chemical, and a dropper filled with potassium iodide. You are then told that when the potassium iodide is mixed with one or more of the four chemicals, it produces a bright yellow solution. Your task is to determine which chemicals to mix. Faced with this problem, the typical nine- or ten-year-old child will arbitrarily begin to mix chemicals, trying one combination after another until stumbling upon the solution. In contrast, the typical thirteen-year-old will plan a systematic course of action, first adding potassium iodide to each beaker, then trying other combinations of chemicals and keeping track of outcomes until the problem is solved (Inhelder & Piaget, 1958).

Unlike Piaget's first three stages, which appear roughly on schedule in different cultures, the **formal operational stage** does not characterize all adults. As we saw in Chapter 7, many Western adults are not necessarily formal operational in their problem solving, often falling back on rules of thumb known as heuristics. Piaget's point, however, is that adolescents and adults are cognitively *capable* of formal operations, whereas children are not. It's interesting that, in France, adolescents tested in the 1990s scored higher on measures of formal operational thought than those tested twenty to thirty years earlier—when fewer teenagers attended secondary school. Piaget may have been right about the age at which children first become capable of formal operational thought, but performance is also influenced by schooling, culture, and other variable experiences (Flieller, 1999).

**Piaget's Legacy**    Piaget was an astute observer of children, and his writings brought the study of cognitive development to life (Beilin, 1992; Brainerd, 1996; Flavell, 1996). Important practical lessons also stem from his theory—like the idea that a child may not be developmentally "ready" for reading, writing, arithmetic, taking turns, and other cognitive and social tasks. Today, many parents try to "jumpstart" their children by enrolling them in academically rigorous preschools or by training them for athletics and other types of competition. Thanks to Piaget, however, many child development experts are quick to warn that children should not be pushed too early—before they have matured to the necessary stage of development (Elkind, 1989; Zigler, 1987).

Many of Piaget's writings have stirred both criticisms and vigorous defenses of his theory (Lourenco & Machado, 1996). Neo-Piagetian researchers are revising and extending his work in important ways. One criticism is that Piaget's interview method was crude by today's standards. As a result, he underestimated young children's cognitive abilities and taxed their capacity to process task-relevant information (Case, 1992). Some studies have shown that babies even have an intuitive grasp of simple laws of physics. For example, they look longer at a ball that appears to roll through a solid object or at one that appears to stop in midair than at one that does *not* produce an unexpected physical outcome (Spelke et al., 1992; Baillargeon, 1994).

Other examples illustrate the point. Piaget said that object permanence did not develop until eight months of age, when babies first try to retrieve toys that have been hidden from view. But what if a more sensitive measure were used? Renee Baillargeon (1986) recorded eye movements and found that six-month-olds reacted

*Although Piaget estimated the ages at which certain cognitive skills develop, experience plays an important role. As with other children who work with clay or with liquid quantities, this young Indian potter is likely to understand the concept of conservation sooner than might be expected.*

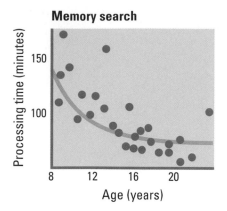

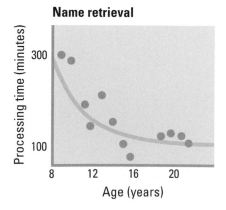

FIGURE 9.14  **Speed of information processing**

In general, response times decline between the ages of seven and twelve, then level off. This same pattern appears in many tasks, including mental addition, memory search, and name retrieval (Kail, 1991).

with surprise when an object temporarily hidden from view seemed to disappear. This experiment, and others like it, suggests that an out-of-sight object may not be out of mind at this age (Meltzoff & Moore, 1998). Similarly, Piaget thought that three- and four-year-olds are egocentric, unable to take the perspective of another person. Yet children at these ages speak more simply to babies than to adults and show pictures to others with the front side facing the viewer (Gelman, 1979). Three- and four-year-olds understand that someone else will see a visible object only if that person's eyes are open and aimed in the right direction—and only if there are no vision-blocking obstacles in the way (Flavell, 1999).

Were Piaget's timetables wrong? Yes and no. Yes, it's clear that young children are more precocious than Piaget had realized. But no, his developmental sequences—for example, the hypothesis that object permanence precedes conservation, which in turn precedes formal logic—have stood up well. Piaget may have underestimated the overall *rate* of development, but he was right about the *sequence* of achievements.

A second question is often raised that goes right to the heart of Piaget's theory: Does cognitive development progress through distinct stages, like a staircase, or is it more gradual, like a ramp? Or, as Robert Siegler (1996) has suggested, should cognitive development be depicted in waves, with the flow of new strategies overlapping with the ebb of old strategies? Robert Thatcher and others (1986) measured electrical brain activity in 577 humans ranging from two months old to young adulthood and spotted distinct growth spurts that corresponded roughly to the emergence of Piaget's stages. Yet Piaget's all-or-none view of development has been challenged inasmuch as children often master a concept in some tasks but not in others. Four-year-olds can order colors from light to dark, but they can't order sticks by length. Six-year-olds understand conservation in the pennies problem before they can solve the liquid or clay problems. These kinds of inconsistencies tell us that cognitive concepts don't burst into mind all at once but, instead, are used for one task at a time. What, then, are we to conclude? Once again, Piaget was only partly correct. The pace of development is more rapid at some ages and in some cultures than others. But within these periods of rapid growth, it takes time for new skills to reach their full maturity.

**Information-Processing Perspectives**  Many cognitive-development researchers examine age-related changes in the way that information is processed. From this perspective, cognitive development is characterized not by a transition from one qualitative stage of logic to another but by gradual increases both in the ability to attend selectively to one stimulus and in the ability to encode, store, and retrieve information from memory. These information-processing skills are refined throughout childhood. From this perspective, young children may fail a Piagetian task not because of how they think or the logic they use but because their attention wanders, they get distracted, and they forget elements of the problem (Kail & Bisanz, 1992; Siegler, 1996). Consider the finding that preoperational children cannot distinguish appearance and reality. Catherine Rice and her colleagues (1997) presented three-year-olds with a sponge that looked like a rock. As in past studies, they could not separate the appearance from reality (if it looked like a rock, they thought it was a rock; if it felt like a sponge, they thought it looked like a sponge). But when a real rock and a normal-looking sponge were placed alongside the target object—which enabled the children to keep in mind both its apparent and its real identities—they were able to make the distinction and realize that the object was a sponge that looked like a rock.

One highly consistent change that takes place in childhood is in memory. On tests of short-term memory span, the average adult can recall about seven items of information (see Chapter 6). Among young children, this number increases steadily with age. Why? Some researchers have found that young children do not use the kinds of encoding, storage, and retrieval strategies common among adults. When you or I have to recall a phone number or grocery list, we try to repeat the items over and over. Not so among young children. In one experiment, children of varying ages were instructed to memorize objects in pictures, while a trained lip reader watched for signs of silent rehearsal. The result: The number who rehearsed increased from 10 percent among five-year-olds to 60 percent among seven-year-olds, to 85 percent among ten-year-olds (Flavell et al., 1966). The memory abilities of young children are currently the subject of heated controversies in the courtroom. (See *Psychology and Law*.)

The use of strategies may partly explain age differences in memory, but researchers also find that the initial limitations and later increases in memory are also related to maturation of the brain and the efficiency with which information is processed. Robert Kail (1991) has found that there is a consistent age-related decline in performance *speed* at cognitive tasks. In a series of experiments, he recorded the amount of time it took for seven- to twenty-one-year-old subjects to do various simple tasks. They were asked to name pictured objects, judge whether two letters on a screen were the same, mentally rotate objects, move pegs from one side of a pegboard to the other, add two numbers, or press a button the moment they detected a target stimulus. The result: On all tasks, responses became quicker with age—and followed the same pattern of change. As depicted in Figure 9.14, information processing speeded up between the ages of seven and twelve, and then leveled off. According to Kail, this general increase in speed stems from the biological maturation of the brain—specifically, perhaps, from the increased myelination of axons, which facilitates the transmission of neural impulses. This increase may account for some of the stagelike performance increments typically found in cognitive-development research. It may also account for age differences in children's ability to read (Kail & Hall, 1994).

## SOCIAL DEVELOPMENT

Born completely helpless, equipped with reflexes that orient them toward people, responsive to human faces and voices, and prepared to mimic facial expressions on cue, the newborn is an inherently social animal. For eager parents, the baby's first smile is the warmest sign of all. It's funny sometimes how nature finds ways to lubricate a parent–newborn bond. If you gently stroke or blow on a newborn baby's face, it reacts to this stimulation by contracting its muscles and pulling back its mouth into what looks like—you guessed it—a smile (Emde et al., 1976). Like adults, infants exhibit different types of smiles—some that last longer than others, and some with the mouth open rather than closed (Messinger et al., 1999). In fact, babies don't crinkle up their eyes and flash "social smiles" at people until they are at least six weeks old (Bower, 1982).

**The Parent–Child Relationship**   Many developmental psychologists believe that a baby's first relationship to the mother or another caretaker sets the stage for social development. Clearly, it is critical in certain species of animals. Newly hatched ducks and geese, for example, will automatically follow their mother—an instinctive form of attachment called **imprinting**, which serves the purpose of keeping the young birds in proximity to each other and to their mother. Intrigued by how automatic the process is, Konrad Lorenz (1937) suspected that any moving, honking stimulus (whether it is the mother or not) will trigger this response. So he squatted, clucked, and moved about in front of birds hatched in an incubator, and it worked like a charm. One of Lorenz's favorite pictures shows him strolling through high grass trailed by a line of geese imprinted by his actions. In

**imprinting**   Among newly hatched ducks and geese, an instinctive tendency to follow the mother.

*Soon after hatching, ducklings will follow the first moving object they see. In this photograph, the imprinted object was ethologist Konrad Lorenz.*

## Psychology and Law

# ARE CHILD WITNESSES COMPETENT TO TESTIFY?

On August 2, 1988, Margaret Kelly Michaels, a twenty-six-year-old preschool teacher, was found guilty of 115 counts of sex abuse committed at the Wee Care Nursery School in New Jersey. The charges against her were shocking. For a period of more than seven months, the jury was told, she had danced nude in the classroom, forced children to drink her urine, stripped the children, licked peanut butter off their genitals, and raped them with kitchen utensils and Lego blocks.

Were the children's stories accurate? On the one hand, there were striking consistencies in the testimonies of nineteen witnesses. On the other hand, social workers and investigators who conducted the interviews prompted the children with highly suggestive questions, told them that Michaels was a bad person, offered bribes for disclosures, and pressured those who claimed ignorance. Except for this testimony, there was no physical evidence of abuse and no witnesses—even though the acts were supposed to have occurred during school hours in an open classroom. Michaels was found guilty and sentenced to prison. After serving five years, she was released when an appeals court overturned the conviction because the children's testimony could not be trusted. "One day you're getting ready for work and making coffee, minding your business," said Michaels, "and the next minute you are an accused child molester."

Can suggestive interviews cause young children to confuse appearance and reality? Some children are more suggestible than others—and more likely to change their reports in response to negative feedback (Scullin & Ceci, 2001). In general, however, with so many child sex-abuse charges filed in recent years against preschool teachers, babysitters, and family members, judges must decide: Are preschoolers competent to take the witness stand, or are they too suggestible, prone to confuse reality and fantasy? To provide guidance to the courts, researchers have studied children's eyewitness memory (Bruck & Ceci, 1999).

This research has evolved through stages. At first, simple laboratory experiments showed that preschoolers are more

*Stephen Ceci has published many pivotal studies of child witnesses. When asked how he started, he recalled the first time that a judge, in a murder trial, asked his advice about a child's testimony. "I remember being frustrated, being unable to tell the judge anything I considered helpful. I went into my lab the next day, determined to redesign a memory study I had started, to shed light on the question the judge had asked. That marked a watershed. From that day forward I added context to memory studies so that they would not only be theoretically interesting but useful to practitioners."*

fact, geese will follow all sorts of first-seen moving objects—decoys, rubber balls, wooden blocks, and even a striped metal pipe (Hess, 1959).

If baby birds are to follow the mother, they must be exposed to her within the first day or so, during a **critical period** for the development of imprinting. In humans, attachment is less automatic, the mother plays a more active role, and there is no "critical" period. Still, the infant does form a very deep and affectionate emotional bond called an **attachment.**

**The First Attachment** Beginning in the second half of the first year, accompanying the development of object permanence, infants all over the world form an intense, exclusive bond with their primary caretaker. This first relationship is highly charged with emotion and emerges with consistency from one culture to the next.

**critical period** A period of time during which an organism must be exposed to a certain stimulus for proper development to occur.

**attachment** A deep emotional bond that an infant develops with its primary caretaker.

likely than older children and adults to incorporate misleading "trick" questions into their memories (Ceci et al., 1987). In fact, interviewers were able to get young children to change their memories, or at least their answers, simply by repeating a question over and over—which implies that the answer given is not acceptable (Poole & White, 1991). But are young children suggestible about real-life, sometimes stressful, experiences? And what kinds of interview procedures are the most biasing?

In one study, Leichtman and Ceci (1995) told nursery-school children about a clumsy man named Sam Stone who always broke things. A month later, the man visited the classroom and then left without incident. The next day, the children were shown a ripped book and a soiled teddy bear and were asked what happened. Reasonably, no one accused Stone. Over the next ten weeks, however, they were asked leading questions ("I wonder if Sam Stone was wearing long pants or short pants when he ripped the book?"). The result: When a new, naive interviewer asked the children to describe what happened, 72 percent blamed Stone for the damage—and 45 percent said they saw him do it. One child "recalled" that Stone painted melted chocolate on the bear. Others "saw" him spill coffee, throw toys, and rip a book and soak it in warm water until it fell apart.

Further research shows that suggestibility effects are not limited to low-stress situations. Maggie Bruck and others (1995) interviewed five-year-old children who had visited their male pediatrician a year earlier for a physical examination and an immunization shot. Also during that visit, a female research assistant showed each child a poster, read a story, and gave out treats. Four interviews were conducted in a one-month period. During the first three sessions, half the children were falsely "reminded" about the day when the male doctor showed them the poster, read the story, and gave them treats while the female assistant gave them the examination, oral vaccine, and shot. During the fourth interview, when asked to recall what happened, those who were not misled were highly accurate in their recollections. But those given misinformation incorporated many false suggestions into their reports. Many even embellished the stories with nonsuggested new events.

False memories in young children are not just an evil byproduct of biased questioning procedures. Research shows that even when interviews of children are fair and neutral, false reports can stem from children's exposure to misinformation from outside sources—such as television (Principe et al., 2000), parents (Poole & Lindsay, 2001), and classmates (Principe & Ceci, 2002).

To summarize, research shows that repetition, misinformation, leading questions, and outside sources of information can bias a child's memory report—and that preschoolers are most vulnerable. In dozens of studies, these procedures have led children to falsely report that they were touched, hit, and kissed; that a thief entered the classroom; that something "yukky" was put into their mouth; and even that a doctor had cut a bone from their nose to stop it from bleeding. Somehow, the legal system must distinguish between true and false claims on a case-by-case basis. To assist in this endeavor, psychologists have proposed interviewing guidelines so that future child witnesses be questioned in an objective and nonbiased manner. When problems do arise, psychologists sometimes testify as expert witnesses—to inform judges and juries about potential problems (Ceci & Helmbrooke, 1998).

What motivates the infant? Some years ago, psychologists assumed that infants would become attached to anyone who feeds them and satisfies their basic physiological needs. That assumption was then put to rest by a classic series of dramatic experiments by Harry Harlow (1958, 1971).

In the 1950s, Harlow was breeding rhesus monkeys to study learning. Infant monkeys were separated from their mothers, fed regularly, and housed in cages equipped with a blanket. At one point, Harlow noticed that the infants had become passionately attached to their blankets—as they would be to their mothers. It is interesting that, like Linus of the old comic strip *Peanuts,* many normal children in the United States, Sweden, New Zealand, and elsewhere clutch security blankets (Passman, 1987). At any rate, this observation sparked in Harlow an interest in the

*In his classic studies with rhesus monkeys, Harlow found that the babies clung to soft cloth "mothers"—and preferred this contact comfort to wire-mesh mothers that provided milk.*

origins of attachment: Are infants drawn to mother for the comfort of her warm and cuddly body or for the food and nourishment she provides? To answer this question, Harlow placed newborn monkeys into a cage that contained two substitute mothers—one was a wire-mesh cylinder with a wooden head; the other was covered with soft terrycloth. Both provided a bottle of milk with a nipple. It was no contest. The infant monkeys spent almost all of their time with the terrycloth doll. In fact, they clung to the cloth substitute even when it did not contain a bottle for feeding. Given the choice, the infant monkeys preferred "contact comfort" over food. In later variations of this study, Harlow found that warmth and rocking motions further intensified the contact comfort provided by a cloth mother. Infants need more from parents than milk and a clean diaper.

Sadly, Harlow found that the infant monkeys raised with inanimate cloth substitutes grew into unhealthy adults, fearful in new settings, socially awkward, and sexually unable to function. But the discovery that contact comfort has therapeutic benefits for the isolated infant has proved useful. For example, consider the predicament of a typical premature baby—kept in an incubator without physical contact and at risk for a host of problems later in life. Working in the maternity ward of a hospital, Saul Schanberg and Tiffany Field (1987) treated premature babies with forty-five minutes of body massage for ten days, then compared their progress to others not receiving massage. The two groups drank the same amount of formula, but the massaged infants gained 47 percent more weight; were more alert, active, and coordinated; and left the hospital an average of six days earlier—for a savings of $10,000 per infant in expenses. Similar interventions show that massage therapy has beneficial effects on premature infants, cocaine-exposed infants, and full-term infants born to depressed mothers. According to Field (2001), touch is a valuable therapeutic tool—not only for premature infants, but also for children and adults, many of whom are "touch-deprived."

**Styles of Attachment** Watch different parents and infants, and you'll notice that some attachments seem more intense than others. Is it possible to measure the intensity of this first relationship? How much of it depends on the parent and how much on the child? And does an infant's first attachment foreshadow his or her social relationships later in life? Developmental psychologists are actively researching questions such as these about the attachment process (Cassidy et al., 1999).

Drawing on evolutionary theory and on Harlow's studies with primates, psychiatrist John Bowlby (1969) theorized that infants are born with a repertoire of behaviors (like sucking, gazing, clinging, and crying) designed to elicit nurturance from parents and lay a foundation for a strong relationship. Bowlby (1988) further argued that this attachment provides a secure base from which children can explore their surroundings and develop their cognitive and social skills. The impact of this first relationship, he said, influences future relationships and lasts a lifetime.

Is it possible to measure the quality of the infant–parent attachment? To study the process systematically, Mary Ainsworth and her colleagues (1978) created the **strange-situation test** in which the parent (usually the mother) brings the baby into an unfamiliar laboratory playroom and proceeds through a routine whereby the parent and a stranger come and go according to a set script. Based on how the infants react to the separations and reunions with the parent, they are classified as having either a secure or an insecure attachment. Infants with a **secure attachment** wander and explore when the mother is present, react with distress when she leaves, and beam with sheer delight when she returns. These babies shower the returning parent with smiles, laughter, hugs, and kisses. Infants having an **insecure attachment** are classified into two types. Some are *anxious* and resistant, clinging to the mother,

**strange-situation test** A parent–infant "separation and reunion" procedure that is staged in a laboratory to test the security of a child's attachment.

**secure attachment** A parent–infant relationship in which the baby is secure when the parent is present, distressed by separation, and delighted by reunion.

**insecure attachment** A parent–infant relationship in which the baby clings to the parent, cries at separation, and reacts with anger or apathy to reunion.

crying when she leaves, and reacting with anger or indifference when she returns. These babies often push the returning mother away, stiffen up, squirm, or even cry when picked up. Others are more detached and *avoidant*, not caring if the mother leaves and ignoring her when she returns. Although a majority of babies worldwide are classified as having secure attachments, the percentage varies from culture to culture. In the United States, about two-thirds of infants tested are securely attached (Lamb et al., 1992; Van IJzendoorn & Kroonenberg, 1988)—and the classifications are generally the same whether the mother and child are tested in an unfamiliar setting or at home (Pederson & Moran, 1996).

It's hard to know for sure what causes a secure or insecure attachment. Clearly, parenting style is important. Mothers and fathers of securely attached babies are more sensitive to their needs, more affectionate, and more playful (Isabella & Belsky, 1991). The infant's temperament also plays a role, though, as securely attached babies are by nature less fussy and more easygoing than those who are not securely attached (Goldsmith & Lansky, 1987; Kagan et al., 1992). After several months, as you can imagine, the personalities of the parent and child become so tangled up that trying to separate the effects of one on the other is like trying to untie a twisted knot.

How important is this first relationship? Does a secure and trusting attachment provide a foundation for close friendships later in life? What is the long-term fate of an insecurely attached infant? According to Bowlby, secure and insecure infants form "internal working models" of attachment figures—and these models influence their perceptions of others and their relationships later in life. Indeed, research shows that infants classified as securely attached at twelve months are later more positive in their outlook toward others (Cassidy et al., 1996)—and have somewhat better peer relations in school (Schneider et al., 2001). Some researchers are further exploring the possibility that our attachments in infancy exert long-term effects on our romantic relationships as adults (Shaver & Clark, 1996). It's important, however, not to overstate the case by concluding that our future relationships are predetermined in the first year of life. The infant-to-child-to-adult correlation is far from perfect, and early attachments per se may not *cause* the differences that appear later in life. Responsive parents and easygoing infants may well continue in their positive ways long after the first-year attachment period has ended. These later interactions may prove to be just as important (Lamb, 1987; Schneider et al., 2001).

**The Day-Care Controversy**  If you've seen black-and-white reruns of *Leave It to Beaver, Father Knows Best,* or other TV shows produced in the 1950s, you are no doubt familiar with the image of the "traditional" all-American family: a working father and a mother who stays home to take care of the house and kids. The typical twenty-first-century American child grows up in a vastly different environment, consisting of either a single parent or two parents who both work outside the home. As a result, many infants in the United States spend much of their "attachment time" with babysitters, in day-care centers, or at home with other relatives. This scenario is not true of all societies. In China and Russia, mothers are encouraged to work full time while their children are cared for in state-supported institutions. In Israel, mothers who live on rural collective settlements called *kibbutzim* work on the farm while child-care specialists raise the children in groups. Does nonmaternal child care for infants disrupt the security of attachment? Should new parents—starting careers or struggling to make ends meet—worry about harmful long-term effects? As the research evidence mounts, professional opinion is divided.

Some psychologists fear that full-time maternal employment puts infants at risk for insecure attachments and minor adjustment problems. Studies using the strange-situation test show that day-care infants whose mothers work full time are somewhat

"He'll have abandonment issues."

more likely than home-raised infants to be insecurely attached (36 percent to 29 percent). As young children, they are also somewhat more aggressive with peers and less obedient with parents (Belsky, 2001; Goldberg et al., 1996). There is also evidence to suggest that babies of mothers who work full time during the first nine months score lower at three years old on a school-readiness test that measures their knowledge of colors, letters, shapes, numbers, and comparisons (Brooks-Gunn et al., 2002). On the positive side, day-care infants are more outgoing and independent. Studies in the United States, Norway, Sweden, New Zealand, and Great Britain also suggest that enriched infant day care does not have negative long-term effects on cognitive or social development (Andersson, 1992; Clarke-Stewart et al., 1994; Broberg et al., 1997; Harvey, 1999)—provided it is safe, healthy, stimulating, and supportive (Scarr, 1998).

To summarize, there is no "bottom line." Day care and home care seem to foster different personal styles, though neither is necessarily better for healthy development. If an only parent has to work or if both parents work outside the home, day care is a viable option that does not have harmful effects. What matters is not the *quantity* of time spent in one setting or the other but the *quality* of that time. Just as some parents are more attentive, loving, and stimulating than others, so too are some other child-care situations. Those that are spacious, well equipped, and adequately staffed to provide warm, individual attention and stimulating activities offer an excellent alternative to parents who work outside the home.

**Beyond Attachment** Attachment is just the first step in a long and complex relationship among mothers, fathers, sons, and daughters. At the age of two or three, children become more autonomous, independent, and even defiant. They stray from parents, test the limits of authority, and spend more time playing with siblings. Through TV and other cultural influences, boys and girls learn about sex roles and other stereotypes. The "terrible twos," sibling rivalry, the first day of school, outside friendships, homework, and the facts of life are among the challenges that confront the growing child. Through it all, the parents—their behavior, attitudes, and discipline styles, whether they are married or divorced, whether they value obedience or independence, whether they are strict or permissive, and so on—exert a marked influence on the child's social development (Bornstein, 1995).

**Peer Relationships** The mother–child attachment is only one factor in social development, as children form key relationships with grandparents, siblings, teachers, classmates, and neighbors. The older the child is, the more important are *horizontal relationships*—friendships among peers, or equals.

The growth of friendships may not pass through stages, but certain patterns are evident. At a year old, infants show little interest in each other and come together only if drawn to the same person or toy. At first, these interactions breed friction, but with experience infants learn to take turns and minimize conflict. By age two, children play near each other rather than alone. By four or five, they begin to prefer some playmates over others. Although these relationships are quickly formed, quickly broken, and based on convenience, they mark the beginning of what can be called friendship (Bukowski et al., 1996; Hartup & Stevens, 1999; Ladd, 1999).

It is interesting that almost all child relationships are between members of the same sex—not only in our culture but in others as well. Watch children on a school playground, and you will see that four-year-olds spend three times as much time with playmates of the same sex than of the opposite sex. By the age of six, this ratio is 11 to 1 (Maccoby & Jacklin, 1987). Why is gender segregation common? According to Eleanor Maccoby (1998), it's because boys and girls prefer different

"Come pick me up. This is going nowhere."

kinds of activities. Boys like competitive, rough-and-tumble play that takes up lots of space and involves large groups; girls like to congregate at home with one or two close friends. These differences may have a socializing impact on children: the more boys and girls play with same-sex peers, the more "boyish" and "girlish" their behavior becomes over time (Martin & Fabes, 2001).

Just as attachments inside the home are important to healthy social development, so is the formation of friendships outside the home. To study this aspect of development, researchers ask schoolchildren to rate themselves and to nominate the classmates they like the most and the least. They may also get ratings from teachers and parents, observe behavior firsthand, and combine the results for each child. Using these methods, researchers have identified four types of school-age children—compared to those in the average majority—based on their "sociometric" status among peers. As described by Andrew Newcomb and others (1993), children can be classified as *popular* (sociable, skilled, and liked), *rejected* (aggressive or withdrawn, lacking in social skills, and disliked), *controversial* (sociable but often aggressive, both liked and disliked), or *neglected* (less sociable and less aggressive than average, and seldom mentioned by peers).

As you might expect, popular children have the most friends (George & Hartmann, 1996) and derive social and emotional benefits of these friendships (Newcomb & Bagwell, 1995). In contrast, children who are rejected by classmates are the most "at risk." Longitudinal studies show that they are lonely and are more likely to drop out of school, have academic and drug problems, and have social-adjustment problems as adults (Parker & Asher, 1987; Asher & Coie, 1990). It's hard to know from these correlations if peer rejection is just part of a deeper problem or if it's the problem itself. And it's hard to know how possible it is to escape the peer rejection trap once caught in it. Some children, once rejected, are always rejected, but others manage over time to gain acceptance from peers. So what distinguishes the two groups? Marlene Sandstrom and John Coie (1999) studied forty-four rejected schoolchildren over a two-year period. They found that those who believed they were partly to blame for their social difficulties, who took part in extracurricular social activities, and who had concerned parents who played an active role in their social lives, were ultimately the most likely to gain acceptance.

Importantly, it also helps to have a friend. In a one-year longitudinal study of French-Canadian schoolchildren in the fourth and then fifth grades, Ernest Hodges and others (1999) identified those who, according to classmates, had been hit, pushed, threatened, called names, or otherwise victimized. They found that those victimized children who had a friend adjusted better and were less likely to behave in self-defeating ways. It's no wonder that Willard Hartup (1989) referred to childhood friendships as "developmental advantages" (p. 125).

## REVIEW QUESTIONS

■ *Describe the biological changes that occur during the first few years of life.*

■ *What four stages of cognitive development did Piaget propose? Describe the achievements and limitations that characterize each stage.*

■ *Describe the general sequence of language acquisition.*

■ *What does the research of Harry Harlow tell us about social development during infancy?*

■ *Distinguish between secure and insecure styles of attachment. What impact do they have on social development?*

## ADOLESCENCE

■ *Why is the timing of puberty important in the transition to adolescence?*
■ *What happens in parent–teenager relationships—and how do they change?*
■ *Are peer influences good or bad?*
■ *Why has adolescence been described as a period of "storm and stress"—and what's the evidence to support it?*

Many cultures have initiation rites to celebrate the passage from childhood to adulthood. Among the African Thongas, boys who reach puberty are beaten with clubs, shaved, stripped, exposed to cold, forced to eat unsavory foods, circumcised,

*Many cultures celebrate the passage from childhood to adulthood. Dressed in buckskin and jewelry, an Apache girl is honored for her first menstrual period in a four-day ritual (left). At age thirteen, Jewish boys achieve their manhood in a religious ceremony known as a bar mitzvah (right).*

and secluded for three months. Among certain Native American groups of North America, girls who menstruate for the first time are bathed, their bodies are painted red by older women, and they are isolated for four days. The ritual may vary, but most cultures have ways of marking adolescence. Confirmation, bar mitzvah, and the move into junior high school are some of the ways that Westerners recognize this transitional time of life (Cohen, 1964).

**Adolescence** is to adulthood what infancy is to childhood: the dawn of a new era, like a second birth. Beginning with a biological event (puberty) and culminating in a social event (independence from parents), adolescence in the United States corresponds roughly to the teen years, thirteen to twenty. No longer a child but not yet an adult, the adolescent is in an important transitional phase of life—a time characterized by biological, cognitive, and social changes (Steinberg & Morris, 2001; Adams & Berzonsky, 2003).

## PUBERTY

The biological motor of adolescence is **puberty,** the gradual onset of sexual maturation brought on by rising hormone levels—estrogen and progesterone in females, and testosterone in males. Plus or minus two years, girls reach puberty between the ages of eleven and thirteen, and boys between the ages of thirteen and fifteen. This sex difference can be seen in the rapid growth that propels children to almost their full adult height. Look at Figure 9.15, and you will see that the growth spurt begins a bit earlier for girls but lasts longer for boys, eventually leaving adult men an average of five inches taller than women. For girls, puberty is highlighted by the first menstrual period, called **menarche.** A girl's development during puberty is a continuous process, and her first period is only a single event in a continuum of hormonal and psychological changes that take place (Dorn et al., 1999). Still, it is often a memorable event in a girl's life, one that she experiences with a mixture of pride, nervousness, and embarrassment (Greif & Ulman, 1982).

A girl's reaction to puberty is influenced in part by her age. When Anne Petersen (1984) interviewed hundreds of adolescents, she found that girls who mature early

**adolescence**   The period of life from puberty to adulthood, corresponding roughly to the ages of thirteen to twenty.

**puberty**   The onset of adolescence, as evidenced by rapid growth, rising levels of sex hormones, and sexual maturity.

**menarche**   A girl's first menstrual period.

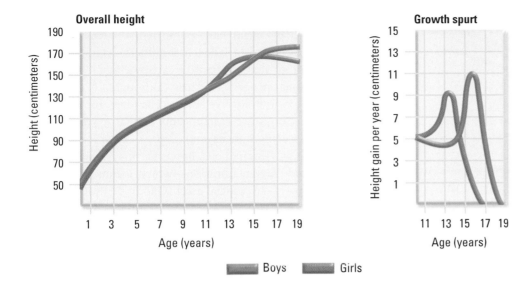

**FIGURE 9.15**  **Adolescent growth spurts in height**

tend to be dissatisfied with their size, weight, and figure. A mature seventh-grade girl may tower over classmates and get teased about her appearance. As shown in Figure 9.16, girls who reach puberty early rather than "on time" or late are the most negative about their own body image and are more likely to diet and develop eating disorders (Graber et al., 1994).

Early puberty presents additional adjustment problems. Girls who attain menarche early become more likely to spend time with older peers, have sex at an earlier age, get lower grades, and engage in norm-breaking behaviors (Stattin & Magnusson, 1990). They are also more likely to become depressed and abuse drugs (Stice et al., 2001). Early onset is particularly problematic for girls with a history of behavior problems. In a longitudinal study in New Zealand, Avshalom Caspi and Terrie Moffitt (1991) collected information from 348 girls nine to fifteen years old, their parents, and their teachers. They found that those who had difficulties before puberty *and* who reached it early were the most likely adolescents to get into trouble (such as getting drunk, stealing items from classmates, getting into fights, sneaking into R-rated movies, cutting classes, and making prank phone calls).

It's interesting that the timing of menarche is highly influenced by environmental factors. In the 1800s, the average American girl didn't begin to menstruate until the age of seventeen. As a likely result of improved nutrition, the average girl now menstruates at a much younger age, twelve or thirteen. In fact, recent pediatric studies in the United States show that today's girls are starting puberty even younger, typically at eleven (Herman-Giddens et al., 1997; Rosenfield et al., 2000)—a trend that concerns parents and pediatricians, and prompted *Time Magazine* to run a cover story, "Teens before their time" (Lemonick, 2000). There are, however, vast individual differences. Models, gymnasts, and ballet dancers who exercise hard, diet, and lack body fat tend to reach menarche later in their teens (Brooks-Gunn & Warren, 1985). At the other extreme, an alarming number of girls are reaching puberty as young as eight or nine years old—particularly if they are overweight (Kaplowitz et al., 2000; Wang, 2002).

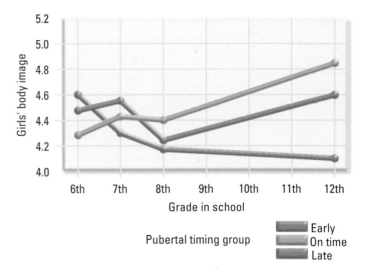

**FIGURE 9.16**  **The timing of puberty and body images in girls**
On ratings of their own body image, early-maturing girls are more negative than others.

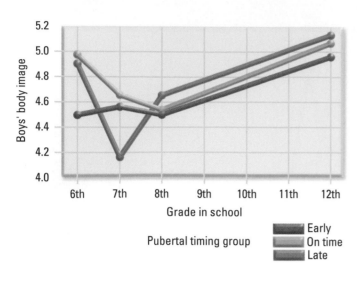

**FIGURE 9.17 The timing of puberty and body images in boys**
On ratings of their own body image, late-maturing boys are the most negative, but they recover quickly.

*"The teenage brain is a work in progress."*
—SANDRA WITELSON

For boys, puberty is marked by the growth of the penis and testes, accompanied by facial hair, pubic hair, increased muscle mass, a lowered voice, and broadened shoulders. Akin to menarche, the high point of male puberty is a boy's first ejaculation, which occurs at about the age of fourteen (although it is not until a year later that the semen holds live sperm cells ready for reproduction). As with girls, boys are reaching puberty at a younger age than in the past (Herman-Giddens et al., 2001)—with some maturing earlier than others. Among boys, however, this is a wholly positive experience, and early maturation—which means being taller and stronger than peers—is a social asset (Gaddis & Brooks-Gunn, 1985; Stein & Reiser, 1994). Consistently, research has shown that early-maturing males excel in sports, are popular among peers, take on leadership roles, and are more self-confident than those who mature later (Jones, 1957; Petersen, 1988). As shown in Figure 9.17, boys who reach puberty early have a generally positive body image during these early years (Petersen, 1984).

## COGNITIVE DEVELOPMENT

Paralleling the physical growth spurt brought on by puberty is what might be called a cognitive growth spurt. You may recall Piaget's observation that adolescents are capable of logic and abstract reasoning—hallmarks of the *formal operational* stage of cognitive development. This capacity for abstraction spurs teenagers to think critically and to challenge parents and societal norms. Eliot Turiel (1983) found that at the age of twelve or thirteen, adolescents begin to see various social conventions—for example, appropriate clothing, hairstyle, or the proper way to address a teacher—as arbitrary and unreasonable.

Despite the significant cognitive gains made at this stage, it's important to keep in mind that even as young adolescents start to flex their newly strengthened intellectual muscles, they are still somewhat *egocentric* in the way they think—and are highly self-conscious. Research shows that eighth- and ninth-graders always seem to think they are on "center stage," the focus of everyone's attention and unique among their peers (Elkind, 1967; Elkind & Bowen, 1979).

**Moral Reasoning** According to Piaget (1932), the adolescent's capacity for abstraction gives rise to a more mature form of **moral reasoning.** Building on the idea that moral reasoning requires cognitive sophistication, Lawrence Kohlberg (1981, 1984) argued that adolescence is a particularly rich time of life for moral development. Kohlberg presented stories containing moral dilemmas to children, adolescents, and adults and asked them how these dilemmas should be resolved. To illustrate, consider the following classic story:

> In Europe, a woman was near death from cancer. One drug might save her, a form of radium that a druggist in the same town had recently discovered. The druggist was charging $2,000—10 times what the drug cost him to make. The sick woman's husband, Heinz, went to everyone he knew to borrow the money, but he could only get together about half of what it cost. He told the druggist that his wife was dying and asked him to sell it cheaper or let him pay later. But the druggist said, "No." The husband got desperate and broke into the man's store to steal the drug for his wife. (Kohlberg, 1969, p. 379)

**moral reasoning** The way people think about and try to solve moral dilemmas.

What do you think: Should Heinz have stolen the drug? Were his actions morally right or wrong, and why? Based on responses to stories like this one, Kohlberg proposed that people advance through three levels of moral thought, further divided into six stages. First, there is a *preconventional* level, in which moral dilemmas are resolved in ways that satisfy self-serving motives—so an act is moral if it enables someone to avoid punishment or obtain reward. Second is a *conventional* level, in which moral dilemmas are resolved in ways that reflect the laws of the land or norms set by parents and other sources of authority. Thus, an act is moral if it meets with social approval or maintains the social order. Third, adolescents and adults who attain Piaget's formal operational stage of cognitive development may also reach a *postconventional* level of moral thought, one that is based on abstract principles such as equality, justice, and the value of life. At this level, an act is moral if it affirms one's own conscience—even if it violates the law.

Is this theory of moral development valid? Over the years, it has drawn an enormous amount of attention, support, and criticism. To Kohlberg's credit, he and others have found that as children and adolescents mature, they climb his moral ladder in the predicted order, step by step, with periods of transition in between steps (Colby et al., 1983; Walker, 1989; Thoma & Rest, 1999). Research shows that although most seven- to ten-year-olds are preconventional in their moral thinking, many thirteen- to sixteen-year-olds reason in conventional terms, and few adolescents—or even mature adults, for that matter—resolve moral issues on a postconventional level (see Figure 9.18).

There are three criticisms of Kohlberg's theory. The first is that it is culturally biased. This is partly true. John Snarey (1985) reviewed studies in twenty-eight countries and found that most children and adolescents advanced at the same rate and in the same sequence through the first two levels. He also found, however, that only educated middle-class adults from urban societies consistently exhibited postconventional forms of morality. In Kohlberg's dilemmas, many non-Westerners—including Tibetan Buddhist monks and respected village leaders from Papua New Guinea—do not reason at this third level. Why? In cultures that value traditions, rules, and authority over individualism and personal rights, conventional moral reasoning is common and desirable.

A second criticism is that the model is gender biased. When Kohlberg first constructed his dilemmas, he tested only males and used their responses as a moral yardstick. Yet according to Carol Gilligan (1982), women address moral issues "in a different voice." Concerned more about compassion for others than about abstract rules, the female voice may be different—but not morally inferior. Gilligan's point has some intuitive appeal, but it lacks empirical support. Public opinion pollsters do find that women care more than men about social issues and relations. But moral development researchers find that women and men obtain similar scores on Kohlberg's dilemmas (Rest, 1986; Walker, 1984). Also contradicting the assumption that people resolve moral dilemmas in set ways, as defined either by Kohlberg or Gilligan, is that men and women are flexible in their reasoning. The kinds of moral judgments we make in real life depend on the situations we're in and the kinds of dilemmas we face (Krebs et al., 1991; Wark & Krebs, 1996).

Finally, many developmental psychologists have argued that Kohlberg's model is limited because morality consists of more than just an ability to think about hypothetical dilemmas in ways that are intellectually sophisticated. There are two criticisms of Kohlberg's model in this regard. John Haidt (2001) argues that people

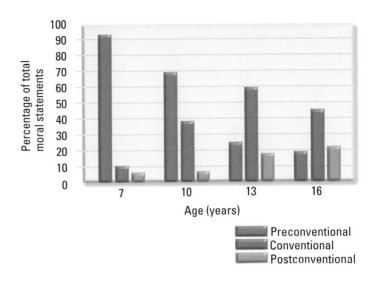

**FIGURE 9.18   Levels of moral reasoning**
On standard moral dilemmas, most seven- to ten-year-olds are preconventional in their reasoning, whereas most thirteen- to sixteen-year-olds are conventional. Very few participants resolved these dilemmas on a postconventional level (Colby et al., 1983).

**empathy**  A feeling of joy for others who are happy and distress for those who are in pain.

**identity crisis**  An adolescent's struggle to establish a personal identity, or self-concept.

make moral judgments intuitively, in a process that is fast, effortless, and without awareness, like a learned reflex—not through slow, hard, and conscious process of cognitive reasoning. A second criticism concerns the assumption that moral reasoning breeds moral conduct. But are postconventional thinkers kinder, more caring, or more virtuous in their daily affairs than those lower on the cognitive ladder? Moral actions speak louder than words, which is why William Damon (1999) asks, "Regardless of how children develop their initial system of values, the key question is: What makes them live up to their ideals?" (p. 75).

According to Martin Hoffman (1984), morality is rooted in **empathy,** a capacity to feel joy for others who are happy and distress for those who are in pain—as seen in a toddler he observed who offered his mother his security blanket when she seemed upset. By this account, morality is present early in life. In the crib, infants often cry when they hear another baby crying. They feel no pain of their own, yet they are distressed, a possible sign of empathy. At less than two years old, babies have been observed giving food, toys, hugs, and kisses to others who are visibly distressed—again, a possible sign of empathy (Zahn-Waxler et al., 1992). At the sight of a homeless person curled up on the floor of a bus station, even the young preconventional child reacts with sorrow and a desire to help (Damon, 1988; Eisenberg & Mussen, 1989).

It's a sad and ironic postscript that Kohlberg—who had a chronic parasitic infection that caused him excruciating stomach pain—committed suicide in 1987, before his sixtieth birthday. He had discussed his predicament with a close friend and concluded that someone with social responsibilities to others ought morally to go on. But overcome with pain and deeply depressed, he drowned himself in Boston Harbor (Hunt, 1993).

## SOCIAL AND PERSONAL DEVELOPMENT

To many people, the word *teenager* is synonymous with floppy jeans, loud music, pierced body parts, long phone conversations, and sleeping past noon. The teen years are a curious time of life. Absorbed in closer-than-ever friendships, newly aroused by sexual urges, needing to fit in and yet wanting to stand out, feeling caught between parents and peers, and anxious about the future, teens are fraught with mixed emotions. The highs are high, the lows are low, and the changes are frequent.

According to Erik Erikson (1963), all people pass through a series of life stages, each marked by a "crisis" that has to be resolved in order for healthy development to occur. During the transitional period of adolescence, the central task is to form an *identity*, or self-concept—hence, the term **identity crisis.** Some teenagers pass through this stage easily—clear about who they are, what values they hold, and what they want out of life. Others drift in confusion as they struggle to break from their parents, find the right friends, establish their sexual orientation, and set career goals for the future. For Erikson, this identity crisis is best described by a sign he once saw in a cowboy bar: "I ain't what I ought to be, I ain't what I'm going to be, but I ain't what I was" (1959, p. 93).

Whatever identity issues adolescents have, there are three aspects of social and personal development that all must come to grips with: parent relationships, peer influences, and sexuality.

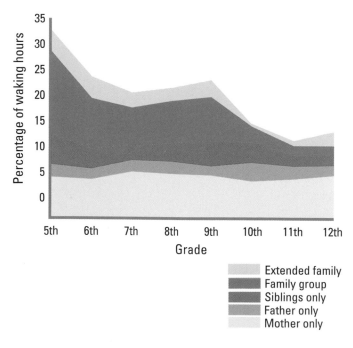

**FIGURE 9.19  Patterns of adolescent "disengagement" from the family**
This study revealed that over the course of adolescent development, the amount of time spent with the family decreased by an average of 2.74 percent per year. As you can see, there was not a similar decline in time spent alone with parents (Larson et al., 1996).

**Parent Relationships**  For the mother or father of a cuddly new baby, it's hard to imagine that the intense emotional bond could ever be broken, or even cracked. To the parent of a teenager, it's no longer so hard to imagine. Whether the topic is a blaring stereo, school grades, money, or dirty laundry, it seems that parents and adolescents engage in a power struggle, involved in one squabble after another. As described by the mother of an eleven-year-old daughter, "It's like being bitten to death by ducks" (Steinberg, 1987, p. 36).

As children mature, what happens to their relationship with parents, and what is the effect? Through questionnaires and interviews, and by observing interactions in the laboratory and in the home, researchers are coming to answer these questions. What emerges from these studies is a portrait of parents and teenagers characterized by two changes. First, coinciding with the onset of puberty and physical maturation, there is a rise in tension between twelve- and thirteen-year-olds asserting their independence and parents, especially the mother. Young adolescents and parents argue about twice a week—but over routine household matters such as taking out the garbage, not about explosive issues such as sex, religion, or politics (Smetana, 1988). Despite cultural differences, similar interaction patterns have been observed between Chinese parents and adolescents in Hong Kong (Yau & Smetana, 1996).

A second change is that adolescents undergo a period marked by both *disengagement* and *transformation* in their family relationships. Reed Larson and his colleagues (1996) studied more than two hundred Chicago-area boys and girls from fifth to eighth grades, then returned four years later when they were in high school. For one week at a time, each subject carried an electronic pager and was signaled several times a day during normal waking hours. Whenever they were signaled, the subjects had to indicate where they were, whom they were with, what they were doing, and how they felt. Together, the students provided a total of 16,477 reports. There were two key results. First, there was a steady decline in the sheer amount of waking time spent with family members—from 35 percent in the fifth grade to 14 percent in the twelfth grade. Interestingly, the students spent the same number of hours alone with mothers and fathers but "disengaged" from family group situations, siblings, and other relatives (see Figure 9.19). Second, there were marked changes in the way the students felt during family interactions. Most felt worse during the early adolescent years. But boys then became positively "transformed" within the family setting during the ninth and tenth grades, and girls followed suit in the eleventh and twelfth grades (see Figure 9.20).

It may seem as if parents and their young teens are at war or in a state of truce, like government and rebel forces, but most research shows that the so-called generation gap has been blown out of proportion. To be sure, there are minor skirmishes and some disengagement—which is hard on parents while it lasts, increasing stress and straining marital relations (Silverberg & Steinberg, 1990). But typically there is peace, and seldom does the bickering leave a permanent scar on the family. Indeed, most teenagers say they admire their parents and accept their political and religious values (Adelson, 1986; Offer & Schonert-Reichl, 1992).

It's clear that the onset of puberty coincides with various changes and transformations. It's not clear, however, what to make of this correlation. From an evolutionary perspective, Laurence Steinberg

*"When I was a boy of 14, my father was so ignorant I could hardly stand to have the man around. But when I got to be 21, I was astonished at how much he had learnt in 7 years."*

—MARK TWAIN

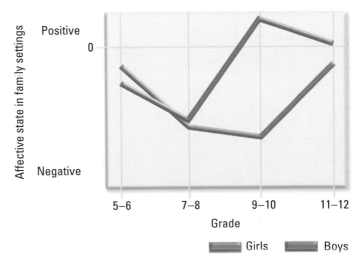

**FIGURE 9.20**   **Patterns of adolescent "transformation" within the family**
Adolescents in the seventh and eighth grades felt worse while with the family, but affect was better among ninth- and tenth-grade boys and eleventh- and twelfth-grade girls (Larson et al., 1996).

"Quit parentalizing me!"

(1989) argues that tensions within the family are triggered not by the adolescent's chronological age but by puberty. If it comes early, so does conflict. If puberty is late, then the conflict is delayed. To clarify the complex link between the biology of adolescence and social relations at home, Steinberg notes that in many primate species living in the wild—gibbons and chimpanzees, for example—it's common for males and females at puberty to depart their group, search elsewhere for a mate, and reproduce outside the family. Even among humans, there is historical precedence for separating parents and teenagers. Before many countries became industrialized, adolescents lived in a state of semiautonomy (living with parents but working to earn money), and in some cultures they were even subject to "extrusion" (sent to live in other households).

The problem that exists today may stem from the fact that sexually mature offspring spend more time in the company of parents than ever before. A hundred years ago, adolescents left home at sixteen or seventeen, roughly the age they became mature. Now adolescents reach puberty at twelve or thirteen but live at home until the eighteen or older. So what does this tell us about parent–child relations? According to Steinberg (1987), everyone should feel reassured: "Telling parents that fighting over taking out the garbage is related to the reproductive fitness of the species provides little solace—and doesn't help get the garbage out of the house, either. But parents need to recognize that quarreling with a teenager over mundane matters may be a normal part of family life during adolescence" (p. 39).

Although the biological changes that come with puberty may play a role in parent–adolescent relations, the "chill" often felt in the home is not universal or inevitable. Many years ago, anthropologists Margaret Mead (1928) and Ruth Benedict (1959) observed that adolescents do not disengage from the family in all cultures. Confirming the point, Alice Schlegel and Herbert Barry (1991) studied 186 preindustrial societies and found that the more traditional a society is, the less tension exists between parents and their adolescent sons and daughters. Apparently, in the more traditional cultures, adolescents are not expected to assert their autonomy, so conflicts over this issue do not arise. There are also differences among Western countries, depending on the cultural emphasis placed on families (Claes, 1998).

As children reach adolescence, peer relationships become more important and developmentally influential, relative to parents.

**Peer Influences** Another important aspect of adolescent social development is the heightened significance of peer groups and relations outside the home—long phone conversations, flirtation, and dating. For the first time, the child becomes primarily oriented to the outside world and may not even want to be seen with parents. Compared to childhood friendships, adolescent relationships are highly intimate. It's not unusual for best friends to talk freely about their thoughts and feelings and to reveal some of their deepest secrets (Berndt, 1996).

Compared to the gender segregation found in childhood friendships, adolescents begin for the first time to explore friendships with peers of the opposite sex. In the electronic pager study described earlier, the children exhibited a steady increase—from grades five through eight to grades nine through twelve—in the amount of time they spent thinking about, and then being alone with, members of the opposite sex (Richards et al., 1998). They even make the distinction that adults do between opposite-sex friends and romantic heterosexual "boyfriends" and "girlfriends" (Furman & Shaffer, 1999).

Although most adolescents retain the fundamental values of their parents, they look to peers for guidance on how to dress or wear their hair, what music to listen to, how to speak, and how to behave in ways that are acceptable. As social beings, we all have a tendency to conform. Is this tendency more pronounced in adolescence? The answer is *yes,* especially in the early stages. Thomas Berndt (1979) asked students in grades three, six, nine, and twelve how they'd react if their friends tried to influence them to see a certain movie, go bowling, help a new kid on the block, or cheat on a test. The result: Conformity rose steadily with age, peaked in the ninth grade, then declined. The tendency to conform is much weaker for actions that are immoral or illegal, but younger adolescents are the most likely followers, wanting desperately to fit in (Brown et al., 1986; Gavin & Furman, 1989).

Whether conforming to a new generation means eating live goldfish, shaving the head, piercing an ear, watching MTV, or burning tattoos onto the skin, conformity satisfies important needs in a teenager's life. Importantly, the socializing influence of peers—particularly close friends—can have both positive and negative effects on teenagers (Berndt, 1996). In a one-year longitudinal study, one thousand high-school students and their friends were asked about their school grades as well as their use of alcohol, marijuana, and other drugs. The result: Even after taking into account the fact that people are drawn to others who are similar, teenagers became more like their friends over time. After one year, those whose friends did well in school raised their grades more than others who started with a similar academic record but whose friends did not do well. On the negative side, those whose friends were frequent drug users increased their own usage—again, compared to peers who were similar at first but whose friends were less frequent users. Interestingly, students with warmer and more demanding parents were less vulnerable to the influence of friends (Mounts & Steinberg, 1995).

**Sexuality**   Triggered by rising hormone levels and physical maturation, adolescent boys and girls are sexual beings, curious and easily aroused. Whether teenagers act on these impulses, however, depends, in part, on social factors. National surveys of sexual practices—beginning with those conducted by Kinsey and his associates (1948, 1953)—have shown that there has been a constant 50 to 70 percent rate of sexual activity among boys but that the number of sexually active girls climbed from a low of 10 percent in the 1940s to a high of over 50 percent in the 1980s. Yet since that time, sex rates have declined—to 48 percent among teenage boys and 43 percent among teenage girls (Brener et al., 2002).

Although American teenagers are sexually more active today than at the time of Kinsey's survey, they are not always better informed about the health risks or more diligent in the use of contraceptives. In the United States, more than 80 percent of pregnancies of girls under eighteen are unplanned and unwanted (Brown & Eisenberg, 1995). All too often, the result is an abortion, a hasty and unhappy marriage, or an out-of-wedlock birth that forces the mother out of school and plunges her into poverty. Thankfully, after many years of rising teenage pregnancy rates, the numbers in the United States are on the decline (National Center for Health Statistics, 1999).

Unwanted teenage pregnancies may be part of a bigger problem: that adolescents are risk takers. Across a range of problem behaviors—such as smoking, drinking, abusing drugs, driving too fast, or having unsafe and unprotected sex—it seems that teenagers are more reckless in health-related matters than adults (Jessor, 1998; Lightfoot, 1999). Why does adolescence bring risk taking? Why, for example, did 63 percent of female college students surveyed and 57 percent of college men admit

*Debunking the Myth*

# THAT ADOLESCENCE BRINGS INEVITABLE STORM AND STRESS

Following Aristotle, Socrates, and Hall, most people seem to think that adolescence is a time of emotional turmoil. Christy Buchanan and Grayson Holmbeck (1998) surveyed mothers, fathers, and college students, and found that they rated the typical adolescent as more likely than the typical school child to have problems with moodiness, anxiousness, confusion, insecurity, and depression. The stereotype is clear, but is it accurate?

To some extent, it is. In a massive cross-national study, Daniel Offer and others (1981) gave questionnaires to more than twenty thousand junior- and senior-high-school students from different countries and found that most were happy and well adjusted. That was the good news. The bad news was that roughly 20 percent did develop emotional problems—which is high compared to younger children and roughly the same percentage as in adults. In this survey, teenagers thirteen to nineteen years old also responded to statements from a self-image questionnaire. Some of the results are shown in Table 9.2. Other researchers have found that adolescents have greater mood swings, from high to low, than their parents do, and they often feel lonely, embarrassed, and self-conscious (Larson & Richards, 1993). There's also a slight "midadolescence peak" in rates of depression, with roughly a third of adolescents being depressed at a given point in time (Petersen et al., 1993). In some cases, the tragic result is an attempted suicide (Lewinsohn et al., 1994).

So what are we to conclude? Despite the transitional growing pains and mood swings that accompany adolescence, turmoil is not inevitable or widespread (Buchanan et al., 1992). Storm and stress is not a myth without foundation. But the popular image of the prototypical disturbed adolescent is exaggerated—much like a cartoon caricature. As Arnett (1999) put it, "Storm and stress in adolescence is not something written indelibly into the human life course. On the contrary, there are cultural differences in storm and stress, and within cultures there are individual differences" (p. 324).

It's important for parents, teachers, and others to have accurate beliefs about adolescent mental health. Many unhappy teenagers do grow up to become maladjusted later in life. Offer (1998) retested adult men who had been in his study thirty years earlier as teenagers, and he found that those identified as having mental-health problems at the ages of fourteen and nineteen were later more likely to have problems in their forties. For that reason, he has urged us all to abandon the old storm-and-stress view of youth and to understand that a teenager who cries for help may be in real trouble, not just "passing through a stage."

### TABLE 9.2   COMMON CONCERNS AMONG THE WORLD'S TEENAGERS

**PERCENTAGE WHO AGREE**

|  | Australia | Bangladesh | Hungary | Israel | Italy | Japan | Taiwan | Turkey | United States | West Germany | International Average |
|---|---|---|---|---|---|---|---|---|---|---|---|
| I feel so lonely | 22 | 43 | 14 | 17 | 20 | 39 | 33 | 32 | 18 | 11 | 25 |
| I frequently feel sad | 27 | 36 | 24 | 28 | 25 | 55 | 26 | 34 | 25 | 17 | 29 |
| My parents are ashamed of me | 11 | 7 | 4 | 3 | 4 | 15 | 10 | 08 | 7 | 2 | 07 |

*Source:* Test items by D. Offer, E. Ostrov, & I. Howard (1981). *The adolescent: A psychological self-portrait.* New York: Basic Books.

that neither they nor their partners had used a contraceptive the first time they had sex (Darling et al., 1992)? One theory is that recklessness and delinquency stems from the fact that the early onset of puberty makes adolescents biological adults before they are accepted into the adult world. As such, they engage in sex, alcohol, and other "adult" activities available to them (Moffitt, 1993). An alternative theory is that adolescents engage in risk-taking behaviors not to join the adult world but to set themselves apart from it, as a form of rebellion (Harris, 1995).

Offering an important perspective, Frederick Gibbons, Meg Gerrard, and their colleagues (1998) find that one key to understanding adolescents' risk taking is to realize that they often do not intend or plan these behaviors, but rather find themselves having to react to social situations that call for risk. The party where cigarettes are passed around, the friend who wants to drive home after too many beers, and the date who is eager to have sex are the kinds of situations that often lead adolescents to engage in behaviors they did not plan. As one sixteen-year-old girl put it about her first sexual experience, "The first time, it was like totally out of the blue. . . I mean, you don't know it's coming, so how are you to be prepared?" (Stark, 1986, p. 28). When it comes to sex, of course, it's possible that teenagers do not make the necessary arrangements because they feel guilty about their desires. After all, if you're ambivalent, it's easier to justify getting "swept off your feet" and "carried away" than it is to have premeditated sex (Gerrard, 1987; Byrne et al., 1993).

## ADOLESCENCE AND MENTAL HEALTH

Aristotle referred to youth as "heated by Nature as drunken men by wine." Socrates saw adolescents as inclined to "contradict their parents" and "tyrannize their teachers." In 1904, G. Stanley Hall—the founder of the American Psychological Association—described adolescence as a time of "storm and stress." Hall's remarks echoed a long-held belief, still popular today, that teenagers by nature suffer inner conflict and turmoil. Mood swings, identity crises, anxiety, rebelliousness, depression, drug use, and suicide are some of the stereotypic images of the adolescent overcome by raging hormones.

Is there any truth to this image? According to Jeffrey Arnett (1999), there are three perceived sources of difficulty: conflict with parents, risk-taking behavior, and mood disruptions. We've seen that there is some truth to the first two claims, though neither is inevitable. But what about mood disruptions and the notion that adolescents are in a state of distress—emotionally vulnerable and prone to serious mental-health problems? Research shows that this image is exaggerated. (See *Debunking the Myth that Adolescence Brings Inevitable Storm and Stress.*)

### REVIEW QUESTIONS

- *How do the consequences of early maturation differ for boys and girls?*

- *Compare and contrast Kohlberg's three stages of moral development.*

- *Describe the changes in parent relationships, peer relationships, and sexuality that characterize adolescence.*

## ADULTHOOD AND OLD AGE

- *What is the human life span, and how does it differ from the life expectancy?*
- *What physical changes mark adult development?*
- *In memory and intelligence, do people become more capable with age, or less?*
- *What's the evidence for a midlife crisis and for despair in old age?*

For many years, it was assumed that our individual life scripts were written in infancy and childhood, waiting only to be acted out during our adult years. Freud felt that personality is largely formed by the sixth birthday, whereas Piaget claimed that the ultimate stage of cognitive development typically blossoms with puberty. These narrow views of the early years of life as critical may well describe changes in height, whereby early growth spurts are followed by a leveling off in adulthood. But such views do not yield an accurate picture when it comes to the full range of biological, cognitive, and social development. In this section, we will see that even though the early years are in some ways formative, each of us continues to change

*There are no bright lines separating the ages of adulthood. In 2002, at the age of 53, Bruce Springsteen and his E Street Band appeared before more than a million fans in cities throughout North America and Europe. Despite the "Boss's" age, these high-energy performances lasted two and a half to three hours.*

**life span** The maximum age possible for members of a given species.

**life expectancy** The number of years that an average member of a species is expected to live.

in important ways when we mature in our adulthood and old age. As our ancestors told us, development is a lifelong process.

In all species of animals, there is a maximum **life span** that sets an upper limit on the oldest possible age of an organism under ideal conditions. Scientists have long held that just as a time clock has twenty-four hours in a day, our biological clocks contain a finite number of years in a life—about 120 among humans. Although this assumption still prevails, it is becoming a subject of controversy. In recent years, some biologists have managed to extend the life span of fruit flies, roundworms, and mice through selective breeding, genetic manipulation, and alterations in diet (Fossell, 1996; Hayflick, 1996; Medina, 1996).

In most species, the **life expectancy**—the actual number of years lived by an average member—is shorter than the maximum life span. On average, guinea pigs live to the tender age of 3; dogs, 10 to 15; chimpanzees, 15 to 20; elephants, 30 to 40; and eagles, 105 (Lansing, 1959). Among humans, the life expectancy is influenced not only by genetics but also by personality, nutrition, health practices, the environment, health care, and other factors. The average Roman in the year 1 CE lived to the age of 22. In the United States, the life expectancy rose from 36 in the nineteenth century to 47 in the year 1900 and to 76.9 in 2000. Women outlive men by an average of five to six years.

Cultural variation is also common. According to the World Health Organization, the average life expectancy is 38 in Mozambique, 40 in Sierra Leone, 53 in Bolivia, 58 in India, 69 in Mexico, 80 in Sweden, and 81 in Japan. In the United States, there is also a racial gap, as white Americans outlive African Americans—on average, 77 years compared to 72.

## PHYSICAL CHANGES IN ADULTHOOD

At birth, a human infant has more than 100 billion brain cells. From that point, however, there is a steady process of attrition: Neurons die without replacement, and those that survive thin out. However, not all parts of the brain age at the same rate. In the brainstem, which controls many simple reflexes, there is little or no cell loss over time. Yet in the motor cortex and frontal lobes, which control motor and cognitive activity, thousands of neurons a day are lost, especially after the age of fifty. By the time people are eighty, the brain weighs 8 percent less than it did during the peak of adulthood. What's fascinating about this aspect of development is that the aging brain is simultaneously in a process of growth and decline. A newborn has a surplus of brain cells, so maturation involves the death of cells that are not used, coupled with the formation of new synaptic connections among those that remain. As we saw in Chapter 2, the human brain has great plasticity, a capacity to change as a result of experience. In the mature adult, then, more can be accomplished with less (Creasey & Rapoport, 1985; Scheibel, 1995).

**The Adult Years** In addition to changes within the brain and nervous system, aging brings other physical changes to adults. Muscle strength, heart and lung capacity, speed of reflexes, and vision increase during the twenties, peak at about the age of thirty, then gradually start to decline. Also at that time, metabolism slows down, leading men and women to lose their youthful physique and to gain weight. Does this mean that young adults who rely on physical skills are over the hill by the age of thirty? No, it depends on one's diet, health, and exercise habits and on the physical demands of a particular activity.

Baseball statistician Bill James and others (1998), as well as Richard Schulz and his colleagues (1994), analyzed the career records of major-league ballplayers and found that batters and pitchers peaked at the age of twenty-six. Football, basketball, and tennis players follow a similar age pattern. Yet world-class sprinters and swimmers peak in their teens and early twenties, and professional bowlers and golfers reach the top of their game in their thirties. It all depends on whether a sport requires speed and agility, endurance, or power—which decline at different rates. Age sets limits on what the body can do, but adults who keep in shape can minimize the effects of aging and stretch performance beyond the average.

One inevitable biological event for women is **menopause,** the end of menstruation, which signals the end of fertility. At about the age of fifty, a woman's ovaries stop producing estrogen. The most common symptoms of this change are "hot flashes" (sudden feelings of warmth usually in the upper body) and sometimes profuse sweating, dizziness, nausea, and headaches. Some women get moody, depressed, or anxious, but most are not terribly bothered by menopause. In a survey of more than eight thousand middle-age women, 70 percent said they felt relieved, liberated, or unaffected by the change (McKinlay et al., 1987). Among those who do suffer, it's not clear whether the experience is linked to lowered estrogen levels or other aspects of aging, such as a fear of illness or the children leaving home. Consistently, large-scale studies have shattered the myth that menopause is a traumatic negative event in a woman's life (Matthews, 1992).

For men, there is no biological equivalent to menopause. Testosterone levels (which peak during adolescence) diminish only gradually, and even though the sperm count may drop, there is little loss of fertility. As with some women, some men pass through a difficult midlife period in which they question their marriage and career, worry about their health and sexual vigor, and feel frustrated about goals they did not achieve. For men and women alike, aging is not just a biological process but a psychological one as well.

**menopause**   The end of menstruation and fertility.

*"When 1,200 Americans were asked when middle age begins, 41% said it's when you worry about health care, 42% said it was when the last child moves out, and 46% said it was when you no longer recognize the names of music groups on the radio."*
—NEWSWEEK (1992)

## Old Age

As people enter their sixties and seventies, the cumulative effects of age begin to show, and the process seems to accelerate. Inside the body, brain cells die at a faster rate, the reflexes continue to slow, muscles continue to lose strength, the immune system begins to fail, bones become more brittle, joints stiffen, and the sense of taste and smell is reduced. Resulting from a steady loss of visual acuity, many older people are farsighted—and some have difficulty adapting to brightness or darkness. There are also noticeable auditory losses, as many older people report having trouble hearing high-pitched sounds, normal speech, and background noises. Perhaps most obvious are the effects of chronological age on appearance—including the wrinkles, stooped posture, thinned white hair, and shrinkage, as the average man loses about an inch in height, the average woman two inches. These physical changes and others are reviewed in two comprehensive books on the aging process (Birren & Schaie, 2001; Whitbourne, 2002).

When Ponce de León left Spain in 1513 and landed in what is now the state of Florida, he was looking for the legendary and mythical fountain of youth. Biologists say that it's impossible to reverse the aging process, but can it be slowed? Can longevity be increased? According to current estimates, only one in a thousand readers of this textbook will live to celebrate a one hundredth birthday—and there's no secret formula for the rest of us. Osborn Segerberg (1982) interviewed twelve hundred centenarians and found that many of them cited peculiar reasons for their longevity ("because I sleep with my head to the north," "because I don't believe in germs"). In fact, what you need is a mixture of healthy genes, a healthy lifestyle, and luck (Palmore, 1982). Having a good attitude about aging may help too. In a

*Jeanne Calment of Arles, France, was the oldest living human ever recorded. Biologists see 120 as the upper limit of the human life span. In February 1997, six months before her death, Calment celebrated her 122nd birthday.*

study of 660 adults, Becca Levy and her colleagues (2002) found that men and women who had positive views of aging, when measured up to twenty-three years earlier, lived seven and a half years longer than those with less positive views of aging. Apparently a positive attitude about aging—which is accompanied by a strong will to live—is more predictive of longevity than gender, wealth, cholesterol level, blood pressure, weight, smoking, and exercise.

## AGING AND INTELLECTUAL FUNCTIONS

The human body peaks at thirty, and then gradually declines. What about the trajectory of *cognitive* development through adulthood? Does a weakened body signal a feeble mind, or are the two paths separate? At what age do "growth" and "maturity" turn to "aging" when it comes to memory, intelligence, and the ability to be productive at one's work?

**Memory and Forgetting** Many people believe that as we age, we inevitably begin to forget names, numbers, the car keys, and whatever else is important. According to this stereotype, people who are ready to retire are forgetful and absentminded. A deterioration of cognitive abilities is not, however, a necessary part of aging. Listen to the nostalgic remembrances of a grandparent and you will marvel at the ease with which he or she can vividly describe the details of an experience that took place a half-century ago. Certain experiences leave an imprint on a person's memory, never to be erased. Sports, politics, wars, disasters, entertainment, and crime are topics that leave clear traces of newsprint on the mind (Howes & Katz, 1988). So do friends from earlier in life. Studies show that although elderly adults often cannot free-recall the names of high-school classmates, they have an uncanny ability to recognize names, recognize faces, and match them up (Bahrick et al., 1975).

Clearly, there is much about our past that we tend not to forget, even as we get older. But studies have shown that although the elderly are as capable as younger adults of recognizing stimuli they have seen before, there is a decline in the ability to free-recall nonsense syllables, word lists, written prose, series of numbers, map directions, names of people just introduced, geometric forms, faces, and other newly learned material (Light, 1991; Craik, 1992).

There are two neurocognitive bases for this age-related decline in memory. The first is related to sensory acuity—that as people age, their eyesight and hearing become impaired. When very old people are tested on cognitive tasks, their performance depends largely on their sensory acuity (Baltes & Lindenberger, 1997; Frieske & Park, 1999). The second change has to do with neural speed. In tightly controlled experiments, Timothy Salthouse (1996) and others have discovered that as people get older they process information and react more slowly—and that this loss of neural speed impairs performance on a range of cognitive tasks, including those used to test memory. The reason that slowness in the nervous system creates problems is that the more time it takes to process information, the less time people have to rehearse the material or attend to items that appear later in the sequence—like getting "backed up" on an assembly line.

**Alzheimer's Disease** Although the brain and nervous system slow gradually as a natural part of aging, there are, sadly, many bright adults with brain damage that causes dementia—a mental disorder that causes severe cognitive impairments. Dementia can occur at any time during adulthood, but it is most likely to happen after age sixty-five and to strike about 10 percent of the elderly population. It is not a normal part of the aging process but, rather, stems from brain damage caused by a

For medical and research information on Alzheimer's disease, as well as caregiver resources, you can visit the Alzheimer's Association at http://www.alz.org/.

stroke, a tumor, the cumulative effects of alcohol, or certain diseases (Parks et al., 1993).

The most common cause of dementia is **Alzheimer's disease (AD)**, a progressive and irreversible brain disorder that afflicts mostly the elderly and kills brain cells at a terrifying pace. When the German psychiatrist Alois Alzheimer first described the disease in 1906, it was rare because most people died young enough to avoid it. As the human life expectancy has increased, however, so has the prevalence of the disease (see Figure 9.21). Today, the statistics on it are staggering. Worldwide, the Alzheimer's Association estimates that AD claims as victims about 5 percent of adults by age 65, 10 to 15 percent by age 75, 20 to 40 percent by age 85, and nearly half of those over 85. At present, about four million Americans have AD, which accounts for nearly half of all nursing-home admissions. As of 2003, the estimated annual cost of AD in the United States exceeded $100 billion.

In patients with AD, the brain tissue contains wads of sticky debris, called plaques, which exterminate brain cells. Although researchers do not know what sets the process in motion, they are in hot pursuit of clues (Terry et al., 1999). Many believe that AD results from a slow virus that invades the nervous system or from an accumulation of environmental toxins in the brain. Others focus on the fact that the disease destroys brain cells that produce acetyl-choline, a neurotransmitter that plays an important role in memory. Still others find that both early and late onset forms of the disease are linked to genetic characteristics. Whatever the root causes of AD, the effects are devastating. It begins with simple lapses in memory and is soon followed by attention problems and an overall loss of cognitive functions. As the disease worsens over time, there are periods of disorientation, bursts of anger, depression, changes in mood and personality, and a deterioration of physical functions. Alzheimer's patients may lose track of a conversation, neglect to turn off a faucet or the stove, forget where they parked the car, or forget the name of a loved one. To make matters worse, they sometimes do not realize the extent of their problem (McGlynn & Kaszniak, 1991). Once diagnosed, people with Alzheimer's live an average of eight more years.

Drugs have been developed that ease the symptoms, though only for some people and only temporarily, by boosting the action of acetylcholine. Looking ahead, some researchers are trying to develop drugs that would stop the destruction of neurons, and others are seeking a vaccine that would inoculate people from the disease. At present, however, there is no means of prevention and no cure for Alzheimer's disease. But there are adult day-care centers designed to help victims and provide relief and social support for the beleaguered families. For patients still in the early stages of AD, there are also memory-retraining programs to teach them how to use mnemonic devices and external memory aids. For doctors, patients, and family members alike, managing this disease is not easy (Mulligan et al., 2003).

**Intelligence**   Psychologists used to believe that intelligence—a concept, as we'll see in Chapter 10, that is not easily defined—peaks during the twenties, declines gradually to the age of fifty, and then takes a dramatic downward turn. This view of development did not arise out of thin air, nor was it proposed by researchers extolling the virtue of youth. David Wechsler (1972), the psychologist who devised the most widely used adult intelligence test, was seventy-six when he wrote that "the decline of mental ability with age is part of the general process of the organism as a whole."

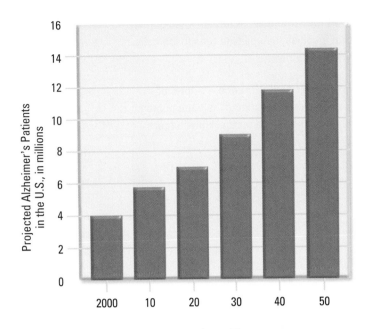

**FIGURE 9.21**   **The Alzheimer's problem**
As the U.S. population ages, so does the projected number of Alzheimer's patients—from 4 million in 2000 to an estimated 14 million in 2050 (*Newsweek*, 2000).

**Alzheimer's disease (AD)**   A progressive brain disorder that strikes older people, causing memory loss and other symptoms.

**fluid intelligence** A form of intelligence that involves the ability to reason logically and abstractly.

**crystallized intelligence** A form of intelligence that reflects the accumulation of verbal skills and factual knowledge.

In light of numerous studies, we now know that old age does not necessarily signal diminished intelligence. The reason today's researchers are more optimistic about intellectual development later in life is that they realize that intelligence is not a single general trait. Rather, psychologists distinguish among different forms of intelligence—and although some forms decline with age, others do not. For example, Raymond Cattell (1963) and, later, John Horn (1982) distinguished between fluid and crystallized intelligence. **Fluid intelligence** is the ability to reason quickly and abstractly, solve problems of logic, detect letter or number sequences, or mentally orient objects in two-dimensional space. In contrast, **crystallized intelligence** reflects an accumulation of factual knowledge, skill, or expertise—as measured, for example, by the sheer size of one's vocabulary or the ability to add and subtract. More and more, psychologists find that this distinction helps us to understand why some intellectual abilities are vulnerable to decline with age, whereas others are maintained (Baltes et al., 1999; Kaufman, 2001).

The distinction between fluid and crystallized intelligence is important because, when both are tested separately, two different developmental patterns are found. In one large-scale study, for example, K. Warner Schaie and Sherry Willis (1993) tested more than sixteen hundred adults in age groups that ranged from twenty-nine to eighty-eight years old. As predicted, the fluid-intelligence test scores started to decline steadily through middle and late adulthood, but the measures of crystallized intelligence remained relatively stable—at least until subjects were in their seventies and eighties (see Figure 9.22). The maintenance of crystallized intelligence comes, in part, from reading books, newspapers, and magazines (Stanovich et al., 1995).

The fluid/crystallized distinction is related to another developmental change: that people lose mental *speed* as they get older. Whether a task involves folding paper, recognizing pictures, solving arithmetic problems or verbal analogies, dialing a telephone, proofreading, assembling cubes, or reading a story, we get slower and slower over the life span (Birren & Fisher, 1995; Salthouse, 1996; Frieske & Park, 1999)—and no one is immune, not even senior university professors and others who are intellectually active and stimulated (Shimamura et al., 1995; Salthouse et al., 2002). This helps to explain why the declines are greater on tests that are timed rather than untimed (Hertzog, 1989; Schaie, 1989) and on mental problems that are complex rather than simple (Salthouse, 1992). To illustrate the point, let's reconsider the Schaie and Willis (1993) study of adults who were twenty-nine to eighty-eight years old. Three vocabulary tests were given to measure verbal ability, a form of crystallized intelligence: a standard untimed test, an untimed test consisting of difficult items, and a standard test that was timed. Figure 9.23 shows that scores declined with age only in the timed test. Without time pressure, the older subjects matched the performance of those half their age. It's worth noting, by the way, that older people can regain some of their diminished skills—even on tests of fluid intelligence—through cognitive training and practice (Willis, 1990; Schaie, 1996).

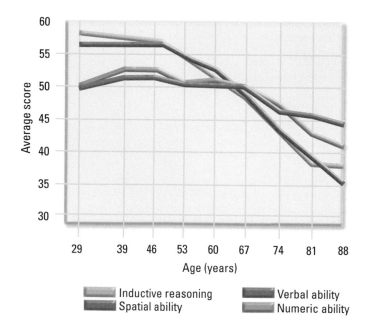

**FIGURE 9.22 Age trends in measures of intelligence**
In this cross-sectional study, 1,628 adults took a battery of tests. Shown on the right are the results of four measures: two involving fluid intelligence (spatial ability and inductive reasoning) and two involving crystallized intelligence (verbal ability and numeric ability).

## SOCIAL AND PERSONAL DEVELOPMENT

Psychologists who study infants and young children are impressed by how accurately chronological age can be used to mark the milestones of social development. The first social smile is seen at six weeks and is predictably followed by attachment behaviors, separation anxiety, crawling, walking, first words, and so on. Do adults similarly pass through an orderly succession of stages? Can chronological age be used to predict changes in self-concept, social relationships, or life satisfaction? Some say *yes*, others *no*.

**Ages and Stages of Adulthood**   In contrast to the once-prevailing view that life patterns are set in early childhood, Erik Erikson (1963) proposed a life-span theory of development. According to Erikson, people mature through eight psychosocial stages, each marked by a crisis that has to be resolved. Stages 1 to 4 unfold in infancy and childhood; stage 5, in adolescence; and stages 6 to 8 in the years of adulthood.

In Erikson's view, those who emerge from adolescence with a sense of identity enter young adulthood, a time when it's critical to fuse with someone else, to find *intimacy* through meaningful close friendships or marriage. The next stage is middle adulthood, a time when people feel the need to achieve *generativity*, by contributing to the welfare of a new generation—at work, at home, or in the community. Research shows that most middle-age adults are more generative in their orientation than college students and young adults—and that generativity can be expressed in different ways (McAdams & de St. Aubin, 1998). Among middle-age women, those who were the most generative were more politically active and cared more about others at work or their children at home (Peterson & Stewart, 1996). The final stage is late adulthood, a time when it's important to gain a sense of *integrity*, a feeling that one's life has been worthwhile. Those fortunate enough to resolve their early crises enjoy a sense of serenity and self-fulfillment. Those not so fortunate live their final years in regret and despair (see Table 9.3).

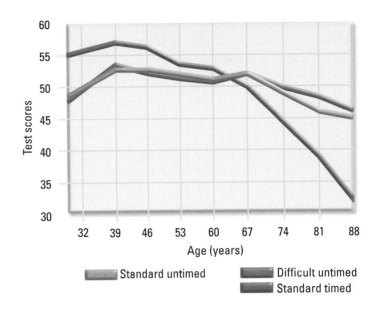

**FIGURE 9.23   Timed vs. untimed vocabulary tests**
To measure verbal ability, Schaie and Willis (1993) administered (1) a standard untimed test, (2) a difficult untimed test, and (3) a standard timed test. As you can see, scores declined with age only in the timed test. Performance on the two untimed tests peaked at the age of sixty-seven.

| TABLE 9.3   ERIKSON'S EIGHT STAGES OF DEVELOPMENT | |
| --- | --- |
| **Stages and Ages** | **The Primary "Crisis"** |
| Infancy (0–1 year) | *Trust vs. mistrust* |
| Toddler (1–2 years) | *Autonomy vs. shame and doubt* |
| Preschool (3–5 years) | *Initiative vs. guilt* |
| Elementary school (6–12 years) | *Industry vs. inferiority* |
| Adolescence (13–19 years) | *Identity vs. role confusion* Adolescents struggle to break from parents and form an identity, or self-concept. |
| Young Adulthood (20–40 years) | *Intimacy vs. isolation* Having resolved the identity crisis, young adults seek intimacy in meaningful relationships and marriage. |
| Middle Adulthood (40–65 years) | *Generativity vs. stagnation* Having achieved intimacy, middle-age adults seek to mentor a new generation at work, at home, and in the community. |
| Late Adulthood (65 and over) | *Integrity vs. despair* Reflecting on life, older adults seek integrity, a sense that their lives were worthwhile. |

***Source:*** E. H. Erikson (1963). *Childhood and society.* New York: Norton.

**social clock** A set of cultural expectations concerning the most appropriate age for men and women to leave home, marry, start a career, have children, and retire.

Building on Erikson's model, other theorists have tried to describe the stages of adulthood in finer detail, with a special emphasis on the middle years, the so-called prime of life (Gould, 1978; Vaillant, 1977). Perhaps the best known of the theories was proposed by Daniel Levinson. Based on extensive interviews with forty successful middle-age men and forty-five women, he proposed that just as there are four seasons in a year, there are four eras in a person's life: preadulthood, followed by early, middle, and late adulthood (Levinson et al., 1978; Levinson, 1996). According to this theory, our lives run in cycles that alternate from periods of stress and upheaval *between* eras to periods of relative calm *within* eras. Thus, each of us is likely to encounter rough times when we cross the transitional bridges to early adulthood (seventeen to twenty-two), middle adulthood (forty to forty-five), and late adulthood (sixty to sixty-five).

In the transition to early adulthood, says Levinson, people shed their adolescence, build dreams, set goals for the future, and make choices that seem permanent—about a job, a spouse, a place to live. These choices are often reevaluated before people settle down. At 40, men and women reach a second turning point in which they may question the paths they have taken and realize that the dreams of their youth are slipping away. Levinson described the early forties as a time when many people undergo a midlife crisis. The final transition to late adulthood begins at sixty to sixty-five. Levinson only speculated about this era, but others have found that this time can prove gratifying to those who are healthy and active. Edwin Shneidman (1989) interviewed male professionals in their seventies and found that they had a positive outlook to their eighties. The same is found in older women (Holahan, 1988). In the seasons of life, says Shneidman, the seventies are like "an Indian Summer."

**Critical Events of Adulthood** Erikson, Levinson, and other age-and-stage theorists believe that adults change in predictable ways and that these changes are linked to chronological age. But in light of the diversity of lifestyles across cultures and within a culture, which often lead people to take different developmental paths, others believe that the course of adult development follows critical events—regardless of the age at which they occur. What are these events? Ask people about turning points in their lives, and they inevitably mention starting school, graduation, their first job, getting married, having children, moving from one home to another, the death of a loved one, health changes, and world events (Ryff, 1989).

For certain milestones, timing seems critical. According to Bernice Neugarten (1979), people are sensitive to the ticking of a **social clock**—the set of culturally shared expectations, known to us all, concerning the best age for men and women to leave home, marry, start a career, have children, retire, and complete other life tasks. Social clocks differ from one culture to the next and from one generation to the next. In the 1950s, for example, most Americans believed that men and women should marry at the ages of nineteen and twenty-four and start a career at twenty-four and twenty-six. Yet today, it seems more appropriate to attend college, then marry and settle down later. In Neugarten's view, social clocks gives us a developmental guideline, and people who are "out of sync" (for example, leaving home too late or marrying too young) feel more stress than those who are "on time."

Not only are expected transitions important, but the fickle finger of fate can alter the course of development in unanticipated ways. Writing on the psychology of chance encounters, Albert Bandura (1982) noted that life paths are often twisted and turned by fortuitous events—as when a student is inspired to choose a career by a professor whose class happened to meet at a convenient hour or when a talented young athlete is permanently injured and sidelined by a hit-and-run driver. Such events cannot be anticipated, but autobiographers who reflect on their own lives are often struck by the powerful influence of these chance encounters (Handel, 1987).

**Life Satisfaction**   How happy are you today compared to when you were fifteen? How satisfied with life do you expect to be in twenty-five years? And what about others: Do you think men and women in general are happier at twenty, forty-five, or seventy? We saw earlier that adolescence is not inevitably filled with storm and stress. But consider other common assumptions. Are the twenties and thirties carefree and exciting? Are people in their forties tormented by midlife crisis? Are the fifties calm? Do the autumn years of retirement ring in sadness? Recent studies cast new light on many of our beliefs.

Surveys of thousands of people from different cultures around the world have shown that 75 to 80 percent are satisfied with life—and this percentage does not vary with age (Inglehart, 1990; Diener et al., 1999). As illustrated in Figure 9.24, this similarity across the life span is interesting, and maybe a bit surprising, for two reasons. First, there's no evidence whatsoever for the turbulent midlife crisis popularized by Levinson, no dip in satisfaction in middle age. In fact, the rates of divorce, marital discord, job change, admission for psychiatric care, and suicide do *not* increase among forty-something adults (Hunter & Sundel, 1989). Robert McCrae and Paul Costa (1990) administered to 350 men, thirty to sixty years old, a "Midlife Crisis Scale" that measured feelings of emptiness, inner turmoil, mortality, confusion, and unhappiness with job and family. Scores did not peak, or even show a blip, in the midlife years. Next, they administered an anxiety questionnaire to 10,000 adults and again found no sign of the so-called midlife crisis.

Let's be clear about what these results mean—and don't mean. First, while we all have ups and downs, the downs are not more likely to occur in our forties than in our twenties, thirties, fifties, or sixties. Second, while most middle-aged adults do not undergo a turmoil-filled "crisis" that transforms who they are, many do make modest changes in their lives. For example, Abigail Stewart and Elizabeth Vandewater (1999) studied college-educated women at thirty-six and forty-seven years old and found that two-thirds made changes between these ages, like returning to school or switching careers; some took steps to make modest "midcourse corrections." A third point is that middle age is an experience that can change from one moment in history to the next. Thus, women who were in college during the 1960s, at the start of the women's movement, may have been more likely than those of other generations to reflect on opportunities lost and try to catch up (Stewart & Ostrove, 1998). Television news anchor Tom Brokaw (1998) made this point in *The Greatest Generation*, a book about American men and women of all racial and ethnic groups, who lived through, fought in, sacrificed for, and were shaped by the events of World War II. Each generation of adults is different, each one unique.

When it comes to life satisfaction, another "surprise" is that it does not decline later in life—in sharp contrast to the stereotypic image of the elderly as sad, demoralized, and chronically worried. Although it's true that people have more medical problems as they age, older people are not as a group more prone to complain about their health or become depressed (Aldwin et al., 1989; Kessler et al., 1992;

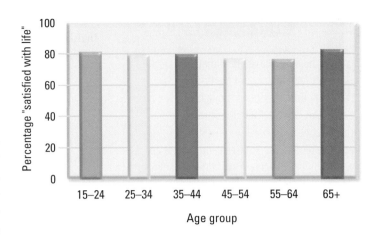

**FIGURE 9.24**   **Life satisfaction**
As shown, ratings of life satisfaction do not vary with age (Inglehart, 1990).

Psychologists have found that life satisfaction does not predictably vary from childhood through adulthood. But what about self-esteem, the extent to which we see ourselves in positive terms? Does self-esteem increase as we get older, or decrease, or is there a nonlinear developmental pattern? In an Internet survey, Richard Robins and others (2002) asked people to rate their self-esteem on a 5-point scale. From a third of a million respondents, nine to ninety years old, these researchers were able to plot the developmental trajectory of self-esteem. Given what you know about biological, cognitive, and social development, what do you think they found? Look at Figure 9.25 and you'll see that self-esteem fluctuates a great deal—it is highest in childhood, from 9 to 12, drops sharply during adolescence, increases gradually throughout adulthood, peaks in the sixties, and declines sharply in old age.

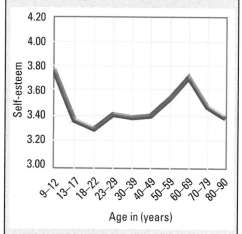

**FIGURE 9.25**

Newmann, 1989). Cross-national studies conducted in Europe have also disconfirmed the stereotype of old people as overly depressed (Copeland et al., 1999).

You may wonder why life satisfaction remains stable with age. Most psychologists agree that being happy requires two main ingredients: *love* and *work*. What's interesting is that these aspects of life are like bottles of wine that seem to get better with age. To be sure, every person's life path is unique. Some people get married; others do not. Some are promoted at work; others get laid off. But there are general tendencies. At home, for example, marital satisfaction tends to decline when a couple first has children (Belsky & Pensky, 1988) and continue to drop until the kids leave home, at which point husbands and wives report *increasing* levels of happiness (White & Edwards, 1990). Having children is an enriching experience, and many parents are saddened by the departure of their youngest child—the so-called empty nest syndrome. But raising a family is also stressful and drains time, energy, and money from a marriage. So relationships are often strained when the nest is full and rejuvenated when it is empty. Job satisfaction also follows an upward pattern later in life—as people report high levels of job satisfaction just before retirement (Rhodes, 1983; Warr, 1992). As workers age, they advance to higher positions, get paid more, and feel more committed. In short, life satisfaction has more to do with the state of one's life at home and at work than with chronological age.

**Changing Perspectives on Time**   As people get older, something happens to the way they perceive and manage time. In an article on "taking time seriously," Laura Carstensen and her colleagues (1999) theorized that people have an underlying sense about the amount of future that awaits them. As people age—and see their time as limited—they become more motivated to enjoy the present and less concerned with building bridges to the distant future. Compared to young adults on the lookout for new friends, social contacts, educational and job opportunities, and acquisitions, older adults are less willing to sacrifice the precious moments of the present for the future. Indicating this orientation toward time, research has shown that older people become narrower and more selective about whom they choose to spend time with, preferring an inner circle of family and close friends to all others (Lang & Carstensen, 2002).

It's interesting what changes with one's orientation to the present relative to the future. Among newly married couples, the initial honeymoon period is often followed by a decline in satisfaction for four years. Yet long-married couples—those who survive the post-honeymoon blues, the children, the empty nest, and other strains—grow closer. Over time, husbands and wives come to enjoy each other more, being less concerned with impressing, dominating, or molding one another (Levenson et al., 1993). At work, too, people who have spent many years on a job are most satisfied with it as they get older and more experienced. As with marriage, older workers care less about climbing the organizational ladder and focus on enjoying the job itself and their coworkers (Hoyer et al., 1999).

## DYING AND DEATH

Humans are probably the only animals who know they are going to die or think about what it means. Many Westerners view death as a transition point in which the body ceases to exist but a soul lives on. Hindus and Buddhists believe in reincarnation. Still others view death as a final parting, period. The ways in which death is viewed, the intense emotions it elicits, the ways dying people are treated, and how the dead are mourned all vary from one person, time, and culture to the next.

Whatever their beliefs, people must cope with the experience of dying and the terrifying prospect of their own demise. After interviewing hundreds of terminally ill patients, psychiatrist Elisabeth Kübler-Ross (1969) proposed that when people know they're dying, they pass through five stages in the coping process: (1) *denial* of their terminal condition ("It's not possible, it must be a mistake"); (2) *anger* and resentment, often directed at physicians and family members ("Why me? It isn't fair!"); (3) *bargaining* for more time ("God, let me live longer, and I'll be virtuous"); (4) *depression* accompanied by crying and refusal to see visitors ("Now I've lost everything I ever cared for"); and finally (5) *acceptance* of one's fate, often marked by a sense of peace and calm ("Oh well, what has to be, has to be").

Kübler-Ross's observations offer a glimpse at some of the ways that people cope with dying. Not everyone passes in sequence through all the stages, however, and the experience can be different from one person to the next. Some patients struggle to the bitter end, whereas others accept death with quiet resignation (Kalish, 1981; Shneidman, 1984). For that reason, Kübler-Ross's stages should not be taken too literally. It may be reassuring for family members and friends to know that irrational denial and anger are common reactions, but it's also important to respect the uniqueness of the process. When a dying patient lashes out or bursts into tears of depression, these feelings should be treated with sensitivity, not dismissed as signs of a person "just going through a stage."

> *"We do not count a man's years until he has nothing else to count."*
>
> —RALPH WALDO EMERSON

## REVIEW QUESTIONS

- *In what ways do our bodies and brains change as we age?*

- *How does age influence memory?*

- *Distinguish between fluid intelligence and crystallized intelligence.*

- *Summarize Erikson's theory of social development. What primary crises occur during adulthood and old age?*

- *What is the relationship between life satisfaction and old age?*

## THINKING LIKE A PSYCHOLOGIST ABOUT HUMAN DEVELOPMENT

For the sake of convenience, developmental psychologists tend to separate the biological, cognitive, and social aspects of development. It's important to realize, however, that the way human beings mature, how they think, and how they interact socially with others are intertwined. For example, only when the brain is sufficiently developed for infants to be capable of object permanence do they experience separation anxiety. A baby must have a capacity to be conscious of its absent mother and father in order to be distressed by their absence. Similarly, as suggested by Piaget, social relations inspire cognitive growth. By talking, sharing, playing, arguing, and watching one another, young children learn from peer interactions to shed their egocentric ways and acquire logical skills such as conservation. In short, the various aspects of development are intimately linked.

Long past infancy and childhood, development continues across the entire life span. Adolescence is not a mere extension of childhood but a time of rapid change—Then there are the various stages of adulthood and old age. Physically, humans are in their prime at thirty, and then lose speed, power, sensory acuity, strength, and endurance. Cognitively, there are two courses of development. A small but steady decline occurs in mental speed, the ability to recall new information, and fluid intelligence. Yet autobiographical memories do not fade, and both crystallized intelligence and wisdom are relatively stable, if not incremental, with age. On the social and personal front, the trajectories of development are more difficult to plot because they are influenced more by critical life events. The one pattern that remains clear is that life satisfaction peaks in late adulthood and doesn't diminish until we are very old, nearing death.

There's one last point worth making about continuity and its relationship to how old we feel. I know someone in his fifties going on sixty, and someone else who is in his forties going on eighteen. It's often said that age is a state of mind. There is some truth to this statement. There is no denying chronology, which provides a rough measure of adult development. But as we saw in the study that opened this chapter, *subjective age*—that is, how old each of feels—is, in some ways, as psychologically important as how old we really are.

## SUMMARY

Developmental **psychology** studies how people grow, mature, and change through the stages of the human life span.

## BASIC DEVELOPMENTAL QUESTIONS

Focused on stability and change from infancy to old age, researchers use two approaches in the study of human development. In **cross-sectional studies,** people of different ages are examined at the same time and their responses compared. In **longitudinal studies,** the same subjects are retested at different times in their lives. Cross-sectional studies reveal differences between groups, but only longitudinal studies measure change as a function of age.

## PRENATAL DEVELOPMENT

### THE GROWING FETUS

In the germinal stage (the first two weeks after conception), the fertilized ovum, or **zygote,** divides into a cluster of cells that pass out of the Fallopian tube and attach to the uterine wall. At this point, the zygote becomes an **embryo.** During the embryonic stage (third to ninth weeks), body parts form and organs start to function. After the ninth week, the embryo becomes a **fetus,** which develops movement, circulation, and even the ability to recognize its mother's voice.

**Teratogens** are toxic substances that can harm the embryo or fetus. Babies of alcoholic mothers often show a pattern of birth defects known as **fetal alcohol syndrome (FAS).** Even small doses of teratogens may be harmful.

## THE REMARKABLE NEWBORN

To investigate how infants distinguish among stimuli, researchers often measure **habituation,** the tendency for attention to a novel stimulus to wane over time, and **recovery,** the tendency for a different stimulus to arouse new interest. These studies and others reveal that infants have remarkable abilities.

### REFLEXES

Babies are born with many adaptive reflexes, such as the **grasping reflex,** the **rooting reflex,** sucking, and swallowing.

### SENSORY CAPACITIES

Though nearsighted, newborns can distinguish between light and dark, follow movements, notice facelike patterns, and mimic adult gestures. Though hard of hearing, they respond to the human voice, especially high pitches and melodic patterns.

### SENSITIVITY TO NUMBER

Using the habituation and recovery method, studies show that six-month-old infants have a rudimentary sense of numbers, including the concepts of addition and subtraction.

## THE INFANT AND GROWING CHILD

### BIOLOGICAL DEVELOPMENT

Babies grow rapidly in the first year. The brain and nervous system develop more synaptic connections and increased myelination. Motor skills also advance in a predictable sequence. Yet these biological aspects of development are influenced by environmental factors.

### COGNITIVE DEVELOPMENT

According to Piaget, infants and children form **schemas** in order to make sense of the world. Through **assimilation,** they try to fit new information into their existing schemas. Through **accommodation,** they modify existing schemas to fit new information.

Piaget described four stages in cognitive development. In the **sensorimotor stage** (birth to two years), infants learn through sensory and motor contact. They develop **object permanence,** an awareness that objects continue to exist after they disappear from view, and **separation anxiety,** a fear reaction to the absence of a caretaker. In the **preoperational stage** (two to six years), children begin to reason in an intuitive, prelogical way. They are still **egocentric,** however, and they do not understand **conservation**—the concept that an object's physical properties stay the same despite superficial changes in appearance. The **concrete operational stage** (six to twelve years) brings logical reasoning but not abstract thought. Finally, at the **formal operational stage** (twelve years to adulthood), people learn to reason at an abstract level.

Piaget may have underestimated the rates of development, but he was right about the sequence. Likewise, he was only partly right about the sharp distinctions between stages. Researchers who study age-related changes in information processing have found that short-term memory and processing speed increase as children grow older.

### SOCIAL DEVELOPMENT

Some animals exhibit **imprinting,** an instinctive tendency to follow the mother during a **critical period** just after birth. In humans, the process is less automatic, but infants form an **attachment,** a deep emotional bond, with the primary care-taker. Studies of humans and monkeys show that "contact comfort" is an important source of attachment. The **strange-situation test** is used to distinguish between **secure attachment** and **insecure attachment,** a difference that results from both parenting style and the infant's own temperament. Although securely attached infants are later more indepen-dent and socially skilled, it isn't clear that the early attach-ment causes these results.

On the effects of day care, recent evidence shows that enriched high-quality day care has more benefits than draw-backs. Horizontal (peer) relationships—mostly between chil-dren of the same sex—become more important as the child grows older. Popular children enjoy the social and cognitive benefits of many friendships, while children rejected by their peers are most at risk for later adjustment problems.

## ADOLESCENCE

**Adolescence** is a transition from childhood to adulthood that corresponds roughly to ages thirteen to twenty in our society.

### PUBERTY

Adolescence begins with **puberty,** the onset of sexual matura-tion marked by rising levels of sex hormones and rapid growth. For girls, puberty brings **menarche,** the first men-strual period. Cultural practices and the timing of menarche influence a girl's reaction. Those who reach puberty early face embarrassment, adjustment problems, and a poor body image. For boys, puberty brings the first ejaculation, as well as growth of the sexual organs and other physical changes. For boys, early maturation is a positive experience.

### COGNITIVE DEVELOPMENT

Adolescence is also a time of rapid cognitive growth. Enter-ing what Piaget called the formal operational stage, teenagers begin to think critically and abstractly. In **moral reasoning,** they show more flexibility in interpreting rules than they did as children.

According to Kohlberg, moral reasoning develops in three stages: preconventional, conventional, and postconventional. But some critics see both cultural and gender bias in this theory, and others question how moral reasoning relates to behavior. Scores on Kohlberg's reasoning tasks correlate only modestly with prosocial behavior, and young children can act morally without the sophisticated reasoning. Children's morality is based on **empathy** for others. As illustrated by the recent controversy concerning euthanasia, or assisted suicide, people often confront moral dilemmas in legal contexts.

## SOCIAL AND PERSONAL DEVELOPMENT

An adolescent's struggle to establish a personal identity, or self-concept, is called an **identity crisis.** Young adolescents typically experience a rise in tension with parents character-ized by bickering and disengagement from family activities. At the same time, peer relationships become more important. In early adolescence, peer pressure brings conformity, which can have both positive and negative effects. Sexuality is a nat-ural part of adolescent development, but it can sometimes bring confusion and harmful consequences. American adoles-cents are sexually more active today than two generations ago, though there has been a recent decline.

### ADOLESCENCE AND MENTAL HEALTH

Severe emotional distress is not more common among adoles-cents than among adults. Nevertheless, unhappy teenagers often become maladjusted adults, so parents should not dis-miss mental-health struggles as just a passing stage.

## ADULTHOOD AND OLD AGE

Biologists agree that each species has a maximum possible **life span,** which is greater than its average **life expectancy.** Among humans, the life expectancy varies across cultural and ethnic groups. In addition, women consistently outlive men.

### PHYSICAL CHANGES IN ADULTHOOD

The number of brain cells diminishes steadily after birth. Muscle strength and reflexes peak at about age thirty, then decline; also at that age, metabolism begins to slow, so that people tend to gain weight. For women, middle age brings **menopause,** the end of menstruation and fertility but without psychological effects. For men, there's only a gradual decline in fertility after adolescence, but no abrupt end.

When people are in their sixties and seventies, the aging process accelerates. The senses decline sharply, and the bones, joints, and immune system begin to deteriorate. Yet Langer's experiment suggests that a youthful state of mind can slow the rate at which people exhibit the symptoms of old age.

### AGING AND INTELLECTUAL FUNCTIONS

Aging need not mean cognitive decline. Autobiographical memories, for instance, survive into old age. Although exper-iments show an age-related decline in ability to free-recall new material, there is no comparable decline in recognition performance. The memory problems that do exist are largely due to a general slowing of neural processes. Older people also lack confidence needed for short-term memory tasks.

Dementia, a disorder resulting in severe cognitive damage, strikes 10 percent of the elderly population. The most common cause is **Alzheimer's disease (AD)**, which progressively destroys brain cells, causing memory loss and other symptoms.

Studies show that **fluid intelligence**, the ability to reason logically and abstractly, declines steadily in middle and late adulthood. However, **crystallized intelligence**, reflecting the accumulation of skills and factual knowledge, remains relatively stable over the life span. Similarly, mental speed decreases with age, but the ability to solve practical problems does not. Finally, although older workers find it harder to learn new skills, objective measures of job performance do not decline with age.

## SOCIAL AND PERSONAL DEVELOPMENT

Theorists such as Erikson and Levinson have described adulthood in terms of distinct stages. In this view, the stages are linked to chronological age, and the transitions produce stress. Other theorists believe that social development has less to do with age than with critical events such as marriage and having children. The **social clock** sets the expected times when major life events should occur. People are also influenced by fate in the form of chance encounters that change a person's life.

Despite prevailing stereotypes, recent research has found no evidence for a turbulent midlife crisis or demoralization of the elderly. Life satisfaction remains stable with age and depression rates decrease, at least until the very late years. The critical ingredients—love and work—both seem to improve with age.

## DYING AND DEATH

Kübler-Ross proposed five stages that people go through in coping with the knowledge of impending death: denial, anger, bargaining, depression, and acceptance. However, not everyone experiences these stages.

## KEY TERMS

developmental psychology (**p. 341**)

cross-sectional study (**p. 341**)

longitudinal study (**p. 341**)

zygote (**p. 342**)

embryo (**p. 342**)

fetus (**p. 342**)

teratogens (**p. 343**)

fetal alcohol syndrome (FAS) (**p. 344**)

habituation (**p. 345**)

recovery (**p. 346**)

grasping reflex (**p. 346**)

rooting reflex (**p. 346**)

schemas (**p. 353**)

assimilation (**p. 353**)

accommodation (**p. 353**)

sensorimotor stage (**p. 353**)

object permanence (**p. 354**)

separation anxiety (**p. 354**)

preoperational stage (**p. 355**)

egocentric (**p. 355**)

conservation (**p. 355**)

concrete operational stage (**p. 356**)

formal operational stage (**p. 356**)

imprinting (**p. 359**)

critical period (**p. 360**)

attachment (**p. 360**)

strange-situation test (**p. 362**)

secure attachment (**p. 362**)

insecure attachment (**p. 362**)

adolescence (**p. 366**)

puberty (**p. 366**)

menarche (**p. 366**)

moral reasoning (**p. 368**)

empathy (**p. 370**)

identity crisis (**p. 370**)

life span (**p. 376**)

life expectancy (**p. 376**)

menopause (**p. 377**)

Alzheimer's disease (AD) (**p. 379**)

fluid intelligence (**p. 380**)

crystallized intelligence (**p. 380**)

social clock (**p. 382**)

## THINKING CRITICALLY ABOUT HUMAN DEVELOPMENT

1. Summarize the evidence suggesting that a fetus can make auditory discriminations during the last three months of pregnancy. What are some of the implications of this work? Do you think these findings indicate that fetuses have "memory"?

2. Compare and contrast Piaget's theory of cognitive development with more recent information-processing approaches. Describe the evidence supporting each perspective. Which theory do you believe best describes cognitive development?

3. Consider the two controversies surrounding language development. To what extent do genetic and environmental factors influence the development of language?

4. Given what you now know about the limitations of early sensory experience and the developmental changes that occur early in life, what kind of toys would you select (or design) for an infant to foster biological, cognitive, and social development? Why would these be effective?

5. Consider the arguments for and against day care. What are the advantages and disadvantages, developmentally? In selecting a day-care program for your child, what sorts of qualities would you look for?

6. Research suggests that child witnesses are specially susceptible to bias. Describe the kinds of biases that children are likely to exhibit. Use what you have learned about development to explain why these biases might occur.

# Intelligence

# ARE PEOPLE SMARTER TODAY THAN IN THE PAST?

## THE SITUATION

Just about everyone is curious about intelligence and the tests that are used to measure it. Most of the tests were created early in the twentieth century, and since then IQ scores have been used to determine academic potential in schools throughout the world. Hmm. The fact that people have been taking IQ tests for many years—and that you may have taken a test very similar to one taken by your parents and grandparents—raises a fascinating question: Have scores changed over time? Are people today more or less smart than a few years ago, or is human intelligence too stable a trait to change in so short a time?

Being trained in psychology, you're accustomed to conducting experiments, often in the laboratory. To answer the question about IQ trends across generations, however, you'll need to use different methods. You'll need to gather old scores from IQ tests that were taken at different times by comparable groups of people. So you contact researchers all over the world and ask if they would send you test scores that have been compiled over the years. In particular, you want scores from tests that were never altered over time and were given to large groups of adults of different generations. You receive the data you need from a number of developed countries, including Australia, Austria, Belgium, Brazil, Canada, China, France, Germany, Great Britain, Israel, Japan, the Netherlands, New Zealand, Norway, Switzerland, and the United States. Now it's time to analyze the results.

## MAKE A PREDICTION

As we'll see shortly, IQ tests are set so that the average score in the population is always 100. This means that if raw scores were to rise or fall over time, the scale would have to be readjusted like a thermostat in order to keep that average. The question is, what has happened to *raw scores* over the past seventy or so years? To make your prediction, look at Figure 10.1 and use the year 1920 as a starting point. Based on 1920 standards, which set the average IQ at 100, what do you think the raw, nonadjusted scores were in 1930, 1940, and other decades up to 1990? Has IQ steadily increased over time, decreased, fluctuated in response to historical events, or stayed essentially the same? Think carefully about the problem. Then, using Figure 10.1, plot your predicted trend for each decade before looking at the actual results.

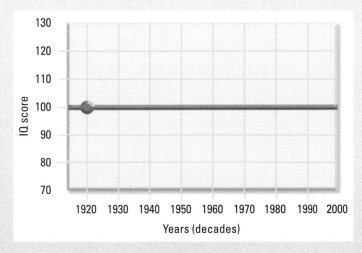

FIGURE 10.1    **Your predictions**

## THE RESULTS

When James Flynn (1987) first compiled the IQ scores in fourteen developed nations (he then added six more), the worldwide trend was unmistakable. Look at Figure 10.2 and you'll see that from one generation to the next, without exception, there have been steady and massive gains in IQ scores—so much so that today's average adult scores twenty-four points higher than in 1920. Named after its discoverer, this phenomenon is now known as the Flynn effect.

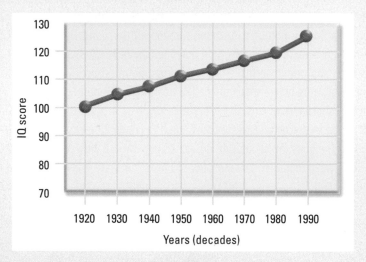

FIGURE 10.2 **The actual results**

## WHAT DOES IT ALL MEAN?

For years, psychologists have hotly debated the nature of intelligence, the validity of standard IQ tests, and the extent to which being smart is the product of nature or nurture. Flynn's discovery that IQ scores have risen sharply over the years has provoked new discussion of these core issues. Is it possible that while IQ has risen, "intelligence" has not? What does the rise in IQ over such a short period imply about the genetic basis for intelligence? What environmental factors could have caused the increase—could it be more time spent in school, parents with more education, better nutrition, or exposure to radio, TV, and computers? And what might we project through the twenty-first century? Researchers are trying to answer these questions (Neisser, 1998; Flynn, 1999). As we'll see in this chapter, the subject of intelligence is fascinating, complex, and frequently controversial.

---

*"Intelligence consists in recognizing opportunity."*
—CHINESE PROVERB

Brace yourself, take a deep breath, and try to answer the following questions: How many miles apart are New York City and Los Angeles? In what ways are a lion and tiger alike? What does the word *disparate* mean? Why is copper used in electric wires? Now read the following series of numbers and, without taking a second look, try to repeat it backwards: 4 7 5 2 8 6. If these questions seem familiar, it's because they are like those that are widely used to measure intelligence. The faster and more accurate you are, the higher your "IQ" will be. But what is an IQ, and what does the score mean? This chapter examines the controversial subject of human intelligence—what it is, how it's defined, how it's measured, the debates it has sparked, and the implications it has for educational policy. As we'll see, this facet of human development raises many profound, challenging questions (Neisser et al., 1996; Sternberg, 2000; Sternberg et al., 2003).

*There are many conceptions of intelligence. One is to associate it with the kind of general knowledge that is needed to play and win* Jeopardy! *Intelligence can also be defined as the capacity to adapt to one's environment. Micronesians and other South Pacific islanders define intelligence in part by the ability to navigate long distances using information from ocean currents and the stars.*

Let's start with a definition: What really is intelligence? In 1921, fourteen prominent psychologists and educators were invited to answer this question, and they came up with fourteen different definitions, such as "the ability to carry on abstract thinking," "the capacity to learn or profit by experience," and "the capacity to acquire capacity" (Thorndike et al., 1921). How do these sound to you? When commuters, supermarket shoppers, and college students were handed a blank sheet of paper and asked to write down the characteristics of intelligence, they produced a long list of traits, including: reasons logically, makes sound decisions, sizes up situations well, speaks fluently, reads widely, is an expert on a particular subject, has many good ideas, accepts others for what they are, has an interest in world events, and thinks before speaking (Sternberg et al., 1981).

Clearly, the term **intelligence** means different things to different people. In fact, it's important to realize that your definition is influenced by the culture and generation in which you live. Many students I talk to are impressed by the combination of speed and general knowledge that enables contestants on TV game shows like *Jeopardy!* to win large sums of money. For some South Pacific islanders, however, intelligence is defined by your ability to navigate the ocean from one island to the next. For the Kalahari Bushmen in Africa, it means having the skills needed for productive hunting and gathering. For gang members of an inner city, "street smarts" is what matters most. To accommodate the many ways in which people all over the world exhibit their intelligence, many psychologists prefer to define the concept in general terms, as *a capacity to learn from experience and adapt successfully to one's environment.*

## INTELLIGENCE TESTS

- *What is intelligence, and why is it measured?*
- *What does IQ stand for, and how are IQ tests constructed?*
- *Are these tests accurate?*
- *Why do some people believe that the tests are biased?*

**intelligence**   The capacity to learn from experience and adapt successfully to one's environment.

*Galton's laboratory at the London Health Exhibition in 1884.*

The study of intelligence began with the instruments used to measure it. Like much of psychology, intelligence testing is long on tradition but short on history. About four thousand years ago, the Chinese used civil-service exams to measure aptitude. But it was not until the end of the nineteenth century that modern forms of assessment were born. The first psychologist to devise such "mental tests" was Francis Galton (1883), Charles Darwin's cousin. Noticing that great achievements run in families like his own, Galton believed that intelligence was inherited. Like it or not, he said, all men and women are *not* created equal. Taking a page from Darwin's book on evolution, Galton went on to suggest that if intelligence could be objectively measured, then the normally slow processes of "natural selection" and "survival of the fittest" could be hastened through *eugenics,* selective-breeding policies that encourage only the brightest of adults to reproduce.

How did Galton measure intelligence? If you had visited the Chicago World's Fair in 1883 or London's International Health Exhibition in 1884, you could have been one of thousands to find out. For a small fee, a technician using Galton's state-of-the-art equipment would measure biologically rooted abilities such as your muscular strength; the size of your head; your speed at reacting to signals; and, most importantly, your ability to detect slight differences between two weights, lights, and tones. Afterward, you would receive an intelligence score printed on a card (Johnson et al., 1985).

Galton's measures are intriguing, and one recent study suggests that the ability to make fine discriminations among colors and tones is somewhat correlated with general intelligence (Acton & Schroeder, 2001). Still, by today's standards these measures are crude and largely without validity. Indeed, even Galton found that bright, highly accomplished adults did *not* get higher-than-average scores. Galton's elitist proposal for increasing the native intelligence of the human species through selective breeding laid the groundwork for what would become a bumpy road for the intelligence-testing movement that followed (Weinberg, 1989). What's worse, he founded a eugenics movement that spawned involuntary sterilization laws in a number of states and later provided justification for the Holocaust in Nazi Germany—a development that would have distressed Galton (Gillham, 2001).

## THE STANFORD–BINET

Across the English Channel, French psychologist Alfred Binet sought to measure intelligence for humane reasons: to enhance the education of children needing special assistance. In 1904, a few years after a law was passed requiring all French children to attend school, the Minister of Public Instruction hired Binet to develop an objective means of identifying children who would have difficulty with normal class work. With the help of Théophile Simon, Binet (1905) developed a test that contained questions on problem solving, numbers, vocabulary, logical reasoning, general knowledge, and memory—the kinds of skills that are necessary in an academic setting. Binet and Simon wrote hundreds of questions, administered them to students in Paris, and recorded the average performance of children at different ages. Questions for the test were retained if answered correctly by an increasing number of children from one grade level to the next.

Once the test was complete, questions were arranged in order of increasing difficulty and administered by someone trained to score and interpret the results. Assuming that children develop in similar ways but at different rates, Binet and

Simon used their test to determine a student's **mental age,** the average age of children who pass the same number of items. In other words, the average ten-year-old would have a mental age of ten. Those who are exceptionally bright would have a mental age that is higher (like an average older child), whereas those who are slow to develop would have one that is lower (like an average younger child). Practically speaking, mental age was a convenient way to score a child's intelligence because it suggested an appropriate grade placement in school.

After Binet died in 1911, the scale was translated into English and imported to the United States by Stanford University psychologist Lewis Terman (1916). The age norms in California were different from those in Paris, so Terman revised many of the questions, added items suitable for adults, published a set of American norms, and gave the test a new name, the **Stanford-Binet.** This test has since been revised four more times (in 1937, 1960, 1986, and 2003). The most recent, the Stanford-Binet V, contains a number of subtests for use between the ages of two and twenty-three, and takes about an hour to administer. Ironically, Binet's work was barely known in France until the Stanford-Binet caught on in the United States. In 1971, sixty years after Binet's death, he and Simon were honored by a commemorative plaque installed at the school in Paris where it all began.

Back at Stanford, Terman was busy developing tests that could be administered in groups (including the popular *Stanford Achievement Test*), theorizing about the roots of intelligence (he favored nature over nurture as an explanation), and initiating a massive longitudinal study of gifted children (to be discussed later). Yet his most notable contribution was the concept of **IQ,** which stands for **intelligence quotient.** Basing his concept on an idea first offered by German psychologist William Stern, Terman proposed that performance on the Stanford-Binet test be converted to a single score—a ratio derived by dividing mental age (MA) by the person's chronological age (CA), then multiplying the result by 100 to eliminate the decimal point. The concept is elegantly simple, yet powerful: $IQ = (MA/CA) \times 100$. Using this formula, you can see that people who are average (that is, those whose MA and

**mental age**    In an intelligence test, the average age of the children who achieve a certain level of performance.

**Stanford-Binet**    An American version of Binet's intelligence test that yields an IQ score with an average of 100.

**intelligence quotient (IQ)**    Originally defined as the ratio of mental age to chronological age, it now represents a person's performance relative to same-age peers.

*Materials used in the Stanford-Binet. (Depiction of the Stanford-Binet Intelligence Scales, Fifth Edition by G.H. Roid reproduced from The Riverside Publishing Company catalog with permission of the publisher. Copyright © 2003. All rights reserved.)*

CA are exactly the same) have an IQ of 100. A ten-year-old child with an MA of twelve has an IQ of 120, and a twelve-year-old with an MA of 10 has an IQ of 83.

Although IQ is a convenient way to represent a child's intelligence, it makes little sense for adults. The problem is that mental age does not continue to increase with chronological age but levels off as we get older. An average ten-year-old may be two MA years ahead of the average eight-year-old, but you can't really say the same for someone who is twenty rather than eighteen or thirty rather than twenty-eight. When you consider specific examples, you can see that the results are ludicrous: If at eighteen you get the same score as the average thirty-six-year-old, your IQ would be 200; but if at thirty-six you had the same score as an average eighteen-year-old, your IQ would be 50. The solution was to drop Terman's quotient and assign IQ-like scores based instead on a person's performance *relative to the average of their same-age peers.*

## THE WECHSLER SCALES

*In schools and other settings, the WISC is the most widely used individually administered IQ test for children.*

Galton, Binet, and Terman all developed tests that reduced intelligence to a single score. But is that necessarily the most informative approach? David Wechsler (1939) didn't think so, so he constructed a test for adults that considers different aspects of intelligence. The most current version of Wechsler's test has fourteen sub-tests grouped within two major scales—one yielding a *verbal* score, and the other a nonverbal *performance* score useful for people who have language problems. He improved the test in 1955 and called it the **Wechsler Adult Intelligence Scale,** or **WAIS** (the test was revised in 1981and 1997, and is abbreviated WAIS–III). He also created similar tests that have since been revised for different age groups. For children six to sixteen years old, there is the *Wechsler Intelligence Scale for Children* (WISC–III), and for preschoolers there is the *Wechsler Preschool and Primary Scale of Intelligence–Revised* (WPPSI–III).

Because the IQ scale was so deeply ingrained in public consciousness, Wechsler kept the same scoring system, setting the average at 100. Keep in mind, however, that if you took the WAIS, you would get three separate scores—one verbal, one performance, and the total (the most recent version of the Stanford-Binet also yields more than one score). To appreciate the kinds of skills measured on the test, try the questions in Figure 10.3. You'll notice that the verbal items call for comprehension, arithmetic, vocabulary, general information, analogies, and the ability to recall strings of digits. In contrast, the items in the nonverbal performance scale ask you to find missing picture parts, arrange cartoons in a logical sequence, reproduce block designs, assemble pieces of a jigsawlike puzzle, and copy symbols onto paper. The Wechsler scales are relatively easy to administer and score, and they are used in many schools and clinics (Kaufman & Lichtenberger, 1999).

**Wechsler Adult Intelligence Scale (WAIS)** The most widely used IQ test for adults, it yields separate scores for verbal and performance subtests.

For more information about SATs, GREs, and other tests, including practice questions and links to education sites, visit the Educational Testing Service: http://www.ets.org/

## GROUP APTITUDE TESTS

The Stanford-Binet and the Wechsler scales are used to test one person at a time and take about an hour to administer. This procedure enables the examiner to interact with the test taker and observe whether he or she has trouble with instructions, loses attention, gets frustrated, or gives up too quickly. The disadvantage is that individualized tests are not practical for quick, large-scale assessment. During World War I, for example, the United States military needed an efficient way to screen recruits for service. With help from psychologists, two group tests were developed and administered to 1.7 million men—the Army Alpha Test, given in writing to those who could read English; and the Army Beta Test, given orally to those who could not (Lennon, 1985).

## VERBAL SCALE

**General Information**
How many hours apart are Eastern Standard and Pacific time?

**Similarities**
In what way are boats and trains alike?

**Arithmetic Reasoning**
If eggs cost 96 cents a dozen, what does 1 egg cost?

**Vocabulary**
What does the word "procrastinate" mean?

**Comprehension**
Why do people buy automobile insurance?

**Digit Span**
Listen carefully to the following numbers. When I am through, I want you to repeat the numbers backwards: 4 8 7 5 2.

## PERFORMANCE SCALE

**Picture Completion**
I'm going to show you a picture with an important part missing. Tell me what's missing:

**Block Design**
Using the sixteen blocks on the left, make the pattern shown on the right:

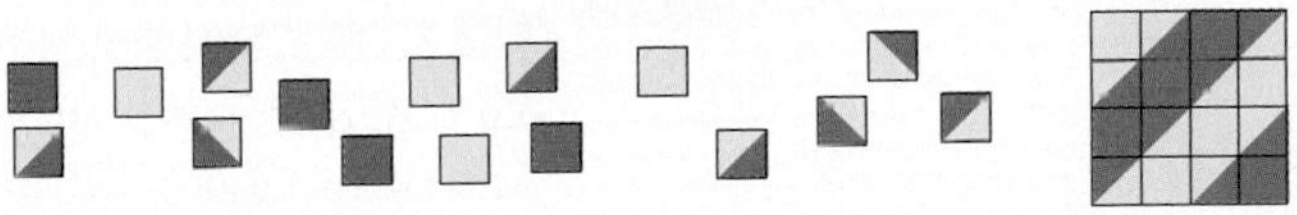

**Object Assembly**
If these pieces are put together correctly, they make something. Put them together as quickly as you can:

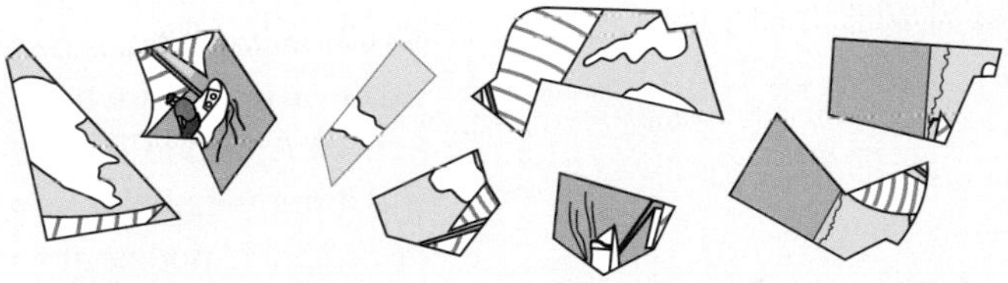

**Picture Arrangement**
The pictures tell a story. Put them in the right order to tell the story:

**Coding**
As quickly as you can, put the appropriate code symbols in the blank spaces:

| Code | ● | □ | ★ | △ | ⁄ |
|------|---|---|---|---|---|
|      | 1 | 2 | 3 | 4 | 5 |

| Test | | | | | | | | | | | | | | |
|---|---|---|---|---|---|---|---|---|---|---|---|---|---|---|
| | 3 | 5 | 2 | 4 | 1 | 2 | 4 | 3 | 5 | 2 | 1 | 4 | 3 | 5 |

FIGURE 10.3   **Simulated items similar to those in the WAIS**

Today, group testing is a regular part of our lives. You are no doubt familiar with the Scholastic Assessment Test (SAT), a national rite of passage that many have learned to fear. Administered by the Educational Testing Service (ETS), the SAT is a grueling two-and-a-half-hour college entrance exam taken by more than a million college-bound seniors every year. The test, which was developed in 1926, was designed to measure both verbal and mathematical reasoning in a multiple-choice format. As a historical matter, it's interesting that the SAT first came into use as a college admission tool in the 1930s. At the time, Harvard president James Conant was unhappy that Harvard was a regional college, easy to get into, and filled with privileged young men from New England boarding schools. Looking to identify and recruit outstanding students from diverse regions and modest backgrounds, and needing a way to make comparisons across a national pool of high-school seniors, he turned to the SAT. In light of criticisms today that these tests favor some segments of society over others, it's ironic that the SAT was first used for a noble purpose: to level the playing field for bright students from modest backgrounds (Lemann, 1999).

Now referred to as SAT-I, the test was revised in 1994 to include math questions that call for write-in answers (students can now use calculators), sentence-completion vocabulary items, and an increased emphasis on critical reading. To be inaugurated by the Class of 2006, there will be a new SAT-I test designed to test reasoning abilities in ways that are more closely linked to high-school and college curricula. The math test will add more algebra content, the verbal test will drop the analogies and focus even more on critical reading, and a writing section will be added to test word choice, grammar, sentence construction, and essay writing (Barnes, 2002; www. collegeboard.com).

In addition to the SAT-I reasoning tests, a number of SAT-II subject tests are available to assess knowledge of specific sciences, social studies, literature, and languages. The SATs are designed to supplement school grades as an objective predictor of academic performance. Instead of or in addition to the SAT, many students take the American College Test (ACT), a rival exam developed in 1939 that tests abilities in English, math, reading, and science reasoning. Comparable tests are also used to screen applicants for advanced education. If you choose to go on to graduate school, you'll have to take the Graduate Record Exam, or GRE. For other more specialized professions, you would take the Medical College Admission Test (MCAT), the Law School Aptitude Test (LSAT), or the Graduate Management Admission Test (GMAT).

Underlying these standardized tests is the assumption that they measure a student's *aptitude,* a potential for academic learning. Psychologists have hotly debated the extent to which this aptitude is influenced by innate potential as opposed to specific experiences at home and in school. For colleges and universities that use these tests for admissions purposes, the issue is irrelevant so long as the test scores can help to predict performance in college. But for students planning to take these exams, this issue has great practical relevance. Students want to know: Can you significantly boost your score by taking a six-week preparation course? As with the SAT itself, there is an interesting history behind the preparation courses. Shortly after the SAT became a routine part of the college application process, a man by the name of Stanley Kaplan, from Brooklyn, New York, set up an SAT tutoring business. Whenever the test was given, Kaplan threw a party afterward for students, each of whom had been instructed to memorize one question from the test and tell it to Kaplan. Between the hamburgers, French fries, and root beer, Kaplan would accumulate actual questions and later review them with the next group of students to be tested. This marked the birth of SAT-preparation courses, which are now common—and led the Educational Testing Service, for decades, to insist that their tests were uncoachable (Lemann, 1999).

Do test-preparation courses raise scores? Research on their actual impact tells us that they are effective, but only to a limited degree. Some ads have claimed that such courses can raise a student's score by 100 points or more. Yet according to the College Board, which administers the SAT, the test measures "developed abilities" acquired from an accumulation of life experiences both inside and outside the classroom. Supporting this latter position is research showing that cramming for the SAT or taking a crash course can increase scores by an average of only 30 to 50 points on the 400–1600 scale. Claims of additional improvement are inflated by the fact that students who take SAT-preparation courses are generally motivated, more

"You're kidding! You count S.A.T.s?"

likely to practice on their own, and more likely to take the test a second time—which by itself tends to raise scores (Kulik et al., 1984; Powers & Rock, 1999).

## ARE INTELLIGENCE TESTS ACCURATE?

Every year, millions of dollars are spent on intelligence testing. But what is the bottom line? Are the tests "accurate"? To answer this question fully, it's important to know that all psychological tests—including those that are designed to measure intelligence—must have three ingredients: standardization, reliability, and validity (Anastasi & Urbina, 1997; Groth-Marnat, 2003).

**Standardization** means that a test provides a standard of existing norms that can be used to interpret an individual's score. Suppose you took a 150-item SAT and then received a letter indicating that you had correctly answered 115 of the questions. How would you feel? Would you celebrate your success or lament your failure? As you can see, a raw score does not provide you with enough information. To interpret the number, you would need to compare it to the performance of others. Standardization is achieved by administering a test to thousands of people similar to those for whom the test is designed. For the Wechsler scales, the average was arbitrarily set at 100, with test scores distributed in a normal, bell-shaped curve where roughly 68 percent of all scores fall between 85 and 115, 95 percent fall between 70 and 130, and 99 percent fall between 55 and 145. The SATs were first standardized in 1941, using a sample of more than ten thousand college-bound students. The verbal and math scores were each put on a scale ranging from 200 to 800, with their averages set at 500. In any case, regardless of whether a test's average is set at 100, 500, or 12 million, your *raw score*—the sheer number of correct answers—must be converted into a standardized *test score* that reflects the distance between your performance and the norm (see Figure 10.4).

The second ingredient is **reliability,** which refers to the consistency of a test's results. Two types of consistency are sought. One is **test-retest reliability,** the extent to which a test yields similar results on different occasions. Just as you would not trust a bathroom scale that shows moment-to-moment fluctuations in your weight, psychologists would not trust an IQ test that shows radical changes from one session to the next. Intelligence is thought to be a relatively stable trait, not one that varies much over a short period. To ensure that a scale has test-retest reliability, researchers test the same subjects on two occasions—say, a month or two apart—and calculate the correlation between their test and retest scores: the higher the correlation, the more reliable the scale.

The second kind of consistency is **split-half reliability,** the extent to which different forms of a test produce similar results. If you had two bathroom scales of the same brand and model, you would expect them to provide identical estimates of your weight. Likewise, alternate forms of an IQ test (often created by dividing it into odd and even items) should produce similar results. Using the test-retest and split-half methods, it's clear that the Stanford-Binet, WAIS, and SAT are reliable measures, all yielding correlations of about +.90. In fact, a study of twenty-three thousand college seniors applying for graduate school showed a very high correlation of +.86 between their scores on the GRE (an exam much like the SAT) and their SAT performances four or more years earlier (Angoff, 1988).

**standardization**   The procedure by which existing norms are used to interpret an individual's test score.

**reliability**   The extent to which a test yields consistent results over time or using alternate forms.

**test-retest reliability**   The degree to which a test yields consistent results when readministered at a later time.

**split-half reliability**   The degree to which alternate forms of a test yield consistent results.

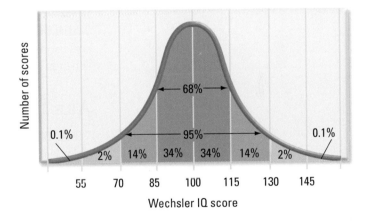

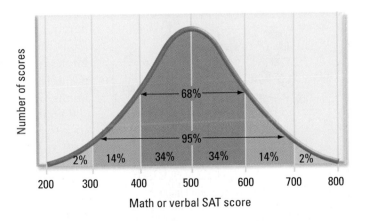

FIGURE 10.4   **Distribution of scores on the WAIS and SAT**

**validity** The extent to which a test measures or predicts what it is designed to.

**content validity** The extent to which a test measures what it's supposed to measure.

**criterion validity** The extent to which a test can predict a concurrent or future outcome.

The U.S. Department of Education (1993) estimates that 90 million Americans lack competence at practical life tasks such as reading a bus schedule, computing the cost to carpet a room, writing a business letter, and balancing a checkbook.

"You can't build a hut, you don't know how to find edible roots and you know nothing about predicting the weather. In other words, you do *terribly* on our IQ test."

The third essential ingredient is **validity,** a test's ability to measure or predict what it's supposed to. IQ tests may yield consistent scores, but do they indicate intelligence? Do college entrance exams measure aptitude? Better yet, are these tests able to predict academic success? Two kinds of validity are necessary. The first is **content validity,** which means that test items should adequately measure what they are designed to measure. Just as a science exam has science questions and a history exam has history questions, an IQ test should contain items that correspond to our definitions of intelligence. The second kind of validity is **criterion validity,** a test's ability to predict a concurrent or future outcome. For intelligence tests, the bottom line is the prediction of academic achievement.

Are IQ tests valid? It depends on what you're trying to predict. If the goal is to assess *academic performance,* then the tests receive a passing grade, particularly in the earlier school years. In elementary school, there is a high correlation among IQ, class grades, and achievement-test scores. There is a somewhat lower correlation between SAT scores and performance in college, but the combination of high-school grades and SAT scores is highly predictive of a student's grade-point average (Jensen, 1980; Linn, 1982). However, if the goal is to predict achievement in nonacademic walks of life, then IQ tests are limited in their validity. Some psychologists believe that although these tests assess academic performance, they do not adequately measure the ability to adapt to life outside the classroom. The complex decisions made by corporate executives, the mental arithmetic used by hurried supermarket shoppers, and the handicapping strategies used by gamblers at a racetrack are common instances of practical, real-world intelligence not predictable by an IQ score. David McClelland (1998) found that the most outstanding executives in a multinational corporation could be distinguished from their more ordinary peers—not by IQ, but by their performance in a "behavioral events interview" in which they were asked to describe how they'd react in various practical, job-related situations. As we'll see later, success in business, sales, the military, and other life settings is predicted by more than IQ scores (Sternberg et al., 2000).

## ARE INTELLIGENCE TESTS BIASED?

When Binet and Simon (1905) constructed their scale, they were trying to identify slow learners for placement in special classes. It soon became clear, however, that IQ tests can too easily be used as instruments of prejudice and discrimination. One of the darkest episodes in psychology's history occurred just prior to World War I when immigrants from overseas arrived at Ellis Island, in the shadow of the Statue of Liberty. Just off the boat and exhausted from their long journey, the new arrivals were immediately tested—and in English, a language many of them could barely understand. Lo and behold, psychologist Henry Goddard (1917) concluded from the results that European Jews, Italians, Russians, and Hungarians were far less intelligent than the average American. Sadly, claims like this one fueled prejudice and contributed, at the time, to the passage of laws designed to restrict immigration.

Critics charge that intelligence tests are culturally biased, in that they favor some social groups over others. To the extent that a test calls for specific cultural knowledge, it *is* biased. That's why Terman had to "Americanize" Binet's French test. But what about IQ testing in the United States, where Americans don't all share a common cultural heritage? Consider an issue that has deeply troubled many psychologists. Ever since cognitive ability tests were first administered, African Americans as a group have averaged 15 points lower than whites on IQ tests and 100 points lower on the SAT verbal and math tests (Jensen, 1994; Miele, 2002). Nobody disputes the fact that the difference exists. However, disagreements arise as to what it means and what the social implications are.

Later, we'll see that there are many possible reasons for this difference. But for now, we'll examine one criticism in particular: that the question content within the tests favors the cultural and educational experiences of the white middle class (Garcia, 1981; Miller-Jones, 1989). If you take the Stanford-Binet or Wechsler test, for example, you may be asked: What is the color of rubies? What does C.O.D. mean? Who was Thomas Jefferson? To answer these questions, one needs to have knowledge of the dominant culture. It's also important to realize that a person's racial and ethnic background may also guide his or her perception of the testing situation, understanding of the task instructions, motivation to succeed, trust in the examiner, and other aspects of the experience (Helms, 1992). There are many subtle ways in which test scores can be influenced by a person's background—independent of his or her intelligence.

Advocates of IQ testing have replied to this criticism in two ways. The first is that group differences are found even on test items that are deemed "culture-fair" (see Figure 10.5)—namely, nonverbal items that do not require extensive knowledge of a particular culture, tasks such as reciting a series of letters or digits, classifying objects, forming a pattern with blocks, or putting together the pieces of a picture puzzle (Cattell, 1949; Raven et al., 1985). Second, intelligence and aptitude tests are statistically valid predictors of performance within the schools of a particular culture, the purpose for which they were designed—regardless of whether students are African American, white, Latino, or Asian (Kaplan, 1985).

In the past, test bias was debated not only in the laboratory but also in the courtroom (Elliott, 1987). In the 1979 case of *Larry P. v. Wilson Riles*, the parents of six African American students in San Francisco claimed that the school had harmed their children by placing them in "dead-end" classes for the educable mentally retarded (EMR), placements influenced by the results of IQ tests culturally biased against African Americans. To bolster their case, the parents noted that 27 percent of all EMR children in California were African American, even though as a group they constituted only 10 percent of the school population. On the opposing side, the school board maintained that IQ tests were administered only to students who had already fallen behind and that the tests were valid—that is, they were predictive of the academic performance of African American children as well as whites. The trial lasted six months, generated ten thousand transcript pages, and included testimony from more than fifty witnesses, most of them psychologists. In the meantime, a nearly identical dispute reached center stage in the Chicago case of *P.A.S.E. v. Hannon* (1980). Once again, African American parents argued that IQ tests administered to their children were biased, local school officials defended the measures, and experts testified on both sides.

Mirroring the disagreements within psychology (Snyderman & Rothman, 1987), the judges in these two cases reached opposite decisions. In San Francisco, the judge concluded that IQ tests were culturally biased and banned their use in the California schools for placement purposes—ironically, for the very reason they were designed. Yet the Chicago judge concluded from the same evidence that intelligence tests are not discriminatory and that they offer a valid way to place children into appropriate classes. So are IQ tests culturally biased or not? Both sides are right. Disadvantaged minorities are handicapped on standardized measures—but they are also handicapped in the classroom. If IQ tests are culturally biased, it is precisely because they are meant to predict success in schools that are themselves part of the dominant culture. Thus, some experts have said that blaming IQ tests for reflecting society's problems is like killing the messenger who delivers the bad news. In this regard, there may also be some good news. In the most recent version of the Stanford-Binet, the race difference was only 10 to 13 points, not 15, as in the past (Thorndike et al., 1986).

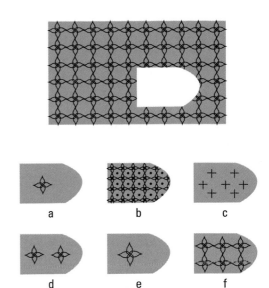

**FIGURE 10.5    Sample item from Raven's "culture-fair" intelligence test**
In this test, the person is given a series of matrices and must complete each one by selecting the appropriate symbol from the accompanying choices.

## REVIEW QUESTIONS

- *Define the concepts of mental age and intelligence quotient.*

- *Distinguish between achievement and aptitude tests.*

- *Summarize the three important characteristics that any psychological instrument should have.*

- *In what ways can IQ tests be culturally biased?*

**general intelligence (g)** A broad intellectual-ability factor used to explain why performances on different intelligence-test items are often correlated.

**factor analysis** A statistical technique used to identify clusters of test items that correlate with one another.

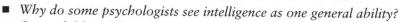

# THE NATURE OF INTELLIGENCE

- *Why do some psychologists see intelligence as one general ability?*
- *Can a child's IQ be predicted in infancy?*
- *Can intelligence be "seen" in the brain?*
- *Why do some psychologists believe that there are multiple human intelligences?*
- *How do analytic, creative, and practical intelligences differ?*

From the beginning, intelligence tests were constructed for strictly practical purposes—to identify slow learners in school, assign new military recruits, and select strong college applicants from modest backgrounds. Unfortunately, the initial emphasis on tests and measurements may have stunted the growth of theories concerning the very nature of intelligence—what it is, where it comes from, and how it is developed. As one psychologist put it, "Intelligence is whatever an intelligence test measures" (Boring, 1923).

One of the most unsatisfying aspects of IQ tests is that they reduce intelligence to a single uncomplicated number. But does that number tell a rich enough story about any one person's intellect? For me, it certainly does not. I can write a decent sentence, I have more inventive research ideas than I can manage, I can hold my own in a game of Trivial Pursuit, and I can cut to the heart of a logical argument in a matter of seconds. But I can't for the life of me solve a Rubik's Cube, I have a lousy sense of direction, and it takes an embarrassing amount of time for me to assemble the pieces of a child's toy. It's amazing how a person can feel so smart and yet so dense all at once. The point is that you have to wonder whether a person's intelligence can really be summarized by a single IQ score or even by two scores, as in the WAIS and SAT.

## GENERAL INTELLIGENCE

Psychologists have long disagreed about whether there is one intelligence or many. Some theorists can be called "lumpers," in that they view different aspects of intelligence as part of a general underlying capacity. Others are "splitters" who divide intelligence into two or more specific abilities (Weinberg, 1989). Following in Binet's footsteps, all test developers make it a point to include many tasks and derive an IQ score by averaging a subject's performance on the different items. But is it then meaningful to calculate an average level of intelligence? Yes, according to the lumpers, some people are generally smarter and more capable than others, regardless of whether they are trying to design a Web page, memorize a poem, learn a foreign language, solve a complex equation, or fix a car.

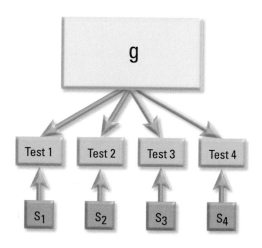

**FIGURE 10.6** **Spearman's theory of intelligence**
To explain why people who score high on one mental test also tend to score high on others, Spearman theorized that individuals differ in general intelligence (g). To explain why the correlations among tests is not perfect, he theorized that each test score is also affected by the specific ability or abilities being tested (S).

**Factor Analysis** Charles Spearman (1904) was the first to propose that **general intelligence** (abbreviated as g) underlies all mental abilities. Spearman noticed that people who excel at one task—say, verbal analogies—also tend to perform well on mazes, block designs, and other seemingly unrelated tasks. To demonstrate the point, Spearman developed **factor analysis**, a statistical technique that is used to identify clusters of test items that correlate with one another. He administered different kinds of tests to subjects, calculated the between-item correlations, and found that although individuals may be more skilled in some areas than in others, the intellectual abilities are highly correlated. This pattern suggests that there is a general intelligence factor, g, which underlies our more specific abilities (see Figure 10.6). As far as Spearman was concerned—and many others as well—a person's intelligence can, at least in a general way, be summarized by a single IQ score (Eysenck, 1982; Jensen, 1998).

**Infant Measures and IQ**   One intriguing source of evidence for the concept of general intelligence comes from infancy-research laboratories. Until just a few years ago, psychologists had tried but failed to devise infant "intelligence tests" that could predict performance later in life. The ages at which babies smile, turn the head toward a voice, inspect their fingers, track moving objects with their eyes, or start babbling, for example, are not related to measures of intelligence taken later in their early childhood (Bayley, 1949).

Thanks to the sophistication that today's researchers bring to the study of infants, it's now possible to make modest predictions of intelligence from certain types of behavior. Specifically, recent longitudinal studies have shown that three- to six-month-old infants who are responsive to changes in a stimulus—as measured by their tendency to look longer at stimuli that are new and different rather than old and familiar—score higher on standard IQ tests in early and middle childhood (Bornstein, 1989; Colombo, 1993; McCall & Carriger, 1995; Dougherty & Haith, 1997). These results—coupled with the fact that children's performance on preschool intelligence tests are even more predictive of IQ scores obtained in high school—suggest that a common ability may underlie the different measures of performance.

**Neural Speed and Efficiency**   A second source of evidence is derived from research that equates general intelligence with mental speed and efficiency. Studies have shown that people with high IQs on standardized tests are quicker than average (in milliseconds) on a range of tasks—such as inspecting stimuli, reacting to flashing lights, matching letters, solving certain types of problems, and retrieving general information from memory (Hunt, 1983; Vernon, 1987; Grudnik & Kranzler, 2001).

These findings have led some researchers to claim that intelligent people are equipped with a nervous system that relays signals rapidly—thus enabling them to learn quickly and accumulate more knowledge. In fact, recent experiments have shown that neural transmission in certain parts of the brain is faster and more efficient in people with higher IQ scores. In one study, for example, Edward Reed and Arthur Jensen (1992) showed male college students black-and-white patterns while monitoring electrical activity in the visual pathway of their brains. In each subject, they recorded the average latency, or amount of time, it took for the brain to react once the stimulus was presented. Then they divided that figure by the length of the subject's head to get a more precise estimate of the speed at which neural impulses were conducted. The result: As shown in Figure 10.7, those with quicker neural reactions also had higher scores on a written test of intelligence. On the basis of these findings, some have speculated that it may be possible in the future to devise neurological measures of intelligence (Matarazzo, 1992; Vernon, 1993). Taking a step in that direction, one team of researchers is using fMRI to monitor activation in the brain as people process information (Deary et al., 2001). Speculating on the neural correlates of general intelligence, others have suggested that human brains differ in their "plasticity"—that is, in the ease with which neural connections are strengthened by stimulation and experience (Garlick, 2002).

**Multifactor Models**   Shortly after Spearman uncovered g, Louis Thurstone (1938) administered fifty-six different tests to college students, used factor analysis to analyze the results, and concluded that human intelligence consists of seven factors, which he called primary mental abilities. For Thurstone, a person's intellectual profile cannot fully be captured by a single number. Other psychologists agree with this emphasis on specific abilities but disagree on how many. John Horn and Raymond Cattell (1966) and Paul Kline (1991) said there are two types of intelligence. J. P. Guilford (1967) believed that intelligence consists of 120 different factors—a number he later increased to 150 (Guilford, 1985).

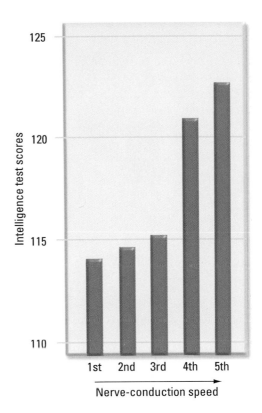

**FIGURE 10.7   Neural speed and intelligence**
Reed and Jensen (1992) recorded the time it took for each subject's brain to react to visual stimuli, then ordered the subjects from the slowest (1) on this measure to the fastest (5). As you can see, the faster subjects also had higher scores on a written test of intelligence.

*According to Gardner, there are many types of intelligence. Landscape artist Elizabeth Sutton uses visual-spatial intelligence* (left), *best-selling crime novelist Patricia Cornwell exhibits linguistic intelligence in her writing* (top center), *basketball legend Michael Jordan exhibited extraordinary bodily-kinesthetic intelligence* (right), *and nuclear physicist Albert Einstein combined mathematical and spatial intelligences* (bottom).

At this point, research provides evidence for both a general intelligence and specific abilities. Scores on the fourteen WAIS subscales are correlated (those who do well on one subscale also tend to do well on others)—evidence for a general intelligence. At the same time, it's not unusual for someone to score high on some of the subscales and low on some others, as correlations are far from perfect (usually in the .30 to .70 range)—evidence of separate mental abilities. So what does an IQ score tell us about the nature of intelligence? Were Albert Einstein, Jane Austen, and King Solomon similarly able individuals, or is that like comparing apples, oranges, and cherries? Many psychologists now believe that there's more to intelligence than IQ scores derived from paper-and-pencil tests. Two theories offer a broader view.

## GARDNER'S "FRAMES OF MIND"

In his 1983 book, *Frames of Mind,* Howard Gardner presents provocative evidence for the existence of **multiple intelligences,** each linked to a separate and independent system within the human brain. Gardner's main point is simple but revolutionary: The word *intelligence* is too narrowly used to describe cognitive abilities and does not adequately encompass the kinds of genius found in great musicians, poets, orators, dancers, athletes, and inspirational leaders all over the world. When former basketball star Michael Jordan soared gracefully toward a hoop, evading blockers and shooting with laserlike precision, didn't he exhibit a form of intelligence? Can't the same be said of Patricia Cornwell, the forensic murder novelist who freezes readers on the edge of their seats with her masterful use of language? And what about Martin Luther King, Jr., the civil-rights leader who stirred millions of Americans with his speeches and inspired massive social change?

Like a detective searching for fingerprints, smoking guns, and other clues, Gardner used converging lines of evidence to marshal support for his theory. He studied brain structures, diverse cultures, evolution, child development, and individuals with

**multiple intelligences** Gardner's theory that there are seven types of intelligence (linguistic, logical-mathematical, spatial, musical, bodily-kinesthetic, interpersonal, intrapersonal).

exceptional abilities—in other words, not just IQ tests. For example, the existence of **prodigies** (children who are normal in general but are highly precocious in a specific domain) and **idiot savants** (people who are mentally retarded yet are extraordinarily talented in some way) tells us that it's possible to have one kind of intelligence and lack another. Similarly, brain-damaged patients who lose certain abilities but retain others tell us that different intelligences can be traced to autonomous systems in the brain. In all, Gardner proposed that there are seven types of intelligence: linguistic, logical-mathematical, spatial, musical, bodily-kinesthetic, interpersonal, and intrapersonal. The first three fit easily within existing conceptions of intelligence. The last four represent a radical departure from tradition. Most recently, Gardner (2000) proposed that the list be expanded to include naturalistic intelligence, and perhaps spiritual and existential intelligences as well.

**prodigy**  Someone who is highly precocious in a specific domain of endeavor.

**idiot savant**  Someone who is mentally retarded but is extraordinarily talented in some ways.

1. *Linguistic intelligence* is a verbal aptitude that is rooted in the auditory and speech centers of the brain and consists of the skills involved in speaking, listening, reading, and writing. Storytellers and poets who are sensitive to shades of meaning, syntax, sounds, inflections, and rhythm are linguistic geniuses. So are politicians, evangelists, and successful trial lawyers who know how to use language for persuasive purposes.

2. *Logical-mathematical intelligence* is the abstract reasoning skill necessary for solving puzzles and equations and programming computers. This form of intelligence blossoms early in childhood and is often displayed by "human calculators" who can perform rapid-fire mental arithmetic. In 1987, for example, an Indian woman named Shakuntala Devi stunned mathematicians, and earned a place in the *Guinness Book of Records*, by multiplying in her head two thirteen-digit numbers randomly dealt by a computer. It took her twenty-eight seconds to calculate the correct product: 18,947,668,177, 995,426,462,773,730.

3. *Spatial intelligence* is rooted in the right hemisphere of the brain and consists of the ability to visualize objects, find one's orientation in space, and navigate from one location to another (if you ever tried to find your way through a fun-house maze, you'll know the skill it takes). A Vietnamese refugee named Minh Thai was a spatial genius. He solved the Rubik's Cube, a highly complex three-dimensional puzzle, in twenty-three seconds—a world record. Great pilots, architects, chess masters, mechanics, and visual artists also exhibit spatial intelligence.

4. *Musical intelligence* is found in all cultures, has existed throughout history, flowers early in childhood, and involves an ability to appreciate the tonal qualities of sound, compose, and play an instrument. The concept of a "musical IQ" is supported by numerous case studies. The most prolific musical prodigy of all was Wolfgang Amadeus Mozart, who learned to play a harpsichord at the age of three, composed at four, and performed in public at five. Then there's Noel Patterson, an autistic man with an IQ of 61 who can memorize melodies at the drop of a hat and play complex classical pieces by ear on the piano (Radford, 1990).

5. *Bodily-kinesthetic intelligence* is the ability to control gross and fine movements of the body. This kind of ability is rooted in the motor cortex and probably evolved in humans for running, climbing, swimming, hunting, and fighting. This form of intelligence can be seen in the figure skater who varies the timing and speed of her jumps, flips, and spins with clocklike

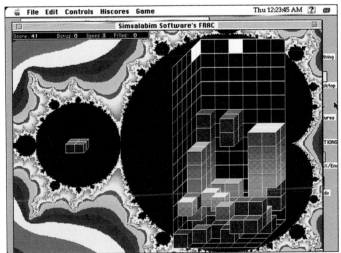

*In computer games modeled after the original Tetris, players use spatial skills to rotate and orient different squared shapes to create a solid block.*

*Tiger Woods was a prodigy and now the best golfer in the world. At three years old (and with two years of experience), Woods scored a 48 in nine holes on a course in California. At fifteen, he was the youngest player ever to win a junior amateur title. At twenty he turned pro. At 21, he became the youngest golfer ever to win the coveted Masters Tournament. He broke the course record in doing so.*

precision, and lands softly on the blade of her skate. It can also be seen in skilled dancers, athletes, and surgeons.

6. *Interpersonal intelligence* is the ability to understand other people—how they feel, what motivates them, what they like, and what they don't like. A person with these abilities can predict how others will act and, in turn, can interact smoothly. This form of intelligence can be found in successful politicians, salespersons, psychotherapists, and others with keen social skills. In *Leading Minds*, Gardner (1995) argued that great leaders have interpersonal intelligence.

7. *Intrapersonal intelligence* is the ability to have insight into one's own thoughts and feelings, to understand the causes and consequences of one's own actions, and, as a result, to make effective decisions. Self-insight is a highly adaptive form of intelligence.

Gardner's theory is controversial. Some psychologists agree that intelligence should be defined broadly enough to encompass musical genius, exquisite use of the body, and personal insight. Others feel that the theory stretches the concept too far. To his critics, Gardner says that there is nothing magical about the word *intelligence*— that to define it narrowly is to place cognitive and academic endeavors on a pedestal. The point is that all kinds of intelligence should be valued—on tests, in school, and elsewhere in life. Whether you agree or not, Gardner has raised consciousness about what it means to have intelligence—a broadened notion that could effectively be used in the classroom. Thus, Colorado kindergarten teacher Niki Mitchell tells her children that there are different ways to be smart: "Maybe you like to draw pictures. That means you're picture-smart." Similarly, she describes how one might be word-smart, number-smart, music-smart, body-smart, or people-smart (Collins, 1998). Gardner's theory has a certain appeal to parents and educators. What remains is to devise tests to measure the different intelligences, to determine if they are truly independent of one another, and to more formally study the impact of this approach for educational reform. Further research is needed to evaluate his provocative ideas.

## STERNBERG'S TRIARCHIC THEORY

"I knew exactly what our school psychologist looked like. Whenever she entered the classroom, I would panic: Her grand entry meant that we were about to take an IQ test, and the mere thought of it left me petrified. She was cold, impersonal, and as scary to me as the Wicked Witch of the West must have been to Dorothy. I really stunk on IQ tests" (quoted in Trotter, 1986, p. 56). Remarkably, this personal story is told by Robert Sternberg, now a psychology professor at Yale University and a leading expert on—you guessed it—intelligence.

Sternberg's initial poor performance piqued his curiosity about IQ tests. He overcame his test anxiety in the sixth grade, performed exceedingly well, and designed his own test of mental abilities as part of a science project. He then found a copy of the Stanford-Binet test in a library book and administered it to some of his classmates. The chief school psychologist found out and threatened to burn the book if Sternberg brought it back to class, so he didn't. After graduating from high school, however, Sternberg worked summers as a research assistant at Educational Testing Service in New Jersey, home of the SAT. "Thus began my lifelong interest in intelligence. Call it the lure of the forbidden; or perhaps it was the experience of flunking those earlier tests. Whatever the impetus, my interest had been sparked, and it would continue throughout my life" (Sternberg, 1988).

In *The Triarchic Mind*, Sternberg proposed that there are three kinds of human intelligence: (1) analytic, (2) creative, and (3) practical. To bring this theory to life,

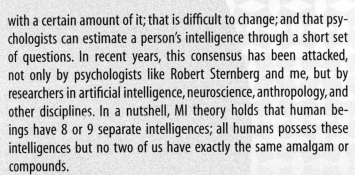

## THE PROCESS OF DISCOVERY

# HOWARD GARDNER
### *Multiple Intelligences Theory*

**Q:  How did you first become interested in psychology?**

**A:** As a teenager, I received a psychology textbook from a favorite uncle. Being color-blind I was fascinated by the text's discussion of this condition. At Harvard in the 1960s, I started out as a history major, but had the good fortune to encounter Erik Erikson, the great psychoanalyst who was writing history from a psychological point of view.

As a result of my work with Erikson, I became interested in child development. But I discovered my true calling as a cognitive-developmental psychologist when I first read Jean Piaget and took a summer job with his younger colleague, Jerome Bruner. Bruner also stimulated my lifelong interest in education and educational reform.

**Q:  How did you come up with your important discovery?**

**A:** In the 1970s, I divided my time equally between the Boston VA Medical Center, where I studied the effects on cognition of brain damage, and a research group called Harvard Project Zero, where I studied the development of various abilities in normal and gifted students. I was struck by the fact that, as a consequence of brain damage, people may lose one ability and retain others; that in young children, gifts in one area (such as music) do not necessarily correlate with gifts in other areas (such as language, athletics, or social skills). This insight became the nub of the theory of multiple intelligences. Colleagues and I received a sizeable grant to study the nature of human potential from a social science point of view. Our work provided the intellectual and empirical foundation for MI theory (as it is now called). Initial results appeared in the 1983 book *Frames of Mind.*

**Q:  How has the field you inspired developed over the years?**

**A:** For nearly a century, there has been consensus among psychologists that there is a single thing called intelligence; that we are born with a certain amount of it; that is difficult to change; and that psychologists can estimate a person's intelligence through a short set of questions. In recent years, this consensus has been attacked, not only by psychologists like Robert Sternberg and me, but by researchers in artificial intelligence, neuroscience, anthropology, and other disciplines. In a nutshell, MI theory holds that human beings have 8 or 9 separate intelligences; all humans possess these intelligences but no two of us have exactly the same amalgam or compounds.

My theory has had some influence in psychology—otherwise it would not be described in this textbook—but it has exerted its chief influence in education. There are now MI schools and programs all over the United States and in countries abroad.

**Q:  What's your prediction on where the field is heading?**

**A:** Experts will continue to debate whether intelligence is single or multiple; how much it is under genetic control; how best to assess it; and how it relates to other human capacities and virtues. I believe that intelligence is too important to be left to those who develop tests; and that the area will be enhanced in the future by the contributions of geneticists, neuroscientists, computer scientists, anthropologists, and experts on the skills needed in a global society. I hope these new "owners" of psychology will be open to the possibility of multiple intelligences.

*Howard Gardner is a John H. and Elisabeth A. Hobbs Professor at the Harvard Graduate School of Education. He is also an Adjunct Professor of Psychology at Harvard and of Neurology at Boston University's School of Medicine.*

Sternberg described three graduate students—Alice, Barbara, and Celia. *Alice* was smart by conventional criteria and was admitted to Yale as a top pick. She had an undergraduate grade-point average of 4.0, high scores on the GRE, and solid letters of recommendation. Yet Alice did *not* prove to be a strong graduate student. She did well enough on tests and was a sharp analytical thinker, but she lacked insight and could not generate creative research ideas. *Barbara* was different. Her GRE scores and grades were nothing to write home about, but her college professors raved about her insight and creativity. Barbara was not accepted into Yale, but

Sternberg hired her as a research associate and found her exceptional: "Some of the most important work I've done was in collaboration with her," he said. *Celia* was the third student. Her grades, GRE scores, and letters were not the best, but they were good enough for admission. Celia lacked Alice's analytical ability and Barbara's creativity. Four years later, however, she was the most successful student on the job market. The reason: Celia had practical intelligence, or "street smarts." She did the kind of research that was in demand, sent her papers to the right journals, made the right contacts, and learned how to satisfy the requirements of her new profession. Like Barbara's creativity, hers was a form of intelligence that does not show up on IQ tests.

To summarize, Sternberg (1986) argues that there are different ways to be smart: "What you want to do is take the components (Alice's analytic intelligence), apply them to your experience (Barbara's creative intelligence), and use them to adapt to, select, and shape your environment (Celia's practical intelligence)" (p. 62). This **triarchic theory of intelligence,** which provides a blueprint for "successful intelligence" (Sternberg, 1997), is depicted in Figure 10.8.

**Analytic Intelligence**  Alice's intelligence—what you might call school smarts—is characteristic of people who test well. Seeing intelligence in *analytic terms,* Sternberg and others have tried to understand how people answer the kinds of questions that regularly appear on traditional IQ tests—specifically, in terms of the mental steps or "components" they use to solve math problems, syllogisms, analogies, and so on.

What does it mean to process information intelligently? In our culture, as we have seen, it is common to equate intelligence with computer-like mental speed. Thus, smart people are often described as quick-witted and as fast learners. Indeed, we saw earlier that people with high IQ scores respond quickly to various cognitive tasks. Sternberg (1980) believes it's not that simple. He asked subjects to solve multiple-choice analogies such as "*Spouse* is to *husband* as *sibling* is to ____ (father, brother, uncle, son)." To answer these kinds of questions, a problem solver must first *identify* the meaning of each term and then *compare* the terms to each other. In the sample problem, you have to recognize that *spouse* is a generic term for married person, that a husband is a male spouse, that *sibling* refers to persons born of the same parents, and so on. Next, you have to match what you know about these terms to each other. To separate the two components of this task, Sternberg put subjects through a timed two-step procedure. First, they read the question part of

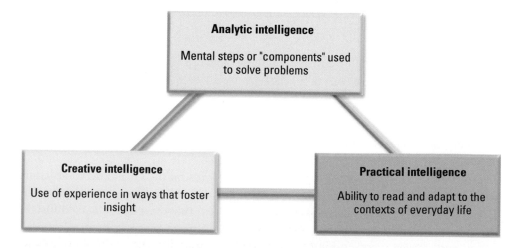

FIGURE 10.8  **Sternberg's triarchic theory of intelligence**

the analogy and pressed a button to signal when they were ready to move on. Next, they saw the multiple choices and pressed a button to select a response option. It turned out that subjects with higher IQ scores spent *more* time than others on the initial identification part of the task but were then quicker at making the necessary comparisons to find the answer. This study suggests that performance on complex thought tasks cannot be equated with sheer mental speed. People who excel on IQ tests seem to realize that the trick is to invest more time up front to comprehend the problem, then to pick up the pace (Galotti, 1989).

**Creative Intelligence**  Barbara did not have classic academic school smarts, but she was gifted with a creative mind—the second facet of Sternberg's (1988) theory. According to one dictionary of psychology, **creativity** refers to "mental processes that lead to solutions, ideas, conceptualizations, artistic forms, theories or products that are unique and novel" (Reber & Reber, 2001). For psychologists who study actors, artists, musicians, scientists, writers, chefs, fashion designers, advertisers, and others with great imagination, creativity is an active subject of research (Runco & Pritzer, 1999; Sternberg, 1999).

To Sternberg, the key to creative intelligence is *insight*—an ability to determine what information is relevant, find connections between old and new, combine facts that seem unrelated, and see the "big picture"—which enables people to create products and ideas that are novel and high in quality (Sternberg, 2001). It's easy to come up with a list of creative geniuses who have used these skills in ways that have transformed our lives. Thomas Edison, who held more than a thousand patented inventions, is an obvious choice. So are Rachel Carson (who pioneered the environmental movement in the United States), the dancer-choreographer Martha Graham (who created a distinctive new style of modern dance), Steve Jobs (the founder of Apple Computers, who first came up with the idea of making personal computers for the home), and Dean Kamen (a modern-day Edison who holds more than 150 patents, and whose invention, the Segway, may revolutionize the way people transport themselves short distances).

Over the years, psychologists have tried to develop tests to measure our capacity for creative insight (Sternberg & Lubart, 1991). J. P. Guilford (1967) suggested that the critical factor is **divergent thinking,** the ability to think flexibly and to open the mind to a range of possible solutions. Several tests have been devised to measure divergent thinking. Guilford asked people to name as many uses as they could for common objects such as a brick. Skilled divergent thinkers came up with unconventional answers—like use it to prop a door open, use it as a paperweight, break a window with it if you're locked out of the house, and so on. A second measure is the Symbolic Equivalents Test, which asks people to produce "symbolic equivalents" for various images. In response to the image of a candle burning low, for example, the divergent thinker is likely to imagine such analogous events as dying, a sunset, and water trickling down a drain (Barron, 1988). A third measure is the Remote Associates Test, in which people are shown three words and asked to come up with a fourth that links all the others. For example, the words *piano, record,* and *baseball* are all linked to player. For *stool, powder,* and *ball,* the answer is *foot* (Mednick, 1962).

However, creativity requires more than just the divergent thought processes that promote insight. Creativity is also an attitude, an approach to a task. To be truly creative requires a personality that lends itself to being open-minded, adventurous, unconventional, and willing to take risks. Individuals differ in this regard, but certain situations can help to bring out open-minded and unconventional thinking. Speculating on how to promote creativity in the corporate world, one business

**creativity**  Intellectual and motivational processes that lead to novel solutions, ideas, artistic forms, or products.

**divergent thinking**  The ability to think flexibly and entertain a wide range of possible solutions.

*Dean Kamen is a modern-day Thomas Edison. Among his more than 150 patents is his most recent invention, the Segway— a self-balancing, battery-powered scooter that may revolutionize the way people transport themselves short distances.*

**practical intelligence** The ability to size up new situations and adapt to real-life demands.

school professor said, "If you're open and honest with each other, you're more willing to propose things that are out of the box" (Lee, 2000).

Creativity also requires a high level of inner drive, curiosity, interest, involvement, and passion—in other words, an intrinsically motivated state (see Chapter 11). In a series of studies, Teresa Amabile (1996) and others had subjects write poems, write stories, draw pictures, make paper collages, paint, and give creative solutions to business dilemmas. Consistently, they found that people are more creative when they feel interested and challenged by the work itself than when they feel pressured to make money, fulfill obligations, win competitions, meet deadlines, or impress others. In one study, Amabile had art experts rate the works of professional artists and found that their commissioned work (art they were contracted for) was judged as lower in quality than their noncommissioned work. To be most creative, it helps to be intrinsically motivated in relation to the task.

Psychologists are a long way from understanding creativity. It's clear that to compose music, design clothing, solve a difficult crime, or discover a chemical process, one needs the ability to process information and think in ways that spark flashes of insight. But it's also clear that creative achievements do not flow from great minds without a willingness to take risks and lots of motivation, commitment, and hard work. Reflecting on his own prolific career, Thomas Edison thus concluded that "genius is one percent inspiration and ninety-nine percent perspiration." (See *How to Strive to Become an Expert*.)

**Practical Intelligence** According to Sternberg (1988), Celia epitomized the reason IQ tests are limited in their ability to predict success outside the classroom. Celia, you may recall, was the student who was weakest on paper but then the most successful on the job market. The reason is that she had street smarts, or **practical intelligence**—the ability to size up new situations, figure out the unspoken "rules of the game," and do what is necessary to adapt to life's demands. Whether you are trying to start a career, buy a house, or make friends, says Sternberg, you need practical intelligence, not just IQ points.

Consider the following example to illustrate the point. The recent television show, *Who Wants to Be a Millionaire?*, with Regis Philbin as the host, had a simple format. Qualified contestants were asked a series of increasingly difficult, general-knowledge questions in a multiple-choice format. Except for the random luck of the draw in questions, people won money if they had knowledge in a broad range of topics and could deduce correct answers by a process of elimination. But there was more to the story. During their climb to $1 million, contestants had available to them three "lifelines"—outside sources of help they could use, once each, as needed: They could call a friend, poll the studio audience, or have two of the four multiple-choice options eliminated. I watched the show several times and noticed that some contestants invoked their lifelines very effectively, knowing, for example, when to turn to the collective audience as opposed to the friend. In contrast, I can still recall one smart contestant who foolishly wasted a precious lifeline early in his climb on an easy question. "I'm 99 percent sure," he said, but then he used the audience to confirm his answer—and thus did not later have that resource available when he really needed it. I'd guess that this contestant was an "A" student in school. But with $1 million at stake, he exhibited a puzzling lack of practical intelligence.

I know a brilliant college professor with an intimidating intellect who eats the *New York Times* crossword puzzle for breakfast every morning. Yet he has terrible social skills, lacks common sense, and can barely balance his checkbook. Clearly, he lacks practical, down-to-earth street smarts. More and more, psychologists are coming to appreciate the importance of practical intelligence in both academic and nonacademic settings (Sternberg et al., 2000).

# THE PROCESS OF DISCOVERY

## ROBERT J. STERNBERG
*Triarchic Theory of Intelligence*

**Q: How did you first become interested in psychology?**

**A:** I first became interested in psychology when, as a child, I did poorly on group IQ tests. I would freeze up on these tests, and that would be the end of that. At least in part as a consequence of my poor IQ test scores, my teachers during my first three years of school treated me as though I wasn't very bright. When I was in fourth grade, I had a teacher who believed in my abilities, despite my low IQ scores, and that teacher turned around my life. I decided to study psychology to try to figure out why I had done so poorly on the tests.

**Q: How did you come up with your important discovery?**

**A:** Early in my career, I studied the mental processes that I theorized were involved in performance on intelligence-test items, such as analogies. But in trying to understand how people solved IQ test items, I was assuming that all there is to intelligence is what IQ tests test. Yet, I knew many students whose performance in school and life outside of school did not seem to match their test scores.

Some years later, as a teacher, I formulated a "theory of successful intelligence." Like all my theories, the theory arose from everyday experiences. I simultaneously was teaching three students whose skill patterns seemed very different. One student, "Alice," did very well on conventional tests, in getting high school grades, and in conventional classroom activities. She succeeded by virtue of her memory and analytical skills. A second student, "Barbara," was very creative and imaginative. She came up with wonderful ideas. A third student, "Celia," excelled in practical endeavors. She knew how to get along with people, how to figure out what teachers expected, and how to advance her career.

So my theory of intelligence came to be based around the notion that people differ in analytical, creative, and practical skills, but that, unfortunately, most of the tests our society uses emphasize only the analytical. Thus the educational system is heavily stacked in favor of Alices, at the expense, I believe, of Barbaras and Celias.

**Q: How has the field you inspired developed over the years?**

**A:** Since I first proposed the theory, we have done a substantial amount of research showing that analytical, creative, and practical skills really are somewhat distinct, and moreover, that one needs all three, in greater or lesser degree, to succeed in school and life. The most successfully intelligent people are those who figure out their pattern of strengths and weaknesses, then think and act in ways that enable them to make the most of their strengths and correct or compensate for their weaknesses. So an important thing in life is to figure out what you do and do not do well, and then make the most of the abilities you have.

**Q: What's your prediction on where the field is heading?**

**A:** We are trying in our research to figure out ways to help people to make the most of their abilities and continue to develop these abilities throughout their lives. I see researchers, today and in the future, helping people to identify and maximize their unique abilities.

*Robert Sternberg is IBM Professor of Psychology and Education at Yale University.*

---

What skills are involved? Some psychologists believe that what's most critical is *social competence*—like Gardner's social or interpersonal intelligence, an ability to know the feelings, thoughts, and actions of other people (Cantor & Kihlstrom, 1987). In a related vein, other psychologists focus more narrowly on *emotional intelligence*, an ability to know how people are feeling, including yourself, and the ability to use that information to guide your own thoughts and actions—qualities that are highly adaptive in social settings (Bar-On & Parker, 2000; Mayer et al., 2001; Matthews et al., 2003). Still others believe that underlying practical intelligence are *wisdom* and *common sense*—an unspoken knowledge that grows with age and experience and enables us to make sound judgments in important life matters. When faced with problems such as how to resolve a conflict between two coworkers

### REVIEW QUESTIONS

- *What is the evidence for the g-factor theory of intelligence?*
- *Describe the seven types of intelligence identified by Gardner's (1983) "frames of mind" theory.*
- *Compare and contrast Sternberg's (1988) three kinds of intelligence.*

or family members, or what to say to a friend who talks of suicide, some people exhibit more wisdom than others (Baltes & Staudinger, 2000; Sternberg, 1998).

Practical intelligence may even boost success in school, typically the domain of analytic intelligence. Wendy Williams and others (2002) had elementary school teachers in Connecticut and Massachusetts train students in "Practical Intelligence for School," a program that taught them to identify what is expected of them, to know their own strengths and weaknesses, and to use effective work habits. Compared to students in control-group classrooms, those assigned to this program became better at reading, writing, homework, and test taking. Apparently, the insights that come with practical intelligence can be taught, resulting in greater scholastic achievement.

## THE GREAT DEBATES

- *Why is debate about the nature and nurture of intelligence politically loaded?*
- *What does research tell us about genetic and environmental influences?*
- *What do Head Start programs try to accomplish, and how successful are they?*
- *What group differences are found in test scores, and how might these differences be interpreted?*

Intelligence testing is a "numbers game" with profound consequences for real people. IQ and aptitude scores help to determine which young children in need of parents are adopted first and which students are accepted into prestigious private schools. They determine whether a child is labeled as retarded or gifted, whether placed in the "bluebirds" or "cardinals" group at school. Later, these scores help to determine which students are admitted into elite colleges, are offered scholarships, and then have the best job prospects. As Richard Weinberg (1989) put it, "IQ tests play a pivotal role in allocating society's resources and opportunities" (p. 100). With the stakes so high, it's easy to see why psychologists who study and measure intelligence find themselves in one emotional debate after another. In this section, we consider three heated issues: nature and nurture, racial and cultural differences, and sex differences.

### NATURE AND NURTURE

To what extent is intelligence determined by the forces of nature (genetics) and nurture (the environment)? How much does each factor contribute, and in what ways do they interact? These questions loom over all others and are the most explosive. To see why this issue generates such furor, let's step back in time and consider some of its social and political implications.

**The Politics** In the nineteenth century, Galton argued that intelligence was an inherited characteristic—and that only bright adults should be encouraged, or even allowed, to reproduce. Many years later, Henry Goddard (1917) tested new European immigrants to the United States, judged many as genetically inferior, and recommended that they be deported. In 1969, Arthur Jensen argued that IQ score differences between black and white Americans were genetically rooted. Jensen, whose views were called "Jensenism," was accused of being a racist and was jeered on campuses across the country. His writings influenced physicist William Shockley (the winner of a Nobel prize for inventing the transistor), who urged the U.S. government to institute a voluntary sterilization program by offering to pay citizens with low IQ scores to undergo sterilization at a rate of $1,000 for each IQ point below 100. Along with some other Nobel prizewinners, Shockley deposited his sperm in a "sperm bank," to be used by women of superior intelligence.

In contrast, nurture advocates have attributed low IQ scores to nongenetic factors such as poverty, maternal drug use, poor nutrition, inadequate schooling, a lack of academic focus in the home, low expectations, and feelings of helplessness and despair. Focused on change, they have promoted social policies designed to enrich the educational experiences of disadvantaged children. In 1905, Binet wanted to identify slow learners so that they could receive special services (Binet & Simon, 1905). Sixty years later, in the United States, psychologists studying the effects of early experience on intelligence helped to inspire **Project Head Start,** a nationwide preschool program for children born of poor families. Similar intellectual-enrichment projects can now be found in other countries as well.

In light of the political stakes, it is perhaps not surprising that the nature–nurture debate has been mired in scandal. When Jensen (1969) argued that racial differences were inherited and that educational-enrichment programs were doomed to fail, he based these conclusions in part on the research of Cyril Burt, an eminent British psychologist who died in 1971. In a series of three studies published in 1943, 1955, and 1966, Burt had reported that the correlation in IQ scores was higher between identical twins reared apart than between fraternal twins reared together—convincing evidence for the role of genetics. When these data were closely inspected, however, they revealed a remarkable story. In *The Science and Politics of IQ*, Leon Kamin (1974) found that even though Burt kept adding new twins to his sample, the IQ correlations he reported never changed—a nearly impossible statistical outcome. Two years later, an article appeared in the *London Times* under the headline "Crucial Data Was Faked by Eminent Psychologist" (Gillie, 1976), followed by a rash of letters to the editor by other well-known researchers. Some claimed that Burt not only fudged his statistics, but also made up names for research assistants and subjects who did not exist. Others discredited Burt's results but concluded merely that he was careless, or even that he was framed. Among historians of psychology, the Burt affair remains a lively topic of discussion (MacKintosh, 1995).

Whatever the truth may be, this episode stands as a tall reminder that on politically tender topics, the conclusions drawn from research data should be made with caution. This brings us to *The Bell Curve* (1994), a highly controversial book by Richard Herrnstein, a psychologist who died just before the book was released, and Charles Murray, a political scientist. After reviewing past research, these authors claimed that intelligence is a largely inherited trait, that it can be measured by standard IQ tests, and that IQ differences within society have created a caste-like division between the intelligent "cognitive elite" and a lesser "cognitive underclass." Herrnstein and Murray argued that low IQ is the root cause of failure in school, poverty, welfare, crime, and other problems. They further argued that because IQ is so influenced by genetic factors, social programs designed to help the poor are doomed to fail. Although the book is not about race or ethnicity, the implication is that the existing IQ gap between African Americans and whites in the United States cannot be closed.

*The Bell Curve* aroused strong and instant public reaction. *Newsweek* called it "frightening stuff." *Time* described it as "845 pages of provocation with footnotes." Yet the *Wall Street Journal* decried those in the media who were engaged in "a frantic race to denounce and destroy Charles Murray." Among psychologists, some critics argued that Herrnstein and Murray overestimated the role of genetic factors. Others noted that correlations between IQ and social class should not be taken to mean that IQ causes poverty. Some other third factor could give rise to both outcomes—or the causal arrow could point in the opposite direction. Thus,

**Project Head Start**    A preschool intellectual-enrichment program for children born of poor families.

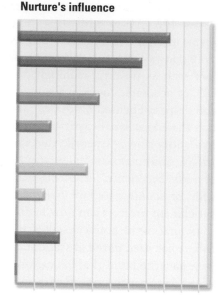

FIGURE 10.9 **Nature's influence on IQ scores**
Studies reveal that the greater the genetic similarity between individuals, the more similar are their IQ scores (evidence for nature). These same studies reveal that individuals reared together have more similar IQ scores than those reared apart (evidence for nurture).

Stephen Ceci (1996) asked, "Is it better to be born rich or smart?" Finally, others challenged the pessimistic assumption that intelligence is a rigid trait that can be altered only minimally by environmental intervention. So, complex as it is, what is the scientific evidence?

**The Science**    After many years of debate, most experts now agree that intelligence is influenced but not entirely determined by genetic factors. In support of this conclusion, Figure 10.9 summarizes the results of 111 studies of more than 100,000 twins and other relatives (Bouchard & McGue, 1981). You can see that genetically identical twins growing up in the same home get highly similar scores on IQ tests—almost as if the same person had taken the test twice. But how much of this similarity is rooted in nature?

To estimate the role of genetic factors, let's compare people who share a similar environment but differ in genetic relatedness. Three comparisons are worth noting: (1) Identical twins who are reared together (in fact, even those reared apart) are more similar than fraternal twins also reared together; (2) siblings who grow up together are more similar than unrelated individuals who grow up in the same home (even biological siblings reared apart show some degree of similarity); and (3) children are more similar to their biological parents than to adoptive parents. Additional research ties the genetic knot around IQ even tighter. Longitudinal studies show that the similarities do not diminish as blood relatives grow older, but get stronger—and that the similarities exist in verbal, mathematical, and spatial abilities; school grades; and vocational interests (McCartney et al., 1990; Plomin, 1988). There is also far more similarity among biological twins than among "virtual twins"—unrelated siblings of the same age who grew up together as a result of adoption (Segal, 2000).

Nobody disputes the role of genetics, but it's clear that the same studies provide strong evidence for environmental influences. This pro-nurture conclusion is based on comparisons of people who have the same genetic relatedness but who live in different environments. As you can see in Figure 10.9, whenever they live together rather than apart there's more similarity between (1) identical twins, (2) siblings, (3) biological parents and children, and (4) unrelated individuals. In all instances, different environments reduce the impact of genetic relatedness. From all the results, it appears that heredity accounts for 60 to 75 percent of the population variation in intelligence, with environmental factors responsible for the rest. Be clear about what this result means. It does not mean that 60 to 75 percent of your IQ is inherited—it means only that genetic factors are responsible for that portion of the differences among individuals in the population.

Wait. Don't these results, which suggest a primary influence of heredity, contradict the finding described at the start of this chapter, that IQ scores all over the world have risen sharply and consistently since 1920? Human genes cannot change from one decade to the next, so the increased IQ presumably reflects changes in the environment—such as better nutrition, more schooling, and advances in technology that increase access to information.

As discussed in Chapter 8, William Dickens and James Flynn (2001) recently proposed a theory that helps to reconcile the apparent discrepancy on the powers of nature and nurture. Dickens and Flynn argue that genetic dispositions and environments are not independent. According to their theory, boys and girls who are brighter than average at birth will have initial success in school, which will bring praise from parents and teachers, motivate them to work hard, draw them to peers who are studious, and encourage them to prepare for college, all of which breeds intellectual success. In contrast, boys and girls who are not as bright at birth will have less initial success, receive less praise, care less about schoolwork, and affiliate with other weak students, all of which breeds failure. In other words, genes create environments, which in turn, multiplies the influence of genes. This theory explains how identical twins separated at birth can live in different homes but experience similar environments. It also explains the consistent but puzzling finding that genetic influences on intelligence seem to increase, not decrease, with age (see Figure 10.10).

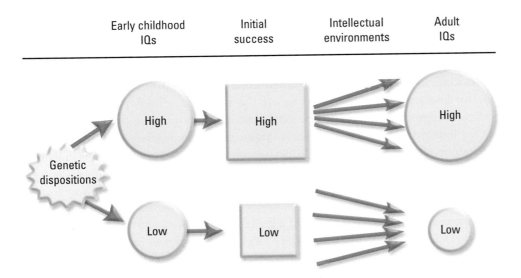

**FIGURE 10.10   How environments magnify genetic influences**
Dickens and Flynn (2001) theorize that genes predispose young children toward varying degrees of initial success in school. These early experiences then steer the children into environments that later constrain or facilitate intellectual development, which increases the differences by adulthood. In this way, genes create environments, which in turn, multiply the influence of genes.

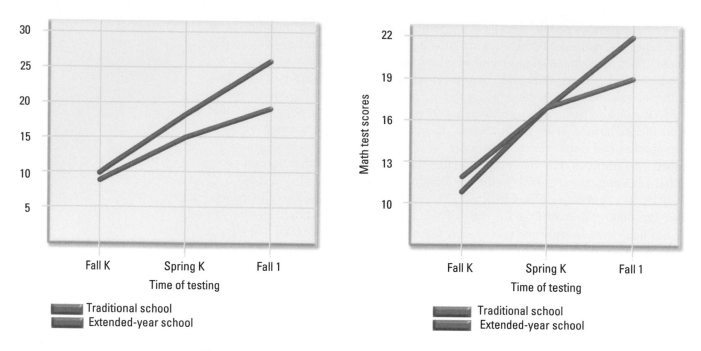

**FIGURE 10.11**

Frazier and Morrison (1998) tested children from two comparable schools, one with a traditional 180-day year, the other with an extended-year program of 210 days. As shown, children coming off the extended school year outperformed the others in both reading (*left*) and math (*right*) tests.

Clearly, environments influence intelligence. So, what environmental factors in particular are important? The possibilities are numerous: prenatal care, exposure to alcohol and other toxins, birth complications, malnutrition in the first few months of life, intellectual stimulation at home, stress, high-quality education, and so on. Just the sheer amount of time spent in school is important—which may account for why test scores drop during summer vacation and rise again during the school year (Ceci, 1991). Julie Frazier and Frederick Morrison (1998) compared kindergarten children at two closely matched schools, one of which was experimenting with an extended-year program consisting of 210 school days instead of the usual 180 (in other words, a shortened summer vacation). All the children were tested in the fall of their kindergarten year, again in the spring, and a third time in the fall of the first grade. Look at the scores on reading and math tests in Figure 10.11, and you'll see that by first grade, children coming off the extended school year outpaced the others on all measures. Simply put, more time in school produced better students.

One interesting variable is *family configuration*—the number and birth order of children in a home. According to Robert Zajonc (1976), a family's intellectual environment consists of the average absolute intelligence levels of all its members. Say, for example, that a family consisting of two adults with average IQs has an intellectual environment of 100. If the couple has a newborn baby (whose mental age is zero), the family average drops to 67 (200/3). If a second baby is born a year later, the average drops even lower, to 50. As children get older, their mental ages increase and raise the family's average. Consistent with this model, Zajonc and Mullally (1997) found that IQ scores are slightly higher among first-borns and children from small families (because they spend much of their time in the company of adults) than among later-borns and those in large families (because they are surrounded by other children, unless their siblings are much older). So, are children from smaller families, and first-borns, intellectually advantaged in their upbringing? It's still not clear. According to Joseph Lee Rodgers and others (2000), the correlations are an "illusion" brought

## Debunking the Myth

# THAT LISTENING TO MOZART MAKES YOU SMARTER

Throughout human history, parents have wanted their children to be intelligent. Today, whole industries claim to offer parents a way to give their infants and young children an intellectual head start. Several years ago, researchers discovered that infants were most visually stimulated not by color but by high-contrast black-and-white patterns. An enriched environment facilitates brain development, so parents went out and bought newly created black-and-white mobiles and hung them in their infants' cribs. Other studies led parents to talk nonstop to their fetuses, play tapes of Dr. Seuss stories, and later prop their toddlers up to the family computer for games that teach counting, reading, and other skills.

The most recent home education fad stemmed from experiments on the so-called "Mozart effect." It all started when Frances Rauscher and others (1993) reported that exposure to music by Mozart improves spatial reasoning, an ability measured in all tests of intelligence. First, they had college students spend ten minutes listening to Mozart's *Sonata for Two Pianos in D Major*, listening to a relaxation tape, or sitting in silence. Then the students completed a set of spatial reasoning tests—for example, imagining what shapes are produced by certain paper foldings and cuttings, or putting together the pieces of a jigsaw puzzle. The authors predicted that exposure to Mozart facilitates abstract spatial reasoning because its musical structure is complex, not simple and repetitive. Sure enough, students who listened to Mozart got the highest test scores.

As you might expect, these provocative results attracted lots of attention from the media. As often occurs when science makes news, the tendency is to hype, overstate, and jump to conclusions not supported by the research. In this case, the "effect" was found in college students and lasted for only a few minutes. Yet it led anxious new parents—eager to provide an enriched intellectual environment—to purchase Mozart CDs for their babies. Companies then sprouted up to exploit the claim by selling specially packaged collections of Mozart. One company, which I won't name, stated: "The evidence is in: Music is not just entertainment." It then promises an offering of Mozart that will "stimulate and inspire young minds, improve intelligence, and help develop IQs." Also influenced by this finding, Georgia Governor Zell Miller,

*Wolfgang Amadeus Mozart (1756–1791)*

who is now a U.S. senator, budgeted to provide CDs to every new mother in the state. In Florida, a law was passed requiring that toddlers in state-run schools listen to classical music every day (Goode, 1999).

Does the evidence support the hype? People with extensive training in music do perform better than most at certain spatial reasoning tasks, suggesting that there may be a link (Gardiner et al., 1996). But psychologists have not studied the Mozart effect in infants and toddlers, and the adult study is under attack on two fronts. First, some researchers have been unable to replicate the basic finding (Steele et al., 1999). Others soon discovered that the effect had little to do with Mozart. For example, Kristin Nantais and Glenn Schellenberg (1999) found that compared to ten minutes of silence, Schubert's *Fantasia for Piano* also increased spatial test scores. Listening to "The Last Rung on the Ladder," a short story by Stephen King, similarly boosted performance, particularly for students who preferred a story to music. William Forde Thompson and others (2001) found that the effect was an artifact of the pleasant mood state aroused by certain types of music. Apparently, there's nothing special about Mozart. The effect can be produced by any auditory stimulation that engages the mind and makes people upbeat and alert while being tested, not bored and drowsy.

For information about government education programs and services, studies, statistics, and press releases, visit the U.S. Department of Education site: http://www.ed.gov/

about by the fact that high-IQ parents have fewer children than low-IQ parents. From their own studies, these investigators conclude that small families don't make high-IQ children; rather, high-IQ parents make small families. (See *Debunking the Myth That Listening to Mozart Makes You Smarter*.)

**Head Start Programs**   Parents who provide an enriched and stimulating home—by hanging mobiles in the crib, reading bedtime stories, playing games, family traveling, and so on—foster a child's intellectual growth. Children deprived of these learning experiences begin life at a tremendous disadvantage. It's like the old chicken-and-egg problem: Poverty lowers intelligence, and low intelligence leads people into poverty. Somehow, the vicious cycle must be broken.

In 1965, as part of President Lyndon Johnson's War on Poverty, Project Head Start was launched with psychologist Edward Zigler as the program's first director. Head Start is a group of preschool programs for children, mostly three and four years old, born into low-income families. In some programs, teachers make house calls to train parents and engage children in playing with building blocks, reading books, and other cognitive activities. In other programs, the children attend special preschools outside the home. Dedicated to helping those who are born into disadvantaged families—two-thirds of whom are minorities—Head Start serves hundreds of thousands of families across the country each year (Zigler & Muenchow, 1992). As of 2002, according to the U.S. Department of Health and Human Services, the average cost was $6,633 per child.

Skeptics wonder if it's worth the money, but research shows that the program has been reasonably successful. It cannot boost IQ scores into the gifted range, but in other ways, Head Start alumni surpass comparable others who don't take part. Entering school, they score about 10 points higher on IQ tests, are more confident, and are quicker to adjust to the demands of sitting in a classroom. Although initial gains in IQ may wear off over time, Head Start children in high-quality programs are later less likely to repeat grades or to be put into remedial classes—and are more likely to graduate from high school and hold after-school jobs (Woodhead, 1988; Lee et al., 1990). In addition, research shows that the younger children are when they get into Head Start, the better. In programs that target infants who are "at risk" due to low birth weight, low income, or low parental IQ, intelligence-test scores increase by as much as nine points by the age of three (Ramey, 1999) and the initial gains in reading and math persist into adulthood (Campbell et al., 2001).

When it comes to academic success and failure, getting off on the right foot can make a difference. Reflecting on Head Start, Edward Zigler and Susan Muenchow (1992) noted: "Head Start is the nation's most successful educational and social experiment. It was a pioneer in providing comprehensive services in a family-centered context, and it continues to offer the only real two-generational assault on poverty. Over 11 million children are better off today because of Head Start—in some cases, dramatically better off" (pp. 244–245).

## THE RACIAL GAP

One reason the nature–nurture debate is so filled with emotion is that certain racial and cultural groups score higher than others on measures of ability and achievement, and these differences ignite blunt claims concerning genetic superiority and inferiority. Let's start with an often-cited empirical fact: African Americans as a group have averaged 15 points lower than whites on IQ tests and 100 points lower on the SAT verbal and math tests (Jensen, 1998).

Why has this gap occurred? If heredity contributes to variations among individuals, does it also account for differences found among groups? No, not necessarily. To be sure, a few psychologists have speculated that differing evolutionary pressures in Europe, Asia, and Africa have, over time, produced measurable differences among humans in brain size and intelligence (Rushton & Ankney, 1996). But as critics of *The Bell Curve* were correct to note, genetic variation among *individuals* within a group does not mean that differences among *groups* are genetically based. Compared to the average African American, white Americans grow up in more affluent homes and with better educational opportunities—differences that can account for the IQ gap (see Figure 10.12).

Three sets of research findings support this point. The first is from a study that asked: What would happen to the IQ scores of black children adopted into white middle-class homes? Sandra Scarr and Richard Weinberg (1976) studied 99 such cases in Minneapolis and found that the average IQ score was 110—well above the African American average and comparable to that of white children from similar families. When the adoptees were retested ten years later, similar results were found (Weinberg et al., 1992).

The second set of findings involves cross-cultural comparisons and historical trends. The cultural perspective reveals that the racial gap in IQ within the United States is not unique. Low scores in disadvantaged groups are found all over the world, including the Maori of New Zealand, the "untouchables" in India, non-European Jews in Israel, and the Burakumin in Japan (Ogbu, 1978). From a historical perspective, it's clear that as a result of school desegregation and social programs such as Head Start, African Americans have had more educational doors opened in recent years than in the past. Paralleling these new opportunities, the racial gap in the Stanford-Binet has diminished somewhat (Thorndike et al., 1986)—and differences in reading and math achievement have substantially narrowed (Jones, 1984; Grissmer et al., 1998).

A third, particularly important, research finding concerns the effect of a college education on the racial gap in IQ. Joel Myerson and others (1998) examined data from a longitudinal study that tracked thousands of young men and women from the ages of fourteen to twenty-one. Specifically focusing on black and white college graduates, these researchers analyzed the scores these students had received on tests taken after the eighth (pre-high school) through twelfth (post-high school) and sixteenth (post-college) grades. If the racial gap in IQ was immutable, as Herrnstein and Murray had suggested in *The Bell Curve,* then the difference in standardized test scores would be little affected by a level educational playing field. Yet it was. Look at Figure 10.13, and you'll see that although the racial gap remained through high school, and even widened somewhat, it was substantially narrowed by the time the students were finished with college. Everyone gained from the experience, but the black students gained more—and cut the gap in half.

## CULTURAL INFLUENCES

As a consequence of the nature–nurture controversy, researchers have also compared people from different ethnic, social, and cultural groups. Most recently, the career achievements of Asian American

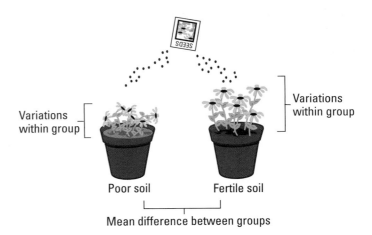

**FIGURE 10.12 Explaining group differences**
To understand how genes can affect the variation among individuals but not account for differences among groups, imagine having an assortment of different seeds, with some more likely than others to grow into tall plants. Now take the mixture, randomly divide it into two groups, and plant one group in a pot of fertile soil and the other in a pot of barren soil. Among the seeds sown *within* a pot, the differences in growth may reflect genetic differences. Yet the average growth difference between the two pots will be largely due to their differing environments.

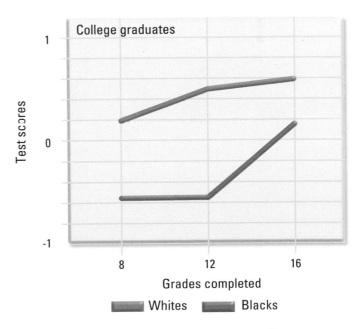

**FIGURE 10.13 Education: The great equalizer**
These are the cognitive test scores of future college graduates as they moved from grades 8 through 16. Indicating the vital equalizing role of education, the initial gap between black and white students was narrowed by the time they completed college (Myerson et al., 1998).

*Lenny Ng was a son of Chinese immigrants. At ten, he scored 800 on the math SAT. At sixteen, he entered Harvard University. Julian Stanley, who founded the Center for Talented Youth at Johns Hopkins University, called him "the most brilliant math prodigy I've ever met."*

immigrants—particularly in high-tech industries—raised the nature–nurture questions once again. Relative to other groups, Asian American students get higher grades and SAT math scores, are more likely to graduate from college, and are more likely to win National Merit Scholarships, Westinghouse Science Talent Searches, and Presidential Scholarships. The news media thus have referred to Japanese, Chinese, Korean, Vietnamese, Filipino, and Indian students collectively as "The New Whiz Kids" (Sue & Okazaki, 1990).

Are Asian Americans, in general, smarter than other groups? Flynn (1991) analyzed more than a dozen IQ studies and found that despite the remarkable record of Asian Americans, their test scores were about average, like everyone else. Looking at IQ and employment statistics, Flynn went on to calculate that Chinese Americans as a group are just as successful as white Americans would be if they had an average IQ of 120—a pattern of "overachievement" that begs for an explanation.

Researchers are struggling to understand this phenomenon. Although some have suggested that the achievements of the Asian American community are the product of genetic factors (Anderson, 1982), most attribute the success to cultural values that emphasize hard work, discipline, and respect for education. The support for this explanation is particularly strong when it comes to academic disparities in mathematics. In a series of studies, Harold Stevenson and others (1990, 1993) compared children in a wide range of schools in Taiwan, Japan, and the United States and found that by the fifth grade, Asian students were superior in number concepts, computation, word problems, and other aspects of math. However, the Asian students also found the schoolwork more difficult, were less confident of their own skills, and were less favorably evaluated by parents and teachers. In other words, American children and adults were more satisfied than Asians were despite lower levels of achievement (Crystal & Stevenson, 1991).

Additional studies have shown that the Asian advantage in math continues into high school, where Taiwanese and Japanese students outperform Americans in algebra, geometry, trigonometry, and calculus (Chen & Stevenson, 1995). Even at the high-school level, there are marked cultural differences in the values placed on academics. When high-school students in the three countries were asked to account for their time, the differences were striking: Students in Taiwan and Japan, relative to those in the United States, spend more time in school and more time studying, whereas the American students spend more time working, socializing, taking part in extracurricular activities, and dating (Fuligni & Stevenson, 1995).

When you put the pieces together, it seems that Americans set lower standards and place a lower value on academic pursuits. Also consistent with this cultural explanation, Philip Ritter and Sanford Dornbusch (1989) surveyed thousands of high-school students in California and found that those of Asian descent were more likely than others to believe that success in life is linked to what they do in school. They also found that the longer an Asian family has lived in the United States, the lower is its level of achievement. Ironically, the cultural values that promote success for new Asian immigrants seem to erode as they become settled in their new homeland.

## GENDER DIFFERENCES

When intelligence tests are constructed, a concerted effort is made to remove questions that prove more difficult for one sex than for the other—or at least to balance items favoring one sex with items favoring the other. The result is that total IQ scores are comparable for males and females. But what about specific abilities? Is there any truth to traditional gender stereotypes that depict math and spatial relations as masculine enterprises and language as the art of women? Several years ago, Eleanor Maccoby and Carol Jacklin (1974) reviewed the research and found that it supported the stereotype. Even today, among high-school students who take the Advanced Placement (AP) and SAT-II subjects tests, males score higher on average in physics, economics, computer science, chemistry, U.S. government, biology, and calculus; females score higher in Spanish, French, German, art history, studio art, and English literature (Stumf & Stanley, 1998).

Because the issue of gender differences has profound implications for how parents treat their sons and daughters—and for how teachers treat male and female students—psychologists have been eager to understand the nature and extent of these differences. Here is what we know at this point.

- **Verbal abilities.** On verbal-aptitude tests, Janet Hyde and Marcia Linn (1988) analyzed data from millions of students tested between 1947 and 1980 and found that girls outscored boys but that the gender gap had narrowed. Currently, there are no gender differences in verbal SAT scores. On average, however, girls are better spellers. They also score slightly higher than boys on tests of reading comprehension, writing, and foreign languages (Hedges & Nowell, 1995; Stumpf & Stanley, 1996).

- **Mathematical abilities.** Girls are better at arithmetic in grade school, but boys surpass them in junior high school—a difference that continues past college and is found in other countries. On the math portion of the SAT-I, males have a 30- to 40-point edge (in 2002, according to the College Board, the male and female averages were 534 and 500). This gap is most evident among the highest-level math students (Benbow, 1988; Hyde et al., 1990) and on unconventional problems that require flexible problem-solving strategies (Gallagher et al., 2000). This difference may underlie the fact that males score higher on high-school achievement tests in physics, chemistry, and computer science (Stumpf & Stanley, 1996).

- **Spatial abilities.** Consistently, males outperform females on spatial tasks such as mentally rotating objects to determine what they look like from another perspective, as depicted in Figure 10.14, and tracking moving objects in space (Linn & Petersen, 1985; Masters, 1998). These skills are used in architecture, mechanical engineering, flight navigation, and certain other types of work. The sex difference is early to develop, and is apparent from test scores at the ages of four and five years old (Levine et al., 1999). In a longitudinal study that followed up on 563 thirteen-year-olds, those who initially had high spatial test scores, compared to those with high verbal scores, were more likely, twenty years later, to have careers in engineering and computer science (Shea et al., 2001).

Why are there gender disparities in math and spatial relations? As you might expect, this question awakens the debate on the relative importance of nature and nurture. On the *biological* side, some researchers have argued on the basis of animal and human studies that sex differences in spatial abilities stem from the prenatal effects of sex hormones on the brain. According to Camilla Benbow (1988) and Doreen Kimura (1999), the male hormone testosterone slows the fetal development of the left hemisphere, thereby enhancing the growth of the more spatial right

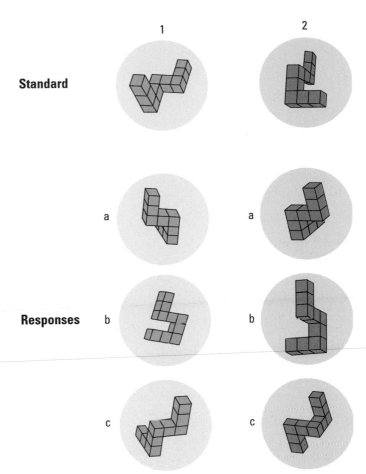

**FIGURE 10.14**  **The mental-rotation test of spatial ability**
For each standard shown on top, which of the three responses on the bottom shows a different view of the same object? The answers appear on page 422.

*Studies show that experience with these games increases spatial test scores—for girls as well as boys.*

## REVIEW QUESTIONS

- *Describe the evidence supporting the role of genetic factors in intelligence.*

- *Describe the evidence supporting the role of environmental factors in intelligence.*

- *What factors contribute to the racial gap in IQ scores?*

- *In what ways do men and women differ in intelligence? How can these differences be explained?*

hemisphere. That is why highly talented math students are also more likely to be left-handed, nearsighted, and allergy sufferers—traits seen as linked to high prenatal levels of testosterone exposure. David Geary (1996) further speculated that the male spatial advantage evolved over time to support navigation, warfare, hunting, and other activities that require movement in three-dimensional space.

On the *social* side, Jacquelynne Eccles (1985) and others attribute at least part of the gender gap to stereotypes of math as a masculine subject, less encouragement of girls by parents and teachers, and different experiences in childhood. For example, boys use spatial skills more often through contact sports, action-packed video games, construction sets, and Transformers (plastic toys that can be "transformed" from one object to another). Consistent with this hypothesis, two studies have shown that playing action video games improves spatial-test performance—in girls as well as in boys (Okagaki & Frensch, 1994; Subrahmanyan & Greenfield, 1994).

## EDUCATION

- *How are giftedness and mental retardation defined, and what education issues do they raise?*
- *What is the self-fulfilling prophecy, and how might the process influence the performance of students in the classroom?*

Now that we have examined the major IQ tests, theories of intelligence, and the debates that have arisen, let's return to where it all started: the classroom. Ever since Binet's work in the schools of Paris, many psychologists have had uneasy feelings about the link between their conceptions of intelligence and education.

There are two principal questions. First, by focusing on the prediction of academic performance, have we adopted too narrow a conception of intelligence? Many influential theorists think so. Gardner complains that IQ tests completely ignore and devalue the musical, bodily-kinesthetic, and personal intelligences. Likewise, Sternberg says that these tests, like the school systems they service, don't recognize the potential for achievement inherent in people who have creative and practical intelligence. The second question concerns the impact of IQ testing on the quality of

**Answer to mental rotation test:**
The correct answers are 1(*a*) and 2(*b*).

education. Once a child is identified as a fast, slow, or average learner, what next? Do those with unusually high or low IQ scores benefit from being identified as "special"? What are the educational implications? Because schools rely heavily on IQ tests to sort children into academic categories, it's important to raise these kinds of critical questions.

## GIFTEDNESS

Popular stereotypes of gifted children include unflattering images of eccentric nerds, geeks, and social misfits doomed to a life of failure—hence the expression "Early ripe, early rot." The story of William James Sidis, considered the world's greatest child prodigy, is a case in point. Sidis was born in 1898 in New York City, to Russian-immigrant parents. He was reading by the age of two, using a typewriter at three, and speaking Russian, French, German, and English at five. Sidis started school at the age of six and whizzed through seven grades in less than twelve months. That year, he devised a new table of logarithms and knew enough about human anatomy to pass a medical-school exam. At the age of eleven, Sidis was admitted into Harvard, where he astonished the Harvard Mathematical Club with a lecture on the fourth dimension. Despite this prodigious start, however, Sidis soon fizzled into obscurity. He dropped out of graduate school and spent most of his life in low-paying clerical jobs. When Sidis died at the age of forty-six, he was living in a rooming house alone, unemployed and penniless (Wallace, 1986).

Researchers have found that many gifted children—particularly those at the very top of the distribution—feel isolated, have social and emotional problems, and fail to realize their creative potential as adults (Winner, 2000). Yet this biographical pattern is not typical or inevitable. In 1921, Lewis Terman (the Stanford psychologist who imported Binet's IQ test) launched what was to become the most extensive longitudinal study of "genius" ever conducted. Terman studied 1,528 California schoolchildren, all with IQs over 135. He and later researchers then followed the progress of their lives for years to come and found that as a group these men and women were healthy, well adjusted, happily married, and highly successful in school and in their careers. Many of the "Termites" went on to become eminent doctors, lawyers, authors, scientists, and professors. At retirement, many were happy and satisfied with their lives (Holahan & Sears, 1995). In a second research program, Camilla Benbow and Julian Stanley (1980) identified through a nationwide "talent search" thousands of mathematically gifted children who took the SAT in the seventh and eighth grade and whose math scores placed them in the top 1 percent of the population. Twenty years later, in a follow-up study of 1,975 of these gifted adolescents, Benbow and her colleagues (2000) found that the men and women in this group were highly educated, successful in their careers, and satisfied with the state of their lives. In a third study, David Lubinski and others (2001) followed up a "profoundly gifted" group of 320 children whose SAT scores placed them, for their age, in the "top 1 in 10,000" of the population. Ten years later, restudied in their early twenties, these men and women "were off to an exciting start"—receiving academic awards, pursuing doctoral degrees at fifty times the normal rate, and making important literary, scientific, and technical achievements. Other new studies of gifted people are also now underway, so more will be known in the years to come (Heller et al., 2002).

It's impossible to know why some gifted individuals, like William Sidis, flounder while so many others, as shown by recent studies, are very successful. From an educational standpoint, however, it's important to know what it means to be "gifted" and how we can educate our bright and talented children. When Terman conducted his study, he selected subjects according to standardized IQ tests. Today, giftedness is

Mensa is an international organization for people with a high IQ (top 2%). There are 100,000 Mensans in the world. Among its members are high-school dropouts and people with advanced degrees, welfare recipients and millionaires, professors, glassblowers, and truck drivers—you name it. For information and a 30-minute "Mensa workout," you can visit its Web site at: http://www.mensa.org

viewed in broader terms. Several years ago, for example, Joseph Renzulli (1986) proposed a three-ring conception of giftedness as the product of above-average intelligence, task commitment, and creativity. Following in the footsteps of Gardner and Steinberg, others maintain that giftedness is not a global trait but, rather, one that is specific to a particular domain. Thus, many high-school students who get perfect scores on one academic subtest of the ACT do not fall within the gifted range on other subtests (Colangelo & Kerr, 1990). You can be a brilliant economist, physicist, writer, or computer programmer without being an intellectual jack-of-all-trades.

As a matter of policy, society has mixed feelings about how gifted children should be treated. On the one hand, we are troubled by a sense that it's fundamentally unfair to provide special opportunities for an elite, chosen group of children, to the exclusion of others. On the other hand, we recognize that it's important to challenge bright minds and harvest their full potential in order to build a better future for everyone. Special resource rooms, an accelerated curriculum, and after-school programs are some ways to enrich the educational experience (Robinson et al., 2000).

In 1972, Julian Stanley of Johns Hopkins University pioneered what is now a nationwide talent search for gifted math students. By administering the math portion of the SAT to bright seventh graders, Stanley and others identified as "mathematically precocious" those boys and girls with scores over 500 (a higher-than-average score for twelfth graders; the top 1 percent of seventh graders). These students were given advanced summer programs in mathematics and science, accelerated college courses, and counseling for their parents. The participants enjoyed the program and benefited from the experience—without showing signs of social or emotional stress (Stanley & Benbow, 1986; Richardson & Benbow, 1990). Focused in nineteen states and seventy countries, this Center for Talented Youth now offers summer programs for school children of all grades—for writing, drama, music, law, history, psychology, and other subjects besides math and science. To date, the Center has identified a million students and has served more than one hundred thousand through its programs. The goal: "To inspire young people by offering distinctive educational opportunities that nurture intellectual abilities, advance academic achievement, and enhance personal development" (http://www.jhu.edu/~gifted/index.html).

## MENTAL RETARDATION

At the opposite end of the continuum, children whose IQ scores are below 70 are evaluated to see if they are mentally retarded. **Mental retardation** is a term used to describe people with limited intellectual ability. It used to be the case that anyone who scored in the lowest 3 to 5 percent was identified as mentally retarded. Since test performance has little to do with the ability to function in nonacademic settings, however, the American Psychiatric Association (1994) raised its criteria. To be diagnosed as mentally retarded, a person must now have (1) an IQ score below 70, and (2) difficulty adapting to routine needs of life, such as self-care and social interactions. Other causes of poor test performance—such as physical illness or impaired vision or hearing—also have to be ruled out. Only about 1 percent of the population meets these criteria, with males outnumbering females (Burack et al., 1998; American Association on Mental Retardation, 2002).

There are four categories of mental retardation, varying in severity. As shown in Table 10.1, most retarded people are only mildly retarded. They have IQ scores in the 50 to 70 range and are sometimes referred to as "educable" because they are capable of achieving a sixth-grade level in reading and math. Usually, mildly retarded children live at home and attend public schools. Once diagnosed, they are

**mental retardation** A diagnostic category used for people with IQ scores below 70 who have difficulty adapting to the routine demands of life.

| TABLE 10.1 | | MENTAL RETARDATION: DEGREES OF SEVERITY | |
|---|---|---|---|
| Level | Percentage of Retarded Persons | Typical IQ Scores | Adaptation to Demands of Life |
| **Mild** | 85% | 50–70 | May learn academic skills up to a sixth-grade level. Adults may, with assistance, achieve self-supporting social and vocational skills. |
| **Moderate** | 10% | 35–49 | May progress to a second-grade level. Adults may contribute to their own support by labor in sheltered workshops. |
| **Severe** | 4% | 20–34 | May learn to talk and to perform simple work tasks under close supervision, but are generally unable to profit from vocational training. |
| **Profound** | 1% | Below 20 | Require constant aid and supervision. |

given individualized education programs that are designed to meet their academic, social, and emotional needs, while keeping them as much as possible within the regular classroom (Robinson et al., 2000). As Alfred Binet had hoped, these students can be taught at their own pace, enabling them to learn better and live more fulfilling lives. Unfortunately, the use of IQ tests for placement purposes can be risky—and may even backfire. The problem is this: Since the tests are not the perfect crystal ball, what happens to a child whose ability is underestimated? What happens if expectations are set too low?

## THE SELF-FULFILLING PROPHECY

In 1948, sociologist Robert Merton told a story about Cartwright Millingville, president of the Last National Bank during the Depression. Although the bank was solvent, a rumor began to spread that it was floundering. Within hours, hundreds of depositors lined up to withdraw their savings, until there was no money left. The rumor was false, but the bank eventually failed. Using stories such as this, Merton proposed that a person's expectation can actually lead to its own fulfillment—a phenomenon known as the **self-fulfilling prophecy.** As we'll see, this can influence the educational process in three ways.

**Teacher Expectancies**   Using Merton's hypothesis, Robert Rosenthal and Lenore Jacobson (1968) wondered about the possible harmful effects of IQ testing. What happens to the educational experience of the child who receives a low score? Would it leave a permanent mark on his or her record, arouse negative expectations on the part of the teacher, and impair future performance? To examine the possible outcomes, Rosenthal and Jacobson told teachers in a San Francisco elementary school that certain pupils were on the verge of an intellectual growth spurt. The results of an IQ test were cited, but in fact the pupils were randomly selected. Rosenthal and Jacobson administered real tests eight months later and found that the so-called late bloomers (but not children assigned to a control group) had actually improved their scores and were evaluated more favorably by their classroom teachers.

When this study was published, it was greeted with chagrin. If high teacher expectations can increase student performance, can low expectations have the opposite effect? Could it be that children who get high scores are destined for success, whereas those who get low scores are doomed to failure, in part because educators hold different expectations of them? To this day, many researchers have been critical of the study and skeptical about the generality of the results (Spitz, 1999). But

**self-fulfilling prophecy**   The idea that a person's expectation can lead to its own fulfillment (as in the effect of teacher expectations on student performance).

*Claude Steele's work on stereotype threat shows that "invisible" sociocultural factors are at work in the classroom. When asked how he discovered this effect, Steele said, "My students and I had been struggling to understand the immeasurable processes that seemed to undermine the academic performance of certain groups in society. . . . Gradually, we were able to describe how people can become intimidated by the prospect of being reduced to a group stereotype in a domain where a stereotype about one's group could apply. When the stereotype is about something important—like intelligence or, for some, athletic ability—it can put a great deal of pressure on the person."*

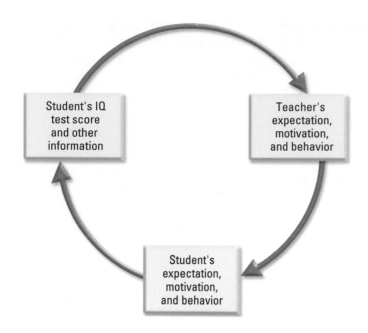

**FIGURE 10.15** **Three-step model of a self-fulfilling prophecy**

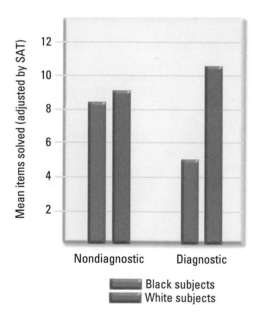

**FIGURE 10.16** **Stereotype threat effect on test performance** Steele and Aronson (1995) compared the performances (adjusted for their own ability) of African American and white students on a thirty-item verbal-reasoning test. When the significance of the test was underplayed, there were no differences (*left*). When the test was presented as diagnostic of verbal ability, the African American students performed worse (*right*). This result is consistent with the stereotype-threat hypothesis.

the phenomenon is potentially too important to be swept under the proverbial rug. After reviewing other tests of the hypothesis, Rosenthal (1985) concluded that teacher expectations significantly predicted student performance 36 percent of the time. Mercifully, the predictive value of teacher expectancies seems to wear off, not accumulate, as children advance from one grade to the next (Smith et al., 1999).

How might teacher expectations be transformed into reality? There are two points of view. According to Rosenthal, the self-fulfilling prophecy can be viewed as a three-step process. First, the teacher forms an impression of the student early in the school year. This impression may be based on IQ-test scores or other information. Second, the teacher behaves in ways that are consistent with that first impression. If the expectations are high rather than low, the teacher gives the student more praise, attention, and challenging homework. Third, the student unwittingly adjusts his or her own behavior according to the teacher's actions. If the signals are positive, the student may become energized. If negative, he or she may lose interest and self-confidence. As depicted in Figure 10.15, the cycle is thus complete and the teacher's expectations confirmed. Importantly, self-fulfilling prophecies like this are at work in many settings—not only in schools but in a range of organizational settings, including the military (McNatt, 2000).

While conceding that the teacher-expectations effect can occur, Lee Jussim and his colleagues (1996) question whether teachers in real life are so likely in the first place to form erroneous impressions of their students. In many naturalistic studies, the expectations teachers have at the start of a school year are later confirmed by their students—a result that is consistent with the notion that the teachers had a hand in producing that outcome. But wait. That same result is also consistent with a more innocent possibility: Perhaps the expectations that teachers form of their students are often *accurate*. There are times, Jussim admits, when teachers may stereotype a student and, without realizing it, behave in ways that create a self-fulfilling prophecy. But there may also be times when teachers can predict how their students will perform without necessarily influencing that performance. In one study, teacher ratings of preschoolers were statistically predictive of these children's school grades fourteen years later, as they graduated from high school (Alvidrez & Weinstein, 1999).

**Stereotype Threat** There's a second way in which expectations can set in motion a self-fulfilling prophecy. According to Claude Steele (1997), African Americans are painfully aware of the negative stereotypes people hold regarding their intelligence. As a result, scholastic test situations make African American students feel threatened by the stereotype and anxious about performance. Research on this hypothesis is still in the early stages, but the results suggest that this process is at work. To make matters worse, notes Steele, this threat can eventually become chronic, causing African American students to tune out and "disidentify" from academic pursuits.

Steele and Aronson (1995) administered a thirty-item verbal test to African American and white college students. Half the subjects were told that the items were merely a device that psychologists use to study the way people solve problems—a "nondiagnostic" instruction that was given to underplay the testlike nature of the task. The other half were told that the same items measured verbal-reasoning ability—a "diagnostic" instruction designed to make stereotype-threatened subjects anxious. As shown in Figure 10.16, African American and white subjects did not differ much when given the low-key nondiagnostic instruction (their scores were statistically adjusted according to each subject's past verbal SAT in order to equalize initial differences in their actual abilities). In the diagnostic condition, however, the African American subjects exhibited a decrease in their own performance. With the task defined as an ability test, those feeling vulnerable to the stereotype, sadly, helped to confirm it. How can this happen? One possibility is suggested by a recent psychophysiological study showing that African Americans in the "diagnostic" condition exhibit an increase in blood pressure during and after the test (Blascovich et al., 2001).

Other research indicates that **stereotype threat** effects are general and can interfere with other groups and other domains of ability. In one study, Steven Spencer and others (1999) found that women performed poorly relative to men in a math test when led to believe that it was the type of test in which there were sex differences favoring men. Importantly, women performed better, and the male-female difference disappeared, when they were simply told beforehand that the test was gender-neutral. In another study, Jeff Stone and others (1999) tested the hypothesis that in the domain of athletic performance, white students would feel threatened by the popular stereotype that African American athletes are superior—an image portrayed in the movie *White Men Can't Jump*. Black and white college students were told they'd be putting on a miniature golf course as part of a sports aptitude test. Some students were told that performance required natural athletic ability, whereas others were told it required intelligence. Performance was measured by the number of strokes subjects needed to complete the course. Can you predict the result? When the task was presented as a test of natural athletic ability, black students performed better—and white students performed worse. It seems that everyone is vulnerable. When a stereotype is "in the air," people fear they will fail, which makes them more likely to do just that (Steele et al., 2002).

## Ability Grouping

A third way in which IQ tests might influence (not just reflect) academic performance is by steering students onto a fast or slow track in the school curriculum. If you've ever read Aldous Huxley's *Brave New World*, you may recall the opening scene in the "Hatchery and Conditioning Centre," where human embryos only a few hours old are transformed into Alphas, Betas, Gammas, Deltas, or Epsilons and are programmed accordingly for a high-class or low-class future. In the foreword to this novel, Huxley (1932) expressed his personal fear that a "science of human differences" could be used to sort people early in life into fixed, immutable social ranks. This may sound like fanciful science fiction, but critics charge that intelligence tests are too often used in the same manner to separate children according to their IQs (Tobias, 1989).

To cope with the tremendous diversity of children who attend public schools, educators try to group students who have similar academic abilities (Dornbusch et al., 1996). Teaching is easier when all students are on the same "wavelength." There are two general ways to reduce student heterogeneity. One is *between-classroom grouping*, in which all the students in a grade are assigned to separate high-, average-, or low-level classes. A second way is *within-classroom grouping*, in which students mixed in the same classroom are put in separate instructional groups, usually for reading and math. What happens to students who are tracked at a young age, often based on a test score? What difference does it make to a child's education and self-esteem to belong to the fast "sharks" rather than the slow "goldfish"?

The main argument for between-classroom grouping is that by separating whole groups of children by ability, a teacher can prepare one curriculum to meet the needs of all students. The level and pace of instruction can be raised for those in the high class and lowered for those in the low class. Yet, as reasonable as this policy

**stereotype threat**   The tendency for positive and negative performance stereotypes about a group to influence its members when they are tested in the stereotyped domain.

seems, this practice can harm students who are put into slow classes because they don't test well. In elementary school, teachers in low-ability classes spend much of their time managing disruptive students, to the detriment of the others (Eder, 1981). In junior and senior high schools, high-track students read great literature, use computers, and learn critical thinking, expository writing, and other skills valuable for college. But in low-track classes, instructors are content to teach "functional literacy" (how to read signs, fill out forms, and so on), basic arithmetic, and rote memorization (Oakes, 1986). In short, a school's curriculum can be either enriched or watered down, depending on a student's placement—a placement that may constrain future performance. Ultimately, the rich get richer and the poor get poorer.

The alternative is within-classroom ability grouping, in which, as noted, mixed students from the same class are separated into groups assembled for math and reading. Most schools favor this approach, though the issue is complicated. After reviewing numerous studies, Robert Slavin (1995) concluded that students who are in heterogeneous classes achieve more when they are grouped for instruction than when the class is taught as a whole and that between-class grouping is not similarly effective. So far, so good. But it's also important to consider the effects of such grouping on self-esteem. For many years, researchers were baffled by the fact that children in disadvantaged schools had higher academic self-esteem than those from more affluent schools. Apparently, children compare themselves to one another and feel smarter when they are surrounded by classmates who are relatively weak academically. In this respect, it's better to be a large fish in a small pond than a small fish in a large pond (Marsh & Parker, 1984).

In terms of classroom composition, heterogeneity is like a two-edged sword: High-ability students gain confidence by being in the presence of weaker peers, but low-ability students lose confidence alongside their stronger peers. These results led David Reuman (1989) to conclude, "choosing within-classroom versus between-classroom grouping policies involves complicated tradeoffs" (p. 187). That's why the current trend among educators, particularly in classrooms with lots of diversity, is toward flexible grouping, as needed—in pairs, small groups, and other arrangements (Caldwell & Ford, 2002).

## REVIEW QUESTIONS

- *How is mental retardation defined? What are the four categories of mental retardation?*

- *How do teacher expectations influence student performance in school?*

- *What is stereotype threat? How can it affect academic performance?*

## THINKING LIKE A PSYCHOLOGIST ABOUT INTELLIGENCE

For about a century now, psychologists have been trying to define, measure, understand, and enhance intelligence, an elusive concept. You can tell by the frequent use of the Stanford-Binet, Wechsler scales, SAT, and other instruments that ability testing is a booming enterprise. It's also one that should be viewed with a critical eye to safeguard against possible abuses. Intelligence is a many-splendored concept—more than just IQ, a magical number used to predict school performance. Intelligence shows up in one person's flair for writing, in a second person's ability to wheel-and-deal in business, and a third person's fluent mastery of five languages. It's the ability to process information with efficiency, generate creative ideas, and use one's skills to get ahead in life.

Underlying much of the tension that surrounds the study of intelligence is the nature–nurture debate. It is clear that both genetic and environmental factors contribute to an individual's intelligence. It's also clear that because racial and cultural groups have distinct life experiences, intellectual differences at the group level are hard to interpret. The same is true of the small differences that exist between men and women. Finally, it's important to consider the educational implications of using IQ tests for identification and placement purposes. On the one hand, objective measures of intelligence help us to predict academic potential and develop programs suitable for individual students. On the other hand, IQ tests can set in motion a self-fulfilling prophecy and steer students onto a fast or slow track in school. Either way, it's important to keep in mind that intelligence is not a tangible object but a word that describes the skills that enable you to make a better life for yourself and others.

# SUMMARY

Many psychologists define **intelligence** as a capacity to learn from experience and adapt successfully to one's environment.

## INTELLIGENCE TESTS

### THE STANFORD–BINET

In the early 1900s, Binet and Simon developed a test to determine a student's **mental age**—the average age of children who achieve a given level of performance. Terman revised the test and renamed it the **Stanford-Binet**. He also scored the test by means of an **intelligence quotient (IQ)**: mental age divided by chronological age and multiplied by 100. Today, an IQ represents a person's performance relative to the average of same-age peers.

### THE WECHSLER SCALES

To distinguish between different aspects of intelligence, the **Wechsler Adult Intelligence Scale (WAIS)** yields separate verbal and performance scores. There are also Wechsler scales for children.

### GROUP APTITUDE TESTS

In contrast to the Stanford-Binet and Wechsler measures, which are individually administered, aptitude tests like the SAT and ACT are given in groups. Although these tests seek to distinguish aptitude from achievement, the two factors are difficult to separate.

### ARE INTELLIGENCE TESTS ACCURATE?

To be accurate, a test must be standardized, reliable, and valid. **Standardization** means that the test provides a standard of norms that can be used to interpret a given score. **Reliability** means that the results are consistent. **Test-retest reliability** ensures that a test will yield similar results at different times; **split-half reliability** ensures that different forms of the test will produce similar results. **Validity** is the extent to which the test measures or predicts what it is supposed to. **Content validity** refers to whether test questions adequately measure the quality they were designed to measure (intelligence). **Criterion validity** concerns the test's ability to predict a concurrent or future outcome (academic achievement). These tests correlate highly with grades in school but are less predictive of adaptation to life outside.

### ARE INTELLIGENCE TESTS BIASED?

Some say that intelligence tests are culturally biased because scores are influenced by such background factors as the test taker's racial or ethnic group. Advocates of testing note that race differences occur even on "culture-fair" items and that intelligence tests do predict academic performance.

## THE NATURE OF INTELLIGENCE

### GENERAL INTELLIGENCE

Spearman was the first to speak of **general intelligence (g)**, a broad factor underlying all mental abilities. By developing **factor analysis,** a statistical technique used to identify clusters of test items that correlate with one another, Spearman found that all intellectual abilities are linked to g. Recent studies show that childhood IQ scores are somewhat predictable from measures of infant responsiveness and that people with high IQ scores process information quickly and efficiently. Other researchers have divided intelligence into various components.

### GARDNER'S "FRAMES OF MIND"

Partly because of the existence of **prodigies** and **idiot savants,** Gardner proposed a theory of **multiple intelligences.** According to Gardner, different systems in the brain produce seven different types of intelligence: linguistic, logical-mathematical, spatial, musical, bodily-kinesthetic, interpersonal, and intrapersonal. The last four types stretch the concept of intelligence beyond traditional notions.

### STERNBERG'S TRIARCHIC THEORY

According to Sternberg's **triarchic theory of intelligence,** a theory of successful intelligence, there are three basic types of intelligence. Analytic intelligence is the kind of skill exhibited on traditional IQ tests and by school grades. It may relate to the sheer speed of neural transmission in the brain.

**Creativity** refers to the mental processes that lead to unique and novel solutions, ideas, artistic forms, or products. One key to creative insight is **divergent thinking,** the ability to think flexibly and entertain a wide range of possible solutions. Another key is intrinsic motivation, an inner drive and enthusiasm for a task.

**Practical intelligence,** the last of Sternberg's three types, is the ability to size up situations and adapt to real-life demands. This ability consists of social competence, wisdom, and emotional intelligence.

## THE GREAT DEBATES

Because test scores affect so many aspects of our lives, debates about intelligence testing have been heated.

## NATURE AND NURTURE

People have long disputed the extent to which intelligence is determined by nature (genetics) and by nurture (environment). Studies of twins and other family members appear to show that heredity accounts for 60 to 75 percent of the population variation in intelligence. Others now suggest that environmental factors multiply the effects of genes. The recent publication of *The Bell Curve* brought this issue into the limelight.

The relationship between intelligence and poverty is a vicious cycle. Research indicates that programs such as **Project Head Start**, which intervenes early in a child's life to break the cycle, have a measurable impact on IQ and school success.

## THE RACIAL GAP

Are group differences in average IQ and SAT scores brought about by nature or by nurture? This issue is politically loaded. But research suggests that environmental factors can help to explain the relatively low scores by African Americans and the relatively high scores by Asian Americans.

## GENDER DIFFERENCES

Whereas girls score somewhat higher on verbal tests, boys on average perform better in mathematical and visual-spatial tasks. Some researchers suggest the difference is biologically rooted, perhaps traceable to the prenatal effects of sex hormones. But others point to social explanations, such as gender differences in the spatial experiences of boys and girls.

## EDUCATION

### GIFTEDNESS

Contrary to stereotypes, gifted children as a group do well in later life. Today, many children identified as gifted are offered special programs. It appears that these students benefit from these programs.

### MENTAL RETARDATION

For students with varying severity levels of **mental retardation**, individualized education programs can help meet special needs. On the other hand, test results may lead educators to underestimate a child's ability.

### THE SELF-FULFILLING PROPHECY

According to studies of the **self-fulfilling prophecy**, teacher expectations influence student performance. If teachers expect little of a child because of a low IQ score, that child will likely perform accordingly.

Recent studies of **stereotype threat** also show that social and cultural groups feel threatened by negative stereotypes about them, which make them anxious and impairs performance.

Finally, grouping, or tracking, often based on intelligence tests, can harm students assigned to the slower groups, yet boost the confidence of students who fare well as "fish in a small pond." Today, most educators favor flexible within-classroom grouping policies.

## KEY TERMS

intelligence (**p. 393**)

mental age (**p. 395**)

Stanford-Binet (**p. 395**)

intelligence quotient (IQ) (**p. 395**)

Wechsler Adult Intelligence Scale (WAIS) (**p. 396**)

standardization (**p. 399**)

reliability (**p. 399**)

test-retest reliability (**p. 399**)

split-half reliability (**p. 399**)

validity (**p. 400**)

content validity (**p. 400**)

criterion validity (**p. 400**)

general intelligence (g) (**p. 402**)

factor analysis (**p. 402**)

multiple intelligences (**p. 404**)

prodigy (**p. 405**)

idiot savant (**p. 405**)

triarchic theory of intelligence (**p. 408**)

creativity (**p. 409**)

divergent thinking (**p. 409**)

practical intelligence (**p. 410**)

Project Head Start (**p. 413**)

mental retardation (**p. 424**)

self-fulfilling prophecy (**p. 425**)

stereotype threat (**p. 427**)

## THINKING CRITICALLY ABOUT INTELLIGENCE

1. Discuss the debate concerning one intelligence versus multiple intelligences. Which view do you believe?

2. Discuss the controversy surrounding the use of IQ and other standardized tests of intelligence. Explain how IQ tests might be both biased and accurate. In what ways might IQ scores influence intelligence rather than simply reflect it?

3. What are the advantages and disadvantages of using IQ scores to label children as "gifted" or "mentally retarded"? Would you want your own child to be labeled by an IQ score? Why or why not?

4. In what ways do genetic and environmental forces interact to determine intelligence? What practical implications does this have for the way in which we educate our children?

5. Is greatness born or made? Defend your position with psychological research.

# Motivation

# WHAT DOES IT TAKE TO MOTIVATE PEOPLE AT WORK?

## THE SITUATION

The year was 1927. Calvin Coolidge was president, Babe Ruth hit sixty home runs, Charles Lindbergh flew across the Atlantic for the first time, and the American economy seemed sound, though it would soon become depressed. Just outside Chicago, the Hawthorne plant of the Western Electric Company employed close to thirty thousand men and women in the manufacture of telephones, wires, cables, and office equipment. As in other large companies, management wanted to boost the morale, motivation, and productivity of its employees. The bottom line was important.

At first, the Industrial Relations Branch of Western Electric thought that they could make workers at the plant more productive by altering the illumination levels in their factory. Proceeding in logical fashion, they increased the lighting for one group of workers in a special *test room*, kept the lighting unchanged in a *control room*, and compared the effects on their productivity. Western Electric then brought in a team of experts to vary other conditions in the factory. Over the next five years, groups of employees from various departments were selected to do their work in a test room where, at different times, they were given additional rest periods, coffee breaks, a free midmorning lunch, shorter workdays, shorter weeks, a new location, overtime payments, personal financial incentives, dimmer lights, or just a different method of payment. At one point, the researchers even went back and merely reinstated the original prestudy conditions inside the test room.

## MAKE A PREDICTION

The researchers involved in this project wanted to know how to increase the motivation and productivity of workers, as measured by their hourly output. Using existing performance levels at the plant as a basis for comparison, they asked what changes in the workplace would have a positive impact. Consider the conditions listed below and check off those that, in your opinion, increased worker productivity.

Brighter lighting　　　　　　＿＿＿＿＿＿＿
Dimmer lighting　　　　　　　＿＿＿＿＿＿＿
Two 5-minute rest periods　　＿＿＿＿＿＿＿
1-hour-shorter workday　　　＿＿＿＿＿＿＿
1/2-day-shorter week　　　　　＿＿＿＿＿＿＿
15-minute rest + free lunch　＿＿＿＿＿＿＿
Financial incentives　　　　　＿＿＿＿＿＿＿
Back to original conditions　＿＿＿＿＿＿＿

## THE RESULTS

If you thought that adding financial incentives boosted worker productivity, you were right. This change was accompanied by a 12.6 percent increase in hourly output. If you thought that a shorter workday or a shorter workweek or a free lunch had positive effects, you were right again. Brighter lighting? Yes. Dimmer lighting? Yes again. In fact, productivity rates increased no matter what the researchers did—even when they dimmed the lights and even when they merely reinstated the original prestudy conditions. So the correct prediction was to check off *all* conditions.

## WHAT DOES IT ALL MEAN?

The Hawthorne project, described in the book, *Management and the Worker* (Roethlisberger & Dickson, 1939), has had a profound influence on the study of motivation in the workplace. At first, the researchers were puzzled and discouraged. With positive effects being observed among all test-room workers (even when the original pretest conditions were in place), it seemed that the project had failed. Think for a moment about the results, however, and you'll see why these studies are important. With striking consistency, workers became more motivated and more productive not because of the specific changes made but because they had been singled out for special assignment. Workers assigned to the test rooms knew they were being studied, and they enjoyed the added attention. This phenomenon, known as the **Hawthorne effect**, laid a foundation for the study of behavior in the workplace and the realization that people are motivated not only by money and other objective states but also by their own needs and social relationships. The Hawthorne plant no longer exists, but the study conducted there has helped psychologists to understand an important practical side of human motivation.

John was the son of Frank Lindh, a Catholic lawyer, and Marilyn Walker, a health-care worker who became a Buddhist. He grew up in Maryland and was the second of three children. When John was 10, his family moved to Marin County, California—an affluent, socially liberal community north of San Francisco—where he attended an alternative school for self-directed students. At 16, John became interested in Islam and joined a local mosque. After graduating from high school, he moved to the Middle East. Two years later, in November 2001, he was a captured Taliban prisoner of war in Afghanistan, charged with bearing arms against American troops. What led this young man to surrender all that was familiar in search of a new religion and culture? At a time when his peers were consumed by sports, music, school, and romance, what inspired him to leave his family, his home, and his country, and dedicate his life to Islam?

At about the same time, news of a business scandal rocked Houston, Texas. Enron was one of the world's largest energy trading companies, marketing electricity and natural gas. In 2000, Enron's revenues topped $101 billion. One year later, the company filed for bankruptcy, forcing CEO Kenneth Lay to resign and causing thousands of workers to lose their life savings in retirement plans. Government investigators soon alleged that some company executives engaged in illegal transactions, broke basic rules of accounting, misled investors, and shredded documents as part of a cover up. Why would millionaires who already have more money than they could reasonably spend in a lifetime break the law and harm others for financial gain?

On a lighter note, but also puzzling, I cannot help but wonder about the behaviors that seemingly ordinary people display on "reality" TV shows such as *Survivor*,

*Big Brother,* and *Temptation Island.* When it comes to human motivation, some particularly bizarre behaviors in need of an explanation appear on *Fear Factor,* a show in which contestants compete in their ability to endure gross and hair-raising experiences. In one stunt, contestants bobbed for apples in a water tank filled with snakes. In another, contestants inserted their heads into a small plastic box containing large rats. Some were required to strip naked and parade along a runway in front of spectators. Still others rode bulls, ate roaches or ants, hung from bridges, walked on the wing of an airplane in flight, and jumped from one city building roof to another—all begging the obvious question, why?

To answer the questions raised about Lindh, the Enron executives, and survival TV show contestants, and about other human endeavors that result in triumph or defeat, we need to understand the psychology of human motivation. **Motivation** is an inner state that energizes an individual toward fulfillment of a *goal.* In this chapter, we'll explore various domains of human motivation, including hunger and eating; sex and sexuality; the social needs for affiliation, intimacy, achievement, and power; and behavior in the workplace. As we'll see, words such as *want, try, wish, urge, intent, desire, drive, goal, energy,* and *ambition* provide the language used to describe motivation.

> **motivation** An inner state that energizes people toward the fulfillment of a goal.

> **instinct** A fixed pattern of behavior that is unlearned, universal in a species, and "released" by specific stimuli.

## WHAT MOTIVATES US?

- *Are there general principles that explain what motivates us?*
- *Are people driven by instincts, a need to achieve a certain level of bodily tension, or a desire for attractive rewards?*
- *Do all people want to satisfy the same basic needs? If so, what are those needs?*

Over the years, psychologists have approached the subject of motivation in two ways. Some have proposed general theories to explain what all human motives have in common. Others have focused on specific motives such as hunger, sex, affiliation and belonging, and achievement. Let's begin with the first approach.

### GENERAL THEORIES OF MOTIVATION

Early in the twentieth century, as Darwin's theory of evolution gained prominence, many psychologists believed that human behavior, like the behavior of other animals, was biologically rooted in instincts. As we saw in Chapter 5 on Learning, an **instinct** is a fixed pattern of behavior that is unlearned, universal within a species, and "released" by a specific set of conditions. Thus, canaries sing, spiders weave webs, and beavers build dams—specific acts that are "hard-wired" by evolution. But is complex human behavior similarly programmed? In 1908, motivation theorist William McDougall argued that a whole range of human behaviors is instinctually based. He went on to compile a long list of instincts—including those for acquisition, jealousy, mating, parenting, pugnacity, greed, curiosity, cleanliness, and self-assertion.

Instinct theories of human motivation were soon rejected. One problem was that they explained human behavior through a flawed process of circular reasoning: "Why are people aggressive? Because human beings possess a powerful instinct to aggress. How do we know humans have this instinct? Because there is so much aggression." Notice the circularity in the logic: Behavior is attributed to an instinct that, in turn, is inferred from the behavior. A second problem with instinct theory is that many so-called instinctual behaviors are learned, shaped by experience, subject to individual differences, and influenced by culture.

*When snow falls, children in all parts of the world make snowballs. Instinct theorists of the past would attribute this universal behavior to an instinct for play. Young Japanese macaques also make snowballs, carry them around as play objects, and even roll them along the ground. But here's where the similarity ends: No one has ever seen a macaque throw a snowball.*

**Drive Theory**   With the demise of instinct-based accounts, psychologists turned to a **drive theory** of human motivation. According to drive theory, physiological needs that arise within the body create an unpleasant state of tension, which motivates or *drives* the organism to behave in ways that reduce the need and return the body to a balanced, less tense state (Hull, 1943). In its original form, drive theory was used to explain various biological functions such as eating, drinking, sleeping, and having sex. The hunger-eating cycle illustrates a presumed chain of events: food deprivation → hunger (drive) → seeking food and eating → drive reduction.

Clearly, drive theory can be used to explain certain biologically driven behaviors. But today, psychologists agree that it cannot explain what motivates the eating-disordered adolescent or the late-night workaholic—or the greedy corporate executive. In particular, drive theory cannot explain why people often engage in activities that increase rather than reduce tension, as when we explore new surroundings just to satisfy our curiosity, skip a snack to save our appetite for dinner, or run miles with our hearts pounding in order to stay in shape. Nor can drive theory explain the behavior of contestants on *Fear Factor* or the popularity of such high-risk activities as ice climbing, extreme skiing, and skydiving.

**Arousal Theory**   To account for the fact that people often seek to increase rather than reduce tension, many psychologists turned to the **arousal theory** of motivation. According to arousal theory, all human beings are motivated to achieve and maintain an *optimum* level of bodily arousal—not too little, not too much (Fiske & Maddi, 1961). Studies show that people who are put into a state of sensory restriction (blindfolded, ears plugged, and unable to move) or into a highly monotonous situation quickly become bored and crave stimulation. Studies also show that when people are bombarded with bright lights, blaring music, and other intense stimuli,

**drive theory**   The notion that physiological needs arouse tension that motivates people to satisfy the need.

**arousal theory**   The notion that people are motivated to achieve and maintain an optimum level of bodily arousal.

they soon withdraw in an effort to lower their level of arousal. In Chapter 15, we'll see that individuals differ in the amount of stimulation they find "optimal" (Aron & Aron, 1997; Eysenck & Eysenck, 1985; Zuckerman, 2003). We'll also see, however, that people are generally happier and more motivated when they engage in activities that are challenging in relation to their ability—not too easy, which is boring, and not too difficult, which triggers anxiety (Csikszentmihalyi, 1997).

**Incentive Theory**   In contrast to the notion that people are "pushed" into action by internal need states, many motivation psychologists believe that people are often "pulled" by external goals, or incentives. According to **incentive theories** of motivation, any stimulus object that people have learned to associate with positive or negative outcomes can serve as an incentive—grades, money, respect, ice cream, a romantic night out, a pat on the back, or relief from pain. People are motivated to behave in certain ways when they *expect* that they can gain the incentive through their efforts and when they *value* that incentive. Recognizing that human beings set goals, make plans, and think about the outcomes they produce, motivation theorists today believe that there is a strong cognitive component to many of our aspirations (Atkinson, 1964; McClelland, 1985; Weiner, 1989).

**incentive theory**   The notion that people are motivated to behave in ways that produce a valued inducement.

**hierarchy of needs**   Maslow's list of basic needs that have to be satisfied before people can become self-actualized.

## THE PYRAMID OF HUMAN MOTIVATIONS

Now that we have considered general theories of motivation, let us examine some of the specific motives that direct and energize our behavior. In other words, what is it that we want most in life? In response to this question, Abraham Maslow (1954) proposed that human beings are motivated to fulfill a **hierarchy of needs,** from those that are basic for survival up to those that promote growth and self-enhancement (see Figure 11.1).

At the base of the hierarchy are the physiological needs for food, water, oxygen, sleep, and sex. Once these needs are met, people seek safety, steady work, financial security, stability at home, and a predictable environment. Next on the ladder are the social needs for affiliation, belongingness and love, affection, close relations, family ties, and group membership (if these needs are not met, we feel lonely and alienated). Next are the esteem needs, which include our desires for social status, respect, recognition, achievement, and power (failing to satisfy this need, we feel inferior and unimportant). In short, everyone strives in their own way to satisfy all the needs on the hierarchy. Once these needs are met, said Maslow, we become ready, willing, and able to strive for self-actualization—a distinctly human need to fulfill one's potential. As Maslow (1968) put it, "A musician must make music, an artist must paint, a poet must write, if he is ultimately to be at peace with himself. What a man *can* be, he *must* be" (p. 46).

By arranging human needs in the shape of a pyramid, Maslow claimed that the needs at the base take priority over those at the top. In other words, the higher needs become important to us only after more basic needs are satisfied. Research generally confirms this prediction that motives lower in the pyramid take precedence, though there are occasional exceptions, as when people starve themselves to death in order to make a political statement. Research also shows that not everyone climbs Maslow's hierarchy in the same prescribed order. Some people seek love and romance before fulfilling their esteem motives, but others who are more achievement-oriented may

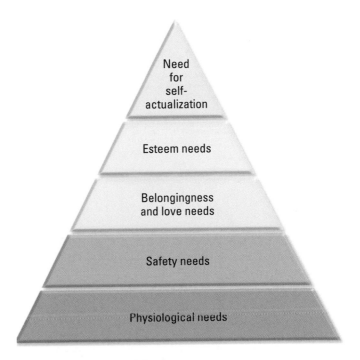

**FIGURE 11.1   Maslow's pyramid of needs**
Maslow theorized that everyone is motivated to fulfill a hierarchy of needs ranging from those most basic to survival up to those that promote self-enhancement.

## REVIEW QUESTIONS

■ *What is the Hawthorne effect? What does it tell us about human motivation?*

■ *Why were instinct theories of human motivation eventually rejected?*

■ *Compare and contrast the general theories of human motivation.*

■ *What is Maslow's hierarchy of needs and how does it relate to human motivation?*

"Sadly, no food was produced after they all became motivational speakers."

try to establish a career before a family (Goebel & Brown, 1981). In this regard, culture can also shape our motivational priorities. Shigehiro Oishi and others (1999) surveyed more than six thousand people living in thirty-nine countries and found that the fulfillment of esteem needs was more satisfying to people from "individualist" Western cultures that value independence and autonomy than to those from "collectivist" cultures that value interdependence and social connections.

Maslow's theory may not accurately describe the motivational path all people take. It does not, for example, account for our need to feel capable, autonomous, and socially secure in our endeavors (Ryan & Deci, 2000; Sheldon et al., 2001). But his distinctions—and the notion that the various needs form a hierarchy—provide a convenient framework for the study of motivation. In the coming pages, we'll begin at the base of Maslow's pyramid with hunger and sexuality, then we'll work our way up to the needs for affiliation, intimacy, achievement, and power. Finally, we'll put the psychology of motivation to work, literally, in a discussion of what motivates people on the job.

## BASIC HUMAN MOTIVES

■ *How do we regulate eating?*
■ *Is hunger a strictly biological state, or is it influenced by psychological factors?*
■ *What causes obesity and eating disorders, and what can be done to correct them?*
■ *In sexual and reproductive behavior, are men and women similarly motivated?*
■ *What influences sexual orientation?*

### HUNGER AND EATING

It has been said that "A hungry stomach has no ears" (Jean de La Fontaine), that "Nobody wants a kiss when they are hungry" (Dorothea Dix), and that "Even God cannot speak to a hungry man except in terms of bread" (Mahatma Gandhi). It seems that when it's time to eat, all other urges, desires, and ambitions fade into the background.

Hunger is a powerful sensation that sets in motion the search for and consumption of food. It's interesting that our commonsense notions about hunger are often incorrect. Sometimes, after working nonstop for several hours, I'll hold my stomach, feel the growling, and just know that I'm hungry. On empty. Time to eat. Breakfast, lunch, dinner, a morning coffee break, an afternoon snack, even a late-night raid on the refrigerator are part of the daily routine. At other times, after a big meal, I'll put my hand over my stomach, feel bloated and stuffed, and complain that I'm full. Time to stop. It's as if sensations from the belly were sending "eat" and "stop" messages straight to the brain. But is this the way hunger works?

**The Biological Component**  The biological mechanisms underlying hunger are complex. Following common sense, early researchers believed that hunger was triggered by sensations in the stomach. In an initial experiment, A. L. Washburn, working with physiologist Walter Cannon, swallowed a long tube with a balloon that was then partially inflated and specially designed to rest in his stomach. Whenever the stomach contracted, the balloon compressed. At the same time, Washburn pressed a key each time he felt hungry. Using this device, and testing other participants, Cannon and Washburn (1912) observed a link between stomach contractions and reports of hunger. In fact, the participants reported feeling hungry at the height of a contraction, not at the beginning—thus suggesting that the contractions had caused the hunger and not the other way around (see Figure 11.2). Indeed, more recent research shows that people begin to feel hungry when the stomach is about 60 percent empty (Sepple & Read, 1989).

A correlation between stomach contractions and hunger may exist, but additional observations soon discredited Cannon and Washburn's theory. The fatal blow came when studies revealed that even after people had had cancerous or ulcerated stomachs surgically removed, they continued to feel hunger. Clearly, if hunger can be felt without a stomach, then stomach contractions cannot be the cause of hunger. Another blow to the Cannon and Washburn theory comes from a clever study of two amnesia patients unable to form memories of new events. Within thirty minutes of eating a full lunch, these patients were offered a second meal, soon to be followed by a third. Their stomachs were full, but because they could not remember having so recently eaten, both patients consumed the meals that were offered (Rozin et al., 1998).

Confronted with the realization that stomach contractions are not the cause of hunger, researchers have focused on the brain and central nervous system. According to one theory, the brain monitors fluctuating levels of glucose (a simple sugar that provides energy) and other nutrients that circulate in the bloodstream. When glucose drops below a certain level, people become hungry and eat. When the glucose level in the blood exceeds a certain point, they feel satiated and stop eating (see Figure 11.3). A good deal of evidence supports this thermostat-like mechanism. In one study, for example, researchers continuously monitored the glucose levels of human participants and found that momentary decreases were accompanied by subjective reports of hunger and requests for food (Campfield et al., 1996).

How and where in the body is blood glucose monitored? Although different regions of the brain may be involved in the process, two distinct areas of the *hypothalamus* play a key role (as we saw in Chapter 2, the hypothalamus is a tiny structure that regulates body temperature, the autonomic nervous system, and the release of hormones). Initially, researchers saw the *lateral hypothalamus* (LH) as the

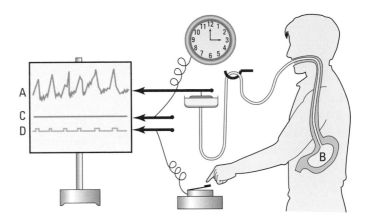

**FIGURE 11.2   Cannon and Washburn's hunger study**
In this study, participants swallowed a balloon, which rested in the stomach. Recorded over time (A) is the volume of the balloon (B) in minutes (C). Participants pressed a key whenever they felt hungry (D). Participants reported feeling hungry at the height of their stomach contractions.

**FIGURE 11.3   The hunger-regulation cycle**
When blood glucose levels are low, people become hungry and eat. The food then raises glucose levels, which lessens hunger and eating. The "thermostat" that monitors glucose levels is in or near the hypothalamus. Other factors as well control hunger and eating.

## WHAT'S YOUR PREDICTION

Eating can be such a social activity that you may wonder: What effect does the holiday season have on our eating habits and weight? If you were to recruit some research volunteers and weigh them before (September-October) during (November-December), and after (January-February) the holiday season, then again the following September, would you observe weight gain, loss, or no change during the holiday season, from Thanksgiving to New Year's Eve? Make a prediction: Would people gain or lose 0, 1, 5, or 10 pounds? And what would their weight be one year later? Make a prediction. Jack Yanovski and others at the National Institutes of Health (2000) followed 195 research volunteers for a year and reported both good news and bad. The good news was that although people did add holiday weight, the average gain was only about a pound. The bad news was that the pound was still there one year later, as people "settled in" at their new higher weight (see Figure 11.4).

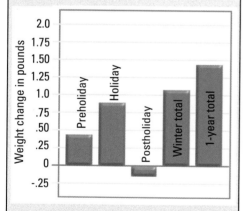

FIGURE 11.4 **Weight gain through the holiday season**

"hunger center": When its neurons are stimulated, an animal will eat, and eat, and eat—even after it's full. When the LH is destroyed, the animal will not eat—and may even starve to death unless it is force-fed (Anand & Brobeck, 1951; Teitelbaum & Epstein, 1962). At about the same time, researchers identified the *ventromedial hypothalamus* (VH) as a "satiation center": When it is stimulated, an animal will not eat, even if it has been deprived of food. When this same area is destroyed, an animal will consume larger quantities than usual, eventually tripling its own body weight (Hetherington & Ranson, 1942; Wyrwicka & Dobrzecka, 1960).

At first, these findings suggested that the hypothalamus monitors blood glucose levels and has an on-off switch for eating (Stellar, 1954). But more recent studies indicate that the mechanism is far more complicated. It turns out, for example, that certain nerves form a tract that runs up from the brainstem through the lateral hypothalamus—and these nerves are somehow involved. In fact, such areas may be part of a more general motor-activation system that, when stimulated, motivates an animal to "Do something!" This general command triggers eating if food is present, drinking if water is present, or running if neither food nor water is present (Berridge et al., 1989). Research also shows that other factors control hunger and eating as well—including levels of protein, fat, and insulin and other hormonal activities associated with the liver, pancreas, and intestines. In short, the body is equipped with a complex biochemical system for the regulation of hunger and eating (Logue, 1991; Woods et al., 2000).

**Psychological Influences** Hunger may be biologically driven, but researchers have learned that other factors such as taste, smell, and visual cues also play an important role—and that eating patterns, which are learned, can also be unlearned (Capaldi, 1996).

Among the influences on eating is taste. In Chapter 3, we saw that there are four primary tastes: sweet, sour, salty, and bitter. It turns out that people all over the world seek out sweet-tasting foods such as cookies, ice cream, soda, ripe fruit, and candy, as well as salty foods such as pretzels and potato chips. Some of these preferences appear to be innate and universal. Thus, studies with newborns show that sugar-sweetened and artificially sweetened water, compared to unsweetened water, has a soothing effect and can stop infants from crying (Barr et al., 1999) and leads them to form a preference for the adult who fed them (Blass & Camp, 2001). A person's state of mind may also influence his or her preference for certain types of food. For example, college students who were asked about their eating habits reported that during times of stress they eat more "snack-type" foods such as cake and chocolates and fewer "meal-type" foods such as meat, fish, fruit, and vegetables (Oliver & Wardle, 1999).

In other ways, our tastes for food are shaped by personal and cultural experience. In China, food is flavored primarily with soy sauce, rice wine, and ginger root; in Greece, olive oil, lemon juice, and oregano are used; Moroccan food is seasoned with coriander, cumin, cinnamon, onion, and fruit; and in Mexico, tomatoes and hot chilies are common ingredients (Barer-Stein, 1999). Consistently, people and most other animals prefer foods that are familiar rather than exotic. Perhaps this is why most Americans react with disgust to such culinary "treats" from other parts of the world as sheep's eyes, dog meat, snakes, sea urchins, and insects. Interestingly, taste preferences and aversions that are learned can also be unlearned through repeated exposure to new foods and food-eating models (Pliner et al., 1993; Hobden & Pliner, 1995).

External food cues can also entice us into eating. If you've ever inhaled the yeasty aroma of pastries in a bakery, popcorn in a movie theater, or garlic in an Italian restaurant, or if you've ever had a sudden urge for beer and a hot dog while sitting in a ball park, you know that we're sometimes drawn into eating by external cues, or incentives. Research shows that people are naturally attracted to the tastes, smells, and textures of fatty foods such as hamburgers, French fries, mozzarella cheese pizzas, crispy bacon, and ice cream (Schiffman et al., 1998). In what is likely an adaptive preference, people also eat more when there is variety in the food supply, as in a multicourse meal (Raynor & Epstein, 2001). Time of day can also be a powerful food cue. For example, Stanley Schachter and Larry Gross (1968) brought participants into a laboratory, rigged the clock on the wall so that it ran fast or slow, then offered crackers as a snack. Not wanting to spoil their appetite, most participants of normal weight ate fewer crackers when they thought it was late than when they thought it was early in the afternoon.

Finally, it's important to realize that eating is a social activity and is often subject to social influences. At times, the presence of others can inhibit us from eating—as when young women consume less food in front of others than when alone in order to present themselves as appropriately "feminine" (Mori et al., 1987; Pliner & Chaiken, 1990; Roth et al., 2001). As a general rule, however, people eat more rather than less in the company of others. Eating-diary studies show that the more people we're with, the longer time we spend at the table and the more food we consume (de Castro & Brewer, 1992; Bellisle et al., 1999). This effect is especially pronounced when the people we're with are family and friends (de Castro, 1994) and when we're in a noticeably good or bad mood (Patel & Schlundt, 2001).

**Obesity** With all the talk that surrounds us about dieting and exercise, you'd think that Americans were obsessed with losing weight. In fact, they spend an estimated $33 billion a year on weight-loss products and services. Yet ongoing Harris polls show that among American adults over 25, a staggering 80 percent are now overweight, with 33 percent being so overweight as to be considered **obese** (Taylor, 2002). This problem has worsened in recent years, as obesity rates rose from the 1980s to the present—among men and women, young and old, black and white, college-educated and uneducated, and smokers and nonsmokers (Mokdad et al., 1999). What's particularly puzzling about this trend is that it comes at a time when Americans are otherwise health conscious—for example, smoking less and using seat belts more than in the past (see Figure 11.5). That's why the World Health Organization and others describe today's obesity problem, observed in many developed countries, as a "global epidemic" (Friedrich, 2002; Wadden et al., 2002).

Obesity is defined as an excess of body fat, which normally accounts for about 25 percent of weight in women and 18 percent in men. Measurements of obesity have varied somewhat, but people are generally classified according to the "body mass index," or BMI, a standard measure derived from a formula that adjusts weight according to height (see Table 11.1). Being slightly overweight does not pose a health risk. But statistically, obese people are more likely to suffer from diabetes, heart disease, high blood pressure, high cholesterol, respiratory problems, arthritis, strokes, depression, pregnancy complications, sleep apnea, certain forms of cancer—and an increased risk of death (Kopelman & Stock, 1998; Calle et al.,

**obesity** The state of having a surplus of body fat that causes a person to exceed his or her optimum weight by 20 percent.

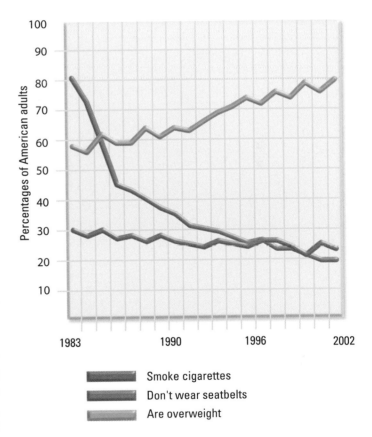

**Smoke cigarettes**
**Don't wear seatbelts**
**Are overweight**

**FIGURE 11.5 U.S. health trends, 1983–2002**
An ongoing Harris poll has shown that the number of Americans who are overweight has risen steadily from the 1980s to the present. Oddly, this problem comes at a time when people are, in other ways, more health conscious. As you can see, fewer Americans today smoke or drive without seat belts.

| TABLE 11.1 | | | BEING OVERWEIGHT: HOW HEAVY IS TOO HEAVY? | | | | | | | | |
|---|---|---|---|---|---|---|---|---|---|---|---|
| **BMI** | 22 | 23 | 24 | 25 | 26 | 27 | 28 | 29 | 30 | 31 | 32 |
| **Height** | | | | | | **Weight (in pounds)** | | | | | |
| 4'11" (59") | 109 | 114 | 119 | 124 | 128 | 133 | 138 | 143 | 148 | 153 | 158 |
| 5'1" (61") | 116 | 122 | 127 | 132 | 137 | 143 | 148 | 153 | 158 | 164 | 169 |
| 5'3" (63") | 124 | 130 | 135 | 141 | 146 | 152 | 158 | 163 | 169 | 175 | 180 |
| 5'5" (65") | 132 | 138 | 144 | 150 | 156 | 162 | 168 | 174 | 180 | 186 | 192 |
| 5'7" (67") | 140 | 146 | 153 | 159 | 166 | 172 | 178 | 185 | 191 | 198 | 204 |
| 5'9" (69") | 149 | 155 | 162 | 169 | 176 | 182 | 189 | 196 | 203 | 209 | 216 |
| 5'11" (71") | 157 | 165 | 172 | 179 | 186 | 193 | 200 | 208 | 215 | 222 | 229 |
| 6'1" (73") | 166 | 174 | 182 | 189 | 197 | 204 | 212 | 219 | 227 | 235 | 242 |
| 6'3" (75") | 176 | 184 | 192 | 200 | 208 | 216 | 224 | 232 | 240 | 248 | 256 |

The body mass index (BMI) converts weight adjusted by height to a single number. Inserting your measurements into the grid above, you can calculate your own BMI (for example, if you're 5'1" tall and weigh 137 pounds, then your BMI is 26). As a general rule, people are classified as "healthy" with a BMI of 24 or less, "overweight" with a BMI of 27 and up, and as "obese" with a BMI of 30 and up.

*Source:* National Center for Health Statistics.

1999; Must et al., 1999). In the United States alone, obesity is implicated in an estimated 300,000 deaths per year (Allison et al., 1999). To make matters worse, obese people are subject to stereotyping, ridicule, and discrimination when they seek college admissions, jobs, or places to live (Wadden et al., 2002). Research shows that obese people are assumed to be slow, lazy, sloppy, and lacking in willpower (Ryckman et al., 1989)—a prejudice that has its roots in a conservative ideology that values self-control and personal responsibility (Crandall, 1994). In a study of long-term social and economic consequences, researchers followed a group of overweight sixteen- to twenty-four-year-old women and found that those who were still obese after seven years made less money than their peers and were less likely to be married (Gortmaker et al., 1993).

People tend to think of obesity as an objective physical condition, measurable by body fat, body mass index, and other numbers. Yet to some extent our beliefs about what constitutes an ideal weight are shaped by culture, race, and other factors. In some cases, geographical and economic conditions play a role. For example, Judith Anderson and others (1992) looked at female body size preferences in fifty-four cultures and found that heavy women are considered more attractive than slender women in places where food is frequently in short supply. Others too have found that being overweight is considered desirable in some developing countries, perhaps because it signals an ability to survive food shortages, stay healthy, and reproduce (Cassidy, 1991). Even within a culture, people of different racial or ethnic groups may differ in their concern about weight and the stigma they attach to obesity. Consider North American culture, which is preoccupied by thinness, especially in women. On average, African American women are heavier than white women of the same age. But are these groups equally concerned about their weight? To answer this question, Delia Smith and others (1999) had more than thirty-seven hundred men and women, both black and white, indicate how satisfied they were with their own body size and appearance. In general, they found that women were less satisfied with their own bodies than men were—and that white men and women were less self-satisfied than blacks were.

Sixty percent of Americans surveyed said they would like to lose weight. (Harris Poll, 2002)

**What Causes Obesity?** Why do some people but not others fight a chronic battle against gaining weight? As with other aspects of hunger and eating, both biological and psychological factors play a role. Physiologically speaking, getting fat is easy to explain. People gain weight when they *consume* more calories than their bodies *metabolize*, or burn up. The excess calories are stored as fat. Evidence for the role of biological factors begins with the fact that obesity runs in families and is influenced by genetics. In one study, Albert Stunkard and others (1990) compared the body mass indexes of genetically identical twins and fraternal twins who were raised together or apart. As illustrated in Figure 11.6, two results provided strong evidence for the role of genetics: (1) The identical twins were more similar in their BMI than were fraternal twins, and (2) identical twins were similar even when raised apart, in separate homes. The same conclusion emerges from adoption studies, which show that in body weight, adoptees resemble their biological parents more than their adoptive parents (Grilo & Pogue-Geile, 1991). Overall, researchers estimate that genes account for 25 to 40 percent of the BMI differences among people (Price, 2002).

So what, specifically, is inherited? Do obese people inherit a tendency to consume large quantities of food or a tendency toward physical *in*activity, or are they born with a particularly slow metabolism, making it difficult for them to burn up calories? These are all possibilities. According to one theory, each of us has a **set point**, a level of weight toward which our own bodies gravitate, and obese people are programmed to maintain a high set-point weight (Keesey, 1995). The set point itself may be genetic or it may stem from eating habits established early in life. Either way, set points are relatively stable—which explains why it's hard to lose massive quantities of weight and why, after dieting, it's so hard to maintain the loss over time (Garner & Wooley, 1991; Vogel, 1999).

Not everyone agrees, however, that hunger and eating are driven by a precise set point—or that people who are too heavy are doomed to stay that way despite their best efforts to lose weight. Considering the research on hunger and weight regulation, John Pinel and others (2000) believe that the human body does not have a fixed set point, but rather a loose *settling point* that drifts upward and downward over time in response to changes in behavior. According to this model, permanent changes in diet and activity level, or energy intake and output, can move a settling point—and keep it there.

Genetic predispositions may help to explain why some people battle the bulge more than others do, but they cannot explain why the world's population has gained dangerous amounts of weight in recent years. Most health experts agree that the global obesity epidemic reflects recent changes in our eating and activity habits, not in our gene pool (Price, 2002). Some researchers blame the epidemic on a "toxic environment" filled with fatty fast foods, all-you-can-eat buffets, minimarkets in gasoline stations, vending machines stocked with sugar-filled soft drinks and snacks, sedentary office work, too little emphasis on physical education in schools, and too much time spent watching television (Horgen & Brownell, 2002; Wadden et al., 2002). Reflecting the possible impact of environmental factors is the comparison between Pima Indian women who moved to Arizona and those who stayed in Mexico. In Pima women of Arizona, fat comprises 41 percent of their caloric intake and they weigh an average of 198 pounds. Among their relatives in Mexico, fat comprises only 23 percent of their diet and they average 154 pounds. Other researchers note, more simply, that obesity results from overeating. Pinel and his

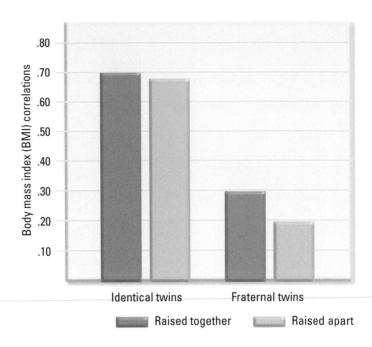

**FIGURE 11.6  Body weight of identical and fraternal twins**

Indicating the role of genetic factors in body weight, identical twins (left) had more similar body weights than did fraternal twins (right). Note also that this same pattern was found regardless of whether the twins were raised together or apart (Stunkard et al., 1990).

*When it comes to the nature and nurture in the origins of obesity, notes George Bray (1998), "Genes load the gun, the environment pulls the trigger."*

**set point**  A level of weight toward which a person's body gravitates.

Forty percent of U.S. adults say they never engage in exercises, sports, or physically active hobbies. (National Center for Health Statistics, 1999)

colleagues (2000) maintain that humans and other warm-blooded animals are programmed by evolution to consume more food than they may need, building a reservoir of excess energy in case of future shortages in the food supply. The problem today is that we still have a relentless drive to eat—but at a time when many people enjoy continuous if not unlimited access to a wide variety of good tasting foods.

**How to Lose Weight** Stroll the aisles of any bookstore and you'll see that the weight-reduction industry is alive and well. There are many approaches to losing weight, including behavioral changes in diet, exercise and activity, medication, and surgery (Wadden & Stunkard, 2002). Some people resort to high-risk medical procedures such as gastric-restriction surgery to shrink the stomach and diet drugs that suppress appetite or increase energy expenditure. For most, however, weight reduction can be achieved through alterations in behavior. In this regard, the key to success is to realize that a change in diet must be sustained and permanent—and that it must be accompanied by a steady regimen of physical exercise (Brownell & Wadden, 1992; Jakicic et al., 1999).

Two factors must be present for someone to sustain the dieting effort: information and motivation. First, a person must have an accurate sense of his or her caloric intake and exercise. This sounds easy, but Steven Lichtman and his colleagues (1992) had a group of failed dieters keep a diary and discovered that they unwittingly underreported the amount of food they had consumed and overestimated their daily exercise. Second, a person's motivation for losing weight is critical. Research shows that people are more likely to succeed in a long-term weight-reduction program when motivated by their own desires than when motivated by external incentives such as the wishes of a spouse (Williams et al., 1996).

**Eating Disorders** Psychological influences on hunger and eating are most evident when it comes to serious eating disorders. **Anorexia nervosa** is a disorder in which a person, typically an adolescent girl or young woman, becomes so fearful of gaining weight that she ignores her hunger pangs, limits her eating, becomes emaciated, and sometimes even starves to death. Many become compulsive about running and exercising. Approximately 95 percent of anorexics are female, and anorexia's worldwide incidence has risen sharply in recent decades. Closely related is **bulimia nervosa,** an eating disorder also found among young women that is marked by cycles of extreme binge eating followed by self-induced vomiting and the overuse of laxatives. A woman with bulimia may eat a whole pizza, a box of cookies, a bucket of fried chicken, or a half-gallon of ice cream—all in one sitting—then purge the food. These binge-and-purge episodes may occur two to fourteen times a week. Bulimia is seldom life threatening (most sufferers are normal in weight, which makes it easy for them to hide their condition), but the repeated vomiting can cause erosion of tooth enamel, dehydration, damage to the intestines, nutritional imbalances, and other medical problems (American Psychiatric Association, 1994).

How common are eating disorders? Although estimates vary, recent studies indicate that less than 1 percent of all women suffer from anorexia, though estimates among fifteen- to twenty-nine-year-olds are higher, at 3 to 10 percent. Twice as many women have bulimia than anorexia, and these rates are higher among female college students than among nonstudents. The future for people with eating disorders is uncertain. More than half show improvement after five years of being treated, but a third continue to have a problem, and 5 to 8 percent die from starvation, suicide, or complications (Fairburn & Brownell, 2002; Polivy & Herman, 2002; Striegel-Moore & Smolak, 2001).

**anorexia nervosa** An eating disorder in which the person, usually an adolescent girl or young woman, limits her eating and becomes emaciated.

**bulimia nervosa** An eating disorder found usually among young women that is marked by cycles of binge eating followed by purging.

As to the possible causes of eating disorders, psychologists have speculated about genetics, hormone imbalances, low set points, overly perfectionistic mothers, and traumas such as sexual abuse. At this point, two findings are clear. First, the problem is most prevalent in weight-conscious cultures in which food is abundant and in which diet centers, exercise videos, and shapely supermodels make aspiring women feel pressured to have a slender appearance (Brumberg, 1988; Ruderman & Besbeas, 1992). Looking at the female actresses who appear on TV situation comedies, for example, researchers found that most were thin or average in weight—and that overweight women were underrepresented in relation to the population at large (Fouts & Burggraf, 1999). A second important finding is that many women with eating disorders have negative, distorted images of their own bodies, often seeing themselves as overweight when in fact they are not (Phillips, 1998; Thompson et al., 1999; Thompson & Smolak, 2001). Look at the drawings in Figure 11.7. Which do you think is ideal for your sex? And which do you think represents *your* body type? Using this task and others like it, researchers have found that girls who have a negative body image (as measured by the discrepancy between their self-image and ideal body types) are most at risk to develop an eating disorder (Attie & Brooks-Gunn, 1989).

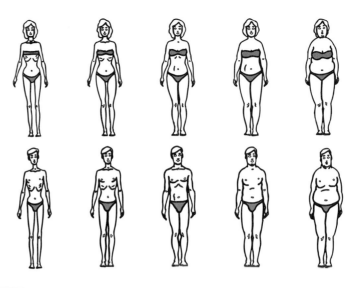

**FIGURE 11.7 Ideal body image**
Which image do you think is ideal for your sex? And which comes closest to your body? This task is commonly used to assess whether a person has a positive or negative body image.

As for the role of cultural ideals, researchers have found that exposure to slender female models in the media leads women who are dissatisfied with their own bodies to become even more anxious about their own weight (Posavac et al., 1998). Trying to measure up to the ultra-thin multimillion-dollar supermodel can only prove frustrating to most. The cultural ideal for thinness may even be set early in childhood. When Kevin Norton and others (1996) projected the life-size dimensions of the world-popular Ken and Barbie dolls, they found that both were unrealistically thin compared to the average young adult. In fact, the estimated odds of a young woman having Barbie's classic shape are about 1 in 100,000.

*Ken and Barbie are the most popular-selling dolls in the world. Yet both are unrealistically thin compared to the average young adult.*

## SEXUAL MOTIVATION

One hundred years ago, Sigmund Freud shocked the scientific community by proposing psychoanalysis, a theory that placed great emphasis on sexual gratification as a driving force in human development. As we'll see in Chapter 15, many of Freud's closest colleagues rejected his focus on sexual motivation. But was he wrong? Although sex is essential to the survival of a *species*, it is not—like hunger, thirst, or the need for sleep—vital to the survival of an *individual*. Yet the sexual motive is a force to be reckoned with. Sexual images and themes appear, literally, in our dreams, in the "dirty" jokes we tell, in the TV shows we watch, in the novels we read, and in the music we hear. It's no wonder that so many public figures become mired in sex scandals. It's also no wonder that advertisers use sex to sell everything from mouthwash to jeans, cars, soft drinks, and shaving cream.

**Surveys of Sexual Practices**   With sex being the most private and intimate aspect of human relations, it is difficult to study systematically. During the 1940s, biologist Alfred Kinsey and his colleagues (1948, 1953) conducted the first large-scale survey of sexual practices in the United States. Based on extensive confidential interviews of more than seventeen thousand men and women, these researchers

## WHAT'S YOUR PREDICTION

What does it mean to say you had sex? For sex researchers, it's important to know how people interpret this deceptively simple question. In an article published in the *Journal of the American Medical Association,* Stephanie Sanders and June Reinisch (1999) asked college students from twenty-nine states, "Would you say you *had sex* with someone if the most intimate behavior you engaged in was . . .?" Make some predictions. What percentage of students, male and female combined, said *yes* with regard to: Deep kissing, oral contact with breasts, touching genitals, oral contact with genitals, penile-anal intercourse, penile-vaginal intercourse? Now look at the results and you'll see that most students agreed that vaginal and anal intercourse constitute having sex—and that deep kissing, oral contact with breasts, and manual contact with genitals do not. Note, however, that there was little consensus about oral contact with genitals. At the time this study was published, former President Clinton, mired in scandal, claimed that he did not have "sexual relations" with Monica Lewinsky despite oral-genital contact. This result suggests that there may be some ambiguity.

| | |
|---|---|
| Deep kissing | 2% |
| Oral contact with breasts | 3% |
| Touching genitals | 14% |
| Oral contact with genitals | 40% |
| Anal intercourse | 81% |
| Vaginal intercourse | 99% |

sought for the first time to describe what nobody would openly talk about: patterns of sexual activity. Kinsey's goal was to uncover the hidden norms for all aspects of sexual behavior, including masturbation, homosexuality, and premarital and extramarital sex. Some of Kinsey's results were shocking, as he revealed that sexual activity was more frequent and more varied than anyone had expected. Among Kinsey's findings: 90 percent of all men and nearly half of all women had premarital sex, virtually all men and a majority of women masturbated, 50 percent of married men and 26 percent of married women had extramarital affairs, and 40 percent of all college-educated couples said they engaged in oral sex. Kinsey's books became instant best sellers. Certain aspects of his methodology were criticized. For example, most participants were young, white, urban, and middle class—hardly a representative sample. He also asked leading questions to enable respondents to report on sexual activities—or make up stories for the interview (Jones, 1997). Despite the flaws, Kinsey's findings are still often used as a basis for comparison. He died in 1954, but his Institute for Sex Research at Indiana University remains a major center for the study of human sexuality.

Since Kinsey's groundbreaking study, many sex surveys have been conducted, and form part of the fascinating research history chronicled in the book, *Kiss and Tell: Surveying Sex in the Twentieth Century* (Ericksen & Steffen, 1999). Regardless of whether these self-reports are taken in face-to-face interviews, telephone surveys, or over the Internet, we can never know for sure how accurate the results are. Part of the problem is that respondents may not be honest in their disclosures, but also problematic is that people differ in their interpretations of survey questions. For example, research shows that survey participants do not agree over what specific acts constitute "having sex." Everyone agrees that vaginal intercourse between two partners who reach orgasm is sex. But would you say that you had sex about vaginal intercourse when one or neither partner reached orgasm? What about other types of contact? For many scenarios tested, people differ in their interpretations (Bogart et al., 2000; Sanders & Reinisch, 1999).

Despite the limitations of self-report, it does appear that societal norms have changed over time. For example, sexual activity levels peaked during the "sexual revolution" of the 1960s and 1970s, but these numbers appear to have declined since that time (Robinson et al., 1991). Recent studies suggest that sexual practices today, at least in the United States, are relatively tame (Leigh et al., 1993). In the recent National Health and Social Life Survey, involving 3,432 Americans, ages eighteen to fifty-nine, researchers found that husbands and wives were more faithful to each other than was expected—and that the vast majority preferred "traditional" vaginal sex over oral, anal, and group sex, bondage, and other "kinky" activities (Laumann et al., 1994; Laumann & Michael, 2001).

One consistent finding to emerge from all surveys over time is that men and women differ in certain aspects of their sexual motivation. When people were asked to select ten private wishes from a list, most men and women similarly wanted love, health, peace on earth, unlimited ability, wealth, and social recognition. There was one major difference: More men than women wanted "to have sex with anyone I choose" (Ehrlichman & Eichenstein, 1992). This finding is common. Surveys consistently show that men are sexually more permissive and promiscuous than women (Oliver & Hyde, 1993). They are also more likely to think about sex spontaneously, seek out erotic materials, initiate sex with or without emotional commitment, make sacrifices for sex, and fantasize about having sex with multiple partners—all leading Roy Baumeister and his colleagues (2001) to conclude that "men desire sex more than women" (p. 270).

**The Evolution of Desire** Why do these differences exist and what do they mean? In *The Evolution of Desire,* David Buss (1994) argues that the answer can be derived from evolutionary psychology, the subdiscipline that uses the principles of evolution to understand human social behavior. According to this perspective, human beings all over the world exhibit mate-selection patterns that favor the conception, birth, and survival of their offspring—and women and men employ different strategies to achieve that common goal.

According to Buss, women must be highly selective because they are biologically limited in the number of children they can bear and raise in a lifetime. Thus, a woman must search for a mate who possesses (or who has the potential to possess) economic resources and a willingness to commit those resources to support her offspring. The strategic result is that women in general should be attracted to men who are older and financially secure or who have intelligence, ambition, stability, and other traits predictive of future success.

In contrast, a man can father an unlimited number of children. He is restricted, however, by his ability to attract a reproductively capable partner and by his uncertainty as to whether the children born are actually his own. With these motives springing from their evolutionary past, men desire women who are young and physically attractive (having smooth skin, full lips, lustrous hair, good muscle tone, and other youthful features—attributes that signal health and reproductive fertility). To minimize paternal uncertainty, they should also seek women who are likely to be sexually faithful rather than promiscuous.

To test his theory of sexual motivation, Buss (1989) and a team of researchers surveyed 10,047 men and women in thirty-seven cultures within North and South America, Asia, Africa, Eastern and Western Europe, and the Pacific. All respondents were asked to rate the importance of various attributes in choosing a mate. The results were consistent with predictions. Both men and women gave equally high ratings to certain characteristics, such as "having a pleasant disposition." But in the vast majority of countries, "good looks" and "no previous experience in sexual intercourse" were valued more highly by men, whereas "good financial prospect" and "ambitious and industrious" were more important to women. Personal ads appearing in magazines and newspapers also reveal that women tend to offer beauty and seek wealth, while men seek beauty and offer wealth (Rajecki et al., 1991; Sprecher et al., 1994).

Also consistent with the evolutionary perspective is a universal tendency for men to seek younger women (who are most likely to be fertile) and for women to desire older men (who are most likely to have financial resources). Buss (1989) found this age preference discrepancy in all the cultures he studied, with men on average wanting to marry women who were 2.7 years younger, and women wanting men who were 3.4 years older. Based on an analysis of personal ads, Douglas Kenrick and Richard Keefe (1992) found that men in their twenties are equally interested in younger women and slightly older women still of fertile age. But men in their thirties seek women who are five years younger, while men in their fifties prefer women ten to twenty years younger. In contrast, women of all ages sought older men. This pattern can also be seen in marriage statistics collected from different cultures and historical generations. There is one interesting exception: Adolescent boys say that they are most attracted to women who are slightly *older* than they are, women in their fertile twenties (Kenrick et al., 1996).

A third line of research consistent with evolutionary theory concerns sexual jealousy, a negative emotional state arising from a perceived threat to one's sexual relationship. Although jealousy is a normal human reaction, men and women are

"If you want sex, just ask—there's no need to preface everything with 'In light of recent events.'"

[© The New Yorker Collection 2001, Alex Gregory from cartoonbank.com. All Rights Reserved.]

*This young man spies through his sunglasses at women lying on the beach. According to the evolutionary perspective in psychology, his attraction is biologically and unconsciously motivated by the search for a fertile reproductive partner.*

aroused by different triggering events. According to the theory, men should be particularly upset by *sexual* infidelity because the woman who has an extramarital affair increases the risk that the children he supports are not his own. In contrast, women should feel threatened more by *emotional* infidelity because the husband who falls in love with another woman might withdraw his financial support (Buss, 2000).

A number of studies support this hypothesis. In one, male and female college students were asked whether they'd be more upset if their romantic partner had formed a deep emotional attachment or had sexual intercourse with another person. Think for a moment about this awful choice. Which situation would *you* find more distressing? The results revealed a striking sex difference: 60 percent of the men said they would be more upset by a partner's sexual infidelity, but 83 percent of women felt that emotional infidelity was worse (Buss et al., 1992).

In a second study, male and female college students were asked to imagine their girlfriend or boyfriend at a party flirting with someone of the opposite sex—someone depicted as physically attractive or unattractive, and as socially dominant or submissive. All subjects were then asked how jealous they would be. The result: men were the most jealous when their male rival was dominant, while women were most jealous when their female rival was attractive (Dijkstra & Buunk, 1998).

In a third study, newly married husbands and wives were interviewed about how they would react if they were to suspect their partner of cheating. Interestingly, the men were most likely to say that they would use various "mate-retention" tactics (concealing or threatening the wife; taking violent action against the male rival) when their wives were young and attractive. In contrast, women were more likely to say they would use mate-retention tactics (being more watchful; enhancing their appearance) when the men they were married to strived for status and had a higher income (Buss & Shackelford, 1997). In short, men and women may differ in their sexual motives, as the evolutionary psychologist predicts, but both react strongly when these motives are threatened.

The differences between sexes are intriguing, and many researchers are adopting an evolutionary perspective (Buss, 1999; Plotkin, 1998; Simpson & Kenrick, 1997). However, critics of this approach argue that the results can be interpreted in terms that are more "psychological" than "evolutionary." One argument is that women trade youth and beauty for money not for reproductive purposes but rather because they often lack *direct* access to economic power. Another argument is that men are more upset over sexual infidelity not because of uncertain paternity but because they assume that the married woman having a sexual affair is also likely to be forming intimate feelings for her extramarital partner (DeSteno & Salovey, 1996; Harris & Christenfeld, 1996). A third argument is that despite the observed differences, men and women are similar in many ways. In Buss's cross-cultural study, both men and women gave their highest ratings to such traits as dependability, kindness, and a pleasant disposition. Also, women want physical attractiveness as much as men do—in a short-term sexual partner (Regan & Berscheid, 1997).

Finally, it's important to realize that the sex differences often observed are not entirely predictable or universal. Human societies are remarkably flexible in the way people adapt to their environments—and there are revealing exceptions to the rules that are supposed to govern how people play on the evolutionary field. For example, David Geary (2000) points out that while human fathers spend less time at childcare than mothers do, they are unique among

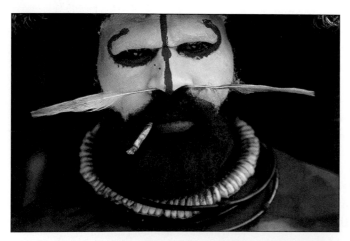

*This Huli warrior from Papua New Guinea paints his face for festivities. In this culture, men are objects of beauty. The purpose: When it comes to marriage, Huli men are free to take as many wives as they can attract and afford (women are allowed only one husband at a time).*

mammals—including chimpanzees, our evolutionary cousins—in the amount of care they give to their offspring. Geary speculates that human men care for their children in part because they enjoy more paternal certainty than do other male primates. Consider, too, the puzzling observation that most women of the Bari tribe in Venezuela are highly promiscuous. From an evolutionary standpoint, this pattern does not seem adaptive since women who "sleep around" may scare off potential mates fearful of wasting their resources on children not their own. So why is promiscuity the female norm in this culture? In *Cultures of Multiple Fathers,* anthropologists Stephen Beckerman, Paul Valentine, and others note that the Bari—and other aboriginal people in lowland South America—believe that a baby can have multiple fathers and that all men who have sex with a pregnant woman make a biological contribution to the unborn child (some groups assume that more than one father, or at least more than one insemination, is *required* to form a fetus). Thus, by taking many lovers a woman can increase the number of men who provide for her child. The strategy appears to work. A multiple-fathered Bari child is 16 percent more likely than a single-fathered child to survive to the age of 15 (Beckerman & Valentine, 2002).

To sum up, evolutionary psychology offers a provocative but controversial new perspective on human sexual motivation. Untangling the influences of culture from those of evolution is challenging and ensures that these dueling perspectives on human sexual motivation will continue to provoke debate in the years to come.

**The Sexual-Response Cycle** Survey-based population statistics, analyses of personal ads, questionnaires, and laboratory experiments provide only a glimpse into human sexual behavior, so more intensive research is also needed. Enter obstetrician/gynecologist William Masters and psychologist Virginia Johnson. As they described in their 1966 book, *Human Sexual Response,* Masters and Johnson filmed and measured physiological activity in 312 male and 382 female volunteers who engaged in over ten thousand acts of masturbation or sexual intercourse in the laboratory. Masters and Johnson's goal was to understand what happens to people *physically* while having sex. Using various recording devices to monitor changes in bodily functions (including an artificial penis equipped with a camera that recorded physiological reactions in the vagina), they found that despite the sex differences in anatomy, evolutionary heritage, socialization, and attitudes, there are striking physiological *similarities* in the male and female sexual response. More recent research on the neurobiology of the sexual response—in studies of humans and animals—has confirmed Masters and Johnson's basic observations and probed the additional influences of the brain and nervous system, testosterone and other hormones, and neurotransmitters (Meston & Frohlich, 2000).

The **sexual-response cycle** has four stages, which are much the same for men and women (see Figure 11.8). In the *excitement* stage, a stimulus sparks sexual arousal marked by increased blood flow to the pelvic region, which then causes the genitals to become engorged with blood. During this phase, the man's penis becomes partially erect, while the woman's vagina secretes a lubricant and her nipples harden and become erect. This phase lasts from just a few minutes to well over an hour.

The excitement then builds to a *plateau* phase, when breathing and heart rates increase. The man's penis fills with a fluid that may contain live sperm, some of which may appear at the tip of the penis, and his erection becomes firmer. For men who have difficulty maintaining an erection, the highly publicized drug Viagra

*The Bari tribeswomen of Venezuela are sexually promiscuous. The Bari believe that a baby can have multiple fathers, so by being promiscuous a woman can ensure child support from many men. This apparent exception to the norm illustrates that human behavior is flexible—and that men and women develop mating strategies to suit the cultural environment.*

**sexual-response cycle** The four physiological stages of sexual responding: excitement, plateau, orgasm, and resolution.

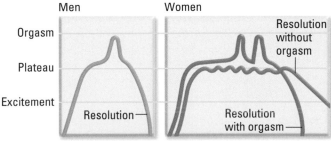

**FIGURE 11.8 The sexual-response cycle**
Research by Masters and Johnson revealed that both men and women experience excitement, plateau, orgasm, and resolution phases in their sexual responses.

## THE PROCESS OF DISCOVERY

# DAVID M. BUSS
### *Evolutionary Psychology of Human Mating*

**Q: How did you first become interested in psychology?**

**A:** What gripped me were the "big" questions—the origins of the universe, the evolution of life, and the nature of human nature. I concluded that the human mind is probably the most complex organic entity in the known universe, so psychology became the most compelling choice.

**Q: How did you come up with your important discovery?**

**A:** When I brought up the possibility of applying evolutionary theories to psychology to my graduate mentors at Berkeley, my suggestion encountered no resonance. Most psychologists lacked a deep knowledge of evolutionary biology. Many viewed it with skepticism and hostility. No one did empirical studies using evolutionary ideas. The field now known as evolutionary psychology did not exist. It was not until my first year teaching at Harvard University, in 1981, that I felt the freedom to test my ideas.

My interest was in human mating. At the time, existing theories of mating were woefully inadequate. All were extraordinarily simplistic, typically positing a single process that determines who mates with whom. All failed to explain why humans are motivated to mate in the directions theorized. All assumed that men and women were identical in their mating psychology. And all assumed that mating tendencies stayed the same regardless of circumstances.

What I regard as my most important discoveries are subsumed by *Sexual Strategies Theory,* which I proposed in the 1980's, and which provided the first theory of human mating. My colleagues and I also gathered empirical support for the theory, which gained it attention—as in a thirty-seven culture study of male and female mate preferences.

**Q: How has the field you inspired developed over the years?**

**A:** The field of human mating has mushroomed since my early work, producing hundreds of articles. Although I believe that the core ideas remain the foundation for understanding human mating, the field has developed in ways more complex than I ever envisioned. Among topics now generating exciting discoveries are the link between women's sexual strategies and ovulation cycles; the role of extramarital affairs; the importance of jealousy; and the cognitive biases in cross-sex "mind reading." There is much gold yet to be discovered.

**Q: What's your prediction on where the field is heading?**

**A:** Human mating research will continue to explode as researchers come to recognize its place in nearly all aspects of human life. Many traditional topics in psychology—such as motivation, emotion, various aspects of social influence—cannot be understood deeply without recognizing that human mating strategies infuse them all. For this reason, I predict that the field will gain increasing acceptance and that historians of science will come to view the initial resistance to evolutionary psychology with bewilderment—much as we now view the previous resistance to the ideas of Copernicus, Galileo, and Darwin.

*David Buss is Professor of Psychology at the University of Texas, Austin.*

(sildenafil) may be prescribed. The woman's vagina becomes wetter, there is a tightening of the vaginal entrance, her breasts become engorged with blood, and a "climax" feels moments away. For both sexes, arousal will fluctuate according to the length and nature of foreplay.

During the *orgasm,* rhythmic genital contractions give rise to an intensely pleasurable feeling of sexual release, accompanied in men by the ejaculation of semen. For both men and women, the contractions are spaced at about 8/10 of a second, with the first five or six being the most intense. The feeling seems to be the same for both sexes. So when people give written descriptions of what their orgasms feel like, those who read the descriptions can't tell which were written by men and which by women.

Afterward, the body slowly returns to its normal pre-aroused state and enters the *resolution* phase. In men, orgasm is followed by a refractory period, during which males are largely unresponsive to further stimulation, making another orgasm impossible. This "downtime" can last from just a few minutes to several hours and increases with age. Women do not have this lengthy refractory period. If restimulated, they are capable of experiencing a succession of orgasms.

Despite the similarities, there are some notable differences in the sexual experiences reported by men and women. One is that men of all ages are two to three times more likely than women to reach orgasm during sexual intercourse. To be more precise, Laumann and others (1994) found that only 75 percent of married women and 62 percent of single women usually or always had orgasm during sexual intercourse. This gender difference may reflect the workings of evolution and biology, as men but not women must achieve orgasm in order to procreate, or it may reflect socialized differences in attitudes that cause many women to feel guilty and inhibited about sex. A second difference, which seems contradictory, is that women but not men are multiorgasmic, capable of climaxing more than once within a brief period of time.

## REVIEW QUESTIONS

■ *What are the biological mechanisms that underlie hunger? What are the psychological influences?*

■ *What are the specific factors that can lead to obesity? Which factors contribute to eating disorders?*

■ *Describe the evidence suggesting that men and women seek different characteristics in a mate.*

■ *Describe the stages of the sexual-response cycle. Is it the same for men and women?*

# SOCIAL MOTIVES

■ *After biological needs are satisfied, what do we strive for?*
■ *Do people actually need other people?*
■ *Is the desire for social relationships a fundamental human motivation?*
■ *What drives individuals who are highly motivated to achieve?*
■ *What about the need for power—does it promote good leadership or bad?*

Satisfying the body's appetite for food or the urge for sex helps propel the biological human engine. But people are not content merely to survive. Most of us want more out of life, much more. In varying degrees, we want to be part of a community, to love and be loved, and to achieve recognition, status, fame, wealth, and power. Whether one's goal is to raise a family, travel the world, earn a million dollars, climb the highest mountain, care for those in need, or paint a masterpiece, to be human is to strive for more than a mere satisfaction of basic drives. Using Maslow's motivational pyramid as a framework, we'll examine two broad classes of motives: belongingness needs and esteem needs.

## BELONGINGNESS MOTIVES

Although born helpless, human infants are equipped at birth with reflexes that orient them toward people. They are responsive to faces, turn their head toward voices, and are prepared to mimic certain facial gestures on cue. Much to the delight of parents, the newborn seems an inherently social animal. If you reflect on the amount of time you spend talking to, being with, pining for, or worrying about other people, you'll realize that we all are. People need people.

Recognizing the power of our social impulses, Maslow ranked belongingness and love needs third in his hierarchy. Being part of a family or community, playing on a sports team, joining a social or religious or professional group, making friends, falling in love, and having children—all service this important motive. So just how important is it? Do people really *need* other people?

According to Baumeister and Leary (1996), the need to belong is a fundamental human motive. As they put it, "human beings have a pervasive drive to form and

**need for affiliation** The desire to establish and maintain social contacts.

**need for intimacy** The desire for close relationships characterized by open and intimate communication.

maintain at least a minimum quantity of lasting, positive, and significant interpersonal relationships" (p. 497). This conclusion is supported by a great deal of research. All over the world, people experience joy when they form new social attachments and react with loneliness, grief, and anxiety when these bonds are broken—as when separated from a loved one by distance, divorce, or death. The need to belong runs deep, which is why people react with distress when they are neglected by others, rejected, excluded, stigmatized, or ostracized, all forms of "social death" (Leary, 2001; Williams et al., 2002). As we'll see in Chapter 18, people who have a network of close social contacts—in the form of lovers, friends, and relatives—tend to be happier and more satisfied with life than those who are more isolated (Diener et al., 1999). In fact, we'll see that people who are more socially connected are also healthier and less likely to die a premature death (House et al., 1988; Uchino et al., 1996).

Dan McAdams (1989) notes that Maslow's belongingness motive is actually composed of two distinct needs. The first is the **need for affiliation,** which is defined as a desire to establish and maintain social contacts. The second is a **need for intimacy,** defined as a further desire for close relationships characterized by an openness of communication. Let's consider each of these needs in turn.

**The Need for Affiliation** Do you ever crave the company of others? Do you ever enjoy being alone? Chances are that you answered *yes* to both questions. Research shows that individuals differ in the strength of their need for affiliation. As you might expect, people with a high need for affiliation are socially more active than lows. They prefer to be in contact with others more often and are more likely to visit friends or even make phone calls and write letters as a way to maintain social contact at a distance (McAdams & Constantian, 1983).

Although individuals differ, even the most gregarious among us wants to be alone at times. In fact, it seems that people are motivated to establish and maintain an *optimum* balance of social contact (not too much, not too little) the way the body maintains a certain level of caloric intake. In an interesting study, Bibb Latané and Carol Werner (1978) found that laboratory rats were more likely to approach others of their species after a period of isolation and were less likely after prolonged social contact. These researchers suggested that like many other animals, rats have a built-in "sociostat" (a social thermostat) to regulate their affiliative tendencies. Is there any evidence of a similar mechanism in humans? Shawn O'Connor and Lorne Rosenblood (1996) recently had college students carry portable beepers for four days. Whenever the beeper went off (on average, every hour), the students wrote down whether at the time they were *actually* alone or in the company of other people, and whether, at the time, they *wanted* to be alone or with others. The results showed that the students were in the state they desired two-thirds of the time—and that the situation they wished they were in on one occasion predicted their actual situation the next time they were signaled. Whether it was solitude or social contact that the students were craving, they successfully managed to regulate their own personal needs for affiliation.

People may differ in the strength of their affiliative needs and in the overall amount of social contact they find satisfying, but there are times when we would all rather be with other people. Take, for example, the scene at Yankee Stadium in October 1999, the night when the New York Yankees won the World Series. There were some sixty thousand fans at the game, and when it ended nobody wanted to go home. Nobody rushed for the parking lot or raced to the subway. For nearly half an hour, no fans even left their seats. Out in the street, jubilant pedestrians sang "New York, New York" and exchanged high-fives, slaps on the back, hugs, and kisses. Even in this city of strangers, people wanted to celebrate together rather than alone.

Affiliating can be satisfying for other reasons as well. From other people, we get energy, attention, stimulation, information, and emotional support (Hill, 1987). One condition that strongly arouses our need for affiliation is stress. It's always amazing to see how neighbors who otherwise never stop to say hello come together in snowstorms, hurricanes, fires, power failures, and other major crises. People under stress may even seek each other out online—as when stock market investors jam into Internet message boards to talk and support each other after their stocks tumble. Many years ago, Stanley Schachter (1959) theorized that external threat triggers fear and motivates us to affiliate—particularly with others who are facing a similar threat. In a laboratory experiment, Schachter found that participants expecting to receive painful electric shocks chose to wait with other nervous participants rather than alone.

Why do we affiliate in times of stress? Recent research suggests that people under stress seek each other out in order to gain *cognitive clarity* about the danger they are in. In one study, James Kulik and Heike Mahler (1989) found that hospital patients awaiting open-heart surgery preferred to have roommates who were postoperative rather than preoperative, presumably because they were in a position to provide information about the experience. Indeed, patients in a second study who were assigned postoperative rather than preoperative roommates became less anxious about the experience and were later quicker to recover from the surgery (Kulik et al., 1996). Even in a laboratory setting, Kulik and his colleagues (1994) found that participants awaiting the painful task of soaking a hand in ice-cold water (compared to those told that the task would not be painful) also preferred to wait with someone who had completed the task than with one who had not—and they asked more questions of these experienced peers. Under stress, we adaptively become motivated to affiliate—not with just anybody but with others who can help us cope with an impending threat.

**The Need for Intimacy**  Affiliating with other people, even superficially, satisfies part of our need for social contact. But in varying degrees, people also have a need for close and intimate relationships. Research shows that individuals who score high rather than low on measures of the need for intimacy are seen by peers as warm, sincere, and loving. They also look at others more, smile more, laugh more, and confide more in their friends. People who score high rather than low on intimacy may also be happier and healthier (McAdams, 1989).

In looking at close relationships and the deep affection that grows between friends or lovers, psychologists have found that the key ingredient is **self-disclosure**, the sharing of intimate, often confidential details about oneself with another person (Jourard, 1971; Derlega et al., 1993). Self-disclosure tends to follow three predictable patterns. The first is that we typically reciprocate another person's self-disclosure with one of our own—and at a comparable level of intimacy. Bare your soul to someone and that person is likely to react by doing the same (Berg, 1987). Second, there are sex differences in openness of communication. Compared to men, women tend to self-disclose more than men *to* others (both male and female), and, in turn, they elicit more self-disclosure *from* others (Dindia & Allen, 1992). Third, people reveal more and more to each other as relationships grow over time. In the early stages, people give relatively little of themselves to others and receive comparably little in return. If these encounters are rewarding, however, the communication becomes more frequent and more intimate (Altman & Taylor, 1973). This increase in self-disclosure can be seen in the fact that the more intimate a relationship

"At this point, my privacy needs are interfering with my intimacy goals."

**self-disclosure**  The sharing of intimate details about oneself with another person.

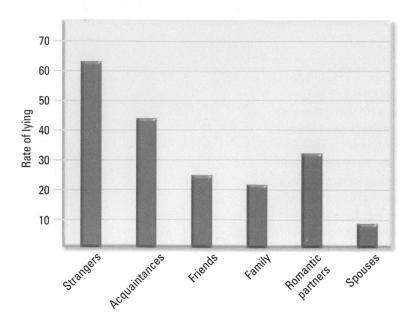

**FIGURE 11.9  To whom do people lie?**
For one week, people recorded every instance in which they tried to mislead someone. As shown, they lied most to strangers, followed by acquaintances, family members, and friends. Also shown is that people lied more often to unmarried romantic partners than to spouses. Consistent with research on self-disclosure, it seems that the closer two people are, the less likely they are to lie to each other (DePaulo & Kashy, 1998).

people have, the less likely they are to lie to each other. In a naturalistic study that illustrates this point, Bella DePaulo and Deborah Kashy (1998) asked people to keep a one-week diary of all social interactions and record every instance in which they tried to mislead someone, including white lies told to spare another person's feelings. They found that lying rates decreased according to the closeness of a relationship. These results are presented in Figure 11.9.

To summarize, self-disclosure is the glue that binds our most intimate relations. The more of it there is among friends, dating partners, and married couples, the more they like each other, the happier they are in the relationship, and the more inclined they are to stay together (Hendrick, 1981; Collins & Miller, 1994). Thus, among pairs of college students brought together to a laboratory for brief getting-acquainted conversations, the more they self-disclosed, the better they felt about each other afterward (Vittengl & Holt, 2000).

## ESTEEM MOTIVES

Have you ever met someone so single-mindedly driven to succeed that you couldn't help but wonder why? One individual who pops to mind is Bill Gates—the cofounder and chair of Microsoft. Gates is the richest man in the world and seems to have an insatiable appetite for more. By his own admission, Gates wants to achieve worldwide domination of the computer industry. Another individual driven to the top of his competitive field is Tiger Woods. Already the winningest and wealthiest golfer of his generation, Woods continues to practice long hours, determined to break all records. Still other images that come to mind are that of the politician who runs for president and the workaholic scientist who spends weekends alone in his or her laboratory. What fuels the drive we often have to succeed, excel, and advance in our work? For years, psychologists have examined two motives that play a role in this regard: the need for achievement and the need for power.

**The Need for Achievement**  In a classic book entitled *The Achievement Motive*, David McClelland and his colleagues (1953) sought to identify people with high levels of **achievement motivation**—defined as a strong desire to accomplish difficult tasks, outperform others, and excel. There was no question that individuals differ in the intensity of their achievement strivings. The question was how this important and perhaps unconscious motive could be measured. Seeking what he would later call a "psychic X ray," McClelland believed that our motives are revealed in our fantasies. To bring these fantasies out, he asked participants to make up stories about a series of ambiguous pictures. Look at the sample photo in Figure 11.10. What's your interpretation? Who is the boy, what is he thinking about, and what will happen to him? Assuming that participants will naturally identify with the main character (some are male, others female), pictures like this provide a screen on which people can project their own needs. If you used the scoring system devised by McClelland and his colleagues, you'd be classified as high in

**achievement motivation**  A strong desire to accomplish difficult tasks, outperform others, and excel.

the need for achievement if you say that the boy in Figure 11.10 is recalling with pride an exam he aced, thinking about how to win a prize or scholarship, or dreaming of becoming a doctor—and if these types of concerns are a recurring theme in your stories.

From the start, this fantasy measure proved intriguing. For example, it proved to be a reasonably sensitive measure of the need for achievement. To demonstrate this, McClelland and his colleagues (1953) had participants solve word puzzles before responding to the pictures. Some participants were told that the puzzles were not that important; others were told that the puzzles tested intelligence and leadership ability—an instruction used to arouse performance concerns. Sure enough, participants who were induced into a heightened state of achievement need told more achievement-relevant stories. Yet research soon showed that scores from this fantasy measure of achievement do not correlate with the way participants described their own achievement needs on questionnaires. The reason: It appears that the story-based measure uncovers deeply ingrained, enduring, unconscious motives that predict a person's behavior over long periods of time, whereas questionnaires measure only conscious, self-attributed motives relevant to the way a person is likely to behave in the immediate situation (McClelland et al., 1989).

As you might expect, there are strong links among a person's motivation, behavior, and level of accomplishment. Those who score high rather than low in the need for achievement work harder and are more persistent, innovative, and future-oriented. They also crave success more than they fear failure (Atkinson, 1964) and then credit success to their own abilities and efforts rather than to external factors (Weiner, 1989). One particularly interesting difference between the highs and lows concerns their level of aspiration. You might think that individuals driven by a need to achieve would take on exceedingly difficult tasks. Not so. When college students playing a ring-toss game could choose where to stand, those high rather than low in the need for achievement stood a moderate distance from the peg—not so close that success would come easy but not so far that they would fail (Atkinson & Litwin, 1960). People who are truly motivated to succeed set goals that are challenging but realistic (McClelland & Koestner, 1992). They are also more interested in mastering a task than they are fearful of failure (Elliot & Church, 1997).

Clearly, hard work and realistic goal setting pay off in life. Individuals high in the need for achievement get better grades in school, are more successful in their careers, and are more upwardly mobile. Over the years, McClelland (1985) and other researchers have often found a positive correlation between the achievement orientation of a whole society (which they measure by analyzing magazine articles and other popular writings) and overall levels of economic growth, scientific progress, and productivity. For example, fluctuating levels of achievement motivation in the United States—as derived from children's readers during the years 1800 and 1950—closely paralleled inventiveness as measured by the per capita number of patents issued during those same years. Thus, the more productive a society is, the more likely it is that parents read hard-work-breeds-success tales to their children, such as *The Little Engine That Could* ("I think I can, I think I can . . . "). These correlations are open to interpretation with regard to cause and effect, but it's clear that the more achievement-oriented a society is at a given point in time, the more productive it is likely to be.

People of achievement set high but realistic goals and then exert enough effort to reach those goals. But what about the *process* of achievement? How are people in pursuit of long-term goals affected by the successes and failures that they will

**FIGURE 11.10  Fantasy measure of achievement**
Who is the boy, what is he thinking about, and what will happen to him? Using ambiguous pictures like this one, researchers get people to tell stories and then code the stories for achievement imagery.

*Exhibiting the work ethic at its best, retired Baltimore Oriole star Cal Ripken, Jr. set an all-time major-league baseball record for playing in 2,632 consecutive games without a single absence. What motivated Ripken? "I want to be remembered as an ironman, a player who went out there and put it on the line every day," he said.*

# BECOME AN EXPERT

Very few people manage to climb to the very top of a skilled domain to become experts, among the best in the world. Those who do reach these heights often dazzle us with their achievements. How do the great ones reach this level? Are they specially gifted, endowed at birth with brains and bodies uniquely suited to their talent? Are they, in other words, born, not made? Is the pursuit of excellence similar from one skill to another? How do people make it, as they say, to the top of their game?

To answer these questions, psychologists have looked at the development of expertise across a broad range of achievement domains. In *The Road to Excellence,* K. Anders Ericsson (1996) brought together researchers who have studied great musicians, visual artists, medical doctors, memory experts, inventors, chess masters, bridge players, and typists, as well as golfers, tennis players, gymnasts, and other athletes. Together, these studies have converged on some core principles—providing answers that are in some ways surprising. To begin with, you don't have to be born with special attributes to become expert in a particular domain. When people see a brilliant performer—as when watching Tiger Woods play golf—they are quick to assume that he or she was specially endowed at birth. Thus, Ericsson noted that when people watch someone memorize a string of fifty-plus rapidly presented digits they assume that this person has a so-called photographic memory. In fact, this person was most likely to have spent hundreds of hours practicing digit-recalling techniques. Ask

highly gifted children about their achievements, and they'll be the first to attribute what they've done to "hard work and effort, not luck and genes" (Winer, 1996, p. 213).

So what does it take to become among the best? First, to become an expert at anything one must make a long-term commitment. The great ones do not emerge all at once in a sudden burst of expertise. In fact, quite the opposite is true. Studying chess masters, Simon and Chase (1973) concluded that it takes at least ten years of playing to reach the international level in chess. Looking at experts in other domains, Ericsson and his colleagues (1993) concluded that no matter how much talent someone has, this same ten-year rule applies to becoming an expert in music composition, science, the arts, and sports—which is the reason that most professionals don't peak until their twenties in most sports or until their thirties and forties in most arts and sciences. Yet so few of us make such a sustained effort, they note, that we never touch the upper limit of our potential.

Time spent on a task is necessary for greatness, but it's not enough. There are plenty of weekend golfers who enjoy hours on driving ranges, putting greens, and fairways, who quickly become good but never great. The reason is that time must be used for intense, concentrated, purposeful activities specifically designed to improve performance—what Ericsson and others call *deliberate practice* (as opposed to mere mindless repetition). The great billiards players tirelessly try to perfect particular strategies; chess masters analyze moves previously made by other

invariably encounter along the way? Focused on children, developmental psychologist Carol Dweck notes that people can attribute their own positive and negative outcomes to intelligence, athleticism, or other natural abilities they see as fixed or immutable. Or, she notes, people can attribute outcomes to preparation, practice, persistence, and other factors within their power to control. Does it matter? Is one type of attribution more adaptive than the other? Yes. In a series of studies, Mueller and Dweck (1998) gave a test with some easy problems to elementary-school children. In giving positive feedback to the students, they told some that "You must be smart at these problems," and others that "You must have worked hard at these problems." In a second phase, the students were given tough problems to solve. Their reaction: Those earlier praised for their effort, compared to those praised for intelligence, stayed more focused, were willing to take on difficult problems, and persisted longer in the face of failure. When the "going gets tough," as they say, it helps to believe that you have the capacity to improve.

masters; major-league baseball hitters study videotapes of pitchers; hockey goalies study the tendencies of shooters. One can only imagine the number of hours Wayne Gretzky used to spend skating, or Michael Jordan did shooting hoops. The finest pianists and violinists in the world play alone, for at least four hours a day, including weekends. By the age of twenty, these musicians have spent over ten thousand hours practicing, which is hundreds of hours more than is spent by less accomplished musicians (Krampe & Ericsson, 1996; Lehman & Ericsson, 1999).

*At four years old, Itzhak Perlman's legs were paralyzed by polio. After dedicating countless hours to practice as a child, and then studying music at the Juilliard School in New York City, he became one of the greatest violinists of all time.*

Over the long haul, intense practice will alter the body's anatomy in ways that improve performance. If you repeatedly push yourself at running, swimming, or lifting weights, you'll expand your capacity. The same is true of other activities. From years of practice, athletes increase the size of their hearts so more oxygen-rich blood is pumped through the muscles. Among the top tennis players of the world, the arm they use to swing the racket forms larger muscles and thicker, wider bones (Ericsson & Lehmann, 1996). As we saw in Chapter 2, even neural connections in the brain are strengthened by usage—as when highly practiced musicians exhibit the growth of extra neural connections in music-sensitive parts of the brain (Schlaug et al., 1995).

Like sheer time spent, deliberate practice may be necessary, but it too is not enough. No one makes it to the top alone. Case studies show that, as children, great achievers in mathematics, swimming, sculpture, and other domains had received guidance from highly skilled teachers who instructed them, set goals for them, designed practices and programs, and set their competitive schedules. With support from dedicated parents, many of the elite, as children, were actually relocated just so they could be close to a desired teacher and training facility (Bloom, 1985).

To sum up, great talents are made, not born. To be sure, some people are more innately talented in some ways than others. But the real key is tireless if not obsessive motivation, hard work, and assistance from an expert. Practice may not make you perfect, but you can't become perfect without it.

According to Steven Heine and others (2001), cultural ideologies and practices influence our approach to success, failure, and motivation. As we'll see in Chapter 14, North Americans tend to see the self as independent, stable, and autonomous—and are strongly motivated to judge themselves in positive, self-enhancing terms. In contrast, people of East Asian cultures tend to see the self as interdependent, part of different social networks, and fluid according to one's role in a situation—and are motivated toward self-improvement for the sake of family, coworkers, teammates, friends, and others. Wondering whether the motivations for self-enhancement and self-improvement color our reactions to success and failure, these researchers compared Canadian students from the University of British Columbia to Japanese students from Kyoto University. All students took a test in which they were given sets of three words and asked to come up with a fourth that relates to the other three (for example, *sleep, fantasy,* and *day* are related to *dream*). Randomly, the students were given either an easy test and told that they scored well

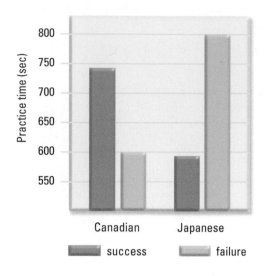

**FIGURE 11.11 Motivating effects of success and failure: Matters of culture**
Canadian and Japanese college students took a test that led them to succeed or fail. Prior to taking a second test, they were given time to relax or practice. As you can see, Canadian students practiced more after success, which made them feel good about themselves—but the Japanese students practiced more after failure, which motivated them to improve (Heine et al., 2001).

---

## REVIEW QUESTIONS

- *Distinguish between the need for affiliation and the need for intimacy.*

- *What is self-disclosure? Describe three characteristics of self-disclosure in relationships.*

- *What is achievement motivation and how does it differ from the need for power?*

**need for power** A strong desire to acquire prestige and influence over other people.

above the fiftieth percentile—or a difficult test and told that they scored well below the fiftieth percentile. Soon afterward, the students were given fifteen minutes alone to relax or practice new problems before taking another test. What effect did success or failure have on their work ethic? Look at Figure 11.11 and you'll see that the Canadian students practiced more after success, a sign of strength that made them feel good about themselves—but that the Japanese students practiced more after failure, a sign of weakness that motivated them to improve.

**The Need for Power**   Related but not identical to achievement motivation is what David Winter (1973) has called the **need for power,** a strong desire to acquire prestige and influence over other people. As you might expect, men and women who are high rather than low in the need for power are more likely to run for public office and strive for other positions of authority. In a study that followed women for fourteen years after they graduated from college, those who had scored high in the need for power as seniors were later more likely to plan on, enter, and remain in careers that involved the exercise of power (Jenkins, 1994).

The need for power provides the fuel for great leadership. To be truly effective, however, leaders must also exercise self-control and use their power for social goals, not personal gain. William Spangler and Robert House (1991) analyzed the inaugural speeches written by thirty-three U.S. presidents, from George Washington to Ronald Reagan, to determine their need for power and other motives. Using complex measures of presidential effectiveness (which took into account their record on war, peaceful solutions to crises, and other decisions made), they discovered that more effective presidents had higher needs for power and a greater motivation to use that power for social rather than personal objectives. It's interesting that a leader's power motivation can change over time. After analyzing speeches given by President Clinton in his first term in office, Winter (1998) found that Clinton's need for power increased as he gained experience on the job. Can a leader's power motivation alter the course of world events? Perhaps. In a series of studies, Winter (1993) analyzed four hundred years of British history, the outbreak of World War I, and the 1962 Cuban Missile Crisis involving the United States and the former Soviet Union. In each study, he derived power-motivation scores for the leaders involved by using government documents and speeches given before, during, and after each conflict. The result: The leaders' need for power was statistically predictive of war and peace. As Winter put it, "When it rises, war is likely; when it falls, war is less likely and ongoing wars are likely to end" (p. 542).

## MOTIVATING PEOPLE AT WORK

- *What motivates us on the job? Are we driven by strictly economic concerns?*
- *Does offering rewards for performance, as in corporate incentive programs, increase or undermine a worker's intrinsic motivation?*
- *How do people react when they feel overpaid or underpaid for their work?*

In any organization—from Microsoft, Toyota, Wal-Mart, and the F.B.I. to your school and library—one of the critical challenges for industrial/organizational (I/O) psychologists is to determine what motivates individuals to work hard and to work well. Think about it. What drives *your* on-the-job performance? Are your concerns strictly economic, or do you have other needs to fulfill? There is no single answer. At work, as in the rest of life, our behavior often stems from the convergence of multiple motives.

# REWARD-BASED MOTIVATION

Out of necessity, people work for money and other economic benefits such as vacation time, sick leave, health insurance, and retirement plans (Heneman & Schwab, 1985; Judge & Welbourne, 1994). Some of the rewards people get at work are not monetary but symbolic—for example, titles, large offices, windows, and access to parking (Becker, 1981; Sundstrom, 1986).

The most popular theory of worker motivation is Victor Vroom's (1964) expectancy theory. According to Vroom, people are rational decision makers who analyze the benefits and costs of their possible courses of action. Specifically, he states, people are motivated to work hard whenever they expect that their efforts will improve performance, believe that good performance will be rewarded, and value the rewards they expect to receive. Over the years, expectancy theory has been used with some success to predict worker attendance, productivity, and other job-related behaviors (Mitchell, 1974). In addition, research has shown that people perform better at work and are more productive when they're given specific goals and a clear standard for success and failure than when they're simply told to "do your best" (Locke & Latham, 1990). Financial incentives, in particular, can effectively increase worker productivity—without compromising the quality of the work (Jenkins et al., 1998).

*"If you pay peanuts, you get monkeys."*

—JAMES GOLDSMITH

"We reward top executives at the agency with a unique incentive program. Money."

## INTRINSIC AND EXTRINSIC MOTIVATION

Although people strive for tangible reward, there's more to money than just economics and more to motivation than just the size of a paycheck. Novelist Mark Twain (1876) seemed to realize this in *The Adventures of Tom Sawyer*, where he quipped, "There are wealthy gentlemen in England who drive four-horse passenger coaches twenty or thirty miles on a daily line, in the summer, because the privilege costs them considerable money; but if they were offered wages for the service that would turn it into work then they would resign." Twain's hypothesis—that reward for an enjoyable activity can undermine interest in that activity—seems to defy intuition and a great deal of psychological research. After all, aren't we all motivated by reward, as declared by B. F. Skinner and other behaviorists? The answer depends on how "motivation" is defined.

As a keen observer of human behavior, Twain anticipated a key distinction between intrinsic and extrinsic motivation. **Intrinsic motivation** originates in factors within a person. People are said to be intrinsically motivated when they engage in an activity for the sake of their own interest, the challenge, or sheer enjoyment. Eating a fine meal, listening to music, and working on a hobby are among the activities you might find intrinsically motivating. In contrast, **extrinsic motivation** originates in factors outside the person. People are said to be extrinsically motivated when they engage in an activity for money, recognition, or other tangible benefits. As the behaviorists have always said, people do strive for reward. The question is: What happens to *intrinsic* motivation once that reward is no longer available? It's clear that business leaders want their employees to be intrinsically motivated, loyal, satisfied, and committed to their work. So where does money fit in? Is tangible reward the bottom line or not?

Research shows that when people start getting paid for a task they already enjoy, they sometimes lose interest in it. In the first test of this effect, Edward Deci (1971) recruited college students to work for three one-hour sessions on some fun block-building puzzles. During the first and third sessions, all participants were treated in the same way. In the second session, however, half the participants were paid

**intrinsic motivation**  An inner drive that motivates people in the absence of external reward or punishment.

**extrinsic motivation**  The desire to engage in an activity for money, recognition, or other tangible benefits.

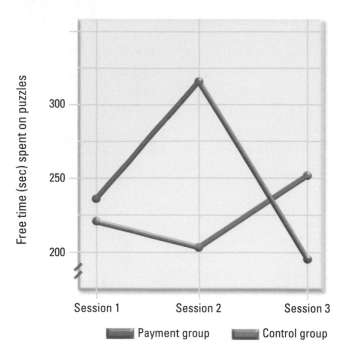

**FIGURE 11.12** **Effects of payment on intrinsic motivation**

In this study, participants worked three times on fun puzzles. Half were paid for completing puzzles during session 2, half were not. As measured by the amount of free time spent on the puzzles after each session, those who had been paid later had less interest in the puzzles when the money was no longer available (Deci, 1971).

"Productivity is up nine percent since I made everyone a vice president."

**equity theory** The notion that people want the ratio between input and outcome to be roughly the same for themselves as for others.

for each puzzle that they completed. To measure their intrinsic motivation, Deci left participants alone during breaks and secretly recorded the amount of free time they spent on the puzzles when other fun activities were available. Compared to participants in the no-reward group, those paid in the second session later showed less interest in the puzzles when the payment was no longer available (see Figure 11.12). The moral: Receive money for a leisure activity, and before you know it what used to be "play" comes to feel like "work."

This paradoxical effect—that tangible rewards can undermine intrinsic motivation—has been observed in studies with preschoolers through adults, using rewards and other extrinsic incentives such as money, deadlines, competition, and evaluation (Deci et al., 1999; Lepper & Greene, 1978; Tang & Hall, 1995). In the long run, rewards may even have adverse effects on creativity and performance. In one study, Teresa Amabile (1996) found that participants who were paid for artistic activities, compared to others who were not paid, produced work that was later judged to be less creative by independent raters. To be maximally productive, people should feel internally driven, not compelled by outside forces.

But wait. If money undermines intrinsic motivation, should employers *not* use monetary incentives? Are pay-for-performance programs often used in the workplace doomed to fail, as some have suggested (Kohn, 1993)? No, not necessarily. To answer this question, it's important to realize that a reward can be interpreted in two ways, depending on how it is presented. On the one hand, being offered payment can make a person feel bribed, bought off, and *controlled*, which can result in the detrimental effects just described. On the other hand, rewards often provide people with positive *information* about the quality of their performance—as when people earn bonuses, scholarships, and verbal praise from others they respect. Research now shows that just as controlling rewards lower intrinsic motivation, informational rewards have the opposite, positive effect—on motivation (Eisenberger & Cameron, 1996) and on creativity (Eisenberger & Rhoades, 2001). Studying an office-machine company, Deci and others (1989) found that the less controlling the managers were, the more satisfied workers were with the company as a whole. People want to feel competent, autonomous, and socially secure, so reward enhances intrinsic motivation if it promotes these motives (Ryan & Deci, 2000).

## EQUITY MOTIVATION

A second aspect of payment that influences motivation is the perception that it is *fair*. According to **equity theory**, people want rewards to be equitable, meaning that the ratio between inputs and outcomes should be roughly the same for us as for others. Relative to coworkers, then, the better your performance is, the more money you think you should earn. If you think you're being overpaid or underpaid, however, you'll feel distressed and try to relieve that unhappy state either by restoring actual equity—say, through working less or seeking a raise—or by convincing yourself that equity already exists (Cropanzano, 1993; Greenberg, 1982).

Equity theory has fascinating implications for behavior in the workplace. Consider Jerald Greenberg's (1988) study of workers in a large insurance firm. To allow for refurbishing, some two hundred employees had to be moved temporarily from one office to another. Randomly, they were assigned to offices that belonged to others who were higher, lower, or equal in their rank (the higher the rank, the more spacious the office). Would these random assignments influence job performance? By keeping track of the number of cases processed and the quality of the decisions made, Greenberg measured each worker's job performance before, during, and after the office switch. To restore equity, he reasoned, the workers given higher-status offices would feel overcompensated and improve their performance, whereas those sent to lower-status offices would feel undercompensated and lower their performance. That is exactly what happened. In a later study, Greenberg (1993) found that many participants who were underpaid for their participation in an experiment went on to restore equity by stealing from the experimenter. When it comes to pay and other aspects of work—such as being praised and treated with respect—people are most dedicated to their jobs when they believe they are being treated fairly (Donovan et al., 1998).

## REVIEW QUESTIONS

- *Define reward-based motivation. In what situations are rewards effective?*

- *Distinguish intrinsic and extrinsic motivation. How is each type of motivation affected by external rewards?*

- *What is equity motivation and how is it affected by the receipt of monetary rewards?*

## THINKING LIKE A PSYCHOLOGIST ABOUT MOTIVATION

When we stop to reflect on our own motivations, we see just how varied they are. From the constant short-term need to stuff our face with food or satisfy the urge to have sex, to the desire to be with others or form close relationships, to the burning ambition to achieve excellence or gain power over others, it's clear that we are energized in many ways and toward many goal objects. Is there more that we want from life? Is achieving the "American Dream" of prosperity truly fulfilling? If not, is there some other "ultimate" motivation? Perhaps. If you've ever met someone who seems to have it all—money, a successful career, good friends, a loving partner, and wonderful children—and yet yearns for more, you will appreciate what's at the very peak of Maslow's pyramid. As we'll see in Chapter 15, Maslow theorized that once our biological and social needs are met, we strive to fulfill all of our potential—toward a state that he called self-actualization.

## SUMMARY

Displaying the **Hawthorne effect,** workers who were put into a special experimental room became more productive regardless of what changes were made.

**Motivation** is an inner state that energizes people toward the fulfillment of a goal. The question psychologists ask is: What motivates us?

### WHAT MOTIVATES US?

Over the years, some psychologists have proposed general theories to account for commonalities among all human motives. Others have studied specific motives such as hunger, sex, affiliation, and achievement.

### GENERAL THEORIES OF MOTIVATION

**Instinct** theories of motivation used to be common but were soon rejected. According to **drive theory,** physiological needs that arise within the body create tension, which motivates us toward its reduction. To account for the fact that people often seek to increase tension, **arousal theory** posits that people are driven to maintain an optimum level of arousal—not too low, not too high. And in **incentive theory,** people behave in ways that they expect will gain a valued external incentive.

### THE PYRAMID OF HUMAN MOTIVATIONS

According to Maslow, all human beings are motivated to fulfill a **hierarchy of needs.** At the base are physiological needs for food, water, and so on. Next, in order, are safety and security needs, the need for belonging, and esteem needs. Once all needs are met, people strive for self-actualization.

### BASIC HUMAN MOTIVES

Among the basic human needs at the base of Maslow's pyramid are hunger and sexual motivation.

## HUNGER AND EATING

Hunger is a sensation that motivates food search and consumption. The brain monitors glucose in the blood. When glucose drops below a certain level, people experience hunger. Eating then raises the glucose and reduces the motivation to eat. The glucose levels are monitored in or near the hypothalamus. Psychological factors such as personal and cultural tastes, and external food cues such as time and the company of other people also play a role in hunger and eating.

People are considered **obese** when they have a surplus of body fat that causes them to exceed their optimum weight by 20 percent. There is a strong genetic component to obesity, which may determine **set point**, a level of weight toward which our body gravitates. Most people can achieve long-term weight loss through changes in diet and exercise. Psychological influences on eating are most evident in the disorders **anorexia nervosa** and **bulimia nervosa**. Both are most common among adolescent girls and young women, particularly in weight-conscious cultures and in women with negative body images.

## SEXUAL MOTIVATION

Surveys show that men and women differ in aspects of their sexual motivations, with most men being more permissive, promiscuous, and driven than most women.

Despite gender differences, there are striking similarities in the **sexual-response cycles** of men and women. Among men and women, the cycle is similarly characterized by four phases: excitement, plateau, orgasm, and resolution.

With regard to **sexual orientation**, about 5 percent of men and 2 to 3 percent of women are homosexual in their orientation. A tiny nucleus in the hypothalamus is larger in heterosexual men than in women and homosexual men. Twin studies involving gay men and lesbians reveal that there is some genetic component. It is not clear, however, whether genes predispose sexual orientation per se or gender-typed behavior in childhood that later gives rise to a sexual orientation.

## SOCIAL MOTIVES

People are not content merely to satisfy biological needs. In addition, there are social motives for belongingness and esteem.

## BELONGINGNESS MOTIVES

Maslow's belongingness motives are composed of two distinct needs. In varying degrees, people enjoy being with others, a **need for affiliation.** Research shows that we seek an optimum balance of social contact but that we affiliate more under stress in order to gain cognitive clarity about the situation we're in. People also have a **need for intimacy,** for close relationships that are characterized by open and confidential communication known as **self-disclosure.**

## ESTEEM MOTIVES

People differ in their level of **achievement motivation,** which is defined as the desire to accomplish difficult tasks and to excel. To assess the strength of this motive, researchers use a fantasy measure in which participants tell stories about the characters in ambiguous pictures and code these stories for achievement themes. Research has shown that people who score high rather than low on this measure work harder, set more realistic goals, and achieve more.

Related to the achievement motive is the **need for power,** a desire to gain prestige and influence over others. There are links between the strength of this need and various indexes of leadership.

## MOTIVATING PEOPLE AT WORK

I/O psychologists seek to determine what motivates people to work hard and well.

## REWARD-BASED MOTIVATION

According to expectancy theory, people work hard when they expect their efforts to improve performance and produce a valued reward. Thus, many corporations use incentive-based programs to motivate workers.

## INTRINSIC AND EXTRINSIC MOTIVATION

Psychologists have distinguished between two types of motivation. **Intrinsic motivation** originates within a person out of interest, challenge, and sheer enjoyment. **Extrinsic motivation** originates in factors outside the person (reward, recognition). Research shows that although reward increases extrinsic motivation, it can lower intrinsic motivation, which becomes evident once the reward is no longer available. Reward has this effect when it is seen as a bribe, but it has the opposite effect when presented as positive feedback.

## EQUITY MOTIVATION

**Equity theory** maintains that people want rewards to be linked in a fair way to performance relative to others. Thus, when people feel overpaid, they work harder to restore equity. Feelings of underpayment lead people to slack off.

## KEY TERMS

Hawthorne effect (**p. 434**)

motivation (**p. 435**)

instinct (**p. 435**)

drive theory (**p. 436**)

arousal theory (**p. 436**)

incentive theory (**p. 437**)

hierarchy of needs (**p. 437**)

obesity (**p. 441**)

set point (**p. 443**)

anorexia nervosa (**p. 444**)

bulimia nervosa (**p. 444**)

sexual-response cycle (**p. 449**)

need for affiliation (**p. 452**)

need for intimacy (**p. 452**)

self-disclosure (**p. 453**)

achievement motivation (**p. 454**)

need for power (**p. 458**)

intrinsic motivation (**p. 459**)

extrinsic motivation (**p. 459**)

equity theory (**p. 460**)

## THINKING CRITICALLY ABOUT MOTIVATION

1. Former Congressman Newt Gingrich once proposed that in order to increase literacy rates among American children, the government should fund a program that pays children $2.00 for each book they read. Many psychologists thought that such a program might actually discourage reading. What do you think the effect would be?

2. Psychologists have approached the study of human motivation in two ways. Compare and contrast these two approaches. Which approach do you believe is better?

3. According to the evolutionary perspective, how can we explain current gender differences in sexual motives and behavior? Can you propose alternative explanations that would account for these differences?

4. How would each of the general theories of human motivation explain altruistic behaviors? Which theory best accounts for such behavior?

5. In some cultures, being overweight does not have the same negative connotation that it does in American culture. In addition, the desire for extreme thinness is a relatively recent phenomenon. Do you think the incidence of eating disorders would change if the popular image of attractive men and women moved closer to normal American weight patterns?

# Emotion

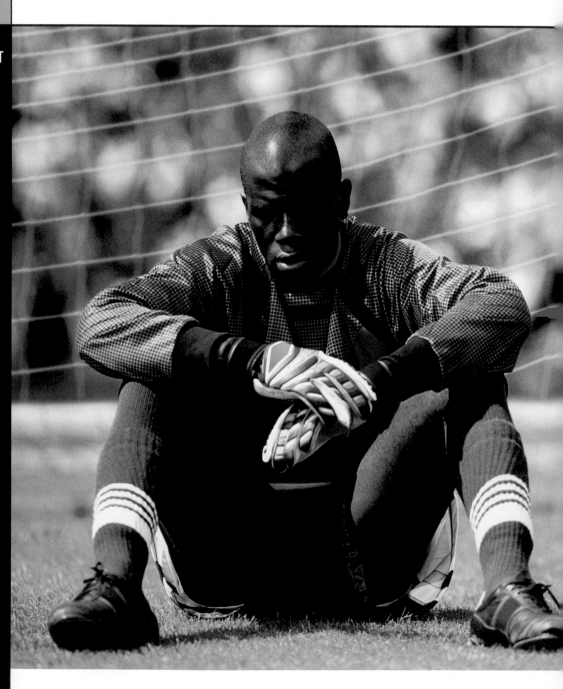

# CAN CULTURE INFLUENCE EMOTION?

## THE SITUATION

Imagine that you are working as part of a research team that is studying cultural influences. The goal of the project is to examine the effects of culture on the way people interpret facial expressions. Do human beings all over the world show joy, sadness, and other emotions in the same way, or are there differences in facial expressions as there are in the languages we speak?

To answer this question, you collect portrait photographs of adult men and women smiling, frowning, pouting, and expressing other emotions on the face. Your goal is to get pictures of people experiencing, or pretending to experience, six emotional states: happiness, sadness, anger, fear, surprise, and disgust. Then you contact colleagues from other countries and arrange for them to translate the words and show the pictures to natives of their culture. In all, you're able to test more than five hundred people from Estonia, Germany, Greece, Hong Kong, Italy, Japan, Scotland, Sumatra, Turkey, and the United States.

The testing procedure is straightforward. Your experimenters schedule "observers" for group sessions. In total, eighteen pictures are shown on slides, for ten seconds each and in random order, and each slide depicts one of the six emotions. Participants are given a response sheet on which they are asked to check off the emotion being displayed in each picture.

## MAKE A PREDICTION

The data that you collect in this study are interesting in two ways. The first question you want to answer is: Are emotions universally recognized, or are there cultural differences? In other words, to what extent do people in general (as represented in the ten cultures) *agree* on the emotions displayed by various facial expressions? Second, do some expressions elicit a higher agreement rate across cultures than others? As you prepare to analyze the results, what are your hypotheses? The table below lists the six emotions represented in this study. On a scale of 0 to 100 percent, what percentage of the participants, across all the ten cultures, do you think recognized each type of emotion?

| Happiness | _____ % | Sadness | _____ % | Anger | _____ % |
| Fear | _____ % | Surprise | _____ % | Disgust | _____ % |

## THE RESULTS

You receive a total of 547 response forms in the mail, tally the results, and notice two key findings. Look at the table below and you'll see, first, that a majority of observers in *all* cultures interpreted facial expressions in the same way. The total agreement rate was far from perfect, but over all cultures and emotions it was quite high, at 82 percent. The second finding is that some emotions elicited more agreement than others. As you can see, people in general were most likely to agree on expressions of happiness and surprise and least likely to agree on anger and disgust.

| | |
|---|---|
| Happiness | 90% |
| Sadness | 85% |
| Anger | 74% |
| Fear | 80% |
| Surprise | 90% |
| Disgust | 73% |

## WHAT DOES IT ALL MEAN?

When Paul Ekman and his colleagues (1987) conducted the study just described, they were addressing a recurring debate in psychology concerning the "universality" of emotional states. On the one hand, emotion is so basic to the human experience that one would expect people all over the world to express their feelings in similar ways. On the other hand, there are cultural differences in the way people think about and interpret each other's behavior. Both positions are partly correct. Ekman's cross-cultural study showed that certain facial expressions are similarly interpreted by people all over the world. But what about other aspects of emotion? There is no simple answer. We'll see in this chapter that emotions are a product of physiological, behavioral, and cognitive factors and that although some aspects are universal, others are shaped by cultural forces.

*The Sum of All Fears. Minority Report. Moulin Rouge. Swordfish. Spider-Man. Chicago. Star Wars.* Go to the movies on a Saturday night, and you'll witness firsthand the power of human emotion. In darkened theaters all over the world, audiences laugh hysterically, cry in sorrow, gasp in fear, bite their fingernails in suspense, clench their jaws in anger, and tingle with sexual delight. Cheers, tears, sweaty palms, tense muscles, and a pounding heart are a vital part of the entertainment experience.

When scientists compare human beings and other animals, they are quick to point to our superior intellect; to the cognitive processes of learning, memory, thought, and language; and to the ability to formulate plans in order to pursue our goals. However, we humans are also intensely emotional, warm-blooded creatures. Love, hate, joy, sadness, pride, shame, hope, fear, lust, boredom, surprise, embarrassment, guilt, jealousy, and disgust are among the powerful feelings that color and animate our daily lives.

**Emotion** is a difficult concept to define, in part because there are so many different emotions in the repertoire of human feelings. Some are universal; others are found only in certain cultures. Some are intense; others are mild. Some are positive;

**emotion** A feeling state characterized by physiological arousal, expressive behaviors, and a cognitive interpretation.

others are negative. Some move us to take action; others do not. Despite these vast differences, however, psychologists agree that emotions in general consist of three interacting components: (1) internal physiological arousal, (2) expressive behavior in the face, body, and voice, and (3) a cognitive appraisal (see Figure 12.1). This chapter examines each of these components as well as various theories on how they combine to produce the conscious sensations we call emotions.

## THE PHYSIOLOGICAL COMPONENT

- *Why is emotion considered a physiological event, and what roles do the brain and nervous system play?*
- *Are all emotions accompanied by a state of general arousal, or does each emotion have its own unique set of symptoms?*
- *What is a polygraph, how can it be used as a lie-detector test, and is it accurate?*

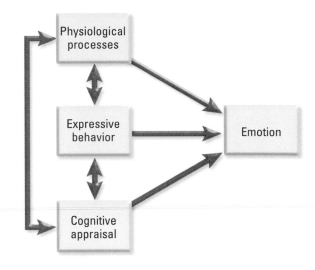

**FIGURE 12.1 Three components of emotion**
Based on many years of research, psychologists agree that emotions are triggered by a combination of factors.

The first time I gave a talk at a professional conference, while in graduate school, I was more nervous than I thought I would be. The symptoms were unmistakable. As I stepped to the podium and looked up at the audience, I had a knot in the pit of my stomach. My heart pounded, my hands shook, cold sweat dripped down my arms, and my mouth was bone dry. If that wasn't bad enough, my voice quivered the moment I started to speak. My body was sending me a message I did not want to hear and could not control. Was this a rare and unique experience? Not at all. Imagine what it feels like to fall head-over-heels in love, to be stranded on a dangerous street at night, to suffer the death of a loved one, or to get cheated out of something you desperately wanted and felt you deserved. The physical sensations may vary, but the body is intimately involved in feelings of intense emotion.

## A HISTORICAL PERSPECTIVE

William James was the first psychologist to theorize about the role of bodily functions in emotion. Common sense tells us that we smile because we're happy, cry because we're sad, clench our fists because we're angry, and tremble because we're afraid. So, if you're crossing the street and see a car speeding toward you, that stimulus will trigger fear, which in turn will cause your heart to pound as you try to escape. This seems reasonable, but in 1884, James turned common sense on its head by proposing what he thought was a radical new idea (philosopher René Descartes had made a similar proposal in the seventeenth century): that people feel happy because they smile, sad because they cry, angry because they clench their fists, and afraid because they tremble. In other words, the *perception* of danger causes your heart to pound as you run for cover—and it's this physiological and behavioral reaction that causes you to become afraid. This proposed chain of events, which was also suggested by a Danish physician named Carl Lange, is known as the **James-Lange theory** of emotion (see Figure 12.2).

In 1927, physiologist Walter Cannon challenged the James-Lange theory on three grounds. First, said Cannon, bodily sensations alone cannot produce

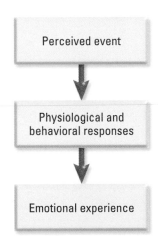

**FIGURE 12.2 The James-Lange theory of emotion**

**James-Lange theory** The theory that emotion stems from the physiological arousal that is triggered by an emotion-eliciting stimulus.

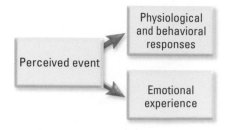

**FIGURE 12.3 The Cannon-Bard theory of emotion**

emotion. Indeed, when people are injected with epinephrine—a hormone that energizes the body—they report feeling "pumped up" and aroused but do not experience any specific emotion. Second, said Cannon, we sometimes feel fear, anger, and other emotions instantly, before all the systems of the body have had time to react. Third, the physical changes that do occur are often too general for us to distinguish between different emotions. Fear may make the heart beat faster, but so do anger and love.

As an alternative to the James-Lange theory, Cannon and a colleague named Philip Bard proposed that emotion originates in the thalamus, the part of the brain that simultaneously relays messages from the sensory organs to the autonomic nervous system (arousal), skeletal muscles (motor behavior), and cerebral cortex (conscious thought). According to the **Cannon-Bard theory**, the body and "mind" are activated independently in the experience of emotion. Thus, if you see a car swerving in your direction, your heart will start to pound, you'll run, and you'll become afraid—all at the same time (see Figure 12.3).

The debate between the James-Lange and Cannon-Bard theories was never resolved, and emotion researchers today are not quite as focused on the precise timing and sequence of the internal stream of events (Ellsworth, 1994). Equipped with sophisticated measurement devices, many physiologically oriented researchers seek instead to understand the role in emotion played by different brain structures, neural pathways, and autonomic arousal (Rolls, 1999). We now consider each of these topics.

## BRAIN CENTERS OF EMOTION

What role does the brain play in the experience of emotion? To begin with, research shows that some emotions are regulated by the *limbic system*—an evolutionarily primitive set of neural structures (including the thalamus, hypothalamus, hippocampus, and amygdala) that surrounds the brainstem and is found in lower mammals (see Figure 2.14). If you stimulate one part of the limbic system in a cat, the cat will pull back in fear; stimulate an adjacent area, and the cat will become enraged-snarling, hissing, and ready to pounce. Electronic stimulation of limbic structures in humans, as is sometimes used in the treatment of epilepsy, has similar effects (Panskepp, 1986).

Research points directly to the *amygdala* as a center for fear responses. For example, Ralph Adolphs and others (1999) encountered a patient who had a rare brain disorder in which excessive amounts of calcium were deposited in her amygdala. The structure was damaged, but other parts of her brain were unaffected. The deficits she exhibited were strikingly specific. When shown pictures of people with different facial expressions, she could identify most of their emotions, but not fear. She also had difficulty identifying emotions that were highly intense or arousing. This case study parallels findings in animal research. In experiments with rats, LeDoux (1996) found that when the amygdala was destroyed, the rats lost the ability to react to harmful stimuli with fear—which they typically do by freezing in place. In other experiments, LeDoux chemically traced the pathways in the brain that are activated in threatening situations and found that fear cut a path from the thalamus, where sensory input is sent, straight to the amygdala, without involvement of the "thinking" cerebral cortex. As we'll see later, this research indicates that fear, and perhaps other raw emotions, too, are triggered instantly—before information reaches the cortex and before we have had time to appraise the situation and formulate a response.

**Cannon-Bard theory** The theory that an emotion-eliciting stimulus simultaneously triggers physiological arousal and the experience of emotion.

Certain emotions may be quick and automatic, but others involve the *cerebral cortex*, the seat of human intellect. One cannot pinpoint a single region of the cortex that regulates all of our feelings because different emotions involve distinct patterns of neural activity. At the very least, research reveals two basic types of emotions: mostly positive feeling states such as joy, interest, and love, that motivate a tendency to *approach* people and situations (though anger, a negative emotion, also prompts approach), and negative feeling states such as sadness, fear, and disgust that motivate the tendency to *withdraw* from people and situations (Cacioppo & Gardner, 1999; Davidson et al., 2000; Watson et al., 1999).

Approach and withdrawal emotions appear to activate different parts of the brain. In a number of experiments, researchers have found that approach emotions evoke more electrical activity in the left cerebral hemisphere, whereas the withdrawal emotions elicit more activity in the right hemisphere. In one study, Davidson and others (1990) had participants watch films that evoked either pleasure (a puppy playing with flowers, a gorilla taking a bath in a zoo) or disgust (a gruesome leg amputation, a burn victim), videotaped their facial expressions with a hidden camera, and took EEG recordings in the brain. The result: Pleasure films increased neural activity in the left hemisphere, and disgust films did so in the right hemisphere. In another study, James Coan and others (2001) activated the left and right hemispheres by having people use the face to "act out" various approach (joy, anger) and withdrawal (sadness, fear, disgust) emotions. Similar results have been found in infants. When newborn babies taste sugared water or when ten-month-olds see their mom, the left hemisphere is primarily activated. When the taste is sour, however, or when the adult seen is a stranger, there is greater activity in the right hemisphere (Fox, 1991).

If approach and withdrawal *behaviors* are associated with the left and right hemispheres, respectively, could there be a link between brain activity and a person's *temperament*? Is it possible, using EEG measures, to distinguish between people who are characteristically outgoing and those who are shy and withdrawn? Yes, it appears so. In one study, four-year-old children interacted in play groups, and then, two weeks later, their EEGs were recorded as they attended to a visual stimulus. Those who were sociable in their playgroups later exhibited more relative activity in the left hemisphere, whereas those who were more isolated and withdrawn exhibited more relative activity in the right hemisphere (Fox et al., 1995). Other research, too, shows that children and adults with a more active left hemisphere tend to be interested, enthusiastic, and joyful, whereas those with a more active right hemisphere are timid, fearful, avoidant, and depressed (Davidson, 1998; Tomarken et al., 1992). This asymmetry is illustrated in Figure 12.4.

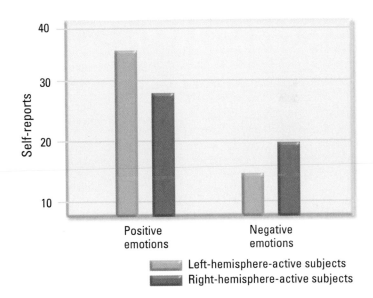

*Emotions evoke specific patterns of EEG activity. In the experiment depicted here, researcher Nathan Fox records brain waves in a four-month-old infant stimulated by toys.*

**FIGURE 12.4    Brain centers of emotion**
Compared to participants who exhibited greater EEG activity in the right hemisphere, those with a more active left hemisphere had emotions that were more positive (left) and less negative (right) (Tomarken et al., 1992).

## GENERALIZED AUTONOMIC AROUSAL

When an event prompts an emotional response, the human body prepares for action. To mobilize us for "fight" or "flight," the hypothalamus activates the **sympathetic nervous system**—the branch of the autonomic nervous system (ANS)

**sympathetic nervous system**  A branch of the autonomic nervous system that controls the involuntary activities of various organs and mobilizes the body for fight or flight.

*Riding a roller coaster activates the sympathetic nervous system. When the ride is over, the parasympathetic nervous system restores the body to its calm state.*

that controls involuntary activities of the heart, lungs, and other organs. Specifically, the adrenal glands secrete more of the hormones epinephrine and norepinephrine (commonly known as adrenaline and noradrenaline), which increase the heart rate and blood pressure and heighten physiological arousal. Then all at once, the liver pours extra sugar into the bloodstream for energy, the pupils dilate to let in more light, the breathing rate speeds up to intake more oxygen, perspiration increases to cool down the body, blood clots faster to heal wounds, saliva flow is inhibited, and digestion slows down to divert blood to the brain and skeletal muscles. Epinephrine and norepinephrine supply the physiological fuel for our many passions.

After an emotional event, the **parasympathetic nervous system** takes over and restores the body to its premobilized calm state. The heart stops racing, blood pressure is lowered, the pupils contract, breathing slows down, saliva flows again, the digestive system resumes its normal functions, and energy is conserved. As the levels of epinephrine and norepinephrine in the bloodstream slowly diminish, and the intensity of our feelings gradually decrease, enabling us to relax, cool down, and get on with our normal functions. This aspect of emotion is illustrated in Figure 12.5.

**12.1** Live! psych

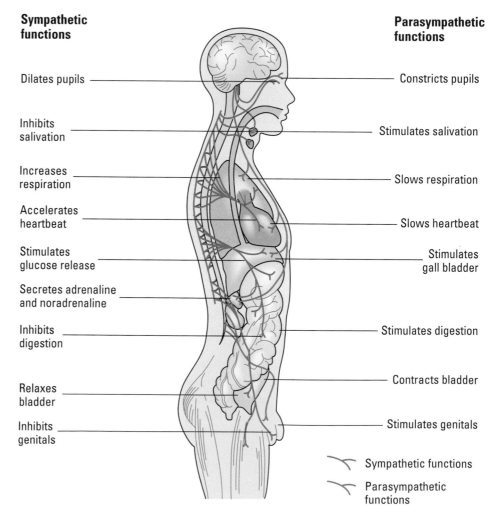

**Sympathetic functions**

- Dilates pupils
- Inhibits salivation
- Increases respiration
- Accelerates heartbeat
- Stimulates glucose release
- Secretes adrenaline and noradrenaline
- Inhibits digestion
- Relaxes bladder
- Inhibits genitals

**Parasympathetic functions**

- Constricts pupils
- Stimulates salivation
- Slows respiration
- Slows heartbeat
- Stimulates gall bladder
- Stimulates digestion
- Contracts bladder
- Stimulates genitals

Sympathetic functions

Parasympathetic functions

**parasympathetic nervous system** The division of the autonomic nervous system that reduces arousal and restores the body to its pre-energized state.

FIGURE 12.5 **The autonomic nervous system**
Note the differing functions of the sympathetic (arousing) and parasympathetic (calming) divisions of the autonomic nervous system.

# SPECIFIC PATTERNS OF AROUSAL

Clearly, physiological arousal intensifies an emotional experience. But are all emotions accompanied by the same general state of arousal, or does each emotion have its own unique set of symptoms? Scholars have been debating this question for many years. William James (1884) and others have argued that each emotion feels different to us because each is associated with its own specific pattern of autonomic activity. Noting that love, rage, and fear all make the heart beat faster, however, Walter Cannon (1927) and, later, others have maintained that all emotions spark the same physiological arousal. Who is right? Does each emotion have its own autonomic "fingerprint," or do they all feel basically the same?

Research suggests there is a bit of truth to both positions. In one study, Paul Ekman and others (1983) trained participants (many of whom were actors) to tense up the facial muscles that express happiness, anger, surprise, fear, sadness, or disgust. Using a mirror, participants held each face for ten seconds and the researchers took various measures of autonomic arousal. As it turned out, the posed expressions produced physiological differences. For example, heart rate increased for both anger and fear, but anger increased skin temperature, whereas fear had the opposite effect. Other studies have since confirmed this point (Levenson, 1992): Many emotions make the heart beat faster, but this similarity masks important differences—differences that are betrayed in the language we use to describe our feelings. Thus, in anger, we say that we're "hot under the collar," that our "blood is boiling," and that we need to "cool off" and "simmer down." In contrast, we describe fear as a "bone-chilling" emotion in which we "freeze" or get "cold feet" (Kovecses, 1990). Even more distinctive is the all-too-familiar pattern of arousal that signals embarrassment, a highly social emotion. When people feel ashamed or embarrassed in front of others, they blush, an involuntary reflex characterized by redness in the cheeks and ears and a rise in body temperature (Shearn et al., 1990). How our bodies react when we lie also has serious implications—for the legal system (see *Psychology and Law*).

*"Man is the only animal that blushes . . . Or needs to."*

—MARK TWAIN

**Culture and Arousal Patterns**   Clearly, autonomic nervous system activity is biologically programmed into the human organism—regardless of whether one lives in North America, South America, Europe, Asia, Africa, or the Pacific Islands. But are the *specific* patterns of arousal similarly universal? Is anger accompanied by increased heart rate and skin temperature in all cultures? What about the link between fear and cooled skin temperature? To test the cross-cultural generality of Ekman's results, Robert Levenson and his colleagues (1992) studied the Minangkabau people of West Sumatra, an island of Indonesia. This culture is different from ours in many ways. Its members are Muslims and farmers, they live in extended matrilineal families, and they forbid the public display of negative emotions. Yet despite these differences, the Levenson team found that the Minangkabau exhibited patterns of autonomic arousal similar to those of American participants.

In fact, people all over the world seem to know intuitively how the body reacts in different emotions. Klaus Scherer and Harald Wallbott (1994) asked three thousand students from thirty-seven countries (including the United States, Canada, Brazil, France, Norway, Greece, Poland, Botswana, Malawi, Israel, India, Hong Kong, and New Zealand) to describe various emotional experiences and found that there was widespread agreement about the primary sensations. To be sure, there were some cultural differences as well. For example, Japanese participants reported fewer symptoms than did American and European participants—perhaps because they are

To learn more about lie-detector tests, you can visit the Web site of the American Polygraph Association at **http://www.polygraph.org**.

## Psychology and Law

# READING EMOTION IN THE LIE-DETECTOR TEST

In *The Truth Machine*, futurist James Halperin (1997) depicts a twenty-first-century world in which a human colony is founded on Mars. There, terminal patients are frozen in liquid nitrogen and later revived, artificial gills that convert water to oxygen allow people to breath underwater—and there exists the "Armstrong Cerebral Image Processor," a wholly foolproof truth machine. Although the power to discern truth and deception seems like fanciful science fiction, the desire is constant. Currently, for example, you can purchase software that purports to turn your home PC into a truth machine by measuring vocal stress (Meyer, 1998).

For centuries, people have known that lying is an emotional experience revealed in involuntary physiological changes in stress levels. The Bedouins of Arabia used to make crime suspects lick a hot iron. In India and China, the suspects were forced to chew rice powder and then spit it out. Because lying was assumed to produce dryness in the mouth, those who burned their tongues or spit out dried powder were judged to be dishonest (Kleinmuntz & Szucko, 1984).

The modern lie-detector test is also based on the assumption that lying heightens autonomic arousal. Because this activity is not observable, law-enforcement officials use the **polygraph**—an electronic instrument that can simultaneously record multiple channels of arousal. The physiological signals are picked up by sensors that are attached to different parts of the body. For example, rubber tubes are strapped around the subject's torso to measure breathing, or respiration; blood pressure cuffs are wrapped around the upper arm to measure pulse rate and other cardiovascular activity; and electrodes on the hand are used to monitor changes in sweat-gland activity, or perspiration. These signals are then boosted by amplifiers and converted into a visual display.

The polygraph itself is merely a physiological recording device. It becomes a lie-detector test only when combined with an oral examination. Here's how it usually works. First, the examiner conducts a pretest interview to get the subject's baseline level of arousal and convince the subject that the polygraph works. Next, the examiner compares the subject's reaction to arousing crime-relevant questions ("Did you steal the car last night?") and control questions

*When Chandra Levy disappeared, the police learned that she was having an affair with Gary Condit, the Congressman for whom she interned. Trying to locate her, the police asked Condit to take an FBI polygraph. He refused but then announced that he had passed a privately administered polygraph. Reflecting the assumption that examiners can influence the results, the police rejected the offer and asked again for an FBI polygraph—which Condit never agreed to take. In May 2002, the remains of Levy's body were found in DC's Rock Creek Park.*

**polygraph** An electronic device that records multiple channels of autonomic arousal and is often used as a lie-detector test.

that are arousing but not relevant to the crime ("Did you steal anything when you were younger?"). In theory, crime-relevant questions should evoke more arousal than the control questions among participants who are lying but not among those who are telling the truth (see Figure 12.6).

Does the lie-detector test work? Many laypeople think that it is foolproof, but scientific opinion is split (Iacono & Lykken, 1997). Some researchers report accuracy rates of up to 90 percent (Horvath, 1984; Raskin, 1986). Others say that these claims are exaggerated and that the test is fraught with serious problems (Lykken, 1981). One problem is that truthful persons too often "fail" the test. For example, a study of polygraph records taken from police files revealed that although 98 percent of suspects later known to be guilty were correctly identified as such, 45 percent of those eventually found innocent were also judged deceptive (Patrick & Iacono, 1991). A second problem is that the test can be passed through faking. Studies show that you can beat the polygraph by tensing your muscles, biting your

tongue, or squeezing your toes during the control questions. Think through the logic of this strategy. By artificially inflating our responses to these "innocent" questions, we can mask the stress that is aroused by lying to the crime-relevant questions (Honts et al., 1994).

What, then, are we to conclude? After carefully reviewing research for the Congressional Office of Technology Assessment, Leonard Saxe and others (1985) concluded that there is no simple answer. Under certain conditions—for example, when a suspect is naive and the examiner well trained—it is possible for polygraphers to make accurate judgments of truth and deception. Still, the problems are hard to overcome—which is why the United States Supreme Court ruled, about a military court martial, that polygraph test results should not be admitted into evidence (*United States v. Scheffer*, 1998). As an alternative, researchers are now trying to develop tests that can distinguish between truth and deception by measuring involuntary electrical activity in the brain (Bashore & Rapp, 1993), pupil dilation when the subject is asked to lie, which requires more cognitive processing effort than telling the truth (Dionisio et al., 2001), and involuntary muscle movements in the face that betray grimaces and other expressions too subtle to detect with the naked eye (Bartlett et al., 1999). Research suggests it may even be possible to judge truth and deception by measuring how long it takes people to react to crime-relevant information, with guilty suspects taking longer to react than innocents (Seymour et al., 2000).

Until recently, many companies used the polygraph to screen employees and uncover theft in the workplace. Those who use it argue that it sharpens their ability to hire employees who are honest. Opponents, however, argue that the test is an invasion of an individual's privacy, that it is often misused, and that the results are not sufficiently accurate. In light of these problems, the U.S. government in 1988 passed a law that prohibits the use of the lie-detector test except when it comes to matters of security and public safety—such as screening scientists who work at nuclear testing facilities (Beardsley, 1999).

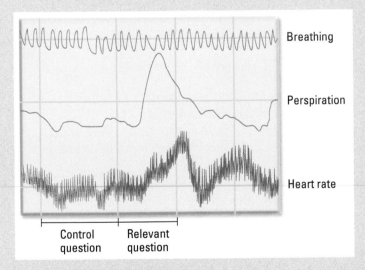

**FIGURE 12.6    Lie-detector test**
This polygraph recording depicts the physiological reactions of a crime suspect judged guilty. Note that heart rate and perspiration increased more in response to a crime-relevant question than to a control question.

## REVIEW QUESTIONS

- *Distinguish between the James-Lange and Cannon-Bard theories of emotion.*

- *What brain structures are involved in the physiology of emotion? How do we know?*

- *Can particular emotional states be identified by specific patterns of arousal? Why or why not?*

- *Are the physiological symptoms associated with different emotions universal, or do they vary from culture to culture?*

**TABLE 12.1    CULTURE AND THE EXPERIENCES OF EMOTION**

People from thirty-seven countries described various emotional experiences. As shown, certain symptoms were commonly described across cultural groups.

| Emotions | Symptoms | Percentage Reported | Emotions | Symptoms | Percentage Reported |
|---|---|---|---|---|---|
| Joy | Feeling warm | 63 | Sadness | Lump in throat | 56 |
| | Fast heartbeat | 40 | | Crying | 55 |
| | Relaxed muscles | 29 | | Tense muscles | 27 |
| Fear | Fast heartbeat | 65 | | Fast heartbeat | 27 |
| | Tense muscles | 52 | | Feeling cold | 22 |
| | Rapid breathing | 47 | Shame | Feeling hot | 40 |
| | Perspiration | 37 | | Fast heartbeat | 35 |
| | Feeling cold | 36 | | Perspiration | 26 |
| | Lump in throat | 29 | Guilt | Lump in throat | 28 |
| | Stomach trouble | 22 | | Fast heartbeat | 27 |
| Anger | Fast heartbeat | 50 | Disgust | Tense muscles | 25 |
| | Tense muscles | 43 | | Fast heartbeat | 23 |
| | Rapid breathing | 37 | | Stomach trouble | 21 |
| | Feeling hot | 32 | | | |
| | Lump in throat | 25 | | | |

less self-focused and less likely to attend to their own inner states. Still, the sensations that Japanese participants did report were very similar to those described by other cultural groups. Table 12.1 shows the most frequently reported bodily symptoms of the various emotions.

## THE EXPRESSIVE COMPONENT

- *What functions are served by our outward expressions of emotion?*
- *Are some emotions "basic" and, if so, which ones?*
- *What is the evidence that facial expressions are inborn and universal?*
- *What's the facial-feedback hypothesis, and why does it predict that smiling can make you happy?*

Emotion may be an internal, purely subjective experience, but it also has an observable behavioral component. The links between inner feelings and outward expressions are numerous: We smile when we're happy, cry when we're sad, blush when we're embarrassed, stand tall when we feel proud, drag our feet when we're down, press our lips in anger, bow our heads in shame, and wrinkle our faces in disgust.

These behavioral expressions of emotion serve two functions. First, they provide us with a means of *nonverbal communication*. People often use words to tell others how they're feeling. But by smiling, frowning, turning bright red in the face, shrugging the shoulders, or winking an eye, we also communicate our feelings nonverbally—which encourages others to approach us, or stay away. Thus, Alan Fridlund (1994) has argued that our expressive behaviors serve more as *signals* to other people than as *symptoms* of how we feel, making the display of emotion an inherently social experience (see Figure 12.7). The second effect of behavioral expression is to provide us with *sensory feedback*. In 1872, Darwin theorized that the expressions that we make clarify and intensify emotional experiences by providing us

*"The face is like a switch on a railroad track. It affects the trajectory of social interaction the way the switch would affect the path of the train."*

—ALAN FRIDLUND

with bodily feedback about how we feel. In short, the expressive component of emotion has two audiences: other people and ourselves.

## NONVERBAL COMMUNICATION

Knowing how another person is feeling can be tricky because people sometimes try to hide their true emotions. Think about it. Have you ever had to suppress your rage at someone, mask your disappointment after failure, feign surprise, or pretend to like something just to be polite? Sometimes we come right out and tell people how we feel. But often we actively try to conceal our true feelings. In instances like these, observers tune in to a silent language—the language of nonverbal behavior.

**Facial Expression**   What kinds of nonverbal cues do people use to judge how someone is feeling? In *The Expression of the Emotions in Man and Animals*, Charles Darwin (1872) argued that the *face* communicates emotion in ways that are innate and are understood by people all over the world. Contemporary research provides strong support for this proposition. In

| Wink | Smirk | Said smiling | Said frowning | Sardonic incredulity |
|------|-------|--------------|---------------|----------------------|
| '-) | :-, | :-) | :-( | ;-) |
| :-I | :-X | :*) | I-( | :-J |
| Disgusted | Kiss, kiss | Clowning around | Said late at night | Said tongue-in-cheek |

**FIGURE 12.7   Some common email "emoticons"**
The social value of the face is evident to those who communicate online. When email first became popular, the written word was often misinterpreted (especially when the writer was trying to be funny) because it lacked the expressions that normally animate and clarify live interactions. To fill in the facial gap, emailers created smiley faces and other "emoticons" (emotion icons) from standard keyboard characters. Meant to be viewed with one's head tilted 90 degrees to the left, some routinely used emoticons are shown above. (Sanderson, 1993).

*Look at the photographs above and try to match each with one of the following emotions: (1) surprise, (2) anger, (3) disgust, (4) fear, (5) joy, and (6) sadness. People from a diversity of cultures exhibit high levels of agreement on this task.*

*Chelsey Thomas was known as the little girl who could not smile. She was born with Moebius syndrome, a rare neurological disorder that impairs activity in the facial muscles. "She always smiled, really, on the inside," said her mother. But with the face playing a vital role in communication, one can only imagine what a social price she paid for her outward blank expression. So Chelsey had corrective surgery and then had to learn how—and when—to smile. At the age of seven, she smiled for the first time.*

12.2

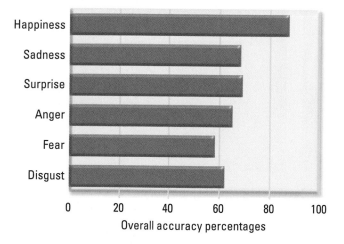

**FIGURE 12.8** **How good are people at identifying emotions in the face?**
A meta-analysis of emotion recognition studies involving 22,148 participants from forty-two countries confirmed that people all over the world can recognize the six basic emotions from posed facial expressions (Elfenbein & Ambady, 2002).

**facial electromyograph (EMG)** An electronic instrument used by emotion researchers to record activity in the facial muscles.

a groundbreaking study, Ekman and Friesen (1974) showed thirty photographs like those on page xxx to participants from New York to New Guinea—including Argentina, Borneo, Brazil, and Japan—and asked them to guess the emotion being portrayed in each photo. The results of this study, and of many others like it, indicate that people can reliably identify six emotions: joy, fear, anger, sadness, surprise, and disgust. In the experiment described at the start of this chapter, people from ten different countries exhibited high levels of agreement in their recognition of these same emotions (Ekman et al., 1987).

Not everyone agrees that the results are strong enough to support the claim that basic emotions are "universally" recognized in the face (Russell, 1994). In general, however, from one end of the world to the other, a smile is a smile and a frown is a frown, and just about everyone knows what they mean—even when the expressions are "put on" by actors and not genuinely felt (Gosselin et al., 1995). As you might expect, people are better at this task when they see videotaped faces in action rather than in "frozen" snapshots (Wehrle et al., 2000). Supporting the view that certain expressions are inborn—and universally recognized—is that even humans who are too young to speak and have yet to fully learn the lessons of their culture make faces that are associated with basic emotions. Thus, when Carroll Izard and his colleagues (1980) analyzed the facial expressions of young infants, they were able to identify several states, each necessary for nonverbal infants to "communicate" from birth with their caretakers. They found that in pleasant and nonpleasant interactions with their mothers, infants as young as ten weeks old made facial expressions that signaled joy, interest, sadness, and anger (Izard et al., 1995).

So what have researchers concluded? Hillary Elfenbein and Nalini Ambady (2002) meta-analyzed ninety-seven emotion recognition studies involving a total of 22,148 people from forty-two different countries. As shown in Figure 12.8, they confirmed the main result that people can generally identify certain basic emotions from facial expressions. By comparing performances across different studies, they also discovered that people are 9 percent more accurate when they judge members of their own national, ethnic, or regional groups than when they judge members of other less familiar groups. In other words, we enjoy an "in-group advantage" when it comes to knowing how those who are closest to us are feeling. We also react to some emotional displays more than others. From an evolutionary standpoint, it is more adaptive to beware of someone who is angry, and likely to lash out in violence, than someone who is happy, a nonthreatening emotion. Studies have shown that angry faces arouse us and cause us to frown even when presented subliminally—without our awareness (Dimberg & Ohman, 1996; Dimberg et al., 2000).

Emotion is accompanied by changes in facial expression—even when these changes are subtle and cannot be seen with the naked eye. The human face has eighty muscles that can create more than seven thousand different expressions. To measure the spontaneous activity of these muscles and their links to emotion, many researchers use a physiological device known as the **facial electromyograph (EMG)**. In facial EMG studies, participants are shown images that evoke positive or negative emotions, while electrodes attached to the face record the activity of various muscles (see Figure 12.9). This research shows that images that elicit positive emotions such as joy, interest, and attraction increase activity in the cheek muscles; those that arouse negative emotions such as anger, distress, and fear spark activity in the forehead and brow area. Evidently, the muscles in the human face reveal smiles, frowns, and other expressions that are otherwise hidden from view (Dimberg, 1990; Tassinary & Cacioppo, 1992).

Using the facial EMG, researchers have also discovered two distinct types of smiles—one more genuine than the other. In a series of experiments, Ekman and others found that when people experience real joy, they beam smiles that raise the cheeks high enough to wrinkle up the skin around the eyes and they exhibit increased electrical activity in the left hemisphere of the brain. But when people wear false, "unfelt" smiles—say, to be polite or to pose for a photograph—the muscle activity in the lips and lower cheeks does not extend up to the eyes or trigger a predominance of left-hemisphere activity in the brain (Ekman & Davidson, 1993; Ekman et al., 1990; Frank et al., 1993).

**Body Language**   Other nonverbal cues also communicate emotion, enabling us to make quick and often accurate judgments of how others are feeling based on "thin slices" of expressive behavior (Ambady & Rosenthal, 1992). One common form of expression is *body language*—the way people stand, sit, walk, and gesture. For example, people who have a youthful walking style—who sway their hips, bend their knees, pick up their feet, and swing their arms in a bouncy rhythm—are seen as happier and more powerful than those who walk slowly, take shorter steps, and stiffly drag their feet (Montepare & McArthur, 1988).

*Gaze,* or eye contact, is also a common and powerful form of communication. The eyes have been called windows of the soul. In many cultures, people assume that someone who avoids looking them in the eye is evasive, cold, fearful, shy, or apathetic; that frequent gazing signals intimacy, sincerity, and confidence; and that the person who stares is tense, angry, or unfriendly. In fact, eye contact is often interpreted in light of preexisting relationships. Among friends and lovers, frequent gaze means warmth and affection. Among enemies, it signals cold hostility. Thus, it has been said that if two people lock eyes for more than a few seconds, they are either going to make love or kill each other (Kleinke, 1986; Patterson, 1983).

Another nonverbal cue is touch—a congratulatory high-five, a sympathetic pat on the back, a joking elbow in the ribs, and a warm loving embrace are just a few examples. Physical touch is generally considered an expression of friendship, caring, and sexual interest. But it may also serve other functions. Several years ago, Nancy Henley (1977) observed that men, older persons, and those of high status are more likely to touch women, younger persons, and others of lower status than the other way around. Henley's interpretation: that touching is an expression not only of intimacy but also of dominance and control. Simple forms of touch, as when people greet each other, also provide us with thin slices of behavioral evidence. Think about the handshakes you've received in your life—and whether the grips were firm or limp, strong or weak, dry or clammy, brief or lingering. Research suggests that the first impressions we form of others may be influenced by these qualities of a simple handshake (Chaplin et al., 2000).

*How happy are these athletes? When genuinely happy, our smiles raise the cheeks high enough to wrinkle up the eyes (when we wear false smiles, the muscle activity in the lips does not extend up to the eyes). This picture was taken during the 2002 Olympics, shortly after Canadian figure skaters David Pelletier and Jamie Sale, thinking they had won a gold medal, received the silver medal instead. As a result of a judging scandal, the International Olympic Committee soon awarded these skaters a second gold medal.*

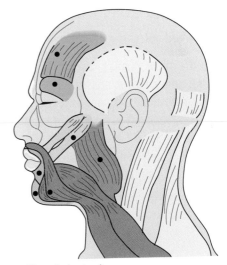

• Site of electrode

**FIGURE 12.9   The facial electromyograph (EMG)**
Electrodes placed on the face record activity in various muscles. These recordings reveal that positive emotions increase activity in the cheek muscles, and negative emotions increase activity in the forehead and brow areas (Cacioppo & Petty, 1981).

# PAUL EKMAN
## *Universals in Facial Expressions*

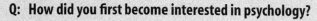

**Q: How did you first become interested in psychology?**

**A:** I became interested in psychology after reading Freud's *New Introductory Lectures* in a humanities course at the University of Chicago in 1949. In class we considered Freud's book as rhetoric, but I found it applicable to my own life. I read all that I could find in English that Freud had written and decided I would pursue a career as a psychoanalyst.

In graduate school at Adelphi University, I started to study gesture and expression, as it would help me understand the psychotherapeutic process. I shifted to full time research after obtaining my Ph.D. in 1958, when I was drafted into the Army and served as chief psychologist at Ft. Dix. There was little opportunity to do psychotherapy, but incredible research opportunities. I obtained a grant from the Surgeon General and studied the psychological changes produced by infantry basic training and the Army's treatment of those who went AWOL. My findings led to more humane and effective disposition of AWOLs. Excited by the impact that research could have, I took a few years out from doing psychotherapy to learn more about research on a post doctoral fellowship. I never got back to psychotherapy.

**Q: How did you come up with your important discovery?**

**A:** In the middle 1960's I was asked by a government agency if I would examine how expressions and gestures differed or were the same across cultures. Although initially reluctant—I was not trained as an anthropologist—I could not resist the opportunity to try to resolve a century old question about this issue. I consulted with the experts: Ray Birdwhistell, Margaret Mead, Ned Hall, Charles Osgood, and Silvan Tomkins. For the next five years I focused on this issue,

eventually publishing a number of books and articles. My most important work was in a visually isolated, stone-age culture in New Guinea, where people could not have learned their expressions from the media or contact with outsiders.

**Q: How has the field you inspired developed over the years?**

**A:** I believe that my work, and that of Carrol Izard, who also found evidence of universals in the facial expressions of half a dozen or so emotions, served to reawaken interest in the field of emotion. Now it is a vital field, at the center of psychology, with studies on many different aspects of emotion: neurophysiology, development, cognition, and social influence. More research is still needed in the study of emotion in natural or quasi-experimental settings.

**Q: What's your prediction on where the field is heading?**

**A:** It is very hard to say where emotion research is going now. Certainly the work on emotion and the brain is blossoming and will continue to thrive. Emotional disturbances in marriage, in parent-child interactions, and the role of emotion in physical health are all growing fields of study and practice. I hope my latest book, published in April 2003, will also help people improve their emotional life.

*Paul Ekman is Professor of Psychology in the Department of Psychiatry at the University of California Medical School, San Francisco.*

## SENSORY FEEDBACK

Draw the corners of your mouth back and up and wrinkle your eye muscles. Relax. Now raise your eyebrows, open your eyes wide, and let your mouth drop open slightly. Relax. Now pull your brows down and together and clench your teeth. Relax. If you followed each of these directions, you would have appeared to others to be feeling first happy, then fearful, and finally angry. The question is, do these expressions affect how you actually feel?

According to the **facial-feedback hypothesis**, an expression does more than simply reflect one's emotion—it actually triggers an emotional experience. In an

**facial-feedback hypothesis** The hypothesis that changes in facial expression can produce corresponding changes in emotion.

interesting first test of this hypothesis, James Laird (1974) told college students that they would take part in an experiment on the activity of the facial muscles. After attaching electrodes to the face, he showed them a series of cartoons and asked them before each one to contract certain facial muscles in ways that made them smile or frown. The result: the students thought the material was funnier and reported feeling happier when they wore a smile than a frown. Similarly, other posed-expression studies show that people can also be induced to experience fear, anger, sadness, and disgust (Duclos et al., 1989). Together, this research suggests that facial expressions—though not *necessary* for the experience of emotion—can evoke and magnify certain emotional states (McIntosh, 1996).

Why does this occur? Laird believes that facial expressions activate emotion through a process of self-perception: "If I'm smiling, I must be happy." To test this hypothesis, Chris Kleinke and his colleagues (1998) asked people to emulate either the happy or angry facial expressions that were depicted in a series of pictures. Half the participants saw themselves in a mirror during the task; the others did not. Did these manipulations affect mood states? Yes. Compared to participants in a no-expression control group, those who put on happy faces felt better—and those who put on angry faces felt worse. As Laird would predict, these effects were most pronounced among participants who saw themselves in a mirror.

Other researchers speculate that there is a second possible reason for this effect, that perhaps expressions trigger an emotional experience by causing physiological changes in the brain (Izard, 1990). For example, Robert Zajonc (1993) proposed that smiling causes facial muscles to increase the flow of air-cooled blood to the brain, which has a pleasant effect by lowering the brain's temperature. Conversely, frowning decreases blood flow, which produces an unpleasant state by raising brain temperature. To demonstrate this mechanism, Zajonc and his colleagues (1989) asked participants to repeat certain vowels twenty times each, including the sounds *ah, e, u,* and the German vowel *ü.* As they uttered the sounds, temperature in the forehead was measured and participants reported on how they felt. The result: *ah* and *e* (vowel sounds that cause speakers to mimic smiling) lowered forehead temperature and elevated mood, whereas *u* and *ü* (vowels that cause speakers to mimic frowning) raised temperature and dampened mood. In other words, movement of the facial muscles influenced emotion even though participants didn't realize that they were wearing an expression. The lesson: If you want an emotional lift, just put on a happy face.

Other expressive behaviors such as body posture also provide us with sensory feedback and influence how we feel. When people feel proud, they stand erect with the shoulders raised, chest expanded, and head held high (*expansion*). When people feel sad and dejected, however, they slump over with their shoulders drooping and head bowed (*contraction*). Clearly, your emotional state is revealed in the way you carry yourself. Is it also possible that the way you carry yourself affects your emotional state? Can people lift their spirits by expanding their posture or lower their spirits through contraction? Yes. Sabine Stepper and Fritz Strack (1993) arranged for participants to sit in a slumped or upright position by varying the height of the table they had to write on. Those forced to sit upright reported feeling more pride after succeeding at a task than did those who were put into a slumped position. In another study, participants who were instructed to lean forward with their fists clenched during the experiment reported feeling anger, whereas those who sat slumped with their heads down said they felt sadness (Duclos et al., 1989; Flack et al., 1999).

*"Refuse to express a passion and it dies."*

—WILLIAM JAMES

## REVIEW QUESTIONS

- *What are the two primary functions of emotional expression?*

- *Describe the evidence that facial expressions of emotion are universal?*

- *How do expressions of emotion (such as facial expressions, body posture, and vocal behavior) influence emotional state?*

**two-factor theory of emotion** The theory that emotion is based both on physiological arousal and a cognitive interpretation of that arousal.

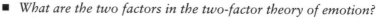

# THE COGNITIVE COMPONENT

- *What are the two factors in the two-factor theory of emotion?*
- *What role does thought play in the experience of emotion?*
- *Which Olympic athlete feels better—the silver medalist or the bronze medalist—and why?*
- *What evidence is there to suggest that cognition is not a necessary ingredient of emotion?*

"Let's do it, let's fall in love."

*Many researchers emphasize the role of cognitive factors in the experience of love and other emotions.*

Emotion is much more than physiological sensations and expressive behaviors. After all, the heart pounds in fear, but it also pounds in anger. We cry out in grief over the death of a loved one, but we also shed tears of joy at weddings and other happy occasions. We laugh when we're amused, but sometimes we laugh out of nervousness. In other words, there has to be more to grief, joy, amusement, and nervousness than arousal and expression. The missing link is cognitive appraisal.

Psychologists have long been embroiled in debate over the role of cognitive factors in emotion. Are your feelings, like inborn reflexes, triggered by stimuli without conscious thought or awareness, or does the way you feel depend largely on how you perceive, interpret, and evaluate the situation you're in? Do you think first and feel second, or is it the other way around? Theories of emotion suggest different answers to these questions.

## SCHACHTER'S TWO-FACTOR THEORY OF EMOTION

When I was nineteen, my girlfriend and I were sitting upstairs in her home late at night. Her parents were away for the weekend and nobody else was in the house. The TV was on and we were on the verge of falling asleep. Then suddenly we heard scraping, clicking, the front door opening, and footsteps downstairs. There was an intruder in the house, and we were terrified. My heart pounded so hard that I could feel my chest throb with every beat. Except for the trembling, I was frozen in place like a statue. The emotion we experienced that night was raw fear, plain and simple. How did I "know" that I was feeling afraid and not sad, angry, disgusted, or ill?

According to Stanley Schachter (1964), two factors are necessary to have a specific emotion. First, the person must experience a heightened state of *physiological arousal,* such as a racing heart, sweaty palms, tightening of the stomach, rapid breathing, and so on—the kind of jitteriness you might feel after drinking too much coffee. Second, the person must find a *cognitive label* or attribution to explain the source of that arousal. The night that my girlfriend and I heard an intruder, I had such an obvious explanation for my symptoms that labeling the emotion as fear was easy. In fact, I was shaky for quite some time afterward. (We called the police, and they arrived minutes later to find the front door wide open. They searched the house with flashlights, but it was too late; the intruder had left.) The same is true when people watch intensely emotional films. When moviegoers saw *Silence of the Lambs,* and its sequel *Hannibal,* they knew they were feeling disgusted rather than ashamed, angry, or sad, because the stimulus itself was unambiguous. At times, however, people become generally excited without knowing why—and must examine their surroundings in order to identify the emotion (see Figure 12.10).

To test this **two-factor theory of emotion,** Schachter and Jerome Singer (1962) injected male participants with epinephrine, the hormone that produces physiological arousal. The participants in one group were warned in advance about the side effects (they were drug-informed), but those in a second group were not (they were drug-uninformed). In a third group, the participants were injected with a harmless placebo (this was the placebo control group). Before the drug—which was described as a vitamin supplement—actually took effect, participants were left alone with a male confederate introduced as another subject who had received the same injection. In some cases, the confederate's behavior was euphoric: He bounced around happily, doodled on paper, sank jump shots into the waste basket, flew paper airplanes across the room, and swung his hips in a hula hoop. In the presence of other participants, the same confederate behaved angrily. At one point, for example, he ridiculed a questionnaire they were filling out and, in a fit of rage, ripped it up and hurled it into the wastebasket.

Think for a moment about the various situations. In the *drug-informed* group, participants began to feel their hearts pound, their hands shake, and their faces flush. Led to expect these side effects, however, they did not have to search very far for an explanation. In the *placebo* group, the participants did not become aroused in the first place, so they had no symptoms to explain. But now consider the predicament of the participants in the *drug-uninformed* group, who suddenly became aroused without knowing why. Trying to identify the sensations, these participants—according to the theory—would take their cues from others who are in the same situation, namely the confederate. The results generally supported this prediction. The drug-uninformed participants reported that they felt more happy or angry depending on the confederate's actions. In some cases, they even displayed similar behavior. For example, one subject "threw open the window and, laughing, hurled paper basketballs at passersby." Those in the drug-informed group, who attributed their arousal to the epinephrine, were not as influenced by these social cues. Neither were participants in the no-drug placebo group—who, after all, were not physiologically aroused.

Schachter's (1964) two-factor theory has attracted a good deal of attention. Not all the research has confirmed the result, but one general conclusion can be drawn: When people are aroused and do not know why, they try to identify their own emotions by observing the situation they're in and making an attribution for their arousal (Reisenzein, 1983). This conclusion has interesting implications. One is that if people attribute their arousal to a *non*emotional source, they will experience less emotion (this is what happened in the drug-informed group, where participants blamed their autonomic symptoms on the epinephrine). Another is that if people attribute their arousal to an emotional source, they will experience more of that emotion (which was the experience of those in the drug-uninformed group). In short, once people are stimulated, they can cognitively intensify, diminish, and alter their own emotions.

**Misattribution**   One particularly intriguing implication of this theory is that the arousal produced by one source can be "misattributed" or "transferred" to another source. Suppose you had just run two miles, spent a full hour playing basketball, or danced hard at a party. Chances are, you would be sweating and gasping for breath. You would realize, of course, that these symptoms had been caused by physical exertion. But what if you went on to another activity? Because it takes time for the autonomic functions to return to normal, you might later attribute the residual arousal to a new source.

Research supports this misattribution hypothesis. Studies have shown that after strenuous physical exercise, participants are angrier when provoked by an insult and more sexually aroused when they meet someone of the opposite sex. Autonomic arousal from one event thus spills over and enhances feelings toward another event (Zillman, 1983; Allen et al., 1989). Donald Dutton and Arthur Aron (1974) demonstrated this spillover effect in a field study conducted on two bridges above British Columbia's Capilano River. One was a narrow, wobbly suspension bridge with a low rail that sways 230 feet above rocky rapids. The other was wide, sturdy,

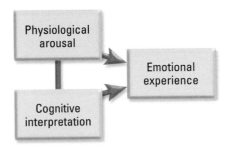

**FIGURE 12.10**   **Two-factor theory of emotion**

**misattribution** An explanation that shifts the perceived cause of arousal from the true source to another one.

and only 10 feet from the ground. As young men walked over these bridges, they were met by a young woman who introduced herself as a research assistant, asked them to fill out a questionnaire, and gave her phone number in case they wanted more information on the project. As predicted, participants who walked over the scary bridge—a highly stressful experience that could be misattributed to the research assistant—were more likely than those who crossed the stable bridge to call the woman later. Perhaps terror can fan the hot flames of romance.

If it is possible to intensify an emotion by the transfer of arousal, it should be possible to diminish emotion in the same way. Consider stage fright, or public-speaking anxiety—an unwanted emotion that claims many victims. As if the dry throat and quivering voice were not embarrassing enough, those who suffer from this common problem get even more anxious because they are anxious. But what if they had an alternative explanation for the symptoms? Is it possible to calm people with speech anxiety by providing face-saving attributions for their arousal? Using the technique of **misattribution**, James Olson (1988) led some participants but not others to believe that a "subliminal noise" would make them feel anxious while speaking. The result: Those who thought that noise made them more anxious gave smoother, more fluent speeches. By prompting these participants to attribute their arousal to an external event rather than to their own anxiety, Olson was able to calm them down and improve their performance. "What, me nervous? My heart may be racing, but thank goodness it's not me—it's just the noise."

## DIMENSIONS OF APPRAISAL

According to cognitively oriented theorists, the emotions we feel are determined by the way we appraise the situation we're in—and certain types of appraisals are particularly important in this regard. To appreciate the cognitive approach, think about the last time you experienced a particular emotion—say, joy. Picture the scene in your mind and answer the following questions. Why were you happy? How pleasant was the experience? Did you feel as if you were in control? Were you responsible for what happened? How well did you understand the situation you were in? Did you know how things would turn out? Were you thinking about how you felt, or were you trying to shut your feelings out? Was the situation important to you? By asking people to answer questions like these about emotion experiences, researchers have found some clear links between our cognitive appraisals and emotional reactions (Frijda, 1986). Even emotions that seem similar on the surface—like embarrassment, shame, and guilt—can be distinguished upon reflection (Tangney et al., 1996).

The cognitive dimensions of appraisal that are most closely linked to emotion are the *pleasantness* of the situation (whether or not it's enjoyable), *attention* (whether we are focused on what's happening), *agency* (the belief that we are in control), and *certainty* (the clarity of the situation and whether the outcome is predictable). Research thus shows that various emotions can be distinguished by the cognitive appraisals people make on these dimensions (Smith & Ellsworth, 1985)—and that these dimensions are relevant not only in the United States but in other countries as well (Mauro et al., 1992; Mesquita & Frijda, 1992). Consider the following examples:

- *Happiness* is a pleasant state that involves high levels of attention, control, and certainty (partying with friends, attending a graduation ceremony).

- *Surprise* is a pleasant, effortless state characterized by a high level of attention but low certainty and control (getting an A in a course when a C was expected, getting an unannounced visit from an old friend).

- *Shame* is an unpleasant state characterized by a desire to avoid thinking about the situation, by moderate levels of certainty, and by a high level of personal control in the form of self-blame (getting caught cheating, gossiping about someone).

- *Anger* is an intensely unpleasant state that involves moderate levels of certainty and attention. Its most prominent aspect is the belief that one's misfortune is controlled by others (having a car stolen, being insulted in public).

- *Sadness* is a highly unpleasant state of uncertainty coupled with a desire to minimize attention to the situation. Unlike situations that spark anger, sadness events are usually blamed on circumstances rather than on other people (illness, divorce, the death of a loved one).

- *Fear* is also a highly aversive state. Like surprise, it is associated with high levels of uncertainty and low levels of personal control, particularly about one's ability to escape or avoid a dreaded outcome (being held at knife point, skidding on an icy winter road).

## COUNTERFACTUAL THINKING

As thoughtful and curious beings, we often are not content to accept the outcomes in our lives without wondering, at least in private, "What if . . . ?" According to Daniel Kahneman and Dale Miller (1986), people's emotional reactions to events are colored by **counterfactual thinking**, the tendency to imagine alternative outcomes that might have occurred but did not. If the imagined result is better than the actual result, we're likely to suffer from feelings of disappointment, frustration, and regret. If the imagined result is worse, then we may react with emotions that range from mild relief to elation. True to the cognitive perspective, then, the emotional impact of positive and negative events depends on the way we think about "what might have been" (Roese, 1997; Roese & Olson, 1995). Importantly, the bridge that connects our cognitive and emotional states holds two-way traffic. Just as counterfactual thoughts can alter our mood, the mood we are in can influence the kind of counterfactual thinking we do. When people feel good, they imagine how much worse things could be; when down in the dumps, they imagine how much better they could be (Sanna et al., 1999).

People don't immerse themselves in counterfactual thought after every experience, obviously. But we do tend to wonder "what if"—often with feelings of regret—after negative outcomes that result from actions we take rather than inactions (Byrne & McEleney, 2000; Gilovich & Medvec, 1995). According to Victoria Medvec and Kenneth Savitsky (1997), certain situations—such as being on the verge of a better or worse outcome, just above or below some cutoff point—make it particularly easy to conjure up images of what might have been. The implications are intriguing. Imagine, for example, that you are an Olympic athlete and have just won a silver medal, a truly remarkable feat. Now imagine that you have just won the bronze medal. Which situation would make you feel better? Rationally, it seems that you should feel more pride and satisfaction with the silver medal. But what if your achievement had prompted you to engage in counterfactual thinking? What alternative would preoccupy your mind if you had finished in second place? And where would your focus be if you had placed third? Is it possible that the athlete who is better off objectively will feel worse?

To examine this question, Medvec and others (1995) videotaped forty-one athletes in the 1992 summer Olympic Games the moment they realized that they had won a silver or bronze medal and again later, during the medal ceremony. Then they showed these tapes, without sound, to participants who did not know the order of

**counterfactual thinking** Imagining alternative scenarios and outcomes that might have happened but did not.

What if Germany had won World War II? What if U.S. intelligence agencies had foiled the attacks on the World Trade Center? Historians often presume that the past was inevitable. But in a fascinating book entitled *Virtual History,* historians ask "what if?" about a number of decisive moments in modern history (Ferguson, 1997).

During the 1996 summer Olympics, Nike ran a counterfactual—and controversial—advertisement: "You don't win silver, you lose gold."

finish. The participants were asked to watch the medalists and rate their emotional states on a scale ranging from "agony" to "ecstasy." The intriguing result, as you might expect, was that the bronze medalist, on average, looked happier than the silver medalist. Was there any direct evidence of counterfactual thinking? In a second study, participants who watched interviews with many of these same athletes rated the silver medalist as more negatively focused on finishing second rather than first and the bronze medalist as more positively focused on finishing third rather than fourth. For these great athletes, feelings of satisfaction were based more on their thoughts of what might have been than on the reality of what was.

## IS COGNITION NECESSARY?

Schachter's two-factor theory, as well as the theories of excitation transfer and cognitive appraisal, are based on the assumption that emotion requires thought. Cognitive-emotion theorists would tell my intruder story as follows: I heard a noise (stimulus) and attributed that noise to someone in the house (cognition), which caused me to feel scared (emotion) and to freeze (behavior). We've seen that many psychologists believe that cognition plays a vital role in the experience of emotion. This claim is a source of controversy, however, and was the topic of a spirited exchange between Robert Zajonc (1984), who wrote an article on "the primacy of affect," and Richard Lazarus (1984), who countered with one on "the primacy of cognition."

According to Zajonc, people sometimes react with emotion instantly and without prior appraisal. In other words, sometimes we feel before we think. If you've ever banged your toe into a table, only to explode in anger and pound your fist, you know that the link between pain and rage seems automatic—that you reacted with an angry outburst before realizing just how ridiculous it is to be mad at a piece of furniture. If you've ever sipped milk that was old and curdled, only to gag and spit it out, you likewise know that the link between aversive tastes and disgust may also be automatic. This primacy of affect may help to explain why people develop intense, irrational, persistent fears of objects that are not inherently dangerous. It may also help to explain why infants make reflexlike facial expressions of pain, interest, joy, distress, disgust, and anger before they have the brain capacity to make the proposed cognitive appraisals (Izard, 1990). It may also help to explain the research finding that our affective states influence the way we process information (Ashby et al., 1999), which reinforces the widespread assumption that rational thought "can be hijacked by the pirates of emotion" (Cacioppo & Gardner, 1999, p. 194).

Zajonc (1984) argued that human emotions and thoughts are controlled by separate anatomical structures within the brain. In support of this argument, animal research shows that certain emotions are triggered instantly—before it is even possible to appraise the situation and formulate a response. From the studies described earlier that were aimed at tracing the neural pathways of emotion, Joseph LeDoux (1996) found in rats that conditioned fear is aroused in a primitive, subcortical pathway within the limbic system—a pathway that connects the eyes and ears through the thalamus directly to the amygdala. This result is significant because it shows that the fear response does not involve the cerebral cortex—which means that it need not entail an initial processing of information. According to LeDoux (1996), this primitive pathway serves as an early warning system, so that the amygdala is activated quickly. When we're confronted with pain, noxious food substances, and other threats, this direct pipeline between sensation and emotion enables us to make a rapid-fire defensive motor response without having to stop for a cognitive appraisal (see Figure 12.11).

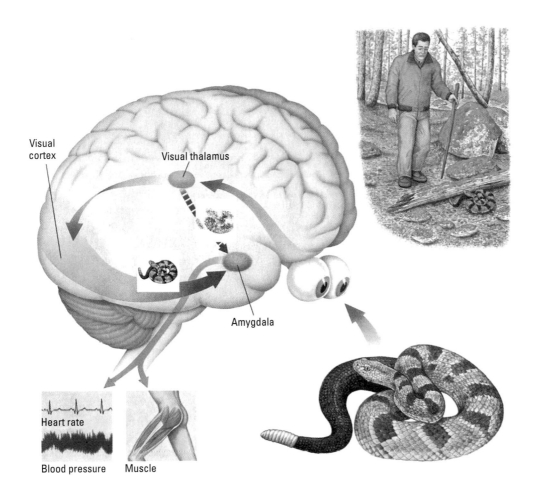

Visual cortex

Visual thalamus

Amygdala

Heart rate

Blood pressure   Muscle

FIGURE 12.11   **Pathway of fear without "thought"**
According to LeDoux (1996), the sensation of a threat can reach the amygdala by way of direct pathways from the thalamus (a quick "low road") or from the thalamus through the cerebral cortex (a slow "high road"). The direct path permits an instantaneous reaction to danger. This initial response may be overridden after the threat is more fully appraised in the cortex, but "the time saved by the amygdala . . . may be the difference between life and death" (p. 166).

Representing the cognitive approach, Richard Lazarus (1991) agrees that emotions can spring up quickly and without awareness, but he maintains that it's just not possible to have an emotion without some kind of thought—even a thought that is quick, effortless, and unconscious. "Without cognitive activity to guide us," says Lazarus, "we could not grasp the significance of what's happening in our adaptational encounters with the environment, nor could we choose among alternative values and courses of action" (p. 353). According to Lazarus (1993), emotion is an individual's response to the perceived harms and benefits of a given situation. Is cognition necessary to emotion? The debate rages on.

Ever since Charles Darwin's (1872) *The Expression of Emotions in Man and Animals,* psychologists, zoologists, and ethologists have debated a related question: Do animals, like humans, have emotions? In *When Elephants Weep,* Jeffrey Masson and Susan McCarthy (1995) argue that they do. Animals may lack the language to describe feelings, they note, but anecdotes from zookeepers and pet owners suggest that animals betray emotional states without words, in vocalizations, gestures, and other expressive behaviors. The most noticeable examples are found when it comes to fear, perhaps the most primitive of emotions. Across a range of species, the

*Do animals experience emotions? Is this playful eight-week-old wolf pup* happy? *(left). Is the growling dog* angry? *(center)? What about the crab-eating macaque whose baby just died—would you say that she is* sad? *(right)*

frightened animal's hair stands on end, its mouth and eyes open wide, and it runs, freezes, or cowers. The terrified gorilla's leg shakes and the dolphin's teeth chatter. The mountain goat flattens its ears, crouches, and points its tail upward. Some would say that animals also feel sadness or grief—as when elephant mothers become lethargic after the death of a calf, or when pet dogs sulk, or don't eat, after being separated from their owners. Nobody disputes these observations. But do the behaviors betray emotions—and their cognitive underpinnings? Is it possible that animals experience "noncognitive" emotions like fear and rage, but not others, like pride and shame?

Demonstrating the vexing nature of the debate, Mark Blumberg and Greta Sokoloff (2001) asked, do infant rats cry? Over the years, animal researchers have observed that many mammal infants, including rat pups, emit ultrasonic "distress vocalizations" when removed from their nest. This cry can be seen as an expression of distress or as a form of communication, a signal designed to elicit care from the mother. In studying these vocalizations, however, these investigators found that the "cry" is an involuntary reaction to a lowered body temperature that serves to increase the flow of warm blood to the heart. They concede that the vocalization serves a communicative purpose and draws the mother back, but they note that it is not intentional—much like a child's sneeze that brings the offer of a tissue. Is the rat pup's cry an expression of emotional distress? Blumberg and Sokoloff argue that there is no proof *for* an underlying emotional state—or *against* it. What do you think?

## CAN PEOPLE PREDICT THEIR FUTURE EMOTIONAL STATES?

Imagine that you just won a million-dollar lottery, or that your favorite sports team just won a championship game. Can you anticipate how happy you'd be one month from now, or six? How sad would you be next year if you just were injured in an automobile accident, or if a close friend moved away to a distant location? What about the emotional aftereffects of graduation, relocation, the start of a new romantic relationship, a breakup or divorce, the death of a loved one, or the birth of a child?

When it comes to anticipating our own emotional states, research shows that people have difficulty projecting forward and predicting how they would feel in response to future emotional events—a process known as **affective forecasting**. In a series of experiments, Timothy Wilson, Daniel Gilbert, and their colleagues (2000) asked research participants to predict how they would feel after various positive and negative life events and then compared the predictions to how others experiencing those same events said they actually felt. Consistently, they found, people overestimated the duration of their emotional reactions, a phenomenon they call the *durability bias*. In

**affective forecasting** The process by which people predict how they would feel in the future, after various positive and negative life events.

one study, junior professors predicted that receiving tenure would increase their levels of happiness for several years, yet those who actually received tenure were not happier at that point than those not granted tenure. In another study, voters predicted they would be happier a month after an election if their candidate were to win than to lose. In actuality, supporters of the winning and losing candidates did not differ in their overall happiness levels one month after the election. Again, people overestimated the impact on themselves of future emotional events.

There are two possible reasons for the durability bias in affective forecasting. First, when it comes to negative life events—such as an injury, illness, or financial loss—people do not fully appreciate the power of their own coping mechanisms, which provide a "psychological immune system" to help cushion the blow. In the face of adversity, human beings can be quite resilient, not as devastated as we fear we will be (Gilbert et al., 1998). A second reason for the durability bias is that when we reflect on the emotional impact of a future event, say the breakup of a close relationship, we become so focused on that one event that we neglect to take into account the effects of other life experiences. To become more accurate in our self-predictions, then, we need to think more broadly about *all* the plusses and minuses that impinge upon us. In one study, college students were asked to predict their emotional reactions to their school football team's winning or losing an important game. As usual, they overestimated how long it would take them to recover from victory or defeat. This bias disappeared, however, when the students first wrote a "prospective diary" in which they estimated the amount of future time they will spend on everyday activities like going to class, talking to friends, studying, and eating meals (Wilson et al., 2000).

## REVIEW QUESTIONS

- *According to Schachter's two-factor theory of emotion, how do we come to experience an emotion?*

- *Describe three implications of Schachter's theory.*

- *Identify the cognitive dimensions of appraisal that are most closely linked to emotion.*

- *What is counterfactual thinking, and how can it influence emotional experience?*

## HUMAN EMOTION: PUTTING THE PIECES TOGETHER

- *Can the range of human emotions be categorized into a small number of types?*
- *Is there any evidence for the notion that every emotional state triggers its opposite?*
- *Are joy, grief, and other emotions universally felt or subject to cultural definition?*
- *Are women more emotional than men?*
- *Who is happy—and why?*

Knowing that emotions stem from physiological sensations, expressive behaviors, and cognitive activities is only a first step. The next step is to determine how the different pieces of this puzzle fit together to produce an emotional experience.

## TYPES OF EMOTIONS

The English language contains more than two thousand words for categories of emotions. Are some of these universal, felt by people in all cultures? Over the years, psychologists have tried to classify human emotions in various ways. Today, as we've seen, there is widespread agreement that fear, anger, joy, disgust, surprise, and sadness are "basic": Each is accompanied by a distinct facial expression, each is shown by infants and young children, and each is found in the words that people of diverse cultures and regions use to describe their feelings. Some researchers believe that interest, acceptance, contempt, pride, shame, and guilt should be added to the list.

*Certain emotions such as intense joy and grief are "basic" to the human experience. Here, members of the Brazilian soccer team celebrate moments after winning the 2002 World Cup, and Israeli women react with grief after loved ones were killed in a suicide terrorist attack.*

If there are only a few basic emotions, what accounts for the vast array of other feelings we often experience? One possibility suggested by Robert Plutchik (1980) is that basic emotions provide the building blocks for more complex emotions in the way that the three primary colors combine to form the hues of the color wheel. According to Plutchik, the richness of human emotions is accounted for in three ways. First, there are eight basic types of emotions (he adds interest and acceptance to the original six). Second, each type comes in varying "shades," or levels of intensity (for example, intense disgust may be felt as hatred or loathing, and mild disgust as boredom). Third, new emotions are formed through mixtures of the eight basic ones (for example, love blends joy and acceptance, contempt blends disgust and anger, and nostalgia blends joy and sadness).

It's easy to come up with a list of emotions. The trick is to classify and compare the emotions along a small number of common dimensions. Perhaps the most obvious way to classify emotions is according to whether they involve positive or negative affect. Most people assume that positive feelings are the opposite of negative feelings—that someone who is happy, for example, cannot at the same time be sad. Research confirms this intuitive assumption about the bipolarity of emotion. So, "Is a human being a pendulum betwixt a smile and a tear? Apparently so" (Russell & Carroll, 1999).

Using this positive-negative distinction as a starting point, James Russell (1980) proposed the circumplex model, a taxonomy that divides all human emotions along two independent dimensions: pleasantness and intensity. According to Russell, emotions are either (1) pleasant or unpleasant, and (2) mild or intense. As illustrated in Figure 12.12, the result is a fourfold circle of emotions that are pleasant and intense ("delighted"), pleasant and mild ("relaxed"), unpleasant and mild ("bored"), and unpleasant and intense ("alarmed"). Research shows that when people are asked to rate emotion words or sort them into piles, this circular ordering consistently appears—not only in English but also in Chinese, Croatian, Estonian, Greek, Hebrew, Japanese, Polish, Swedish, and German (Larsen & Diener, 1992; Reisenzein, 1994). People's ratings of the emotions triggered by images of other human beings,

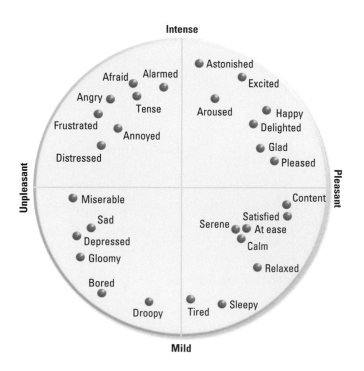

**FIGURE 12.12 Russell's circumplex model**
According to this circumplex model, there are four types of emotions: pleasant-intense, pleasant-mild, unpleasant-intense, and unpleasant-mild (Russell, 1980).

animals, nature, objects, scenes, and events can similarly be classified (Lang, 1995). Over the years, many psychologists have theorized about the structure of human emotions and have come up with similar two-dimensional models (Russell & Barrett, 1999; Watson et al., 1999).

## DYNAMICS OF EMOTION

I have always loved roller coasters. I find the speed and sharp turns frightening, the loops make me dizzy, and my neck muscles are often strained after tensing up for so long. But the feeling of relief that rushes through me when the terror-filled experience has ended is alone worth the price of admission. The scarier the ride, the greater the pleasure.

This common paradoxical experience illustrates an important point about emotion: It is dynamic, complex, and ever changing—not easily captured in a snapshot. To explain this type of paradox, Richard Solomon (1980) proposed the *opponent-process theory* of emotion. According to Solomon, an event triggers (1) a "primary state"—an unlearned, automatic response, which in turn, triggers (2) an "opponent state"—a learned response that is the emotional opposite of the primary state. Thus, danger activates fear often followed by relief, whereas happy events activate joy followed by sadness. The key difference between the two reactions is that the opponent state, compared to the primary state, starts later and lasts longer. It also gets stronger with repetition and experience. Thus, every positive emotional state is balanced in time by its negative counterpart—and vice versa (see Figure 12.13).

Solomon cited various animal and human studies that support this point. One such study concerned the emotional reactions of skydivers. Right before their first jump, they were terrified: Their bodies stiffened, their pupils dilated, their eyes bulged, and breathing became irregular. Then, after their feet hit the ground, there was an initial stunned silence followed by relief, chatter, laughter, even a sense of exhilaration. From their normal baseline state, fear had turned to elation. Research on the effects of mind-altering drugs also supports this point. At first, opiate drugs (if the dosage is not excessive) produce a pleasurable "high," followed by a less intense state of euphoria. As the drug wears off, however, the user suffers through an agonizing state of withdrawal that is far less pleasant than his or her predrug state. Skydivers thus find that their fear subsides after several jumps, and drug users find that they must increase their dosage to get high.

The opponent-process theory offers some interesting insights into our changing emotional states. The notion that every emotion triggers its opposite, perhaps to keep us emotionally balanced, may help to explain why women sometimes experience a "letdown" after the joy of childbirth or why health enthusiasts enjoy hard physical exercise, hot and dry saunas, and other types of "good pain." Contemplating the implications, Solomon was quick to note that the opponent-process theory is a puritan's theory: Pleasure will enlarge the appetite for reward and make joy more elusive, whereas pain and suffering will enhance one's later sense of well-being. Pleasure has its costs; pain its benefits.

## ARE THERE GENDER DIFFERENCES IN EMOTION?

When people are asked to compare the typical man and woman, they consistently say that women are more emotional (or, to put it another way, that men are less

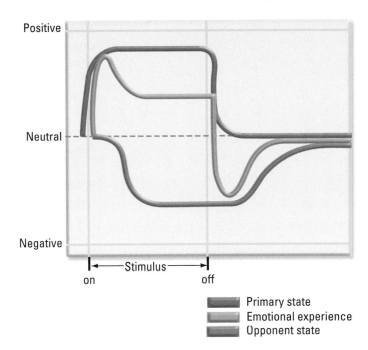

**FIGURE 12.13    Opponent-process theory of emotion**
According to this theory, every primary emotional state triggers its opposite. The result is a more balanced experience in which a positive state is soon followed by a negative state, and vice versa.

emotional). This belief is found among children and adults from many different cultures (Fabes & Martin, 1991; Williams & Best, 1982). In a study that illustrates just how deeply ingrained this stereotype is, adult participants were shown a videotape of a nine-month-old baby. Half were told that they were watching a boy; the other half thought the baby was a girl. In fact, everyone saw the same tape. Yet when the baby burst into tears over a jack-in-the-box, participants were gender-biased in the way that they interpreted the child's emotional state: *he* was *angry,* but *she* was *frightened* (Condry & Condry, 1976).

Are there gender differences in emotion or is the perception of difference a mere illusion? The research is mixed, but certain differences do seem to emerge with regularity (Brody & Hall, 1993; Grossman & Wood, 1993; LaFrance & Banaji, 1992). On the one hand, women describe themselves as more emotional—or men as less emotional—when asked direct questions about their emotionality. On the other hand, there is little support for the conclusion that the sexes differ in their actual feelings. Both men and women become happy when they achieve something that they have strived for. Similarly, both sexes become saddened by the loss of a loved one, angry when frustrated, fearful when in danger, and embarrassed when they slip up in front of others. Men and women also exhibit similar facial expressions and autonomic reactions to emotion-triggering events. People surely differ in their propensity for certain types of feelings, but these differences say more about us as individuals than as men or women.

So in what ways are women more emotional than men? One clear finding is that regardless of how men and women actually feel, they often differ in their public expressions of emotion. After reviewing 205 studies involving more than 23,000 participants, Kathryn Dindia and Mike Allen (1992) concluded that women disclose their feelings to others more than men do. Women also exhibit more emotion on the face and more muscle activity on the facial EMG (Dimberg, 1990). The result is that people in general can "read" women better than they can men. In one study, for example, male and female participants saw slides that evoked emotions ranging from joy to disgust. As they watched, their faces were recorded with a hidden camera. Observers who later watched these tapes were better at judging the emotions felt by the expressive female participants (Wagner et al., 1986).

Why are women more open and expressive than men? One explanation is that girls more than boys are socialized at an early age to talk about their feelings. Researchers who analyze parent-child conversations in the home find that parents talk more about the emotional aspect of events with their daughters than with their sons ("That music was scary, wasn't it?" "You were happy, weren't you?")—even with children who are only two or three years old (Dunn et al., 1987; Kuebli & Fivush, 1992). Another reason, at least in American culture, is that although women are permitted to be expressive (except when it comes to rage and anger, emotions that men are allowed to express and women are supposed to contain), men are taught to be stoic—to fulfill the ideal of the strong, silent type. Masculinity norms demand that men publicly suppress their own fears and sorrows. As the saying goes, "Big boys don't cry" (Tavris, 1992).

## ARE THERE CULTURAL DIFFERENCES IN EMOTION?

Certain aspects of human emotion seem universal. We saw earlier that people from diverse cultures react to emotion-filled events with similar physiological symptoms and facial expressions. In fact, certain events trigger the same emotions everywhere in the world. In all cultures, for example, friendship and achievement elicit joy; insult and injustice elicit anger; novelty and risk taking elicit fear; death and separation from a loved one elicit sadness. Yet there are regional differences as well in the types of antecedent events that stir our various passions. Among the Utku Eskimos, fear is triggered by thin ice, rough seas, dangerous animals, and evil spirits. Among Israelis—for whom the fear of terrorism and war are constant—fear is awakened most often by interactions with strangers (Mesquita & Frijda, 1992).

Culture also shapes the way people categorize their feelings. Consider the words we use to describe various emotions. Based on ethnographies and cross-cultural studies of language, James Russell (1991) uncovered some striking differences. For example, although the English language contains more than 2,000 words for categories of emotion, there are only 1,501 emotion words in Dutch, 750 in Taiwanese, 58 among the Ifalukian of Micronesia, and 7 among the Chewong of Malaysia. Among the Ilongot, a head-hunting people of the Philippines, the word *liget* is used to describe both anger and grief-intense feelings. Japanese does not have a word for "disappointed," Tahitian lacks a word for "sadness," and Gujarati, a language spoken in India, lacks a word for "excited."

Ralph Hupka and others (1999) combed through the dictionaries of sixty major languages from all regions of the world and found that certain basic emotions—such as joy, grief, affection, fear, anger, and disgust—are universally represented in words. Some languages, however, have precise emotion words that have no clear counterpart in English. For example, the German word *Schadenfreude* specifically refers to the pleasure derived from another person's suffering. In Indonesia, a distinction is made between *malu,* a feeling of shame brought on by one's own actions, and *dipermalukan,* a feeling of shame caused by someone else's deeds. Among the Baining of Papua New Guinea, *awumbuk* is an emotion that combines sadness, tiredness, and boredom that is brought on specifically by the departure of visiting friends or relatives. Among the Utku Eskimos, *naklik* refers to the love of babies, sick people, and others in need of protection, whereas *niviuq* is a form of love felt toward those who are charming or admired.

Finally, some striking cultural differences can be seen in the display rules that determine when it's appropriate for people to express certain feelings. The release of anger sparked by insult, frustration, or a physical attack is a prime example. People all over the world exhibit similar patterns of autonomic arousal, but cultures teach us whether to manage that arousal by exploding or by suppressing our rage. Among the Kung Bushmen of the Kalahari Desert, nomadic hunters and gatherers who forage as a group and share food, people must control their fury in order to survive. Japanese people also practice restraint, often masking anger with a polite smile. In Japan, an angry outburst is seen as a shameful loss of control, so it is better to publicly "grin and bear it" (Matsumoto & Ekman, 1989). Yet among the Yanomamo of the Amazon jungle, public displays of anger are common. As anthropologists have observed, Yanomamo who are angry sometimes scream at the top of their lungs and launch into a barrage of personal and public insults: "You scaly ass, you bucktooth, you protruding fang, you caiman skin!" (Good & Chanoff, 1991, p. 71).

## PLEASURE AND THE PURSUIT OF HAPPINESS

Long before psychology was born into science, philosophers regarded happiness to be the ultimate state of being. In the Declaration of Independence, Thomas Jefferson cited life, liberty, and "the pursuit of happiness" as the most cherished of human rights. But what is happiness, and how is it achieved? Aristotle said it was the reward of an active life. Freud pointed to both work and love. Others have focused on money, power, health and fitness, religion, beauty, the satisfaction of basic desires, and the achievement of goals. According to some, a sense of well-being springs from an ability to derive pleasure and avoid pain in the events of everyday life (Kahneman et al., 1999). According to others, our well-being emerges from leading a life that enables us to realize our talents, values, potentialities, and sense of self (Ryan & Deci, 2001).

To study happiness—or, as many psychologists now call it, "subjective well-being"—one must be able to measure it. How do researchers know if someone is happy? Simple: They ask. Better yet, they use such brief questionnaires as the Satisfaction with Life Scale, in which participants respond to statements such as "If I could live my life over, I would change almost nothing" (Diener et al., 1984; Pavot & Diener, 1993). As Marcus Aurelius said, "No man is happy who does not think himself so."

Consistently, surveys show that 75 percent of Americans describe themselves as happy—and that in 86 percent of all nations sampled, the mean ratings are more positive than neutral (Diener, 2000). In general, people who are happy also have cheerful moods, high self-esteem, physical and mental health, a sense of personal control, more memories for positive than negative events, and optimism about the future (Myers & Diener, 1995). It's no secret that our outlook on life becomes rosy right after we win a game, fall in love, land a great job, or make money. Nor is it a secret that the world seems gloomy right after we lose, fall out of love, or suffer a personal tragedy or financial setback. Predictably, the events of everyday life trigger fluctuations in mood. For example, people are most happy on Fridays and Saturdays and least happy on Mondays and Tuesdays (Larsen & Kasimatis, 1990). Even during the day, happiness levels fluctuate like clockwork. For example, David Watson and his colleagues (1999) asked college students to rate their mood states once a day for 45 days, always at a different hour. They found, on average, that the students felt best during the middle of the day (noon to 6 PM) and worst in the early morning and late evening hours.

**The Roots of Happiness** What determines our long-term satisfaction, and why are some people happier in general than others? Seeking the roots of happiness, Ed Diener and others (1999) reviewed many years of research and found that subjective well-being is not meaningfully related to demographic factors such as age, sex, race, ethnic background, IQ, education level, or physical attractiveness. Contrary to popular belief, people are not less happy during the so-called crisis years of midlife or in old age than in their "peak" young-adult years. Men and women do not differ, and in the United States African Americans are as happy as white Americans.

There are three predictive indicators of happiness: (1) *social relationships* (people with an active social life, close friends, and a happy marriage are more satisfied than those who lack these intimate connections), (2) *employment status* (employed people are happier than those who are out of work—regardless of income), and (3) *physical health* (people who are healthy are happier than those who are not). Reflecting the impact of these and other factors, research shows that happiness levels vary, and remain relatively stable, from one culture to the next (Diener & Suh, 2000). As shown in Figure 12.14, national happiness and life satisfaction ratings are highest in Iceland and lowest in Bulgaria. On the basis of more than 100,000 survey respondents from forty-four countries, the United States ranked ninth in the world and Canada ranked twentieth (Veenhoven, 2000).

**Does Money Buy Happiness?** Perhaps the most interesting relationship is between income and subjective well-being.

*Money may buy summer homes, convertible sports cars, pearl necklaces, and other luxuries, but research suggests that among those whose basic needs are already satisfied, money does not buy long-term happiness.*

**social-comparison theory** The theory that people evaluate themselves by making comparisons with others.

| Nations | Average ratings | Nations | Average ratings | Nations | Average ratings |
|---|---|---|---|---|---|
| Iceland | 3.39 | Finland | 3.09 | Israel | 2.88 |
| Netherlands | 3.38 | Philippines | 3.08 | South Korea | 2.86 |
| Denmark | 3.36 | Turkey | 3.08* | Portugal | 2.83 |
| Sweden | 3.36 | Argentina | 3.07* | South Africa | 2.82 |
| Ireland | 3.36 | Canada | 3.05 | India | 2.81* |
| Belgium | 3.31 | Spain | 3.04 | Greece | 2.77 |
| Switzerland | 3.30 | Chile | 3.03* | Hungary | 2.72 |
| Australia | 3.30 | Germany | 3.00 | Czech Republic | 2.69 |
| United States | 3.28 | Japan | 3.00 | Romania | 2.63 |
| Britain | 3.28 | Italy | 2.98 | Slovenia | 2.62 |
| Norway | 3.23 | Poland | 2.97 | Estonia | 2.58 |
| Austria | 3.20 | Mexico | 2.95 | Russia | 2.53 |
| New Zealand | 3.18 | Brazil | 2.94 | Bulgaria | 2.33 |
| Luxembourg | 3.18 | Nigeria | 2.93 | | |
| France | 3.16 | China | 2.92* | | |

\* Due to an under-representation of poor rural populations, averages with an asterisk are somewhat inflated.

**FIGURE 12.14    National Happiness Ratings**
Would you say that you are: very happy (4), quite happy (3), not very happy (2), or not at all happy (1)? From surveys conducted in the 1990s, many of the world's countries were ranked according to the average happiness ratings of their people.

Everyone knows the saying "Money can't buy happiness." But personally, I know very few people—particularly among those who are financially strapped—who believe it. Is wealth a key to happiness? The evidence is mixed (Diener et al., 1999).

Cross-national studies have revealed a positive association between a nation's prosperity and the subjective well-being of its people. There are some exceptions, but as a general rule the more prosperous a country is, the happier its citizens are. The reason for this association is not clear. It may be that affluence brings pleasure through the satisfaction of basic needs and material possession— or by affording freedom, which makes life more enjoyable (Veenhoven, 2000). Within a given country, however, the differences between wealthy and middle-income people are more modest. In one survey, a group of the wealthiest Americans said they were happy 77 percent of the time—which was only moderately higher than the 62 percent figure given by those of average income. And when we make comparisons within a single culture over time, there is no connection between affluence and happiness. Americans on average are more than twice as rich now as they were fifty years ago—before we had wall-sized color TVs, cell phones, microwave ovens, and personal computers that brought the Internet into the home. Yet during that time period, the number of respondents who said they were "very happy" was 35 percent in 1957 and only 32 percent in 1993 (see Figure 12.15). So what are we to conclude? It looks as though having shelter, food, and safety are essential for subjective well-being, but once these basic needs are met, increased affluence does not appreciably raise levels of happiness.

Why doesn't money contribute more to subjective well-being? One reason is that our perceptions of wealth are not absolute but relative to certain *standards* (Parducci, 1995). According to **social-comparison theory**, people naturally compare themselves to others

*"It matters little whether one is rich or poor, successful or unsuccessful, beautiful or plain: Happiness is completely relative . . . the pleasantness of any particular experience depends on its relationship to a context of other experiences, real or imagined."*

—ALLEN PARDUCCI

**adaptation-level theory** The theory that people evaluate experiences in relation to current levels to which they have become accustomed.

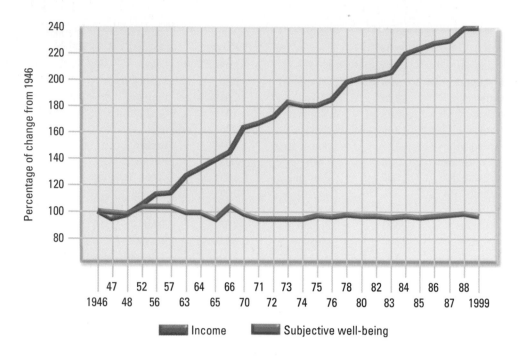

**FIGURE 12.15** **Changes in national wealth and subjective well-being**
Over more than forty years, Americans became twice as wealthy, but no happier.

"Remember how I said I was happiest when we had nothing?"

and feel contented or deprived depending on how they fare in this comparison. To demonstrate, Ladd Wheeler and Kunitate Miyake (1992) asked college students to keep for two weeks a written record of every time they mentally compared their grades, appearance, abilities, possessions, or personality to someone else's. Consistently, these diaries revealed that "upward comparisons" (to others who are better off) triggered negative feelings, and "downward comparisons" (to others who are worse off) triggered positive feelings. In fact, other research shows that happy people make more downward comparisons in their lives than do unhappy people (Lyubomirsky & Ross, 1997). These results may shed light on why there's only a modest relationship between income and happiness. The middle-class worker whose friends and neighbors can't pay their bills feels successful. Yet the upper-class social climber who moves into an affluent suburb and rubs elbows with the rich and famous feels relatively deprived. The key is to avoid looking to the top of the ladder at others who are better off.

People also use their own recent past as a basis of comparison. According to **adaptation-level theory**, our satisfaction with the present depends on the level of success to which we are accustomed. Get married, buy a new house, or make a killing in the stock market, and you'll surely enjoy a wave of euphoria. Before long, however, the glitter will wear off, and you will adapt to your better situation and raise your standard of comparison. Thus, Philip Brickman and others (1978) interviewed twenty-two people who had won between $50,000 and $1 million in a lottery and found that they did not rate themselves as happier than in the past. Compared to others from similar backgrounds, the winners said that they now derived less pleasure from such routine activities as shopping, reading, and talking to a friend. Perhaps the more money you have, the more you need to stay happy. A Chicago public-opinion poll showed that although people who earned less than $30,000 a year said that $50,000 would fulfill their dreams, those who earned more than $100,000 said it would take $250,000 to make them happy (Csikszentmihalyi, 1999).

There is another possible explanation for why money is not more important to the happiness equation: Perhaps each of us, as a result of biological and environmental factors, has a set baseline level of happiness toward which we gravitate. This notion is supported by three recent findings. One is that ratings of happiness are higher among pairs of identical twins raised together or apart than among fraternal twins (Lykken & Tellegen, 1996)—leading David Lykken (2000) to speculate that there may be a genetic basis for being happy and content. A second finding is that the fluctuations in mood that accompany positive and negative life events wear off over time. Eunkook Suh and others (1996) studied participants for two years and found that only experiences occurring within the last three months correlated with subjective well-being. Getting engaged or married, breaking up, starting a new job, and being hospitalized are the kinds of high-impact experiences that people assume to have lasting if not permanent effects on happiness (Gilbert et al., 1998). But their impacts were only temporary. A third finding is that happiness levels, like personalities, are relatively stable over time and place, leading to the conclusion that some people, in general, are happier than others (DeNeve & Cooper, 1998).

## REVIEW QUESTIONS

- *What six emotions do psychologists consider the "basic" emotions?*

- *According to Russell's circumplex model, all emotions can be classified along what two dimensions?*

- *Explain the opponent-process theory of emotion advanced by Solomon.*

- *What three factors seem to best predict long-term happiness?*

# THINKING LIKE A PSYCHOLOGIST ABOUT EMOTION

Now that we have explored the psychology of emotion, let us step back and reflect on what it contributes to our understanding of human competence and rationality. You will recall that many cognitive psychologists compare human beings to computers, noting the ease with which we are able to learn, recall, reason, and communicate our knowledge. At the same time, however, research shows that performance often falls short of competence. Sometimes people fail to learn (or, instead, learn to behave in maladaptive ways), forget or distort their memories of past events, and use cognitive heuristics that steer them into making poor judgments. This two-headed portrait characterizes our emotional lives as well. In this chapter, for example, we saw that although emotion often follows from a rational interpretation of events, it may also arise instantly and without conscious thought, perhaps leading us to feel before we think. In addition, we sometimes attribute our arousal sensations to the wrong source, causing us to mislabel our own emotions. In matters of the heart and mind, human beings are not entirely competent or incompetent but a complex and fascinating mixture of both.

# SUMMARY

Although **emotion** is a difficult concept to define, most psychologists agree that emotions consist of three interacting components: (1) physiological arousal, (2) expressive behavior, and (3) a cognitive appraisal.

## THE PHYSIOLOGICAL COMPONENT

The body is intimately involved in feelings of joy, fear, anger, and other emotions. The question is, in what capacity?

### A HISTORICAL PERSPECTIVE

According to the **James-Lange theory**, emotion follows from one's reactions to an emotion-eliciting stimulus (you're afraid because you are trembling). In contrast, the **Cannon-Bard theory** states that a stimulus elicits various reactions and emotion at the same time (perceiving a danger causes you to tremble and feel afraid). Today, physiologically oriented emotion researchers seek to understand the role played by different brain structures, neural pathways, and autonomic arousal.

## BRAIN CENTERS OF EMOTION

Many emotions are regulated by the limbic system—an evolutionarily primitive set of neural structures. Certain emotional reactions are automatic (triggered instantly by the amygdala); others involve the processing of information in the cerebral cortex. We cannot pinpoint a single region of the cortex that regulates all feelings, but research shows that approach emotions evoke higher levels of EEG activity in the left hemisphere, whereas withdrawal emotions elicit more activity in the right.

## GENERALIZED AUTONOMIC AROUSAL

When an event prompts an emotional response, the **sympathetic nervous system** mobilizes the body for an adaptive fight-or-flight response. Afterward, the **parasympathetic nervous system** restores the body to its premobilized calm state.

## SPECIFIC PATTERNS OF AROUSAL

Are all emotions associated with the same state of arousal, or does each emotion have unique symptoms? Research supports the latter alternative. For example, heart rate increases for both anger and fear, but anger increases skin temperature, whereas fear has the opposite effect. Assuming that lying increases stress, law-enforcement officials often use the **polygraph,** an instrument that records multiple channels of arousal. Participants who exhibit more arousal to crime-relevant questions than to control questions are judged to be lying. Many professionals claim that lie-detector tests work, but researchers have uncovered some serious problems with such tests.

## THE EXPRESSIVE COMPONENT

Behavioral expressions of emotion serve two functions. They provide us not only with a means of nonverbal communication to others but also with sensory feedback for the self.

## NONVERBAL COMMUNICATION

The face communicates emotion in ways that are understood by people from different countries of the world. Further suggesting that these expressions are innate is the fact that even young infants make the faces that are associated with basic emotions. To measure the activity of facial muscles and their links to emotion, researchers use the **facial electromyograph (EMG)**. This device has revealed two distinct types of smiles, one more genuine than the other. Additional nonverbal behaviors that communicate emotion are body language, gaze, and touch.

## SENSORY FEEDBACK

According to the **facial-feedback hypothesis,** an expression not only reflects one's emotion but triggers an emotional state as well. Although psychologists disagree over the reason for this effect, research indicates that it does occur.

## THE COGNITIVE COMPONENT

Psychologists have long debated the role of cognitive factors in emotion. Different theories of emotion provide different points of view.

## SCHACHTER'S TWO-FACTOR THEORY OF EMOTION

According to the **two-factor theory of emotion,** two factors are necessary to have a specific emotion: (1) a heightened state of arousal and (2) a cognitive label. When people are aroused and do not know why, they determine their emotions by scanning the situation and making an attribution. Through a process of **misattribution,** arousal from one event can spill over and fuel our emotional reaction to another event.

## DIMENSIONS OF APPRAISAL

According to cognitive theorists, the emotions we experience are determined by our appraisals of the situation we are in.

## COUNTERFACTUAL THINKING

Sometimes our emotional reactions to outcomes are influenced by **counterfactual thinking**—as when bronze medalists feel better by imagining a fourth-place finish, whereas silver medalists feel worse by imagining a first-place finish.

## IS COGNITION NECESSARY?

Some psychologists argue that people sometimes react with emotion instantly and without cognitive appraisal and that our emotions and thoughts are controlled by separate anatomical structures within the brain. Others maintain that it is not possible to have emotion without thought, even thought that is quick, effortless, and unconscious. This debate remains unresolved and touches on the related controversy over whether nonhuman animals experience emotions.

## CAN PEOPLE PREDICT THEIR FUTURE EMOTIONAL STATES?

People have difficulty predicting how they'd feel in response to future emotional events, a process known as **affective forecasting.** Exhibiting a durability bias, people consistently overestimate the future emotional impact on them of positive and negative events.

## HUMAN EMOTION: PUTTING THE PIECES TOGETHER

Knowing that emotions stem from physiological, expressive, and cognitive activities is only a first step. The next step is to determine how these elements combine to produce an emotional experience.

## TYPES OF EMOTIONS

There is widespread agreement that fear, anger, disgust, joy, surprise, and sadness are basic human emotions. Some researchers speculate that other emotions are derived from mixtures of these or that all emotions can be classified along two independent dimensions: pleasantness and intensity.

## DYNAMICS OF EMOTION

According to the opponent-process theory of emotion, an event triggers a "primary state" (an unlearned response), which in turn activates an "opponent state" (a learned response that is the emotional opposite of the primary state). The opponent state starts later, lasts longer, and gets stronger with repetition. Every positive emotional state is thus balanced in time by its negative counterpart, and vice versa.

## ARE THERE GENDER DIFFERENCES IN EMOTION?

Many people believe that women are more emotional than men, and certain differences do emerge. Women describe themselves as more emotional (or men as less emotional), are more self-disclosing to others, and are more facially expressive. Socialization practices may well account for these sex differences.

## ARE THERE CULTURAL DIFFERENCES IN EMOTION?

Certain aspects of human emotion seem universal, as when people from diverse cultures react to emotion-filled events with similar bodily reactions and facial expressions. Clearly, however, cultures shape the way people categorize their feelings as well as the display rules that determine when it's appropriate to express these feelings.

## PLEASURE AND THE PURSUIT OF HAPPINESS

Most people report being relatively happy, but there are marked individual differences. Three important factors are having social relationships, being employed, and being healthy. Although more affluent nations are happier, the evidence for an association between income level and happiness is mixed. As suggested by **social-comparison theory** and **adaptation-level theory**, one reason is that our perceptions of wealth are relative—to what others have and to what we are accustomed to. It has also been suggested that people have a certain dispositional level of happiness toward which they gravitate over time.

## KEY TERMS

emotion (**p. 466**)

James-Lange theory (**p. 467**)

Cannon-Bard theory (**p. 468**)

sympathetic nervous system (**p. 469**)

parasympathetic nervous system (**p. 470**)

polygraph (**p. 472**)

facial electromyograph (EMG) (**p. 476**)

facial-feedback hypothesis (**p. 478**)

two-factor theory of emotion (**p. 480**)

misattribution (**p. 482**)

counterfactual thinking (**p. 483**)

affective forecasting (**p. 486**)

social-comparison theory (**p. 493**)

adaptation-level theory (**p. 494**)

## THINKING CRITICALLY ABOUT EMOTION

1. The polygraph is generally referred to as a "lie detector." Is this an accurate label? Why or why not?

2. Consider what life would be like without emotions (like Mr. Spock from *Star Trek* or Data from *Star Trek: The Next Generation*). What would be the advantages of not having emotions? What about the disadvantages?

3. Gyms and health clubs are often likened to singles bars. In what way might the misattribution of arousal be contributing to the romantic pairings such places seem to foster?

4. Compare and contrast Zajonc's (1984) views on the primacy of affect with those of Lazarus (1984), who argues for the primacy of cognition. Which view do you support?

5. In what ways are men and women similar when it comes to emotions? In what ways are they different? How might these differences be explained?

# Social Influences

# HOW FAR CAN PEOPLE BE PUSHED?

## THE SITUATION

You see a newspaper ad for a psychology experiment that pays well, so you sign up. As you arrive at the laboratory, located at Yale University, you meet two men. One is the experimenter, a young man dressed in a white lab coat. The other is a pleasant middle-age man named Mr. Wallace. After introductions, the experimenter explains that you will be taking part in a study on the effects of punishment on learning. By a drawing of lots, it is determined that you'll serve as the "teacher" and Mr. Wallace as the "learner." So far, so good.

Before you know it, however, the situation takes on a more ominous tone. You find out that your job is to test the learner's memory and administer electric shocks of increasing intensity whenever he makes a mistake. You are taken to another room, where the experimenter straps Mr. Wallace into a chair, rolls up his sleeve, tapes electrodes onto his arm, and applies "electrode paste" to prevent blisters and burns. You overhear Mr. Wallace say that he has a heart problem and the experimenter reply that although the shocks are painful, they will not cause permanent damage. You then go back to the main room, where you're seated in front of a shock generator—a machine with thirty switches that range from 15 volts (labeled "slight shock") to 450 volts (labeled "XXX").

Your task is easy. First, you read a list of word pairs to Mr. Wallace through a microphone. Blue—phone. Girl—hat. Fish—spoon. Then, you test his memory with a series of multiple-choice questions. The learner answers each question by pressing one of four switches that light up on the shock generator. If his answer is correct, you go to the next question. If it's incorrect, you announce the correct answer and shock him. As you press the shock switch, you can hear a buzzer go off in the learner's room. After each wrong answer, you're told, the shock intensity should be increased by 15 volts.

You don't realize it, but the experiment is rigged, and Mr. Wallace—who works for the experimenter—is not receiving any shocks. As the session proceeds, the learner makes more and more errors, leading you to work your way up the shock scale. As you reach 75 volts, you hear the learner grunt in pain. At 120 volts, he shouts. If you're still in it at 150 volts, he complains about his heart and cries out, "Experimenter! That's all. Get me out of here. I refuse to go on!" Screams of agony and protest follow. If you reach 300 volts, he absolutely refuses to go on. By the time you surpass 330 volts, the learner falls silent and is not heard from again. 360 volts. Zap. Not a peep. 420, 435, 450. Zap. Still no response. At some point, you turn to the experimenter. What should I do? Shouldn't we check on him? But in answer to your inquiries, the experimenter calmly repeats his commands: "Please continue." "The experiment requires that you continue." "You have no other choice, you must go on."

## MAKE A PREDICTION

What do you do? Feeling caught between a rock and a hard place, do you follow your conscience or obey the experimenter? Do you stop at 45 volts? 150? 300? How would other participants react? Would anyone in their right mind keep shocking the hapless Mr. Wallace all the way to 450 volts? Based on what you know about people, try to predict the point at which most participants stopped and defied the experimenter. Make your prediction by circling a voltage level.

| 15 | 45 | 75 | 105 | 135 | 165 | 195 | 225 |
|----|----|----|-----|-----|-----|-----|-----|
| 255 | 285 | 315 | 345 | 375 | 405 | 435 | 450 |

## THE RESULTS

Forty years ago, social psychologist Stanley Milgram (1963) staged this situation to examine obedience to authority. When Milgram described the study to college students, adults, and a group of psychiatrists, they predicted that, on average, they would stop at 135 volts—and that almost nobody would go all the way. They were wrong. In Milgram's initial study, twenty-six out of forty men—that's 65 percent—delivered the ultimate punishment of 450 volts.

## WHAT DOES IT ALL MEAN?

Why did so many participants obey the experimenter, even while thinking they were hurting a fellow human being? One possible explanation for these scary results is that Milgram's participants—all of whom were male—were unusually cruel and sadistic. Who were these guys? Or maybe the result says something about men in general. What if the participants were women instead? How far up the shock scale would they go? In a follow-up study, Milgram examined this question by putting forty women in the same situation. The result: 65 percent of the women tested administered 450 volts, identical to the number of men.

Hmm. Males and females, perhaps people in general, are willing if not eager to harm a fellow human being. As a sad commentary on human nature, perhaps Milgram's study says more about aggression than obedience. But how far would participants go if not ordered to do so? What if the experimenter did not constantly prod the participants to raise the voltage level? In this situation, Milgram found that only one participant out of forty (2.5 percent) pressed the last switch. Most stopped at 75 volts.

Milgram's participants had acted out of obedience, not cruelty. In fact, most were visibly tormented by the experience. Many of those who administered 450 volts perspired, stuttered, trembled, bit their lips, and even burst into fits of nervous laughter. It was as if they wanted to stop but felt powerless to do so. What does it mean? When Nazis were tried for war crimes after World War II, their defense was: "I just followed orders." Intrigued by the power of authority implied by this statement, Milgram devised a laboratory situation to mimic the forces that operate in real-life crimes of obedience. As we'll see throughout this chapter, this classic research cries out the message of social psychology loud and clear: Other people can have a profound impact on our behavior.

Every now and then, an event comes along that lays bare aspects of human social behavior that seem to defy explanation. Bringing out the best in people, and the worst, the September 11, 2001, terrorist attack was an event like no other.

In New York City, the morning was sunny, bright, and clear. Then at 8:46 A.M., a Boeing 767 headed from Boston to Los Angeles was hijacked by Middle Eastern terrorists fueled with hatred, and crashed into the north tower of the World Trade Center. Eighteen minutes later, a second jumbo jet plunged into the south tower. Nobody knew it at the time, but both towers would soon collapse, amputating the skyline of lower Manhattan. Moments later, a third hijacked jet slammed into the Pentagon outside of Washington, D.C. A fourth jet, which may have been headed for the White House, then dove into a wooded area in Pennsylvania when passengers—hearing of the other attacks—battled their hijackers and forced the plane down. All domestic flights were grounded, bridges and tunnels leading into New York were closed, and the U.S. military was placed on high alert. Overall, more than three thousand people from eighty-two countries were killed. It was the single most destructive enemy attack in American history.

*In New York City, on September 11, 2001, tragic scenes illustrated the range of human social behavior. On September 11, 2001, a jumbo jet hijacked by terrorists slammed into the south tower of the World Trade Center, the second attack of the morning. As workers fled the building, heroic firefighters climbed up the stairs, many to their own death, looking for survivors. On the streets below, people, covered in soot and ash, were dazed. Nearby, families of missing victims posted fliers of their loved ones on walls that would later become memorials.*

In downtown Manhattan, gray smoke billowed up into a blue city sky as glass, metal, and paper rained onto the ground below. Inside the twin towers, where thousands of people were at work, the upper floors filled with fire, heat, smoke, and fumes. People trapped in the building screamed for help, tried to escape, and made last-minute cell-phone calls to helpless loved ones. Many jumped to their deaths. Remarkably, fleeing workers said afterward that they had crossed paths with firefighters who climbed *up* the stairs, many to their own deaths, looking for survivors.

On the street, sirens blared everywhere. When the buildings collapsed, daylight turned to night. It was pitch black. Looking like statues but gasping for air, people were covered in thick gray soot and ash. The streets themselves were a bed of ash, littered with body parts, blown-out windows, slabs of cement, steel beams, eyeglasses, shoes, cell phones, and confettilike papers. Everyone was dazed, shaking and crying. Chased by an avalanche of powder and rubble, people dropped everything, covered their mouths, and ran as fast as they could. New York City Mayor Rudolph Guiliani, pale and somber, maintained his poise and resolve on camera to address a shaken city and nation.

Away from this site, which would later be dubbed "ground zero," worried friends and relatives flooded phone lines and used email to communicate. Families of missing victims posted fliers about their loved ones on walls and tried to get their pictures on TV. Some people were gripped by such paranoia that they feared terrorism in every airplane, van, briefcase, and person with olive-toned skin. Still, thousands of New Yorkers rallied to offer a helping hand. They brought towels, aspirins, t-shirts, bandages, ice, water bottles, and other necessities. Over the next few weeks, crowds gathered to cheer police, firefighters, and rescue workers. All over the country, people donated thousands of pints of blood and over a billion dollars in relief funds. In an outburst of patriotism, millions of Americans hung flags from their houses and cars. Although some targeted Arab and Muslim citizens for retaliation, most showed restraint. And although some segments of the world population celebrated the attack, the vast majority expressed sadness, sympathy, outrage, and support.

This entire episode—from the attack to the ensuing acts of human kindness, the ethnic group tensions, and the resulting war—raises profound questions about human social behavior. What could possibly have triggered the deliberate execution

**social psychology**   The study of how individuals think, feel, and behave in social situations.

**social perception**   The processes by which we come to know and evaluate other persons.

**attribution theory**   A set of theories that describe how people explain the causes of behavior.

of a plot by nineteen suicide-driven terrorists to kill innocent men, women, and children? Were they intensely frustrated and enraged, or did they blindly follow orders from a leader in whom they believed? In the chaos that ensued, what inspired heroic firefighters, rescue workers, and the passengers who took down the plane in Pennsylvania to sacrifice their lives? Why, afterward, did Americans come together rather than break apart, gathering in groups at candlelight vigils and patriotic ceremonies, and displaying the Stars and Stripes wherever they went? These questions—about aggression, altruism, group pride, intergroup conflict, and perceptions of others—are all questions of **social psychology**: the study of how individuals think, feel, and behave in social situations.

## SOCIAL PERCEPTION

- *How do we come to know other people?*
- *What is the fundamental attribution error—and is it really "fundamental"?*
- *Why are we so slow to revise our first impressions in the light of new evidence?*
- *In liking, do birds of a feather flock together, or do opposites attract?*
- *Is physical beauty an objective characteristic or strictly in the eye of the beholder?*

As social beings, humans are drawn to each other. We work together, play together, live together, and often make lifetime commitments to grow old together. In all our interactions, we engage in **social perception**, the process of knowing and evaluating other persons. People are complex, not transparent, and it's not easy to form accurate impressions of them. So how do we do it? What kinds of evidence do we use? We cannot actually "see" inner dispositions or states of mind any more than a detective can see a crime that has already been committed. So, like the detective who tries to reconstruct events from physical traces, witnesses, and other clues, we observe the way people behave, try to explain that behavior, then put all the pieces together to form an impression.

### MAKING ATTRIBUTIONS

Why did the suicide terrorists commit such a vicious act against human beings they did not know? Were they evil by nature, frustrated and enraged, or driven by the quest of a holy war? Or were they somehow set up, provoked, or under orders from a revered leader, trapped in circumstances they could not control? In trying to make sense of people from their actions, we must understand what caused their behavior. What kinds of explanations do we come up with, and how do we go about making them? In *The Psychology of Interpersonal Relations*, Fritz Heider (1958) proposed that we are all "intuitive scientists" in the way we determine why people behave as they do. According to Heider, the explanations we come up with are called attributions, and the theory that describes the process is called **attribution theory**.

**Attribution Theory**   Although the events of human behavior can be explained in many ways, Heider found it useful to group our attributions into two major categories: personal and situational. In the case of 9/11, for example, it was natural to wonder: Was the attack caused by characteristics of the hijackers (a *personal attribution*), or were these individuals somehow coerced or, as some suggested, induced by the promise of a better afterlife (a *situational attribution*)? For attribution theorists, the goal is not to determine the true causes of this event but, rather, to understand our *perceptions* of the causes.

Following Heider, Harold Kelley (1967) theorized that people often make attributions, logically, on the basis of three types of information: consensus, distinctiveness, and consistency. To illustrate these concepts, imagine that you're standing on a street corner one hot, steamy evening, when all of a sudden a stranger bursts out of a cool, air-conditioned movie theater and blurts out, "Great movie!" Looking up, you don't recognize the film title, so you wonder what to make of this candid appraisal. Was the behavior (the rave review) caused by something about the person (the stranger), the stimulus (the film), or the unique circumstances (perhaps the cool and comfortable theater)? Because you're possibly interested in spending an evening at the movies, how do you explain this incident?

Thinking like a scientist, you would probably seek *consensus information* to see how other persons react to the same stimulus. In other words, how do other moviegoers feel about this film? If others also rave about the film, the stranger's behavior is high in consensus and is thus attributed to the stimulus. If others are critical of the same film, the behavior is low in consensus and is attributed to the person.

"It's not you, Frank, it's me—I don't like you."

*People make attributions all the time in an effort to make sense of their social world.*

Still thinking like a scientist, you might want to have *distinctiveness* information to see how the same person reacts to different stimuli. In other words, how does this raving moviegoer react to other films? If this stranger is critical of many other films, then this rave review is highly distinctive and is attributed to the stimulus. If the stranger gushes about everything, then this review is low in distinctiveness and is attributed to the person, not to the film.

Finally, you might seek *consistency* information to see what happens to the behavior at another time when the person and the stimulus both remain the same. How does this moviegoer feel about this same film on another night? If the stranger raves about the film on video as well as in the theater, then the behavior is consistent. But if the stranger does not always enjoy the film, then the behavior is low in consistency. According to Kelley, behavior that is consistent is attributed to the stimulus when consensus and distinctiveness are also high, and to the person when they are low. Behaviors that are low in consistency are attributed to fleeting circumstances, such as the temperature of the movie theater. The theory and its predictions are represented in Figure 13.1.

Kelley's attribution theory is logical, but does it describe the way that you and I analyze the behavior of others? To some extent, it does. Research shows that when people are asked to make attributions for someone's behavior, they often follow this logic and make attributions on the basis of consensus, distinctiveness, and consistency information (McArthur, 1972; Cheng & Novick, 1990; Fosterling, 1992). But as social perceivers, do we really analyze behavior in the way one might expect of a computer? Do we have the time, the desire, or the cognitive capacity for such mindful processes? Not always. With so much to explain and not enough time in a day, we often take mental shortcuts, make culturally appropriate assumptions, cross our fingers, and get on with life (Fiske & Taylor, 1991). The problem is that with speed comes bias and perhaps a loss of accuracy. Let's examine some of the biases in attribution.

**The Fundamental Attribution Error**   By the time you complete this chapter, you will have learned the cardinal lesson of social psychology: Human beings are influenced in profound ways by situations. This point seems obvious, right? Why, then, are parents often so astonished to hear that their mischievous child, the family monster, is a perfect angel in school? And why are students often surprised to

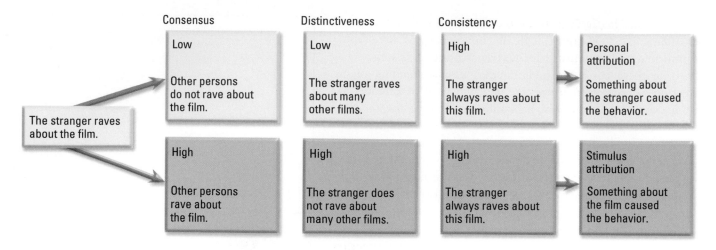

**FIGURE 13.1 Kelley's attribution theory**
For behaviors that are consistent over time, attribution theory predicts that people make personal attributions under conditions of low consensus and distinctiveness (top row), and situational attributions under high consensus and distinctiveness (bottom row). Behaviors that are low in consistency (not shown) are attributed to passing circumstances.

see that a favorite professor, an eloquent lecturer, is awkward in casual conversation? These reactions are symptoms of a well-documented aspect of social perception: When people try to explain the behavior of others, they typically overestimate the role of personal factors and underestimate the role of the situation. This bias is so pervasive, and often so misleading, that it has been called the **fundamental attribution error** (Ross, 1977).

The fundamental attribution error was first discovered in a study by Edward Jones and Victor Harris (1967). In that study, participants read a speech presumably written by a college student that was either for or against Fidel Castro, the communist leader of Cuba. Some participants were told that the student had freely chosen his or her position; others were told that he was assigned the position by an instructor. What was the student's true attitude? In response to this question, participants sensibly judged the student's attitude from the speech when the position was freely chosen. So far, so good. But even when participants knew that the student had no choice, they still inferred his or her attitude from the speech. Thus, the student who wrote for rather than against Castro was seen as more favorable toward the Cuban leader—whether that essay position was freely chosen or not. This finding has been repeated many times, with the same result: Except when participants are highly motivated and have the time to make a careful judgment, they attribute the speaker's position to his or her attitude—regardless of the situation (Jones, 1990).

A fascinating study by Lee Ross and others (1977) exposed the fundamental attribution error in a familiar setting, the TV quiz show. By the flip of a coin, participants were randomly assigned to play the role of questioner or contestant in a quiz game, while spectators looked on. In front of the contestant and spectators, the experimenter instructed the questioner to write ten challenging questions from his or her own store of general knowledge. If you're a trivia buff, you can imagine how esoteric these questions could be: Who was the first governor of Idaho? What team won the NHL Stanley Cup in 1968? It's no wonder that contestants correctly answered less than 40 percent of the questions asked. When the game was over, everyone rated the questioner's and contestant's general knowledge on a scale of 0 to 100.

Picture the events that occurred. The questioners appeared more knowledgeable than the contestants—after all, they knew all the answers. But a moment's reflection

**fundamental attribution error** A tendency to overestimate the impact of personal causes of behavior and to overlook the role of situations.

should remind us that the situation put the questioner at a huge advantage. Did spectators take this into account, or did they conclude that the questioners actually had more knowledge? As shown in Figure 13.2, the results were startling. Spectators rated the questioners as above average in general knowledge and the contestants as below average. The contestants even rated themselves as inferior to their partners. Like the spectators, they too were fooled by the loaded situation.

What's going on here? Why do we make unwarranted attributions for behavior to persons and fail to appreciate the impact of situations? According to Daniel Gilbert and Patrick Malone (1995), the problem stems from *how* attributions are made. Theorists used to assume that people survey all the evidence and then decide on either a personal or situational attribution. Instead, claims Gilbert, there is a two-step process: First, we identify the behavior and make a quick personal attribution; then we try to correct or adjust that inference to account for situational influences. The first step is simple, natural, and automatic—like a reflex; the second step requires attention, thought, and effort.

**Attributions as Cultural Constructions**   Why is it natural to attribute behavior to persons rather than to the situations they are in? Is this tendency universal, or is it limited to Western cultures in which individuals are seen as autonomous and responsible for their own actions? Indeed, many non-Western cultures take a more holistic view that focuses on the relationship between persons and their social roles. To see if these differing worldviews relate to attributions, Joan Miller (1984) asked people of various ages from the United States and from India to describe what caused certain positive and negative behaviors they observe in their lives. Among young children, there were no cultural differences. With increasing age, however, the American participants made more personal attributions, whereas the Indian participants became more situational. These findings suggest that the fundamental attribution error may be unique to Western cultures (see Figure 13.3).

According to Ara Norenzayan and Richard Nisbett (2000), these cultural differences in attribution are founded on different folk theories about human causality. Western cultures, they argue, emphasize the individual person and his or her attributes, whereas East Asian cultures focus on the background or "community" that surrounds that person. To test this hypothesis, they showed American and Japanese college students underwater scenes that contained a cast of small fish, small animals, plants, rocks, and coral—and one or more large, fast-moving *focal* fish, the stars of the show. Moments later, when asked to recount what they saw, both groups recalled details about the focal fish about equally, but the Japanese reported far more details about the supporting, background cast. Other researchers too have observed this difference. Compared to the inhabitants of most Western cultures, people from East Asia tend to see "the person as being situated in a broad social context" (Choi et al., 1999, p. 47).

Today, the world's nations are becoming more and more intertwined. As people migrate from one country to another, many are *bicultural*, keeping their ancestral heritage while adopting some of the values of their new homeland. How do bicultural individuals make attributions? When shown a picture of one fish swimming ahead of a group and asked why, Americans tend to see the lone fish as *leading* the others (a personal attribution), whereas Chinese see the same fish as being *chased*

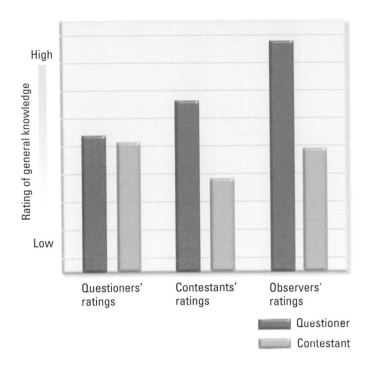

**FIGURE 13.2   Fundamental attribution error in a TV quiz show**

The simulated quiz show put questioners at an advantage over contestants, yet observers still saw the questioners as more knowledgeable (right). Although questioners did not overrate their own general knowledge (left), contestants, like the observers, rated themselves as inferior (middle). These results illustrate the fundamental attribution error.

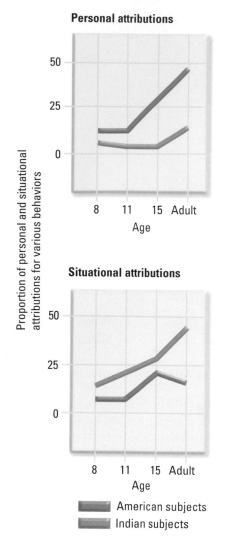

**FIGURE 13.3 Fundamental attribution error: a Western bias?**
Participants from the United States and India described the causes of various behaviors. Among young children, there were almost no cultural differences. With age, however, the Americans made more personal attributions and Indian participants made more situational attributions.

by the others (a situational attribution). What about bicultural social perceivers? In a study of China-born students attending college in California, researchers presented images that symbolized one of the two cultures (such as the U.S. and Chinese flags) and administered the fish test. As shown in Figure 13.4, students exposed to the Chinese images—compared to those who saw the American images—made more situational attributions, seeing the lone fish as being chased rather than as leading. Apparently, people can simultaneously hold differing cultural worldviews and perceive others within either frame, depending on which culture is brought to mind (Hong et al., 2000).

**Self-Serving Attributions** As objective as we try to be, our social perceptions are sometimes colored by personal needs, wishes, and preferences. This tendency showed itself in the officiating controversies of the 2002 Winter Olympics. When the Canadian figure-skating pair of Jamie Sale and David Pelletier performed a flawless program and beamed smiles to the cheering crowd, they "knew" they had won the gold medal over Elena Berezhnaya and Anton Sikharulidze of Russia. Yet when the judges' scores came up, moments later, the Russian pair was granted first place, unleashing a torrent of disapproval from the Salt Lake Ice Center crowd. Soon, a French judge admitted that she had been pressured in her vote, leading the International Olympic Committee to award a second gold to the Canadian skaters. The reaction: Canadian fans saw the decision as fair and just; but many Russians were outraged, insisting that Berezhnaya and Sikharulidze had won outright. This conflict illustrates a powerful exception to the rule that people are objective in their social perceptions: sometimes we see what we want to see.

People have an underlying need to maintain and enhance their self-esteem—and this motive can bias their attributions. Time and again, research has shown that when students receive their exam grades, those who do well take credit for the success; those who do poorly complain about the instructor and test questions. When professors have articles accepted for publication, they assume it reflects on the high quality of their work; when articles are rejected, they blame the editor or the reviewers. In a whole range of situations, it seems that we are biased in the attributions we make for our own outcomes—taking credit for success but distancing ourselves from failure (Schlenker et al., 1990).

Other motives can also influence our attributions about others. William Klein and Ziva Kunda (1992) showed participants the score on a practice quiz of another participant, a male target, who was later expected to become either their partner or their opponent in a competition. In all cases, the target answered the practice questions correctly. What was the reason for his success? Hoping he was not too competent, participants who thought that the target was to be their opponent perceived him as less able than those who thought he was their prospective partner. To justify their wishful thinking, the participants reasoned that the task was easy and that luck was a contributing factor.

## FORMING IMPRESSIONS

In forming an impression of a person, making attributions is only the first step. A second step is to combine and integrate all the evidence into a coherent picture. Studies show that the impressions we form of people are generally based on a "weighted averaging" of all the evidence (Anderson, 1981; Kashima & Kerekes, 1994). This same research also shows, however, that once we do form an impression of someone, we become less and less likely to revise our opinion in light of new evidence, even if it's contradictory. Thus, first impressions are powerful.

**Cognitive-Confirmation Biases**  It's often said that first impressions stick, and social psychologists are inclined to agree. In a classic demonstration, Solomon Asch (1946) told a group of research participants that a hypothetical person was "intelligent, industrious, impulsive, critical, stubborn, and envious." He then presented a second group with exactly the same list, but in reverse order. Logically, the two groups should have formed the same impression. Instead, however, participants who heard the first list—in which the positive traits came first—were more favorable in their evaluations than those who heard the second list. The reason: People are influenced more by information they receive early in an interaction than by information that appears later. This finding is known as the **primacy effect.**

The primacy effect occurs for two reasons. The first is that we become somewhat less attentive to later behavioral evidence once we have already formed an impression. Thus, when participants in one study read a series of statements about a person, the amount of time they spent reading each statement declined steadily as they proceeded through the list (Belmore, 1987). Does this mean that we are doomed to a life of primacy? Not necessarily. If we are tired or unstimulated, our attention may wane. Donna Webster and others (1996) found that college students "leaped to conclusions" about a person on the basis of preliminary information when they were mentally fatigued from having just taken a two-hour exam. But when the students were alert and sufficiently motivated to keep from tuning out, this bias was diminished.

More unsettling is the second reason for primacy, known as the change-of-meaning hypothesis. Once people form an impression, they later interpret inconsistent information in light of that impression. Asch's research shows how malleable the meaning of a trait can be. When people are told that a kind person is *calm*, they assume that he or she is gentle, peaceful, and serene. When a cruel person is said to be *calm*, however, the same word is interpreted to mean cool, shrewd, and calculating. There are many examples to illustrate the point. Depending on your first impression, the word *proud* can mean self-respecting or conceited; *critical* can mean astute or picky; and *impulsive* can mean spontaneous or reckless (Hamilton & Zanna, 1974; Watkins & Peynircioglu, 1984).

A study by John Darley and Paget Gross (1983) illustrates this point in an educational setting. In their study, participants were asked to evaluate the academic potential of a fourth-grade girl named Hannah. Half the participants were led to believe that she was from an upper-middle-class home with educated, professional parents (high expectations). Others were told that she lived in a run-down neighborhood and had uneducated working parents (low expectations). As illustrated in Figure 13.5, participants in the first group were somewhat more positive in their ratings of Hannah's ability than were those in the second group. Within each of these groups, however, half the participants watched a videotape of Hannah taking an academic test. Her performance on the tape was about average—she correctly answered some hard questions but missed others that were easy. With all participants seeing the same objective-test performance, you would think that the difference between the high- and low-expectation groups would be completely wiped out. Yet among participants who saw the tape, Hannah received even lower ability ratings from those with low expectations and even higher ratings from those with high expectations. Presenting a body of evidence did not extinguish the first-impression bias; it reinforced it.

In events that are ambiguous enough to support contrasting interpretations, people see what they expect to see. In fact, research shows that people will sometimes flatly discredit the evidence that contradicts the conclusions they want to reach (Ditto & Lopez, 1992; Kunda, 1990). Thus, five full months after the terrorist attack on the World Trade Center, the Gallup Organization interviewed some ten

*"It is a capital mistake to theorize before you have all the evidence. It biases the judgment."*

—ARTHUR CONAN DOYLE

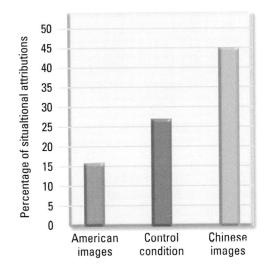

**FIGURE 13.4  Attributions within cultural frames**

When one fish swims ahead of others in a group, Americans see that fish as *leading* (a personal attribution), and Chinese see it as being *chased* (a situational attribution). In a study of bicultural Chinese students in California, Ying-Yi Hong and others (2000) displayed American or Chinese symbols and then administered the fish test. As shown, compared to students in a no-image control group (center), the students made more situational attributions after exposure to Chinese images (right) and fewer situational attributions after exposure to American images (left). For people familiar with both worldviews, social perceptions were fluid, dependent on which culture was brought to mind.

**primacy effect**  The tendency for impressions of others to be heavily influenced by information appearing early in an interaction.

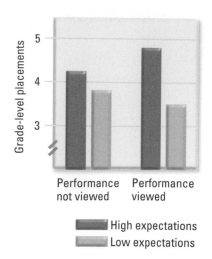

FIGURE 13.5    **Mixed evidence: does it extinguish or reinforce first impressions?**
Participants rated the potential of a schoolgirl. Without seeing her test performance, those with high expectations rated her slightly higher than did those with low expectations. Among participants who watched a tape of the girl taking a test, the expectations effect was even greater.

thousand residents of nine Muslim countries and found that 61 percent did *not* believe—as virtually all Westerners did—that the attacks were carried out by Arab men (Gallup Organization, 2002).

**Behavioral-Confirmation Biases**    As social perceivers, we interpret new information in light of our existing beliefs and preferences. At times, we may even unwittingly *create* support for these beliefs and preferences. In Chapter 12, we saw, in a classic study by Robert Rosenthal and Lenore Jacobson (1968), that teachers who are given positive or negative expectations of a student, perhaps based on an IQ score, alter their behavior toward that student, setting into motion a self-fulfilling prophecy. This teacher expectations study inspired—and continues to inspire—a great deal of research. As a result, we now know that the process is at work not only in schools, but in other organizational settings, too, including the military (McNatt, 2000).

In a study of corporate managers who interviewed job applicants, Amanda Phillips and Robert Dipboye (1989) found that when the managers had positive expectations, they spent more time trying to impress rather than evaluate the applicant—and were more likely to make a favorable hiring decision. Interviewers with positive rather than negative expectations are also warmer, more outgoing, and more cheerful in their demeanor (Dougherty et al., 1994).

Behavioral-confirmation bias is also found in the criminal justice system when police interrogate suspects. In one study, Kassin and others (2002) had some college students but not others commit a mock crime, stealing $100 from a laboratory. All suspects were then questioned over headphones by student interrogators who were led to believe that their suspect was probably guilty or innocent. The result: the interrogators who presumed guilt asked more incriminating questions, conducted more coercive interrogations, and tried harder to get the suspect to confess. In turn, this more aggressive style made the suspects sound defensive and led observers who later listened to the tapes to judge them guilty. In short, interrogators who presumed guilt were more intense in their questioning, which made the suspects sound guilty to neutral observers—even when they were innocent.

How does this self-fulfilling prophecy work? How do social perceivers transform beliefs into reality? As shown by research on teacher expectations, the process involves a three-step chain of events (see Figure 13.6). First, a perceiver forms an opinion of a target person—based on the target's physical appearance, reputation, gender, race, or initial interactions. Second, the perceiver behaves in a manner that is consistent with that first impression. Third, the target unwittingly adjusts his or her behavior to the perceiver's actions. By steering interactions with others along a path narrowed by our beliefs, we engage in a "behavioral-confirmation" bias that keeps us from judging others objectively. Fortunately, this bias is not inevitable. If the problem is conceptualized as a three-step process, it is possible to identify two links in the chain that can be broken to prevent a vicious cycle (Hilton & Darley, 1991; Snyder & Stukas, 1999).

First, there's the link between a perceiver's expectations and his or her behavior toward the target. When perceivers are highly motivated to seek the truth (as when they evaluate the target as a possible teammate or opponent), when they can attend closely to the interaction, and when they are concerned about the way they are being judged by the target, they become more objective—and often do not confirm prior expectations (Copeland, 1994; Harris & Perkins, 1995; Judice & Neuberg, 1998). Next is the link between a perceiver's actions and a target's response. Often, the

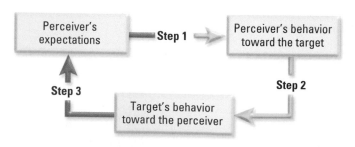

FIGURE 13.6    **The behavioral-confirmation process**
People can create false support for their first impressions through this three-step chain of events.

## THE PROCESS OF DISCOVERY

# ROBERT ROSENTHAL
## *Self-Fulfilling Prophecies*

**Q: How did you first become interested in psychology?**

**A:** Without really understanding what psychology was, I thought about it as a career long before I graduated from high school. Other kids were always telling me their troubles, and I knew psychologists were people who listened to troubles for a living. That turned out to be a good career choice for me. I started out in clinical psychology, at the University of North Dakota and at Harvard University, but my research was really in social psychology. When Harvard offered me a tenured professorship in social psychology I accepted very happily. I enjoyed my early clinical career, but I guess, in truth, I had transmuted into a social psychologist.

**Q: How did you come up with your important discovery?**

**A:** I think it all started when I ruined the results of my doctoral dissertation at UCLA, in 1956. My experiment on Freud's defense mechanism of projection showed that the research participants responded as they were expected to even *before* they received the experimental treatment. My only explanation for this odd result was that since I knew which treatment each participant was to receive, I treated them differently so as to bring about, quite unintentionally, the results I had hoped and expected to obtain.

Perhaps because misery loves company, I began a program of research on the unintended effects of psychology experimenters' expectations on the results of their research. With the help of my many superb students I found that when we created expectations for certain results in the minds of our experimenters, they tended to obtain those results. Experimenter expectations came to serve as *self-fulfilling prophecies*, not only with humans but with animals too. Rats learned faster in mazes and in Skinner boxes when experimenters were given more favorable expectations for their learning.

These rat learning experiments led us to wonder whether children might also learn better when expected to by their teachers. Lenore Jacobson, a school principal and a doctoral student at Berkeley, and I created, in the minds of eighteen teachers, especially favorable expectations for the intellectual performance of some of their students. We found that these randomly selected students later gained more IQ points than did children for whom no special expectations had been created.

**Q: How has the field you inspired developed over the years?**

**A:** For the first twenty years or so, much effort was devoted to learning in what areas of laboratory research and in what areas of everyday life these effects could be found and with what strength. To date, some 500 studies have been conducted, and many quantitative procedures of meta-analysis were applied and further developed to summarize all the findings.

**Q: What's your prediction on where the field is heading?**

**A:** Having documented the effects of interpersonal expectations, researchers are now focused—and will continue to focus—on the variables that influence the effect in classrooms, courtrooms, the military, and other organizations. They are also studying personal characteristics of "expectors" and "expectees" as well as their verbal and nonverbal behavior. We found that teachers with favorable expectations treat students with greater warmth. They also teach them *more material*. So when your psychology professor gives you a reading list longer than you think you can endure, keep in mind that it is nothing more than a reflection of his or her high regard for your intellectual ability!

---

*Robert Rosenthal is a Distinguished Professor of Psychology at University of California, Riverside.*

---

targets of our perceptions are not aware of the expectations that we have of them. But what if they were? How would you react if *you* knew that you were being cast in a particular light? When it happens to participants in social-perception studies—especially when they think they are being misjudged—they often try to behave in ways that contradict the perceiver's initial beliefs (Hilton & Darley, 1985; Swann & Ely, 1984; Smith et al., 1997). Clearly, the persons we perceive have their own prophecies to fulfill.

## Psychology and Law

# BIASES IN JURY DECISION MAKING

Every year, it seems, an American courtroom serves as a theater for a "trial of the century." In 1995, it was the double murder trial of former football star O. J. Simpson. More recently, there were the trials of Andrea Yates (the Houston mother who drowned her five children), Thomas Junta (the Boston "hockey dad" who beat his son's coach to death in a brawl), and Zacarias Moussauoi (the alleged twentieth hijacker charged with conspiracy to commit terrorism).

Regardless of how one felt about each of these trials, they illustrated the importance of social psychology at work in the legal system. Every day, ordinary people are brought into a courtroom and empowered to make decisions of utmost importance. The trial consists of three stages. First, members of the local community are summoned to court, questioned, and selected. Next comes the presentation of testimony, arguments, and the judge's instructions. Third, jurors deliberate as a group and strive to reach a common verdict. By law, juries are told to base their decisions only on evidence presented in court—not on extraneous factors. But is this ideal achieved? Over the years, social psychologists have examined some possible sources of bias (Devine et al., 2001).

### PRETRIAL PUBLICITY

When cases are featured in the newspapers and on TV, does the pretrial publicity corrupt the jury? Public-opinion surveys have shown that the more people know about a case, the more likely they are to presume the defendant guilty (Moran & Cutler, 1991). This result is not hard to explain. The information appearing in the news tends to come from the police and district attorney's office, so it typically reveals facts unfavorable to the defense. The question for jury researchers, and for the legal system, is whether this exposure overwhelms the evidence—and the jury (Fulero, 2002).

Norbert Kerr and his colleagues (1991) played a videotaped simulation of an armed-robbery trial to hundreds of participants who took part in 108 mock juries. Beforehand, they were exposed to news clippings about the case. Some read material that was neutral, but others received information that implicated the defendant in another crime. As in court, mock jurors were told to base their decisions solely on the evidence. But the pretrial publicity had a marked effect. In groups exposed to the neutral story, 33 percent of the participants voted guilty after the trial and deliberations. In groups exposed to an incriminating story, that figure increased to 48 percent. Why is pretrial publicity so harmful? Part of the problem is that it is revealed before the evidence—bringing first-impression biases into play.

Equally important, jurors may also be influenced by *general* publicity—not about the case they are deciding, but about other similar cases. Think about it. Would a jury

To this point, we have discussed the way people form and maintain their impressions of each other. It's important to recognize, however, that the process begins with a warm-blooded, motivated, emotional human being whose impressions are often positive or negative, not neutral. We now examine this evaluative aspect of social perception. First, we look at some of the factors that promote positive evaluations, or attraction. Later, in Chapter 14, we turn to the problem of prejudice, the dark side of social perception. (See *Psychology and Law*.)

## ATTRACTION

When you meet someone for the first time, what are you drawn to? Common sense is filled with contradiction: Does familiarity breed fondness or contempt? Do birds of a feather flock together, or do opposites attract? And is beauty the object of our desire, or do we think appearances are deceiving? Over the years, researchers have

judging an alleged terrorist, or a possibly corrupt corporate CEO, be influenced by news stories about terrorism, or corporate wrongdoing? In a series of studies, Margaret Bull Kovera (2002) preexposed mock jurors in a rape trial to brief portions of a network news story about date rapes on college campuses. Some jurors watched a proprosecution story that featured a candlelight vigil for rape victims. Others saw a prodefense story that preached caution about prosecuting men accused of rape without corroboration. Neither story pertained to the case the mock jurors were to decide. Yet those who saw the prodefense story—compared to those exposed to the proprosecution story—set a higher standard for conviction, saying they would need more evidence for a guilty verdict.

## INADMISSIBLE EVIDENCE

Just as jurors can be biased by news stories, they occasionally receive extralegal information within the trial itself. By law, a judge may exclude from evidence any items that are inflammatory, are unreliable, or have been illegally obtained. If such information is disclosed at trial, the judge instructs jurors to disregard it. But can people strike information from the mind the way a court reporter can strike it from the record? Can jurors resist the forbidden fruit of inadmissible testimony? Common sense suggests not, and so does the research.

In one study, Kassin and Sommers (1997) had mock jurors read a transcript of a double murder trial based on evidence that was relatively weak, leading only 24 percent to vote guilty. Three other groups read the same case except that the state's evidence included a wiretapped phone conversation in which the defendant had confessed to a friend. In all cases, the defense lawyer objected to this disclosure. When the judge admitted the tape into evidence, the conviction rate rose considerably, to 79 percent. But when the judge excluded the tape and instructed jurors to disregard it, their reaction depended on the reason for the tape being excluded. When told to disregard the tape because it was inaudible and could not be trusted, participants mentally erased the information, as they should, and delivered the same verdict as in the no-tape control group. But when told to disregard the item because it was illegally obtained, 55 percent voted guilty. Despite the judge's warning, these participants were unwilling to ignore testimony they found relevant just because of a legal "technicality." It is not easy for jurors to ignore information they find useful (Lieberman & Arndt, 2000). However, additional studies have shown that they will comply with an instruction to disregard when the technicality involves a serious violation of the defendant's constitutional rights (Fleming et al., 1999).

identified various determinants of attraction (Berscheid & Reis, 1998; Brehm et al., 2001). Two of the most powerful are similarity and physical attractiveness.

**Similarity and Liking**   Time and again, studies have revealed a basic principle of attraction: The more exposure we have to a stimulus, and the more familiar it becomes—whether it's a face, a foreign word, a melody, or a geometric form—the more we like it (Zajonc, 1968; Bornstein, 1989; Harmon-Jones & Allen, 2001). In Chapter 4, we saw that this **mere-exposure effect** occurs even when stimuli are presented subliminally, without a participant's awareness. Mere exposure can also influence our self-evaluations. Imagine, for example, that you had a photograph of yourself developed into two pictures—one that depicted your actual appearance, the other a mirror-image copy. Which picture would you prefer? Which would your friends prefer? Theodore Mita and others (1977) tried this experiment with female college students and found that most preferred their own mirror images, whereas

**mere-exposure effect**   The attraction to a stimulus that results from increased exposure to it.

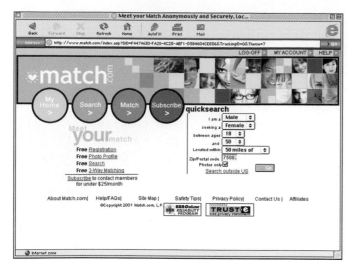

*In a survey of forty-five hundred single men and women, Internet dating service match.com asked, "What attribute do you find most attractive in a potential partner?" What do you predict would be most important? The top pick, as chosen by a third of all respondents: a good sense of humor.*

*"Cyberdating works because the courting process is reversed; people get to know each other from the inside out."*

—TRISH MCDERMOTT, MATCH.COM

their friends liked the actual photos. In both cases, the preference was for the view of the face that was most familiar.

Although exposure tends to increase liking, interactions provide us with additional information about others. Imagine that you meet someone for the first time and strike up a conversation about politics, sports, restaurants, or your favorite band—only to realize that the two of you have a lot in common. Now imagine the opposite experience, of meeting someone who is very different in his or her interests, values, and outlook on life. Which of these strangers would you want to see again: the one who is similar or the one who is different?

As a general rule, people prefer to associate with others who are similar to themselves. According to Donn Byrne and others (1986), this effect on attraction is a two-step process: (1) We avoid others who are very different; then (2) among those who are left, we seek out those people who are the most similar to us. As a result, friends and couples are more likely than are randomly paired persons to share common attitudes and interests. They are also more likely to be similar in their age, race, religion, education level, intelligence, height, and economic status. The more similar two individuals are, the better are the chances that the relationship will last (Byrne, 1971; 1997). Commenting on the magnetlike appeal of similarity, even in diverse multicultural societies, sociologist John Macionis (2001) notes, "Cupid's arrow is aimed by society more than we think." One unfortunate result, as we'll see in Chapter 14, is that by associating only with similar others, people form social niches that are homogeneous—and divided along the lines of race, ethnic background, age, religion, level of education, and occupation (McPherson et al., 2001).

**Physical Attractiveness** When we first encounter people, our perceptions are influenced in subtle ways by their height, weight, skin color, hair color, clothing, and other aspects of outward appearance. Among North Americans, blonds are considered fun-loving and sociable, and obese people are seen as weak-willed and lazy. Whether these perceptions are accurate or not, people connect outward appearance and personality (Bruce & Young, 1998; Zebrowitz, 1997).

The most influential aspect of appearance is physical attractiveness. As children, we were told that "beauty is only skin deep." Yet as adults, we like others who are good looking. Inspiring Nancy Etcoff's (1999) book *Survival of the Prettiest*, studies have shown that in the affairs of our social world, attractive people fare better in the way they are treated by teachers, employers, judges, juries, and others (Langlois et al., 2000). Through interviews conducted in the United States and Canada, for example, economists discovered that across occupational groups, good-looking men and women earned more money than others who were comparable—except less attractive (Hamermesh & Biddle, 1994). But wait. What is meant by the term *attractiveness*? Is beauty an objective and measurable quality, like height and weight? Or is beauty subjective, existing in the eye of the beholder?

Some psychologists believe that some faces are inherently more attractive than others (Rhodes & Zebrowitz, 2001). This "objective" view of beauty has two sources of evidence. First, when people rate faces on a 10-point scale, there are typically high levels of agreement over which are more or less attractive (Langlois et al., 2000). It appears that people prefer faces with eyes, noses, lips, and other features that are not too different from the average. Judith Langlois and Lori Roggman (1990) showed actual yearbook photographs to college students as well as computerized facial composites that "averaged" the features in these photos. Time and again, participants preferred the averaged composites to the actual faces. Other studies have since confirmed this effect (Langlois et al., 1994; Rhodes et al., 1999). Still other studies have shown that people are attracted to faces that are symmetrical—in other words, faces in which the right and left sides closely mirror each other (Grammer & Thornhill, 1994; Mealey et al., 1999).

A second source of evidence comes from the infant research laboratory, which shows that even babies who are too young to have learned their culture's standards of beauty exhibit a measurable preference for faces seen as attractive by adults. Judging from their eye movements, young infants spend more time gazing at attractive faces than at unattractive ones—regardless of whether the faces are young or old, male or female, or black or white (Langlois et al., 1991). Other studies have similarly revealed that infants look longer at faces that are "averaged" in their features (Rubenstein et al., 1999). "These kids don't read *Vogue* or watch TV," notes Langlois, "yet they make the same judgments as adults" (Cowley, 1996, p. 66).

Other researchers argue that beauty is subjective and is influenced by culture, time, and the circumstances of our perception. People from different cultures enhance their appearance with face painting, makeup, plastic surgery, hairstyling, scarring, tattooing, the molding of bones, the filing of teeth, braces, and the piercing of body parts—all contributing to "the enigma of beauty" (Newman, 2000). Even within a culture, standards change from one generation to the next. Brett Silverstein and others (1986) examined measurements of female models appearing in women's magazines between 1901 and 1981, and they found that "curvaceousness" (as measured by the bust-to-waist ratio) varied over time, with a boyish slender look becoming most desirable in recent years. Finally, judgments of beauty can be inflated or deflated by various circumstances. For example, we evaluate others as more attractive after we have grown to like them (Gross & Crofton, 1977). In contrast, participants who viewed nude *Playboy* models later lowered their ratings of the attractiveness of average-looking women—the result of a contrast effect (Kenrick et al., 1989).

The bias for beauty seems so shallow, so superficial. Why, then, are we drawn to people who are physically attractive? One explanation is that it's rewarding to be in the company of others who are aesthetically appealing, that we derive pleasure from beautiful men and women the same way we enjoy breathtaking scenery. A second explanation is that we associate beauty with other desirable qualities. Over the years, studies have shown that good-looking people are also assumed to be smart, successful, well adjusted, happy, confident, assertive, socially skilled, and popular (Dion et al., 1972; Eagly et al., 1991).

This perceived link between beauty and goodness is not hard to understand. Think about children's fairy tales, where Snow White and Cinderella are portrayed as beautiful *and* kind, and where the witch and stepsisters are depicted as ugly *and* cruel. This association between beauty and goodness can even be seen in Hollywood movies. Stephen Smith and others (1999) had people watch and rate the main characters appearing in the hundred top-grossing movies from the years 1940 to 1990. They found that the more attractive the characters were, the more they were

*Consistent with the notion that beauty is in the eye of the beholder, people from different cultures enhance their appearance in different ways. Pictured here are a Mejecodoteri woman from Amazon Venezuela (top left), a Tuareg woman from Niger (top right), a woman from the state of Gujarat in India (bottom left), and a Russian woman named Anna Kournikova (bottom right).*

*"Beauty as an objective and universal entity does not exist."*

—NAOMI WOLF

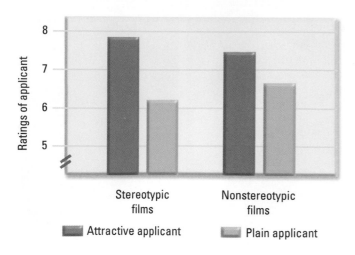

**FIGURE 13.7** **Media influences on the attractiveness stereotype**

In this study, participants evaluated graduate school applicants who differed in their physical attractiveness. Indicating the power of the media to influence us, those who had first watched a stereotypic film in which beauty was associated with goodness were more likely to favor the attractive applicant than those who had first seen a nonstereotypical film (Smith et al., 1999).

## REVIEW QUESTIONS

- *Distinguish between personal and situational attributions. What three types of information do we consider when making attributions?*

- *What is the fundamental attribution error and why does it occur?*

- *What is the primacy effect in impression formation? Why does it occur?*

- *Describe the chain of events involved in behavioral confirmation.*

- *How do similarity and physical attractiveness influence liking?*

portrayed as virtuous, romantically active, and successful. In a second study, these investigators showed college students a film that depicted either a strong or weak link between the beauty and goodness of the characters. In what was supposed to be an unrelated experiment, these students were then asked to evaluate graduate school applicants who had equivalent credentials but whose photographs differed in attractiveness. The result was both interesting and disturbing: students who watched a film that depicted the beautiful-is-good stereotype were more likely than those who watched a nonstereotypic film to favor the physically attractive student applicant in their evaluations (see Figure 13.7). This study suggests that the entertainment industry unwittingly may help to foster and perpetuate our tendency to judge people by their physical appearance.

Is the physical-attractiveness stereotype accurate? Only to a limited extent. Research shows that good-looking people have more friends and a more active sex life, but that beauty is *not* related to measures of intelligence, personality, personal adjustment, or self-esteem. In these ways, it seems that popular perceptions exaggerate the reality (Feingold, 1992). It also seems that the specific nature of the stereotype depends on our cultural conceptions of what is "good." Ladd Wheeler and Youngmee Kim (1997) asked people in Korea to rate photos of various men and women and found that people seen as physically attractive were also assumed to have "integrity" and "a concern for others"—traits that are highly valued in that culture. In contrast to what is considered desirable in most Western cultures, attractive people in Korea were not assumed to be independent or assertive. What is beautiful is good, but what is good is culturally defined.

So why, you might wonder, does the physical-attractiveness stereotype endure? One possibility is that social perceivers create support for their biased impressions. Think about the three-step model of the *self-fulfilling prophecy* described earlier. Snyder and others (1977) demonstrated this phenomenon in a classic study of interpersonal attraction. The participants were unacquainted pairs of male and female college students. All were given a background sketch of their partners, with each man also receiving a photograph of an attractive or unattractive woman, supposedly his partner. At that point, the men rated their partners and then had a conversation with them over headphones. The result: Men who thought that their partner was physically attractive formed more positive impressions of her personality and were friendlier in their conversational behavior. And now for the clincher: Female participants whose partners had seen the attractive photograph were later rated by listeners to the conversation as warmer, more confident, and more animated. Fulfilling their own prophecies, men who expected an attractive partner actually created one. This finding calls to mind the Greek myth of Pygmalion, who fell in love with the statue he had carved—and brought it to life.

## SOCIAL INFLUENCE

- *What's the difference between public and private conformity?*
- *Just how far can people be pushed to obey the commands of an authority?*
- *What makes for a persuasive communication?*
- *Why is it that a change in behavior can elicit a change in attitude?*
- *When do groups arouse us, when do they relax us, and why do they sometimes make bad decisions?*

Advertisers hire celebrities and supermodels to sell soft drinks, sneakers, and other products. Sports fans spread the "wave" and chant "de-fense" in a spectacular show of unison. Protestors, lost in a sea of anonymous faces, shed their inhibitions and become transformed into an unruly mob. Performers with stage fright tremble, turn pale, and freeze before appearing in front of an audience. These examples illustrate that people influence one another in various ways. As we'll see, the source of influence may be a person or a group, its effect may be on behavior or attitude, and the change may be socially hurtful or helpful to others. In all the forms that it takes, social influence is pervasive (Cialdini & Trost, 1998).

## SOCIAL INFLUENCE AS "AUTOMATIC"

As social animals, human beings are vulnerable to a host of subtle, almost reflexlike influences. Without realizing it, we yawn when we see someone else yawn and laugh when we hear others laughing. Knowing that people imitate others, TV producers infuse their situation comedies with canned laughter to make viewers think the shows are funny, political candidates trumpet their own inflated poll results to attract new voters, and bartenders stuff dollar bills into empty tip jars to draw more money from customers. As they say, "Monkey see, monkey do."

Research demonstrates the compelling nature of this automatic and nonconscious social response (Dijksterhuis & Bargh, 2001). In one study, Milgram and others (1969) had research confederates stop on a busy street in New York City, look up, and gawk at a sixth-floor window of a nearby building. Films shot from behind the window showed that 80 percent of passersby stopped and gazed up when they saw the confederates. In another study, Tanya Chartrand and John Bargh (1999) set up participants to work with a partner, a confederate who exhibited a habit of rubbing his face or shaking his foot. Hidden cameras revealed that, without realizing it, the participants mimicked these motor behaviors, rubbing their face or shaking a foot to match their partner's behavior. Chartrand and Bargh called this finding "the chameleon effect," after the lizard that changes colors according to its physical environment (see Figure 13.8).

The impulse to mimic others is even found in nonsocial situations. In one study, Ulf Dimberg and others (2000) exposed people to rapid-fire subliminal pictures of happy or angry faces. Participants were not conscious of having seen the images. Yet by recording facial muscle activity through the use of electrodes (as described in Chapter 12, the facial EMG can be used to record subtle changes in facial expression that cannot be seen with the naked eye), these researchers found that the happy and angry faces evoked the muscle reactions associated with smiling and frowning. In another study, Roland Neumann and Fritz Strack (2000) had people listen to an abstract philosophical speech that was recited on tape in either a happy, sad, or neutral voice. Afterward, participants rated their own mood as more positive when they heard the happy voice and as more negative when they heard the sad voice. Apparently, the speaker's emotional state was socially contagious—an effect that can be described as a form of "mood contagion."

Sometimes, the automatic social influences on us are not funny but potentially hazardous to our health—as when people commit suicide while under the influence of certain fanatic cults (Galanter, 1999). Consider the less extreme but still unusual events that occurred in a Tennessee high school. It all started when a teacher

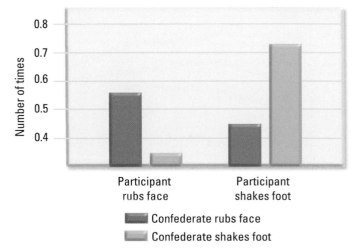

**FIGURE 13.8 The chameleon effect**

This study shows the number of times per minute participants rubbed their faces and shook their feet when with a confederate who was rubbing his face or shaking his foot (Chartrand & Bargh, 1999).

**conformity** A tendency to alter one's opinion or behavior in ways that are consistent with group norms.

noticed a gaslike smell in her classroom and then came down with a headache, nausea, shortness of breath, and dizziness. Word spread, others reported the same symptoms, and soon the school was evacuated, with eighty students and nineteen staff members taken to a local emergency room. Nothing showed up in blood tests, urine tests or other medical procedures; nor were gases, pesticides, or other toxins detected in or near the building. What the investigation did turn up was that students who reported feeling ill that day were more likely than others to have seen someone with symptoms, heard about someone with symptoms, or knew a classmate who was ill. The researchers, who reported the findings in the *New England Journal of Medicine*, concluded that the problems were the product of "mass psychogenic illness"—a profound form of social influence (Jones et al., 2000).

## CONFORMITY

**Conformity**, defined as the tendency for people to bring their behavior in line with group norms, is a fact of social life. Cast in a positive light, it promotes harmony, group solidarity, and peaceful coexistence—as when people assume their places in a waiting line. Cast in a negative light, conformity has harmful effects—as when people drink too much at parties or tell offensive ethnic jokes because others are doing the same. For social psychologists, the goal is not to make moral judgments, but to determine the factors that promote conformity and the reasons for it.

**The Early Classics** In 1936, Muzafer Sherif published a classic laboratory experiment on how norms develop in small groups. The participants in his study, thinking their visual perception was being tested, sat in a dark room, saw a beam of light, and then estimated the distance the light had moved. This procedure was repeated several times. The participants didn't realize it, but the light never moved. The movement they thought they saw was merely an optical illusion. At first, each participant sat alone and reported his or her perceptions only to the experimenter (most estimates stabilized in the range of one to ten inches). During the next few days, they returned to work in three-person groups. Each time a beam of light was flashed, participants stated their estimates one by one. As shown in Figure 13.9, initial estimates varied considerably, but the individuals eventually converged on a common perception, each group establishing its own set of norms.

Fifteen years after Sherif's experiment, Solomon Asch (1951) constructed a different situation. Imagine yourself in the following study. You sign up for a psychology experiment, and when you arrive you find six other students waiting around a table. You take an empty seat, and the experimenter explains that he is measuring people's ability to make visual discriminations. As a warm-up, he asks you and the others to indicate which of three comparison lines is identical in length to a standard line (see Figure 13.10). That seems easy enough. The experimenter then asks you all to take turns in order of your seating position. Starting on his left, he asks the first person for a judgment. Seeing that you are in the next-to-last position, you patiently await your turn. The opening

*Realizing the power of social influence, the photographer who took this picture anticipated that when one schoolgirl climbed the wall at the Tower of London, others would soon follow.*

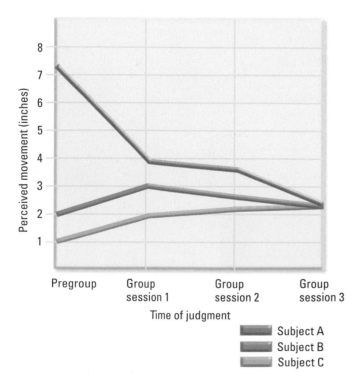

FIGURE 13.9 **A classic case of suggestibility**
This group in Sherif's study illustrates how participants' estimates of the apparent movement of light converged over time. Gradually, the group established its own set of norms.

moments pass uneventfully. The task is clear and everyone agrees on the answers. On the third set of lines, however, the first participant selects the wrong line. Huh? What happened? Did he suddenly lose his mind, his eyesight, or both? Before you know it, the next four participants choose the same wrong line. Now it's your turn. Faced with what seems like an easy choice, you rub your eyes and take another look. What do you think? Better yet, what do you do? As you may have guessed by now, the other "participants" were actually confederates trained to make incorrect judgments on certain trials. The right answers were clear. In a control group, where participants made their judgments alone, performance was virtually errorless. Yet those in the experimental group went along with the incorrect majority 37 percent of the time. This result may seem surprising, but recent studies too have shown that people conform to others on a variety of cognitive tasks (Larsen, 1990; Schneider & Watkins, 1996).

Both Sherif and Asch found that people are influenced by the behavior of others. But there is an important difference in the types of conformity exhibited in these studies. Sherif's participants were literally "in the dark"—uncertain of their own perceptions. Wanting to be correct, they looked to others for guidance and adopted the average of the group's estimates as their own. In Asch's study, however, the task was simple enough for participants to see the lines with their own eyes. Most knew that the majority was wrong but went along to avoid becoming social outcasts. In short, there are two very different types of social influence: informational and normative (Deutsch & Gerard, 1955; Campbell & Fairey, 1989). **Informational influence** leads people to conform because they assume that the majority is correct. In **normative influence**, people conform because they fear the social rejection that accompanies deviance. This decision is made for good reason. Research shows that people who stray from the norm are disliked and often are ridiculed and laughed at (Levine, 1989). These types of negative social reactions are hard to take. In fact, Kipling Williams and his colleagues (2002) conducted a series of controlled experiments in which they found that when people are socially *ostracized*—that is, neglected, ignored, and excluded in a live or Internet chat room conversation—they react by feeling hurt, angry, alone, and, in some cases, helpless.

The distinction between the two types of social influence is important because they show different types of conformity—private and public. Like beauty, conformity may be skin-deep or may penetrate beneath the surface. In *private conformity*, we change not only our behavior but our opinions as well. To conform at this level is to be genuinely persuaded that the majority is right. In contrast, *public conformity* refers to a temporary and superficial change in which we outwardly comply with the majority in our behavior but privately maintain our own beliefs.

In a demonstration of both processes, Robert S. Baron and others (1996) had participants, in groups of three (the other two were confederates), act as eyewitnesses: First, they observed a picture of a person, then they tried to pick that person out of a lineup. In some groups, the task was difficult, like Sherif's, as they saw each picture only once, for half a second. For other participants, the task was easier, like Asch's, as they saw each picture twice for a total of ten seconds. How often did participants conform when confederates made the wrong identification? It depended on how motivated they were. When the experimenter downplayed the task as only a "pilot study," the conformity rates were 35 percent when the task was difficult and 33 percent when it was easy. But when participants were offered a

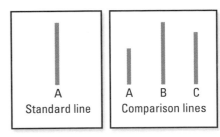

**FIGURE 13.10    Line-judgment task in Asch's study**
Which comparison line—A, B, or C—is the same length as the standard line?

*After two uneventful rounds in Asch's line-judgment study the subject faces a dilemma. Confederates 1 through 5 all gave the same wrong answer. Should he give his own or conform to theirs?*

**informational influence**    Conformity motivated by the belief that others are correct.

**normative influence**    Conformity motivated by a fear of social rejection.

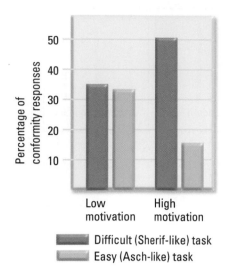

**FIGURE 13.11  Private and public conformity**

Regardless of whether the task was difficult or easy, there were moderate levels of conformity when participants had a low motivation (left). But when motivated (right), with pride and money on the line, the participants conformed more when the task was difficult, as in Sherif's study, and less when it was easy, as in Asch's study (Baron et al., 1996).

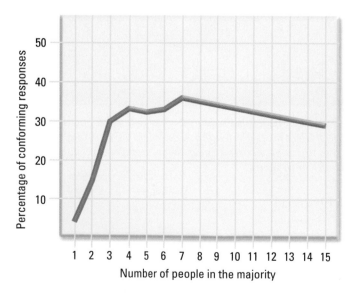

**FIGURE 13.12  Group size and conformity**

By varying the number of confederates, Asch found that conformity increased with the size of the majority, but only up to a point. As you can see, fifteen had no more impact than did four.

financial incentive to do well, conformity went up to 51 percent when the task was difficult—and down to 16 percent when it was easy (see Figure 13.11). With pride and money on the line, the Sherif-like participants conformed more, and the Asch-like participants conformed less.

**Majority Influence**  With more and more people communicating over the Internet, you may wonder: Do the social forces that influence people in face-to-face groups also operate in virtual groups, where the members are anonymous? Yes. McKenna and Bargh (1998) observed behavior in a number of Internet newsgroups in which people with common interests post and respond to messages on a range of topics such as obesity, sexual orientation, and the stock market. The social medium in this situation is relatively "remote." Still, these researchers found that in newsgroups that bring together people with "hidden identities" (for example, gays and lesbians who have concealed their sexual orientation from others in their lives), members were highly responsive to social feedback. Those who posted messages that were met with approval rather than disapproval later became more active participants of the newsgroup. When it comes to social support and rejection, even virtual groups have the power to shape our behavior (Williams et al., 2000).

Realizing that people can be pressured by others is only the first step in understanding the process of social influence. The next step is to identify the situational factors that make us more or less likely to conform. One obvious factor is the size of a group. Common sense suggests that as a majority increases in size, so does its impact. Actually, it is not that simple. Asch (1956) varied the size of his groups by using one, two, three, four, eight, or fifteen confederates, and he found that conformity rose only up to a point. After four confederates, the amount of *additional* influence was negligible, subject to the law of diminishing returns. Bibb Latané (1981) likened this impact on an individual to the way lightbulbs illuminate a surface. Add a second bulb in a room, and the effect is dramatic. Add a tenth bulb, and its impact is barely noticed (see Figure 13.12).

In Asch's initial study, participants were pitted against a unanimous majority. But what if they had an ally, a partner in dissent? Put yourself in this situation: How do you think having an ally would affect *you?* Varying this aspect of his experiment, Asch found that the presence of just one confederate who gave the correct answer reduced conformity by almost 80 percent. In fact, any dissenter—even one whose competence is called into question—can break the spell cast by a unanimous majority and reduce the pressure to conform (Allen & Levine, 1971).

Although the size of a majority and the presence of an ally influence the amount of pressure that is felt, people are most likely to conform when their attention is drawn to social norms (Cialdini et al., 1991). Of course, we must know what the norms are in a group in order to conform. This may sound like an obvious point, but people often misperceive what is normative—in part because others are afraid or embarrassed to publicly present their true views or behaviors. One common example concerns perceptions of alcohol usage. In universitywide surveys, Deborah Prentice and Dale Miller (1996) found that many students overestimated how comfortable their peers were with the drinking level on campus. They also found that the more positive students thought others were at the start of the school year, the more likely they were, eventually, to conform to this misperception in their own attitudes and behavior. The point is that we are affected not by social norms per se but by our *perceptions* of those norms.

Finally, cultural factors play an invisible but certain role. In many Western cultures—notably, the United States, Australia, Great Britain, Canada, and the Netherlands—independence and autonomy are highly valued. In contrast, many cultures of Asia, Africa, and Latin America place a value on social harmony and "fitting in" for the sake of the community. Among the Bantu of Zimbabwe, for example, an African people in whom deviance is scorned, 51 percent of those placed in an Asch-like study conformed to the majority's wrong answer, which is more than the number typically obtained in the West (Triandis, 1994; Bond & Smith, 1996). Not surprisingly, many anthropologists—interested in how cultures shape individuals—study the processes of conformity and conflict (Spradley et al., 2000).

**Minority Influence**   It is not easy for individuals who express unpopular views to enlist support from others. Philosopher Bertrand Russell said that "conventional people are roused to frenzy by departure from convention, largely because they regard such departure as criticism of themselves." Russell may have been right. People who challenge the status quo may be perceived as competent, but they are intensely disliked (Bassili & Provencal, 1988).

Maintaining independence in the face of social pressure is difficult but not impossible. Think about it. Asch's original participants conformed in 37 percent of the trials, but this means that they refused to acquiesce in the other 63 percent—a result that bears witness to the human spirit of independence (Friend et al., 1990). The question is, how do nonconformists withstand the pressure to change? Better yet, how do they ever manage to sway the majority? According to Serge Moscovici (1985), majorities exert power by sheer numbers, but those in a minority derive their power by sticking to their positions in a persistent, unwavering, and self-confident manner. By holding firm, dissenters can get others to sit up, take notice, and rethink their own positions. Does it work? Yes. Many studies have shown that dissenters who take a position and remain clear and consistent over time can produce minority influence (Clark, 2001; Crano, 2000; Wood et al., 1994).

Moscovici and his colleagues (1969) first noticed this phenomenon by confronting people with a *minority* of confederates who made incorrect judgments. In groups of six, participants took part in what was believed to be a study of color perception. They viewed a series of blue slides and, for each, took turns naming the color. The task was simple—until two confederates described the slides as green. When these confederates were *consistent*—that is, when both made incorrect green judgments for all slides—one-third of all participants incorrectly reported seeing at least one green slide. People can be influenced in important but subtle ways by minority opinion. Because of social pressures, we may be too intimidated to admit or even to recognize the influence. But it exists, and it is especially likely to materialize when participants give their answers anonymously or in an indirect way (Clark & Maass, 1990; Wood et al., 1996)—and when individual members in the initial majority begin to defect (Clark, 2001).

**Obedience to Authority**   Allen Funt, creator of the TV program *Candid Camera,* used to spend as much time observing people as most psychologists do. His conclusion: "The worst thing is how easily people can be led by any kind of authority figure, or even the most minimal signs of authority." Funt went on to

*Taken to extreme, blind obedience can have tragic results. In World War II, Nazi officials killed millions of Jews in the Holocaust. Were these Germans willing participants, as suggested by Daniel Goldhagen in his 1996 book,* Hitler's Willing Executioners, *or were they just following orders, as subjects did in Milgram's research?*

describe the time he put up a road sign that read DELAWARE CLOSED TODAY. What was the reaction? "Motorists didn't question it. Instead they asked, 'Is Jersey open?'" (Zimbardo, 1985, p. 47).

Blind obedience may seem funny, but as the pages of history attest, the implications are sobering. In World War II, Nazi officials participated in the deaths of millions of Jewish men, women, and children. When they came to trial for these crimes, their defense was always the same: "I was just following orders." Was this episode a fluke, or an historical aberration? In *Hitler's Willing Executioners,* historian Daniel Goldhagen (1996) argues on the basis of past records that many ordinary German people were willing accomplices in the Holocaust—not just following orders. On the other hand, human crimes of obedience are not unique to Nazi Germany and are committed all over the world (Kelman & Hamilton, 1989). On one most extraordinary occasion, such obedience was carried to its limit: In 1978, 912 men and women of the People's Temple cult obeyed an order from the Reverend Jim Jones to kill themselves and their children.

To study the power of authority, Stanley Milgram conducted the dramatic experiments described at the start of this chapter. In his 1974 book, *Obedience to Authority,* Milgram reported on the results of having put one thousand participants into a situation in which they were ordered by an experimenter to administer painful electric shocks to a confederate. Recall that participants thought they were "teachers" testing the effects of punishment on learning and that each time the "learner" made a mistake, they were to deliver a shock of increasing intensity. The participants could not see the learner, but they could hear grunts of pain, objections, loud screams, and eventual silence. Yet at each step, they were ordered to continue up the shock scale. Despite the pain participants thought they were inflicting, and despite the guilt and anguish they were experiencing, 65 percent in Milgram's initial study delivered the ultimate punishment of 450 volts.

At first, these grim results led people to conclude that Milgram's participants were heartless and cruel, not "normal" like you and me. On the contrary, most participants were tormented by the experience—and comparable levels of obedience were also then found among men, women, and college students all over the world, leading one author to ask, *Are We All Nazis?* (Askenasy, 1978). Indeed, high levels of obedience were found just a few years ago in studies much like Milgram's that were conducted in the Netherlands (Meeus & Raaijmakers, 1995).

The lesson of Milgram's research is clear. Although some people are more obedient than others, even decent human beings can be pushed to behave in ways that violate the conscience. Think about it. To me, the most striking aspect of Milgram's findings is that a psychology experimenter, unlike one's boss or military superior, cannot ultimately enforce any commands. Can you imagine the power that is wielded by real-life figures of authority? Not content merely to demonstrate obedience, Milgram altered aspects of his experimental situation in order to identify the factors that bring out obedience. Three types of factors were systematically varied:

■ **The authority.** When Milgram moved his experiment from the prestigious campus of Yale University to a run-down city office building, arranged for the experimenter to issue his commands by telephone, or replaced the experimenter with an ordinary person, obedience levels dropped.

■ **The victim.**   In Milgram's main experiment, participants were physically separated from the learner, so they could distance themselves emotionally from his pain and suffering. When the participant and learner were seated in the same room, however, especially when participants had to touch the learner, levels of obedience declined.

■ **The situation.**   Two aspects of the experimental situation fueled the high levels of obedience: (1) The experimenter explicitly assumed responsibility for the victim's welfare, and (2) full obedience was reached gradually, each step requiring only 15 volts more than the last one. As Milgram (1965) said, people become "integrated in a situation that carries its own momentum. The subject's problem . . . is to become disengaged from a situation which is moving in an altogether ugly direction" (p. 73).

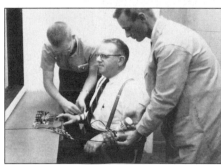

*Milgram's subjects used the shock generator shown here to seemingly deliver up to 450 volts to a confederate who was strapped into his chair.*

Today, with the air we breathe filled with threats of global conflict and terrorism, obedience to authority is a social issue of such massive importance that social psychologists all over the world continue to ponder and debate the ramifications of Milgram's studies (Blass, 2000). Before we leave the topic, consider an awkward but important moral question: By providing a situational explanation for such evils as Nazi Germany, are social psychologists unwittingly excusing the perpetrators? Does blaming what they did on the situation let them off the responsibility hook? In a series of studies, Arthur Miller and others (1999) found that after people were asked to come up with explanations for acts of wrongdoing, they tended to be more forgiving of the individuals who committed those acts—and were seen as more forgiving by others. This appearance of forgiveness was certainly not Milgram's intent, nor is it the intent of other researchers who seek to understand cruelty, even while continuing to condemn it. Miller and his colleagues were thus quick to caution, "To explain is not to forgive" (p. 265).

## ATTITUDES AND ATTITUDE CHANGE

People often change their behavior in response to social pressure from a group or figure of authority. These changes, however, are typically limited to one act in one situation at one fleeting moment in time. For the effects to endure, it is necessary to change attitudes, not just behaviors. An **attitude** is a positive, negative, mixed, or indifferent reaction toward a person, object, or idea. People hold quite passionate attitudes about a whole range of issues—from abortion rights, political correctness, and the way to approach the war on terrorism to whether they prefer America Online or Yahoo! as an Internet search engine. Thus, whether the goal is to win votes on Election Day, get consumers to buy a product, raise funds for a worthy cause, or combat sexual harassment in the military, attitude change is the key to a deeper, more lasting form of social influence (Ajzen, 2001; Eagly & Chaiken, 1998; Petty et al., 1997; Wood, 2000).

### Persuasive Communications   Persuasion, which is the process of changing attitudes, is a part of everyday life. The most common approach is to make a persuasive communication. Appeals made in person and through the mass media rely on the spoken word, the written word, and the picture that is worth a thousand words. What determines whether an appeal succeeds or fails? To understand why some approaches work and others do not, we need a road map of the persuasion process.

It's a familiar scene in American politics: Every four years, presidential candidates launch extensive campaigns for office. In a way, if you've seen one election, you've seen them all. The names and dates change, but over and over again opposing candidates accuse each other of ducking the issues and turning the election into

**attitude**   A positive, negative, or mixed reaction to any person, object, or idea.

**central route to persuasion** A process in which people think carefully about a message and are influenced by its arguments.

**peripheral route to persuasion** A process in which people do not think carefully about a message and are influenced by superficial cues.

a popularity contest. Whether or not the accusations are true, they show that politicians are keenly aware that they can win votes by two very different methods. They can stick to the issues, or they can base their appeal on slogans, jingles, flag-waving crowds, and other grounds.

To account for these varying approaches, Richard Petty and John Cacioppo (1986) proposed a two-track model of persuasion. When people have the ability and motivation to think critically about the contents of a message, they take the **central route to persuasion.** In these instances, people are influenced by the strength and quality of the arguments. When people do not have the ability or motivation to pay close attention to the issues, however, they take mental shortcuts along the **peripheral route to persuasion.** In this case, people may be influenced by a speaker's appearance, slogans, one-liners, emotions, audience reactions, and other superficial cues. This two-track model helps to explain how voters, consumers, juries, and other targets of persuasion can seem so logical on some occasions, yet so illogical on other occasions (Petty & Wegener, 1999).

To understand the conditions that produce change on one route or the other, it's helpful to view persuasion as the outcome of three factors: a *source* (who), a *message* (says what), and an *audience* (to whom). If a speaker is clear, if the message is relevant and important, if there is a bright and captive audience that cares deeply about the issues, then that audience will take the effortful central route. But if the source speaks too fast to comprehend, if the message is trivial, or if the audience is distracted, pressed for time, or just not interested, then the less strenuous peripheral route is taken. Particularly important is whether the target audience is personally involved in the issue under consideration. High involvement leads us to take the central route; low involvement, the peripheral route (Johnson & Eagly, 1989; Petty & Cacioppo, 1990). This model is illustrated in Figure 13.13.

**The Source**   The communicator, or source of a message, is the first important consideration in changing attitudes. What makes some communicators more persuasive than others? There are two key characteristics: credibility and likability. To have credibility, a communicator must be perceived as *competent*. Doctors, scientists, corporate CEOs, film critics, and other experts can thus have a disarming effect on us by virtue of their status. A credible communicator must also be someone who is seen as *trustworthy*—that is, willing to state a position honestly and without compromise. If a source has been bought and paid for, has an ax to grind, or has something to gain, then he or she will lose credibility. Using both competence and trustworthiness to create high- and low-credibility sources, Shelly Chaiken and Durairaj Maheswaran (1994) thus found that participants were more impressed by,

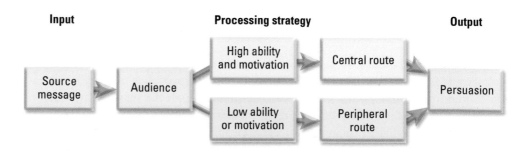

**FIGURE 13.13   Two routes to persuasion**
Based on aspects of the source, message, and audience, people take either a "central" or a "peripheral" route to persuasion. On the central route, we are influenced by strong arguments and evidence. On the peripheral route, we are influenced more by superficial cues.

and willing to purchase, a consumer product when they read a favorable review attributed to *Consumer Reports* rather than to a Kmart promotional pamphlet.

A second important characteristic is likability. As Dale Carnegie (1936) implied in the title of his classic, *How to Win Friends and Influence People,* being liked and being persuasive go hand in hand. The speaker who is similar to us or physically appealing has an advantage. In one study, Diane Mackie and others (1990) found that college students were more influenced by a speech on the SATs when the speaker was said to be from their own university than from another school. In another study, Chaiken (1979) had male and female assistants try to get students on campus to sign a petition and found that the more attractive the assistants were, the more signatures they were able to collect. It's no wonder that advertisers spend multiple millions of dollars a year on celebrity endorsements from Britney Spears, Halle Berry, Jerry Seinfeld, Russell Crowe, Derek Jeter, Tiger Woods, and other popular stars.

*Although she was only 19 at the time, pop star Britney Spears signed a multimillion dollar contract, one of the largest ever, to promote Pepsi. Can attractive sources help to sell products? Targeting the peripheral route to persuasion, the advertising industry seems to think so.*

**The Message**   Does the source hold the key to success? Are we so impressed by experts and so drawn to beautiful models that we uncritically embrace whatever they have to say? In light of what social psychologists know about the central and peripheral routes to persuasion, the answer is that it depends. When the target audience has a low level of involvement, superficial source characteristics make a difference. Under high involvement, however, a lack of substance cannot so easily be masked by style (Petty & Wegener, 1999). So how can a message be constructed for maximum impact? Should it be crammed with facts or short and to the point? What about using one-sided versus two-sided arguments, and visual versus auditory media? Despite many years of research, there are no specific formulas—but there are answers. To illustrate, let us consider two strategic questions that confront all communicators.

Before making an appeal, the astute communicator knows that audience members are not blank slates but human beings endowed with preexisting values. Knowing this, how discrepant a position should one advocate from that of an audience? Is it better to stake out an extreme position to stimulate the most change or to preach moderation in order to avoid being rejected outright? Research shows that communicators should take positions that are only moderately discrepant from that of the audience. A study by Kari Edwards and Edward Smith (1996) helps explain why taking a more extreme, counterattitudinal position is counterproductive. These investigators first measured people's attitudes on a number of hot social issues—for example, whether gay and lesbian couples should adopt children, whether employers should give preference in hiring to minorities, and whether the death penalty should be abolished. Weeks later, they asked these same participants to read, think about, and rate arguments that were either consistent or inconsistent with their own prior attitudes. The result: When given arguments to read that preached attitudes that were discrepant from their own, the participants spent more time scrutinizing the material and judged the arguments to be weak. Apparently, people are quick to refute persuasive messages they don't agree with. In fact, the more personally important the issue is to us, the more stubborn and resistant to change we become (Zuwerink & Devine, 1996).

A second common question concerns the arousal of emotion. Is it better to recite only facts and rational arguments or to stir up primitive emotions? This issue is often raised about the persuasive effects of fear, a common device. Magazine ads for condoms often use fear appeals—the most extreme being "I enjoy sex but I don't want to die for it" (Struckman-Johnson et al., 1990). Similarly blunt ads tell us that smoking "is a matter of life and breath" and that "this [a fried egg] is your brain on drugs." Does fear persuade? If so, is it better to arouse just a little nervousness or a full-blown anxiety attack? Over the years, researchers have measured the amount of attitude change produced by messages varying in fearfulness. The results suggest that high-fear messages produce more change than low-fear messages—as long as they provide reassurance coupled with instructions on how to avoid the threatened danger (Gleicher & Petty, 1992; Keller, 1999; Leventhal, 1970). Without guidance on how to cope, people tune out. But when clear instructions are given, fear arousal is effective. Antismoking films thus work better when they show gory scenes of lung-cancer patients rather than charts filled with dry statistics. Similarly, driving-safety films have more impact when they show bloody human victims instead of crash dummies (Rogers, 1983).

It's interesting that just as fear sparks change, so does positive emotion. Food, drinks, a soft reclining chair, tender memories, pleasant music, and a breathtaking view can all lull us into a positive emotional state—ripe for persuasion. Why? One reason is that when people are in a good mood, they want to savor the moment and get mentally lazy, uncritically accepting of persuasive arguments (Isen, 1987). A second reason is that a good mood can be distracting, causing the mind to wander and making it more difficult to scrutinize a persuasive message (Mackie & Worth, 1989). Weakened in the motivation and the ability for critical thinking, people are easier to persuade when they're in a positive emotional state (Schwarz et al., 1991).

**The Audience**  Source and message factors are important, but no persuasion strategy is complete without a consideration of the audience. Presentations that work on some people may fail with others. Are some individuals easier to persuade than others? Not as a general rule. But people are responsive to different types of messages. For example, some people are more likely than others to take the central route to persuasion—and, therefore, to be focused on content. According to Cacioppo and Petty (1982), individuals differ in terms of how much they enjoy and engage in effortful cognitive activities or, as they call it, the *need for cognition*. Research shows that people with a high need for cognition are influenced by strong informational messages, whereas those who are low in the need for cognition are swayed more by a speaker's reputation, the applause of an audience, and other peripheral cues (Cacioppo et al., 1996; Kaufman et al., 1999).

According to Mark Snyder (1987), people who are highly concerned about their public image exhibit *self-monitoring:* a tendency to modify their behavior from one social situation to the next. As measured by the Self-Monitoring Scale, high self-monitors tend to say that "in different situations and with different people, I often act like different persons." As targets of influence, high self-monitors are thus drawn to messages that promise a desirable social image. In one study, Snyder and Kenneth DeBono (1985) had participants read information-oriented or image-oriented magazine ads and found that high self-monitors were willing to pay more for products that were presented in the image-oriented ads. To be most persuasive, a message should meet the psychological needs of its audience (DeBono, 1987; Lavine & Snyder, 1996).

**Self-Persuasion**  Anyone who has ever acted on stage knows how easy it is to become so absorbed in a role that the experience seems real. Forced laughter can make an actor feel happy, and fake tears can turn to sadness. Even in real life, the effect can be dramatic. In 1974, Patty Hearst—a sheltered young college student from a wealthy family—was kidnapped by a revolutionary group. By the time she was arrested months later, she was carrying a gun and calling herself Tania. How could someone be so totally converted? In Hearst's own words, "I had thought I was humoring [my captors] by parroting their clichés and buzzwords without believing in them. In trying to convince them I convinced myself."

The Patty Hearst case reveals the powerful effects of role playing. Nonetheless, you don't have to be terrorized to be coaxed into doing something that contradicts your inner convictions. People often engage in attitude-discrepant behavior—as part of a job, for example, or to please others. This raises a profound question: What happens when people behave in ways that do not follow from their attitudes? We know that attitudes influence behavior. But can the causal arrow be reversed? That is, can a forced change in behavior spark a change in attitude?

**Cognitive-Dissonance Theory**   The answer to this question was provided by Leon Festinger's (1957) cognitive-dissonance theory. According to Festinger, people hold numerous cognitions about themselves and the world around them—and sometimes these cognitions clash. For example, you say you're on a diet, and yet you just dove headfirst into a chocolate mousse. Or you waited in line for hours to get into a concert, but then the band was disappointing. Or you baked under the hot summer sun, even though you knew of the health risks. In each case, there is inconsistency and conflict. You committed yourself to a course of action, but you realize that your behavior contradicts your attitude.

According to Festinger, these kinds of discrepancies often produce an unpleasant state of tension that he called **cognitive dissonance**. Attitude-discrepant behavior doesn't always arouse dissonance. If you broke a diet for a holiday dinner or if you thought that the mousse you ate was low in calories, you would be relatively free of tension. Attitude-discrepant behavior that is performed freely and with knowledge of the consequences, however, does arouse dissonance—and the motivation to reduce it. There are different ways to cope with this unpleasant state. Often the easiest is to change your attitude so that it becomes consistent with your behavior.

To understand dissonance theory, imagine for a moment that you are a participant in the classic study by Leon Festinger and J. Merrill Carlsmith (1959). The experimenter tells you that he is interested in various measures of performance. He hands you a wooden board containing forty-eight pegs in square holes and asks you to turn each peg to the left, then to the right, then back to the left, and again to the right. The routine seems endless. After thirty minutes, the experimenter comes to your rescue. Or does he? Just when you think things are looking up, he hands you another board, another assignment. For the next half-hour, you are to take twelve spools of thread off the board, put them back on, take them off, and so on. By now, you're just about ready to tear your hair out. As you think back over better times, even the first task begins to look good.

Finally, you've finished. After one of the longest hours of your life, the experimenter lets you in on a secret: There's more to this study than meets the eye. You were in the control group. To test the effects of motivation on performance, the experimenter will tell other participants that the experiment is fun. You don't realize it, but you're being set up for a critical part of the study. Would you tell the next participant that the experiment is enjoyable? Just as you hem and haw, the experimenter offers to pay for your lie. Some participants, like you, are offered a dollar; others, twenty dollars. Before you know it, you're in the waiting room trying to dupe an unsuspecting fellow student.

By means of this staged presentation, participants were goaded into an attitude-discrepant behavior, an act that contradicted their private attitudes. They knew the

**cognitive dissonance**   An unpleasant psychological state often aroused when people behave in ways that are discrepant with their attitudes.

> **WHAT'S YOUR PREDICTION**
>
> Cognitive-dissonance theory makes another interesting prediction: that we will change our attitudes to justify our effort, money spent, time, or suffering. In a classic study, Eliot Aronson and Judson Mills (1959) invited female students to join a discussion group about sex. But first they had to pass an "embarrassment test." Some underwent a severe test (they had to read obscene passages out loud), others underwent a mild test (they read only mildly erotic words), and still others were admitted without initiation. All passed, only to find that the discussion group was dreadfully boring. Afterward, the women were asked to rate how interesting they found the group. Make a prediction: Who saw the boring group as fun: those put through a *severe initiation* (and had to justify their suffering), *mild initiation* (creating positive feelings for the group), or *no initiation* (it was all new to them)? As predicted by dissonance theory, women who endured a severe initiation liked the group the most. Apparently, we have to justify our efforts—leading us to like what we suffer for.

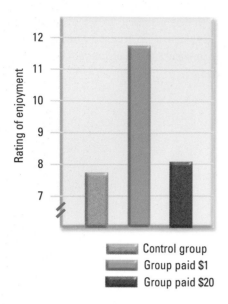

**FIGURE 13.14 Festinger and Carlsmith's classic dissonance study**
How interesting is a boring task? Compared to participants who did not have to lie and those paid twenty dollars to do so, those paid only one dollar later rated the task as more enjoyable. Having engaged in an attitude-discrepant behavior, these latter participants reduced dissonance by changing their attitude.

experiment was dull, but they raved. Was cognitive dissonance aroused? It depended on how much participants were paid. Suppose you were one of the lucky ones offered twenty dollars. Even by today's standards, that amount provides sufficient justification for telling a little white lie. Being well compensated, these participants did not feel dissonance. But wait. Suppose you were offered only one dollar. Surely your integrity is worth more than that, don't you think? In this case, you do not have sufficient justification for going along. So you cope by changing your view of the task. If you can convince yourself that the experiment was interesting, then there is no conflict.

When the experiment was presumably over, participants were asked to rate the peg-board tasks. Control-group participants, who did not mislead a confederate, admitted the tasks were boring. So did those in the twenty-dollar condition who had ample justification for what they did. Those paid only one dollar, however, rated the tasks as more enjoyable. After engaging in an attitude-discrepant behavior without sufficient justification, these participants felt internally pressured to change their attitudes in order to reduce cognitive dissonance (see Figure 13.14). In an interesting replication of this provocative study, Eddie Harmon-Jones and others (1996) found that participants who were asked to lie about the good taste of a Kool-Aid beverage laced with vinegar later rated that drink as more pleasing to the palette than it actually was.

**Alternative Routes to Self-Persuasion** Following Festinger, generations of social psychologists have studied and refined his basic theory (Harmon-Jones & Mills, 1999). Nobody disputes the fact that when people are coaxed into performing an attitude-discrepant behavior, they often go on to change their attitudes. In fact, people who have a high need for consistency are most likely to show the effect (Cialdini et al., 1995). But under what conditions will people feel and reduce dissonance, and why? According to Joel Cooper and Russell Fazio (1984), four conditions are necessary for change to occur: (1) The behavior has *negative consequences;* (2) the person feels *responsible* for these consequences; (3) the person becomes *physiologically aroused,* experiencing tension that needs to be reduced; and (4) the person *attributes* that arousal to his or her behavior.

The "why" question is still a matter of controversy. Some theorists argue that the attitude change is not fueled by a need to justify our actions but instead occurs as a rational process through which people draw conclusions about how they feel by observing their own behavior. In other words, participants who lied about the boring task for a dollar reflected on their actions and concluded that the task must have been interesting—or else why would they have said so (Bem, 1967). Other theorists claim that the predominant motive is not to be consistent but to *appear* consistent, or favorable, to others. In this view, the participants who lied simply did not want the experimenter to think they had sold out for a paltry sum of money (Tedeschi et al., 1971). Still others claim that the change in attitude is necessary for one's self-concept—that the participants who lied had to view the task as fun in order to repair the damage done to their self-esteem (Steele, 1988; Stone et al., 1997; Aronson, 1999).

## GROUP PROCESSES

When individuals assemble in groups, profound changes sometimes take place. Examples include the random violence and vandalism of street gangs, avid sports fans who scream at the top of their lungs and sometimes riot after victory, high-powered corporate groups that make unusually risky decisions, and angry and militant mobs seeking revenge. It's as if the group casts a spell over the individuals who compose it.

## Social Facilitation

First things first. How does the mere presence of others affect behavior? Appropriately, this most basic question in social psychology was also the first to be tested. In 1898, Norman Triplett studied bicycle-racing records and discovered that the cyclists were faster when they competed alongside others than when they pedaled alone against the clock. Intrigued by this finding, Triplett had forty children simply wind a fishing reel—sometimes alone, other times in pairs. Again, performance was faster among those who worked together than alone. Triplett's conclusion: The presence of others triggers "nervous energy," thereby enhancing performance.

Subsequently, many researchers confirmed that the presence of others speeds up performance on various cognitive and motor tasks (even ants excavate more and chickens eat more when they are in the company of other members of their species). At the same time, however, other researchers were observing performance declines. Why did the presence of others have such different effects on task performance? In 1965, Robert Zajonc solved the problem. He noted that (1) the presence of others increases arousal, and (2) arousal enhances the "dominant" response—that is, whatever response is most likely to occur. Zajonc reasoned that the dominant response is more likely to be the correct one when a task is easy (such as adding two numbers) but to be incorrect when the task is more difficult (such as solving a complex equation). The presence of other people should thus improve our performance on simple tasks but impair performance on tasks that are difficult. To demonstrate, Zajonc found that participants who tried to memorize simple word associations (*mother—father*) performed better in the presence of others than alone, but those who tried to learn difficult associations (*mother   algebra*) did worse. This phenomenon is known as **social facilitation** (see Figure 13.15).

Is the mere presence of co-actors or observers sufficient to produce social facilitation, as Zajonc suggested? Research has confirmed that the presence of others increases cardiovascular arousal among individuals working on some tasks (Blascovich et al., 1999). But what is the source of that arousal? Some social psychologists argue that we are aroused by others only when they are in a position to *evaluate* our performance. Others claim that we are aroused only when others *distract* us. Either way, one fact is clear: In the company of other people, we perform better on tasks we're

**social facilitation**   The tendency for the presence of others to enhance performance on simple tasks and impair performance on complex tasks.

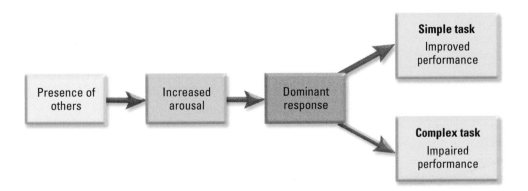

**FIGURE 13.15   Social facilitation**
Zajonc theorized that the mere presence of others increases our arousal, which strengthens the "dominant" response. As a result, the presence of others improves performance on simple tasks but impairs performance on tasks that are complex.

# WHY ATHLETES SOMETIMES "CHOKE" UNDER PRESSURE

Heading to the 2002 Winter Olympics, 21-year-old American figure skater Michelle Kwan was favored to win her first gold medal. An accomplished skater, she had already won four world championships and six U.S. titles. True to form, she entered the final four minutes of competition at a distinct advantage—she was in first place and in front of a home crowd rooting for her to win. She proceeded, however, to skate a cautious program. Uncharacteristically, she then two-footed her triple toe loop jump and fell to the ice on her triple flip. She finished third. In sharp contrast, 16-year-old Sarah Hughes had very low expectations. As she put it, "I skated for pure enjoyment." Yet she proceeded through a highly challenging program and skated flawlessly through seven triple jumps, five in combination. Hughes said it was the best performance of her life. In the end, she won the gold. What happened? Was Kwan feeling too pressured? Could an arena filled with supportive and expectant fans have made it worse, causing her to choke under the pressure? Was Hughes loose, fearless, and fluid in her skating precisely because of her low expectations?

Although many athletes rise to the occasion, the pages of sports history are filled with stories of basketball players who lose their touch in the final minute of a championship game, of golfers who lose the pin while putting for tournament victory, and of tennis players who lose

*Michelle Kwan*

*Sarah Hughes*

good at but worse on those we find difficult (Guerin, 1986). This basic social reaction can affect us in many life settings—as in the workplace, where some companies monitor the performance of employees from a remote location using computers (Aiello & Douthitt, 2001). (See *Psychology and Sports*.)

**Social Loafing** Social facilitation effects are found for *individual* tasks such as running a race, solving a problem, or memorizing a word list. In these types of activities, one's own performance is easy to identify. But what about cooperative *joint* activities for which individual contributions are pooled? In a tug-of-war, say, or in a cooperative class project, does each person exert more effort when they participate as part of a team or alone? To find out, Alan Ingham and others (1974) asked blindfolded participants to pull on a rope "as hard as you can" and found that participants pulled 18 percent harder when they knew they were alone than when they thought that three other participants were pulling with them. Bibb Latané and others (1979) then asked participants to clap or cheer "as loud as you can"—either alone or in groups of two, four, or six. The result: As individuals, participants produced less noise when they thought they were part of a group than when they thought they were alone.

their serve, all when it matters most. "Choking" seems to be a paradoxical type of failure caused by thinking too much. When you learn a new motor activity for the first time, like how to throw a curve ball, land a jump, or hit a backhand, you think through the mechanics in a slow and cautious manner. As you get better and more experienced, however, your movements become automatic, as you do not have to think about timing, breathing, the position of your head and limbs, the distribution of your weight, and other aspects of play. You relax and just do it. Unless trained to perform while self-focused, athletes under pressure often try their hardest not to fail, become self-conscious, and think too much—which disrupts the fluid nature of their performance (Beilock & Carr, 2001).

Where does an audience fit in? Social facilitation studies have shown that performance is affected in complex ways by the eyes of watchful spectators. But does it matter if the spectators are friends as opposed to adversaries? Isn't it comforting to perform in front of fans and others who root for us to win? You'd think so. But Jennifer Butler and Roy Baumeister (1998) found that people perform worse, not better, in front of supportive audiences. They had participants play Sky Jinks, a video game with a joystick in which the object is to steer an airplane through an obstacle course containing red and blue pylons. After twenty minutes of practice, participants were offered a financial reward for

reaching a certain score—which requires high speed without many crashes. But there was a hitch: They would be observed by a stranger who either had no vested interest in the participant's performance or stood to win money if the participant were to post the necessary score. Being observed increases the pressure to perform, but does it help if the audience is rooting for you? The participants in this study reported feeling less stressed when they thought that their audience was supportive rather than neutral. As measured by speed and crash frequency, however, they performed worse in this situation.

Why might people "choke" in front of supportive others? Butler and Baumeister believe that an audience of friendly faces increases the pressure—and our fear of failure (we hate to disappoint those who root for us). It also makes us more self-conscious, a state of mind that can cause athletes to stiffen up. Either way, these results seem at odds with the home-field advantage known to exist in professional sports. Across the board, statistics show that home teams tend to win. Perhaps the added pressure in these situations is offset by other advantages—such as living at home rather than in a hotel, being familiar with the physical conditions of the field, and a possible officiating bias that favors home teams.

The Latané team (1979) coined the term **social loafing** to describe this group-produced reduction in individual effort. As illustrated in Figure 13.16, social loafing increases with group size: The more others there are, the less effort each individual participant exerts. In the clapping and cheering study, for example, two-person groups performed at only 71 percent of their individual capacity, four-person groups at 51 percent, and six-person groups at 40 percent.

Why do people slack off when others are there to pick up the slack? There are a few reasons. One is that people see their own contribution as unessential to the group's success. A second is that people are less concerned about being personally evaluated—in part because individual performance standards within a group are unclear. A third possibility is that people slack off in order to guard against looking like the "sucker" who works harder than everyone else. Putting all the pieces together, researchers have concluded that social loafing occurs because individuals often do not see the connection between their own effort and the desired outcome (Sheppard, 1993).

Social loafing threatens work groups throughout Western society and, to a lesser extent, in Eastern cultures as well (Gabrenya et al., 1983). Studies have shown that people retain less information when they anticipate being in a collaborative work

The Home-Team Advantage in Professional Sports
54% baseball
57% football
61% hockey
64% basketball
69% soccer

**social loafing** The tendency for people to exert less effort in group tasks for which individual contributions are pooled.

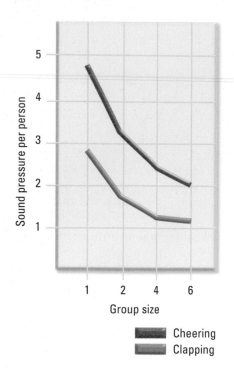

**FIGURE 13.16 Social loafing**
Participants were told to clap or cheer "as loud as you can"—either alone or in groups of two, four, or six. The more others there were, the less effort was exerted by each individual participant (Latané et al., 1979).

group, such as a deliberating jury, than when they expect to make their decisions alone (Henningsen et al., 2000). This decline in performance is not, however, inevitable. Based on a meta-analysis of seventy-eight social-loafing studies, Steven Karau and Kipling Williams (1993) concluded that people are less likely to take a "free ride" when they think their individual performance can somehow be separated from the group's performance, when their own effort is needed for the group to succeed, when success will be amply rewarded, when the task is personally meaningful, or when the group consists of friends rather than strangers.

**Groupthink** In 1961, President Kennedy and his top advisers set into motion a half-baked plan to attack the Bay of Pigs in Cuba with fourteen hundred CIA-trained Cuban exiles. The invasion resulted in a quick and humiliating defeat, leaving Kennedy to wonder how such poor judgment could have come about. Curious for an answer, Irving Janis (1972, 1989) studied the decision-making procedures leading up to the Bay of Pigs fiasco, along with other serious miscalculations (such as the decision to escalate the Vietnam War, the Watergate cover-up, and NASA's fatal decision to launch the space shuttle *Challenger*). What happened in the groups that made these blundering decisions? Was the process rational or irrational?

According to Janis, decision-making groups in politics, business, education, and other settings often fall prey to **groupthink**—a concurrence-seeking process in which the members convince themselves that their policies are correct. Insulated, tightly knit groups that value harmony and have a strong leader are most vulnerable to this conspiracy of silence. Groupthink seems to operate at two levels. In some cases, members suppress personal doubts on their own, often without realizing they are doing so; in other cases, they are openly and actively pressured into submission by a majority intolerant of dissent (McCauley, 1989). Researchers disagree on the specific conditions that put decision-making groups "at risk" for groupthink (Choi & Kim, 1999; Tetlock, 1998). But the adverse consequences are clear. In the Netherlands, Tom Postmes and others (2001) assembled groups of college students for two unrelated tasks. In the first task, they created a poster or discussed a matter of public policy—and were instructed either to be critical of each other or to strive to reach a group consensus. Later, in what was supposed to be another experiment, the same students were given different job applicant folders to read and were then brought together to make a hiring decision. Groups that had earlier established a consensus norm rather than a critical norm shared less information during their discussion and made lower-quality decisions.

The behavioral symptoms of groupthink are seen in three ways. First, the group tends to overestimate its own capacity. Group members harbor an illusion of invulnerability, an illusion of unanimity, and an exaggerated belief in the morality of their views. Second, group members become closed-minded, rationalizing their actions and stereotyping the targets of these actions. And third, there is great pressure toward uniformity. In the interests of group unity, members censor their thoughts and act as "mind guards" to prevent expressions of dissent. By inviting the pathological decision-making process outlined in Figure 13.17, groupthink raises the odds of a miscalculation and failure.

Can groups inoculate themselves against this problem? After the Bay of Pigs fiasco, President Kennedy took active steps to make his decision-making process more constructive. Using the safeguards Kennedy had adopted, Janis (1989) gave the following advice: (1) To avoid isolation, experts should be brought in and members should consult with impartial outsiders; (2) to reduce conformity pressures, the leader should not take a strong public stand early in the group discussion; and (3) to

**groupthink** A group decision-making style by which group members convince themselves that they are correct.

establish a norm of critical review, subgroups should separately discuss the same issue, a member should be assigned to play devil's advocate, and a "second-chance" meeting should be held to reconsider the preliminary decision.

## SOCIAL RELATIONS

- *What kinds of aversive events predispose people to behave aggressively?*
- *Does alcohol spark or inhibit aggression?*
- *And what situational cues serve as "triggers"?*
- *In contrast to aggression, what is altruism—and why is it so difficult to define?*
- *Why do bystanders to an emergency seldom intervene?*
- *And what situational factors influence helping behavior?*

People relate to one another in different ways. Sometimes our interactions and the decisions we make are negative, hostile, and antisocial. At other times, we are helpful, charitable, and prosocial in our behavior. Let's examine these two contrasting tendencies and the situations that bring them out in us.

## AGGRESSION

In the summer of 2000, at a hockey rink in Reading, Massachusetts, Thomas Junta attacked Michael Costin, his son's hockey coach. Enraged by the way his son was treated during a rough scrimmage, and in front of all the boys on the team, Junta threw Costin to the ground, pummeled him with his fists, and left him dead with a ruptured artery in his neck. One year later, in Houston, Texas, Andrea Yates—who was suffering from postpartum depression—drowned her children Noah, 7, John, 5, Luke, 3, Paul, 2, and Mary, 6 months. One by one, she pushed and held them in a tub of water until they lay breathless and motionless. Her oldest boy pleaded and tried to escape but she chased him down, dragged him to the bathroom, and drowned him too. In Karachi, Pakistan, during the winter of 2002, terrorist Ahmad Omar Saeed Sheikh and others lured *Wall Street Journal* reporter Daniel Pearl into a trap and abducted him. Several weeks later, despite public pleas from his pregnant wife, Mariane, Pearl's captors beheaded him—and videotaped the barbaric act. These examples serve as a sad reminder that the attacks on the World Trade Center and the Pentagon were, unfortunately, not isolated acts of human aggression. From the terrorist suicide bombers of the Middle East to the violent episodes of road rage that flare up on highways to the child bullies who abuse their classmates in schoolyards, the list of violent incidents occurring daily all over the world seems endless.

In some ways, these acts are so deviant that they shed little light on "normal" human nature. In other ways, however, they serve to remind us that **aggression**— behavior that is intended to inflict harm on someone motivated to avoid it—is a common and contagious social disease. Every day, people all over the world are victims of wars between nations, conflicts between ethnic and religious groups, racism, street gangs, drug dealers, sexual assaults, domestic violence, police brutality, and suicide. Aggression is so prevalent that psychologists have desperately tried to pinpoint its origins. Some argue that aggression is programmed into human nature by instincts, genes, hormones, and other biological factors. Others emphasize the role of culture, social learning, and environmental stressors. As always, human behavior is not the product of either nature or nurture but the interaction of many factors (Anderson & Bushman, 2002; Berkowitz, 1993).

## REVIEW QUESTIONS

- *Distinguish between normative and informational social influence, and describe an empirical demonstration of each.*

- *Describe Milgram's famous study of obedience. What does this study tell us about human nature?*

- *Distinguish between the central and peripheral routes to persuasion. How do source, message, and audience factors influence persuasion?*

- *What is cognitive dissonance and how does it lead to attitude change?*

- *Describe the phenomena of social facilitation and social loafing.*

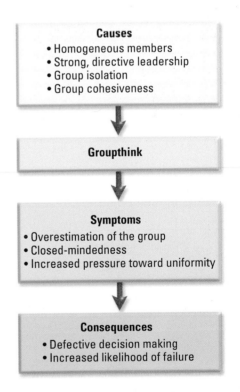

**FIGURE 13.17   Groupthink**

**aggression**   Behavior intended to inflict harm on someone who is motivated to avoid it.

*Thomas Junta, the Massachusetts "hockey dad," was found guilty and sentenced for six to ten years in prison for killing his son's hockey coach in a brawl. Human violence is all too common in the world, especially among people who are predisposed and provoked.*

"It's a guy thing."

**Biological Roots** On November 11, 1918, World War I ended. Shell-shocked, covered in mud, with lungs blasted by gas, millions of soldiers had died on the battlefields of Europe. What sinister forces of human nature could possibly explain the bloodshed? For Sigmund Freud (1920), who had earlier proposed that people were motivated by powerful life instincts, the war suggested that human beings are also unconsciously driven by a self-destructive "death instinct." In the conflict of these opposing forces, said Freud, the death instinct is redirected—from oneself to others.

Drawing on his observations of animal behavior, Konrad Lorenz (1966) also saw aggression as an inborn and adaptive instinct. According to Lorenz, successful aggressors gain access to food, water, and desirable mates. Thus, natural selection favors the evolution of an aggressive instinct. So are wars, crimes, and other acts of violence inevitable? Not necessarily. Both Freud and Lorenz argued that instinctual aggressive impulses can be channeled into hunting, contact sports, intellectual debates, and other socially acceptable outlets.

Instinct theories—which are based on the assumption that aggression is hard wired, unlearned, and characteristic of the whole species—have relatively little influence today. One problem is that instinct-based explanations are logically circular: People are aggressive because of an instinct—which we know exists because people are aggressive. A second problem is that some vast cultural differences cannot be explained by instinct. The Yanomamo of the Amazon jungle are known ferocious warriors, for example, but the Arapesh of New Guinea, the Ifaluk of Micronesia, the Chewong of the Malay Peninsula, and the Zapotec of southern Mexico live quite peacefully (Bonta, 1997).

Whether or not human aggression is fixed by instinct, it is subject to biological influences (Renfrew, 1997). Twin and adoption studies have suggested that genetic factors play a role, though it's not clear how large that role is (DiLalla & Gottesman, 1991; Miles & Carey, 1997). There are also consistent sex differences in aggression. Among children and adolescents, boys are more physically aggressive than girls in the way they play and fight (Loeber & Hay, 1997). Similarly, among adults, men behave more aggressively in laboratory experiments than women (Eagly & Steffen, 1986; Bettencourt & Miller, 1996). In every country that has kept criminal records, men commit more violent crimes than women. According to the FBI, the ratio of male to female murderers in the United States is about 10 to 1.

Aggression can also take more subtle forms. Research conducted in many countries has shown that female children and adults exhibit more *indirect*, or *relational*, aggression than do their male counterparts—by criticizing others, for example, or spreading hurtful gossip behind their back (Oesterman et al., 1998). This type of aggression can be seen in *Odd Girl Out*, a book in which Rachel Simmons (2002) describes, drawing on interviews of girls from thirty schools, such acts of indirect aggression as the silent treatment, note passing, glaring, gossiping, ganging up, and making fun of others' clothes and bodies.

What explains the sex difference in direct physical aggression? One possibility is that aggression is linked to the male sex hormone testosterone. Although both men and women are endowed with testosterone, men have higher levels on average than women do. What is the effect? In rats, mice, and other animals, injections of testosterone increase levels of aggression, whereas castration, which lowers testosterone, has the opposite effect (Breuer et al., 2001). In humans, correlational studies show that people with high levels of testosterone tend to be bold, courageous, energetic, competitive, rambunctious, and yes—aggressive (Dabbs, 2000). Among teenagers and adults, the use of anabolic steroids is linked to unprovoked acts of violence, or as it is sometimes called, "roid rage" (Pope et al., 2000). Most interesting in this regard are studies of fifty transsexuals who voluntarily altered their sex hormone levels by undergoing sex-change treatments. The result: female-to-male transsexuals became more aggressive after treatment, whereas male-to-female transsexuals became less aggressive (van Goozen et al., 1995; Cohen-Ketteinis & van Goozen, 1997).

Finally, strong evidence implicates alcohol in the commission of homicides, stabbings, child abuse, and other violent crimes (Greenfeld, 1998). Laboratory experiments too have shown that alcohol fuels aggression (Bushman, 1993)—particularly when participants are frustrated (Ito et al., 1996). In one study, for example, individuals delivered more painful shocks, supposedly to another person, after drinking beverages spiked with 100-proof vodka or bourbon than after consuming nonalcoholic beverages (Taylor & Leonard, 1983). Why does alcohol bring this tendency out in us? According to Claude Steele and Robert Josephs (1990), people self-disclose more, take more risks, and behave more aggressively when they are drunk than when they are sober. The reason, they say, is that alcohol leads us to lose touch with our values and become short-sighted about the consequences of our actions—thus evoking a state of "drunken excess."

**Aversive Stimulation**   Aggression may have biological roots, but it is also learned from experience and then is triggered by factors in the environment. What kinds of events unleash our aggressive impulses? How can social influences be used to promote peace and nonviolence?

Put two rats in a cage together, subject them to painful shocks, loud noise, or intense heat, and a fight is likely to break out. Put people together in unpleasant conditions—an overcrowded ghetto, intense heat, a noisy construction site, a room filled with cigarette smoke, the stench of body odor, or the company of an obnoxious coworker—and they too become more likely to lash out. As a general rule, aversive stimulation sparks aggression (Berkowitz, 1983).

One type of aversive event that we all experience at times is frustration. In 1939, John Dollard and others proposed the hypothesis that frustration leads to aggression either against the source of frustration or against an innocent but vulnerable substitute, or scapegoat. According to the U.S. Department of Transportation, this is all too often seen on highways and city streets, where motorists obstructed by traffic scream, honk, tailgate, and hurl obscene gestures at other drivers, as they erupt in fits of "road rage." The effects of frustration are exhibited by passengers in the not-so-friendly skies of commercial airlines, where long lines, cramped spaces, schedule delays, overbooked planes, stale air, and battles for the armrest have frayed nerves and increased incidents of "air rage," often directed at flight attendants (Zoroya, 1999).

Testing the implications of this **frustration-aggression hypothesis**, Carl Hovland and Robert Sears (1940) examined the link between economic hard times and racial violence. They analyzed records from fourteen southern states during the years 1882 to 1930 and discovered a strong negative correlation between the value of cotton and lynchings: As the price of cotton fell, the number of lynchings increased. Although this correlation cannot be interpreted in causal terms, experiments have confirmed that frustration sparks aggression by arousing anger, fear, and other negative emotions (Berkowitz, 1989). Ervin Staub (1996) believes that historical acts of genocide—as in the Holocaust of World War II—often stem from societal frustration, poor economic conditions, and the need to find a scapegoat. A meta-analysis of forty-nine studies showed that people who are frustrated do, at times, *displace*

**frustration-aggression hypothesis**   The theory that frustration causes aggression.

their aggression by lashing out against innocent others (Marcus-Newhall et al., 2000). For example, Jean Twenge and others (2001) found that college students who thought they had been socially excluded from a research group later reacted more aggressively toward a critical fellow student.

The high temperatures of a "long, hot summer" also seem to spark violence. Correlational analyses of worldwide weather records and crime statistics reveal a strong link between heat and aggression. More violent crimes occur in the summer than in the winter, during hot years than in cooler years, and in hot cities than in cooler cities. As you can see in Figure 13.18, the numbers of political uprisings, riots, homicides, assaults, rapes, and reports of family violence all peak in the months of June, July, and August (Anderson, 1989). Indirect acts of aggression also increase in excessive heat. As temperatures rise above 90°F, laboratory research participants become more likely to interpret ambiguous events in hostile terms (Rule et al., 1987), drivers in cars without air conditioning are more likely to honk at other motorists (Kenrick & MacFarlane, 1984), and major-league baseball pitchers are more likely to hit batters with a pitch (Reifman et al., 1991). When we are "hot under the collar"—or when we are uncomfortably cold and unable to find relief—tempers flare (Anderson et al., 2000).

> "By far, the worst thing about the firehouse was the heat. It got really, really hot inside there the last few weeks of shooting. We had no air conditioning, and the hotter it got, the angrier we got."
> —JASON, ON HIS EXPERIENCE IN MTV's THE REAL WORLD: BOSTON

In this regard, cultural factors may also play a role—even within the same country. In a book entitled *Culture of Honor*, Richard Nisbett and Dov Cohen (1996) analyzed crime statistics in the United States and found that rates of violence, over time, are consistently higher in the South than in all other regions. They speculate that this pattern reveals the workings of a culture in which men are highly protective of valued possessions, quick to defend against intruders, and anxious to project an image of strength. As a historical matter, they note that while northern towns were being settled mostly by farmers, the South was being settled by herders, whose "manly honor" was necessary to protect their flocks. Can this history be used to explain current violence rates? Nisbett and Cohen examined public-opinion surveys and found that southern respondents were more likely to agree that "a man has the right to kill" in order to defend his family and house. They were also more likely to own guns, favor capital punishment, and retaliate for an insult hurled in a laboratory experiment. At this point, you may be wondering, is it possible that violence in the South says more about the climate, which is hot, than the culture? Craig Anderson and Katherine Anderson (1996) used various statistical techniques to sort out these influences. They found that heat is associated with aggression regardless of regional factors and that the presumed effect of southern culture results primarily, though not entirely, from the generally high temperatures of the region.

**Situational Cues** Frustration, extreme heat, and other aversive events predispose us to aggression by arousing negative affect. Once we are in this state of readiness, the presence of people and objects associated with aggression may then prompt us to act on this predisposition. Aversive events "load the gun," so to speak, but situational cues get us to "pull the trigger." What situational cues have this effect?

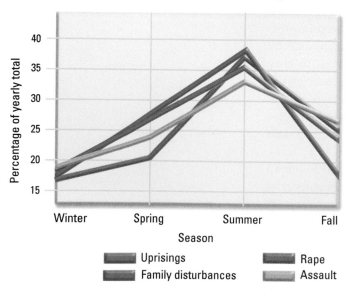

**FIGURE 13.18 The link between heat and violence**
Worldwide weather records and crime statistics reveal that more violent crimes are committed during the summer than in the other seasons (Anderson, 1989).

**Weapons** The sights and sounds of violence are everywhere. In the United States, millions of adults own handguns. Daily TV news reports flood us not only with graphic images of street violence but also with talk of nuclear, chemical, and biological weapons of mass destruction. Does any of this matter? Yes. According to Leonard Berkowitz, the mere sight of an aggressive stimulus can influence behavior. In a classic demonstration of this point, Berkowitz and Anthony LePage (1967) had male participants administer electric shocks to a confederate who had insulted half the participants right before the session. In one condition, only the shock-generating apparatus was present in the lab. In a second condition, a .38-caliber pistol and a 12-gauge shotgun were on the table near the shock button—supposedly left from an earlier previous experiment. As measured by the number of shocks given, aggression was increased by the sight of these guns. Participants who were angered and primed to be aggressive, retaliated more in the presence of the weapons than in their absence.

This provocative "weapons effect" has been observed in other, more recent experiments. As to why it occurs, Anderson and others (1998) theorized that because weapons are commonly associated with violence, the mere sight of a pistol, a club, or a sword automatically brings aggression-related thoughts to mind. To demonstrate, they presented participants with pictures of weapons or plants and then recorded the amount of time it took those participants to read aloud as quickly as possible various words flashed on a screen. The result: After seeing images of weapons as opposed to plants, participants were quicker to read aggression-related words such as *punch, choke, butcher,* and *shoot.* So do guns kill, or are people the problem? As Berkowitz puts it, "The finger pulls the trigger, but the trigger may also be pulling the finger."

**Media Violence**   As if reality did not provide enough of a stimulus, the entertainment industry adds fuel to the fire. Estimates suggest that there are more television sets in the United States than there are toilets (Bushman & Huesmann, 2001). Over the years, analyses of television shows have revealed what you might have suspected: depictions of violence are common in news shows, movies, TV dramas, music videos, commercials, and worst of all, children's cartoons—where heroes, villains, and other creatures fight dozens of battles an hour. Research has shown that roughly 60 percent of all programs contain some violence. What's worse, the perpetrators are often "good guys," the context is often humorous, the violence is almost never punished, and it is seldom depicted as bloody, painful, or harmful in the long run (*National Television Violence Study,* 1998).

Does exposure to TV violence promote aggression? Literally hundreds of studies have addressed this important question, with alarming results. Correlational studies reveal a link between the amount of TV violence watched by young boys and their subsequent level of aggression—a link commonly observed in the United States and Europe (Huesmann & Eron, 1986; Geen & Donnerstein, 1998). In a longitudinal development study, for example, Leonard Eron (1987) found that a boy's exposure to TV violence at eight years of age predicted criminal activity twenty-two years later. Critics are quick to note that these correlations cannot be used to draw conclusions about cause and effect. Perhaps exposure to TV violence causes aggression, as it seems, or perhaps aggressiveness causes children to seek out violence on TV, or perhaps poverty and other external conditions cause the tendency both to watch and to commit acts of aggression (Freedman, 1988). Whatever the explanation, the link between TV violence exposure and aggressive behavior is almost as strong as the correlation between cigarette smoking and lung cancer (Bushman & Huesmann, 2001).

To pin down cause and effect, researchers have observed participants who are randomly assigned to watch violent or nonviolent events. Controlled laboratory studies of this sort show that exposure to aggressive models, either live or on

Television provides a major outlet for commercial persuasion. The average American watches 30 hours of TV per week—and views roughly 37,822 commercials per year.

*Playing violent video games, like watching violence on TV, may increase aggression in children.*

film, has negative effects. In the first of these experiments, Albert Bandura and others (1961) found that preschool children were more likely to attack an inflated doll after watching an aggressive adult model than after watching a nonaggressive model. Among children and adolescents, exposure to violent models increases aggression—not just in laboratories but also in classrooms, playgrounds, and other settings (Wood et al., 1991). More recently, in light of the popularity today of the Xbox, Play Station, Nintendo, and other high-tech video game systems, Craig Anderson and Karen Dill (2000) randomly assigned college students to play a video game that was violent (*Wolfenstein 3D*) or nonviolent (*Myst*). One week later, those who had played the violent game had more hostile thoughts and were more aggressive in their behavior, blasting an opponent with noise louder and for a longer time. Even outside the laboratory, students who said they played more violent video games at home were more aggressive in their own lives.

When it comes to popular Hollywood movies, unfortunately, life often imitates art—as when films such as *Money Train, The Basketball Diaries*, and *Scream* inspired violent acts that were nearly identical to those depicted on the big screen. Similarly, the terrifying news stories of 2001, about postal letters laced with the deadly chemical anthrax, triggered several copycat hoaxes. Is there a solution? The evening news cannot be censored, but the American television industry does offer a rating system for TV shows, modeled after the one used for movies, so that parents can regulate what shows their children watch. Perhaps this policy will help curb the violence.

**Deindividuation**  Earlier, we saw that the presence of others can arouse us (social facilitation) or relax us (social loafing), depending on the situation. At times, the effect of a group is even more profound and more troubling. Hidden in a faceless crowd, people tend to shed their normal inhibitions—sometimes resulting in violent acts of racism, looting, vandalism, sexual assaults, and riots. How can normal, law-abiding citizens turn into frenzied mobs that take the law into their own hands? The problem is that in large groups, people lose their sense of individuality, which results in a breakdown of their internal controls against deviant behavior. This depersonalized state of mind is called **deindividuation.**

Large groups promote deindividuation in two ways. First, people feel anonymous, if not "invisible," and less accountable for their actions. Anonymity has powerful effects. In one study, participants who were dressed in white coats and Ku Klux Klan-style hoods that marked their bodies and faces punished a confederate with longer electric shocks than did participants who wore their regular clothing and name tags (Zimbardo, 1970). In a second study, Halloween trick-or-treaters who were invited to take one candy from a bowl were more likely to grab extras when they were nameless and in groups than when they appeared alone and were asked for their names (Diener et al., 1976). If you've ever entered an online chat room, you no doubt have noticed that when people communicate with strangers in cyberspace, they often disclose stunningly intimate details about themselves and, in contrast, often engage in "flaming"—a bold, hostile, offensive style of communication. Being anonymous, online chatters shed their normal inhibitions, at times behaving in antisocial ways (Douglas & McGarty, 2002; Gackenbach, 1998). As one teenager admitted, "I would totally say so many things online I would never say to someone's face" (*U.S. News & World Report*, 1999).

A second aspect of deindividuation is a loss of self-consciousness. Have you ever been at a concert or a party with music blaring so loud that you could feel the room vibrate and your identity slipping away? When attention is diverted away from the

**deindividuation**  A loss of individuality, often experienced in a group, that results in a breakdown of internal restraints against deviant behavior.

self by intense environmental stimulation, people momentarily lose track of their own values, morals, and internal standards of conduct—resulting in behavior that is impulsive, uninhibited, and often aggressive (Prentice-Dunn & Rogers, 1989). This effect may grow with the size of the group. When Brian Mullen (1986) analyzed newspaper accounts of sixty lynchings that had occurred between 1899 and 1946, he discovered that the more people there were in the lynch mob, the more vicious were their actions. Deindividuation does not always unleash violence, but it does make us vulnerable to getting swept up in the momentum of a social situation (Postmes & Spears, 1998).

# ALTRUISM

Few of us will ever forget the horrific images of the World Trade Center under attack, the fire, fuel, and smoke that engulfed the sky, or the towers collapsing onto the streets of New York City. Yet this same tragedy exposed the brightest side of human nature, as firefighters without hesitation climbed *up* the twin buildings—many to their own deaths—to rescue their fellow humans, strangers who were trapped (Smith, 2002). Stories of raw heroism had also peeked out from the horrors of Nazi Germany, where a number of German citizens risked their lives to hide their Jewish friends and neighbors (Schneider, 2000). Why did all these heroes try to rescue those in need? Why do some people faced with a crisis not intervene?

Focusing on prosocial aspects of human interaction, many social psychologists study **altruism**, helping behavior that is motivated primarily by a desire to benefit a person other than oneself. When people are asked to list instances of helping in their own lives, they cite helping a classmate with homework, listening to a friend's problems, giving moral support, lending out CDs or DVDs, giving directions to someone who seems lost, giving rides, and so on (McGuire, 1994). Everyday examples are not hard to find. Yet psychologists ask: Does altruism really exist, or is helping always selfishly motivated? And why do we sometimes fail to come to the aid of someone who needs it? These are just some of the puzzling questions asked about helping and the factors that influence it (Schroeder et al., 1995; Batson, 1998).

**The Altruism Debate**    On the surface, altruism—as an act of self-sacrifice—seems personally maladaptive. The hero who risks life and limb to save a victim and the philanthropist who donates large sums of money come out losers in the exchange. Or do they? Evolutionary psychologists claim that in the fight for survival, helpfulness can perpetuate our own "selfish" genes (Dawkins, 1989). One way this may operate is that people of all cultures follow the norm of reciprocity—a moral code that directs us to help, not hurt, those who have helped us. Helping can thus be considered a long-term investment in the future. Evolutionary psychologists also point out that people are quick to help their own offspring, followed by other family members in proportion to their genetic relatedness and strangers who are similar to themselves. The result: self-sacrificing behavior that, paradoxically, promotes one's own genetic immortality (Rushton, 1989; Burnstein et al., 1994).

*In March of 1999, this two-year-old Kosovar Albanian boy was passed between family members in a refugee camp. According to evolutionary psychologists, people often sacrifice their own lives to assist in the survival of genetically related family members.*

It is often said that helpfulness serves short-term personal interests as well. According to some theorists, people decide whether to intervene by weighing the costs (time, stress, the risk of injury) against the benefits (financial reward, praise, social

**altruism**    Helping behavior that is motivated primarily by a desire to benefit others, not oneself.

**empathy-altruism hypothesis** The proposition that an empathic response to a person in need produces altruistic helping.

approval, a feeling of satisfaction). This decision making may not be conscious, but if the anticipated benefits exceed the anticipated costs, we help; if not, we stay put. In other words, helping is motivated not by altruism but by self-serving goals—such as financial reward, praise, recognition, a desire for a "helper's high," or even a desire to avoid feeling guilty for not helping (Cialdini et al., 1973; Fritzsche et al., 2000; Piliavin et al., 1981).

Are humans ever truly altruistic, or is our behavior always selfishly motivated? C. Daniel Batson (1991) argues that an act of assistance is altruistic when the helper's main goal is to benefit someone in need—regardless of the consequences for the helper. According to Batson's **empathy-altruism hypothesis**, diagrammed in Figure 13.19, people have two emotional reactions to someone in need: *personal distress* (guilt, anxiety, and discomfort) and *empathy* (perspective-taking, sympathy, and compassion for the other person). When the first reaction predominates, we help primarily to relieve our own discomfort—a self-centered, "egoistic" motivation. When the second reaction predominates, however, people help in order to alleviate the other's suffering—an altruistic motivation. In other words, says Batson, helping can often satisfy both selfish and noble motives.

If Batson is correct, then empathy—a genuine gut-level compassion for another person, as was evident in the World Trade Center rescue efforts—is the engine that drives pure altruism. Can empathy inspire helping? How can the two helping motives be distinguished? According to Batson, people who come face to face with a needy person—say, a beggar on the street or an accident victim—can relieve their *own* distress by offering help or by escaping the situation (out of sight, out of mind). For people with empathy for the victim, however, there is no mental escape. The *victim's* distress can be reduced only by helping.

To demonstrate, Batson and others (1981) devised a situation in which participants watched a female accomplice, posing as another participant, receive electric shocks as part of an experiment. Over closed-circuit TV, they saw that she was upset and heard her say that she had suffered an electrical accident as a child. What next? Given a choice, would participants leave the experiment, having already completed their part in it (escape), or would they volunteer to trade places with the accomplice (help)? As predicted by Batson, the choice participants made depended on their feelings of empathy for the woman. Among those low in empathy (because her values were different from theirs), only 18 percent agreed to trade places. But

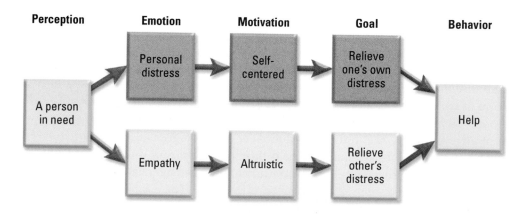

FIGURE 13.19 **Two pathways to helping**
In response to someone needing help, people feel a combination of personal distress and empathy. Accordingly, there are two paths to helping: One is self-centered (aimed at the relief of one's own discomfort), and the other is altruistic (designed to alleviate the other's suffering).

among participants who were high in empathy (because she shared similar values), 91 percent agreed to the trade. These latter participants could have made themselves feel better by leaving, but instead they stayed to help the other person. Does this mean pure altruism exists? Some say *yes* (Batson et al., 1989; Dovidio et al., 1990; Schroeder et al., 1995); others say *no* (Cialdini et al., 1987; Schaller & Cialdini, 1988).

**Bystander Intervention**    This debate about human nature is fascinating, but what inspired social psychologists to study helping in the first place were hair-raising news stories about bystanders who fail to take action even when someone's life is in danger. The problem first made headlines in March 1964. Kitty Genovese was walking home from work in Queens, New York, at 3:20 in the morning. As she crossed the street from her car to her apartment, a man with a knife appeared. She ran, but he caught up and stabbed her. She cried frantically for help and screamed, "Oh my God, he stabbed me! . . . I'm dying, I'm dying!"—but to no avail. The man fled but then returned, raped her, and stabbed her eight more times, until she was dead. In the still of the night, the attack lasted for over half an hour. Thirty-eight neighbors heard the screams, turned lights on, and came to their windows. One couple even pulled chairs up to the window and turned out the light to see better. Yet nobody came down to help. Until it was over, nobody even called the police.

What happened? How could people have been so heartless and apathetic? How could they have remained passive while a neighbor was being murdered? Rather than blame the bystanders, Bibb Latané and John Darley (1970) focused on the social factors at work in this situation. In a series of important experiments, they staged emergencies, varied the conditions, and observed what happened. In one study, Darley and Latané (1968) took participants to a cubicle and asked them to discuss the kinds of adjustment problems that college students face. For confidentiality purposes, they were told, participants would communicate over an intercom system and the experimenter would not be listening. The participants were also told to speak one at a time and to take turns. Some were assigned to two-person discussions, others to larger groups. Although the opening moments were uneventful, one participant (an accomplice) mentioned in passing that he had a seizure disorder that was triggered by pressure. Sure enough, when it came his turn to speak again, this participant struggled and pleaded for help:

> "I could really-er-use some help so if somebody would-er-give me a little . . . h-help-uh-er-er-er . . . c-could . . . somebody-er-er-help er-uh-uh-uh (choking sounds) . . . I'm gonna die-er-er-I'm . . . gonna die-er-help-er-er-seizure-er."

If you were in this situation, how would you react? Would you stop the experiment, dash out of your cubicle, and seek out the experimenter? As it turned out, the response was strongly influenced by the size of the group. Actually, all participants participated alone, but they were led to believe that others were present and that there was a real crisis. Almost all participants who thought they were in a two-person discussion left the room for help immediately. In the larger "groups," however, participants were less likely to intervene and were slower to do so when they did. In fact, the larger the group was supposed to be, the less helping occurred (see Figure 13.20). This pattern of results was labeled the **bystander effect:** The more bystanders there are, the less likely a victim is to get help. In an emergency, the presence of others paradoxically inhibits helping.

At first, this pioneering research seemed to defy all common sense. Isn't there safety in numbers? Don't we feel more secure rushing in to help when others are there for support? To understand fully what went wrong, Latané and Darley (1970) provided a careful, step-by-step analysis of the decision-making process in

**bystander effect**    The finding that the presence of others inhibits helping in an emergency.

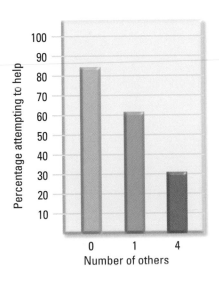

**FIGURE 13.20    The bystander effect** When participants thought that they alone heard a seizure victim in need, the vast majority sought help. As the number of bystanders increased, however, they became less likely to intervene (Darley & Latané, 1968).

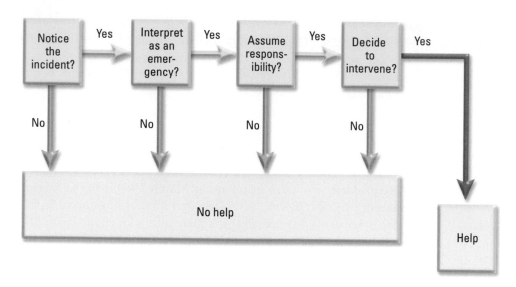

FIGURE 13.21    **A model of bystander intervention**
This step-by-step analysis suggests several reasons for the fact that bystanders often do not help in emergencies.

emergency situations. According to their scheme, bystanders help only when they *notice* the event, *interpret* it as an emergency, *take responsibility* for helping, *decide* to intervene, and then *act* on that decision (see Figure 13.21).

This analysis of the intervention process sheds light on the bystander effect, in that the presence of others can inhibit helping at each of the five steps. Consider, for example, the second requirement, that bystanders interpret an event as an emergency. Have you ever heard screaming from a nearby house and the sound of crashing objects, only to wonder if you were overhearing an assault or just a family quarrel? Cries of pain may sound like shrieks of laughter, and heart-attack victims may be mistaken for drunk. How do other bystanders influence our interpretation? Faced with a sudden, possibly dangerous event, everyone pretends to stay calm. As each person sees that others seem indifferent, they shrug it off. As a result, the event no longer feels like an emergency.

This process was observed in a study in which Latané and Darley (1970) had participants fill out questionnaires alone or in groups of three. After the experimenter left, white smoke was pumped into the room through a vent. Alone, most participants worried that there was a fire and quickly reported the smoke to the experimenter. Yet in the company of others, most participants did not seek help. In some groups, the smoke was so thick that participants rubbed their eyes and waved fumes away from their face as they worked on the questionnaires, but they did not call for help. Why not? In postexperiment interviews, they said they assumed the smoke was harmless steam, air-conditioning vapor, or even "truth gas"—but not a fire.

The presence of others also inhibits helping by causing a **diffusion of responsibility,** a belief that others will intervene. Thirty-eight people watched from their apartments and did nothing while Kitty Genovese was killed. Participants in the group conditions of the seizure experiment also did not intervene. When participants thought that they alone could hear the victim, making them solely responsible for his welfare, they took action. Many of those who thought that others were also present, however, behaved like the neighbors of Kitty Genovese: They stayed put

**diffusion of responsibility**    In groups, a tendency for bystanders to assume that someone else will help.

## THE PROCESS OF DISCOVERY

# JOHN M. DARLEY
## *The Bystander Effect*

**Q: How did you first become interested in psychology?**

**A:** My mom and dad were both academic psychologists. When I was a teenager, my dad was directing the Laboratory for Research in Human Relations, which was then the home for the Kurt Lewin Group Dynamics Lab. During that time period, Leon Festinger, Stan Schachter, and Hank Reicken had joined an "end of the world" cult that they later wrote about from a social psychological perspective, and so our living room was host to the first discussions of their amazing observations. Clearly, psychology could be an enormously exciting career, so I majored in psychology at Swarthmore and went on to receive my Ph.D. from Harvard.

**Q: How did you come up with your important discovery?**

**A:** In 1964, just after I started teaching at NYU, all of New York City was discussing the "Kitty Genovese incident" in which a young woman had been stabbed to death while all who witnessed failed to intervene. Toward the end of that week, Bibb Latané and I met for a long-scheduled dinner. Like everyone else, we discussed the incident and the prevailing "pop psychology" reactions to it—which were that a randomly chosen set of Queens dwellers were somehow all "alienated," "apathetic," or secretly harboring hostile impulses from the frustrations of living in the city. At first rather idly, but then with increasing excitement, we talked through the social psychological processes that could cascade to produce non-responding even from bystanders who were normal, decent people. The design for our research project emerged on the paper tablecloth of a Greenwich Village restaurant!

**Q: How has the field you inspired developed over the years?**

**A:** Since our initial studies, other researchers have done elegant work in what I suppose is now recognized as a research field of bystander intervention. Related work has also given us the overarching field of helping and cooperation, or "prosocial behavior." Perhaps the discoveries made in this work have contributed to recent efforts to develop a more complete account of human thinking and action, in which positive impulses are present as well as the negative ones. (I think, for example, of the studies of altruism that ask whether people are motivated to help by self-serving motives or by other-oriented values.) Keeping one's eye on these positive impulses in the shadow of the Holocaust and the World Trade Towers is a difficult task, but a necessary one.

**Q: What is your prediction on where the field is heading?**

**A:** Our studies of the "spontaneous dynamics" of bystander intervention generated many other studies, and the bystander stream has flowed together with research on more considered acts of helping, such as donating money and even willingness to make blood, kidney, and bone marrow donations. In general terms, this now is the study of prosocial behavior. Colleagues and I are now considering what makes citizens voluntarily expend the efforts necessary to make their societies prosper and succeed, again a form of positive voluntary behavior that is broadly "pro-societal" in nature.

*John M. Darley is Warren Professor of Psychology at Princeton University.*

because they assumed someone else was helping. Indeed, laboratory research has confirmed that individuals working in groups diffuse the responsibility for their collective performance, with each member assuming less responsibility as the number of others present increases from two to eight (Forsyth et al., 2002).

The bystander effect is powerful and scary. Over the years, researchers have observed behavior in different kinds of staged crises. Would participants report a theft or a possible fire? Would they stop for a stranded motorist, help a person who faints or sprains an ankle, or try to break up a fight? Would they rush to the aid of a seizure victim, a subway passenger who staggers and falls to the ground, or an

1. When the bystander is in a good mood
2. When the bystander feels guilty or needs a self-esteem boost
3. When the bystander observes someone else helping
4. When the bystander is not pressed for time
5. When the bystander is male and the victim female
6. When the victim makes a direct request for help
7. When the victim is physically attractive
8. When the victim appears to deserve help
9. When the victim is similar in some way to the bystander
10. In a small town or rural area, not a large city

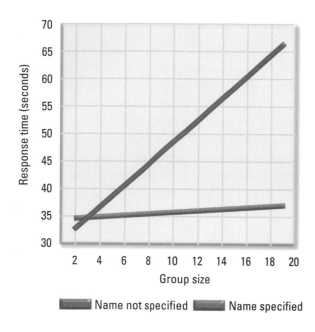

FIGURE 13.22  **Cyberhelping**
In this study, individuals participating in an online chat room saw a plea for help. Illustrating the bystander effect, the more others thought to be present, the slower people were to respond. If the individual's name was identified in the request for help, however, the inhibiting effect of other bystanders on helping was eliminated.

## REVIEW QUESTIONS

- *Summarize the biological and environmental factors that influence aggression.*

- *What is deindividuation, and how does it contribute to aggression?*

- *According to Batson's empathy-altruism hypothesis, when are people likely to help?*

- *What is the bystander effect, and how can it be explained?*

experimenter having an asthma attack? What are the odds that a person in need will actually receive help? Clearly, helping depends in complex ways on various characteristics of the victim, the bystanders, and the situation (see Table 13.1). The fact remains, however, that a person is less likely to intervene in a group than when alone. Even more remarkable is that victims are more likely to get help from someone when their welfare rests on the shoulders of a single potential helper than when many others are present (Latané & Nida, 1981).

If ever you are in need of help in public, is there anything you can do to get someone to step out from the shadow of the crowd? Consider the necessary steps to intervention, and you will see that a person in need should draw attention to himself or herself, make it clear that help is needed, and single out an individual bystander—through eye contact, by pointing, or even by making a direct request. In a recent extension of Latané and Darley's research to "cyberhelping," a plea for help was made to nearly five thousand participants in some four hundred Internet chat rooms. As shown in Figure 13.22, the more others that were assumed to be on line, the slower the participants were to help. When the person in need addressed participants by name, however, the bystander effect was eliminated. In this case, the helping response was quick—regardless of how many others were supposedly in the chat room (Markey, 2000).

The study of bystander intervention raises important social policy questions. In deciding whether to intervene, bystanders are responsive to the perceived costs and benefits of their actions. Some governments have thus sought to encourage helping among its citizens by enacting "Good Samaritan" laws that require people to offer or summon aid in an emergency. After the tragic car accident in Paris that killed Princess Diana, her companion, and their driver, French authorities arrested the photographers who had arrived at the crash scene and allegedly took pictures of the accident victims rather than come to their aid. In French law, it is a crime not to provide assistance in this type of situation. In the final 1998 episode of the TV show *Seinfeld*, the four main characters were arrested, convicted, and sentenced to prison for callously failing to help someone in need. In reality, Good Samaritan laws—which use the threat of punishment to increase the cost of not helping—are rare. But some states have enacted "immunity from liability" laws designed to lower the cost of helping by protecting Good Samaritans against possible lawsuits. To the extent that people weigh costs and benefits in deciding to intervene, perhaps it is possible to encourage helpfulness among people as a matter of policy.

# THINKING LIKE A PSYCHOLOGIST ABOUT SOCIAL INFLUENCES

Let's step back for a moment and revisit Milgram's studies of obedience to authority. This counterintuitive if not shocking research cries out the message of social psychology: that people are influenced in profound ways by their social surroundings. At the core, human beings are highly social creatures. We need each other, sometimes desperately. This is precisely why we have the power to influence others—and why we are sometimes so vulnerable to manipulation by others.

Think about the 9/11 attack on the World Trade Center and on the material presented in this chapter, and you'll see

that human social behavior is filled with contradiction and that social psychology's focus on the power of the situation comes across for a wide range of behaviors—and in a wide range of settings. Studies of social perception, interpersonal attraction, conformity, persuasion, group processes, aggression, and altruism clearly show that each of us is influenced and even changed, for better and for worse, by the words and actions of other people.

# SUMMARY

Social psychology is the study of how individuals think, feel, and behave in social situations. The principal message is that people can influence one another's behavior in profound ways.

## SOCIAL PERCEPTION

Social perception refers to the processes of coming to know and evaluate other people. To a large extent, the impressions we form of others are based on our observations of their behavior.

### MAKING ATTRIBUTIONS

People make attributions for other people's behavior. According to **attribution theory**, people analyze a person's behavior and its situational context in order to make a personal attribution or a situational attribution. According to Kelley, people use three types of information in making attributions: consensus (how other people react in the situation), distinctiveness (how the target person reacts in other situations), and consistency (how the target person reacts at different times).

Other studies point to attribution errors and biases. In explaining the behavior of others, we typically overestimate the role of personal factors, the **fundamental attribution error**. This tendency may be unique to cultures that value individualism. Attributions can also be biased by self-serving motivations, as people are more likely to make self-attributions for success than for failure.

### FORMING IMPRESSIONS

In perceiving others, people are subject to a **primacy effect** by which first impressions weigh heavily and are highly resistant

to change. Through various cognitive-confirmation biases, first impressions guide the way they interpret later contradictory evidence. Through behavioral-confirmation biases, we often alter our behavior and unwittingly shape others in ways that confirm our impressions.

## ATTRACTION

Several factors spark a positive impression, or attraction. The first is familiarity. Through the **mere-exposure effect**, exposure to a person increases liking. A second factor is physical attractiveness. People like others who are physically attractive and behave more warmly toward them. Third, people like others who are similar in attitudes and interests.

## SOCIAL INFLUENCE

### SOCIAL INFLUENCE AS "AUTOMATIC"

As social animals, human beings are vulnerable to a host of subtle, almost reflexlike influences. This was demonstrated in studies showing that, in both social and nonsocial situations, people unconsciously mimic each other's behaviors.

### CONFORMITY

**Conformity** is the tendency to change one's opinion or behavior in response to social norms. Classic studies by Sherif and Asch revealed two types of social influence. People demonstrating **informational influence** go along with the group and change their opinions because they believe the others are correct. **Normative influence** leads people to conform only in their public behavior because they fear social rejection.

Conformity increases with group size (up to a point) and with the salience of social norms. Conformity decreases when an ally is present. Cultural factors are also important, as more conformity is found in cultures that value social harmony. Nonconformists are unpopular, but they can influence majorities by sticking to their positions with consistency and confidence.

History offers many examples of crimes committed in the name of obedience. Milgram's research showed that even decent people can violate the conscience on command. By varying characteristics of the authority, victim, and situation, he was able to determine what factors increase the likelihood of obedience.

## ATTITUDES AND ATTITUDE CHANGE

To have lasting effects, social influence must change not just behavior but **attitudes**. Attitude change, or persuasion, can occur in two ways. On the **central route to persuasion**, people think carefully about a message and are influenced by its arguments. On the **peripheral route to persuasion**, they rely on superficial cues. The central route requires the ability and motivation to process the communication carefully.

Persuasive communication is the outcome of three factors: source, message, and audience. Source credibility and likability increase persuasiveness. Messages are persuasive if the position taken is moderately discrepant and if it uses fear to motivate change or arouses positive emotions. Audience factors are also important, such as the need for cognition and self-monitoring.

Just as attitudes influence behavior, behavior can influence attitudes. Festinger argued that behaving in attitude-discrepant ways can create an unpleasant state of **cognitive dissonance**. This leads us to change our attitudes to match or justify our behavior. The evidence supports this basic effect and the conditions in which it occurs. Theorists continue to debate the reasons for it.

## GROUP PROCESSES

People behave differently in groups than when alone. Through **social facilitation**, the presence of others enhances performance on simple tasks but impairs performance on complex tasks. Zajonc explained that the mere presence of others increases arousal and triggers our dominant response. Others have proposed different interpretations. In joint activities, people often exert less effort than they would alone.

This **social loafing** increases with group size because people do not see the link between their own effort and the desired group outcome.

**Groupthink**, a process in which members convince themselves that they are correct, is especially likely in groups that are isolated, cohesive, and homogeneous and have strong leadership. This process occurs because members feel invulnerable, become closed-minded, and are pressured toward uniformity. Groupthink raises the odds of miscalculation and failure.

## SOCIAL RELATIONS

### AGGRESSION

**Aggression** is rooted in both human biology and social factors. Although instinct theories do not account for differences among cultures, there are biological influences, perhaps even a genetic component. Men are more physically aggressive than women, and aggression is also increased by alcohol.

In general, aversive stimulation sparks aggression. Studies of the **frustration-aggression hypothesis** show that frustration correlates with aggressive behavior. Intense summer heat is also linked to aggression. Once aversive stimulation arouses negative emotion, situational cues—such as the presence of weapons and exposure to violence—prompt us to turn the feeling into action. Aggression is also increased by **deindividuation**, a loss of individuality that people sometimes experience in large groups.

### ALTRUISM

Does **altruism**—helping behavior primarily motivated by a desire to benefit others—really exist? Evolutionary psychologists theorize that by helping others we selfishly promote the long-term success of our own genes. Others say helping is motivated by short-term gains. According to Batson's **empathy-altruism hypothesis**, however, people react to someone else's need with both personal distress and empathy. When the latter reaction predominates, we have altruistic motivation.

Studies demonstrate a **bystander effect** in which the presence of others inhibits helping. The bystander effect can reduce our tendency to interpret an event as an emergency and create a **diffusion of responsibility**, a belief that others are providing the necessary help.

## KEY TERMS

social psychology (p. 502)

social perception (p. 502)

attribution theory (p. 502)

fundamental attribution error (p. 504)

primacy effect (p. 507)

mere-exposure effect (p. 511)

conformity (p. 516)

informational influence (p. 517)

normative influence (p. 517)

attitude (p. 521)

central route to persuasion (p. 522)

peripheral route to persuasion (p. 522)

cognitive dissonance (p. 525)

social facilitation (p. 527)

social loafing (p. 529)

groupthink (p. 530)

aggression (p. 531)

frustration-aggression hypothesis (p. 533)

deindividuation (p. 536)

altruism (p. 537)

empathy-altruism hypothesis (p. 538)

bystander effect (p. 539)

diffusion of responsibility (p. 540)

## THINKING CRITICALLY ABOUT SOCIAL INFLUENCES

1. Explain how behavioral confirmation biases could contribute to the perseverance of stereotypes.

2. Given what you now know about influence and persuasion, design a campaign to curb teenage smoking. Would you attempt to persuade via the central or peripheral route? How would you incorporate source, message, and audience characteristics to increase the effectiveness of your campaign? How might you use cognitive dissonance to your advantage?

3. Imagine that you are the leader of a group that must make an important decision. You would like to make sure that your group does not fall prey to groupthink. What symptoms of groupthink will you look for? What specific actions could you take to avoid it?

4. Most students, at one time or another, have experienced social loafing firsthand when working in groups for a class project. What policies could a professor implement to reduce the incidence of social loafing on group projects?

5. Is aggression innate, learned, or both? Support your position with empirical evidence. What does this imply about the most effective method(s) of reducing violence?

6. Are there any truly altruistic behaviors? What criteria did you use to define altruistic?

# CHAPTER 14

# Social and Cultural Groups

# DOES CULTURE SHAPE SOCIAL BEHAVIOR?

## THE SITUATION

Having read some social psychology, you're interested in social interaction. Most of the studies you've read about took place in North America, and you're curious about the influences of culture both here and in other parts of the world. You already know that compared to most North Americans, people from Japan maintain a longer "polite" distance while interacting and that people from other countries, such as Venezuela, set a closer, more "intimate" distance. You assume that these different norms must cause occasional misunderstanding in cross-cultural interactions, and you want to explore this question.

You're at a large university and have access to students from different countries, all of whom speak English. What if students from Japan were to converse, in Japanese, as part of an American psychology experiment? Would they adopt the usual polite distance or behave more like North Americans? What if they were to converse in English? Would that bring them even closer? Next, you wonder about students from Venezuela interacting in Spanish. Would they "crowd" each other or increase the distance according to North American norms? Again, what if they were to converse in English?

To put these questions to the test, you recruit 105 male and female Japanese, Venezuelan, and American students for a study of conversations. You want to carefully control who they talk to, so you hire six confederates (two from each country) and arrange for all the participants to interact for five minutes with a same-sex partner from their own country. You also want to standardize the situation, so you train the confederates to behave in set ways and to discuss sports and hobbies. All the foreign students and confederates are bilingual, so you instruct half to speak in their native tongue and the other half in English. In each session, you then escort the participant and confederate into a room with a one-way mirror. The confederate sits first and you prompt the participant to pull up a chair. You then leave the room and videotape the conversation from behind the mirror. Later, you review the tape and measure to the nearest inch the distance of the participant's chair from the confederate's.

## MAKE A PREDICTION

Two questions are being tested. First, will students from Japan, Venezuela, and the United States—talking to partners of the same sex and nationality—differ in the amount of distance they set? You might think that culturally ingrained interaction styles, like habits, are tough to break. On the other hand, you would not be surprised to find that people alter their behavior according to the situation they're in. Second, will students vary the distance according to the language they speak? Look at the table below and predict the number of inches from the confederate the participants set themselves. Here are two items to help guide your predictions: (1) The range is thirty to forty-five inches, and (2) on average, American participants set a distance of thirty-five inches.

| | SPEAKING NATIVE LANGUAGE | | SPEAKING ENGLISH | |
| --- | --- | --- | --- | --- |
| | Japanese | Venezuelan | Japanese | Venezuelan |
| Distance | _____ | _____ | _____ | _____ |

## THE RESULTS

The actual results are presented below. On the question of whether differences would be found among students speaking in their native tongue, the answer is *yes* (left). Compared to the American students, who were at thirty-five inches, the Japanese students sat farther and the Venezuelan students sat closer. On the question of what would happen when all participants interacted in English, you can see that the differences between the Japanese and Venezuelan participants vanished (right).

| | SPEAKING NATIVE LANGUAGE | | SPEAKING ENGLISH | |
| --- | --- | --- | --- | --- |
| | Japanese | Venezuelan | Japanese | Venezuelan |
| Distance | 40 | 32 | 39 | 40 |

## WHAT DOES IT ALL MEAN?

Like world travelers, psychologists have long known that just as people around the world speak different languages, they also differ in nonverbal aspects of communication—such as eye contact, the use of gestures, touching, and physical distance. In the study just described, Nan Sussman and Howard Rosenfeld (1982) found that the interaction styles people exhibit in their own cultures can be observed in a controlled laboratory setting—a finding that reveals the subtle ways in which culture shapes our everyday behavior. They also found, however, that people alter their interaction styles, without being told to do so, in order to suit the situation they are in—a finding that is consistent with the message of social psychology. As we'll see in this chapter, both types of influences are important—not only in studies of different cultures but also in comparisons among ethnic groups and between men and women within a culture.

The National Geographic Society surveyed eighty thousand people from 178 countries in its Survey 2000. Among the results, 80 percent believe that "people are kind" and pizza is the most popular food. To view the survey, go online to http://survey2000.nationalgeographic.com

The first time I heard the song was at the 1964 World's Fair in Queens, New York. I was eleven years old at the time, and the exhibit was called "It's a Small World." After waiting in line, my family and I were seated in a "boat" that transported us from one large room of the exhibit to another and treated us to a fantasy-like display that left a lasting imprint in my memory. There were hundreds of animated dolls colorfully dressed as children from all the continents of the world. As the dolls circled and moved about on mechanical platforms, you could hear children's voices singing in their native languages. The message of the exhibit: "There's so much that we share that it's time we're aware, it's a small world after all."

It's now some forty years later, and millions of people continue to tour this exhibit in the Disney parks of Florida, California, Paris, and Tokyo. And the message—that it's a small world—rings truer today than ever before. This smallness was evident on the eve of January 1, 2000, as millions of people all over the world watched live, via satellite, the jubilant Millennium New Year celebrations in New York, Paris, Mexico City, Beijing, Sydney, Alexandria, and other great cities. It was also tragically evident on the morning of September 11, 2001, when the attack on New York City's World Trade Center claimed victims from eighty-two countries.

This global village of ours is shrinking, bringing us all in closer contact. All over the world, people watch the Olympics broadcast on TV via satellite. Similarly, we witness live terrorist attacks, outbreaks of wars, natural disasters, royal weddings, and state funerals. People all over the world now communicate online, sharing information seamlessly over the Internet. Thanks to various international trade agreements, you can wear Levi's jeans, watch MTV, drink Coke, and eat McDonald's burgers in Moscow. In the United States, you can drive a Japanese car, fill the tank with oil from Saudi Arabia, wear clothes made in Taiwan, and eat in restaurants that serve enchiladas, lasagna, wonton soup, pita bread, sushi, curried lamb, and other international delights.

As the people of the world come into greater contact with each other, one wonders: What challenges lie ahead in the twenty-first century? Will the "smallness" of the world homogenize different cultures and ethnic and religious groups, or will it sharpen our awareness of human diversity? What about migration patterns *within* countries? Consider the changes in the American landscape resulting from recent influxes of immigrants. In the coming years, ethnic minorities will constitute a majority of the population in many cities in the United States. Will this greater heterogeneity breed tolerance of others who are different, or will it fuel conflict, prejudice, and discrimination?

Over the years, social psychologists have found that people are deeply affected by the situations they are in. Milgram's obedience experiments illustrate this point in a dramatic way (see Chapter 13). We'll also see that social and cultural groups to which we belong and, as a result, the ways that we are similar to others and different, play a prominent role. The various issues addressed in this chapter converge on another important point: For people to get along, they must have mutual tolerance, understanding, and an appreciation of the diversity of human life. If I had to sum up all of psychology—and the theme of this chapter—in just one sentence, it would be this: *Everyone is basically the same, yet no two people are alike.*

The similarities among us are so self-evident that they are invisible, taken for granted. Regardless of whether you are male or female; regardless of whether the color of your skin is black, white, brown, yellow, or olive; and regardless of where in the world you live, you squint your eyes in bright sunlight, prefer sweet foods to bitter, get lightheaded when you drink too much alcohol, smile when you're happy, have the capacity to hold seven or so items in short-term memory, forget events that took place when you were two years old, repeat behaviors that produce reinforcement, seek the company of others who are similar, respond to social pressure from peers, and react to trauma with anxiety or depression. Similarly, babies all over the world babble before uttering a word, fear strangers in the first year of life, think concretely before using abstract logic, and start yearning for sex in adolescence.

Despite the "universals" of human behavior, there are some differences—both *among* cultures and between racial and ethnic groups *within* cultures. As we'll see, these differences are largely rooted in the various physical, economic, and social environments in which people live.

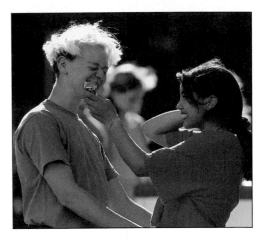

*Despite cultural diversity, there are many similarities among the people of the world. Teenagers flirt and think about sex regardless of where they live.*

## CROSS-CULTURAL PERSPECTIVES

- *What are individualism and collectivism, and how do cultures differ on this dimension?*
- *Is one orientation better, or more adaptive, than the other?*
- *Do cultures differ in the extent to which they breed conformity?*
- *Can cultures influence the way people see themselves in relation to others?*

For every two ticks of the second hand on your watch, 9 new babies are born and 3 people die. The net increase of roughly 3 human lives per second means that the world's population grows by 10,600 per hour, 254,000 per day, 1.8 million per week, 7.7 million per month, and 93 million per year. According to the United Nations,

For information on the world's populations, you can cyber-visit the United Nations at http://www.un.org/

| TABLE 14.1 | WHERE IN THE WORLD PEOPLE LIVE |
|---|---|
| **Of Every 100 People** | **Live in** |
| 21 | China |
| 16 | India |
| 5 | United States |
| 5 | Former Soviet Union |
| 4 | Indonesia |
| 3 | Brazil |
| 2 | Bangladesh |
| 2 | Japan |
| 2 | Mexico |
| 2 | Nigeria |
| 2 | Pakistan |
| 36 | All remaining countries |

there are more than 6 billion people in the world's total population, a number that is projected to reach 9 to 10 billion by the year 2050. Increasingly, people will need to live peacefully and cooperatively.

Immersed in our own ways of life, we can all too easily overlook an important fact: There is no dominant world culture. Look at Table 14.1, for example, and you'll see that of every hundred people in the two hundred or so nations of the world, the U.S. Census Bureau estimates that twenty-one live in China, sixteen live in India, and only five live in the United States. We humans are a heterogeneous lot. As a matter of *geography*, some of us live in large, heavily populated cities, whereas others live in small towns, affluent suburbs, rural farming or fishing communities, hot and humid jungles, expansive deserts, high-altitude mountains, tropical islands, and icy arctic plains. Excluding the dialects, more than sixty-eight hundred different *languages* are spoken—including Chinese, English, Hindi, Spanish, Russian, Arabic, Malay, Bengali, Portuguese, French, German, and Japanese (Grimes & Grimes, 2000). There are also hundreds of *religions* that people identify with—the most popular being Christianity (33 percent), Islam (22 percent), Hinduism (15 percent), and Buddhism (6 percent), with Judaism (0.4 percent) and others claiming fewer adherents. Roughly 15 to 20 percent of the world's population is not affiliated with a religion.

In light of the many ways in which cultures differ, psychologists make cross-cultural comparisons in order to fully understand the commonalities and boundaries of human behavior (Berry et al., 2002; Shiraev & Levy, 2001). This research is important and necessary—but also tricky. North Americans are used to answering personal questions, for example, but people in some cultures are reluctant to talk about themselves because it makes them feel uncomfortable (Fiske, 2002). It can also be difficult for researchers to translate verbal research materials from one language into another. The goal is not to create literal translations but to create materials that are equivalent in their meaning. This process involves having one bilingual person translate an item—say, from English to Spanish—then having another bilingual person "back-translate" the item from Spanish into English. If there are discrepancies in meaning, the process is repeated until linguistic equivalence is achieved. Table 14.2 presents examples—from signs displayed around the world—of what can go wrong when simple sentences are poorly translated (Triandis, 1994).

## CULTURAL DIVERSITY: A FACT OF LIFE

Linked together by space, language, religion, and historical bonds, each cultural group has its own ideology, folklore,

*After China, India is the second most populous country in the world. This scene shows a Hindu woman at the holy river Ganges.*

| TABLE 14.2 | TRANSLATION "BLOOPERS" |
|---|---|

- "Drop your trousers here for best results" (a dry cleaner in Thailand).
- "You are invited to take advantage of the chambermaid" (a hotel in Japan).
- "Ladies are requested not to have children in the bar" (a cocktail lounge in Norway).
- "The manager has personally passed on the water served here" (a hotel in Mexico).
- "Take one of our horse-driven city tours—we guarantee no miscarriages" (a tourist agency in Czechoslovakia).
- "We take your bags and send them in all directions" (an airline in Denmark).

*Source:* H. C. Triandis. (1994). *Culture and social behavior.* New York: McGraw-Hill.

music, political system, family structure, sexual mores, fashions, and foods. As governments and world travelers come to learn, sometimes the hard way, local customs and laws also vary in significant ways.

Cultural differences are sometimes striking to tourists. Visit an outdoor market in Iraq, and you should expect to barter or negotiate the price of everything you purchase. Plan a meeting with a native of Brazil, and don't be surprised if your appointment is late. It's nothing personal. In North America, it's common to sit casually opposite someone with your legs outstretched. Yet in Nepal, it's an insult to point the bottoms of your feet at someone. In Turkey, heterosexual men can embrace and kiss on the cheek. Yet in certain other parts of the world, public displays between men are considered unmanly. In Iran, Muslim women cover the lower part of the face; in European countries nearby, women paint their lips, shadow their eyes, and powder their faces. People in some parts of the world eat with forks and knives; others use chopsticks, bread, or bare hands. Some people exchange greetings by shaking hands or waving; others lower the head and bow. Even the way we space ourselves while interacting is culturally determined. Americans, Germans, the British, and most northern Europeans maintain a polite distance between themselves and others—and feel "crowded" by the closer, nose-to-nose style of the French, Greeks, Arabs, Mexicans, and people of Latin America. In the affairs of day-to-day living, each culture operates by its own implicit rules of conduct, or social norms. **Social norms** can be so different from one country to the next that people who travel for business or for pleasure should be armed with an awareness of local customs. (See *How to Avoid Social Blunders When Traveling in Foreign Cultures.*)

Just as cultures differ in their social norms, so too they differ in the extent to which people are expected to adhere to those norms. As an example, compare the United States and China. In the United States, parents teach their children to be self-reliant, independent, and assertive. In China, however, children are taught the values of conformity, loyalty, and harmony within the community. As we'll see, this comparison indicates that there are two very different cultural orientations toward persons and the groups to which they belong. One orientation centers on the individual, the other on the group.

"In the interest of cultural diversity, we've hired Jason, here, who owns a number of hip-hop CDs."

*Immersed in our own way of life we often fail to acknowledge the richness and diversity of other cultures.*

*Cultures differ in their unique, often colorful norms. Here, Spanish revelers in Pamplona hold up their bandanas before the start of the San Fermin Festival, where six fighting bulls run through the crowded streets in the center of town every morning for nine days.*

## INDIVIDUALISM AND COLLECTIVISM: A TALE OF TWO CULTURAL WORLDVIEWS

Over the years, social psychologists have observed that cultures differ in the extent to which they value **individualism** and the virtues of independence, autonomy, and self-reliance or **collectivism** and the virtues of interdependence, cooperation, and social harmony. Under the banner of individualism, personal goals take priority over group allegiances. In collectivist cultures, however, the person is, first and foremost, a loyal member of a family, team, company, church, state, and other groups

**social norms**   Implicit rules of conduct according to which each culture operates.

**individualism**   A cultural orientation in which personal goals and preferences take priority over group allegiances.

**collectivism**   A cultural orientation in which cooperation and group harmony take priority over purely personal goals.

# AVOID SOCIAL BLUNDERS WHEN TRAVELING IN FOREIGN CULTURES

Anyone who has traveled in foreign countries for business or for pleasure knows just how different local customs and laws can be. To avoid cultural misunderstandings, it helps to know some of the unspoken but powerful norms that guide the perceptions and behaviors of people in different parts of the world.

Consider something as simple as the management of time, an aspect of social life we all take for granted. Interested in the pace of life, Robert Levine and Ara Norenzayan (1999) had teams of researchers in thirty-one cities of the world measure the walking speed of pedestrians, the amount of time it took postal workers to fill a request for stamps, and the accuracy of the clocks on downtown banks. In general, they found the fastest pace of life in the cities of Western Europe and Japan and the slowest pace in the Middle East, Africa, and South America (in North America, Canada and the United States were in the middle of the list, and Mexico was last).

When the pace of life changes, you feel it. In *A Geography of Time*, Levine (1997) tells about Mexican psychologist Vicente Lopez, who spent years commuting from Tijuana to San Diego. Every time he crossed the border, he said, he had to switch into rapid clock-time mode, walking faster, talking faster, and driving faster. Then coming home at the end the day, his body would slow and relax the moment he saw the Mexican customs agent. If you do business in foreign lands, it also helps to know that cultures also differ in the way that time is spent at the office. For Americans, 80 percent of the workday is spent on task; 20 percent is spent chatting with coworkers. In India, the split is closer to 50–50.

Being able to interact smoothly with inhabitants of other cultures is not just about time. Sometimes it's about the law. For example, if you visit Saudi Arabia, an Islamic country, you'll find that it's against the law for unmarried couples to share a hotel room—and that desk clerks will

*From the Middle East to Japan, world travelers come to realize that people set different interpersonal distances and greet each other in culturally appropriate ways.*

(see Table 14.3). In what countries are these differing orientations most extreme? In a worldwide study of 116,000 employees of IBM, Geert Hofstede (1980) found that the most fiercely individualistic people were from the United States, Australia, Great Britain, Canada, and the Netherlands, in that order. The most collectivist people were from Venezuela, Colombia, Pakistan, Peru, Taiwan, and China. What is *your* orientation? Read the statements in Table 14.3 and see whether you agree or disagree

demand a marriage license as proof. Every culture also has its own customs for greetings, nonverbal communication, dining, and giving gifts. As described in Roger Axtell's (1993) *Do's and Taboos Around the World*, here are some helpful tips for the world traveler:

■ **GREETINGS.** Waving and shaking hands may seem universal, but there are different rules for greeting. In Finland, you should give a firm handshake; in France, you should loosen the grip; in Zambia, you should use your left hand to support the right; and in Bolivia, you should extend your arm if your hand is dirty. In Japan, people bow; in Thailand, they put both hands together in a praying position on the chest; and in Fiji, they smile and raise their eyebrows. In Venezuela, Paraguay, and certain other parts of Latin America, it is common for people to embrace and kiss upon meeting. In most Arab countries, men greet one another by saying, *salaam alaykum,* ("May the peace and blessings of Allah be upon you"), then shaking hands and saying, *Kaif halak,* ("How are you?") and kissing each other on the cheek.

■ **NONVERBAL COMMUNICATION.** When you don't speak the native language, it's natural to use gestures. Watch out. In Bulgaria, nodding your head means "no" and shaking your head sideways means "yes." In Germany and Brazil, the American "okay" sign (forming a circle with your thumb and forefinger) is an obscene gesture. Personal space habits also vary across cultures. Japanese people prefer to keep a comfortable distance while talking. But in Puerto Rico and much of Latin America, people stand very close—and backing off is considered an insult. Also beware of what you do with your eyes. In Latin America, locking eyes is a must, yet in Japan too much eye contact shows a lack of respect. If you're in the habit of stroking your cheek, you should know that in Italy, Greece, and Spain it means you find the person you're talking to attractive. And whatever you do, don't ever touch someone's head in a Buddhist country, especially Thailand. The head is sacred.

■ **DINING.** So much human social activity revolves around eating that it's important to accept local foods and table manners. First, be prepared for foods you may consider "exotic." For example, you may be served sheep's eyes in Saudi Arabia, raw fish in Japan, bear's paw soup in China, and lobster in the United States. Be mindful of strict religious prohibitions, and don't ask for beef in India or pork in Islamic countries. Table etiquette is also tricky. In Zambia, the guest should ask to be served, because it's impolite for the host to offer food first. In Saudi Arabia, you show your appreciation of a meal by stuffing yourself. As a dinner guest in Bolivia, you should clean your plate to prove you enjoyed the meal, but in India you should leave some food to signal to the host that you've had enough to eat. In parts of Pakistan, India, and Indonesia, you should never pass, accept, or touch food with your left hand.

■ **GIVING AND RECEIVING GIFTS.** Giving and accepting gifts are customary parts of social interaction. They also present an opportunity for misunderstanding. In Japan, gift giving is used to express friendship, gratitude, and respect. But beware: If you receive a gift, you should reciprocate—so don't get caught empty-handed. When you give a gift in Japan, however, make sure it is not wrapped in white paper, because white is associated with death. In China, avoid using red ink because messages written in red imply the severing of a relationship. Of course, what you give is as important as how you present it. Never present a bottle of wine to a Muslim, because Islam prohibits alcohol. In Hong Kong, avoid giving clocks (which symbolize death) and sharp objects (which signify the breakup of a relationship). Flowers are nice, but in Guatemala white flowers are reserved for funerals, and in Chile yellow flowers signify contempt. If you visit someone in Greece, Morocco, and many Arab countries, be careful not to admire or praise any possession too much or your host will feel obligated to give it to you.

with them. People from collectivist cultures tend to agree more with the *C* statements; those from individualistic cultures tend to agree more with the *I* statements.

Why are some cultures individualistic and others collectivistic? Speculating about the origins of these orientations, Harry Triandis (1995) suggests that there are three key factors. The first is the *complexity* of a society. As people live in more complex industrialized societies—for example, compared to a life of hunting and food

| TABLE 14.3 | INDIVIDUALISTIC AND COLLECTIVIST ORIENTATIONS |
|---|---|

1. If the group is slowing me down, it is better to leave it and work alone. (I)
2. I like my privacy. (I)
3. I can count on my relatives for help if I find myself in any kind of trouble. (C)
4. If you want something done right, you've got to do it yourself. (I)
5. It is reasonable for a son to continue his father's business. (C)
5. In the long run, the only person you can count on is yourself. (I)
7. I enjoy meeting and talking to my neighbors every day. (C)
8. I like to live close to my good friends. (C)
9. The bigger the family, the more family problems there are. (I)
10. There is everything to gain and nothing to lose for classmates to group themselves for study and discussion. (C)

*Source:* H. C. Triandis. (1995). *Individualism and collectivism.* Boulder, CO: Westview Press.

*One needs to cultivate the spirits of sacrificing the* little me *to achieve the benefits of the* big me.

—A CHINESE SAYING

*These photographs were taken of "average income" families posing in front of their homes and material possessions. Representing the individualistic orientation common in affluent societies is the Skeen family of Pearland, Texas (top). From the collectivistic orientation found in more impoverished societies is the Natoma family of Kouakourou, Mali (bottom).*

gathering among desert nomads—they have more groups to identify with (family, hometown, alma mater, church, place of employment, political party, sports teams, social clubs, and so on), which means less loyalty to any one group and a greater focus on personal rather than collective goals. Second is the *affluence* of a society. As people prosper, they gain financial independence from one another, a condition that promotes social independence, mobility, and, again, a focus on personal rather than collective goals. The third factor is *heterogeneity*. Societies that are homogeneous or "tight" (where members share the same language, religion, and social customs) tend to be rigid and intolerant of those who veer from the norm. In contrast, societies that are culturally diverse or "loose" (where two or more cultures coexist) tend to be more permissive of dissent—thus allowing for greater individual expression. Other psychologists have speculated that these cultural orientations are rooted in religious ideologies—as in the link between Christianity and individualism (Sampson, 2000).

It's important to realize that orientations toward individualism and collectivism are not set in stone within cultures and may change over time. Consider this question: If you were a parent, what traits would you like your child to develop? When this question was asked of American mothers in 1924, many chose "obedience," "loyalty," and "good manners"—key characteristics of collectivism. But when American mothers were asked the same question fifty-four years later, in 1978, they cited "independence" and "tolerance of others"— important aspects of individualism. Due, perhaps, to the greater complexity, affluence, and diversity of Western life in general, similar trends were also found in Germany, Italy, and England (Remley, 1988)—and in laboratory experiments, where conformity rates are somewhat lower today than in the past (Bond & Smith, 1996).

It's also important to realize that individualism and collectivism are not simple opposites on a continuum, and that the similarities and differences between countries do not fill a simple pattern. Daphna Oyserman and others (2002) conducted a meta-analysis of many thousands of respondents in eight-three studies. Within the United States, they found that African Americans were the most individualistic subgroup and that Asian and Latino Americans were the most collectivistic. Comparing nations, they found that Americans as a group are relatively individualistic. Collectivist orientations varied within Asia, however, as the Chinese were more collectivistic than Japanese and Korean respondents.

**Conceptions of the Self**  Individualism and collectivism can be so deeply ingrained in a culture that they mold our very self-conceptions and identities. According to Hazel Markus and Shinobu Kitayama (1991), people who grow up in individualistic countries see themselves as entities that are *independent*—distinct, autonomous, and endowed with unique dispositions. By contrast, people from more collectivist countries hold *interdependent* views of the self as part of a larger social network that includes family, coworkers, friends, and others with whom they are socially connected. People with independent views say that "The only person you can count on is yourself" and "I enjoy being unique and different from others." Those with interdependent views are more likely to agree that "I'm partly to blame if one of my family members or coworkers fails" and "My happiness depends on the happiness of those around me" (Rhee et al., 1995; Singelis, 1994; Triandis et al., 1998). These contrasting orientations—one focused on the personal self, the other on the collective self—are depicted in Figure 14.1.

Research confirms a close link between culture and conceptions of the self. David Trafimow and others (1991) had American and Chinese college students complete twenty sentences beginning with "I am ____." He found that the Americans were more likely to fill in the blank with personal trait descriptions ("I am shy"), whereas the Chinese were more likely to identify themselves by group affiliations ("I am a college student"). It's no wonder that in China, the family name comes *before* one's personal name.

These differing conceptions of the self can influence the way people perceive themselves and others. Markus and Kitayama (1991) identified two interesting differences between East and West. The first is that people in individualistic cultures strive for personal achievement, whereas those living in collectivist cultures derive more of their self-esteem through the status of a valued group. Thus, whereas North Americans overestimate their own contributions to a team effort, take credit for success, and blame others for their own failure, people from collectivist cultures underestimate their own role and present themselves in more modest, self-effacing terms in relation to others in the group (Akimoto & Sanbonmatsu, 1999; Heine et al., 2001).

A second consequence of these differing conceptions of the self is that American college students see themselves as less similar to others than do Asian Indian students. This finding reinforces the idea that people with independent conceptions of the self believe they are unique. In fact, our cultural orientations toward conformity or independence may even lead us to favor all things similar or unique. Heejung Kim and Hazel Markus (1999) showed abstract figures to participants from the United States and Korea. Each figure contained nine parts. Most of the parts were identical in shape, position, and direction. One or more were different. Look at Figure 14.2. Which of the nine subfigures within each group do you like most? The American participants liked the

*Exhibiting a collectivist orientation, two hundred Amish men and women come together for a barn raising. After an arsonist set fire to several barns in this Pennsylvania community, the men built new structures, while the women prepared lunch. This barn was rebuilt in ten hours.*

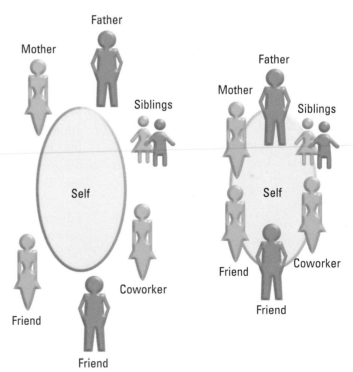

**FIGURE 14.1  Self-conceptions**
Markus and Kitayama (1991) find that people from individualistic cultures see themselves as independent and distinct from others (left). In contrast, people in collectivist cultures see themselves as interdependent, as part of a larger social network (right).

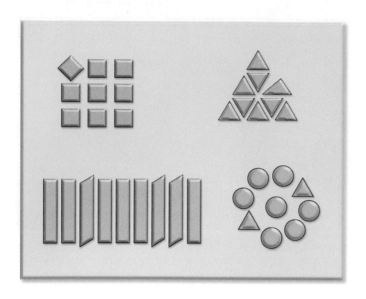

**FIGURE 14.2**
Which subfigure within each set do you prefer? Kim and Markus (1999) found that Americans tend to like subfigures that "stand out" as unique or in the minority, whereas Koreans tend to like subfigures that "fit in" with the surrounding group.

subfigures that were unique or in the minority, whereas Korean participants preferred those that "fit in" as part of the group.

In another study, Kim and Markus approached people of American and East Asian heritage at San Francisco's International Airport to fill out a questionnaire. Afterward, as a gift, they offered participants a choice of one pen from a handful of pens, three or four of which had the same color barrel, green or orange. The result: 74 percent of Americans chose a uniquely colored pen, and 76 percent of East Asians selected one of the commonly colored pens. It seems that our culturally ingrained orientations to conformity or independence leave a mark on us, leading us to form preferences for things that either "fit in" or "stand out."

Are people from disparate cultures locked into thinking about the self in either personal or collective terms, or are both aspects of the self present in everyone, to be expressed according to the situation? Recall the study described earlier, in which American students described themselves more in terms of personal traits, and Chinese students cited more group affiliations. In a follow-up, Trafimow and others (1997) studied high school and college students from Hong Kong, all of whom spoke English as a second language. Half of the participants were given the "Who am I?" test in Chinese, and the other half took it in English. Did this variation influence the results? Yes. Among these Hong Kong students, those who described themselves in English focused more on personal traits, whereas those who took the test in Chinese focused more on group affiliations. It appears that people have both personal and collective aspects of the self to draw on. The part that comes to mind depends on the situation.

**Developmental Influences** Culturally prescribed socialization practices that breed independence or interdependence begin soon after a baby is born. In the United States, a vast majority of middle-class parents who can afford it put their babies to bed in a separate room. Indeed, pediatrician Benjamin Spock (1945)—author of the best-selling child-care book ever—advised that it is better "not to take the child into the parents' bed for any reason" (p. 101). Most parents never think twice about it. Separate sleeping arrangements are just a part of independence training. Yet in most other countries of the world, it is common for young children to sleep in the same room, and even in the same bed, with parents (Whiting & Edwards, 1988). Perhaps that is part of *inter*dependence training. To many non-Americans, it's cruel to force babies to lie alone in a dark room. When Mayan mothers from Guatemala were told of this practice, they reacted with shock, disapproval, and pity. As one disbelieving mother asked, "But there's someone else with them there, isn't there?" (Morelli et al., 1992).

Socialization fosters different cultural orientations in other ways, too. In individualistic cultures, parents are quick to wean infants from the breast and to toilet train their toddlers out of diapers. Teenagers fight to separate from parents, and adults struggle to resolve the "identity crisis" that seems to plague us all. With all the focus on "me," the individual, it's no wonder that bookstore shelves are lined with paperbacks on how to "get in touch with your feelings," "speak your mind," "fulfill your potential," and become "self-actualized." In many ways, we take our cultural orientations for granted. Consider the vital issue of marriage, a lifetime commitment, and ponder this question: If a man or woman had all other qualities you desired, would you marry this person if you were not in love? In North America, only 4 percent

# HAZEL ROSE MARKUS
*Cultural Influences on the Self*

**Q: How did you first become interested in psychology?**

**A:** My family moved from London to Los Angeles when I was just entering school. I always paid close attention to everyone around me and saw that there were differences in how to behave in different places. I was also surprised at how people in what appeared to be similar conditions often behaved so differently.

**Q: How did you come up with your important discovery?**

**A:** Maybe it was because I was in graduate school during the "me" decade of the 1970s but it always seemed obvious to me that the *self* was of central importance to people. The self is the place where the person meets society. If people engage different social contexts and environments, they will have different selves.

When I taught at the University of Michigan, we had an exchange program with Osaka University in Japan. I gave lectures there about the importance of self-esteem. One day my colleague and friend Shinobu Kitayama said, "Did you realize that nothing you say about the self makes sense in Japan?" He probably said it more politely, but this is what I remember. His remark was disconcerting, but it was not really shocking. If selves differ depending on the situation, then it made sense. Since Japanese and American worlds were so different, it was hardly surprising that Japanese and American selves would also differ.

At the time, my daughter was small and we were listening to Sesame Street tapes. I remember one song in which Grover sang: "I am very proud of me/ I think I will sing out loud of me/ There ought to be a crowd of me/ Because I am so special!" Grover's positive, self-oriented view fit well with our studies showing that American college students think they are smarter, more social, more athletic, and more moral than their peers. Yet my Japanese colleagues were amazed by Grover's song. Praising the self is not common in Japan, and we found that Japanese college students do not show these self-enhancing tendencies.

**Q: How has the field you inspired developed over the years?**

**A:** Many psychologists are now interested in cultural variations in cognition, emotion, motivation, personality, development, psychopathology, stereotyping and prejudice, intergroup processes, and organizational behavior. We now know that it is important to attend to a person's significant social and cultural contexts.

**Q: What is your prediction on where the field is heading?**

**A:** Many students from diverse ethnic, religious, and socioeconomic backgrounds within North America and around the world are now entering psychology. They bring with them perspectives that differ from those of their middle-class European and American predecessors who had organized the field. It is an exciting time for psychology. We are now beginning to reveal important differences and universals in human social behavior. My prediction is that the field will become increasingly interested in the human capacity to make meaning, share ideas, and build distinct worlds according to these ideas.

*Hazel Rose Markus is Professor of Psychology and Davis-Brack Professor of Behavioral Sciences at Stanford University.*

of respondents say they would. Yet that number is 8 percent in England and up to 49 percent in India and 51 percent in Pakistan. In parts of India, even today, families arrange for the future marriage of their children (Levine, 1993). The influence of culture on love is interesting. At first, you might think that the rugged individualism found in Western cultures would inhibit the tendency to become intimate and interdependent with others. But in cultures that value individual rights, people feel free to make marital decisions according to their own feelings —not family concerns, social obligations, religious constraints, income, and the like (Dion & Dion, 1996).

**The Social Consequences**   Try as they do to be objective, cross-cultural researchers cannot help but make value judgments about the individualist and collectivist orientations. Is one orientation better, more adaptive, more productive, or more humane? There is no quick and simple answer. Predictably, individualists are less likely than collectivists to follow social norms. In Chapter 13, we saw that when American participants were confronted with confederates who made incorrect perceptual judgments, they conformed to this incorrect majority 37 percent of the time (Asch, 1951). When similar tasks were given to participants from collectivist cultures, conformity rates were even higher. Among the Bantu of Zimbabwe, where deviance is punished, 51 percent conformed. John Berry (1979) compared participants from seventeen cultures and found that conformity rates ranged from a low of 18 percent among Inuit hunters of Baffin Island to a high of 60 percent among village-living Temne farmers of West Africa. More recent analyses have shown that conformity rates are generally higher in cultures that are collectivistic rather than individualistic in their orientation (Bond & Smith, 1996).

There is a drawback to individualism. If everyone focuses on personal goals, then the group as a whole suffers. The baseball player who worries more about his batting average than the team's winning percentage is a case in point. We saw in Chapter 13 that people often exert less effort, or "loaf" on the job, when they work as part of a group than when they work alone (Latané et al., 1979). To many of us, it seems natural to slack off when others are there to pick up the slack. But social loafing is not equally strong all over the world. For example, research shows that Chinese participants in Taiwan work harder in a group than they do for themselves alone (Gabrenya et al., 1983). In collectivist cultures, what's good for the group is good for the individual.

Ironically, the benefit of collectivism may also be its main flaw. Intimately connected to groups, collectivists are loyal and team-spirited, willing to risk personal gain for the group's long-term well-being, and sometimes even willing to fight and die for their group. But how do collectivists behave toward members of other groups? Because they identify so strongly with their own, collectivists tend to see their own norms as universal and exploit outsiders for competitive gain. In a study of interpersonal conflict, Kwok Leung (1988) found that Chinese participants were less likely than Americans to pursue a conflict with a friend, but they were more likely to confront a stranger. As Triandis put it, "While collectivists are very nice to those who are members of their own groups, they can be very nasty, competitive, and uncooperative toward those who belong to other groups" (quoted in Goleman, 1990, p. 41). The result: The collective "we" may fuel intergroup tensions and promote ethnic, regional, national, and religious conflict against the collective "them."

---

## REVIEW QUESTIONS

- *Provide examples of different cultural norms.*

- *Distinguish between individualism and collectivism. What three factors contribute to these different cultural orientations?*

- *How do individualistic and collectivistic orientations influence the self-concept?*

- *Describe some of the socialization practices that foster cultural orientation.*

---

## MULTICULTURAL PERSPECTIVES

- *Is immigration a worldwide phenomenon, or is it largely restricted to the United States?*
- *What is acculturation, and why is the process often stressful?*
- *How do immigrants cope with the formation of an ethnic identity?*

In Beijing in March 2002, twenty-five North Korean citizens rushed past Chinese guards and burst into the Spanish Embassy. Complaining of food shortages and poor living conditions, the group sought asylum—which they were granted—in neighboring South Korea. "We are now at the point of such desperation and live in such fear of persecution within North Korea," they said, "that we have come to the decision to risk our lives for freedom rather than passively await our doom." Upset by the political and economic climate at home, these men, women, and children desperately wanted to start a new life.

## ETHNIC DIVERSITY: A FACT OF LIFE

The names, dates, and places may change, but this script is replayed time after time. A few years ago, thousands of Albanians seeking political freedom stole into the night and sailed across the Adriatic Sea to Italy. Most but not all were sent back. Similarly, thousands of Haitian refugees received political asylum in neighboring countries, Mexicans crossed the border into the United States, Afghans escaped war to Pakistan, Pakistanis moved to Great Britain, Turks sought employment in Germany, and Russian Jews moved from their homeland to Israel. Immigration is not the only source of ethnic diversity within a culture. In some cases, ethnic groups inhabit a country because they don't have their own homeland. Thus, many Sikhs live in Pakistan and India; Kurds inhabit Turkey and Iraq; Basques live in Spain; Tamils live in Sri Lanka; Palestinians are scattered throughout the Middle East; and Navajo, Sioux, and other Native Americans live within the United States (Times Books, 2000; Turner, 2002).

*Illustrating a collectivist orientation, employees of Celcom—Malaysia's first private telecommunications company—march in corporate cadence.*

Like most countries, the United States has a culturally and ethnically mixed population—and it is becoming even more so with time. According to the U.S. Census Bureau, out of approximately 287 million U.S. citizens, 28 million were born in another country. As self-categorized, 77 percent of the population are of European descent or Middle Eastern descent; 13 percent are of African descent; 13 percent are of Hispanic origin and trace their roots to Mexico, Puerto Rico, Central America, Cuba, and other Spanish-speaking countries; 4 percent are from Asia or the Pacific Islands, the largest group being Chinese; 1.5 percent are Native Americans, Eskimos, and Aleuts; and 4 percent are from other groups. These figures total more than 100 percent because some people identify with more than one ethnic category.

Growing racial and ethnic diversity within many countries of the world presents us all with new challenges and an uncertain future. How do the different groups within a culture coexist? Why, so often, is there animosity and conflict? More specifically, what are the causes and effects of discrimination, and how can this chronic social disease be treated? These and other questions have triggered, in recent years, an examination of multicultural research, the study of racial and ethnic groups within a culture.

## ACCULTURATION AND ETHNIC IDENTITY

When people migrate from one country to another, they bring with them a cultural heritage and lifestyle that reach deep into the past. The result is that each racial or ethnic group is unique—similar to the dominant culture in some ways, different in others. For example, African American psychologist James Jones (1991) argues that compared to white Americans, African Americans tend to be more present-oriented, improvisational, expressive, spiritual, and emotional. With ancestors in Africa or among slaves of the American South, many black people have a colorful and conspicuous behavior style—as seen in a certain slow, casual, and rhythmic walk; in handshakes such as the "high five" and "thumb grasp"; and in sports, where athletes spike footballs into the end zone and slam dunk basketballs through the hoop (Majors, 1991).

Regardless of where racial or ethnic groups come from, how they get there, or why they leave their land of origin, all face the same core dilemma: whether to blend

In 1976, there were sixty-seven Spanish-language radio stations in the United States. Now there are more than three hundred (Market Segment Research, Inc.).

*Many cultural and ethnic groups in the United States retain the traditions of their homeland. Chinese Americans honor the Chinese New Year, Mexican Americans celebrate Cinco de Mayo, and Muslim Americans pray in a local mosque.*

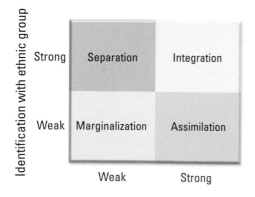

**FIGURE 14.3 Acculturation strategies**

**acculturation** The process by which individuals are changed by their immersion in a new culture.

into the new culture or retain a separate identity, language and all. There are two radically different historical perspectives on how this conflict between old and new should be managed. One is the romantic American ideal that all immigrant groups discard their heritage culture and blend into the American way of life. This assimilationist view is captured by the image of a *melting pot* in which all ethnic groups are mixed together to produce one harmonious mainstream culture. In the United States, this ideal is formalized in the laws that require immigrants to renounce other citizenships, pass a test of American history, and take an oath of loyalty.

The second approach encourages immigrants to retain their ancestral heritage, producing an ethnically diverse culture. In 1971, Canada adopted a policy of multiculturalism, in which the image of a melting pot was replaced by one of a colorful mosaic whereby each cultural group takes pride in its own unique identity and tolerates differences among groups. Research shows, for example, that many recent Greek, Arab, and Italian immigrants to North America want their children to retain their own cultural identity (Moghaddam et al., 1993).

Torn between the need to fit in and a desire to retain their own heritage, ethnic-group members differ in how they manage **acculturation**—the process by which persons are changed by their immersion in a new culture. John Berry (1997) notes four types of coping strategies. At one extreme is *assimilation,* in which the person abandons the old for the new and completely embraces his or her host culture—its language, customs, identity, and ways of life. At the opposite extreme is *separation,* a pattern characterized by a desire to maintain one's ethnic traditions and not become part of the host culture. Native American Indians who live on reservations and the Amish who live in Lancaster, Pennsylvania, are good examples. A third strategy is *integration,* a bicultural pattern in which the person tries to make the best of both worlds by retaining old traditions while adapting to the new way of life. The fourth strategy is *marginalization,* in which the person has no desire to maintain traditional ties or adopt the new host culture, perhaps due to prejudice and discrimination. These four types of acculturation strategies are summarized in Figure 14.3.

This conflict is poignantly illustrated in Eric Liu's (1998) *The Accidental Asian.* In this book, Liu describes what it feels like to be pulled by two worlds and how he has resolved the conflict. Liu is the son of Chinese immigrants from Taiwan. After growing up in a small town in New York, he went to Yale University, wrote speeches for President Clinton after he graduated, married a white American woman, and attended Harvard Law School. Despite his outward appearance, Liu says he doesn't feel particularly *Asian* American and that he sees the dual identity as largely unnecessary. Although they represent only 4 percent of the U.S. population, Asian Americans have the highest median income of all racial groups, including whites. Thus, "Asian Americans are only as isolated as they want to be," Liu writes. "They—we—do not face levels of discrimination and hatred that demand an enclave mentality." Liu admits that he is sometimes jolted from complacency by incidents of anti-Asian hate crimes, college-admission quotas that limit Asian American attendance, and other forms of discrimination. But he sees these as exceptions to the rule. Liu's book set off a storm of controversy in the Asian American community. Some applauded Liu's success and courage in speaking out against identity politics, but others were infuriated by his apparent lack of ethnic pride. For many Americans, Liu's dilemma is theirs as well. So what's the process by which this dilemma is resolved?

Because of acculturation pressures, people who are caught between cultures come to identify with one or both of these cultures in the formation of an **ethnic identity**. Thus, French-speaking residents of Quebec may think of themselves as French, Canadian, French Canadian, or none of those; Irish Americans identify themselves as Irish, American, or Irish American. Jean Phinney (1996) notes that our ethnic identities are revealed in the way we label ourselves; in our sense of belonging to and pride in a group; and in the extent to which we speak the language, study the history, follow the customs, and enjoy the food, music, dance, literature, holidays, and traditions. Phinney also notes that ethnic-identity formation typically begins in adolescence with a passive acceptance of the dominant culture, is followed in early adulthood by an awakening of interest in one's roots, and culminates later on in an ethnic identification. As you might expect, ethnic-group identification is stronger among immigrants who enter the host country as adults than it is among those who arrive at a younger, more formative age. For people who adopt a new homeland—particularly for those who belong to a stigmatized minority group— ethnic identity is fundamental to their self-concept (Phinney, 2000).

Acculturation is so important for the way people adapt to a change in homeland that researchers are seeking to measure the extent to which people identify with their ethnic and host cultures. For example, Margaret Stephenson (2000) developed a "multigroup" test for use with minorities in the United States. This questionnaire independently asks respondents to report on their orientation both toward their native culture ("I think in my native language," "I like to listen to music of my ethnic group") and toward their new host culture ("I feel at home in the United States," "I like to eat American foods").

Regardless of how immigrants, refugees, displaced natives, and other minorities adapt to the cultural landscape, some individuals and groups have a more difficult time than others in making the adjustment. The problem used to be called "culture shock." Now the term **acculturative stress** is used. Either way, studies show that entering a new culture may bring about anxiety, depression, and other mental-health problems—and that these problems are linked to language barriers, lack of familiarity with the host culture, lack of education, rejection of one's group, prejudice, the absence of social-support services, and other factors (Berry et al., 2002). Is there a healthy, optimum way for new Americans to cope with being strangers in a strange land, like fish swimming outside of the mainstream? Consider the acculturation strategies described earlier. Is it better to become "integrated" and bicultural, or should people shed their native past in an effort to become fully "assimilated" into the host culture?

Juan Sanchez and Diana Fernandez (1993) sought to answer this question in a study of Hispanic Americans in Miami. They administered questionnaires to 164 college students who were born in Cuba, Puerto Rico, Latin America, Central America, or the United States. One questionnaire measured the extent to which participants identified with their ethnic group ("I have a sense of belonging to

**ethnic identity**  The part of a person's identity that is defined by an ethnic heritage, language, history, customs, and so on.

**acculturative stress**  The stress and mental-health problems often found in immigrants trying to adjust to a new culture.

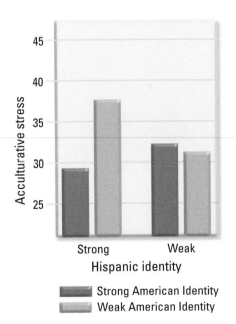

**FIGURE 14.4  The link between cultural identity and acculturative stress**
In Miami, Hispanic American students answered questions about their Hispanic and American identities and acculturative stress. As shown, students who were "integrated" (leftmost bar) reported less stress than those who did not identify with one or both cultures.

Hispanic heritage"), a second measured the extent to which they identified with North American culture ("I consider myself an American"), and the third assessed feelings of acculturative stress ("People look down on me if I practice customs of my culture," "It is difficult to show off my family"). As shown in Figure 14.4, students who were classified as integrated—those who had a strong ethnic identification *and* who embraced American culture—reported less acculturative stress than students who did not identify with one or both cultures. Similar results were found in a study of Chinese, Japanese, Korean, Vietnamese, and other Asian college students in British Columbia, Canada (Ryder et al., 2000).

These correlations should be interpreted with caution. They may mean that identification with the host culture reduces stress—or that a lack of acculturative stress promotes identification. Either way, the correlations are consistent with the increasingly popular notion that bicultural competence is psychologically adaptive, as it enables a person to alternate, without tension, between cultures (LaFromboise et al., 1993).

It's also important to realize that not all immigrant groups face exactly the same challenges, and that the integrated bicultural ideal is more or less difficult to achieve, depending on the fit between native and adopted homelands. In a book on Asian Americans, for example, Laura Uba (1994) notes that immigrants from Korea, China, Japan, and the Southeast Asian countries find that the values they learned at home clash in fundamental ways with those they encounter in the United States. Taught to be respectful, contained, and obedient, they feel pressured by teachers and peers to be more open, vocal, emotionally expressive, and assertive. Making the clash of cultures even more prominent is that many first-generation Asian American parents urge their children not to become too Americanized. In doing so, they often prohibit dating and restrict other social activities. According to Uba, the result of these pressures is that "in the short run, biculturality can create cultural conflicts and stress for Asian-American children who are trying to forge an identity" (pp. 126–127).

## REVIEW QUESTIONS

- *What basic dilemma confronts members of all ethnic groups?*
- *Define acculturation, and summarize four different acculturation strategies.*
- *Discuss the evidence concerning the adaptiveness of the different acculturation strategies.*

## INTERGROUP DISCRIMINATION

- *How is prejudice a by-product of the way we think?*
- *Is stereotyping inevitable, or can it be controlled?*
- *What motives seem to fuel prejudice all over the world?*
- *What are some social-psychological symptoms of racism in our society?*
- *In an ideal world, how can the problem be treated?*

Minority groups of the world face unique challenges in their formation of an ethnic identity—and may need to cope in different ways. Of the many obstacles that confront ethnic minorities in many cultures, the most disheartening is **discrimination**: behavior directed against persons because of their affiliation with a "different" social, racial, ethnic, or religious group. Instances of discrimination can be seen all over the world, causing its victims to be avoided, excluded, rejected, belittled, and attacked. The victims of discrimination often receive less-than-equal treatment in the pursuit of jobs, housing, educational opportunities, and other resources. In the United States, historically, African Americans have been uniquely targeted victims of racist discrimination—a source of stress that takes a toll on a people's health and longevity (Clark et al., 1999).

Discrimination has both cognitive and motivational-emotional roots. From a cognitive standpoint, it can often be traced to *stereotypes*—generalized beliefs

**discrimination** Behavior directed against persons because of their affiliation with a social group.

that associate whole groups of people with certain, sometimes unflattering, traits. Stereotypes have a depersonalizing effect on the way people perceive ethnic minorities. In addition, discrimination is often motivated by deep-seated *prejudice,* feelings of disdain toward others based on their membership in a social or cultural group. Unfortunately, stereotypes and prejudice are pervasive—and often hurtful.

## STEREOTYPES: THE COGNITIVE ROOTS

To some extent, discrimination is a by-product of the beliefs we hold and the way we think. The beliefs are called stereotypes, and the cognitive processes that promote stereotyping are social categorization and the outgroup-homogeneity bias (Hilton & von Hippel, 1996).

### How Stereotypes Are Formed   A **stereotype** is a belief that associates a whole group of people with certain traits. When you stop to think about it, the list of common, well-known stereotypes seems endless. Consider some examples: The Japanese are sneaky, blondes are ditzy, Italians are emotional, Jews are materialistic, Californians are laid back, accountants are dull, college professors are absent-minded, black people have rhythm, white men can't jump, and used-car salespeople cannot be trusted as far as you can throw them. Now, truthfully, how many of these images ring a bell? More important, how do they influence our evaluations of each other? There are many theories on how such stereotypes are born within a culture. But social psychologists ask a different question: How do stereotypes operate in the minds of individuals, and how do they affect our judgments of others?

From a cognitive perspective, the formation of stereotypes involves two related processes. The first is that people naturally divide each other into groups based on sex, race, age, nationality, religion, and other attributes. This process is called **social categorization.** In some ways, social categorization is natural and adaptive. By grouping human beings the way we group foods, animals, furniture, and other objects, we make judgments quickly and easily and use past experience to guide interactions with people we've never met (Macrae & Bodenhausen, 2000). The problem is that categorization may lead us to magnify the differences *between* groups and overlook the differences among individuals *within* groups (Wilder, 1986; Stangor & Lange, 1994).

The second process that promotes stereotyping follows from the first. Although grouping people is like grouping objects, there's a key difference: In social categorization, the perceivers themselves are members or nonmembers of the categories they employ. Groups that you identify with—your country, religion, political party, or even your hometown sports team—are called *ingroups,* whereas groups other than your own are called *outgroups.* The tendency to carve the world up into "us" and "them" has important psychological and social consequences.

One consequence is the pervasive tendency to assume that "they" are all alike—a phenomenon known as the **outgroup-homogeneity bias** (Linville & Jones, 1980). This bias is shown in three types of research evidence. First, when people are asked to estimate how many group members share a certain stereotyped characteristic, percentage estimates are higher in ratings of outgroups than of ingroups. Second, when people are asked to estimate the range of differences within a population, that range is seen as narrower when the population being considered comes from an outgroup rather than an ingroup. Third, when people are asked to rate a group of individuals for how alike they are, outgroup members are seen as being more similar to each other than are ingroup members (Ostrom & Sedikides, 1992).

These effects are common—and there are many real-life examples. Americans who arrive from Korea, China, Vietnam, Taiwan, and the Philippines see themselves

"Why is it we never focus on the things that unite us, like falafel?"

**stereotype**   A belief that associates a group of people with certain traits.

**social categorization**   The classification of persons into groups based on common attributes.

**outgroup-homogeneity bias**   The tendency to assume that "they" (members of groups other than our own) are all alike.

as quite different from one another, but to the Western eye they are all Asian. Likewise, the people of Mexico, Puerto Rico, Central America, and Cuba distinguish among themselves, but others refer to them all as Hispanic. Business majors talk about "engineering types," engineers lump together "business types," conservatives see liberals as all peas of the same pod, and although the natives of New York City proclaim their cultural and ethnic diversity, outsiders talk of the typical New Yorker. This phenomenon is also seen in studies of visual memory, which show that eyewitnesses find it relatively difficult to recognize members of a racial or ethnic group other than their own (Meissner & Brigham, 2001). When it comes to "them," apparently, "If you've seen one, you've seen them all."

**Is Stereotyping Inevitable?** As generalized beliefs, stereotypes offer us quick and convenient summaries of social groups. Yet as *over*generalized beliefs, they cause us to overlook the diversity within groups and form mistaken impressions of specific individuals. It's important to realize that our stereotypes may be positive or negative, accurate or inaccurate (Judd & Park, 1993; Lee et al., 1995). Sadly, many stereotypes cast groups in unfavorable light, sometimes with hurtful consequences. If we assume that these beliefs are born of the human tendency to categorize all objects, it's easy to justify the result as an innocent by-product of the way we think. But is this true? Is stereotyping inevitable? There are two points of view.

According to Anthony Greenwald and Mahzarin Banaji (1995), stereotypes are often activated without our awareness and operate at an unconscious or implicit level. It just happens. Various experiments illustrate the point. In one study, participants worked on a computer while words such as *Harlem, slavery,* and *jazz* flashed across the screen so rapidly that they were not aware of the exposure. Yet moments later, in an unrelated task, they were more likely to see a fictional male target person as aggressive—consistent with the negative stereotype of African Americans (Devine, 1989). In a second study, participants were instructed to complete word fragments such as *rice* and *polite.* When the items were presented on tape by an Asian woman, participants who were also distracted by another task created words that are stereotypic of Asians, words such as *rice* and *polite* (Gilbert & Hixon, 1991). And in a third study, participants worked at unscrambling sentences that depicted acts of aggression ("cuts off other drivers") or dependence ("won't go alone"). Later, ostensibly as part of a different experiment, participants read about Donald or Donna, a male or female target person. Consistent with popular images of men and women, participants exposed to the aggression phrases saw Donald as more aggressive, and those exposed to dependence phrases saw Donna as more dependent (Banaji et al., 1993). Sometimes, it seems as if the stereotypes we hold are "irrepressible" (Nelson et al., 1996).

Clearly, we can bring stereotypes to mind automatically, without trying, and without awareness, and they can color our judgments of others. But this does not mean that each of us is inevitably trapped into evaluating people on the basis of social categories. Studies have shown that people are most likely to form a quick impression based on simple stereotypes when they're busy or distracted (Gilbert & Hixon, 1991), pressed for time (Pratto & Bargh, 1991), mentally tired (Bodenhausen, 1990), under the influence of alcohol (von Hippel et al., 1995), or elderly and set in their ways (von Hippel et al., 2000).

Thankfully, recent studies have also shown that we can stop ourselves from judging others in stereotyped ways just as we can learn to break other bad habits—as long as we are informed, alert, and motivated to do so. Thus, researchers have found ways to inhibit the use of stereotypes, at least in the laboratory. In a study conducted in the Netherlands, participants were trained over the course of

"You look like this sketch of someone who is thinking about committing a crime"

hundreds of trials to press a key labeled *NO* whenever they saw a picture of a skin-head paired with a word normally associated with skinheads (such as "violent"). In a second laboratory session, up to twenty-four hours later, these trained participants were less likely than others to respond reflexively to the skinhead stimulus (Kawakami et al., 2000). In a study of racial stereotypes, European and Asian American college students were exposed to pictures of black individuals who are admired (Denzel Washington, Colin Powell) or detested (Mike Tyson, O. J. Simpson) as part of a general knowledge test. Other participants saw control pictures of flowers and insects. Later, on a test that measures "implicit" racial associations by the speed at which people associate blacks and whites with positive and negative words, participants who were exposed to problack images were less stereotypical than those exposed to antiblack or neutral images (Dasgupta & Greenwald, 2001). Still other studies have shown that stereotyping can be controlled by encouraging people to take the perspective of someone from a stereotyped outgroup (Galinsky & Moskowitz, 2000) or simply to imagine individuals who don't fit the stereotype (Blair et al., 2001).

## PREJUDICE: THE MOTIVATIONAL ROOTS

As people interact with others who are different in their culture, social class, and ethnic and religious background, tolerance of diversity becomes a social necessity. Too often, however, people evaluate others negatively because they are members of a particular group. This problem was illustrated in December 1999, when major-league baseball pitcher John Rocker openly stated, in an interview for *Sports Illustrated*, that "The biggest thing I don't like about New York are the foreigners. I'm not a very big fan of foreigners." This statement—which reveals a dislike of others because they are members of a particular group—is an expression of **prejudice.**

Stories of prejudice today are not hard to find. In Germany, neo-Nazis terrorize Turkish immigrants. In Northern Ireland, political conflict fuels street violence between Protestants and Catholics. In the Middle East, Israelis and Palestinians fight what seems like an eternal battle. And in what used to be the Soviet Union, raging ethnic conflicts erupt on a regular basis. The streets of America are also witness to bigotry. In Laramie, Wyoming, two men pistol-whipped, tortured, and killed a male college student because he was gay. In Jasper, Texas, three white men chained a black man by the ankles to the back of a pickup truck and dragged him to his death. And on a regular basis, the Equal Opportunity Employment Commission receives complaints from minorities who say they are harassed in the workplace by co-workers who leave knotted hangman's nooses—a symbol of racial hatred and intimidation—in stockrooms, lunchrooms, offices, lockers, and closets (Siwolop, 2000). Stories like these make the news on an all too regular basis, bringing to life an important point: People often dislike and resent others simply because they are different. Throughout history, and in all parts of the world, prejudice is one of the most tenacious social problems of modern times.

From a cognitive perspective, stereotypes spring from the process of social categorization and the distinctions people make between ingroups and outgroups. In other words, stereotypes are a by-product of the way people think. But is that all there is to it? If people could somehow be prevented from categorizing one another, would all the prejudice in the world be eliminated? Doubtful. The way we *think* about social groups is important, but there's another factor to consider: how we *feel* about the groups we encounter, and perhaps even our *need* to perceive them in a particular light.

*Prejudice is one of the most tenacious social afflictions of our time. The problem, as shown by this young white supremacist, is that the hatred is passed from one generation to the next.*

 **14.1**

**prejudice**    Negative feelings toward others based solely on their membership in a certain group.

*In one of the world's most volatile areas of conflict involving nations armed with nuclear weapons, there is intense competition for the bordering areas that separate the primarily Hindu population of India and the Muslim population of Pakistan.*

**Realistic-Conflict Theory** There are two major motivational theories of prejudice. The first is **realistic-conflict theory**, which begins with a simple observation: Many intergroup conflicts in the world today stem from direct competition for valuable but limited resources (Levine & Campbell, 1972). As a matter of economics, one group may fare better than a neighboring group in a struggle for land, jobs, or power. The losers become frustrated, the winners feel threatened, and before long the conflict heats to a rapid boil. Chances are that a good deal of prejudice in the world—such as the hostility often directed at immigrants—is driven by the realities of competition (Stephan et al., 1999; Taylor & Moghaddam, 1994).

Realistic conflict clearly accounts for part of the problem, as frustration evokes hostility, aggression, and the search for a scapegoat. From the years 1882 and 1930, for example, the number of black Americans lynched in the Deep South increased as cotton prices fell—a sign of economic frustration (Hovland & Sears, 1940; Beck & Tolnay, 1990). The realities of conflict over valuable but limited natural resources may pose a challenge to the future of international relations. In *Resource Wars*, Michael Klare (2001) argues that future wars will most likely erupt over the competition for oil in the Persian Gulf and the Caspian and South China Seas; for water in the Nile Basin and other river systems; and for timber in Liberia, diamonds in Angola, copper in Papua New Guinea. In the near term, for example, he predicts inevitable conflict between Israel, Jordan, and Syria over the outflow of water from the River Jordan.

The premise of realistic-conflict theory in the study of prejudice seems compelling, but there's more to the story—much more. Research has shown that people are often prejudiced even when the quality of their lives is *not* directly threatened by the outgroup they despise, and that people are sensitive about the status of their ingroups relative to rival outgroups even when personal interests are *not* at stake. Is it possible that personal interests really *are* at stake, that our protectiveness of ingroups is nourished by a concern for the self? If so, might that explain why people all over the world seem to think that their own nation, culture, and religion are better and more deserving than others?

**Social-Identity Theory** Questions about ingroups and outgroups were initially raised in a series of laboratory studies. In the first of these, Henri Tajfel and his colleagues (1971) showed participants a sequence of dotted slides and asked them to estimate the number of dots on each. The slides were flashed in rapid-fire succession, so the dots could not be counted. The experimenter then told participants that some people are chronic "overestimators" and others are "underestimators." As part of a second, separate task, participants were then divided, supposedly for the sake of convenience, into groups of overestimators and underestimators (in fact, the assignments were random). Knowing who was in their group, the participants allocated points to each other for various tasks, points that reflected favorable judgments and could be cashed in for money. This procedure was designed to create *minimal groups* of persons categorized by trivial similarities. The overestimators and underestimators were not bitter rivals, they had no history of antagonism, and they did not compete for a limited resource. Yet they allocated more points to members of their own group than to those of the outgroup. This pattern of discrimination, which is known as **ingroup favoritism**, has been observed in experiments conducted all over the world (Capozza & Brown, 2000).

**realistic-conflict theory** The theory that prejudice stems from intergroup competition for limited resources.

**ingroup favoritism** The tendency to discriminate in favor of ingroups over outgroups.

Our preference for ingroups is so powerful that its effects can be measured by the language we use. According to Charles Perdue and others (1990), ingroup pronouns such as *we, us,* and *ours* trigger positive emotions, and outgroup pronouns such as *they, them,* and *theirs* elicit negative emotions. These investigators presented participants with numerous pairs of letter strings on a computer—each pair containing both a pronoun and a nonsense syllable ("we-xeh," "they-yof"). Their task was to decide as quickly as possible which letter string in each pair was a real word. They didn't realize it, but one nonsense syllable was always paired with ingroup pronouns, another with outgroup pronouns. Afterward, participants were asked for their reactions to each of the nonsense syllables. The result: Those previously paired with ingroup words were seen as more pleasant than those paired with outgroup words. The ingroup-outgroup distinction has such emotional meaning for people that it can bias their views of an unfamiliar string of letters—or a person. What's more, this process occurs quickly, automatically, and without awareness, as soon as others are perceived as "them" rather than "us" (Ashburn-Nardo et al., 2001).

To explain ingroup favoritism in the absence of realistic conflict, Tajfel (1982) and John Turner (1987) proposed **social-identity theory.** According to this theory, each of us strives to enhance our self-esteem, which has two components: a *personal* identity and various collective or *social* identities that are based on the groups to which we belong. In other words, people can boost their self-esteem through their personal achievements or by affiliating with successful groups. What's nice about the need for social identity is that it leads us to derive pride from our connections with others. What's sad, however, is that often we feel the need to belittle "them" in order to feel secure about "us." Religious fervor, racial and ethnic conceit, and patriotism may all fulfill this darker side of our social identity. In this way, prejudice is nourished by a concern for oneself. The theory is summarized in Figure 14.5.

Social-identity theory makes two predictions: (1) Threats to self-esteem should heighten the need to exhibit prejudice, and (2) expressions of prejudice should, in turn, restore one's self-esteem. Research generally supports these predictions (Brewer & Brown, 1998; Capozza & Brown, 2000; Hogg & Abrams, 1990; Turner et al., 1994).

**social-identity theory**  The theory that people favor ingroups and discriminate against outgroups in order to enhance their own self-esteem.

*See that man over there?*
*Yes.*
*Well, I hate him.*
*But you don't know him.*
*That's why I hate him.*

—ALLPORT, 1954

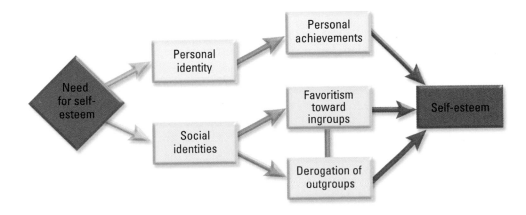

**FIGURE 14.5    Social-identity theory**
According to social-identity theory, people strive to enhance self-esteem, which has two components: a personal identity and various social identities derived from the groups to which we belong. Thus, people can boost their self-image by viewing and treating ingroups more favorably than outgroups.

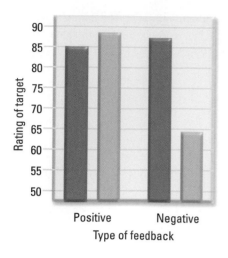

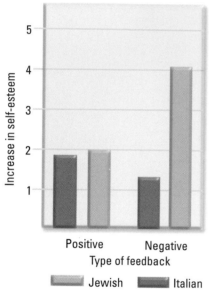

**FIGURE 14.6** **Derogation in the service of self-esteem**
Participants received positive or negative feedback and then evaluated a female job applicant believed to be Italian or Jewish. There were two key results: (1) Participants whose self-esteem had been lowered by negative feedback evaluated the woman less favorably when she was Jewish than Italian (top); and (2) negative-feedback participants given the opportunity to belittle the Jewish woman showed a postexperiment increase in self-esteem (bottom) (Fein & Spencer, 1997).

**racism** A deep-seated form of prejudice that is based on the color of a person's skin.

In a study that tested both components of social-identity theory, Steven Fein and Steven Spencer (1997) gave participants positive or negative feedback about their performance on a test of social and verbal skills—feedback that temporarily raised or lowered their self-esteem. These participants then took part in what was supposed to be a second experiment in which they evaluated a job applicant. All participants received a snapshot of a young woman, her résumé, and a videotaped job interview. In half the cases, the woman was named Maria D'Agostino and was depicted as Italian; in the other half, she was Julie Goldberg and was depicted as Jewish (on the campus where the study was conducted, students had a negative stereotype of the "Jewish American Princess" that was evoked by upper-middle-class Jewish women from New York). When this task was complete, participants were retested for their self-esteem.

As shown in Figure 14.6, there were two main results, both consistent with social-identity theory. First, among participants whose self-esteem had been lowered by negative feedback, Julie Goldberg was rated more negatively than Maria D'Agostino—even though their pictures and credentials were the same. Second, negative-feedback participants given an opportunity to belittle the Jewish woman later exhibited a postexperiment increase in self-esteem. A blow to one's self-image evokes prejudice—and the expression of prejudice helps to restore that image. This effect has also been found by other researchers (Branscombe & Wann, 1994). Also important, some individuals in particular harbor prejudice for social-identity purposes. People differ in the extent to which they want their social ingroups to dominate others. In studies conducted in Israel, the Palestinian West Bank and Gaza Strip, China, Taiwan, New Zealand, the former Soviet Union, the United States, and Canada, people who are motivated by a need for social dominance exhibit more ingroup favoritism and endorse more cultural values that favor "us" over "them" (Pratto et al., 2000; Sidanius et al., 2000; Whitley, 1999).

So far, we have seen that stereotypes are overgeneralized, easily activated beliefs that lead us to overlook the diversity within social outgroups and to rush to judgment about specific individuals. We have also seen that prejudice can stem from a competition for resources or the need to favor ingroups in the service of self-esteem. We now put these problems into concrete terms by focusing on racism, a common form of prejudice.

## RACISM IN AMERICA

The slave trade. The Deep South. Abolitionists. The Civil War. Lynch mobs. Separate but equal. The Ku Klux Klan. Jackie Robinson. Sitting in the back of the bus. Martin Luther King, Jr. Civil rights. Malcolm X. School busing. *Roots.* Muhammad Ali. Affirmative action. The Reverend Jesse Jackson. The Confederate flag. Race relations in the United States have had a checkered, troubled, and emotional history—a history marked by both hatred and guilt, riots and peace marches, tolerance and intolerance, advances and setbacks. At the heart of it all, **racism:** a deep-seated form of prejudice that is based on the color of a person's skin. In the United States, this conflict is multidirectional, with all groups exhibiting prejudice in one form or another.

**The Problem** I have been told, and I believe it, that because I am white I'll never really understand what it feels like to be a black person living in the United States—and what it felt like many years ago, in the segregated South. In a powerful and revealing book, *Remembering Jim Crow,* historian William Chafe and others (2002) interviewed twelve hundred elderly African Americans who lived in ten states of the segregated South during the first half of the twentieth century. These witnesses to history recalled separate drinking fountains and restrooms, backdoor entries to public facilities, separate platforms at the train station. Some recalled rapes, beatings, and harrowing escapes in the middle of the night from lynch mobs. All recall how carefully they had to move about in an unpredictable land—where some whites were friendly and helpful, others hostile and prejudiced.

In *Race,* a book on contemporary America, Studs Terkel (1992) interviewed ordinary people, both black and white, about what he calls "the American obsession." In some cases, Terkel tells penetrating real-life stories about overt, old-fashioned prejudice—for example, the construction worker who complained bitterly about affirmative action because, as he put it, "they live like low lifes." Yet in other cases, he observed a prejudice that was more subtle—as when Terkel's friend's wife, who is white and who sees herself as color blind, drove through a black neighborhood in Chicago: "The people at the corners were all gesticulating at her. She was very frightened, turned up the windows, and drove determinedly. She discovered after several blocks, she was going the wrong way on a one-way street and they were trying to help her. Her assumption was they were blacks and were out to get her." One story involved Terkel himself. He boarded a bus one morning and deposited his fare, only to have the driver, a young black man, say he was a dime short. Terkel was sure he had paid the right amount and was upset. But he fished into his pocket and dropped another dime into the box. "Oh, I understood the man," he thought. "I know the history of his people's bondage. It was his turn—a show of power, if only in a small way. If that's how it is, that's how it is. Oh, well." Then it happened. "As I was about to disembark, I saw a dime on the floor. My dime. I held it up to him. 'You were right.' He was too busy driving to respond. I waved: 'Take it easy.' 'You, too,' he replied. I've a hunch he'd been through something like this before" (p. 6).

This subtle form of racism may seem invisible, but it can be humiliating to its victims. In *Color-Blind,* writer Ellis Cose (1997), who is African American, tells a story about how he was treated in a job interview some twenty years ago. He was an award-winning newspaper reporter at the time and was hoping to land a job with a national magazine. The editor he had met with was pleasant and gracious, but he said that the magazine did not have many black readers. "I don't know whether the editor had bothered to read my clippings, but then, the clips were somehow superfluous. . . . All the editor saw was a young black guy, and since *Esquire* was not in need of a young black guy, they were not in need of me . . . he had been so busy focusing on my race that he was incapable of seeing me or my work" (p. 150). Then a few years later, and in the light of affirmative action, Cose was asked if he was interested in a position as a corporate director of equal opportunity. "I was stunned, for the question made no sense. I was an expert neither on personnel nor on equal employment law; I was, however, black, which seemed to be the most important qualification" (p. 156).

*Although racism is still a serious problem in the United States, it is from an historical perspective on the decline. Looking back, America has come a long way from the forced segregation common in the first half of the twentieth century (top) to an historic evening, in March of 2002, when African Americans Denzel Washington and Halle Berry won Oscar awards for best actor and actress (bottom).*

**The Symptoms**   Racism in the twenty-first century is a problem that poisons social relations between black and white people. Detecting racism is not as easy as it may seem. In 1933, Daniel Katz and Kenneth Braly found that many white college students believed that black Americans were lazy, happy-go-lucky, aggressive, and ignorant. Follow-up surveys and public opinion polls taken in 1951, 1967, 1982, 1993, and up to the present have shown that although the negative stereotypes have not completely disappeared, these images have largely faded (Dovidio & Gaertner, 1998).

Or have they? Research suggests that many people today are racially ambivalent. They want to see themselves as fair and are reluctant to express racist sentiments,

but they still harbor feelings of anxiety and discomfort in the presence of people from other racial groups (Hass et al., 1992). So can public-opinion polls be trusted, or has racism simply gone underground? And what about the distrust of white people that many African Americans harbor? If people will not admit their biases to pollsters, or even to themselves, how can we know that this chronic social disease still exists? What are the symptoms? Better yet, what is the cure?

People may not openly express their prejudices, but racism can be subtle, distorting our perceptions and our behavior. In an old and classic demonstration of this point, Gordon Allport and Leo Postman (1947) showed white participants a picture of a subway train filled with passengers. In the picture were a black man dressed in a suit and a white man holding a razor (see Figure 14.7). One participant viewed the scene briefly and described it to a second person who had not seen it. The second participant communicated the description to a third person and so on, through six rounds of communication. The result: The final participant's report often indicated that the black man, not the white man, had held the razor. Some participants even reported that he was waving the weapon in a threatening manner.

Needing to measure prejudice in order to study it, social psychologists sought to develop indirect tests that can detect negative feelings that people are not willing or able to admit to a pollster. Several years ago, researchers found that reaction time—the speed it takes to answer a question—can be used to uncover hidden prejudices. In one study, white participants read word pairs and pressed a button whenever they thought the words fitted together. In each case, the word *blacks* or *whites* was paired with either a positive trait (*clean, smart,* etc.) or a negative trait (*stupid, lazy,* etc.). The results were revealing. Participants did not openly associate *blacks* with negative terms or *whites* with positive terms. And they were equally quick to reject negative terms in both cases. However, participants were quicker to respond to the positive words when they were paired with *whites* than with *blacks*. Because it takes

Racial gap in perceptions of discrimination (ABCNEWS.com, 2002)

Q: Do taxi drivers avoid picking up blacks?

A: Whites 19%, Blacks 42%

Q: Do sales clerks in expensive stores make blacks feel unwelcome?

A: Whites 25%, Blacks 66%

Q: Are police more likely to pull over black motorists?

A: Whites 33%, Blacks 75%

**FIGURE 14.7** **How racist beliefs distort perceptions**
After looking at this drawing, one participant described it to a second, who described it to a third, and so on. After six rounds of communication, the final report often placed the razor blade held by the white man into the black man's hand (Allport & Postman, 1947).

less time to react to information that fits existing beliefs, this finding suggests that participants were unconsciously predisposed to associate positive traits with *whites* more than with *blacks* (Gaertner & McLaughlin, 1983; Dovidio et al., 1997).

Picking up on the use of reaction time to betray a person's unconscious feelings, Anthony Greenwald, Mahzarin Banaji, and their colleagues developed the **Implicit Association Test,** or **IAT.** The IAT measures how readily people can associate pairs of concepts (Greenwald et al., 1998). To see how it works, try visiting the IAT Web site by typing "Implicit Association Test" in a search engine or http://implicit.harvard.edu/implicit/demo/.

Take the test to measure your implicit racial attitudes, and you'll go through a series of stages. First, you will be asked to categorize black or white faces as quickly as you can, for example, pressing a left-hand key in response to black and a right-hand key for white. Next, you will be asked to categorize a set of words, for example, pressing a left-hand key for positive words (*love, laughter, friend*) and a right-hand key for negative words (*war, failure, evil*). After these two stages, you'll be familiar with the categorization task. In a third stage, faces and words are combined. You may be asked, for example, to press the left-hand key if you see a black face or positive word and a right-hand key if you see a white face or negative word. Then in the fourth stage, the opposite pairings are presented—black or negative, white or positive. Black and white faces will then be interspersed in a quick sequence of trials, each time paired with a positive or negative word. In rapid-fire succession, you will have to press one key or another in response to stimulus pairs such as *black—wonderful, black—failure, white—love, black—laughter, white—evil, white—awful, black—war,* and *white—joy.* As you work through the list, you may find that some pairings are harder—and take longer to respond to—than others. In general, people are quicker to respond when liked faces are paired with positive words and disliked faces are paired with negative words than the other way around. The IAT thus detects your implicit attitudes about African Americans by the speed it takes you to respond to *black-bad/white-good* pairings relative to *black-good/white-bad* pairings. When you're done, you will receive the results of your test and what it means (see Figure 14.8).

**Implicit Association Test (IAT)**   A measure of stereotyping that is derived from the speed at which people respond to pairings of concepts (such as *blacks* or *whites* with *good* or *bad*).

What nonconscious stereotypes do you hold? If interested, you can take the *Implicit Association Test,* free of charge. It takes ten minutes to complete, and right afterward you'll receive a score. Visit http://implicit.harvard.edu/implicit/demo/

**FIGURE 14.8   The Implicit Association Test (IAT)**
Through a sequence of tasks, the IAT measures implicit racial attitudes toward, for example, African Americans, by measuring how quickly people respond to *black-bad/white-good* word pairings relative to *black-good/white-bad* pairings. Suggesting they harbor negative associations, most white Americans are quicker to respond to the first type of pairings than to the second.

*Psychology and Education*

# USING SCHOOLS TO COMBAT RACISM

About fifty years ago, the United States Supreme Court launched a bold and historic experiment in race relations. In the case of *Brown v. Board of Education of Topeka,* the Court ruled that racially separate schools were unequal, in violation of the Constitution. This opinion was informed by research suggesting that segregation had an adverse effect on the self-esteem and academic performance of black students and on prejudice itself (Allport et al., 1953).

At the time, the Court's decision was controversial. Many Americans opposed school desegregation and argued that forcing interracial contact would only worsen matters. Others pinned their hopes on the **contact hypothesis,** which

*In Topeka, Kansas, in 1954, Linda Brown was forced to attend a segregated school after being denied admission to an all-white school. In* Brown v. Board of Education, *the Supreme Court ruled that this separation of the public schools was unconstitutional.*

states that under certain conditions, direct contact between members of different groups will improve relations. For contact to have this effect, it was proposed, four conditions must be met: (1) The two groups should be of equal status in the contact situation, (2) there should be personal interactions among the individual members, (3) the groups should have a common goal that requires their cooperation, so that "they" can become part of "us," and (4) the contact should be supported by social norms and people in authority.

Despite the Court's ruling, desegregation proceeded slowly. Many schools remained untouched until the 1970s. Then as the dust began to settle, research brought the sad news that there was little improvement in race relations (Stephan, 1986). Was the contact hypothesis wrong? It's hard to say. School desegregation had not produced all the desired changes, but the conditions necessary for effective intergroup contact had not been met. Nobody ever said that deeply rooted racism would be erased overnight just by throwing black and white schoolchildren together. In fact, the four conditions necessary for contact to succeed did not exist in the schools.

First, the two groups did not come together on equal-status terms. When public schools were desegregated, the white children were from more affluent families and were better prepared than their black peers (Cohen, 1984). Second, personal interactions among black and white children were uncommon. Schools are not a melting pot, and desegregation does not ensure true integration. After the bus arrives, students gravitate toward members of their own race in the cafeteria and on the playground (Epstein, 1985; Schofield, 1982). Third, the typical classroom is filled with competition for a teacher's attention, grades, and so on—not the kinds of cooperative activities that bring people together to achieve a common goal. Fourth,

**contact hypothesis** The proposition that in certain conditions, direct contact between members of rival groups will improve relations.

Starting in 1998, for the next three or so years, visitors to this site completed 1.5 million tests. In questionnaires, interviews, and public-opinion polls, people don't tend to reveal their own stereotypes or prejudices. Yet on the IAT, respondents have exhibited an average implicit preference for self over other, white over black, young over old, and the stereotype that links males with careers and females with family (Nosek et al., 2002).

school desegregation was not supported by social norms. Many principals, teachers, and state officials objected, and many parents boycotted busing—hardly an ingredient for success.

Although problems have plagued school-desegregation efforts, research shows that prejudice *can* be reduced in situations that truly satisfy the chief requirements of the contact hypothesis (Cook, 1985). In a recent meta-analysis of studies involving ninety thousand people from twenty-five different countries, Thomas Pettigrew and Linda Tropp (2000) found that when intergroup contact satisfies all or even some of these requirements, it brings on a measurable reduction in prejudice.

Perhaps the most successful demonstration of this point took place on the baseball diamond. On April 15, 1947, Jackie Robinson played first base for the Brooklyn Dodgers—and became the first black man to break the color barrier in Major League Baseball. In a story told by Anthony

*Jackie Robinson and Branch Rickey discuss Robinson's contract with the Brooklyn Dodgers. This deal had great historical significance. The two men also went on to become good friends.*

Pratkanis and Marlene Turner (1994), Robinson's opportunity came through Dodger owner Branch Rickey, who felt that integrating baseball was both moral and good for the game. Rickey knew about the contact hypothesis and was assured by a social-scientist friend that a team can furnish the conditions for it to work: equal status among teammates, one-on-one interactions, dedication to a common goal, and a positive climate from the owner and coaching staff. The rest is history. Rickey signed Robinson and created the situation necessary for success. Baseball was integrated. In 1947, Jackie Robinson was named Rookie of the Year, and in 1962 he was elected into the Hall of Fame. At his induction ceremony, Robinson asked three people to stand beside him: his mother, his wife, and his friend Branch Rickey.

Can similar results be achieved in a school setting? Back in the classroom, Elliot Aronson and others developed a cooperative-learning method called the "jigsaw classroom" (Aronson & Platnoe, 1997). In newly desegregated elementary schools in Texas and California, they assigned fifth graders to small, racially and academically mixed groups. The material to be learned within each group was divided into subtopics, much the way a jigsaw puzzle is broken into pieces. Each student was responsible for learning one piece of the puzzle, after which all members took turns teaching their material to one another. Under this system, everyone—regardless of race, ability, or self-confidence—needed everyone else if the group as a whole was to succeed. The method produced impressive results. Compared to schoolchildren in traditional classes, those in jigsaw classrooms grew to like one another more, were more tolerant, liked school more, and had higher self-esteem. On the academic front, test scores improved for minority students and remained the same for white students. As in interracial sports teams, the jigsaw classroom offers a promising way to create a truly integrated educational setting. It also provides a model of how to use personal contact to promote tolerance of diversity among children of all colors.

Reaction-time tests may seem subtle, but the results suggest that certain associations are so deeply ingrained in our culture that the negative images are as difficult to break as a bad habit (Devine, 1989). That's why Terkel jumped to the conclusion that the black bus driver who said he was a dime short was being difficult when in fact the dime had fallen on the floor. To be sure, many nonprejudiced white Americans admit they are not always fair to African Americans—an insight

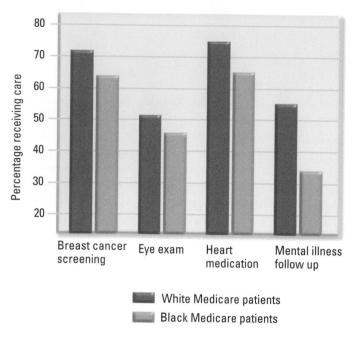

FIGURE 14.9 **Racial disparities in medical care**

that causes them to feel embarrassed, guilty, and ashamed of themselves (Devine et al., 1991).

Our subtle prejudices may be more common than we realize, and they can have grave consequences. Consider the possible risks in a medical setting. One team of researchers showed video-taped interviews of a patient complaining of chest pains to 720 physicians who were asked to recommend a course of action. The interviews were actually staged using black or white actors as patients. The result: All patients presented the same symptoms, but physicians were less likely to recommend cardiac catheterizations for black patients than for white (Schulman et al., 1999). A second research group examined existing medical records of eleven thousand elderly adults diagnosed with a form of lung cancer that is often curable through surgery. The survival rate among blacks in the sample was 26 percent, compared to 34 percent among whites. One possible reason: The black patients were 13 percent less likely to receive the surgical treatment (Bach et al., 1999). A third research group examined the records of forty thousand heart attack patients and found that black patients were nearly 10 percent less likely than whites were to receive an angiogram, a nonsurgical procedure used to assess a patient's cardiac condition. This difference in treatment was found regardless of whether the attending physician was black or white (Chen et al., 2001). A fourth group studied the health records for three hundred thousand senior citizens enrolled in Medicare-managed health-care plans. Figure 14.9 shows that black patients were less likely than whites to receive breast-cancer screening, beta blocker medications after heart attacks, follow-up visits after hospitalization for mental illness, and eye examinations for those with diabetes. These disparities in medical care were significant even after socioeconomic differences were accounted for (Schneider et al., 2002). No matter how subtle, innocent, or unintended the discrimination, the effect can mean the difference between life and death.

**The Treatment** In the United States, black and white people openly disagree about the extent to which racism still exists. Surveys show that most white Americans believe that racial discrimination is on the decline in housing, education, and employment, but that many black Americans maintain that the problem still exists (Schuman et al., 1997; Sigelman & Welch, 1991). Not too long ago, differences of opinion were also found among highly paid athletes. *Sports Illustrated* surveyed three hundred athletes from the NFL, the NBA, and major-league baseball. Sixty-three percent of black respondents, compared to only 2 percent of their white teammates, believed that black athletes in their sport were the victims of discrimination—in salaries, fan support, treatment by coaches, commercial endorsements, and management opportunities (Johnson, 1991). Similarly, the U.S. military surveyed forty thousand service members and found that although most whites did not perceive prejudice to be a problem, three-quarters of all African Americans and other minorities said they had experienced at least one racially offensive behavior (Suro & Fletcher, 1999). In a story on "Perception vs. Experience," an ABC News poll revealed that substantially more blacks than whites believe that police, taxi drivers, and sales clerks in expensive stores discriminate against black Americans (ABCNEWS.com, 2002).

Racism is a social disease that gets transmitted from one generation to the next and afflicts millions of people from all groups. One wonders if it can be treated. Can people be joined cooperatively, perhaps, to foster a redrawing of the boundaries between "us" and "them"? In a laboratory study, Samuel Gaertner and others (1990) brought six participants into the laboratory and divided them into two three-person groups. Each group took a name, wore color-coded ID tags, and worked on a decision-making task. Next, the groups were brought together and either listened to others discussing a problem (a neutral interaction) or joined forces to solve the problem themselves (a cooperative encounter). The strategy worked like a charm in two ways. First, despite initial allegiances, 58 percent of the participants in the cooperative condition said they felt like one large group rather than two separate groups, an increase compared to only 28 percent in the neutral condition. Second, when participants rated each other, those in the cooperative condition did not show the usual ingroup bias. Rather than derogate former outgroup members, they saw them as more likable, honest, and similar to "self." Other research has confirmed the point: Thanks to cooperation and the development of a common identity "they" become part of "us" (Gaertner et al., 2000).

Is it possible to produce these kinds of effects on a large scale between racial or ethnic groups? Does it help to expose children to diversity at a young age? A large-scale "experiment" of this nature has been in progress, all across the country, in programs designed to desegregate the public schools. (See *Psychology and Education*.)

### REVIEW QUESTIONS

- *What basic cognitive processes contribute to prejudice?*

- *Describe the evidence suggesting that stereotypes operate automatically.*

- *Explain prejudice from the perspectives of realistic-conflict theory and social-identity theory.*

- *Describe some of the subtle forms of racism that occur today.*

## THINKING LIKE A PSYCHOLOGIST ABOUT SOCIAL AND CULTURAL GROUPS

When you stop to consider the ways in which all humans are similar and share a common fate, the differences seem small and unimportant. Yet as we come into more and more contact with people from other cultures, as our society becomes increasingly diverse, and as tensions between black and white Americans stubbornly persist, it seems clear that we must recognize the differences among social and cultural groups if we are to understand, communicate, and be tolerant if not appreciative of one another.

But what should be the goal? Should the differences among individuals and groups be ignored or acknowledged? One view is that people should strive to become "blind" to cultural, racial, and ethnic heritage—categorizations that should have no bearing on the way we treat each other. In an ideal color-blind society, for example, healthy relations among European, African, Latino, Asian, and Native Americans demand that individuals be perceived, evaluated, and treated on a strictly personal basis. An alternative view is that people derive pride and a sense of belonging from their social identities—that although everyone should be treated equally and without discrimination, cultural, racial, and ethnic diversity should be celebrated, not ignored. Clearly, there are similarities among us, and there are differences. The trick, I suppose, is not to focus exclusively on one or the other but to strike a sensible balance.

## SUMMARY

As the world becomes a global village, it's important to know the ways in which people from different cultural and ethnic groups are similar and different.

### CROSS-CULTURAL PERSPECTIVES

#### CULTURAL DIVERSITY: A FACT OF LIFE

People vary in their language, religion, geography, and **social norms**—a culture's implicit rules of conduct—and in the degree to which they conform to these norms.

### INDIVIDUALISM AND COLLECTIVISM: A TALE OF TWO CULTURAL WORLDVIEWS

Cultures differ in their orientation toward **individualism** and **collectivism**. Individualistic cultures value independence and self-reliance, whereas collectivist cultures stress interdependence and cooperation. According to Triandis, societies that are complex, affluent, and heterogeneous are most likely to be individualistic.

Individualism and collectivism influence the extent to which we see the self as encompassing other people and groups with which we identify. In individualistic cultures, socialization practices are designed to foster independence; in collectivist cultures, the emphasis is on interdependence.

Each orientation has advantages and disadvantages. In collectivist societies, people are more likely to follow social norms, which promote harmony and loyalty and discourage social loafing. But collectivism can also produce narrow-mindedness and a confrontational attitude toward outsiders.

## MULTICULTURAL PERSPECTIVES

### ETHNIC DIVERSITY: A FACT OF LIFE

As ethnic diversity increases in the United States and elsewhere, more attention is being paid to multiculturalism, the study of diverse racial and ethnic groups within a culture.

### ACCULTURATION AND ETHNIC IDENTITY

All ethnic groups face the dilemma of how to adapt to the larger society. Should they blend into a single "melting pot" or retain their heritage as part of a cultural "mosaic"? **Acculturation,** the process of change that occurs when people are immersed in a new culture, can occur in four ways: assimilation (abandoning the old culture for the new), separation (retaining the old and rejecting the new), integration (retaining the old and adapting to the new), or marginalization (identifying with neither culture).

Through acculturation, people form an **ethnic identity,** which is revealed in language, customs, and a sense of belonging. But immigrants may also experience **acculturative stress,** resulting in various mental-health problems. The strategy of integration seems to correlate with less acculturative stress than the other three strategies, but different immigrant groups face different adjustment problems.

## INTERGROUP DISCRIMINATION

A difficult obstacle for ethnic minorities is **discrimination,** behavior directed against people because of their affiliation with a social or cultural group. Discriminatory behaviors stem from stereotypic beliefs and feelings of prejudice.

### STEREOTYPES: THE COGNITIVE ROOTS

The cognitive roots of prejudice involve **stereotypes**—beliefs that associate a group of people with certain traits. Through

a process of **social categorization,** we divide people into groups based on common attributes. We also distinguish among ingroups (those we identify with) and outgroups (groups not our own). Although this process is natural and adaptive, the **outgroup-homogeneity bias** leads us to assume that members of outgroups are all alike.

Research suggests that stereotypes come to mind automatically, without effort, and, at times, without conscious awareness. Studies also show that although stereotyping is cognitively inevitable, people who are informed, alert, and motivated, can learn to overcome the effects and judge others on a more individualized basis.

### PREJUDICE: THE MOTIVATIONAL ROOTS

**Prejudice** refers to negative feelings toward others based solely on their membership in a certain group. Certain motivations fuel intergroup hostility and prejudice.

**Realistic-conflict theory** holds that prejudice often stems from intergroup competition for limited resources. But this explanation does not account for **ingroup favoritism** that appears even when groups are not in competition and resources are not limited.

According to **social-identity theory,** the self contains not only a personal component but also various social identities. Thus, people can boost their self-esteem by discriminating against outgroups. Research generally confirms that threats to self-esteem raise the need for prejudice and that expressions of prejudice in turn enhance self-esteem.

### RACISM IN AMERICA

**Racism,** a deep-seated form of prejudice based on the color of a person's skin, is not as overt in the United States as it used to be, but studies find evidence of it in many settings. Racism can influence our perceptions and our interpretations of events. People are reluctant to admit having a negative racial attitude in their self-reports, but it can be detected through use of the **Implicit Association Test (IAT)** and other indirect measures.

As described by the **contact hypothesis,** the most effective way to combat prejudice is through personal, equal-status, cooperative contact between rival-group members in a situation in which the social norms for contact are favorable. The goal is to get people to recategorize outgroup members so that "they" become part of "us."

## KEY TERMS

social norms (**p. 551**)

individualism (**p. 551**)

collectivism (**p. 551**)

acculturation (**p. 560**)

ethnic identity (**p. 561**)

acculturative stress (**p. 561**)

discrimination (**p. 562**)

stereotype (**p. 563**)

social categorization (**p. 563**)

outgroup-homogeneity bias (**p. 563**)

prejudice (**p. 565**)

realistic-conflict theory (**p. 566**)

ingroup favoritism (**p. 566**)

social-identity theory (**p. 567**)

racism (**p. 568**)

Implicit Association Test (IAT) (**p. 571**)

contact hypothesis (**p. 572**)

## THINKING CRITICALLY ABOUT SOCIAL AND CULTURAL GROUPS

1. Discuss some of the strengths and weaknesses of collectivistic and individualistic cultural orientations. In what ways might the formation of an ethnic identity be influenced by a conflict of cultural orientations?

2. Imagine that you had been born as a member of a different race or ethnic group. Do you think you would be essentially the same person you are now? In what ways would you be the same? In what ways would you be different?

3. Are stereotyping, prejudice, and discrimination inevitable? Why or why not?

4. Suppose you are in charge of student relations at a large ethnically and culturally diverse university. What specific things can you do to foster positive interactions and tolerance for diversity among all students?

# Personality

# HOW STABLE IS PERSONALITY?

## THE SITUATION

From research you've read, you know that an individual's personality consists of various, presumably enduring traits. You also know that many psychologists find it useful to describe personality by comparing people along five broad dimensions: (1) *neuroticism* (a proneness to anxiety and distress), (2) *extraversion* (a desire for social interaction, stimulation, and activity), (3) *openness* (a receptiveness to new experiences), (4) *agreeableness* (a selfless concern for others), and (5) *conscientiousness* (a tendency to be reliable, disciplined, and ambitious). Does one's relative standing on these traits stay basically the same over time, or does personality change with age, life experience, and other factors? If you're generally calm, outgoing, and open-minded now, will that be your profile later in life? What about the fact that people's behavior differs from one situation to another?

To determine the stability of personality, you decide to contact a large group of adults who had completed a personality test six years ago as part of another study. The test they had taken was designed to measure the top three of the five major traits (neuroticism, extraversion, openness). Overall, 635 people had taken the test—365 men and 270 women, ranging in age from twenty-five to ninety-one. In the original experiment, each person was given the test two times, with a six-month interval. Your goal now is to retest these same people on a newer version of the same scale. Most agree to take part in your study. But others, you come to learn, have died, moved, become disabled, or lost interest. In the end, you are able to recruit 398 of the original subjects. To each one, you mail the questionnaire, the instructions, and a stamped self-addressed envelope.

The questionnaire you use is called the Neuroticism-Extraversion-Openness Personality Inventory, or NEO-PI. This test is the one most often used in research (Costa & McCrae, 1992). The NEO-PI contains 181 statements ("I am usually cheerful," "I really like most people I meet," "I have a very active imagination"). Next to each one, subjects rate on a 5-point scale how much they agree or disagree. The items measuring neuroticism, extraversion, and openness are dispersed throughout the test, but afterward you total the scores separately for each "subscale"—a procedure that yields three scores per subject. Once all tests are scored, the data are ready to be analyzed.

So what next? To determine the stability of the traits you measured, you need to take a longitudinal approach by comparing each subject's scores in the first and second tests. What is the *correlation* between the two sets of scores? If personality, like mood, were to fluctuate wildly from one moment to the next or if you were to pair the scores of one subject with those of another, randomly selected subject, the correlation would be 0 (remember, a correlation coefficient ranges from 0 to +1 or −1). At the other extreme, if personality were completely set in stone or if the same subjects were retested only six days, weeks, or months apart, the two sets of scores should be strongly and positively correlated, in the .90 range. The question is: How strongly correlated would the two sets of scores be after six *years*?

## MAKE A PREDICTION

Six years ago, your 398 subjects took the test, which yielded three trait scores: one for neuroticism, another for extraversion, and a third for openness to experience. Now you have tested them again. How high do you think the correlations are between the two sets of scores? To give you a basis of comparison, the correlation coefficients that were found in earlier research when the test was readministered after only six months appear in the left-hand column of the table below. On a scale ranging from 0 (no correlation, no stability) to +1 (a perfect correlation, total stability), and using the six-month numbers as a guideline, predict the correlations that are found after six full years:

| TRAIT | SIX MONTHS | SIX YEARS |
|---|---|---|
| Neuroticism | .87 | _____ |
| Extraversion | .91 | _____ |
| Openness | .86 | _____ |

## THE RESULTS

The research just described is based on studies of adult personality that were conducted by Robert McCrae and Paul Costa (1990). So what did you predict? Does one's personality stay basically the same, or does it change over time? As shown below, the results revealed an extraordinary degree of stability—comparable, in fact, to that found after only six months.

| TRAIT | SIX MONTHS | SIX YEARS |
|---|---|---|
| Neuroticism | .87 | .83 |
| Extraversion | .91 | .82 |
| Openness | .86 | .83 |

## WHAT DOES IT ALL MEAN?

Think for a moment about your own personality—your basic feelings, attitudes, and ways of relating to others. Have you changed at all or stayed pretty much the same? When McCrae and Costa (1990) asked their subjects this question, 51 percent said they had stayed the same, 35 percent said they had changed a little, and 14 percent said they had changed a good deal. Were the self-perceptions of those who said they had changed accurate? Not according to the test scores. Costa and McCrae recalculated the test-retest correlations for only those subjects who said they had changed a lot—and the numbers were just as high.

As a general rule, personality is stable over time. Indeed, if it were not, you could not predict the kind of person you would be tomorrow, set a future career goal, or commit yourself to a marriage partner. This is not to say that we all stay the same as we get older. As we saw in Chapter 9, the aging process itself is accompanied by physical, sensory, and cognitive changes. As a result of life experiences, we may also change certain habits, attitudes, and behaviors. Even subtle shifts in personality are possible. When adults of different age groups are tested, for example, those who are older tend to score slightly lower on neuroticism, extraversion, and openness.

For clinical psychologists who work at helping people in distress, this research addressed a particularly critical question: Can people who suffer from anxiety, depression, or other types of mental disorders be helped? In Chapter 17, we'll see that they can. But as to the question of how much change is possible—and how difficult it is to facilitate that change—we'll see in this chapter that the answer you come up with will depend, in part, on your theoretical orientation.

Visit Amazon.com's online bookstore and type in "personality." How many related books pop up? When I did it in the spring of 2002, a total of 4,970 entries appeared.

Browse through any bookstore and you will notice that the shelves are lined with pop-psych books that promise to reveal your true hidden personality. All you have to do, they say, is analyze your diet (you are what you eat), color preferences (if you like red, you're said to be emotional), handwriting (short, clipped strokes mean that you're stingy), astrological signs (I've been told that I have a

Taurus-like stubborn streak), facial characteristics (people with eyes set close together cannot be trusted), and body shape ("round" people are outgoing party animals). Self-insight is not the only reason for all the interest in personality. Marketing experts categorize consumers so they can develop advertisements that appeal to certain segments of the market. Trial lawyers hire consultants to select jurors personally disposed to favor their case. Insurance companies generate profiles of high-risk clients prone to driving accidents. The FBI employs psychologists to probe the minds of terrorists and serial killers. Guidance counselors give tests to tell whether someone is suited to working alone or with people. Even novelists use vivid personality sketches to develop their characters.

So what is **personality**? Although the word comes from the Latin *persona*, which means "mask," personality is more than just a face we wear in public. It's also what lies behind the mask—an enduring "inner core" that embodies every individual's distinct pattern of thoughts, feelings, motives, values, and behaviors. The study of personality seeks to describe individuals, the ways in which they are similar to one another, and the ways in which each is unique (Funder, 2001).

This chapter presents four major approaches to the study of human personality: (1) psychoanalysis, (2) the cognitive social-learning approach, (3) the humanistic approach, and (4) the trait approach. Each perspective contains a set of theories that share certain assumptions about human nature—how personality forms and then develops; whether people are inherently good, bad, or neutral; the relative importance of biological and environmental factors; the role of unconscious determinants of behavior; and the question of stability and change. As we'll see, the scientific study of personality integrates theory, testing, and an interest in the clinical implications.

*You might say that this woman "has personality." But then we all do. Individuals differ not in the amount of personality they have but in their distinctive patterns of thoughts, feelings, motives, and behaviors.*

## PSYCHOANALYSIS

- *What experiences inspired Freud to formulate psychoanalysis?*
- *What do dreams, jokes, and slips of the tongue have in common?*
- *Who were Jung and Adler, and how did these theorists differ from Freud?*
- *What are projective tests—and how are they used?*
- *What is Freud's greatest legacy?*

On the evening of May 6, 1856, at 6:30 PM, a baby boy was born in what is now the Czech Republic to Jakob and Amalie Freud. The boy arrived in a caul, a membrane that sometimes covers the infant's head at birth. Superstition had it that to be born in a caul is a good-luck omen—a sign that the baby will one day achieve fame and fortune. After one year of marriage, Jakob and Amalie had little money, but they were thrilled. They named the first of their six children Sigmund.

The boy grew up to be strong, healthy, and bright, at the top of his class in school. He enrolled at the University of Vienna at the age of seventeen, received a medical degree eight years later, and became a practicing neurologist. By his own admission, Freud was a driven young man, one who sorely wanted to make his mark on the world. In 1884, however, his desire for fame took a downward turn. He had heard about a "magic drug" with anesthetic powers, tried it, and enjoyed the uplifting effects it had on his mood and work. Thinking he was on the verge of a medical breakthrough, Freud prescribed the drug to a friend, who became hopelessly addicted and died of an overdose. The drug was cocaine. Having lost a friend, a patient, and a measure of respect in the medical community, Freud abandoned the drug and pursued other interests.

**personality** An individual's distinct and relatively enduring pattern of thoughts, feelings, motives, and behaviors.

*Sigmund Freud and his daughter Anna—who went on to become a psychoanalyst in her own right.*

## THE BIRTH OF PSYCHOANALYSIS

In 1885, Freud moved to Paris to study with Jean Charcot, an eminent French neurologist. Charcot was studying *hysteria,* a "conversion disorder" in which the patient experiences symptoms such as paralysis of the limbs, blindness, deafness, convulsions, and the like—without an organic basis (see Chapter 16). What's fascinating about hysteria is that the patient is not faking, yet there's nothing physically wrong. Charcot found that hysterical disorders often started with a traumatic event in the patient's childhood and that he could make the symptoms vanish by putting the patient under hypnosis. You can imagine how dazzled Freud was by the sight of "paralyzed" patients suddenly able to walk and of those who were "blind" suddenly able to see. Demonstrations like these filled Freud with a profound regard for the power of unconscious forces.

Back in Vienna, Freud became intrigued by the case of Anna O., a patient who suffered from hysterical paralysis of three limbs, impaired vision and speech, and a nervous cough. With the help of her physician, Josef Breuer, Anna was able to recall the events that precipitated her symptoms. As if a large block had been removed from her mind, Anna's symptoms slowly disappeared. Breuer had invented a *talking cure.* But something else happened that would also prove significant. After many sessions, Anna had become emotionally attached to Breuer. Freud was puzzled by the intensity of Anna's feelings, until one day when he had the same experience. Without provocation, a female patient lovingly threw her arms around Freud's neck. Freud had not sought the patient's affection, he said, and assumed he was not the real target of her passion. He thought that this patient, without realizing it, must have transferred her feelings for someone else (maybe her father) onto him, a phenomenon Freud called *transference.*

Freud went into private practice but did not have much luck using hypnosis. He realized that not everyone could be hypnotized and that the so-called cures produced in hypnosis often did not last. To help patients recall and talk freely about their past, Freud came up with his first technique of psychotherapy, *free association.* The procedure is simple: The patient lies on a couch, relaxes, and says whatever comes to mind, no matter how trivial, embarrassing, or illogical it may seem. After many sessions, Freud noticed something curious. Although patients would produce streams of ideas leading to the unconscious, many seemed unable to talk or even think about painful and unpleasant memories. In fact, once on the brink of an important insight, they would often stop, go blank, lose their train of thought, or change the subject. Freud called this phenomenon *resistance* and concluded that it was part of an unconscious defensive process designed to keep unwanted thoughts under lock and key—and out of awareness.

## FREUD'S THEORY OF PERSONALITY

Freud's clinical experiences laid a foundation for the theory he later developed. He was convinced that the traumas and conflicts of early childhood can have lasting effects, that we are ruled by unconscious forces, that what's unconscious can be brought out through free association, that we resist painful self-insights, and that we often transfer our feelings for one object onto another. Slowly but surely, the pieces were falling into place. In 1896, Freud used the term **psychoanalysis** for the first time. Then in 1900, he published *The Interpretation of Dreams,* the first of his twenty-four books and the one that marked the birth of what would become one of the broadest, most influential theories in modern history. The theory is summarized in Freud's (1940) last book, *An Outline of Psychoanalysis,* published one year after his death.

**psychoanalysis** Freud's theory of personality and method of psychotherapy, both of which assume that our motives are largely unconscious.

**The Unconscious**   Underlying psychoanalysis is the assumption that personality is shaped largely by forces that act within a person's *unconscious*. To illustrate, Freud compared the human mind to an iceberg. Like the small tip of the iceberg that can be seen above the water, the conscious part of the mind consists of all that a person is aware of at a given moment. Below the surface is the vast region of the unconscious, which contains thoughts, feelings, and memories that are hidden from view. Part of this region lies just beneath the surface, in an area Freud called the preconscious. Preconscious material is not threatening, just temporarily out of awareness and easy to bring to mind. The rest of the unconscious, however, is a deep, dark sea of secret urges, wishes, and drives. According to Freud, the mind keeps these unacceptable impulses out of awareness. Still, they rumble, make waves, and surface for air—in our dreams, our slips of the tongue, the jokes we tell, the people we're attracted to, and the anxieties we feel. In other words, only through psychoanalysis can we achieve meaningful insight into our personality.

What's in the unconscious? According to Freud, two major instincts motivate all of human behavior. The first is collectively referred to as the *life instincts*, which include the need for food, water, air, and sex. At the time of Freud's writing, the sex part raised eyebrows. But Freud felt it was critical because many of the childhood stories that his patients described were sexual in nature. Years later, after living through the stark destruction of World War I, Freud also proposed that there is a second, darker side of human nature—that buried in the unconscious is a *death instinct*, a need to reduce all tensions by returning to a calm lifeless state. Because these self-destructive impulses conflict with the more powerful life forces, reasoned Freud, they are turned away from the self and directed instead toward others. The fated result of the death instinct, then, is aggression—a problem that has plagued humans throughout history.

**The Structure of Personality**   Have you ever had a burning urge to kiss or embrace someone you're attracted to or to hit someone who has angered you, only to be stopped by the haunting voice of your conscience? If so, how do you resolve these dilemmas? Based on his clinical experiences, Freud believed that people are perpetually driven by inner conflicts (conscious vs. unconscious, free association vs. resistance, life vs. death)—and that compromise is a necessary solution. Freud thus divided the human personality into three interacting parts: the id, ego, and superego. These parts are not presumed to be actual structures in the brain. Rather, they are concepts that Freud used to represent the different aspects of personality.

The **id** is the most primitive part of personality. Present at birth, it is a reservoir of instincts and biological drives that energize us. According to Freud, the id operates according to the **pleasure principle,** motivating us to seek immediate and total gratification of all desires. When a person is deprived of food, water, air, or sex, a state of tension builds until the need is satisfied. Thus, the id is a blind, pleasure-seeking part of us that aims for the reduction of all tension. If the impulsive, id-dominated infant could speak, it would scream: "I want it, and I want it *now*!"

The **superego** is a socially developed aspect of personality that motivates us to behave in ways that are moral, ideal, even perfect. Whereas the id pushes people to seek immediate gratification, the superego is a prude, a moralist, a part of us that shuns sex and other innate sources of pleasure. Where does the superego come from? According to Freud, children learn society's values from their parents. Through repeated experiences with reward for good behavior and punishment for

*"Every man has reminiscences which he would not tell to everyone but only to his friends. He has other matters in mind which he would not reveal even to his friends, but only to himself, and that in secret. But there are other things which a man is afraid to tell even to himself, and every decent man has a number of such things stored away in his mind."*
—FYODOR DOSTOYEVSKY

**id**   In psychoanalysis, a primitive and unconscious part of personality that contains basic drives and operates according to the pleasure principle.

**pleasure principle**   In psychoanalysis, the id's boundless drive for immediate gratification.

**superego**   In psychoanalysis, the part of personality that consists of one's moral ideals and conscience.

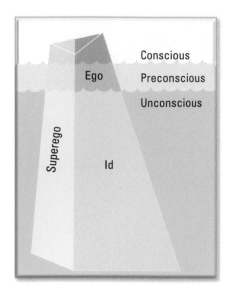

FIGURE 15.1 **The structure of personality according to Freud**

**ego** In psychoanalysis, the part of personality that operates according to the reality principle and mediates the conflict between the id and superego.

**reality principle** In psychoanalysis, the ego's capacity to delay gratification.

**psychosexual stages** Freud's stages of personality development during which pleasure is derived from different parts of the body (oral, anal, phallic, and genital).

**Oedipus complex** In psychoanalysis, a tendency for young children to become sexually attracted to the parent of the opposite sex and hostile toward the parent of the same sex.

bad, children eventually develop their own internal standards of what's right and wrong. The superego has two components. One is the *ego-ideal,* an image of the ideals we should strive for. The other is the *conscience,* a set of prohibitions that define how we should not behave. Once the superego is developed, people reward themselves internally for moral acts by feeling pride, and they punish themselves for immoral acts by suffering pangs of guilt.

The third aspect of personality is the **ego,** which mediates the conflict between the "wants" of the id and the "shoulds" of the superego. According to Freud, the ego is a pragmatic offshoot of the id, the part of personality that helps us achieve realistic forms of gratification. In contrast to the id (which strives for immediate gratification) and the superego (which seeks to inhibit the same impulses), the ego operates according to the **reality principle**—the goal being to reduce one's tensions, but only at the right time, in the right place, and in a socially appropriate manner. The ego is thus a master of compromise, a part of us that tries to satisfy our needs without offending our morals. The ego, said Freud, is the executive officer of the personality, the part that controls our behavior. Freud's model is illustrated in Figure 15.1.

**Psychosexual Development** According to Freud the physician, many of his patients told wild tales about childhood traumas—tales involving sexual and aggressive encounters with mothers, fathers, neighbors, and dirty old uncles. Eventually he came to believe that although some of the stories he heard were true, others were sheer fantasies, a product of overactive imaginations. In recent years, a number of psychologists have combed through Freud's clinical records and writings like detectives in search of a crime. Some now question whether his patients had ever talked of child sexual abuse, suggesting instead that Freud made the stories up or suggested them to his patients (Esterson, 2001). Others believe that these reformulations of Freud's work are unwarranted (Gleaves & Hernandez, 1999).

According to Freud, his clinical work led him to draw two conclusions about human development: (1) that personality is shaped in the first few years of life, and (2) that the resolution of "psychosexual" conflicts is the key contributor. He went on to propose that all children pass through an odyssey of **psychosexual stages** of development, with each stage defined by a different "erogenous zone," a part of the body that's most sensitive to erotic stimulation.

First in this theory comes the *oral stage,* which occurs in the first year of life, a time when the baby's mouth is the pleasure-seeking center of attention. Oral activity begins with the sucking of nipples, thumbs, and pacifiers, then moves on to biting, chewing, cooing, and other oral activities. In this stage, the infant is totally dependent on caretakers, feeding is a key activity, and weaning (the transition away from the breast or bottle) is a major source of conflict. Next comes the *anal stage,* which occurs during the second and third years of life, when the baby derives pleasure in the sensation of holding in and letting go of feces. There is a regular and enjoyable cycle of tension buildup and release. In this stage, however, toilet training brings the parent ("Wait!") and child ("I don't want to!") into sharp conflict. Between the ages of four and six, the child then enters the *phallic stage,* a time when pleasure is felt in the genital area. In this stage, children become fascinated with the body and can often be seen playing with their own sex organs in public, a habit that once again brings them into conflict with parents. To Freud, the single most dramatic conflict in psychosexual development takes place at this point.

There's a famous Greek tragedy in which the hero, an abandoned infant who goes on to become King Oedipus, returns as a young man to kill his father and marry his mother, both without realizing who they are. According to Freud, this legend exposes an unconscious human wish he called the **Oedipus complex**—a

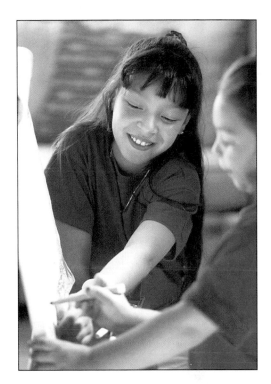

*According to Freud, psychosexual development progresses through stages, each one of which is defined by a part of the body that is most sensitive. In the oral stage (top left), everything is put into the mouth. During the anal stage (top center), toilet training brings the child and parents into conflict. Middle childhood is considered a calm latency period (top right) when sexual urges lie dormant. Beginning at puberty, the genital stage (bottom right) is marked by the emergence of adultlike sexual desires.*

tendency for children to become sexually attracted to the parent of the opposite sex and to develop feelings of jealousy and rage toward the rival parent of the same sex. Freud's theory of male development is clear: The young boy wants his mother and hates his father for standing in the way. Because the father is bigger and more powerful, however, the boy develops *castration anxiety,* a fear that the father will retaliate by cutting off his son's prized genitals. For defensive reasons, the boy represses his sexual urge for the mother and tries to emulate the father, in a process known as **identification**. As a result, the boy becomes less anxious, derives partial satisfaction of his repressed wish for his mother, and adopts his father's moral values. Freud admitted that his theory of female development is less clear. At some point, he says, the girl notices that her father has a penis but that she and her mother do not. Unconsciously, the girl blames and resents her mother for this deficiency, develops *penis envy,* and seeks to become daddy's little girl. Eventually, she realizes the futility of these feelings, represses her envy, and identifies with her mother. For both boys and girls, then, the identification part of the process is important: It means that the superego springs full blown from the Oedipus complex.

Once Oedipal conflicts are resolved, the child enters a long *latency period,* which lasts roughly between the ages of seven and twelve. In these middle years of childhood, sexual impulses lie dormant, as boys and girls concentrate on friends of the same sex and schoolwork. As parents come to appreciate, this is a time of calm between storms. Indeed, it precedes the fourth and final stage of psychosexual development—the *genital stage.* Starting at puberty, boys and girls emerge from their latency shells and feel the stirring of adultlike sexual urges for the first time. Once again, the ego must cope with an undeclared state of war between biological drives and social prohibitions.

According to Freud, one must pass successfully through all psychosexual stages in order to form a healthy personality and enjoy mature adult relationships. If

**identification** In psychoanalysis, the process by which children internalize their parent's values and form a superego.

**fixation** In psychoanalysis, a tendency to get "locked in" at early, immature stages of psychosexual development.

**defense mechanisms** Unconscious methods of minimizing anxiety by denying and distorting reality.

**repression** A defense mechanism in which personally threatening thoughts, memories, and impulses are banned from awareness.

**denial** A primitive form of repression in which anxiety-filled external events are barred from awareness.

children receive *too much* or *too little* gratification at an earlier stage, they will become stuck or "fixated" at that stage. **Fixation** is thus responsible for the development of the following personality types:

■ **Oral.** If you were weaned too early or too late as an infant, you would become fixated at the oral stage and feel the need to smoke, drink, bite your nails, chew on pencils, or spend hours talking on the phone. You might also seek symbolic forms of oral gratification by becoming passive, dependent, and demanding— like a nursing infant.

■ **Anal.** If, as a toddler, you were toilet trained in a harsh and rigid manner, you would become anally fixated and react in one of two ways—either by becoming tight, stubborn, punctual, and overcontrolled (the holding-on, "anal-retentive" type) or by becoming rebellious, messy, and disorganized (the letting-go, "anal-expulsive" type).

■ **Phallic.** If you masturbated freely during the preschool years or if all genital contact was prohibited, resulting in frustration, you would develop a phallic personality—one that is entirely self-centered, vain, arrogant, and in constant need of attention. The man who seems obsessed with building his muscles, wearing expensive clothing, and conquering women is a classic example.

**The Dynamics of Personality** Influenced by the science of physics, Freud believed that the human mind has a constant, finite amount of "psychic energy"— energy that cannot be created or destroyed, only transformed from one state to another. What this means for personality is that even though the id's instinctual impulses can be temporarily suppressed, its energy must find an outlet, a way to leak out. According to Freud, the ego searches for safe and normal outlets for these needs.

> *"Every impulse we strive to strangle broods in the mind, and poisons us."*
>
> —OSCAR WILDE

You may recall from Chapter 4 that in Freud's theory, the dreams you remember in the morning are a disguised, nonthreatening expression of your unconscious wishes. Pent-up energy is released while you're asleep, but in ways that are confusing, and therefore nonthreatening. The same is true of the so-called Freudian slips of the tongue and, as we'll see later, a defense mechanism known as sublimation. Even humor can serve as an outlet, as when people tell ethnic jokes to relieve hostile impulses and erotic jokes to ease their sexual tension. Disguised wish fulfillment—it's the compromise we strike with ourselves (see Figure 15.2).

To help minimize the anxiety that results from the clash between our wishes, morals, and reality, the ego uses powerful weapons: unconscious defense mechanisms that deny and distort our self-perceptions. Here are some common **defense mechanisms** described by Freud. See if you recognize any of them:

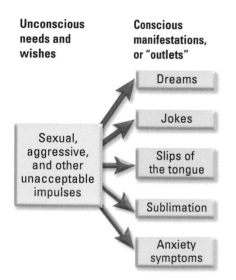

**FIGURE 15.2 The psychodynamics of personality**
In psychoanalysis, unconscious sexual and aggressive impulses find acceptable forms of expression.

■ **Repression** occurs when anxiety-provoking thoughts and memories are "forgotten" and pushed out of awareness. Freud believed that people repress unacceptable sexual and aggressive urges, traumas, and guilt feelings. A few years ago, a woman jogging in Central Park, in New York, was raped, beaten, and left for dead by a gang of teenagers. She later testified that she could barely remember the attack—a possible sign of repression. According to Freud, this defense mechanism is a necessary prerequisite for all the others but is seldom an ultimate solution.

■ **Denial** is a primitive form of repression in which anxiety-filled external events not only are forgotten but also are barred from awareness in the first place (see no evil, hear no evil). Denial is common among terminally ill patients and in families that sometimes refuse to admit that a loved one is dying. It is also characteristic of smokers who refuse to recognize the health risks of their habit, husbands and wives who ignore signs of marital conflict, and politicians who manage to overlook corruption that takes place right under their noses.

■ **Projection** occurs when people attribute or "project" their own unacceptable impulses onto others. In Freud's view, a person who is sexually attracted to a friend's spouse, or to anyone else who is "off limits," might repress those feelings and consciously come to believe that the friend's spouse is attracted to him or her. In this way, "I lust for this person" is transformed into "This person lusts after me." Similarly, people who are prejudiced against certain racial or ethnic groups are quick to attribute their own hostile impulses to "them."

■ **Reaction formation** involves converting an unacceptable feeling into its opposite. Someone who brags may be masking feelings of inadequacy. Similarly, hatred can be transformed into love, and sadness into joy. Compared to true feelings, reaction formations often appear exaggerated. Examples include the mother who smothers with affection an unwanted child she secretly resents, the schoolboy who goes out of his way to taunt a girl he really likes, the antipornography crusader who deep down inside is aroused by sexually explicit material, and the vocal antigay activist who fights to cover up his own homosexual impulses.

■ **Rationalization** involves making excuses for one's failures and shortcomings. The fox in Aesop's fable who refused the grapes he could not reach "because they were sour" used rationalization. So do failing students who say they don't really care about their grades, gamblers who justify their massive losses as entertainment costs, and scorned lovers who find fault with those who reject them.

■ **Sublimation** is the channeling of the id's repressed urges into socially acceptable substitute outlets. Freud saw this as the healthiest defense mechanism because it represents a genuine compromise among the id, ego, and superego. Thus, a person with pent-up hostile impulses may derive satisfaction by becoming a surgeon, football player, or critic. Similarly, a person may sublimate sexual needs by listening to others talk about sex or through music, art, dance, and other activities. Freud believed that civilization's greatest achievements spring from the wells of sexual and aggressive energies. He suggested, for example, that Leonardo da Vinci painted the famous *Mona Lisa* as a sublimation of his need for intimacy with a mother from whom he was separated at an early age. As for other men, the lyrics of an old song hint at how substitute gratification for repressed Oedipal urges can be achieved: "I want a girl just like the girl that married dear old dad!"

## FREUD'S LEGACY

Freud was born and raised in the prudish Victorian era, so his theory was met with skepticism. Unconscious conflicts, dreams, jokes, and slips of the tongue that hold hidden meaning, erotic impulses churning in the innocent newborn baby, repression and other defense mechanisms that keep us from falling apart at the seams—it all seemed pretty wild. Still, Freud's legacy is remarkable. As we'll see, his ideas gave rise to other psychoanalytic theories and a whole class of personality tests. He also provided something for psychologists of other theoretical persuasions to shoot at— and build upon.

**Neo-Freudian Theorists**   Despite the controversy, Freud's emerging theory immediately attracted a group of followers, many of whom went on to propose competing theories. Make no mistake about it, these dissenters were psychoanalytically

"But if I say I'm in denial then, by definition, I'm *not* in denial."

**projection**   A defense mechanism in which people attribute or "project" their own unacceptable impulses onto others.

**reaction formation**   A defense mechanism in which one converts an unacceptable feeling into its opposite.

**rationalization**   A defense mechanism that involves making excuses for one's failures and shortcomings.

**sublimation**   In psychoanalysis, the channeling of repressed sexual and aggressive urges into socially acceptable substitute outlets.

*Carl Jung*

*Alfred Adler*

**collective unconscious** As proposed by Jung, a kind of memory bank that stores images and ideas that humans have accumulated over the course of evolution.

oriented. Following Freud, they assumed that unconscious factors play a critical role, that people need to resolve inner conflicts, and that personality is formed early in childhood. The main sticking point was—and still is, for many—Freud's emphasis on s-e-x as a driving force.

Carl Jung was a favorite within Freud's inner circle, heir apparent to the throne of psychoanalysis. Jung (1928), however, complained that Freud viewed the brain "as an appendage to the genital glands," and he sought to change the theory in two ways. First, Jung maintained that the unconscious consists not only of repressed material from one's personal life but also of universal symbols and memories from our ancestral past—an inherited **collective unconscious**. That's why, said Jung, so many humans are born with an irrational fear of snakes; why we're drawn like magnets to fire, water, wind, and other natural elements; and why certain common themes appear in cultural myths and legends around the world. Jung's second shift in emphasis concerned the subject of personality development. He agreed that people strive for the satisfaction of biological drives. But he also felt that at the age of forty or so, we undergo a midlife transition, a time during which the youthful and vigorous pursuit of biological needs is replaced by deeper, more cerebral, even spiritual concerns. As far as Jung was concerned, personality development continues into adulthood.

Alfred Adler was another major theorist within Freud's inner circle. Like the others, Adler was trained in medicine. He broke with Freud, however, because he felt that personality was formed more from social conflicts than from sexual tension. According to Adler (1927), all humans feel small, helpless, and weak in the first few years of life, symptoms of what he termed an *inferiority complex*. As a result, we grow up trying unconsciously to compensate for these feelings and strive for superiority, while at the same time taking an interest in the welfare of others. Adler felt that Freud was so focused on the triangle of relationships among mother, father, and child that he neglected other family influences. Adler wrote, for example, about the impact of being first-, middle-, or later-born within the family, and he coined the term *sibling rivalry*.

Later generations of psychoanalytic theorists either viewed themselves as classical Freudians (Brenner, 1982) or extended the theory in two directions. One group followed in Adler's path by emphasizing that humans are inherently social animals. Erich Fromm (1941) maintained that as Western civilization abandoned the caste system, people felt freer and more independent but also more alone and isolated. Fromm argued that we unconsciously seek to "escape from freedom" by falling in love, getting married, having children, joining religious groups, and rallying behind powerful leaders. What distinguishes individuals from one another, he proposed, are the ways in which they resolve the conflict between freedom and unity. Karen Horney (1945) similarly claimed that all humans need love and security and become highly anxious when they feel isolated and alone. According to Horney, people have different ways of coping with this anxiety: Some are unconsciously driven to be loved, others to be feared, and still others to be admired. Again, the goal is to satisfy needs that are social, not biological.

A second group of psychoanalysts known as ego psychologists enlarged the role of the ego in personality. For Freud, the ego existed in order to accommodate the id and yet operate within the boundaries of reality, appease the superego, and ward off anxiety through the use of defense mechanisms. But according to daughter Anna Freud, Heinz Hartmann, David Rapaport, Erik Erikson, and other theorists, the ego is more than simply the id's brainy assistant. In their view, the ego is present at birth, is as basic as the id, and is the reason why people are thoughtful as well as passionate. This ego helps to organize our thoughts, feelings, and memories, and it leads us to grow and pursue creative activities for the sake of enjoyment, not simply the reduction of tension. As ego psychologist Robert White (1975) put it, "Human beings have intrinsic urges which make them want to grow up."

**Projective Personality Tests**   Psychoanalysis is founded on the assumption that meaningful parts of one's personality are locked away in an unconscious part of the mind. What this means is that one cannot truly get to know someone by asking direct questions. Searching for the key to this warehouse of personal secrets, Freud tried hypnosis, free association, and the interpretation of dreams—the "royal road to the unconscious." Is it possible to explore the mind without psychotherapy? Seeking a shortcut to the unconscious, psychoanalytic researchers and practitioners devised what's known as **projective tests**. A projective test asks people to respond to an ambiguous stimulus—a word out of context, an incomplete sentence, an inkblot, a fuzzy picture. The assumption they make is that if a stimulus has no inherent meaning and can accommodate a multitude of interpretations, then whatever people see must be a *projection* of their own needs, wishes, hopes, fears, and conflicts.

The most popular of the projective tests is the **Rorschach**, introduced in 1921 by Swiss psychiatrist Hermann Rorschach, which consists of a set of ten symmetrical inkblots—some in color, others in black and white. Look, for example, at the inkblot in Figure 15.3. What do you see? Is it a man with a beer belly wearing a bow tie? Two bats hanging from a wall? Two women bending over a pot? An upside-down frog? A bearskin rug? A butterfly? As you can imagine, stimuli like this can evoke wildly different interpretations. You may see crawling insects, animals, humans, sexual organs, or weapons or other inanimate objects. You may see a single large image, or you might dissect the inkblot into many smaller images. In fact, the examiner is interested not only in what you see but also in how you approach the task—whether you take two seconds per card or five minutes; whether you're sensitive to form or to color; and whether the images you report are common or uncommon. I'll never forget the time a graduate school friend of mine was learning to work with the Rorschach as part of her clinical training and used me as a guinea pig. Following a series of black-and-white inkblots, she turned over a bright, multicolored design. "Wow, nice!" was my immediate reaction, at which point my friend raised an eyebrow and quickly jotted down some notes. Later, I was told that not everyone reacts as I did to the color—that my animated reaction meant I'm an emotional person.

Over the years, many elaborate systems have been developed for scoring the Rorschach, which is still widely used in clinical practice. Critics say there are two problems. The first is that it lacks reliability, which means that two examiners often reach different conclusions from the same set of responses. The second is that the test lacks validity, which means that it does not discriminate well among groups known to have different personalities. In a scathing critique, Robyn Dawes (1994) called the Rorschach a "shoddy" instrument and suggested that it "is not a valid test of anything" (p. 146).

Despite these criticisms, Rorschach users are now becoming more sophisticated. Using past research, John Exner, Jr. (1993) developed a computerized scoring system. Studies have shown that, as a general rule, there are higher levels of reliability and validity than in the past (Parker et al., 1988)—but that these levels are still lower than those found in the kinds of "objective" tests to be described later (Garb et al., 1998). According to many Rorschach users, however, skillful examiners can employ the test to understand how people think and to explore depths of personality that do not otherwise surface in questionnaires, interviews, or observations of behavior (Exner, 1996). To this day, researchers are split in their opinions and continue to debate the value of this inkblot test as a measure of personality (Hunsley & Bailey, 2001; Meyer & Archer, 2001; Wood et al., 2002).

**FIGURE 15.3   Sample Rorschach card**
According to psychoanalytically oriented psychologists, what you see in this inkblot—and how you see it—can be used to assess your personality.

**projective tests**   Psychoanalytic personality tests that allow people to "project" unconscious needs, wishes, and conflicts onto ambiguous stimuli.

**Rorschach**   A projective personality test in which people are asked to report what they see in a set of inkblots.

**FIGURE 15.4   Sample TAT picture**
This ambiguous picture is used in the Thematic Apperception Test.

Reprinted by permission of the publishers from Henry A. Murray, THEMATIC APPERCEPTION TEST, Cambridge, Mass.: Harvard University Press, © 1943 by the President and Fellows of Harvard College, © 1971 by Henry A. Murray.

**Thematic Apperception Test (TAT)**   A projective personality test in which people are asked to make up stories from a set of ambiguous pictures.

A second popular projective instrument is the **Thematic Apperception Test,** or **TAT,** introduced by Henry Murray. In 1938, Murray formulated a personality theory that distinguishes people by the kinds of psychological needs that motivate their behavior—such as the needs for power, achievement, nurturance, and affiliation. We saw in Chapter 11, in our discussion of achievement motivation, that to measure these needs, Murray (1943) developed a set of drawings of characters in ambiguous situations (plus one blank card, the ultimate projective test!) and asked subjects to tell a story about the "hero." Look, for example, at the picture presented in Figure 15.4. What do you see going on? Who are the characters, and what's their relationship? What led up to this situation, and how will it all turn out? You can see that the possibilities are limitless—like a blank page awaiting your personal signature. The last time I showed this card to my students, I received a wide range of stories. Some said the woman in the shawl is the girl's mother, disappointed in her daughter's choice of a husband or career or in the fact that she's a lesbian. Others said that the girl is looking into the mirror, seeing herself as an old woman, alone and without a family. Still others said that the young woman is angry at her mother for driving her father out of the house.

The TAT is based on the assumption that people identify with the heroes and project their own needs into their responses. If someone tells one story after another about the loss of a loved one, resistance to authority, the struggle to achieve success, or fear of rejection, chances are that the particular theme is an important one for the person. As with the Rorschach, the TAT has been criticized for lacking high levels of reliability and validity (Anastasi & Urbina, 1997). At the same time, certain TAT pictures have been reliably used to identify specific motives and predict behavior. As we saw in Chapter 11, for example, people whose TAT stories reveal a high rather than low *need for intimacy* think more often about their social relationships and spend more time talking, smiling, and making eye contact when engaged in conversation (McAdams et al., 1984). In contrast, people whose stories reveal a high rather than low *need for achievement* set realistic goals, persist more in the face of failure, are more likely to succeed at work, and derive more pride from their accomplishments (Atkinson, 1957; McClelland, 1985; Spangler, 1992). Not all TAT cards will activate a person's need state, but when they do, the fantasy stories people tell, and the themes they emphasize, reveal their personalities (Cramer, 1996; Gieser & Stein, 1999; Tuerlinckx et al., 2002).

**Current Perspectives on Psychoanalysis**   In 1993, *Time* magazine had a picture of Sigmund Freud on the cover, accompanied by three words: "Is Freud Dead?" It has now been more than a hundred years since Freud started putting together the pieces of psychoanalysis, a theory that would alter the course of psychology as a discipline. Needless to say, Freud and his fellow psychoanalysts have always attracted their share of critics, as new research developments within psychology lead us to modify or reject some propositions and to accept others. To this day, Freud remains a subject of biography, analysis, and controversy (Breger, 2000; Gay, 1988).

There are three major criticisms of psychoanalysis. One is that as a theory of personality it paints too bleak a portrait of human nature. It was bad enough when Copernicus exposed the myth that earth is at the center of the universe and when Darwin said that human beings were descended from apes. But when Freud claimed that we are driven, even as infants, by lustful, incestuous desires and antisocial, aggressive impulses and that we are all at the mercy of unconscious forces beyond our control, some felt he went too far. The theory was simply too pessimistic for many people to accept. Before World War II, physicist Albert Einstein wrote Freud and asked if he thought that war could be avoided. Freud wrote back a fourteen-page letter. The essence of his answer was *no*, war is inevitable.

The second criticism of psychoanalysis is that it does not meet acceptable standards of science. From the start, Freud based his whole theory on observations he made of his Vienna patients, hardly a representative group of human beings. He then proceeded to use the theory to explain family dynamics, mental illness, love and attraction, homosexuality, war, religion, suicide, crime and punishment, and the course of human history. Of course, after-the-fact explanations are easy, very much like betting on a horse after the race has been run. But can Freud's theory predict these kinds of events in advance?

The critics say *no*, which leads to the third major criticism of psychoanalysis: Carefully controlled research fails to support many of its propositions. One important example concerns the assumption that personality is completely formed in the first few years of life. In light of recent research, we now know that although early childhood experiences are formative, and can have a lasting impact on us, development is a lifelong process (see Chapter 9). Freud's theory that childhood conflicts cause people to become fixated at certain psychosexual stages has also not stood the test of time. Research has shown that although oral, anal, and phallic personality types can be identified, they don't necessarily arise from difficulties experienced in weaning, toilet training, masturbation, or other psychosexual experiences. Even the Oedipus complex, the centerpiece of Freud's development theory, receives little support. Young boys and girls often do favor the opposite-sex parent and identify with the same-sex parent—but there's little evidence for castration anxiety, penis envy, or other sex-related motives (Fisher & Greenberg, 1977; Daly & Wilson, 1990).

So is Freud dead? The man is, but his influence clearly is not—leading Drew Westen (1998) to note that Freud's "repeated burials lie on shaky grounds" (p. 333). In its classic form, psychoanalysis has shortcomings and relatively few adherents. But many of its concepts have become so absorbed into mainstream psychology—not to mention popular culture—that it is very much alive and continues to inspire new theories and research. In fact, some researchers believe that recent advances in neuroscience may make it possible to uncover the biological bases for some of Freud's ideas (Kandel, 1999).

As a physician, Freud helped to convince the world that mental disorders are often psychological, not medical, in origin. As a personality theorist, he drew attention to the profound importance of the attachment bond between parents and the growing young child, the powerful unconscious filled with inner turmoil, and our arsenal of nonrational coping mechanisms. The theory may paint an unflattering portrait, psychoanalysts will admit, but one must recognize the dark shadows of human nature in order to deal with them. Freud had the courage to expose this side of us and to penetrate beneath the surface of our behavior.

Perhaps the most enduring of Freud's ideas is his view of the mind as an iceberg. Today, virtually everyone agrees that the unconscious is vast and important—and that people have a limited awareness of why they think, feel, and behave as they do (Singer, 1990). Psychologists disagree, however, about the nature of the human unconscious. Some maintain that it contains thoughts, wishes, impulses, memories, and other information actively blocked from awareness for self-protective reasons (Erdelyi, 1992; Bowers & Farvolden, 1996). Others maintain that the unconscious consists of innocent material that is not attended to, or else is forgotten, for strictly cognitive reasons (Greenwald, 1992; Kihlstrom et al., 1992).

As we have seen in previous chapters, psychologists today are busily studying a wide range of unconscious processes such as perception without awareness, implicit learning and memory, subliminal influences, and implicit social stereotypes. Two

"And then I say to myself, 'If I really wanted to talk to her, why do I keep forgetting to dial 1 first?'"

recent lines of research illustrate the vitality of Freud's observations concerning the power of unconscious forces. In one set of experiments, Susan Andersen and Michele Berk (1998) have found, just as Freud had observed, that when someone we meet for the first time reminds us of a significant other in our lives, without realizing it we "transfer" our feelings from the significant other onto this new person—and assume that he or she has other resemblances as well. In another set of experiments, Tom Pyszczynski, Jeff Greenberg, and Sheldon Solomon (1999) have found that when people are confronted with fleeting thoughts of death—a source of anxiety that Freud wrote about—they engage in a host of defensive processes, desperately trying to suppress thoughts about their own mortality. According to their provocative *terror-management theory,* this deeply rooted fear of death highly motivates people to see themselves as valuable members of society, to see their own cultural worldviews as good and correct, and to harbor contempt and prejudice for others who are different.

This leads us to a second enduring legacy of Freud's theory: his analysis of defense mechanisms. Based on the resistance shown by so many of his patients, Freud argued that people distort reality to ward off anxiety. Research shows that he was absolutely right. Some of us may be more defensive than others, but everyone harbors illusions about the self. We see ourselves in inflated terms, we have an exaggerated sense of control over uncontrollable events, we compare ourselves to others who are less fortunate, and we think more optimistically than we should about our own future—and these illusions may help us cope with adversity (Taylor & Armor, 1996). These forms of coping are defense mechanisms much like those Freud had described (Baumeister et al., 1998; Cramer, 1998). Indeed, Phebe Cramer (2000) notes that Freud's view of unconscious defense mechanisms is now supported throughout psychology in various studies of attention, thinking, feeling, memory, and coping without awareness. This part of Freud's theory can shed light on some of the most irrational and atrocious acts of humankind. For example, Robert Jay Lifton (1986) interviewed twenty-eight Nazi doctors who aided in the murder of millions of concentration-camp victims in World War II, and he found that these men covered their psychological tracks through denial, rationalization, "psychic numbing," and other unconscious forms of self-deception.

If he were alive, Freud would have liked Lifton's analysis of the Nazi doctors. Freud himself had to escape Vienna when the Nazis stormed his hometown. He died in 1939, in London, at the age of eighty-three. Sixteen years later, a statue was unveiled in the courtyard of the University of Vienna, where he used to walk as a student. The inscription on the statue reads: "Sigmund Freud: who divined the famed riddle and was a man most mighty."

## REVIEW QUESTIONS

- *Define transference, free association, and resistance.*

- *Describe the three different parts of the personality identified by Freud.*

- *Summarize the psychosexual stages of personality development. What role does fixation play in this model?*

- *What purpose do defense mechanisms serve? Describe the various defense mechanisms.*

- *In what way did neo-Freudians expand on traditional Freudian theory?*

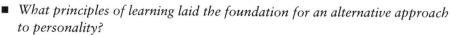

# THE COGNITIVE SOCIAL-LEARNING APPROACH

- *What principles of learning laid the foundation for an alternative approach to personality?*
- *What is locus of control, and how do internals and externals differ?*
- *What is reciprocal determinism?*

**cognitive social-learning theory** An approach to personality that focuses on social learning (modeling), acquired cognitive factors (expectancies, values), and the person-situation interaction.

In contrast to psychoanalysis, **cognitive social-learning theory** is an approach that views personality as the product of a continuous interaction between persons and their environments. This theory has its roots in the behavioral principles of classical and operant conditioning, social-learning theory, and cognitive psychology. Let's trace the evolution of this important second approach.

# PRINCIPLES OF LEARNING AND BEHAVIOR

As psychoanalysis was emerging in Europe, a second movement was being conceived in animal laboratories in the United States and Russia. At the time, animal researchers were discovering some very powerful principles of learning and were spreading the new word of behaviorism—a scientific approach to psychology that focuses on environmental determinants of observable behavior. To the hard-core behaviorist, personality was a nonscientific figment of the Freudian imagination. After all, behaviorists had refused to muddy the scientific study of behavior by speculating about inner states of "mind." As we saw earlier in this book, the first spokesperson for this countermovement was John Watson, whose message was loud and clear:

> Give me a dozen healthy infants, well-formed, and my own specified world to bring them up in, and I'll guarantee to take any one at random and train him to become any type of specialist I might select—doctor, lawyer, artist, merchant-chief and, yes, even beggarman and thief, regardless of his talents, penchants, tendencies, abilities, vocations, and race of his ancestors. (1925, p. 104)

At the same time that Freud was writing his classic book on dreams, animal researchers were discovering five simple but very powerful principles of learning: classical conditioning, operant conditioning, stimulus generalization, discrimination, and extinction (these are more fully described in Chapter 5).

The first, classical conditioning, was based on Ivan Pavlov's finding that the dogs in his laboratory would start to salivate before they were fed, in anticipation of the meal they were about to eat. By repeatedly sounding a buzzer before the presentation of food, Pavlov found that eventually the dogs would salivate as soon as the buzzer was sounded. Thus, the animals were trained to react to a neutral stimulus that was associated with food, which is an unconditioned stimulus that naturally elicits the reaction. The second major principle was operant conditioning, first shown by Edward Thorndike's finding that organisms repeat behaviors that are rewarded. Working with cats and, later, with humans, Thorndike found that whatever solution succeeded for a subject on one puzzle was later tried on other puzzles as well. A few years later, B. F. Skinner tested the effects of reinforcement schedules on behavior by training rats to press bars and pigeons to peck at keys for food.

Both classical- and operant-conditioning researchers made parallel discoveries not yet relevant to the study of personality. The first was stimulus generalization, the principle that once a response is learned in one situation, it may also be evoked in other, similar situations—as when Pavlov's dogs learned to salivate to tones that were similar but not identical to the conditioned stimulus. The second, opposite principle is discrimination: the learned tendency to distinguish between a conditioned stimulus and other stimuli—as when a child learns that having tantrums works on parents but not on teachers and friends. The third principle is extinction, the tendency for a conditioned response to diminish if not reinforced. Pavlov's dogs eventually stopped salivating to the buzzer if it was no longer followed by meat, and Skinner's animals stopped pressing bars when food pellets were no longer forthcoming.

These principles of learning and behavior were momentous discoveries in psychology, the new science of behavior. But what did drooling dogs, puzzled cats, and key-pecking pigeons have to do with personality? In a crude first attempt to answer this question, John Watson and Rosalie Rayner (1920) conducted a well-known but ethically questionable demonstration. As you may recall from Chapter 5, Watson and Rayner brought an eleven-month-old boy named Albert into contact with a harmless white rat, then repeatedly made a loud sound every time the boy reached for the animal. Soon poor Albert was terrified not only of the rat but of rabbits, dogs, and a white furry coat. What was the point? Poking fun at Freud and his followers,

Watson declared that some day a psychoanalyst would meet a man named Albert with a fur-coat phobia, analyze his dreams, and conclude that his fear is related to a scolding he received from his white-haired mother. Such were the pitfalls of a non-scientific approach to personality, said Watson. Looking back, Mark Rilling (2000) notes an interesting paradox: That despite Watson's anti-Freudian bias, Watson popularized psychoanalysis and pioneered the scientific study of its concepts.

Picking up where Watson left off, B. F. Skinner emerged as behaviorism's most forceful and dedicated proponent. He coined the term *operant conditioning*, studied different schedules of reinforcement, and wrote about how these principles could be used to socialize children, increase worker productivity, extinguish behavioral disorders, and build a better society. As far as Skinner was concerned, personality is nothing more than a collection of behavior patterns acquired, maintained, and—if necessary—modified by one's unique history of reinforcement.

## SOCIAL-LEARNING THEORY

Although Skinner offered a change of pace from psychoanalysis, many psychologists found his pointed focus on behavior too narrow and rejected his unwillingness to explore thoughts, feelings, motivations, and the richness and texture of the human personality. At the very least, it seemed that behaviorism had to be extended in two ways. Enter social-learning theory, an approach that examines the social and cognitive factors involved in learning and the development of personality. Leading the way were Albert Bandura, Julian Rotter, and Walter Mischel.

The first problem was to account for the fact that people often acquire new behavior patterns without personal experience with reward and punishment. According to Bandura (1977), people learn by observing and imitating others, a process called **modeling.** Children, for example, absorb what their parents say and how they act, pay close attention to TV characters and sports heroes, and emulate peers whom they admire. Research shows that modeling is a multistep process: We look, we learn, and we store in memory (learning). Then, if we are capable and motivated, and if the time is right, we imitate (performance). Bandura thus reminded us that learning takes place in a social context and that people can learn to become aggressive, helpful, fearful, moral, and so on by observing others (see Chapter 5).

The second important extension of behaviorism was to examine how our thoughts can influence the effects of reinforcement on behavior. Skinner had insisted that behavior is determined by actual reinforcement contingencies, but Julian Rotter (1954) argued that what really matters is how we perceive, interpret, and value the rewards in our lives. According to Rotter, human behavior in any given situation is determined by two broad factors: (1) our subjective *expectancy* that a specific act will be reinforced, and (2) the *value* to us of that reinforcement. If you expect that reading the rest of this book will help you learn psychology and earn a high grade for the course—and if these strike you as desirable outcomes—you'll probably read on. If you don't expect to learn from this book or if you don't really care, this may be the last paragraph you read. As far as personality is concerned, Rotter and his colleagues (1972) found that individuals differ both in the amount of control they expect to have over outcomes in their lives and in the kinds of outcomes they value.

Expanding on Rotter's model, Walter Mischel (1973) proposed a *cognitive social-learning theory.* According to Mischel, it is important to consider five "person variables" to understand how individuals interact with their environment. These person variables are (1) *competencies*—our mental and physical abilities, social skills, and creative talents, all of which influence what we strive for and what we can do; (2) *encoding strategies*—how we process information about other

**modeling** The social-learning process by which behavior is observed and imitated.

people and situations (for example, whether we tend to evaluate others in terms of their intelligence, friendliness, power, or physical appearance); (3) *expectancies*—our beliefs about the causes of success and failure and other possible consequences of our actions (there are two types of expectancies: whether we can perform a particular behavior, and whether it will be reinforced); (4) *subjective values*—the kinds of outcomes we find more or less rewarding (for example, whether we strive for love, security, respect, or dominance); and (5) *self-regulatory systems*—our ability to set goals, monitor and evaluate our progress, delay our short-term needs for gratification, and plan for the future.

Self-regulation is an important, highly adaptive person variable. In many years of research, Mischel and others (1989) have found that preschoolers who show they can defer their gratification in the laboratory, say, by waiting for a larger but delayed reward, grow up to become more competent, attentive, deliberate, and able to cope with real frustrations later in life. In fact, the number of seconds a preschool child is willing to wait for two marshmallows—rather than settling for the one that is immediately available—is predictive of his or her SAT scores in high school. Metcalfe and Mischel (1999) have suggested that to exercise such self-control, or willpower, we must learn to use various cognitive strategies that enable us to override the "go" impulses that can lure us away from our long-term goals. One way to do this is by working on some task rather than waiting passively for a future reward. In a study of preschool boys and girls, researchers found that those who worked on a Baby Bird feeding task while waiting for a desirable but delayed reward were more patient and willing to wait (Peake et al., 2002).

*An internal orientation is adaptive—except in situations that are not truly controllable.*

**Locus of Control**   According to cognitive social-learning theory, human behavior is influenced not by actual reinforcements, as Skinner had maintained, but by our perceptions of control. Think about it. Is there a connection between how hard you study and the grades you receive, or does grading seem arbitrary? Does getting ahead require hard work and persistence, or is it simply a matter of being in the right place at the right time? Can individuals influence government policies or global conflicts, or are we at the mercy of powerful leaders? And what about the quality of your health, friendships, and financial well-being—are you in control?

According to Rotter (1966), individuals differ in their **locus of control,** defined as a generalized expectancy for the control of reinforcement. People who have an *internal* locus of control believe they are in charge of their own destiny. Those who have an *external* locus of control feel they are at the mercy of luck, fate, and powerful others. To assess these contrasting orientations, Rotter constructed the I-E Scale (see Table 15.1). Immediately, psychologists grasped the implications of having an internal or external locus of control. Over the years, many hundreds of studies using the I-E Scale were published. Studying people of different ages, cultures, and ethnic backgrounds, researchers found that internals, compared to externals, are more inquisitive, active, hardworking, and persistent. They are also more likely to take preventive health measures, play an active role in social and political affairs, get high grades in school, and cope actively with stressful life events (Lefcourt, 1982; Strickland, 1989; Rotter, 1990).

To see whether you are an internal or an external, look at the six items from the I-E Scale in Table 15.1. For each item, circle the letter (a or b) of the statement you agree with more. Give yourself one point for each of the following answers: 1 (a), 2 (b), 3 (a), 4 (b), 5 (b), 6 (a). Next, add up your total number of points (from 0 to 6).

**locus of control**   A term referring to the expectancy that one's reinforcements are generally controlled by internal or external factors.

| TABLE 15.1 | ARE YOU AN INTERNAL OR AN EXTERNAL? |
| --- | --- |

1. a. No matter how hard you try, some people just don't like you.
   b. People who can't get others to like them don't understand how to get along with others.

2. a. One of the major reasons we have wars is because people don't take enough interest in politics.
   b. There will always be wars, no matter how hard people try to prevent them.

3. a. Sometimes I can't understand how teachers arrive at the grades they give.
   b. There is a direct connection between how hard I study and the grades I get.

4. a. The average citizen can have an influence in government decisions.
   b. This world is run by a few people in power, and there is not much the little guy can do about it.

5. a. Becoming a success is a matter of hard work; luck has little or nothing to do with it.
   b. Getting a good job depends mainly on being in the right place at the right time.

6. a. Most people don't realize the extent to which their lives are controlled by accidental happenings.
   b. There really is no such thing as "luck."

**Source:** J. B. Rotter (1966). Generalized expectancies for internal versus external control of reinforcement. *Psychological Monographs, 80* (Whole No. 609).

The higher your score is, the more *external* is your generalized expectancy for control.

Although people differ in their locus of control, there are two important qualifications. The first is that it is entirely possible to have an internal orientation in some life situations but an external orientation in others. Look again at Table 15.1, and you'll see that the I-E Scale asks about control expectancies for a wide range of domains—including health, academics, career pursuits, friendships, and remote political and social events. The second is that individuals also differ in the extent to which they *want* control. Some of us care more deeply than others about making our own decisions or having an influence over others. People with a strong desire for control—regardless of whether they are internal or external in their expectancies—are more likely to become stressed and upset in situations that make them feel helpless (Burger, 1991).

Is an expectation for control adaptive? At first glance, it seems that an internal orientation is the key to health, success, and emotional well-being—and there is a great deal of research to support this point (Marshall, 1991). In a study of nursing-home patients, for example, 93 percent of those who by random assignment were given more control over minor daily affairs were happier, more active, and more alert when tested eighteen months later (Rodin, 1986). "No doubt about it," I tell my kids, "you need to believe in yourself, take charge of your life, open doors, and make things happen. As they say, the buck stops here" (point to yourself). But wait. Is an internal orientation *always* adaptive, or are there times when it's better to see life's reinforcements as beyond our command?

This is a tough question because there are two exceptions to the rule that it's better to be internal than external. First, an internal orientation can cause problems when we don't carefully distinguish between truly controllable and uncontrollable events. For example, people with an inflated sense of control are at risk to lose money gambling on games of pure chance (Langer, 1975). And victims of rape and other crimes suffer more distress when they blame themselves for having been careless or done something to provoke their attack (Janoff-Bulman, 1989; Frazier & Schauben, 1994). Second, an internal orientation can cause problems if it leads us to develop an overcontrolling, stress-inducing style of behavior—whether that means always having the last word in an argument, driving from the back seat of a car, or planning every detail of a leisurely vacation. Sometimes it is better to just let go (Wright et al., 1990). On this point, Japanese psychologist Hiroshi Azuma (1984) offers these Japanese proverbs: "Willow trees do not get broken by piled-up snow" and "The true tolerance is to tolerate the intolerable."

**Self-Efficacy**   As noted, locus of control refers to the expectation that our behaviors can produce satisfying outcomes. But people also differ in the extent to which they think they can perform these reinforced behaviors in the first place. These concepts seem related, but in fact they refer to different beliefs, both of which are necessary for us to feel that we control the outcomes in our lives (Skinner, 1996). According to Bandura (1997), the latter expectations are based on feelings of competence, or **self-efficacy.** Although some people are generally more confident than others, Bandura believes that self-efficacy is a state of mind that varies from one task and situation to another. In other words, you may have a high self-efficacy about meeting new people but not about raising your grades. Or you may have a high self-efficacy about solving a math problem but not about writing a paper.

"Amazing, three failed marriages, scores of disastrous relationships, many financial reversals, and countless physical ailments, but through it all I've always had good luck parking."

*It's common for people to have feelings of self-efficacy in some life domains but not in others.*

Bandura (1997) believes that with life full of impediments, adversities, setbacks, and frustrations, a personal sense of self-efficacy is essential for success. How do we gain a belief in our own efficacy? Bandura cites four sources: (1) our own past experiences at successfully overcoming obstacles and failures; (2) our observations of similar others who overcome obstacles to succeed; (3) words of encouragement from family, friends, and others in our lives who urge us forward; and (4) feelings of relaxation and calm rather than tension during performance.

Numerous studies of self-efficacy indicate that the more of it you have at a particular task, the more likely you are to take on an activity, try hard, persist in the face of failure, and succeed. The implications for health are particularly striking. Research shows that people who have a high level of self-efficacy about their ability to cope with stress also exhibit an enhanced functioning of the immune system (Wiedenfeld et al., 1990). People with a high self-efficacy on health-related matters are more likely to succeed, if they want, to stop smoking, abstain from alcohol, or overcome other forms of substance abuse (Maddux, 1991; Bandura, 1999).

# PERSPECTIVES ON COGNITIVE SOCIAL-LEARNING THEORY

Cognitive social-learning theorists believe that personality is rooted in the basic principles of learning. In contrast to psychoanalysis, this approach rests on the assumption that human behavior is derived more from external factors than from instincts and that personality is shaped by reinforcement, observation, and the development of learned abilities, expectancies, values, and information-processing strategies.

Although all learning-based theories of personality share this assumption, the more recent approach has come a long way from that taken by the hard-core behaviorists. In his facetious call for a dozen healthy infants, Watson claimed that he could mold people like clay through the use of reward and punishment. Years later, Skinner similarly argued that human behavior is shaped by external forces, by reinforcement contingencies beyond our awareness and control. Yet cognitive social-learning theorists maintain that personality emerges from an ongoing mutual

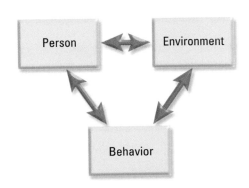

**FIGURE 15.5   Reciprocal determinism**

**self-efficacy**   The belief that one is capable of performing the behaviors required to produce a desired outcome.

## REVIEW QUESTIONS

- *In what ways did social-learning theory extend behaviorist notions of learning?*

- *Describe the five person variables identified by Mischel's (1973) cognitive social-learning theory.*

- *Distinguish internal and external locus of control. What are the advantages and disadvantages associated with each?*

- *What is self-efficacy, and what factors contribute to it?*

interaction among persons, their actions, and their environments, a concept that Bandura calls **reciprocal determinism** (see Figure 15.5). The point is that environmental forces may help shape personalities, but we can also choose and alter the situations we encounter and we can interpret these situations in light of our own points of view. In fact, Bandura (2001) sees human beings as not just reactive to outside forces, but as generative, creative, proactive, and reflective agents of change. "The capacity to exercise control over the nature and quality of one's life," he states, "is the essence of humanness" (2001, p. 1).

To measure personality, cognitive social-learning theorists use fairly direct forms of assessment. One method is behavioral observation, in which subjects are observed either in real-life settings or in the laboratory. Another involves asking subjects to report on their own expectancies, values, and past behaviors using standardized interviews or questionnaires like the I-E Scale. Whatever the specific technique may be, information about an individual is measured in ways that are direct and to the point. No inkblots, no fuzzy pictures. To those in hot pursuit of the unconscious, the cognitive social-learning approach is doomed to shed light on only the tip of the iceberg. To others, this approach permits the study of personality in a more straightforward manner.

## THE HUMANISTIC APPROACH

- *What are the tenets of a humanistic approach to personality?*
- *What clinical observations inspired Carl Rogers to theorize about the self?*
- *What are self-discrepancies and how do they affect our emotional well-being?*
- *What does it mean to be self-actualized—and what does it feel like?*

Faced with a choice between psychoanalysis and behaviorism, many personality psychologists in the 1940s and 1950s had the uneasy feeling that something was missing, something vital about human nature. Freud had drawn attention to the darker forces of the unconscious, and Skinner was interested only in the effects of reinforcement on observable behavior. But what about the conscious mind, free will, subjective experiences, and the capacity for self-reflection? If we want to know about someone, can't we just ask? Are people really that mechanical? And isn't there a brighter side to human nature? In short, where's the *person* as we know it in personality? To fill the void, a "third force" was born—the **humanistic theory** of personality. Inspired by Carl Rogers and Abraham Maslow, a group of psychologists founded the Association of Humanistic Psychology and adopted four basic principles: (1) The experiencing person is of primary interest; (2) human choice, creativity, and self-actualization are the preferred topics of investigation; (3) meaningfulness must precede objectivity in the selection of research problems; and (4) ultimate value is placed on the dignity of the person.

**reciprocal determinism** The view that personality emerges from a mutual interaction of individuals, their actions, and their environments.

**humanistic theory** An approach to personality that focuses on the self, subjective experience, and the capacity for fulfillment.

## CARL ROGERS

Carl Rogers was the first self-proclaimed humanistic theorist. Born into a religious family in a Midwest farming town, Rogers attended a theological seminary for two years before he decided to become a clinical psychologist. He received his degree in 1931, the same year that B. F. Skinner got his. Like Freud, Rogers spent his early years as a therapist treating emotionally troubled "clients." Yet unlike Freud, who was impressed by his patients' efforts to resist their own cures, Rogers was struck by how often his clients reflected on who they were ("I'd like to be more independent, but that just isn't me," "I just haven't been myself lately") and by their natural will to get better and reach their full potential. True, Rogers saw signs of temporary resistance and other ego defense mechanisms. But he was much more impressed by the self-concept—and by the underlying will to improve. If therapists provide warmth, a gentle, guiding hand, and a climate of uncritical acceptance, he said, clients will ultimately solve their own problems and find the road to health, happiness, and fulfillment. As far as Rogers was concerned, there is in each of us an inner wisdom.

**Rogers's Theory**   The seeds of a new and different approach to personality were planted in fertile ground. From a humanist's standpoint, Rogers went on to develop client-centered therapy (1951) and a theory of personality, as described in his book *On Becoming a Person* (1961). According to Rogers, all living organisms are innately endowed with an actualizing tendency, a forward drive not only to survive but also to grow and reach their full genetic capacity. For thinking and feeling humans, there is also a natural need for self-actualization—a drive to behave in ways that are consistent with one's conscious identity, or self-concept. So far, so good. But problems arise because we are social animals, born helpless and dependent on others for approval, support, and love. In other words, there also develops within us a competing need, a need for positive regard. And therein lies the potential for conflict in the development of personality. Rogers, who was born and raised on a farm, saw many parallels among humans, plants, and other forms of life. He summarized his portrayal of the human drive for actualization in the following passage:

> During a vacation weekend some months ago I was standing on a headland overlooking one of the rugged coves which dot the coastline of Northern California. Several large rock outcroppings were at the mouth of the cove, and these received the full force of the great Pacific combers which, beating upon them, broke into mountains of spray before surging into the cliff-lined shore. As I watched the waves breaking over these large rocks in the distance, I noticed with surprise what appeared to be tiny palm trees on the rocks, no more than two or three feet high, taking the pounding of the breakers. Through my binoculars, I saw that these were some type of seaweed, with a slender "trunk" topped off with a head of leaves. As one examined a specimen in the interval between the waves it seemed clear that this fragile, erect, top-heavy plant would be utterly crushed and broken by the next breaker. When the wave crunched down upon it, the trunk bent almost flat, the leaves were whipped into a straight line by the torrent of the water, yet the moment the wave had passed, here was the plant again, erect, tough, resilient. It seemed incredible that it was able to take this incessant pounding hour after hour, day after night, week after week, perhaps for all I know, year after year, and all the time nourishing itself, extending its domain, reproducing itself; in short, maintaining and enhancing itself in this process which, in our shorthand, we call growth. Here in this palm-like seaweed was the tenacity of life, the forward thrust of life, the ability to push into an incredibly hostile environment and not only hold its own, but to adapt, develop, become itself. (1974, pp. 1–2)

Because humans are driven by the need for self-actualization *and* the need for positive regard, one of two general outcomes is possible. If you're fortunate enough to get **unconditional positive regard** from parents and significant others—that is, if the important people in your life are loving and respectful despite your failures and setbacks, no ifs, ands, or buts—then life is rosy. Your need for positive regard is met, giving you the green light to pursue the all-important need for self-actualization. However, if you are subject to **conditional positive regard**—that is, if your parents, spouse, and close friends withdraw their love when your actions and life choices don't meet with their approval—then you get hung up trying to strike a balance between your true self and the kind of person others want you to become. The result:

**unconditional positive regard**   A situation in which the acceptance and love one receives from significant others is unqualified.

**conditional positive regard**   A situation in which the acceptance and love one receives from significant others is contingent upon one's behavior.

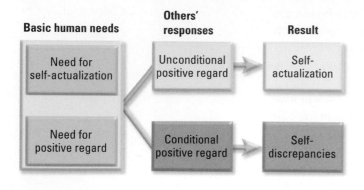

| Basic human needs | Others' responses | Result |
|---|---|---|
| Need for self-actualization | Unconditional positive regard | Self-actualization |
| Need for positive regard | Conditional positive regard | Self-discrepancies |

**FIGURE 15.6    The personality theory of Carl Rogers**
According to Rogers, the needs for self-actualization and positive regard present a potential for conflict. Unconditional positive regard permits self-actualization, but conditional positive regard can result in self-discrepancies.

**self-schemas**    Specific beliefs about the self that influence how we interpret self-relevant information.

**self-esteem**    A positive or negative evaluation of the self.

frustration, anxiety, and feelings of incongruence or "discrepancy" within the self. This theory is illustrated in Figure 15.6.

**Self-Esteem**    From the start, Rogers sought empirical verification for his newly formulated theory. To evaluate the importance of the self-concept, he taped, transcribed, and analyzed many of his therapy sessions and found that, as treatment progressed, clients made more and more positive statements about themselves. Whatever self-discrepancies that existed tended to diminish. More recent research confirms that people have clear, often complex beliefs about the self. According to Hazel Markus (1977), these beliefs are made up of a collection of **self-schemas**, which are specific beliefs about the self that influence how we interpret self-relevant information. It also appears that we think about—and are guided by—images of what we might become, would like to become, and are afraid of becoming in the future (Markus & Nurius, 1986; Ruvolo & Markus, 1992).

When it comes to the self, we are not mere cool and dispassionate observers. Rather, we evaluate ourselves in positive and negative terms, opinions that comprise a person's **self-esteem** (Coopersmith, 1967). Some individuals have higher opinions of themselves than others do. However, self-esteem is not a single trait etched permanently in stone. Rather, it is a state of mind that varies in response to success, failure, changes in fortune, social interactions, and other life experiences (Heatherton & Polivy, 1991). Also, because self-concepts are made up of many self-schemas, people may have higher self-esteem in some life domains than others (Pelham, 1995; Pelham & Swann, 1989). In fact, some people consistently have high or low regard for themselves, but others seem to fluctuate up and down as a result of daily experiences—which makes them highly responsive to praise and overly sensitive to criticism (Kernis & Waschull, 1995; Baldwin & Sinclair, 1996; Schimel et al., 2001).

In many ways, satisfying the need for self-esteem is critical to our entire outlook on life (Brown, 1998). People with positive rather than negative self-images tend to be happy, healthy, productive, and successful. They are also confident, bringing to new challenges a winning and motivating attitude—which leads them to persist longer at difficult tasks, sleep better at night, maintain independence in the face of peer pressure, and suffer fewer ulcers. In contrast, people with negative self-images tend to be more depressed, pessimistic about the future, and prone to failure. Lacking confidence, they bring to new tasks a losing attitude that traps them in a self-defeating cycle. Expecting to fail, and fearing the worst, they become anxious, exert less effort, and "tune out" on important challenges. Then when they do fail, people with low self-esteem blame themselves, which makes them feel even worse (Brockner, 1983; Brown & Dutton, 1995). Low self-esteem may well be hazardous to your health. Some research suggests that becoming aware of one's own negative attributes adversely affects the activity of certain white blood cells in the immune system, thus compromising the body's capacity to ward off disease (Strauman et al., 1993).

Just as individuals differ in their self-esteem, so too do social and cultural groups. Think about it. If you were to administer a self-esteem test to thousands of people all over the world, would you find that some segments of the population score higher than others? Believing that self-esteem promotes health, happiness, and success, and concerned that some social groups are disadvantaged in this regard, researchers have made these types of comparisons. Consider the possibility of a gender gap. Over the years, much has been written in the popular press about the inflated but fragile "male ego" and the low self-regard among adolescent girls and women. Does research support this assumption? To find out, Kristin Kling and others (1999) statistically combined the results of 216 studies involving 97,000 respondents, then analyzed the surveys of 48,000 American students conducted by the National Center for Education Statistics. The result: among adolescents and young adults, males outscore females on general measures of self-esteem. Contrary to popular belief, however, the difference is very small, particularly among older adults.

Researchers have also wondered if low self-esteem is a problem for stigmatized minority groups, historical victims of prejudice and discrimination. Does being part of a minority group—such as being African American—deflate one's sense of self-worth? Based on the combined results of studies involving more than half a million respondents, Bernadette Gray-Little and Adam Hafdahl (2000) reported that black American children, adolescents, and young adults tend to score higher, not lower, than their white counterparts on measures of self-esteem. In a meta-analysis of hundreds of studies that compared all age groups and other American minorities, Jean Twenge and Jennifer Crocker (2002) confirmed the African American advantage in self-esteem relative to whites but found that Hispanic, Asian, and Native American minorities have lower self-esteem scores. These differences, as illustrated in Figure 15.7, are not easy to interpret. Surprised by the high African American scores, some researchers have suggested that perhaps African Americans—relative to other minorities—are able to preserve their self-esteem in the face of adversity by attributing negative outcomes to the forces of discrimination and using this adversity to build a sense of group pride. In this regard, it would be interesting to see whether the self-esteem of black Americans, relative to whites, has risen over time—from the pre–civil rights days of the 1950s to the 1980s and 1990s. What do *you* think?

Variations in self-esteem have also been observed among people from different parts of the world. Earlier we saw that inhabitants of individualistic cultures tend to view themselves as distinct and autonomous, whereas those in collectivist cultures view the self as part of a larger, interdependent social network. Do these different orientations have implications for self-esteem? Steven Heine and others (1999) believe that they do. They compared the distribution of self-esteem scores in Canada and Japan and found that whereas most Canadians' scores clustered in the high-end range, the average Japanese respondent scored in the center of that same range. This result has led researchers to wonder: Do the Japanese truly have less inflated self-esteem than do North Americans, which can be seen in their tendency to speak in self-effacing terms? Or, do Japanese respondents, high in self-esteem, simply feel compelled by the collectivist need to "fit in" rather than "stand out" to present themselves modestly to others? To answer this question, researchers have tried to develop indirect, "implicit" tests that would measure a person's self-esteem without his or her awareness. In a timed word-association study, for example, Anthony Greenwald and Shelly Farnham (2000) found that despite their noninflated scores on self-esteem tests, Asian Americans—like their European American counterparts—were quicker to associate themselves with positive words such as *happy* and *sunshine* than with negative words such as *vomit* and *poison*. Does this mean that collectivists think highly of themselves but don't admit it? It's too early to tell. At this point, researchers still debate the question of whether the implicit word-association test actually measures self-esteem (Bosson et al., 2000; Greenwald & Farnham, 2000).

In general, what determines how people feel about themselves? Picking up where Carl Rogers left off, E. Tory Higgins (1989) has confirmed the hypothesis that

Self-esteem scores compared to whites

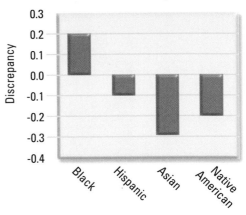

**FIGURE 15.7   Self-esteem in U.S. minorities**
Through a meta-analysis, Twenge and Crocker (2002) found that African Americans score higher on self-esteem tests relative to whites, but that Hispanic-, Asian-, and Native-American minorities score lower.

**WHAT'S YOUR PREDICTION**

Research shows that black Americans score higher on self-esteem tests than do white Americans. Has this difference always existed, or is it a recent phenomenon helped along, perhaps, by the civil rights movement? What's your prediction? Twenge and Crocker (2002) looked at self-esteem scores over the past forty years and found that there was no racial difference in the 1960s. Rather, as shown in the figure below, the black advantage has risen over time. It appears that self-esteem (and maybe other personality traits, too) are influenced by historical changes occurring within a culture.

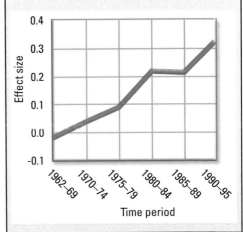

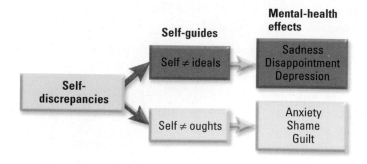

**FIGURE 15.8** **Self-discrepancy theory**
According to Higgins (1989), the emotional and mental-health consequences of self-discrepancy differ according to whether we fall short of our ideal or ought selves.

self-discrepancies breed emotional turmoil. According to his **self-discrepancy theory**, our self-esteem is defined by the match between how we see ourselves and how we want to see ourselves. To demonstrate, try the following exercise. On a blank sheet of paper, write down ten traits that describe the kind of person you think you *actually* are (smart? easygoing? sexy? excitable?). Next list ten traits that describe the kind of person you *ought* to be, traits that would enable you to meet your sense of duty, obligation, and responsibility. Then make a list of traits that describe an *ideal* of what you would like to be, an ideal that embodies your hopes, wishes, and dreams. If you follow these instructions, you should have three lists: your actual self, ought self, and ideal self.

Research shows that these trait lists can be used to predict your emotional well-being. The first list is your self-concept. The others represent your personal standards, or *self-guides*. To the extent that you fall short of meeting these standards, you will have a lowered self-esteem, negative emotions, and in extreme cases a psychological disorder. The specific consequence depends on which self-guides you don't achieve. If there's a discrepancy between your actual and ought selves, you'll feel guilty, ashamed, and resentful. You might even suffer from excessive fears and anxieties. If the discrepancy is between your actual and ideal selves, you'll feel disappointed, frustrated, sad, and unfulfilled. In extreme cases, you might become depressed. These emotional and mental-health effects of self-discrepancies are summarized in Figure 15.8 (Boldero & Francis, 2000; Scott & O'Hara, 1993; Strauman, 1989).

Carl Rogers believed that we form a self-concept from repeated interactions with the significant others in our lives. But are our self-discrepancies stable aspects of personality? Timothy Strauman (1996) examined this question. He tested college students twice, three years apart. In both sessions, he asked them to write down the kind of person they are, the kind of person they would like to be, and the kind of person they ought to be. The students exhibited some changes in how they described themselves. But the amount of their self-discrepancies—between the actual self on the one hand and their ideal and ought selves on the other—stayed very much the same.

## ABRAHAM MASLOW

Abraham Maslow was the second influential spokesperson for the humanistic approach to personality. Oddly enough, Maslow started out as a behaviorist conducting learning experiments with monkeys. Then came the birth of his first child. As most parents would agree, this was an eye-opening experience. Said Maslow, "I was stunned by the mystery and by the sense of not really being in control. I felt small and weak and feeble before all this. I'd say anyone who had a baby couldn't be a behaviorist." Over the years, Maslow (1954, 1968) went on to formulate a motivational theory of personality, focusing on how people strive to fulfill their utmost potential.

**Maslow's Theory** Have you ever met someone who seems to have it all—great looks, money, successful career, nice home, loving spouse, and wonderful children—and yet seems unsatisfied, searching for more? If so, then you'll appreciate the essence of Maslow's theory. As we saw in Chapter 11, Maslow (1954) theorized that all people are motivated to fulfill a hierarchy of needs, from the physiological needs basic to survival to the needs for safety and security, belongingness and love, and esteem-related needs for achievement, status, and recognition. In short, said Maslow, each of us strives in our own way to be biologically content, safe, loved, and respected. Only when these needs are met are we ready, willing, and able to

**self-discrepancy theory** The notion that discrepancies between one's self-concept and "ideal" and "ought" selves have negative emotional consequences.

strive for **self-actualization**—the distinctly human need to become everything one is capable of becoming.

Maslow's primary interest was in self-actualization, which he considered the ultimate state. Thus, he went out of his way to study happy, healthy, and productive individuals who embody the best that human nature has to offer. He interviewed a select group of acquaintances, and he used biographies to examine the lives of great historical figures such as Ludwig van Beethoven, Abraham Lincoln, Albert Einstein, and Eleanor Roosevelt. What did these self-actualized people have in common? Maslow (1968) saw self-actualization as a rare state of being in which a person is open to new experiences, spontaneous, playful, loving, realistic, accepting of others, creative, energetic, independent rather than conforming, and problem-focused rather than self-centered. If this set of traits sounds almost too good to be true, you're right. Maslow estimated that less than 1 percent of the world's adults are truly self-actualized. The rest of us are too busy trying to overcome obstacles in order to satisfy lower, more basic needs.

**The State of Self-Actualization**  How self-actualized are you? Based on Maslow's theory, Everett Shostrom (1965) developed the Personal Orientation Inventory, a lengthy questionnaire designed to assess various aspects of self-actualization—such as the capacity for intimate contact, spontaneity, and self-acceptance (see Table 15.2). This scale was endorsed by Maslow and used in clinical settings. Research shows that people with high scores are psychologically healthier than those who receive low scores (Campbell et al., 1989; Knapp, 1976). A sample of ten statements from the Personal Orientation Inventory is given in Table 15.2. How many of the values thought to be associated with self-actualization do you possess?

If you're wondering what it feels like to be self-actualized, at least temporarily, try this: "Think about the most wonderful experiences of your life; happiest moments, ecstatic moments, moments of rapture, perhaps from being in love, or from listening to music or suddenly 'being hit' by a book or a painting, or from some great creative moment" (Maslow, 1968, p. 71). Maslow claimed that self-actualized individuals have more moments like these than other people do. Still, each of us enjoys an occasional **peak experience**, defined as a fleeting but intense moment of self-actualization in which we feel happy, absorbed, and capable of extraordinary performance. Music, sexual love, religion, nature, running, sports, creative pursuits, childbirth, and reminiscing are the most common situations people cite when asked about their peak experiences (Privette, 1983).

Working from Maslow's writings, Mihaly Csikszentmihalyi (1990) has studied a pleasant state of engagement he calls *flow*, an "optimal experience." Under what

*Self-actualization is a state of mind that we achieve on a temporary basis—during peak experiences.*

| TABLE 15.2 | HOW SELF-ACTUALIZED ARE YOU? |
|---|---|

1. I live in terms of my wants, likes, dislikes, and values.
2. I believe that man is essentially good and can be trusted.
3. I don't feel guilty when I'm selfish.
4. I believe it is important to accept others as they are.
5. I am not afraid of making mistakes.
6. I believe in saying what I feel in dealing with others.
7. I often make decisions spontaneously.
8. I welcome criticism as an opportunity for growth.
9. I enjoy detachment and privacy.
10. For me, work and play are the same.

*Source:* E. Shostrom (1965). An inventory for the measurement of self-actualization. *Educational and Psychological Measurement, 24,* 207–218.

**self-actualization**  In humanistic personality theories, the need to fulfill one's unique potential.

**peak experience**  A fleeting but intense moment of self-actualization in which people feel happy, absorbed, and extraordinarily capable.

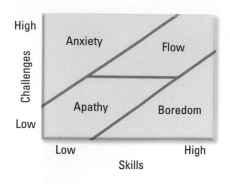

High

Challenges

Low

Anxiety      Flow

Apathy      Boredom

Low           High

Skills

FIGURE 15.9 **Flow, the optimal experience**
A state of "flow" arises when we engage in activities that we are skilled at and at levels that are challenging but not too difficult (Csikszentmihalyi, 1990).

conditions, Csikszentmihalyi asks, do we tend to become so fully immersed in an activity that we lose all track of time and all awareness of the self, forget our worries, and concentrate our energy on what we're doing, much to our benefit and enjoyment? I sometimes have this exquisite experience when I write, play baseball, or listen to music. Csikszentmihalyi interviewed athletes, dancers, rock climbers, artists, factory workers, chess masters, surgeons, sailors, elderly Korean women, Japanese motorcyclists, Navajo shepherds, and farmers in the Italian Alps. He found that people from all parts of the world and all walks of life describe a similar kind of experience—when what they're doing seems effortless and perfect, when they're so completely tuned in that nothing else seems to matter. In a demonstration of this point, Regina Conti (2001) found that college students who scored high rather than low on a measure of their intrinsic motivation checked time less often during the day, lost track of time more often, and perceived time as passing more quickly. Apparently, time does fly when you're having fun—and "in the zone."

What precipitates flow? From his research, Csikszentmihalyi theorizes that this state arises when people engage in activities at which they are skilled and at levels that are challenging in relation to their ability. As depicted in Figure 15.9, tasks that are too easy result in boredom, whereas those that are too difficult cause anxiety. Also important is the capacity of these activities to present clear goals and immediate feedback. In some studies, for example, subjects carried portable beepers for a period of time and stopped to record on paper what they were doing, thinking, and feeling whenever the beeper went off. Supporting the flow model, subjects reported feeling more excited, more motivated, and more engaged at those times when they were involved in high-skill, high-challenge activities.

These findings can be applied to many domains, including sports. In all sports, it seems, athletes who are hot and playing at the top of their game often talk about being focused in mind and body, and "in the zone." In studies of amateur tennis players, basketball players, and golfers, for example, researchers found that this state occurs in all sports ("My attention was focused entirely on what I was doing," "I felt in control of my game," "My performance felt effortless") and that the conditions that produce it vary—depending on the competitive nature of the activity and the importance of winning. When good athletes are motivated but relaxed, their performance is fluid, almost without conscious thought or effort (Beilock et al., 2002). Thus, people may be able to create for themselves the conditions that will unleash this optimal state of performance (Jackson & Csikszentmihalyi, 1999).

## PERSPECTIVES ON THE HUMANISTIC APPROACH

When Carl Rogers (1974) looked back on his career and on his impact on psychology, counseling, and education, he concluded that "I expressed an idea whose time had come." The idea he referred to was that people are inherently good, that conscious mental experience is important, and that the self-concept lies at the heart of personality.

Humanistic psychologists have received praise for drawing our attention to this idea, for providing an alternative perspective on personality, and for sparking interest among researchers in previously neglected topics related to the self. At the same time, they have been severely criticized for naively taking people's self-report statements at face value and for painting too rosy a picture of human nature while ignoring our demonstrated capacity for evil. Focused on the quest for self-actualization, humanistic psychologists have also been accused of inadvertently promoting the self-indulgent, "be true to yourself" approach to life. Sure, the self is important, say the critics, but where does the rest of the world fit in?

## REVIEW QUESTIONS

- *Summarize the four principles of humanistic psychology.*

- *According to Rogers, personality development is shaped by the conflict between what two needs?*

- *Distinguish the ideal, ought, and actual selves. According to self-discrepancy theory, how do discrepancies among these selves affect us?*

- *Define Maslow's concept of self-actualization.*

# THE TRAIT APPROACH

- *What are the main goals in a trait approach to personality?*
- *What are the "Big Five"?*
- *How are personality tests like the MMPI constructed, and what are their strengths and weaknesses?*
- *What evidence is there for the role of genetic factors in personality?*
- *What's an introvert, what's an extravert, and how do they differ?*

In 1919, a twenty-two-year-old psychology student from Indiana handwrote a letter to Sigmund Freud to say he'd be traveling in Europe and would like to meet. Freud was the master, known worldwide, and the student, a fan, wanted to meet him. A time was arranged, so the student took a train to Vienna, arrived on schedule, and entered the master's inner office. But Freud just sat there in silence, staring, waiting for his young, wide-eyed admirer to state his mission. Desperate to break the awkward stalemate, the student told about an incident he witnessed on the train that day involving a young boy who appeared to have a "dirt phobia." The boy complained that the seats were soiled and pleaded with his mother to keep dirty passengers from sitting nearby. The mother, it turned out, was a dominant, "well-starched" woman. Isn't that an interesting case? When the student finished telling his story, Freud paused, then leaned over and said in a soft voice, "And was that little boy *you?*"

Freud's young admirer was terribly embarrassed. Wishing he could disappear, he nervously changed the subject, babbled a bit, then excused himself and left. How could Freud have been so wrong? Was he so accustomed to analyzing the hidden motives of his anxious patients that he couldn't appreciate a man's simple curiosity? It turns out that the student was Gordon Allport, who went on to become one of the most important personality psychologists of all time. In an autobiography published the year he died, Allport (1967) said that this experience convinced him that before personality theorists search for deep and analytical explanations, they should start by trying to *describe* and *measure* the basic units of personality. In other words, first things first. This rule now guides what is known as the trait approach.

## THE BUILDING BLOCKS OF PERSONALITY

Working from the ground up, Allport and his colleague Henry Odbert (1936) combed through an unabridged English dictionary and came up with a list of eighteen thousand words that could be used to describe people. By eliminating synonyms, obscure words and words referring to moods and other temporary states, they brought the list down to forty-five hundred, and then grouped words that were similar into about two hundred clusters of related traits. For Allport, these **traits** were the building blocks of personality (though he was quick to point out that not all traits are relevant to all people, nor do they all have an influence on behavior).

To reduce Allport's list to a more manageable size and construct a science of personality, Raymond Cattell (1965) used *factor analysis*, a statistical technique designed to identify clusters of items that correlate with one another. You may recall from Chapter 12 that this technique was used to distinguish among different aspects of intelligence. Cattell, who majored in chemistry in college, wanted to uncover the basic units of personality, much like chemistry's periodic table of elements. Are individuals who are passive also thoughtful, calm, and even-tempered? Do those who describe themselves as sociable also say they're easygoing, lively, and talkative? How many trait clusters are needed to fully describe personality? To answer these

**trait**   A relatively stable predisposition to behave in a certain way.

**five-factor model** A model of personality that consists of five basic traits: neuroticism, extraversion, openness, agreeableness, and conscientiousness.

questions, Cattell collected people's ratings of themselves and others on various attributes, crunched the numbers through factor analysis, and found that personality consists of sixteen distinct units, which he called *source traits*. What distinguishes one individual from another, said Cattell, is that each of us has a unique combination of traits—high levels of some, and low levels of others—a pattern that is summarized by a personality "profile." To derive this profile, Cattell devised the Sixteen Personality Factors Questionnaire (16 PF), a 187-item scale that yields sixteen separate scores, one for each factor.

As factor analysis became more sophisticated, researchers began to notice that Cattell's model (and other models as well) could be simplified even further—and that five major factors often seemed to emerge from self-ratings, ratings of others, and an assortment of personality questionnaires. This **five-factor model** of personality has emerged consistently in studies of children, college students, and older adults; in men and women; in different languages; and in testing conducted in the United States, Canada, Finland, Germany, Japan, Poland, China, the Philippines, and other countries. Hence, these factors have been nicknamed the Big Five (De Raad, 2000; McCrae & Costa, 1997; Paunonen et al., 1992; Wiggins, 1996).

Not everyone agrees with the five-factor model. Cattell thought five factors were too few. Hans Eysenck, whom we will meet shortly, thought five was too many. Others see five as the right number but disagree about how the factors should be described. For the most part, however, evidence is mounting in support of the five-factor model represented in Table 15.3. Most researchers are now convinced that the best way to characterize individual differences in personality is to find where people stand on the following broad traits: (1) *neuroticism* (a proneness to anxiety and negative affect); (2) *extraversion* (a desire for stimulation, activity, and social interaction); (3) *openness* (a receptiveness to new experiences and ideas); (4) *agreeableness* (a selfless concern for others); and (5) *conscientiousness* (a tendency to be reliable, disciplined, and ambitious).

*"N, E, O, A, and C are not inventions of Western psychologists; they are part of human nature—dimensions of enduring dispositions that somehow find expression in every culture."*

—ROBERT R. MCCRAE

| TABLE 15.3 | THE BIG FIVE PERSONALITY FACTORS |
|---|---|
| **Factor** | **Description of Traits** |
| **Neuroticism** | Anxious vs. relaxed |
| | Insecure vs. secure |
| | Emotional vs. calm |
| | Self-pitying vs. content |
| **Extraversion** | Sociable vs. withdrawn |
| | Fun-loving vs. sober |
| | Friendly vs. aloof |
| | Adventurous vs. cautious |
| **Openness** | Original vs. conventional |
| | Imaginative vs. down-to-earth |
| | Broad interests vs. narrow interests |
| | Receptive vs. closed to new ideas |
| **Agreeableness** | Good-natured vs. irritable |
| | Soft-hearted vs. ruthless |
| | Courteous vs. rude |
| | Sympathetic vs. tough-minded |
| **Conscientiousness** | Well-organized vs. disorganized |
| | Dependable vs. undependable |
| | Hardworking vs. lazy |
| | Ambitious vs. easygoing |

New tests have been developed to measure these five broad factors and to use the scores to predict behavior (Costa & McCrae, 1992; De Raad & Perugini, 2002). In one study, for example, researchers tested large numbers of college students and recruits from a temporary employment agency. They found that those who scored low on the conscientiousness trait were more likely to get a speeding ticket and be involved in an automobile accident (Arthur & Graziano, 1996). As we'll see on page 615, the Big Five can be used to predict aspects of performance in the workplace.

## CONSTRUCTION OF MULTITRAIT INVENTORIES

As Allport had noted, the study of personality must begin not only with description but also with measurement. And so it did. One of the important contributions of trait psychology is the construction of personality inventories, questionnaires designed to assess a whole multitude of traits. Cattell's Sixteen Personality Factors Questionnaire is one such instrument. There are many others. The most widely used is the **Minnesota Multiphasic Personality Inventory,** or **MMPI,** a 550-item questionnaire originally developed in the 1940s to help in the diagnosis of psychological disorders (Hathaway & McKinley, 1983).

The MMPI is to personality measurement what the Stanford-Binet was to intelligence testing. Taking an empirical approach, Alfred Binet developed his test by generating a large number of problems, testing schoolchildren, and retaining those problems that were solved differently by fast and slow learners. The MMPI developers used a similar strategy. They wrote hundreds of true-false statements, gave them to both normal adults and clinical patients with varying psychiatric diagnoses (depressed, paranoid, and so on), and then included in the final test only those items that were answered differently by the two groups—even if the content made little sense. The MMPI is filled with discriminating but odd items (for example, hysterical patients are more likely than others to answer *True* to "My fingers sometimes feel numb"). Indeed, satirist Art Buchwald once wrote a spoof of MMPI-like personality tests by creating his own items. Among them: "I think beavers work too hard," "Frantic screams make me nervous," and "My mother's uncle was a good man."

These MMPI scales have been used for more than fifty years. Many of the original items became dated, however, and the norms had been based on a predominantly white, rural, middle-class group of subjects. To bring the test up to date, new items were written and a more diverse cross-section of the United States was sampled. The result was a newer 567-item version known as MMPI-2 (Butcher & Williams, 2000; Graham, 2000). Like the original test, the MMPI-2 contains the ten *clinical scales* shown in Table 15.4. Eight of these are designed to distinguish between "normals" and diagnostic groups. Two other scales are used to measure masculinity-femininity and social introversion. The MMPI-2 also contains fifteen *content scales* that measure work attitudes, family problems, and other characteristics. In addition, the MMPI and MMPI-2 contain a set of *validity scales* designed to expose test takers who are evasive, confused, lying to make a good impression, or defensive. Someone who answers *True* to many socially desirable but implausible statements such as "I never get angry" is assumed to be trying too hard to project a healthy image. Less-than-honest responses may be a problem when the stakes are high (Baer & Miller, 2002)—as when the test results will have a bearing on whether the test taker wins legal custody of a child (Bagby et al., 1999) or will be used to classify a criminal offender for placement and treatment purposes (Megargee et al., 2001).

The MMPI-2 is easy to administer, and in contrast to the Rorschach and TAT, in which two examiners may reach different conclusions, MMPI scoring is perfectly objective. Thus, a test taker's responses can be converted into a personality profile

## WHAT'S YOUR PREDICTION

Thousands of people all over the world have been tested for their standing on the Big Five traits. Do you think there are gender differences in personality, or are men and women basically the same? What's your prediction: Are men more *neurotic* than women, are women more neurotic, or is there no average difference? What about *extraverted, open, agreeable,* and *conscientious*? Based on the test scores of twenty-three thousand respondents from twenty-six cultures, Paul Costa and others (2001) found some small but consistent differences: Women are more neurotic and agreeable than are men. Women are more extraverted when it comes to people; men are more extraverted when it comes to risk taking. Women are more open about aesthetics and feelings; men are more open to new ideas. Men and women are similarly conscientious. It is not clear to what extent the observed differences are genetically determined or the product of cultural factors.

**Minnesota Multiphasic Personality Inventory (MMPI)**   A large-scale test designed to measure a multitude of psychological disorders and personality traits.

| TABLE 15.4 | CLINICAL AND VALIDITY SCALES OF THE MMPI | |
|---|---|---|
| **Clinical Scales** | **Descriptions** | **Sample Items** |
| 1. *Hypochondriasis* | Excessive concern about self and physical health, fatigue, a pattern of complaining | "I have a great deal of stomach trouble." |
| 2. *Depression* | Low morale, pessimistic about the future, passive, hopeless, unhappy, and sluggish | "I wish I could be as happy as others seem to be." |
| 3. *Hysteria* | Use of physical symptoms to gain attention from others or avoid social responsibility | "I have had fainting spells." |
| 4. *Psychopathic deviation* | Disregard for social rules and authority, impulsive, unreliable, self-centered, has shallow relationships | "In school I was sometimes sent to the principal for cutting up." |
| 5. *Masculinity/ Femininity* | Identification with masculine and/or feminine sex roles | "I enjoy reading love stories." |
| 6. *Paranoia* | Feelings of persecution and/or grandeur, suspiciousness, hypersensitivity, use of blame and projection | "I am sure I get a raw deal from life." |
| 7. *Psychasthenia* | Anxiousness as exhibited in fears, self-doubt, worries, guilt, obsessions and compulsions | "I feel anxiety about something or someone almost all of the time." |
| 8. *Schizophrenia* | Feelings of social alienation, aloofness, confusion and disorientation, bizarre thoughts and sensations | "I often feel as if things were not real." |
| 9. *Mania* | Hyperactivity, excitement, flakiness, elation, euphoria, and excessive optimism | "At times my thoughts race ahead faster than I could speak them." |
| 10. *Social introversion* | Withdrawal from social contact, isolation, shyness, a reserved, inhibited, self-effacing style | "Whenever possible I avoid being in a crowd." |
| **Validity Scales** | **Descriptions** | **Sample Items** |
| *Cannot say* | Evasiveness, as indicated by a high number of noncommittal, "Cannot say" responses | (None; this score consists of the number of "Cannot say" responses) |
| *Lie scale* | Tendency to present oneself favorably, not honestly, to fake a good impression | "I always tell the truth." |
| *Infrequency scale* | Tendency to "fake bad" by reporting unusual weaknesses and problems | "Everything tastes the same." |
| *Correction* | Subtle test-taking defensiveness, or lack of self-insight | "I have never felt better in my life than I do now." |

by computer. That's one reason why the test has been translated into more than a hundred languages and is popular in both clinical and research settings. Test administrators must be cautious, however, about how to use the test and how to interpret the results. The test has good reliability and validity, but it is far from perfect. Psychologists need to be particularly careful in interpreting the responses of test takers from cultural and subcultural groups that share different beliefs, values, ideals, and experiences. A pattern of responses may be normal in one culture and deviant in another (Church, 2001). With Internet-based assessment and mental-health services becoming popular, psychologists must also be cautious at interpreting the personality tests that people take online, as the results may be different in this anonymous and impersonal format (Buchanan, 2002).

## BIOLOGICAL ROOTS OF PERSONALITY

Many trait theories, even those that predate psychology's birth as a discipline, assume that a link exists between biological and personal dispositions. In the fifth century BCE, the Greek physician Hippocrates argued that people could be classified into four temperament types, depending on which of their "humors," or body fluids, predominated: An excess of blood was associated with cheerfulness, black bile with sadness, yellow bile with anger, and phlegm with sluggishness. In the nineteenth century, German physician Franz Gall introduced phrenology, the pseudoscience that tried to link personality to brain structures that could be seen in bumps on the head. Others used physiognomy, the idea that a person's character is revealed in the features of the face (for example, people with thin lips were said to be conscientious; those with thick lips, emotional).

Although these early theories were rejected, there is renewed interest in the connections between biology and personality. In 1954, William Sheldon studied thousands of adult men and concluded that there are three kinds of physique, each linked to a distinct type of personality. The *ectomorph*, said Sheldon, has a thin, frail body and a restrained, anxious, shy disposition. The *endomorph* has a soft, plump body and is relaxed, sociable, and easygoing. And the *mesomorph* has a strong, muscular build and is bold, assertive, and energetic. Sheldon reported high correlations between body types and personality, but his methods were flawed, and later research produced less impressive results.

Are there biological underpinnings to personality? Yes, absolutely. In *Heroes, Rogues, and Lovers,* James Dabbs (2000) describes a number of provocative studies that link levels of the male sex hormone testosterone to stable patterns of behavior. The average man produces eight to ten times as much testosterone as the average woman, but individuals differ and the effect is the same in both sexes. In studies of college students, athletes, actors, lawyers, construction workers, military veterans, strippers, prison inmates, and others, Dabbs and his colleagues have found that people who are high in testosterone—which can be measured in blood or saliva samples—are bold, competitive, energetic, dominant, sexually active, rambunctious, impulsive, and aggressive. The result: people high in testosterone are more likely than lows both to commit violent crimes and to risk their lives in death-defying acts of heroism.

Whatever the biological mechanisms, it is clear that there is a genetic component to personality. Recall the nature–nurture debate and the twins study method presented in Chapter 10. For a wide range of traits, these studies have shown that (1) identical twins raised together are more similar than fraternal twins, and (2) twins raised apart are as similar as those raised in the same home. Taken together, then, a growing body of research suggests that personality differences in the population are 40 to 50 percent genetically determined (Loehlin, 1992; Plomin, 1997). As shown in Figure 15.10, this estimate is consistent with the results of a recent German study in which the Big Five personality factors were measured in 168 pairs of identical twins and 132 pairs of fraternal twins (Borkenau et al., 2001).

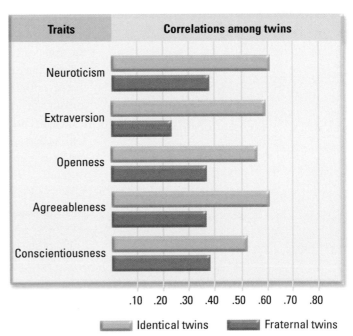

**FIGURE 15.10    Genetic influences on personality**
Based on twin studies, these correlations provide estimates of the degrees to which various personality characteristics are inherited. Note that some traits have stronger genetic roots than others (Bourkenau et al., 2001).

*Identical twins Gerald Levey and Mark Newman were separated after birth and raised by different families. When reunited at the age of 31, they discovered that they were similar on a range of traits—and that both had become firefighters. Implicating the role of genetics in personality, studies have shown that identical twins are similar whether raised together or apart.*

To the surprise of many psychologists, twin studies have revealed that there are also genetic links to characteristics that would seem to be determined entirely by personal experience. Specifically, identical twins are more similar than fraternal twins of the same sex in their attitudes toward sexuality, sports, religion, abortion, and the death penalty (Olson et al., 2001; Tesser, 1993); in their vocational and personal interests (Lykken et al., 1992); and in their risk of getting divorced (McGue & Lykken, 1992). Apparently, certain personality traits for which there is a genetic component predispose us to have certain types of experiences more than others. For example, people who score high on measures of neuroticism, or anxiousness—for which there's a genetic basis—are more likely to get divorced than those who are low on this trait (Jockin et al., 1996).

## INTROVERSION AND EXTRAVERSION

Psychologists may disagree over whether personality consists of 2, 5, 16, or 200 traits, but they all agree that one of the most powerful dimensions—one that can be seen in infants as well as adults, in cultures all over the world, and in written questionnaires as well as behavior—is introversion–extraversion, one of the Big Five traits. The ancient Greeks and Romans noticed it, as have philosophers, physicians, and creative writers through the ages. Carl Jung wrote about individual differences on this dimension. So did Allport and Cattell. Even Pavlov said that some of the dogs in his classical-conditioning laboratory were more outgoing than other dogs. But it was British psychologist Hans Eysenck who most clearly defined the trait, constructed a test to measure it, and proposed a provocative theory to explain its origin.

As described by Eysenck (1967), the typical **extravert** is someone who has many friends, likes parties, craves excitement, seeks adventure, takes chances, acts on the spur of the moment, and is uninhibited. In contrast, the typical **introvert** is low-keyed, has just a few close friends, shies away from stimulation, acts cautiously, and distrusts the impulse of the moment. Based on past writings, personal observations, and factor analyses of trait questionnaires, Eysenck developed a test that includes a measure of introversion and extraversion (see Table 15.5). Using this instrument, and others, researchers have found that extraverts are generally more talkative, prefer occupations that involve social contact, and take greater risks (Eysenck & Eysenck, 1985). The question is, what accounts for this broad and pervasive aspect

**extravert** A kind of person who seeks stimulation and is sociable and impulsive.

**introvert** A kind of person who avoids stimulation and is low-key and cautious.

| TABLE 15.5   ARE YOU AN INTROVERT OR AN EXTRAVERT? |
| --- |
| 1. Are you usually carefree? |
| 2. Do you generally prefer reading to meeting people? |
| 3. Do you often long for excitement? |
| 4. Are you mostly quiet when you're with others? |
| 5. Do you often do things on the spur of the moment? |
| 6. Are you slow and unhurried in the way you move? |
| 7. Would you do almost anything for a dare? |
| 8. Do you hate being in a crowd that plays jokes on one another? |
| 9. Do you enjoy wild parties? |
| 10. Do you like the kind of work you need to pay attention to? |

*Source:* H. J. Eysenck & S. G. B. Eysenck. (1964). *Manual of the Eysenck Personality Inventory.* London: University of London Press.

of personality? To see whether you are an introvert or an extravert, go to Table 15.5 and answer the questions for yourself. If you said *yes* on most odd-numbered questions and *no* on the even-numbered ones in Table 15.5, you are relatively extraverted. If you answered the other way around, then you're more introverted. Many people fall somewhere in the middle of the continuum.

Eysenck argues that individual differences are biologically rooted and that introverts have central nervous systems that are more sensitive to stimulation. According to Eysenck, people seek a moderate, comfortable level of CNS arousal. Introverts are easily aroused, so they avoid intense sources of excitement. In contrast, extraverts are not easily aroused, which leads them to approach high levels of excitement. Thus, it takes a more potent stimulus for the extravert to feel the "buzz." Research generally supports this hypothesis (Bullock & Gilliland, 1993; Eysenck, 1990). For example, one study showed that when drops of natural lemon juice are placed on the tongue, most introverts salivate more than most extraverts (Deary et al., 1988). Others have shown that introverts are more easily aroused by caffeine and other stimulants—and are less easily relaxed by alcohol and other depressants (Stelmack, 1990). A recent PET scan study also shows that introverts exhibit more blood flow activity in the frontal lobes than extraverts do (Johnson et al., 1999). In short, says Eysenck, each of us is born with a nervous system that predisposes us to either love or hate large crowds, bright lights, blaring music, fast cars, roller coasters, suspenseful movies, spicy foods, and other, more social stimulants.

As you can see, extraverts are not just more sociable and people oriented than introverts. According to Marvin Zuckerman (1994), they are also more *sensation seeking*—a trait that leads people to drink, smoke, and use other drugs; seek out novel experiences; enjoy dangerous sports and other intense forms of stimulation; and gamble and take other risks for the thrill of it. As for the introvert, Elaine and Arthur Aron (1997) note that avoiding stimulating social situations is a smart and adaptive strategy for people sensitive to stimulation. In a series of studies, they

If you crave self-assessment, you can take and score yourself on a number of serious and not-so-serious personality tests at: http://www.2h.com/Tests/personality.phtml.

*New Year celebrations in New York City's Times Square are wild and raucous events. With throngs of people screaming, champagne spouting, horns and music blaring, confetti raining, lights flashing, and fireworks booming overhead, this is the type of sensory experience that extraverts crave and introverts avoid.*

*Reflecting their desire for sensory stimulation and arousal, extraverts are also more likely to take extreme risks—as in ice climbing.*

| TABLE 15.6 WHAT'S YOUR ORIENTATION TO STIMULATION? |
| --- |

**SENSATION-SEEKING SCALE (Zuckerman, 1994)**

1. I would like to try parachute jumping.
2. I like "wild" uninhibited parties.
3. I often like to get high.
4. I get bored seeing the same old faces.
5. I enjoy the company of people who are free and easy about sex.

**HIGHLY SENSITIVE PERSON SCALE (Aron & Aron, 1997)**

1. Do you startle easily?
2. Are you easily overwhelmed by strong sensory input?
3. Are you made uncomfortable by loud noises?
4. Do changes in your life shake you up?
5. Do you get rattled when you have a lot to do in a short amount of time?

found that subjects who described themselves as "highly sensitive" were more likely to report feeling overwhelmed by strong sensory input. Compared to others, they cry more easily, are more sensitive to daylight, are less tolerant of pain, are affected more by emotional films, and prefer country living to the city. Table 15.6 presents sample items from the tests that are used to measure both sensation seeking and sensitivity.

Interestingly, the rudiments of adult introversion and extraversion can be seen in the predispositions of infants shortly after birth. Over the years, Jerome Kagan (1994) and others have studied children who are *inhibited* and *uninhibited* in their temperament (most fall between these two extremes). At sixteen weeks old, inhibited infants—compared to those who are uninhibited—are more easily distressed and cry more in response to hanging mobiles, human speech, intense odors, and other types of stimulation. At two years old, inhibited children are fearful, wary of strangers, and avoidant of novel situations, whereas their uninhibited peers are adventurous, outgoing, and quick to approach new people and situations. At five years old, socially inhibited children are shy and more easily aroused by mildly stressful tasks—as measured by increases in heart rate, dilation of the pupils, and a rise in norepinephrine. They often have more tension in the face muscles and are more likely to have higher-than-average levels of cortisol, a hormone associated with physiological arousal during stress. Even at ten to twelve years of age, they are more excitable and sensitive to stimulation (Woodward et al., 2001).

Not all inhibited infants grow up to become inhibited adults. But longitudinal research indicates that there is continuity—that some aspects of adults' personalities are predictable from their temperament and behavior as young children. For example, toddlers who were observed to be highly irritable, impulsive, and hard to control at age three were more likely to have drug problems, problems at work, and relationship conflicts by the time they were twenty-one. In contrast, those who were highly inhibited, fearful, and shy at age three were more likely to become socially isolated and depressed at age twenty-one (Caspi, 2000).

Two lines of research suggest that temperament is a biological predisposition. First, Stephen Suomi (1991) observed that infant rhesus monkeys also differ in their behavior at birth. Suomi calls the inhibited monkeys "uptight" and the uninhibited ones "laid back." He found that the uptight monkeys, who are shy and anxious, also have the same physical attributes as Kagan's inhibited human infants. Second, Janet DiPietro and others (1996) monitored heart rate and motor activity in thirty-one human fetuses for twenty weeks prior to their birth. They found, through follow-up reports provided by the mothers, that the most active fetuses were later fussier, more difficult, and less adaptable as six-month-old babies. It appears that certain aspects of an infant's temperament can be detected even before birth.

## THE PROCESS OF DISCOVERY

# JEROME KAGAN
### *Origins of Human Temperament*

**Q: How did you first become interested in psychology?**

**A:** The decision to become an academic psychologist had a dual origin for me based upon my personal characteristics and my history. Youths vary with respect to the natural phenomena that evoke a passionate curiosity. For some, the stars excite the soul; for others, rocks. For me, the fascination fixed on the thoughts of others, but I do not understand the reasons why the human mind had this powerful attraction.

The historical conditions are easier to describe. In the middle of the twentieth century, when I was deciding what to become, American psychologists had persuaded themselves and the media that discovery of the early environmental conditions that produced crime, psychosis, depression, and anxiety were almost within reach. If that premise were true, investigators who discovered the critical experiences that led to these undesirable outcomes could communicate their insights to parents and the problems would become extinct. Most 18-year olds who believed that ingenuous idea would be attracted to studying the psychology of the child.

**Q: How did you first come up with your important discovery?**

**A:** I remember the moment when the origins of the temperamental category we call the *high-reactive infant* pierced consciousness. Nancy Snidman and I had collected behavioral data on a group of four-month old infants and, closeted in a room, I was looking at the videotapes of the first few dozen. One infant girl was distinctly different from the others I had watched. She pumped her arms and legs, arched her back, and cried in distress whenever a colorful mobile was moved back and forth across her face. It seemed obvious that this child was born with a temperamental bias favoring extreme arousal to simple but unfamiliar stimuli. The concept of the high reactive infant was born that afternoon.

**Q: How has the field you inspired developed over the years?**

**A:** The study of human temperaments has become popular thanks to the work of many scientists. It is relatively clear that most social scientists now acknowledge the contribution of each individual's temperament to later development.

**Q: What's your prediction on where the field is heading?**

**A:** Two predictions seem likely to prove true. First, psychologists will discover a large number of temperaments, many more than the nine hypothesized by Thomas and Chess in their original, bold work, published almost fifty years ago. Some of the temperamental categories will be common, some rare. I also suspect that most of the temperaments will be derivatives of variation in the concentration of—as well as the placement and density of—receptors for neurochemicals in the human brain. Variation in neurochemistry will be the root basis for the temperamental bias; hence, future temperamental categories will be defined by both behavior and biology, rather than behavior alone.

However, we will also learn that no temperamental bias is deterministic. The experiences of the child sculpt each temperament into one of a limited number of possible outcomes. All high reactive infants will not be shy adolescents, but very few will become exuberant, fearless risk-takers. It is not possible to predict the final resting-place of a small stone that has begun its descent down a mountain. Thus, although a temperamental bias pushes a child in a particular direction initially, no specific outcome is knowable because of the unpredictable contingencies that the future holds.

*Jerome Kagan is Daniel and Amy Starch Professor of Psychology at Harvard University.*

## PERSPECTIVES: DO TRAITS EXIST?

Intuitively, we are all trait psychologists. We use trait terms to describe ourselves and others, and we have preconceptions about how various characteristics relate to one another and to behavior. We assume that people who are unpredictable are also dangerous and that those who talk slowly are also slow-witted. We're surprised when a polite and unassuming coworker erupts in violence or when the sweet "girl next door" turns out to be the "other woman." Each of us notices some traits more than others. One person may measure everyone by an intellectual yardstick, whereas others look for physical beauty, friendliness, a sense of humor, or a firm handshake. When I was younger, I used to think I could instantly tell all about people—whether they were relaxed or intense, competitive or cooperative, cautious or adventurous, and so on—by the way they played board games like Scrabble, Risk, and Monopoly.

Although it seems natural to think about people and their behavior in terms of traits, some critics complain that the approach is limited. Psychoanalysts say it's superficial, cognitive social-learning theorists say it neglects situational factors, and humanists say it's cold and impersonal. By far the most serious attack, however, was Walter Mischel's (1968) startling claim that traits simply do not exist. After reviewing years of research, Mischel concluded that (1) personality test scores are not predictive of behavior, and (2) people do not act with traitlike consistency from one situation to the next. To illustrate, he cited a classic study by Hugh Hartshorne and Mark May (1928) in which they observed the moral conduct of thousands of children in school, at home, at parties, and so on. Seeking evidence of a trait for honesty, Hartshorne and May found that the children exhibited strikingly little cross-situational consistency in behavior. A child might pass up a chance to cheat in class or steal money from a dropped wallet but then be quick to cheat in an athletic event or lie to parents. Thus, said Mischel (1968), traits—as measured by personality tests—cannot reliably predict behavior.

Mischel's critique whipped up a tremendous controversy among personality psychologists wondering whether traits were a mere figment of the imagination. After many years of debate and additional research, three main conclusions can be drawn. First, as noted by Seymour Epstein (1979), traits are highly informative—but only when they're used to predict an *aggregation* of behaviors. To measure personality, psychologists derive test scores by combining answers to several related questions. Similarly, says Epstein, behavior should be measured by combining several trait-related acts. Just as an IQ score is not expected to predict a grade in a particular class during a particular semester, your score on an introversion—extraversion scale cannot be expected to predict whether you will tell jokes at your next party. By the same token, just as an IQ score can predict grade point *averages*, a personality test can predict general behavior tendencies (Epstein & O'Brien, 1985; Moskowitz, 1982). (See *Psychology and Business*.)

The second important conclusion is that behavior springs from complex *interactions* between persons and situations (Magnusson & Endler, 1977; Snyder & Ickes, 1985; Mischel & Shoda, 1995; Cervone & Shoda, 1999). This interaction can take many forms. First, personality traits are expressed only in relevant situations. If you're the anxious type, you may break out in a cold sweat before a first date or public presentation but not when at home watching TV. Second, traits are expressed only in situations that do not constrain our behavior. Just about everyone is quiet and reserved in churches, libraries, and crowded elevators, but our unique personalities are free to emerge at home, at a party, or in the street. Third, people influence the situations they are in. The way we treat our friends, family, and others, for example, steers the treatment we receive in turn. Thus, child-development researchers who used to write about how parents shape their children now realize that children, even infants, shape their parents as well. Fourth, people choose settings that are compatible with their own personalities. Extraverts craving excitement are likely to visit amusement parks and casinos, but introverts seek out quiet restaurants, hiking trails, and other out-of-the-way places. Fifth, our personalities color the way we interpret and react to situations. Optimists see the proverbial glass as half-full, whereas pessimists see the same glass as half-empty. As Allport (1961) said, "The same fire that melts the butter hardens the egg" (p. 102).

## *Psychology and Business*

# USE OF PERSONALITY TESTS IN THE WORKPLACE

Anyone who has applied for a desirable job knows that you sometimes have to climb hurdles and jump through hoops to get hired. It's a familiar routine. You submit a résumé and a list of references, fill out an application, and maybe even take the "hot seat" in a face-to-face interview. You may even be asked to bring in samples of your work or take a standardized test of intelligence, vocational interests, or personality. When it comes to personnel selection in business and industry, there are many methods—all designed to predict performance in the workplace (Hough & Oswald, 2000).

The use of personality tests for employment purposes is controversial. Can scores on trait inventories be used to predict worker productivity, motivation, satisfaction, loyalty, or other aspects of job performance? For many years, the MMPI was used to assess a candidate's personality—even though it had been developed for the purpose of diagnosing mental disorders, and even though there was no clear link between MMPI scores and work performance (Guion, 1965). Questions were also raised about whether it was ethical, or a violation of privacy, to require the testing of all prospective employees. People are free to refuse to take a test as part of an application process, but 52 percent of personnel managers surveyed said they automatically reject applicants who refuse to take a test (Blocklyn, 1988).

Despite the initial problems and occasional misdirections, it's now clear that certain personality tests can be used to predict a whole range of worker outcomes, including leadership potential, helpfulness, absenteeism, and petty theft (Goffin et al., 1996; Hogan et al., 1996). In particular, many researchers have found that perfor-

mance across different occupations can be significantly predicted by questionnaires that measure the Big Five personality factors. Among both skilled and unskilled workers, for example, research shows that people who score high in the trait of conscientiousness—which means being dependable, responsible, organized, and persistent—are more likely to perform well on the job. Even more specific a prediction is that people who score as highly extraverted rather than introverted are more likely to succeed as business managers and salespersons (Hurtz & Donovan, 2000; Hogan et al., 1996; Salgado, 1997)—and emerge as inspirational leaders (Judge & Bono, 2000). Clearly, the measurement of personality traits is useful for predicting success and failure in the workplace (Goldberg, 1993; Hogan et al., 1996).

One criticism of personality testing for employment purposes is that, as motivated test takers, job candidates can fake their responses in order to present themselves in a positive light. This is a serious possible drawback. Imagine having applied for a job you really wanted, and all that stands in your way are the results of a personality questionnaire. Isn't it possible that you would cover up your flaws, consciously or not, according to what you think is desirable? And wouldn't this render your test results invalid? The answer is yes to the first question, but no to the second. Industrial/organizational psychologists have found that people do bias their responses in a socially desirable direction—but this does not diminish the value of the tests. Apparently, the ability to present oneself favorably is a sign of emotional stability and conscientiousness—traits that are predictive of success at work (Barrick & Mount, 1996; Ones et al., 1996).

A third general conclusion is that our personalities have stability over time. That is not to say that we do not change as we age. We do. Research on the Big Five personality factors has shown that as people get older—from their late teens to their fifties—they predictably become less extraverted, less anxious, and less open to new experiences, but more agreeable and more conscientious. This pattern of change was found among both men and women in Germany, Italy, Portugal, Croatia, and South Korea (McCrae et al., 1999). Despite these changes that come with age, however, the differences among us are highly consistent. Let's say you're more extraverted than your best friend. Twenty years from now, you'll probably be less extraverted than you are now—but you're still likely to be more extraverted than

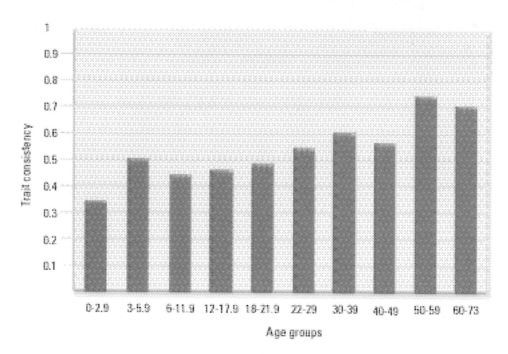

FIGURE 15.11 **Personality consistency across the lifespan**
Is personality more consistent at some points in life than others? By testing people of different ages on two or more occasions, researchers can estimate how stable (as opposed to changing) personality is. Taken together, these studies reveal that our personalities are the least stable during childhood, somewhat more stable in early adulthood, and the most stable after the age of fifty (Roberts & DelVecchio, 2000).

## REVIEW QUESTIONS

- *What traits can best be used to describe personality according to the five-factor model of personality?*

- *Describe the evidence demonstrating biological influences on personality.*

- *Distinguish between introversion and extraversion.*

- *What are the major criticisms of the trait approach? How have trait theorists responded?*

the friend. Does personality remain more consistent during some periods in life than in others? To answer this question, Brent Roberts and Wendy DelVecchio (2000) combined the results of 152 longitudinal studies in which various traits were measured at two or more points in time. They found that personalities undergo the most change during childhood, change less in early adulthood, and become most stable after the age of fifty. Personalities form loosely at first but gradually harden through adulthood (see Figure 15.11).

## THINKING LIKE A PSYCHOLOGIST ABOUT PERSONALITY

Now that you are familiar with the four major approaches to personality, you are in a position to evaluate each perspective for yourself. If you were to stop and think about your own life—say, to write your autobiography—which of the four approaches would best describe your personality and explain how you got that way?

To summarize, psychoanalysis emphasizes unconscious conflicts, sex and aggression, defensive behavior, anxiety, and early childhood influences. Cognitive social-learning theory views personality as a socially acquired pattern of behavior, a learned response to how people perceive, interpret, and value the external reinforcements in their lives. Humanists believe that people are inherently good, that we have self-insight,

and that personality springs from the desire and struggle to reach our full potential. The trait approach makes few value judgments about human nature, but it assumes that everyone can be compared on a standard set of dispositions that are consistent over time and, at least to some extent, genetically determined.

The four approaches also differ in their perspectives on change and in their approaches to the treatment of psychological disorders. Beginning with Freud, most psychoanalysts see the early years of childhood as formative, if not critical, to the development of personality—with relatively little room for change in adulthood. In fact, psychoanalytic therapists say that patients unconsciously resist the recovery process.

The trait approach, with its emphasis on genetic factors and the stability of core dispositions, also takes a relatively dim view of change. In the trait approach, people are biologically introverted or extraverted, and calm or anxious—thus leaving little room for variation. In contrast, the behavioral and cognitive social-learning theorists see people as flexible and influenced by environmental factors. According to this view, psychological disorders are learned—and can be unlearned just as well. The humanistic approach is equally clear in its view that people have not only the capacity but also the will to change and, specifically, to strive toward self-actualization.

Although we have discussed the four approaches as distinct, you don't necessarily have to choose a favorite or accept any one approach completely. Many personality psychologists are *eclectic*, which means that they accept bits and pieces of different theories. Mix in some of Freud's unconscious, hold the sex, add a dash of reinforcement and a pinch of self-actualization, then administer a multitrait personality inventory, and you will have formed a new perspective from a blending of existing ingredients. It is also instructive to consider the possibility that each approach may better account for some aspects of personality than for others. Psychoanalysis may shed light on why we inexplicably feel troubled and anxious, cognitive social-learning theory may explain why having control is often so important to us, humanism may capture the experience of pursuing and catching lifelong dreams, and the trait approach may offer the best way to measure our unique predispositions. The human personality is so complex and multifaceted that all perspectives are necessary.

## SUMMARY

The study of **personality**—an individual's distinct and relatively enduring pattern of thoughts, feelings, motives, and behaviors—shows that personality characteristics are stable over time. There are four major approaches to personality.

### PSYCHOANALYSIS

#### THE BIRTH OF PSYCHOANALYSIS

Just before the turn of the twentieth century, Freud used his clinical experience with hysteria to formulate **psychoanalysis**.

#### FREUD'S THEORY OF PERSONALITY

Psychoanalysis assumes that unconscious conflicts play a large part in shaping personality. Freud divided personality into three parts. The **id**—a primitive, unconscious reservoir of basic drives—operates according to the **pleasure principle**. The personality's moral part, the **superego**, consists of the ego-ideal and the conscience. The **ego** mediates between the id's "wants" and the superego's "shoulds" and follows a **reality principle** that allows for gratification of needs in a socially appropriate manner.

Freud believed that personality is shaped by conflicts that arise during the **psychosexual stages** of development. Young children pass through the oral, anal, and phallic stages. During the phallic stage (ages four to six), children experience the **Oedipus complex**, a tendency to become attracted to the parent of the opposite sex and hostile to the parent of the same sex. Children resolve this complex, however, and form an **identification** with the same-sex parent, internalizing the parent's values. At puberty, the genital stage begins. Too much or too little gratification in any of the first three stages can result in **fixation** at that stage and a distinct type of personality.

According to Freud, we feel anxiety when our impulses clash with morals, so the ego uses unconscious **defense mechanisms** that deny and distort reality. **Repression** helps us "forget" threatening thoughts, memories, and impulses by pushing them out of awareness. In **denial**, we bar anxiety-provoking thoughts from awareness in the first place. Through **projection**, we attribute our own unacceptable impulses to others. Through **reaction formation**, we convert an unacceptable feeling into its opposite. **Rationalization** involves making excuses for failures and shortcomings. And in **sublimation**, the healthiest defense mechanism, we channel repressed urges into socially acceptable substitute outlets.

#### FREUD'S LEGACY

Freud's followers continued to focus on unconscious factors, inner conflicts, and early-childhood influences. Jung proposed that people are influenced by a **collective unconscious** consisting of memories from our ancestral past, and he argued that personality development continues into adulthood. Adler stressed social conflicts and developed the notions of sibling rivalry and the inferiority complex. More recent theorists have emphasized social needs or the role of the ego.

Psychoanalytic researchers also developed **projective tests** to reveal the unconscious through responses to ambiguous stimuli. The **Rorschach** uses inkblots. The **Thematic Apperception Test (TAT)** asks people to make up stories from a set of pictures.

Critics say that psychoanalysis takes too bleak a view of human nature and that its propositions are not supported by controlled research. Yet Freud's ideas, particularly those about the unconscious and defense mechanisms, have become an integral part of psychology.

## THE COGNITIVE SOCIAL-LEARNING APPROACH

Unlike psychoanalysis, **cognitive social-learning theory** sees personality as the result of a continuous interaction between persons and environments.

### PRINCIPLES OF LEARNING AND BEHAVIOR

Early behaviorists investigated classical conditioning, operant conditioning, and other key principles of learning. Watson and Skinner applied these principles to the study of personality.

### SOCIAL-LEARNING THEORY

Social-learning theory extended behaviorism to include social and cognitive factors. Through **modeling,** people can learn behavior by observing and imitating. Rotter and Mischel further showed that thoughts influence the link between reinforcement and behavior.

According to cognitive social-learning theory, people differ in **locus of control**—expectations about the control of reinforcement. Internals, who believe they can control their own fate, tend to be healthier and more successful. People also differ in **self-efficacy,** the belief that they can perform the behaviors needed for a desired outcome. The more self-efficacy people have for a task, the more likely they are to succeed.

### PERSPECTIVES ON COGNITIVE SOCIAL-LEARNING THEORY

Cognitive social-learning theory emphasizes **reciprocal determinism,** the notion that personality emerges from an ongoing interaction among individuals, their actions, and environments. Environmental forces shape our personalities, but we can choose, alter, and interpret the situations we encounter. To assess personality, cognitive social-learning theorists use direct methods such as behavioral observations and self-reports.

## THE HUMANISTIC APPROACH

By the 1940s, some psychologists began to develop a **humanistic theory** of personality.

### CARL ROGERS

Impressed by his patients' self-insight and will to improve, Rogers theorized that we all have a natural need for self-actualization—that is, a drive to behave in ways consistent with our self-concepts. The self-concept is made up of various

self-schemas, specific beliefs about the self. As social beings, however, we also have a competing need for positive regard. **Unconditional positive regard** from significant others frees us to pursue self-actualization. But if we receive **conditional positive regard,** we experience frustration, anxiety, and **self-discrepancies.** Studies have shown that individuals as well as social and cultural groups differ in their **self-esteem,** the extent to which they evaluate themselves favorably.

### ABRAHAM MASLOW

Maslow believed that people are motivated to fulfill a hierarchy of needs en route to **self-actualization,** the distinctly human need to become everything one is capable of becoming. Few people reach this state, though it is common to have momentary **peak experiences.**

### PERSPECTIVES ON THE HUMANISTIC APPROACH

Humanistic psychologists have been praised for focusing on the good in human beings, the self-concept, and conscious experience. They have been criticized for ignoring the darker side of human nature and relying too heavily on people's self-reports.

## THE TRAIT APPROACH

### THE BUILDING BLOCKS OF PERSONALITY

To study the basic units of personality, Gordon Allport compiled a list of two hundred personality **traits.** With factor analysis, Raymond Cattell reduced these to sixteen source traits. Now, researchers have condensed the list to a **five-factor model** consisting of five traits: neuroticism, extraversion, openness, agreeableness, and conscientiousness.

### CONSTRUCTION OF MULTITRAIT INVENTORIES

The trait approach gave rise to the construction of personality inventories such as the **Minnesota Multiphasic Personality Inventory (MMPI).**

### BIOLOGICAL ROOTS OF PERSONALITY

Different traits show different degrees of genetic linkage. According to recent estimates, many personality factors are 40 to 50 percent genetically determined in the population.

### INTROVERSION AND EXTRAVERSION

One of the most powerful trait dimensions is introversion and extraversion. An **extrovert** is sociable and impulsive and seeks stimulation. An **introvert** is low-keyed, cautious, and avoidant of stimulation. Research suggests that extraverts are sensation seekers, whereas introverts are overly sensitive to stimulation. Recent studies reveal similar differences in temperament between inhibited and uninhibited infants and children.

## PERSPECTIVES: DO TRAITS EXIST?

Debates about trait theory lead to two major conclusions. First, traits can predict an aggregation of behaviors but not specific acts. Second, behavior springs from an interaction between traits and situations.

## KEY TERMS

personality (**p. 581**)

psychoanalysis (**p. 582**)

id (**p. 583**)

pleasure principle (**p. 583**)

superego (**p. 583**)

ego (**p. 584**)

reality principle (**p. 584**)

psychosexual stages (**p. 584**)

Oedipus complex (**p. 584**)

identification (**p. 585**)

fixation (**p. 586**)

defense mechanisms (**p. 586**)

repression (**p. 586**)

denial (**p. 586**)

projection (**p. 587**)

reaction formation (**p. 587**)

rationalization (**p. 587**)

sublimation (**p. 587**)

collective unconscious (**p. 588**)

projective tests (**p. 589**)

Rorschach (**p. 589**)

Thematic Apperception Test (TAT) (**p. 590**)

cognitive social-learning theory (**p. 592**)

modeling (**p. 594**)

locus of control (**p. 595**)

self-efficacy (**p. 597**)

reciprocal determinism (**p. 598**)

humanistic theory (**p. 598**)

unconditional positive regard (**p. 599**)

conditional positive regard (**p. 599**)

self-schemas (**p. 600**)

self-esteem (**p. 600**)

self-discrepancy theory (**p. 602**)

self-actualization (**p. 603**)

peak experience (**p. 603**)

trait (**p. 605**)

five-factor model (**p. 606**)

Minnesota Multiphasic Personality Inventory (MMPI) (**p. 607**)

extravert (**p. 610**)

introvert (**p. 610**)

## THINKING CRITICALLY ABOUT PERSONALITY

1. Compare the four approaches to personality (psychoanalytic, cognitive social-learning, humanistic, and trait). What are the implications of these differences for the way in which personality is measured? Give examples of the different measurement instruments advocated by each approach.

2. Take a few moments to write down a description of your own personality, and then use each of the four approaches to explain it. Which of the four approaches do you think best accounts for your personality?

3. What are the major criticisms of Freudian theory? What Freudian concepts continue to endure? What would you say is Freud's most enduring legacy?

4. Csikszentmihalyi's research seems to suggest that anyone can have "optimal experiences." Identify a domain in which you have experienced, or would like to experience, flow. What did this experience feel like (or what do you think it would feel like)? Suggest some ways that you would increase the likelihood of experiencing flow.

5. Discuss the evidence that introversion is biologically based. What are the implications of this work for personality change? That is, can an introvert become more extraverted, or vice versa? If so, how might this be accomplished?

# Psychological Disorders

# HOW COMMON ARE PSYCHOLOGICAL DISORDERS?

## THE SITUATION

In clinical psychology, it's difficult but important to know the mental-health status of the nation and the kinds of problems most in need of attention. How common are different types of disorders? Are some segments of the population more "at risk" than others? And how can we make estimates that can be trusted?

Imagine that you have extensive experience at conducting personal interviews and that you get a call from the University of Michigan's National Research Center. Apparently, the center is planning a massive nationwide study to determine the prevalence in the United States of certain psychological disorders and wants to know whether you can help conduct the interviews. You say yes, but first you need to attend a seven-day training program along with 157 other experienced interviewers recruited for the same study.

Using a standard set of questions, interviewers in forty-eight states (excluding Hawaii and Alaska) get responses from a total of 8,098 men and women, fifteen to fifty-four years old—and carefully sampled to represent the national population. Some 75 percent are white, 12 percent black, 9 percent Hispanic, and 4 percent from other groups. With all respondents, your goal is to find out whether they have suffered from certain mental disorders during their lives.

You ask about five types of disorders. One type is characterized by high and persistent levels of *anxiety*. Included in this category are people who are chronically anxious, who have panic attacks, who have intense fears of common objects and social situations, or who are afraid to leave the house. A second type are mood disorders, characterized primarily by *depression*. Included here are people who have suffered a bout of clinical depression or are chronically sad and "down in the dumps." The third type of disorder involves *substance abuse*. In this category are people who are addicted to alcohol or other drugs—or who abuse drugs in ways that cause physical, social, or legal harm. The fourth type is *schizophrenia*, a severe disorder marked by hallucinations, grossly distorted thoughts, bizarre behavior, and loss of contact with reality. Fifth is the *antisocial personality*, characterized by a blatant disregard for other people. Those having this disorder repeatedly lie, steal, cheat, fight, assault others, and break the law—without feelings of remorse.

You interview people in your area from a list you're given. After you complete each interview, you send it to your regional supervisor, who checks to make sure that all the necessary questions were asked and answered. If responses are incomplete or unclear, the form is returned for you to go back and collect the missing information. If it is complete, the interview data are sent to the national office, where all the results are compiled and analyzed.

## MAKE A PREDICTION

Think carefully about the five types of disorders described above. How prevalent are they? Are men and women equally at risk? For each disorder, use the table below to predict the percentages of men and women (from 0 to 100) who have ever suffered from it during their lives.

PERCENTAGE WHO HAVE EVER SUFFERED

| Types of Disorder | Men | Women |
|---|---|---|
| Anxiety | _____ % | _____ % |
| Depression | _____ % | _____ % |
| Substance abuse | _____ % | _____ % |
| Schizophrenia | _____ % | _____ % |
| Antisocial personality | _____ % | _____ % |

## THE RESULTS

When the responses were tallied, the results were consistent with previous research. Look at the table below, and you'll see, first, that the lifetime prevalence rate for both sexes combined is highest for substance abuse—followed, in order, by anxiety, depression, antisocial personality disorder, and schizophrenia. Second, notice that although men and women are equally vulnerable overall, they differ in the types of disorders they exhibit. Men are more likely to have substance abuse and antisocial personality problems, whereas women are more likely to suffer from anxiety and depression.

PERCENTAGE WHO HAVE EVER SUFFERED

| Types of Disorder | Men | Women |
|---|---|---|
| Anxiety | 19% | 31% |
| Depression | 15% | 24% |
| Substance abuse | 35% | 18% |
| Schizophrenia | .6% | .8% |
| Antisocial personality | 6% | 1% |

## WHAT DOES IT ALL MEAN?

In this study, Ronald Kessler and others (1994) conducted extensive interviews with a large national sample of respondents and provided much-needed information about the mental-health status of American men and women in the 1990s. For now, three aspects of these results are worth noting.

First, the numbers were somewhat higher than those found in an earlier national study (Robins & Regier, 1991). In fact, a reanalysis of these data has shown that when only "clinically significant" disorders are considered—those that interfered with everyday life, or required professional help or medication—the prevalence estimates were much lower (Narrow et al., 2002). Second, these numbers represent *lifetime* prevalence rates. When Kessler and colleagues (1994) asked respondents about the past twelve months, the numbers, again, were much lower. In other words, someone might experience anxiety, depression, or substance abuse at one point in life but then recover. The third important point is that the number of Americans likely to have a problem is less than the sum for the different types of disorders. Add the percentages in the above table and it will appear that roughly three-quarters of all men and women will have a psychological disorder. Not so. As we'll see later in this chapter, people who have one problem often have others too—so that many of the respondents in this study were counted in more than one row. In fact, the lifetime rate for having at least one disorder was only 48 percent.

In this chapter, we'll discuss these disorders, and others that are less common, in greater detail. We will look not only at their incidence in the population but also at the possible causes, symptoms, and likely outcomes.

Have you ever lost a loved one to death, only to be stricken by grief, despair, and the numb feeling that life is just not worth living? Have you ever been so nervous before making a speech or going on a date that your heart raced, your voice trembled, and your stomach tightened up? Have you ever been the victim of a car accident and blocked out the whole experience? Have you ever jumped out of bed in the middle of the night, startled by a terrifying nightmare you couldn't shake or by creaking noises you imagined were the sound of an intruder? Have you ever been haunted by a tune you kept humming and couldn't get out of your mind, no matter how hard you tried? And have you ever heard the sound of laughter as you entered a room, only to wonder for a moment if everyone was looking and laughing at *you*?

Chances are that one or more of these descriptions will ring a familiar bell and provide you with a personal glimpse into the unhappy, disturbing, and sometimes frightening world of psychological disorders. You don't have to be "crazy" to have these kinds of episodes. For some of us, they are rare and last for brief periods. But for others, they are frequent, prolonged, and intense. Based on nationwide surveys, it is estimated that in the course of a lifetime, one-third to one-half of all Americans will suffer from a problem serious enough to be diagnosed as a psychological disorder (Kessler et al., 1994; Regier et al., 1993). In any given one-year period, 28 percent of the adult population in the United States will have some form of psychological distress—and 19 percent will suffer from a disorder significant enough to interfere with their everyday lives or require professional help or medication (Narrow et al., 2002).

These surveys, supplemented by clinical case studies, tell us that psychological disorders are often a temporary condition. Most people are resilient in their capacity for recovery. But no one is invulnerable in times of great stress, a fact that was acutely evident in the large numbers of Americans—particularly New York City residents—who suffered anxiety, nightmares, sleep loss, and other stress symptoms after the traumatic 9/11/01 terrorist attacks (Galea et al., 2002; Schuster et al., 2001). For the clinical psychologist, the key point is that people undergo changes in their mental-health status, sometimes for the better, at other times for the worse. In this chapter, we examine the negative form of change—the causes and effects of psychological disorders.

For information on mental-health disorders and statistics, you can visit the National Institute of Mental Health (NIMH) Web site at http://www.nimh.nih.gov/.

## PSYCHOLOGICAL DISORDERS: A GENERAL OUTLOOK

- *In matters of mind and behavior, what separates normal from abnormal?*
- *What is the medical perspective on psychological disorders?*
- *What is the sociocultural perspective?*
- *What are the pitfalls of diagnosis, and why is it necessary?*

Before we discuss the wide array of mental-health problems that plague people all over the world, three general questions must be asked. First, when are thoughts, feelings, and behaviors defined as disordered? That is, when does a person cross the invisible line between health and illness, psychology and psycho*pathology*, normal and *ab*normal? Second, what biological and environmental factors put our psychological well-being at risk? Third, how can different problems be distinguished for the sake of treating those in need of assistance?

### DEFINING NORMAL AND ABNORMAL

In a journey through a subway station in New York City, I passed by a middle-aged man in a neatly pressed blue suit who stood on a bench, waved his arms, and urged commuters to repent for their sins because the planet was due to explode. On the same bench, an older bearded man in a heavy wool coat lay all curled up, with his arms folded together and his eyes cast down to the ground. Once on the train, I watched a man who switched his seat several times during the ride. Crazy? For all I know, the other passengers—who slept, hid behind walls of newspapers, tuned

*"Enigma" controls his gag reflex and the muscles down to his stomach in order to swallow two feet of steel. What does this behavior reveal about him—is he normal or abnormal? What more information would you need to make such a judgment?*

into headphones, read books, and minded their own business—were wondering about me, the nosy guy who couldn't stop spying on everyone else.

People-watching experiences like this one demonstrate how tricky it can be to determine whether someone has a psychological disorder. Various criteria have been proposed over the years, and many are still being proposed—and all have sparked controversy (Clark, 1999). A frequently cited definition is one provided by the American Psychiatric Association (APA). According to the APA (1994), a pattern of behavior can be considered a **psychological disorder** if, and only if, it satisfies three conditions:

1. The person experiences significant pain or distress, an inability to work or play, an increased risk of death, or a loss of freedom in important areas of life.

2. The source of the problem resides within the person, due to biological factors, learned habits, or mental processes, and is not simply a normal response to specific life events such as the death of a loved one.

3. The problem is not a deliberate reaction to conditions such as poverty, prejudice, government policy, or other conflicts with society.

These criteria suggest some key points about a definition. One is that the term *abnormal* means more than just "different from the norm" in a statistical sense. Nobel Prize winners and Olympic gold medalists are also atypical, but most are not clinically troubled. Also, what's normative in one cultural or ethnic group may be deviant in another. A second point is that normal and abnormal are merely points along a continuum, not distinct conditions separated by a bright line. Think about it. At what point should nervousness be called "anxiety," or sadness "depression"? How much pain, distress, or impairment is too much? When is a person who is deeply but reasonably upset by a tragic life event in need of psychological assistance? And when it comes to people who are poverty-stricken or homeless, how can we tell that their actions are not a normal response to a cruel and hostile environment? These difficult questions can be addressed only on a case-by-case basis. A third point is that certain behavior patterns are considered abnormal not because they are disabling to the individual but because they threaten the safety and welfare of others. The model citizen who has a well-paying job but is abusive to his wife or children is an all-too-familiar example.

Finally, the criteria used to identify psychological disorders do not in themselves explain the source of those disorders or imply a certain form of treatment. As we'll see, the unhealthy mind is sometimes the product of an unhealthy body and, thus, is treatable with drugs. Yet often the problem stems from deep-seated personal conflicts, bad habits, negative life experiences, daily stress, faulty processing of information, and sociocultural factors. Before describing the kinds of disorders from which so many of us suffer, let's examine these theoretical models.

## MODELS OF ABNORMALITY

When archaeologists unearth human bone fragments from thousands of years ago, they sometimes find a small hole that was drilled into the skull. The reason, some experts speculate, is that our prehistoric ancestors believed that mental disorders were caused by the intrusion of evil spirits into the body and that these spirits needed an opening to escape. In more recent times, these disorders were variously attributed to witchcraft, demonic possession, full moons, and other supernatural forces. Evil spirits were thus "driven out" through exorcism, torture, primitive forms of surgery, noise making, bloodletting, bitter potions, and starvation. Today, we have more enlightened, naturalistic perspectives on abnormality—medical, psychological, and sociocultural.

**psychological disorder** A condition in which a person's thoughts, feelings, or behavior is judged to be dysfunctional.

**The Medical Perspective**   Within the **medical model,** disordered thoughts, feelings, and behaviors are caused by physical disease. In 400 BCE, Greek physician Hippocrates, the founder of modern medicine, proposed that psychological disorders are caused by body-fluid imbalances. This perspective is an important one today, as researchers try to identify genetic links, damage to parts of the brain and nervous system, hormone imbalances, and neurotransmitter activity that is associated with various problems. The medical model is powerfully evoked by the language used to describe abnormality. Thus, it is common to speak of *diagnosing* mental *illness* as opposed to *health* in *patients* so that *treatment, hospitalization,* and *therapy* will relieve the *symptoms* and produce a *cure*. In short, a strictly medical model holds that although mental disorders take on a psychological appearance, the underlying problems are physical in nature.

The medical approach is more humane than demonology but it is not without critics. In *The Myth of Mental Illness,* psychiatrist Thomas Szasz (1961) argued that mental illness is a socially defined, relative concept used to cast aside people who are deviant ("If you talk to God, you are praying; if God talks to you, you have schizophrenia"). Szasz (1987) charged that psychologists, psychiatrists, and other mental-health experts are too quick to guard society's norms and values. What's worse, he claims, the label *sick* invites those with real problems to become passive—dependent on doctors and drugs rather than relying on their own inner strengths.

These criticisms raise provocative questions, but they are misguided. Thanks to recent advances in genetics and with the help of new brain-imaging technologies, it has become clear that mental illness is *not* a myth—and it would be cruel to deny treatment to people whose psychological disorders have biological as well as environmental origins and consequences. Describing how a neurobiological approach helps to destigmatize mental illness, Nancy Andreasen (2001) says, "I wanted people to understand that the human sufferers should be accorded the same compassion and respect as we accord people with other illnesses such as cancer or diabetes" (p. ix).

**The Psychological Perspective**   A second major approach to abnormal behavior is based on the **psychological model,** which holds that psychological disorders are caused and then maintained by a person's past and present life experiences. The list of negatively impactful events is a long one. Examples include prolonged illness, natural disasters, war, physical and sexual abuse, domestic violence, divorce, poverty, the death of a loved one, a lack of friendships, and persistent failure. This perspective was first born of Freud's interest in hysteria, a disorder in which the patient experiences bodily symptoms in the absence of physical damage. Freud and others believed that this disorder usually began with a traumatic event in childhood and that it could be treated successfully with *psycho*therapy, a form of "talking cure."

Today, there is not one psychological model of abnormality but many. Paralleling the major approaches to personality described in Chapter 15, there are three broad perspectives. The first is psychoanalysis, which emphasizes the role of parental influences, unconscious conflicts, guilt, frustration, and an array of defense mechanisms used to ward off anxiety. According to this view, psychological disorders spring from inner conflicts so intense that they overwhelm our normal defenses. The second perspective is rooted in behaviorism and cognitive social-learning theories. In this view, abnormal behavior is a learned response to reward and punishment, further influenced by our perceptions, expectations, values, and role models. The third perspective is humanistic, which holds that mental disorders arise when we are blocked in our efforts to grow and achieve self-actualization. In this view, the self-concept is all-important.

**medical model**   The perspective that mental disorders are caused by biological conditions and can be treated through medical intervention.

**psychological model**   The perspective that mental disorders are caused and maintained by one's life experiences.

"Here I was, all this time, worrying that maybe I'm a selfish person, and now it turns out I've been suffering from compassion fatigue."

*Critics of DSM-IV argue that it pathologizes "everyday" human imperfections.*

**The Sociocultural Perspective** Whether one prefers to think in medical or psychological terms, it is important to realize that the social and cultural context in which we live affects the kinds of stresses we're exposed to, the kinds of disorders we're likely to have, and the treatment we're likely to get. Particularly impressive evidence for a **sociocultural model** comes from the fact that different disorders, or symptoms, appear in different cultures (Lopez & Guarnaccia, 2000). For example, John Weisz and others (1993) studied behavioral and emotional problems among teenagers in the United States and Thailand and found that although problems are evident in both countries, they take very different forms. In the United States, troubled teens tend to act out by bullying others, getting into fights, or running afoul of teachers. But in the predominantly Buddhist country of Thailand, where children are taught to inhibit expressions of negative emotion, troubled teens are more likely to sulk, go silent, sleep too much, or become constipated.

Additional evidence of sociocultural influence comes from the fact that some disorders are found almost exclusively in specific regional groups. We saw in Chapter 11 that *anorexia nervosa* and *bulimia nervosa* (eating disorders that tend to afflict adolescent girls and young women) strike primarily middle- and upper-class women of Westernized cultures—presumably because they feel most pressured to sport a slender appearance (Brumberg, 1988; Hesse-Biber, 1996). Indeed, many women with eating disorders have negatively distorted images of their own bodies, often seeing themselves as overweight (Thompson et al., 1999).

Over the years, medical anthropologists and psychologists have identified a number of **culture-bound syndromes,** folk illnesses characterized by alterations in behavior. One that is particularly well known is *amok,* a brief period of brooding followed by a violent outburst, often resulting in murder. This disorder is frequently triggered by a perceived insult and is found only among men in Malaysia, Papua New Guinea, the Philippines, Polynesia, and Puerto Rico and among the Navajo. Another culture-bound syndrome is *pibloktoq,* a brief period of intense excitement that is often followed by seizures and a coma lasting up to twelve hours. During an attack of this condition, which is found only among arctic and subarctic Eskimo communities, the person may tear off his or her clothing, break furniture, shout obscenities, and eat feces—acts that are later reportedly forgotten. Psychological disorders are a universal aspect of the human condition, but the forms they take may vary from one culture to the next (American Psychiatric Association, 2000; Lopez & Guarnaccia, 2000; Simons & Hughes, 1986; Tseng, 2001).

**Combining Perspectives in a "Synthetic" Model** As you read through this chapter, you'll see that no single perspective can fully explain the array of psychological disorders that people encounter. Whereas some problems are largely biological, and perhaps genetic, in origin, others are based more on personal and developmental experiences embedded within a context of time, place, and culture. Further complicating matters is that most mental disorders spring from a combination of factors, as when individuals who are genetically vulnerable suffer intense life stress—as we'll see later, a dangerous combination. To understand mental health and illness, one cannot think in either-or terms about all the possible influences— or treatment alternatives. To capture the complexity of the problem, Andreasen

**sociocultural model** The perspective that psychological disorders are influenced by cultural factors.

**culture-bound syndromes** Recurring patterns of maladaptive behavior that are limited to a specific cultural group or location.

(2001) offers instead a "synthetic model" of mental illness, one that recognizes the interaction of multiple biological, psychological, and sociocultural influences.

## DIAGNOSIS: A NECESSARY STEP

In science, as in other pursuits, it often helps to group people, objects, and situations that share similar properties. Biologists classify animals into species, archaeologists divide time into eras, and geographers split the earth into regions. Likewise, mental-health professionals find it enormously useful—for the sake of prediction, understanding, and treatment—to categorize mental disorders that involve similar patterns of behavior, or syndromes. This process of grouping and naming mental disorders is referred to as **diagnosis.**

Today, the most widely used classification scheme in the United States is the American Psychiatric Association's *Diagnostic and Statistical Manual of Mental Disorders* (4th Edition), known by its acronym, **DSM-IV** (American Psychiatric Association, 2000). Written for mental-health professionals, this manual provides a comprehensive list of psychological disorders that are grouped into seventeen broad categories. (Those discussed in this chapter are previewed in Table 16.1.) For each disorder, the prominent symptoms are described in concrete behavioral terms. Also presented are the prevalence rates for men and women, predisposing factors, the normal age of onset, and the expected outcome. Accompanying the manual are books with illustrative case studies and standardized interviews for use in making a diagnosis—all updated in light of recent research (Spitzer et al., 2001).

It is important to realize that DSM-IV, which was released in 1994, is only one link in an evolving chain of diagnostic schemes and was preceded by four earlier versions. DSM was first published in 1952, was substantially revised in 1968 (DSM-II), was substantially revised again in 1980 (DSM-III), and was updated in 1987 (DSM-III-R). In this context, it's interesting that more and more psychological disorders are identified today than in the past. DSM-I listed 60 disorders, DSM-II listed 145, and DSM-IV has 410. What does this increase mean? Some would say that psychologists and psychiatrists have become more sophisticated in their ability to detect and then treat problems. Others would argue that they have become overly sensitive to human frailties and imperfections—and that they "pathologize"

**diagnosis**   The process of identifying and grouping mental disorders with similar symptoms.

**DSM-IV**   Acronym for the American Psychiatric Association's *Diagnostic and Statistical Manual of Mental Disorders* (4th Edition).

| TABLE 16.1 | DSM-IV MENTAL DISORDERS DESCRIBED IN THIS CHAPTER |
|---|---|
| **Anxiety disorders** | Disorders in which intense anxiety is the main symptom. This category includes generalized anxiety and panic disorders, phobias, obsessive-compulsive disorder, and posttraumatic stress disorder. |
| **Somatoform disorders** | Disorders involving physical symptoms, such as paralysis or sensory loss, that are psychological in origin. This category includes hypochondriasis and conversion disorder (formerly known as hysteria). |
| **Dissociative disorders** | Disorders in which part of one's experience is detached from consciousness. This category includes amnesia, fugue states, and dissociative identity disorder (formerly known as multiple personality disorder). |
| **Mood disorders** | Disorders marked by severe mood disturbances, such as major depression, mania (elation), or an alternating pattern of both. |
| **Schizophrenic disorders** | A group of psychotic disorders characterized by a loss of contact with reality, hallucinations, delusions, disorganized thought and affect, and bizarre behavior. |
| **Personality disorders** | Long-term, inflexible, maladaptive patterns of behavior. This category includes the borderline and antisocial personality disorders. |

## Psychology and Education

# ATTENTION-DEFICIT HYPERACTIVITY DISORDER

This chapter is focused on adult psychological disorders. Among the diagnostic categories in DSM-IV, however, is one that pertains to problems that arise in infancy, childhood, or adolescence—often with adverse effects on performance in school.

Almost every elementary school classroom has at least one child, usually a boy, who is always on the go, lacks patience, and cannot sit still or sustain attention for an extended time. Parents and teachers label children who fit this description as "hyperactive." Because these children also tend to be distractible and find it difficult to stay focused on a single task, they are diagnosed in DSM-IV as having *attention-deficit hyperactivity disorder*, or *ADHD*. What's the problem? As described by Sally Smith, founder of a private school for children with learning disabilities, "It's not that they are not paying attention. They are paying too much attention to too many things" (Hancock, 1996).

Research shows that the average two-year-old can attend to a constant stimulus for about seven minutes, and that three-year-olds can do so for nine minutes, four-year-olds for thirteen minutes, and five-year-olds for fifteen minutes. The average first-grader can be expected to sit and work for up to an hour. Yet children with ADHD have three distinctive symptoms: they are inattentive, impulsive, and hyperactive. Thus, they are easily distracted, easily stimulated, quick to move from one task to another, and constantly on the lookout for new activities. In school, these children can't seem to stay in their seats, listen to the teacher, stand in line, or follow instructions. They constantly blurt out answers, wiggle their feet, climb on furniture, tap their pencils, lose things, and act as if being driven by a motor (Barkley, 1998).

ADHD affects an estimated 3 to 7 percent of all children of elementary school age in North America and is more prevalent among boys than girls by about a 3 to 1 ratio. Among children diagnosed with ADHD, the problem persists into adolescence for 50 to 80 percent and into adulthood for 30 to 50 percent (Weiss & Hechtman, 1993). In fact, it's estimated that over 15 million American adults have had attentional disorders that are often not diagnosed—but that are significant enough to disrupt their lives (Resnick, 2000).

Many children with ADHD have behavioral and learning disabilities and have trouble adjusting to structured settings such as a classroom. They tend to do poorly in school and have difficulty at reading, complex problem solving, and tasks that require fine motor coordination. These problems often continue into adolescence, resulting in low grades, and expulsion or early withdrawal from school (Klein & Mannuzza, 1991). As adults, they often have

everyday behaviors (Kutchins & Kirk, 1997). The proposition that teenagers who spend too much time on the Internet be labeled "Internet addicts" may be a case in point (Griffiths, 1998).

*"The scientific basis of DSM is credible. But it is not infallible. Because DSM has become institutionalized in training programs . . . it is revered too much and doubted too little."*

—NANCY ANDREASEN

Over the years, critics of psychiatric diagnosis have voiced three concerns. The first was that the system lacked reliability. If two mental-health experts interview the same person, what are the chances that they will independently come up with the same diagnosis? Research on the earliest versions of DSM revealed low levels of reliability. However, more recent versions, most notably, DSM-IV, base classifications on observable behavior and thus provide a checklist of specific, objective items to guide the diagnosis. As in medicine, the system is still not perfect, but reliability estimates are higher now than in the past (Nathan & Langenbucher, 1999).

A second concern is that clinical judgments, like all other judgments that people make, may be biased by stereotypes about a person's gender, race, age, socioeconomic status, ethnic and cultural background, and other factors (Mezzich et al., 1996). Gender provides a common example. In general, men and women suffer equally from mental disorders, but some specific problems are more common

problems in marriage, relationships, and jobs (Barkley, 1997).

There are many theories about the causes of ADHD. According to one theory, children with ADHD exhibit unusually low levels of arousal in the central nervous system, so they seek stimulation in order to raise that arousal level (Zentall & Zentall, 1983). Other researchers have found that the problem is one of "disinhibition," and that children with ADHD are unable to stop themselves from acting on their impulses (Nigg, 2001). Still others have examined differences in brain activity, diet, neurotransmitters, parenting styles, and social learning. Whatever its origins, most ADHD children can be successfully treated—though not cured—with Ritalin and other stimulant drugs that increase arousal and the production of the neurotransmitters norepinephrine and dopamine (Greenhill & Osman, 2000; Solanto et al., 2001). Nicknamed "Vitamin R," and more potent a stimulant than caffeine, Ritalin is prescribed for about 600,000 children a year in the United States alone—the equivalent of 1 to 2 percent of the school-age population. Most ADHD children on Ritalin enjoy short-term gains in attention span, reductions in motor activity, and improvements in classroom behavior and performance (Greenhill & Osman, 1999).

It's important to be cautious in diagnosing ADHD—and not identify as disordered children who are merely active and somewhat rambunctious. It's also important, if Ritalin is prescribed, to combine its use with psychologically oriented therapy and classroom teaching strategies aimed at modifying the child's behavior and problem-solving skills. When she talks to her students about Ritalin, teacher Sally Smith holds up a ruler, points to the one-inch mark, and says, "This is how much Ritalin does for you. It makes you available to learn. You and your parents and teachers have to work on all the rest" (Hancock, 1996, p. 56). In this intersection of clinical psychology and education, it's clear that parents, teachers, psychologists, and physicians must collaborate in their efforts (Pelham et al., 1993).

*In the classroom, children with ADHD have difficulty staying focused.*

among men, others among women (Hartung & Widiger, 1998). Is it possible that these well-known differences influence a mental-health expert's judgment? We saw in Chapter 13 that people tend to see what they expect to see. Could the same be said of clinical diagnosis?

To examine this possibility, Maureen Ford and Thomas Widiger (1989) mailed a case history of a fictitious male or female adult to 354 clinical psychologists and asked each for a diagnosis. For some, the case depicted a classic "antisocial personality," a mostly male disorder characterized by self-centered behavior and reckless disregard for rules. For other subjects, the case portrayed a "histrionic personality," a mostly female disorder characterized by excessive attention seeking, emotionality, and flirtatiousness. The result: the diagnoses that were made were clearly biased by gender. Regardless of which case history was read, the male patient was more likely to be labeled antisocial, and the female histrionic. Similar research suggests the possibility that African American patients are more often diagnosed—or misdiagnosed—as schizophrenic than are white patients with the same general symptoms (DelBello, 2002).

A third concern is that diagnostic labels can adversely affect the way we perceive and treat people who suffer from mental disorders. In a provocative demonstration

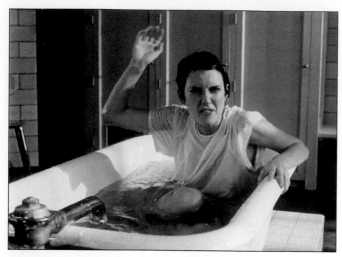

*"What exactly is crazy?"* In Girl, Interrupted, *Winona Ryder played Susanna Kaysen, an eighteen-year-old girl who checked into a mental hospital for being depressed, lazy, and apathetic. While there, Susanna was surrounded by a pathological liar, a laxative addict, and someone who purposely burned herself with gasoline and a match—all of whom made her feel "normal" by comparison.*

of how a label can take on a life of its own, psychologist David Rosenhan (1973) and seven colleagues visited twelve mental hospitals in five states, gave false names and occupations, and complained of hearing an unfamiliar disembodied voice say the words *thud, empty,* and *hollow.* Based on these reports, all the pseudopatients were diagnosed as schizophrenic and admitted for treatment. From that point on, however, they answered all questions truthfully, behaved normally, followed instructions, and reported hearing no voices. Yet it took an average of nineteen days for Rosenhan and the others to get released (one was held for fifty-two days), and not a single psychiatrist, psychologist, social worker, or nurse uncovered the fraud (ironically, several real patients suspected that the researchers were journalists or investigators). Written case reports revealed that staff members sometimes interpreted normal behaviors in abnormal ways. When one pseudopatient paced the halls out of boredom, he was said to be "anxious." Another who was seen taking notes was said to be "paranoid." Like first impressions, a diagnostic label can be hard to remove. In ways that are felt by those who are stigmatized by mental illness, we tend to see people who are labeled mentally ill through different eyes—as dangerous, irresponsible, and childlike—and we treat them accordingly (Farina et al., 1992; Corrigan & Penn, 1999). (For a glimpse at the diagnosis of childhood disorders, see *Psychology and Education.*)

Thanks to the objective criteria provided in DSM-IV and the use of structured interviews and careful assessments of a patient's social and occupational functioning, diagnostic reliability has never been better. The critics are correct in noting that clinical diagnosis is an imperfect human enterprise. As in medicine, mental-health professionals sometimes disagree on a patient, their judgments may subtly be influenced by stereotypes, and there is the ever-present danger that the labels will color the way people with disorders are perceived. Yet diagnosis is necessary. Just as physicians have to distinguish among heart disease, cancer, and pneumonia in order to prescribe an effective treatment, mental-health professionals must distinguish among different psychological disorders. To ease the stigma associated with diagnostic categories, the American Psychiatric Association (2000) recommends that the labels be applied to *behaviors,* not to *individuals.* It's better to say that someone has schizophrenia or alcohol dependence than to call that person a schizophrenic or an alcoholic—terms that imply permanence.

In the remainder of this chapter, we consider some of the most common as well as some of the most bewildering disorders identified in DSM-IV. But first a word of caution: Watch out for "medical student's disease," the tendency to see in yourself the disorders described in this chapter. If you are troubled or find it hard to function on a day-to-day basis, see someone about your problems. Otherwise, don't be alarmed. Normal and abnormal are points on a continuum—and everyone experiences some of the symptoms some of the time.

## REVIEW QUESTIONS

- *What conditions must be met for a pattern of behavior to be considered a psychological disorder?*

- *Identify the three models of abnormality. How does each model explain psychological disorders?*

- *Provide some examples of culture-bound syndromes. What do these tell us about psychological disorders?*

- *What is the DSM? How has it changed since 1952?*

## ANXIETY DISORDERS

- *What do cross-cultural studies tell us about the anxiety disorders?*
- *What is panic, and what are its biological and psychological origins?*
- *What's the difference between a simple and social phobia?*
- *Why do some people wash their hands hundreds of times a day?*

Anyone who has faced military combat, the interview of a lifetime, a championship game, major surgery, or the menacing sound of a prowler in the house knows what anxiety feels like. On occasion, we all do. It's a nervous, jittery feeling of apprehension accompanied by a pounding heart, trembling hands, cold and sweaty palms, a quivering voice, a dry mouth, dizziness, light-headedness, fatigue, a shortness of breath, an upset stomach, or diarrhea.

## GENERALIZED ANXIETY DISORDER

Anxiety is a normal response to threatening and stressful situations. As we saw earlier, however, about 25 percent of all Americans will at some time in life experience anxiety that is so intense, persistent, and disabling that it is considered to be a disorder (Kessler et al., 1994). Over the course of a lifetime, an estimated 5 percent of adults suffer what is known as **generalized anxiety disorder (GAD)**—a persistent, gnawing undercurrent of "free-floating" (not linked to an identifiable source) anxiety. Feeling aroused and not knowing why, the person with a generalized anxiety disorder is highly sensitive to criticism, has difficulty making decisions, dwells on past mistakes, and worries constantly and excessively about money, work, family matters, and illness (Barlow, 2001). What is not clear, however, is whether these are effects or causes of the disorder. Research suggests that people with generalized anxiety disorder are hypersensitive and anxious before they seek treatment—and remain so after the disorder is in remission (Brown, O'Leary et al., 2001).

Many people have anxiety attacks that are more focused than GAD. In particular, three such disorders are described in this section: panic, phobias, and obsessive-compulsive disorders. Before you read on, however, two points are worth noting. First, although the different anxiety disorders are in some ways distinct, most people who have one type are likely to exhibit the symptoms of at least one other type as well (Brown & Barlow, 1992; Sanderson et al., 1990). Second, although people all over the world suffer from intense anxiety, the specific symptoms they experience are molded by their cultural upbringing (Good & Kleinman, 1985).

## PANIC DISORDER

Norwegian artist Edvard Munch (1863–1944) was a troubled man who knew all too well the meaning of the word *panic*. In 1893, Munch painted *The Scream*, a nightmarish portrait of a terrified person standing on a bridge under a blood-streaked sky, covering his or her ears, and screaming in anguish as two ominous, shadowy people approach from behind. Said Munch, this image was inspired one day when "I was walking . . . and I felt a loud, unending scream piercing nature." Sometimes a picture really is worth a thousand words.

People who are diagnosed with **panic disorder** experience frequent, sudden, and intense rushes of anxiety, usually lasting for several minutes. The symptoms of a panic attack include chest pains and heart palpitations, hyperventilation, shortness of breath, choking and smothering sensations, and fainting. These symptoms are often accompanied by feelings of unreality and detachment from one's body and by a fear of going crazy, losing control, or dying. Table 16.2 presents the percentages of panic-disordered patients who experience various symptoms. An attack is considered "panic" if it includes four or more of these symptoms (Craske & Barlow, 2001).

Research shows that panic strikes most often during the day but that it also frequently occurs between the hours of 1:30 and 3:30 AM, while people are asleep; that heart rates increase an

**generalized anxiety disorder** A psychological disorder that is characterized by a constant state of anxiety not linked to an identifiable source.

**panic disorder** A disorder characterized by sudden and intense rushes of anxiety without an apparent reason.

The Scream. *(Edvard Munch*, The Scream. *Oslo, National Gallery. Scala/Art Resource, NY. © 1998 Artists Rights Society (ARS), New York/ADAGP, Paris )*

*"A man who fears suffering is already suffering from what he fears."*

—MICHEL DE MONTAIGNE

| TABLE 16.2 | THE PANIC BUTTON: SYMPTOMS |
| --- | --- |
| **Symptoms** | **Percentages** |
| Heart palpitations | 87 |
| Dizziness or faintness | 87 |
| Trembling or shaking | 86 |
| Fear of losing control | 76 |
| Shortness of breath | 75 |
| Hot flashes or chills | 74 |
| Excessive sweating | 70 |
| Numbness or tingling sensations | 58 |
| Depersonalization | 57 |
| Nausea or abdominal distress | 56 |
| Fear of dying | 52 |
| Choking sensation | 50 |
| Chest pains | 38 |

**Source:** D. H. Barlow (2001). *Anxiety and its disorders.* New York, Guilford Press.

*"In between attacks there is this dread and anxiety that it's going to happen again. I'm afraid to go back to places where I've had an attack. Unless I get help, there soon won't be anyplace where I can go and feel safe from panic."*

—ANONYMOUS PATIENT

**agoraphobia**   An anxiety disorder in which the main symptom is an intense fear of public places.

**phobic disorder**   An anxiety disorder characterized by an intense and irrational fear.

**simple phobia**   An intense, irrational fear of a specific object or situation.

**social phobia**   An intense fear of situations that invite public scrutiny.

average of thirty-nine beats per minute; and that the episodes last for approximately sixteen minutes, followed by exhaustion (Taylor et al., 1986). What's worse, those who get frequent panic attacks worry so much about embarrassing themselves in front of others—by fainting, vomiting, gasping for air, or losing bladder control—that they very often develop **agoraphobia,** a fear of being in public places that are hard to escape. People with agoraphobia frequently become prisoners in their own homes, afraid to stray into shopping malls, restaurants, sports arenas, theaters, airports, or train stations. The word itself comes from a Greek term meaning "fear of the marketplace."

Approximately one-third of all adults report having experienced panic during the past year (Norton et al., 1992). However, only one or two out of every hundred—a majority of them women—suffer from panic disorder at a given point in time (Narrow et al., 2002). What causes panic disorder? There are two major perspectives—one biological, the other psychological (McNally, 1994). Supporting a biological point of view, research shows that panic attacks tend to strike without warning or provocation, that the attack is accompanied by changes in the prefrontal cortex, and that the experience can be induced and treated with drugs (Gorman et al., 1989; Bremner et al., 2000).

The psychological approach is supported by three kinds of evidence. First, many patients report that their first attack struck shortly after an illness, miscarriage, or other traumatic event. Through the processes of classical conditioning described in Chapter 5, they may then become anxious in response to situational cues innocently associated with that first attack—such as the time, place, and people who were present (Bouton et al., 2001). Second, people with panic disorder are highly attuned to bodily sensations and are prone to misinterpret the signals in ways that are "catastrophic." Feeling aroused, for example, they are quick to fear that they are having a heart attack, stroke, or some other life-threatening ordeal—and this belief fuels the fire (Clark et al., 1997; Ehlers & Breuer, 1992; Schmidt & Trakowski, 1997). Among people prone to panic, for example, inhaling carbon dioxide—or air that contains a shortage of oxygen—sets off a false "suffocation-alarm" (Klein, 1993; Beck et al., 1999). Even during sleep, people with panic disorder are quick to make catastrophic attributions for "normal" but unexpected sensations (Craske et al., 2002). Third, psychological forms of therapy—such as exposure and relaxation training, breathing exercises, and various behavioral and cognitive techniques—can help to alleviate panic attacks without the use of drugs (Craske & Barlow, 2001; McNally, 1994; Rachman & Maser, 1988). To sum up: The human panic button can be activated by biological or psychological means.

## PHOBIC DISORDER

Once a week during football season, John Madden broadcasts a National Football League game on television. From one Monday night to the next, regardless of whether the game is played in Philadelphia, Cleveland, Green Bay, or San Diego, Madden drives hundreds of miles in his own private bus. As inconvenient as this may seem, it is the only way Madden will travel. The reason? Despite his 260-pound, 6'4" frame and rough exterior, Madden is terrified of flying on airplanes.

Whereas panic attacks strike suddenly and without warning, phobias are more focused and predictable. A **phobic disorder** is one in which a person reacts to an object or event with high levels of anxiety, knows that the reaction is irrational, and copes by avoidance. The word *phobia* comes from the name of the Greek god Phobos, who instilled fear in his enemies. One out of eight Americans experiences this disorder (Magee et al., 1996).

There are two types of phobias. A **simple phobia** is an intense and irrational fear of a specific object or situation. The most common are fear of heights, airplanes, closed spaces, blood, snakes, and spiders. But there are other, more idiosyncratic phobias as well. I once had a friend who would grip his car seat, stiffen up, and break into a cold sweat whenever we drove over a drawbridge with a metal-grating surface. Table 16.3 presents a partial list of simple phobias that have been identified and named over the years. Some names may sound familiar; others you may be able to figure out from the prefix (Maser, 1985). The severe and less severe frequencies of the most prevalent phobias are shown in Figure 16.1.

A second type of phobic disorder is the **social phobia**, an exaggerated fear, in children or adults, of situations that invite public scrutiny (Beidel & Turner, 1998; Heimberg et al., 1995; Leary & Kowalski, 1995; Turk et al., 2001). Social phobias are among the most prevalent of psychological disorders. Probably the most familiar example is public-speaking anxiety, or stage fright—a performer's worst nightmare. If you've ever had to make a presentation, only to feel weak in the knees and hear your voice quiver, you will have endured at least a hint of this disorder. What is there to fear in public speaking? When people were asked this question, the most common responses were: shaking and showing other signs of anxiety, going blank, saying something foolish, and being unable to continue (Stein et al., 1996). For the social phobic, unbearable levels of self-consciousness may also be evoked by other situations. Examples include eating at a public lunch counter, signing a check in front of a store clerk, and, for males, urinating in a crowded men's room. In private, these behaviors pose no problem. In front of others, however, they arouse so much fear that the situations are avoided and escaped at all costs. In extreme cases, the reaction becomes so debilitating that the person just stays at home. Because social phobias are so pervasive and so disabling, Cynthia Turk and others (2001) are lobbying for the problem to be renamed "social *anxiety* disorder" in future editions of DSM.

What's interesting about social phobias is that the anticipation may be far worse than the reality, the bark worse than the bite. In a recent study, researchers recruited socially phobic and nonphobic adults. After getting baseline measures of heart rate and self-reported anxiety, the experimenter told subjects that they would have to prepare and give a speech to a live audience of professionals, after which they went on to give the speech. Look at Figure 16.2, and you'll see that heart rates increased for all subjects as they neared the dreaded event—but those with a social phobia felt much more anxious (Davidson et al., 2000).

What causes phobic disorders? Many years ago, Freud argued that people with phobias are anxious about hidden impulses and

| TABLE 16.3 | PARTIAL LIST OF SIMPLE PHOBIAS |
|---|---|
| **Phobia** | **Feared Object or Situation** |
| Acrophobia | Heights |
| Aerophobia | Flying |
| Agoraphobia | Public places |
| Aichmophobia | Sharp pointed objects |
| Aquaphobia | Water |
| Arachnophobia | Spiders |
| Brontophobia | Thunderstorms |
| Claustrophobia | Closed spaces |
| Entomophobia | Insects |
| Hematophobia | Blood |
| Homilophobia | Sermons |
| Monophobia | Being alone |
| Mysophobia | Dirt and germs |
| Nyctophobia | Darkness |
| Ophidiophobia | Snakes |
| Parthenophobia | Virgins |
| Porphyrophobia | The color purple |
| Triskaidekaphobia | The number 13 |
| Xenophobia | Strangers |
| Zoophobia | Animals |

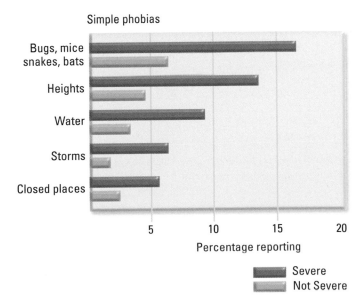

**FIGURE 16.1    Frequency of the most prevalent simple phobias**

*Steve Fox's social anxiety was so severe in high school that cheerleaders would say "hello" just to make him blush. Fox (left) was successfully treated and is now married to one of the girls who used to tease him. "Imagine being allergic to people" is part of an education campaign to raise public awareness of social phobias and how they can be treated (right).*

cope by displacing their anxiety onto substitute objects that are less threatening and easier to avoid. To illustrate, he wrote about the classic case of Little Hans, a five-year-old boy who would not leave home because he was terrified of being bitten by a horse. According to Freud (1909), Hans was in the midst of an Oedipal conflict and had converted an unconscious fear that his father would castrate him into a conscious fear of getting bitten by a horse. From a psychoanalytic perspective, then, the phobic object is merely a symbol for a deeper, more troubling problem.

In reaction to Freud's case study, behaviorist John Watson demonstrated with a baby named Little Albert that phobias can develop through conditioning (see

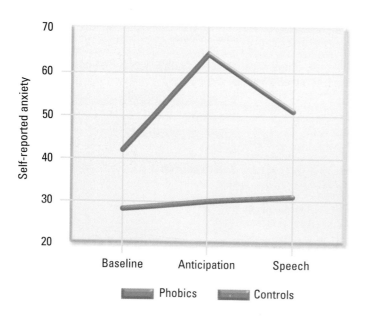
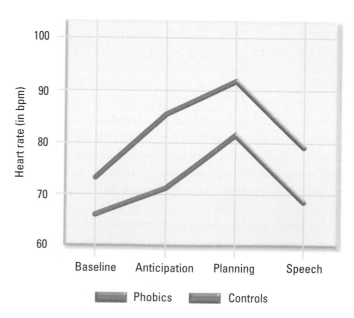

**FIGURE 16.2** **Reactions of people with social phobias**
Socially phobic and nonphobic adults prepared and gave a speech to a live audience. As shown, heart rates increased for both groups in anticipation of the dreaded event (left), but only those with a social phobia reported feeling more anxious (right) (Davidson et al., 2000).

Chapter 5). Since that time, researchers have found that phobias may be learned by classical conditioning (Ost, 1992) or by the observation of someone else's fear reaction to an object. For example, Susan Mineka and Michael Cook (1993) found that when laboratory-raised rhesus monkeys saw wild monkeys of their species react fearfully to a snake, they too became distressed and acquired an intense fear of snakes. To the behaviorist, then, phobias originate in a personal experience or observation and then spread through a process of stimulus generalization. Thus, if a child is locked in a closet at a tender young age, he or she may acquire a specific fear of closets or a more general case of claustrophobia. In this view, the reason phobias last long after the precipitating experience is forgotten is that we tend to avoid phobic objects, denying ourselves an opportunity to unlearn the fear. Also consistent with this view, research shows that people whose phobias are extinguished in treatment are later less likely to suffer a relapse when reexposed to the phobic object in exactly the same situation (Mineka et al., 1999).

*Certain phobic disorders occur with greater frequency than others. One of the most common is acrophobia (a fear of heights).*

A third view, also described in Chapter 5, is that humans are genetically programmed through evolution, or "prepared," to develop certain kinds of phobias. People all over the world fear darkness, heights, snakes, insects, and other harmless objects, some of which they may never encounter. The reason, according to Seligman (1971), is that human beings, like other animals, are prepared by evolution to fear and avoid objects and situations that were harmful to their prehistoric ancestors. Many psychologists embrace this view that aversions are part of our human nature, which is why people react with fear to certain potentially lethal stimuli (such as the proverbial "snake in the grass")—an affective reaction that is quick, automatic, easy to learn, and hard to control (Ohman & Mineka, 2001).

## OBSESSIVE-COMPULSIVE DISORDER

Howard Hughes had it all. He was a billionaire, a famous pilot, an entrepreneur, and a Hollywood producer. There was just one hitch: Hughes was tormented by an uncontrollable preoccupation with germs, eventually causing him to live the life of a hermit. He sealed all windows and doors with tape and spent many hours a day washing himself. His aides had to open doors with their feet to avoid contaminating doorknobs, wear white cotton gloves before serving his food, and deliver newspapers in stacks of three so he could slide the middle one out with a tissue. Toward the end of his life, Hughes became so overwhelmed by his own routines that he could not take care of himself. When he died at the age of sixty-nine his body was filthy and emaciated, his beard was scraggly, his teeth were rotted, and his fingernails were so long that they curled in on themselves—a sad and ironic ending for a man who had once said, "I want to live longer than my parents, so I avoid germs" (Fowler, 1986, p. 33).

Along with an estimated four million other Americans, Howard Hughes suffered from **obsessive-compulsive disorder (OCD)**—a crippling anxiety ailment characterized by constant *obsessions* (the intrusion into consciousness of persistent, often disturbing thoughts) and *compulsions* (behavior rituals performed in response to the obsessions). OCD usually begins in late adolescence and early adulthood, affects men and women equally, and is found in India, England, Norway, Egypt, Nigeria, Japan, Hong Kong, and other countries around the world (Insel, 1984). Most people with OCD know that their habits are crazy, but they just can't stop themselves. Fearing shame and humiliation, many of them try to keep their actions a secret and wait years before seeking treatment.

**obsessive-compulsive disorder (OCD)** An anxiety disorder defined by persistent thoughts (obsessions) and the need to perform repetitive acts (compulsions).

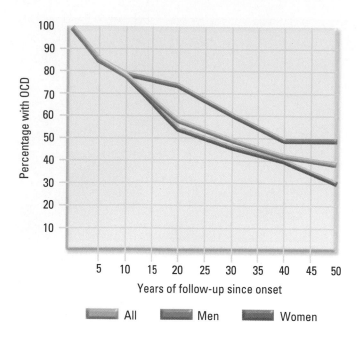

FIGURE 16.3 **What happens to people with OCD**
A long-term follow-up study of untreated OCD patients revealed that two-thirds improved after ten years and four-fifths improved after forty years. Unfortunately, very few fully recovered—and some even got worse (Skoog & Skoog, 1999).

If they are left untreated, what happens to people with OCD? Gunnar and Ingmar Skoog (1999) conducted a long-term follow-up study of 144 patients diagnosed as having OCD in the 1950s and then reexamined by the same psychiatrist in the 1990s. Very few of these patients had received the treatments known today to be effective. The results were mixed. The good news was that two-thirds of the patients had improved within ten years of the onset of OCD, and four-fifths had improved within forty years. The bad news was that only one-fifth of the original patients were *fully* recovered, with two-thirds continuing to experience some of the symptoms. After forty years, one-tenth of them showed no improvement—and another tenth got worse (see Figure 16.3).

What kinds of thoughts and behaviors haunt OCD patients? In *The Boy Who Couldn't Stop Washing,* psychiatrist Judith Rapoport (1989) described one boy who washed his hands so much they became raw and bloodied from all the scrubbing; another boy who ran up and down a flight of stairs exactly sixty-three times a day; and a woman who was so determined to keep her eyebrows symmetrical that she plucked out each and every hair. Similarly, in *The Sky Is Falling,* Raeann Dumont (1996) described a woman who spent eight hours a day bathing; a man who couldn't leave a subway station without picking up all the litter; and a man whose apartment was stacked to the ceiling with dirty old clothes, dishes, and other objects he had collected but could not bring himself to throw away. As bizarre as these stories seem, research shows that OCD sufferers constantly check, doubt, wash, hoard, order, obsess, and mentally neutralize their unacceptable thoughts and behaviors (Foa et al., 1999). The most common themes, as reported in interviews with one hundred OCD patients, are presented in Table 16.4. Most patients have multiple obsessions and compulsions (Jenicke et al., 1986).

Everyone has a few mild obsessions and compulsions. You may double- and triple-check your alarm clock at night, or try to avoid stepping on sidewalk cracks, or feel a burning need to straighten out crooked wall hangings. Professional athletes are especially well known for their compulsive rituals. Many baseball players, for example, adjust their caps, tug at their shirts, bang their shoes, and run through a complicated sequence of superstitious gestures before every pitch. If these examples don't apply to you, try this: Do not imagine a white bear. Seriously, put this book down, and try not to think about white bears. See the problem? Daniel Wegner (1989) finds that when people actively try to suppress a thought, that thought intrudes into consciousness with remarkable frequency—like a newly developed obsession. What distinguishes these mild quirks from OCD is the intensity of the accompanying anxiety and the extent to which it interferes with one's life. Wegner and Zanakos (1994) devised a questionnaire they called the *White Bear Suppression Inventory,* and they found that individuals who agree with such statements as "I have thoughts I cannot stop" and "There are images that come to mind I cannot erase" are prone to obsessional thinking.

There are different theories about the causes of OCD. Psychoanalysts maintain that obsessive thoughts leak forbidden sexual and aggressive urges into consciousness, compelling the person to devise elaborate rituals as a countermeasure. In this view, compulsive

| TABLE 16.4 | OBSESSIVE-COMPULSIVE DISORDER |
|---|---|
| **Themes OCD Sufferers Obsess About** | **Percentage** |
| Dirt, germs, contamination | 55 |
| Aggressive impulses | 50 |
| Need for symmetry | 37 |
| Bodily concerns | 35 |
| Forbidden sexual impulses | 32 |
| **Rituals OCD Sufferers Perform** | **Percentage** |
| Checking | 79 |
| Washing | 58 |
| Counting | 21 |

*Source:* M. A. Jenicke et al. (1986). *Obsessive-compulsive disorders: Theory and management.* Littleton, MA: PSG.

washing symbolizes a person's need to cleanse the soul of dirty impulses. Behaviorally oriented theorists note that the compulsions endure because they help to reduce the anxiety aroused by obsessive thoughts. Indeed, many compulsions can be extinguished in a few weeks by exposing patients to the source of the obsession but preventing them from responding to it—for example, no washing allowed despite the buildup of anxiety (Foa & Franklin, 2001).

Biological factors also play a role, as indicated by the fact that antidepressant drugs help most sufferers of OCD to terminate their rituals (Rapoport, 1989). Also, PET scans of the brains of OCD patients have revealed abnormally high levels of activity in a group of nuclei that are involved in the control of habitual behaviors. In a PET study of eighteen OCD patients, Jeffrey Schwartz and others (1996) found that this area became less active after behavioral and cognitive therapy. For about ten weeks, patients were prevented from acting on their obsessions. Struck with the urge to wash for the umpteenth time of the day, for example, they were trained to label the urge a mere brain-triggered obsession and refocus their attention on a constructive activity such as gardening or golf. As Schwartz (1996) describes in his book, *Brain Lock,* this refocusing procedure is designed to engage a new part of the brain, and this helps to "unlock" the area that had become stuck in its pattern. When it comes to OCD, it appears that the mind can change the brain.

## CULTURAL INFLUENCES ON ANXIETY DISORDERS

Anxiety is a universal human affliction but the specific forms it takes may vary according to cultural beliefs. Consider the case of a twenty-five-year-old Chinese American patient. Shortly after having sex with a prostitute, he complained of a sudden burning pain in his penis, accompanied by a fear that his genitals were shrinking. He became terrified that his penis would retract into his abdomen, causing him to suffer and die. In a state of panic, he tried to masturbate in order to assure himself that all was well, but he could not achieve an erection. The young man became so desperate that he contemplated suicide.

This case may sound idiosyncratic, like one of a kind, but it's not: The man was suffering from *Koro* (also called *suo-yang* in some Chinese medical books), an anxiety disorder that has existed for hundreds of years in Southeast Asia. Typically found among young males, Koro is characterized by an acute panic attack lasting for days or weeks and by a fear that one's sexual organs will disappear into the body, causing death. A Koro epidemic swept through Singapore in 1967. Shortly after the Vietnam War, another thousand cases were reported in Thailand. Then in the 1980s, two waves of Koro spread through China. Many patients link the onset of this disorder to a sexual escapade, and treatment often consists of wearing a clamp that prevents retraction of the penis (Bernstein & Gaw, 1990).

Koro is only one example of an anxiety disorder that is restricted to a cultural group. There are others. In Mexico and certain Latin American cultures, people are sometimes afflicted with *susto*—an intense fear reaction, insomnia, and irritability, believed to be brought on by the "evil eye" of voodoo or black magic. In Japan, there is *shinkeishitsu*—an emotional disorder in which people become so self-conscious and perfectionistic that they feel too inadequate to interact with others. In China, there is *paleng*—a disorder in which sufferers wear several layers of clothing, even in the summer, because of a morbid fear that they will die from a loss of body heat. In Ethiopia, Sudan, Egypt, and certain other North African and Middle Eastern cultures, there is *zar,* a term used to describe the uncontrollable fits of laughter, shouting, crying, blacking out, and head-banging that people exhibit when they are said to become possessed by spirits.

## ■ REVIEW QUESTIONS

- *What is generalized anxiety disorder?*

- *What types of symptoms are associated with panic disorder? What causes it?*

- *Distinguish between a simple phobia and social phobia. How do phobias develop?*

- *Distinguish between obsessions and compulsions. What causes obsessive-compulsive disorder?*

Three important lessons can be learned from these cross-cultural comparisons. First, anxiety is universal, and the *physiological* symptoms are the same from one culture to the next. Regardless of where you are born and raised, anxiety is a bodily reaction characterized by such symptoms as a shortness of breath, a racing heart, trembling, sweating, dry mouth, and weak knees. Second, culture influences the *cognitive* component of anxiety, so the symptoms people worry about, how they interpret those symptoms, and their beliefs about the causes of anxiety all depend on the values and ideologies to which they are exposed (Barlow, 2001; Good & Kleinman, 1985; Simons & Hughes, 1986; Tseng, 2001). The third lesson concerns treatment. Precisely because our cultural heritage can influence the source of our anxiety and the way it's expressed, mental-health workers must self-consciously step outside the boundaries of their way of thinking in order to counsel those who are culturally different (Sue & Sue, 1999).

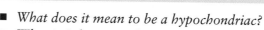

# SOMATOFORM DISORDERS

- *What does it mean to be a hypochondriac?*
- *What is "glove anesthesia," and what is its psychological significance?*

Long before psychology became a discipline, physicians struggled with the problem of treating people who complained of muscular aches and pains, upset stomachs, and other ailments for which an organic basis could not be found. According to DSM-IV, many of these patients suffer from a **somatoform disorder** (the word *somatoform* means "bodylike"), in which they experience bodily symptoms that are psychological, not medical, in origin. Somatoform disorders are not easy to diagnose. People who complain of an illness are not consciously faking (a condition known as malingering), nor does their psychological distress cause physiological damage (the way stress can cause ulcers, migraine headaches, and other "psychosomatic" conditions). Illustrating that mind and body are interlocked are two types of somatoform disorder: hypochondriasis and conversion disorder.

## HYPOCHONDRIASIS

While on his famed *Beagle* voyage around the world, naturalist Charles Darwin (1809–1882) was constantly seasick. Then, at about the time that his wife, Emma, became pregnant with the first of their ten children and continuing for the rest of his life, he complained of nausea, numbness in the fingertips, indigestion, dizzy spells, chest pains, and other assorted ailments. Darwin was so pampered by his family that "the whole day was planned out to suit him, to be ready for reading aloud to him, to go on his walks with him, and to be constantly at hand to alleviate his daily discomforts" (Colp, 1977, p. 92).

If Darwin were alive today, he would likely be diagnosed as having **hypochondriasis,** a disorder involving a chronic and unwarranted preoccupation with one's own physical health. Hypochondriacs are highly sensitive to normal bodily sensations. Equipped with do-it-yourself medical books, thermometers, blood-pressure kits, and shelves lined with vitamins, they become alarmed the moment they sneeze, cough, feel warm, feel cool, get an itch, pull a muscle, or skip a heartbeat. Not wanting to hear words of reassurance, they jump from one doctor to the next until they find one who takes their complaints seriously (Baur, 1988; Kellner, 1987). Hypochondriacs tend to set many health-related goals such as losing weight, relaxing, and managing

*"Nothing is more fatal to Health, than the Over Care of it."*

—BENJAMIN FRANKLIN

**somatoform disorder**   A type of mental disorder in which a person experiences bodily symptoms that are psychological rather than medical in nature.

**hypochondriasis**   A disorder characterized by an unwarranted preoccupation with one's physical health.

stress (Lecci et al., 1996). They are also quick to agree with such statements as, "When one sweats a lot it can be due to an overburdened heart" and "A tingling sensation in the legs can be a serious sign of a nerve disorder" (Rief et al., 1998). Gene Weingarten (1998), who describes himself as a recovered hypochondriac, notes that he used to worry about the most harmless sensations, from hiccups to nosebleeds, stiff necks, skin rashes, and the sniffles.

Some psychologists have speculated that hypochondriasis is a reaction to separation anxiety and the desire to stay helpless, or that it is symptomatic of society's preoccupation with health. Others believe it is caused by an oversensitive nervous system. But are hypochondriacs more sensitive, prone to amplify bodily sensations? To test this hypothesis, Sandra Gramling and her colleagues (1996) used the MMPI to identify fifteen high-scoring hypochondriacal women and fifteen female controls. Each participant was asked to place her foot into a tub of ice water for three minutes—or until she could no longer tolerate it. Before, during, and afterward, heart rate and hand temperature were recorded. There were two telling results. First, the hypochondriacal women kept their feet in the tub for less time and rated the sensation as more unpleasant. In fact, only seven went the distance—compared to thirteen in the control group. Second, among those who did, hypochondriacal participants had more elevated heart rates and lowered hand temperatures during the ice-water task and afterward, during a posttask recovery period. People with hypochondriasis may be highly reactive to stimulation not just in their self-reports and behavior but also at a deeper physiological level (see Figure 16.4).

Whatever the causes of this somatoform disorder, two points are clear. The first is that hypochondriasis can easily become a lifelong pattern nourished by attention and sympathy, relief from work, excuse for failure, and other social rewards. Even Darwin realized before he died that "my head would have failed years ago had not my stomach saved me from a minute's over-work" (Colp, 1977, p. 70). Second, our sensitivity to bodily sensations falls on a continuum on which both extremes are maladaptive. Just as the hypochondriac is too health-conscious, others are not attuned enough to the symptoms of illness, choosing instead to deny the body's warning signals, often to their own detriment (Strauss et al., 1990).

## CONVERSION DISORDER

A second somatoform disorder is **conversion disorder,** in which the person temporarily loses a bodily function without a physical cause. This problem is primarily found in young women, which is why Hippocrates in 400 BCE called it *hysteria* (from the Greek word for "uterus")—and prescribed marriage as the cure. In the nineteenth century, Freud theorized that hysteria arose from traumas or deep-seated sexual conflicts and that the resulting anxiety was "converted" into physical ailments. The classic symptoms mimic neurological disorders such as paralysis, blindness, deafness, epilepsy, and anesthesia (a loss of feeling in a limb). This disorder was seen in a wave of cases in the 1970s, after a reign of terror in Cambodia. Many women who had been tortured—or worse, had seen their own children tortured and murdered—became psychologically blind. One woman, a refugee whose family was killed before she managed to escape to the United States, said, "I cried for four years. When I stopped crying, I was blind" (Rozee & Van Boemel, 1989).

How can one tell the difference between conversion disorder and actual nerve damage? It's not always easy. One clue is that the reported symptoms are sometimes not anatomically possible, as in the case of "glove anesthesia," shown in Figure 16.5. Another is that the symptoms may suddenly disappear—as when a "blind" patient manages to walk right through the doctor's office without bumping into furniture or

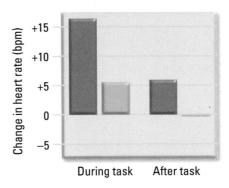
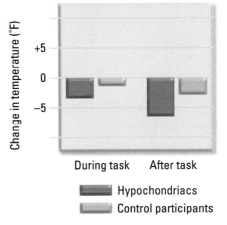

**Hypochondriacs**
**Control participants**

**FIGURE 16.4   Sensitivity in people with hypochondriasis**
Hypochondriacal and control participants put their feet into ice-cold water for three minutes. Relative to their baseline levels, hypochondriacal participants had more elevated heart rates during the task—and later, in a posttask recovery period (top). They also had lowered hand temperatures during and after the task (bottom). These results suggest that hypochondriacs may be physiologically more reactive to stimulation than others (Gramling et al., 1996).

**conversion disorder**   A disorder in which a person temporarily loses a bodily function in the absence of a physical cause.

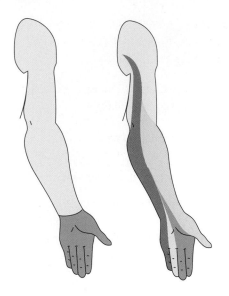

**FIGURE 16.5    Glove Anesthesia: A conversion disorder**
A person with "glove anesthesia" reports numbness in the hand from the wrist to the fingertips but continued sensation in other parts of the arm (left). This complaint can be diagnosed as a conversion disorder because it is anatomically impossible. If there is actual nerve damage, the sensory loss would extend to upper parts of the arm as well (right).

## REVIEW QUESTIONS

■ *How do somatoform disorders differ from psychosomatic symptoms?*

■ *What is hypochondriasis and what factors contribute to the development of this disorder?*

■ *What is conversion disorder and how is it influenced by culture?*

a "paralyzed" patient walks in his or her sleep. How can a conversion disorder be distinguished from conscious faking? No diagnosis is foolproof, but there is one clue: Whereas people who fake ailments are always evasive and defensive about examination, true conversion patients tend to display *la belle indifference,* a nondefensive and curious lack of concern about their condition (Ford & Folks, 1985).

Sociocultural context seems to play an important role in the outbreak of somatoform disorders. Cases of hysterical paralysis, which Freud and his contemporaries reported at the turn of the century, are today rare. Perhaps it's because Western society is less sexually repressive than in Freud's era. Or perhaps we have become too sophisticated about psychological matters to believe that a person could be paralyzed for no apparent reason. Whatever the explanation, conversion-disorder cases are now rare. As a result, the subject has captured the imagination of many historians—including Mark Micale (1995), whose book, *Approaching Hysteria,* chronicles the curious "disease and its interpretations" from the ancient Greeks through the Middle Ages, nineteenth-century Europe, and today.

# DISSOCIATIVE DISORDERS

■ *What is a dissociative disorder, and how does it differ from simple "tuning out"?*

■ *What is dissociative identity disorder—and why does it arouse skepticism?*

Have you ever found yourself listening to someone talk, only to realize that you missed most of what was said? Were you ever in a place that was familiar but could not remember having been there before? Did you ever have trouble figuring out whether an experience that you had was real or just a dream? Like absentmindedness and other lapses of awareness, these phenomena are possible signs of dissociation—a process by which a portion of one's experience becomes separated or detached from one's identity or conscious memory. Look at the items listed in Table 16.5, taken from the Curious Experiences Survey (Goldberg, 1999). How many of these have

| TABLE 16.5 | TYPES OF DISSOCIATIVE EXPERIENCES |
|---|---|

This list contains ten dissociative experiences—some that are common, others that are rare. Which have you had, at least on occasion? The numbers alongside each item represent the percentage of nonclinical respondents who report having had the experience.

| | |
|---|---|
| 1. Was listening to someone talk and suddenly realized I did not hear part or all of what was said. | 94 |
| 2. Talked out loud to myself. | 85 |
| 3. Found that I sometimes sit staring off in space, thinking of nothing, and am not aware of the passage of time. | 55 |
| 4. Drove or rode somewhere without remembering later what happened during all or part of the trip. | 52 |
| 5. Found that I had become so involved in a fantasy or daydream that it felt as if it were really happening to me. | 27 |
| 6. Found that I had no memory for some important event in my life (for example, a wedding or graduation). | 22 |
| 7. Felt as if I were disconnected from my body. | 18 |
| 8. Felt as if I were looking at the world through a fog, so that people or objects appeared far away or unclear. | 13 |
| 9. Found myself in a place and had no idea how I had gotten there. | 08 |
| 10. Found myself dressed in clothes I didn't remember putting on. | 02 |

*Source:* Goldberg, 1999, p. 136.

you had, and how often? Some are common. In a survey of hundreds of adults, for example, 94 percent said they had at least occasionally "spaced out" on chunks of a conversation and 52 percent said they had driven somewhere without later recalling details of the drive. In Japan, Belgium, the Netherlands, and the United States, studies have shown that people consistently report having such experiences (Ray, 1996; Ross, 1997).

In contrast to these normal episodes that we all experience, people diagnosed with a **dissociative disorder** have serious long-term memory gaps. In essence, it is believed, these people have learned to cope with intense trauma and stress by mentally erasing unwanted parts of life from their memory. There are three types of dissociative disorders: amnesia, fugue state, and dissociative identity disorder (Michelson & Ray, 1996).

## AMNESIA AND FUGUE STATES

The most common dissociative disorder is **amnesia,** which involves a partial or complete loss of memory. Amnesia can last for varying periods of time and can be caused by physical trauma such as a hard blow to the head or alcohol intoxication. Alternatively, the problem can sometimes be traced to a stressful event such as a car accident, a rape, or a physical beating. In these cases of dissociative amnesia, only self-relevant memories are blocked. Amnesia victims may forget who they are and where they live, but they remember clearly how to speak, read, drive a car, and recite information from general knowledge (Weingartner et al., 1983).

Dissociative **fugue states** (*fugue,* as in the word *fugitive,* means "flight") are more extensive than simple amnesia. In extreme cases, someone who slips into a fugue state not only forgets his or her name but also wanders from home, takes on a new identity, remarries, gets a new job, and starts a new life. Then, just as suddenly, the person will "wake up"—disoriented and confused, oblivious to what has transpired, and eager to return home as if no time has passed. Fugue states may last for hours or for years. Sometimes, the victim's new life is more exciting and uninhibited than the old routine. At other times, it provides an escape from responsibility and danger. Fugue states are quite common, for example, among soldiers bound for combat. Either way, it is difficult, if not sometimes impossible, to tell whether a fugue victim has a genuine dissociative disorder or is faking (Schacter, 1986).

## DISSOCIATIVE IDENTITY DISORDER

The most dramatic instance of dissociation is **dissociative identity disorder (DID),** an extremely rare condition in which a person displays two or more distinct identities (until DSM-IV was published in 1994, this condition was called *multiple personality disorder*). Sometimes, two opposing identities battle for control, as in the classic tale of Dr. Jekyll and Mr. Hyde. Sometimes there are three personalities, as in *The Three Faces of Eve*, a film about a woman who alternated among Eve White, a timid housewife; Eve Black, a sexually promiscuous woman; and Jane, a balanced blend of the other two. In other cases, one dominant identity is accompanied by a host of subordinate personalities, as in the case of Sybil Dorsett, whose sixteen personalities were portrayed in the film *Sybil.*

Dissociative identity disorder is such a strange phenomenon that you might think it springs from the imaginative minds of playwrights and novelists. What are the facts and fictions about DID?

**dissociative disorder**  A condition marked by a temporary disruption in one's memory, consciousness, or self-identity.

**amnesia**  A dissociative disorder involving a partial or complete loss of memory.

**fugue state**  A form of amnesia in which a person "forgets" his or her identity, wanders from home, and starts a new life.

**dissociative identity disorder (DID)**  Formerly known as multiple personality disorder, it is a condition in which an individual develops two or more distinct identities.

*Chris Sizemore was the subject of* The Three Faces of Eve, *a 1957 film about a woman with multiple personality disorder. Eventually, Sizemore had twenty-two different personalities to cope with "traumatic death experiences" she had when she was two years old.*

| TABLE 16.6 | SYMPTOMS OF DISSOCIATIVE IDENTITY DISORDER |
|---|---|
| **Symptoms** | **Percentages** |
| Another person existing inside | 90 |
| Voices talking | 87 |
| Amnesia for childhood | 83 |
| Referring to self as "we" or "us" | 74 |
| Blank spells | 68 |
| Being told by others of unremembered events | 63 |
| Feelings of unreality | 57 |
| Strangers know the patient | 44 |
| Noticing that objects are missing | 42 |
| Coming out of a blank spell in a strange place | 36 |
| Objects are present that cannot be accounted for | 31 |
| Different handwriting styles | 28 |

*Source:* C. A. Ross et al. (1990). Structured interview data on 102 cases of Multiple Personality Disorder from four centers. *American Journal of Psychiatry, 147,* p. 599.

According to DSM-IV, it is nine times more prevalent among women than men and is ordinarily preceded by a childhood history of repeated abuse. Summarizing five major studies of 843 DID patients, for example, Colin Ross and his colleagues (1990) found that more than 88 percent reported having been victims of sexual, physical, or emotional child abuse—a striking statistic that was confirmed in a later study in the Netherlands (Boon & Draijer, 1993). This finding suggests the hypothesis that children who are abused and are utterly defenseless learn early in life to cope by tuning out, divorcing a part of themselves from the pain and suffering, and constructing alternative persons within which to live. Ross (1977) thus described DID as "a little girl imagining that the abuse is happening to someone else" (p. 59).

In almost all cases, at least one personality is unable to recall what happens to the others (Putnam et al., 1986). Thus, nine DID patients who were presented with words to learn while in a particular identity were better able to recall those words within the same identity than while in an alternate identity state (Eich et al., 1997). Clinical reports suggest that, at times, the differences among personalities can be extraordinary, as each may have its own voice, speech pattern, motor habits, memories, clothing, and handwriting. Some reports suggest that physical changes may also occur, as when two personalities coexisting within the patient exhibit different brain-wave patterns, blood-pressure readings, eyeglass prescriptions, allergies, or reactions to medicine (Kluft, 1996). Based on interviews with 102 people with DID, which yielded the percentages associated with various symptoms, Table 16.6 presents the most common symptoms of DID.

If you find the notion of multiple personalities hard to believe, you are not alone. Since the first case was reported in 1817, fewer than two hundred appeared in psychiatric journals up to the year 1970. Since that time, however, thousands of new cases have been reported, virtually all in North America. To be sure, DID can be found in most societies, but the frequency of the disorder and the form it takes vary from one generation and culture to another (Spanos, 1996; Lilienfeld et al., 1999). All this has skeptics wondering: Is the disorder really on the rise? There are three possible explanations. One is that many patients are faking multiple personalities for personal gain, and therapists are simply unable to distinguish between true and false cases. A second is that therapists used to miss or misdiagnose the problem and are now more sensitive to the symptoms. A third possible explanation is that therapists are now overdiagnosing the disorder or, worse, are suggesting and reinforcing its presence in patients, thus producing a "psychiatric growth industry" (Weissberg, 1993).

If you saw the 1996 thriller *Primal Fear,* you'd appreciate this diagnostic dilemma. In that film, actor Richard Gere plays a lawyer who defends a man, played by Edward Norton, who murdered a priest. The defendant has enormous gaps in his memory and undergoes dramatic transformations in his demeanor, so Gere—and most viewers—come to believe that he has multiple personalities. Not until the film ends, however, and the defendant is found not guilty by reason of insanity, does he tell Gere that he had faked the disorder.

As bizarre as this situation may seem, it actually occurred several years ago in the case of Kenneth Bianchi, otherwise known as the Hillside Strangler. Based on convincing evidence, Bianchi was charged, along with his cousin, with brutally murdering ten California women. At first, he denied the charges. But then a psychologist hypnotized Bianchi and uncovered hidden personalities. During the hypnosis session, the psychologist said, "I've talked a bit to Ken, but I think perhaps there might be another part of Ken that I haven't talked to . . . Would you please come, Part, so I can talk to you too?" Lo and behold, a completely new personality named Steve Walker came out. Ranting and raving, using foul language, and smoking nonfilter cigarettes, Steve confessed to the crimes and said he hated Ken because he was a "goodie two-shoes." According to Steve, Ken was innocent.

Was Steve a real personality, or was he born of convenience just to help Ken escape punishment for his crimes? The dissociative disorders are a serious problem, one that inflicts profound suffering on those who have it. In this case, however, the local police were suspicious, so they hired psychiatrist Martin Orne to conduct further tests. At one point, Orne casually said to Bianchi that real multiples usually have three or more personalities, not just two. The trap was set, and Ken fell in: The next time he was under hypnosis, Ken produced a third personality. Orne's trick—along with the discovery that Bianchi owned numerous books on hypnosis and multiple personality—was convincing evidence. The jury that tried Bianchi found him guilty of murder (Orne et al., 1984; Schwarz, 1981). Can defendants who claim DID-related amnesia for their crimes be believed? Currently, researchers are hoping to develop psychophysiological measures of memory, much like a lie-detector test, to help evaluate such claims (Allen & Iacono, 2001).

A scene from Primal Fear, *a film about a cold-blooded murderer who fakes a multiple personality to escape punishment for his crime.*

## REVIEW QUESTIONS

- *Distinguish between amnesia and fugue states.*

- *Define dissociative identity disorder (DID) and describe the symptoms associated with it.*

- *Why does DID appear to be on the rise?*

# MOOD DISORDERS

- *Why is depression often called the "common cold" of mental disorders?*
- *What are the biological and psychological causes of depression?*
- *Do people who commit suicide leave clues of their intention?*
- *What is bipolar disorder, and why might it be linked to artistic creativity?*

Personal experience tells us that mood can powerfully shade our view of ourselves, the world, and the future. On the roller coaster of life, the range of feelings is familiar to all of us: The exhilarating highs are on one end of the continuum, and the depths of despair are on the other. Land the job of your dreams, fall head over heels in love, or win a lottery, and you fly elatedly "on cloud 9." Lose a job or money, break up with a lover, or struggle in school or at work, and you become sad, even depressed. These fluctuations are normal. Problems arise, however, when someone's mood state is so intense and so prolonged that it profoundly impairs the

**mood disorder** A condition characterized by prolonged emotional extremes ranging from mania to depression.

**depression** A mood disorder characterized by sadness, despair, feelings of worthlessness, and low self-esteem.

*"Depression is the flaw in love. To be creatures who love, we must be creatures who despair."*

—ANDREW SOLOMON

ability to function. There are two main types of **mood disorders:** major depression and bipolar disorder.

## MAJOR DEPRESSIVE DISORDER

A chronic sufferer of depression, Winston Churchill referred to his condition as the "black dog" that followed him around. He was not alone. Comparisons of family members born at different times show that the incidence of depression has risen dramatically in recent years (Klerman & Weissman, 1989). An estimated nineteen million Americans—12 percent of American males and 21 percent of females—will suffer a major depression at some point in life (Kessler et al., 1994). In a given year, 4 to 5 percent of Americans will experience depression that is bad enough to interfere with their daily lives and require treatment (Narrow et al., 2002).

Depression is so widespread that Churchill's black dog has been called the common cold of mental disorders. It appears that no one is immune from an occasional bout with depression—not even the rich and famous. Halle Berry, who won the 2002 Academy Award for Best Actress, was so depressed after a prior divorce that she was suicidal. Others include Drew Carey, Jim Carrey, Sheryl Crow, Ellen DeGeneres, Carrie Fisher, Harrison Ford, Tipper Gore, Anthony Hopkins, Janet Jackson, Elton John, Ashley Judd, Dave Matthews, Rosey O'Donnell, Ozzy Osbourne, Monica Seles, Ben Stiller, and Ted Turner.

**Depression** is a mood disorder characterized by deep sadness and despair. Because these feelings are sometimes an appropriate and normal reaction to tragedy, someone is considered clinically depressed only if the episode arises without a discernible cause and lasts for two or more weeks. In addition to the effects on mood, symptoms include (1) diminished pleasure or interest in food, sex, social banter, and other joys; (2) intense feelings of worthlessness, guilt, and self-blame; (3) restlessness and agitation, marked by difficulty sleeping, concentrating on work, and making decisions; (4) fatigue, slowness, and a lack of energy (in extreme cases, there is such a paralysis of the will that the person has to be pushed out of bed, washed, dressed, and fed by others); and (5) recurring thoughts of suicide and death. Indeed, up to 15 percent of people who are clinically depressed go on to kill themselves (American Psychiatric Association, 1994). In *Noonday Demon,* Andrew Solomon (2001) offers a poignant first-hand glimpse into the despair that envelops people in a state of depression, from the "breakdowns" to the attempts at suicide.

For now, consider some quick facts and numbers about this disorder.

- Age is a relevant factor. Depression is seldom identified for the first time in someone's life before early adolescence. As you can see in Figure 16.6, the age of first onset rises sharply during the teen years, increases through adulthood, peaks at middle age, and declines (Lewinsohn et al., 1986).

- People all over the world get depressed, though the form it takes may differ. For example, depressed people complain of headaches and "nerves" in Latino cultures, of "imbalance" in Chinese and Asian cultures, and of problems of the "heart" in Middle Eastern cultures (American Psychiatric Association, 1994).

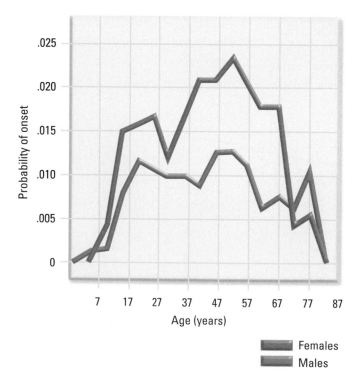

FIGURE 16.6 **Depression: ages of first onset**

- The depression rate has been rising with each successive generation—a trend found not only in the United States and Canada but also in France, Germany, Italy, Lebanon, New Zealand, Puerto Rico, and Taiwan (Cross-National Collaborative Group, 1992).

- About twice as many women as men seek treatment for depression—a disparity that first appears in adolescence, at about the age of thirteen (Nolen-Hoeksema & Girgus, 1994; Cyranowski et al., 2000). This may occur because adolescent girls (1) encounter more adversity than boys do (physical appearance, sexuality, and relationships become major sources of stress); (2) ruminate more about negative events (boys, and later men, tend to use physical activity, alcohol, and other distractions); and then (3) become needy when depressed, which causes friends to withdraw, further worsening the problem (Hankin & Abramson, 2001).

- Some people get depressed on a seasonal basis, a condition known as *seasonal affective disorder,* or *SAD* (Rosenthal, 1998). Every year, during the short, dark days of winter, people with SAD who live in colder regions of the world become listless and withdrawn. They sleep more, eat more, crave carbohydrates, gain weight, lose interest in sex, and falter at work and in social relationships. Two hours a day of exposure to bright light is an effective treatment for many SAD sufferers.

- Regardless of one's sex, age, culture, or generation, it's reassuring to know that depressive episodes often last only a few weeks. However, 50 to 60 percent of those who suffer one major depression later have a recurrence that is longer lasting and more severe (Maj et al., 1992; Winokur et al., 1993).

## THEORIES OF DEPRESSION

Why, one wonders, does depression afflict so many millions of people in the world? From an evolutionary standpoint, shouldn't the processes of natural selection have lessened the survival odds of humans prone to depression? Randolph Nesse (2000) asked this very question and speculated that the deflated mood that blankets the body and mind in depression can be a useful form of adaptation. Nesse noted that depression-like symptoms are often seen in apes and monkeys who are doomed to stay in subordinate positions within their social groups. To survive, they withdraw rather than compete, and appear lonely and depressed, a strategy that helps them to survive within the group. In a similar manner, he suggests, human beings may have adapted depression—the low mood, the lack of energy, and the lack of initiative and activity—as a way to cope with life situations that are difficult, futile, or too dangerous to confront.

Psychologists have tried for many years to find a cure for this common cold of mental disorders. To treat and prevent depression, however, one must first understand where it comes from and what factors serve to maintain it.

**Biological Factors**   Ernest Hemingway killed himself with a shotgun. So did his father and brother. Then many years later, in June 1996, his granddaughter Margaux Hemingway committed suicide with a drug overdose. Clearly, say researchers, the depression that triggers suicide runs in families. But does this mean that depression is inherited? Or is it the product of shared environments?

*Vincent van Gogh's* Crows over the Wheatfield *is an intense and haunting portrayal of the French countryside under troubled skies. This may have been Van Gogh's last painting before he committed suicide in 1890. (Gogh, Vincent Van "Wheatfield with Crows," 1890. Van Gogh Museum, Amsterdam, Netherland. Art Resource, NY.)*

Research shows that if one fraternal twin suffers a major depression, there is a 20 percent chance that at some point the other will too. Yet the rate for identical twins is about 50 percent, a comparison that reveals a clear genetic linkage (Tsuang & Faraone, 1990; Kendler et al., 1993; McGuffin et al., 1996). This finding suggests two compatible conclusions: (1) There is a genetic basis of depression, but (2) environmental factors also play a prominent role.

In all likelihood, genes influence mood disorders by acting on neurotransmitters, the biochemicals that relay impulses from one neuron to another. In the 1950s, doctors noticed that drugs used to treat blood pressure and tuberculosis often had dramatic side effects on a patient's mood—sometimes causing depression, at other times euphoria. Researchers then found that the same drugs also increase the supply of norepinephrine and serotonin, neurotransmitters that regulate moods and emotions. So what does it all mean? When the two strands of evidence were put together, it became apparent that depression is associated with lower-than-normal levels of these neurotransmitters—and that mania is caused by an overabundance. As we'll see in Chapter 17, the practical benefit of this discovery was the development of antidepressant drugs such as Prozac, Zoloft, and Paxil.

It is now clear that the link between biological states and mood is more complicated than was once believed. Antidepressants are effective for many people but not for everyone, and some drugs work without altering norepinephrine or serotonin levels (Depue & Iacono, 1989; McNeal & Cimbolic, 1986). Other biological factors may also play a role. For example, certain infectious diseases, neurological disorders, and even vitamin deficiencies can have mood-altering effects (Hollandsworth, 1990); many depressed people have higher-than-normal levels of cortisol, a stress hormone (Nemeroff, 1989); people who suffer the chronic pain of rheumatoid arthritis are also prone to be depressed (G. K. Brown, 1990); the brains of depressed people are smaller and less active in the left frontal lobe and other interconnected emotion-regulating structures (Davidson et al., 2002). Researchers are currently trying to understand how and why these biological states are linked to depression—and whether they are causes or effects in the chain of events.

**Psychological Factors** In a 1917 paper entitled "Mourning and Melancholia," Sigmund Freud noted similarities between depression and the kind of grief that accompanies the death of a loved one. According to Freud, melancholia, like mourning, is a reaction to *loss*. The loss may involve the breakup of a relationship, financial ruin, or failure to reach an important goal. Not everyone overreacts to these kinds of events. Among those who were abandoned or neglected as children, however, even a minor setback may cause them to retreat into a passive, dependent, childlike state. It can also awaken intense anger that is turned inward, or "internalized"—which is why people who are depressed often punish themselves with self-blame, feelings of worthlessness, and suicide.

Behaviorally oriented psychologists trace depression to one's history of reinforcement and perception of control. According to Peter Lewinsohn (1974), people get depressed when they are unable to produce for themselves a high rate of positive reinforcement. Similarly, Martin Seligman (1975) argued that depression is a form of **learned helplessness,** an expectation that one cannot control important outcomes in life. In a series of experiments during the 1960s, Seligman found that dogs strapped into a harness and exposed to painful electric shocks soon became passive and gave up trying to escape—even in new situations where escape was possible. As applied to humans, this finding suggests that prolonged exposure to uncontrollable outcomes may similarly cause apathy, inactivity, a loss of motivation, and pessimism.

Realizing that perception is more important than reality, most psychologists now focus on *social-cognitive* aspects of depression. Some years ago, psychiatrist

"It's a new anti-depressant—instead of swallowing it, you throw it at anyone who appears to be having a good time."

**learned helplessness** A learned expectation that one cannot control important life outcomes, resulting in apathy and depression.

**depressive explanatory style** The tendency for depressed people to attribute negative events to factors that are internal, stable, and global.

Aaron Beck (1967) noticed that his depressed patients viewed themselves, their world, and the future through dark glasses. According to Beck, these patients distorted reality by focusing more attention on negative events than on positive ones—a pattern consistently found in research (Haaga et al., 1991). This bleak, self-defeating outlook is pervasive. Research shows that depressed people are not only down on themselves but also down on their parents and romantic partners (Gara et al., 1993).

Lynn Abramson, Gerald Mctalsky, and Lauren Alloy (1989) proposed that depression is a state of *hopelessness* brought on by the negative self-attributions that people make for failure. Specifically, they note, some people have a **depressive explanatory style**, a tendency to attribute bad events to factors that are internal rather than external ("It's my fault"), stable rather than unstable ("It will not change"), and global rather than specific ("It affects other parts of my life"). Many studies now provide support for this proposition. Whether people are trying to explain social rejection, a sports defeat, low grades, or inability to solve an experimenter's puzzle, those who are depressed are more likely than others to blame factors that are within the self, unlikely to change, and broad enough to impair other aspects of life. The result: pessimism, hopelessness, and despair (Metalsky et al., 1993; Seligman, 1991).

Does having a negative explanatory style signal a person's vulnerability to depression? Perhaps it does. Alloy and her colleagues (1999) recently measured the explanatory styles of nondepressed first-year college students. They then followed up on these students in their junior year and found that those who had a negative explanatory style in their first year—compared to classmates who had a more positive style—were more likely to suffer their first major or minor depressive disorder (see Figure 16.7).

Finally, humanistic theorists believe that people become depressed if they fail to achieve self-actualization. Consistent with this hypothesis, studies show that people feel unfulfilled and depressed when they perceive that a discrepancy exists between their actual and ideal selves (Higgins, 1989)—particularly when the discrepancy is large and the spotlight of attention is focused on the self (Strauman, 1989; Pyszczynski & Greenberg, 1987).

## THE VICIOUS CYCLE OF DEPRESSION

It's one of the sad ironies for men and women with depression: They desperately need social support and a shoulder to cry on, yet they tend to behave in ways that drive away the most important people in their lives. As illustrated in Figure 16.8, the result is a vicious, self-perpetuating cycle: Depression elicits social rejection, which in turn worsens the depression (Joiner & Coyne, 1999).

Do depressed people really elicit negative reactions and rejection? Are we all so cold-hearted that we turn our backs on those in need of emotional support? Sometimes, yes. When people are severely depressed, friends do try to cheer them up and offer a sympathetic ear, a shoulder to lean on, and advice. As psychotherapists are the first to admit, however, these efforts usually fail and

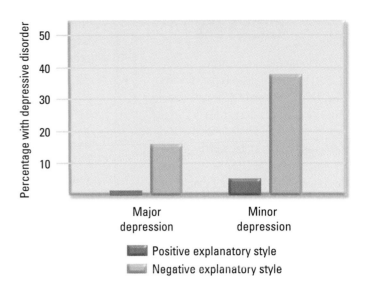

**FIGURE 16.7  Explanatory styles and depression**
In this study, researchers measured explanatory styles among first-year college students. Two years later, those with a negative as opposed to positive style were more likely to experience a major or minor depressive disorder (Alloy et al., 1999).

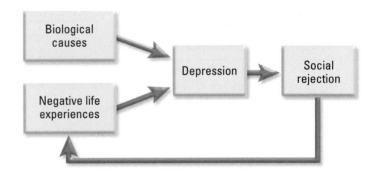

**FIGURE 16.8  The vicious cycle of depression**

*These teenagers have all attempted suicide. Among the reasons most often cited in such cases are loneliness, depression, problems with boyfriends and girlfriends, grades, money, and feelings of helplessness.*

Concerned about the mental health of teenagers, Susan Furr and others (2001) surveyed 1,455 students at four American colleges and universities about whether they had felt depression while in school and whether they had thought about or attempted suicide. How prevalent are these problems? Think about yourself, your friends, and acquaintances, and make a prediction: What percentage of students, from 0 to 100, said that they had (1) experienced depression, (2) thought about suicide, and (3) actually attempted suicide? For mental-health professionals, the results were sobering. Of the students surveyed, 53 percent said they had experienced depression at some point, 9 percent said they had thought about suicide, and 1 percent actually attempted to commit suicide. Why is depression so common? When asked, students most frequently cited grade problems, loneliness, money problems, and boyfriend or girlfriend problems.

*"The thought of suicide is a great source of comfort; with it a calm passage is to be made across many a bad night."*

—FRIEDRICH WILHELM NIETZSCHE

Question: In the United States, what's more common: Suicide or homicide?
Answer: Suicide, by a 5 to 3 margin.

**bipolar disorder**   A rare mood disorder characterized by wild fluctuations from mania (a euphoric, overactive state) to depression (a state of hopelessness and apathy).

the depression persists. The suffering person is filled with complaints, regrets, and expressions of self-pity, which makes social interaction unpleasant. What's worse, studies have shown that people who are depressed avoid eye contact, speak softly, are slow to respond, wear sad or blank facial expressions, and are negative in their demeanor—a pattern of behavior that is seen as rude, detached, and nonresponsive (Segrin & Abramson, 1994). The result is that people react to those who are depressed with mixed emotions—sorrow laced with frustration, anger, and a desire to avoid future contact (Coyne, 1976; Gurtman, 1987; Sacco & Dunn, 1990). This vicious cycle may help to explain why strained friendships are common among people with depression—and why their social interactions are generally less intimate and rewarding (Nezlek et al., 1994). Depression takes a toll on marriage too. Studies show that in married couples in which the wife is depressed, she and her husband have more conflict, more complaints, and less physical and emotional affection (Benazon & Coyne, 2000; Coyne et al., 2002).

## SUICIDE: THE ULTIMATE "SOLUTION"

"I don't believe it. I just saw him and he looked fine." "I knew she was depressed, but I had no idea it was this bad. Why didn't she call me?" These statements are typical of how people react when someone they know commits suicide.

The World Health Organization estimates that roughly one million people a year die from suicide. In the United States, that number is thirty thousand, for an average of one suicide every half-hour. Remarkably, for every one person who actually commits suicide, there are ten to twenty others who try. To many of us, nothing about human behavior seems more puzzling, tragic, or senseless. Yet to those who are depressed and in a state of mental pain and anguish, it often seems like the only solution (Maltsberger & Goldblatt, 1996; Jamison, 1999).

Who tries to commit suicide, and why? Suicidology researchers are providing answers (Hawton & van Heeringen, 2000; Maris et al., 2001). In the United States, statistics show that women are three times more likely to attempt suicide, but men are four times more likely to succeed. This difference reflects the fact that most men use firearms, whereas women are more likely to overdose on sleeping pills—a slower and less certain method. Either way, about 75 percent of suicides are committed by people who are depressed. In fact, the single best predictor of suicide potential is a sense of hopelessness. In one study, more than two thousand psychiatric outpatients were tested and followed for up to seven years. Of the seventeen who went on to commit suicide, sixteen had initially gotten high scores on a "hopelessness scale" (Beck et al., 1990).

When do people who feel hopeless resort to suicide? Roy Baumeister (1990) theorized that the main purpose of suicide is to "escape from self." In his view, people think about suicide when they fail to achieve an important life goal, blame themselves for the failure, focus too much attention on the self, become sad and depressed, think in short-sighted terms as a way to escape mentally from the anguish, and, as a result, shed the inhibitions that normally prevent people from contemplating such drastic measures. In other words, suicide is a last resort, with the goal being "oblivion"—a complete loss of self-consciousness. Although it is impossible to test this theory directly, Baumeister presented an array of suicide research statistics compatible with his propositions. For example, consistent with the hypothesis that people who kill themselves are highly self-focused, he finds that compared to the farewell notes written by people who face death from illness, suicide notes contain more first-person pronouns (*I* and *me*).

Shocked friends and relatives always wonder: Should I have known? Could I have done something to prevent it? These are tough personal questions. Suicide is difficult to predict, and nobody should feel guilty about getting caught by surprise. But there are patterns to watch for (Shneidman, 1996). (See *How to Help a Friend Who Is Suicidal.*) First, people who are depressed and who use drugs are particularly vulnerable—not while they are in the depths of despair, as you may think, but afterward, as they start to regain their energy and spirit. Second, about 90 percent of all suicides are preceded by remarks about one's death or departure—such as "Sometimes I wonder if life is worth living" or "You won't see me again" (note that only 2 or 3 percent of people who talk about suicide make the attempt, but of those who commit suicide, almost all had talked about it). Third, people preparing to kill themselves often leave telltale behavioral clues. They might start to put their papers in order, for example, pull back from prior commitments, take unusual risks, or give away prized possessions. Fourth, it helps to know that people who attempt suicide once are at a higher-than-average risk to do so again, even much later in life.

Is there a way to prevent suicide? If you are concerned about someone you know, Edwin Shneidman (1996) recommends taking certain actions. Stay close and communicate openly. If the person alludes to death, gives away valued possessions, or leaves other hints, it's best to inquire as to what's happening and, if necessary, ask directly, "Are you thinking about suicide?" Offer sympathy, suggest options, and most important of all—make sure the person gets professional help. In case of a crisis, call for help yourself.

**FIGURE 16.9   Brain activity in bipolar disorder**
The PET scans shown here were taken from the brain of a bipolar-disorder patient who alternated every twenty-four to forty-eight hours from depression (top) to mania (middle), and back to depression (bottom). Note that dark blues and greens mark low levels of activity; red, orange, and yellow mark higher levels of activity.

## BIPOLAR DISORDER

In contrast to major depression, a *unipolar* disorder in which moods range from neutral to depressed, **bipolar disorder** produces wild fluctuations that range from *manic* (a euphoric, overactive state) to *depressed* (a state of hopelessness and apathy). Having what used to be called "manic depression," bipolar-disorder patients alternate uncontrollably between the two extremes, in cycles that last from a few days to several months. One week, they are flying as high as a kite, bursting with energy and optimism. The next week, they have sunk to the depths of despair (see Figure 16.9).

What does the manic phase of this disorder feel like? What are the symptoms? In its early stages, mania is an exhilarating state of mind that many of us have enjoyed from time to time. The mildly manic person is boundless in energy, filled with self-esteem, and confident that no challenge is too daunting. With the mind racing at full speed, the manic person is entertaining, witty, imaginative, quick to see connections between ideas, and filled with ambitious and creative schemes.

More than a hundred years ago, the German psychiatrist Emil Kraepelin (1883; reprinted 1923) observed that manic excitement "sets free powers that otherwise would be constrained by inhibition." The pages of history suggest he may have been right. In *Touched with Fire*, Kay Redfield Jamison (1993) notes that among the many creative geniuses who had bipolar disorder were composers Robert Schumann and George Frideric Handel, artist Vincent van Gogh, and writers Edgar Allan Poe, Ernest Hemingway, Eugene O'Neill, Sylvia Plath, F. Scott Fitzgerald, Mark Twain, Walt Whitman, Tennessee Williams, and Virginia Woolf. In *The Price of Greatness*, Arnold Ludwig (1995) reported on a biographical survey of more than a thousand

*Professor of Psychiatry Kay Redfield Jamison, who has bipolar disorder, describes the experience in a memoir. An Unquiet Mind: "When you're high it's tremendous. The ideas and feelings are fast and frequent like shooting stars . . . But, somewhere, this changes. The fast ideas are far too fast, and there are far too many . . . you are irritable, angry, frightened, uncontrollable, and enmeshed totally in the blackest caves of the mind." (p. 67)*

## *How To*

# HELP A FRIEND WHO IS SUICIDAL

Everyone feels sad and discouraged from time to time. How can you tell whether a friend is simply feeling blue or sliding into a serious depression, even planning to commit suicide? There is no "typical" suicide victim. But by analyzing attempted and actual suicides, psychologists have identified some risk factors—and common warning signs to look for. Suicide is preventable. So if you have a friend you're worried about, know that by reaching out you *can* make a difference.

## WARNING SIGNS

■ **LOSS OR FAILURE.** Particularly among students, suicides are often triggered by events that leave them feeling alone or humiliated, such as the death of a family member or close friend, the separation or divorce of parents, a breakup with a girl- or boyfriend, an accident or injury for which they feel responsible, or disappointing results on an important test.

■ **TALK ABOUT SUICIDE.** Nearly every young person who attempts or commits suicide tells someone beforehand, even if only indirectly. Listen for hints such as "I'd be better off dead" or "I won't be a problem for you much longer" or "Nothing matters; it's no use."

■ **DRAMATIC CHANGES IN MOOD OR BEHAVIOR.** An outgoing student may suddenly become uncommunicative and withdrawn, or a shy student may suddenly become hyperactive and flamboyant.

■ **PROBLEMS WITH SLEEPING, EATING, AND PERSONAL HYGIENE.** Suicidal students may spend most of their time sleeping or complain of insomnia; they may "forget" to eat and lose weight, or eat all the time and gain weight; they may stop taking showers or caring about their own appearance.

■ **DIFFICULTIES WITH SCHOOL.** Problems with school or work may be a cause of, or a symptom that, a person is contemplating suicide. So when a conscientious student loses interest in studying and skips classes, often for days at a time, consider this a warning sign.

■ **LOSS OF INTEREST IN ENJOYABLE ACTIVITIES.** Watch out for the person who withdraws from friends, hobbies, and social activities, drops out of sports teams and clubs, avoids social gatherings, and spends most of the time alone.

■ **PREOCCUPATION WITH DEATH.** Beware of the friend who suddenly becomes drawn to art, music, movies, books, or Internet sites focusing on death.

■ **INCREASED RISK-TAKING, AS IN THE USE OF DRUGS AND ALCOHOL.** Depressed students may try to "medicate" themselves through drugs and/or engage in risky and destructive behavior. These coping mechanisms may alleviate pain temporarily, but they also signal a person's vulnerability.

■ **"CLEANING HOUSE."** Like adults who learn that they are terminally ill, students who plan suicide frequently straighten out their affairs. They may clean their rooms, throw things out, give away prized possessions, and

---

famous people of the twentieth century. He discovered that writers, poets, and artists were two to three times more likely to have bipolar disorder than successful professionals in business, science, sports, and public life. But he also found that they were more likely to suffer from alcoholism and other drug abuse, anxiety disorders, depression, and schizophrenic disorders (see Figure 16.10). As the philosopher Nietzsche once said, "One must harbor chaos within oneself to give birth to a dancing star."

Before jumping to the conclusion that bipolar disorder is worth having, you should know that there is a much darker side. As the disorder progresses, the mania accelerates out of control, and "high" becomes "too high." The person becomes easily distracted, moves from one project to another, stays awake at night, and is extremely sensitive to stimulation. It has been said that to the manic person, a gentle

arrange for the care of a pet as if planning a long trip. In effect, they are writing a will.

- **"SAYING GOODBYE."**   After a long spell of depression, suicidal students may appear to "snap out of it." Suddenly, they seem cheerful again. This does not necessarily mean they have recovered; on the contrary, it may mean that they feel relieved because they have made the decision to end their lives. Calls or visits to family members and old friends after an extended period of self-isolation may mean "goodbye"—forever.

## WHAT TO DO

If you spot several of the warning signs in a friend you're worried about, don't wait to see what happens. Take action yourself or communicate your concern to someone else, such as a mental-health counselor or teacher. Don't worry that you are betraying a friend in any way. If the friend had a serious injury or illness, you'd take him or her to a doctor. The same urgency applies here. The question is, what should you do?

- **TALK OPENLY TO YOUR FRIEND.**   Tell your friend you care, ask what's going on, and listen matter-of-factly, without judging. If your friend doesn't respond, reassure him or her that there are others to turn to—that family, friends, doctors, and teachers are willing to listen. Your friend needs to know that he or she is not alone.
- **BRING UP SUICIDE.**   Contrary to popular belief, mentioning suicide will not put ideas into a person's head or encourage the act. If your friend has considered suicide, don't lecture or talk about all the reasons to live.

Instead, point out that depression is an illness that can be treated.

- **GET SPECIFIC.**   If your friend admits to thoughts of suicide, ask concrete questions. Do you have a plan? Have you bought a gun or stockpiled pills? If not, make a contract: "Promise not to do anything without talking to me first, okay?" Then get help. Speak to someone you trust, maybe someone from a mental-health center. If your friend has planned his or her suicide, treat the situation as an emergency.
- **CRISIS INTERVENTION.**   First, do not leave your friend alone. Try to find out where the gun or pills are and take them away. If you must leave, remove all potential hazards (knives, razors, ropes, poisonous household products) before you go. Second, get professional help immediately. Don't imagine you can handle the problem yourself. Try to convince your friend to go with you to a local help center—now, not tomorrow. If he or she refuses, call the center and follow their advice. If no one is available, dial 1-800-SUICIDE, a national hotline staffed with trained counselors.
- **DO NOT KEEP TALK OF SUICIDE SECRET.**   All suicide threats and attempts are cries for help. People who plan suicide want to end the pain they are feeling, not end their lives. The reasons they do not seek help on their own are that they fear ridicule or anger, do not want to "burden" others with their problems, or do not think that anyone can help them.

*Source:* American Psychiatric Association Joint Commission on *Public Information: Teen Suicide,* APA Web site, March 2000.

breeze feels like a slap on the face and the dropping of a pin sounds like a clanging noise. People in an advanced state of mania also harbor delusions (false beliefs) of grandeur. They make promises they cannot keep, buy things they cannot afford, start new sexual relationships, and drag others into risky moneymaking schemes that are bound to fail. Socially, the charm and wit give way to behavior that embarrasses others. Fitting the stereotype of the "raving maniac," the person becomes loud, fast-talking, frenzied, and explosive. Even mild criticism may trigger anger and hostility. This manic phase is sometimes then followed by major depression. Illustrating that what goes up must come down, bipolar-disorder sufferers either return to normal or hit the ground in a crash landing. A remarkable number of creative geniuses who reaped the benefits of their manic energy later killed themselves while depressed (Goodwin & Jamison, 1990; Ludwig, 1995).

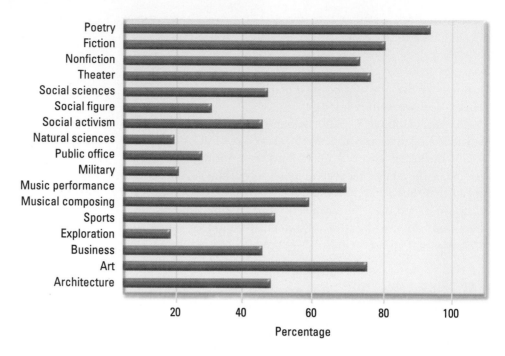

**FIGURE 16.10** **Is there a connection between creativity and mental illness?**
In a study of 1,005 successful twentieth-century people, Ludwig (1995) found that the lifetime rate of mental illness in general (not just bipolar disorder) was higher among those in the arts than in other professions. How can this phenomenon be explained?

**REVIEW QUESTIONS**

- *How do psychologists distinguish clinical depression from normal sadness?*

- *Describe the symptoms associated with major depression. How does culture influence this experience?*

- *Summarize the biological and psychological factors that contribute to depression.*

- *What is bipolar disorder, and what are some of its symptoms?*

Although bipolar disorder is a close relative of depression, the two are quite different. To begin with, bipolar disorder has a stronger genetic component. Thus, if one twin has it, the odds are about 72 percent that an identical twin will have it too, compared to only 13 or 14 percent for a fraternal twin of the same sex (Blehar et al., 1988). Thus, there is overwhelming evidence for the role of genetic factors in bipolar disorder (National Institute of Mental Health's Genetics Workgroup, 1999; Meltzer, 2000). As we'll see in Chapter 17, bipolar patients can be treated with the drug lithium.

## SCHIZOPHRENIC DISORDERS

- *What does the word* schizophrenia *mean?*
- *What are the five major symptoms of the schizophrenic disorders?*
- *What's the difference between a delusion and a hallucination?*
- *What evidence is there for the genetic and environmental roots of schizophrenia?*

When you stop to think about "madness" or "insanity," what comes to mind? For many of us, the words alone evoke stereotyped images of people who stare blankly into space, talk in gibberish to themselves, see imaginary pink animals, walk in circles, and erupt in fits of rage and violence. These images are not generally accurate, as we'll see, but they come closest to describing schizophrenia—the most dreaded of psychological disorders (Lenzenweger & Dworkin, 1998). Over the course of the illness, between 4 and 6 percent of people with schizophrenia commit suicide (Hyman, 2000).

**Schizophrenic disorders** are marked by gross distortions of thought and perception and by a loss of contact with reality. In some cases, the disorder strikes suddenly between the ages of seventeen and twenty-five and is followed by a full recovery. In other cases, the disorder develops slowly, causes the person to deteriorate over a period of years and casts a life sentence on its victim—no parole, no time off for good behavior. Schizophrenia is found in all cultures of the world and affects men and women equally. It is estimated that slightly less than 1 percent of all Americans will exhibit a schizophrenic disorder—in the course of a lifetime (Regier et al., 1988) or within a given year (Narrow et al., 2002). The most likely age of first onset is eighteen to twenty-five for men, twenty-six to forty-five for women. This sex difference in the age of onset shows up all over the world and has researchers puzzled (Gottesman, 1991; Straube & Oades, 1992).

*"I felt a cleaving in my mind—*
*As if my brain had split—*
*I tried to match it seam by seam—*
*But could not make them fit.*
*The thought behind, I strove to join*
*Unto the thought before—*
*But sequence reveled out of Sound*
*Like Balls—upon a Floor."*

—EMILY DICKINSON
"POEM 937"

## THE SYMPTOMS OF SCHIZOPHRENIA

Translated from Greek, the word *schizophrenia* means "split brain." The so-called split is not between two or more inner selves, as in dissociative identity disorder, but rather between thoughts, beliefs, perceptions, emotions, motor behavior, and other brain functions. To people with schizophrenia, it's like being stuck in a "Twilight Zone" (Torrey, 1988).

**schizophrenic disorders** Disorders involving gross distortions of thoughts and perceptions and by loss of contact with reality.

*The thoughts and emotions of people with schizophrenia can often be seen in their creative expressions. In the words of artist Sandra Milne, "This painting was done in response to my doctor's suggestion that I paint who I really was. Each person represents a side of me" (left). A second artist says, "This is a picture of what happens when you have a nervous breakdown: the world explodes and the powers of cosmic destruction overwhelm your mind and soul with the screech of panic, fear of nonexistence, loud voices, bright lights, chaos, and confusion" (right).*

**delusions** False beliefs that often accompany schizophrenia and other psychotic disorders.

**hallucinations** Sensory experiences that occur in the absence of actual stimulation.

*In the 2001 film, A Beautiful Mind, Russell Crowe plays an eccentric mathematical genius, John Nash Jr., who won a Nobel Prize for work he did in the 1940s. Early in his career, Nash was diagnosed with paranoid schizophrenia and overwhelmed by delusions, hallucinations, and other incapacitating symptoms. Remarkably, after thirty years, the schizophrenia lifted in what some have called a "miraculous remission," enabling Nash to re-engage with people and his work.*

Five major symptoms are found in people with a schizophrenic disorder. First and foremost, many of them exhibit *incoherent thinking*. The person may be mentally disorganized and confused, on a different wavelength than the rest of us. This problem is most evident in speech. Listen to people with this symptom talk, and you may well hear them create new words and drift illogically from one topic to another, making their statements sound like something of a "word salad." Often, for example, they will string together utterances that are only loosely associated. Eugen Bleuler (1911), the Swiss psychiatrist who gave schizophrenia its name, cited an example from one of his patients: "I wish you a happy, joyful, healthy, and fruitful year, and many good wine years to come as well as a healthy and good apple-year, and sauerkraut and cabbage and squash and seed year." In this sample of speech, the word fruitful set off a chain of food-related associations. The reason is that schizophrenic patients who exhibit disorganized thinking tend to have difficulty focusing attention on one stimulus and filtering out distractions (McGhie & Chapman, 1961; Freedman et al., 1987). In the autobiographies of fifty former patients, concentration problems were the most frequent thought-related complaint (Freedman, 1974).

A second symptom is the presence of **delusions,** or false beliefs. In schizophrenic minds all over the world, certain delusional themes appear with great frequency (Appelbaum et al., 1999). Among the most common are delusions of *influence*—the belief that one's thoughts are being broadcast in public, stolen from one's mind, or controlled by evil forces. Thus, one patient was convinced that his thoughts were publicized to others on a "mental ticker-tape," another spoke of having her thoughts "sucked out of my mind by a phrenological vacuum extractor," and a third believed "a radio was implanted in my skull." Also common are delusions of *grandeur* (that one is famous or powerful, capable of controlling weather, planets, and other people), delusions of *reference* (that one is the primary recipient of other peoples' actions), and delusions of *persecution* (that one is a target of secret plots by others).

A third symptom is the presence of **hallucinations,** sensory experiences that occur without actual stimulation. To hallucinate is to see, hear, smell, taste, or feel something that does not exist. The most common hallucinations are auditory. Many people with schizophrenia report that they "hear" the swishing or thumping sound of a heartbeat, musical choirs, or disembodied voices that comment on their lives, make accusations, and issue commands. "Son of Sam" David Berkowitz, who terrorized New York City in the 1970s by killing young women, claimed he was ordered to stalk and shoot his victims by the demonic voice of a barking dog. Sometimes, but less often, hallucinations occur in other sensory systems as well. People may "see" heavenly visions, "smell" foul body odors, "taste" poison in their food, or "feel" a tingling, burning, or pricking sensation on their skin. Other perceptual distortions are also evident. According to some reports, lights seem brighter, colors more vibrant, and sounds more intense. And people's bodies often appear longer, shorter, smaller, rounder, or otherwise deformed—like viewing the world through a funhouse mirror.

The fourth symptom is a *disturbance of affect*, or emotional experience. Some people with schizophrenia have a flattened affect. They sit still for hours, wear a blank expression on the face, speak in a low and monotonic voice, avoid eye contact, and show little interest or concern in anything. As one psychiatrist noted, "It is uncannily like interacting with a robot" (Torrey, 1988). Others express feelings that are highly animated and exaggerated or are inappropriate to the situation—crying at happy news, laughing at tragedy, or screaming in anger without external provocation.

The fifth symptom is *bizarre behavior*. Absorbed in an inner world of stimulation, perhaps confused by distorted perceptions of the outer world, people with schizophrenia often withdraw, go into social exile, and cease to function effectively at work. They may talk to themselves, repeat like parrots what others say, spend

## THE PROCESS OF DISCOVERY

# NANCY ANDREASEN
## *The Symptoms of Schizophrenia*

**Q:  How did you first become interested in psychology?**

**A:**  I cannot really point to a time when I first became interested. My interest in psychiatry began when I was a young English professor at the University of Iowa. Troubled students tended to seek me out for advice and consolation. A serious illness at that time also stimulated my interest in medicine and led to my decision to become a physician. My first encounter with people suffering from schizophrenia hooked me on the specialty. "How could the human brain produce such profound disruptions?" I asked myself.

**Q:  How did you come up with your important discovery?**

**A:**  The knowledge about language that I brought from my career in English combined naturally with an interest in human thought and speech in people with psychotic illnesses such as schizophrenia. Some of my earliest research emphasized the study of "thought disorder," long considered the hallmark of schizophrenia. This was fundamentally correct, although I also found empirically that manic patients may display significant thought disorder as well. Science dictates that we cannot study what we cannot measure, so I wanted to develop rating scales for thought disorder. I always liked challenges and enjoyed figuring out how to measure signs and symptoms that people said were difficult to measure reliably. This led me to produce scales for rating thought disorder and later scales for rating positive and negative symptoms.

My clinical experience led me to appreciate the importance of negative symptoms. In the '70s, when I was a young clinician, it became obvious that medications reduced or even eliminated psychotic symptoms such as delusions or hallucinations but that my patients remained chronically ill. They were ill because they lacked volition, emotional richness, fluency of thought and speech, or social involvement with others. I referred to these lost capacities as "negative symptoms," borrowing the term from Hughlings Jackson, a 19th Century British neurologist. My Scale for the Assessment of Negative Symptoms (SANS) is now widely used.

**Q:  How has the field you helped inspire developed over the years?**

**A:**  In the 1980's a new group of tools became available for studying mental illness—the tools of neuroimaging, like computerized tomography (CT), magnetic resonance (MR), and positron emission tomography (PET). I quickly recognized that these tools would permit us to directly visualize and measure the structure and activity of the brain, and I did a number of pioneering studies using them. Now, these techniques are crucial to cognitive neuroscience and to psychiatry.

**Q:  What's your prediction on where the field is heading?**

**A:**  Increasingly, the boundaries between cognitive neuroscience, psychology, psychiatry, and neurology are blurring, since all share an interest in the mind and brain. An even more important future development will be the integration of neuroimaging with studies conducted at the cellular and molecular level. Even as I write this, we are seeing the beginning of an era when mind and molecule meet and merge. Increasingly, we will understand human behavior on multiple levels—an exciting development that may be useful in finding new treatments for serious mental illnesses.

*Nancy Andreasen is Andrew H. Woods Chair of Psychiatry and Director of the Mental Health Clinical Research Center at the University of Iowa.*

hours in statue-like poses, walk backward or in circles, take their clothes off in public, and so on. Remarkably, they also lack self-insight. People with schizophrenia often think that their word salads are coherent, their delusions and hallucinations real, and their emotions appropriate. As one former patient (quoted below) said, "I felt I was the only sane person in the world gone crazy."

A little knowledge, people say, is a dangerous thing. My problems first started when I decided to go back to college at the age of 27. After taking a psychology course, I recognized signs of stress in myself and went for help. I was taking 16 credits, working full time in my business which was a day-care center, and taking care of my children in the absence of their father. He was working out of town and came home on weekends. During that school term, certain remarks made by my professors led me to the conclusion that they were working to rescue me from what they thought was an abusive marriage. And I, contrarily, was convinced that I wanted to stay married.

I felt particularly influenced by a foreign language instructor. I was convinced that this professor and I had a private means of communication and, because of this, interpreted what he said in class as personally relating to me. Sometimes the things I heard in class had no relation to the class purpose. One time, the professor asked the room at large, "So your husband used to be a minister?" I had not divulged that information to him, but because I had recently told my baby-sitter that, I felt the incident was more than coincidence. I felt that there was a large network of people finding out about me, watching me on the street for some unknown reason. This feeling of lack of privacy soon grew into thinking my house was bugged, a fear I would have off and on for the next eight years. The bizarre and illogical things I heard people say were later dismissed as auditory hallucinations. They seemed very real to me, however.

On one occasion, I saw a personal experience of mine written on the blackboard in French and English. I did not recognize it as a hallucination at that time. This caused me considerable anguish, but I continued to act as normal as I could for fear that any bizarre behavior would cause me to lose my job. I did not talk about these things, so the only noticeable signs of my illness were that I became silent and withdrawn, not my usual ebullient and smiling self. I did not think I was sick, but that these things were being done to me. I was still able to function though I remember getting lunch ready very slowly as if working in molasses, each move an effort.

By Christmas, I heard an actor call me a liar over the TV, and I felt sure the media also knew about me. When I went to the store, I bought things that symbolically meant something else to me; each fruit, flavor, or color had a meaning that tied in with my delusion. For example, I would not buy Trix cereal, because it was associated with prostitution in my mind, but I bought a lot of Cheerios to make my day happier. The world of delusion soon became a world of imagined depravities that were a torment to my moralistic mind. I felt I was the only sane person in the world gone crazy. (Anonymous, 1990, pp. 547–548)

## TYPES OF SCHIZOPHRENIA

Even before Bleuler named the disorder, it was obvious that there were different kinds of schizophrenia, with each featuring different combinations of symptoms. In DSM-IV, five major types are distinguished (McGlashan & Fenton, 1991):

- **Disorganized.** A category used to describe those who exhibit signs of illogical thinking, incoherent speech, a neglect of personal hygiene, exaggerated displays of emotion, and mannerisms that are silly and childish.

- **Catatonic.** A rare form of the disorder that features extremes in motor behavior ranging from motionless "stupors" to bursts of hyperactivity.

- **Paranoid.** A form in which the main symptom is being preoccupied with one or more delusions or hallucinations, often with extreme suspiciousness and hostility.

- **Undifferentiated.** A catchall category for cases that exhibit a mixture of symptoms and do not clearly fit into another type.

- **Residual.** A diagnostic category that is used for people who had prior episodes of schizophrenia but are currently not experiencing the major symptoms.

In recent years, many clinical researchers have sought to determine which of the various symptoms of schizophrenia tend to appear together—in the same people and at the same time. Although somewhat different classification schemes have been proposed, it's clear that there are at least two major types of symptoms (McGlashan

*A catatonic stupor is an extreme form of withdrawal. While in this state, the person does not move or speak. In fact, the person may hold an uncomfortable statue-like pose for so long that the limbs become stiff and swollen.*

| TABLE 16.7 | POSITIVE AND NEGATIVE SYMPTOMS OF SCHIZOPHRENIA |
|---|---|

| Positive Symptoms | Percentage |
|---|---|
| Delusions | 84 |
| Hallucinations | 69 |
| Thought disorders | 43 |
| Bizarre behavior | 26 |

| Negative Symptoms | Percentage |
|---|---|
| Apathy | 90 |
| Flattened affect | 88 |
| Social withdrawal | 88 |
| Inattention | 66 |
| Slowed or no speech | 53 |

*Source:* N. C. Andreasen (1987). The diagnosis of schizophrenia. *Schizophrenia Bulletin,* 13, pp. 1–8.

& Fenton, 1992; Andreasen et al., 1995; Arndt et al., 1995). *Positive symptoms* consist of cognitive, emotional, and behavioral *excesses.* Those that tend to appear together include delusions and hallucinations, which are exaggerations in beliefs and perceptions, as well as incoherent speech, inappropriate displays of emotion, and grossly bizarre behavior. In contrast are *negative symptoms* that are characterized by cognitive, emotional, and behavioral *deficits* such as apathy, blank looks, blunted affect, slowed movement and speech, and social withdrawal. As seen in a study of 111 schizophrenic outpatients in an Iowa hospital, the estimated prevalence of both positive and negative symptoms is presented in Table 16.7. Note that delusions were the most common positive symptom and apathy the most common negative symptom.

Can people with schizophrenia be classified into the two general types? Not neatly. On the one hand, research suggests that people with positive symptoms have a better predisorder state and a greater chance of recovery than those suffering from the negative symptoms. On the other hand, many patients exhibit both kinds of symptoms, so the two disorders often coexist (McGlashan & Fenton, 1992).

## THEORIES OF SCHIZOPHRENIA

Can anyone stressed by adverse life circumstances "catch" a schizophrenic disorder, or are some of us more prone than others? Can the outbreak of schizophrenia in a young adult be predicted in childhood? Indeed, are the causes biological, psychological, or a combination of both?

**Biological Factors** Family, twin, and adoption studies reveal a strong genetic basis for schizophrenic disorders (Holzman & Matthysse, 1990; Meltzer, 2000). You may recall that about 1 percent of the American population is diagnosed as having schizophrenia at some point in life. However, the more closely related you are to someone with schizophrenia, the greater the risk (see Figure 16.11). When one fraternal twin has it, the odds are 17 percent for the other. With an identical twin, however, the odds increase even further, to 48 percent—a number that remains high regardless of whether the twins are raised together or apart (Gottesman & Shields, 1982; Gottesman, 1991).

Searching for the biological origins of schizophrenia, many researchers have found that many positive symptoms are associated with overactivity of the neurotransmitter dopamine. Three kinds of evidence support this linkage. First, antipsychotic drugs that block the activity of dopamine in the brain also lessen hallucinations, delusions, and other behavioral excesses. Second, amphetamines both increase dopamine activity and intensify these same symptoms (long-term usage or overdoses can even trigger

| Relationship | Genetic relatedness | Risk |
|---|---|---|
| Identical twins | 100% | 48% |
| Offspring of two schizophrenic parents | 100% | 46% |
| Fraternal twins | 50% | 17% |
| Offspring of one schizophrenic parent | 50% | 17% |
| Sibling | 50% | 9% |
| Nephew or niece | 25% | 4% |
| Spouse | 0% | 2% |
| Unrelated person | 0% | 1% |

FIGURE 16.11    **Genetic relationships and schizophrenia**
As shown, the lifetime risk of schizophrenia increases as a function
of how genetically related a person is to someone else who is known
to have schizophrenia (Gottesman, 1991, p. 96).

schizophrenic-like episodes in normal people). Third, autopsies on the brains of schizophrenic patients often reveal an excess of dopamine receptors (Wong et al., 1986; Seeman et al., 1993).

The negative symptoms of schizophrenia are not as predictably affected by antipsychotic drugs or amphetamines. But like the excesses, these symptoms—the flat affect, apathy, lack of speech, attention problems, immobility, and withdrawal—may be linked to structural defects in the brain. Brain-imaging studies of people with schizophrenia reveal an enlargement of fluid-filled spaces called cerebral ventricles and a corresponding shrinkage of cerebral tissue (Shelton & Weinberger, 1986; Raz & Raz, 1990). The greater the shrinkage, the worse the symptoms tend to be. In fact, the schizophrenic brain may well deteriorate with age. In a five-year longitudinal study of twelve teenagers with schizophrenia, MRI researchers discovered a progressive loss of gray matter over time—particularly among those with the worst symptoms (Thompson et al., 2001). In another study that compared 159 schizophrenia patients and 158 healthy controls, all between the ages of sixteen and seventy, researchers observed that the schizophrenia patients' brains were smaller. This difference became more pronounced with age, suggesting that schizophrenia involves a progressive loss of gray matter (Hulshoff et al., 2002).

Thanks to recent discoveries, it now appears that schizophrenia is a *neurodevelopmental disorder,* one that is caused by various disruptions in the normal process of brain development before and at birth. According to the view, insults to the brain during early sensitive periods of development can cause subtle brain damage, increasing a person's vulnerability to schizophrenia in adolescence and early adulthood. These problems may be caused by viral infections, malnutrition, fetal exposure to alcohol and other toxins, or complications during the birth process (Brown, 1999).

**Psychological Factors**  Although there is a genetic basis for schizophrenia, 54 percent of those people born to two schizophrenic parents do *not* themselves develop the disorder. In other words, heredity may increase the risk, but it does not by itself predetermine one's fate. This notion has given rise to the **diathesis-stress model,** which states that people with a genetic or acquired vulnerability, or "diathesis," develop schizophrenia when exposed to high levels of stress (Meehl, 1962; Fowles, 1992; Walker & Diforio, 1977). What experiences act as triggering mechanisms?

To identify factors that predict the onset of schizophrenia, researchers in the United States, Canada, Israel, Finland, Denmark, and Sweden are conducting longitudinal studies in which high-risk children (those who have at least one schizophrenic parent) are followed closely as they grow older. The life experiences of the children who go on to develop schizophrenia are then compared to those of children who do not. So far, the results show that high-risk subjects who become schizophrenic were more likely to have had complications at birth and low birth weight. They were also more likely to have been separated from their mothers at an early age, to have fathers hospitalized for a mental disorder, to grow up in conflict-filled homes, to have a short attention span, and to have social problems in school (Asarnow, 1988). Can the future of a high-risk child be predicted? Perhaps. When psychology graduate students were shown old home movies of future schizophrenic patients and their healthy siblings—all of whom were normal while growing up— 78 percent guessed correctly which of the children in the films went on to develop the disorder (Walker & Lewine, 1990).

As always, it is easier to identify factors that *predict* the onset of a disorder than to pinpoint its psychological *causes*. To see why, consider two classic findings that are interesting but hard to interpret. First, schizophrenia is most prevalent in the lowest socioeconomic classes of society. This pattern appears in studies all over the world and is sometimes taken to mean that poverty causes schizophrenia. Or is it the other way around? Perhaps schizophrenia—precisely because it is characterized by massive cognitive and social impairment—leads its sufferers to drop out of school, lose jobs, and drift downward into poverty. A second example is the well-publicized observation that parents of schizophrenics communicate to their offspring in ways that are inconsistent and confusing. This finding is often taken to suggest that faulty communication patterns at home cause schizophrenia. Again, however, it is equally possible that the behavior of parents is not a cause but a *response* to the problem of communicating with preschizophrenic children. Which comes first, the chicken or the egg? Either way, it seems that biological and environmental forces combine to produce this devastating disorder.

## PERSONALITY DISORDERS

- *What are personality disorders, and what one feature do they have in common?*
- *What does it mean to have a borderline personality?*
- *Why is there so much interest in antisocial personality disorder?*

You have a unique personality. So do I. We all do. You may be sloppy or meticulous, calm or emotional, self-centered or altruistic, cautious or impulsive, a loner or a social butterfly. However, if someone has a personality that is highly inflexible

**diathesis-stress model**  The theory that certain mental disorders (such as schizophrenia) develop when people with a genetic or acquired vulnerability are exposed to high levels of stress.

### REVIEW QUESTIONS

- *Describe the five major symptoms of schizophrenia.*

- *Identify and describe the major types of schizophrenia.*

- *What is the evidence that schizophrenia has a biological component?*

- *According to the diathesis-stress model, why does schizophrenia occur? Describe evidence consistent with this model.*

## *Psychology and Law*

# THE INSANITY DEFENSE

In Houston, Texas, 36-year-old Andrea Yates drowned her five children—Noah, 7, John, 5, Luke, 3, Paul, 2, and Mary, 6 months. One by one, she put and held them in a bathtub of water until they lay breathless and motionless. Her oldest boy pleaded with his mother and tried to escape but she chased him down, dragged him to the bathroom, and drowned him too. She then dialed 911, and when the police arrived she confessed. In an emotionless, zombie-like manner, Yates said she killed her children to rid herself of Satan and save them from going to hell. As it turned out, Yates had suffered from severe postpartum depression, which worsened after the birth of her last child. She had been hospitalized in the past, and on antipsychotic medications, and had twice attempted suicide. Yates went to trial and pleaded not guilty by reason of insanity. The trial lasted for four weeks and included expert testimony on both sides from psychologists and psychiatrists. Then on March 12, 2002, a jury of four men and eight women voted that Yates was sane—and guilty. She was sentenced to life in prison.

Was Andrea Yates sane or *insane*? What do these terms mean in law? To begin with, it's important to realize that *insanity* is a legal concept, not a psychological one. Insanity is not a diagnostic category and does not appear in DSM-IV. But it is a fundamental concept in criminal law. Individuals who are charged with a crime can plead guilty or not guilty, or they can argue that they should not be held responsible due to extraordinary circumstances. The law provides a variety of excusing conditions for this purpose. If a person commits a crime by accident, was coerced, or acted in self-defense, then he or she may argue for a verdict of not guilty. In a similar manner, the law permits an insanity defense, to protect from punishment those who cannot

morally be faulted for their actions because they were mentally impaired while committing the crime (Golding, 1992).

Over time, the courts have defined insanity in different ways. In the nineteenth century, Great Britain and the United States adopted the rule that defendants were legally insane if, as a result of mental illness, they did not know what they were doing—or that it was wrong. Critics argued that this definition too narrowly focused on a defendant's cognitive state and excluded those who knew what they were doing but could not control themselves. Some states thus added the "irresistible impulse" test by which defendants are considered insane if they lack the capacity to control their actions. Throughout the years, other definitions have been proposed. Today, the most common is one that combines three key elements. As defined by the Model Penal Code, defendants are not responsible for a criminal act if (1) as a result of mental disorder, (2) they cannot

---

**personality disorders**   A group of disorders characterized by a personality that is highly inflexible and maladaptive.

and maladaptive and that causes distress, the person is diagnosed as having a **personality disorder** (Livesley, 2001; Millon, 1995).

Among the disorders classified in DSM-IV, these are among the most controversial. People diagnosed with personality disorders—an estimated 5 to 10 percent of the population—are not swamped with anxiety, depression, or confusion, nor have they lost touch with reality. In fact, they are not particularly motivated to change. The problem is that they are trapped by their own rigid ways in self-defeating patterns of behavior, patterns that begin to form in adolescence and then harden like plaster for the rest of their lives.

appreciate the wrongfulness of their conduct, or (3) they cannot conform their actions to the law. In the state of Texas, where Yates was tried, juries are given a narrower test of insanity: A defendant is insane if—and only if—she did not know right from wrong.

The insanity plea is a constant source of controversy. In 1843, a Scot named Daniel M'Naughten tried to assassinate British Prime Minister Robert Peel and mistakenly killed Peel's secretary. M'Naughten suffered from delusions of persecution and believed that Peel had plotted against him. He went to trial but was found not guilty by reason of insanity. The public was outraged. In 1981, John Hinckley, Jr., shot and wounded President Reagan and was quickly apprehended. The shooting was witnessed by millions of TV viewers. Hinckley was tried in the District of Columbia, but this jury, too, returned a verdict of not guilty by reason of insanity. Again, the public was outraged (Low et al., 2000).

Understandably, many people fear that the insanity defense opens up a loophole through which massive numbers of criminals can use "designer defenses" to escape punishment for their crimes (Kirwin, 1997). But is that fear justified? Consider these three questions: (1) What percentage of criminal defendants enter a plea of insanity? (2) Of those who do, what percentage succeed? (3) Of those who succeed, what percentage are set free? Eric Silver and others (1994) compared public opinions on these questions to the actual figures gathered from forty-nine counties in eight different states and found that respondents, on average, vastly overestimated the overall impact of the insanity defense in criminal justice. Specifically, the public estimated that 37 percent of all criminal defendants plead insane, that 44 percent are acquitted, and that 26 percent of those acquitted are set free. In actuality, less than 1 percent of all defendants plead insanity, 26 percent are acquitted, and 15 percent of those acquitted are set free (the others are committed to a mental hospital). Put these numbers together, and you'll see that public opinion is highly distorted. For every 1,000 cases, people estimate that 163 defendants are acquitted by reason of insanity, and that 47 are set free. In actuality, 2 defendants in 1,000 are acquitted by reason of insanity, and only 3 in 10,000 are set free. In most cases, the person found to be insane spends as much time confined to a hospital as he or she would have spent in prison. Other studies too have confirmed the point: The insanity defense is rarely used and seldom successful—despite what people think (Lymburner & Roesch, 1999).

Despite the moral underpinnings of the insanity defense and the reassuring odds concerning the frequency of its usage, there are problems in its implementation. One is that many defendants who are evaluated for insanity engage in some form of malingering, or faking. To overcome this problem, psychologists have developed tests and interview methods to try to detect such faking (Hall & Pritchard, 1996; Rogers, 1997). A second problem is that judges often turn for expert opinion to clinical psychologists and psychiatrists who are trained to diagnose mental disorders—not to resolve disputes about criminal responsibility. Predictably, many insanity trials feature a battle of opposing experts who disagree in their opinions (Dawes et al., 1989; Hagen, 1997).

Is there a solution to the insanity dilemma? On the one hand, it seems inhumane to punish people who cannot be held responsible for their actions. On the other hand, it seems repugnant to provide a loophole for violent criminals. In recent years, many courts have reformed their laws to discourage acquittals by reason of insanity (Borum & Fulero, 1999). Although it remains to be seen what effect these changes will have on judges and juries, controversy will clearly continue to surround this awkward relationship between clinical psychology and the law.

There are eleven personality disorders listed in DSM-IV, many of them quite colorful in their character. For example, there is the socially isolated and emotionally detached *schizoid personality,* the perfectionistic *obsessive-compulsive personality,* the overly sensitive and suspicious *paranoid personality,* the melodramatic and attention-seeking *histrionic personality,* the self-centered and ego-inflated *narcissistic personality,* and the *avoidant personality,* who so fears rejection that he or she does not start new relationships or make social commitments. Two others in particular have attracted widespread attention: (1) the borderline personality, which is quite common; and (2) the antisocial personality, which is socially destructive.

**borderline personality disorder**    A type of personality characterized by instability in one's self-image, mood, and social relationships and a lack of clear identity.

**antisocial personality disorder**    A personality disorder involving a chronic pattern of self-centered, manipulative, and destructive behavior toward others.

Comorbidity is the rule rather than the exception. Researchers don't yet know why, but there is an association between heavy smoking and depression.

## THE BORDERLINE PERSONALITY

Marilyn Monroe was famous for her beauty and her tremendous success in Hollywood. She was also known for being unpredictable, impulsive, insecure, impossible to live with, and yet desperately afraid to be alone. At the age of thirty-six, she shocked the world by killing herself with an overdose of sleeping pills. From what is known about her life, Marilyn Monroe did not have a serious anxiety, somatoform, conversion, or dissociative disorder, nor was she schizophrenic. At times, she was depressed. If she were alive today, however, she might well be diagnosed, along with 20 percent of all psychiatric patients and 3 to 5 percent of everyone else, as having a **borderline personality disorder.**

Borderline personality disorder features a lack of identity and a pattern of instability in self-image, mood, and social relationships. People with this disorder (about two-thirds of whom are women) are uncertain of who they are in terms of their career goals, friends, values, and sometimes sexual orientation. They complain of feeling empty and bored, can't stand to be left alone, and are desperate for the company of others. Unhappily, people with a borderline personality cling to others with such fierce dependence that their relationships are stormy and do not last. They are impulsive and in the habit of running away, getting into fights, and jumping into bed with strangers. As a way to get attention, they are also notorious for committing acts of self-destruction. In a study of the lives of fifty-seven borderline patients, there were forty-two suicide threats, forty overdoses, thirty-eight cases of drug abuse, thirty-six acts of self-mutilation (slashing wrists, banging heads, burning skin with cigarettes, pulling out hair), thirty-six cases of sexual promiscuity, and fourteen automobile accidents caused by reckless driving (Gunderson, 1984, 2001). As for what motivates these acts, women with borderline personality disorder say they had committed nonsuicidal self-injury to punish themselves, distract themselves, experience emotions, and vent anger—but that they had attempted suicide to benefit others whom they burden (Brown et al., 2002).

## THE ANTISOCIAL PERSONALITY

The brutally cold, calculating, and callous individual is often depicted in books and in films such as *Silence of the Lambs*. Unfortunately, the characters depicted in art come from real life. Every now and then, a crime story appears on the news that is so horrible it sends chills up my spine. Three high school students pour gasoline on their teacher and set her on fire. A man slashes the face of a model with a razor blade in exchange for $200. What kind of person is capable of these atrocities? Who are these monstrous creatures? In the nineteenth century, they were described as morally insane. More recently, they were called psychopaths, then sociopaths. Today, the term **antisocial personality disorder** is used to describe people who have "ice in their veins" and who behave in ways that are self-centered, irresponsible, destructive, and completely without regard for the welfare of others.

According to DSM-IV, the antisocial personality (ASP) is a disorder that applies to people who, as children, would cut school, run away from home, set fires, harm animals, steal, cheat, and get into fights—and who, as adults, drive recklessly, borrow money and do not return it, get into fights, behave irresponsibly as spouses or parents, drink excessively, and engage in unlawful activities.

As you might expect, a person with ASP cannot hold a job or a close relationship. But the most striking feature is that he (80 percent are men) lacks a conscience and feels no guilt, remorse, or empathy for his victims. He uses others for pleasure or profit and then discards them. When intelligent, the person with ASP is not a common street criminal but a cool, manipulative, charming, and clever con artist who

MOB PSYCHOLOGIST

"So, while extortion, racketeering, and murder may be bad acts, they don't make you a bad person."

can seduce romantic companions with empty words of love, lie to business partners with a straight face, and sweet-talk his way out of trouble (Cleckley, 1976; Hare, 1993; Lykken, 1995; Millon et al., 1998). In light of all this, it comes as no surprise that surveys in twelve countries have revealed that 47 percent of male prisoners and 21 percent of female prisoners have ASP—which is ten times more than in the general population (Fazel & Danesh, 2002).

For many years, researchers have speculated about the causes of ASP. Some have tried to trace the disorder in childhood to broken homes, neglectful parents, and faulty role models that impede the formation of a superego and moral development. Others have measured brain-wave patterns and heart rates, and they have found that people with antisocial personalities are less excitable than the average person and are not as easily startled. They remain physiologically calm in the face of electric shock, tense situations, and images of children screaming and crying, an attribute that makes them fearless (Blair et al., 1997; Patrick et al., 1993). In fact, boys who are referred for their antisocial behavior have lower-than-average levels of cortisol, a stress hormone normally released in situations that arouse fear (McBurnett et al., 2000). Still others find that people diagnosed with ASP lack the ability to control their impulses, a problem that is worsened by their tendency to abuse alcohol and other disinhibiting drugs (Myers et al., 1998). Society can take some comfort in the fact that individuals with antisocial personalities who go on to become criminals tend to burn out and commit fewer crimes after age forty (Hare et al., 1988). (See *Psychology and Law*).

**comorbidity**   The tendency for people diagnosed with one mental disorder to exhibit symptoms of other disorders as well.

## REVIEW QUESTIONS

- *Identify the various kinds of personality disorders. What do all of these have in common?*

- *What symptoms are associated with borderline personality disorder?*

- *What are the major features of antisocial personality disorder? What factors are believed to contribute to it?*

# THINKING LIKE A PSYCHOLOGIST ABOUT PSYCHOLOGICAL DISORDERS

Psychological disorders keep people from adapting in the most effective way to their environment. In this chapter, six types of disorders were described, each featuring different primary symptoms: intense anxiety, physical ailments and complaints, dissociation of the self from memory, extreme moods ranging from depression to euphoria, schizophrenic devastation of mental functions, and self-defeating patterns of behavior. Yet there are many more—such as disorders involving sleep, sex, impulse control, substance abuse, and development. Clearly, no aspect of our existence is immune to breakdown.

Now that you've seen the list of psychological disorders, you should note two ways in which the picture is more complicated than it appears. First, although each disorder is presented separately in its own neat and tidy package, people diagnosed with one disorder often have symptoms of others as well, a common phenomenon known as **comorbidity** (Kendall & Clarkin, 1992; Kessler et al., 1994). It turns out, for example, that 57 percent of people diagnosed with an anxiety disorder and 81 percent of those with a mood disorder have at least one other DSM problem as well (Brown et al., 2001). Thus, people with phobias often suffer too from obsessive-compulsive disorder, many of those with generalized anxiety disorder are also depressed, those who are depressed often have sleep disorders, and people with schizophrenia often abuse drugs. In a similar vein, psychological disorders do not exist in caricature-like terms. Depression may be considered a mood disorder, but it also has cognitive symptoms; schizophrenia is considered a thought disorder, but it has a marked impact on emotion.

The second complication is that "normal" and "abnormal" are not distinct, well-defined categories but, rather, points on a continuum. Hence, people who are otherwise happy, healthy, and well adjusted may experience some symptoms of psychological disorders. On occasion, most of us have felt panic, phobic anxiety, mania, and depression. Most of us know what it's like to lose sleep when we're nervous or to worry excessively about our health when a contagious disease or threat of terrorism begins to spread. Most of us know what it's like to tune out for short periods of time and dissociate mentally from our surroundings. Sometimes we even catch brief, mild glimpses of schizophrenic symptoms. For example, the new parent who "hears" his or her newborn cry, only to see that the baby is fast asleep, is having an auditory hallucination. And the person who dines alone in a restaurant and self-consciously thinks everyone is watching is under some kind of delusion. In short, psychological order and disorder are not always black-and-white categories, but shades of gray.

At times, diagnosis is a judgment call based on how intense, frequent, prolonged, and disabling the symptoms are.

Once psychological disorders are identified and diagnosed, and once we understand their causes, what next? At this point, we must return our attention to the underlying challenge of clinical psychology: the potential for positive *change*. As we saw in Chapter 15, personality remains relatively stable throughout adulthood. But what about the problems that afflict so many people? What about episodes of anxiety or depression? For those needing professional help, the answer is to seek treatment through drugs, counseling and psychotherapy, and other forms of intervention. Reflecting the hope and the reality that people can help other people change, the next chapter addresses these topics.

# SUMMARY

## PSYCHOLOGICAL DISORDERS: A GENERAL OUTLOOK

Because psychological disorders are widespread, it's important to define them, make distinctions among different types of problems, and know what factors put us at risk.

### DEFINING NORMAL AND ABNORMAL

The term **psychological disorder** has been defined in various ways. The APA definition stresses significant pain or dysfunctional behavior and an internal, involuntary source. Whatever definition is used, there is no strict line between normal and abnormal.

### MODELS OF ABNORMALITY

The **medical model** attributes mental disorders to biological conditions. The **psychological model** locates the cause of disorder in past and present experiences. The **sociocultural model** stresses the importance of cultural context, as seen in **culture-bound syndromes**, recurring patterns of maladaptive behavior that are limited to a specific cultural group or location.

### DIAGNOSIS: A NECESSARY STEP

Today, the process of **diagnosis**—the grouping and naming of mental disorders—is based on **DSM-IV**. Although diagnosis is more reliable than in the past, stereotypes can bias judgments, and diagnostic labels can then affect the way people are perceived and treated.

## ANXIETY DISORDERS

Anxiety is a nervous feeling of apprehension accompanied by physical symptoms, such as a pounding heart and trembling hands.

### GENERALIZED ANXIETY DISORDER

A constant state of anxiety not linked to an identifiable source is the mark of **generalized anxiety disorder**. Cross-cultural studies show that the physiological symptoms of anxiety are universal but that the cognitive component (the particular set of worries and interpretations) varies with the culture.

### PANIC DISORDER

**Panic disorder**—characterized by frequent, sudden, intense rushes of anxiety for no apparent reason—is often accompanied by **agoraphobia**, a fear of public places. There is evidence for both biological and psychological causes.

### PHOBIC DISORDER

A **phobic disorder** is an intense and irrational fear. A **simple phobia** involves a fear of a specific object, and a **social phobia** is a fear of a situation that invites public scrutiny. Freud attributed phobias to anxiety over hidden impulses; behaviorists stress conditioning and learning; others have linked common phobias to evolutionary programming or "preparedness."

### OBSESSIVE-COMPULSIVE DISORDER

In **obsessive-compulsive disorder** (OCD), the person is plagued by obsessions (persistent thoughts) and compulsions (the need to perform repetitive acts or rituals). Psychoanalysts, behaviorists, and biological psychologists have all offered explanations and possible therapies. For many people, OCD can be treated with antidepressants.

### CULTURAL INFLUENCES ON ANXIETY DISORDERS

Anxiety is a universal human affliction but the specific forms it takes may vary according to cultural beliefs. Thus, certain anxiety disorders are found in some cultures but not others.

## SOMATOFORM DISORDERS

People with a **somatoform disorder** have bodily symptoms that are psychological rather than medical in origin.

### HYPOCHONDRIASIS

A disorder involving unwarranted preoccupation with one's physical health, **hypochondriasis** can become a lifelong pattern. People with this disorder may be acutely sensitive to stimulation.

### CONVERSION DISORDER

**Conversion disorder** is a temporary loss of a bodily function without a physical cause. It mainly affects young women but is far less common today than it was a hundred years ago, when it was called "hysteria."

## DISSOCIATIVE DISORDERS

Many people have experiences in which they lose their memory for a portion of their lives or identity. A severe condition of this sort is known as a **dissociative disorder**.

### AMNESIA AND FUGUE STATES

**Amnesia** is a partial or complete loss of memory. Causes include physical trauma, alcohol, and stressful events. In the rarer forms known as **fugue states**, people forget their identity, wander away, and start a new life.

### DISSOCIATIVE IDENTITY DISORDER

In **dissociative identity disorder** (DID), which used to be called multiple personality disorder, the person develops two or more distinct personalities. Women exhibit this disorder more often than men and often have a history of abuse as children. Reported cases of DID are on the rise, a situation that has triggered controversy.

## MOOD DISORDERS

People normally have many fluctuations of mood. But prolonged emotional extremes that impair the ability to function are diagnosed as **mood disorders**.

### MAJOR DEPRESSIVE DISORDER

**Depression**, a widespread mood disorder, brings feelings of deep sadness and despair without a discernible cause and lasts for two weeks or more. Other symptoms include loss of sleep and appetite, feelings of worthlessness, hopelessness, and a lack of energy.

### THEORIES OF DEPRESSION

Twin studies show a genetic foundation for depression. Early research stressed the role of neurotransmitters, but now it appears that the connection between biology and mood is more complicated.

Psychological factors have also been noted. Freud considered depression a reaction to loss. Behaviorists link it to **learned helplessness**, an expectation that we cannot control important life outcomes. Social-cognitive theorists say that depressed people have a **depressive explanatory style**, a tendency to attribute negative events to factors that are internal, stable, global—and to assume that things will not change. Humanistic theories see depression as the result of the failure to reach self-actualization.

### THE VICIOUS CYCLE OF DEPRESSION

Depressed people often behave in ways that alienate others. Social rejection then intensifies the depression—a vicious cycle.

### SUICIDE: THE ULTIMATE "SOLUTION"

Three-quarters of suicides are committed by depressed people. Baumeister sees suicide as an "escape from self" into oblivion. Clinically, scales of hopelessness are the best predictor. Among friends or relatives, signs of potential suicide include depression and drug use, remarks about death, and previous attempts.

### BIPOLAR DISORDER

People with **bipolar disorder** experience wild mood swings from depression at one extreme to mania (a euphoric, overactive state) at the other. Many famous artists had bipolar disorder, and their manic phases may have contributed to their brilliance. But mania may also spiral out of control, producing delusions and risky and embarrassing behavior. Though related to simple depression, bipolar disorder has a stronger genetic component.

## SCHIZOPHRENIC DISORDERS

Marked by gross distortions of thought and perception and a loss of contact with reality, **schizophrenic disorders** are equally common in women and men all over the world, though they tend to strike women at a later age.

### THE SYMPTOMS OF SCHIZOPHRENIA

Schizophrenia's major symptoms are incoherent thought and speech, **delusions** (false beliefs), **hallucinations** (sensory experiences without actual stimulation), disturbance of affect (flattened, exaggerated, or inappropriate emotion), and bizarre behavior.

## TYPES OF SCHIZOPHRENIA

DSM-IV lists five major types of schizophrenia: disorganized, catatonic, paranoid, undifferentiated, and residual. Researchers have found that two types of symptoms tend to appear together. Positive symptoms are behavioral *excesses* (such as delusions and hallucinations), and negative symptoms consist of behavioral *deficits* (such as flat affect and social withdrawal). Many patients exhibit symptoms of both kinds.

## THEORIES OF SCHIZOPHRENIA

Twin, family, and adoption studies reveal a genetic basis for schizophrenia, linked to the neurotransmitter dopamine or to structural brain defects. But psychological factors also play a role. Some evidence supports the **diathesis-stress model**, which holds that people with genetic or acquired vulnerability develop schizophrenia when exposed to a high level of stress.

## PERSONALITY DISORDERS

A person with a highly inflexible and maladaptive personality is said to have a **personality disorder**.

## THE BORDERLINE PERSONALITY

People with **borderline personality disorder** lack identity, cling to others, act impulsively, and are prone to self-destruction.

## THE ANTISOCIAL PERSONALITY

Of those who have **antisocial personality disorder**, 80 percent are men. The condition produces a chronic pattern of self-centered, manipulative, and destructive behavior toward others. Its most notable feature is lack of conscience.

Although the disorders presented in this chapter are treated separately, people diagnosed with one disorder often have symptoms of other disorders too, a phenomenon known as **comorbidity**.

# KEY TERMS

psychological disorder (p. 624)

medical model (p. 625)

psychological model (p. 625)

sociocultural model (p. 626)

culture-bound syndromes (p. 626)

diagnosis (p. 627)

DSM-IV (p. 627)

generalized anxiety disorder (p. 631)

panic disorder (p. 631)

agoraphobia (p. 632)

phobic disorder (p. 632)

simple phobia (p. 632)

social phobia (p. 632)

obsessive-compulsive disorder (OCD) (p. 635)

somatoform disorder (p. 638)

hypochondriasis (p. 638)

conversion disorder (p. 639)

dissociative disorder (p. 641)

amnesia (p. 641)

fugue state (p. 641)

dissociative identity disorder (DID) (p. 641)

mood disorder (p. 644)

depression (p. 644)

learned helplessness (p. 646)

depressive explanatory style (p. 646)

bipolar disorder (p. 648)

schizophrenic disorders (p. 653)

delusions (p. 654)

hallucinations (p. 654)

diathesis-stress model (p. 659)

personality disorders (p. 660)

borderline personality disorder (p. 662)

antisocial personality disorder (p. 662)

comorbidity (p. 663)

# THINKING CRITICALLY ABOUT PSYCHOLOGICAL DISORDERS

1. Discuss the major criticisms of psychiatric diagnosis. Why does the psychological community continue to use diagnosis? How can the problems be minimized?

2. Is the desire to take one's own life necessarily a sign of poor mental health? Should individuals be allowed to commit suicide if they so desire? Why or why not?

3. The majority of individuals with borderline personality disorder are women, whereas the vast majority of those with antisocial personality disorder are men. Why might this gender difference exist?

4. Use the three perspectives of abnormality to explain the high incidence of comorbidity.

5. Think back to the theories of personality that you learned about in the previous chapter. How would these theories account for dissociative identity disorder (DID)?

6. Discuss the controversy surrounding the use of the insanity defense. What is your position on this controversy?

# Treatment

# CONSUMER REPORTS ASKS,
# DOES PSYCHOTHERAPY HELP?

■

## THE SITUATION

People who have personal problems—such as being anxious or depressed, drinking too much, having marital trouble, or feeling generally unhappy without knowing why—wonder where they can turn for help. Sometimes people turn to friends, relatives, clergy, or family doctors; at other times, they seek help from psychologists, psychiatrists, and other mental-health specialists. Do the specialists really help? Do psychotherapy and other forms of mental-health intervention produce the kind of improvement we all hope for?

To answer to this question, *Consumer Reports (CR)* added a survey about psychotherapy to its annual questionnaire, in which readers are asked to rate laundry detergents, breakfast cereals, home appliances, automobiles, and other products and services. *CR* asked readers to fill out a special mental-health section "if at any time over the past three years you experienced stress or other emotional problems for which you sought help." The survey was mailed to 184,000 randomly selected subscribers; and 22,000 responded, a 12 percent response rate that is typical of *CR* surveys. Of those who did return it, 35 percent said they had a mental-health problem. Within this group, 40 percent sought some kind of professional help. Specifically, 2,900 readers sought help from a psychologist, psychiatrist, social worker, or marriage counselor; the others saw family doctors or self-help or support groups.

All respondents were asked to indicate the nature and severity of their distress and to provide background information about cost, insurance, type of therapy they had, and other matters. Then they rated the extent to which their treatment helped with the specific problem they had (and, more generally, with their work and social lives and sense of personal fulfillment). They also indicated their overall level of satisfaction or dissatisfaction with the therapy.

## MAKE A PREDICTION

On the question regarding improvement, respondents indicated whether the treatment made things a lot worse, somewhat worse, no different, somewhat better, or a lot better. The question is, How many reported improvement? Specifically, what percentage of the respondents do you think said that they were somewhat better or a lot better after treatment? Was it 10 percent? 25, 50, 90 percent? Next, consider the respondents' level of satisfaction with the therapy they received. What percentage do you think said they were highly satisfied? And what percentage were fairly satisfied? Using the table below, make predictions for both sets of measures.

| Measures | Overall responses |
|---|---|
| Improvement | ___% Somewhat better |
|  | ___% A lot better |
| Satisfaction | ___% Fairly satisfied |
|  | ___% Highly satisfied |

## THE RESULTS

In November 1995, *Consumer Reports* published the results of this survey (the largest ever conducted on the topic) and concluded that patients in general derive substantial benefit from psychotherapy. Just how substantial was the overall level of improvement? Combining all the respondents—regardless of the type of problem they had, the type of therapist they saw, or the amount of time they spent in treatment—the percentages of those who said they were a lot better and satisfied were striking. As you can see in the table below, a total of 86 percent felt they were improved after therapy and 89 percent were satisfied with the experience.

| Measures | Overall responses |
| --- | --- |
| Improvement | 44% Somewhat better |
| | 42% A lot better |
| Satisfaction | 27% Fairly satisfied |
| | 62% Highly satisfied |

## WHAT DOES IT ALL MEAN?

Over the years, the number of people seeking professional help for psychological problems has climbed. In light of soaring medical costs and the limits imposed by managed care and other health-insurance policies, those in need of help—the consumers of psychological treatments—need to know whether the treatments work. *Consumer Reports* has a reputation for being fair and objective in its evaluations. But are the survey results valid? Are *CR* subscribers representative of the population? Is it possible that people who were satisfied with the experience were more likely to take part in the survey than those not satisfied or that they would have felt better, eventually, without outside help? Is it possible that the self-reported improvements, which could not be verified, were exaggerated? Or is it possible that psychotherapy truly helps those in need?

When psychologist Martin Seligman (1995) presented the results to psychologists, he set off a wave of debate on Internet bulletin boards. In October 1996, the *American Psychologist* devoted an entire issue to commentary and debate about this study and what it meant. Some were critical of the study and its methods. Others, including Seligman, defended it and stood by the results. We'll revisit this controversy later in this chapter. We'll also see from more controlled studies that psychological therapies (as well as medical interventions) *are* generally effective—and that for people in distress, they offer hope, social support, and an opportunity to open up.

In *Love's Executioner and Other Tales of Psychotherapy*, Irvin Yalom (1989) tells the story of Betty, a twenty-seven-year-old female patient who was 5'2" and weighed 250 pounds. A few moments into the first meeting, Yalom asked his standard opening question, "So what ails?" Betty's reply: "Everything." She worked sixty hours a week, had no friends, cried every night, had frequent headaches, and spent weekends at home eating in front of the TV. According to Betty, she was too heavy for people to accept yet too depressed to lose weight. Had she sought professional help before? Yes, but without much success.

Throughout the first few weeks of therapy, Betty did not really open up. According to Yalom, she droned on about trivial work problems, giggled constantly, and put on silly accents—but she revealed nothing truly intimate about herself. To break the ice, Yalom confronted Betty with her avoidant tactics. Soon she began to open up (a frightening prospect, she said, "like jumping out of a plane without a parachute"). She became more engaged in the sessions and more interesting to talk to, but she was also more anxious. To speed up the process and provide a supportive social network, Yalom then put Betty into a therapy group, which worked wonders. She enrolled in a weight-reduction program, joined a bowling league, devoured her last honey-glazed doughnut, and went on a diet. As the months passed, Betty lost a great deal of weight. And with each new low, she would have flashbacks of emotionally charged events that had occurred when she was at that particular weight. At 150, for example, she recalled the death of her father. Swarms of painful memories poured out—her father's affectionate manner, his fight with cancer, how alone she felt when he died, and how afraid she was of dying the same way. There was one insight after another, until Betty became a happier, healthier, more confident woman. After fifteen months, the therapist and patient had their final session together. They reminisced about the past, looked forward to the future, embraced, and said good-bye. As this story illustrates, the treatment of psychological distress is not only a science but also an art. Other poignant tales of what goes on in psychotherapy—and with what effect—also illustrate the point (Briddell, 2000). Whereas some psychologists study the human mind and behavior in research, practicing clinical psychologists help people cope with real-life problems. Sometimes the goal is to treat the symptoms of a specific disorder or to help people cope with a stressful life event; at other times, it is to foster growth in those of us who are "normal" but not content with the state of our lives. Whatever the problem, this chapter addresses three questions: (1) What treatments are available to people in need of psychological help? (2) Are these treatments effective? (3) And if so, why?

The methods for treating psychological disorders are far from perfect, and are not always successful, but they've come a long way in a few short years (Gamwell & Tomes, 1995; Stone, 1997). Our prehistoric ancestors believed that people afflicted with psychological disorders were inhabited by evil spirits—so they drilled holes in the skull large enough for these spirits to escape. In the seventeenth century, the same disorders were attributed to witchcraft and demonic possession and were "treated" with exorcism, noise making, bloodletting, beating, bitter potions, starvation, and torture. By the eighteenth century, people with mental disorders were considered ill but were hidden from public view—often chained to the walls of dark, dungeon-like hospitals called "asylums" (see Figure 17.1). Then during the nineteenth century, a

**FIGURE 17.1    Old-fashioned "cures" for mental illness**
In the eighteenth century, many crude devices were used to treat mental illness. Among the more popular were the crib (used to restrain patients who would not stay in bed), the tranquilizing chair (used to calm those who were manic or violent), and the circulating swing (used to treat depression through high-speed rotation). Twentieth-century methods included cold packs, hot-steam showers, vibrating helmets, infrared-lightbulb cabinets, and electric "mummy bags."

spirit of humanitarian reform swept through many institutions in the United States and Europe. The inmates were unchained, housed in clean rooms with windows, and permitted to walk outside on hospital grounds.

At the turn of the twentieth century, major advances were made on two fronts. One was the finding that the symptoms of *hysteria* (such as paralysis of a limb or blindness) could be treated with hypnosis. The other was the discovery that a schizophrenia-like disorder called *general paresis*—which is marked by hallucinations, delusions, personality changes, and death—was caused by syphilis, a sexually transmitted genital infection. These developments now stand as symbols for the two predominant models of treatment: one psychological, the other medical. Today, as we'll see, these two models complement rather than compete with each other.

# PSYCHOLOGICAL THERAPIES

- *What is psychoanalysis, and what is its goal for treatment?*
- *What principles underlie behavioral therapy, and what techniques are used?*
- *What are the main features of cognitive therapies?*
- *What is the humanistic approach?*
- *Why do therapists sometimes prefer to treat people in groups?*

The term **psychotherapy** is used to describe all forms of treatment in which a trained professional uses psychological techniques to help persons in need of assistance. Psychotherapy comes in many different forms. The trained professional may be a *clinical psychologist* (who attends graduate school, earns a Ph.D. in psychology, and conducts testing, diagnosis, treatment, and research), a *psychiatrist* (who attends medical school, receives an M.D., does a residency in psychiatry, and is the only mental-health professional who can prescribe drugs), a *counseling psychologist* (who receives a Ph.D. in counseling to help people with marital, family, and minor adjustment problems), or a *psychiatric social worker* (who earns a two-year master's degree in social work and has had special training in counseling). The person in need of assistance also varies from one case to another. He or she may suffer from one of the psychological disorders listed in DSM-IV or may simply feel inadequate, lonely, unimportant, or unloved and may just want more from life.

Psychotherapists can choose from a vast array of techniques—about four hundred in all (American Psychological Association Task Force, 1995). A small number of therapists, who get too much attention from the media, use "faddish" techniques—for example, insulting patients to shake them up, having patients scream at the top of their lungs, or "regressing" them to infancy and into the womb. But the vast majority of therapists are professionals who work with individual children or adults, families, and groups—and who are trained in one of four major approaches: psychoanalytic, behavioral, cognitive, and humanistic. These approaches are described in the following pages.

## PSYCHOANALYTIC THERAPIES

Imagine you are lying outstretched on a couch, with a soft pillow tucked underneath your head. You stare at the walls and ceiling, noticing subtle streaks of white paint, shadows, hairline cracks in the plaster, and dust on the drapes. You fixate on a small, neatly drilled hole in the wall from which a picture must have been hung. As your eyes scan every nook and cranny, however, your mind is elsewhere, in another time and place. You recall the tantrum you had on your first day of school, the fight your parents had after putting you to bed one night, the moment you were

**psychotherapy** A term used to describe any treatment in which a trained professional uses psychological techniques to help someone in need of assistance.

told that your favorite grandfather died, the peculiar dream you had the night before, or the way the family used to get together on Thanksgiving to eat, drink, and watch the parade on TV. As an image comes to mind, you talk about it and relive the emotions you felt. You laugh, you cry, you clench your teeth in anger as you become reabsorbed in the events of your own life. But you're not alone. Sitting behind you—listening to every word you say, commenting from time to time, and passing the Kleenex—is your "analyst."

**Orthodox Psychoanalysis** Ever since Josef Breuer and Sigmund Freud (1895) found that people often feel better after purging their minds of material buried in the unconscious, psychoanalysis has had a marked influence on the treatment of mental disorders. You may recall from Chapter 15 that Breuer treated a young patient named Anna O., who suffered from hysterical blindness, paralysis of an arm, a nervous cough, and other symptoms of conversion disorder. This case was important in three ways. First, Breuer found that when Anna talked about herself, she sometimes stumbled upon memories that had been repressed for many years. Second, these insights often brought about a relief of her symptoms. Third, Anna became intensely attached to Breuer, eventually causing him, a married man, to terminate their sessions.

Some historians and writers have questioned the actual nature and success of Breuer's treatment of Anna (Borch-Jacobsen, 1996; Guttmann, 2001). Nevertheless, Freud went on to use this case, and others like it, to develop psychoanalysis, the first systematic method of "talking cure"—a term coined by Anna herself. Psychoanalysis is designed to achieve two goals: *catharsis,* a release of bottled-up psychic tension, and *insight,* or self-understanding. As we will see, these goals are achieved through the therapist's interpretation of three types of behavior: free association, resistance, and transference.

**Free Association** For Freud, the principal technique of psychoanalysis was born in 1892 with a patient named Elisabeth. At first, Freud had her lie down, close her eyes, think hard about a symptom, and try to recall the moment it started. Meanwhile, he asked pointed questions and pressed his hand against her forehead to help her concentrate. Then at one point, after many futile attempts, Elisabeth had an insight—but concerning a part of her life that was unrelated to the symptom she was trying to recall. Freud was taken by surprise. Why had she waited so long to reveal something so important? "I could have told you that the first time, but I didn't think that it was what you wanted," she said (quoted in Jones, 1953, p. 243). Humbled by this turn of events, Freud came up with a new set of rules. From now on, he said, follow your own train of thought. Elisabeth was agreeable but, in turn, asked Freud to stop asking so many irrelevant questions. This episode marked the first use of **free association**, the backbone of psychoanalysis. In free association, the patient lies back, relaxes, and talks about thoughts, wishes, memories, fantasies, physical sensations, dreams, and whatever else comes to mind—no matter how trivial, embarrassing, or crazy it may seem. No censorship. No interruption. In the meantime, the analyst listens attentively, trying to put together the pieces of an emerging puzzle.

Beginning with Freud's (1900) work on dreams, psychoanalysts have encouraged patients to free-associate about their dreams—the "royal road to the unconscious." As we saw in Chapter 4, this emphasis is based on the theory that pent-up psychic energy from repressed sexual and aggressive impulses is released when we're

**free association** A basic technique of psychoanalysis in which the patient says whatever comes to mind—freely and without censorship.

*Treated by Breuer in the 1880s, Anna O. played a pivotal role in the birth of psychoanalysis. In relating her dreams and "fairy tales," she coined the term talking cure to describe the process. Her symptoms (which appeared when she was twenty-one years old and her father became terminally ill) were only temporarily relieved under Breuer's care, but she did eventually recover. Seventy years later, a biographer of Freud revealed her true identity for the first time. Her name was Bertha Pappenheim. When she died in 1936, she was an internationally renowned social activist, writer, and feminist (Guttmann, 2001).*

*To encourage patients to relax, Freud had them recline on the couch in his study while he sat out of view. You can see this couch if you visit Freud's historic home in Vienna.*

"Look, call it denial if you like, but I think what goes on in my personal life is none of my own damn business."

[© The New Yorker Collection 2000, Robert Mankoff from cartoonbank.com. All Rights Reserved.]

*"In a sonata all the themes that are going to appear are stated at the beginning. . . . One might think of one's first relationships as the themes of one's interpersonal life and all subsequent relationships as the development and recapitulation of those themes."*

—MICHAEL KAHN

**resistance**   In psychoanalysis, the tendency for patients to actively block, or "resist," psychologically painful insights.

**transference**   In psychoanalysis, the tendency of patients to displace intense feelings for others onto the therapist.

asleep, but in ways that are confusing and hard to interpret. According to Freud, the dreams you remember in the morning are well-disguised expressions of deep, hidden impulses. Thus, as patients describe the conscious *manifest content* of dreams, their analysts are busy trying to unmask the underlying *latent content*—what the dreams "really" mean.

**Resistance**   Free association was only the beginning. Right from the start, Freud noticed something curious. His patients could talk for long periods of time and produce endless streams of ideas, but they often would not face unpleasant thoughts and memories. On the brink of an important but painful insight, patients would stop, go blank, lose their train of thought, change the subject, argue with the therapist, "forget" the next appointment, make jokes, call it quits, or seek another therapist. Freud called this pattern of avoidance **resistance** and concluded that it was part of an unconscious defensive process designed to keep threatening personal insights out of awareness.

In psychoanalysis, resistance is a double-edge sword. On the one hand, it slows down the course of therapy and may even bring it to a grinding halt. On the other hand, it signals that the patient is on the verge of exposing a psychic raw nerve and that therapy is moving in the right direction. Where there's smoke, there's fire; where there's resistance, there's emotional turmoil. The analyst's goal is to make the patient aware of the resistance by carefully interpreting what it means. "I notice you never want to talk about your mother" and "Why do you always make jokes when you discuss your illness?" are the kinds of interpretive statements analysts make in order to get at underlying problems and nudge patients toward difficult self-insights.

**Transference**   Also critical to psychoanalysis is the therapist–patient relationship. Just as Anna O. became attached to Breuer, many of Freud's patients developed intense, unsolicited feelings toward him. Freud assumed that he was not the real target of these passions, so he speculated that people have an unconscious tendency to transfer feelings for parents, siblings, lovers, and other significant persons onto the therapist—a phenomenon he called **transference**. Sometimes the patient reacts with passionate love and affection (positive transference) but at other times with hatred, anger, and hostility (negative transference). Either way, the therapist is merely a convenient substitute for the person for whom these feelings are really meant. In fact, said Freud, therapists need to beware of their own tendency to "countertransfer" feelings they have for others onto their patients. In *Love's Executioner,* for example, Yalom (1989) freely admitted that when he started to treat Betty, the obese woman, he had to fight a lifelong aversion to people who are overweight, an aversion he traced to his own childhood.

Like resistance, transference is a welcomed disruption in psychoanalysis. It may slow down and complicate matters, but it also provides a window to the unconscious. When deeply rooted feelings are awakened in therapy, patients can more easily slip into the past and recall events from childhood. Again, the goal is for people to gain insight into current relationships—to understand why they are attracted to certain kinds of people or why they shy away from commitments, need constant reassurance, or become fiercely possessive and jealous. To foster these kinds of transference-related insights, the psychoanalyst sits behind the patient, maintains a shadowy presence, and then interprets the transference reaction. Examples include: "You always seem to want my approval, the way you must have needed your mother's approval" and "You're angry because I won't tell you how to run your life, and you think I don't care. Is that why you're always upset with your boyfriend? He isn't bossy, so you think he doesn't care?"

| TABLE 17.1 | PSYCHOANALYSIS IN ACTION |
|---|---|

Taken from an actual therapy session, this dialogue illustrates one psychoanalyst's use of interpretation (Baker, 1985, pp. 41–42).

**Patient:** You know, I really didn't want to come today. I just don't seem to have very much to talk about. (long silence) I'm just not really sure what to say; maybe you can suggest a topic.

**Therapist:** You'd like for me to tell you what to talk about, to give you some structure?

**Patient:** Sure, after all, that's what I'm paying you for. (pause) It seems that you just sit there all the time not saying anything. I'm not really sure this is helping very much.

**Therapist:** Perhaps we should talk about your feeling that I'm not giving you what you want.

**Patient:** It's not so much want, it's what I need. You always just sit there; you never give me advice; you never tell me what to do. I thought therapy would be different from this.

**Therapist:** You expected more?

**Patient:** I expected something. You know, it's a little irritating to pay out good money and feel like you're not getting your money's worth.

**Therapist:** So it feels as if I'm cheating or depriving you in some way. Perhaps that is why you're feeling so angry today.

**Patient:** I'm not feeling angry. (pause) Well . . . I guess I am a little. In fact, I really didn't even want to come.

**Therapist:** Perhaps there's a relationship between those feelings . . . feeling angry and then wanting to withdraw.

**Patient:** You know, I think I do that a lot. I feel uncomfortable being angry at you. It doesn't seem justified somehow and yet I do feel angry and feel like I just want to not come and not talk; or not pay my bill or do something to get even. I guess I do that a lot. I mean, when I get angry, I get quiet and I just don't talk.

**Therapist:** Perhaps that is why you were so quiet at the beginning of the hour. It was a way of indirectly letting me know that you were angry, while at the same time protecting yourself and me from that anger and your fears of what it might do.

**Patient:** I guess you are right. I am afraid of anger and I have a lot of difficulty letting people know directly when I feel they have done something bad or hurt me in some way. So I just . . . withdraw.

Based on material that is provided by free association, resistance, and transference, psychoanalysts seek insight through a process of interpretation (see Table 17.1). One key factor in this endeavor is timing. Someone who is emotionally prepared to face painful ideas will feel relieved and enlightened by an interpretation. But for someone who is not, the technique will backfire, heightening anxiety and resistance. Psychoanalysis is thus a long, hard, and expensive process—typically requiring four or five fifty-minute sessions a week and lasting for some number of years. It's interesting that Freud's patients seldom stayed in psychoanalysis for more than a year. Since then, however, the process has become longer and more drawn out (it's been said that analysis used to last a year and marriage a lifetime but that now it's the opposite). If you ever saw the classic movie *Sleeper*, you'll recall that after having been frozen for two hundred years, Woody Allen wakes up and says, in a semiserious tone, "If I had kept seeing my analyst, I'd almost be cured by now!"

**Brief Psychoanalytic Therapies** Inspired by neo-Freudian theorists such as Jung, Adler, Fromm, Horney, and Erikson (see Chapter 15) and by a practical need for shorter-term, less costly methods of treatment, most psychoanalytic therapists today use modified, nonorthodox techniques. They still share key aspects of Freud's approach—such as an appreciation for the importance of past experiences and unconscious processes. In general, however, these newer therapies are briefer, less intense, and more flexible. Sessions are usually scheduled once a week and for a limited period of time, usually just a few months rather than years. To accelerate the therapy process, many analysts now sit face-to-face with their patients and take a more active conversational role, often asking direct questions and prompting certain lines of inquiry. Unconscious resistance is still interpreted, and transference is still considered a useful vehicle for insight, but today's analyst tries to minimize these reactions or else to facilitate the process through role-playing exercises. Analysts also spend less time plunging into the past and more time addressing current life problems (Alexander & French, 1946; Crits-Christoph & Barber, 1991; Henry et al., 1994; Luborsky, 1984). Some have even suggested that analysts can facilitate the therapy process by occasionally self-disclosing personal experiences or feelings to their patients, a practice once regarded as off limits (Jacobs, 1999).

**Controversies in Psychoanalysis** Ever since Freud claimed that from birth, people are driven by lustful desires and aggressive impulses and that they are at the mercy of unconscious forces beyond their control, psychoanalysis as a theory has been steeped in controversy. It is also controversial as a form of treatment. There are three main criticisms. The first, aimed at orthodox psychoanalysis, is that it takes too long and is too expensive, available only to those who are affluent. The second is that psychoanalytic interpretations can never be disproved. If a therapist interprets a patient's late arrival as a sign of resistance and the patient accepts this interpretation, it stands confirmed. If the patient emphatically denies the interpretation, the denial itself becomes proof of resistance, also "confirming" the initial interpretation ("heads I win, tails you lose"). A third criticism is that psychoanalysis is not truly therapeutic, that people are no better off after they come out than before they went in. We'll see later that this claim is unfair. Studies show that psychoanalytic therapy, like other types of psychotherapy, is generally effective. But must people dive head first into the past and open old wounds in order to solve current life problems? Many psychologists and psychiatrists do not think so. Thus, psychoanalysis has been on the decline, leaving some of its adherents in the United States wondering, "Is there a future for American psychoanalysis?" (Kirsner, 1990).

Despite the criticisms, psychoanalysis has left a permanent imprint on clinical theories, practice, and research (Nersessian & Kopff, 1996). Therapists from all orientations agree that resistance is a typical behavior among psychotherapy patients (Mahoney, 1991). Indeed, research shows that defensiveness and self-deception in general are normal, if not adaptive, parts of human nature. Many practitioners also agree that transference and other aspects of the therapist–patient relationship are key to success (Kahn, 1991). In addition, studies support Freud's claim that patients bring into therapy unique, consistent, and largely unconscious interaction styles from past relationships (Luborsky & Crits-Christoph, 1998). As such, patients may unwittingly be influenced by gender, responding differently to male and female therapists (Kalb, 2002). Even in laboratory experiments, participants have been shown to react positively or negatively toward neutral strangers depending on whether they resembled liked or disliked others from their own lives (Berk & Andersen, 2000). Finally, many of us now take for granted the psychoanalytic assumptions that mental disorders are often rooted in childhood, that trauma triggers defensive mechanisms, that we often avoid thinking about deep-seated conflicts, and that insight has therapeutic value. (For an interesting perspective on the application of psychoanalysis, see *Psychology and the Law*.)

## BEHAVIORAL THERAPIES

Psychoanalysis is an intensive form of therapy in which people are opened up, taken apart, and reassembled before they can be cured. In this approach, analysts have to get to the root of the "problem" in order to eliminate the "symptoms." Then along came Pavlov, Watson, Skinner, and other behaviorists. Armed with the principles of classical and operant conditioning, they argued that psychological disorders consist of maladaptive behaviors that are learned by reinforcement and can be unlearned in the same manner. Afraid to fly? Depressed? Think everyone is out to get you? Well, said the behaviorists, forget the past, ignore your dreams, keep unconscious urges in the closet, and stop waiting for pearls of wisdom to fall from the lips of your all-knowing analyst. Instead, tell me what it is you want to change about yourself. Then we'll make a list of concrete behavioral goals and try to achieve these goals as quickly as we can. Eliminate the symptom and you have solved the problem.

Whether people have a phobia, test anxiety, a sexual disorder, or an inability to stop smoking, they can often be treated using classical and operant conditioning and other well-established principles of learning. In a book on behavioral techniques, 158 specific procedures were described, including "anger-control therapy," "verbal-satiation therapy," and "implosion therapy" (Bellack & Hersen, 1985). Together, these various techniques are known as **behavioral therapy** (Kazdin, 2001) or, in some forms, **cognitive-behavioral therapy** (Dobson, 2000).

**Classical-Conditioning Techniques** As we saw in Chapter 5, *classical conditioning* is the Pavlovian process by which a once-neutral stimulus (a bell) comes to elicit an emotional or behavioral response (salivation) after being paired repeatedly with an unconditioned stimulus (food) that already has the power to elicit that reaction. In 1920, Watson and Rayner used this model to train a baby boy to react with fear to a white rat by pairing the rat with an aversive loud noise. If phobias and other disorders develop through classical conditioning, suggested Watson, then perhaps they can be erased in the same manner.

**Flooding** If Watson was right, it should be possible to treat certain disorders through *extinction*. After repeated presentations of a bell without food, Pavlov's dogs eventually stopped salivating in response to the sound. Similarly, people who confront a fearful situation without a negative consequence should see that the fear is unfounded. This idea gave rise to **flooding**—a technique in which a person is exposed to, or "flooded," with an anxiety-provoking stimulus until the anxiety is extinguished. Sometimes the person is guided to imagine the dreaded stimulus; at other times, the experience is firsthand. Someone with agoraphobia (a fear of being in public places), for example, might be taken by a reassuring therapist into a crowded shopping mall and kept there for hours until the fear subsides. This procedure is repeated several times until the anxiety is completely diminished. Flooding is sometimes effective, but success is not guaranteed. Some people can't bring themselves to confront their feared situation; others agree to but then panic, escape, and become even more anxious; still others complete the program but later experience a relapse (Barlow, 1988).

**Systematic Desensitization** Another powerful and more reliable antidote to anxiety is *counterconditioning*—a procedure in which a person is trained to react to

**behavioral therapy or cognitive-behavioral therapy** Techniques used to modify disordered thoughts, feelings, and behaviors through the principles of learning.

**flooding** A behavioral therapy technique in which the patient is saturated with a fear-provoking stimulus until the anxiety is extinguished.

## Psychology and Law

# Putting Repressed Memories on Trial

It is sometimes ironic how history repeats itself. It was the year 1900. While formulating his theory of psychoanalysis, Freud reported hearing his patients recount horrifying tales of early childhood abuse. One after another, they told of incest and other traumas, often sexual in nature. But Freud soon came to believe that at least some of the stories told were false, the figments of overactive imaginations. This notion seemed a terrible blow, but Freud later concluded that the patients were not really lying—that they truly believed that the incidents they recounted had happened. To this day, psychologists debate the validity of Freud's reports and interpretations (Esterson, 2001; Gleaves & Hernandez, 1999).

Turn the clock forward to the year 1990. In Redwood City, California, fifty-one-year-old George Franklin stood trial for the murder of an eight-year-old girl that had taken place more than twenty years earlier. For years, the crime was left unsolved. Then Eileen Franklin, the victim's friend—who was eight years old at the time of the girl's death—came forward to implicate the defendant, her father. According to Eileen, she had forgotten the incident and just recently had started to have flashbacks. She now remembers playing with her friend in the family van when the attack took place. She remembers seeing her father sexually assault the girl and raise his hands up, holding a rock. She remembers screams, a struggle, and the sight of her friend covered with blood, with a smashed silver ring on her finger. Solely on the basis of her testimony, Franklin was convicted of first-degree murder and sentenced to prison. It was the first time ever that someone was tried and convicted of murder on the basis of a newly recovered repressed memory.

The Franklin conviction was followed by a barrage of new charges. Alleged victims soon appeared in courtrooms and on daytime TV talk shows to tell horrifying tales of abuse, at times as part of satanic-cult rituals. In some states, statutes of limitations that had kept people from bringing cases forward after long periods of time were modified for those who recovered long-lost memories. As a result, thousands of men and women filed multimillion-dollar lawsuits against family members and others in their distant past, leaving the courts to decide how to treat this evidence. In one case, a federal court ruled to allow a sixty-eight-year-old woman to sue her cousin who, she alleged, sexually abused her when they were teenagers, a memory recovered fifty years later in therapy. Yet in another case, a federal court disallowed the testimony of a woman in her thirties who sued her aunt, uncle, and many others for repeatedly drugging her, raping her, and forcing her to drink blood from as early as the age of three—memories she recovered in hypnosis (Ewing, 1996).

These cases went on to trigger a backlash against the use of repressed memories. Accused mothers, fathers, grandparents, and others sought each other out and formed the

In 2002, John Geoghan, a former priest from Boston, was found guilty and sentenced for molesting a boy eleven years earlier. Since then, 130 others claimed that they too were molested by him as children. Many of the allegations are undoubtedly true. But had the victims previously repressed the incidents, or had they chosen consciously not to come forward?

False Memory Syndrome Foundation, a nationwide support group. These people, too, had stories to tell about having their families and reputations torn apart by false accusations. Many repressed-memory accusers later withdrew their claims—some even joined their families in suing the therapists who brought the so-called memories out in the first place (de Rivera, 1997).

Childhood sex abuse is a real crime, can have devastating and lasting consequences for mental health, and may be more common than was previously realized. Some psychotherapists point to cases in which patients had "forgotten" traumatic events until the memories surfaced years later, to be corroborated by independent evidence. But what should be done when there is no independent evidence? On one side of the debate are Ellen Bass and Laura Davis (1988), authors of *The Courage to Heal,* a book that has been described as the "bible" for the survivors of incest and childhood sex abuse. Though not trained in psychology, Bass and Davis provide readers with a list of symptoms to watch for—such as anxiety, depression, intimacy problems, dependence, and loss of appetite. And when a reader is in doubt? "If you are unable to remember any specific instances . . . but still have a feeling that something abusive happened to you, it probably did" (p. 21).

On the other side of the debate, Elizabeth Loftus (1993) warns that a person's memories for remote-past events are often not memories at all but images and ideas suggested by therapists eager to find the source of a patient's distress. Is it possible for one person to plant a false trauma memory into the mind of another? Loftus (1997) described some compelling demonstrations. In one, she and Jacqueline Pickrell arranged for a fourteen-year-old boy named Chris to be told by his older brother Jim that he got lost in a mall when he was five years old and that he was found crying by a tall older man wearing a flannel shirt. The story was false. Yet a few days later, Chris "recalled" being scared, being asked by an older man if he was lost, and being scolded afterward by his mother. Two weeks later, he described even more fully what had happened: "I was with you guys for a second and I think I went over to look at the toy store. . . . I thought I was never going to see my family again. I was really scared, you know. And then this old man, I think he was wearing blue flannel, came up to me . . .

he was kind of old. He was kind of bald on top . . . he had like a ring of gray hair . . . and he had glasses."

As judges and juries struggle to sort facts from fictions, it is important to balance our concerns for both the victims of abuse and the victims of false accusations. Research suggests that people often avoid certain thoughts, and that events once forgotten can sometimes be recalled (Erdelyi, 1996). But is there any evidence that this can occur for high-impact personal events? Can repressed-and-recovered memories of blunt trauma be trusted? In psychology, the controversy has become highly emotional and divisive (Pezdek & Banks, 1996). Seeking a resolution, the American Psychological Association assembled a task force to examine the issue, a mixed group composed of both researchers and therapists. The group could agree on little, however, except the following:

- Sexual abuse is a pervasive problem.
- Most people abused as children remember all or part of what happened.
- It is possible to recall old memories that have been forgotten over time.
- It is possible to construct false memories of events that did not occur.
- There are many unanswered questions about what leads to accurate versus inaccurate childhood memories.

Finally, let's return to the case of George Franklin. After Franklin spent five years in prison, his conviction was overturned by an appeals court on a matter of evidence. Franklin was freed and granted a new trial. It was later revealed that Eileen had reported the event in therapy, that she had undergone hypnosis, that the details she recounted had been published in the newspaper, that her reports had changed during the investigation, and that she had falsely accused her father of another murder. To this day, there is no way to know whether her memory was true or false. In 1996, however, the prosecutor was concerned enough about Eileen's credibility as a witness that he chose not to retry Franklin. As the debate rages on, it is clear that these questions can be answered only on a case-by-case basis—and with the help of independent evidence.

**systematic desensitization** A behavioral therapy technique used to treat phobias and other anxiety disorders by pairing gradual exposure to an anxiety-provoking situation with relaxation.

a feared stimulus with a positive response that is incompatible with anxiety. Mary Cover Jones (1924), a student of Watson's, sought to demonstrate that anxiety could be erased by associating a feared stimulus with a pleasurable experience. Jones treated a three-year-old boy named Peter, who had become intensely fearful of rabbits and other furry animals. One afternoon, Jones took Peter into a room with a caged rabbit, sat him at a table, and fed him milk and crackers. This routine was repeated several times, and each time the rabbit was moved closer as the boy devoured his snack. After a few weeks, Peter was holding the rabbit on his lap, stroking it with one hand, and eating with the other. Through the process of stimulus generalization, he shed his fear of other animals as well.

Thirty-four years after Jones reported on this case, Joseph Wolpe (1958) devised **systematic desensitization**, a technique that is now widely used in the treatment of phobias and other anxiety disorders. Based on the fact that a person cannot simultaneously feel anxious and relaxed, systematic desensitization is designed to condition people to respond to a feared stimulus with calm, not anxiety. There are three steps in this procedure: (1) relaxation training, (2) the construction of an anxiety hierarchy, and (3) gradual exposure. To see how systematic desensitization works, imagine that you are afraid to fly and that whenever you see an airplane on a runway, hear the thunderous noise of its engines, smell the fuel, or feel the vibrations, your heart races and you break into a cold sweat. You make an appointment with a behavior therapist, and before you know it you're ready to begin.

The first step is to learn how to relax in response to a cue from the therapist. This is accomplished through *relaxation training*—a procedure in which you are taught to concentrate on what it feels like to tighten and then relax various muscle groups throughout the body. Try it. Really. Sit back comfortably, loosen your clothing, take your shoes off, take a deep breath, and let your muscles get loose and heavy. Now wrinkle up your forehead, wrinkle it tighter, tighter again. Hold it for a few seconds. Now stop tensing, relax, and smooth it out. Picture your entire forehead and scalp becoming smoother. Now frown and crease your brows. Close your eyes, tighter and tighter. Feel the tension. Now relax, and let go. Keep your eyes closed gently, and notice the relaxation. Now clench your jaw and purse your lips, tighter and tighter. Press your tongue hard against the roof of your mouth, and feel the tension. All right, now relax. Relax your jaw, loosen your lips, let your mouth hang open, and let your tongue return to a comfortable position. Notice how relaxed you are all over. Let all your muscles go limp and feel the smoothness in your forehead, scalp, eyes, mouth, and lips. See how it feels to be relaxed.

The next step is to come up with an *anxiety hierarchy*, a graduated sequence of fear-provoking situations that you rate on a 100-point scale, ranging from mild to terrifying. In your case, the hierarchy might begin with "You see a newspaper ad for discount airfares" and progress to "You look out the window as the plane leaves the ground" (see Table 17.2).

Prepared with an ability to relax on cue and with a hierarchy of fear-provoking situations, you brace yourself for the third and final step. At this point, the therapist talks you into a state of relaxation and guides you through a gradual series of *exposures*. You're instructed to close your eyes and imagine the mildest fear-provoking situation in the hierarchy. If you keep your cool while visualizing this scene, you move on to the next item on the list. If you begin to get anxious, however, the therapist will instruct you to stop and relax. The scene is then revisited until it ceases to arouse anxiety. Lasting several sessions, this same routine is repeated for all items in the hierarchy until you are "cured" of the fear. This technique, in which the person mentally confronts the anxiety-provoking stimulus, is known as *imaginal exposure*. To ensure long-term success, however, many

## TABLE 17.2   A SAMPLE ANXIETY HIERARCHY

The scenes in this hierarchy are typical of those used in the systematic desensitization of a fear of flying. The numbers to the left of each item represent one patient's subjective rating of how anxiety-provoking a situation is, on a scale from 0 to 100.

| | |
|---|---|
| 5 | You see a newspaper ad for discount airfares. |
| 10 | You see a TV commercial for an airline. |
| 20 | A group of friends talks about arranging a trip that requires flying. |
| 30 | You visit a travel agent to make plane reservations. |
| 35 | The week before the trip, you get your plane tickets in the mail. |
| 40 | The night before the trip, you pull out your suitcase to pack. |
| 55 | You park your car near the departure terminal. |
| 60 | You check in, and the agent asks if you want a window or aisle seat. |
| 65 | The announcement is made that your flight is ready for passenger boarding. |
| 70 | You're in line, with ticket in hand, ready to board. |
| 80 | You're in your seat, and the flight attendant says, "Fasten your seatbelts for takeoff." |
| 90 | You feel the plane begin to roll down the runway. |
| 95 | You look out the window as the plane leaves the ground. |

therapists prefer to use *in vivo exposure*—in which the person confronts the feared situations in real life. The ultimate test of whether you have conquered the fear of flying is in your ability to board an airplane, stay calm during the flight, and make the return trip later on.

In an intriguing new development, behavioral therapists have been experimenting with exposure through the use of virtual reality. Imagine being fearful of heights and peering down from the top edge of the Empire State Building. To achieve this sensation, the patient wears a helmet with an electromagnetic sensor. The therapist programs the helmet with a computer-generated 3-D view of a virtual environment that changes with head and body movements. Thus, as part of systematic desensitization, patients can realistically experience what it feels like to stand on the roof of a virtual skyscraper, speak in front of a virtual audience, fly in a virtual airplane, or handle a virtual snake, all without leaving the therapist's office. Research shows that this technique is highly successful—and that the gains made are lasting. In a controlled study of patients with a fear of flying, Barbara Rothbaum and others (1995) found that a virtual exposure treatment was effective. Importantly, a twelve-month follow-up revealed that 92 percent of those flew on a real airplane, on their own, since their "graduation flight" (Rothbaum et al., 2002).

Systematic desensitization is a common and highly effective form of therapy and has been used to treat fears of dogs, snakes, blood, heights, open spaces, crowds, balloons, feathers, violins, dentists, tunnels, needles, and eating in public (Marks, 1987)—sometimes in a single session (Ost, 1989; Zinbarg et al., 1992). According to Wolpe (1982), systematic desensitization works via counterconditioning, by associating a new response (relaxation) to the feared stimulus. However, others find that exposure alone is all that's needed, with or without the relaxation (Rachman, 1990). Many home-bound agoraphobics, for example, benefit from an in vivo exposure treatment in which they are taken by their therapist, a spouse, or a companion into crowded streets, shopping malls, and other progressively difficult situations (Foa & Kozak, 1986).

As shown in Figure 17.2, behavior therapists have used this technique with success to treat people with obsessive-compulsive disorder by exposing them to the situations that evoke obsessive thoughts but then preventing them from carrying out their compulsive rituals (Meyer, 1966). This technique has also been used to help women with bulimia, an eating disorder that is characterized by cycles of binge

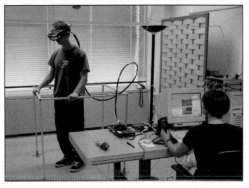

*Some behavioral therapists now use virtual reality to expose patients to phobic objects and situations—like the cabin of an airplane. As part of systematic desensitization, this patient receives exposure to anxiety-provoking visual displays through a virtual reality headset.*

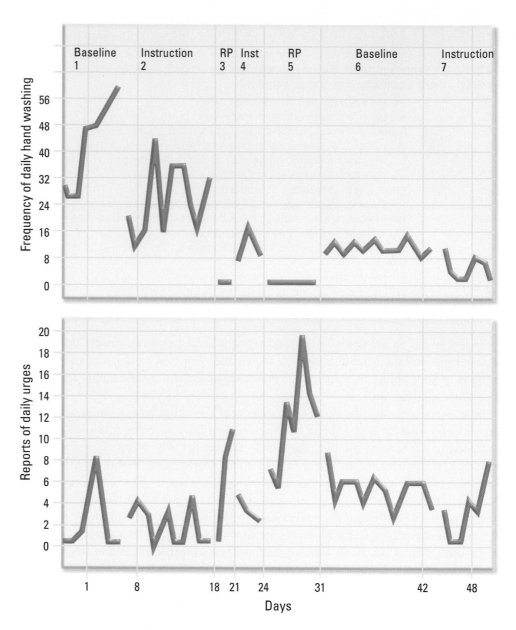

**FIGURE 17.2** **Therapeutic effects of exposure and response prevention**
A woman with a compulsive hand-washing ritual was hospitalized and permitted for a week to wash as desired (baseline). During the next week, she was told to try to break the habit (instruction). This was followed by three days of denied access to running water (response prevention), another instruction, and more response prevention. This treatment was highly effective. After a few weeks, the woman was washing less often and getting fewer urges (Mills et al., 1973).

eating and purging. Thus, the women are fed but prevented from vomiting (Wilson et al., 1986). In all cases, exposure-and-response-prevention causes an initial buildup of anxiety that eventually subsides, often with lasting success (Foa & Franklin, 2001).

Sometimes it helps to watch the harmless exposure of others to an anxiety-provoking situation. In a study on the therapeutic effects of *modeling*, Albert Bandura and others (1969) had persons with snake phobias observe a filmed or live model handling snakes and found that these exposures—especially to a live model—increased the extent to which subjects were able to approach a snake without anxiety.

In another study, medical patients who needed "hyperbaric oxygen therapy" (a stressful procedure in which they are locked for an hour in a narrow chamber containing pressurized oxygen) were more relaxed, completed more prescribed treatments, and required fewer days in the hospital when they first watched a filmed model coping with the same situation than when they did not (Allen et al., 1989). Even more effective is *participant modeling*, which combines passive exposure to a model with gradual practice (Ost et al., 1991; Mineka et al., 1999).

**Aversive Conditioning**    The aim of systematic desensitization is to get people to stay calm in safe situations. But when people are attracted to activities that are harmful—such as smoking, drinking, overeating, and other destructive habits—the opposite effect is sought. In these cases, behavioral therapists often use **aversion therapy**, a technique designed to elicit an aversive rather than pleasurable reaction to a harmful stimulus.

In the treatment of alcoholism, the goal of aversion therapy is to cause heavy drinkers to feel sick to the stomach at the sight, smell, and taste of liquor (see Figure 17.3). This objective can be achieved in a number of ways. In one technique, the alcoholic drinker is given Antabuse (a drug that causes nausea when combined with certain other drugs, including alcohol) and then is taken to a darkened room (one designed to look much like a bar) and served beer, wine, gin, whiskey, or other favorite drinks. After a few minutes, the person vomits uncontrollably. This treatment has, in some cases, resulted in abstinence after five or six visits, followed by occasional booster sessions (Cannon et al., 1981). In a study of 685 hospitalized alcoholics treated with aversion therapy, 63 percent were still "dry" after one year, and 33 percent were still dry after three years (Wiens & Menustik, 1983).

By itself, aversion therapy is not a sufficient treatment for alcoholism. With people who are desperate and willing, however, this technique is sometimes used in conjunction with other forms of therapy (those being treated as such take an Antabuse pill every day, so if they drink they get sick). There are also nonchemical aversion methods as well—such as having the problem drinker imagine unpleasant and disgusting scenes along with vivid images of drinking. As part of a larger treatment program, the goal of this conditioning technique is to suppress the urge to drink (Rimelle et al., 1995).

## Operant-Conditioning Techniques

While some behaviorists were discovering the principles of reinforcement by training animals to peck keys, press bars, and jump over barriers for food, water, or the termination of electric shock, others began using the methods of operant conditioning for clinical purposes. On the assumption that all the world's a Skinner box, reinforcement can be used to promote behaviors that are desirable and to extinguish those that are not.

**Reward and Punishment**    It is sometimes necessary to establish clear reinforcement programs to treat people who are severely disordered. In one case, a female patient with schizophrenia wore twenty-five pounds of clothing, including several dresses, sweaters, shawls, turbans, stockings, and coats. To control this bizarre behavior, the therapist in charge required this woman to weigh in at the door of the dining room before meals. Whether she was then allowed to enter and eat was contingent on a steadily decreasing clothing weight. After thirteen weeks, the problem was solved (Ayllon, 1963). Sometimes, in an institutional setting, the staff establish

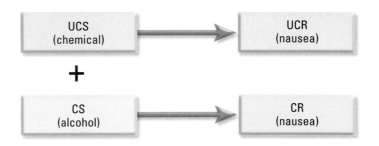

**FIGURE 17.3**    **Aversion therapy to treat alcoholism**
In aversion therapy, the goal is to eliminate the urge to drink by pairing alcohol with a chemical that causes nausea and vomiting. When used, this conditioning-based technique is typically accompanied by other forms of treatment.

*Illustrating aversive conditioning, behavioral therapists use the "rapid smoking technique" by forcing smokers who can't break the habit to puff continuously, every few seconds. For a period of time, this procedure is repeated over and over again until the urge to smoke is suppressed.*

**aversion therapy**    A behavioral therapy technique for classically conditioning people to react with aversion to alcohol and other harmful substances.

a large-scale reinforcement program called a **token economy.** In a token economy, patients earn plastic chips or "tokens" for engaging in desirable behaviors (such as prompt attendance at group-therapy meetings). Like money, the tokens can then be used to purchase candy, TV privileges, weekend passes, books, and other commodities (Ayllon & Azrin, 1968). This is an effective way to shape behavior—not only in psychiatric hospitals but also in classrooms, homes for juvenile delinquents, and other settings (Kazdin, 1982, 2001).

Reward usually produces impressive changes, but punishment is sometimes necessary to eliminate dangerous or self-destructive behavior. In one study, punishment was used on nineteen autistic preschoolers who were uncommunicative and who injured themselves by pulling out hair, biting chunks of skin, and banging their heads against the wall. With help from their parents, these children were put into a two-year home-treatment program in which they were ignored, interrupted, or slapped on the thigh whenever they engaged in violent, self-abusive acts. By the first grade, nine of them functioned normally in school—a remarkable accomplishment compared to those not treated with punishment and in light of previous failures with similar children (Lovaas, 1987).

**Biofeedback**  Yoga practitioner Swami Rama once astonished psychologists by proving in controlled laboratory tests that he could voluntarily slow down or speed up his pulse rate, stop his heart from pumping blood for seventeen seconds, raise or lower the temperature in his hand, and alter his brain-wave patterns. But is it possible? Can people control their physiological behavior? Yes, absolutely. In 1969, Neil Miller found that he could condition heart rates in animals to increase or decrease in response to rewarding, pleasurable brain stimulation.

As an outgrowth of this research, psychologists developed **biofeedback,** a procedure by which people learn to control their own autonomic processes by receiving continuous, moment-to-moment information, or feedback, in the form of visual or auditory displays. With the aid of electronic sensors attached to parts of the body and an instrument that records and amplifies the various signals, people can monitor and eventually regulate not only their heart rate but also their blood pressure, skin temperature, gastric acidity, hormone secretions, and muscle tension. Today, behavior therapists use biofeedback to treat hypertension, chronic back pain, ulcers, bedwetting, headaches, and other health problems (Blanchard et al., 1982; Hatch et al., 1987). For people with sleep problems, attentional problems, migraine headaches, or certain types of seizures, some psychologists now use neurofeedback, a similar procedure that trains people to alter their brain waves through feedback about their own EEG activity (Evans & Abarbanel, 1999). It's no wonder that these techniques have been referred to as the "Yoga of the West" and as "electronic Zen" (Schwartz et al., 1999). (See *How to Use Biofeedback to Treat Headaches.*)

**Social-Skills Training**  For people who are painfully shy, unresponsive, or socially awkward, there is **social-skills training**—lessons on how to speak clearly, make eye contact, maintain a comfortable amount of social distance, and respond appropriately to questions (Curran & Monti, 1982). In social-skills training, the therapist models the desired behaviors, the patient imitates and rehearses these behaviors in role-playing exercises, and the therapist responds with a combination of praise and constructive criticism. This reinforcement-based therapy produces impressive results. Studies show, for example, that it helps people with schizophrenia to interact with others more easily and to feel more comfortable in public situations (Benton & Schroeder, 1990).

**token economy**  A large-scale behavior-change program in which the participants earn valuable tokens for engaging in desired target behaviors.

**biofeedback**  An operant procedure in which people learn to control physiological responses with the help of "feedback" about their internal states.

**social-skills training**  A form of behavioral therapy used to teach interpersonal skills through modeling, rehearsal, and reinforcement (e.g., assertiveness training).

## How To

# USE BIOFEEDBACK TO TREAT HEADACHES

Have you ever had a pulsating headache so painful that you had to just lie down and close your eyes? If so, you're not alone. Surveys reveal that more than 90 percent of all adolescents and young adults have at least one such headache per year (Linet et al., 1989). In fact, in one survey 10 to 20 percent of respondents said *yes* to the question "Do you have a headache today?" (Rasmussen et al., 1991). For most people, headaches are infrequent, mild, and easily treatable with aspirin and rest in a dark, quiet room. But an estimated twenty-eight million Americans suffer from headaches that are frequent, severe, and disabling (Lipton et al., 2001).

There are more than hundred different kinds of headaches (Oleson et al., 2000). The two most common are migraines and tension types. *Migraine headaches* tend to strike several times a month, usually on one side of the head, and often around the eyes. They may be accompanied by throbbing pain, nausea and vomiting, and a heightened sensitivity to noise, bright light, and physical exertion. In contrast, *tension headaches* are characterized by feelings of muscle tightness on both sides, often in the back of the neck or forehead. Studies show that headaches are more common among women than among men. They may be caused by such factors as high blood pressure, stress, too much or too little sleep, heat or cold, eyestrain, food allergies, alcohol, menstruation, physical injury, and high altitude. Mild tension headaches can usually be treated with analgesics. For people who suffer from a chronic barrage of headaches, however, overuse of aspirin and other painkillers can trigger even more headaches as the medicines lose some of their impact over time.

Searching for an alternative, behaviorally oriented psychologists have successfully trained headache sufferers in the use of progressive muscle-relaxation and biofeedback. In one series of studies, for example, Edward Blanchard and his colleagues showed that biofeedback can help people with tension-type headaches. In some cases, the patients are provided with electromyographic (EMG) recordings of muscle tension in the face and scalp. For example, they may watch a light on an instrument panel that brightens as the muscles in the forehead, neck, or upper back tighten and dims as these muscles relax. Over time, this feedback enables patients to control the EMG displays as they learn to relax the right muscles (see Figure 17.4).

Another approach, which is typically used in the treatment of migraine headaches, is to provide patients with thermal biofeedback. In this procedure, sensors are attached to a finger and a beeping signal slows in rhythm as temperature rises. With experience, people learn to warm the finger, or even a hand or foot, thus bringing greater blood flow to that limb and away from the head. Overall, biofeedback has benefited more than 50 percent of tension-headache sufferers who tried it on a permanent, long-term basis (Blanchard, 1994). These results compare favorably with those produced by drug treatments—without the adverse side effects.

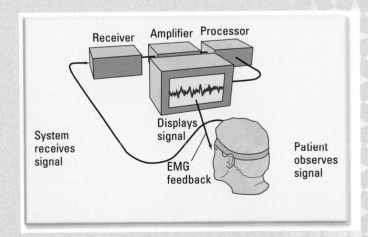

FIGURE 17.4 **Biofeedback and the tension headache**
Using biofeedback, a headache sufferer learns to relax the forehead muscles by monitoring EMG recordings of tension in this region.

One type of social-skills training that is currently popular is *assertiveness training* (Alberti & Emmons, 1986). Imagine that you are waiting in a long line for concert tickets and someone cuts in front of you. Or you are in a movie theater and the people behind you talk so loudly that you can't concentrate. Or a friend asks you for a lift to the airport, but you're too busy at the time. Or you take your car in for repairs, but when you pick it up you get a bill that is twice the estimated cost. How

**cognitive therapy** A form of psychotherapy in which people are taught to think in more adaptive ways.

**rational-emotive behavior therapy (REBT)** A form of cognitive therapy in which people are confronted with their irrational, maladaptive beliefs.

would you react in these situations? Would you speak up and assert yourself or hold your tongue and say nothing? For people who feel easily manipulated, assertiveness training—through the use of modeling and reinforcement—teaches them how to protect their own self-interests, resulting in treatment gains that may be enduring (Baggs & Spence, 1990).

## COGNITIVE THERAPIES

Behaviorists seek to modify maladaptive behavior through the use of classical and operant conditioning. But what matters most, stimulus–response connections and reinforcement per se, or the way we perceive these events? Reflecting psychology's interest in mental processes, many therapists use a more cognitive, rational approach. The result is **cognitive therapy**, a form of treatment designed to alter the maladaptive ways in which people interpret significant events in their lives. To the cognitive therapist, "As you think, so shall you feel" (McMullin, 2000).

There are different brands of cognitive therapy and many techniques, but all have certain features in common. Based on the assumption that anxiety, depression, and other emotional disorders spring from the way we think, cognitive therapists try to get people to open their minds, challenge their assumptions, and think about old problems in new ways. Cognitive therapy is short term, often limited to twenty sessions, and the therapist acts as a partner, friend, and teacher all rolled into one. Sessions are centered on concrete problems, and the therapist maintains a brisk, businesslike pace. Among the most prominent pioneers of this approach are Albert Ellis and Aaron Beck.

**Rational-Emotive Behavior Therapy** Though initially trained in psychoanalysis, Albert Ellis (1962) went on to develop what he now calls **rational-emotive behavior therapy**, or **REBT** (Ellis, 1999). His basic proposition is this: Mental distress is caused not by upsetting events per se but by the rigid and maladaptive ways in which we construe these events. In other words, A (activating events) gives rise to B (beliefs), which triggers C (emotional consequences). This A-B-C model is illustrated in Figure 17.5. The problem, said Ellis, is that too many of us hold beliefs that set us up for emotional turmoil. "I have to be liked by everyone," "I have to be perfect at whatever I do," and "Everyone gets what they deserve" are common beliefs that Ellis sees as irrational. What's the solution? Said Ellis, "My approach to psychotherapy is to zero in as quickly as possible on the client's basic philosophy of life; to get him to see exactly what this is and how it is inevitably self-defeating; and to persuade him to work his ass off, cognitively, emotively and behaviorally, to profoundly change it" (quoted in Warga, 1988, p. 57).

It's not easy for people to get rid of their lifelong assumptions or open their minds to new ways of thinking. To meet the task, REBT therapists use blunt, confrontational techniques. "Why do you always have to make mountains out of

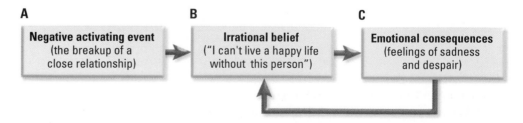

**FIGURE 17.5 Ellis's A-B-C theory of emotional distress**
According to Ellis, emotional distress is caused by irrational thoughts and the assumptions people make. This distress, in turn, helps to sustain the irrational beliefs.

tiny molehills?" "Where is it written that life is supposed to be fair?" "Who says you'll die if your marriage breaks up?" "What makes you think you'll be happier with more money?" are some of the argumentative questions typically asked. REBT therapists also encourage their clients to step out of character, try new behaviors, and engage in "shame exercises." In one case, for example, Ellis instructed a shy young woman to sing at the top of her lungs in the subway, strike up conversations in the supermarket, flirt with men she liked, and even ask them for dates—so she could see that these actions did not bring life to a crashing end. Another part of REBT is "psychoeducation," in which clients are lectured on the ABCs of emotional distress and given tapes of their own therapy sessions to review at home, along with booklets and audiotapes that teach the cognitive approach. Ellis himself made a series of self-help tapes, with straight-shooting titles such as "How to Stubbornly Refuse to Be Ashamed of Anything" (Bernard & DiGiuseppe, 1989).

Ellis's approach to psychotherapy may seem unconventional, but as a pioneer of the cognitive approach, he has had substantial impact on the practice of psychotherapy. Although it's difficult to know precisely the extent to which patients benefit from REBT (Haaga & Davison, 1993), studies designed to measure its effects on a patient's later adjustment and well-being have generally revealed positive results (Engels et al., 1993; Lyons & Woods, 1991). Reflecting immodestly on his own approach, Ellis (1996) said, "Most therapies help many clients to *feel better* . . . but only a few therapies help them *get better*" (p. 150).

### Beck's Cognitive Therapy

Like Ellis, Aaron Beck was trained in psychoanalysis, but he went on to devise a cognitive therapy when he noticed that his patients were filled with self-defeating beliefs (Beck, 1991). People who are depressed, for example, view themselves, their world, and the future through dark-colored glasses and make statements like "It's my fault," "I can't do anything right," "It's the story of my life," and "I'm a hopeless case" (Beck et al., 1979). People with anxiety disorders also think in ways that are maladaptive. They exaggerate the likelihood that they will fall victim to fatal accidents or diseases, and they engage in catastrophic thinking about their own bodies. When panic-disorder sufferers get aroused, for example, they often assume that they're having a heart attack or a stroke—beliefs that further heighten anxiety. Whether the problem is depression, an eating disorder, a sexual disorder, obsessive-compulsive disorder, drug abuse, schizophrenia, or a fear of speaking in public, there exists an element of irrational thinking that can and should be changed. Recently, Beck (1999) has applied his cognitive approach to understanding and treating "prisoners of hate," people whose dysfunctional beliefs lead them to become angry, hostile, and violent.

All cognitive therapists share the same objectives, but they differ in style. Following Ellis, REBT therapists forcefully confront clients with their irrational beliefs. In contrast, Beck—who has a soft, folksy manner—uses a gentler, more collaborative approach, helping people restructure the way they interpret events by means of a Socratic style of questioning. Beckian cognitive therapists commonly ask such questions as "What's the evidence for this idea?" "Are these facts, or your interpretation of the facts?" "Is there another way to look at the situation?" and "What's the worst that could happen?" (see Table 17.3).

Many techniques play an important role in Beck's cognitive therapy. One is to get clients to experience their distress in therapy. In one case, an eighteen-year-old woman who had frequent panic attacks was instructed to hyperventilate, which heightened her physiological arousal and triggered a state of panic. The therapist then helped her to interpret her bodily sensations in noncatastrophic terms. After four sessions, the woman's attacks subsided: "Every time my heart rate increased,

| TABLE 17.3    BECK'S COGNITIVE THERAPY IN ACTION |
| --- |

The following dialogue between Beck and a client epitomizes his approach to therapy. When the client came in, he was upset over the poor job he did wallpapering a kitchen. Note how Beck gets the client to realize that he was exaggerating his negative appraisal (Beck et al., 1979, pp. 130–131).

**Therapist:** Why didn't you rate wallpapering the kitchen as a mastery experience?

**Patient:** Because the flowers didn't line up.

**Therapist:** You did in fact complete the job?

**Patient:** Yes.

**Therapist:** Your kitchen?

**Patient:** No, I helped a neighbor do his kitchen.

**Therapist:** Did he do most of the work?

**Patient:** No, I really did almost all of it. He hadn't wallpapered before.

**Therapist:** Did anything else go wrong? Did you spill paste all over? Ruin the wallpaper? Leave a big mess?

**Patient:** No, the only problem was that the flowers didn't line up.

**Therapist:** Just how far off was this alignment of the flowers?

**Patient:** (holding his fingers about an eighth of an inch apart) About this much.

**Therapist:** On each strip of paper?

**Patient:** No . . . on two or three pieces.

**Therapist:** Out of how many?

**Patient:** About twenty or twenty-five.

**Therapist:** Did anyone else notice it?

**Patient:** No, in fact my neighbor thought it was great.

**Therapist:** Could you see the defect when you stood back and looked at the whole wall?

**Patient:** Well, not really.

I'd say, it's okay, it's no big deal" (Alford et al., 1990, p. 232). Keeping a diary is another important part of Beck's approach. Clients are encouraged to keep a daily log in which they describe the situation they were in, how they felt, what they were thinking, and how rational these thoughts were when they became upset. These assignments provide a basis for discussion and learning from one session to the next. Assigned reading, or bibliotherapy, is a third important technique. Clients are given books that explain the cognitive basis of psychological distress. Indeed, research shows that people benefit from reading cognitive-therapy self-help books that communicate the message "You feel the way you think" (Jamison & Scogin, 1995).

Cognitive therapy is popular among clinical psychologists. As noted, Ellis and Beck are the pioneers of the approach, but there are others as well. For example, Donald Meichenbaum (1985) uses stress-inoculation training, in which people are taught to make optimistic, positive self-statements—to insulate them from stress the way vaccines inoculate us against medical disease. Others within the cognitive tradition focus on problem-solving skills, feelings of self-efficacy, and behavioral self-control. Whatever the specific technique may be, cognitive therapy is now the most frequently taught orientation in American clinical-psychology graduate programs (Nevid et al., 1987) and is an effective form of treatment for a wide range of problems (McMullin, 2000).

## THE PROCESS OF DISCOVERY

# AARON T. BECK
*Cognitive Therapy*

**Q: How did you first become interested in psychiatry?**

**A:** I came to the field somewhat by accident. Although I was interested in psychiatry when I first entered medical school, I soon lost interest because I found the evidence for the then dominant psychoanalytic formulations to be weak. When I entered my residency in neurology, there was a shortage of psychiatry residents, so the neurology residents had to spend a rotation in psychiatry. During this rotation I became more interested in psychoanalytic thinking and I started conducting scientific experiments to put psychoanalytic theory on firmer ground. However, when I tested some of the ideas, I found that many of the basic propositions were not well supported. This experience got me thinking about simpler, more straightforward explanations of depression and other psychopathology.

**Q: How did you come up with your important discovery?**

**A:** My original formulations began when I was working with depressed patients in psychoanalytic psychotherapy. At one point I observed, to my surprise, that my patients experienced specific types of thoughts of which they were only dimly aware and did not generally report on during their free associations. These cognitions, which I came to term "automatic thoughts," seemed to arise quickly, as though by reflex. When I directed the patients to focus their attention on these automatic thoughts with a probe such as "What is going through your mind right now?" I found that they would frequently report a string of such thoughts. I also discovered these thoughts were biased against the patient and intimately tied to the emotion he or she was experiencing. For example, if someone had the automatic thought that she was "boring me," she would feel sad. I further noted that people could become aware of these thoughts and examine their validity—and even adjust the thoughts to conform to logic and reality. Finally, I observed that once the biased thinking changed, the person's emotional tenor changed as well.

**Q: How has the field you inspired developed over the years?**

**A:** In 1976, I posed the question "Can a fledging psychotherapy challenge the giants in the field—psychoanalysis and behavior therapy?" The work over the past four decades seems to have answered that question in the affirmative. Cognitive therapy for depression has developed into a very sophisticated model that has demonstrated superiority or equivalence to other forms of treatment, including drug treatments. Further research has found that the risk of relapse is less for depressed individuals who receive cognitive therapy compared with individuals who receive antidepressants. Cognitive therapy for anxiety has also seen tremendous growth—for panic disorder, social phobia, generalized anxiety disorder and posttraumatic stress disorder. More recent work has focused on personality disorders. Current work in the United Kingdom and Canada also applies cognitive principles to schizophrenia with surprisingly successful results.

**Q: What is your prediction on where the field is heading?**

**A:** I think cognitive therapy will become increasingly specialized and will develop more specified treatments for each of the particular disorders. For example, in our own unit we are working on specialized treatments for suicide attempters, Parkinson's disease, auditory hallucinations and delusions, and Borderline Personality Disorder. I also hope that a stronger effort will be made in ensuring that practitioners in the community are educated on delivering empirically supported treatments such as cognitive therapy.

*Aaron Beck is a University Professor Emeritus of Psychiatry. He is also President and founder of the Beck Institute for Cognitive Therapy and Research.*

## HUMANISTIC THERAPIES

When Carl Rogers was a young therapist, he noticed that his clients had a strong sense of self and an inner drive to grow, improve, and fulfill their potential. All the therapist has to do, he said, is provide warmth, a gentle, guiding hand, and a climate of uncritical acceptance, and clients will find the way to happiness and personal fulfillment.

**person-centered therapy** A humanistic psychotherapy in which a warm and accepting environment is created to foster self-insight and acceptance.

**Gestalt therapy** A humanistic form of psychotherapy in which clients are aggressively prompted to express their feelings.

With this simple advice, the humanistic approach to psychotherapy was born. This approach (1) trusts a client's growth instincts; (2) focuses on feelings, not cognitions or behavior; (3) is oriented in the here-and-now, not in the distant past; and (4) makes the client responsible for change. Over the years, two types of humanistic therapy have had a marked impact on clinical practice: person-centered therapy and Gestalt therapy.

**Person-Centered Therapy**   When 415 psychotherapists were asked to name the person who most influenced their work, Carl Rogers was cited more often than anyone else (Smith, 1982). The reason? In a profound way, Rogers redefined the role that a therapist should play: not detective, teacher, or adviser but a facilitator for the client. As Rogers put it, "Therapy is not a matter of doing something to the individual or inducing him to do something about himself. It is instead a matter of freeing him for normal growth and development" (1942, p. 7). Believing that people know what's right for themselves, Rogers let his clients call the shots. At various times, he referred to this approach as *nondirective, client-centered,* and *person-centered* (Farber et al., 1996).

Person-centered therapy is designed to provide a safe haven for people to clarify their feelings, their sense of who they are, and their hopes for what they would like to become, without fear of punishment or disapproval. To foster this process of self-exploration and discovery, person-centered therapists create a warm and caring relationship with the client. Specifically, they need to exhibit *empathy* (an ability to take the client's perspective in order to understand how he or she feels) and to offer *unconditional positive regard* (an unwavering respect for the client as a person—and these qualities have to be genuine, not put on) for people to open up and reveal themselves. Believing that counselors should not preach what's right and wrong, interpret problems, or give Dear Abby-like advice, person-centered therapists also use *reflection,* a nondirective, minimum-intervention technique in which the therapist actively listens to a client's statements, responding by paraphrasing what was said and seeking clarification. No interruption, no analysis, no evaluation. In this way, the therapist serves as a human mirror into which clients can see their feelings reflected clearly and without distortion. If psychotherapy were a dance, the person-centered client would lead, and the therapist would follow (see Table 17.4).

Underlying the Rogerian approach is the fundamental belief that the client, not his or her therapist, is ultimately responsible for making positive changes. As such, one would expect that Rogers would play a less directive role than, say, cognitive therapists who seek to effect change through various interventions. Is there any evidence of this difference in therapist–client interactions? Interestingly, yes. Nathaniel Raskin (1996) examined published case transcripts and counted the number of lines spoken by therapists and their clients. He found that although cognitive therapists Ellis and Beck did 67 percent of the talking in their sessions, Rogers accounted for only 29 percent of the lines spoken in his sessions. His technique truly was "person-centered."

**Gestalt Therapy**   Have faith in human nature, encourage people to introspect, listen with a sympathetic ear, and guide with a gentle hand, and you are a humanistic psychologist in the mold of Carl Rogers. Focus on feelings that are unconscious, show an interest in dreams, and use techniques that are dramatic and confrontational, and you have **Gestalt therapy**, which was devised by humanistic psychologist Frederick (Fritz) Perls.

Like Rogers, Gestalt therapists try to make people feel singly responsible for their own growth and development. In other ways, however, there is little resemblance.

## TABLE 17.4   PERSON-CENTERED THERAPY IN ACTION

The following dialogue between Carl Rogers and a young man who is upset over his relationship with his mother illustrates the technique of reflection. Note how skillfully Rogers helped his client clarify his feelings toward his stepfather. Without prompting, he moved from a blunt statement of mutual hatred, to one of unilateral hatred, to an expression of respect (Raskin, 1985, pp. 167–168).

**Client:**    You see I have a stepfather.

**Therapist:**    I see.

**Client:**    Let's put it this way. My stepfather and I are not on the happiest terms in the world. And so, when he states something and, of course, she goes along, and I stand up and let her know that I don't like what he is telling me, well, she usually gives in to me.

**Therapist:**    I see.

**Client:**    Sometimes, and sometimes it's just the opposite.

**Therapist:**    But part of what really makes for difficulty is the fact that you and your stepfather, as you say, are not . . . the relationship isn't completely rosy.

**Client:**    Let's just put it this way, I hate him and he hates me. It's that way.

**Therapist:**    But you really hate him and you feel he really hates you.

**Client:**    Well, I don't know if he hates me or not, but I know one thing, I don't like him whatsoever.

**Therapist:**    You can't speak for sure about his feelings because only he knows exactly what those are, but as far as you are concerned . . .

**Client:**    . . . he knows how I feel about it.

**Therapist:**    You don't have any use for him.

**Client:**    None whatsoever. And that's been for about eight years now.

**Therapist:**    So for about eight years you've lived with a person whom you have no respect for and really hate.

**Client:**    Oh, I respect him.

**Therapist:**    Ah. Excuse me. I got that wrong.

**Client:**    I have to respect him. I don't have to, but I do. But I don't love him, I hate him. I can't stand him.

**Therapist:**    There are certain things you respect him for, but that doesn't alter the fact that you definitely hate him and don't love him.

**Client:**    That's the truth. I respect anybody who has bravery and courage, and he does.

**Therapist:**    . . . You do give him credit for the fact that he is brave, he has guts or something.

**Client:**    Yeah. He shows that he can do a lot of things that, well, a lot of men can't.

**Therapist:**    M-hm, m-hm.

**Client:**    And also he has asthma, and the doctor hasn't given him very long to live. And he, even though he knows he is going to die, he keeps working and he works at a killing pace, so I respect him for that, too.

**Therapist:**    M-hm. So I guess you're saying he really has . . .

**Client:**    . . . what it takes.

---

Forget about nondirective beating around the bush, Perls used to say. Instead, put clients on the "hot seat." When they speak in ways that are not brutally honest—by slipping into the past to avoid the present or by talking in general, abstract terms rather than in first-person—they should be challenged. "Do you really *need* to stay in

**group therapy** The simultaneous treatment of several clients in a group setting.

this dysfunctional relationship, or do you *want* to?" "Do you *have* to work for seven days a week, or do you *choose* to?" "Is it that you *can't* say no, or that you *won't*?" "Why do you squirm in your seat, fold your arms, and cross your legs every time you say your sex life is fine?" "When you say it's hard for *people* to express anger, what you really mean is that you find it hard to show *your* anger. If that's what you mean, say so!" (Perls et al., 1951; Perls, 1969). To help clients confront unresolved issues, Perls developed some specific techniques—such as the *empty chair dialogue* in which the therapist guides the person through an imaginary conversation with a significant other. Typically, in this "dialogue," the client airs his or her complaint, venting, and blaming the significant other, often shifting roles to imagine and understand the other's likely response. A study of twenty-six clients who underwent Gestalt therapy for interpersonal problems revealed that those who expressed previously unmet needs in an empty chair dialogue felt better and improved more than those who did not (Greenberg & Malcom, 2002).

## GROUP-THERAPY APPROACHES

In the case study described at the start of this chapter, Yalom (1989) put Betty, his patient, into a therapy group. She felt isolated, craved companionship, and needed a fresh perspective. Betty resisted the idea at first, but went along. It worked like a charm. At one point, a young man named Carlos revealed to the group that he was dying of cancer, the disease that had terrified Betty ever since it took the life of her father. At first, these encounters with Carlos made Betty acutely anxious. She became physically ill and obsessed with the fear that she too would get cancer, lose weight, and shrivel away. No wonder Betty was obese, they all thought—she was fighting the skin-and-bones image of her father before he died. Whether it's true or not, this insight was a key to Betty's problems. Soon she began to diet, with her therapy group acting as a supportive community, rooting her on with every pound she shed. One male member half-jokingly said he would take her to Hawaii for the weekend if she lost a hundred pounds. It was the first time a man had ever shown an interest in her.

As this story illustrates, **group therapy** provides a valuable alternative to individual psychotherapy. Typically, one or two therapists work with four to ten clients at a time, and often the clients have similar problems. The benefits are numerous, as groups furnish social support and encouragement, new outlooks on old problems, and interpersonal experience for those who are shy or socially awkward. There are different types of group therapy. The format and goals depend on the therapist's theoretical orientation (Brabender, 2002).

In psychoanalytic groups, therapists interpret each member's interactions with the others in the same way that resistance and transference are interpreted in individual sessions. One psychoanalytic form of group therapy is *transactional analysis* (TA), in which the therapist analyzes the interactions between group members for clues concerning the individuals. In contrast, behavioral and cognitive groups seek to modify thoughts and behaviors, using members who have the same problem as both models and reinforcers. For example, social-skills training is often conducted in groups, as is systematic desensitization for people who have the same anxiety disorder (as when a group of people with agoraphobia are taken on a trip away from home). Among humanistic psychologists, groups are brought together to enhance personal development. One outgrowth of this approach is the *sensitivity-training* group, in which business executives, teachers, and others, in groups ranging in size from twelve to twenty persons, are taught to interact openly and with sensitivity. A close cousin of this is the *encounter group*, developed by Carl Rogers. In an encounter group, members express themselves with complete and brutal honesty—crying, yelling, laughing, and so on.

Encounter groups are not popular now, as they were in the 1960s and 1970s, but still popular today are specialized *self-help groups* in which people who share a common problem come together for mutual help and social support. The best known is Alcoholics Anonymous, or AA. AA was founded in 1935 and now has two million members worldwide. Many other groups are available for people with AIDS, battered women, parents without partners, compulsive gamblers, teenage mothers, drug addicts, rape victims, weight watchers, smokers, newly arrived immigrants, families of cancer victims, and so on. It's estimated that twenty-five million Americans will participate in thousands of self-help groups in the course of a lifetime (Kessler et al., 1997). People coming together for information and mutual support is a promising idea that no one can oppose. But are self-help groups effective? To date, these programs have not been extensively evaluated, so firm conclusions cannot be drawn (Christensen & Jacobson, 1994).

People often enter therapy because of problems that arise at home so many psychologists prefer to treat families, not individuals. There is no single approach, but **family therapies** in general treat the family as an interdependent social "system" in which the whole is greater than the sum of its parts (Cox & Paley, 1997). The therapist observes family members together—how they relate, what roles they play, and what alliances they form. Indeed, researchers have tried to analyze these therapy interactions in systematic ways (Friedlander & Heatherington, 1989). Problems within the family vary— a boy acts out to get attention from two busy working parents; a husband and wife don't get along and use their daughter as a scapegoat; a child reaches adolescence, but the parents don't recognize her need for independence; a father drinks too much, but everyone denies it and says that "he's just under the weather." Whatever the problem, whole families are gathered in an effort to heal old wounds and prevent further conflict (Minuchin, 1974; Hazelrigg et al., 1987; Glick et al., 2000).

*Alcoholics Anonymous is a successful self-help group that ensures anonymity—which is why these members turn their backs to the camera. Meetings held in community settings usually begin with a reading of the AA Preamble: "Alcoholics Anonymous is a fellowship of men and women who share their experience, strength, and hope with each other that they may solve their common problem and help others to recover from alcoholism. The only requirement for membership is a desire to stop drinking. . . ."*

## PERSPECTIVES ON PSYCHOTHERAPY

- *How can the effectiveness of psychotherapy be measured, and does it work?*
- *Are some forms of therapy more effective than others?*
- *What do all therapies have in common?*
- *And what does it mean to be "eclectic" in approach?*

At the heart of psychotherapy is the assumption that people have a capacity for change. Thus, two questions loom over the entire enterprise: Can humans help humans change? And are some forms of helping better than others? (Mahoney, 1991). For those interested in the answers to these questions, Allen Bergin and Sol Garfield's (1994) *Handbook of Psychotherapy and Behavior Change* provides a comprehensive review of much of this research.

### THE BOTTOM LINE: DOES PSYCHOTHERAPY WORK?

Read case studies written by psychotherapists, and you'll have the impression that success is guaranteed. Ask people who have undergone psychotherapy, and three

### REVIEW QUESTIONS

- *Define psychotherapy. What kinds of professionals use psychotherapy?*

- *Describe the roles of free association, resistance, and transference in psychoanalytic therapy.*

- *Describe the various behavioral therapy techniques.*

- *What assumptions underlie all cognitive therapies?*

- *What are the primary features of humanistic therapy?*

**family therapy**   Form of psychotherapy that treats the members of a family as an interactive system.

For an extensive online list of support groups and support-related services, from Aarskog syndrome (look it up!) to Yoga, visit http://www.support-group.com/

*"Two strangers meet by prearrangement; their purpose, to wrestle with life itself; their goal, to win from deadness more life for one of them; their risk, that one or both of them will find life filled with pain and anxiety for some period of time; their certainty, that if they persist in good faith with their struggle both will be changed in some measure."*

—JAMES F. T. BUGENTAL

## WHAT'S YOUR PREDICTION

People join social-support groups for hundreds of life problems. But do all problems trigger this need for social support, or are some problems "needier" than others? Kathryn Davison and her colleagues (2000) asked this question in a survey of thousands of social-support group members in New York, Los Angeles, Chicago, and Dallas. Look at the list below of eight support groups and make a prediction: Out of twenty health problem groups surveyed, adjusted for populations of sufferers, which four were the *most* heavily enrolled (M) and which were the *least* enrolled (L)?

| | | | |
|---|---|---|---|
| AIDS | ____ | Migraines | ____ |
| Chronic pain | ____ | Anorexia | ____ |
| Alcoholism | ____ | Breast cancer | ____ |
| Ulcers | ____ | Hypertension | ____ |

What kinds of illnesses lead people to seek each other out? In order, the top four illness groups were alcoholism, AIDS, breast cancer, and anorexia. In order, the least enrolled groups were for hypertension, migraine headaches, chronic pain, and ulcers. Do you notice a pattern in these results? What does it all mean? According to the researchers, people are most likely to affiliate for illnesses that are socially embarrassing or stigmatizing. Hence, AIDS patients are 250 times more likely to participate in a support group than are hypertension patients.

out of four will say they were "satisfied" or "very satisfied" with the outcome (Lebow, 1982). With such glowing reports, is there any reason for doubt?

Let's return to the *Consumer Reports* survey that opened this chapter. In that survey, 86 percent of those who saw a mental-health specialist reported feeling better after therapy and 89 percent were satisfied with the experience. In addition, psychiatrists, psychologists, and social workers were all equally effective—more so than family doctors. On the basis of these findings, Seligman (1995) concluded that psychotherapy works. Yet many psychotherapy researchers were critical of the study, which was based solely on the self-reports of a nonrepresentative group of former clients (Jacobson & Christensen, 1996; Strupp, 1996). Steven Hollon (1996) said, "I am curious what the magazine would have found had it surveyed the readers of supermarket tabloids regarding their experiences with psychics and faith healers. My suspicion is that people who make use of such 'professionals' are generally pleased with their services. . . . I doubt that I would be prepared to believe that psychic healing works" (p. 1026). In response, Seligman (1996) noted that in a similar *CR* survey on lawyers, consumers were much more negative. "In fact, the devout reader of *CR* would do well to scan any of their articles on service professions; he or she will have a hard time finding any profession rated as highly as mental health professionals" (p. 1075).

As in the past, there are two reasons that researchers are cautious when it comes to using personal endorsements from clients—or therapists, for that matter—to measure the effectiveness of psychotherapy. First, both therapists and clients are motivated to believe that their efforts were successful. Therapists want to affirm their professional value and integrity, and clients need to justify their investment of time and money. Researchers thus seek independent and objective measures of improvement—for example, pre- to posttreatment changes in test scores, behavior, or third-party evaluations. The second problem is that people often get better on their own—without treatment. This improvement may occur as a result of support received from friends and family members or simply because "Time heals all wounds." (You know what they say about the common cold: "Take medicine and your stuffy nose will disappear in seven days; do nothing and it will last a whole week.") If psychotherapy is to be judged effective, those who are treated should improve more than comparable others who are not. The question is whether they do.

In 1952, Hans Eysenck reviewed twenty-four psychotherapy studies and found that roughly two-thirds of all patients showed improvement. So far, so good. But there was a hitch: About two-thirds of people who were on waiting lists for therapy but were never actually treated also improved in the same time frame, on their own. Eysenck's blunt and pessimistic conclusion was that psychotherapy is worthless. His article stirred a major debate. Psychologists attacked the studies Eysenck had cited as well as his analysis of the results. It turned out, for example, that many of the control-group subjects were healthier initially than those who were treated, that some controls were taking drugs prescribed by physicians, and that they improved less than Eysenck believed (Bergin & Lambert, 1978).

Despite its shortcomings, Eysenck's article inspired an active, sophisticated generation of clinical researchers determined to evaluate psychotherapy outcomes. By 1980, when Mary Lee Smith and others reviewed the available research, there were 475 published studies involving literally thousands of patients. Using meta-analysis to statistically combine the results of these studies, they found that psychotherapy was effective for a whole range of problems—including anxiety disorders, low self-esteem, social problems, and addiction. As shown in Figure 17.6, the average psychotherapy patient improved more than did 80 percent of no-treatment controls. Smith and her colleagues (1980) concluded that "psychotherapy benefits people of all ages as reliably as schooling educates them, medicine cures them, or business turns a profit" (p. 183).

Although some psychologists still question the benefits of psychotherapy (Dawes, 1994), others have drawn similarly positive conclusions from the research evidence (Shapiro & Shapiro, 1982; Lipsey & Wilson, 1993; Russell & Orlinsky, 1996; Shadish et al., 1997). Today, many clinical researchers are exploring the links between processes and outcomes (Kopta et al., 1999). If a person started psychotherapy today, for example, how long would it take to feel better? Is there a timetable? Reviewing fifteen studies involving more than twenty-four hundred clients, Kenneth Howard and others (1986) found that the percentage of people who improved increased with the number of therapy sessions *up to a point*. After six months, or twenty-six sessions, 70 percent of the outcomes were successful. From then on, however, the improvement rate leveled off and additional sessions contributed only little more to the final outcome (see Figure 17.7). In follow-up studies, Howard and others (1996) found that different aspects of a person's well-being change at different rates during the course of therapy. The improvement appears to occur in three stages. First, patients report that they "feel better," then they experience relief from the specific symptoms that drove them into therapy, and finally, they begin to function more effectively at work, at home, and in their social relationships.

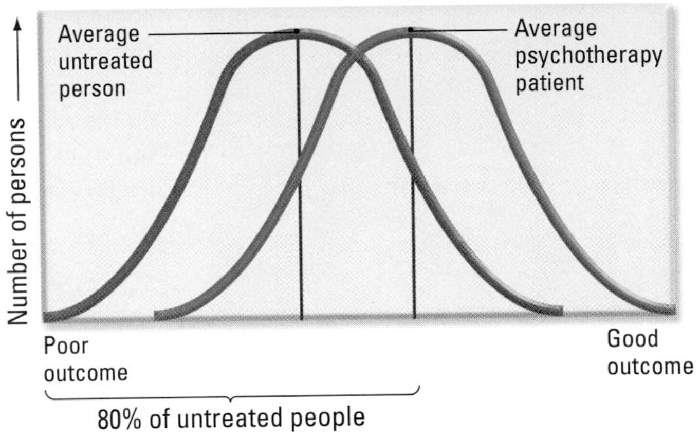

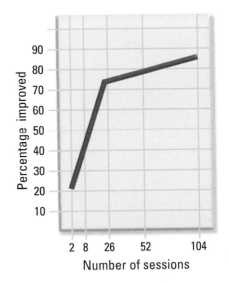

**FIGURE 17.6   The benefits of psychotherapy**
Summarizing the results of 475 studies, Smith and others (1980) found that the average psychotherapy client shows more improvement than 80 percent of the no-treatment controls.

## ARE SOME THERAPIES BETTER THAN OTHERS?

Some 80 percent of all therapy patients improve more than no-treatment controls; and 70 percent of those who improve do so within six months. These figures are interesting, you may think, but they're just averages, generalities. Don't some people derive more or less benefit than the average? Aren't some problems more amenable to change than others? What about the differences among the psychoanalytic, behavioral, cognitive, and humanistic approaches? Interestingly, Smith and her colleagues (1980) did compare the different types of therapies, and they found a surprising result: All approaches were effective, and all were *equivalent*—that is, despite radical differences in techniques, no single approach was consistently superior to another. This conclusion, supported in other studies as well, has been called the "Dodo bird verdict" after the *Alice in Wonderland* character who declared, after a race, that "everyone has won, and all must have prizes" (Stiles et al., 1986; Wampold et al., 1997).

The Dodo bird verdict poses a puzzling question: How can such different forms of treatment—ranging from a probing analysis of unconscious childhood conflicts, to a hard-nosed modification of behaviors or cognitions, to warm and nondirective reflection and acceptance—produce the same results? There are three answers to this question. First, specific techniques are less critical to the final outcome than are personal characteristics of the client and therapist (Lambert & Bergin, 1994). Second, the different approaches may well be equivalent on average, but the value of any one technique depends on the problem to be solved. Behavioral forms of therapy are ideal for extinguishing phobias, compulsions, a fear of public speaking, and other specific anxiety-related ailments (Bowers & Clum, 1988). But person-centered therapy is ideally suited to raising self-esteem (Smith et al., 1980), and cognitive therapy is particularly potent in the battle against depression (Dobson, 1989; Ablon & Jones, 2002). Perhaps with so many disorders listed in DSM-IV, psychotherapists

**FIGURE 17.7   Improvement in psychotherapy: the more the better?**
A summary of fifteen studies indicates that there is continued improvement over twenty-six sessions but that the rate of improvement then levels off. At one session per week, six months seems to be an ideal amount of time.

*On the island of Bali, people with mental disorders are often seen as victims of witchcraft and are sent for treatment to a balian, like the one shown here. Using massage, healing smoke, holy water, and other rituals, the balian would drive evil wind spirits from the patient's body. Like healers and shamans in other cultures, balians are often successful. Perhaps nonspecific factors that contribute to psychotherapy—such as hope and social support—are also at work in these rituals.*

should act as "matchmakers" and use different techniques with different clients. A third explanation is that all psychological therapies are more similar in important ways than one might think. In other words, despite the surface differences, all psychotherapies have much in common at a deeper level—and these common factors, not the specific techniques, provide the active ingredients necessary for change (Stiles et al., 1986; Strupp, 1989).

## WHAT ARE THE ACTIVE INGREDIENTS?

Regardless of differences in theoretical orientations and techniques, there are three common, "nonspecific" factors at work in all brands of psychotherapy.

**A Supportive Relationship**  First, all therapists provide a *supportive relationship* that contains warmth, trust, concern, encouragement, reassurance, acceptance, a shoulder to cry on, and agreement on treatment goals and processes. Indeed, the better the "working alliance" is between a therapist and client, the more favorable the outcome (Horvath & Symonds, 1991; Horvath & Luborsky, 1993; Stiles et al., 1998). In one study, for example, schizophrenic patients who had a good rapport with their therapists were more likely than those who did not to remain in therapy, take their prescribed drugs, and improve in the end (Frank & Gunderson, 1991).

Why is this one-on-one human relationship so important? Hans Strupp (1996) believes that people find it immensely gratifying to be listened to with concern, empathy, and respect. "The simple and incontrovertible truth," he says, "is that if you are anxious or depressed, or if you are experiencing difficulties with significant people in your life, chances are that you feel better if you talk to someone you can trust" (p. 1017). Support is a key to a healthy alliance between psychotherapist and patient, but it's also important that the therapist understand that the patient belongs to a specific cultural group. In the United States, for example, African, Asian, Hispanic, European, and Native Americans bring to therapy different family backgrounds, religious beliefs, values, worldviews—and problems. Therefore, mental-health workers must seek to become "multiculturally competent" when working with patients from cultural groups other than their own (Sue & Sue, 1999).

**A Ray of Hope**  Second, all therapies offer a ray of *hope* to people who are unhappy, demoralized, and down on themselves. In all aspects of life, we are motivated by positive expectations, faith, and optimism (Seligman, 1991). The same is true in psychotherapy. It's even been suggested that high expectations alone are sufficient to produce change even when they are not justified (Prioleau et al., 1983). This suggestion is based on the **placebo effect**, an established medical phenomenon whereby patients will show more improvement when they are given an inactive drug, or placebo, than when they are not. Somehow, believing can help make it so—which is how faith healers, shamans, and witch doctors all over the world have been known to perform "miracle cures" with their rituals. So is that *all* there is to psychotherapy, just one big placebo effect? No, carefully controlled studies have shown that although people randomly assigned to receive a placebo therapy (bogus exercises, group discussions, self-help tapes, and sugar pills) are often better off than those who do not, they typically do not improve as much as those who undergo psychotherapy (Barker et al., 1988). Hope may be necessary, but it's not sufficient.

**An Opportunity to Open Up**  A third common ingredient is that all psychotherapies offer an ideal setting for *opening up*, a chance for people to confide in

**placebo effect**  The curative effect of an inactive treatment that results simply from the patient's belief in its therapeutic value.

someone and talk freely about their troubles—maybe for the first time. In a series of controlled studies on the healing power of opening up, James Pennebaker (1997b) brought college students into a laboratory and asked them to write for twenty minutes about either past traumas or trivial events. He found that when people wrote about having been mistreated, the divorce of their parents, the death of a family pet, and other traumas, their systolic-blood-pressure levels rose during disclosure but then dipped below preexperiment levels. Afterward, they felt better, had a more positive outlook, and exhibited a decline in the number of visits to the campus health center over the next six months. Other studies, too, have shown that keeping secrets is stressful and that "letting it out" has therapeutic effects on our mental and physical health—effects that are especially strong when the events being described are highly traumatic (Smyth, 1998).

Why does it help to open up? Why do *you* sometimes feel the need to talk out your problems? One possibility, recognized many years ago by Freud, is that the experience itself provides a much-needed *catharsis*, a discharge of psychic tension—like taking the lid off a boiling pot of water to slow the boiling. Another interpretation, favored by most therapists, is that talking about a problem helps you to sort out your thoughts, understand the problem better, and gain *insight*, in cognitive terms. Whatever the reason, it's clear that psychotherapy provides an ideal setting for self-disclosure: The listener is patient, caring, and nonjudgmental, and what's said is kept in confidence. This last point is critical because despite the potential for gain, opening up can also cause great distress when the people we choose to confide in react with rejection or unwanted advice, or worse, disclose to others what was said (Kelly & McKillop, 1996).

## WHAT'S THE FUTURE OF PSYCHOTHERAPY?

The twenty-first century will place urgent new demands on the practice of psychotherapy. The terrorist attack of 9/11 and the stress it unleashed have left no doubt of the need for mental-health professionals to help those traumatized by violence. Because of increasing mobility in the world, it's also clear that more immigrants will need help adjusting to new cultures. The average life expectancy continues to climb, forcing an increasingly elderly population to cope with the mental-health toll of aging and illness. Prevalence rates for depression have never been higher. Yet as health costs skyrocket, and as people turn for insurance reasons to managed-health-care programs, it's clear that the consumer demand is for psychological therapies that are quick, inexpensive, and proven effective. If Charles Dickens were alive today, he might well say of the profession, "It was the best of times, it was the worst of times."

Two trends are evident—and will continue—at least partly in response to the pragmatic need for quick, cheap, and effective treatment. One trend is for therapists to be flexible in their approach and *eclectic*, borrowing ideas and techniques, as needed, from different orientations rather than identify themselves with a single orientation. This blurring of boundaries has been occurring for years. Psychoanalysis first emerged from the medical model, behaviorists and humanists came forward in response to psychoanalysis, and cognitive therapies evolved from a desire to soften up hard-core behaviorism. Each approach had staked out a position that seemed radically different from others. Yet today, psychoanalytic therapists are playing a more active and interpersonal role than in the past. Behavioral and cognitive approaches have formed a hybrid known as cognitive-behavior therapy—and some of them now talk about unconscious processes and self-concepts. Person-centered therapists are more directive than they used to be, while many behaviorists are less directive.

"I utilize the best from Freud, the best from Jung and the best from my uncle Marty, a very smart fellow."

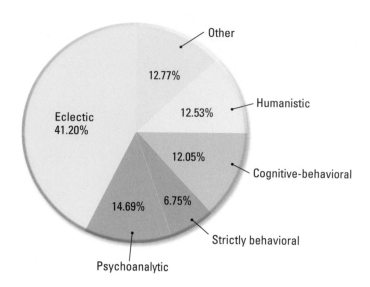

**FIGURE 17.8** **Orientations of psychotherapists**
Presented here are the results of a national survey in which 422 practicing clinical and counseling psychologists were asked to describe their theoretical orientations (Smith, 1982). The trend toward eclecticism continues today.

## REVIEW QUESTIONS

- *Why are researchers cautious about personal endorsements from clients and therapists?*

- *Describe evidence for the effectiveness of psychotherapy. How is it that all forms appear equally effective?*

- *Describe the three factors that contribute to an effective therapy experience.*

- *What does it mean for a psychologist to take an eclectic approach?*

- *What are two trends in treatment today?*

As illustrated in Figure 17.8, national surveys show that more psychotherapists describe themselves as *eclectic* than identify themselves with a single orientation (Smith, 1982; Beitman et al., 1989). More recent surveys suggest that this percentage has risen even higher over the past few years, leading sixty-two of the most prominent psychotherapy researchers in the United States to predict more of the same in the future (Norcross et al., 2002). According to this model, specific treatment techniques should be chosen on a case-by-case basis, depending on the client, his or her problem, and the desired outcome (Norcross, 1991). In this vein, Arnold Lazarus (1996) describes the ideal clinician as an "authentic chameleon." Reflecting on his forty-plus years of experience, Lazarus concludes that "a therapist must decide when and how to be directive, supportive, reflective, cold, warm, tepid, formal or informal. He/she must determine when and when not to be confrontational; when and whether to be earthy, chummy, or casual; when to self-disclose or remain enigmatic; when to be soft-nosed, gentle and tender, and when to come on like gangbusters" (pp. 143–144).

A second trend born of economic necessity is to identify, through research, "empirically supported treatments" that therapists can choose from. As noted earlier, there are roughly four hundred techniques used in the practice of psychotherapy. Although the Dodo bird verdict suggested that all therapies are generally effective, there is reason to believe that some approaches are better than others—depending on the problem. On the basis of controlled studies, in which patients getting a certain treatment are compared to placebo- and no-treatment controls, an APA Task Force (1995) came up with a preliminary list of twenty-five types of intervention that pass the research test. These efforts enable clinical psychologists to offer clear, practical recommendations in manuals such as *A Guide to Treatments That Work* (Nathan & Gorman, 1998). This trend toward the standardization, derisively referred to as "manualization," is highly controversial, and therapists are evenly split in their opinion on it (Addis & Krasnow, 2000). Some psychologists applaud the effort to impose scientific standards on practice; others say it is too inflexible and fear it will take the "art" out of—and dehumanize—psychotherapy. Indeed, the good therapist can be seen as "a disciplined improvisational artist, not a manual-driven technician" (Bohart et al., 1998, p. 145). With all the pressure on mental-health workers to provide a service that is cost effective, it will be interesting to see how this trend develops in years to come (Beutler, 2000; Chambless & Ollendick, 2001; Kendall & Chambless, 1998).

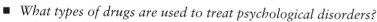

## MEDICAL INTERVENTIONS

- *What types of drugs are used to treat psychological disorders?*
- *What are the advantages of these drugs, and what are the drawbacks?*
- *What is electroconvulsive therapy, what is psychosurgery, and when, if ever, are these treatment methods used?*

For people who suffer from severe anxiety, mood disorders, and schizophrenia, medical interventions may provide an alternative or supplement to psychotherapy. Based on established links among the brain, the mind, and behavior, three types of medical treatment are available: drug therapy, electroshock therapy, and psychosurgery.

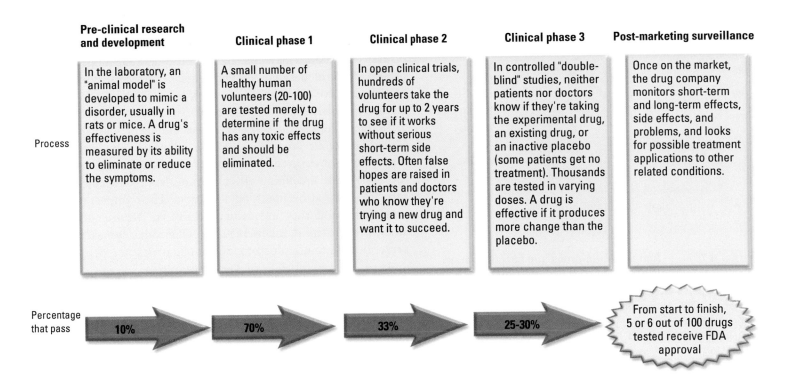

**FIGURE 17.9** **What it takes to bring a new drug to market**
Pharmaceutical companies are constantly creating new compounds whose chemical structures suggest they may treat anxiety, depression, schizophrenia, or other disorders. Once a drug company identifies a compound with promise, it must undergo a rigorous process to test its efficacy and safety. It takes five to ten years to complete the process and bring a new drug to market (U.S. Food and Drug Administration).

## DRUG THERAPIES

In 1952, French psychiatrists Jean Delay and Pierre Deniker eliminated the symptoms of a schizophrenic patient with a wonder drug called *chlorpromazine*. David Healy (2002) argues that this discovery is as important in the history of medicine as the discovery of penicillin. From then on, the use of medications in the treatment of psychological disorders has skyrocketed in popularity. As a result, pharmaceutical companies find themselves in a race against time—and against each other—to create, test, gain government approval, and market newer and better drugs (see Figure 17.9).

Today, in the booming area of **psychopharmacology**, a vast array of drugs is used for psychotherapeutic purposes (Schatzberg & Nemeroff, 1998). Most of them work by acting on neurotransmitters, the biochemicals that relay impulses between neurons. For the hundreds of thousands of people who used to languish in psychiatric wards and hospitals, these drugs opened doors to life in the community—for better and for worse (see Figure 17.10). Michael Gitlin's (1996) book, *The Psychotherapist's Guide to Psychopharmacology*, describes these drugs in clear, nontechnical language—their trade names, purposes, dosage levels, effects on the brain and behavior, the benefits, potential side effects, and dangers. The main types are summarized in Table 17.5.

**Antianxiety Drugs** Whether the cause is internal or external, and whether the condition is chronic or acute, there are many possible sources of anxiety and many people who at times suffer through it. Thus, it's no wonder there has always

*"The goal of the twenty-first century is to find a 'penicillin' for mental illness."*

—NANCY ANDREASEN (2001)

**psychopharmacology** The study of the effects of drugs on psychological processes and disorders.

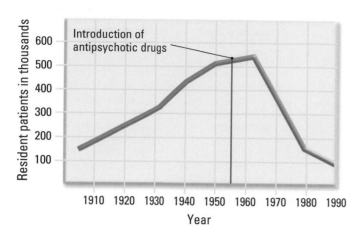

**FIGURE 17.10** **Antipsychotic drugs and hospitalization trends**
The inpatient population in U.S. mental hospitals has declined sharply since 1960, putting the treatment emphasis on outpatient community care. This trend resulted from the widespread use of antipsychotic drugs, which were introduced in the 1950s. Some benefited greatly from deinstitutionalization. Others—without families or a capacity to cope on their own—were left homeless.

"Of course your daddy loves you. He's on Prozac—he loves everybody."

been a great demand for—and abuse of—**antianxiety drugs,** or tranquilizers. During the 1950s, many doctors prescribed *barbiturates* for anxious patients. Barbiturates combat anxiety by depressing central nervous system activity. They are effective but highly addictive. They help us to relax but also cause us to become clumsy and drowsy.

In the 1960s, a new class of tranquilizers was developed. Called *benzodiazepines,* they include chlordiazepoxide (Librium), diazepam (Valium), and alprazolam (Xanax). These drugs have the same desired calming effect and are less likely than barbiturates to cause drowsiness or addiction. Their impact is almost immediate, and they are most effective in treating generalized anxiety disorder, if taken regularly. Benzodiazepines are often prescribed by family doctors, not psychiatrists, for people in the midst of a stressful time of life. These drugs are not as safe as once thought, however. They are dangerous when combined with alcohol, and they may produce temporary side effects such as slurred speech, dry mouth, lightheadedness, and diminished psychomotor control. When a regular user stops taking them, the result may be a two-week "rebound anxiety" more intense than ever (Julien, 1992). A drug called *buspirone,* which was first released in 1986, provides an alternative. It acts more slowly, usually taking a few days or weeks to have an effect, but it is also less likely to promote dependence or have unpleasant side effects.

**Antidepressants**     In the 1950s, doctors noticed that drugs being used to treat high blood pressure and tuberculosis had dramatic side effects on mood—sometimes causing depression, other times euphoria. At about the same time, researchers found that these drugs also increased levels of the neurotransmitter norepinephrine, a chemical cousin of adrenaline found in a part of the brain that regulates mood and emotion. Together, these strands of evidence suggested that depression is associated with lower-than-needed norepinephrine levels. Later research also linked

| TABLE 17.5 | TYPES OF DRUG TREATMENTS | |
|---|---|---|
| **Drug Type** | **Trade Name** | **Beneficial Effects** |
| **Antianxiety Drugs** | | |
| chlordiazepoxide | Librium | Act as tranquilizers and, if taken |
| diazepam | Valium | regularly, can be used in the treatment |
| alprazolam | Xanax | of generalized anxiety disorder. |
| buspirone | BuSpar | |
| **Antidepressants** | | |
| imipramine | Tofranil | Have mood-elevating effects and |
| fluoxetine | Prozac | can relieve depression. |
| **Mood Stabilizer** | | |
| lithium | Lithium Carbonate | Calms mania and, if continuously taken, may reduce bipolar mood swings. |
| **Antipsychotic Drugs** | | |
| chlorpromazine | Thorazine | Reduce hallucinations, delusions, and other |
| clozapine | Clozaril | positive symptoms of schizophrenia. |
| risperidone | Risperdal | |

**antianxiety drugs**     Tranquilizing medications used in the treatment of anxiety.

depression to serotonin. The practical result was the development of **antidepressants** such as *imipramine* (Tofranil), drugs that tend to increase the supply of norepinephrine or serotonin and elevate mood. Studies have shown that the antidepressants are effective. They are not addictive and cause only minor side effects such as dry mouth, constipation, blurred vision, and fatigue.

Today, psychiatrists are most likely to prescribe a new class of antidepressants, called selective serotonin reuptake inhibitors (SSRIs). The best known of these drugs is *fluoxetine*—better known by its trade name, Prozac. By blocking the absorption and removal of serotonin from neural synapses without affecting other neurotransmitters, Prozac is effective with only mild side effects. So are its younger cousins Luvox, Paxil, Celexa, and Zoloft. Prozac is the most widely used antidepressant in the world. A large-scale survey of trends in the treatment of depression, from 1987 to 1997, revealed that the proportion of treated individuals who used antidepressants doubled, from 37 to 74 percent, an increase attributable to the arrival of Prozac and the other SSRIs (Olfson et al., 2002).

Prozac has also been the subject of controversy. Many psychiatrists have observed that in some patients, Prozac can relieve not only depression but also certain anxiety disorders and eating disorders. It also seems to transform the personality, making users happier, more self-confident and productive at work, and more engaged and relaxed in social situations. As a result, this "wonder drug" in a little green-and-white capsule is sometimes prescribed for people who are not clinically depressed. This last development is unsettling and raises hard ethical questions concerning the proper use of psychoactive drugs (Kramer, 1993). Some psychiatrists have also expressed concern that this new breed of antidepressants is indiscriminately overprescribed and not without risk (Breggin, 2001). (For a nonmedical approach to seasonal depression, see *How To Beat the Winter Blues*.)

"Discouraging data on the antidepressant."

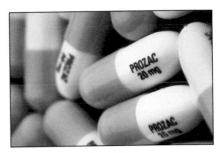

*Encased in a small green-and-white capsule, Prozac is the most widely prescribed antidepressant in the world. There are 24 million users in 197 countries.*

### Mood Stabilizers

For bipolar disorder—which is characterized by wild manic-depressive mood swings—different, mood-stabilizing drugs are used. The best known of these is **lithium**—an inexpensive mineral found in rocks, water, plants, and animals. Taken on a continuous basis, lithium can usually prevent moods from reeling out of control and is considered the most effective treatment for bipolar disorder (Schou, 1997). Common side effects include dry mouth, thirst, weight gain, excessive urination, fatigue, and tremors. Taken in dosages that are too high, lithium can prove dangerous, even life-threatening. For bipolar patients who don't respond to lithium or who can't tolerate the side effects, other mood-stabilizing drugs can be used instead (Rivas-Vazquez et al., 2002).

### Antipsychotic Drugs

In the past, people with schizophrenia who exhibited hallucinations, delusions, confused speech, exaggerated displays of emotion, paranoia, and utterly bizarre behavior were dismissed as lost causes. All that changed in the 1950s, however, with the discovery of **antipsychotic drugs**, which reduce the intensity of these positive "uncontrollable" symptoms. As noted earlier, the first in this class of drugs was *chlorpromazine*, better known as Thorazine. By blocking the activity of dopamine, the neurotransmitter that has been linked to schizophrenia, antipsychotic drugs enable many people previously confined to hospital wards to live relatively normal lives.

Chlorpromazine has two drawbacks. The first is that it often does not relieve the negative symptoms of schizophrenia—symptoms such as flat affect, apathy, immobility, and social withdrawal, which may be linked to structural defects in the brain, not to dopamine (see Chapter 16). The second drawback is that very unpleasant

**antidepressants** Drugs that relieve depression by increasing the supply of norepinephrine, serotonin, or dopamine.

**lithium** A drug used to control mania and mood swings in people with bipolar disorder.

**antipsychotic drugs** Drugs that are used to control the positive symptoms of schizophrenia and other psychotic disorders.

# BEAT THE WINTER BLUES

People who live in a four-season climate have a sense that their emotional states can be influenced by the weather. Have you ever had a case of the "blues" after a succession of overcast days, only to be rejuvenated by a cheerful dose of sunshine? After a dreary winter, have you ever caught "spring fever" the first time the sun and air were warm enough for you to shed your coat? If so, you have company. And lots of it.

Over the past few years, psychologists and psychiatrists have discovered that although everyone is affected to a greater or lesser extent, some people suffer from **seasonal affective disorder**, or **SAD**—a form of depression that strikes during the short, dark, cold days of late autumn and winter (see Figure 17.11). Every year, people with SAD who live in relatively cool regions of the world fall into a lethargic emotional state that resembles hibernation. They become listless, drowsy, and withdrawn. They also sleep more, eat more, crave pasta and other carbohydrates, gain weight, lose interest in sex, and falter in their work and social relationships. Consistent with the hypothesis that SAD is related to climate, surveys show that both SAD sufferers and people in general report feeling worse during the winter months and that the prevalence of SAD increases with a region's distance north of the equator. SAD is far more common, for example, in Alaska and New Hampshire than in Maryland and Florida (Booker & Hellekson, 1992).

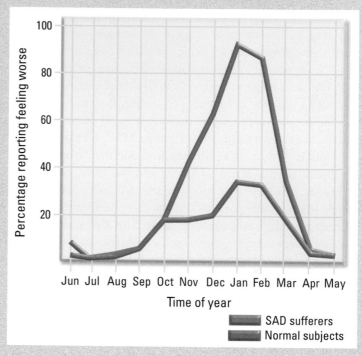

**FIGURE 17.11   Seasonal differences in SAD**
This graph depicts the percentage of sufferers and "normal" subjects who report feeling blue each month of the year. Most people feel worse in winter, a pattern that is exaggerated among those with SAD (Kasper & Rosenthal, 1989).

---

**seasonal affective disorder (SAD)** A form of depression that strikes during the short, dark days of late autumn and winter.

side effects are common. In the worst of cases, these include Parkinson disease–like symptoms such as shaking and a loss of control over voluntary movements, stiff muscles, sluggishness, blunted affect, weight gain, and sexual impotence in men. These symptoms can often be treated with other drugs. Still, psychiatrists and patients must weigh the benefits of relief from the symptoms of schizophrenia against the costs of drug-induced side effects (Gitlin, 1996).

Recent research suggests that *clozapine* (Clozaril), an antipsychotic medication first released in 1990, may be more effective than its predecessors. Clozapine operates through a different mechanism. It is effective at controlling hallucinations and other psychotic symptoms (even in some patients who do not respond to Thorazine) without the undesirable side effects on motor functions. Yet for about 2 percent of those who take it, clozapine has a toxic effect on the white blood cells and increases the risk of a rare but fatal blood disorder. Released in 1994, an even newer drug, *risperidone* (Risperdal), seems to provide all the benefits of clozapine without the severe toxic effects. "In many ways, risperidone seems destined to become *the* first-line antipsychotic medication" (Gitlin, 1996, p. 394).

*During the winter months, daily exposure to bright fluorescent light helps some people to combat their SAD.*

It's not yet clear why the winter months cause SAD or why some people are affected more than others. One theory traces the problem to the pineal gland—a tiny structure in the brain that secretes melatonin, the hormone that causes drowsiness (light inhibits its secretion). Another theory is that the circadian rhythms, the internal biological clocks, of SAD sufferers are disrupted by the relative lack of sunshine. Whatever the specific cause, there is, for many sufferers, a simple and often effective solution: light therapy.

Relying on controlled studies, Norman Rosenthal (1998) and others recommend one to two hours a day, at a time that is convenient, in front of intensely bright fluorescent lights with your eyes open (Lam, 1998; Rosenthal & Blehar, 1999). After one to two weeks, the clouds of gloom should begin to lift and you should feel more energetic. This treatment should be repeated until spring season brings in an abundance of natural sunshine. Then put the lights away until the autumn leaves start to fall (a portable head-mounted light visor is also now available). When researchers from the National Institute of Mental Health conducted a long-term follow-up study of fifty-nine former patients who had been treated with light therapy, they found after an average of eight years that many still suffered from SAD. Overall, 41 percent continued to use the light treatment with positive results, but for others with more severe cases, the light treatment alone was often not sufficient (Schwartz et al., 1996).

## PERSPECTIVES ON DRUG THERAPIES

"There's a place for drugs for some people, but they are overrated and overprescribed. In comparisons of psychotherapy and drugs, by and large drugs do not appear to be the superior treatment." "To say that psychiatric drugs are overrated is a stupid statement. . . . For a wide range of psychiatric disorders, it's well documented that these drugs are the most effective treatments." The first remark was made by psychologist Roger Greenberg, the second by psychiatrist Paul Bender (in Goleman, 1989). Which of these statements is more accurate? Is psychological therapy preferable to drug therapy, or is it the other way around?

*"No pill can help me deal with the problem of not wanting to take pills; likewise, no amount of psychotherapy alone can prevent my manias and depressions. I need both."*

—KAY REDFIELD JAMISON

The debate over psychotherapy and drugs is as old as the split between psychology and medicine. But there is no winner, no right or wrong answer, no contest. In the spirit of taking an eclectic approach to the treatment of disorders, mental-health professionals are advised to make their judgments on an individual case basis and not exclude either approach as a matter of principle. Clearly, the drugs have helped

**electroconvulsive therapy (ECT)** Electric-shock treatments that often relieve severe depression by triggering seizures in the brain.

hundreds of thousands of people once hidden away in psychiatric institutions, and they will continue to do so in years to come. And clearly, there are people whose disorders do not respond as well to psychological forms of treatment. There are reasons for caution, however. One is that some drugs produce side effects that are unpleasant and, at times, dangerous under high dosage levels. A second is that some drugs produce a physical or psychological dependence, relegating patients to play a passive role in their own healing process. The person who gets into the habit of popping a Valium at the first sign of tension learns how to control the aversive symptoms of anxiety but not how to cope with the source of the problem.

In an effort to match treatments to specific disorders, many researchers are currently evaluating the relative effectiveness of psychological and drug therapies. So far neither approach has emerged as uniformly more effective. In one large-scale study, for example, the National Institute of Mental Health compared cognitive therapy, an interpersonal form of psychotherapy that focuses on social relations, an antidepressant, and a placebo control group in which the patients were given an inactive pill, attention, and encouragement. A total of 239 patients of twenty-eight therapists in Oklahoma, Pennsylvania, and Washington, D.C., were randomly assigned to receive one form of treatment for a total of sixteen weeks. Among those in the placebo group, 29 percent were no longer depressed when the "treatment" was ended. In the other groups, that number was near 50 percent—and the psychological and drug therapies were equally effective (Elkin et al., 1989). Other research shows that the outcome changes over time and that for those who are depressed, cognitive therapy may be slower than antidepressants to take effect but is then more likely to last (Dobson, 1989; Hollon et al., 1991). With drugs that are used to combat depression and those used in the treatment of anxiety, patients are often kept for long periods of time on a "maintenance" dosage to lower the risk of a relapse (Thase & Kupfer, 1996; Lydiard et al., 1996).

## ELECTROCONVULSIVE THERAPY

It used to be a terrifying experience, a Frankenstein-like nightmare come to life. The patient would be dragged kicking and screaming to a hospital table and strapped down by the arms and legs, lying helpless as a white-coated physician leaned over to administer the pain. The patient would then be jolted by 100 volts of electricity to both sides of the skull, triggering seizures, unconsciousness, and muscle spasms so violent that they sometimes resulted in broken bones. The shock also had a mind-scrambling effect, causing confusion and amnesia for chunks of time before and after the treatment.

**Electroconvulsive therapy (ECT)** has a curious history. In the nineteenth century, an "electric machine" was used to stimulate the nerves. But it was not until 1938 that an Italian doctor, Ugo Cerletti, introduced ECT—and the notion that mental illness could be cured by quite literally shocking the system. From the start, it was clear that ECT provided relief from depression. It was widely used in the 1950s and 1960s but fell out of favor when antidepressant drugs became available. Eventually, it made a quiet comeback when procedures were made safer and more humane. Today, consenting ECT patients are given a general anesthetic and a muscle relaxant to prevent injury from convulsions. They then receive briefer, milder shock to the head, which sets off a brain seizure that lasts for a minute or so. As in surgery, patients regain consciousness within minutes, unable to remember what happened. The entire process consists of ten or so sessions administered over a two-week period.

Although ECT has always stirred controversy, and is often misunderstood, it is now a viable alternative for people who are deeply and chronically depressed, and

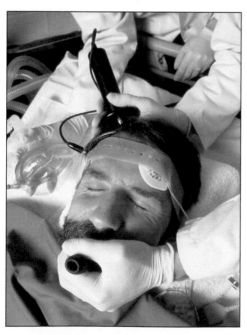

*A person receiving electroconvulsive therapy. In this case, the shock is delivered to the side of the head.*

suicidal, and not responsive to psychological or drug therapies (Abrams, 2002; American Psychiatric Association Task Force, 2001; Fink, 1999). It has also been used with some success to treat mania in people with bipolar disorder and some of the symptoms of schizophrenia. The convulsions triggered by electrical current to the brain provide quick, sometimes permanent, relief. ECT is also safe, as it results in only 2 deaths per 100,000 treatments, a mortality rate lower than that for childbirth (Abrams, 1988; Endler & Persad, 1988). Brain scans of ECT patients show no signs of structural brain damage (Coffey et al., 1991; Devanand et al., 1994). As far as side effects are concerned, however, they undergo a temporary state of confusion. When ECT patients regain consciousness, they often cannot recall events of the recent past and are disoriented about where they are and how they got there.

ECT techniques continue to be refined for the more than 100,000 patients per year who receive it. For example, researchers recently found that better clinical results are produced when shocks are delivered to the forehead than to the temple (Bailine et al., 2000). It's still not clear why ECT is effective—that is, whether it works by stimulating seizures in inactive parts of the brain, inhibiting overactive parts, or triggering the release of scarce neurotransmitters. What is clear is that despite its therapeutic value, there is a stigma that follows those who use it. In the words of one patient who describes the treatment as lifesaving, "You should see the look in people's eyes when I tell them. They think I'm a freak, like Frankenstein, so I've learned to keep it a secret" (Fischer, 2000, p. 46).

## PSYCHOSURGERY

The most controversial of interventions is **psychosurgery,** the removal of portions of the brain for the purpose of treating psychological disorders. In 1935, Portuguese neurologist Egas Moniz performed the first *lobotomy,* a surgical procedure in which he cut the nerves that connect the frontal lobes to the rest of the brain, in order to tame patients who were agitated, manic, and violent. Moniz based this procedure on his belief that pathological mental activity occurred in the frontal lobes, which needed to be severed "to cut off the flow of morbid ideas." The operation was so highly regarded that in 1949 Moniz was awarded a Nobel Prize in medicine. As reported in *The New York Times* (1949), "Hypochondriacs no longer thought they were going to die, would-be suicides found life acceptable, sufferers from persecution complex forgot the machinations of imaginary conspirators. . . . Surgeons now think no more of operations on the brain than they do of removing an appendix."

Was the lobotomy all that it was cracked up to be? In a book entitled *Great and Desperate Cures,* Elliot Valenstein (1986) described how thousands of mentally ill patients around the world were mutilated on the operating table: "After drilling two or more holes in a patient's skull, a surgeon inserted into the brain any of various instruments—some resembling an apple corer, a butter spreader, or an ice pick—and, often without being able to see what he was cutting, destroyed parts of the brain" (p. 3). The results were often tragic. The lobotomy was supposed to relieve patients of crippling emotions, but it also profoundly altered their core personalities, creating people who were like robots: lethargic, flat, emotionless, unmotivated, and without aim or purpose. Talking about her lobotomized husband, one woman said, "His soul appears to be destroyed; he is not the man I once knew." These lobotomies were not merely the work of incompetent or evil physicians, but were practiced within the mainstream medical community (Pressman, 1998). Mercifully, the procedure was virtually extinguished when antipsychotic drugs came into use (Swayze, 1995).

Psychosurgery is more sophisticated today than in the past, enabling neurosurgeons to "damage the brain to save the mind" (Rodgers, 1992). Specific regions

**psychosurgery**   The surgical removal of portions of the brain for the purpose of treating psychological disorders.

### REVIEW QUESTIONS

■ *Describe the drug therapies available today. What are the advantages and disadvantages associated with them?*

■ *What is electroconvulsive therapy (ECT) and for what disorders is it effective?*

■ *Summarize the history of psychosurgery. When is it likely to be used?*

of the brain can now be destroyed with precision through ultrasonic irradiation or by sending electrical currents through fine wire electrodes. For people who are stricken with uncontrollable seizures, for example, the nerve fibers involved can be deactivated. Psychosurgery is also used sparingly, but with some success, on people incapacitated by chronic anxiety and depression or by severe obsessive-compulsive disorders that are not responsive to other forms of treatment (Baer et al., 1995). Still, there is debate over the science and ethics of psychosurgery, a treatment of last resort. After all, whether the outcome is positive or negative, the effect is irreversible.

## THINKING LIKE A PSYCHOLOGIST ABOUT TREATMENT

Over the years, the number of people seeking professional help for psychological problems has climbed dramatically. The helpers are psychiatrists, clinical psychologists, psychiatric nurses, social workers, and marital and family counselors (see Figure 17.12). The kinds of help provided range from the most intensive one-on-one psychoanalysis to behavioral, cognitive, humanistic, and group therapies. In a small number of cases, obscure techniques are practiced, as in mandala therapy, electric-sleep therapy, alpha-wave therapy, deprivation therapy, and the Zaraleya Psychoenergetic Technique. In a growing number of cases, people are turning to nonprofessionals, such as the many self-help and support groups that are widely available (Christensen & Jacobson, 1994). And in the newest development, some people are seeking psychotherapy and counseling by computer, at home, online, and anonymous—on a "virtual couch" (Hamilton, 1999). There is only a smattering of research on the uses of online therapy, but the results so far are encouraging (Jacobs et al., 2001).

Faced with an overwhelming array of treatment alternatives, people in the market for professional help have choices to make and problems to solve. One problem is that although someone must have a professional degree and supervised training to become licensed as a psychologist, anyone can hang up a shingle, offer a service, and call it therapy. From among those who are qualified, how do you select someone, and what kind of experience can you expect to have? Should you set your sights on psychotherapy or medical treatment?

If you need help and don't know where to turn, it's probably best to start with personal recommendations from a close friend, relative, family doctor, or teacher. Or you might check with the college counseling service, which is free, or a local community mental-health center. If you have a health

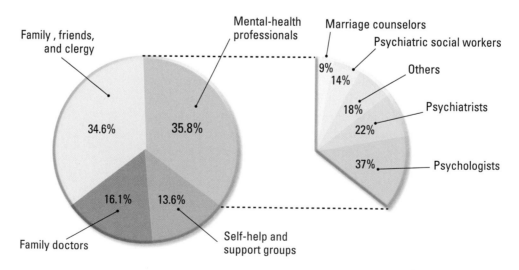

FIGURE 17.12 **Where people turn for help**
The *Consumer Reports* study revealed that among respondents who had a psychological problem, many turned for help to friends, relatives, clergy, and family doctors. Among those who sought help within the mental-health profession, psychologists were seen more frequently than other types of specialists.

*Anyone needing psychological assistance can check with the American Psychological Association's Help Center at http://helping.apa.org/, or call 1-800-964-2000.*

insurance policy that covers psychological services, find out whether the policy covers what you want. If not, the hourly rates vary. Shop around and talk to two or three therapists until you are satisfied that you have found one you like, respect, and can work with. Talk openly about your goals and ask about fees, credentials, orientations, and values, to determine whether the two of you are on the same wavelength. Remember: The working relationship between therapist and client is an essential first step on the road to successful treatment.

All this brings us back to an important theme in the study of psychological disorders and treatment: the possibility of change. Under normal conditions, our personalities remain relatively stable throughout our adult lives. Individuals who are outgoing at one point in time are likely to remain that way later in life. But changes in behavior can be made, as when someone seeks to overcome shyness. When people suffer through a mental disorder, the need for change takes on an added dimension of importance. Some problems are relatively easy to overcome, others more difficult. Through psychological and medical forms of therapy, however, the possibilities for improvement are real. Whether the specific goal is to overcome a fear, lower anxiety, lift depression, or clear the mind of illogical thoughts and perceptions, there is reason for hope, which is necessary for change.

# SUMMARY

T reatment raises the basic question of the possibilities and limits of human change. The two primary models of treatment are psychological and medical.

## PSYCHOLOGICAL THERAPIES

The term **psychotherapy** refers to all forms of treatment in which a trained professional uses psychological techniques to help people who are distressed. The four major approaches are psychoanalytic, behavioral, cognitive, and humanistic.

### PSYCHOANALYTIC THERAPIES

Orthodox psychoanalysis aims for catharsis and insight. Its key technique, pioneered by Freud, is **free association,** in which patients say whatever comes to mind without censoring it. Often, the patient free-associates about dreams while the therapist tries to get behind the manifest content to the latent content. **Resistance**—a patient's tendency to block painful thoughts—can be an obstacle but can also signal that therapy is heading in the right direction. The same is true of **transference,** whereby the patient displaces intense feelings for others onto the therapist. On the basis of these behaviors, the therapist offers interpretations to help the patient gain insight.

In briefer psychoanalytic therapies, the analyst plays a more active role, focuses less on the patient's past, and puts more emphasis on current life problems. The psychoanalytic approach has been criticized on various grounds. Yet despite the criticisms, it has left a strong mark on therapeutic practice.

### BEHAVIORAL THERAPIES

Rather than search for deep problems, **behavioral therapies** use learning principles to modify the symptoms. Classical-conditioning techniques include **flooding** the patient with an anxiety-provoking stimulus until the anxiety is extinguished. **Systematic desensitization,** a form of counterconditioning, pairs gradual exposure to an anxiety-provoking stimulus with relaxation training. **Aversion therapy** is designed to produce an aversive reaction to a harmful stimulus.

Other behavioral therapies use the principles of operant conditioning. **Token economies** reward patients for desirable behaviors; for dangerous behavior, punishment may be necessary. **Biofeedback**—learning to use feedback from the body to control physiological processes—is useful for health problems such as tension-related headaches. Assertiveness training and other types of **social-skills training** use the techniques of modeling, rehearsal, and reinforcement.

## COGNITIVE THERAPIES

**Cognitive therapies** focus on maladaptive perceptions and thoughts. Developed by Ellis, **rational-emotive behavior therapy (REBT)** bluntly confronts people with their irrational beliefs and provides "psychoeducation" on ways to change. Beck's cognitive therapy takes a more collaborative approach, giving clients homework assignments and role-playing exercises. These and other cognitive approaches are now the most common approaches to psychotherapy.

## HUMANISTIC THERAPIES

Acting as a facilitator, Rogers developed **person-centered therapy,** which creates a warm, caring environment to promote self-insight. Person-centered therapists offer empathy and unconditional positive regard. Through reflection, the therapist becomes an emotional mirror for the client. **Gestalt therapy,** developed by Perls, also makes clients responsible for their own change, but it focuses more on unconscious feelings and dreams, and it aggressively challenges clients to express their feelings.

## GROUP-THERAPY APPROACHES

An alternative to individual therapies, **group therapy** involves working with several clients simultaneously and together. In transactional analysis, a psychoanalytic therapist analyzes the interactions among group members. Behavioral and cognitive therapies can also take place in groups. Humanistic psychology has spawned sensitivity-training groups, encounter groups, and various self-help groups. In **family therapies,** the members of a family are treated together as an interdependent social system.

# PERSPECTIVES ON PSYCHOTHERAPY

Is psychotherapy effective? Are some approaches better than others? What are the active ingredients of effective psychotherapy? These are among the important questions raised over the years.

## THE BOTTOM LINE: DOES PSYCHOTHERAPY WORK?

As the reaction to the recent *Consumer Reports* mental-health survey showed, psychologists have long argued about the effectiveness of psychotherapy. Meta-analysis has shown that psychotherapy patients experience more improvement, on average, than people who are not treated. After about six months of therapy, however, improvement rates appear to level off.

## ARE SOME THERAPIES BETTER THAN OTHERS?

Overall, the different forms of psychotherapy are about equally effective. Some work better on particular problems than others, but all share certain features in common that make them more similar in their effects than different.

## WHAT ARE THE ACTIVE INGREDIENTS?

There are three common attributes of all therapies that constitute the active ingredients for a successful outcome: (1) a supportive relationship; (2) hope, which, as the **placebo effect** demonstrates, can itself produce improvement; and (3) an ideal setting in which the patient is able to open up and confide in another person.

## WHAT'S THE FUTURE OF PSYCHOTHERAPY?

In need of speedy and effective forms of treatment, most therapists today use a pragmatic, flexible, eclectic strategy. Thus, they borrow ideas and techniques from the various approaches. There is also a trend toward standardization in the use of techniques shown empirically to be effective for certain disorders.

# MEDICAL INTERVENTIONS

Medical interventions take three major forms: drug therapy; electroconvulsive, or shock, therapy; and psychosurgery.

## DRUG THERAPIES

**Psychopharmacology** is concerned with the effects of certain drugs on mental processes and disorders. **Antianxiety drugs** include buspirone and the widely used class of benzodiazepines. Research linking depression to neurotransmitters led to the development of **antidepressants,** such as the controversial new drug fluoxetine (Prozac). The mood stabilizer **lithium,** a mineral found in nature, can control mood swings in bipolar disorder. For schizophrenia and other psychotic disorders, **antipsychotic drugs** often reduce the positive symptoms, though often with side effects.

## PERSPECTIVES ON DRUG THERAPIES

In the debate about the relative merits of psychoactive drugs and psychotherapy, there is no one answer. On the one hand, drugs have helped hundreds of thousands of patients; on the other, they can have unpleasant or dangerous side effects, and some produce physical or psychological dependence.

## ELECTROCONVULSIVE THERAPY

Though once a nightmare-like experience, **electroconvulsive therapy (ECT)** now provides milder electric shock that can relieve severe depression by triggering seizures in the right side of the brain.

## PSYCHOSURGERY

**Psychosurgery**, the most controversial medical intervention, involves removing portions of the brain to treat a psychological disorder. The technique of lobotomy, once popular, has fallen into disrepute. Today's psychosurgery is more sophisticated, targeting specific regions of the brain with ultrasonic irradiation or electrical currents. But safer methods are available, and the effects of psychosurgery are irreversible.

## KEY TERMS

psychotherapy (**p. 672**)

free association (**p. 673**)

resistance (**p. 674**)

transference (**p. 674**)

behavioral therapy (**p. 677**)

cognitive-behavioral therapy (**p. 677**)

flooding (**p. 677**)

systematic desensitization (**p. 680**)

aversion therapy (**p. 683**)

token economy (**p. 684**)

biofeedback (**p. 684**)

social-skills training (**p. 684**)

cognitive therapy (**p. 686**)

rational-emotive behavior therapy (REBT) (**p. 686**)

person-centered therapy (**p. 690**)

Gestalt therapy (**p. 690**)

group therapy (**p. 692**)

family therapy (**p. 693**)

placebo effect (**p. 696**)

psychopharmacology (**p. 699**)

antianxiety drugs (**p. 700**)

antidepressants (**p. 701**)

lithium (**p. 701**)

antipsychotic drugs (**p. 701**)

seasonal affective disorder (SAD) (**p. 702**)

electroconvulsive therapy (ECT) (**p. 704**)

psychosurgery (**p. 705**)

## THINKING CRITICALLY ABOUT TREATMENT

1. Imagine yourself as a therapist. Which type of therapy do you think you would practice? Why? Now imagine yourself as a client. Which type of therapy would you prefer to experience? Why?

2. Browse your local bookstore, and you will probably find a large section devoted to self-help books. What types of therapies are likely to be addressed in such books? Are particular disorders more amenable to such self-treatment?

3. In many states, people with psychiatric diagnoses are required by law to receive drug therapy (often, but not always, antipsychotic drugs). Discuss the ethics of such court-ordered medication. Do people have the right to be psychotic?

4. The role of culture in psychological disorders was discussed in the previous chapter. Speculate as to the role of culture in the treatment of disorders. In what ways might cultural factors affect the therapeutic relationship? Are all therapies equally effective for all cultures?

# Health and Well-Being

## DOES STRESS LOWER RESISTANCE?

### THE SITUATION

This time you really outdid yourself. You're one of 420 volunteers in a medical experiment for which you agreed to risk exposure to a common-cold virus. You'll be reimbursed for all travel expenses, and for nine days you'll receive free room and board in the clinic. So you pack your bags, check in, and sign an informed-consent statement.

The first two days are hectic. First you're given a complete medical examination that includes a blood test. Then you fill out a stack of questionnaires. You answer questions about your mood, personality, health practices, and recent stressful experiences (such as a death in the family, pressures at work, or the breakup of a relationship). Then it happens. To simulate the person-to-person transmission of a virus, an attendant drops a clear liquid solution into your nose. If you're lucky, you were randomly assigned to the control group and receive only saline. If not, then you're in an experimental group and receive a low dose of a cold virus—just what you need. These exposures tend to produce illness at rates of 20 to 60 percent.

You are now quarantined in a large apartment for seven days—alone or with one or two roommates. Every day, you're examined by a nurse who takes your temperature, extracts a mucus sample, and looks for signs of a cold: sneezing, watery eyes, stuffy nose, hoarseness, sore throat, and cough (you don't know it, but the nurse also keeps track of the number of tissues you use). Basically, the researchers are interested in two results: (1) Are you infected (is there a virus in your system)? (2) Do you have a cold (as judged by the various symptoms)? What you don't realize is that the researchers are trying to see if there is a link between the recent stress in your life and your susceptibility to illness.

### MAKE A PREDICTION

On the basis of the questionnaires initially filled out, you and others are classified as having a high or low level of stress in your life. Does this psychological factor make a person more or less vulnerable to viral infection? Among those who are infected, does recent life stress elevate the risk of catching a cold? All participants were healthy at the start of the project—and not a single saline control subject developed a cold. Among those exposed to the virus, however, 82 percent became infected, and 46 percent caught a cold, symptoms and all. A virus is a virus, and there is no escape. But were the rates significantly different among the high- and low-stress groups? What do you think?

1. Were high-stress participants more likely to become infected?     YES     NO
2. Were high-stress participants more likely to catch a cold?     YES     NO

### THE RESULTS

In 1985, the prestigious *New England Journal of Medicine* published a study that failed to find a link between psychological factors and medical outcomes. In an accompanying note, the journal's editor took the opportunity to scoff at the very notion that a person's mental state can affect physical health. Six years later, Sheldon Cohen and others (1991) published the study just described in the same *New England Journal of Medicine*—an event that marked a "turning point in medical acceptance of a mind/body connection" (Kiecolt-Glaser & Glaser, 1993).

The results of this study were convincing. Life stress was not correlated with the rate of infection. Among those exposed to a virus, 85 percent of the high-stress participants and 81 percent of the low-stress participants became infected. Among those who were infected, however, high-stress participants were more likely to catch a cold than were the low-stress participants—53 percent compared to 40 percent. In fact, when participants who had been housed with infected roommates were eliminated from the analysis (because of the risk that they had been reexposed), the high-stress participants were still more likely to catch a cold than their low-stress counterparts—45 percent to 28 percent. Thus, once infected, people whose lives are filled with stress are particularly vulnerable to illness.

## WHAT DOES IT ALL MEAN?

This study reveals that there is a correlation between life stress and susceptibility to illness. Correlations do not prove causality, however, so we cannot conclude from this study alone that stress *per se* has this effect (it's theoretically possible, for example, that they are under stress because they are physically vulnerable). However, other researchers are finding that stress lowers resistance and compromises the immune system, the body's first line of defense against illness. Studies show that the activity of the immune system's white blood cells can be altered temporarily in participants who are exposed to even a mildly stressful laboratory experience—such as a difficult mental task, a gruesome film, the recollection of bad memories, loud noise, or a bad social interaction (Kiecolt-Glaser et al., 1992; Martin, 1998).

This research has profound implications. Until recently, psychological and medical researchers believed that the human brain and immune system were separate and noninteracting. Not so. We now know that the organs of the immune system are richly endowed with nerve fibers, providing a direct pipeline to the brain—and that psychological factors such as stress can play an important role. The result is a new field that focuses on the seamless interplay of mental and physical health. This new field is called **psychoneuroimmunology (PNI)**: *psycho* for mind, *neuro* for the nervous system, and *immunology* for the immune system (Ader et al., 2001). Later in this chapter, we'll see that PNI is generating a great deal of excitement in all areas of psychology.

We've seen throughout this textbook that psychology is a remarkably diverse and eclectic discipline. Some psychologists define what they do as the study of the mind; others prefer to focus on behavior. Some are interested in the evolutionary and biological roots of human nature; others are interested more in cognitive and affective processes, growth and development, social and cultural factors, personality, or clinical disorders. Some of us build theories and conduct research to understand basic human processes; others want to apply what is known to improve health, education, law, life in the workplace, and other aspects of the human condition. It has all become so diversified that Sigmund Koch (1993)—a prominent psychology historian—believes the discipline should be renamed the Psychological Studies.

Koch may have a point. A more important point, however, is that although psychology appears fragmented on the surface, many researchers in different areas of specialization unite in sharing a common objective: *to help improve our health and well-being and to enhance the quality of our lives.* In this chapter, we'll try to put psychology's puzzle pieces together. Beginning with the concept of the self and moving to the link between the mind and the body, we'll examine some of the new and exciting health-related questions that are captivating researchers at the start of this twenty-first century.

# MIND OVER MATTER

- *In what ways has the study of psychology revealed the power of the human mind?*
- *What is the placebo effect, and what does it tell us?*

Australian Aborigines believe that sorcerers have the power to cause death by pointing a bone at a person. The !Kung of Africa believe that malaria can be caused by the death of a loved one. Many Western religious leaders maintain that faith heals all wounds. Shortly after the death of their wives, men die at a rate three times greater than others of the same age. Natives of Fiji and other Pacific islands walk barefoot over beds of glowing hot coals without pain, blisters, or burns. Some doctors say they can prolong the lives of terminally ill patients through visualization (close your eyes, concentrate on the cancer in your body, and imagine that your disease-fighting white blood cells are gobbling up the cancer cells like Pac-Man). Still others advocate the power of positive thinking, laughter, confession, psychotherapy, prayer, meditation, yoga, jogging, subliminal self-help tapes, hypnosis, biofeedback, neurofeedback, massage, acupuncture, social support, family pets, and screaming at the top of your lungs. Some of this advice is without merit. But as we'll see, a good deal of research supports the general point that we can improve our own health by learning to control not only our behavior but our minds as well.

In *The Healing Brain*, Robert Ornstein and David Sobel (1987) contend that "the brain minds the body," for the brain's primary function is not perception, consciousness, learning, thought, language, memory, motivation, or emotion—but health maintenance. According to Ornstein and Sobel, "The brain is the largest organ of

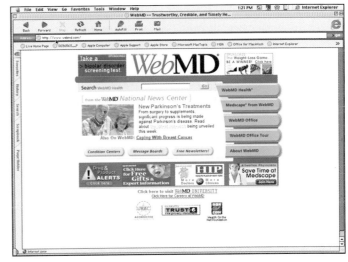

*Today, a wealth of health-related information is available on Internet sites such as WebMD.*

*Walking barefoot on red-hot coals is an annual event at Mount Takao, Japan. This ritual may seem to demonstrate the power of mind over matter, but actually the wood coals are poor conductors of heat—and fire walkers often wet their feet before walking.*

## *Debunking the Myth*

# THAT PLACEBO EFFECTS ARE "ALL IN THE MIND"

A classic and profound illustration of the theme that people can use the mind to heal the body can be seen most clearly in the placebo effect, the observation that all sorts of interventions can improve a person's health through the powers of suggestion, faith, and reassurance (Harrington, 1997). For a wide range of ailments, people often feel better simply because they *think* they have received an effective treatment. Estimating that 30 to 40 percent of patients experience relief from symptoms after taking a placebo, psychiatrist Walter Brown (1998) asks, "Should doctors be prescribing sugar pills?"

It is common for people to think that placebo effects are all in the mind—that although inactive treatments can make us feel better, the physical improvements are imagined, not real. This is not true. In an early demonstration of the placebo effect, Robert Sternbach (1964) gave to volunteer participants a white sugar pill that contained no active ingredients. At first, participants were told that the pill contained a drug that would stimulate a strong churning sensation in the stomach. The next time they were told that it would reduce their stomach activity and make them feel full. On a third occasion, they were informed that the pill was only a placebo. The result: Participants always swallowed the same tablet, yet they exhibited measurable changes in stomach activity consistent with their expectations. Other research has shown that placebos can influence a wide range of physical changes, including changes in cholesterol levels and hair loss (Ernst & Abbot, 1999).

Over the years, placebos have been used to treat allergies, headaches, insomnia, constipation, skin rashes, upset stomachs, chronic pain, and other ailments. That is why, in order to test the effectiveness of a new drug or other form of treatment, researchers must demonstrate that the participants who received that drug improved more than others who *believed* they had received it but did not. Only then can the actual effect of the treatment be separated from the power of suggestion. Somehow, in the seamless interplay of mind and body, beliefs transform reality.

*"Your body hears everything your mind says."*

—NAOMI JUDD

secretion in the body, and the neuron, far from being like a chip within a computer, is a flesh-and-blood little gland, one that produces hundreds of chemicals. These chemicals do not, for the most part, serve thought or reason. They serve keeping the body out of trouble" (p. 11). Taking the argument one step further, Howard Friedman (1991), author of *The Self-Healing Personality,* notes that although he never saw a death certificate marked "death due to unhealthy personality," there is a link to such chronic conditions as headaches, ulcers, asthma, arthritis, and even cancer. In *Mind-Body Deceptions,* Steven Dubrovsky (1997) argues that in "the psychosomatics of everyday life," the mind can often be used to heal the body. It all rings familiar the expression "Mind over matter."

The power we all have to shape and alter our own experiences is a recurring theme in psychology. Elsewhere in this book, we saw that the perception of an object's size is determined not just by the size of its retinal image but also by the perceiver's knowledge of what the object is and its distance from the eye. We saw that accident victims who have an arm or leg amputated often feel pain in the missing limb even though no pain receptors are stimulated. And we saw that people often develop intense fears of harmless objects, construct memories of past events that did not occur, cure headaches with biofeedback, elevate their mood by smiling, and create self-fulfilling prophecies by behaving in ways that confirm their own beliefs.

Is the placebo effect real? Danish researchers Asbjorn Hrobjartsson and Peter Gotzsche (2001) reviewed 114 medical studies that compared patients who received placebos for various illnesses with those who received no treatment and concluded that the two groups did not differ much in their treatment outcomes. When this review was published in *The New England Journal of Medicine,* the Boston Globe wrote of the placebo effect, "It's a scam;" the *New York Times* called it "More myth than science." In fact, powerful placebo effects are found all the time—*for some conditions* (even the Danish researchers admitted that placebos have proved effective for pain-killing purposes). As Walter Brown put it, "If you tested penicillin on 40 different clinical conditions, you would get similar results: it works for some infections but it won't do anything for arthritis" (quoted in Gibbs, 2001).

The placebo effect is not a magical occurrence, or a miracle, or even a purely mental phenomenon. And psychologists would not accept the claims made in the medical community solely on the basis of stories, anecdotes, and case studies. So is there a way to explain what Norman Cousins (1989) described as the biology of hope? The process is not well understood—probably because there is not one process, but many. Some have suggested that the positive expectations communicated by a confident and optimistic doctor can trigger the release of endorphins, naturally occurring morphine-like substances in the brain that provide temporary relief from pain (Levine et al., 1978). Others speculate that placebos reduce people's anxiety about being sick, which dampens the release of stress hormones that lower the body's resistance (Taylor, 1998). In a study of male depressed patients, those given a placebo exhibited some of the same changes in glucose metabolism activity in the brain as those who received a common antidepressant (Mayberg et al., 2002). In a PET-scan study of Parkinson's patients—whose loss of motor control is caused by a shortage of the neurotransmitter dopamine—those injected with a placebo showed a measurable pick-up in the release of dopamine (Fuente-Fernandez et al., 2001). When it comes to placebos, the question is not *if* they work, but *when* and *how* they work.

One of the most profound illustrations of this theme is in the widely documented *placebo effect*—a psychological form of treatment routinely observed in medical circles (see Chapter 17). A placebo is any medical intervention (including inactive drugs, counseling, or surgery) designed to improve one's condition merely through the power of suggestion. In past years, sick people were forced to consume potions made of frog sperm, lizard tongues, crocodile dung, fly specks, unicorn horns, and ground snake. They were also subjected to shock treatments, bloodletting, forced vomiting, freezing, and blistering. It seems a miracle anyone survived. Yet accounts of early medical practices indicate that many people were "cured" by these peculiar remedies. The reason: The patient's faith and hope are important parts of the healing process (Harrington, 1997; Brown, 1998). (See *Debunking the Myth That Placebo Effects Are "All in the Mind."*)

This chapter describes recent developments in the psychology of health and well-being on two fronts. First, we'll explore the topic of the self—the ways in which we think and feel about ourselves and the consequences of self-awareness for our mental and physical health. Next, we'll examine the topic of stress—what causes it, what effects it has on the body, and what coping mechanisms are most adaptive. As we'll see, people can use their minds to improve the quality of their lives.

*"For a wide range of afflictions, 30 to 40 percent of patients experience relief after taking a placebo."*

—WALTER A. BROWN

## REVIEW QUESTIONS

- *Describe some examples that illustrate the power of the human mind.*

- *Are placebo effects all in the mind, or do they produce real change?*

- *How have psychologists attempted to explain the placebo effect?*

## THE SELF AND WELL-BEING

- *In what ways do people with high and low self-esteem differ?*
- *What role does self-awareness play?*
- *Is it more adaptive to harbor positive illusions or accurate perceptions of ourselves?*

You and I and just about everyone else are motivated by a need for self-esteem, and satisfying that need is critical to our entire outlook on life. People with high self-esteem tend to be happy, healthy, productive, and successful. They tend to persist longer at difficult tasks, sleep better at night, and have fewer ulcers. They are also more accepting of others and less likely to conform to peer pressure. In contrast, people with low self-esteem are more anxious, depressed, pessimistic about the future, and prone to failure (Brown, 1991).

People with high self-esteem are confident and bring to new challenges a winning and motivating attitude. In contrast, people lacking in self-esteem also lack confidence, so they bring to new tasks a losing attitude that traps them in a vicious, self-defeating cycle. Expecting to fail, they become anxious, exert less effort, and "tune out" on life's important challenges. Then when they fail, people who are low in self-esteem blame themselves—which makes them feel worthless and even more incompetent (Brockner, 1983; Brown & Dutton, 1995). People with low self-esteem may also be prone to illness. Research suggests that making people aware of their negative self-evaluations has adverse effects on the immune system, the body's capacity to ward off disease (Strauman et al., 1993).

### THE SELF-AWARENESS "TRAP"

If you carefully review your daily routine—classes, work, leisure activities, social interactions, meals, and so on—you'll probably be surprised at how little time you actually spend thinking about yourself. In a study that illustrates this point, more than one hundred people, ranging in age from nineteen to sixty-three, were equipped for a week with electronic beepers that sounded on average every two hours between 7:30 AM and 10:30 PM. Each time the beepers went off, participants interrupted whatever they were doing, wrote down what they were thinking at that moment, and filled out a questionnaire. Out of forty-seven hundred observations, only 8 percent of all recorded thoughts were about the self. Even more interesting is that when participants did think about themselves, they reported feeling relatively unhappy and wished they were doing something else (Csikszentmihalyi & Figurski, 1982).

This is an interesting correlation. Is it really unpleasant to think about ourselves? Is self-awareness a mental trap from which we need to escape? Perhaps. Many psychologists have found that self-focus brings out our personal shortcomings the way staring into a mirror draws our attention to every blemish on the face. According to **self-awareness theory**, certain situations predictably force us to turn inward and become the object of our own attention. When we talk about ourselves, glance in a mirror, stand before an audience or camera, watch ourselves on videotape, or behave in a conspicuous manner, we enter a state of heightened self-awareness that leads us to compare our behavior to some standard. This comparison often results in a negative discrepancy and a drop in self-esteem as we discover that we fall short of our ideals (Wicklund, 1975).

**Is Self-Consciousness an Adaptive Trait?**  In *Escaping the Self*, Roy Baumeister (1991) argued that contemporary Western culture places so much

**self-awareness theory**  The theory that self-focused attention leads people to notice their shortcomings, thus motivating a change in behavior or an escape from self-awareness.

**FIGURE 18.1    Self-awareness theory**
Focusing attention on the self makes us aware of our self-discrepancies. This awareness pressures us either to match our behavior to ideal standards or else to tune out.

emphasis on selfhood and identity that it is a constant burden to keep up. To maintain a positive image for ourselves and others, we read books on how to make a good impression, replace clothing when it is no longer fashionable, starve ourselves thin, spend countless dollars on cosmetic surgery, rationalize failure and rejection, and blush when we say something foolish in front of others. The more energy we invest in the self, the more we have to lose. Society is so enamored of, obsessed with, and addicted to the self, writes Baumeister, that "maintaining self-esteem can start to seem like a full-time job!" (p. 12).

If focusing on the self is a problem, what's the solution? Self-awareness theory suggests there are two ways to cope with the discomfort: (1) behave in ways that might reduce one's self-discrepancies, or (2) withdraw from self-awareness. According to Charles Carver and Michael Scheier (1981), the solution chosen depends on whether you expect that you can successfully reduce the self-discrepancy—and whether you're satisfied with the progress you make once you try (Duval et al., 1992). If you are, you'll match your behavior to the standard; if not, you'll tune out, seek distractions, and turn attention away from the self. This process is depicted in Figure 18.1.

In general, research supports these predictions of self-awareness theory (Gibbons, 1990). When people are self-focused, they are more likely to behave in ways that are consistent with their values and socially accepted ideals. When the prospects for discrepancy reduction seem grim, however, they take the second route: escape from self-awareness. In one experiment, for example, participants worked on a task in a room that did or did not have a full-length mirror facing them. Participants who received negative feedback about their task performance were quicker to leave the room when it had a mirror to remind them of their failure than when it did not (Duval & Wicklund, 1972).

Using escape as a coping strategy has some disturbing health-related implications. One concerns the use of alcohol. According to Jay Hull, people often drown their sorrows in a bottle as a way to flee mentally from the negative effects of self-awareness. To demonstrate this process, Hull and Richard Young (1983) administered what was supposed to be an IQ test to male participants and then gave them false feedback suggesting they had either succeeded or failed. Supposedly as part of a separate study, participants were then asked to taste and rate different wines. They did not realize it, but the experimenters kept track of how much wine they drank during the fifteen-minute tasting period. As predicted, participants who had high scores on the Self-Consciousness Scale drank more after failure than after success, presumably to escape from the negative implications for their self-esteem. Among those who were low in self-consciousness, there was no difference in alcohol

"More wine! Less truth!"

*This college student sits drunk on a Texas beach during spring break. People may drink heavily to escape from past failure—and to set up a face-saving excuse for future failure.*

consumption. Similar results were obtained in a study of men who had been hospitalized for alcoholism and then released. After three months, those who both were high in self-consciousness and were under stress were the most likely to relapse into heavy drinking (Hull et al., 1986). These results come as no surprise. Many people expect alcohol to grant this type of relief and to help us manage our emotional highs and lows (Leigh & Stacy, 1993; Cooper et al., 1995).

## POSITIVE ILLUSIONS

Self-awareness can force us to notice our shortcomings, so we turn away from unpleasant truths. We must be pretty good at it, because research consistently shows that most people tend to think and speak highly of themselves. Time and again, people see positive traits as more self-descriptive than negative ones, they rate themselves more highly than they rate others, they rate themselves more highly than they are rated by others, they overestimate their contribution to team efforts, and they exaggerate their control over life events (Taylor, 1989).

People also overestimate their own intellectual and social abilities across a whole range of domains. What's interesting about this tendency is that those who are least competent may be the most likely to overrate their own performance. In a series of studies, Justin Kruger and David Dunning (1999) found that college students with the lowest scores on tests of logic, grammar, and humor were the ones who most grossly overestimated their abilities (on average, their scores were in the lowest 12 percent among peers, yet they estimated themselves to be in the top 38 percent). Perhaps ignorance, as they say, is bliss.

Most people also exhibit "unrealistic optimism," a tendency to predict a uniquely bright and rosy future for themselves. As presented in Figure 18.2, college

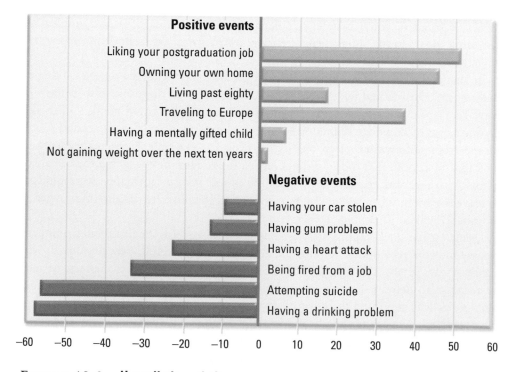

**FIGURE 18.2** **Unrealistic optimism**
When students were asked to predict their own future compared to that of their same-sex classmates, they rated their own chances as above average for positive events and as below average for negative events.

students asked to predict their own future compared to that of their classmates believed, on average, that they were more likely to graduate higher in their class, get a better job, earn a higher salary, have a happier marriage, and bear a gifted child. They also believed that they were less likely to get fired, get divorced, have a drinking problem, become depressed, become involved in a car accident, or suffer from a heart attack (Weinstein, 1980). Many other examples illustrate this point—as when voters predict that their favored candidate will prevail and sports fans bet on their favorite teams to win. In one study, students set their odds of getting divorced at only 20 percent, even while knowing that the divorce rate for new marriages is close to 50 percent (Kunda, 1987).

We can't all be better than average, nor can we all have a rosier future than everyone else. So how do we maintain such a generally positive outlook? How do we cope with our own faults, inadequacies, and an uncertain future? Simple. Using cognitive strategies like the unconscious defense mechanisms described by Freud, we harbor positive illusions about ourselves.

**Are Positive Illusions Adaptive?**   Psychologists used to agree that an accurate perception of reality is vital to mental health. More and more, however, this view is being challenged by research on positive illusions. Are these illusions a sign of well-being or symptoms of disorder?

When Shelley Taylor and Jonathon Brown (1988) reviewed the relevant research, they noticed that people who are mildly depressed or low in self-esteem have less inflated—and more realistic—views of themselves than do others who are better adjusted. Their self-appraisals are more likely to match appraisals of them made by neutral others, they are less likely to exaggerate their control over uncontrollable events, and they make more balanced predictions about the future. These results led Taylor and Brown to draw the provocative conclusion that when it comes to the self, positive illusions, not accurate perceptions of reality, promote health and well-being. In their words, "these illusions help make each individual's world a warmer and more active and beneficent place in which to live" (p. 205). In fact, research involving people under stress—such as men infected with HIV—shows that perceived control, optimism, and other positive beliefs are "health protective" psychological resources that help people cope with adversity (Taylor et al., 2000).

Others are not so sure that people are better off being eternal optimists than hard realists. Baumeister and Scher (1988) argue that positive illusions can give rise to chronic patterns of self-destruction—as when people escape from self-awareness through the use of drugs and deny health-related problems until it's too late for treatment. From an interpersonal point of view, C. Randall Colvin and others (1995) found that people with inflated rather than realistic views of themselves were rated less favorably on certain dimensions by their own friends. In their studies, self-enhancing men were seen as assertive and ambitious, which are okay, but also as boastful, condescending, hostile, and inconsiderate. Self-enhancing women were seen as more hostile, more defensive and sensitive to criticism, more likely to overreact to minor setbacks, and less well liked by others. Consistent with these findings, other research shows that people with high self-esteem are more likely to lash out after criticism, rejection, and other bruises to the ego (Baumeister et al., 1996).

In a study that illustrates the dark side of high self-esteem, Todd Heatherton and Kathleen Vohs (2000) administered a standard self-esteem test to pairs of unacquainted college students and then brought them together for a brief conversation. Just before meeting, one student within each pair took a "Remote Associates Test" that involved finding one word that connects sets of three seemingly unrelated words (for example, *lick, sprinkle,* and *mines* are linked by the word *salt*). For half of these target students, the test was pitched as experimental and the problems they were given were easy to solve. Others were told that the test measured achievement potential and were given very difficult problems—leading them to perform, supposedly, worse than average. Did this ego-threatening feedback affect the students' behavior and the impressions they made on their interaction partners? In the no-threat group, high and low self-esteem students were equally well liked. In the ego-threat situation, however, those with high self-esteem became less likeable and were rated by their partners as rude, unfriendly, and arrogant. It appears that when high self-esteem people feel threatened, they try to assert their competence, which comes across as boastful and abrasive.

Realism or illusion—which orientation is more adaptive? As psychologists debate the short-term and long-term consequences of positive illusions, it's clear that there is no simple answer. For now, the picture that has emerged is this: People who harbor positive illusions about themselves are likely to enjoy the benefits and achievements of high self-esteem. But these same individuals may pay a price in other ways, as in their relations with others. So what are we to conclude? Is it possible that positive illusions motivate us to personal achievement but alienate us socially from others? Could it be that it's adaptive to see oneself in ways that are slightly inflated, but not too much? As psychologists speculate about the costs and benefits of positive illusions, it will be interesting to see what research uncovers in the years to come (Robins & Beer, 2001; Schneider, 2001).

## REVIEW QUESTIONS

- *In what ways do people with high self-esteem differ from those with low self-esteem?*

- *According to self-awareness theory, what types of situations increase self-awareness, and why does it often lower self-esteem?*

- *Describe the effects of alcohol on perceptions of the self.*

- *Describe two strategies that help us maintain positive illusions about ourselves.*

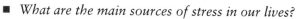

# STRESS AND HEALTH

- *What are the main sources of stress in our lives?*
- *What are the effects of stress on the body?*
- *What is the Type A personality, and why is it bad for the heart?*
- *How does the immune system work, and how is it affected by stress and other psychological states?*

The reason psychologists are interested in mental health is obvious. But the field has also had a long-standing interest in physical health, a domain normally associated with medicine. Influenced by psychoanalysis, clinical psychologists used to study *psychosomatic* ailments such as asthma, ulcers, headaches, and constipation—conditions thought to result from unconscious conflicts. Working from a behavioral perspective, others later referred to these same ailments as *psychophysiological* disorders. Either way, it's long been clear that psychological states can influence physical well-being.

Over the past few years, increasing numbers of researchers have become interested in the emerging area of **health psychology**, the application of psychology to the promotion of physical health and the prevention and treatment of illness (Baum & Posluszny, 1999; Friedman, 2002; Salovey et al., 1998; Schneiderman et al., 2001; Taylor, 2002a). You may wonder: What does psychology have to do with catching a cold, having a heart attack, or being afflicted with cancer? If you could turn the clock back a few years and ask your family doctor, his or her answer would be "very little." In the past, illness was considered a purely biological event. But this strict medical perspective has given way to a broader model that holds that health is a joint product of biological and psychological factors.

Part of the reason for this broadened view is that illness patterns over the years have changed in significant ways. In the year 1900, the principal causes of death

For constantly updated health and disease statistics, and advice for travelers, visit the World Health Organization (WHO) at **http://www.who.org/**. For news, frequently asked questions, and information about health in the United States, visit the National Center for Health Statistics at **http://www.cdc.gov/nchs/**.

**health psychology** The study of the links between psychological factors and physical health and illness.

were contagious diseases—polio, smallpox, tuberculosis, typhoid fever, malaria, influenza, pneumonia, and the like. Today, one century later, none of these infectious illnesses is currently a leading killer. Instead, Americans are most likely to die, in order of risk, from heart disease, cancer, strokes, and accidents (AIDS is fifteenth on the list)—problems that are often preventable through changes in lifestyle, outlook, and behavior (see Figure 18.3).

Although it's not possible to quantify the extent of the problem, psychological stress is a known potent killer. Regardless of who you are, when you were born, or where you live, you have no doubt experienced stress. Sitting in a rush-hour traffic jam, getting married or divorced, losing hours of work to a computer crash, getting into an argument with a close friend, worrying about an unwanted pregnancy or the health of your child, being stranded at an airport, living in a noisy neighborhood, struggling to make financial ends meet, and caring for a loved one who is sick—these are the kinds of stresses and strains we all must learn to live with. Whether they are short term or long term, serious or mild, no one is immune and there is no escape. But there are ways to cope.

In this section, we examine three interrelated questions of relevance to your health and well-being: (1) What are some of the primary sources of stress? (2) What are the effects of stress on the body? (3) What are the most adaptive ways of coping with stress? Together, the answers to these questions provide a useful model of the stress-and-coping process (see Figure 18.4).

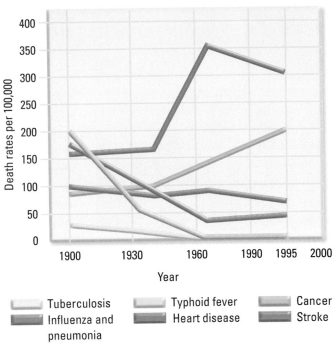

FIGURE 18.3   **Leading causes of death, 1900–2000**
Across the twentieth century, heart disease, cancer, and strokes have replaced infectious diseases as the major causes of death in the United States.

## THE SOURCES OF STRESS

**Stress** is an unpleasant state of arousal that arises when we perceive that an event threatens our ability to cope effectively. There are many different sources of stress, or *stressors*. Try writing down the stressors in your own life, and you'll probably find that the items in your list can be divided into three major categories: catastrophes, major life events, and daily hassles.

**Catastrophes**   The terrorist assault on the World Trade Center and the Pentagon on September 11, 2001, was a national trauma no one old enough to witness will ever forget. Most profoundly touched were those at work in those buildings or

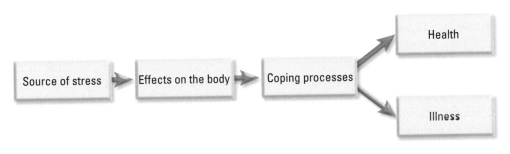

FIGURE 18.4   **Stress and coping**
Advances in health psychology show that although stressful events have effects on the body, the way we cope with stress can promote health or illness.

**stress**   An aversive state of arousal triggered by the perception that an event threatens our ability to cope effectively.

In New York City, calls to the mental-health helpline Lifenet, which averaged 3,000 per month, more than doubled after September 11, 2001, to a record of 6,600 in January 2002.

*Tornadoes have such devastating power that those who survive often exhibit posttraumatic stress disorder.*

*It has long been recognized that combat leaves psychological scars and the symptoms of posttraumatic stress disorder.*

**posttraumatic stress disorder (PTSD)** An anxiety disorder triggered by an extremely stressful event, such as combat.

nearby, those with friends and family in the vicinity, and rescue workers called to the scene. In fact, however, Americans all over the world took the attack personally and were affected by it—whether they were present or not. In a nationwide telephone survey of 560 adults conducted later that week, 90 percent said they were experiencing some symptoms of stress—and 44 percent reported "substantial" symptoms such as recurring thoughts, dreams, and memories; difficulty falling or staying asleep; difficulty concentrating on work; and unprovoked outbursts of anger (Schuster et al., 2001).

Other events can have similarly traumatic effects—such as motor vehicle accidents, plane crashes, violent crimes, physical or sexual abuse, the death of a loved one, and natural disasters such as hurricanes, tornadoes, floods, earthquakes, and fires (Kubany et al., 2000). The harmful effects of catastrophic stressors on physical health are well documented. Paul and Gerald Adams (1984) examined the public records in Othello, Washington, before and after the 1980 eruption of the Mount Saint Helens volcano, which spewed thick layers of ash all over the community. They discovered that there were posteruption increases in calls made to a mental-health crisis line, police reports of domestic violence, referrals to the alcohol treatment center, and visits to the local hospital emergency room. In a study of disasters involving 377 counties, a team of researchers found that, compared to the years preceding each disaster, the suicide rate increased—by 14 percent after floods, by 31 percent after hurricanes, and by 63 percent after earthquakes (Krug et al., 1998).

War in particular leaves deep and permanent psychological scars. Soldiers who experience combat see horrifying injuries, death, and destruction on a routine basis, leaving them with images and emotions that do not fade. In World War I, the problem was called shell shock. In World War II, it was called combat fatigue. It's now called **posttraumatic stress disorder (PTSD)** and is identified by such symptoms as recurring anxiety, sleeplessness, nightmares, vivid flashbacks, intrusive thoughts, attentional problems, and social withdrawal. To evaluate the extent of the problem, the Centers for Disease Control (1988) compared seven thousand Vietnam combat veterans with seven thousand noncombat veterans who served in the military at the same time, that is, more than twenty years before the study. They found that although the Vietnam War was a distant memory to most Americans, 15 percent of those who saw combat—twice as many as were in the comparison group—reported lingering symptoms of posttraumatic stress disorder. Those who had the most traumatic of experiences (crossing enemy lines, being ambushed or shot at, handling dead bodies) were five times more likely to have nightmares, flashbacks, startle reactions, and other problems. Similar results have been found among older veterans of World War II and the Korean War (Fontana & Rosenheck, 1994; Spiro et al., 1994).

PTSD, a form of anxiety disorder, can be caused by traumas off the battlefield as well. Conducting a nationwide survey of nearly six thousand Americans, fifteen to fifty-four years old, Ronald Kessler and his colleagues (1995) estimated that 8 percent of the population (5 percent among men, 10 percent among women) have posttraumatic stress disorder in the course of a lifetime—and that the symptoms often persist for many years. This research shows that such traumas can be caused by a range of experiences—such as life-threatening accidents, fires, natural disasters, combat, being raped or attacked, and witnessing an injury or murder. In a study of Miami residents caught in a major hurricane, Gail Ironson and others (1997) found that after a few months, one-third exhibited symptoms of PTSD and that the more injury, property damage, and loss they suffered from the storm, the more severe their symptoms were.

**Major Life Events**  Some people are lucky enough to avoid major catastrophes. But nobody can avoid stress. The reason, say some psychologists, is that change of any kind causes stress because it forces us to adapt to new circumstances. This hypothesis was first proposed by Thomas Holmes and Richard Rahe (1967), who interviewed hospital patients and found that their illnesses were often preceded by major changes in some aspect of their lives. Some of the changes were negative, others were positive. To measure life stress, Holmes and Rahe devised the Social Readjustment Rating Scale (SRRS)—a checklist of forty-three major life changes, which they ranked on the basis of how much readjustment they require. The events listed include the death of a spouse, divorce, imprisonment, getting married, losing a job, moving to a new residence, starting a new job, being promoted, having a baby, and even taking a vacation.

You may have seen a questionnaire like the SSRS in a book or magazine. The claim made is that the number of stress points or "life-change units" you accumulate in a recent period of time indicates the amount of stress you are under. I recall filling out such a questionnaire the year I finished graduate school. I received my Ph.D. One week later, my wife and I got married, moved fifteen hundred miles to a new state, rented a new apartment, and started new jobs. For the first and only time in her life, my wife had an ulcer. Her doctor's first question: "Has anything changed in your life?"

The simple notion that change is inherently stressful has an intuitive ring about it. Indeed, research shows that people with high scores on the SRRS are more likely to come down with physical illnesses (Dohrenwend & Dohrenwend, 1978; Maddi et al., 1987). But is change per se necessarily harmful? There are two problems with this notion. First, although there is a statistical link between negative events and illness, research does not similarly support the claim that positive "stressors"—taking a vacation, graduating, winning a lottery, starting a new career, or getting married—are similarly harmful (Stewart et al., 1986). The second complicating factor is that the impact of any change depends on who the person is and how the change is interpreted. Moving to a new country, for example, is less stressful to immigrants who can speak the new language (Berry et al., 1992); having an abortion is less stressful to women who have the support of family, partners, and friends (Major et al., 1990); a diagnosis of infertility is less devastating to married men and women who want children when they confront the issue, emotionally, rather than avoid it (Berghuis & Stanton, 2002). The amount of change in a person's life may provide crude estimates of stress and future health, but the predictive equation is more complex.

**Microstressors**  Think again about the sources of stress in your life, and catastrophes or exceptional events spring to mind. Researchers have found, however, that the most significant source of stress arises from the hassles that irritate us on a daily basis. Environmental irritants such as population density, loud noise, extreme heat or cold, and cigarette smoke are all possible sources of stress. Car problems, waiting in lines, losing keys, arguments with friends, nosy neighbors, bad workdays, money troubles, and other "microstressors" also place a constant strain on us. Table 18.1 shows the events that most routinely stress children, college students, and adults (Kanner et al., 1981; Kanner et al., 1991; Kohn et al., 1990). However, there is nothing "micro" about the impact of these stressors on health and well-being. Studies show that the accumulation of daily hassles contributes more to illness than do major life events (Kohn et al., 1991).

**WHAT'S YOUR PREDICTION**

Based on studies on the stress effects of catastrophes, it's reasonable to expect that the attack on the World Trade Center increased the population of New Yorkers with PTSD and depression. But did location *within* the city matter? Make a prediction: Were Manhattan residents who lived downtown, close to ground zero, scarred more than those further away—or was proximity irrelevant in the face of this assault? In October and November of 2001, Sandro Galea and others (2002) interviewed a thousand Manhattan adults and compared those living north versus south of Canal Street, near ground zero. The result: North of Canal Street, 7 percent had severe symptoms of PTSD and 9 percent were clinically depressed. Among those south of Canal Street, however, an astonishing 20 percent had PTSD and 17 percent were depressed. In human terms, these numbers translate into hundreds of thousands of emotionally distraught New Yorkers—and yes, the closer they were, the more scarred they were by the experience (see Figure 18.5).

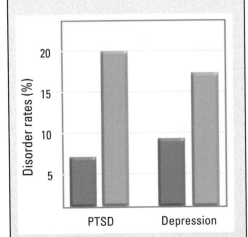

**FIGURE 18.5**
(Galea et al., 2002)

| TABLE 18.1 | COMMON DAILY HASSLES |
|---|---|

**Children and Early Adolescents**

Having to clean up your room
Being bored and having nothing to do
Seeing that another kid can do something better
Getting punished for doing something wrong
Having to go to bed when you don't want to
Being teased at school

**College Students**

Conflicts with a boyfriend or girlfriend
Dissatisfaction with your athletic skills
Having your trust betrayed by a friend
Struggling to meet your own academic standards
Not having enough leisure time
Gossip concerning someone you care about
Dissatisfaction with your physical appearance

**Middle-Aged Adults**

Concerns about weight
Health of a family member
Social obligations
Inconsiderate smokers
Concerns about money
Misplacing or losing things
Home maintenance
Job security

*Waiting helplessly in traffic is one of the most common microstressors in daily life.*

One source of stress that plagues many people in the workplace is *burnout*—a prolonged response to job stress characterized by emotional exhaustion, cynicism, disengagement, and a lack of personal accomplishment. Teachers, doctors, nurses, police officers, social workers, and others in human-service professions are particularly at risk for burnout. Under relentless job pressures, those who are burned out describe themselves as feeling drained, frustrated, hardened, apathetic, and lacking in energy and motivation (Maslach, 1982; Maslach et al., 2001).

On the homefront, economic pressure is another common source of stress. In a three-year study of over four hundred married couples, researchers found that those who are strained by a tight budget and have difficulty paying the bills experience more distress and conflict in their marriages (Conger et al., 1999). A follow-up study of African American families further showed that economic hardship spells emotional distress for parents—and adjustment problems for their children (Conger et al., 2002).

## THE PHYSIOLOGICAL EFFECTS OF STRESS

The term *stress* was popularized by Hans Selye (1936, 1976), an endocrinologist. As a young medical student, Selye noticed that patients who were hospitalized for different illnesses often had similar symptoms, such as muscle weakness, a loss of weight and appetite, and a lack of ambition. Maybe these symptoms were part of a generalized response to an attack on the body, he thought. In the 1930s, Selye tested this hypothesis by exposing laboratory rats to various stressors, including heat, cold, heavy exercise, toxic substances, food deprivation, and electric shock. As anticipated, the different stressors all produced a similar physiological response: enlarged adrenal glands, shrunken lymph nodes, and bleeding stomach ulcers. Selye borrowed a term from engineering and called the reaction stress, a word that quickly became part of everyday language.

According to Selye, the body naturally responds to stress in a three-stage process he called the **general adaptation syndrome** (see Figure 18.6). Sparked by the recognition of a threat, any threat—predator, enemy soldier, speeding automobile, or virus—the body has an initial alarm reaction. To meet the challenge, adrenaline and other hormones are poured into the bloodstream, thus heightening physiological arousal. Heart rate, blood pressure, and breathing rates increase, while slower, long-term functions such as growth, digestion, and the operation of the immune system are inhibited. At this stage, the body mobilizes all its resources to ward off the threat. Next comes a resistance stage, during which the body remains aroused and on the alert. There is a continued release of stress hormones, and local defenses are activated (if there is a virus, for example, immune-system antibodies are called into action). But if the stress persists for a prolonged time (as in a failing marriage, high-pressure job, or poverty), the body will fall into an exhaustion stage. According to Selye, the body's natural antistress resources are limited. Eventually, resistance breaks down, putting us at risk for illness and even death.

Research has since revealed that different types of stressors elicit somewhat different bodily responses—and that exhaustion occurs not because the body's stress-fighting resources are limited but because the overuse of these resources causes other systems in the body to break down. Still, Selye's basic model makes an important point: Stress may be an adaptive short-term reaction to threat, but over time it compromises our health and well-being. As we'll see in the coming pages, stress is linked to coronary heart disease and the workings of the immune system.

A stress response is found in all mammals. So why, asks neuroscientist Robert Sapolsky (1994), don't zebras get ulcers? Sapolsky notes that the physiological stress response is superbly designed through evolution to help animals mobilize to fight or escape in an acute emergency. For the zebra, this occurs when a hungry lion leaps out from a bush and sprints at top speed across the savanna. For humans, it occurs in combat or in competitive sports—maybe even on first dates and job interviews. But make a mental list of the situations you find stressful, and you'll see that people become anxious over things that would make no sense to a zebra. "We humans live well enough and long enough, and are smart enough, to generate all sorts of stressful events purely in our heads," notes Sapolsky. "From the perspective of the evolution of the animal kingdom, psychological stress is a recent invention" (p. 5). The reason that stress causes ulcers and other illnesses, then, is that the response is designed for acute physical emergencies, yet we turn it on often and for prolonged periods as we worry about taxes, mortgages, family members, public speaking, career goals, and the inevitability of death.

All humans respond bodily to stress, which is what enables us to mount a defense. Physiologically, the sympathetic nervous system is activated and more adrenaline is secreted, which increases the heart rate and heightens arousal. Then all at once the liver pours extra sugar into the bloodstream for energy, the pupils dilate to let in more light, breathing speeds up for more oxygen, perspiration increases to

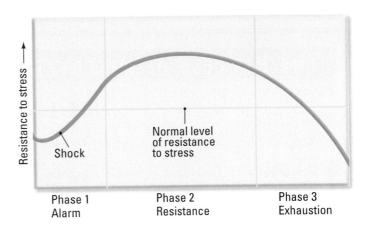

**FIGURE 18.6**   **The general adaptation syndrome**
According to Selye, the human body responds to threat in three phases: alarm, resistance, and exhaustion.

   18.1

**general adaptation syndrome**   A three-stage process (alarm, resistance, and exhaustion) by which the body responds to stress.

# THE PROCESS OF DISCOVERY

## SHELLEY TAYLOR
### *How People Cope with Stress*

**Q: How did you first become interested in psychology?**

**A:** I decided to become a psychology major literally the first day I attended Introductory Psychology at Connecticut College. Although the instructor was a bit intimidating, the material resonated with my thinking about how the world works in ways that nothing had previously or has since. I continued in the field, and in 1972 I received my Ph.D. in social psychology at Yale University.

**Q: How did you come up with your important discovery?**

**A:** In the early 1980's, having studied how people think about the social world, I became interested in how people cope with stress—especially stressors that have the potential to shake up their beliefs about themselves and the world. I found that people who hold positive illusions about their personal resources, their future, and their ability to control the events that befall them, help to create a self-fulfilling prophecy. In work with people infected with HIV, for example, I found that those with positive expectations about their disease course and their ability to stave off AIDS in fact did so for longer.

Among my observations about coping with stress was that women and men diverge somewhat in their coping strategies. While men are likely to take on a stressor directly or withdraw from it (behaviors that fit the classic "fight-or-flight" formulation that has guided stress research for decades), women seem to turn to their families and their friends instead. My colleagues and I put forth the "tend-and-befriend" model of coping in which we argued that stress often produces not just tendencies to fight or flee but, especially in women, impulses to tend to offspring and protect them from harm. Women also turn to friends, especially female friends, for help in this process. Guided by evolutionary theory and by animal research on the biology of affiliation, I argue in my book, *The Tending Instinct*, that this inclination to tend-and-befriend is guided by specific hormones that are released in response to stress and prompt these affiliative reactions.

**Q: How has the field you inspired developed over the years?**

**A:** Studying the social psychology of health, I am gratified to see how the field is maturing. Health psychology has its own division in the American Psychological Association, with membership numbering in the thousands. My work represents an early contribution to positive psychology as well, a field that emphasizes how positive emotions and thoughts may actively contribute to physical and mental health—a far cry from traditional models that emphasize negative states such as anxiety, depression, and their guiding role in human behavior.

**Q: What's your prediction on where the field is heading?**

**A:** I predict for the future of health psychology that psychology's liaisons with biology will grow stronger, with each field informing the contributions of the other. As biologists explore the molecular mechanisms underlying the influence of psychological states on mental and physical health processes, psychologists can help to craft the big picture of how biological, social, and psychological forces interact to produce the kinds of people we turn out to be.

*Shelley Taylor is Professor of Psychology at the University of California, Los Angeles.*

cool down the body, blood clots faster to heal wounds, saliva flow is inhibited, and digestion slows down to divert blood to the brain and skeletal muscles. In the face of threat, the body readies for action. But what, behaviorally, is the nature of the defense? Many years ago, Walter Cannon (1932) described the body as prepared for "fight or flight." To be sure, men often lash out aggressively when under siege. But do women similarly respond? In her book *The Tending Instinct*, Shelley Taylor (2002b) argues that while men exhibit the classic fight-or-flight reaction to stress, women exhibit a very different "tend-and-befriend" response. Prepared by evolution—and necessity—to enhance the survival of their offspring, she argues, women adapt to hardship by caring for their children and seeking out other people who might help. Consistent with this argument, studies have shown that, under stress, women become more nurturing than men—and more affiliative.

**Coronary Heart Disease**   Coronary heart disease (CHD) is a narrowing of the blood vessels that carry oxygen and nutrients to the heart muscle. It is currently the leading cause of death in the United States. An estimated sixty-nine million Americans suffer from CHD. For many, the result is a heart attack, which occurs when the blood supply to the heart is blocked. This causes an uncomfortable feeling of pressure, fullness, squeezing, or pain in the center of the chest—and sometimes also sweating, dizziness, nausea, fainting, and a shortness of breath. Every year, 1.5 million Americans have heart attacks. One-third of them do not survive.

Several factors are known to increase the risk of CHD. The three most important are hypertension, or high blood pressure; cigarette smoking; and high cholesterol (others include a family history of CHD, obesity, and a lack of exercise). People with one of these three major risk factors are twice as likely to develop CHD, those with two risk factors are 3.5 times as likely, and those with all three are six times as likely. These statistics are compelling and should not be taken lightly. But combined, these factors account for fewer than half the known cases of CHD. What's missing from the equation is the fourth major risk factor: stress.

In 1956, cardiologists Meyer Friedman and Ray Rosenman were studying the relationship between cholesterol and coronary heart disease. After noticing that husbands were more likely than their wives to have CHD, they speculated that work-related stress might be the reason (at the time, most women did not work outside the home). To test this hypothesis, Friedman and Rosenman interviewed three thousand healthy middle-aged men. Those who seemed to be the most hard-driving, competitive, impatient, time conscious, and quick to anger were classified as having a **Type A personality.** Roughly an equal number of those who were easygoing, relaxed, and laid back were classified as having a **Type B personality.** Interestingly, out of 258 men who eventually had heart attacks over the following nine years, 69 percent had been classified as Type As and only 31 percent were Type Bs (Rosenman et al., 1975).

The Type A personality of the so-called workaholic is made up of many traits, including competitive drive, a sense of time urgency, and a dangerous mix of anger, cynicism, and hostility (Friedman & Booth-Kewley, 1987; Matthews, 1988). In interviews and questionnaires, Type A people say they tend to walk fast and talk fast, work late hours, interrupt other speakers in mid-sentence, get angry with people who are late, detest waiting in lines, race through yellow lights when they drive, lash out at others when frustrated, strive to win at all costs, and save time by doing many things at once. In contrast, "there are those who breeze through the day as pleased as park rangers—despite having deadlines and kids and a broken-down car and charity work and scowling Aunt Agnes living in the spare bedroom" (Carey, 1997, p. 75).

Over the years, researchers have found that not all the Type A personality traits are bad. Being time-pressured, competitive, and driven to achieve do not put us at risk. However, the one trait that is toxic and is related to an individual's proneness to CHD is *hostility*—as seen in people who are constantly angry, cynical, and mistrustful of others (see Table 18.2). People who are often in a negative emotional state are besieged by stress. But because the heart is just a dumb pump and the

For news, risk-assessment tests, and other useful information about heart disease, visit the American Heart Association at **http://www.americanheart.org/.**

**Type A personality**   A personality characterized by an impatient, hard-driving, and hostile pattern of behavior.

**Type B personality**   A personality characterized by an easygoing, relaxed pattern of behavior.

| TABLE 18.2  HOW "HOSTILE" IS YOUR PATTERN OF BEHAVIOR? |
| --- |
| • When in the express checkout line at the supermarket, do you often count the items in the baskets of the people ahead of you to be sure they aren't over the limit? |
| • When an elevator doesn't come as quickly as it should, do your thoughts quickly focus on the inconsiderate behavior of the person on another floor who's holding it up? |
| • When someone criticizes you, do you quickly begin to feel annoyed? |
| • Do you frequently find yourself muttering at the television during a news broadcast? |
| • When you are held up in a slow line in traffic, do you quickly sense your heart pounding and your breath quickening? |

*Source:* R. Williams (1993). *Anger kills.* New York: Times Books.

blood vessels merely hoses, "The cardiovascular stress-response basically consists of making them work harder for a while, and if you do that on a regular basis, they will wear out, just like any pump or hoses you could buy at Sears" (Sapolsky, 1994, p. 42). In the long run, a pattern of hostility and anger can be lethal (Siegman & Smith, 1994; Miller et al., 1996). In fact, people who have a lot of anger and suppress it are as likely to develop high blood pressure as those who have anger and express it. It's the felt anger that is toxic—not whether you hold it in or let it go (Everson et al., 1998).

The strength of the link between Type A behavior and coronary heart disease depends on how people are diagnosed. After Friedman and Rosenman's early study, many psychologists—in their haste to pursue this vital line of research—tried to identify Type A people by using quick, easy-to-administer questionnaires instead of time-consuming interviews. The questionnaires, however, were not as predictive. Apparently, the Type A personality is more evident from a subject's interview *behavior* (whether he or she constantly checks the time, speaks quickly, and interrupts the interviewer) than from his or her *self-reports.* As shown in Figure 18.7, recent research confirms that when interviews are used to make the diagnosis, 70 percent of men who have CHD have a Type A personality—compared to only 46 percent of those who are healthy (Miller et al., 1991).

What explains the connection between Type A behavior and coronary heart disease? As shown in Figure 18.8, one explanation is that Type As are less health-conscious than Type Bs. They tend to smoke more, drink more caffeine and alcohol, exercise less, sleep less, eat less healthy foods, and also be less likely to comply with health advice from doctors (Leiker & Hailey, 1988; Siegler, 1994). A second explanation is that Type A people are physiologically more reactive than Type Bs are. In

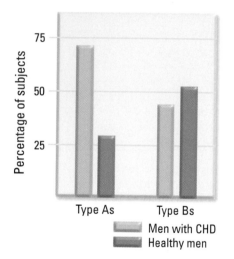

FIGURE 18.7  **Personality and coronary heart disease**
Studies of middle-aged men reveal that Type As are more likely than Type Bs to suffer from CHD (Miller et al., 1991).

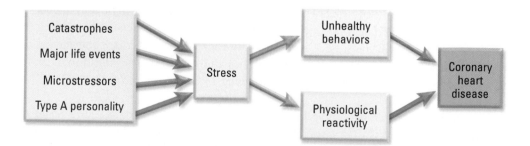

FIGURE 18.8  **Pathways from stress to CHD**
Under stress, people (1) engage in less healthy behaviors (they smoke more, sleep less, and consume more caffeine and alcohol), and (2) are physiologically more reactive (they exhibit larger increases in pulse rate, blood pressure, and adrenaline level).

tense social situations, they react with greater increases in pulse rate, blood pressure, and adrenaline—a hormone that accelerates the build-up of fatty plaques on the artery walls, causing a hardening of the arteries (Krantz & McCeney, 2002). In fact, research shows that people who are hostile exhibit more intense cardiovascular reactions not only during the event that makes them angry—say, being involved in a heated argument (Davis et al., 2000)—but long afterward as well, when asked to relive the event (Frederickson et al., 2000).

## THE IMMUNE SYSTEM

When it comes to the interaction between mind and body, the link between stress and the heart is just the tip of the iceberg. It now appears that stress also increases the risk of chronic back pain, diabetes, arthritis, appendicitis, upper respiratory infections, herpes, gum disease, the common cold, and some forms of cancer. How can stress have this wide range of disabling effects? Answer: by compromising the body's immune system—the first line of defense against illness (Ader et al., 2001; Glaser & Kiecolt-Glaser, 1994; Schedlowski & Tewes, 1999).

The **immune system** is a complex surveillance system that fights bacteria, parasites, viruses, fungi, and other "nonself" substances that invade the body (Sompayrac, 1999). The system consists of more than a trillion specialized white blood cells called **lymphocytes** that originate in the bone marrow (*B cells*) and thymus (*T cells*), migrate to various organs, circulate through the bloodstream, and secrete chemical antibodies. These sharklike search-and-destroy cells protect us by patrolling the body twenty-four hours a day and attacking trespassers. Yet on occasion, they overreact and strike at benign material. This can result in "autoimmune" diseases such as multiple sclerosis, trigger allergic reactions to harmless pollen and ragweed, and cause the body to reject transplanted organs. The immune system is also equipped with large scavenger cells known as *macrophages* ("big eaters") and *natural killer cells* (NK cells) that zero in on viruses and cancerous tumors. Serving as a "sixth sense" for foreign invaders, the immune system continually renews itself. During the few seconds it takes to read this sentence, your body will have produced ten million new lymphocytes (see Figure 18.9).

Many health psychologists—specializing in psychoneuroimmunology, or PNI—are now studying connections among the brain, behavior, the immune system, health, and illness. Before we get into some of the fascinating results, let's pause for a moment and consider three of the methods that these researchers use to spy on the operations of the immune system. One method is to take blood samples from animal or human participants exposed to varying degrees of stress and simply count the numbers of lymphocytes and other white blood cells circulating in the bloodstream. A second is to extract blood, add cancerous tumor cells to the mix, and measure the extent to which the NK cells destroy the tumors. A third method is to "challenge" the living organism by injecting a foreign agent into the skin and measuring the amount of swelling that arises at the site of the injection. The more swelling there is, the more potent the immune reaction is assumed to be (Ader et al., 2001).

**What Stress Does to the Immune System**   It's now clear that stress can adversely affect the immune system, at least temporarily, and that psychological interventions can help matters. The medical community used to reject the idea, but most are now convinced. What changed? At first, animal experiments showed that rats exposed to noise, overcrowding, or inescapable shocks, and that primates separated from their social companions, exhibit a drop in immune-cell activity compared to nonexposed animals (Coe, 1993; Moynihan & Ader, 1996). A link was

**immune system**   A biological surveillance system that detects and destroys "nonself" substances that invade the body.

**lymphocytes**   Specialized white blood cells that secrete chemical antibodies and facilitate the immune response.

 **18.2**

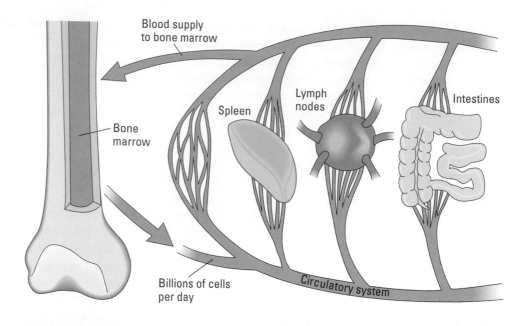

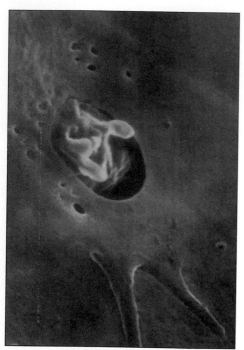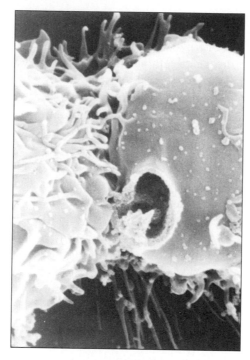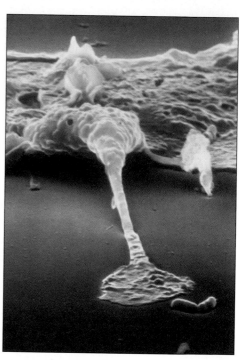

FIGURE 18.9    **The immune system**
Originating in the bone marrow, lymphocytes move into certain organs and circulate continuously through the bloodstream. As pictured, a B cell migrates from the bone marrow to a blood vessel (left), a killer T cell locates and attacks a tumor cell (center), and a large macrophage prepares to trap and ingest a tiny bacterium (right).

also observed in human participants. Intrigued by the fact that people often become sick and die shortly after they are widowed, R. W. Barthrop and his colleagues (1977) took blood samples from twenty-six men and women whose spouses had just died. Compared to nonwidowed controls, these grief-stricken spouses exhibited a weakened immune response, as measured by T-cell activity. This was the first demonstration of its kind.

Additional studies soon revealed weakened immune responses in NASA astronauts after their reentry into the atmosphere and splash-down, in participants who were deprived of sleep for a prolonged period of time, in students in the midst of final exams, in men and women recently divorced or separated, in people who are caring for a family member with Alzheimer's disease, in snake phobics exposed to a live snake, and in workers who had lost their jobs (O'Leary, 1990). Even in the laboratory, participants who are given complex arithmetic problems to solve or painful stimuli to tolerate exhibit changes in immune-cell activity—and these changes last for one or more hours after the stress has subsided (Cohen & Herbert, 1996).

In a particularly intriguing study, Arthur Stone and others (1994) paid forty-eight adult volunteers to take a harmless but novel protein pill every day for twelve weeks—a substance that would lead the immune system to respond by producing an anti-body. Every day, the participants completed a diary in which they reported on their moods and on experiences at work, at home, in financial matters, in leisure activities, and in relationships with their spouses, children, and friends. Participants also gave daily saliva samples that were later used to measure the amount of the antibody that was produced. The results were striking, as are their implications: The more positive events participants had in a given day, the more of the antibody was produced. The more negative the events, the less of that antibody that was produced. In many ways, it's now clear that negative experiences—and the emotions they elicit—can weaken our immune system's ability to protect us from injuries, infections, and a wide range of illnesses (Kiecolt-Glaser et al., 2002). However, on the question of whether positive psychological interventions can be used to reinvigorate immune responses, more research is needed (Miller & Cohen, 2001).

We have seen that psychological states can "get into" the immune system. But how? To be sure, certain organs that play a key role in the immune system (the thymus, bone marrow, and lymph nodes) are richly endowed with nerve fibers, providing a direct pipeline to the brain. But what explains the link between stress and the activity of lymphocytes? As illustrated in Figure 18.10, there are two possible ways this can happen. First, as described earlier, people who are stressed tend to

*Following their nine days in orbit, these NASA astronauts pose soon after touching ground. Given what is known about the link between stress and immunity, their immune responses may have been in a weakened state when this picture was taken.*

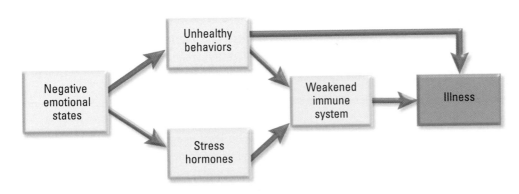

FIGURE 18.10    **Pathways from stress to illness**
Negative emotional states may cause illness in two ways: (1) by promoting unhealthful behaviors (more alcohol, less sleep, and so on) and (2) by triggering the release of hormones that weaken the immune system by suppressing activity of the lymphocytes.

## THE PROCESS OF DISCOVERY

# JANICE KIECOLT-GLASER
## *Stress Effects on Immune Function*

**Q: How did you first become interested in psychology?**

**A:** I first became interested in psychology as an undergraduate; I was fascinated by the mysteries of personality and human behavior, and I decided to become a psychology major even before taking my first course. My introductory psychology cemented my interest.

**Q: How did you come up with your important discovery?**

**A:** My key discoveries are the happy result of my marriage to my collaborator, Ronald Glaser, the person responsible for the immunological side of our interdisciplinary research program. In our early years together we joked about collaborating, which did not seem to be a serious prospect in the face of our obvious differences. (His research program centered on basic science studies with Epstein-Barr virus, while my early work was in assertion training.) When Ron's father died, a friend told him to be careful about his health because a recent study had suggested that bereavement was associated with alterations in immune function. That comment made us think seriously about collaborating. We began by using medical students as subjects, and we found that students showed adverse immunological changes during academic examinations compared to lower stress periods when they didn't have tests; moreover, lonelier students had poorer immune function than their student colleagues who were not as lonely.

**Q: How has the field you inspired developed over the years?**

**A:** The explosive growth in both animal and human studies was stimulated by Robert Ader and Nicholas Cohen's seminal 1975 finding that immune function could be classically conditioned in mice. The interdisciplinary field, named psychoneuroimmunology (PNI) by Ader and Cohen, addresses the interactions among the central nervous system, the endocrine system, and the immune system. Few PNI studies appeared prior to the 1980s; indeed, when we began our research program in 1982, the scant literature with human subjects addressed immunological change in response to extreme and novel events such as bereavement, seventy-seven hours of noise and sleep deprivation, or the space flights of astronauts. In contrast, we began by looking at commonplace events like examinations. Subsequently we and other researchers have shown that psychological stress can have significant consequences for health—it can impair one's ability to fight off an infection from colds or flu, to respond to a vaccine, and to heal wounds, to name only a few key findings.

**Q: What's your prediction on where the field is heading?**

**A:** PNI stands to be one of the "growth" areas in health psychology, related to the medical community's enhanced appreciation of how central a role the immune system plays in a variety of diseases. Indeed, there is now excellent evidence that the immune system is an important player in the genesis of cardiovascular disease, the leading cause of mortality. Immune dysregulation has also been linked to a host of other age-related diseases, including osteoporosis, arthritis, type 2 diabetes, certain cancers, periodontal disease, and frailty and functional decline. I think we have just begun to appreciate the extent to which emotions and behavior influence health.

*Janice Kiecolt-Glaser is Professor and Director of the Division of Health Psychology, Department of Psychiatry, Ohio State University College of Medicine.*

smoke more, use more alcohol and drugs, sleep less, exercise less, and have poorer diets—behaviors that compromise the immune system. For example, one study showed that when healthy male adults were kept awake between 3:00 and 7:00 AM, natural-killer-cell activity diminished—and returned to normal only after a full night of uninterrupted sleep (Irwin et al., 1994). Second, stress triggers the release of adrenaline and other stress hormones into the bloodstream, and these hormones suppress lymphocyte activity (Dhabhar & McEwen, 1995). The result is a temporary lowering of the body's resistance and increased susceptibility to illness (Cohen & Williamson, 1991).

**The Link between Stress and Illness** At the start of this chapter, we saw that participants who had reported high rather than low levels of everyday stress were more likely to catch a common cold after exposure to a cold virus. In one follow-up of this experiment, Sheldon Cohen and others (1998) interviewed 276 volunteers about recent life stressors, infected them with a cold virus, and then measured whether or not they developed a cold. These researchers found that some types of stress were more toxic than others. Specifically, people who had experienced *chronic* stress that lasted for more than a month (such as ongoing marital problems or unemployment) were more likely to develop a cold than those who had experienced acute short-term stress (such as having a fight with a spouse or being reprimanded at work). As illustrated in Figure 18.11, the longer a stressor had lasted, the more likely a person was to catch a cold. In a second follow up, Cohen and his colleagues (2002) found that people who reacted to a stressful lab task with high levels of the stress-related hormone cortisol were more likely to get sick than those who did not react as strongly. Over time, stress breaks down the body's immune system.

The common-cold studies are important because they demonstrate not only that stress can weaken the immune system but also, as a result, that it can leave us vulnerable to illness. Does stress have similar effects on more serious illnesses? Can it, for example, hasten the spread of cancer? In an early test of this hypothesis, Madeline Visintainer and others (1982) implanted tumorous cancer cells into laboratory rats, some of whom were then repeatedly exposed to shocks they could not escape. After one month, 50 percent of the animals not shocked died of cancer. Yet relative to that baseline, the death rate climbed to 73 percent among those subjected to the inescapable shock. This study was among the first to show that psychological states—such as a feeling of helplessness— can influence the spread of cancer.

The growth of tumors in helpless white laboratory rats is interesting, but does the same principle apply to people? For obvious ethical reasons, researchers cannot fill human participants with despair or inject lethal tumors into their bodies to test the cause-and-effect chain directly. But they can examine the medical records of people whose lives are struck by tragedy. Studies of this sort have revealed that cancer appears more often than normal in people prone to being in a negative emotional state (Sklar & Anisman, 1981). In one large-scale study, investigators looked up two thousand male workers of the Western Electric Company in Chicago whose personalities had been assessed in 1958. At the time, test scores indicated that some of the men were low in self-esteem, unhappy, and depressed. The result? Some twenty years later, these men were more likely than their coworkers to have died of cancer (Persky et al., 1987). Let's be clear about what these results mean. Nobody disputes the notion that cancer is caused by exposure to toxic substances and other biological factors. But individuals who are clinically depressed or under great stress have weakened immune systems—which, in some cases, may result in a higher death rate from cancer and other killer diseases (Herbert & Cohen, 1993; Andersen et al., 1994).

Toward the end of his life, Albert Schweitzer was asked for his opinion of traditional African medicine and the witch doctors who practice it. His reply: "The witch doctor succeeds for the same reason all the rest of us succeed. Each patient carries his own doctor inside him." More recently, Robert Ornstein and David Sobel (1987) referred to the human brain as an "internal pharmacy dispensing a

*"The most important thing in illness is never to lose heart."*

—Nikolai Lenin

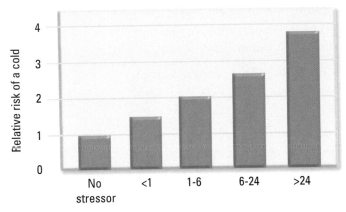

Duration of life stressor (in months)

**FIGURE 18.11  Stress duration and illness**
Two hundred seventy-six volunteers were interviewed about recent life stress, then infected with a cold virus. As shown above, the longer a stressor had lasted, in months, the more likely a person was to catch the cold. Over time, stress breaks down the body's immune system.

## REVIEW QUESTIONS

- *Summarize the various sources of stress in our lives. What are the physiological effects?*

- *Distinguish between Type A and Type B personalities. Discuss the link to coronary heart disease.*

- *What methods are used to examine the impact of stress on the immune system?*

- *Describe the evidence that stress weakens the immune system and explain how it has that effect.*

stream of powerful drugs" (p. 89). Whether it involves pharmacists or doctors, psychoneuroimmunology research suggests that the key is to find ways for each of us to tap our own inner resources.

## COPING WITH STRESS

- *Is it adaptive to block unwanted thoughts and emotions from awareness?*
- *Are relaxation and exercise truly healthful?*
- *What is the role played by feelings of control and optimism?*
- *Why is it said that friendships and other forms of social support are vital to our health and well-being?*

Stress is inevitable. No one can prevent it. But we can try to minimize its harmful effects on our health. To understand how some people keep their composure while others crumble under the pressure, it is useful to examine the coping process and ask the question: What are some adaptive ways to cope with stress?

### COPING STRATEGIES

Leaving home. Taking exams. Breaking up with my college girlfriend. Working long nights on my thesis. Seeking employment in a competitive job market. Having children. Raising children. Facing academic pressures to publish or perish. Struggling to meet the deadline to complete this text. I could have coped with these sources of stress in any number of ways. In each case, I might have focused on solving the problem, talked to friends, invited distractions to pass the time, drunk myself silly, smiled and pretended that all was well—or I could have just freaked out.

Richard Lazarus and Susan Folkman (1984) distinguished two general types of coping strategies. The first is *problem-focused coping,* designed to reduce stress by overcoming the problem. Difficulties in school? Study harder, hire a tutor, or reduce your workload. Marriage on the rocks? Talk it out or see a counselor. Problems at work? Talk to your boss or look for another job. The goal is to attack the source of your stress. A second approach is *emotion-focused coping,* in which one tries to manage the emotional turmoil, perhaps by learning to live with the problem. If you're struggling at school, at work, or in a relationship, you can keep a stiff upper lip and ignore the situation or make the best of it. People probably take an active problem-focused approach when they think they can overcome a stressor but fall back on an emotion-focused approach when they see the problem as out of their control. According to Lisa Aspinwall and Shelley Taylor (1997), there is a yet third alternative: *proactive coping,* which consists of up-front efforts to ward off or modify the onset of a stressful event. Coping, they say, is thus an ongoing process by which we try to prevent—not just react to—the bumps and bruises of daily life.

**Thought Suppression** One emotion-focused strategy people often use is to block stressful thoughts and feelings from awareness. I have used this strategy myself. As I reclined in the dentist's chair with my mouth wide open and a bright light blinding my eyes, the sound of the drill and the grinding on my teeth used to send chills up my spine. To cope, I tried to lock eyes with a gigantic toothbrush hanging on the wall or imagine that I was lying on a warm, sunny beach. Ignore the noise and the pain, I said to myself. Think about something else.

This strategy, a form of *thought suppression,* can have a peculiar and paradoxical effect. Daniel Wegner (1994) conducted a series of experiments in which he had people say whatever came to mind into a microphone—and he told half of them not to think about a white bear. As described in Chapter 4, Wegner found that people could not keep the image from popping to mind. What's more, he found that when permitted later to think about a white bear, those who had earlier tried to suppress the image were unusually preoccupied with it, providing evidence of a "rebound" effect. It's difficult to follow the command "Don't think about it"—and the harder you try, the less likely you are to succeed. The solution: focused self-distraction. When people were told to imagine a tiny red Volkswagen whenever the forbidden white bear intruded into consciousness, the rebound effect vanished (Wenzlaff & Wegner, 2000).

What do white bears and red cars have to do with coping? Lots. When people try to force stressful thoughts or painful sensations out of awareness, they are doomed to fail. In fact, the problem may worsen. That's where focused self-distraction comes in. In a study of pain tolerance, Delia Cioffi and James Holloway (1993) had participants put a hand into a bucket of ice-cold water and keep it there until they could no longer bear the pain. One group was instructed to avoid thinking about the sensation. A second group was told to form a mental picture of their room at home. Afterward, participants who had coped through suppression were slower to recover from the pain than were those who used focused self-distraction. To manage stress—whether it's caused by physical pain, a strained romance, final exams, or problems at work—distraction ("think about lying on the beach") is a better coping strategy than mere suppression ("don't think about the dentist's drill").

It may be particularly maladaptive to keep secrets and hold in strong emotions. More than hundred years ago, Breuer and Freud (1895) theorized that emotional inhibition, or what they called strangulated affect, can cause mental illness. Current studies suggest it may be physically taxing as well. James Gross and Robert Levenson (1997) showed female students funny, sad, and neutral films. Half the time, they instructed participants to not let their feelings show. From a hidden camera, videotapes confirmed that when asked to conceal their feelings, participants were less expressive. But physiological recordings revealed that as they watched the funny and sad films, participants had a greater cardiovascular response when they tried to inhibit their feelings than when they did not. Physiologically, the effort to suppress the display of emotion backfired.

A study by Steve Cole and others (1996) pushes this point a suggestive but profound step further. These investigators identified eighty gay men in the Los Angeles area who were newly infected with the HIV virus but had no symptoms, administered various psychological tests, and monitored their progress every six months for nine years. They found that in men who were partly "in the closet"—compared to those who were completely open about their sexuality—the infection spread more rapidly, causing them to die sooner. By itself, this correlation does not prove that "coming out" is healthier than "staying in." In a controlled laboratory experiment, however, participants who were instructed to suppress rather than express turbulent emotional thoughts exhibited a temporary decrease in the activity of certain immune cells (Petrie et al., 1998). It appears that actively concealing your thoughts and feelings can be hazardous to your health.

**Relaxation**    There are also ways to manage the physical symptoms of stress. One popular technique is *relaxation*. Years ago, cardiologist Herbert Benson (1975) recruited experienced meditators for a study and fitted them with various physiological measurement devices—including catheters in the veins and arteries. Participants spent twenty minutes in a quiet resting state, then meditated, then returned to a normal state. There were no observable changes in their posture or level of physical activity. But the physiological results were striking. While meditating,

*Try not to think of a white bear, and this image is likely to intrude upon consciousness with remarkable frequency.*

participants consumed 17 percent less oxygen and produced less carbon dioxide. Breathing slowed from fourteen or fifteen breaths per minute to ten or eleven breaths per minute. Blood tests showed there was a marked drop in the amount of lactate, a chemical typically associated with anxiety. Finally, brain-wave patterns were slower than those normally found in the waking state.

According to Benson, who went on to establish the Mind/Body Medical Institute at Harvard Medical School, anyone can be taught this "relaxation response." Try it. Sit quietly and comfortably, close your eyes, and relax all the muscles from your feet to your face. Then breathe deeply through the nose, and each time you exhale, silently utter some word (such as "one . . . one . . . one . . . "). As you proceed, let your mind drift freely. If anxiety-provoking thoughts pop into mind, refocus your attention on the word you are chanting and stay calm. Repeat this exercise once or twice a day, for ten to twenty minutes. Says Benson (1993), "By practicing two basic steps—the repetition of a sound, word, phrase, prayer, or muscular activity; and a passive return to the repetition whenever distracting thoughts recur—you can trigger a series of physiological changes that offer protection against stress" (p. 256).

Meditative relaxation can be powerfully effective. In one study, Friedman and Ulmer (1984) randomly assigned hundreds of heart attack patients to one of two treatment groups. In one group, they received standard medical advice on drugs, exercise, work, and diet. In the second group, they were also counseled on how to relax, slow down their pace, smile more, and take time to enjoy the moment. After three years, the relaxation patients had suffered only half as many repeat heart attacks as did those in the control group (see Figure 18.12). In another study, Janice Kiecolt-Glaser and her colleagues (2001) found that relaxation also fortifies the immune system. They took blood samples from medical and dental students—early in the semester, then again just before major exams. Some of the students but not others were trained in relaxation using self-hypnosis. The result: no-treatment control students exhibited a decrease in immune-system activity prior to examinations, but those trained to relax did not. This result offers each of us hope that we can learn to relax—and keep ourselves immunologically protected in the face of stress.

**Aerobic Exercise** A second way to manage stress is through *aerobic exercise*—sustained, vigorous physical activity designed to build heart and lung capacity and enhance the body's use of oxygen. Walking, running, swimming, bicycling, cross-country skiing, and dancing are ideal forms of aerobic exercise. The health benefits seem clear. One large-scale study showed that men who burned at least two thousand calories a week through exercise lived longer than those who were less active (Paffenbarger et al., 1986). Another study of both men and women showed that even a moderate amount of exercise is associated with increased longevity (Blair et al., 1989).

Don't jump from these correlations to the causal conclusion that if you start running you'll live longer. It is possible, for example, that people who exercise regularly are also more health-conscious about eating, smoking, wearing seat belts, and other factors that promote longevity. Still, the effects of exercise on physical health and well-being are extensive. Research shows that exercise strengthens the heart, lowers blood pressure, aids in the metabolism of carbohydrates and fats, boosts self-esteem, elevates

*"Those who think they have no time for bodily exercise will sooner or later have to find time for illness."*

—EDWARD STANLEY

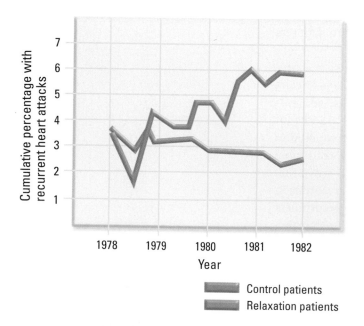

**FIGURE 18.12    Relaxation and the heart**
After three years, heart-attack victims who were taught to relax their pace suffered fewer recurrences than did those who received only standard medical advice (Friedman & Ulmer, 1984).

mood, and improves cognitive functioning (Simon, 1991). In a study involving mildly depressed female students, Lisa McCann and David Holmes (1984) randomly assigned some to take part in a ten-week aerobic-exercise program and others to a ten-week program of relaxation exercises. A third group received no treatment. Afterward, those who exercised were the most improved, scoring lowest on a measure of depression. Other studies have shown that physical fitness can also soften the toxic effects of stress on health (Brown, 1991).

## THE "SELF-HEALING PERSONALITY"

For years, psychologists have speculated about very specific correlations between personality traits and illness. People who are anxious are doomed to get ulcers, we're told, just as angry types are prone to headaches, depressives are prone to cancer, weak and dependent types suffer from asthma, and workaholics die of heart attacks. In light of recent work on psychology and the immune system, others have considered the alternative possibility that there's a generic "disease-prone personality" consisting of a cluster of negative emotional states. According to this view, anger, anxiety, hostility, and depression all lead us to complain of bodily ailments (Watson & Pennebaker, 1989) and perhaps put us at risk for a whole range of illnesses (Friedman & Booth-Kewley, 1987). Whether the links are specific or general is a matter of dispute. However, most health researchers believe that certain traits are healthier and more adaptive than others (Adler & Matthews, 1994)—that there is, in essence, a "self-healing personality" (Friedman, 1991, 2002).

**Hardiness**    Stress affects people differently, an observation that led Suzanne Kobasa (1979) to wonder why some of us are more resilient than others. Kobasa studied two hundred business executives who were under stress. Many said they were frequently sick, affirming the link between stress and illness; others had managed to stay healthy. The two groups were similar in terms of age, education, job status, income, and ethnic and religious background. But from various tests, it was clear that they differed in their attitudes toward themselves, their jobs, and the people in their lives. On the basis of these differences, Kobasa identified a personality style that she called **hardiness** and concluded that hardy people have three characteristics: (1) *commitment,* a sense of purpose with regard to work, family, and other domains; (2) *challenge,* an openness to new experiences and a desire to embrace change; and (3) *control,* the belief that one has the power to influence important future outcomes.

In general, research supports the point that hardiness acts as a buffer against stress (Funk, 1992)—and that control is the active ingredient. Studies have shown that the harmful effects of noise, crowding, heat, and other stressors are reduced when people think they can exert control over these aspects of their environment. Thus, rats exposed to electric shock are less likely to develop ulcers if they are trained to know they can avoid it; children awaiting a doctor's injection cope better when they're prepared with a pain-reducing cognitive strategy; nursing-home residents become healthier and more active when they're given more control over daily events; and patients with cancer, AIDS, and coronary heart disease are better adjusted, emotionally, when they think that they can influence the course of their illness (Rodin, 1986; Helgeson, 1992; Reed et al., 1993; Thompson et al., 1993).

**Optimism and Hope**    A second important trait in the self-healing personality is optimism, a generalized tendency to expect positive outcomes. Are you an optimist or a pessimist? Do you see the proverbial glass as half empty or as half full? Do you expect good things to happen or do you tend to believe in Murphy's Law,

**hardiness**    A personality style that is characterized by commitment, challenge, and control. Hardiness acts as a buffer against stress.

*"Cheerfulness is the very flower of health."*

—JAPANESE PROVERB

that if something can go wrong, it will? By asking questions like these, Michael Scheier and Charles Carver (1985) categorized college students along this dimension and found that dispositional optimists reported fewer symptoms of illness during the semester than did pessimists. Correlations between optimism and health are common. Other studies have shown that optimists are more likely to take a problem-focused approach to coping with stress; complete a rehabilitation program for alcoholics; make a quicker, fuller recovery from coronary-artery bypass surgery; and, among gay men concerned about AIDS, take a more active, less avoidant approach to the threat (Scheier & Carver, 1992). In a study of 1,306 healthy adult men from the Boston area, those reporting high levels of optimism rather than pessimism were half as likely to have coronary heart disease ten years later (Kubzansky et al., 2001).

In a book entitled *Learned Optimism*, Martin Seligman (1991) argues that optimism and pessimism are rooted in our "explanatory styles"—in the ways we explain good and bad events. Based on a large number of studies, Seligman described the typical pessimist as someone who attributes failure to factors that are internal ("It was my fault"), permanent ("I'm washed up"), and global ("I'm bad at everything")—and success to factors that are external ("I lucked out"), temporary ("The task was easy"), and specific ("It was my strength"). This explanatory style breeds despair and low self-esteem. In contrast, the typical optimist is someone who makes the opposite attributions. According to Seligman, the optimist blames failure on factors that are external, temporary, and specific, while crediting success to factors that are internal, permanent, and global—an explanatory style that fosters hope, effort, and a high regard for oneself. Do *you* interpret events as an optimist or pessimist? Imagine the situations described in Table 18.3 and circle cause A or B—whichever you think is the more likely. When you've finished, count the number of points you

---

### TABLE 18.3   EXPLANATORY-STYLES TEST

1. You forget your boyfriend's (girlfriend's) birthday:
   A. I'm not good at remembering birthdays. (0)
   B. I was preoccupied with other things. (1)

2. You stop a crime by calling the police:
   A. A strange noise caught my attention. (0)
   B. I was alert that day. (1)

3. You were extremely healthy all year:
   A. Few people around me were sick, so I wasn't exposed. (0)
   B. I made sure I ate well and got enough rest. (1)

4. You fail an important examination:
   A. I wasn't as smart as the others taking the exam. (0)
   B. I didn't prepare for it well. (1)

5. You ask someone to dance, and he (she) says no:
   A. I am not a good enough dancer. (0)
   B. He (she) doesn't like to dance. (1)

6. You gain weight over the holidays and you can't lose it:
   A. Diets don't work in the long run. (0)
   B. The diet I tried didn't work. (1)

7. You win the lottery:
   A. It was pure chance. (0)
   B. I picked the right numbers. (1)

8. You do extremely well in a job interview:
   A. I felt extremely confident during the interview. (0)
   B. I interview well. (1)

*Source:* M. E. P. Seligman. (1991). *Learned optimism.* New York: Knopf.

earned (in parentheses). A score of 0 indicates a high degree of pessimism; a score of 8 indicates a high degree of optimism.

In the course of a lifetime, everyone has setbacks. Do optimists weather the storms better? Are they happier, healthier, and more successful? Do they have, in the words of Alan McGinnis (1987, p. 16), "the gift for turning stumbling blocks into stepping stones"? To find out, Christopher Peterson and others (1988) collected personal essays that were written in the 1940s by ninety-nine men who had just graduated from Harvard, and they analyzed these materials to determine what each subject's explanatory style was in his youth. Were these men optimists or pessimists? What eventually happened to them? Their health at age sixty was predictable from their explanatory styles thirty-five years earlier. Young optimists were healthier than young pessimists later in life. How can this result be explained? There are two possibilities: one is biological, the other behavioral. In studies that support a biological explanation, researchers have found that pessimists exhibit a weaker immune-system response to stress than optimists (Kamen-Siegel, 1991; Segerstrom et al., 1998). In a study supporting a behavioral explanation, Peterson and his colleagues (1998) scored the explanatory styles of 1,528 healthy young adults from some questionnaires they had filled out between 1936 and 1940. After fifty years, the pessimists (specifically, those who made global rather than specific attributions for bad events) were more likely to have died an accidental or violent death.

There's an old saying "While there's life, there's hope." It's possible that the opposite is also true: "While there's hope, there's life." In a remarkable illustration of this point, Susan Everson and others (1996) studied 2,428 middle-aged men in Finland. Based on the extent to which they agreed with two simple statements ("I feel that it is impossible to reach the goals I would like to strive for" and "The future seems hopeless, and I can't believe that things are changing for the better"), the men were initially classified as having a high, medium, or low sense of hopelessness. When the investigators checked the death records roughly six years later, they found that the more hopeless the men were at the start, the more likely they were to have died of various causes—even when the men were otherwise equated for their age and prior health status. Compared to those who were low in hopelessness, the highs were more than twice as likely to die from cancer and four times more likely to die of cardiovascular disease (see Figure 18.13).

As usual, we should be cautious in interpreting correlations—in this case, between optimism, pessimism, and longevity. Assuming that optimism is adaptive, however, and that it's better to be safe than sorry, Seligman (1991) believes that pessimists can be retrained—not through "mindless devices like whistling a happy tune" but by learning a new set of cognitive skills. According to Seligman, people can train themselves to make optimistic explanations by following three steps: (1) think about situations of adversity (losing in a sports competition, having a friend not return your calls); (2) consider the way you normally explain these events, and if it is pessimistic ("I always choke under pressure," "My friend does not really care about me"); then (3) dispute these explanations by looking closely at the facts ("My opponent played a great game," "My friend has been very busy"). Practice this exercise over and over again. You may find that changing a pessimistic outlook is like breaking a bad habit. Chances are, it will be worth the effort, as "positive expectations can be self-fulfilling" (Peterson, 2000).

## SOCIAL SUPPORT

We hear it all the time: No man (or woman) is an island, human beings are social animals, people need people, and to get by you need a little help from your friends.

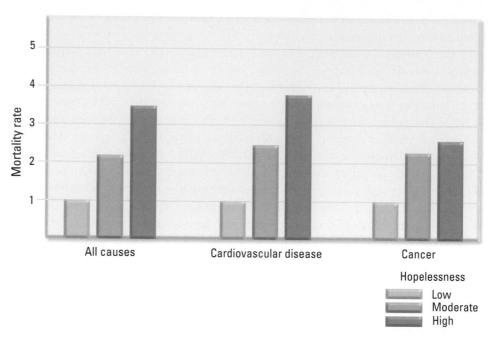

FIGURE 18.13 **Hopelessness and the risk of death**
Among middle-aged men in Finland, those who were initially high rather than low in hopelessness were more likely to die within six years—overall, from cancer, and from cardiovascular disease. On the same measures of mortality, those who were moderate in hopelessness fell between the two extremes (Everson et al., 1996).

Is all this true? Do close family ties, lovers, buddies, community support groups, and relationships at work serve as a buffer against stress? The truth is, yes. An overwhelming amount of evidence now shows that **social support** has therapeutic effects on our psychological and physical well-being (Cohen et al., 2000; Uchino et al., 1996; Wills, 1990).

Psychiatrist David Spiegel, of the Stanford University School of Medicine, came to appreciate the value of social connections several years ago when he organized support groups for women with advanced breast cancer. The groups met weekly in ninety-minute sessions to laugh, cry, share stories, and discuss ways of coping. Spiegel had fully expected the women to benefit, emotionally, from the experience. But he found something else he did not expect: These women lived an average of eighteen months longer than did similar others who did not attend these groups. According to Spiegel (1993), "The added survival time was longer than any medication or other known medical treatment could be expected to provide for women with breast cancer so far advanced" (pp. 331–332).

Similar discoveries were also made by other researchers. In one study, Lisa Berkman and Leonard Syme (1979) surveyed seven thousand residents of Alameda County, California, conducted a nine-year follow-up of mortality rates, and found that the more social contacts people had, the longer they lived. In fact, those who lived alone, had very few close friends or relatives, and did not participate in community groups died at a rate two to five times greater than those with more extensive social networks. This was true of both men and women, young and old, rich and poor, and people from all racial and ethnic backgrounds. James House and his colleagues (1988) then studied 2,754 adults interviewed during visits to their doctors. He found that the most socially active men were two to three times less

**social support** The healthful coping resources provided by friends and other people.

likely to die within nine to twelve years than those of similar age who were more isolated. Socially active women were almost two times less likely to die. According to House, social isolation, statistically, is as predictive of early death as smoking or high cholesterol.

Research findings like these are now common. Married people are more likely than unmarried people to survive cancer for five years (Taylor, 1990), gay men infected with HIV are less likely to contemplate suicide if they have close ties than if they do not (Schneider et al., 1991), and people who have a heart attack are less likely to have a second one if they're living with someone than if they live alone (Case et al., 1992). Among students stressed by schoolwork and among the spouses of cancer patients, more social support is also associated with a stronger immune response (Baron et al., 1990; Jemmott & Magloire, 1988). Based on a review of eighty-one studies, Bert Uchino and others (1996) concluded that in times of stress, social support lowers blood pressure, suppresses the secretion of stress hormones, and strengthens immune responses. There is, however, a vital exception to this rule. Of all the social networks that support us, romantic partnerships, as in marriage, are the most powerful. But while men and women who are happily married live longer than those who are single or divorced, marital conflict breeds stress, elevated blood pressure, ulcers, depression, alcohol and drug abuse, changes in immune function, and other unhealthy effects—especially for women (Kiecolt-Glaser & Newton, 2001).

Our social connections can be therapeutic for many reasons. Friends encourage us to get out, exercise, eat regularly, or seek professional help. Emotionally, friends offer sympathy and reassurance in times of stress. Perhaps having a good friend around boosts our confidence, self-esteem, and sense of security. On an intellectual level, someone to talk to provides a sounding board, new perspectives, and advice as we struggle for solutions to problems. Communicating helps us sort things out in our own minds (Clark, 1993).

It's important to talk about upsetting experiences. As we noted in Chapter 17, James Pennebaker (1997) conducted a number of studies in which he had college students talk to a hidden experimenter or into a tape recorder, or else write about a trauma they had experienced. While speaking, participants were physiologically aroused and upset. Many tearfully recounted accidents, failures, instances of sex abuse, loneliness, rape, the divorce of their parents, shattered relationships, death, and their fears about the future. Soon, however, the participants were feeling better than ever. Blood samples taken afterward revealed a heightened immune response relative to their baseline level, and in the ensuing months participants who had "opened up" made 50 percent fewer visits to the campus health center. A comparison group of students who talked only about trivial matters did not similarly benefit from the experience. The health benefits of opening up—even if only in expressive writing—have now been found in patients with arthritis, asthma, HIV, and other illnesses, leading some to suggest that keeping a diary can serve as a "writing cure" (Smyth & Lepore, 2002).

Finally, religion provides a deeply important source of social and emotional support for many people. Currently more than six billion people in the world belong to hundreds of religions—the most popular, in order, being Christianity, Islam, Hinduism, and Buddhism (Judaism and others have much fewer adherents). Only about 15 to 20 percent of the world's population is unaffiliated with a religious group. Is there a link between religiosity and health? This is an interesting but controversial question. On the one hand, population surveys suggest that people who regularly attend religious services live longer than those who do not (McCullough

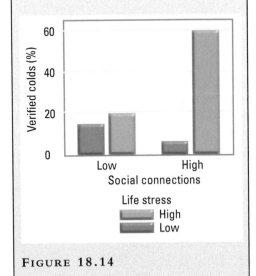

**WHAT'S YOUR PREDICTION**

The health benefits of social support show just how important it is to connect with people. Are there drawbacks to an active social life? Is it possible that the more people we interact with in a day—such as family, friends, classmates, teammates, coworkers, and neighbors—the more exposed we are to catch a cold or flu? Natalie Hamrick and others (2002) asked eighteen- to thirty-year-old adults about recent stressful events and about their social lives, then had them keep a health diary for three months. Based on past research, they expected that participants who were under high stress would get sick more than those under low stress. But what about people with high versus low levels of social contact? Would their social connections make them vulnerable or protect them? Make a prediction. According to the results, the answer is, it depends. Look at Figure 18.14 and you'll see that for people under low stress, social connections did not matter. For people under high stress, however, those with high levels of social contact were *more* likely to catch a cold or flu. It's healthy to be popular . . . except, perhaps, during flu season.

**FIGURE 18.14**

## REVIEW QUESTIONS

- *Distinguish among problem-focused coping, emotion-focused coping, and proactive coping.*

- *How effective are the coping strategies of thought suppression, relaxation, and aerobic exercise?*

- *What three characteristics are associated with hardiness? How do they act as a buffer against stress?*

- *How does social support help people cope with stress?*

et al., 2000). When you think about it, this correlation may make some sense. Religious faith may fill people with hope and optimism rather than despair, offer relaxation in prayer, provide a community of social support to prevent isolation, and promote a safe and healthy way of life by discouraging such toxic habits as drinking and smoking. In analyzing thirty years of health data from twenty-six hundred California adults, for example, William Strawbridge and others (2001) found that men and women who regularly attend religious services drink less, smoke less, and exercise more. On the other hand, some researchers note that the correlations between religiosity and longevity are modest and can be interpreted in different ways. For example, it's possible that nonsmokers, teetotalers, and others who abstain from unhealthful behaviors are more likely to adopt religion as part of their lives than smokers, drinkers, and risk takers—that their survival comes from who they are, not from their attendance at religious services (Sloan et al., 1999).

## THINKING LIKE A PSYCHOLOGIST ABOUT HEALTH AND WELL-BEING

Psychologists from all areas of the discipline are seeking to better understand the factors that promote human health and well-being. With this goal in mind, they have made tremendous strides in recent years. We now know that self-awareness may lower rather than raise our self-esteem, that it may be healthy to harbor some positive illusions, that daily stress can kill us by overworking the heart and weakening the immune system, that it's unhealthy to suppress negative thoughts and emotions, and that certain coping strategies, a sense of control, hope, and social support can be used to restore the body's natural defenses. *The mind is a powerful tool. The more we know about how to use it, the better off we'll be.*

Psychology's latest discoveries are exciting, but it is also important to recognize the limitations. Recently established links among mind, behavior, and the immune system, for example, raise the hope that perhaps each of us has the power to slow the spread of cancer and other diseases. This is not an invitation to believe in miracles, however, nor does it mean that we should reject standard medical treatments and try instead to wish away our illnesses. If we smoke, if we're exposed to radiation, if we breathe polluted air or spend too much time baking in the hot sun, the risk of cancer will be increased—regardless of how relaxed, fit, determined, or upbeat we are and regardless of how many friends we have to support us. Although we should appreciate the powers of the

mind to influence the body, it's also important to guard against blaming the victims of terminal illness for their condition and making them feel guilty—as if dying were the ultimate failure. As Howard Friedman (1991) put it, "We must walk a fine line between blaming patients on the one hand and absolving them of any role in their health on the other" (p. 96).

In no case is this truer than with people who have contracted AIDS. Earlier, we noted that heart attacks, cancers, strokes, and accidents are now more common causes of death in the United States than infectious diseases. But AIDS, the first truly global epidemic, has spread at an alarming rate. AIDS has been described as a recently exploded microbiological time bomb (Mann, 1992). In 1981, five homosexual men in North America were diagnosed with AIDS and were among 189 cases reported that year. By 1996, the number of AIDS cases in North America had skyrocketed to three-quarters of a million—and included heterosexual men, women, and children. Thus far, an estimated 58 million people worldwide have been infected with HIV. The World Health Organization projects that the numbers will climb higher, particularly in Latin America, sub-Saharan Africa, North Africa, the Middle East, Eastern Europe, and parts of Asia (see Figure 18.15).

The AIDS virus is transmitted from one person to another in infected blood, semen, vaginal secretions, and other body fluids. People who are HIV-positive may have no symptoms

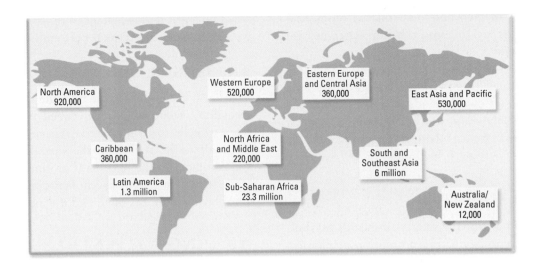

FIGURE 18.15
**Estimated number of adults and children living with AIDS at the start of 2000**

for several years and may not even realize they are infected. Eventually, however, the virus will ravage the immune system by destroying the lymphocytes that help ward off disease. What's frightening about AIDS is that it's fatal, that it's increasing at a rate of fifteen thousand new cases a day, and that there is still no vaccine or reliable treatment for it (Stine, 2002).

At present, the only way to truly control the spread of AIDS is to alter people's beliefs, motivations, and risk-taking behavior (Fisher & Fisher, 1992; Gerrard et al., 1996;

Kalichman, 1998). As we navigate our way through the twenty-first century, in a global village that brings the world's people together as never before, that's where psychology comes in. Psychologists need to design programs that encourage voluntary AIDS testing, provide counseling to assist those who are positively identified, identify possible nonbiological factors that influence the progression of AIDS in those who are infected, educate the public about the disease, and convince everyone to use condoms as a means of protection. As always, we can use our minds to help protect our lives.

# SUMMARY

Although psychology is a diverse field, all its branches share the objective of improving our health and well-being.

## MIND OVER MATTER

The mind's influence on the body, a frequent theme in psychology, can be seen in the placebo effect. Positive expectations increase the release of pain-relieving endorphins and suppress adrenaline and other stress hormones that reduce the body's resistance.

## THE SELF AND WELL-BEING

People strive to maintain a high level of **self-esteem**. Those with high self-esteem tend to be happy, healthy, and successful. Those with low self-esteem are more anxious, pessimistic, and prone to failure. If our self-concept falls short of our

standards, self-esteem declines. The more discrepancy there is and the more accessible it is to awareness, the more discomfort we feel.

## THE SELF-AWARENESS "TRAP"

According to **self-awareness theory**, certain situations raise our self-awareness and prompt us to compare our behavior to standards, often resulting in a loss of self-esteem. Individuals differ, however, in their tendencies toward self-consciousness. We can cope with self-awareness either by reducing self-discrepancies (trying to make our behavior match our standards) or by escaping from self-awareness. The escape strategy sometimes involves harmful actions such as getting intoxicated.

## POSITIVE ILLUSIONS

We also cope with inadequacies through self-deception, distorting and hiding unpleasant truths from ourselves. People tend to see themselves in favorable and inflated terms. Unrealistic optimism leads us to expect better outcomes for ourselves than for others.

Are positive illusions adaptive? Some research indicates that people with positive illusions have higher self-esteem, happiness, and health. Yet certain kinds of self-deception can cause self-destructive behaviors, and recent studies suggest that people with inflated views of themselves are liked less by others.

## STRESS AND HEALTH

Researchers have taken a growing interest in **health psychology,** which applies psychology to the promotion of physical health and the prevention and treatment of illness. Among the influences on health, stress is especially important.

### THE SOURCES OF STRESS

**Stress** is an unpleasant state of arousal that occurs when we perceive that an event threatens our ability to cope. Catastrophes are one major type of stressor. **Posttraumatic stress disorder (PTSD)** among combat veterans and other trauma victims produces long-lasting symptoms ranging from sleeplessness to social withdrawal.

According to one view, major life events such as marriage, divorce, or promotion, cause stress. Research does show a link between negative life events and health problems, but no such connection for positive events. It's also important to recognize that people interpret events differently.

Daily hassles, or microstressors, can have even more impact than major life events. Job pressures may cause burnout. Environmental factors such as crowding also play a role.

### THE PHYSIOLOGICAL EFFECTS OF STRESS

Selye saw the body's response to stress as a **general adaptation syndrome** marked by the stages of alarm, resistance, and exhaustion. This model suggests that stress may be adaptive in the short term but a threat to health in the long term. According to Sapolsky, the problem for humans is that although the stress response is designed for occasional emergencies, psychological stress occurs often and for prolonged periods of time.

Other researchers have linked stress to coronary heart disease (CHD). People with a hostile **Type A personality** make up a greater percentage of those with CHD than people with a more relaxed **Type B personality.**

### THE IMMUNE SYSTEM

Stress also compromises the **immune system,** which relies on specialized white blood cells called **lymphocytes** and other types of cells to fight bacteria, viruses, and other invaders. Stress alters the activity of the various immune-system cells and can increase the likelihood of illness by weakening resistance. The new field of **psychoneuroimmunology** studies this interplay between the mind and the immune system.

## COPING WITH STRESS

Although we cannot prevent stress, we can minimize its effects on our health by means of active coping strategies.

### COPING STRATEGIES

Coping strategies can be divided broadly into problem-focused coping (overcoming the source of the problem) and emotion-focused coping (managing the emotional turmoil). Thought suppression, an emotion-focused strategy, doesn't usually work unless accompanied by focused self-distraction—deliberately thinking about something else. Relaxation techniques have been shown to boost the immune system. Aerobic exercise, which correlates with longevity and physical health, may also reduce the impact of stress.

### THE "SELF-HEALING PERSONALITY"

The personality style known as **hardiness,** which includes a strong sense of control, seems to act as a buffer against stress. Another important trait is optimism, which has been linked with health and a strong immune response. Optimism and pessimism are often related to explanatory style, and some researchers believe that people can train themselves to use optimistic explanations.

### SOCIAL SUPPORT

**Social support** from friends and family members—or even pets—can reduce stress and promote health. Research shows that people with more social contacts survive illness better and live longer. Correlational research also suggests that people who are involved in religion live longer and healthier lives.

## KEY TERMS

psychoneuroimmunology (PNI) (**p. 712**)

self-awareness theory (**p. 716**)

health psychology (**p. 720**)

stress (**p. 721**)

posttraumatic stress disorder (PTSD) (**p. 722**)

general adaptation syndrome (**p. 725**)

Type A personality (**p. 727**)

Type B personality (**p. 727**)

immune system (**p. 729**)

lymphocytes (**p. 729**)

hardiness (**p. 737**)

social support (**p. 740**)

## THINKING CRITICALLY ABOUT HEALTH AND WELL-BEING

1. Discuss the advantages and disadvantages of positive self-illusions. Is it best for your general well-being to be an optimist, a pessimist, or a realist? Support your position with empirical evidence.

2. Distinguish between positive and negative stressors. If both types of life events can result in stress, then why is it that negative life events are related to illness, but positive ones are not?

3. Identify several specific actions that you could implement in your life right now to help you reduce or cope with stress. Why would these actions work?

4. Discuss the implications of the research concerning the impact of stress on the immune system, as well as research concerning coping with stress, to current systems of health care. How could you apply this research to improve the quality of care in hospitals, nursing homes, and the like?

# APPENDIX

## STATISTICS IN PSYCHOLOGICAL RESEARCH

Everyday, we are besieged by claims backed by statistics. In our personal lives and in the news, we are presented with averages, percentages, probabilities, correlations, and margins of error. Whether we are reading *Consumer Reports, Sports Illustrated,* or the *New England Journal of Medicine,* an understanding of statistical concepts is vital to critical thinking.

Understanding and interpreting the results of psychological research also requires an understanding of the statistical methods that are used for describing and drawing conclusions from data. Chapter 1 introduced some terms and concepts associated with *descriptive statistics*—the numbers that psychologists use merely to describe and present their data—and with *inferential statistics*—the mathematical procedures used to draw conclusions from data and to make inferences about what they mean. Here, we present more details about these statistical analyses that will help you to evaluate research results.

## DESCRIBING DATA

Consider a hypothetical experiment on the effects of incentives on performance. The experimenter presents a list of problems to two groups of subjects. Each group must solve these problems within a fixed period of time, but for each correct answer, the low-incentive group is paid ten cents, while the high-incentive group gets one dollar. The hypothesis to be tested is the **null hypothesis,** the assertion that the independent variable manipulated by the experimenter will have no effect on the dependent variable. In this case, the null hypothesis holds that the size of the incentive (the independent variable) will not affect performance on the task (the dependent variable).

Assume that the experimenter has obtained a sample of subjects, assigned them randomly to the two incentive groups, and done everything possible to avoid the problems discussed in Chapter 1. The experiment has been run, and the researcher now has the data: a list of the number of correct answers given by each subject in each group. Now comes the first task of statistical analysis: describing the data in a way that is easy to understand.

### THE FREQUENCY HISTOGRAM

The simplest way to describe the data is to draw up something like Table A.1—test scores obtained by thirteen subjects performing in a low-incentive condition and thirteen in a high-incentive condition—in which all the numbers are presented in a list. After glancing at the table, you might think that the high-incentive group seems to have done better than the low-incentive group, but the difference is not immediately obvious. A picture is worth a thousand words, so a more satisfactory way of presenting the same data is in a picturelike graphic known as a **frequency histogram** (see Figure A.1).

| TABLE A.1 | A SIMPLE DATA SET: TEST SCORES OF TWO CONDITIONS |
|---|---|
| **Low Incentive** | **High Incentive** |
| 4 | 6 |
| 6 | 4 |
| 2 | 10 |
| 7 | 10 |
| 6 | 7 |
| 8 | 10 |
| 3 | 6 |
| 5 | 7 |
| 2 | 5 |
| 3 | 9 |
| 5 | 9 |
| 9 | 3 |
| 5 | 8 |

**null hypothesis** The assertion that the independent variable will have no effect on the dependent variable.

**frequency histogram** A graphic presentation of data in which a set of bars is used to represent how frequently different values occur in a data set.

Construction of a histogram is simple. First, divide the scale for measuring the dependent variable (in this case, the number of correct solutions) into a number of categories, or "bins." The bins in our example are 1–2, 3–4, 5–6, 7–8, and 9–10. Next, sort the raw data into the appropriate bin. (For example, the score of a subject who had 5 correct answers would go into the 5–6 bin, a score of 8 would go into the 7–8 bin, and so on.) Finally, for each bin, count the number of scores in that bin and draw a bar up to the height of that number on the vertical axis of a graph. The set of bars makes up the frequency histogram.

We are interested in comparing the scores of two groups, so two separate histograms are presented in Figure A.1: one for the high-incentive group, the other for the low-incentive group. Now the difference between groups that was difficult to see in Table A.1 becomes more clearly visible: More people in the high-incentive group obtained high scores than in the low-incentive group.

Histograms and other pictures are useful for visualizing and better understanding the "shape" of research data, but in order to analyze the results statistically, more is needed. For example, before we can tell whether two histograms are different statistically or just visually, the data that they represent must be summarized using descriptive statistics.

## DESCRIPTIVE STATISTICS

Descriptive statistics are used for basic purposes: (1) to measure the number of observations made; (2) to summarize the typical value of a set of data; (3) to summarize the spread, or variability, in a set of data; and (4) to express the correlation between two sets of data.

**Sample Size** The easiest statistic to compute, abbreviated as $N$, simply describes the number of observations that make up a data set. In Table A.1, for example, $N = 13$ for each group, or 26 for the entire data set. Simple as it is, $N$ plays a very important role in more sophisticated statistical analyses.

**Measures of Central Tendency** Look at the histograms in Figure A.1, and you'll see that there is a difference in the pattern of scores between the two groups. But how much of a difference is it? What is the typical value, or the *central tendency,* that represents each group's performance? There are three measures of central tendency that capture this typical value: the mode, the median, and the mean. The *mode* is the value or score that occurs most often in the data set. The *median* is the middle score in the data set, the 50th percentile. If you list the scores in order from lowest to highest, half will fall above the median, half below it. The *mean* is the arithmetic average. To find the mean, add the values of all the scores and divide by the number of scores.

**Measures of Variability** The variability, or dispersion, of scores in a set of data can be just as important as its central tendency. Are the scores clumped together or spread out? Basically, there are two ways to quantify the variability of scores. These measures are known as the range and the standard deviation.

The *range* is simply the difference between the highest and lowest values in a data set. For the results in Table A.1, the range for the low-incentive group is $9 - 2 = 7$; for the high-incentive group, the range is $10 - 3 = 7$.

The *standard deviation,* abbreviated as SD, measures the average difference between each score in a sample and the mean. To see how the standard deviation is derived, consider the data in Table A.2 and calculate, in order: (1) the mean of the set (in this example, $20/5 = 4$); (2) the difference, or *deviation* (D), of each score from that mean by subtracting the mean from each score (as in column 2 of

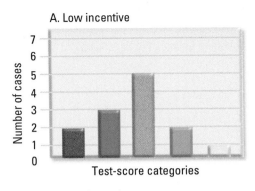

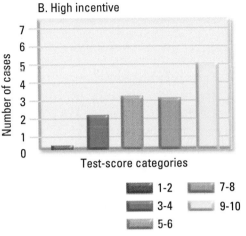

**FIGURE A.1  Frequency histograms**
The height of each bar of a histogram represents the number of scores falling within each range of score values. The pattern formed by these bars provides a visual image of how research results are distributed.

**normal distribution** A symmetrical dispersion of scores in which the mean, median, and mode all have the same value.

| TABLE A.2 | CALCULATING THE STANDARD DEVIATION | |
|---|---|---|
| **Raw Data** | **Difference from Mean = $D$** | **$D^2$** |
| 2 | $2 - 4 = -2$ | 4 |
| 2 | $2 - 4 = -2$ | 4 |
| 3 | $3 - 4 = -1$ | 1 |
| 4 | $4 - 4 = \ 0$ | 0 |
| 9 | $9 - 4 = \ 5$ | <u>25</u> |
| Mean = 20/5 = 4 | | $\Sigma D^2 = 34$ |

$$\text{Standard deviation} = \sqrt{\frac{\Sigma D^2}{N}} = \sqrt{\frac{34}{5}} = \sqrt{6.8} = 2.6$$

Table A.2); and (3) the average of these deviations. Note that if you calculated the average by finding the arithmetic mean, you would sum the deviations and find that the negative deviations exactly balance the positive ones, resulting in a mean difference of 0. Obviously, there is more than zero variation around the mean in the data set. So instead of using the arithmetic mean, we compute the standard deviation by squaring the deviations (which removes all negative values), summing these squared deviations, dividing by $N$, and then taking the square root of the result. These simple steps are outlined in more detail in Table A.2.

### The Normal Distribution

Now that we have described histograms and reviewed some descriptive statistics, we will reexamine how these methods of representing research data relate to some of the concepts discussed elsewhere in the book.

When psychology researchers collect multiple measurements and plot their data in histograms, the pattern that results often resembles that shown for the low-incentive group in Figure A.1. That is, the majority of scores tend to fall in the middle of the distribution, with fewer and fewer occurring as one moves toward the extremes. As more and more data are collected, and as smaller and smaller bins are used (perhaps containing only one value each), the histograms tend to smooth out, until they resemble the bell-shape curve known as the **normal distribution**, or *normal curve*, which is shown in Figure A.2A. When a distribution of scores follows a truly normal curve, its mean, median, and mode all have the same value. If the curve is normal, we can use its standard deviation to describe how any particular score stands in relation to the rest of the distribution.

Intelligence-test scores provide an example. As we saw in Chapter 12, IQ scores are distributed in a normal curve, with a mean, median, and mode of 100 and an SD of 15 (see Figure A.2B). In such a distribution, half of the population will have an IQ above 100, and half will be below 100. The shape of the true normal curve is such that 68 percent of the area under it lies within 1 standard deviation above and below the mean. In terms of IQ, this means that 68 percent of the population has an IQ somewhere between 85 (100 − 15) and 115 (100 + 15). Of the remaining 32 percent of the population, half falls more than 1 SD above the mean, and half falls more than 1 SD below the mean. Thus, 16 percent of the population has an IQ above 115, and 16 percent scores below 85.

A. Normal distribution showing the smoothed approximation to the frequency histogram

B. The normal distribution of IQ

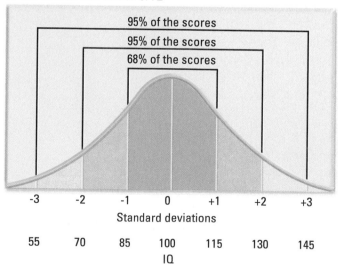

**FIGURE A.2** **The normal distribution**
Many kinds of research data approximate the symmetrical shape of this normal curve, in which most scores fall toward the center of the range.

### TABLE A.3 CALCULATING THE CORRELATION COEFFICIENT

| Subject | Test 1 | Test 2 | [Step B] $(x - M_x)(y - M_y)$ |
|---------|--------|--------|------------------------------|
| A | 1 | 3 | $(1 - 3)(3 - 4) = (-2)(-1) = +2$ |
| B | 1 | 3 | $(1 - 3)(3 - 4) = (-2)(-1) = +2$ |
| C | 4 | 5 | $(4 - 3)(5 - 4) = (1)(1) \quad = +1$ |
| D | 6 | 5 | $(6 - 3)(5 - 4) = (3)(1) \quad = +3$ |
| [Step A] | $M_x = 3$ | $M_y = 4$ | $\Sigma(x - M_x)(y - M_y) \qquad = +8$ |

[Step C] $\quad \Sigma(x - M_x)^2 = 4 + 4 + 1 + 9 = 18$

[Step D] $\quad \Sigma(y - M_y)^2 = 1 + 1 + 1 + 1 = 4$

[Step E] $\quad r = \dfrac{\Sigma(x - M_x)(y - M_y)}{\sqrt{\Sigma(x - M_x)^2 \Sigma(y - M_y)^2}} = \dfrac{8}{\sqrt{18 \times 4}} = \dfrac{8}{\sqrt{72}} = \dfrac{8}{8.48} = +.94$

The normal curve is also the basis for percentiles. A **percentile score** indicates the percentage of people or observations that fall below a given score in a normal distribution. In Figure A.2B, for example, the mean score (which is also the median) lies at a point below which 50 percent of the scores fall. Thus, the mean of a normal distribution is at the 50th percentile. What does this mean for IQ? If you score 1 SD above the mean, your score is at a point above which only 16 percent of the population falls. This means that 84 percent of the population (100 percent − 16 percent) must be below that score; so this IQ score is at the 84th percentile. A score at 2 SDs above the mean is at the 97.5 percentile, because only 2.5 percent of the scores are above it in a normal distribution.

Scores may also be expressed in terms of their distance in standard deviations from the mean, producing what are called **standard scores**. A standard score of 1.5, for example, is 1.5 standard deviations from the mean.

**Correlation** Histograms, measures of central tendency, and measures of variability describe certain characteristics of one dependent variable at a time. However, psychologists are often concerned with describing the *relationship* between two variables. Measures of correlation are often used for this purpose. In Chapter 1, we discussed the meaning of a *correlation coefficient*. Here we describe how to calculate it.

Recall that correlations are based on the relationship between two sets of numbers associated with each subject or observation. The numbers may represent, say, a person's height and weight or the IQ of a parent and child. Table A.3 contains these kinds of data for four subjects from our incentives study who took the test twice. (As you may recall from Chapter 12, the correlation between their scores would be a measure of *test-retest reliability*.) The formula for computing the Pearson correlation, or *r*, is as follows:

$$r = \frac{\Sigma(x - M_x)(y - M_y)}{\sqrt{\Sigma(x - M_x)^2 \, \Sigma(y - M_y)^2}}$$

where:
  $x$ = each score on variable 1 (in this case, test 1)
  $y$ = each score on variable 2 (in this case, test 2)
  $M_x$ = the mean of the scores on variable 1
  $M_y$ = the mean of the scores on variable 2

The main function of the denominator in this formula is to ensure that the coefficient ranges from +1.00 to −1.00, no matter how large or small the values of the

**percentile score** The percentage of people or observations that fall below a given score in a normal distribution.

**standard score** A value that indicates the distance, in standard deviations, between a given score and the mean of all the scores in a data set.

variables being correlated. The "action element" of this formula is the numerator. It is the result of multiplying the amounts by which each of two observations ($x$ and $y$) differ from the means of their respective distributions ($M_x$ and $M_y$). Notice that, if the two variables "go together" (so that, if one is large, the other is also large, and if one is small, the other is also small), then either both will tend to be above the mean of their distribution or both will tend to be below the mean of their distribution. When this is the case, $x - M_x$ and $y - M_y$ will both be positive, or they will both be negative. In either case, their product will always be positive, and the correlation coefficient will also be positive. If, on the other hand, the two variables go opposite to one another, such that, when one is large, the other is small, one of them is likely to be smaller than the mean of its distribution, so that either $x - M_x$ or $y - M_y$ will have a negative sign and the other a positive sign. Multiplying these differences together will always result in a product with a negative sign, and $r$ will be negative as well.

Now compute the correlation coefficient for the data presented in Table A.3. The first step (Step A in the table) is to compute the mean ($M$) for each variable. $M_x$ turns out to be 3, and $M_y$ is 4. Next, calculate the numerator by finding the differences between each $x$ and $y$ value and its respective mean and then multiplying them (as in Step B of Table A.3). Notice, in this example, that the differences in each pair have like signs, so the correlation coefficient will be positive. The next step is to calculate the terms in the denominator; in this case, as shown in Steps C and D in Table A.3, they have values of 18 and 4. Finally, place all the terms in the formula and carry out the arithmetic (Step E). The result in this case is an $r$ of +.94—which is a high and positive correlation, suggesting that performances on repeated tests are very closely related. A subject doing well the first time is very likely to do well again; a person doing poorly at first will probably do no better the second time.

## INFERENTIAL STATISTICS

The descriptive statistics from the incentives experiment tell the experimenter that the performances of the high- and low-incentive groups differ. But there is some uncertainty. Is the difference large enough to be important? Does it represent a stable effect or a fluke? The researcher would like to have a *measure of confidence* that the difference between groups is genuine and reflects the impact of incentive on mental tasks in the real world, rather than the effect of the particular subjects used, the phase of the moon, or other random or uncontrolled factors. One way of determining confidence would be to run the experiment again with a new group of subjects. Confidence that incentives produced differences in performance would grow stronger if the same or a larger between-group difference occurs again. In reality, psychologists rarely repeat, or *replicate*, their experiments in exactly the same way three or four times. But *inferential statistics* provide a measure of how likely it was that results came about by chance. They put a precise mathematical value on the confidence or probability that rerunning the same experiment would yield similar (or even stronger) results.

**Differences between Means: The *t* test**  One of the most important tools of inferential statistics is the **_t_ test.** It allows the researcher to ask how likely it is that the difference between two means occurred by chance rather than as a function of the effect of the independent variable. When the *t* test or other inferential statistic says that the probability of chance effects is small enough (usually less than 5 percent), the results are said to be *statistically significant*. Conducting a *t* test of statistical significance requires the use of three descriptive statistics.

**_t_ test**  A statistical test used to assess the likelihood that differences between two means occurred by chance.

The first component of the *t* test is the size of the observed effect, the difference between the means. Recall that the mean is calculated by summing a group's scores and dividing by the number of scores. In the example shown in Table A.1, the mean of the high-incentive group is 94/13, or 7.23, and the mean of the low-incentive group is 65/13, or 5. Thus, the difference between the means for the high- and low-incentive groups is $7.23 - 5 = 2.23$.

Second, the standard deviation of scores in each group must be known. If the scores in a group are quite variable, the standard deviation will be large, indicating that chance may have played a large role in producing the results. The next replication of the study might generate a very different set of group scores. If the scores in a group are all very similar, however, the standard deviation will be small, which suggests that the same result would probably occur for that group if the study were repeated. Thus, the *difference* between groups is more likely to be significant when each group's standard deviation is small. If variability is high enough that the scores of two groups overlap (in Table A.1, for example, some people in the low-incentive group actually did better on the math test than some in the high-incentive group), the mean difference, though large, may not be statistically significant.

Third, we need to take the sample size, N, into account. The larger the number of subjects or observations, the more likely it is that a given difference between means is significant. This is so because, with larger samples, random factors within a group—the unusual performance of a few people who were sleepy or anxious or hostile, for example—are more likely to be canceled out by the majority, who better represent people in general. The same effect of sample size can be seen in flipping a coin. If you toss a quarter 5 times, you might not be too surprised if heads comes up 80 percent of the time. If you get 80 percent heads after 100 tosses, however, you might begin to suspect that this is probably not due to chance alone—that some other effect, perhaps bias in the coin, produced the results. For the same reason, a relatively small correlation coefficient—say, between diet and grades—might be statistically significant if it was based on 50,000 students. As the number of subjects increases, it becomes less likely that the correlation reflects the influence of a few oddball cases.

To summarize, as the differences between the means get larger, as N increases, and as standard deviations get smaller, *t* increases. This increase in *t* raises the researcher's confidence in the significance of the difference between means.

**Analysis of Variance**  Many psychology experiments are considerably more complex than simple comparisons between two groups. They often involve three or more experimental and control groups. Some experiments also include more than one independent variable. For example, suppose we had been interested not only in the effect of incentive size on performance but also in the effect of problem difficulty. We might then create six groups whose subjects would perform easy, moderate, or difficult problems with low or high incentives.

In an experiment like this, the results might be due to the incentive, the problem difficulty, or the combined effects (known as the *interaction*) of the two. Analyzing the size and source of these effects is typically accomplished through procedures known as *analysis of variance*. The details of analysis of variance are beyond the scope of this book. But for now, note that the statistical significance of each effect is influenced by differences between means, standard deviations, and sample sizes in much the same way as described for the *t* test.

For more detailed information about how analysis of variance and other inferential statistics are used to understand and interpret the results of psychological research, consider taking courses in research methods and statistics.

# SUMMARY

Psychological research generates data. Statistics are methods for describing and drawing conclusions from data.

## DESCRIBING DATA

Researchers often test the **null hypothesis,** which is the assertion that the independent variable will have no effect on the dependent variable.

### THE FREQUENCY HISTOGRAM

Graphic representations such as **frequency histograms** provide visual descriptions of data, making data easier to understand.

### DESCRIPTIVE STATISTICS

Numbers that summarize the data are called descriptive statistics. The easiest statistic to compute is $N$, which gives the number of observations made. Measures of central tendency describe the typical value and include the mean, median, and mode. Variability is measured by the range and standard deviation.

Sets of data often follow a **normal distribution,** which means that most scores fall in the middle of the range, with fewer scores occurring as one moves toward the extremes. In a truly normal distribution, the mean, median, and mode are identical. In a normal distribution, a single observation can be described as a **percentile score,** which indicates the percentage of observations falling below it, and in terms of **standard scores,** which indicate its distance from the mean. Another type of descriptive statistic, a correlation coefficient, is used to measure the association between sets of scores.

## INFERENTIAL STATISTICS

Researchers use inferential statistics to quantify the probability that conducting the same experiment again would yield similar results.

### DIFFERENCES BETWEEN MEANS: THE $t$ TEST

One inferential statistic, the $t$ **test,** assesses the likelihood that differences between two means occurred by chance or reflect the impact of an independent variable. Performing a $t$ test requires using the difference between the means of two sets of data, the standard deviation of scores in each set, and the number of observations or subjects.

### ANALYSIS OF VARIANCE

When more than two groups are compared in an experiment, researchers typically rely on analysis of variance to interpret the results.

# KEY TERMS

null hypothesis (**p. A-1**)

frequency histogram (**p. A-1**)

normal distribution (**p. A-3**)

percentile score (**p. A-4**)

standard score (**p. A-4**)

$t$ test (**p. A-5**)

**absolute threshold**  The smallest amount of stimulation that can be detected.

**accommodation**  In Piaget's theory, the process of modifying existing cognitive structures in response to new information.

**accommodation**  The visual process by which lenses become rounded for viewing nearby objects and flatter for viewing remote objects.

**acculturation**  The process by which individuals are changed by their immersion in a new culture.

**acculturative stress**  The stress and mental-health problems often found in immigrants trying to adjust to a new culture.

**acetylcholine (ACh)**  A neurotransmitter found throughout the nervous system that links the motor neurons and muscles.

**achievement motivation**  A strong desire to accomplish difficult tasks, outperform others, and excel.

**acquisition**  The formation of a learned response to a stimulus through the presentation of an unconditioned stimulus (classical conditioning) or reinforcement (operant conditioning).

**action potential**  An electrical impulse that surges along an axon, caused by an influx of positive ions in the neuron.

**activation-synthesis theory**  The theory that dreams result from the brain's attempt to make sense of random neural signals that fire during sleep.

**adaptation-level theory**  The theory that people evaluate experiences in relation to current levels to which they have become accustomed.

**adaptations**  Advantageous physical and psychological traits that are inherited.

**adolescence**  The period of life from puberty to adulthood, corresponding roughly to the ages of thirteen to twenty.

**adoption studies**  A method of testing nature and nurture by comparing twins and other siblings reared together with those separated by adoption.

**affective forecasting**  The process by which people predict how they would feel in the future, after various positive and negative life events.

**afterimage**  A visual sensation that persists after prolonged exposure to and removal of a stimulus.

**aggression**  Behavior intended to inflict harm on someone who is motivated to avoid it.

**agoraphobia**  An anxiety disorder in which the main symptom is an intense fear of public places.

**algorithm**  A systematic, step-by-step problem-solving strategy that is guaranteed to produce a solution.

**altruism**  Helping behavior that is motivated primarily by a desire to benefit others, not oneself.

**Alzheimer's disease (AD)**  A progressive brain disorder that strikes older people, causing memory loss and other symptoms.

**amnesia**  A dissociative disorder involving a partial or complete loss of memory.

**amygdala**  A limbic structure that controls fear, anger, and aggression.

**analogy**  A problem solving heuristic that involves using an old solution as a model for a new, similar problem.

**anchoring effect**  The tendency to use an initial value as an "anchor," or reference point, in making a new numerical estimate.

**anorexia nervosa**  An eating disorder in which the person, usually an adolescent girl or young woman, limits her eating and becomes emaciated.

**anterograde amnesia**  A memory disorder characterized by an inability to store new information in long-term memory.

**antianxiety drugs**  Tranquilizing medications used in the treatment of anxiety.

**antidepressants**  Drugs that relieve depression by increasing the supply of norepinephrine, serotonin, or dopamine.

**antipsychotic drugs**  Drugs that are used to control the positive symptoms of schizophrenia and other psychotic disorders.

**antisocial personality disorder**  A personality disorder involving a chronic pattern of self-centered, manipulative, and destructive behavior toward others.

**applied research**  Research that aims to solve practical human problems.

**archival research**  A form of research that relies on existing records of past behavior.

**arousal theory**  The notion that people are motivated to achieve and maintain an optimum level of bodily arousal.

**assimilation**  In Piaget's theory, the process of incorporating and, if necessary, changing new information to fit existing cognitive structures.

**association cortex**  Areas of the cortex that communicate with the sensory and motor areas and house the brain's higher mental processes.

**attachment**  A deep emotional bond that an infant develops with its primary caretaker.

**attention**  A state of awareness consisting of the sensations, thoughts, and feelings that one is focused on at a given moment.

**attitude**  A positive, negative, or mixed reaction to any person, object, or idea.

**attribution theory**  A set of theories that describe how people explain the causes of behavior.

**audition**  The sense of hearing.

**auditory localization**  The ability to judge the direction a sound is coming from.

**autobiographical memory**  The recollections people have of their own personal experiences and observations.

**autonomic nervous system**  The branch of the peripheral nervous system that connects the CNS to the internal muscles, organs, and glands.

**availability heuristic**  A tendency to estimate the likelihood of an event in terms of how easily instances of it can be recalled.

**aversion therapy**  A behavioral therapy technique for classically conditioning people to react with aversion to alcohol and other harmful substances.

**axon**  Extension of the cell body of a neuron that sends impulses to other neurons.

**babbling**  Spontaneous vocalizations of basic speech sounds, which infants begin at about four months of age.

**basal ganglia**  Masses of gray matter in the brain that help to initiate and coordinate deliberate movements.

**basic research**  "Pure science" research that tests theories and builds a foundation of knowledge.

**behavioral genetics**  A subfield that examines the role of genetic factors on behavior.

**behavioral neuroscience**  A subfield that studies the links among the brain, nervous system, and behavior.

**behavioral observation**  A form of research that is based on the firsthand observation of a subject's behavior.

**behavioral therapy or cognitive-behavioral therapy**  Techniques used to modify disordered thoughts, feelings, and behaviors through the principles of learning.

**behaviorism**  A school of thought that defines psychology as the scientific study of observable behavior.

**belief perseverance**  The tendency to cling to beliefs even after they have been discredited.

**binocular disparity**  A binocular cue for depth perception whereby the closer an object is to a perceiver, the more different the image is in each retina.

**biofeedback**  An operant procedure in which people learn to control physiological responses with the help of "feedback" about their internal states.

**biological rhythm**  Any periodic, more or less regular fluctuation in a biological organism.

**bipolar disorder**  A rare mood disorder characterized by wild fluctuations from mania (a euphoric, overactive state) to depression (a state of hopelessness and apathy).

**blind spot**  A part of the retina through which the optic nerve passes. Lacking rods and cones, this spot is not responsive to light.

**blindsight**  A condition caused by damage to the visual cortex in which a person encodes visual information without awareness.

**borderline personality disorder**  A type of personality characterized by instability in one's self-image, mood, and social relationships and a lack of clear identity.

**brainstem**  The inner core of the brain that connects to the spinal cord and contains the medulla, pons, and reticular formation.

**Broca's area**  A region in the left hemisphere of the brain that directs the muscle movements in the production of speech.

**bulimia nervosa**  An eating disorder found usually among young women that is marked by cycles of binge eating followed by purging.

**bystander effect**  The finding that the presence of others inhibits helping in an emergency.

**Cannon-Bard theory**  The theory that an emotion-eliciting stimulus simultaneously triggers physiological arousal and the experience of emotion.

**case studies**  A type of research that involves making in-depth observations of individual persons.

**central nervous system (CNS)**  The network of nerves contained within the brain and spinal cord.

**central route to persuasion**  A process in which people think carefully about a message and are influenced by its arguments.

**cerebellum**  A primitive brainstem structure that controls balance and coordinates complex voluntary movements.

**cerebral cortex**  The outermost covering of the brain, largely responsible for higher-order mental processes.

**cerebral lateralization**  The tendency for each hemisphere of the brain to specialize in different functions.

**childhood amnesia**  The inability of most people to recall events from before the age of three or four.

**chromosomes**  Rodlike structures, found in all biological cells, that contain DNA molecules in the form of genes.

**chunking** The process of grouping distinct bits of information into larger wholes, or chunks, to increase short-term-memory capacity.

**circadian rhythm** A biological cycle, such as sleeping and waking, that occurs approximately every twenty-four hours.

**classical conditioning** A type of learning in which an organism comes to associate one stimulus with another (also called Pavlovian conditioning).

**cocktail party phenomenon** The ability to attend selectively to one person's speech in the midst of competing conversations.

**cognition** A general term that refers to mental processes such as thinking, knowing, and remembering.

**cognitive dissonance** An unpleasant psychological state often aroused when people behave in ways that are discrepant with their attitudes.

**cognitive social-learning theory** An approach to personality that focuses on social learning (modeling), acquired cognitive factors (expectancies, values), and the person-situation interaction.

**cognitive therapy** A form of psychotherapy in which people are taught to think in more adaptive ways.

**collective unconscious** As proposed by Jung, a kind of memory bank that stores images and ideas that humans have accumulated over the course of evolution.

**collectivism** A cultural orientation in which cooperation and group harmony take priority over purely personal goals.

**comorbidity** The tendency for people diagnosed with one mental disorder to exhibit symptoms of other disorders as well.

**concept** A mental grouping of persons, ideas, events, or objects that share common properties.

**concrete operational stage** Piaget's third stage of cognitive development, when children become capable of logical reasoning.

**concussion** An alteration in a person's mental state caused by trauma to the head.

**conditional positive regard** A situation in which the acceptance and love one receives from significant others is contingent upon one's behavior.

**conditioned response (CR)** A learned response (salivation) to a classically conditioned stimulus (bell).

**conditioned stimulus (CS)** A neutral stimulus (bell) that comes to evoke a classically conditioned response (salivation).

**conduction hearing loss** Hearing loss caused by damage to the eardrum or bones in the middle ear.

**cones** Cone-shaped photoreceptor cells in the retina that are sensitive to color.

**confirmation bias** The inclination to search only for evidence that will verify one's beliefs.

**conformity** A tendency to alter one's opinion or behavior in ways that are consistent with group norms.

**consciousness** An awareness of the sensations, thoughts, and feelings that one is attending to at a given moment.

**conservation** The concept that physical properties of an object remain the same despite superficial changes in appearance.

**contact hypothesis** The proposition that in certain conditions, direct contact between members of rival groups will improve relations.

**content validity** The extent to which a test measures what it's supposed to measure.

**control group** The condition of an experiment in which participants are not exposed to the independent variable.

**convergence** A binocular cue for depth perception involving the turning inward of the eyes as an object gets closer.

**conversion disorder** A disorder in which a person temporarily loses a bodily function in the absence of a physical cause.

**cornea** The clear outer membrane that bends light so that it is sharply focused in the eye.

**corpus callosum** A bundle of nerve fibers that connects the left and right hemispheres.

**correlation** A statistical measure of the extent to which two variables are associated.

**counterfactual thinking** Imagining alternative scenarios and outcomes that might have happened but did not.

**creativity** Intellectual and motivational processes that lead to novel solutions, ideas, artistic forms, or products.

**criterion validity** The extent to which a test can predict a concurrent or future outcome.

**critical period** A period of time during which an organism must be exposed to a certain stimulus for proper development to occur.

**critical thinking** The process of solving problems and making decisions through a careful evaluation of evidence.

**cross-cultural research** A body of studies designed to compare and contrast people of different cultures.

**cross-sectional study** A method of developmental research in which people of different ages are tested and compared.

**crystallized intelligence** A form of intelligence that reflects the accumulation of verbal skills and factual knowledge.

**CT (computerized tomography) scan** A series of X rays taken from different angles and converted by computer into an image that depicts a horizontal slice of brain.

**culture-bound syndromes** Recurring patterns of maladaptive behavior that are limited to a specific cultural group or location.

**dark adaptation** A process of adjustment by which the eyes become more sensitive to light in a dark environment.

**deception** A research procedure used to mislead participants about the true purposes of a study.

**declarative memory** Stored long-term knowledge of facts about ourselves and the world.

**defense mechanisms** Unconscious methods of minimizing anxiety by denying and distorting reality.

**deindividuation** A loss of individuality, often experienced in a group, that results in a breakdown of internal restraints against deviant behavior.

**delusions** False beliefs that often accompany schizophrenia and other psychotic disorders.

**dendrites** Extensions from the cell body of a neuron that receive incoming impulses.

**denial** A primitive form of repression in which anxiety-filled external events are barred from awareness.

**deoxyribonucleic acid (DNA)** The complex molecular structure of a chromosome that carries genetic information.

**dependent variable** A variable that is being measured in an experiment (the proposed effect).

**depression** A mood disorder characterized by sadness, despair, feelings of worthlessness, and low self-esteem.

**depressive explanatory style** The tendency for depressed people to attribute negative events to factors that are internal, stable, and global.

**depth perception** The use of visual cues to estimate the depth and distance of objects.

**developmental psychology** The study of how people grow, mature, and change over the life span.

**diagnosis** The process of identifying and grouping mental disorders with similar symptoms.

**diathesis-stress model** The theory that certain mental disorders (such as schizophrenia) develop when people with a genetic or acquired vulnerability are exposed to high levels of stress.

**diffusion of responsibility** In groups, a tendency for bystanders to assume that someone else will help.

**discrimination** Behavior directed against persons because of their affiliation with a social group.

**discrimination** In classical and operant conditioning, the ability to distinguish between different stimuli.

**discriminative stimulus** A stimulus that signals the availability of reinforcement.

**displacement** The property of language that accounts for the capacity to communicate about matters that are not in the here-and-now.

**dissociation** A division of consciousness that permits one part of the mind to operate independently of another part.

**dissociative disorder** A condition marked by a temporary disruption in one's memory, consciousness, or self-identity.

**dissociative identity disorder (DID)** Formerly known as multiple personality disorder, it is a condition in which an individual develops two or more distinct identities.

**divergent thinking** The ability to think flexibly and entertain a wide range of possible solutions.

**divided attention** The ability to distribute one's attention and simultaneously engage in two or more activities.

**dopamine** A neurotransmitter that functions as an inhibitor and is involved in the control of voluntary movements.

**drive theory** The notion that physiological needs arouse tension that motivates people to satisfy the need.

**DSM-IV** Acronym for the American Psychiatric Association's Diagnostic and Statistical *Manual of Mental Disorders* (4th Edition).

**dualism** The assumption that the body and mind are separate, though perhaps interacting, entities.

**echoic memory** A brief sensory memory for auditory input that lasts only two to three seconds.

**ego** In psychoanalysis, the part of personality that operates according to the reality principle and mediates the conflict between the id and superego.

**egocentric** Self-centered, unable to adopt the perspective of another person.

**elaborative rehearsal** A technique for transferring information into long-term memory by thinking about it in a deeper way.

**electroconvulsive therapy (ECT)** Electric-shock treatments that often relieve severe depression by triggering seizures in the brain.

**electroencephalograph (EEG)** An instrument used to measure electrical activity in the brain through electrodes placed on the scalp.

**embryo** The developing human organism, from two weeks to two months after conception.

**emotion** A feeling state characterized by physiological arousal, expressive behaviors, and a cognitive interpretation.

**empathy** A feeling of joy for others who are happy and distress for those who are in pain.

**empathy-altruism hypothesis** The proposition that an empathic response to a person in need produces altruistic helping.

**encoding specificity** The principle that any stimulus encoded along with an experience can later jog one's memory of that experience.

**endocrine system** A collection of ductless glands that regulate aspects of growth, reproduction, metabolism, and behavior by secreting hormones.

**endorphin** A morphinelike neurotransmitter that is produced in the brain and is linked to pain control and pleasure.

**epidemiology** The study of the distribution of illnesses in a population.

**equity theory** The notion that people want the ratio between input and outcome to be roughly the same for themselves as for others.

**ethnic identity** The part of a person's identity that is defined by an ethnic heritage, language, history, customs, and so on.

**ethologists** Scientists who study the behavior of animals in their natural habitat.

**evolutionary psychology** A subfield that uses the principles of evolution to understand human social behavior.

**experiment** A type of research in which the investigator varies some factors, keeps others constant, and measures the effects on randomly assigned participants.

**experimental group** Any condition of an experiment in which participants are exposed to an independent variable.

**explicit memory** The types of memory elicited through the conscious retrieval of recollections in response to direct questions.

**extinction** The elimination of a learned response by removal of the unconditioned stimulus (classical conditioning) or reinforcement (operant conditioning).

**extrasensory perception (ESP)** The alleged ability to perceive something without ordinary sensory information.

**extravert** A kind of person who seeks stimulation and is sociable and impulsive.

**extrinsic motivation** The desire to engage in an activity for money, recognition, or other tangible benefits.

**facial electromyograph (EMG)** An electronic instrument used by emotion researchers to record activity in the facial muscles.

**facial-feedback hypothesis** The hypothesis that changes in facial expression can produce corresponding changes in emotion.

**factor analysis** A statistical technique used to identify clusters of test items that correlate with one another.

**family studies** Studies that estimate genetic influences through similarities of family members who vary in their degree of genetic relatedness.

**family therapy** Form of psychotherapy that treats the members of a family as an interactive system.

**feature detectors** Neurons in the visual cortex that respond to specific aspects of a visual stimulus (such as lines or angles).

**fetal alcohol syndrome (FAS)** A specific pattern of birth defects (stunted growth, facial deformity, and mental retardation) often found in the offspring of alcoholic mothers.

**fetus** The developing human organism, from nine weeks after conception to birth.

**field research** Research that is conducted in real-world locations.

**five-factor model** A model of personality that consists of five basic traits: neuroticism, extraversion, openness, agreeableness, and conscientiousness.

**fixation** In psychoanalysis, a tendency to get "locked in" at early, immature stages of psychosexual development.

**fixed action pattern** A species-specific behavior that is built into an animal's nervous system and triggered by a specific stimulus.

**flashbulb memories** Highly vivid and enduring memories, typically for events that are dramatic and emotional.

**flooding** A behavioral therapy technique in which the patient is saturated with a fear-provoking stimulus until the anxiety is extinguished.

**fluid intelligence** A form of intelligence that involves the ability to reason logically and abstractly.

**forgetting curve** A consistent pattern in which the rate of memory loss for input is steepest right after input is received and levels off over time.

**formal operational stage** Piaget's fourth stage of cognitive development, when adolescents become capable of logic and abstract thought.

**fovea** The center of the retina, where cones are clustered.

**framing effect** The biasing effects on decision making of the way in which a choice is worded, or "framed."

**free association** A basic technique of psychoanalysis in which the patient says whatever comes to mind—freely and without censorship.

**free recall** A type of explicit-memory task in which a person must reproduce information without the benefit of external cues (e.g., an essay exam).

**frequency histogram** A graphic presentation of data in which a set of bars is used to represent how frequently different values occur in a data set.

**frustration-aggression hypothesis** The theory that frustration causes aggression.

**fugue state** A form of amnesia in which a person "forgets" his or her identity, wanders from home, and starts a new life.

**functional fixedness** The tendency to think of objects only in terms of their usual functions, a limitation that disrupts problem solving.

**fundamental attribution error** A tendency to overestimate the impact of personal causes of behavior and to overlook the role of situations.

**gate-control theory** The theory that the spinal cord contains a neurological "gate" that blocks pain signals from the brain when flooded by competing signals.

**gender roles** Sex-typed behaviors promoted by social learning.

**gender schemas** A network of beliefs about men and women that influence the way we perceive ourselves and others.

**general adaptation syndrome** A three-stage process (alarm, resistance, and exhaustion) by which the body responds to stress.

**general intelligence (g)** A broad intellectual-ability factor used to explain why performances on different intelligence-test items are often correlated.

**generalizability** The extent to which a finding applies to a broad range of subject populations and circumstances.

**generalized anxiety disorder** A psychological disorder that is characterized by a constant state of anxiety not linked to an identifiable source.

**generativity** The property of language that accounts for the capacity to use a limited number of words to produce an infinite variety of expressions.

**genes** The biochemical units of heredity that govern the development of an individual life.

**genetics** The branch of biology that deals with the mechanisms of heredity.

**genotype** The underlying DNA sequence that an individual inherits.

**Gestalt psychology** A school of thought rooted in the idea that the whole (perception) is different from the sum of its parts (sensation).

**Gestalt therapy** A humanistic form of psychotherapy in which clients are aggressively prompted to express their feelings.

**glial cells** Nervous system cells, also called neuroglia, that provide structural support, insulation, and nutrients to the neurons.

**grasping reflex** In infants, an automatic tendency to grasp an object that stimulates the palm.

**group therapy** The simultaneous treatment of several clients in a group setting.

**groupthink** A group decision-making style by which group members convince themselves that they are correct.

**gustatory system** The structures responsible for the sense of taste.

**habituation** The tendency for attention to a stimulus to wane over time (often used to determine whether an infant has "learned" a stimulus).

**habituation** The tendency of an organism to become familiar with a stimulus as a result of repeated exposure.

**hallucinations** Sensory experiences that occur in the absence of actual stimulation.

**hallucinogens** Psychedelic drugs that distort perceptions and cause hallucinations.

**hardiness** A personality style that is characterized by commitment, challenge, and control. Hardiness acts as a buffer against stress.

**Hawthorne effect** The finding that workers who were put in a special experimental room became more productive regardless of what changes were made.

**health psychology** The study of the links between psychological factors and physical health and illness.

**heritability** A statistical estimate of the percentage of the variability of a trait within a group that is attributable to genetic factors.

**heuristic** A rule of thumb that allows one to make judgments that are quick but often in error.

**hierarchy of needs** Maslow's list of basic needs that have to be satisfied before people can become self-actualized.

**hindsight bias** The tendency to think after an event that we knew in advance what was going to happen.

**hippocampus** A portion of the brain in the limbic system that plays a key role in encoding and transferring new information into long-term memory.

**hormones** Chemical messengers secreted from endocrine glands, into the bloodstream, to various organs throughout the body.

**human genome** The genetic blueprint for making a complete human being.

**humanistic theory** An approach to personality that focuses on the self, subjective experience, and the capacity for fulfillment.

**hypermnesia** A term referring to the unsubstantiated claim that hypnosis can be used to facilitate the retrieval of past memories.

**hypnosis** Attention-focusing procedures in which changes in a person's behavior or mental state are suggested.

**hypnotic susceptibility** The extent to which an individual is characteristically responsive to hypnosis.

**hypochondriasis** A disorder characterized by an unwarranted preoccupation with one's physical health.

**hypothalamus** A tiny limbic structure in the brain that helps regulate the autonomic nervous system, endocrine glands, emotions, and basic drives.

**hypothesis** A specific testable prediction, often derived from a theory.

**iconic memory** A fleeting sensory memory for visual images that lasts only a fraction of a second.

**id** In psychoanalysis, a primitive and unconscious part of personality that contains basic drives and operates according to the pleasure principle.

**identification** In psychoanalysis, the process by which children internalize their parent's values and form a superego.

**identity crisis** An adolescent's struggle to establish a personal identity, or self-concept.

**idiot savant** Someone who is mentally retarded but is extraordinarily talented in some ways.

**illusion of control** The tendency for people to believe that they can control chance events that mimic skill situations.

**image** A mental representation of visual information.

**immune system** A biological surveillance system that detects and destroys "nonself" substances that invade the body.

**Implicit Association Test (IAT)** A measure of stereotyping that is derived from the speed at which people respond to pairings of concepts (such as *blacks* or *whites* with *good* or *bad*).

**implicit memory** A nonconscious recollection of a prior experience that is revealed indirectly, by its effects on performance.

**imprinting** Among newly hatched ducks and geese, an instinctive tendency to follow the mother.

**incentive theory** The notion that people are motivated to behave in ways that produce a valued inducement.

**inclusive fitness** The notion that an organism's genes are preserved not only through its own offspring but also through the offspring of genetic relatives.

**independent variable** Any variable that the researcher manipulates in an experiment (the proposed cause).

**individualism** A cultural orientation in which personal goals and preferences take priority over group allegiances.

**informational influence** Conformity motivated by the belief that others are correct.

**information-processing model** A model of memory in which information must pass through discrete stages via the processes of attention, encoding, storage, and retrieval.

**informed consent** The ethical requirement that prospective participants receive enough information to permit them to decide freely whether to participate in a study.

**ingroup favoritism** The tendency to discriminate in favor of ingroups over outgroups.

**insecure attachment** A parent-infant relationship in which the baby clings to the parent, cries at separation, and reacts with anger or apathy to reunion.

**insight** A form of problem solving in which the solution seems to pop to mind all of a sudden.

**insomnia** An inability to fall asleep, stay asleep, or get the amount of sleep needed to function during the day.

**instinct** A fixed pattern of behavior that is unlearned, universal in a species, and "released" by specific stimuli.

**intelligence** The capacity to learn from experience and adapt successfully to one's environment.

**intelligence quotient (IQ)** Originally defined as the ratio of mental age to chronological age, it now represents a person's performance relative to same-age peers.

**interneurons** Central nervous system neurons that connect sensory inputs and motor outputs.

**intrinsic motivation** An inner drive that motivates people in the absence of external reward or punishment.

**introspection** Wundt's method of having trained observers report on their conscious, moment-to-moment reactions.

**introvert** A kind of person who avoids stimulation and is low-key and cautious.

**iris** The ring of muscle tissue that gives eyes their color and controls the size of the pupil.

**James-Lange theory** The theory that emotion stems from the physiological arousal that is triggered by an emotion-eliciting stimulus.

**just noticeable difference (JND)** The smallest amount of change in a stimulus that can be detected.

**kinesthetic system** The structures distributed throughout the body that give us a sense of position and movement of body parts.

**kinship selection theory** The tendency for organisms to preferentially help others according to their genetic relatedness.

**laboratory research** Research conducted in an environment that can be regulated and in which participants can be carefully observed.

**language** A form of communication consisting of sounds, words, meanings, and rules for their combination.

**latent content** According to Freud, the unconscious, censored meaning of a dream.

**latent learning** Learning that occurs but is not exhibited in performance until there is an incentive to do so.

**law of effect** A law stating that responses followed by positive outcomes are repeated, whereas those followed by negative outcomes are not.

**learned helplessness** A learned expectation that one cannot control important life outcomes, resulting in apathy and depression.

**learning** A relatively permanent change in knowledge or behavior that results from experience.

**lens** A transparent structure in the eye that focuses light on the retina.

**lexical decision making** An experimental task that requires subjects to decide as quickly as possible whether a string of letters briefly presented is a word or nonword.

**life expectancy** The number of years that an average member of a species is expected to live.

**life span** The maximum age possible for members of a given species.

**light adaptation** The process of adjustment by which the eyes become less sensitive to light in a bright environment.

**limbic system** A set of loosely connected structures in the brain that help to regulate motivation, emotion, and memory.

**linguistic-relativity hypothesis** The hypothesis that language determines, or at least influences, the way we think.

**lithium** A drug used to control mania and mood swings in people with bipolar disorder.

**locus of control** A term referring to the expectancy that one's reinforcements are generally controlled by internal or external factors.

**longitudinal study** A method of developmental research in which the same people are tested at different times to track changes related to age.

**long-term memory (LTM)** A relatively permanent memory storage system that can hold vast amounts of information for many years.

**lucid dreaming** A semiconscious dream state in which a sleeper is aware that he or she is dreaming.

**lymphocytes** Specialized white blood cells that secrete chemical antibodies and facilitate the immune response.

**magnetic resonance imaging (MRI)** A brain-scanning technique that uses magnetic fields and radio waves to produce clear, three-dimensional images.

**maintenance rehearsal** The use of sheer repetition to keep information in short-term memory.

**manifest content** According to Freud, the conscious dream content that is remembered in the morning.

**means-end analysis** A problem-solving heuristic that involves breaking down a larger problem into a series of subgoals.

**medical model** The perspective that mental disorders are caused by biological conditions and can be treated through medical intervention.

**medulla** A brainstem structure that controls vital involuntary functions.

**memory** The process by which information is retained for later use.

**menarche** A girl's first menstrual period.

**menopause** The end of menstruation and fertility.

**mental age** In an intelligence test, the average age of the children who achieve a certain level of performance.

**mental models** Intuitive theories about the way things work.

**mental retardation** A diagnostic category used for people with IQ scores below 70 who have difficulty adapting to the routine demands of life.

**mental set** The tendency to return to a problem-solving strategy that worked in the past.

**mere-exposure effect** The attraction to a stimulus that results from increased exposure to it.

**meta-analysis** A set of statistical procedures used to review a body of evidence by combining the results of individual studies.

**microsleep** A brief episode of sleep that occurs in the midst of a wakeful activity.

**Minnesota Multiphasic Personality Inventory (MMPI)** A large-scale test designed to measure a multitude of psychological disorders and personality traits.

**misattribution** An explanation that shifts the perceived cause of arousal from the true source to another one.

**misinformation effect** The tendency to incorporate false postevent information into one's memory of the event itself.

**mnemonics** Memory aids designed to facilitate the recall of new information.

**modeling** The social-learning process by which behavior is observed and imitated.

**monocular depth cues** Distance cues, such as linear perspective, that enable us to perceive depth with one eye.

**mood disorder** A condition characterized by prolonged emotional extremes ranging from mania to depression.

**moon illusion** The tendency for people to see the moon as larger when it's low on the horizon than when it's overhead.

**moral reasoning** The way people think about and try to solve moral dilemmas.

**morphemes** In language, the smallest units that carry meaning (e.g., prefixes, root words, suffixes).

**motivation** An inner state that energizes people toward the fulfillment of a goal.

**motor cortex** The area of the cortex that sends impulses to voluntary muscles.

**motor neurons** Neurons that transmit commands from the central nervous system to the muscles, glands, and organs.

**Müller-Lyer illusion** An illusion in which the perceived length of a line is altered by the position of other lines that enclose it.

**multicultural research** A body of studies designed to compare and contrast racial and ethnic minority groups within cultures.

**multiple intelligences** Gardner's theory that there are seven types of intelligence (linguistic, logical-mathematical, spatial, musical, bodily-kinesthetic, interpersonal).

**mutations** Random gene copying errors that can spark evolution by natural selection.

**myelin sheath** A layer of fatty cells that is tightly wrapped around the axon to insulate it and speed the movement of electrical impulses.

**narcolepsy** A sleep disorder characterized by irresistible and sudden attacks of REM sleep during the day.

**natural selection** The evolutionary process by which some genes in a population spread more than others, causing species to change over time.

**naturalistic observation** The observation of behavior as it occurs naturally in real-world settings.

**nature-nurture debate** The debate over the extent to which human behavior is determined by genetics and the environment.

**need for affiliation** The desire to establish and maintain social contacts.

**need for intimacy** The desire for close relationships characterized by open and intimate communication.

**need for power** A strong desire to acquire prestige and influence over other people.

**neural graft** A technique of transplanting healthy tissue from the nervous system of one animal into that of another.

**neural networks** Clusters of densely interconnected neurons that form and strengthen as a result of experience.

**neurogenesis** The production of new brain cells.

**neurons** Nerve cells that serve as the building blocks of the nervous system.

**neurotransmitters** Chemical messengers in the nervous system that transmit information by crossing the synapse from one neuron to another.

**normal distribution** A symmetrical dispersion of scores in which the mean, median, and mode all have the same value.

**normative influence** Conformity motivated by a fear of social rejection.

**NREM sleep** The stages of sleep not accompanied by rapid eye movements.

**null hypothesis** The assertion that the independent variable will have no effect on the dependent variable.

**obesity** The state of having a surplus of body fat that causes a person to exceed his or her optimum weight by 20 percent.

**object permanence** Developing at six to eight months, an awareness that objects continue to exist after they disappear from view.

**observational learning** Learning that takes place when one observes and models the behavior of others.

**obsessive-compulsive disorder (OCD)** An anxiety disorder defined by persistent thoughts (obsessions) and the need to perform repetitive acts (compulsions).

**Oedipus complex** In psychoanalysis, a tendency for young children to become sexually attracted to the parent of the opposite sex and hostile toward the parent of the same sex.

**olfactory system** The structures responsible for the sense of smell.

**operant conditioning** The process by which organisms learn to behave in ways that produce reinforcement.

**operational definition** A concrete definition of a research variable in terms of the procedures needed to control and measure it.

**opiates** A class of highly addictive drugs that depress neural activity and provide temporary relief from pain and anxiety.

**opponent-process theory** The theory that color vision is derived from three pairs of opposing receptors. The opponent colors are blue and yellow, red and green, and black and white.

**optic nerve** The pathway that carries visual information from the eyeball to the brain.

**outgroup-homogeneity bias** The tendency to assume that "they" (members of groups other than our own) are all alike.

**panic disorder** A disorder characterized by sudden and intense rushes of anxiety without an apparent reason.

**parapsychology** The study of ESP and other claims that cannot be explained by existing principles of science.

**parasympathetic nervous system** The division of the autonomic nervous system that reduces arousal and restores the body to its pre-energized state.

**partial-reinforcement effect** The tendency for a schedule of partial reinforcement to strengthen later resistance to extinction.

**peak experience** A fleeting but intense moment of self-actualization in which people feel happy, absorbed, and extraordinarily capable.

**percentile score** The percentage of people or observations that fall below a given score in a normal distribution.

**perception** The processes by which people select, organize, and interpret sensations.

**perceptual illusions** Patterns of sensory input that give rise to misperceptions.

**perceptual set** The effects of prior experience and expectations on interpretations of sensory input.

**peripheral nervous system (PNS)** The network of nerves that radiate from the central nervous system to the rest of the body. The PNS comprises the somatic and autonomic nervous system.

**peripheral route to persuasion** A process in which people do not think carefully about a message and are influenced by superficial cues.

**personality** An individual's distinct and relatively enduring pattern of thoughts, feelings, motives, and behaviors.

**personality disorders** A group of disorders characterized by a personality that is highly inflexible and maladaptive.

**person-centered therapy** A humanistic psychotherapy in which a warm and accepting environment is created to foster self-insight and acceptance.

**PET (positron emission tomography) scan** A visual display of brain activity, as measured by the amount of glucose being used.

**phenotype** An organism's observable properties, physical and behavioral.

**pheromones** Chemicals secreted by animals that transmit signals-usually to other animals of the same species.

**phobic disorder** An anxiety disorder characterized by an intense and irrational fear.

**phonemes** The basic, distinct sounds of a spoken language.

**phrase** A group of words that act as a unit to convey meaning. Phrases are formed from combinations of morphemes.

**phrenology** The pseudoscientific theory that psychological characteristics are revealed by bumps on the skull.

**physical dependence** A physiological addiction in which a drug is needed to prevent symptoms of withdrawal.

**pituitary gland** A tiny gland in the brain that regulates growth and stimulates hormones in other endocrine glands at the command of the hypothalamus.

**placebo effect** The curative effect of an inactive treatment that results simply from the patient's belief in its therapeutic value.

**plasticity** A capacity to change as a result of experience.

**pleasure principle** In psychoanalysis, the id's boundless drive for immediate gratification.

**polygraph** An electronic device that records multiple channels of autonomic arousal and is often used as a lie-detector test.

**pons** A portion of the brainstem that plays a role in sleep and arousal.

**Ponzo illusion** An illusion in which the perceived length of a line is affected by linear perspective cues.

**posthypnotic amnesia** A reported tendency for hypnosis subjects to forget events that occurred during the induction.

**posthypnotic suggestion** A suggestion made to a subject in hypnosis to be carried out after the induction session is over.

**posttraumatic stress disorder (PTSD)** An anxiety disorder triggered by an extremely stressful event, such as combat.

**practical intelligence** The ability to size up new situations and adapt to real-life demands.

**prejudice** Negative feelings toward others based solely on their membership in a certain group.

**preoperational stage** Piaget's second stage of cognitive development, when two- to six-year-olds become capable of reasoning in an intuitive, prelogical manner.

**primacy effect** The tendency for impressions of others to be heavily influenced by information appearing early in an interaction.

**priming** The tendency for a recently presented word or concept to facilitate, or "prime," responses in a subsequent situation.

**proactive interference** The tendency for previously learned material to disrupt the recall of new information.

**procedural memory** Stored long-term knowledge of learned habits and skills.

**prodigy** Someone who is highly precocious in a specific domain of endeavor.

**Project Head Start** A preschool intellectual-enrichment program for children born of poor families.

**projection** A defense mechanism in which people attribute or "project" their own unacceptable impulses onto others.

**projective tests** Psychoanalytic personality tests that allow people to "project" unconscious needs, wishes, and conflicts onto ambiguous stimuli.

**prosopagnosia** A condition stemming from damage to the temporal lobes that disrupts the ability to recognize familiar faces.

**prototype** A "typical" member of a category, one that has most of the defining features of that category.

**psychoactive drug** A chemical that alters perceptions, thoughts, moods, or behavior.

**psychoanalysis** Freud's theory of personality and method of psychotherapy, both of which assume that our motives are largely unconscious.

**psychological dependence** A condition in which drugs are needed to maintain a sense of well-being or relief from negative emotions.

**psychological disorder** A condition in which a person's thoughts, feelings, or behavior is judged to be dysfunctional.

**psychological model** The perspective that mental disorders are caused and maintained by one's life experiences.

**psychology** The scientific study of behavior and the mind.

**psychoneuroimmunology (PNI)** A new subfield of psychology that examines the interactions among psychological factors, the nervous system, and the immune system.

**psychopharmacology** The study of the effects of drugs on psychological processes and disorders.

**psychophysics** The study of the relationship between physical stimulation and subjective sensations.

**psychosexual stages** Freud's stages of personality development during which pleasure is derived from different parts of the body (oral, anal, phallic, and genital).

**psychosurgery** The surgical removal of portions of the brain for the purpose of treating psychological disorders.

**psychotherapy** A term used to describe any treatment in which a trained professional uses psychological techniques to help someone in need of assistance.

**puberty** The onset of adolescence, as evidenced by rapid growth, rising levels of sex hormones, and sexual maturity.

**punishment** In operant conditioning, any stimulus that decreases the likelihood of a prior response.

**pupil** The small round hole in the iris of the eye through which light passes.

**racism** A deep-seated form of prejudice that is based on the color of a person's skin.

**random assignment** The procedure of assigning participants to conditions of an experiment in an arbitrary manner.

**random sample** A method of selection in which everyone in a population has an equal chance of being chosen.

**rational-emotive behavior therapy (REBT)** A form of cognitive therapy in which people are confronted with their irrational, maladaptive beliefs.

**rationalization** A defense mechanism that involves making excuses for one's failures and shortcomings.

**reaction formation** A defense mechanism in which one converts an unacceptable feeling into its opposite.

**realistic-conflict theory** The theory that prejudice stems from intergroup competition for limited resources.

**reality principle** In psychoanalysis, the ego's capacity to delay gratification.

**receptive field** An area of the retina in which stimulation triggers a response in a cell within the visual system.

**receptors** Specialized neural cells that receive neurotransmitters.

**reciprocal altruism** The tendency for organisms to help members of other species, who may later reciprocate.

**reciprocal determinism** The view that personality emerges from a mutual interaction of individuals, their actions, and their environments.

**recognition** A form of explicit-memory retrieval in which items are represented to a person who must determine if they were previously encountered.

**recovery** Following habituation to one stimulus, the tendency for a second stimulus to arouse new interest (often used to test whether infants can discriminate between stimuli).

**reflex** An inborn automatic response to a sensory stimulus.

**reinforcement** In operant conditioning, any stimulus that increases the likelihood of a prior response.

**reliability** The extent to which a test yields consistent results over time or using alternate forms.

**REM sleep behavior disorder (RBD)** A condition in which the skeletal muscles are not paralyzed during REM sleep, enabling a sleeper to act on his or her nightmares, often violently.

**REM sleep** The rapid-eye-movement stage of sleep associated with dreaming.

**replication** The process of repeating a study to see if the results are reliable enough to be duplicated.

**representativeness heuristic** A tendency to estimate the likelihood of an event in terms of how typical it seems.

**repression** A defense mechanism in which personally threatening thoughts, memories, and impulses are banned from awareness.

**resistance** In psychoanalysis, the tendency for patients to actively block, or "resist," psychologically painful insights.

**reticular formation** A group of nerve cells in the brainstem that helps to control sleep, arousal, and attention.

**retina** The rear, multilayered part of the eye where rods and cones convert light into neural impulses.

**retroactive interference** The tendency for new information to disrupt the memory of previously learned material.

**retrograde amnesia** A memory disorder characterized by an inability to retrieve long-term memories from the past.

**reversible figure** A drawing that one can perceive in different ways by reversing figure and ground.

**rods** Rod-shaped photoreceptor cells in the retina that are highly sensitive to light.

**rooting reflex** In response to contact on the cheek, an infant's tendency to turn toward the stimulus and open its mouth.

**Rorschach** A projective personality test in which people are asked to report what they see in a set of inkblots.

**scatterplot** A graph in which paired scores (X, Y) for many participants are plotted as single points to reveal the direction and strength of their correlation.

**schemas** In Piaget's theory, mental representations of the world that guide the processes of assimilation and accommodation.

**schemas** Preconceptions about persons, objects, or events that bias the way new information is interpreted and recalled.

**schizophrenic disorders** Disorders involving gross distortions of thoughts and perceptions and by loss of contact with reality.

**seasonal affective disorder (SAD)** A form of depression that strikes during the short, dark days of late autumn and winter.

**secure attachment** A parent-infant relationship in which the baby is secure when the parent is present, distressed by separation, and delighted by reunion.

**sedatives** A class of depressant drugs that slow down activity in the central nervous system.

**selective attention** The ability to focus awareness on a single stimulus to the exclusion of other stimuli, as in the cocktail party phenomenon.

**self-actualization** In humanistic personality theories, the need to fulfill one's unique potential.

**self-awareness theory** The theory that self-focused attention leads people to notice their shortcomings,

thus motivating a change in behavior or an escape from self-awareness.

**self-disclosure** The sharing of intimate details about oneself with another person.

**self-discrepancy theory** The notion that discrepancies between one's self-concept and "ideal" and "ought" selves have negative emotional consequences.

**self-efficacy** The belief that one is capable of performing the behaviors required to produce a desired outcome.

**self-esteem** A positive or negative evaluation of the self.

**self-fulfilling prophecy** The idea that a person's expectation can lead to its own fulfillment (as in the effect of teacher expectations on student performance).

**self-report** A method of observation that involves asking people to describe their own thoughts, feelings, or behavior.

**self-schemas** Specific beliefs about the self that influence how we interpret self-relevant information.

**semantic network** A complex web of semantic associations that link items in memory such that retrieving one item triggers the retrieval of others as well.

**semanticity** The property of language that accounts for the communication of meaning.

**sensation** The processes by which our sense organs receive information from the environment.

**sensorimotor stage** Piaget's first stage of cognitive development, from birth to two years old, when infants come to know the world through their own actions.

**sensorineural hearing loss** Hearing loss caused by damage to the structures of the inner ear.

**sensory adaptation** A decline in sensitivity to a stimulus as a result of constant exposure.

**sensory memory** A memory storage system that records information from the senses for up to three seconds.

**sensory neurons** Neurons that send signals from the senses, skin, muscles, and internal organs to the central nervous system.

**sentence** An organized sequence of words that expresses a thought, a statement of fact, a proposition, an intention, a request, or a question.

**separation anxiety** Among infants with object permanence, a fear reaction to the absence of their primary caretaker.

**serial-position curve** A U-shape pattern indicating the tendency to recall more items from the beginning and end of a list than from the middle.

**set point** A level of weight toward which a person's body gravitates.

**sexual orientation** One's sexual preference for members of the same sex, opposite sex, or both sexes.

**sexual-response cycle** The four physiological stages of sexual responding: excitement, plateau, orgasm, and resolution.

**shape constancy** The tendency to see an object as retaining its form despite changes in orientation.

**shaping** A procedure in which reinforcements are used to gradually guide an animal or person toward a specific behavior.

**short-term memory (STM)** A memory storage system that holds about seven items for up to twenty seconds before the material is transferred to long-term memory or is forgotten.

**signal-detection theory** The theory that detecting a stimulus is jointly determined by the signal and the subject's response criterion.

**simple phobia** An intense, irrational fear of a specific object or situation.

**size constancy** The tendency to view an object as constant in size despite changes in the size of the retinal image.

**Skinner box** An apparatus, invented by B. F. Skinner, used to study the effects of reinforcement on the behavior of laboratory animals.

**sleep apnea** A disorder in which a person repeatedly stops breathing during sleep and awakens gasping for air.

**social categorization** The classification of persons into groups based on common attributes.

**social clock** A set of cultural expectations concerning the most appropriate age for men and women to leave home, marry, start a career, have children, and retire.

**social facilitation** The tendency for the presence of others to enhance performance on simple tasks and impair performance on complex tasks.

**social loafing** The tendency for people to exert less effort in group tasks for which individual contributions are pooled.

**social norms** Implicit rules of conduct according to which each culture operates.

**social perception** The processes by which we come to know and evaluate other persons.

**social phobia** An intense fear of situations that invite public scrutiny.

**social psychology** The study of how individuals think, feel, and behave in social situations.

**social support** The healthful coping resources provided by friends and other people.

**social-comparison theory** The theory that people evaluate themselves by making comparisons with others.

**social-identity theory** The theory that people favor ingroups and discriminate against outgroups in order to enhance their own self-esteem.

**social-skills training** A form of behavioral therapy used to teach interpersonal skills through modeling, rehearsal, and reinforcement (e.g., assertiveness training).

**sociocultural model** The perspective that psychological disorders are influenced by cultural factors.

**soma** The cell body of a neuron.

**somatic nervous system** The branch of the peripheral nervous system that transmits signals from the sensory organs to the CNS, and from the CNS to the skeletal muscles.

**somatoform disorder** A type of mental disorder in which a person experiences bodily symptoms that are psychological rather than medical in nature.

**somatosensory cortex** The area of the cortex that receives sensory information from the touch receptors in the skin.

**split brain** A surgically produced condition in which the corpus callosum is severed, thus cutting the link between the left and right hemispheres of the brain.

**split-half reliability** The degree to which alternate forms of a test yield consistent results.

**spontaneous recovery** The reemergence of an extinguished conditioned response after a rest period.

**standard score** A value that indicates the distance, in standard deviations, between a given score and the mean of all the scores in a data set.

**standardization** The procedure by which existing norms are used to interpret an individual's test score.

**Stanford-Binet** An American version of Binet's intelligence test that yields an IQ score with an average of 100.

**statistics** A branch of mathematics that is used for analyzing research data.

**stereotype** A belief that associates a group of people with certain traits.

**stereotype threat** The tendency for positive and negative performance stereotypes about a group to influence its members when they are tested in the stereotyped domain.

**stimulants** A class of drugs that excite the central nervous system and energize behavior.

**stimulus generalization** The tendency to respond to a stimulus that is similar to the conditioned stimulus.

**strange-situation test** A parent-infant "separation and reunion" procedure that is staged in a laboratory to test the security of a child's attachment.

**stress** An aversive state of arousal triggered by the perception that an event threatens our ability to cope effectively.

**stroop test** A color-naming task that demonstrates the automatic nature of highly practiced activities such as reading.

**sublimation** In psychoanalysis, the channeling of repressed sexual and aggressive urges into socially acceptable substitute outlets.

**subliminal message** A stimulus that is presented below the threshold for awareness.

**superego** In psychoanalysis, the part of personality that consists of one's moral ideals and conscience.

**survey** A research method that involves interviewing or giving questionnaires to a large number of people.

**syllogism** A logical problem in which the goal is to determine the validity of a conclusion given two or more premises.

**sympathetic nervous system** A branch of the autonomic nervous system that controls the involuntary activities of various organs and mobilizes the body for fight or flight.

**sympathetic nervous system** The division of the autonomic nervous system that heightens arousal and energizes the body for action.

**synapse** The junction between the axon terminal of one neuron and the dendrites of another.

**synesthesia** A rare condition in which stimulation in one sensory modality triggers sensations in another sensory modality.

**syntax** Rules of grammar that govern the arrangement of words in a sentence.

**systematic desensitization** A behavioral therapy technique used to treat phobias and other anxiety disorders by pairing gradual exposure to an anxiety-provoking situation with relaxation.

*t* **test** A statistical test used to assess the likelihood that differences between two means occurred by chance.

**taste buds** Nets of taste-receptor cells.

**telegraphic speech** Early short form of speech in which the child omits unnecessary words-as telegrams once did ("More milk").

**teratogens** Toxic substances that can harm the embryo or fetus during prenatal development.

**test-retest reliability** The degree to which a test yields consistent results when readministered at a later time.

**thalamus** A limbic structure that relays neural messages between the senses and areas of the cerebral cortex.

**Thematic Apperception Test (TAT)** A projective personality test in which people are asked to make up stories from a set of ambiguous pictures.

**theory** An organized set of principles that describes, predicts, and explains some phenomenon.

**threshold** The level of stimulation needed to trigger a neural impulse.

**token economy** A large-scale behavior-change program in which the participants earn valuable tokens for engaging in desired target behaviors.

**trait** A relatively stable predisposition to behave in a certain way.

**transduction** The process by which physical energy is converted into sensory neural impulses.

**transference** In psychoanalysis, the tendency of patients to displace intense feelings for others onto the therapist.

**trial and error** A problem-solving strategy in which several solutions are attempted until one is found that works.

**triarchic theory of intelligence** Sternberg's theory that there are three kinds of intelligence: analytic, creative, and practical.

**trichromatic theory** A theory of color vision stating that the retina contains three types of color receptors—for red, blue, and green—and that these combine to produce all other colors.

**twin-study method** A method of testing nature and nurture by comparing pairs of identical and fraternal twins of the same sex.

**two-factor theory of emotion** The theory that emotion is based both on physiological arousal and a cognitive interpretation of that arousal.

**Type A personality** A personality characterized by an impatient, hard-driving, and hostile pattern of behavior.

**Type B personality** A personality characterized by an easygoing, relaxed pattern of behavior.

**unconditional positive regard** A situation in which the acceptance and love one receives from significant others is unqualified.

**unconditioned response (UR)** An unlearned response (salivation) to an unconditioned stimulus (food).

**unconditioned stimulus (US)** A stimulus (food) that triggers an unconditioned response (salivation).

**validity** The extent to which a test measures or predicts what it is designed to.

**vestibular system** The inner ear and brain structures that give us a sense of equilibrium.

**visual cliff** An apparatus used to test depth perception in infants and animals.

**visual cortex** Located in the back of the brain, it is the main information-processing center for visual information.

**Weber's law** The principle that the just noticeable difference of a stimulus is a constant proportion despite variations in intensity.

**Wechsler Adult Intelligence Scale (WAIS)** The most widely used IQ test for adults, it yields separate scores for verbal and performance subtests.

**Wernicke's area** A region in the left hemisphere of the brain that is involved in the comprehension of language.

**white noise** A hissing sound that results from a combination of all frequencies of the sound spectrum.

**working memory** Term used to describe short-term memory as an active workspace where information is accessible for current use.

**zygote** A fertilized egg that undergoes a two-week period of rapid cell division and develops into an embryo.

# REFERENCES

AAMR. (2002). *Mental retardation: Definition, classification, and systems of supports* (10th ed.). Washington, DC: American Association on Mental Retardation.

Abbey, A. (1982). Sex differences in attributions for friendly behavior: Do males misperceive females' friendliness? *Journal of Personality and Social Psychology, 42,* 830–838.

Abbey, A. (1987). Misperceptions of friendly behavior as sexual interest: A survey of naturally occurring incidents. *Psychology of Women Quarterly, 11,* 173–194.

ABCNEWS.com. (2002, February 17). Perception vs. experience: ABCNEWS poll on racial discrimination.

Ablon, J. S., & Jones, E. E. (2002). Validity of controlled clinical trials of psychotherapy: Findings from the NIMH Treatment of Depression Collaborative Research Program. *American Journal of Psychiatry, 159,* 775–783.

Abramov, I., & Gordon, J. (1994). Color appearance: On seeing red–or yellow, or green, or blue. *Annual Review of Psychology, 45,* 451–485.

Abrams, R. (1988). *Electroconvulsive therapy.* New York: Oxford University Press.

Abrams, R. (2002). *Electroconvulsive therapy* (4th ed.). New York: Oxford University Press.

Abramson, L. Y., Metalsky, G., & Alloy, L. B. (1989). Hopelessness depression: A theory-based subtype. *Psychological Review, 96,* 358–372.

Ackerman, D. (1990). *A natural history of the senses.* New York: Random House.

Ackerman, P. L., & Rolfhus, E. L. (1999). The locus of adult intelligence: Knowledge, abilities, and nonability traits. *Psychology and Aging, 14,* 314–330.

Acton, G. S., & Schroeder, D. H. (2001). Sensory discrimination as related to general intelligence. *Intelligence, 29,* 263–271.

Adams, G. R., & Berzonsky, M. D. (Eds.). (2003). *Blackwell handbook of adolescence.* Oxford: Blackwell Publishers.

Adams, P. R., & Adams, G. R. (1984). Mount Saint Helens's ashfall: Evidence for a disaster stress reaction. *American Psychologist, 39,* 252–260.

Adams, R. J., & Courage, M. L. (1998). Human newborn color vision: Measurement with chromatic stimuli varying in excitation purity. *Journal of Experimental Child Psychology, 68,* 22–34.

Adams, R. J., & Maurer, D. (1984). Detection of contrast by the newborn and 2-month-old infant. *Infant Behavior and Development, 7,* 415–422.

Addis, M. E., & Krasnow, A. D. (2000). A national survey of practicing psychologists' attitudes toward psychotherapy treatment manuals. *Journal of Consulting and Clinical Psychology, 68,* 331–339.

Adelson, J. (1986). *Inventing adolescence: The political psychology of everyday schooling.* New Brunswick, NJ: Transaction.

Ader, R., & Cohen, N. (1985). CNS-immune system interactions: Conditioning phenomena. *Behavioral and Brain Sciences, 8,* 379–426.

Ader, R., & Cohen, N. (1993). Psychoneuroimmunology: Conditioning and stress. *Annual Review of Psychology, 44,* 53–85.

Ader, R., & Cohen, N. (2001). Conditioning and immunity. In R. Ader, D. L. Felten, & N. Cohen (Eds.), *Psychoneuroimmunology* (3rd ed., Vol. 2, pp. 3–34). San Diego: Academic Press.

Ader, R., Felten, D. L., & Cohen, N. (Eds.). (1991). *Psychoneuroimmunology* (2nd ed.). San Diego: Academic Press.

Ader, R., Felton, D. L., & Cohen, N. (Eds.). (2001). *Psychoneuroimmunology* (3rd ed.). New York: Academic Press.

Adler, A. (1927). *The practice and theory of individual psychology.* New York: Harcourt, Brace & World.

Adler, N., & Matthews, K. (1994). Health psychology: Why do some people get sick and some stay well? *Annual Review of Psychology, 45,* 229–259.

Adolph, K. E., Vereijken, B., & Denny, M. A. (1998). Learning to crawl. *Child Development, 69,* 1299–1312.

Adolphs, R., Russell, J. A., & Tranel, D. (1999). The role for the human amygdala in recognizing emotional arousal from unpleasant stimuli. *Psychological Science, 10,* 167–171.

Aggleton, J. P. (Ed.). (2001). *The amygdala: A functional analysis.* New York: Oxford University Press.

Ahrentzen, S., Joe, G. M., Skorpanich, M. A., & Evans, G. W. (1982). School environments and stress. In G. W. Evans (Ed.), *Environmental stress.* New York: Cambridge University Press.

Aiello, J. R., & Douthitt, E. A. (2001). Social facilitation from Triplett to electronic performance monitoring. *Group Dynamics, 5,* 163–180.

Aiken, L. R. (2000). *Dying, death, and bereavement* (4th ed.). Mahwah, NJ: Erlbaum.

Ainsworth, M. D. S., Blehar, M. C., Waters, E., & Wall, S. (1978). *Patterns of attachment: A psychological study of the Strange Situation.* Hillsdale, NJ: Erlbaum.

Ajzen, I. (1991). The theory of planned behavior. *Organizational Behavior and Human Decision Processes, 50,* 179–211.

Ajzen, I. (2001). Nature and operation of attitudes. *Annual Review of Psychology, 52,* 27–58.

Akerstedt, T. (1988). Sleepiness as a consequence of shift work. *Sleep, 11,* 17–34.

Akil, L. (1982). On the role of endorphins in pain modulation. In A. L. Beckman (Ed.), *The neural bases of behavior* (pp. 311–333). New York: Spectrum.

Akimoto, S. A., & Sanbonmatsu, D. M. (1999). Differences in self-effacing behavior between European and Japanese Americans: Effect on competence evaluations. *Journal of Cross-Cultural Psychology, 30,* 159–177.

Alberti, R. E., & Emmons, M. L. (1986). *Your perfect right: A guide to assertive living* (5th ed.). San Luis Obispo, CA: Impact Publishers.

Alcock, J. (1997). *Animal behavior: An evolutionary approach* (6th ed.). New York: Sinauer.

Aldwin, C. M., Spiro, A., Bosse, R., & Levenson, M. R. (1989). Longitudinal findings from the normative aging study: 1. Does mental health change with age? *Psychology and Aging, 4,* 295–306.

Alessandri, D. M., Sullivan, R. W., Imaizumi, S., & Lewis, M. (1993). Learning and emotional responsivity in cocaine-exposed infants. *Developmental Psychology, 29,* 989–997.

Alexander, F., & French, T. M. (1946). *Psychoanalytic therapy: Principles and application.* New York: Ronald Press.

Alford, B. A., Freeman, A., Beck, A. T., & Wright, F. D. (1990). Brief focused cognitive therapy of panic disorder. *Psychotherapy, 27,* 230–234.

Allan, K., & Burridge, K. (1991). *Euphemism and dysphemism: Language used as shield and weapon.* New York: Oxford University Press.

Allen, J. B., & Iacono, W. G. (2001). Assessing the validity of amnesia in dissociative identity disorder: A dilemma for the DSM and the courts. *Psychology, Public Policy, & Law, 7,* 311–344.

Allen, J. B., Kenrick, D. T., Linder, D. E., & McCall, M. A. (1989). Arousal and attraction: A response-facilitation alternative to misattribution and negative-reinforcement models. *Journal of Personality and Social Psychology, 57,* 261–270.

Allen, J. J. B., Schnyer, R. N., & Hitt, S. K. (1998). The efficacy of acupuncture in the treatment of major depression in women. *Psychological Science, 9,* 397–400.

Allen, K. D., Danforth, J. S., & Drabman, R. S. (1989). Videotaped modeling and film distraction for fear reduction in adults undergoing hyperbaric oxygen therapy. *Journal of Consulting and Clinical Psychology, 57,* 554–558.

Allen, V. L., & Levine, J. M. (1971). Social support and conformity: The role of independent assessment of reality. *Journal of Experimental Social Psychology, 7,* 48–58.

Alliger, G. M., Lilienfeld, S. O., & Mitchell, K. E. (1996). The susceptibility of overt and covert integrity tests to coaching and faking. *Psychological Science, 7,* 32–39.

Allison, D. B., Fontaine, K. R., Manson, J. E., Stevens, J., & Vanltallie, T. B. (1999). Annual deaths attributable to obesity in the United States. *Journal of the American Medical Association, 282,* 1530–1538.

Allison, T., & Cicchetti, D. V. (1976). Sleep in mammals: Ecological and constitutional correlates. *Science, 194,* 732–734.

Alloy, L. B., Abramson, L. Y., & Francis, E. L. (1999). Do negative cognitive styles confer vulnerability to depression? *Current Directions in Psychological Science, 8,* 128–132.

Allport, F. H., et al. (1953). The effects of segregation and the consequences of desegregation: A social science statement. *Minneapolis Law Review, 37,* 429–440.

Allport, G. W. (1937). *Personality: A psychological interpretation.* New York: Holt, Rinehart & Winston.

Allport, G. W. (1961). *Pattern and growth in personality.* New York: Holt, Rinehart & Winston.

Allport, G. W. (1967). Gordon W. Allport. In E. G. Boring and G. Lindzey (Eds.), *A history of psychology in autobiography* (Vol. V). New York: Appleton-Century-Crofts.

Allport, G. W., & Odbert, H. S. (1936). Trait-names: A psycholexical study. *Psychological Monographs, 47* (Whole No. 1).

Allport, G. W., & Postman, L. J. (1947). *The psychology of rumor.* New York: Holt.

Almerigi, J. B., Carbary, T., & Harris, L. J. (2002). Most adults show opposite-side biases for the imagined holding of objects and infants. *Brain and Cognition, 48,* 258–263.

Altman, I., & Taylor, D. A. (1973). *Social penetration: The development of interpersonal relationships.* New York: Holt, Rinehart & Winston.

Alvidrez, A., & Weinstein, R. S. (1999). Early teacher perceptions and later student academic achievement. *Journal of Educational Psychology, 91,* 731–746.

Amabile, T. M. (1996). *Creativity in context.* New York: Westview.

Ambady, N., & Rosenthal, R. (1992). Thin slices of expressive behavior as predictors of interpersonal consequences: A meta-analysis. *Psychological Bulletin, 111,* 256–274.

American Academy of Neurology. (1997). Practice parameter: The management of concussion in sports (summary statement). *Neurology, 48,* 581–585.

American Psychiatric Association. (1989). *Treatments of psychiatric disorders.* Washington, DC: American Psychiatric Association.

American Psychiatric Association. (1994). *Diagnostic and statistical manual of mental disorders* (4th ed.). Washington, DC: American Psychiatric Association.

American Psychiatric Association. (2000). *Diagnostic and statistical manual of mental disorders* (4th ed., rev.). Washington, DC: American Psychiatric Association.

American Psychiatric Association Task Force. (2001). *Practice of electroconvulsive therapy: Recommendations for treatment, training, and privileging* (2nd ed.). Washington, DC: American Psychiatric Association.

American Psychological Association. (1992). Ethical principles of psychologists and code of conduct. *American Psychologist, 47,* 1597–1611.

American Psychological Association Task Force on the Promotion and Dissemination of Psychological Procedures. (1995). *Clinical Psychology, 48,* 3–23.

Amoore, J. E., Johnston, J. W., & Rubin, M. (1964). The stereochemical theory of odor. *Scientific American, 210,* 42–49.

Anand, B. K., & Brobeck, J. R. (1951). Localization of a "feeding center" in the hypothalamus of the rat. *Proceedings of the Society for Experimental Biology and Medicine, 77,* 323–324.

Anastasi, A., & Urbina, S. (1997). *Psychological testing* (7th ed.). Upper Saddle River, NJ: Prentice Hall.

Andersen, B. L., Kiecolt-Glaser, J. K., & Glaser, R. (1994). A biobehavioral model of cancer stress and disease course. *American Psychologist, 49,* 389–404.

Andersen, S. M., & Berk, M. S. (1998). The social-cognitive model of transference: Experiencing past relationships in the present. *Current Directions in Psychological Science, 7,* 109–115.

Anderson, A. (1982). The great Japanese IQ increase. *Nature, 297,* 180–181.

Anderson, C. A. (1989). Temperature and aggression: Ubiquitous effects of heat on occurrence of human violence. *Psychological Bulletin, 106,* 74–96.

Anderson, C. A., & Anderson, K. B. (1996). Violent crime rate studies in philosophical context: A destructive testing approach to heat and Southern culture of violence effects. *Journal of Personality and Social Psychology, 70,* 740–756.

Anderson, C. A., Anderson, K. B., Dorr, N., DeNeve, K. M., & Flanagan, M. (2000). Temperature and aggression. *Advances in Experimental Social Psychology, 32,* 63–133.

Anderson, C. A., Benjamin, A. J., & Bartholow, B. D. (1998). Does the gun pull the trigger? Automatic priming effects of weapon pictures and weapon names. *Psychological Science, 9,* 308–314.

Anderson, C. A., & Bushman, B. J. (2001). Effects of violent video games on aggressive behavior, aggressive cognition, aggressive affect, physiological arousal, and prosocial behavior: A meta-analytic review of the scientific literature. *Psychological Science, 12,* 353–359.

Anderson, C. A., & Bushman, B. J. (2002). The general aggression model: An integrated social-cognitive model of human aggression. *Annual Review of Psychology, 53,* 27–51.

Anderson, C. A., & Dill, K. E. (2000). Video games and aggressive thoughts, feelings, and behavior in the laboratory and in life. *Journal of Personality and Social Psychology, 78,* 772–790.

Anderson, C. A., Lepper, M. R., & Ross, L. (1980). Perseverance of social theories: The role of explanation in the persistence of discredited information. *Journal of Personality and Social Psychology, 39,* 1037–1049.

Anderson, J. L., Crawford, C. B., Nadeau, J., & Lindberg, T. (1992). Was the Duchess of Windsor right? A cross-cultural review of the socioecology of ideals of female body shape. *Ethology and Sociobiology, 13,* 197–227.

Anderson, J. R. (1983). *The architecture of cognition.* Cambridge, MA: Harvard University Press.

Anderson, J. R. (1990). *Cognitive psychology and its implications* (3rd ed.). New York: W. H. Freeman.

Anderson, J. R., & Milson, R. (1989). Human memory: An adaptive perspective. *Psychological Review, 96,* 703–719.

Anderson, J. R., & Schooler, L. J. (1991). Reflections of the environment in memory. *Psychological Science, 2,* 396–408.

Anderson, M. J., Petros, T. V., Beckwith, B. E., Mitchell, W. W., & Fritz, S. (1991). Individual differences in the effect of time of day on long-term memory access. *American Journal of Psychology, 104,* 241–255.

Anderson, N. H. (1981). *Foundations of information integration theory.* New York: Academic Press.

Andersson, B. E. (1992). Effects of day care on cognitive and socioemotional competence of thirteen-year-old Swedish school children. *Child Development, 63,* 20–36.

Andrade, J., Baddeley, A., & Hitch, G. (Eds.). (2002). *Working memory in perspective.* Brighton, UK: Psychology Press.

Andreasen, N. C. (1987). The diagnosis of schizophrenia. *Schizophrenia Bulletin, 13,* 1–8.

Andreasen, N. C. (1988). Brain imaging: Applications in psychiatry. *Science, 239,* 1381–1388.

Andreasen, N. C. (2001). *Brave new brain: Conquering mental illness in the era of the genome.* New York: Oxford.

Andreasen, N. C., Arndt, S., Alliger, R., Miller, D., & Flaum, M. (1995). Symptoms of schizophrenia: Methods, meanings, and mechanisms. *Archives of General Psychiatry, 52,* 341–351.

Angoff, W. H. (1988). The nature-nurture debate, aptitudes, and group differences. *American Psychologist, 43,* 713–720.

Anisfeld, M. (1991). Neonatal imitation. *Developmental Review, 11,* 60–97.

Annett, M. (2002). *Handedness and brain asymmetry: The right shift theory* (2nd ed.). New York: Psychology Press.

Anonymous. (1990). Behind the mask: A functional schizophrenic copes. *Schizophrenia Bulletin, 16,* 547–549.

Antrobus, J. (1991). Dreaming: Cognitive processes during cortical activation of high afferent thresholds. *Psychological Review, 98,* 96–121.

Appelbaum, P. S., Robbins, P. C., & Roth, L. H. (1999). Dimensional approach to delusions: Comparison across types and diagnoses. *American Journal of Psychiatry, 156,* 1938–1943.

Archer, J. (1988). *The behavioural biology of aggression.* Cambridge: Cambridge University Press.

Archer, J. (1991). The influence of testosterone on human aggression. *British Journal of Psychology, 82,* 1–28.

Archer, S. N., Djamgoz, M. B. A., Loew, E. R., Partridge, J. C., & Vallerga, S. (Eds.). (1999). *Adaptive mechanisms in the ecology of vision.* Dordrecht: Kluwer.

Arndt, S., Andreasen, N. C., Flaum, M., Miller, D., & Nopoulos, P. (1995). A longitudinal study of symptom dimensions in schizophrenia. *Archives of General Psychiatry, 52,* 352–360.

Arnett, J. J. (1999). Adolescent storm and stress, reconsidered. *American Psychologist, 54,* 317–326.

Aron, A., Aron, E. N., & Smollan, D. (1992). Inclusion of other in the self scale and the structure of interpersonal closeness. *Journal of Personality and Social Psychology, 63,* 596–612.

Aron, E. N., & Aron, A. (1997). Sensory-processing sensitivity and its relation to introversion and emotionality. *Journal of Personality and Social Psychology, 73,* 345–368.

Aronson, E. (1999). Dissonance, hypocrisy, and the self-concept. In E. Harmon-Jones & J. Mills (Eds.), *Cognitive dissonance: Progress on a pivotal theory in social psychology* (pp. 103–126). Washington, DC: American Psychological Association.

Aronson, E., & Mills, J. (1959). The effect of severity of initiation on liking for a group. *Journal of Abnormal and Social Psychology, S9,* 177–181.

Aronson, E., & Patnoe, S. (1997). *The jigsaw classroom: Building cooperation in the classroom* (2nd ed.). New York: Addison Wesley Longman.

Arthur, W., Jr., & Graziano, W. G. (1996). The five-factor model, conscientiousness, and driving accident involvement. *Journal of Personality, 64,* 593–618.

Asarnow, J. R. (1988). Children at risk for schizophrenia: Converging lines of evidence. *Schizophrenia Bulletin, 14,* 613–631.

Asch, S. E. (1946). Forming impressions of personality. *Journal of Abnormal and Social Psychology, 41,* 258–290.

Asch, S. E. (1951). Effects of group pressure upon the modification and distortion of judgments. In H. Guetzkow (Ed.), *Groups, leadership, and men.* Pittsburgh, PA: Carnegie Press.

Asch, S. E. (1956). Studies of independence and conformity: A minority of one against a unanimous majority. *Psychological Monographs, 70,* 416.

Aserinksy, E., & Kleitman, N. (1953). Regularly occurring periods of eye motility and concomitant phenomena during sleep. *Science, 118,* 273.

Ashburn-Nardo, L., Voils, C. I., & Monteith, M. J. (2001). Implicit associations as the seeds of intergroup bias: How easily do they take root? *Journal of Personality and Social Psychology, 81,* 789–799.

Ashby, F. G., Isen, A. M., & Turken, A. (1999). A neuropsychological theory of positive affect and its influence on cognition. *Psychological Review, 106,* 529–550.

Ashcraft, M. H. (1989). *Human memory and cognition.* Glenview, IL: Scott, Foresman.

Asher, S. R., & Coie, J. D. (1990). *Peer rejection in childhood.* New York: Cambridge University Press.

Askenasy, H. (1978). *Are we all Nazis?* Secaucus, NJ: Lyle Stuart.

Aslin, R. N. (1989). Discrimination of frequency transitions by human infants. *Journal of the Acoustical Society of America, 86,* 582–590.

Aspinwall, L. G., & Taylor, S. E. (1997). A stitch in time: Self-regulation and proactive coping. *Psychological Bulletin, 121,* 417–436.

Atkinson, J. W. (1957). Motivational determinants of risk-taking behavior. *Psychological Review, 64,* 359–372.

Atkinson, J. W. (1964). *An introduction to motivation.* New York: Van Nostrand.

Atkinson, J. W., & Litwin, G. H. (1960). Achievement motive and test anxiety conceived as motive to approach success and motive to avoid failure. *Journal of Abnormal and Social Psychology, 60,* 52–63.

Atkinson, R. C., & Shiffrin, R. M. (1968). Human memory: A proposed system and its control processes. In K. Spence & J. Spence (Eds.), *The psychology of learning and motivation: Advances in research and theory* (Vol. 2). New York: Academic Press.

Atlas, S. W. (2002). *Magnetic resonance imaging of the brain and spine.* Baltimore: Lippincott, Williams, & Wilkin.

Attie, I., & Brooks-Gunn, J. (1989). Development of eating problems in adolescent girls: A longitudinal study. *Developmental Psychology, 25,* 70–79.

Axelrod, S., & Apsche, J. (Eds.). (1983). *The effects of punishment on human behavior.* New York: Academic Press.

Axsom, D. (1989). Cognitive dissonance and behavior change in psychotherapy. *Journal of Experimental Social Psychology, 25,* 234–252.

Axtell, R. E. (1993). *Do's and taboos around the world* (3rd ed.). New York: Wiley.

Ayllon, T. (1963). Intensive treatment of psychotic behaviour by stimulus satiation and food reinforcement. *Behaviour Research and Therapy, 1,* 53–61.

Ayllon, T., & Azrin, N. H. (1968). *The token economy.* New York: Appleton-Century-Crofts.

Azar, B. (1996, January). Why is it that practice makes perfect? *APA Monitor,* p. 18.

Azar, B. (1999, February). McGaugh saw stress hormones as strengtheners of memory. *APA Monitor,* pp. 18–19.

Azuma, H. (1984). Secondary control as a heterogeneous category. *American Psychologist, 39,* 970–971.

Bach, P. B., Cramer, L. D., Warren, J. L., & Begg, C. B. (1999). Racial differences in the treatment of early-stage lung cancer. *The New England Journal of Medicine, 341,* 1198–1205.

Bachman, J. G., O'Malley, P. M., Schulenberg, J. E., Johnston, L. D., Bryant, A. A., & Merline, A. C. (2002). *The decline of substance use in young adulthood: Changes in social activities, roles, and beliefs.* Mahwah, NJ: Erlbaum.

Backlund, E. O., Grandburg, P. O., & Hamberger, B. (1985). Transplantation of adrenal medullary tissue to striatum in Parkinsonianism: First clinical trials. *Journal of Neurosurgery, 62,* 169–173.

Baddeley, A. (1966). Short-term memory for word sequences as a function of acoustic, semantic, and formal similarity. *Quarterly Journal of Experimental Psychology, 18,* 362–365.

Baddeley, A. (1990). *Human memory: Theory and practice.* Boston: Allyn & Bacon.

Baddeley, A. (1992). Working memory. *Science, 255,* 556–559.

Baddeley, A. (1999). *Essentials of human memory.* Philadelphia: Psychology Press.

Baenninger, M., & Newcombe, N. (1989). The role of experience in spatial test performance: A meta-analysis. *Sex Roles, 20,* 327–344.

Baer, L., et al. (1995). Cingulotomy for intractable obsessive-compulsive disorder. *Archives of General Psychiatry, 52,* 384–392.

Baer, R. A., & Miller, J. (2002). Underreporting of psychopathology on the MMPI-2: A meta-analytic review. *Psychological Assessment, 14,* 16–26.

Bagby, R. M., Nicholson, R. A., Buis, T., Radovanovic, H., & Fidler, B. J. (1999). *Psychological Assessment, 11,* 24–28.

Bagemihl, B. (1999). *Biological exuberance: Animal homosexuality and natural diversity.* New York: St. Martin's Press.

Baggs, K., & Spence, S. H. (1990). Effectiveness of booster sessions in the maintenance and enhancement of treatment gains following assertion training. *Journal of Consulting and Clinical Psychology, 58,* 845–854.

Bahill, A. T., & Karnavas, W. J. (1993). The perceptual illusion of baseball's rising fastball and breaking curveball. *Journal of Experimental Psychology: Human Perception and Performance, 19,* 3–14.

Bahrick, H. P. (1984). Semantic memory content in permastore: Fifty years of memory for Spanish learned in school. *Journal of Experimental Psychology: General, 113,* 1–35.

Bahrick, H. P., Bahrick, P. O., & Wittlinger, R. P. (1975). Fifty years of memory for names and faces: A cross-sectional approach. *Journal of Experimental Psychology: General, 104,* 54–75.

Bahrick, H. P., & Hall, L. K. (1991). Lifetime maintenance of high school mathematics content. *Journal of Experimental Psychology: General, 120,* 20–33.

Bahrick, H. P., Hall, L. K., & Berger, S. A. (1996). Accuracy and distortion in memory for high school grades. *Psychological Science, 7,* 265–271.

Bailes, J. E., Lovell, M. R., & Maroon, J. C. (1998). *Sports-related concussion.* St. Louis: Quality Medical Publishing.

Bailey, J. M., Dunne, M. P., & Martin, N. G. (2000). Genetic and environmental influences on sexual orientation and its correlates in an Australian twin sample. *Journal of Personality and Social Psychology, 78,* 524–536.

Bailey, J. M., & Pillard, R. C. (1991). A genetic study of male sexual orientation. *Archives of General Psychiatry, 48,* 1089–1096.

Bailey, J. M., Pillard, R. C., Neale, M. C., & Agyei, Y. (1993). Heritable factors influence sexual orientation in women. *Archives of General Psychiatry, 50,* 217–223.

Bailey, J. M., & Zucker, K. J. (1995). Childhood sex-typed behavior and sexual orientation: A conceptual analysis and quantitative review. *Developmental Psychology, 31,* 43–55.

Bailine, S. H., et al. (2000). Comparison of bifrontal and bitemporal ECT for major depression. *American Journal of Psychiatry, 157,* 121–123.

Baillargeon, R. (1986). Representing the existence and the location of hidden objects: Object permanence in 6- and 8-month-old infants. *Cognition, 23,* 21–41.

Baillargeon, R. (1994). How do infants learn about the physical world? *Current Directions in Psychological Science, 5,* 133–140.

Baird, A. A., Kagan, J., Gaudette, T., Walz, K. A., Hershlag, N., & Boas, D. A. (2002). Frontal lobe activation during object permanence: Data from near-infrared spectroscopy. *NeuroImage, 16,* 1120–1126.

Baker, E. L. (1985). Psychoanalysis and psychoanalytic therapy. In S. J. Lynn & J. P. Garske (Eds.), *Contemporary psychotherapies: Models and methods.* Columbus, OH: Merrill.

Balda, R. P., Pepperberg, I. M., & Kamil, A. C. (Eds.). (1998). *Animal cognition in nature: The convergence of psychology and biology in laboratory and field.* San Diego: Academic Press.

Baldwin, M. W., & Sinclair, L. (1996). Self-esteem and "if-then" contingencies of interpersonal acceptance. *Journal of Personality and Social Psychology, 71,* 1130–1141.

Ballard, C. G. (2002). *Handbook of classical conditioning.* Dordrecht: Kluwer.

Balota, D. A., & Paul, S. T. (1996). Summation of activation: Evidence from multiple primes that converge and diverge within semantic memory. *Journal of Experimental Psychology: Learning, Memory, and Cognition, 22,* 827–845.

Baltes, P. B., Cornelius, S. W., & Nesselroade, J. R. (1979). Cohort effects in developmental psychology. In J. R. Nesselroade & P. B. Baltes (Eds.), *Longitudinal research in the study of behavior and development* (pp. 61–87). New York: Academic Press.

Baltes, P. B., & Lindenberger, U. (1997). Emergence of a powerful connection between sensory and cognitive functions across the adult life span: A new window to the study of cognitive aging? *Psychology and Aging, 12,* 12–21.

Baltes, P. B., & Staudinger, U. M. (2000). Wisdom: A metaheuristic (pragmatic) to orchestrate mind and virtue toward excellence. *American Psychologist, 55,* 122–136.

Baltes, P. B., Staudinger, U. M., & Lindenberger, U. (1999). Lifespan psychology: Theory and application to intellectual functioning. *Annual Review of Psychology, 50,* 471–507.

Banaji, M. R., Hardin, C., & Rothman, A. J. (1993). Implicit stereotyping in person judgment. *Journal of Personality and Social Psychology, 65,* 272–281.

Banaji, M. R., & Steele, C. M. (1989). Alcohol and self-evaluation: Is a social cognition approach beneficial? *Social Cognition, 7,* 137–151.

Bandura, A. (1977). *Social learning theory.* Englewood Cliffs, NJ: Prentice-Hall.

Bandura, A. (1982). The psychology of chance encounters and life paths. *American Psychologist, 37,* 747–755.

Bandura, A. (1986). *Social foundations of thought and action: A social cognitive theory.* Englewood Cliffs, NJ: Prentice-Hall.

Bandura, A. (1997). *Self-efficacy: The exercise of control.* New York: Freeman.

Bandura, A. (1999). A sociocognitive analysis of substance abuse: An agentic perspective. *Psychological Science, 10,* 214–218.

Bandura, A. (2001). Social cognitive theory: An agentic perspective. *Annual Review of Psychology, 52,* 1–26.

Bandura, A., Blanchard, E. B., & Ritter, B. (1969). Relative efficacy of desensitization and modeling approaches for inducing behavioral, affective, and attitudinal changes. *Journal of Personality and Social Psychology, 13,* 173–199.

Bandura, A., Ross, D., & Ross, S. A. (1961). Transmission of aggression through imitation of aggressive models. *Journal of Abnormal and Social Psychology, 63,* 575–582.

Banich, M. T. (1998). Integration of information between the cerebral hemispheres. *Current Directions in Psychological Science, 7,* 32–37.

Banks, M. S., & Salapatek, P. (1983). Infant visual perception. In M. M. Haith & J. J. Campos (Eds.), *Handbook of child psychology: Vol. 2. Infancy and developmental psychobiology* (4th ed., pp. 435–571). New York: Wiley.

Bar, M., & Biederman, I. (1998). Subliminal visual priming. *Psychological Science, 9,* 464–469.

Barasch, M. (1993, August). The mind-body revolution. *Psychology Today,* pp. 58–63, 86, 90, 92.

Barbaro, N. M. (1988). Studies of PAG/PVG stimulation for pain relief in humans. *Progress in Brain Research, 77,* 165–173.

Barber, T. X. (1969). *Hypnosis: A scientific approach.* New York: Van Nostrand Reinhold.

Barer-Stein, T. (1999). *You eat what you are: People, culture, and food traditions.* Buffalo, NY: Firefly Books.

Bargh, J. A., Chen, M., & Burrows, L. (1996). Automaticity of social behavior: Direct effects of trait construct and stereotype activation on action. *Journal of Personality and Social Psychology, 71,* 230–244.

Bar-Hillel, M. (1980). The base-rate fallacy in probability judgments. *Acta Psychologica, 44,* 211–213.

Barker, K., & Kovaleski, S. F. (2002, October 17). Faulty witness reports not unusual. *Washington Post,* p. A10.

Barker, R. A., & Dunnett, S. B. (1999). *Neural repair, transplantation and rehabilitation.* New York: Psychology Press.

Barker, S. L., Funk, S. C., & Houston, B. K. (1988). Psychological treatment versus nonspecific factors: A meta-analysis of conditions that engender comparable expectations for improvement. *Clinical Psychology Review, 8,* 579–594.

Barkley, R. A. (1997). Behavioral inhibition, sustained attention, and executive functions: Constructing a unifying theory of ADHD. *Psychological Bulletin, 121,* 65–94.

Barkley, R. A. (1998). *Attention deficit hyperactivity disorder* (2nd ed.). New York: Guilford Press.

Barlow, D. H. (1988). *Anxiety and its disorders.* New York: Guilford Press.

Barlow, D. H. (Ed.). (2001). *Anxiety and its disorders: The nature and treatment of anxiety and panic* (2nd ed.). New York: Guilford.

Barnes, J. E. (2002, November 11). The SAT revolution. *U.S. News & World Report.*

Barnier, A. J., & McConkey, K. M. (1998). Posthypnotic responding away from the hypnotic setting. *Psychological Science, 9,* 256–262.

Baron, R., & Parker, J. D. A. (2000). *The handbook of emotional intelligence* (pp. 320–342). New York: Jossey Bass.

Baron, R., Logan, H., Lilly, J., Inman, M., & Brennan, M. (1994). Negative emotion and message processing. *Journal of Experimental Social Psychology, 30,* 181–201.

Baron, R. S., Cutrona, C. E., Hicklin, D., Russell, D. W., & Lubaroff, D. M. (1990). Social support and immune function among spouses of cancer patients. *Journal of Personality and Social Psychology, 59,* 344–352.

Baron, R. S., Vandello, J. A., & Brunsman, B. (1996). The forgotten variable in conformity research: Impact of task importance on social influence. *Journal of Personality and Social Psychology, 71,* 915–927.

Baron-Cohen, S., Harrison, J. Goldstein, L. H., & Wyke, M. (1993). Coloured speech perception: Is synaesthesia what happens when modularity breaks down? *Perception, 22,* 419–426.

Barr, R. G., Pantel, M. S., Young, S. N., Wright, J. H., Hendricks, L. A., & Gravel, R. (1999). The response of crying newborns to sucrose: Is it a "sweetness" effect? *Physiology & Behavior, 66,* 409–417.

Barrick, M. R., & Mount, M. K. (1996). Effects of impression management and self-deception on the predictive validity of personality constructs. *Journal of Applied Psychology, 81,* 261–272.

Barron, F. (1988). Putting creativity to work. In R. Sternberg (Ed.), *The nature of creativity* (pp. 76–98). New York: Cambridge University Press.

Barthrop, R. W., Lazarus, L., Luckhurst, E., Kiloh, L. G., & Penny, R. (1977). Depressed lymphocyte function after bereavement. *Lancet, 1,* 834–839.

Bartlett, F. C. (1932). *Remembering: A study in experimental and social psychology.* Cambridge: Cambridge University Press.

Bartlett, M. S., Hagar, J. C., Ekman, P., & Sejnowski, T. J. (1999). Measuring facial expressions by computer image analysis. *Psychophysiology, 36,* 253–263.

Barton, J. (1994). Choosing to work at night: A moderating influence on individual tolerance to shift work. *Journal of Applied Psychology, 79,* 449–454.

Bartoushuk, L. M., & Beauchamp, G. K. (1994). Chemical senses. *Annual Review of Psychology, 45,* 419–449.

Bashore, T. R., & Rapp, P. E. (1993). Are there alternatives to traditional polygraph procedures? *Psychological Bulletin, 113,* 3–22.

Bass, E., & Davis, L. (1988). *The courage to heal.* New York: Harper & Row.

Bassili, J. N., & Provencal, A. (1988). Perceiving minorities: A factor-analytic approach. *Personality and Social Psychology Bulletin, 14,* 5–15.

Batson, C. D. (1991). *The altruism question: Toward a social-psychological answer.* Hillsdale, NJ: Erlbaum.

Batson, C. D. (1998). Altruism and prosocial behavior. In D. T. Gilbert, S. T. Fiske, & G. Lindzey (Eds.), *Handbook of social psychology* (4th ed., Vol. 2, pp. 282–316). New York: McGraw-Hill.

Batson, C. D., Batson, J. G., Griffitt, C. A., Barrientos, S., Brandt, J. R., Sprengelmeyer, P., & Bayly, M. J. (1989). Negative-state relief and the empathy-altruism hypothesis. *Journal of Personality and Social Psychology, 56,* 922–933.

Batson, C. D., Duncan, B. D., Ackerman, P., Buckley, T., & Birch, K. (1981). Is empathic emotion a source of altruistic motivation? *Journal of Personality and Social Psychology, 40,* 290–302.

Bauer, P. J. (1996). What do infants recall of their lives?: Memory for specific events by one- to two-year olds. *American Psychologist, 51,* 29–41.

Baum, A., & Posluszny, D. M. (1999). Health psychology: Mapping biobehavioral contributions to health and illness. *Annual Review of Psychology, 50,* 137–163.

Baumeister, R. F. (1990). Suicide as escape from the self. *Psychological Review, 97,* 90–113.

Baumeister, R. F. (1991). *Escaping the self.* New York: Basic Books.

Baumeister, R. F. (2000). Gender differences in erotic plasticity: The female sex drive as socially flexible and responsive. *Psychological Bulletin, 126,* 347–374.

Baumeister, R. F., Catanese, K. R., & Vohs, K. D. (2001). Is there a gender difference in the strength of sex drive?

Theoretical views, conceptual distinctions, and a review of relevant evidence. *Personality and Social Psychology Review, 5,* 242–273.

Baumeister, R. F., Dale, K., & Sommer, K. L. (1998). Freudian defense mechanisms and empirical findings in modern social psychology: Reaction formation, projection, displacement, undoing, isolation, sublimation, and denial. *Journal of Personality, 66,* 1081–1124.

Baumeister, R. F., & Leary, M. R. (1996). The need to belong: Desire for interpersonal attachments as a fundamental human motivation. *Psychological Bulletin, 117,* 497–529.

Baumeister, R. F., & Scher, S. J. (1988). Self-defeating behavior patterns among normal individuals: Review and analysis of common self-destructive tendencies. *Psychological Bulletin, 104,* 3–22.

Baumeister, R. F., Smart, L., & Boden, J. M. (1996). Relation of threatened egotism to violence and aggression: The dark side of high self-esteem. *Psychological Review, 103,* 5–33.

Baumrind, D., Larzelere, R. E., & Cowan, P. A. (2002). Ordinary physical punishment: Is it harmful? Comment on Gershoff (2002). *Psychological Bulletin, 128,* 580–589.

Baur, S. (1988). *Hypochondria: Woeful imaginings.* Berkeley: University of California Press.

Bayley, N. (1949). Consistency and variability in the growth of intelligence from birth to eighteen years. *Journal of Genetic Psychology, 75,* 165–196.

Bayliss, G. C., Rolls, E. T., & Leonard, C. M. (1985). Selectivity between faces in the responses of a population of neurons in the cortex in the superior temporal sulcus of the monkey. *Brain Research, 342,* 91–102.

Beardsley, T. (1999, October). Truth or consequences. *Scientific American,* pp. 21, 24.

Bechara, A., Tranel, D., Damasio, R., Adolphs, C. R., & Damasio, A. (1995). Double dissociation of conditioning and declarative knowledge relative to the amygdala and hippocampus in humans. *Science, 269,* 1115–1118.

Beck, A. T. (1967). *Cognitive therapy and the emotional disorders.* New York: International Universities Press.

Beck, A. T. (1985). Cognitive therapy. In H. I. Kaplan & J. Sadock (Eds.), *Comprehensive textbook of psychiatry* (4th ed). Baltimore: Williams & Wilkins.

Beck, A. T. (1991). Cognitive therapy: A 30-year retrospective. *American Psychologist, 46,* 368–375.

Beck, A. T. (1999). *Prisoners of hate: The cognitive basis of anger, hostility, and violence.* New York: Harper-Collins.

Beck, A. T., Brown, G., Berchick, R. J., Stewart, B. L., & Steer, R. A. (1990). Relationship between hopelessness and ultimate suicide: A replication with psychiatric outpatients. *American Journal of Psychiatry, 147,* 190–195.

Beck, A. T., Emery, G., & Greenberg, R. L. (1985). *Anxiety disorders and phobias: A cognitive perspective.* New York: Basic Books.

Beck, A. T., Rush, A. J., Shaw, B. F., & Emery, G. (1979). *Cognitive therapy of depression.* New York: Guilford Press.

Beck, E. M., & Tolnay, S. E. (1990). The killing fields of the Deep South: The market for cotton and the lynching of blacks, 1882–1930. *American Sociological Review, 55,* 526–539.

Beck, J. G., Freeman, J. B., Shipherd, J. C., Hamblen, J. L., & Lackner, J. M. (2001). Specificity of Stroop interference in patients with pain and PTSD. *Journal of Abnormal Psychology, 110,* 536–543.

Beck, J. G., Ohtake, P. J., & Shipherd, J. C. (1999). Exaggerated anxiety is not unique to CO2 in panic disorder: A comparison of hypercapnic and hypoxic challenges. *Journal of Abnormal Psychology, 108,* 473–482.

Becker, F. D. (1981). *Workspace.* New York: Praeger.

Beckerman, S., & Valentine, P. (Eds.). (2002). *Cultures of multiple fathers: The theory and practice of partible paternity in lowland South America.* Gainesville: University Press of Florida.

Begley, S., & Ramo, J. C. (1993, November 1). Not just a pretty face. *Newsweek,* pp. 63–67.

Beidel, D. C., & Turner, S. M. (1998). *Shy children, phobic adults: Nature and treatment of social phobia.* Washington, DC: American Psychological Association.

Beilin, H. (1992). Piaget's enduring contribution to developmental psychology. *Developmental Psychology, 28,* 191–204.

Beilock, S. L., & Carr, T. H. (2001). On the fragility of skilled performance: What governs choking under pressure? *Journal of Experimental Psychology: General, 130,* 701–725.

Beilock, S. L., Carr, T. H., MacMahon, C., & Starkes, J. L. (2002). When paying attention becomes counterproductive: Impact of divided versus skill-focused attention on novice and experienced performance of sensorimotor skills. *Journal of Experimental Psychology: Applied, 8,* 6–16.

Beitman, B. D., Goldfried, M. R., & Norcross, J. C. (1989). The movement toward integrating the psychotherapies: An overview. *American Journal of Psychiatry, 146,* 138–147.

Bekoff, M., Allen, C., & Burghardt, G. M. (Eds.). (2002). *The cognitive animal: Empirical and theoretical perspectives on animal cognition.* Cambridge, MA: MIT Press.

Belicki, K. (1985). The assessment and prevalence of nightmare distress. *Sleep Research, 14,* 145.

Bell, A. P., Weinberg, M. S., & Hammersmith, S. K. (1981). *Sexual preference: Its development in men and women.* Bloomington: Indiana University Press.

Bellack, A. S., & Hersen, M. (Eds.). (1985). *Dictionary of behavior therapy techniques.* New York: Pergamon.

Belli, R. F., Lindsay, D. S., Gales, M. S., & McCarthy, T. T. (1994). Memory impairment and source misattribution in postevent misinformation experiments with short retention intervals. *Memory and Cognition, 22,* 40–54.

Bellisle, F., Dalix, A. M., & de Castro, J. M. (1999). Eating patterns in French subjects studied by the "weekly food diary" method. *Appetite, 32,* 46–52.

Belmore, S. M. (1987). Determinants of attention during impression formation. *Journal of Experimental Psychology: Learning, Memory, and Cognition, 13,* 480–489.

Belsky, J. (2001). Developmental risk (still) associated with early child care. *Journal of Child Psychology and Psychiatry, 42,* 845–860.

Belsky, J., & Pensky, E. (1988). Marital changes across the transition to parenthood. *Marriage and Family Review, 12,* 133–156.

Bem, D. J. (1967). Self-perception: An alternative interpretation of cognitive dissonance phenomena. *Psychological Review, 74,* 183–200.

Bem, D. J. (1996). Exotic becomes erotic: A developmental theory of sexual orientation. *Psychological Review, 103,* 320–335.

Bem, D. J. (2000). Exotic becomes erotic: Interpreting the biological correlates of sexual orientation. *Archives of Sexual Behavior, 29,* 531–548.

Bem, D. J., & Honorton, C. (1994). Does Psi exist? Replicable evidence for an anomalous process of information transfer. *Psychological Bulletin, 115,* 4–18.

Bem, S. L. (1981). Gender schema theory: A cognitive account of sex typing. *Psychological Review, 88,* 354–364.

Benazon, N. R., & Coyne, J. C. (2000). Living with a depressed spouse. *Journal of Family Psychology, 14,* 71–79.

Benbow, C. P. (1988). Sex differences in mathematical reasoning ability in intellectually talented preadolescents: Their nature, effects, and possible causes. *Behavioral and Brain Sciences, 11,* 169–232.

Benbow, C. P., Lubinksi, D., Shea, D. L., & Eftekhari-Sanjani, H. (2000). Sex differences in mathematical reasoning ability at age 13: Their status 20 years later. *Psychological Science, 11,* 474–480.

Benca, R. M., Obermeyer, W. H., Thisted, R. A., & Gillin, J. C. (1992). Sleep and psychiatric disorders: A meta-analysis. *Archives of General Psychiatry, 49,* 651–658.

Benedict, R. (1959). *Patterns of culture.* Boston: Houghton Mifflin.

Benjamin, L. T., Jr. (1988). A history of teaching machines. *American Psychologist, 43,* 703–712.

Benjamin, L. T., Jr., Durkin, M., Link, M., Vestal, M., & Acord, J. (1992). Wundt's American doctoral students. *American Psychologist, 47,* 123–131.

Bennett, R. J. (1998). Taking the sting out of the whip: Reactions to consistent punishment for unethical behavior. *Journal of Experimental Psychology: Applied, 4,* 248–262.

Ben-Shakhar, G., Bar-Hillel, M., Bilu, Y., Ben-Abba, E., & Flug, A. (1986). Can graphology predict occupational success? Two empirical studies and some methodological ruminations. *Journal of Applied Psychology, 71,* 645–653.

Benson, H. (1975). *The relaxation response.* New York: Morrow.

Benson, H. (1993). The relaxation response. In D. Goleman & J. Gurin (Eds.), *Mind body medicine: How to use your mind for better health* (pp. 233–257). Yonkers, NY: Consumer Reports Books.

Benson, J. B. (1993). Season of birth and onset of locomotion: Theoretical and methodological implications. *Infant Behavior and Development, 16,* 69–81.

Benton, M. K., & Schroeder, H. E. (1990). Social skills training with schizophrenics: A meta-analytic evaluation. *Journal of Consulting and Clinical Psychology, 58,* 741–747.

Ben-Zeev, T. (1995). The nature and origin of rational errors in arithmetic thinking: Induction from examples and prior knowledge. *Cognitive Science, 19,* 341–376.

Berg, J. H. (1987). Responsiveness and self-disclosure. In V. J. Derlega & J. H. Berg (Eds.), *Self-disclosure* (pp. 101–130). New York: Plenum.

Berghuis, J. P., & Stanton, A. L. (2002). Adjustment to a dyadic stressor: A longitudinal study of coping and depressive symptoms in infertile couples over an insemination attempt. *Journal of Consulting and Clinical Psychology, 70,* 433–438.

Bergin, A. E., & Garfield, S. L. (Eds.). (1994). *Handbook of psychotherapy and behavior change* (4th ed.). New York: Wiley.

Bergin, A. E., & Lambert, M. J. (1978). The evaluation of therapeutic outcomes. In S. L. Garfield & A. E. Bergin (Eds.), *Handbook of psychotherapy and behavior change* (2nd ed., pp. 139–189). New York: Wiley.

Bergman, E. T., & Roediger, H. L. (1999). Can Bartlett's repeated reproduction experiments be replicated? *Memory & Cognition, 27,* 937–947.

Berk, M. S., & Andersen, S. M. (2000). The impact of past relationships on interpersonal behavior: Behavioral confirmation in the social-cognitive process of transference. *Journal of Personality and Social Psychology, 79,* 546–562.

Berkely, K. J. (1997). Sex differences in pain. *Behavioral and Brain Sciences, 20,* 371–380.

Berkman, L., & Syme, S. L. (1979). Social networks, host resistance, and mortality: A nine-year follow-up study of Alameda County residents. *American Journal of Epidemiology, 109,* 186–204.

Berkowitz, L. (1983). Aversively stimulated aggression: Some parallels and differences in research with animals and humans. *American Psychologist, 38,* 1135–1144.

Berkowitz, L. (1989). Frustration-aggression hypothesis: Examination and reformulation. *Psychological Bulletin, 106,* 59–73.

Berkowitz, L. (1993). *Aggression: Its causes, consequences, and control.* New York: McGraw-Hill.

Berkowitz, L., & LePage, A. (1967). Weapons as aggression-eliciting stimuli. *Journal of Personality and Social Psychology, 7,* 202–207.

Bernard, M. E., & DiGiuseppe, R. (Eds.). (1989). *Inside rational-emotive therapy.* New York: Academic Press.

Berndt, T. J. (1979). Developmental changes in conformity to peers and parents. *Developmental Psychology, 15,* 606–616.

Berndt, T. J. (1996). Transitions in friendship and friends' influence. In J. A. Graber, J. Brooks-Gunn, & A. C. Petersen (Eds.), *Transitions through adolescence: Interpersonal domains and context* (pp. 57–84). Mahwah, NJ: Erlbaum.

Bernstein, I. L., & Borson, S. (1986). Learned food aversion: A component of anorexia syndromes. *Psychological Review, 93,* 462–472.

Bernstein, R., & Gaw, A. (1990). Koro: Proposed classification for DSM-IV. *American Journal of Psychiatry, 147,* 1670–1674.

Berridge, A. P., & Valenstein, E. S. (1991). What psychological process mediates feeding evoked by electrical stimulation of the lateral hypothalamus? *Behavioral Neuroscience, 105,* 3–14.

Berridge, K. C., Venier, I. L., & Robinson, T. E. (1989). Taste reactivity analysis of 6-hydroxydopamine-induced aphagia: Implications for arousal and anhedonia hypotheses of dopamine function. *Behavioral Neuroscience, 103,* 3645.

Berry, D. S., & McArthur, L. Z. (1986). Perceiving character in faces: The impact of age-related craniofacial changes in social perception. *Psychological Bulletin, 100,* 3–18.

Berry, D. S., & McArthur, L. Z. (1988). What's in a face? Facial maturity and the attribution of legal responsibility. *Personality and Social Psychology Bulletin, 14,* 23–33.

Berry, J. W. (1979). A cultural ecology of social behavior. *Advances in Experimental Social Psychology, 12,* 177–206.

Berry, J. W. (1997). Immigration, acculturation, and adaptation. *Applied Psychology: An International Review, 46,* 5–68.

Berry, J. W., Poortinga, Y. H., Segall, M. H., & Dasen, P. R. (1992). *Cross-cultural psychology: Research and applications.* New York: Cambridge University Press.

Berry, J. W., Segall, M. H., & Poortinga, Y. H. (Eds.). (2002). *Cross-cultural psychology: Research and applications* (2nd ed.). New York: Cambridge University Press.

Berscheid, E. (1994). Interpersonal relationships. *Annual Review of Psychology, 45,* 79–129.

Berscheid, E., & Reis, H. T. (1998). Attraction and close relationships. In D. T. Gilbert, S. T. Fiske, & G. Lindzey (Eds.), *Handbook of social psychology* (4th ed.). New York: McGraw-Hill.

Berscheid, E., Snyder, M., & Omoto, A. M. (1989). The Relationship Closeness Inventory: Assessing the closeness of interpersonal relationships. *Journal of Personality and Social Psychology, 57,* 792–807.

Berscheid, E., & Walster, E. (1974). A little bit about love. In T. Huston (Ed.), *Foundations of interpersonal attraction* (pp. 356–379). New York: Academic Press.

Best, D. L., & Williams, J. E. (1993). A cross-cultural viewpoint. In A. E. Beall & R. J. Sternberg (Eds.), *The psychology of gender* (pp. 215–248). New York: Guilford Press.

Best, P. J., White, A. M., & Minai, A. (2001). Spatial processing in the brain: The activity of hippocampal place cells. *Annual Review of Neuroscience, 24,* 459–486.

Bettencourt, B. A., & Miller, N. (1996). Gender differences in aggression as a function of provocation: A meta-analysis. *Psychological Bulletin, 119,* 422–447.

Beutler, L. E. (2000). David and Goliath: When empirical and clinical standards of practice meet. *American Psychologist, 55,* 997–1007.

Beyer, S. (1990). Gender differences in the accuracy of self-evaluations of performance. *Journal of Personality and Social Psychology, 59,* 960–970.

Biederman, I. (1987). Recognition-by-components: A theory of human image understanding. *Psychological Review, 94,* 115–147.

Biernat, M. (1991). Gender stereotypes and the relationship between masculinity and femininity: A developmental analysis. *Journal of Personality and Social Psychology, 61,* 351–365.

Biner, P. M., Angle, S. T., Park, J. H., Mellinger, A. E., & Barber, B. C. (1995). Need state and the illusion of control. *Personality and Social Psychology Bulletin, 21,* 899–907.

Binet, A., & Simon, T. (1905). Methodes nouvelles pour le diagnostic du niveau intellectuel des anormaux. *L'Annee Psychologique, 11,* 191–244.

Binson, D., Michaels, S., Stall, R., Coates, T. J., Gagnon, J. H., & Catania, J. A. (1995). Prevalence and social distribution of men who have sex with men: United States and its urban centers. *Journal of Sex Research, 32,* 245–254.

Birren, J. E., & Fisher, L. M. (1995). Aging and speed of behavior: Possible consequences for psychological functioning. *Annual Review of Psychology, 46,* 329–353.

Birren, J. E., & Schaie, K. W. (Eds.). (2001). *Handbook of the psychology of aging* (5th ed.). San Diego: Academic Press.

Bjork, D. W. (1997). *B. F. Skinner: A life.* (Reprint edition). New York: Basic Books.

Bjork, E. L., & Bjork, R. A. (Eds.). (1996). *Memory.* San Diego: Academic Press.

Black, D. W., & Larson, C. L. (1999). *Bad boys, bad men: Confronting antisocial personality disorder.* New York: Oxford University Press.

Blair, I. V., Ma, J. E., & Lenton, A. P. (2001). Imagining stereotypes away: The moderation of implicit stereotypes through mental imagery. *Journal of Personality and Social Psychology, 81,* 828–841.

Blair, R. J. R., Jones, L., Clark, F., & Smith, M. (1997). The psychopathic individual: A lack of responsiveness to distress cues? *Psychophysiology, 34,* 192–198.

Blair, S. N., Kohl, H. W., Paffenbarger, R. S., Clark, D. G., Cooper, K. H., & Gibbons, L. W. (1989). Physical fitness and all-cause mortality: A prospective study of healthy men and women. *Journal of the American Medical Association, 262,* 2395–2401.

Blakeslee, S. (1993, June 1). Scanner pinpoints sites of thoughts as people see or speak. *The New York Times,* pp. C1, C3.

Blakeslee, S. (2000, January 4). A decade of discovery yields a shock about the brain. *The New York Times: Science Times section,* pp. D1, D4.

Blanchard, E. B. (1994). Behavioral medicine and health psychology. In A. E. Bergin & S. L. Garfield (Eds.), *Handbook of psychotherapy and behavior change* (4th ed., pp. 701–733.) New York: Wiley.

Blanchard, E. B., et al. (1982). Biofeedback and relaxation training with three kinds of headache: Treatment effects and their prediction. *Journal of Consulting and Clinical Psychology, 50,* 562–575.

Blanchard, F. A., Lilly, T., & Vaughn, L. A. (1991). Reducing the expression of racial prejudice. *Psychological Science, 2,* 101–105.

Blanchard, R. (1997). Birth order and sibling sex ratio in homosexual versus heterosexual males and females. *Annual Review of Sex Research, 8,* 27–67.

Blanchard, R. (2001). Fraternal birth order and the maternal immune hypothesis of male homosexuality. *Hormones and Behavior, 40,* 105–114.

Blascovich, J., Mendes, W. B., Hunter, S. B., & Salomon, K. (1999). Social facilitation as challenge and threat. *Journal of Personality and Social Psychology, 77,* 68–77.

Blascovich, J., Spencer, S. J., Quinn, D., & Steele, C. (2001). African Americans and high blood pressure: The role of stereotype threat. *Psychological Science, 12,* 225–229.

Blasi, A. (1980). Bridging moral cognition and moral action: A critical review of the literature. *Psychological Bulletin, 88,* 1–45.

Blass, E. M., & Camp, C. A. (2001). The ontogeny of face recognition: Eye contact and sweet taste induce face preference in 9- and 12-week-old human infants. *Developmental Psychology, 37,* 762–774.

Blass, T. (1992). The social psychology of Stanley Milgram. *Advances in Experimental Social Psychology, 25,* 227–329.

Blass, T. (Ed.). (2000). *Obedience to authority: Current perspectives on the Milgram paradigm.* Mahwah, NJ: Erlbaum.

Blehar, M. C., Weissman, M. M., Gershon, E. S., & Hirschfeld, R. M. A. (1988). Family and genetic studies of affective disorders. *Archives of General Psychiatry, 45,* 289–292.

Bleuler, E. (1911). *Dementia praecox oder gruppe der schizophrenien.* Leipzig, Germany: F. Deuticke.

Block, J. (1981). Some enduring and consequential structures of personality. In A. I. Rabin (Ed.), *Further explorations in personality.* New York: Wiley.

Blocklyn, P. L. (1988). Preemployment testing. *Personnel, 65,* 63–65.

Bloom, A. (1981). *The linguistic shaping of thought.* Hillsdale, NJ: Erlbaum.

Bloom, B. S. (1985). *Developing talent in young people.* New York: Ballantine Books.

Bloom, L. C., & Mudd, S. A. (1991). Depth of processing approach to face recognition: A test of two theories. *Journal of Experimental Psychology: Learning, Memory, and Cognition, 17,* 556–565.

Blum, D. (1997). *Sex on the brain: The biological differences between men and women.* New York: Viking Books.

Blumberg, M. S., & Sokoloff, G. (2001). Do infant rats cry? *Psychological Review, 108,* 83–95.

Bodenhausen, G. V. (1990). Stereotypes as judgmental heuristics: Evidence of circadian variations in discrimination. *Psychological Science, 1,* 319–322.

Boer, F., & Dunn, J. (Eds.). (1992). *Children's sibling relationships.* Hillsdale, NJ: Erlbaum.

Bogart, L. M., Cecil, H., Wagstaff, D. A., Pinkerton, S. D., & Abramson, P. R. (2000). Is it "sex"?: College students' interpretations of sexual behavior terminology. *Journal of Sex Research, 37,* 108–116.

Bogen, J. E. (1978). The callosal syndrome. In K. M. Heilman & E. Valenstein (Eds.), *Clinical neuropsychology* (2nd ed., pp. 308–359). New York: Oxford University Press.

Bohart, A. C., O'Hara, M., & Leitner, L. M. (1998). Empirically violated treatments: Disenfranchisement of humanistic and other psychotherapies. *Psychotherapy Research, 8,* 141–157.

Boldero, J., & Francis, J. (2000). The relation between self-discrepancies and emotion: The moderating roles of self-guide importance, location relevance, and social self-domain centrality. *Journal of Personality and Social Psychology, 78,* 38–52.

Bolles, R. C. (1970). Species-specific defense reactions and avoidance learning. *Psychological Review, 77,* 32–48.

Bond, R., & Smith, P. B. (1996). Culture and conformity: A meta-analysis of studies using Asch's (1952b, 1956) line judgment task. *Psychological Bulletin, 119,* 111–137.

Boneau, C. A. (1990). Psychological literacy: A first approximation. *American Psychologist, 45,* 891–900.

Bonta, B. D. (1997). Cooperation and competition in peaceful societies. *Psychological Bulletin, 121,* 299–320.

Booker, J. M., & Hellekson, C. J. (1992). Prevalence of seasonal affective disorder in Alaska. *American Journal of Psychiatry, 149,* 1176–1182.

Boon, S., & Draijer, N. (1993). Multiple personality disorder in the Netherlands: A clinical investigation of 71 patients. *American Journal of Psychiatry, 150,* 489–494.

Booth-Kewley, S., & Friedman, H. S. (1987). Psychological predictors of heart disease: A quantitative review. *Psychological Bulletin, 101,* 343–362.

Borbely, A. (1986). *The secrets of sleep.* New York: Basic Books.

Borch-Jacobsen, M. (1996). *Remembering Anna O.* London: Routledge.

Boring, E. G. (1923). Intelligence as the tests test it. *New Republic, 35,* 35–37.

Borkenau, P., Riemann, R., Angleitner, A., & Spinath, F. M. (2001). Genetic and environmental influences on observed personality: Evidence from the German observational study of adult twins. *Journal of Personality and Social Psychology, 80,* 655–668.

Bornstein, B. H., & Zickafoose, D. J. (1999). "I know I know it, I know I saw it": The stability of the confidence-accuracy relationship across domains. *Journal of Experimental Psychology: Applied, 5,* 76–88.

Bornstein, M. H. (1989). Information processing (habituation) in infancy and stability in cognitive development. *Human Development, 32,* 129–136.

Bornstein, M. H. (Ed.). (1995). *Handbook of parenting* (Vol. 1–4). Mahwah, NJ: Erlbaum.

Bornstein, R. F. (1989). Exposure and affect: Overview and meta-analysis of research, 1968–1987. *Psychological Bulletin, 106,* 265–289.

Bornstein, R. F. (1992). Subliminal mere exposure effects. In R. F. Bornstein & T. S. Pittman (Eds.), *Perception without awareness: Cognitive, clinical, and social perspectives* (pp. 191–210). New York: Guilford Press.

Bornstein, R. F., Kale, A. R., & Cornell, K. R. (1990). Boredom as a limiting condition on the mere exposure effect. *Journal of Personality and Social Psychology, 58,* 791–800.

Bornstein, R. F., & Pittman, T. S. (Eds.). (1992). *Perception without awareness: Cognitive, clinical, and social perspectives.* New York: Guilford Press.

Boroditsky, L. (2001). Does language shape thought?: Mandarin and English speakers' conceptions of time. *Cognitive Psychology, 43,* 1–22.

Borum, R., & Fulero, S. M. (1999). Empirical research on the insanity defense and attempted reforms: Evidence toward informed policy. *Law and Human Behavior, 23,* 117–135.

Bosson, J. K., Swann, W. B., & Pennebaker, J. W. (2000). Stalking the perfect measures of implicit self-esteem: The blind men and the elephant revisited? *Journal of Personality and Social Psychology, 79,* 631–643.

Bouchard, T. J., Jr., Lykken, D. T., McGue, M., Segal, N. L., & Tellegen, A. (1990). Sources of human psychological differences: The Minnesota study of twins reared apart. *Science, 250,* 223–228.

Bouchard, T. J., Jr., & McGue, M. (1981). Familial studies of intelligence. *Science, 212,* 1055–1059.

Bousfield, W. A. (1953). The occurrence of clustering in the recall of randomly arranged associates. *Journal of General Psychology, 49,* 229–240.

Bouton, M. E., Mineka, S., & Barlow, D. H. (2001). A modern learning theory perspective on the etiology of panic disorder. *Psychological Review, 108,* 4–32.

Bovbjerg, D. H., et al. (1990). Anticipatory immune suppression in women receiving cyclic chemotherapy for ovarian cancer. *Journal of Consulting and Clinical Psychology, 58,* 153–157.

Bovbjerg, D. H., et al. (1992). An experimental analysis of classically conditioned nausea during cancer chemotherapy. *Psychosomatic Medicine, 54,* 623–637.

Bower, G. H. (1970). Organizational factors in memory. *Cognitive Memory, 1,* 18–46.

Bower, G. H. (1981). Mood and memory. *American Psychologist, 36,* 129–148.

Bower, G. H., & Winzenz, D. (1970). Comparison of associative learning strategies. *Psychonomic Science, 20,* 119–120.

Bower, T. G. R. (1982). *Development in infancy* (2nd ed.). San Francisco: W. H. Freeman.

Bowers, K. S. (1992). Imagination and dissociation in hypnotic responding. *International Journal of Clinical and Experimental Hypnosis, 40,* 253–275.

Bowers, K. S., & Farvolden, P. (1996). Revisiting a century-old Freudian slip: From suggestion disavowed to the truth repressed. *Psychological Bulletin, 119,* 355–380.

Bowers, K. S., & Woody, E. Z. (1996). Hypnotic amnesia and the paradox of intentional forgetting. *Journal of Abnormal Psychology, 105,* 381–390.

Bowers, T. G., & Clum, G. A. (1988). Relative contribution of specific and nonspecific treatment effects: Meta-analysis of placebo-controlled behavior therapy research. *Psychological Bulletin, 103,* 315–323.

Bowlby, J. (1969). *Attachment and loss: Volume 1. Attachment.* London: Hogarth.

Bowlby, J. (1988). *A secure base.* New York: Basic Books.

Boyd, R., & Silk, J. (2003) *How humans evolved* (3rd ed.). New York: Norton.

Boysen, S. T., & Himes, G. T. (1999). Current issues and emerging theories in animal cognition. *Annual Review of Psychology, 50,* 683–705.

Braaksma, M. A. H., Rijlaarsdam, G., & van den Bergh, H. (2002). Observational learning and the effects of model-observer similarity. *Journal of Educational Psychology, 94,* 405–415.

Brabender, V. (2002). *Introduction to group therapy.* New York: Wiley.

Bradfield, A. L., Wells, G. L., & Olson, E. A. (2002). The damaging effect of confirming feedback on the relation between eyewitness certainty and identification accuracy. *Journal of Applied Psychology, 87,* 112–120.

Bradshaw, J. L., & Nettleton, N. C. (1981). The nature of hemispheric specialization in man. *Behavioral and Brain Sciences, 4,* 51–91.

Brainerd, C. J. (1996). Piaget: A centennial celebration. *Psychological Science, 7,* 191–195.

Branscombe, N. R., & Wann, D. L. (1994). Collective self-esteem consequences of outgroup derogation when a valued social identity is on trial. *European Journal of Social Psychology, 24,* 641–657.

Brasted, P. J., Watts, C., Torres, E., Robbins, T., & Dunnett, S. B. (2000). Behavioral recovery after transplantation into a rat model of Huntington's disease dependence on anatomical connectivity and extensive postoperative training. *Behavioral Neuroscience, 114,* 431–436.

Braun, B. G. (1988). *Treatment of multiple personality disorder.* Washington, DC: American Psychiatric Press.

Brean, H. (1958, March 31). What hidden sell is all about. *Life,* pp. 104–114.

Breedlove, S. M. (1994). Sexual differentiation of the human nervous system. *Annual Review of Psychology, 45,* 389–418.

Breen, R. B., & Zuckerman, M. (1999). "Chasing" in gambling behavior: Personality and cognitive determinants. *Personality and Individual Differences, 27,* 1097–1111.

Breger, L. (2000). *Freud: Darkness in the midst of vision.* New York: Wiley.

Breggin, P. (2001). *The anti-depressant fact book: What your doctor won't tell you about Prozac, Zoloft, Paxil, Celexa, and Luvox.* New York: Perseus Books.

Bregman, A. S. (1990). *Auditory scene analysis.* Cambridge MA: MIT Press.

Brehm, S. S., & Miller, R., Perlman, D., & Campbell, S. M. (2001). *Intimate relationships* (3rd ed.). New York: McGraw-Hill.

Breland, K., & Breland, M. (1961). The misbehavior of organisms. *American Psychologist, 16,* 681–684.

Bremner, J. D., et al. (2000). SPECT [I-123] iomazenil measurement of the benzodiazepine receptor in panic disorder. *Biological Psychiatry, 47,* 96–106.

Bremner, J. G. (2002). The nature of imitation by infants. *Infant Behavior & Development, 25,* 65–67.

Brener, N., Lowry, R., Kann, L., Kolbe, L., Lehnherr, J., Janssen, R., & Jaffe, H. (2002). Trends in sexual risk behaviors among high school students—United States, 1991–2001. *MMWR, 51,* 856–859.

Brenner, C. (1982). *The mind in conflict.* New York: International Universities Press.

Breuer, J., & Freud, S. (1895). Studies on hysteria. In J. Strachey (Ed.), *The standard edition of the complete psychological works of Sigmund Freud.* London: Hogarth Press. (Reprinted in 1955.)

Breuer, M. E., McGinnis, M. Y., Lumia, A. R., & Possidente, B. P. (2001). Aggression in male rats receiving anabolic androgenic steroids: Effects of social and environmental provocation. *Hormones and Behavior, 40,* 409–418.

Brewer, M. B., & Brown, R. J. (1998). Intergroup relations. In D. T. Gilbert, S. T. Fiske, & G. Lindzey (Eds.), *Handbook of social psychology* (4th ed., Vol. 2, pp. 554–594). New York: McGraw-Hill.

Brewer, W. F., & Treyens, J. C. (1981). Role of schemata in memory for places. *Cognitive Psychology, 13,* 207–230.

Brewin, C., Reynolds, M., & Tata, P. (1999). Autobiographical memory processes and the course of depression. *Journal of Abnormal Psychology, 108,* 511–517.

Brickman, P., Coates, D., & Janoff-Bulman, R. J. (1978). Lottery winners and accident victims: Is happiness relative? *Journal of Personality and Social Psychology, 36,* 917–927.

Briddell, D. W. (2000). *The love bug and other tales of psychotherapy.* New York: St. Martin's Press.

Broberg, A. G., Wessels, H., Lamb, M. E., & Hwang, C. P. (1997). Effects of day care on the development of cognitive abilities in 8-year-olds: A longitudinal study. *Developmental Psychology, 33,* 62–69.

Broca, P. (1861). Paul Broca on the speech centers (M. D. Boring, Trans.). In R. J. Herrnstein & E. G. Boring (Eds.), *A source book in the history of psychology.* Cambridge, MA: Harvard University Press. (Reprinted in 1965.)

Brocas, I., & Carillo, J. D. (Eds.). (2003). *Economics and psychology.* New York: Oxford University Press.

Brockner, J. (1983). Low self-esteem and behavioral plasticity: Some implications. In L. Wheeler & P. Shaver (Eds.), *Review of personality and social psychology* (Vol. 4, pp. 237–271). Beverly Hills, CA: Sage.

Brody, L. R., & Hall, J. A. (1993). Gender and emotion. In M. Lewis & J. M. Haviland (Eds.), *Handbook of emotions* (pp. 447–460). New York: Guilford Press.

Brokaw, T. (1998). *The greatest generation.* New York: Random House.

Bronfenbrenner, U., & Ceci, S. J. (1994). Nature-nurture reconceptualized in developmental perspective: A bioecological model. *Psychological Review, 101,* 568–586.

Brooks-Gunn, J., Han, W-J., & Waldfogel, J. (2002). Maternal employment and child cognitive outcomes in the first years of life: The NICHD study of early child care. *Child Development, 73,* 1052–1072.

Brooks-Gunn, J., & Warren, M. P. (1985). The effects of delayed menarche in different contexts: Dance and nondance students. *Journal of Youth and Adolescence, 14,* 163–189.

Broughton, R. S. (1991). *Parapsychology: The controversial science.* New York: Ballantine Books.

Brown, A. S. (1991). A review of the tip-of-the-tongue experience. *Psychological Bulletin, 109,* 204–223.

Brown, A. S. (1999). New perspectives on the neurodevelopmental hypothesis of schizophrenia. *Psychiatric Annals, 29,* 128–130.

Brown, A. S., & Murphy, D. R. (1989). Cryptomnesia: Delineating inadvertent plagiarism. *Journal of Experimental Psychology: Learning, Memory, and Cognition, 15,* 432–442.

Brown, B. B., Clasen, D. R., & Eicher, S. A. (1986). Perceptions of peer pressure, peer conformity dispositions, and self-reported behavior among adolescents. *Developmental Psychology, 22,* 521–530.

Brown, B. B., Larson, R. W., & Saraswathi, T. W. (Eds.) (2002). *The world's youth: Adolescence in eight regions of the globe.* New York: Cambridge University Press.

Brown, C. M., & Hagoort, P. (1999). *The neurocognition of language.* New York: Oxford University Press.

Brown, E. L., Deffenbacher, K. A., & Sturgill, W. (1977). Memory for faces and the circumstances of encounter. *Journal of Applied Psychology, 62,* 311–318.

Brown, G. K. (1990). A causal analysis of chronic pain and depression. *Journal of Abnormal Psychology, 99,* 127–137.

Brown, J. D. (1990). Evaluating one's abilities: Shortcuts and stumbling blocks on the road to self-knowledge. *Journal of Experimental Social Psychology, 26,* 149–167.

Brown, J. D. (1991). Staying fit and staying well: Physical fitness as a moderator of life stress. *Journal of Personality and Social Psychology, 60,* 555–561.

Brown, J. D. (1998). *The self.* New York: McGraw-Hill.

Brown, J. D., & Dutton, K. A. (1995). The thrill of victory, the complexity of defeat: Self-esteem and people's emotional reactions to success and failure. *Journal of Personality and Social Psychology, 68,* 712–722.

Brown, M. Z., Comtois, K. A., & Linhan, M. M. (2002). Reasons for suicide attempts and nonsuicidal self-injury in women with borderline personality disorder. *Journal of Abnormal Psychology, 111,* 198–202.

Brown, P. L. (2003, January 17). Penguins get a new will to swim. *New York Times.*

Brown, R. (1973). *A first language: The early stages.* Cambridge, MA: Harvard University Press.

Brown, R., & Kulik, J. (1977). Flashbulb memories. *Cognition, 5,* 73–99.

Brown, R., & McNeill, D. (1966). The "tip of the tongue" phenomenon. *Journal of Verbal Learning and Verbal Behavior, 5,* 325–337.

Brown, S., & Eisenberg, L. (1995). *The best intentions: Unintended pregnancy and the well-being of children and families.* Washington, DC: National Academy Press.

Brown, T. A., & Barlow, D. H. (1992). Comorbidity among anxiety disorders: Implications for treatment and DSM-IV. *Journal of Consulting and Clinical Psychology, 60,* 835–844.

Brown, T. A., Campbell, L. A., Lehman, C. L., Grisham, J. R., & Mancill, R. B. (2001). Current and lifetime comorbidity of the DSM-IV anxiety and mood disorders in a large clinical sample. *Journal of Abnormal Psychology, 110,* 585–599.

Brown, T. A., O'Leary, T. A., & Barlow, D. H. (2001). Generalized anxiety disorder. In D. H. Barlow (Ed.), *Anxiety and its disorders: The nature and treatment of anxiety and panic* (2nd ed., pp. 154–208). New York: Guilford.

Brown, T. L., Gore, C. L., & Carr, T. H. (2002). Visual attention and word recognition in Stroop color naming: Is word recognition "automatic?" *Journal of Experimental Psychology: General, 131,* 220–240.

Brown, W. A. (1998, January). The placebo effect. *Scientific American,* pp. 90–95.

Brownell, K. D., & Wadden, T. A. (1992). Etiology and treatment of obesity: Understanding a serious, prevalent, and refractory disorder. *Journal of Consulting and Clinical Psychology, 60,* 505–517.

Bruce, V., & Young, A. (1998). *In the eye of the beholder: The science of face perception.* New York: Oxford University Press.

Bruck, M., & Ceci, S. J. (1999). The suggestibility of children's memory. *Annual Review of Psychology, 50,* 419–439.

Bruck, M., Ceci, S. J., Francoeur, E., & Barr, R. (1995). "I hardly cried when I got my shot!" Influencing children's reports about a visit to their pediatrician. *Child Development, 66,* 193–208.

Brumberg, J. J. (1988). *Fasting girls: The emergence of anorexia nervosa as a modern disease.* Cambridge, MA: Harvard University Press.

Bruner, J. S. (1983). *Child's talk: Learning to use language.* New York: Norton.

Bruner, J. S., & Potter, M. C. (1964). Interference in visual recognition. *Science, 144,* 424–425.

Brunner, D. P., Kijk, D. J., Tobler, I., & Borbely, A. A. (1990). Effect of partial sleep stages and EEG power spectra: Evidence for non-REM and REM sleep homeostasis. *Electroencephalography and Clinical Neurophysiology, 75,* 492–499.

Bryan, J. H., & Test, M. A. (1967). Models and helping: Naturalistic studies in aiding behavior. *Journal of Personality and Social Psychology, 6,* 400–407.

Buchanan, C. M., Eccles, J. S., & Becker, J. B. (1992). Are adolescents the victims of raging hormones? Evidence for activational effects of hormones on moods and behavior in adolescence. *Psychological Bulletin, 111,* 62–107.

Buchanan, C. M., & Holmbeck, G. N. (1998). Measuring beliefs about adolescent personality and behavior. *Journal of Youth and Adolescence, 27,* 607–627.

Buchanan, T. (2002). Online assessment: Desirable or dangerous? *Professional Psychology: Research and Practice, 33,* 148–154.

Buck, L. B. (2000). Smell and taste: The chemical senses. In E. R. Kandel, J. H. Schwartz, & T. M. Jessell (Eds.), *Principles of neural science* (4th ed., pp. 625–647). New York: McGraw-Hill.

Buckhout, R. (1974). Eyewitness testimony. *Scientific American, 231*, 23–31.

Buckley, J. T. (1996, November 18). Cold-nosed fleet puts heat on terrorism. *USA Today*, pp. 19A-20A.

Budiansky, S. (1998). *If a lion could talk: Animal intelligence and the evolution of consciousness*. New York: The Free Press.

Bukowski, W. M., Newcomb, A. F., & Hartup, W. W. (Eds.). (1996). *The company they keep: Friendship in childhood and adolescence*. New York: Cambridge University Press.

Bullock, W. A., & Gilliland, K. (1993). Eysenck's arousal theory of introversion-extraversion: A converging measures investigation. *Journal of Personality and Social Psychology, 64*, 113–123.

Burack, J. A., Hodapp, R. M., & Zigler, E. (Eds.). (1998). *Handbook of mental retardation and development*. New York: Cambridge University Press.

Burger, J. M. (1991). Control. In V. Derlega, B. Winstead, & W. Jones (Eds.), *Personality* (pp. 287–312). Chicago: Nelson-Hall.

Burnham, C. A., & Davis, K. G. (1969). The nine-dot problem: Beyond perceptual organization. *Psychonomic Science, 17*, 321–323.

Burnstein, E., Crandall, C., & Kitayama, S. (1994). Some neo-Darwinian decision rules for altruism: Weighing cues for inclusive fitness as a function of the biological importance of the decision. *Journal of Personality and Social Psychology, 67*, 773–789.

Burton, H., & Sinclair, R. (1996). Somatosensory cortex and tactile perceptions. In L. Kruger (Ed.), *Pain and touch* (pp. 105–177). San Diego: Academic Press.

Bushman, B. J. (1993). Human aggression while under the influence of alcohol and other drugs: An integrative research review. *Current Directions in Psychological Science, 2*, 148–152.

Bushman, B. J., & Cooper, H. M. (1990). Effects of alcohol on human aggression: An integrative research review. *Psychological Bulletin, 107*, 341–354.

Bushman, B. J., & Huesmann, L. R. (2001). Effects of televised violence on aggression. In D. G. Singer & J. L. Singer (Eds.), *Handbook of children and the media* (pp. 223–254). Thousand Oaks, CA: Sage.

Buske-Kirschbaum, A., Kirschbaum, C., Stierle, H., et al. (1994). Conditioned manipulation of natural killer (NK) cells in humans using a discriminative learning protocol. *Biological Psychology, 38*, 143–155.

Buske-Kirschbaum, A., Kirschbaum, C., Stierle, H., Lehnert, H., & Hellhammer, D. (1992). Conditioned increase in natural killer cell activity (NKCA) in humans. *Psychosomatic Medicine, 54*, 123–132.

Buss, A. H. (1980). *Self-consciousness and social anxiety*. San Francisco, CA: W. H. Freeman.

Buss, D. M. (1988). The evolution of human intrasexual competition: Tactics of mate attraction. *Journal of Personality and Social Psychology, 54*, 616–628.

Buss, D. M. (1989). Sex differences in human mate preferences: Evolutionary hypotheses tested in 37 cultures. *Behavioral and Brain Sciences, 12*, 1–14.

Buss, D. M. (1994). *The evolution of desire*. New York: Basic Books.

Buss, D. M. (1999). *Evolutionary psychology: The new science of the mind*. Boston: Allyn & Bacon.

Buss, D. M. (2000). *The dangerous passion: Why jealousy is as necessary as love and sex*. New York: Simon & Schuster.

Buss, D. M., Larsen, R. J., Westen, D., & Semmelroth, J. (1992). Sex differences in jealousy: Evolution, physiology, and psychology. *Psychological Science, 3*, 251–258.

Buss, D. M., & Shackelford, T. K. (1997). From vigilance to violence: Mate retention tactics in married couples. *Journal of Personality and Social Psychology*, in press.

Butcher, J. N., & Williams, C. J. (2000). *Essentials of MMPI-2 and MMPI-A interpretation* (2nd ed.). Minneapolis: University of Minnesota Press.

Butler, J. L., & Baumeister, R. F. (1998). The trouble with friendly faces: Skilled performance with a supportive audience. *Journal of Personality and Social Psychology, 75*, 1213–1230.

Byne, W., & Parsons, B. (1993). Human sexual orientation: The biological theories reappraised. *Archives of General Psychiatry, 50*, 228–239.

Byrne, D. (1971). *The attraction paradigm*. New York: Academic Press.

Byrne, D. (1997). An overview (and underview) of research and theory within the attraction paradigm. *Journal of Social and Personal Relationships, 14*, 417–431.

Byrne, D., Clore, G. L., & Smeaton, G. (1986). The attraction hypothesis: Do similar attitudes attract anything? *Journal of Personality and Social Psychology, 51*, 1167–1170.

Byrne, D., Kelley, K., & Fisher, W. A. (1993). Unwanted teenage pregnancies: Incidence, interpretation, and intervention. *Applied and Preventive Psychology, 2*, 101–113.

Byrne, R. M. J., & McEleney, A. (2000). Counterfactual thinking about actions and failures to act. *Journal of Experimental Psychology: Learning Memory, and Cognition, 26*, 1318–1331.

Cabeza, R. (2002). Hemispheric asymmetry reduction in older adults: The HAROLD model. *Psychology & Aging, 17*, 85–100.

Cabeza, R., & Nyberg, L. (2000). Imaging cognition II: An empirical review of 275 PET and fMRI studies. *Journal of Cognitive Neuroscience, 12*, 1–47.

Cacioppo, J. T., & Gardner, W. L. (1999). Emotion. *Annual Review of Psychology, 50*, 191–214.

Cacioppo, J. T., & Petty, R. E. (1982). Eletromyograms as measures of extent and affectivity of information processing. *American Psychologist, 36*, 441–456.

Cacioppo, J. T., & Petty, R. E. (1982). The need for cognition. *Journal of Personality and Social Psychology, 42*, 116–131.

Cacioppo, J. T., Petty, R. E., Feinstein, J. A., Jarvis, W. B. G. (1996). Dispositional differences in cognitive motivation: The life and times of individuals varying in need for cognition. *Psychological Bulletin, 119*, 197–253.

Cairns, R. B., Gariepy, J. L., & Hood, K. E. (1990). Development, microevolution, and social behavior. *Psychological Review, 97*, 49–65.

Caldwell, J., & Ford, M. P. (2002). *Where have all the Bluebirds gone?: How to soar with flexible grouping*. Portsmouth, NH: Heinemann.

Calle, E. E., Thun, M. J., Petrelli, J. M., Rodriguez, C., & Heath, C. W. (1999). Body-mass index and mortality in a prospective cohort of U.S. adults. *The New England Journal of Medicine, 341*, 1097–1105.

Camara, W. J., & Schneider, D. L. (1994). Integrity tests: Facts and unresolved issues. *American Psychologist, 49*, 112–119.

Cameron, C. L., et al. (2001). Persistent symptoms among survivors of Hodgkin's disease: An explanatory model based on classical conditioning. *Health Psychology, 20*, 71–75.

Campbell, D. G. (1997). *The Mozart effect: Tapping the power of music to heal the body, strengthen the mind and unlock the creative spirit*. New York: Avon Books.

Campbell, D. J., & Lee, C. (1988). Self-appraisal in performance evaluation: Development versus evaluation. *Academy Management Review, 13*, 302–313.

Campbell, F. A., Pungello, E. P., Miller-Johnson, S., Burchinal, M., & Ramey, C. T. (2001). The development of cognitive and academic abilities: Growth curves from an early childhood educational experiment. *Developmental Psychology, 37*, 231–242.

Campbell, J. D., & Fairey, P. J. (1989). Informational and normative routes to conformity. *Journal of Personality and Social Psychology, 57*, 457–468.

Campbell, J. M., Amerikaner, M., Swank, P., & Vincent, K. (1989). The relationship between the Hardiness Test and the Personal Orientation Inventory. *Journal of Research in Personality, 23*, 373–380.

Campbell, S. S., & Murphy, P. J. (1998). Extraocular circadian phototransduction in humans. *Science, 279*, 396–399.

Campfield, L., Arthur, S., Francoise, J., Rosenbaum, M., & Hirsch, J. (1996). Human eating: Evidence for a physiological basis using a modified paradigm. *Neuroscience & Biobehavioral Reviews, 20*, 1133–1137.

Campos, J. J., Langer, A., & Krowtiz, A. (1970). Cardiac responses on the visual cliff in prelocomotor infants. *Science, 170*, 196–197.

Canfield, R. L., & Smith, E. G. (1996). Number-based expectations and sequential enumeration by 5-month-old infants. *Developmental Psychology, 32*, 269–279.

Cannon, D. S., Baker, T. B., & Wehl, C. K. (1981). Emetic and electric shock alcohol aversion therapy: Six- and twelve-month follow-up. *Journal of Consulting and Clinical Psychology, 49*, 360–368.

Cannon, W. B. (1927). The James-Lange theory of emotion: A critical examination and an alternative theory. *American Journal of Psychology, 39*, 106–124.

Cannon, W. B. (1932). *The wisdom of the body*. New York: Norton.

Cannon, W. B., & Washburn, A. L. (1912). An explanation of hunger. *American Journal of Physiology, 29*, 441–454.

Cantor, N., & Kihlstrom, J. F. (1987). *Personality and social intelligence*. Englewood Cliffs, NJ: Prentice-Hall.

Capaldi, E. D. (Ed.). (1996). *Why we eat what we eat: The psychology of eating*. Washington, DC: American Psychological Association.

Capozza, D., & Brown, R. (2000). *Social identity processes: Trends in theory and research*. London: Sage.

Caramazza, A., & Hillis, A. E. (1991). Lexical organization of nouns and verbs in the brain. *Nature, 349*, 788–790.

Carey, B. (1997). Don't face stress alone. *Health*, pp. 74–76, 78.

Carlo, G., et al. (1996). A cross-national study on the relations among prosocial moral reasoning, gender role orientations, and prosocial behaviors. *Developmental Psychology, 32*, 231–240.

Carmichael, L., Hogan, H. P., & Walter, A. (1932). An experimental study of the effect of language on the reproduction of visually perceived form. *Journal of Experimental Psychology, 15*, 73–86.

Carnegie, D. (1936). *How to win friends and influence people*. New York: Pocket Books. (Reprinted in 1972.)

Carpenter, S. (1999, July/August). Freud's dream theory gets boost from imaging work. *APA Monitor*, p. 19.

Carpenter, S. (2002, February). Plagiarism or memory glitch? *APA Monitor, 33*, 25–26.

Carroll, M. E., & Overmier, J. B. (2001). *Animal research and human health: Advancing human welfare through behavioral science*. Washington, DC: American Psychological Association.

Carskadon, M. A. (1993). Microsleep. In M. Carskadon (Ed.), *Encyclopedia of sleep and dreaming* (pp. 373–374). New York: Macmillan.

Carson, R. A., Rothstein, M. A., & Bloom, F. E. (Eds.). (1999). *Behavioral genetics: The clash of culture and biology*. Baltimore, MD: Johns Hopkins University Press.

Carstensen, L. L., Isaacowitz, D. M., & Charles, S. T. (1999). Taking time seriously: A theory of socioemotional selectivity. *American Psychologist, 54*, 165–181.

Carston, R. (2002). *Thoughts and utterances: The pragmatics of explicit communication*. London: Blackwell.

Carter, C. S. (1991). Hormonal influences on human sexual behavior. In J. B. Becker, S. M. Breedlove, & D. Crews (Eds.), *Behavioral endocrinology* (pp. 131–142). Cambridge, MA: MIT Press.

Carver, C. S., & Scheier, M. F. (1981). *Attention and self-regulation: A control-theory approach to human behavior*. New York: Springer-Verlag.

Casanova, C., & Ptito, M. (Eds.). (2001). *Vision: From neurons to cognition*. Amsterdam: Elsevier Science.

Case, R. (1992). *The mind's staircase*. Hillsdale, NJ: Erlbaum.

Case, R. B., Moss, A. J., Case, N., McDermott, M., & Eberly, S. (1992). Living alone after myocardial infarction: Impact on prognosis. *Journal of the American Medical Association, 267*, 515–519.

Casey, K. L., & Bushnell, M. C. (Eds.). (2000). *Pain imaging*. Seattle: IASP Press.

Caspi, A. (2000). The child is the father of man: Personality continuities from childhood to adulthood. *Journal of Personality and Social Psychology, 78*, 158–172.

Caspi, A., Lynam, D., Moffitt, T. E., & Silva, P. A. (1993). Unraveling girls' delinquency: Biological, dispositional, and contextual contributions to adolescent misbehavior. *Developmental Psychology, 29*, 19–30.

Caspi, A., & Moffitt, T. E. (1991). Individual differences are accentuated during periods of social change: The sample case of girls at puberty. *Journal of Personality and Social Psychology, 61*, 157–168.

Cassidy, C. M. (1991). The good body: When big is better. *Medical Anthropology: Cross-Cultural Studies in Health and Illness, 13*, 181–214.

Cassidy, J., Kirsh, S. J., Scolton, K. L., & Parke, R. D. (1996). Attachment and representations of peer relationships. *Developmental Psychology, 32*, 892–904.

Cassidy, J., Shaver, P. R., & Main, M. (Eds.). (1999). *Handbook of attachment: Theory, research, and clinical applications*. New York: Guilford.

Cattell, R. B. (1949). *The culture-free intelligence test*. Champaign, IL: Institute for Personality and Ability Testing.

Cattell, R. B. (1963). Theory of crystallized and fluid intelligence: A critical experiment. *Journal of Educational Psychology, 54,* 1–22.

Cattell, R. B. (1965). *The scientific analysis of personality.* Baltimore, MD: Penguin Books.

CBS News. (2002, April 28). Poll: Most believe in psychic phenomena. CBSNEWS.com.

Ceci, S. J. (1991). How much does schooling influence general intelligence and its cognitive components? A reassessment of the evidence. *Developmental Psychology, 27,* 703–722.

Ceci, S. J. (1996). *On intelligence: A bioecological treatise on intellectual development.* Cambridge, MA: Harvard University Press.

Ceci, S. J., & Hembrooke, H. (Eds.). (1998). *Expert witnesses in child abuse cases.* Washington, DC: American Psychological Association.

Ceci, S. J., Leichtman, M., & White, T. (in press). Interviewing preschoolers: Remembrances of things planted. In D. P. Peters (Ed.), *The child witness: Cognitive, social, and legal issues.* Netherlands: Kluwer.

Ceci, S. J., Ross, D. F., & Toglia, M. P. (1987). Suggestibility of children's memory: Psycholegal implications. *Journal of Experimental Psychology: General, 116,* 38–49.

Ceci, S. J., & Williams, W. M. (Eds.). (2000). *The nature-nurture debate: The essential readings.* Oxford, UK: Blackwell.

Centers for Disease Control and Prevention. (1993, July 19). *Newsweek,* p. 8.

Centers for Disease Control Vietnam Experience Study. (1988). Health status of Vietnam veterans: I. Psychosocial characteristics. *Journal of the American Medical Association, 259,* 2701–2707.

Cernoch, J. M., & Porter, R. H. (1985). Recognition of maternal axillary odors by infants. *Child Development, 56,* 1593–1598.

Cervone, D., & Shoda, Y. (Eds.). (1999). *The coherence of personality: Social-cognitive bases of consistency, variability, and organization.* New York: Guilford.

Chafe, W. H., Gavins, R., & Korstad, R. (2002). *Remembering Jim Crow: African Americans tell about life in the segregated south.* New York: Norton.

Chaiken, S. (1979). Communicator physical attractiveness and persuasion. *Journal of Personality and Social Psychology, 37,* 1387–1397.

Chaiken, S., & Maheswaran, D. (1994). Heuristic processing can bias systematic processing: Effects of source credibility, argument ambiguity, and task importance on attitude judgment. *Journal of Personality and Social Psychology, 66,* 460–473.

Chambless, D. L., & Ollendick, T. H. (2001). Empirically supported psychological interventions: Controversies and evidence. *Annual Review of Psychology, 52,* 685–716.

Chandler, C. C. (1991). How memory for an event is influenced by related events: Interference in modified recognition tests. *Journal of Experimental Psychology: Learning, Memory, and Cognition, 17,* 115–125.

Chaplin, W. F., Phillips, J. B., Brown, J. D., Clanton, N. R., & Stein, J. L. (2000). Handshaking, gender, personality, and first impressions. *Journal of Personality and Social Psychology, 79,* 110–117.

Chartrand, T. L., & Bargh, J. A. (1999). The chameleon effect: The perception-behavior link and social interaction. *Journal of Personality and Social Psychology, 76,* 893–910.

Chase, M. H., & Morales, F. R. (1983). Subthreshold excitatory activity and motorneuron discharge during REM periods of active sleep. *Science, 221,* 1195–1198.

Chase, W. G., & Simon, H. A. (1973). Perception in chess. *Cognitive Psychology, 4,* 55–81.

Cheek, J. M., & Briggs, S. R. (1990). Shyness as a personality trait. In W. R. Crozier (Ed.), *Shyness and embarrassment: Perspectives from social psychology* (pp. 315–337). New York: Cambridge University Press.

Chen, C., Lee, S., & Stevenson, H. W. (1995). Response style and cross-cultural comparisons of rating scales among East Asian and North American students. *Psychological Science, 6,* 170–175.

Chen, C., & Stevenson, H. W. (1995). Motivation and mathematics achievement: A comparative study of Asian-American, Caucasian-American, and East Asian high school students. *Child Development, 66,* 1215–1234.

Chen, J., Rathore, S. S., Radford, M. J., Wang, Y., & Krumholz, H. M. (2001). Racial differences in the use of cardiac catheterization after acute myocardial infarction. *The New England Journal of Medicine, 344,* 1443–1449.

Chen, Y., Brockner, J., & Katz, T. (1998). Toward an explanation of cultural differences in in-group favoritism: The role of individual versus collective primacy. *Journal of Personality and Social Psychology, 75,* 1490–1502.

Chen, Z. (2002). Analogical problem solving: A hierarchical analysis of procedural similarity. *Journal of Experimental Psychology: Learning, Memory, and Cognition, 28,* 81–98.

Cheney, D. L., & Seyfarth, R. M. (1990). *How monkeys see the world.* Chicago: University of Chicago Press.

Cheney, D. L., & Seyfarth, R. M. (1992). Precis of How monkeys see the world. *Behavioral and Brain Sciences, 15,* 135–182.

Cheng, P. W., Holyoak, K. J., Nisbett, R. E., & Oliver, L. M. (1986). Pragmatic versus syntactic approaches to training deductive reasoning. *Cognitive Psychology, 18,* 293–328.

Cheng, P. W., & Novick, L. R. (1990). A probabilistic contrast model of causal induction. *Journal of Personality and Social Psychology, 58,* 545–567.

Cherry, E. C. (1953). Some experiments on the recognition of speech, with one and with two ears. *Journal of the Acoustical Society of America, 25,* 975–979.

Chinwalla, A. T., et al. (2002). Initial sequencing and comparative analysis of the mouse genome. *Nature, 420,* 520–562.

Chipman, S. F., Brush, L. R., & Wilson, D. M. (Eds.). (1985). *Women and mathematics.* Hillsdale, NJ: Erlbaum.

Chochinov, H. M., Wilson, K. G., Enns, M., Mowchun, N., Lander, S., Levitt, M., & Clinch, J. J. (1995). Desire for death in the terminally ill. *American Journal of Psychiatry, 152,* 1185–1191.

Choi, I., Nisbett, R. E., & Norenzayan, A. (1999). Causal attribution across cultures: Variation and universality. *Psychological Bulletin, 125,* 47–63.

Choi, J. N., & Kim, M. U. (1999). The organizational application of groupthink and its limitations in organizations. *Journal of Applied Psychology, 84,* 297–306.

Chomsky, N. (1957). *Syntactic structures.* The Hague: Morton Publishers.

Chomsky, N. (1959). A review of B. F. Skinner's "Verbal Behavior." *Language, 35,* 26–58.

Chomsky, N. (1972). *Language and mind.* New York: Harcourt Brace Jovanovich.

Christensen, A., & Jacobson, N. S. (1994). Who (or what) can do psychotherapy: The status and challenge of nonprofessional therapies. *Psychological Science, 5,* 8–14.

Chumlea, W. C. (1982). Physical growth in adolescence. In B. Wolman (Ed.), *Handbook of developmental psychology.* Englewood Cliffs, NJ: Prentice-Hall.

Church, A. T. (2001). Personality measurement in cross-cultural perspective. *Journal of Personality, 69,* 979–1006.

Chynoweth, C. (2002, March 23). Even drunk drivers are not as dangerous as our . . . mobile phone pests. *The Daily Telegraph.*

Cialdini, R. B. (1988). *Influence: Science and practice* (2nd ed.). Glenview, IL: Scott, Foresman.

Cialdini, R. B., Darby, B. L., & Vincent, J. E. (1973). Transgressional altruism: A case for hedonism. *Journal of Personality and Social Psychology, 9,* 502–516.

Cialdini, R. B., Kallgren, C. A., & Reno, R. R. (1991). A focus theory of normative conduct: A theoretical refinement and reevaluation of the role of norms in human behavior. *Advances in Experimental Social Psychology, 24,* 201–234.

Cialdini, R. B., Schaller, M., Houlihan, D., Arps, K., Fultz, J., & Beaman, A. L. (1987). Empathy-based helping: Is it selflessly or selfishly motivated? *Journal of Personality and Social Psychology, 52,* 749–758.

Cialdini, R. B., & Trost, M. R. (1998). Influence, social norms, conformity, and compliance. In D. Gilbert, S. Fiske, & G. Lindzey (Eds.), *The handbook of social psychology* (4th ed). New York: Oxford University Press.

Cialdini, R. B., Trost, M. R., & Newsom, J. T. (1995). Preference for consistency: The development of a valid measure and the discovery of surprising behavioral implications. *Journal of Personality and Social Psychology, 69,* 318–328.

Cioffi, D., & Holloway, J. (1993). Delayed costs of suppressed pain. *Journal of Personality and Social Psychology, 64,* 274–282.

Cipolli, C., Bolzani, R., Cornoldi, C., DeBeni, R., & Fagioli, I. (1993). Bizarreness effect in dream recall. *Sleep, 16,* 163–170.

Claes, M. (1998). Adolescents' closeness with parents, siblings, and friends in three countries: Canada, Belgium, and Italy. *Journal of Youth and Adolescence, 27,* 165–184.

Clark, D. M., Salkovskis, P. M., Ost, L. G., Breitholtz, E., Koehler, K. A., Westling, B. E., Jeavons, A., & Gelder, M. (1997). Misinterpretation of body sensations in panic disorder. *Journal of Consulting and Clinical Psychology, 65,* 203–213.

Clark, H. H. (1985). Language use and language users. In G. Lindzey & E. Aronson (Eds.), *Handbook of social psychology* (3rd ed., pp. 179–231). New York: Random House.

Clark, H. H. (1996). *Using language.* New York: Cambridge University Press.

Clark, L. A. (1999). Introduction to the special section on the concept of disorder. *Journal of Abnormal Psychology, 108,* 371–373.

Clark, L. F. (1993). Stress and the cognitive-conversational benefits of social interaction. *Journal of Social and Clinical Psychology, 12,* 25–55.

Clark, R., Anderson, N. B., Clark, V. R., & Williams, D. R. (1999). Racism as a stressor for African Americans: A biosocial model. *American Psychologist, 54,* 805–816.

Clark, R. D., & Maass, A. (1990). The effects of majority size on minority influence. *European Journal of Social Psychology, 20,* 99–117.

Clark, R. D., III. (2001). Effects of majority defection and multiple minority sources on minority influence. *Group Dynamics: Theory, Research, and Practice, 5,* 57–62.

Clarke-Stewart, K. A., Gruber, C. P., & Fitzgerald, L. M. (1994). *Children at home and in day care.* Mahwah, NJ: Erlbaum.

Classen, C., Howes, D., & Synnott, A. (1994). *Aroma: The cultural history of smell.* London: Routledge.

Clayton, N. S. (2001). Hippocampal growth and maintenance depend on food-caching experience in juvenile mountain chickadees (*Poecile gambeli*). *Behavioral Neuroscience, 115,* 614–625.

Clayton, N. S., & Dickinson, A. (1998). Episodic-like memory during cache recovery by scrub jays. *Nature, 395,* 272–274.

Clearfield, M. W., & Mix, K. S. (1999). Number versus contour length in infants' discrimination of small visual sets. *Psychological Science, 10,* 408–411.

Cleckley, H. (1976). *The mask of sanity* (5th ed.). St. Louis: Mosby.

Coan, J. A., Allen, J. J. B., & Harmon-Jones, E. (2001). Voluntary facial expression and hemispheric asymmetry over the frontal cortex. *Psychophysiology, 38,* 912–925.

Coe, C. L. (1993). Psychosocial factors and immunity in nonhuman primates: A review. *Psychosomatic Medicine, 55,* 298–308.

Coffey, C. E., et al. (1991). Brain anatomic effects of electroconvulsive therapy: A prospective magnetic resonance imaging study. *Archives of General Psychiatry, 48,* 1013–1021.

Cohen, E. G. (1984). The desegregated school: Problems in status power and interethnic climate. In N. Miller & M. B. Brewer (Eds.), *Groups in contact: The psychology of desegregation* (pp. 77–96). New York: Academic Press.

Cohen, J. D., & Schooler, J. W. (Eds.). (1997). *Scientific approaches to consciousness.* Hillsdale, NJ: Erlbaum.

Cohen, S., Frank, E., Doyle, W. J., Skoner, D. P., Rabin, B. S., & Gwaltney, J. M. (1998). Types of stressors that increase susceptibility to the common cold in healthy adults. *Health Psychology, 17,* 214–223.

Cohen, S., Hamrick, N., Rodriguez, M. S., Feldman, P. J., Rabin, B. S., & Manuck, S. B. (2002). Reactivity and vulnerability to stress-associated risk for upper respiratory illness. *Psychosomatic Medicine.*

Cohen, S., & Herbert, T. B. (1996). Health psychology: Psychological factors and physical disease from the perspective of human psychoneuroimmunology. *Annual Review of Psychology, 47,* 113–142.

Cohen, S., Tyrrell, D. A. J., & Smith, A. P. (1991). Psychological stress and susceptibility to the common cold. *New England Journal of Medicine, 325,* 606–612.

Cohen, S., Tyrrell, D. A. J., & Smith, A. P. (1993). Negative life events, perceived stress, negative affect and susceptibility to the common cold. *Journal of Personality and Social Psychology, 64,* 131–140.

Cohen, S., Underwood, L. G., & Gottlieb, B. H. (Eds.). (2000). *Social support measurement and intervention: A guide for health and social scientists.* New York: Oxford University Press.

Cohen, S., & Williamson, G. (1991). Stress and infectious disease in humans. *Psychological Bulletin, 109,* 5–24.

Cohen, Y. (1964). *The transition from childhood to adolescence: Cross-cultural studies of initiation ceremonies, legal systems, and incest taboos.* Chicago: Aldine.

Cohen-Kitteinis, P. T., & van Goozen, S. H. M. (1997). Sex reassignment of adolescent transsexuals: A follow-up study. *Journal of the American Academy of Child and Adolescent Psychiatry, 36,* 263–271.

Coile, D. C., & Miller, N. E. (1984). How radical animal activists try to mislead humane people. *American Psychologist, 39,* 700–701.

Colangelo, N., & Kerr, B. A. (1990). Extreme academic talent: Profiles of perfect scorers. *Journal of Educational Psychology, 82,* 404–409.

Colby, A., Kohlberg, L., Gibbs, J., & Lieberman, M. (1983). A longitudinal study of moral judgment. *Monographs of the Society for Research in Child Development, 48*(1–2, Serial No. 200).

Cole, S. W., Kemeny, M. E., Taylor, S. E., Visscher, B. R., & Fahey, J. L. (1996). Accelerated course of human immunodeficiency virus infection in gay men who conceal their homosexual identity. *Psychosomatic Medicine, 58,* 219–231.

Coleman, R. M. (1986). *Wide awake at 3:00 a.m.: By choice or by chance?* New York: W. H. Freeman.

Coles, R. (1997). *The moral intelligence of children.* New York: Random House.

Collaer, M. L., & Hines, M. (1995). Human behavioral sex differences: A role for gonadal hormones during early development? *Psychological Bulletin, 118,* 55–107.

Collins, A. M., & Loftus, E. F. (1975). A spreading activation theory of semantic processing. *Psychological Review, 82,* 407–428.

Collins, N. L., & Miller, L. C. (1994). Self-disclosure and liking: A meta-analytic review. *Psychological Bulletin, 116,* 457–475.

Collins, W. A., Maccoby, E. E., Steinberg, L. E., Hetherington, E. M., & Bornstein, M. H. (2000). Contemporary research on parenting: The case for nature and nurture. *American Psychologist, 55,* 218–232.

Colombo, J. (1993). *Infant cognition: Predicting later intellectual functioning.* Thousand Oaks, CA: Sage.

Colp, R., Jr. (1977). *To be an invalid: The illness of Charles Darwin.* Chicago: University of Chicago Press.

Coltheart, V. (Ed.). (1999). *Fleeting memories: Cognition of brief visual stimuli.* Cambridge, MA: MIT Press.

Colvin, C. R., & Block, J. (1994). Do positive illusions foster mental health? An examination of the Taylor and Brown formulation. *Psychological Bulletin, 116,* 3–20.

Colvin, C. R., Block, J., & Funder, D. C. (1995). Overly positive self-evaluations and personality: Negative implications for mental health. *Journal of Personality and Social Psychology, 68,* 1152–1162.

Condry, J., & Condry, S. (1976). Sex differences: A study of the eye of the beholder. *Child Development, 47,* 812–819.

Conel, J. L. (1939–1963). *The postnatal development of the human cerebral cortex* (Vols. I–VI). Cambridge, MA: Harvard University Press.

Conger, R. D., Reuter, M. A., & Elder, G. H., Jr. (1999). Couple resilience to economic pressure. *Journal of Personality and Social Psychology, 76,* 54–71.

Conger, R. D., Wallace, L. E., Sun, Y., Simons, R. L., McLoyd, V. C., & Brody, G. H. (2002). Economic pressure in African American families: A replication and extension of the family stress model. *Developmental Psychology, 38,* 179–193.

Conrad, R. (1964). Acoustic confusions in immediate memory. *British Journal of Psychology, 55,* 75–84.

*Consumer Reports.* (1995, November). Mental health: Does therapy help?, pp. 734–739.

*Consumer Reports.* (1999, September). Special report: Noise, pp. 19–22.

Conti, R. (2001). Time flies: Investigating the connection between intrinsic motivation and the experience of time. *Journal of Personality, 69,* 1–26.

Conway, B. R. (2002). *Neural mechanisms of color vision: Double-opponent cells in the visual cortex.* Dordrecht: Kluwer.

Conway, M. (1995). *Flashbulb memories.* Mahwah, NJ: Erlbaum.

Conway, M., Cohen, G., & Stanhope, N. (1991). On the very long-term retention of knowledge acquired through formal education: Twelve years of cognitive psychology. *Journal of Experimental Psychology: General, 120,* 395–409.

Conway, M., Collins, A. F., Gathercole, S. E., & Anderson, S. J. (1996). Recollections of true and false autobiographical memories. *Journal of Experimental Psychology: General, 125,* 69–95.

Cook, M., & Mineka, S. (1990). Selective association in the observational conditioning of fear in monkeys. *Behaviour Research and Therapy, 25,* 349–364.

Cook, S. W. (1985). Experimenting on social issues: The case of school desegregation. *American Psychologist, 40,* 452–460.

Cook, T. D., Cooper, H., Cordray, D. S., Hartmann, H., Hedges, L. V., Light, R. J., Louis, T. A., & Mosteller, F. (1992). *Meta-analysis for explanation: A casebook.* New York: Russell Sage Foundation.

Cooper, J., Bloom, F., & Roth, R. (1995). *The biochemical basis of neuropharmacology* (7th ed.). New York: Oxford University Press.

Cooper, J., & Fazio, R. H. (1984). A new look at dissonance theory. In L. Berkowitz (Ed.), *Advances in experimental social psychology* (Vol. 17, pp. 229–267). New York: Academic Press.

Cooper, J. R., Bloom, F. E., & Roth, R. H. (2002). *The biochemical basis of neuropharmacology* (8th ed.). New York: Oxford University Press.

Cooper, M. L., Frone, M. R., Russell, M., & Mudar, P. (1995). Drinking to regulate positive and negative emotions: A motivational model of alcohol use. *Journal of Personality and Social Psychology, 69,* 990–1005.

Coopersmith, S. (1967). *The antecedents of self-esteem.* San Francisco: Freeman.

Copeland, J. R. M., et al. (1999). Cross-cultural comparison of depressive symptoms in Europe does not support stereotypes of aging. *British Journal of Psychiatry, 174,* 322–329.

Copeland, J. T. (1994). Prophecies of power: Motivational implications of social power for behavioral confirmation. *Journal of Personality and Social Psychology, 67,* 264–277.

Corballis, M. C. (1997). The genetics and evolution of handedness. *Psychological Review, 104,* 714–727.

Corballis, M. C. (1999). Are we in our right minds? In S. D. Sala (Ed.), *Mind myths: Exploring popular assumptions about the mind and brain* (pp. 25–41). London: Wiley.

Corballis, P. M., Funnell, M. G., & Gazzaniga, M. S. (2002). Hemispheric asymmetries for simple visual judgments in the split brain. *Neuropsychologia, 40,* 401–410.

Coren, S. (1993). *The left-hander syndrome.* New York: Vintage Books.

Coren, S. (1996). *Sleep thieves: An eye-opening exploration into science and mysteries of sleep.* New York: Free Press.

Coren, S., & Aks, D. J. (1990). Moon illusion in pictures: A multimechanism approach. *Journal of Experimental Psychology: Human Perception and Performance, 16,* 365–380.

Coren, S., & Halpern, D. F. (1991). Left-handedness: A marker for decreased survival fitness. *Psychological Bulletin, 109,* 90–106.

Corina, D. P., Vaid, J., & Belugi, U. (1992). The linguistic basis of left-hemisphere specialization. *Science, 255,* 1258–1260.

Corrigan, P. W., & Penn, D. L. (1999). Lessons from social psychology on discrediting psychiatric stigma. *American Psychologist, 54,* 765–776.

Cose, E. (1997). *Color-blind.* New York: HarperCollins.

Costa, P. T., Jr., & McCrae, R. M. (1992). *Revised NEO personality inventory: NEO PI and NEO Five Factor Inventory (NEO FFI Professional Manual).* Odessa, FL: Psychological Assessment Resources, Inc.

Costa, P. T., Jr., Terracciano, A., & McCrae, R. R. (2001). Gender differences in personality traits across cultures: Robust and surprising findings. *Journal of Personality and Social Psychology, 81,* 322–331.

Costa, P. T., Jr., & Widiger, T. A. (Eds.). (1994). *Personality disorders and the five factor model of personality.* Washington, DC: American Psychological Association.

Cote, K. A., De Lugt, D. R., & Campbell, K. B. (2002). Changes in the scalp topography of event-related potentials and behavioral responses during the sleep onset period. *Psychophysiology, 39,* 29–37.

Cousins, N. (1989). *Head first: The biology of hope.* New York: Dutton.

Cowan, N. (1988). Evolving concepts of memory storage, selective attention, and their mutual constraints within the human information-processing system. *Psychological Bulletin, 104,* 163–191.

Cowan, N. (2000). The magical number 4 in short-term memory: A reconsideration of mental storage capacity. *Behavioral and Brain Sciences, 24,* 87–185.

Cowan, N., Wood, N. L., & Borne, D. N. (1994). Reconfirmation of the short-term storage concept. *Psychological Science, 5,* 103–106.

Cowey, A., & Stoerig, P. (1991). The neurobiology of blindsight. *Trends in Neuroscience. 14,* 140–145.

Cowey, A., & Stoerig, P. (1992). Reflections on blindsight. In A. D. Milner & M. D. Rugg (Eds.), *The neuropsychology of consciousness.* London: Academic Press.

Cowley, G. (1996, June 3). The biology of beauty. *Newsweek,* pp. 61–69.

Cox, M. J., Owen, M. T., Henderson, V. K., & Margand, N. A. (1992). Prediction of infant-father and infant-mother attachment. *Developmental Psychology, 28,* 474–483.

Cox, M. J., & Paley, B. (1997). Families as systems. *Annual Review of Psychology, 48,* 243–267.

Coyne, J. C. (1976). Depression and the responses of others. *Journal of Abnormal Psychology, 85,* 186–193.

Coyne, J. C., Thompson, R., & Palmer, S. C. (2002). Marital quality, coping with conflict, marital complaints, and affection in couples with a depressed wife. *Journal of Family Psychology, 16,* 26–37.

Crabbe, J. C. (2002). Genetic contributions to addiction. *Annual Review of Psychology, 53,* 435–462.

Craig, J. C., Reiman, E. M., Evans, A., & Bushnell, M. C. (1996). Functional imaging of an illusion of pain. *Nature, 384,* 258–260.

Craig, J. C., & Rollman, G. B. (1999). Somesthesis. *Annual Review of Psychology, 50,* 305–331.

Craik, F., Moroz, T. M., Moscovitch, M., Stuss, D. T., Winocur, G., Tulving, E., & Kapur, S. (1999). In search of the self: A positron emission tomography study. *Psychological Science, 10,* 26–34.

Craik, F. I. M. (1992). In F. Craik & T. A. Salthouse (Eds.), *Handbook of aging and cognition.* Hillsdale, NJ: Erlbaum.

Craik, F. I. M., & Tulving, E. (1975). Depth of processing and the retention of words in episodic memory. *Journal of Experimental Psychology: General, 104,* 268–294.

Cramer, P. (1996). *Storytelling, narrative, and the Thematic Apperception Test.* New York: Guilford Press.

Cramer, P. (1998). Coping and defense mechanisms: What's the difference? *Journal of Personality, 66,* 919–946.

Cramer, P. (2000). Defense mechanisms in psychology today: Further processes for adaptation. *American Psychologist, 55,* 637–646.

Crandall, C. S. (1994). Prejudice against fat people: Ideology and self-interest. *Journal of Personality and Social Psychology, 66,* 882–894.

Crano, W. D. (2000). Milestones in the psychological analysis of social influence. *Group Dynamics: Theory, Research, and Practice, 4,* 68–80.

Craske, M. G., Lang, A. J., Rowe, M., DeCola, J. P., Simmons, J., Mann, C. Yan-Go, F., & Bystritsky, A. (2002). Presleep attributions about arousal during sleep: Nocturnal panic. *Journal of Abnormal Psychology, 111,* 53–62.

Craske, M. G., & Barlow, D. H. (2001). Panic disorder and agoraphobia. In D. H. Barlow (Ed.), *Anxiety and its disorders: The nature and treatment of anxiety and panic* (2nd ed., pp. 1–59). New York: Guilford.

Crawford, H. J., Brown, A. M., & Moon, C. E. (1993). Sustained attentional and disattentional abilities: Differences between low and highly hypnotizable persons. *Journal of Abnormal Psychology, 102,* 534–543.

Crawford, H. J., Kitner-Triolo, M., Clarke, S. W., & Otesko, B. (1992). Transient positive and negative experiences accompanying stage hypnosis. *Journal of Abnormal Psychology, 101,* 663–667.

Creasey, H., & Rapoport, S. I. (1985). The aging human brain. *Annals of Neurology, 17,* 2–11.

Crits-Christoph, P., & Barber, J. (Eds.). (1991). *Handbook of short-term dynamic psychotherapy.* New York: Basic Books.

Crocker, J., & Major, B. (1989). Social stigma and self-esteem: The self-protective properties of stigma. *Psychological Review, 96,* 608–630.

Crocker, J., Voelkl, K., Testa, M., & Major, B. (1991). Social stigma: The affective consequences of attributional ambiguity. *Journal of Personality and Social Psychology, 60,* 218–228.

Crocker, J., & Wolfe, C. T. (2001). Contingencies of self-worth. *Psychological Review. 108,* 593–623.

Cropanzano, R. (Ed.). (1993). *Justice in the workplace: Approaching fairness in human resource management.* Mahwah, NJ: Erlbaum.

Crosby, F., Bromley, S., & Saxe, L. (1980). Recent unobtrusive studies of black and white discrimination and prejudice: A literature review. *Psychological Bulletin, 87,* 546–563.

Cross-National Collaborative Group. (1992). The changing rate of major depression. *Journal of the American Medical Association, 268,* 3008–3015.

Crowder, R. G. (1993). Short-term memory: Where do we stand? *Memory and Cognition, 21,* 142–145.

Crystal, D. S., & Stevenson, H. W. (1991). Mothers' perceptions of children's problems with mathematics: A cross-national comparison. *Journal of Educational Psychology, 83,* 372–376.

Csikszentmihalyi, M. (1990). *Flow: The psychology of optimal experience.* New York: Harper & Row.

Csikszentmihalyi, M. (1997). *Finding flow.* New York: Basic Books.

Csikszentmihalyi, M. (1999). If we're so rich, why aren't we happy? *American Psychologist, 54,* 821–827.

Csikszentmihalyi, M., & Figurski, T. J. (1982). Self-awareness and aversive experience in everyday life. *Journal of Personality, 50,* 15–28.

Cuellar, I., & Paniagua, F. A. (Eds.). (2000). *Handbook of multicultural mental health: Assessment and treatment of diverse populations.* San Diego: Academic Press.

Cumming, B. G., & DeAngelis, G. C. (2001). The physiology of stereopsis. *Annual Review of Neuroscience, 24,* 203–238.

Curran, J. P., & Monti, P. M. (1982). *Social skills training: A practical handbook for assessment and treatment.* New York: Guilford Press.

Cutler, B. L., & Penrod, S. D. (1995). *Mistaken identification: The eyewitness, psychology, and the law.* New York: Cambridge University Press.

Cyranowski, J. M., Frank, E., Young, E., & Shear, M. K. (2000). Adolescent onset of the gender difference in lifetime rates of major depression. *Archives of General Psychiatry, 57,* 21–27.

Cytowic, R. E. (2002). *Synesthesia: A union of the senses* (2nd ed.). Cambridge, MA: MIT Press.

Czeisler, C. A., Johnson, M. P., Duffy, J. F., Brown, E. N., Ronda, J. M., & Kronauer, R. E. (1990). Exposure to bright light and darkness to treat physiologic maladaptation to night work. *New England Journal of Medicine, 322,* 1253–1259.

Dabbs, J. B. (2000). *Heroes, rogues, and lovers: Testosterone and behavior.* New York: McGraw-Hill.

Dabbs, J. M., Jr., with Dabbs, M. G. (2000). *Heroes, rogues & lovers: Testosterone and behavior.* New York: McGraw-Hill.

Dallenbach, K. M. (1927). The temperature spots and end organs. *American Journal of Psychology, 54,* 431–433.

Dalton, P., & Wysocki, C. J. (1996). The nature and duration of adaptation following long-term odor exposure. *Perception and Psychophysics, 58,* 781–792.

Daly, M., & Wilson, M. (1990). Is parent-offspring conflict sex-linked? Freudian and Darwinian models. *Journal of Personality, 58,* 163–189.

Damasio, A. R. (1994). *Descartes' error: Emotion, reason, and the human brain.* New York: Avon Books.

Damasio, H., Grabowski, T., Frank, R., Galaburda, A. M., & Damasio, A. R. (1994). The return of Phineas Gage: The skull of a famous patient yields clues about the brain. *Science, 264,* 1102–1105.

Damon, W. (1988). *The moral child.* New York: Free Press.

Damon, W. (1999, December). The moral development of children. *Scientific American,* pp. 72–78.

Darley, J. M., & Gross, P. H. (1983). A hypothesis-confirming bias in labeling effects. *Journal of Personality and Social Psychology, 44,* 20–33.

Darley, J. M., & Latané, B. (1968). Bystander intervention in emergencies: Diffusion of responsibility. *Journal of Personality and Social Psychology, 8,* 377–383.

Darling, C. A., Davidson, J. K., & Passarello, L. C. (1992). The mystique of first intercourse among college youth: The role of partners, contraceptive practices, and psychological reactions. *Journal of Youth and Adolescence, 21,* 97–117.

Darwin, C. (1859). *The origin of species.* New York: Washington Square Press. (Reprinted in 1963.)

Darwin, C. (1872). *The expression of the emotions in man and animals.* London: John Murray.

Darwin, C. J., Turvey, M. T., & Crowder, R. G. (1972). An auditory analogue of the Sperling partial report procedure: Evidence for brief auditory storage. *Cognitive Psychology, 3,* 255–267.

Dasgupta, N., & Greenwald, A. G. (2001). On the malleability of automatic attitudes combating automatic prejudice with images of admired and disliked individuals. *Journal of Personality and Social Psychology, 81,* 800–814.

Davey, G. C. L. (1995). Preparedness and phobias: Specific evolved associations or a generalized expectancy bias? *Behavioral and Brain Sciences, 18,* 289–325.

Davidson, R. J. (1998). Affective style and affective disorders: Perspectives from affective neuroscience. *Cognition and Emotion, 12,* 307–330.

Davidson, R. J., Ekman, P., Saron, C. D., Senulis, J. A., & Friesen, W. V. (1990). Approach-withdrawal and cerebral asymmetry: Emotional expression and brain physiology I. *Journal of Personality and Social Psychology, 58,* 330–341.

Davidson, R. J., & Hugdahl, K. (Eds.). (1995). *Brain asymmetry.* Cambridge, MA: MIT Press.

Davidson, R. J., Jackson, D. C., & Kalin, N. H. (2000). Emotion, plasticity, context, and regulation: Perspectives from affective neuroscience. *Psychological Bulletin, 126,* 890–909.

Davidson, R. J., Marshall, J. R., Tomarken, A. J., & Henriques, J. B. (2000). While a phobic waits: Regional brain electrical and autonomic activity in social phobics during anticipation of public speaking. *Biological Psychiatry, 47,* 85–95.

Davidson, R. J., Pizzagalli, D., Nitschke, J. B., & Putnam, K. (2002). Depression: Perspectives from affective neuroscience. *Annual Review of Psychology, 53,* 545–574.

Davies, I., Sowden, P., & Jerrett, D. (1998). A cross-cultural study of English and Setswana speakers on a colour triads task: A test of the Sapir-Whorf hypothesis. *British Journal of Psychology, 89,* 1–15.

Davis, M. (1992). The role of the amygdala in fear and anxiety. *Annual Review of Neuroscience, 15,* 353–375.

Davis, M. C., Matthews, K. A., & McGrath, C. (2000). Hostile attitudes predict elevated vascular resistance during interpersonal stress in men and women. *Psychosomatic Medicine, 62,* 17–25.

Davison, K. P., Pennebaker, J. W., & Dickerson, S. S. (2000). Who talks? The social psychology of illness support groups. *American Psychologist, 55,* 205–217.

Dawes, R. M. (1994). *House of cards: Psychology and psychotherapy built on myth.* New York: Free Press.

Dawes, R. M., Faust, D., & Meehl, P. E. (1989). Clinical versus actuarial judgment. *Science, 243,* 1668–1674.

Dawkins, R. (1989). *The selfish gene* (2nd ed.). Oxford: Oxford University Press.

Dawkins, R. (1996). *Climbing Mount Improbable.* New York: Norton.

de Castro, J. M. (1994). Family and friends produce greater social facilitation of food intake than other companions. *Physiology and Behavior, 56,* 445–455.

de Castro, J. M., & Brewer, E. M. (1992). The amount eaten in meals by humans is a power function of the number of people present. *Physiology and Behavior, 51,* 121–125.

De Groot, A. D. (1965). *Thought and chance in chess.* The Hague: Moulton.

De Houwer, J., Thomas, S. & Baeyens, F. (2001). Association learning of likes and dislikes: A review of 25 years of research on human evaluative conditioning. *Psychological Bulletin, 127,* 853–869.

De Raad, B. (2000). *The big five personality factors.* Seattle: Hogrefe & Huber.

De Raad, B., & Perugini, M. (Eds.). (2002). *Big five assessment.* Seattle: Hogrefe & Huber.

de Rivera, J. (1997). The construction of false memory syndrome: The experience of retractors. *Psychological Inquiry, 8,* 271–292.

Deacon, T. W. (1998). *The symbolic species: The co-evolution of language and the brain.* New York: W.W. Norton.

Deary, I. J., Ramsay, H., Wilson, J. A., & Riad, M. (1988). Stimulated salivation: Correlations with personality and time of day effects. *Personality and Individual Differences, 9,* 903–909.

Deary, I. J., Simonotto, E., Marshall, A., Marshall, I., Goddard, N., & Wardlaw, J. M. (2001). The functional anatomy of inspection time: A pilot fMRI study. *Intelligence, 29,* 497–510.

Death Odds. (1990, September 24). *Newsweek,* p. 10.

DeBono, K. G. (1987). Investigating the social-adjustive and value-expressive functions of attitudes: Implications for persuasion processes. *Journal of Personality and Social Psychology, 52,* 279–287.

DeCasper, A. J., & Fifer, W. P. (1980). Of human bonding: Newborns prefer their mothers' voices. *Science, 208,* 1174–1176.

DeCasper, A. J., & Sigafoos, A. D. (1983). The intrauterine heartbeat: A potent reinforcer for newborns. *Infant Behavior and Development, 6,* 19–25.

DeCasper, A. J., & Spence, M. J. (1986). Prenatal maternal speech influences newborns' perception of speech sounds. *Infant Behavior and Development, 9,* 133–150.

Deci, E. L. (1971). Effects of externally mediated rewards on intrinsic motivation. *Journal of Personality and Social Psychology, 18,* 105–115.

Deci, E. L., Connell, J. P., & Ryan, R. M. (1989). Self-determination in a work organization. *Journal of Applied Psychology, 74,* 580–590.

Deci, E. L., Koestner, R., & Ryan, R. M. (1999). A meta-analytic review of experiments examining the effects of extrinsic rewards on intrinsic motivation. *Psychological Bulletin, 125,* 627–668.

DelBello, M. P. (2002). Effects of ethnicity on psychiatric diagnosis: A developmental perspective. *Psychiatric Times, 19.*

DeLoache, J. S., & Brown, A. L. (1983). Very young children's memory for the location of objects in a large-scale environment. *Child Development, 54,* 888–897.

Dement, W. C. (1992). *The sleepwatchers.* Stanford, CA: Stanford Alumni Association.

Dement, W. C., & Kleitman, N. (1957). The relation of eye movements during sleep to dream activity: An objective method for the study of dreaming. *Journal of Experimental Psychology, 53,* 339–346.

Dement, W. C., & Vaughan, C. (1999). *The promise of sleep.* New York: Delacorte.

Dempster, F. N. (1981). Memory span: Sources of individual and developmental differences. *Psychological Bulletin, 89,* 63–100.

Dempster, F. N. (1988). The spacing effect: A case study in the failure to apply the results of psychological research. *American Psychologist, 43,* 627–634.

DeNeve, K. M., & Cooper, H. (1998). The happy personality: A meta-analysis of 137 personality traits and subjective well-being. *Psychological Bulletin, 124,* 197–229.

Denmark, F. L. (1998). Women and psychology: An international perspective. *American Psychologist, 53,* 465–473.

Dennett, D. (1995). *Darwin's dangerous idea: Evolution and the meaning of life.* New York: Simon & Schuster.

DePaulo, B. M., & Kashy, D. A. (1998). Everyday lies in close and casual relationships. *Journal of Personality and Social Psychology, 74,* 63–79.

Depue, R. A., & Iacono, W. G. (1989). Neurobehavioral aspects of affective disorders. *Annual Review of Psychology, 40,* 457–492.

Deregowski, J. B. (1989). Real space and represented space: Cross-cultural perspectives. *Brain and Behavioral Sciences, 12,* 51–119.

Derlega, V. J., Metts, S., Petronio, S., & Margulis, S. T. (1993). *Self-disclosure.* Newbury Park, CA: Sage.

Derlega, V. J., Winstead, B. A., Wong, P. T. P., & Hunter, S. (1985). Gender effects in an initial encounter: A case where men exceed women in disclosure. *Journal of Social and Personal Relations, 2,* 25–44.

D'Esposito, M. (Ed.). (2002). *Neurological foundations of cognitive neuroscience.* Cambridge, MA: MIT Press.

D'Esposito, M., Zarahn, E., & Aguirre, G. K. (1999). Event-related functional MRI: Implications for cognitive psychology. *Psychological Bulletin, 125,* 155–164.

DeSteno, D. A., & Salovey, P. (1996). Evolutionary origins of sex differences in jealousy? Questioning the "fitness" model. *Psychological Science, 7,* 367–372.

Detweiler, J. B., Bedell, B. T., Pronin, E., & Rothman, A. J. (1999). Message framing and sunscreen use: Gain-framed messages motivate beach-goers. *Health Psychology, 18,* 189–196.

Deutsch, M., & Gerard, H. B. (1955). A study of normative and informational social influences upon individual judgment. *Journal of Abnormal and Social Psychology, 51,* 629–636.

Devanand, D. P., Dwork, A. J., Hutchinson, M. S. E., Bolwig, T. G., & Sackeim, H. A. (1994). How does ECT alter brain structure? *American Journal of Psychiatry, 151,* 957–970.

Devine, D. J., Clayton, L. D., Dunford, B. B., Seying, R., & Pryce, J. (2001). Jury decision making: 45 years of empirical research on deliberating groups. *Psychology, Public Policy, & Law, 7,* 622–727.

Devine, P. G. (1989). Stereotypes and prejudice: Their automatic and controlled components. *Journal of Personality and Social Psychology, 56,* 5–18.

Devine, P. G., Monteith, M. J., Zuwerink, J. R., & Elliot, A. J. (1991). Prejudice with and without compunction. *Journal of Personality and Social Psychology, 60,* 817–830.

Dhabhar, F., & McEwen, B. (1995). *Journal of Immunology, 154,* 5511–5527.

Diamond, M. (1993). Homosexuality and bisexuality in different populations. *Archives of Sexual Behavior, 22,* 291–310.

Dickens, W. T., & Flynn, J. R. (2001). Heritability estimates versus large environmental effects: The IQ paradox resolved. *Psychological Review, 108,* 346–369.

Dielenberg, R. A., & McGregor, I. S. (1999). Habituation of the hiding response to car odor in rats. *Journal of Comparative Psychology, 113,* 376–387.

Diener, E. (2000). Subjective well-being: The science of happiness, and a proposal for a national index. *American Psychologist, 55,* 34–43.

Diener, E., Diener, M., & Diener, C. (1995). Factors predicting the subjective well-being of nations. *Journal of Personality and Social Psychology, 69,* 851–864.

Diener, E., Emmons, R. A., Larsen, R. J., & Griffin, S. (1984). The Satisfaction with Life Scale. *Journal of Personality Assessment, 49,* 71–75.

Diener, E., Fraser, S. C., Beaman, A. L., & Kelem, R. T. (1976). Effects of deindividuation variables on stealing among Halloween trick-or-treaters. *Journal of Personality and Social Psychology, 33,* 178–183.

Diener, E., Horwitz, J., & Emmons, R. A. (1985). Happiness of the very wealthy. *Social Indicators Research, 16,* 263–274.

Diener, E., & Suh, E. M. (Eds.). (2000). *Culture and subjective well-being.* Cambridge, MA: MIT Press.

Diener, E., Suh, E. M., Lucas, R. E., & Smith, H. L. (1999). Subjective well-being: Three decades of progress. *Psychological Bulletin, 125,* 276–302.

Dijksterhuis, A., & Bargh, J. A. (2001). The perception-behavior expressway: Automatic effects of social perception on social behavior. *Advances in Experimental Social Psychology, 33,* 1–40.

Dijksterhuis, A., & Smith, P. (2002). Affective habituation: Subliminal exposure to extreme stimuli decreases their extremity. *Emotion, 2,* 203–214.

Dijkstra, P., & Buunk, B. P. (1998). Jealousy as a function of rival characteristics: An evolutionary perspective. *Personality and Social Psychology Bulletin, 24,* 1158–1166.

DiLalla, L. F., & Gottesman, I. I. (1991). Biological and genetic contributions to violence—Widom's untold tale. *Psychological Bulletin, 109,* 125–129.

Dimberg, U. (1990). Facial electromyography and emotional reactions. *Psychophysiology, 27,* 481–494.

Dimberg, U., & Ohman, A. (1996). Behold the wrath: Psychophysiological responses to facial stimuli. *Motivation and Emotion, 20,* 149–181.

Dimberg, U., Thunberg, M., & Elmehed, K. (2000). Unconscious facial reactions to emotional facial expressions. *Psychological Science, 11,* 86–89.

Dindia, K., & Allen, M. (1992). Sex differences in self-disclosure: A meta-analysis. *Psychological Bulletin, 112,* 106–124.

Dinges, D. F., Whitehouse, W. G., Orne, E. C., Powell, J. W., Orne, M. T., & Erdelyi, M. H. (1992). Evaluating hypnotic memory enhancement (hypermnesia and reminiscence) using multitrial forced recall. *Journal of Experimental Psychology: Learning, Memory, and Cognition, 18,* 1139–1147.

Dion, K. K., Berscheid, E., & Walster, E. (1972). What is beautiful is good. *Journal of Personality and Social Psychology, 24,* 285–290.

Dion, K. K., & Dion, K. L. (1996). Cultural perspectives on romantic love. *Personal Relationships, 3,* 5–17.

Dionisio, D. P., Granholm, E., Hillix, W. A., & Perrine, W. F. (2001). Differentiation of deception using pupillary responses as an index of cognitive processing. *Psychophysiology, 38,* 205–211.

DiPietro, J. A., Hodgson, D. M., Costigan, K. A., Hilton, S. C., & Johnson, T. R. B. (1996). Fetal neurobehavioral development. *Child Development, 67,* 2553–2567.

DiPietro, J. A., Hodgson, D. M., Costigan, K. A., & Johnson, T. R. B. (1996). Fetal antecedents of infant temperament. *Child Development, 67,* 2568–2583.

Dittman, R. W., Kappes, M. E., & Kappes, M. H. (1992). Sexual behavior in adolescent and adult females with congenital adrenal hyperplasia. *Psychoneuroendocrinology, 17,* 153–170.

Ditto, P. H., & Lopez, D. F. (1992). Motivated skepticism: Use of differential decision criteria for preferred and nonpreferred conclusions. *Journal of Personality and Social Psychology, 63,* 568–584.

Doblin, R., & Kleiman, M. A. R. (1991). Medical use of marijuana. *Annals of Internal Medicine, 114,* 809–810.

Dobson, K. S. (1989). A meta-analysis of the efficacy of cognitive therapy for depression. *Journal of Consulting and Clinical Psychology, 57,* 414–419.

Dobson, K. S. (Ed.). (2000). *Handbook of cognitive-behavioral therapies* (2nd ed.). New York: Guilford.

Dodson, C., & Reisberg, D. (1991). Indirect testing of eyewitness memory: The (non)effect of misinformation. *Bulletin of the Psychonomic Society, 29,* 333–336.

Dohrenwend, B. S., & Dohrenwend, B. P. (1978). Some issues in research on stressful life events. *Journal of Nervous and Mental Diseases, 166,* 7–15.

Dollard, J., Doob, L. W., Miller, N. E., Mowrer, O. H., & Sears, R. R. (1939). *Frustration and aggression.* New Haven, CT: Yale University Press.

Domhoff, G. W. (1996). *Finding meaning in dreams: A quantitative approach.* New York: Plenum.

Domhoff, G. W. (1999). New directions in the study of dream content using the Hall and Van de Castle coding system. *Dreaming, 9,* 115–138.

Domhoff, G. W. (2001). A new neurocognitive theory of dreams. *Dreaming, 11,* 13–33.

Domjan, M., Blesbois, E., & Williams, J. (1998). The adaptive significance of sexual conditioning: Pavlovian control of sperm release. *Psychological Science, 9,* 411–415.

Domjan, M., & Purdy, J. E. (1995). Animal research in psychology: More than meets the eye of the general psychology student. *American Psychologist, 50,* 496–503.

Donley, R. D., & Ashcraft, M. H. (1992). The methodology of testing naive beliefs in the physics classroom. *Memory and Cognition, 20,* 381–391.

Donnelly, C., & McDaniel, M. (1993). Use of analogy in learning scientific concepts. *Journal of Experimental Psychology: Learning, Memory, and Cognition, 19,* 975–986.

Donnerstein, E., & Berkowitz, L. (1981). Victim reactions in aggressive erotic films as a factor in violence against women. *Journal of Personality and Social Psychology, 41,* 710–724.

Donnerstein, E., Linz, D., & Penrod, S. (1987). *The question of pornography.* New York: Free Press.

Donovan, M. A., Drasgow, F., & Munson, L. J. (1998). The Perceptions of Fair Interpersonal Treatment Scale: Development and validation of a measure of interpersonal treatment in the workplace. *Journal of Applied Psychology, 83,* 683–692.

Dorn, L. D., et al. (1999). Variability in hormone concentrations and self-reported menstrual histories in young adolescents: Menarche as an integral part of a developmental process. *Journal of Youth and Adolescence, 28,* 283–304.

Dornbusch, S. M., Glasgow, K. L., & Lin, I. (1996). The social structure of schooling. *Annual Review of Psychology, 47,* 401–429.

Dostoevsky, F. (1960). *Notes from underground* (R. E. Matlaw, Trans.). New York: Dutton. (Original work published 1864.)

Doty, R. L. (Ed.). (1995). *Handbook of olfaction and gustation.* New York: Marcel Dekker.

Doty, R. L. (2001). Olfaction. *Annual Review of Psychology, 52,* 423–452.

Doty, R. L., Applebaum, S., Zusho, H., & Settle, R. G. (1985). Sex differences in odor identification ability: A cross-cultural analysis. *Neuropsychologia, 23,* 667–672.

Dougherty, T. M., & Haith, M. M. (1997). Infant expectations and reaction time as predictors of childhood speed of processing and IQ. *Developmental Psychology, 33,* 146–155.

Dougherty, T. W., Turban, D. B., & Callender, J. C. (1994). Confirming first impressions in the employment interview: A field study of interviewer behavior. *Journal of Applied Psychology, 79,* 659–665.

Douglas, K. M., & McGarty, C. (2002). Internet identifiability and beyond: A model of the effects of identifiability on communicative behavior. *Group Dynamics, 6,* 17–26.

Douglas, N. J. (1998). The psychosocial aspects of narcolepsy. *Neurology, 50,* S27-S30.

Dovidio, J. F., Allen J. L., & Schroeder, D. A. (1990). Specificity of empathy-induced helping: Evidence for altruistic motivation. *Journal of Personality and Social Psychology, 59,* 249–260.

Dovidio, J. F., & Gaertner, S. L. (1998). On the nature of contemporary prejudice: The causes, consequences, and challenges of aversive racism. In J. L. Eberhardt & S. T. Fiske (Eds.), *Racism: The problem and the response* (pp. 3–32). Thousand Oaks, CA: Sage.

Dovidio, J. F., Kawakami, K., Johnson, C., Johnson, B., & Howard, A. (1997). On the nature of prejudice: Automatic and controlled processes. *Journal of Experimental Social Psychology, 33,* 510–540.

Driskell, J. E., Willis, R. P., & Copper, C. (1992). Effect of overlearning on retention. *Journal of Applied Psychology, 77,* 615–622.

Dubovsky, S. L. (1997). *Mind-body deceptions: The psychosomatics of everyday life.* New York: Norton.

Duclos, S. E., Laird, J. D., Schneider, E., Sexter, M., Stern, L., & Lighten, O. V. (1989). Emotion-specific effects of facial expressions and postures on emotional experience. *Journal of Personality and Social Psychology, 57,* 100–108.

Dudycha, G. J., & Dudycha, M. M. (1941). Childhood memories: A review of the literature. *Psychological Bulletin, 38,* 668–682.

Dumont, R. (1996). *The sky is falling: Understanding and coping with phobias, panic, and obsessive-compulsive disorders.* New York: W. W. Norton.

Duncker, K. (1945). On problem-solving (L. S. Lees, Trans.). *Psychological Monographs, 58* (No. 270).

Dunn, D. S., & Wilson, T. D. (1990). When the stakes are high: A limit to the illusion-of-control effect. *Social Cognition, 8,* 305–323.

Dunn, J., Bretherton, I., & Munn, P. (1987). Conversations about feeling states between mothers and their young children. *Developmental Psychology, 23,* 132–139.

Dunn, J., & Plomin, R. (1990). *Separate lives: Why siblings are so different.* New York: Basic Books.

Dunning, D., Griffin, D. W., Milojkovic, J. D., & Ross, L. (1990). The overconfidence effect in social prediction. *Journal of Personality and Social Psychology, 58,* 568–581.

Dutton, D. G., & Aron, A. P. (1974). Some evidence for heightened sexual attraction under conditions of high anxiety. *Journal of Personality and Social Psychology, 23,* 510–517.

Duval, S., Duval, V. H., & Mulilis, J. P. (1992). Effects of self-focus, discrepancy between self and standard, and outcome expectancy favorability on the tendency to match self to standard or to withdraw. *Journal of Personality and Social Psychology, 62,* 340–348.

Duval, S., & Wicklund, R. A. (1972). *A theory of objective self-awareness.* New York: Academic Press.

Eacott, M. J., & Crawley, R. A. (1998). The offset of childhood amnesia: Memory for events that occurred before age 3. *Journal of Experimental Psychology: General, 127,* 22–33.

Eagly, A. H. (1987). *Sex differences in social behavior: A social-role interpretation.* Hillsdale, NJ: Erlbaum.

Eagly, A. H., Ashmore, R. D., Makhijani, M. G., & Longo, L. C. (1991). What is beautiful is good, but . . . : A meta-analytic review of research on the physical attractiveness stereotype. *Psychology Bulletin, 110,* 107–128.

Eagly, A. H., & Chaiken, S. (1993). *The psychology of attitudes.* Fort Worth, TX: Harcourt Brace Jovanovich.

Eagly, A. H., & Chaiken, S. (1998). Attitude structure and function. In D. Gilbert, S. Fiske, & G. Lindzey (Eds.), *Handbook of social psychology* (4th ed.). New York: McGraw-Hill.

Eagly, A. H., & Steffen, V. J. (1986). Gender and aggressive behavior: A meta-analytic review of the social psychology literature. *Psychological Bulletin, 100,* 309–330.

Eagly, A. H., & Wood, W. (1999). The origins of sex differences in human behavior: Evolved dispositions versus social roles. *American Psychologist, 54,* 408–423.

Eaton, W. W., et al. (1991). Panic and phobia. In L. N. Robins & D. A. Regier (Eds.), *Psychiatric disorders in America* (pp. 155–179). New York: Free Press.

Ebbinghaus, H. (1913). *Memory: A contribution to experimental psychology* (H. Roger & C. Bussenius, Trans.). New York: Teachers College Press. (Original work published 1885.)

Eccles, J. (1965). *The brain and unity of conscious experience: The 19th Arthur Stanley Eddington Memorial Lecture.* Cambridge: Cambridge University Press.

Eccles, J. P. (1985). Sex differences in achievement patterns. In T. B. Sonderegger (Ed.), *Nebraska symposium on motivation: Psychology and gender.* Lincoln: University of Nebraska Press.

Eccles, J. S., Jacobs, J. E., & Harold, R. D. (1990). Gender role stereotypes, expectancy effects, and parents' socialization of gender differences. *Journal of Social Issues, 46,* 183–201.

Eccles, J. S., Wigfield, A., Harold, R. D., & Blumenfeld, P. (1993). Age and gender differences in children's self- and task perceptions during elementary school. *Child Development, 64,* 830–847.

Eccleston, C., & Crombez, G. (1999). Pain demands attention: A cognitive-affect model of the interruptive function of pain. *Psychological Bulletin, 125,* 356–366.

Eder, D. (1981). Ability grouping as a self fulfilling prophecy: A microanalysis of teacher-student interaction. *Sociology of Education, 54,* 151–161.

Edwards, K., & Smith, E. E. (1996). A disconfirmation bias in the evaluation of arguments. *Journal of Personality and Social Psychology, 71,* 5–24.

Efron, R. (1990). *The decline and fall of hemispheric specialization.* Hillsdale, NJ: Erlbaum.

Egan, S. K., & Perry, D. G. (2001). Gender identity: A multidimensional analysis with implications for psychosocial adjustment. *Developmental Psychology, 37,* 451–463.

Ehlers, A., & Breuer, P. (1992). Increased cardiac awareness in panic disorder. *Journal of Abnormal Psychology, 101,* 371–382.

Ehrlichman, H., & Eichenstein, R. (1992). Private wishes: Gender similarities and differences. *Sex Roles, 26,* 399–422.

Eibl-Eibesfeldt, I. (1989). *Human ethology.* New York: Aldine de Gruyter.

Eich, E. (1995). Mood as a mediator of place dependent memory. *Journal of Experimental Psychology: General, 124,* 293–308.

Eich, E., Macaulay, D., Loewenstein, R. J. & Dihle, P. H. (1997). Memory, amnesia, and dissociative identity disorder. *Psychological Science, 8,* 417–422.

Eisenberg, N. (1992). *The caring child.* Cambridge, MA: Harvard University Press.

Eisenberg, N., Carlo, G., Murphy, B., & Van Court, P. (1995). Prosocial development in late adolescence: A longitudinal study. *Child Development, 66,* 1179–1197.

Eisenberg, N., & Mussen, P. H. (1989). *The roots of prosocial behavior in children.* New York: Cambridge University Press.

Eisenberger, R., & Cameron, J. (1996). Detrimental effects of reward: Reality or myth? *American Psychologist, 51,* 1153–1166.

Eisenberger, R., & Rhoades, L. (2001). Incremental effects of reward on creativity. *Journal of Personality and Social Psychology, 81,* 728–741.

Ekman, P., & Davidson, R. J. (1993). Voluntary smiling changes regional brain activity. *Psychological Science, 4,* 342–345.

Ekman, P., Davidson, R. J., & Friesen, W. V. (1990). The Duchenne smile: Emotional expression and brain physiology II. *Journal of Personality and Social Psychology, 58,* 342–353.

Ekman, P., & Friesen, W. V. (1974). Detecting deception from the body or face. *Journal of Personality and Social Psychology, 29,* 288–298.

Ekman, P., Friesen, W. V., O'Sullivan, M., Chan, A., Diacoyanni-Tarlatzis, I., Heider, K., Krause, R., LeCompte, W. A., Pitcairn, T., Ricci-Bitti, P., Scherer, K., Tomita, M., & Tzavaras, A. (1987). Universals and cultural differences in the judgments of facial expressions of emotion. *Journal of Personality and Social Psychology, 53,* 712–717.

Ekman, P., Levenson, R. W., & Friesen, W. V. (1983). Autonomic nervous system activity distinguishes among emotions. *Science, 221,* 1208–1210.

Elbert, T., Pantev, C., Wienbruch, C., et al. (1995). Increased cortical representation of the fingers of the left hand in string players. *Science, 270,* 305–307.

Eldridge, L. L., Masterman, D., & Knowlton, B. J. (2002). Intact implicit habit learning in Alzheimer's disease. *Behavioral Neuroscience, 116,* 722–726.

Elfenbein, H. A., & Ambady, N. (2002). On the universality and cultural specificity of emotion recognition: A meta-analysis. *Psychological Bulletin, 128,* 203–235.

Elkin, I., et al. (1989). National Institute of Mental Health treatment of depression collaborative research program. *Archives of General Psychiatry, 46,* 971–983.

Elkind, D. (1967). Egocentrism in adolescence. *Child Development, 38,* 1025–1034.

Elkind, D. (1989). *Miseducation: Preschoolers at risk.* New York: Knopf.

Elkind, D., & Bowen, R. (1979). Imaginary audience behavior in children and adolescents. *Developmental Psychology, 15,* 38–44.

Elliot, A. J., & Church, M. A. (1997). A hierarchical model of approach and avoidance achievement motivation. *Journal of Personality and Social Psychology, 72,* 218–232.

Elliott, R. (1987). *Litigating intelligence: IQ tests, special education, and social science in the courtroom.* Dover, MA: Auburn House.

Ellis, A. (1962). *Reason and emotion in psychotherapy.* New York: Lyle Stuart.

Ellis, A. (1989). Rational-emotive therapy. In R. J. Corcini & D. Wedding (Eds.), *Current psychotherapies* (4th ed.). Itasca, IL: Peacock.

Ellis, A. (1996). How I learned to help clients feel better and get better. *Psychotherapy, 33,* 149–151.

Ellis, A. (1999). Why rational emotive therapy to rational emotive behavior therapy? *Psychotherapy, 36,* 154–159.

Ellis, L., & Ames, M. A. (1987). Neurohormonal functioning and sexual orientation: A theory of homosexuality-heterosexuality. *Psychological Bulletin, 101,* 233–258.

Ellis, P. J., Marshall, E., Windridge, C., Jones, S., & Ellis, S. J. (1998). Left-handedness and premature death. *The Lancet, 351,* 1634.

Ellsworth, P. C. (1994). William James and emotion: Is a century of fame worth a century of misunderstanding? *Psychological Review, 101,* 222–229.

Emde, R. N., Gaensbauer, T. J., & Harmon, R. J. (1976). Emotional expression in infancy: A biobehavioral study. *Psychological Issues, 10*(Monograph 37).

Endicott, N. A. (1998). Chronic fatigue syndrome in psychiatric patients: Lifetime and premorbid personal history of physical health. *Psychosomatic Medicine, 60,* 744–751.

Endler, N. S., & Persad, E. (1988). *Electroconvulsive therapy: The myths and the realities.* Toronto: Hans Huber Publishers.

Engel, S. (1999). *Context is everything: The nature of memory.* New York: W. H. Freeman.

Engels, G. I., Garnefski, N., & Diekstra, R. (1993). Efficacy of rational-emotive therapy: A quantitative analysis. *Journal of Consulting and Clinical Psychology, 61,* 1083–1090.

Engen, T. (1982). *The perception of odors.* New York: Academic Press.

Enright, R. D., Levy, V. M., Harris, D., & Lapsley, D. K. (1987). *Journal of Youth and Adolescence, 16,* 541–559.

Epstein, H. T. (2001). An outline of the role of brain in the human cognitive development. *Brain and Cognition, 45,* 44–51.

Epstein, J. L. (1985). After the bus arrives: Resegregation in desegregated schools. *Journal of Social Issues, 41,* 23–43.

Epstein, R., Kirshnit, C. E., Lanza, R. P., & Rubin, L. C. (1984). "Insight" in the pigeon: Antecedents and determinants of an intelligent performance. *Nature, 308,* 61–62.

Epstein, S. (1979). The stability of behavior: I. On predicting most of the people much of the time. *Journal of Personality and Social Psychology, 37,* 1097–1126.

Epstein, S., & O'Brien, E. J. (1985). The personsituation debate in historical and current perspective. *Psychological Bulletin, 98,* 513–537.

Erdelyi, M. H. (1985). *Psychoanalysis: Freud's cognitive psychology.* New York: W. H. Freeman.

Erdelyi, M. H. (1992). Psychodynamics and the unconscious. *American Psychologist, 47,* 784–787.

Erdelyi, M. H. (1996). *The recovery of unconscious memories: Hypermnesia and reminiscence.* Chicago: University of Chicago Press.

Ericksen, J. A., & Steffen, S. A. (1999). *Kiss and tell: Sex in the twentieth century.* Cambridge, MA: Harvard University Press.

Ericsson, K. A. (Ed.). (1996). *The road to excellence: The acquisition of expert performance in the arts and sciences, sports and games.* Mahwah, NJ: Erlbaum.

Ericsson, K. A., & Chase, W. G. (1982). Exceptional memory. *American Scientist, 70,* 607–615.

Ericsson, K. A., Chase, W. G., & Faloon, S. (1980). Acquisition of a memory skill. *Science, 208,* 1181–1182.

Ericsson, K. A., Krampe, R. Th., & Tesch-Romer, C. (1993). The role of deliberate practice in the acquisition of expert performance. *Psychological Review, 100,* 363–406.

Ericsson, K. A., & Lehmann, A. C. (1996). Expert and exceptional performance: Evidence for maximal adaptations on task constraints. *Annual Review of Psychology, 47,* 273–305.

Erikson, E. H. (1959). *Identity and the life cycle. Psychological Issues (Monograph 1).* New York: International Universities Press.

Erikson, E. H. (1963). *Childhood and society.* New York: Norton.

Ernst, E., & Abbot, N. (1999). I shall please: The mysterious power of placebos. In S. D. Sala (Ed.), *Mind myths: Exploring popular assumptions about the mind and brain* (pp. 209–213). Chichester, England: Wiley.

Eron, L. D. (1987). The development of aggressive behavior from the perspective of a developing behaviorism. *American Psychologist, 42,* 435–442.

Espie, C. A. (2002). Insomnia: Conceptual issues in the development, persistence, and treatment of sleep disorders in adults. *Annual Review of Psychology, 53,* 215–243.

Esterson, A. (2001). The mythologizing of psychoanalytic history: Deception and self-deception in Freud's accounts of the seduction theory episode. *History of Psychiatry, 12,* 329–352.

Etcoff, N. (1999). *Survival of the prettiest: The science of beauty.* New York: Doubleday.

Ether, J. T., Szuchman, L. T., & Rothberg, S. T. (1990). Everyday memory failure: Age differences in appraisal and attribution. *Psychology and Aging, 5,* 236–241.

Evans, J. R., & Aberbanel, A. (Eds.). (1999). *Introduction to quantitative EEG and neurofeedback.* San Diego: Academic Press.

Everson, C. A. (1995). Functional consequences of sustained sleep deprivation in the rat. *Behavioural Brain Research, 69,* 43–54.

Everson, S. A., et al. (1996). Hopelessness and risk of mortality and incidence of myocardial infarction and cancer. *Psychosomatic Medicine, 58,* 103–121.

Everson, S. A., Goldberg, D. E., Kaplan, G. A., Julkunen, J., & Salonen, J. T. (1998). Anger expression and incident hypertension. *Psychosomatic Medicine, 60,* 730–735.

Ewing, C. P. (1996, July). Judicial notebook: Courts consider repressed memory. *APA Monitor,* p. 14.

Exner, J. E., Jr. (1993). *The Rorschach: A comprehensive system: Vol. 1. Basic foundations* (3rd ed.). New York: Wiley.

Exner, J. E., Jr. (1996). A comment on "The comprehensive system for the Rorschach: A critical examination." *Psychological Science, 7,* 11–13.

Eysenck, H. J. (1952). The effects of psychotherapy: An evaluation. *Journal of Consulting Psychology, 16,* 319–324.

Eysenck, H. J. (1967). *The biological basis of personality.* Springfield, IL: Thomas.

Eysenck, H. J. (1982). *A model for intelligence.* Berlin: Springer Verlag.

Eysenck, H. J. (1990). Biological dimensions of personality. In L. A. Pervin (Ed.), *Handbook of personality theory and research* (pp. 244–276). New York: Guilford Press.

Eysenck, H. J., & Eysenck, M. W. (1985). *Personality and individual differences: A natural science approach.* New York: Plenum.

Eysenck, H. J., & Eysenck, S. G. B. (1964). *Manual of the Eysenck Personality Inventory.* London: University of London Press.

Fabes, R. A., & Martin, C. L. (1991). Gender and age stereotypes of emotionality. *Personality and Social Psychology Bulletin, 17,* 532–540.

Fairburn, C. G., & Brownell, K. D. (Eds.). (2002). *Eating disorders and obesity: A comprehensive handbook.* New York: Guilford Press.

Fantz, R. L. (1961). The origin of form perception. *Scientific American, 204,* 66–72.

Farah, M. J. (1989). The neural basis of mental imagery. *Trends in Neuroscience, 12,* 395–399.

Farah, M. J. (2000). *The cognitive neuroscience of vision.* London: Blackwell.

Faravelli, C., & Pallanti, S. (1989). Recent life events and panic disorders. *American Journal of Psychiatry, 146,* 622–626.

Farber, B. A., Brink, D. C., & Raskin, P. M. (Eds.). (1996). *The psychotherapy of Carl Rogers: Cases and commentary.* New York: Guilford Press.

Farina, A., Fisher, J. D., & Fischer, E. H. (1992). Societal factors in the problems faced by deinstitutionalized psychiatric patients. In P. J. Fink & A. Tasman (Eds.), *Stigma and mental illness.* Washington, DC: American Psychiatric Press.

Farrell, P. A., Gates, W. K., Maksud, M. G., & Morgan, W. P. (1982). Increases in plasma beta endorphin/ beta-lipotropin immunoreactivity after treadmill running in humans. *Journal of Applied Psychology, 52,* 1245–1249.

Fawcett, J., Rosser, A. E., & Dunnett, S. B. (Eds.). (2001). *Brain damage and brain repair.* New York: Oxford University Press.

Fay, R. E., Turner, C. F., Klassen, A. D., & Gagnon, J. H. (1989). Prevalence and patterns of same-gender sexual contact among men. *Science, 243,* 343–348.

Fazel, S., & Danesh, J. (2002). Serious mental disorder in 23,000 prisoners: A systematic review of 62 surveys. *Lancet, 359,* 545–550.

Fechner, G. T. (1860). *Elements of psychophysics* (H. E. Alder, Trans.). New York: Holt, Rinehart & Winston. (Translated edition 1966.)

Fehr, B., & Russell, J. A. (1991). The concept of love: Viewed from a prototype perspective. *Journal of Personality and Social Psychology, 60,* 425–438.

Feifel, H. (1990). Psychology and death: Meaningful rediscovery. *American Psychologist, 45,* 537–543.

Feigenson, L., Carey, S., & Spelke, E. (2002). Infant discrimination of number and spatial extent. *Cognitive Psychology, 44,* 33–66.

Fein, S., Hilton, J. L., & Miller, D. T. (1990). Suspicion of ulterior motivation and the correspondence bias. *Journal of Personality and Social Psychology, 58,* 753–764.

Fein, S., & Spencer, S. (1997). Prejudice as self-image maintenance: Affirming the self through negative evaluations of others. *Journal of Personality and Social Psychology, 73,* 31–44.

Feinberg, R. A. (1986). Credit cards as spending facilitating stimuli: A conditioning interpretation. *Journal of Consumer Research, 13,* 348–356.

Feingold, A. (1992). Good-looking people are not what we think. *Psychological Bulletin, 111,* 304–341.

Feingold, A. (1994). Gender differences in personality: A meta-analysis. *Psychological Bulletin, 116,* 429–456.

Fenigstein, A., Scheier, M. F., & Buss, A. H. (1975). Public and private self-consciousness: Assessment and theory. *Journal of Consulting and Clinical Psychology, 43,* 522–527.

Fennell, M. J. (1989). Depression. In K. Hawton, P. Salkovskis, J. Kirk, & D. Clark (Eds.), *Cognitive behaviour therapy for psychiatric problems* (pp. 167–234). New York: Oxford Medical Publications.

Fenson, L., Dale, P. S., Reznick, J. S., Bates, E., Thal, D. J., & Pethic, S. J. (1994). Variability in early communicative development. *Monographs of the Society for Research in Child Development, 59*(5, Series No. 242).

Fenton, W. S., McGlashan, T. H., Victor, B. J., & Blyler, C. R., (1997). Symptoms, subtypes, and suicidality in patients with schizophrenia spectrum disorders. *American Journal of Psychiatry, 154,* 199–204.

Ferguson, N. (Ed.). (1997). *Virtual history: Alternatives and counterfactuals.* London: Picador.

Fernald, A. (1985). Four-month-old infants prefer to listen to motherese. *Infant Behavior and Development, 8,* 181–195.

Fernald, A., Taeschner, T., Dunn, J., Papousek, M., Boysson-Bardies, B. D., & Fukui, I. (1989). A cross-linguistic study of prosodic modifications in mothers'

and fathers' speech to preverbal infants. *Journal of Child Language, 16,* 477–501.

Ferster, C. B., & Skinner, B. F. (1957). *Schedules of reinforcement.* New York: Appleton-Century-Crofts.

Festinger, L. (1957). *A theory of cognitive dissonance.* Stanford, CA: Stanford University Press.

Festinger, L., & Carlsmith, J. M. (1959). Cognitive consequences of forced compliance. *Journal of Abnormal and Social Psychology, 58,* 203–210.

Field, T. (2001). *Touch.* Cambridge: MIT Press.

Field, T., Cohen, D., Garcia, R., & Greenberg, R. (1984). Mother-stranger face discrimination by the newborn. *Infant Behavior and Development, 7,* 19–25.

Field, T., Woodson, R., Greenberg, R., & Cohen, D. (1982). Discrimination and imitation of facial expressions by neonates. *Science, 218,* 179–181.

Field, T. M. (1998). Massage therapy effects. *American Psychologist, 53,* 1270–1281.

Fifer, W. P., & Moon, C. M. (1995). The effects of fetal experience with sound. In J. Lecanuet, W. P. Fifer, N. A. Krasnegor, & W. P. Smotherman (Eds.), *Fetal development: A psychobiological perspective* (pp. 351–366). Mahwah, NJ: Erlbaum.

Fink, M. (1999). *Electroshock: Restoring the mind.* New York: Oxford University Press.

Firestein, S., & Werblin, F. (1989). Odor-induced membrane currents in vertebrate-olfactory receptor neurons. *Science, 244,* 79–82.

Fischer, J. S. (2000, January 24). Taking the shock out of electroshock. *U.S. News & World Report,* p. 46.

Fischer, K. W. (1987). Relations between brain and cognitive development. *Child Development, 58,* 623–632.

Fischhoff, B. (1975). Hindsight/foresight: The effect of outcome knowledge on judgment under uncertainty. *Journal of Experimental Psychology: Human Perception and Performance, 1,* 288–299.

Fischhoff, B., Slovic, P., & Lichtenstein, S. (1977). Knowing with certainty: The appropriateness of extreme confidence. *Journal of Experimental Psychology: Human Perception and Performance, 3,* 552–564.

Fishbein, M. (1980). A theory of reasoned action: Some applications and implications. In H. E. Howe & M. M. Page (Eds.), *Nebraska symposium on motivation* (Vol. 27, pp. 65–116). Lincoln: University of Nebraska Press.

Fisher, G. H. (1968). Ambiguity of form: Old and new. *Perception and Psychophysics, 4,* 189–192.

Fisher, J. D., & Fisher, W. A. (1992). Changing AIDS-risk behavior. *Psychological Bulletin, 111,* 455–474.

Fisher, S., & Greenberg, R. P. (1977). *The scientific credibility of Freud's theories and therapy.* New York: Columbia University Press.

Fiske, A. P. (2002). Using individualism and collectivism to compare cultures—A critique of the validity and measurement of the constructs: Comment on Oyserman et al. (2002). *Psychological Bulletin, 128,* 78–88.

Fiske, D. W., & Maddi, S. R. (1961). *The functions of varied experience.* Homewood, IL: Dorsey.

Fiske, S. T., & Taylor, S. E. (1991). *Social cognition.* New York: McGraw-Hill.

Fitzgerald, J. M. (1988). Vivid memories and the reminiscence phenomenon: The role of self-narrative. *Human Development, 31,* 261–273.

Fivush, R., Haden, C. A., & Dimmick, J. W. (Eds.). (2003). *Autobiographical memory and the construction of a narrative self: Developmental and cultural perspectives.* Mahwah, NJ: Erlbaum.

Flack, W. F., Jr., Laird, J. D., & Cavallaro, L. A. (1999). Separate and combined effects of facial expressions and bodily postures on emotional feelings. *European Journal of Social Psychology, 29,* 203–217.

Flavell, J. H. (1996). Piaget's legacy. *Psychological Science, 7,* 200–203.

Flavell, J. H. (1999). Cognitive development: Children's knowledge about the mind. *Annual Review of Psychology, 50,* 21–45.

Flavell, J. H., Beach, D. R., & Chinsky, J. M. (1966). Spontaneous verbal rehearsal in a memory task as a function of age. *Child Development, 37,* 283–299.

Flavell, J. H., Green, F. L., & Flavell, E. R. (1986). Development of knowledge about the appearance-reality distinction. *Monographs of the Society for Research in Child Development, 51* (1, Serial No. 212).

Flavell, J. H., Miller, P. H., & Miller, S. A. (1993). *Cognitive development* (3rd ed.). Englewood Cliffs, NJ: Prentice-Hall.

Fleischman, J. (2002). *Phineas Gage: A gruesome but true story about brain science.* Boston: Houghton Mifflin.

Fleming, I. A., Baum, A., & Weiss, L. (1987). Social density and perceived control as mediators of crowding stress in high-density residential neighborhoods. *Journal of Personality and Social Psychology, 52,* 899–906.

Fleming, M. A., Wegener, D. T., & Petty, R. E. (1999). Procedural and legal motivations to correct for perceived judicial biases. *Journal of Experimental Social Psychology, 35,* 186–203.

Flieller, A. (1999). Comparison of the development of formal thought in adolescent cohorts aged 10 to 15 years (1967–1996 and 1972–1993). *Developmental Psychology, 35,* 1048–1058.

Flor, H., et al. (1995). Phantom-limb pain as a perceptual correlate of cortical reorganization following arm amputation. *Nature, 375,* 482–484.

Flynn, J. R. (1987). Massive IQ gains in 14 nations: What IQ tests really measure. *Psychology Bulletin, 101,* 171–191.

Flynn, J. R. (1991). *Asian-Americans: Achievement beyond IQ.* Hillsdale, NJ: Erlbaum.

Flynn, J. R. (1999). Searching for justice: The discovery of IQ gains over time. *American Psychologist, 54,* 5–20.

Foa, E. B., & Franklin, M. E. (2001). Obsessive-compulsive disorder. In D. H. Barlow (Ed.), *Clinical handbook of psychological disorders* (3rd ed., pp. 209–263). New York: Guilford.

Foa, E. B., & Franklin, M. E. (2001). Obsessive-compulsive disorder. In D. H. Barlow (Ed.), *Anxiety and its disorders: The nature and treatment of anxiety and panic* (2nd ed., pp. 209–263). New York: Guilford.

Foa, E. B., & Kozak, M. J. (1986). Emotional processing of fear: Exposure to corrective information. *Psychological Bulletin, 99,* 20–35.

Foa, E. B., Kozak, M. J., Salkovskis, P. M., Coles, M. E., & Amir, N. (1999). The validation of a new obsessive-compulsive disorder scale: The Obsessive-Compulsive Inventory. *Psychological Assessment, 10,* 206–214.

Foertsch, J., & Gernsbacher, M. A. (1997). In search of gender neutrality: Is singular they a cognitively efficient substitute for generic he? *Psychological Science, 8,* 106–111.

Fontana, A., & Rosenheck, R. (1994). Traumatic war stressors and psychiatric symptoms among World War II, Korean, and Vietnam War veterans. *Psychology and Aging, 9,* 27–33.

Ford, C. V., & Folks, D. G. (1985). Conversion disorders: An overview. *Psychosomatics, 26,* 371–374, 380–383.

Ford, M. R., & Widiger, T. A. (1989). Sex bias in the diagnosis of histrionic and antisocial personality disorders. *Journal of Consulting and Clinical Psychology, 57,* 301–305.

Forrest, D. (2001). *Hypnotism: A history.* New York: Penguin USA.

Forsyth, D. R., Zyzniewski, L. E., & Giammanco, C. A. (2002). Responsibility diffusion in cooperative collectives. *Personality and Social Psychology Bulletin, 28,* 54–65.

Fossel, M. (1996). *Reversing human aging.* New York: Morrow.

Foster, J. K., & Jelicic, M. (Eds.). (1999). *Memory: Systems, process, or function?* New York: Oxford University Press.

Fosterling, F. (1992). The Kelley model as an analysis of variance analogy: How far can it be taken? *Journal of Experimental Social Psychology, 28,* 475–490.

Foulke, E. (1991). Braille. In M. A. Heller & W. Schiff (Eds.), *The psychology of touch* (pp. 219–233). Hillsdale, NJ: Erlbaum.

Foulkes, D. (1962). Dream reports from different states of sleep. *Journal of Abnormal and Social Psychology, 65,* 14–25.

Foulkes, D. (1985). *Dreaming: A cognitive-psychological analysis.* Hillsdale, NJ: Erlbaum.

Foulkes, D. (1999). *Children's dreaming and the development of consciousness.* Cambridge: Harvard University Press.

Fouts, G., & Burggraf, K. (1999). Television situation comedies: Female body images and verbal reinforcements. *Sex Roles, 40,* 473–481.

Fouts, R. S., Fouts, D. H., & Van Cantfort, T. E. (1989). The infant Loulis learns signs from cross-fostered chimpanzees. In R. A. Gardner, B. T. Gardner, & T. E. Van Cantfort (Eds.), *Teaching sign language to chimpanzees* (pp. 280–292). Albany: State University of New York Press.

Fowler, M. J., Sullivan, M. J., & Ekstrand, B. R. (1973). Sleep and memory. *Science, 179,* 302–304.

Fowler, R. D. (1986, May). Howard Hughes: A psychological autopsy. *Psychology Today,* pp. 22–33.

Fowles, D. C. (1992). Schizophrenia: Diathesis-stress revisited. *Annual Review of Psychology, 43,* 303–336.

Fox, N. A. (1991). If it's not left, it's right: Electroencephalograph asymmetry and the development of emotion. *American Psychologist, 46,* 863–872.

Fox, N. A., Coplan, R. J., Rubin, K. H., Porges, S. W., Calkins, S. D., Long, J. M., Marshall, T. R., & Stewart, S. (1995). Frontal activation asymmetry and social competence at four years of age. *Child Development, 66,* 1770–1784.

Frank, A. F., & Gunderson, J. G. (1991). The role of the therapist alliance in the treatment of schizophrenia: Relationship to course and outcome. *Archives of General Psychiatry, 47,* 228–236.

Frank, D. A., Augustyn, M., Grant-Knight, W., Pell, T., & Zuckerman, B. (2001). Growth, development, and behavior in early childhood following prenatal cocaine exposure. *Journal of the American Medical Association, 285,* 1613–1625.

Frank, M. G., Ekman, P., & Friesen, W. V. (1993). Behavioral markers and recognizability of the smile of enjoyment. *Journal of Personality and Social Psychology, 64,* 83–93.

Frank, R. H. (1999). *Luxury fever: Why money fails to satisfy in an era of excess.* New York: Free Press.

Frankenburg, W., Dodds, J., Archer, P., Shapiro, H., & Bresnick, B. (1992). The Denver II: A major revision and restandardization of the Denver Developmental Screening Test. *Pediatrics, 89,* 91–97.

Frazier, J. A., & Morrison, F. J. (1998). The influence of extended-year schooling on growth of achievement and perceived competence in early elementary school. *Child Development, 69,* 495–517.

Frazier, P., & Schauben, L. (1994). Causal attributions and recovery from rape and other stressful events. *Journal of Social and Clinical Psychology, 13,* 1–14.

Fredricks, J. A., & Eccles, J. S. (2002). Children's competence and value beliefs from childhood through adolescence: Growth trajectories in two male-sex-typed domains. *Developmental Psychology, 38,* 519–533.

Frederickson, B. L., Maynard, K. E., Helms, M. J., Haney, T. L., Siegler, I. C., & Barefoot, J. C. (2000). Hostility predicts magnitude and duration of blood pressure response to anger. *Journal of Behavioral Medicine, 23,* 229–243.

Freed, W. J. (1999). *Neural transplantation: An introduction.* Cambridge, MA: MIT Press.

Freedman, B. J. (1974). The perceptual experience of perpetual and cognitive disturbances in schizophrenia: A review of autobiographical accounts. *Archives of General Psychiatry, 30,* 333–340.

Freedman, J. L. (1988). Television violence and aggression: What the evidence shows. *Applied Social Psychology Annual, 8,* 144–162.

Freedman, J. L., Cunningham, J. A., & Krismer, K. (1992). Inferred values and the reverse-incentive effect in induced compliance. *Journal of Personality and Social Psychology, 62,* 357–368.

Freedman, R., et al. (1987). Neurobiological studies of sensory gating in schizophrenia. *Schizophrenia Bulletin, 13,* 669–678.

Freud, S. (1900). *The interpretation of dreams.* In Vols. 4 and 5 of the Standard edition. London: Hogarth.

Freud, S. (1905). Fragments of an analysis of a case of hysteria. *Collected papers* (Vol. 3). New York: Basic Books. (Reprinted in 1959.)

Freud, S. (1909). Analysis of a phobia in a five-year-old boy. In *Collected works of Sigmund Freud* (Vol. 10). London: Hogarth. (Reprinted in 1956.)

Freud, S. (1917). Mourning and melancholia. In J. Riviere (Trans.), *Collected papers* (Vol. 4). London: Hogarth Press. (Reprinted in 1924.)

Freud, S. (1920). *Beyond the pleasure principle: A study of the death instinct in human aggression* (J. Strachey, Trans.). New York: Bantam Books. (Reprinted in 1959.)

Freud, S. (1940). *An outline of psychoanalysis.* In Vol. 23 of the Standard edition. London: Hogarth.

Fridlund, A. J. (1994). *Human facial expression: An evolutionary view.* San Diego: Academic Press.

Friedlander, M. L., & Heatherington, L. (1989). Analyzing relational control in family therapy interviews. *Journal of Counseling Psychology, 36,* 139–148.

Friedman, H. S. (1991). *The self-healing personality.* New York: Henry Holt.

Friedman, H. S. (2002). *Health psychology* (2nd ed.). Upper Saddle River, NJ: Prentice-Hall.

Friedman, H. S., & Booth-Kewley, S. (1987). The "disease-prone personality": A meta-analytic view of the construct. *American Psychologist, 42,* 539–555.

Friedman, M., & Rosenman, R. F. (1974). *Type A behavior and your heart.* New York: Knopf.

Friedman, M., & Ulmer, D. (1984). *Treating Type A behavior—and your heart.* New York: Knopf.

Friedman, W. J. (1993). Memory for the time of past events. *Psychological Bulletin, 113,* 44–66.

Friedrich, M. J. (2002). Epidemic of obesity expands its spread to developing countries. *Journal of the American Medical Association, 287,* 1382–1386.

Friend, R., Rafferty, Y., & Bramel, D. (1990). A puzzling misinterpretation of the Asch "conformity" study. *European Journal of Social Psychology, 20,* 29–44.

Frieske, D. A., & Park, D. C. (1999). Memory for news in young and old adults. *Psychology and Aging, 14,* 90–98.

Frijda, N. H. (1986). *The emotions.* New York: Cambridge University Press.

Fritzsche, B. A., Finkelstein, M. A., & Penner, L. A. (2000). To help or not to help: Capturing individuals' decision policies. *Social Behavior and Personality, 28,* 561–578.

Fromm, E. (1941). *Escape from freedom.* New York: Farrar & Rinehart.

Fry, J. M. (1998). Treatment modalities for narcolepsy. *Neurology, 50,* S43–48.

Fu, Q. J., & Shannon, R. V. (1999). Recognition of spectrally degraded and frequency-shifted vowels in acoustic and electric hearing. *Journal of the Acoustical Society of America, 105,* 1889–1900.

Fuente-Fernandez, R., Ruth, T. R., Sossi, V., Schulzer, M., Calne, D. B., & Stoessl, A. J. (2001). Expectation and dopamine release: Mechanism of the placebo effect in Parkinson's disease. *Science, 293,* 1164–1166.

Fulero, S. M. (2002). Empirical and legal perspectives on the impact of pretrial publicity: Effects and remedies. *Law and Human Behavior, 26,* 1–3.

Fuligni, A. J., & Stevenson, H. W. (1995). Time use and mathematics achievement among American, Chinese, and Japanese high school students. *Child Development, 66,* 830–842.

Funder, D. C. (2001). Personality. *Annual Review of Psychology, 52,* 197–221.

Funk, S. C. (1992). Hardiness: A review of theory and research. *Health Psychology, 11,* 335–345.

Furman, W., & Shaffer, L. A. (1999). A story of adolescence: The emergence of other-sex relationships. *Journal of Youth and Adolescence, 28,* 513–522.

Furr, S. R., Westefeld, J. S., McConnell, G. N., & Jenkins, J. M. (2001). Suicide and depression among college students: A decade later. *Professional Psychology: Research and Practice, 32,* 97–100.

Gabrenya, W. K., Jr., Latane, B., & Wang, Y. E. (1983). Social loafing in cross-cultural perspective: Chinese in Taiwan. *Journal of Cross-Cultural Psychology, 14,* 368–384.

Gabrieli, J. D., Desmond, J. E., Demb, J. B., Wagner, A. D., Stone, M. V., Vaidya, C. J., & Glover, G. H. (1996). Functional magnetic resonance imaging of semantic memory processes in the frontal lobes. *Psychological Science, 7,* 278–283.

Gackenbach, J. (Ed.). (1998). *Psychology and the Internet: Intrapersonal, interpersonal, and transpersonal implications.* San Diego: Academic Press.

Gackenbach, J., & Bosveld, J. (1989). *Control your dreams.* New York: Harper & Row.

Gaddis, A., & Brooks-Gunn, J. (1985). The male experience of pubertal change. *Journal of Youth and Adolescence, 14,* 61–69.

Gaertner, S. L., Dovidio, J. F., Banker, B. S., Houlette, M., Johnson, K. M., & McGlynn, E. A. (2000). Reducing intergroup conflict: From superordinate goals to decategorization, recategorization, and mutual differentiation. *Group Dynamics, 4,* 98–114.

Gaertner, S. L., Mann, J. A., Dovidio, J. F., Murrell, A. J., & Pomare, M. (1990). How does cooperation reduce intergroup bias? *Journal of Personality and Social Psychology, 59,* 692–704.

Gaertner, S. L., & McLaughlin, J. P. (1983). Racial stereotypes: Associations and ascriptions of positive and negative characteristics. *Social Psychology Quarterly, 46,* 23–30.

Gage, F. H. (1993). Fetal implants put to the test. *Nature, 361,* 405–406.

Galanter, E. (1962). Contemporary psychophysics. In R. Brown, E. Galanter, H. Hess, & G. Mandler (Eds.), *New directions in psychology.* New York: Holt, Rinehart & Winston.

Galanter, M. (1999). *Cults: Faith, healing, and coercion* (2nd ed.). New York: Oxford University Press.

Galea S., Ahern J., Resnick H., Kilpatrick D., Bucuvalas M., Gold J., & Vlahov D. (2002). Psychological sequelae of the September 11 terrorist attacks in New York City. *The New England Journal of Medicine, 346,* 982–987.

Galinsky, A. D., & Moskowitz, G. B. (2000). Perspective-taking: Decreasing stereotype expression, stereotype accessibility, and in-group favoritism. *Journal of Personality and Social Psychology, 78,* 708–724.

Gallagher, A. M., De Lisi, R., Holst, P. C., McGillicuddy-De Lisi, A. V., & Cahalan, C. (2000). Gender differences in advanced mathematical problem solving. *Journal of Experimental Child Psychology, 75,* 165–190.

Gallant, J. L., Braun, J., & Van Essen, D. C. (1993). Selectivity for polar, hyperbolic, and Cartesian gratings in macaque visual cortex. *Science, 259,* 100–103.

Gallo, D. A., Roberts, M. J., & Seamon, J. G. (1997). Remembering words not presented in lists: Can we avoid creating false memories? *Psychonomic Bulletin and Review, 4,* 271–276.

Gallup Organization. (2002, February 27). *Gallup Poll of the Islamic World.*

Galotti, K. M. (1989). Approaches to studying formal and everyday reasoning. *Psychological Bulletin, 105,* 331–351.

Galton, F. (1883). *Inquiries into human faculty and its development.* London: Dent.

Gamwell, L., & Tomes, N. (1995). *Madness in America: Cultural and medical perceptions of mental illness before 1914.* Ithaca, NY: Cornell University Press.

Gara, M. A., Woolfolk, R. L., Cohen, B. D., Goldston, R. B., Allen, L. A., & Novalany, J. (1993). Perception of self and other in major depression. *Journal of Abnormal Psychology, 102,* 93–100.

Garb, H. N., Florio, C. M., & Grove, W. M. (1998). The validity of the Rorschach and the Minnesota Multiphasic Personality Inventory: Results from meta-analyses. *Psychological Science, 9,* 402–404.

Garcia, J. (1981). The logic and limits of mental aptitude testing. *American Psychologist, 36,* 1172–1180.

Garcia, J., & Koelling, R. A. (1966). The relation of cue to consequence in avoidance learning. *Psychonomic Science, 4,* 123–124.

Gardiner, M. F., Fox, A., Knowles, F., & Jeffrey, D. (1996). Learning improved by arts training. *Nature, 381,* 284.

Gardner, E. P., & Martin, J. H. (2000). Coding of sensory information. In E. R. Kandel, J. H. Schwartz, & T. M. Jessell (Eds.), *Principles of neural science* (4th ed., pp. 411–429). New York: McGraw-Hill.

Gardner, H. (1983). *Frames of mind: The theory of multiple intelligences.* New York: Basic Books.

Gardner, H. (1995). *Leading minds: An anatomy of leadership.* New York: Basic Books.

Gardner, H. (2000). *Intelligence reframed: Multiple intelligences for the 21st century.* New York: Basic Books.

Gardner, R. A., & Gardner, B. I. (1969). Teaching sign language to a chimpanzee. *Science, 165,* 664–672.

Gardner, R. A., & Gardner, B. T. (1978). Comparative psychology and language acquisition. *Annuals of the New York Academy of Science, 309,* 37–76.

Garlick, D. (2002). Understanding the nature of the general factor of intelligence: The role of individual differences in neural plasticity as an explanatory mechanism. *Psychological Review, 109,* 116–136.

Garner, D. M., & Wooley, S. C. (1991). Confronting the failure of behavioral and dietary treatments for obesity. *Clinical Psychology Review, 11,* 729–780.

Gatchel, R. J., & Turk, D. C. (Eds.). (1999). *Psychosocial factors in pain: Critical perspectives.* New York: Guilford Press.

Gathercole, S. E. (Ed.). (2001). *Short-term and working memory.* Brighton, UK: Psychology Press.

Gaulin, S. J. C., & McBurney, D. H. (2000). *Psychology: An evolutionary approach.* Upper Saddle River, NJ: Prentice-Hall.

Gavin, L., & Furman, W. (1989). Age differences in adolescents' perceptions of their peer groups. *Developmental Psychology, 25,* 827–834.

Gay, P. (1988). *Freud: A life for our time.* New York: Norton.

Gazzaniga, M. S. (1967). The split brain in man. *Scientific American,* 24–29.

Gazzaniga, M. S. (1970). *The bisected brain.* New York: Appleton-Century-Crofts.

Gazzaniga, M. S. (1985). *The social brain.* New York: Basic Books.

Gazzaniga, M. S. (1992). *Nature's mind: The roots of thinking, emotions, sexuality, language, and intelligence.* New York: Basic Books.

Gazzaniga, M. S. (1998, July). The split brain revisited. *Scientific American,* 51–55.

Gazzaniga, M., Ivry, R., & Mangun, G. (2002). *Cognitive neuroscience: The biology of the mind* (2nd ed.). New York: Norton.

Gazzaniga, M. S., & LeDoux, J. E. (1978). *The integrated mind.* New York: Plenum.

Geary, D. C. (1996). Sexual selection and sex differences in mathematical abilities. *Behavioral and Brain Sciences, 19,* 229–284.

Geary, D. C. (1999). Evolution and developmental sex differences. *Current Directions in Psychological Science, 8,* 115–120.

Geary, D. C. (2000). Evolution and proximate expression of human paternal investment. *Psychological Bulletin, 126,* 55–77.

Geen, R. G. (1998). Aggression and antisocial behavior. In D. Gilbert, S. Fiske, & G. Lindzey (Eds.), *The handbook of social psychology* (4th ed., Vol. 2, pp. 317–356). New York: McGraw-Hill.

Geen, R. G., & Donnerstein, E. (1998). *Human aggression: Theories, research, and implications for social policy.* San Diego: Academic Press.

Gegenfurtner, K. R., & Sharpe, L. T. (Eds.). (2000). *Color vision: From genes to perception.* New York: Cambridge University Press.

Geldard, F. A. (1972). *The human senses* (2nd ed.). New York: Wiley.

Gelman, R. (1979). Preschool thought. *American Psychologist, 34,* 900–905.

Gentner, D., & Stevens, A. L. (Eds.). (1983). *Mental models.* Hillsdale, NJ: Erlbaum.

George, T. P., & Hartmann, D. P. (1996). Friendship networks of unpopular, average, and popular children. *Child Development, 67,* 2301–2316.

Gerrard, M. (1987). Sex, sex guilt, and contraceptive use revisited: The 1980s. *Journal of Personality and Social Psychology, 52,* 975–980.

Gerrard, M., Gibbons, F. X., & Bushman, B. J. (1996). Relation between perceived vulnerability in HIV and precautionary sexual behavior. *Psychological Bulletin, 119,* 390–409.

Gershkoff-Stowe, L., Thal, D. J., Smith, L. B., & Namy, L. L. (1997). Categorization and its developmental relation to early language. *Child Development, 68,* 843–859.

Gershoff, E. T. (2002). Corporal punishment by parents and associated child behaviors and experiences: A meta-analytic and theoretical review. *Psychological Bulletin, 128,* 539–579.

Gescheider, G. A. (1997). *Psychophysics: The fundamentals* (3rd ed.). Mahwah, NJ: Erlbaum.

Geschwind, N. (1979). Specializations of the human brain. *Scientific American, 241,* 180–199.

Geschwind, N., & Behan, P. (1982). Left-handedness: Association with immune disease, migraine, and left-handed learning disorder. *Proceedings of the National Academy of Sciences, 79,* 5097–5100.

Gesell, A. L. (1940). *The first five years of life: A guide to the study of the preschool child.* New York: Harper.

Gevins, A. S., Leong, J., Smith, M. E., Le, J., & Du, R. (1995). Mapping cognitive brain function with modern high-resolution electroencephalography. *Trends in the Neurosciences, 18,* 429–436.

Gibbons, F. X. (1990). Self-attention and behavior: A review and theoretical update. In M. P. Zanna (Ed.), *Advances in experimental social psychology* (Vol. 23, pp. 249–303). New York: Academic Press.

Gibbons, F. X., Gerrard, M., Blanton, H., & Russell, D. W. (1998). Reasoned action and social reaction: Willingness and intention as independent predictors of health risk. *Journal of Personality and Social Psychology, 74,* 1164–1180.

Gibbs, W. W. (2001, October). Fact or artifact?: The placebo effect may be a little of both. *Scientific American,* p. 1.

Gibson, B., & Sanbonmatsu, D. M. (1997). The effects of selective hypothesis testing on gambling. *Journal of Experimental Psychology: Applied, 3,* 126–142.

Gibson, E., & Walk, R. D. (1960). The visual cliff. *Scientific American, 202,* 80–92.

Gibson, E. J., & Walker, A. S. (1984). Development of knowledge of visual-tactual affordances of substance. *Child Development, 55,* 453–461.

Gibson, H. B. (1991). Can hypnosis compel people to commit harmful, immoral and criminal acts? A review of the literature. *Contemporary Hypnosis, 8,* 129–140.

Gibson, J. J. (1962). Observations on active touch. *Psychological Review, 69,* 477–491.

Gibson, J. J. (1979). *The ecological approach to visual perception.* Boston: Houghton Mifflin.

Gick, M. L., & Holyoak, K. J. (1980). Analogical problem solving. *Cognitive Psychology, 12,* 306–355.

Gieser, L., & Stein, M. I. (1999). *Evocative images: The Thematic Apperception Test and the art of projection.* Washington, DC: American Psychological Association.

Gigerenzer, G., Todd, P. M., & The ABC Research Group. (1999). *Simple heuristics that make us smart.* New York: Oxford University Press.

Gilbert, A. N., & Wysocki, C. J. (1987, October). The smell survey results. *National Geographic,* pp. 514–525.

Gilbert, D. T., & Hixon, J. G. (1991). The trouble of thinking: Activation and application of stereotypic beliefs. *Journal of Personality and Social Psychology, 60,* 509–517.

Gilbert, D. T., & Malone, P. S. (1995). The correspondence bias. *Psychological Bulletin, 117,* 21–38.

Gilbert, D. T., Pinel, E. C., Wilson, T. D., Blumberg, S. J., & Wheatley, T. P. (1998). Immune neglect: A source of durability bias in affective forecasting. *Journal of Personality and Social Psychology, 75,* 617–638.

Gillham, N. W. (2001). *A life of Sir Francis Galton: From African exploration to the birth of Eugenics.* New York: Oxford University Press.

Gillie, O. (1976, October 24). Crucial data was faked by eminent psychologist. *London Sunday Times.*

Gilligan, C. (1982). *In a different voice: Psychological theory and women's development.* Cambridge, MA: Harvard University Press.

Gilovich, T. (1983). Biased evaluation and persistence in gambling. *Journal of Personality and Social Psychology, 40,* 797–808.

Gilovich, T. (1991). *How we know what isn't so: The fallibility of human reason in everyday life.* New York: Free Press.

Gilovich, T., Griifin, D., & Kahneman, D. (Eds.). (2002). *Heuristics and biases: The psychology of intuitive judgment.* New York: Cambridge University Press.

Gilovich, T., & Medvec, V. H. (1995). The experience of regret: What, when, and why. *Psychological Review, 102,* 379–395.

Ginsburg, H., & Opper, S. (1988). *Piaget's theory of intellectual development* (3rd ed.). Englewood Cliffs, NJ: Prentice-Hall.

Gitlin, M. J. (1996). *The psychotherapist's guide to psychopharmacology* (2nd ed.). New York: Free Press.

Glanzer, M., & Cunitz, A. (1966). Two storage mechanisms in free recall. *Journal of Verbal Learning and Verbal Behavior, 5,* 351–360.

Glaser, R. (1990). The reemergence of learning theory within instructional research. *American Psychologist, 45,* 29–39.

Glaser, R., & Kiecolt-Glaser, J. K. (Eds.). (1994). *Handbook of stress and immunity.* San Diego: Academic Press.

Glasgow, R. E., & Lichtenstein, E. (1987). Long-term effects of behavioral smoking cessation interventions. *Behavior Therapy, 18,* 297–324.

Glass, D. C. (1977). *Behavior patterns, stress, and coronary disease.* Hillsdale, NJ: Erlbaum.

Glass, J. D., & Johnson, R. T. (1996). Human immunodeficiency virus and the brain. *Annual Review of Neuroscience, 19,* 1–26.

Gleaves, D. H., & Hernandez, E. (1999). Recent reformulations of Freud's development and abandonment of his seduction theory: Historical/scientific clarification or a continued assault on the truth? *History of Psychology, 2,* 324–354.

Gleicher, F., & Petty, R. E. (1992). Expectations of reassurance influence the nature of fear-stimulated attitude change. *Journal of Experimental Social Psychology, 28,* 86–100.

Glenn, N. D. (1990). Quantitative research on marital quality in the 1980s: A critical review. *Journal of Marriage and the Family, 52,* 818–831.

Glick, I. D., Clarkin, J. F., Rait, D. S., & Berman, E. M. (2000). *Marital and family therapy* (4th ed.). Washington, DC: American Psychiatric Association.

Glick, P., Fiske, S. T., et al. (2000). Beyond prejudice as simple antipathy: Hostile and benevolent sexism across cultures. *Journal of Personality and Social Psychology, 79,* 763–775.

Gluck, M. A., & Myers, C. E. (2000). *Gateway to memory : An introduction to neural network modeling of the hippocampus and learning.* Cambridge, MA: MIT Press.

Gobet, F., & Simon, H. A. (1996). Recall of random and distorted chess positions: Implications for the theory of expertise. *Memory and Cognition, 24,* 493–503.

Goddard, H. H. (1917). Mental tests and the immigrant. *The Journal of Delinquency, 2,* 243–277.

Godden, D. R., & Baddeley, A. D. (1975). Context-dependent memory in two natural environments: On land and underwater. *British Journal of Psychology, 66,* 325–332.

Goebel, B. L., & Brown, D. (1981). Age differences in motivation related to Maslow's need hierarchy. *Developmental Psychology, 17,* 809–815.

Goethals, G. R., & Reckman, R. F. (1973). The perception of consistency in attitudes. *Journal of Experimental Social Psychology, 9,* 491–501.

Goffin, R. D., Rothstein, M. G., & Johnston, N. G. (1996). Personality testing and the assessment center: Incremental validity for managerial selection. *Journal of Applied Psychology, 81,* 746–756.

Golay, M., & Rollyson, C. (1996). *Where America stands 1996.* New York: Wiley.

Gold, P. E. (1995). Role of glucose in regulating the brain and cognition. *American Journal of Clinical Nutrition, 61*(Suppl. 4), 987S–988S.

Goldberg, L. R. (1990). An alternative "description of personality": The big-five factor structure. *Journal of Personality and Social Psychology, 59,* 1216–1229.

Goldberg, L. R. (1993). The structure of phenotypic personality. *American Psychologist, 48,* 26–34.

Goldberg, L. R. (1999). The curious experiences survey, a revised version of the dissociative experiences scale: Factor structure, reliability, and relations to demographic and personality variables. *Psychological Assessment, 11,* 134–145.

Goldberg, L. R., Grenier, J. R., Guion, R., Sechrest, L. B., & Wing, H. (1991). *Questionnaires used in the prediction of trustworthiness in pre-employment selection decisions: An A.P.A. Task Force Report.* Washington, DC: American Psychological Association.

Goldberg, W. A., Greenberger, E., & Nagel, S. K. (1996). Employment and achievement: Mothers' work involvement in relation to children's achievement behaviors and mothers' parenting behaviors. *Child Development, 67,* 1512–1527.

Goldhagen, D. J. (1996). *Hitler's willing executioners: Ordinary Germans and the Holocaust.* New York: Knopf.

Golding, S. L. (1992). The adjudication of criminal responsibility: A review of theory and research. In D. Kagehiro & W. Laufer (Eds.), *Handbook of psychology and law.* New York: Springer-Verlag.

Goldman-Rakic, P. S. (1987). Development of cortical circuitry and cognitive function. *Child Development, 58,* 601–622.

Goldsmith, H. H., & Lansky, J. A. (1987). Maternal and infant temperamental predictors of attachment: A meta-analytic review. *Journal of Consulting and Clinical Psychology, 55,* 805–816

Goldstein, D. G., & Gigerenzer, G. (2002). Models of ecological rationality: The recognition heuristic. *Psychological Review, 109,* 75–90.

Goldstein, J. S. (2001). *War and gender: How gender shapes the war system and vice versa.* Cambridge, UK: Cambridge University Press.

Goldstein, S. R., & Young, C. A. (1996). "Evolutionary" stable strategy of handedness in major league baseball. *Journal of Comparative Psychology, 110,* 164–169.

Goleman, D. (1989, October 17). Critics challenge reliance on drugs in psychiatry. *The New York Times,* p. C1.

Goleman, D. (1990, December 25). The group and the self: New focus on a cultural rift. *The New York Times*, pp. 37, 41.

Golomb, J., de Leon, M. J., Kluger, A., George, A. E., Tarshish, C., & Ferris, S. H. (1993). Hippocampal atrophy in normal aging: An association with recent memory impairment. *Archives of Neurology, 50*, 967–973.

Golombok, S., Hines, M., Johnston, K., Golding, J., et al. (2000). The role of brothers and sisters in the gender development of preschool children. *Journal of Experimental Child Psychology, 77*, 292–303.

Good, B. J., & Kleinman, A. M. (1985). Culture and anxiety: Cross-cultural evidence for the patterning of anxiety disorders. In A. H. Tuma & J. D. Maser (Eds.), *Anxiety and the anxiety disorders*. Hillsdale, NJ: Erlbaum.

Good, K., & Chanoff, D. (1991). *Into the heart*. New York: Simon & Schuster.

Goodall, J. (1986). *The chimpanzees of Gombe: Patterns of behavior*. Cambridge, MA: Harvard University Press.

Goodall, J. (2000, Reissue). *Through a window: My thirty years with the chimpanzees of Gombe*. Boston: Houghton Mifflin.

Goode, E. (1999, August 3). Mozart for baby? Some say, maybe not. *New York Times*, pp. D1, D9.

Goodman, G. S., Aman, C., & Hirschman, J. (1987). Child sexual and physical abuse. In S. Ceci, M. Toglia, & D. Ross (Eds.), *Children's eyewitness testimony* (pp. 1–23). New York: Springer-Verlag.

Goodwin, F. K., & Jamison, K. R. (1990). *Manic depressive illness*. New York: Oxford University Press.

Gopnik, A., Meltzoff, A. N., & Kuhl, P. K. (1999). *The scientist in the crib: Minds, brains, and how children learn*. New York: Morrow.

Gordon, S. (1986, October). What kids need to know. *Psychology Today*, pp. 22–26.

Gorman, J. M., Liebowitz, M. R., Fyer, A. J., & Stein, J. (1989). A neuroanatomical hypothesis for panic disorder. *American Journal of Psychiatry, 146*, 148–161.

Gortmaker, S. L., Must, A., Perrin, J. M., Sobol, A. M., & Dietz, W. H. (1993). Social and economic consequences of overweight in adolescence and young adulthood. *New England Journal of Medicine, 329*, 1008–1012.

Gosling, S. D. (2001). From mice to men: What can we learn about personality from animal research? *Psychological Bulletin, 127*, 45–86.

Gosselin, P., Kirouac, G., & Dore, F. Y. (1995). Components and recognition of facial expression in the communication of emotion by actors. *Journal of Personality and Social Psychology, 68*, 83–96.

Gottesman, I. I. (1991). *Schizophrenia genesis: The origins of madness*. San Francisco: W. H. Freeman.

Gottesman, I. I., & Shields, J. (1982). *Schizophrenia: The epigenetic puzzle*. New York: Cambridge University Press.

Gould, E., Beylin, A., Tanapat, P., Reeves, A., & Shors, T. J. (1999a, March). Learning enhances adult neurogenesis in the hippocampal formation. *Nat. Neurosci. 2*(3): 260–265.

Gould, E., Reeves, A. J., Graziano, M. S., & Gross, C. G. (1999b, October 15). Neurogenesis in the neocortex of adult primates. *Science, 286*(5439), 548–552.

Gould, J. L., & Marler, P. (1987). Learning by instinct. *Scientific American, 256*(1), 74–75.

Gould, R. L. (1978). *Transformations: Growth and change in adult life*. New York: Simon & Schuster.

Gould, S. J. (2001, February 19). Humbled by the genome's mysteries. *The New York Times*.

Gould, S. J. (2002). *The structure of evolutionary theory*. Cambridge, MA: Harvard University Press.

Graber, J. A., Brooks-Gunn, J., Paikoff, R. L., & Warren, M. P. (1994). Prediction of eating problems: An 8-year study of adolescent girls. *Developmental Psychology, 30*, 823–834.

Graffin, N. F., Ray, W. J., & Lundy, R. (1995). EEG concomitants of hypnosis and hypnotic susceptibility. *Journal of Abnormal Psychology, 104*, 123–131.

Graham, J. R. (2000). *MMPI-2: Assessing personality and psychopathology* (3rd ed.). New York: Oxford University Press.

Gramling, S. E., Clawson, E. P., & McDonald, M. K. (1996). Perceptual and cognitive abnormality model of hypochondriasis: Amplification and physiological reactivity in women. *Psychosomatic Medicine, 58*, 423–431.

Grammer, K., & Thornhill, R. (1994). Human facial attractiveness and sexual selection: The role of averageness and symmetry. *Journal of Comparative Psychology, 108*, 233–242.

Grant, B. R., & Grant, P. R. (1989). Natural selection in a population of Darwin's finches. *American Naturalist, 133*, 377–393.

Grant, H. M., Bredahl, L. C., Clay, J., Ferrie, J., Groves, J. E., McDorman, T. A., & Dark, V. J. (1998). Context-dependent memory for meaningful material: Information for students. *Applied Cognitive Psychology, 12*, 617–623.

Gray, J. (1997). *Men are from Mars, women are from Venus*. New York: HarperCollins.

Gray-Little, B., & Hafdahl, A. R. (2000). Factors influencing racial comparisons of self-esteem: A quantitative review. *Psychological Bulletin, 126*, 26–54.

Green, D. M., & Swets, J. A. (1966). *Signal detection theory and psychophysics*. New York: Wiley.

Green, J. P. (1999). Hypnosis and the recall of early autobiographical memories. *International Journal of Clinical and Experimental Hypnosis, 47*.

Greenberg, J. (1982). Approaching equity and avoiding inequity in groups and organizations. In J. Greenberg & R. L. Cohen (Eds.), *Equity and justice in social behavior* (pp. 389–435). New York: Academic Press.

Greenberg, J. (1988). Equity and workplace status: A field experiment. *Journal of Applied Psychology, 73*, 606–613.

Greenberg, J. (1993). Stealing in the name of justice: Informational and interpersonal moderators of theft reactions to underpayment equity. *Organizational Behavior and Human Decision Processes, 54*, 81–103.

Greenberg, J., Solomon, S., & Pyszczynski, T. (1997). Terror management theory of self-esteem and cultural worldviews: Empirical assessments and conceptual refinements. *Advances in Experimental Social Psychology, 29*, 61–139.

Greenberg, L. S., & Malcolm, W. (2002). Resolving unfinished business: Relating process to outcome. *Journal of Consulting and Clinical Psychology, 70*, 406–416.

Greenfeld, L. A. (1998). *Alcohol and crime: An analysis of national data on the prevalence of alcohol involvement in crime*. Washington, DC: Department of Justice, Bureau of Justice Statistics.

Greenhill, L. L., & Osman, B. B. (Eds.). (1999). *Ritalin: Theory and practice* (2nd ed.). New York: Mary Ann Liebert.

Greenough, W. T., Black, J. E., & Wallace, C. S. (1987). Experience and brain development. *Child Development, 58*, 539–559.

Greenough, W. T., Withers, G. S., & Wallace, C. S. (1990). Morphological changes in the nervous system arising from behavioral experience: What is the evidence they are involved in learning and memory? In L. R. Squire & E. Lindenlaub (Eds.), *The biology of memory* (pp. 159–185). Stuttgart: Schattauer.

Greenspan, J. D., & Bolanowski, S. J. (1996). The psychophysics of tactile perception and its peripheral physiological basis. In L. Kruger (Ed.), *Pain and touch* (pp. 25–103). San Diego: Academic Press.

Greenwald, A. G. (1980). The totalitarian ego: Fabrication and revision of personal history. *American Psychologist, 35*, 603–618.

Greenwald, A. G. (1992). New Look 3: Unconscious cognition reclaimed. *American Psychologist, 47*, 766–779.

Greenwald, A. G., & Banaji, M. R. (1995). Implicit social cognition: Attitudes, self-esteem, and stereotypes. *Psychological Review, 102*, 4–27.

Greenwald, A. G., & Farnham, S. D. (2001). Using the Implicit Association Test to measure self-esteem and self-concept. *Journal of Personality and Social Psychology, 79*, 1022–1038.

Greenwald, A. G., McGhee, D. E., & Schwartz, J. L. K. (1998). Measuring implicit differences in implicit cognition: The implicit association test. *Journal of Personality and Social Psychology, 74*, 1464–1480.

Greenwald, A. G., Spangenberg, E. R., Pratkanis, A. R., & Eskenazi, J. (1991). Double-blind tests of subliminal self-help audiotapes. *Psychological Science, 2*, 119–122.

Gregory, R. L. (1998). *Eye and brain: The psychology of seeing* (5th ed.). Princeton, NJ: Princeton University Press.

Greif, E. B., & Ulman, K. J. (1982). The psychological impact of menarche on early adolescent females: A review of the literature. *Child Development, 53*, 1413–1430.

Griffiths, M. (1998). Internet addiction: Does it really exist? In J. Gackenbach (Ed.), *Psychology and the Internet: Intrapersonal, interpersonal, and transpersonal implications* (pp. 61–75). San Diego: Academic Press.

Griggs, R. A., & Cox, J. R. (1982). The elusive thematic-materials effect in Wason's selection task. *British Journal of Psychology, 73*, 407–420.

Grilo, C. M., & Pogue-Geile, M. (1991). The nature of environmental influences in weight and obesity: A behavior genetic analysis. *Psychological Bulletin, 110*, 520–537.

Grimes, B. F., & Grimes, J. E. (Eds.). (2000). *Ethnologue: Languages of the world* (14th ed.). Dallas: SIL International.

Grissmer, D. W., Williamson, S., Kirby, S. N., & Berends, M. (1998). Exploring the rapid rise in black achievement scores in the United States (1970–1990). In U. Neisser (Ed.), *The rising curve: Long-term gains in IQ and related measures* (pp. 251–285). Washington, DC: American Psychological Association.

Gross, A. E., & Crofton, C. (1977). What is good is beautiful. *Sociometry, 40*, 85–90.

Gross, C. G., Rocha-Miranda, F. C., & Bender, D. B. (1972). Visual properties of neurons in the inferotemporal cortex of the macaque. *Journal of Neurophysiology, 35*, 96–111.

Gross, J. J., & Levenson, R. W. (1997). Hiding feelings: The acute effects of inhibiting negative and positive emotion. *Journal of Abnormal Psychology, 106*, 95–103.

Grossman, M., & Wood, W. (1993). Sex differences in intensity of emotional experience: A social role interpretation. *Journal of Personality and Social Psychology, 65*, 1010–1022.

Groth-Marnat, H. (2003). *Handbook of psychological assessment* (4th ed.). New York: Wiley.

Grudnik, J. L., & Kranzler, J. H. (2001). Meta-analysis of the relationship between intelligence and inspection time. *Intelligence, 29*, 523–535.

Grunwald, L., & Goldberg, J. (1993, July). The amazing minds of infants. *Life*, pp. 46–56.

Guerin, B. (1986). Mere presence effects in humans: A review. *Journal of Experimental Social Psychology, 22*, 38–77.

Guilford, J. P. (1967). *The nature of human intelligence*. New York: McGraw-Hill.

Guilford, J. P. (1985). The structure-of-intellect model. In B. B. Wolman (Ed.), *Handbook of intelligence: Theories, measurements, and applications* (pp. 225–266). New York: Wiley.

Guilleminault, C., & Roth, T. (1993). Hypersomnia. In M. A. Carskadon (Ed.), *Encyclopedia of sleep and dreaming* (pp. 287–288). New York: Macmillan.

*Guinness Book of World Records.* (1994). New York: Bantam Books.

Guion, R. M. (1965). *Personnel testing*. New York: McGraw-Hill.

Gump, P. V. (1987). School and classroom environments. In D. Stokols & I. Altman (Eds.), *Handbook of environmental psychology* (Vol. 1). New York: Wiley.

Gumperz, J. J., & Levinson, S. C. (Eds.). (1996). *Rethinking linguistic relativity*. Cambridge, UK: Cambridge University Press.

Gunderson, J. G. (1984). *Borderline personality disorder*. Washington, DC: American Psychiatric Press.

Gunderson, J. G. (2001). *Borderline personality disorder: A clinical guide*. Washington, DC: American Psychiatric Press.

Gur, R. C., Schroeder, L., Turner, T., McGrath, C., Chan, R. M., Turetsky, B. I., Alsop, D., Maldjian, J., & Gur, R. E. (2002). Brain activation during facial emotion processing. *Neuroimage, 16*, 651–662.

Gurtman, M. B. (1987). Depressive affect and disclosures as factors in interpersonal rejection. *Cognitive Therapy and Research, 11*, 87–100.

Guthrie, J. P., Ash, R. A., & Bendapudi, V. (1995). Additional validity evidence for measures of morningness. *Journal of Applied Psychology, 80*, 186–190.

Guttman, N., & Kalish, H. (1956). Discriminability and stimulus generalization. *Journal of Experimental Psychology, 51*, 79–88.

Guttmann, M. G. (2001). *The enigma of Anna O.: A biography of Bertha Pappenheim*. Wickford, RI: Moyer Bell.

Gwynne, S. C. (1999, April 12). Genes and money. *Time*, p. 69.

Haaga, D., & Davison, G. C. (1993). An appraisal of rational-emotive therapy. *Journal of Consulting and Clinical Psychology, 61,* 215–220.

Haaga, D. A., Dyck, M. J., & Ernst, D. (1991). Empirical status of cognitive theory of depression. *Psychological Bulletin, 110,* 215–236.

Haaga, D. A. F. (2002). Introduction to the special section on stepped care models in psychotherapy. *Journal of Consulting and Clinical Psychology, 68,* 547–548.

Haddock, G., Zanna, M. P., & Esses, V. M. (1993). Assessing the structure of prejudicial attitudes: The case of attitudes toward homosexuals. *Journal of Personality and Social Psychology, 65,* 1105–1118.

Hagen, M. A. (1997). *Whores of the court: The fraud of psychiatric testimony and the rape of American justice.* New York: HarperCollins.

Haidt, J. (2001). The emotional dog and its rational tail: The social intuitist approach to moral judgment. *Psychological Review, 108,* 814–834.

Hailman, J. P. (1969). How an instinct is learned. *Scientific American, 221,* 98–106.

Haist, F., Shimamura, A. P., & Squire, L. R. (1992). On the relationship between recall and recognition memory. *Journal of Experimental Psychology: Learning, Memory, and Cognition, 18,* 691–702.

Haith, M. (1980). *Rules that babies look by.* Hillsdale, NJ: Erlbaum.

Haith, M. M. (1998). Who put the cog in infant cognition? Is rich interpretation too costly? *Infant Behavior and Development, 21,* 167–179.

Haldeman, D. C. (2002). Gay rights, patient rights: The implications of sexual orientation conversion therapy. *Professional Psychology: Research and Practice, 33,* 260–264.

Hall, C. S., & Van de Castle, R. (1966). *The content analysis of dreams.* New York: Appleton-Century-Crofts.

Hall, G. S. (1904). *Adolescence.* New York: Appleton-Century-Crofts.

Hall, H. V., & Pritchard, D. A. (1996). *Detecting malingering and deception: Forensic distortion analysis (FDA).* Delray Beach, FL: St. Lucie Press.

Hall, J. A. (1984). *Nonverbal sex differences: Communication accuracy and expressive style.* Baltimore: Johns Hopkins University Press.

Halperin, J. L. (1997). *The truth machine.* New York: Del Ray.

Halpern, A. R. (1986). Memory for tune titles after organized or unorganized presentation. *American Journal of Psychology, 99,* 57–70.

Halpern, A. R., & Deveraux, S. D. (1989). Lucky numbers: Choice strategies in the Pennsylvania number game. *Bulletin of the Psychonomic Society, 27,* 167–170.

Halpern, D. F. (2000). *Sex differences in cognitive abilities* (3rd ed.). Mahwah, NJ: Erlbaum.

Halpern, D. F. (2002). *Thought and knowledge: An introduction to critical thinking* (4th ed.). Mahwah, NJ: Erlbaum.

Halpern, D. F., & Coren, S. (1993). Left-handedness and life span: A reply to Harris. *Psychological Bulletin, 114,* 235–241.

Hamer, D. H., Rice, G., Risch, N., & Ebers, G. (1999). Genetics and male sexual orientation. *Science, 285,* 803.

Hamermesh, D. S., & Biddle, J. E. (1994). Beauty and the labor market. *American Economic Review, 84,* 1174–1195.

Hamilton, A. (1999, May 24). On the virtual couch. *Time,* p. 71.

Hamilton, D. L., & Zanna, M. P. (1974). Context effects in impression formation: Changes in connotative meaning. *Journal of Personality and Social Psychology, 29,* 649–654.

Hampton, R. R., & Shettleworth, S. J. (1996). Hippocampus and memory in a food-storing and in a nonstoring bird species. *Behavioral Neuroscience, 110,* 946–964.

Hamrick, N., Cohen, S., & Rodriguez, M. S. (2002). Being popular can be healthy or unhealthy: Stress, social network diversity, and incidence of upper respiratory infection. *Health Psychology, 21,* 294–298.

Hancock, L. (1996, March 18). Mother's little helper. *Newsweek,* pp. 51–56.

Handel, A. (1987). Personal theories about the life-span development of one's self in autobiographical self-presentations of adults. *Human Development, 30,* 83–98.

Hankin, B. L., & Abramson, L. Y. (2001). Development of gender differences in depression: An elaborated cognitive vulnerability-transactional stress theory. *Psychological Bulletin, 127,* 773–796.

Hanna, E., & Meltzoff, A. N. (1993). Peer imitation by toddlers in laboratory, home, and day-care contexts: Implications for social learning and memory. *Developmental Psychology, 29,* 701–710.

Hansson, B. S. (2002). A bug's smell: Research into insect olfaction. *Trends in Neurosciences, 25,* 270–274.

Hardin, C., & Banaji, M. R. (1993). The influence of language on thought. *Social Cognition, 11,* 277–308.

Hare, R. D. (1993). *Without conscience: The disturbing world of the psychopaths among us.* New York: Pocket Books.

Hare, R. D., McPherson, L. M., & Forth, A. E. (1988). Male psychopaths and their criminal careers. *Journal of Consulting and Clinical Psychology, 56,* 710–714.

Hargadon, R., Bowers, K. S., & Woody, E. Z. (1995). Does counterpain imagery mediate hypnotic responding? *Journal of Abnormal Psychology, 104,* 508–516.

Harkins, D. A., & Uzgiris, I. C. (1991). Hand-use matching between mothers and infants during the first year. *Infant Behavior and Development, 14,* 289–298.

Harley, K., & Reese, E. (1999). Origins of autobiographical memory. *Developmental Psychology, 35,* 1338–1348.

Harlow, H. F. (1958). The nature of love. *American Psychologist, 13,* 673–685.

Harlow, H. F. (1971). *Learning to love.* San Francisco: Albion.

Harlow, J. M. (1868). Recovery from the passage of an iron bar through the head. *Massachusetts Medical Society Publication, 2,* 327–347.

Harmon-Jones, E., & Allen, J. B. (2001). The role of affect in the mere exposure effect: Evidence from psychophysiological and individual differences approaches. *Personality and Social Psychology Bulletin, 27,* 889–898.

Harmon-Jones, E., Brehm, J. W., Greenberg, J., Simon, L., & Nelson, D. E. (1996). Evidence that the production of aversive consequences is not necessary to create cognitive dissonance. *Journal of Personality and Social Psychology, 70,* 5–16.

Harmon-Jones, E., & Mills, J. (Eds.). (1999). *Cognitive dissonance: Progress on a pivotal theory in social psychology.* Washington, DC: American Psychological Association.

Harrington, A. (Ed.). (1997). *The placebo effect: An interdisciplinary exploration.* Cambridge, MA: Harvard University Press.

Harris, B. (1979). Whatever happened to Little Albert? *American Psychologist, 34,* 151–160.

Harris, C. R., & Christenfeld, N. (1996). Gender, jealousy, and reason. *Psychological Science, 7,* 364–366.

Harris, J. R. (1995). Where is the child's environment? A group socialization theory of development. *Psychological Review, 102,* 458–489.

Harris, J. R. (1998). *The nurture assumption: Why children turn out the way they do.* New York: Free Press.

Harris, L. J. (1993). Do left-handers die sooner than right-handers? Commentary on Coren and Halpern's (1991) "Left-handedness: A marker for decreased survival fitness." *Psychological Bulletin, 114,* 203–234.

Harris, L. J. (2002). Lateral biases for holding infants: Early opinions, observations, and explanations, with some possible lessons for theory and research today. *Brain and Cognition, 48,* 392–394.

Harris, M. J., & Perkins, R. (1995). Effects of distraction on interpersonal expectancy effects: A social interaction test of the cognitive busyness hypothesis. *Social Cognition, 13,* 163–182.

Harris, P. L., & Kavanaugh, R. D. (1993). Young children's understanding of pretense. *Monographs of the Society for Research in Child Development, 58*(1, Serial No. 231).

Harris, R. J., & Monaco, G. E. (1978). Psychology of pragmatic implication: Information processing between the lines. *Journal of Experimental Psychology: General, 107,* 1–22.

Harrison, A. A., & Saeed, L. (1977). Let's make a deal: An analysis of revelations and stipulations in lonely hearts advertisements. *Journal of Personality and Social Psychology, 35,* 257–264.

Harrison, J. (2001). *Synaesthesia: The strangest thing.* Oxford, UK: Oxford University Press.

Hartshorne, H., & May, M. (1928). *Studies in deceit.* New York: Macmillan.

Hartung, C. M., & Widiger, T. A. (1998). Gender differences in the diagnosis of mental disorders: Conclusions and controversies of the DSM-IV. *Psychological Bulletin, 123,* 260–278.

Hartup, W. W. (1989). Social relationships and their developmental significance. *American Psychologist, 44,* 120–126.

Hartup, W. W., & Stevens, N. (1999). Friendships and adaptation across the life span. *Current Directions in Psychological Science, 8,* 76–79.

Harvey, A. G. (2002). A cognitive model of insomnia. *Behaviour Research and Therapy, 40,* 869–894.

Harvey, E. (1999). Short-term and long-term effects of early parental employment on children of the National Longitudinal Survey of Youth. *Developmental Psychology, 35,* 445–459.

Hasher, L., & Zacks, R. T. (1984). Automatic processing of fundamental information: The case of frequency. *American Psychologist, 39,* 1372–1388.

Hass, R. G., Katz, I., Rizzo, N., Bailey, J., & Moore, L. (1992). When racial ambivalence evokes negative affect, using a disguised measure of mood. *Personality and Social Psychology Bulletin, 18,* 786–797.

Hassett, J. (1978). *A primer of psychophysiology.* San Francisco: W. H. Freeman.

Hastie, R., & Dawes, R. (2001). *Rational choice in an uncertain world: The psychology of judgement and decision making.* Thousand Oaks, CA: Sage Publications.

Hatch, J. P., Fisher, J. G., & Rugh, J. D. (1987). *Biofeedback: Studies in clinical efficacy.* New York: Plenum.

Hatfield, E. (1988). Passionate and compassionate love. In R. J. Sternberg & M. L. Barnes (Eds.), *The psychology of love.* New Haven, CT: Yale University Press.

Hathaway, S. R., & McKinley, J. C. (1983). *Minnesota Multiphasic Personality Inventory: Manual for administration and scoring.* New York: Psychological Corporation.

Hausmann, M., Slabbekoorn, D., Van Goozen, S. H. M., Cohen-Kettenis, P. T., & Guentuerkuen, O. (2000). Sex hormones affect spatial abilities during the menstrual cycle. *Behavioral Neuroscience, 114,* 1245–1250.

Hawkins, S. A., & Hastie, R. (1990). Hindsight: Biased judgments of past events after the outcomes are known. *Psychological Bulletin, 107,* 311–327.

Hawton, K., & van Heeringen, K. (2000). *The international handbook of suicide and attempted suicide.* New York: Wiley.

Hayes, C. (1951). *The ape in our house.* New York: Harper.

Hayflick, L. (1996). *How and why we age.* New York: Ballantine.

Hazelrigg, M. D., Cooper, H. M., & Borduin, C. (1987). Evaluating the effectiveness of family therapies: An integrative review and analysis. *Psychological Bulletin, 101,* 428–442.

Healy, D. (2002). *The creation of psychopharmacology.* Cambridge, MA: Harvard University Press.

Heatherton, T. F., & Polivy, J. (1991). Development and validation of a scale for measuring state self-esteem. *Journal of Personality and Social Psychology, 60,* 895–910.

Heatherton, T. F., & Vohs, K. D. (2000). Interpersonal evaluations following threats to self: The role of self-esteem. *Journal of Personality and Social Psychology, 78,* 725–736.

Heatherton, T. F., & Weinberger, J. L. (Eds.). (1994). *Can personality change?* Washington, DC: American Psychological Association.

Hecht, H., & Proffitt, D. R. (1995). The price of expertise: Effects of experience on the water-level task. *Psychological Science, 6,* 90–95.

Hedges, L. B., & Nowell, A. (1995). Sex differences in mental test scores, variability, and numbers of high-scoring individuals. *Science, 269,* 41–45.

Heider, F. (1958). *The psychology of interpersonal relations.* New York: Wiley.

Heimberg, R. G., Liebowitz, M. R., Hope, D. A., & Schneier, F. R. (Eds.). (1995). *Social phobia: Diagnosis, assessment, and treatment.* New York: Guilford Press.

Heine, M. K., Ober, B. A., & Shenaut, G. K. (1999). Naturally occurring and experimentally induced tip-of-the-tongue experiences in three adult age groups. *Psychology and Aging, 14,* 445–457.

Heine, S. J., Kitayama, S., Lehman, D. R., Takata, T., Ide, E., Leung, C., & Matsumoto, H. (2001). Divergent consequences of success and failure in Japan and North America: An investigation of self-improving motivations and malleable selves. *Journal of Personality and Social Psychology, 81,* 599–615.

Heine, S. J., Lehman, D. R., Markus, H. R., & Kitayama, S. (1999). Is there a universal need for positive self-regard? *Psychological Review, 106,* 756–794.

Heine, S. J., Takata, T., & Lehman, D. R. (2000). Beyond self-presentation: Evidence for self-criticism among Japanese. *Personality and Social Psychology Bulletin, 26,* 71–78.

Heinrichs, R. W. (2001). *In search of madness: Schizophrenia and neuroscience.* New York: Oxford University Press.

Helgeson, V. S. (1992). Moderators of the relation between perceived control and adjustment to chronic illness. *Journal of Personality and Social Psychology, 63,* 652–666.

Heller, K. A., Monks, F. J., Sternberg, R. J., & Subotnik, R. F. (Eds.). (2002). *International handbook of giftedness and talent* (2nd ed.). New York: Pergamon.

Heller, M. A., & Schiff, W. (Eds.). (1991). *The psychology of touch: Theory and application.* Hillsdale, NJ: Erlbaum.

Hellige, J. B. (2000). Cerebral hemispheric specialization in normal individuals: Experimental assessment. In F. Boller & J. Grafman (Eds.), *Handbook of neuropsychology* (Vol. 1, Part 1, pp. 121–138). Amsterdam: Elsevier.

Helmholtz, H. von. (1852). On the theory of compound colours. *Philosophical Magazine, 4,* 519–534.

Helms, J. E. (1992). Why is there no study of cultural equivalence in standardized cognitive ability testing? *American Psychologist, 47,* 1083–1101.

Henderlong, J., & Lepper, M. R. (2002). The effects of praise on children's intrinsic motivation: A review and synthesis. *Psychological Bulletin, 128,* 774–795.

Hendrick, S. S. (1981). Self-disclosure and marital satisfaction. *Journal of Personality and Social Psychology, 40,* 1150–1159.

Heneman, H. G., & Schwab, D. P. (1985). Pay satisfaction: Its multidimensional nature and measurement. *International Journal of Psychology, 20,* 129–141.

Henley, N. M. (1977). *Body politics: Power, sex, and nonverbal communication.* Englewood Cliffs, NJ: Prentice-Hall.

Henningsen, D. D., Cruz, M. G., & Miller, M. L. (2000). Role of social loafing in pre-deliberation decision making. *Group Dynamics, 4,* 168–175.

Henry, W. A. (1994, June 27). Pride and prejudice. *Time,* pp. 54–59.

Henry, W. P., Strupp, H. H., Schacht, T. E., & Gaston, L. (1994). Psychodynamic approaches. In A. E. Bergin & S. L. Garfield (Eds.), *Handbook of psychotherapy and behavior change* (4th ed., pp. 467–508). New York: Wiley.

Hensel, H. (1981). *Thermoreception and temperature regulation.* London: Academic Press.

Henslin, J. M. (1967). Craps and magic. *American Journal of Sociology, 73,* 316–330.

Hepper, P. G., Shahidullah, S., & White, R. (1990). Origins of fetal handedness. *Nature, 347,* 431.

Herbert, T. B., & Cohen, S. (1993). Depression and immunity: A meta-analytic review. *Psychological Bulletin, 113,* 472–486.

Herdt, G. (1998). *Same sex, different cultures: Exploring gay and lesbian lives.* Boulder, CO: Westview Press.

Herek, G. M. (1988). Heterosexuals' attitudes toward lesbians and gay men: Correlates and gender differences. *Journal of Sex Research, 25,* 451–477.

Hering, E. (1878). *Outlines of a theory of the light sense* ( Hurvich & D. Jameson, Trans.). Cambridge, MA: Harvard University Press.

Herman, L. M., Kuczaj, S. A., & Holder, M. D. (1993). Responses to anomalous gestural sequences by a language-trained dolphin: Evidence for processing of semantic relations and syntactic information. *Journal of Experimental Psychology: General, 122,* 184–194.

Herman, L. M., & Uyeyama, R. K. (1999). The dolphin's grammatical competency: Comments on Kako (1999). *Animal Learning & Behavior, 27,* 18–23.

Herman-Giddens, M. E., et al. (1997). Secondary sexual characteristics and menses in young girls seen in office practice: A study from the Pediatric Research in Office Settings Network. *Pediatrics, 99,* 505–512.

Herman-Giddens, M. E., Wang, L., & Koch, G. (2001). Secondary sexual characteristics in boys. *Archives of Pediatric and Adolescent Medicine, 155,* 1022–1028.

Herrnstein, R. J. (1970). On the law of effect. *Journal of the Experimental Analysis of Behavior, 7,* 243–266.

Herrnstein, R. J., & Murray, C. (1994). *The bell curve: Intelligence and class structure in American life.* New York: Free Press.

Hershenson, M. (Ed.). (1989). *The moon illusion.* Hillsdale, NJ: Erlbaum.

Hertzog, C. (1989). Influences of cognitive slowing on age differences in intelligence. *Developmental Psychology, 25,* 636–651.

Hess, E. H. (1959). Imprinting. *Science, 130,* 133–144.

Hesse-Biber, S. (1996). *Am I thin enough yet?: The cult of thinness and the commercialization of identity.* New York: Oxford University Press.

Hetherington, A. W., & Ranson, S. W. (1942). The spontaneous activity and food intake of rats with hypothalamic lesions. *American Journal of Physiology, 136,* 609–617.

Hetherington, E. M., Reiss, D., & Plomin, R. (Eds.). (1994). *Separate social worlds of siblings: The impact of nonshared environment on development.* Hillsdale, NJ: Erlbaum.

Heyes, C. M., & Galef, B. G., Jr. (1996). *Social learning in animals: The roots of culture.* New York: Academic Press.

Heyser, C. J., Spear, N. E., & Spear, L. P. (1993). Effects of prenatal exposure to cocaine on conditional discrimination learning in adult rats. *Behavioral Neuroscience, 106,* 837–845.

Hibbard, W. S., & Worring, R. W. (1996). *Forensic hypnosis: The practical application of hypnosis in criminal investigation.* Springfield, IL: Charles C. Thomas.

Higgins, E. T. (1989). Self-discrepancy theory: What patterns of self-beliefs cause people to suffer? In L. Berkowitz (Ed.), *Advances in experimental social psychology* (Vol. 22, pp. 93–136). New York: Academic Press.

Higgins, E. T., Bond, R. N., Klein, R., & Strauman, T. (1986). Self-discrepancies and emotional vulnerability: How magnitude, accessibility, and type of discrepancy influence affect. *Journal of Personality and Social Psychology, 51,* 5–15.

Hilgard, E. R. (1982). Hypnotic susceptibility and implications for measurement. *International Journal of Clinical and Experimental Hypnosis, 30,* 394–403.

Hilgard, E. R. (1986). *Divided consciousness: Multiple controls in human thought and action.* New York: Wiley-Interscience.

Hilgard, E. R. (1987). *Psychology in America: A historical survey.* San Diego: Harcourt Brace Jovanovich.

Hilgard, E. R. (1992). Divided consciousness and dissociation. *Consciousness and Cognition, 1,* 16–31.

Hilgard, E. R., Morgan, A. H., & MacDonald, H. (1975). Pain and dissociation in the cold pressor test: A study of "hidden reports" through automatic key-pressing and automatic talking. *Journal of Abnormal Psychology, 84,* 280–289.

Hilgard, J. R. (1979). *Personality and hypnosis: A study of imaginative involvement.* Chicago: University of Chicago Press.

Hill, C. A. (1987). Affiliation motivation: People who need people . . . but in different ways. *Journal of Personality and Social Psychology, 52,* 1008–1018.

Hill, R. M., Hegemeir, S., & Tennyson, L. M. (1989). The fetal alcohol syndrome: A multihandicapped child. *Neuro-Toxicology, 10,* 585–596.

Hilton, D. (1995). The social context of reasoning: Conversational inference and rational judgment. *Psychological Bulletin, 118,* 248–271.

Hilton, J. L., & Darley, J. M. (1985). Constructing other persons: A limit on the effect. *Journal of Experimental Social Psychology, 21,* 1–18.

Hilton, J. L., & Darley, J. M. (1991). The effects of interaction goals on person perception. *Advances in Experimental Social Psychology, 24,* 235–267.

Hilton, J. L., & von Hippel, W. (1996). Stereotypes. *Annual Review of Psychology, 47,* 237–271.

Hilts, P. J. (1995). *Memory's ghost: The strange tale of Mr. M and the nature of memory.* New York: Simon & Schuster.

Hirsch, A. R. (1998). *Scentsational sex: The secret of using aroma for arousal.* New York: Element Books.

Hirsh, I. J., & Watson, C. S. (1996). Auditory psychophysics and perception. *Annual Review of Psychology, 47,* 461–484.

Hobbes, T. (1919). *Leviathan.* London: J. M. Dent. (Original work published 1651.)

Hobden, K., & Pliner, P. (1995). Effects of a model on food neophobia in humans. *Appetite, 25,* 101–113.

Hobson, J. A. (1988). *The dreaming brain.* New York: Basic Books.

Hobson, J. A. (1989). *Sleep.* New York: Scientific American.

Hobson, J. A. (2003). *Dreaming: An introduction to the science of sleep.* New York: Oxford University Press.

Hobson, J. A., & McCarley, R. W. (1977). The brain as a dream state generator: An activational-synthesis hypothesis of the dream process. *American Journal of Psychiatry, 134,* 1335–1348.

Hochberg, J. E. (1978). *Perception* (2nd ed.). Englewood Cliffs, NJ: Prentice-Hall.

Hodges, E. V., Boivin, M., Vitaro, F., & Bukowski, W. M. (1999). The power of friendship: Protection against an escalating cycle of peer victimization. *Developmental Psychology, 35,* 94–101.

Hofbauer, R. K., Rainville, P., Duncan, G. H., & Bushnell, M. V. (2001). Cortical representation of the sensory dimension of pain. *Journal of Neurophysiology, 86,* 402–411.

Hoffman, D. D. (1998). *Visual intelligence: How we create what we see.* New York: W.W. Norton.

Hoffman, E. (1989). *Lost in translation: A life in a new language.* New York: Dutton.

Hoffman, L. W. (1989). Effects of maternal employment in the two-parent family. *American Psychologist, 44,* 283–292.

Hoffman, M. L. (1984). Empathy, its limitations, and its role in a comprehensive moral theory. In J. Gewirtz & W. Kurtines (Eds.), *Morality, moral development, and moral behavior* (pp. 283–302). New York: Wiley.

Hoffner, C., & Badzinski, D. M. (1989). Children's integration of facial and situational cues to emotion. *Child Development, 60,* 411–422.

Hoffstein, V., Mateika, S., & Anderson, D. (1994). Snoring: Is it in the ear of the beholder? *Sleep, 17,* 522–526.

Hofmann, A. (1980). *LSD: My problem child.* New York: McGraw-Hill.

Hofstede, G. (1980). *Culture's consequences.* Beverly Hills, CA: Sage.

Hogan, R., Hogan, J., & Roberts, B. W. (1996). Personality measurement and employment decisions: Questions and answers. *American Psychologist, 51,* 469–477.

Hogg, M. A., & Abrams, D. (1990). Social motivation, self-esteem and social identity. In D. Abrams & M. Hogg (Eds.), *Social identity theory: Constructive and critical advances* (pp. 28–47). New York: Springer-Verlag.

Holahan, C. K. (1988). Relation of life goals at age 70 to activity participation and health and psychological well-being among Terman's gifted men and women. *Psychology and Aging, 3,* 286–291.

Holahan, C. K., & Sears, R. R. (1995). *The gifted group in later maturity.* Palo Alto, CA: Stanford University Press.

Holden, C. (1980, November). Twins reunited. *Science, 80,* 55–59.

Holder, R. W. (2002). *How not to say what you mean: A dictionary of euphemisms* (3rd ed.). New York: Oxford University Press.

Holding, D. H. (1989). *Human skills* (2nd ed.). New York: Wiley.

Hollandsworth, J. G., Jr. (1990). *The physiology of psychological disorders.* New York: Plenum.

Hollins, M., Faldowski, R., Rao, S., & Young, F. (1993). Perceptual dimensions of tactile surface texture: A multidimensional scaling analysis. *Perception and Psychophysics, 54,* 697–705.

Hollon, S. D. (1996). The efficacy and effectiveness of psychotherapy relative to medications. *American Psychologist, 51,* 1025–1030.

Hollon, S. D., Shelton, R. C., & Loosen, P. T. (1991). Cognitive therapy and pharmacotherapy for depression. *Journal of Consulting and Clinical Psychology, 59,* 88–99.

Holmbeck, G. (1996). A model of family relational transformations during the transition to adolescence: Parent-adolescent conflict and adaptation. In J. A. Graber, J. Brooks-Gunn, & A. C. Petersen, (Eds.), *Transitions through adolescence: Interpersonal domains and context* (pp. 167–199). Mahwah, NJ: Erlbaum.

Holmes, T. H., & Rahe, R. H. (1967). The Social Readjustment Rating Scale. *Journal of Psychosomatic Research, 11,* 213–218.

Holtgraves, T., & Skeel, J. (1992). Cognitive biases in playing the lottery: Estimating the odds and choosing the numbers. *Journal of Applied Social Psychology, 22,* 934–952.

Holton, S. D., Shelton, R. C., & Loosen, P. T. (1991). Cognitive therapy and pharmacotherapy for depression. *Journal of Consulting and Clinical Psychology, 59,* 88–99.

Holyoak, K. J., & Spellman, B. A. (1993). Thinking. *Annual Review of Psychology, 44,* 265–315.

Holyoak, K. J., & Thagard, P. (1997). The analogical mind. *American Psychologist, 52,* 35–44.

Holzman, P. S., & Matthysse, S. (1990). The genetics of schizophrenia: A review. *Psychological Science, 1,* 279–286.

Hong, Y., Morris, M. W., Chiu, C., & Benet-Martinez, V. (2000). Multicultural minds: A dynamic constructivist approach to culture and cognition. *American Psychologist, 55,* 709–720.

Honts, C. R., Raskin, D. C., & Kircher, J. C. (1994). Mental and physical countermeasures reduce the accuracy of polygraph tests. *Journal of Applied Psychology, 79,* 252–259.

Hopkins, W. D., & Leavens, D. A. (1998). Hand use and gestural communication in chimpanzees. *Journal of Comparative Psychology, 112,* 95–99.

Hopkins, W. D., & Pearson, K. (2000). Chimpanzee (Pan troglodytes) handedness: Variability across multiple measures of hand use. *Journal of Comparative Psychology, 114,* 126–135.

Hoptman, M. J., & Davidson, R. J. (1994). How and why do the two cerebral hemispheres interact? *Psychological Bulletin, 116,* 195–219.

Horgen, K. B., & Brownell, K. D. (2002). Confronting the toxic environment: Environmental and public health actions in a world crisis. In T. A. Wadden & A. J. Stunkard (Eds.), *Handbook of obesity treatment* (pp. 95–106). New York: Guilford Press.

Horn, J. C. (1987). Bigger pay for better work. *Psychology Today, 21*(1), 54–57.

Horn, J. L. (1982). The aging of human abilities. In B. B. Wolman (Ed.), *Handbook of developmental psychology* (pp. 847–870). Englewood Cliffs, NJ: Prentice-Hall.

Horn, J. L., & Cattell, R. C. (1966). Refinement and test of the theory of fluid and crystallized general intelligences. *Journal of Educational Psychology, 57,* 253–270.

Horne, J. A. (1988). *Why we sleep: The functions of sleep in humans and other animals.* Oxford, England: Oxford University Press.

Horne, J. A., & Reyner, L. A. (1996). Counteracting driver sleepiness: Effects of napping, caffeine, and placebo. *Psychophysiology, 33,* 306–309.

Horner, K. L., Rushton, J. P., & Vernon, P. A. (1986). Relation between aging and research productivity of academic psychologists. *Psychology and Aging, 1,* 319–324.

Horney, K. (1945). *Our inner conflicts.* New York: Norton.

Horvath, A. O., & Luborsky, L. (1993). The role of the therapeutic alliance in psychotherapy. *Journal of Consulting and Clinical Psychology, 61,* 561–573.

Horvath, A. O., & Symonds, B. D. (1991). Relation between working alliance and outcome in psychotherapy: A meta-analysis. *Journal of Counseling Psychology, 38,* 139–149.

Horvath, F. (1984). Detecting deception in eyewitness cases: Problems and prospects in use of the polygraph. In G. Wells & E. Loftus (Eds.), *Eyewitness testimony: Psychological perspectives* (pp. 214–255). New York: Cambridge University Press.

Hothersall, D. (1990). *History of psychology* (2nd ed.). New York: McGraw-Hill.

Hough, L. M., & Oswald, F. L. (2000). Personnel selection: Looking toward the future—remembering the past. *Annual Review of Psychology, 51,* 631–664.

Houk, J. C., Buckingham, J. T., & Barto, A. G. (1996). Models of the cerebellum and motor learning. *Behavioral and Brain Sciences, 19,* 368–383.

House, J. S., Landis, K. R., & Umberson, D. (1988). Social relationships and health. *Science, 241,* 540–545.

Hovland, C. I., & Sears, R. R. (1940). Minor studies in aggression: VI. Correlation of lynchings with economic indices. *Journal of Psychology, 9,* 301–310.

Howard, I. P. (1986). The perception of posture, self-motion, and the visual vertical. In K. R. Boff, L. Kaufman, & J. P. Thomas (Eds.), *Handbook of perception and human performance* (Vol. 1). New York: Wiley.

Howard, K. I., Cornille, T. A., Lyons, J. S., Vessey, J. T., Lueger, R. J., & Saunders, S. M. (1996). Patterns of mental health service utilization. *Archives of General Psychiatry, 53,* 696–703.

Howard, K. I., Kopta, S. M., Krause, M. S., & Orlinsky, D. E. (1986). The dose-effect relationship in psychotherapy. *American Psychologist, 41,* 159–164.

Howard, K. I., Moras, K., Brill, P. L., Martinovich, Z., & Lutz, W. (1996). Evaluation of psychotherapy: Efficacy, effectiveness, and patient progress. *American Psychologist, 51,* 1059–1064.

Howe, M. L., & Courage, M. L. (1993). On resolving the enigma of infantile amnesia. *Psychological Bulletin, 113,* 305–326.

Howes, J. L., & Katz, A. N. (1988). Assessing remote memory with an improved public events questionnaire. *Psychology and Aging, 3,* 142–150.

Hoyer, W. J., Rybash, J. M., & Roodin, P. A. (1999). *Adult development and aging* (4th ed.). New York: McGraw-Hill.

Hrobjartsson, A., & Gotzsche, P. C. (2001). Is the placebo powerless?: An analysis of clinical trials comparing placebo with no treatment. *The New England Journal of Medicine, 344,* 1594–1602.

Hubel, D. H. (1979). The brain. *Scientific American.*

Hubel, D. H. (1996). A big step along the visual pathway. *Nature, 380,* 197–198.

Hubel, D. H., & Wiesel, T. N. (1962). Receptive fields, binocular interaction and functional architecture in the cat's visual cortex. *Journal of Physiology, 160,* 106–154.

Hubel, D. H., & Wiesel, T. N. (1979). Brain mechanisms of vision. *Scientific American, 241,* 150–162.

Hudson, W. (1960). Pictorial depth perception in subcultural groups in Africa. *Journal of Social Psychology, 52,* 183–208.

Hudspeth, A. J. (2000). Hearing. In E. R. Kandel, J. H. Schwartz, & T. M. Jessell (Eds.), *Principles of neural science* (4th ed., pp. 590–613). New York: McGraw-Hill.

Huesmann, L. R., & Eron, L. D. (Eds.). (1986). *Television and the aggressive child: A cross-national comparison.* Hillsdale, NJ: Erlbaum.

Hugdahl, K., Satz, P., Mitrushina, M., & Miller, E. N. (1993). Left-handedness and old age: Do left-handers die earlier? *Neuropsychologia, 31,* 325–333.

Hull, C. L. (1943). *Principles of behavior.* New York: Appleton-Century-Crofts.

Hull, J. G., & Young, R. D. (1983). Self-consciousness, self-esteem, and success-failure as determinants of alcohol consumption in male social drinkers. *Journal of Personality and Social Psychology, 44,* 1097–1109.

Hull, J. G., Young, R. D., & Jouriles, E. (1986). Applications of the self-awareness model of alcohol consumption: Predicting patterns of use and abuse. *Journal of Personality and Social Psychology, 51,* 790–796.

Hulshoff, P., et al. (2002). Volume changes in gray matter in patients with schizophrenia. *American Journal of Psychiatry, 159,* 244–250.

Humphries, S. A., Johnson, M. H., & Long, N. R. (1996). An investigation of the gate control theory of pain using the experimental pain stimulus of potassium iontophoresis. *Perception and Psychophysics, 58,* 693–703.

Hunsley, J., & Bailey, J. M. (2001). Wither the Rorschach? An analysis of the evidence. *Psychological Assessment, 13,* 472–485.

Hunt, E. (1983). On the nature of intelligence. *Science, 219,* 141–146.

Hunt, E., & Agnoli, F. (1991). The Whorfian hypothesis: A cognitive psychology perspective. *Psychological Review, 9,* 377–389.

Hunt, M. (1997). *How science takes stock: The story of meta-analysis.* New York: Russell Sage Foundation.

Hunter, S., & Sundel, M. (Eds.). (1989). *Midlife myths: Issues, findings, and practice implications.* Newbury Park, CA: Sage.

Hupka, R. B., Lenton, A. P., & Hutchison, K. A. (1999). Universal development of emotion categories in natural language. *Journal of Personality and Social Psychology, 77,* 247–278.

Hur, Y. M., & Bouchard, T. J., Jr. (1995). Genetic influences on perceptions of childhood family environment: A reared apart twin study. *Child Development, 66,* 330–345.

Hurt, H. T., Scott, M. D., & McCroskey, J. C. (1978). *Communication in the classroom.* Reading, MA: Addison-Wesley.

Hurtz, G. M., & Donovan, J. J. (2000). Personality and job performance: The Big Five revisited. *Journal of Applied Psychology, 85,* 869–879.

Huttenlocher, J., Levine, S., & Vevea, J. (1998). Environmental input and cognitive growth: A study using time-period comparisons. *Child Development, 69,* 1012–1029.

Huttenlocher, P. R. (2002). *Neural plasticity: The effects of environment on the development of the cerebral cortex.* Cambridge, MA: Harvard University Press.

Huxley, A. (1932). *Brave new world.* London: Chatto & Windus.

Hyde, J. S., Fennema, E., & Lamon, S. (1990). Gender differences in mathematics performance: A meta-analysis. *Psychological Bulletin, 107,* 139–155.

Hyde, J. S., & Linn, M. C. (1988). Gender differences in verbal ability: A meta-analysis. *Psychological Bulletin, 104,* 53–69.

Hyman, I., Husband, T., & Billings, F. (1995). False memories of childhood experiences. *Applied Cognitive Psychology, 9,* 181–198.

Hyman, I. E., & Billings, F. J. (1998). Individual differences and the creation of false childhood memories. *Memory, 6,* 1–20.

Hyman, R. (1989). *The elusive quarry: A scientific appraisal of psychical research.* Buffalo, NY: Prometheus Books.

Hyman, R. (1994). Anomaly or artifact? Comments on Bem and Honorton. *Psychological Bulletin, 115,* 19–24.

Hyman, S. E. (2000). The NIMH perspective: Next steps in schizophrenia research. *Biological Psychiatry, 47,* 1–7.

Iaccino, J. F. (1993). *Left brain–right brain differences: Inquiries, evidence, and new approaches.* Hillsdale, NJ: Erlbaum.

Iacono, W. G., & Lykken, D. T. (1997). The validity of the lie detector: Two surveys of scientific opinion. *Journal of Applied Psychology, 82,* 426–433.

Ingham, A. G., Levinger, G., Graves, J., & Peckham, V. (1974). The Ringelmann effect: Studies of group size and group performance. *Journal of Experimental Social Psychology, 10,* 371–384.

Inglehart, R. (1990). *Culture shift in advanced industrial society.* Princeton, NJ: Princeton University Press.

Ingram, R. E. (1990). Self-focused attention in clinical disorders: Review and a conceptual model. *Psychological Bulletin, 107,* 156–176.

Inhelder, B., & Piaget, J. (1958). *The growth of logical thinking from childhood to adolescence.* New York: Basic Books.

Insel, T. R. (Ed.). (1984). *New findings in obsessive-compulsive disorder.* Washington, DC: American Psychiatric Press.

Intons-Peterson, M. (1993). Imaginal priming. *Journal of Experimental Psychology: Learning, Memory, and Cognition, 19,* 223–235.

Intons-Peterson, M. J., Rocchi, P., West, T., McLellan, K., & Hackney, A. (1999). Age, testing at preferred or nonpreferred times (testing optimality), and false memory. *Journal of Experimental Psychology: Learning, Memory, & Cognition, 25,* 23–40.

Intraub, H., Bender, R. S., & Mangels, J. A. (1992). Looking at pictures but remembering scenes. *Journal of Experimental Psychology: Learning, Memory, and Cognition, 18,* 180–191.

Intraub, H., Gottesman, C. V., & Bills, A. J. (1998). Effects of perceiving and imagining scenes on memory for pictures. *Journal of Experimental Psychology: Learning, Memory, and Cognition, 24,* 186–201.

Ironson, G., et al. (1997). Posttraumatic stress symptoms, intrusive thoughts, loss, and immune function after Hurricane Andrew. *Psychosomatic Medicine, 59,* 128–141.

Irwin, M., Mascovich, S., Gillin, J. C., Willoughby, R., Pike, J., & Smith, T. L. (1994). Partial sleep deprivation reduces natural killer cell activity in humans. *Psychosomatic Medicine, 56,* 493–498.

Isaacson, W. (1997, January 13). In search of the real Bill Gates. *Time,* pp. 45–57.

Isabella, R. A., & Belsky, J. (1991). Interactional synchrony and the origins of infant-mother attachment: A replication study. *Child Development, 62,* 373–384.

Isen, A. M. (1987). Positive affect, cognitive processes, and social behavior. In L. Berkowitz (Ed.), *Advances in experimental social psychology* (Vol. 20, pp. 203–253). New York: Academic Press.

Ito, T. A., Miller, N., & Pollock, V. E. (1996). Alcohol and aggression: A meta-analysis on the moderating effects of inhibitory cues, triggering events, and self-focused attention. *Psychological Bulletin, 120*, 60–82.

Iverson, L. (2000). *The science of marijuana.* New York: Oxford University Press.

Izard, C. E. (1990). Facial expressions and the regulation of emotions. *Journal of Personality and Social Psychology, 58*, 487–498.

Izard, C. E. (1993). Four systems for emotion activation: Cognitive and noncognitive processes. *Psychological Review, 100*, 68–90.

Izard, C. E., Fatauzzo, C. A., Castle, J. M., Haynes, O. M., Rayias, M. F., & Putnam, P. H. (1995). The ontogeny and significance of infants' facial expressions in the first 9 months of life. *Developmental Psychology, 31*, 997–1013.

Izard, C. E., Huebner, R., Risser, D., McGinnes, G., & Dougherty, L. (1980). The young infant's ability to produce discrete emotion expressions. *Developmental Psychology, 16*, 132–140.

Jacklin, C. N. (1989). Female and male: Issues of gender. *American Psychologist, 44*, 127–133.

Jackson, H. J. (1958). In J. Taylor (Ed.), *Selected writings of John Hughlings Jackson.* New York: Basic Books.

Jackson, S. A., & Csikzentmihalyi, M. (1999). *Flow in sports.* Champaign, IL: Human Kinetics.

Jacobs, B., Schall, M., Scheibel, A. B. (1993). A quantitative dendritic analysis of Wernicke's area. II. Gender, hemispheric, and environmental factors. *Journal of Comparative Neurology, 237*, 97–111.

Jacobs, G. H. (1993). The distribution and nature of colour vision among the mammals. *Biological Review, 68*, 413–471.

Jacobs, J. E. (1991). Influence of gender stereotypes on parent and child mathematics attitudes. *Journal of Educational Psychology, 83*, 518–527.

Jacobs, M. K., Christensen, A., Snibbe, J. R., Dolezal-Wood, S., Huber, A., & Polterok, A. (2001). A comparison of computer-based versus traditional individual psychotherapy. *Professional Psychology: Research and Practice, 32*, 92–96.

Jacobs, T. (1999). On the question of self-disclosure by the analyst: Error or advance in technique? *Psychoanalytic Quarterly, 68*, 159–183.

Jacobson, J. L., & Jacobson, S. W. (1996). Methodological considerations in behavioral toxicology in infants and children. *Developmental Psychology, 32*, 390–403.

Jacobson, N. S., & Christensen, A. (1996). Studying the effectiveness of psychotherapy: How well can clinical trials do the job? *American Psychologist, 51*, 1031–1039.

Jacobson, N. S., & Hollon, S. D. (1996). Cognitive-behavior therapy versus pharmacotherapy: Now that the jury's returned its verdict, it's time to present the rest of the evidence. *Journal of Consulting and Clinical Psychology, 64*, 74–80.

Jacobson, S. W., Jacobson, J. L., Sokol, R. J., Martier, S. S., & Ager, J. W. (1993). Prenatal alcohol exposure and infant information processing ability. *Child Development, 64*, 1706–1721.

Jacoby, L. L., Kelley, C. M., Brown, J., & Jasechko, J. (1989). Becoming famous overnight: Limits on the ability to avoid unconscious influences of the past. *Journal of Personality and Social Psychology, 56*, 326–338.

Jacoby, L. L., Toth, J. P., & Yonelinas, A. P. (1993). Separating conscious and unconscious influences on memory: Measuring recollection. *Journal of Experimental Psychology: General, 122*, 139–154.

Jacowitz, K. E., & Kahneman, D. (1995). Measures of anchoring in estimation tasks. *Personality and Social Psychology Bulletin, 21*, 1161–1166.

Jakicic, J. M., Winters, C., Lang, W., & Wing, R. R. (1999). Effects of intermittent exercise and use of home exercise equipment on adherence, weight loss, and fitness in overweight women. *Journal of the American Medical Association, 282*, 1554–1560.

James, B., Dewan, J., Munro, N., & Zminda, D. (1998). *Bill James presents STATS: All-time baseball sourcebook.* Morton Grove, IL: STATS, Inc.

James, W. (1884). What is an emotion? *Mind, 9*, 188–205.

James, W. (1890). *Principles of psychology* (Vols. 1–2). New York: Holt.

Jamison, C., & Scogin, F. (1995). The outcome of cognitive bibliotherapy with adults. *Journal of Consulting and Clinical Psychology, 63*, 644–650.

Jamison, K. R. (1993). *Touched with fire: Manic-depressive illness and the artistic temperament.* New York: Free Press.

Jamison, K. R. (1999). *Night falls fast: Understanding suicide.* New York: Knopf.

Janis, I. L. (1972). *Groupthink.* Boston: Houghton Mifflin.

Janis, I. L. (1989). *Crucial decisions: Leadership in policy-making and crisis management.* New York: Free Press.

Janoff-Bulman, R. (1989). The benefits of illusions, the threat of disillusionment, and the limitations of inaccuracy. *Journal of Social and Clinical Psychology, 8*, 158–175.

Jansari, A., & Parkin, A. J. (1996). Things that go bump in your life: Explaining the reminiscence bump in autobiographical memory. *Psychology and Aging, 11*, 85–91.

Jaroff, L. (1993, November). Lies of the mind. *Time*, pp. 52–59.

Jemmott, J. B., III, & Magloire, K. (1988). Academic stress, social support, and secretary immunoglobin. *Journal of Personality and Social Psychology, 55*, 803–810.

Jenicke, M. A., Baer, L., & Minichiello, W. E. (1986). *Obsessive-compulsive disorders: Theory and management.* Littleton, MA: PSG.

Jenkins, G. D., Jr., Mitra, A., Gupta, N., & Shaw, J. D. (1998). Are financial incentives related to performance? A meta-analytic review of empirical research. *Journal of Applied Psychology, 83*, 777–787.

Jenkins, J. G., & Dallenbach, K. M. (1924). Oblivescence during sleep and waking. *American Journal of Psychology, 35*, 605–612.

Jenkins, S. R. (1994). Need for power and women's careers over 14 years: Structural power, job satisfaction, and motive change. *Journal of Personality and Social Psychology, 66*, 155–165.

Jennings (Walstedt), J., Geis, F. L., & Brown, V. (1980). Influence of television commercials on women's self-confidence and independent judgment. *Journal of Personality and Social Psychology, 38*, 203–210.

Jensen, A. R. (1969). How much can we boost IQ and scholastic achievement? *Harvard Educational Review, 39*, 1–123.

Jensen, A. R. (1980). *Bias in mental testing.* New York: Free Press.

Jensen, A. R. (1998). *The g factor: The science of mental ability.* Westport, CT: Praeger.

Jessell, T. M., & Kelly, D. D. (1991). Pain and analgesia. In E. R. Kandel, J. H. Schwartz, & T. M. Jessell (Eds.), *Principles of neural science* (3rd ed., pp. 385–399). New York: Elsevier.

Jessor, R. (Ed.). (1998). *New perspectives on adolescent risk behavior.* New York: Cambridge University Press.

Jockin, V., McGue, M., & Lykken, D. T. (1996). Personality and divorce: A genetic analysis. *Journal of Personality and Social Psychology, 71*, 288–299.

John, O. P. (1990). The "Big Five" factor taxonomy: Dimensions of personality in the natural language and in questionnaires. In L. A. Pervin (Ed.), *Handbook of personality theory and research* (pp. 66–100). New York: Guilford Press.

Johnson, B. T., & Eagly, A. H. (1989). Effects of involvement on persuasion: A meta-analysis. *Psychological Bulletin, 106*, 290–314.

Johnson, D. (1990). Animal rights and human lives: Time for scientists to right the balance. *Psychological Science, 1*, 213–214.

Johnson, D. L., Wiebe, J. S., Gold, S. M., Andreasen, N. C., Hichwa, R. D., Watkins, G. L., & Ponto, L. L. B. (1999). Cerebral blood flow and personality: A positron emission tomography study. *American Journal of Psychiatry, 156*, 252–257.

Johnson, G. (1995, June 6). Chimp talk debate: Is it really language? *The New York Times*, p. C1.

Johnson, H. M., & Seifert, C. M. (1998). Updating accounts following a correction of misinformation. *Journal of Experimental Psychology: Learning, Memory, and Cognition, 24*, 1483–1494.

Johnson, J. E., Christie, J. F., & Yawkey, T. D. (1987). *Play and early childhood development.* Glenview, IL: Scott, Foresman.

Johnson, J. S., & Newport, E. L. (1989). Critical period effects in second language learning: The influence of maturational state on the acquisition of English as a second language. *Cognitive Psychology, 21*, 60–99.

Johnson, M. H., Dziurawiec, S., Ellis, H. D., & Morton, J. (1991). Newborns' preferential tracking of faces and its subsequent decline. *Cognition, 40*, 1–19.

Johnson, M. K., Hashtroudi, S., & Lindsay, D. S. (1993). Source monitoring. *Psychological Bulletin, 114*, 3–28.

Johnson, R. C., McClearn, G. E., Yuen, S., Nagoshi, C. T., Ahern, F. M., & Cole, R. E. (1985). Galton's data a century later. *American Psychologist, 40*, 875–892.

Johnson, W. O. (1991). How far have we come? *Sports Illustrated, 75*(6), 39–47.

Johnson-Laird, P. N. (1983). *Mental models.* Cambridge, MA: Harvard University Press.

Johnson-Laird, P. N. (1999). Deductive reasoning. *Annual Review of Psychology, 50*, 109–135.

Johnson-Laird, P. N. (2001). Mental models and deduction. *Trends in Cognitive Science, 5*, 434–442.

Joiner, T., & Coyne, J. C. (Eds.). (1999). *The interactional nature of depression.* Washington, DC: American Psychological Association.

Jones, E. (1953). *The life and work of Sigmund Freud.* New York: Basic Books.

Jones, E. E. (1990). *Interpersonal perception.* New York: W. H. Freeman.

Jones, E. E., & Harris, V. A. (1967). The attribution of attitudes. *Journal of Experimental Social Psychology, 3*, 1–24.

Jones, E. E., & Pulos, S. M. (1993). Comparing the process in psychodynamic and cognitive-behavioral therapies. *Journal of Consulting and Clinical Psychology, 61*, 306–316.

Jones, J. H. (1997). *A public/private life.* New York: Norton.

Jones, J. L. (Ed.). (1991). *Black psychology* (3rd ed.). Berkeley, CA: Cobb & Henry.

Jones, K. L., Smith, D. W., Ulleland, C. N., & Streissguth, A. P. (1973). Patterns of malformation in the offspring of chronic alcoholic mothers. *Lancet, 1*, 1267–1271.

Jones, L. V. (1984). White black achievement differences: The narrowing gap. *American Psychologist, 39*, 1207–1213.

Jones, M. C. (1924). A laboratory study of fear: The case of Peter. *Journal of Genetic Psychology, 31*, 308–315.

Jones, M. C. (1957). The late careers of boys who were early- or late-maturers. *Child Development, 28*, 115–128.

Jones, T. F., et al. (2000). Mass psychogenic illness attributed to toxic exposure at a high school. *The New England Journal of Medicine, 342*, 96–100.

Josephs, R. A., Markus, H. R., & Tafarodi, R. W. (1992). Gender and self-esteem. *Journal of Personality and Social Psychology, 63*, 391–402.

Jourard, S. M. (1971). *Self-disclosure: An experimental analysis of the transparent self.* New York: Wiley.

Judd, C. M., & Park, B. (1993). Definition and assessment of accuracy in social stereotypes. *Psychological Review, 100*, 109–128.

Judge, T. A., & Bono, J. E. (2000). Five-factor model of personality and transformational leadership. *Journal of Applied Psychology, 85*, 751–765.

Judge, T. A., & Welbourne, T. M. (1994). A confirmatory investigation of the dimensionality of the pay satisfaction questionnaire. *Journal of Applied Psychology, 79*, 461–466.

Judice, T. N., & Neuberg, S. L. (1998). When interviewers desire to confirm negative expectations: Self-fulfilling prophecies and inflated applicant self-perceptions. *Basic and Applied Social Psychology, 20*, 175–190.

Julien, R. M. (1992). *A primer of drug action* (6th ed.). New York: W. H. Freeman.

Jung, C. G. (1928). *Contributions to analytical psychology.* New York: Harcourt Brace.

Jussim, L., Eccles, J., & Madon, S. (1996). Social perception, social stereotypes, and teacher expectations: The quest for the powerful self-fulfilling prophecy. *Advances in Experimental Social Psychology, 28*, 281–387.

Kagan, J. (1976). Emergent themes in human development. *American Scientist, 64*, 186–196.

Kagan, J. (1984). *The nature of the child.* New York: Basic Books.

Kagan, J. (1994). *Galen's prophecy: Temperament in human nature.* New York: Basic Books.

Kagan, J., Reznick, J. S., & Snidman, N. (1990). Biological bases of childhood shyness. *Science, 240*, 167–171.

Kagan, J., Snidman, N., & Arcus, D. M. (1992). Initial reactions to unfamiliarity. *Current Directions in Psychological Science, 1*, 171–174.

Kahn, M. (1991). *Between therapist and client: The new relationship*. New York: W. H. Freeman.

Kahneman, D., Diener, E., & Schwarz, N. (Eds.). (1999). *Well-being: The foundations of hedonic psychology.* New York: Russell Sage Foundation.

Kahneman, D., & Miller, D. T. (1986). Norm theory: Comparing reality to its alternatives. *Psychological Review, 93,* 136–153.

Kahneman, D., Slovic, P., & Tversky, A. (Eds.). (1982). *Judgment under uncertainty: Heuristics and biases.* New York: Cambridge University Press.

Kahneman, D., & Tversky, A. (1972). Subjective probability: A judgement of representativeness. *Cognitive Psychology, 3,* 430–454.

Kahneman, D., & Tversky, A. (1973). On the psychology of prediction. *Psychological Review, 80,* 237–251.

Kahneman, D., & Tversky, A. (1984). Choices, values, and frames. *American Psychologist, 39,* 341–350.

Kahneman, D., & Tversky, A. (1996). On the reality of cognitive illusions. *Psychological Review, 103,* 582–591.

Kail, R. (1990). *The development of memory in children* (3rd ed.). New York: W. H. Freeman.

Kail, R. (1991). Developmental changes in speed of processing during childhood and adolescence. *Psychological Bulletin, 109,* 490–501.

Kail, R., & Bisanz, J. (1992). The information-processing perspective on cognitive development in childhood and adolescence. In R. J. Sternberg & C. A. Berg (Eds.), *Intellectual development.* New York: Cambridge University Press.

Kail, R., & Hall, L. K. (1994). Processing speed, naming speed, and reading. *Developmental Psychology, 30,* 949–954.

Kaiser, P. K., & Boynton, R. M. (1996). *Human color vision* (2nd ed.). Washington, DC: Optical Society of America.

Kako, E. (1999). Elements of syntax in the systems of three language-trained animals. *Animal Learning & Behavior, 27,* 1–14.

Kalakoski, V., & Saariluoma, P. (2001). Taxi drivers' exceptional memory of street names. *Memory & Cognition, 29,* 634–638.

Kalb, M. B. (2002). Does sex matter? The confluence of gender and transference in analytic space. *Psychoanalytic Psychology, 19,* 118–143.

Kalichman, S. C. (1998). *Understanding AIDS: Advances in research and treatment* (2nd ed.). Washington, DC: American Psychological Association.

Kalish, R. A. (1981). *Death, grief, and caring relationships.* Monterey, CA: Wadsworth.

Kamen-Siegel, L., Rodin, J., Seligman, M. E. P., & Dwyer, J. (1991). Explanatory style and cell-mediated immunity in elderly men and women. *Health Psychology, 10,* 229–235.

Kamin, L. J. (1974). *The science and politics of IQ.* New York: Wiley.

Kandel, E. R. (1979). Small systems of neurons. *Scientific American, 241,* 66–87.

Kandel, E. R. (1999). Biology and the future of psychoanalysis: A new intellectual framework for psychiatry revisited. *American Journal of Psychiatry, 156,* 505–524.

Kandel, E. R., Schwartz, J. H., & Jessell, T. M. (Eds.). (2000). *Principles of neural science* (4th ed.). New York: McGraw-Hill.

Kane, J. M., Honigfeld, G., Singer, J., Meltzer, H., & The Clozaril Collaborative Study Group. (1988). Clozapine for the treatment-resistant schizophrenic. *Archives of General Psychiatry, 45,* 789–796.

Kanner, A. D., Coyne, J. C., Schaefer, C., & Lazarus, R. S. (1981). Comparison of two modes of stress measurement: Daily hassles and uplifts versus major life events. *Journal of Behavioral Medicine, 4,* 1–39.

Kanner, A. D., Feldman, S. S., Weinberger, D. A., & Ford, M. F. (1991). Uplifts, hassles, and adaptational outcomes in early adolescents. In A. Monat & R. S. Lazarus (Eds.), *Stress and coping: An anthology* (pp. 158–181). New York: Columbia University Press.

Kaplan, R. M. (1985). The controversy related to the use of psychological tests. In B. B. Wolman (Ed.), *Handbook of intelligence: Theories, measurements, and applications* (pp. 465–504). New York: Wiley.

Kaplowitz, P. B., Slora, E. J., Wasserman, R. C., Pedlow, S. E., & Herman-Giddens, M. E. (2000). Earlier onset of puberty in girls: Relation to increased body mass index and race. *Pediatrics, 108,* 347–353.

Karau, S. J., & Williams, K. D. (1993). Social loafing: A meta-analytic review and theoretical integration. *Journal of Personality and Social Psychology, 65,* 681–706.

Karl, A., Birbaumer, N., Lutzenberger, W., Cohen, L., & Flor, H. (2001). Reorganization of motor and somatosensory cortex in upper extremity amputees with phantom limb pain. *Journal of Neuroscience, 21,* 3609–3618.

Karni, A., & Ungerleider, L. (1996). Comorbidity and treatment implications. *Journal of Consulting and Clinical Psychology, 60,* 833–834.

Kashima, Y., & Kerekes, A. R. Z. (1994). A distributed memory model of averaging phenomena in person impression formation. *Journal of Experimental Social Psychology, 30,* 407–455.

Kasier, P. K., & Boynton, R. M. (1996). *Human color vision.* Washington, DC: Optical Society of America.

Kasper, S., & Rosenthal, N. E. (1989). Anxiety and depression in seasonal affective disorders. In P. Kendall & D. Watson (Eds.), *Anxiety and depression: Distinct and overlapping features* (pp. 341–375). San Diego: Academic Press.

Kassin, S. M. (1997). The psychology of confession evidence. *American Psychologist, 52,* 221–233.

Kassin, S. M., Goldstein, C. J., & Savitsky, K. (2002). *Behavioral confirmation in the interrogation room: On the dangers of presuming guilt.* Unpublished manuscript.

Kassin, S. M., & Sommers, S. R. (1997). Inadmissible testimony, instructions to disregard, and the jury: Substantive versus procedural considerations. *Personality and Social Psychology Bulletin, 23,* 1046–1054.

Kassinove, J. I., & Schare, M. L. (2001). Effects of the "near miss" and the "big win" on persistence at slot machine gambling. *Psychology of Addictive Behaviors, 15,* 155–158.

Katz, D., & Braly, K. (1933). Racial stereotypes of 100 college students. *Journal of Abnormal and Social Psychology, 28,* 280–290.

Kaufman, A. S. (2001). WAIS-III IQs, Horn's theory, and generational changes from young adulthood to old age. *Intelligence, 29,* 131–167.

Kaufman, A. S., & Lichtenberger, E. O. (1999). *Essentials of WAIS-III Assessment.* New York: Wiley.

Kaufman, D. Q., Stasson, M. F., & Hart, J. W. (1999). Are the tabloids always wrong or is that just what we think? Need for cognition and perceptions of articles in print media. *Journal of Applied Social Psychology, 29,* 1984–1997.

Kaufman, L., & Rock, I. (1962). The moon illusion. (Vol. I). *Science, 136,* 953–961.

Kavanaugh, R. D., Eizenman, D. R., & Harris, P. L. (1997). Young children's understanding of pretense expressions of independent agency. *Developmental Psychology, 33,* 764–770.

Kawakami, K., Dovidio, J. F., Moll, J., Hermsen, S., & Nijmegen, A. R. (2000). Just say no (to stereotyping): Effects of training in the negation of stereotypic associations on stereotype activation. *Journal of Personality and Social Psychology, 78,* 871–888.

Kazdin, A. E. (1982). The token economy: A decade later. *Journal of Applied Behavior Analysis, 15,* 431–445.

Kazdin, A. E. (2001). *Behavior modification in applied settings* (6th ed.). Belmont, CA: Wadsworth.

Kecklund, G., & Akerstedt, T. (1993). Sleepiness in long distance truck driving: An ambulatory EEG study of night driving. *Ergonomics, 36,* 1007–1017.

Keesey, R. E. (1995). A set-point model of weight regulation. In K. D. Brownell & C. G. Fairburn (Eds.), *Eating disorders and obesity* (pp. 46–50). New York: Guilford Press.

Keith, J. R., & McVety, K. M. (1988). Latent place learning in a novel environment and the influences of prior training in rats. *Psychobiology, 16,* 146–151.

Keller, P. A. (1999). Converting the unconverted: The effect of inclination and opportunity to discount health-related fear appeals. *Journal of Applied Psychology, 84,* 403–415.

Kelley, H. H. (1967). Attribution theory in social psychology. In D. Levine (Ed.), *Nebraska symposium on motivation* (Vol. 15, pp. 192–241). Lincoln, NE: University of Nebraska Press.

Kellman, P. J., & Arterberry, M. E. (1998). *The cradle of knowledge: Development of perception in infancy.* Cambridge, MA: MIT Press.

Kellner, R. (1987). Hypochondriasis and somatization. *Journal of the American Medical Association, 258,* 2718–2722.

Kellogg, W. N., & Kellogg, L. A. (1933). *The ape and the child.* New York: McGraw-Hill.

Kelly, A. E., & McKillop, K. J. (1996). Consequences of revealing personal secrets. *Psychological Bulletin, 120,* 450–465.

Kelman, H. C., & Hamilton, V. L. (1989). *Crimes of obedience: Toward a social psychology of authority and responsibility.* New Haven, CT: Yale University Press.

Kempermann, G., & Gage, F. H. (May, 1999). New nerve cells for the adult brain. *Scientific American,* pp. 48–53.

Kendall, P. C., & Chambless, D. L. (Eds.). (1998). Empirically supported psychological therapies. *Journal of Consulting and Clinical Psychology, 66,* 3–167 (special issue).

Kendall, P. C., & Clarkin, J. F. (1992). Introduction to special section: Comorbidity and treatment implications. *Journal of Consulting and Clinical Psychology, 60,* 833–834.

Kendler, K. S., MacLean, C., Neale, M., Kessler, R., Heath, A., & Eaves, L. (1991). The genetic epidemiology of bulimia nervosa. *American Journal of Psychiatry, 148,* 1627–1637.

Kendler, K. S., Neale, M. C., Kessler, R. C., Heath, A. C., & Eaves, L. J. (1993). The lifetime history of major depression in women. Reliability of diagnosis and heritability. *Archives of General Psychiatry, 50,* 863–870.

Kenealy, P. M. (1997). Mood-state-dependent retrieval: The effects of induced mood on memory reconsidered. *Quarterly Journal of Experimental Psychology: Human Experimental Psychology, 50,* 290–317.

Kenrick, D. T. (1994). Evolutionary social psychology: From sexual selection to social cognition. *Advances in Experimental Social Psychology, 26,* 75–121.

Kenrick, D. T., Gabrielidis, C., Keefe, R. C., & Cornelius, J. S. (1996). Adolescents' age preferences for dating partners: Support for an evolutionary model of life-history strategies. *Child Development, 67,* 1499–1511.

Kenrick, D. T., Gutierres, S. E., & Goldberg, L. L. (1989). Influence of popular erotica on judgments of strangers and mates. *Journal of Experimental Social Psychology, 25,* 159–167.

Kenrick, D. T., & Keefe, R. C. (1992). Age preferences in mates reflect sex differences in human reproductive strategies. *Behavioral and Brain Sciences, 15,* 75–91.

Kenrick, D. T., & MacFarlane, S. W. (1984). Ambient temperature and horn-honking: A field study of the heat/aggression relationship. *Environment and Behavior, 18,* 179–191.

Keogh, E., & Herdenfeldt, M. (2002). Gender, coping, and the perception of pain. *Pain, 97,* 195–201.

Kerkhof, G. A. (1985). Inter-individual differences in the human circadian system: A review. *Biological Psychology, 20,* 83–112.

Kernis, M. H., & Waschull, S. B. (1995). The interactive roles of stability and level of self-esteem: Research and theory. *Advances in Experimental Social Psychology, 27,* 93–141.

Kerns, J. G., & Berenbaum, H. (2002). Cognitive impairments associated with formal thought disorder in people with schizophrenia. *Journal of Abnormal Psychology, 111,* 211–224.

Kerr, N. L., Kramer, G. P., Carroll, J. S., & Alfini, J. J. (1991). On the effectiveness of voir dire in criminal cases with prejudicial pretrial publicity: An empirical study. *The American University Law Review, 40,* 665–701.

Kerwin, M. L. E., & Day, J. D. (1985). Peer influences on cognitive development. In J. Pryor & J. Day (Eds.), *The development of social cognition* (pp. 211–228). New York: Springer-Verlag.

Kessler, R. C., Foster, C., Webster, P. S., & House, J. S. (1992). The relationship between age and depressive symptoms in two national surveys. *Psychology and Aging, 7,* 117–126.

Kessler, R. C., McGonagle, K. A., Zhao, S., Nelson, C. B., Hughes, M., Eshleman, S., Wittchen, H. U., & Kendler, K. S. (1994). Lifetime and 12-month prevalence of DSM-III-R psychiatric disorders in the United States. *Archives of General Psychiatry, 51,* 8–19.

Kessler, R. C., Mickelson, K. D., & Zhao, S. (1997). Patterns and correlates of self-help group membership in the United States. *Social Policy, 27,* 27–46.

Kessler, R. C., Sonnega, A., Bromet, E., Hughes, M., & Nelson, C. B. (1995). Posttraumatic stress disorder in the National Comorbidity Survey. *Archives of General Psychiatry, 52,* 1048–1060.

Key, W. B. (1973). *Subliminal seduction.* Englewood Cliffs, NJ: Signet.

Key, W. B. (1989). *The age of manipulation.* New York: Holt.

Keysers, C., Xiao, D. K., Foldiak, P., & Perrett, D. I. (2001). The speed of sight. *Journal of Cognitive Neuroscience, 13,* 90–101.

Kiecolt-Glaser, J. K., Cacioppo, J. T., Malarkey, W. B., & Glaser, R. (1992). Acute psychological stressors and short-term immune changes: What, why, for whom, and to what extent? *Psychosomatic Medicine, 54,* 680–685.

Kiecolt-Glaser, J. K., & Glaser, R. (1992). Psychoneuroimmunology: Can psychological interventions modulate immunity? *Journal of Consulting and Clinical Psychology, 60,* 569–575.

Kiecolt-Glaser, J. K., & Glaser, R. (1993). Mind and immunity. In D. Goleman & J. Gurin (Eds.), *Mind body medicine* (pp. 39–61). Yonkers, NY: Consumer Reports Books.

Kiecolt-Glaser, J. K., Marucha, P. T., Atkinson, C., & Glaser, R. (2001). Hypnosis as a modulator of cellular immune dysregulation during acute stress. *Journal of Consulting and Clinical Psychology, 69,* 674–682.

Kiecolt-Glaser, J. K., McGuire, L., Robles, T. F., & Glaser, R. (2002). Emotions, morbidity, and mortality: New perspectives from psychoneuroimmunology. *Annual Review of Psychology, 53,* 83–107.

Kiecolt-Glaser, J. K., & Newton, T. L. (2001). Marriage and health: His and hers. *Psychological Bulletin, 127,* 472–503.

Kiewra, K. A., et al. (1991). Note-taking functions and techniques. *Journal of Educational Psychology, 83,* 240–245.

Kihlstrom, J. F. (1998). Dissociations and dissociation theory in hypnosis: Comment on Kirsch and Lynn (1998). *Psychological Bulletin, 123,* 186–191.

Kihlstrom, J. F., Barnhardt, T. M., & Tataryn, D. J. (1987). The psychological unconscious: Found, lost, and regained. *American Psychologist, 47,* 788–791.

Kihlstrom, J. F., Barnhardt, T. M., & Tataryn, D. J. (1992). The psychological unconscious: Found, lost, and regained. *American Psychologist, 47,* 788–791.

Kihlstrom, J. F., Schacter, D. L., Cork, R. C., Hurt, C. A., & Behr, S. E. (1990). Implicit and explicit memory following surgical anesthesia. *Psychological Science, 1,* 303–306.

Kilgour, A., & Lederman, S. J. (2002). Face recognition by hand. *Perception & Psychophysics, 64,* 339–352.

Kim, H., & Markus, H. R. (1999). Deviance or uniqueness, harmony or conformity? A cultural analysis. *Journal of Personality and Social Psychology, 77,* 785–800.

Kimball, M. M. (1989). A new perspective on women's math achievement. *Psychological Bulletin, 105,* 198–214.

Kimble, D. P. (1990). Functional effects of neural grafting in the mammalian central nervous system. *Psychological Bulletin, 108,* 462–479.

Kimble, D. P. (1992). *Biological psychology* (2nd ed.). Fort Worth, TX: Harcourt Brace Jovanovich.

Kimmel, A. J. (1991). Predictable biases in the ethical decision-making of American psychologists. *American Psychologist, 46,* 786–788.

Kimura, D. (1999). *Sex and cognition.* Cambridge, MA: MIT Press.

Kinnunen, T., Zamanksi, H. S., & Block, M. L. (1994). Is the hypnotized subject lying? *Journal of Abnormal Psychology, 103,* 184–191.

Kinsey, A. C., Pomeroy, W. B., & Martin, C. E. (1948). *Sexual behavior in the human male.* Philadelphia: W. B. Saunders.

Kinsey, A. C., Pomeroy, W. B., Martin, C. E., & Gebhard, P. H. (1953). *Sexual behavior in the human female.* Philadelphia: W. B. Saunders.

Kirby, K. N. (1997). Bidding on the future: Evidence against normative discounting of delayed rewards. *Journal of Experimental Psychology: General, 126,* 54–70.

Kirby, K. N., Petry, N. M., & Bickel, W. K. (1999). Heroin addicts have higher discount rates for delayed rewards than non-drug-using controls. *Journal of Experimental Psychology: General, 128,* 78–87.

Kirsch, I., Capafons, A., Cardena-Buelna, E., & Amigo, S. (1999). *Clinical hypnosis and self-regulation: Cognitive-behavioral perspectives.* Washington, DC: American Psychological Association.

Kirsch, I., & Lynn, S. J. (1995). Altered state of hypnosis: Changes in theoretical landscape. *American Psychologist, 50,* 846–858.

Kirsch, I., & Lynn, S. J. (1998). Dissociation theories of hypnosis. *Psychological Bulletin, 123,* 100–115.

Kirsch, I., & Lynn, S. J. (1999). Automaticity in clinical psychology. *American Psychologist, 54,* 504–515.

Kirsch, I., Montgomery, G., & Sapirstein, G. (1995). Hypnosis as an adjunct cognitive-behavioral psychotherapy: A meta-analysis. *Journal of Consulting and Clinical Psychology, 63,* 214–220.

Kirsner, D. (1990). Is there a future for American psychoanalysis? *Psychoanalytic Review, 77,* 175–200.

Kirsner, K., Speelman, C., Mayberry, M., O'Brien-Malone, A., Anderson, M., & MacLeod, C. (Eds.). (1998). *Implicit and explicit mental processes.* Mahwah, NJ: Erlbaum.

Kirwin, B. R. (1997). *The mad, the bad, and the innocent: The criminal mind on trial.* Boston: Little Brown.

Kitayama, S., & Markus, H. R. (Eds.). (1994). *Emotion and culture: Empirical studies of mutual influence.* Washington, DC: American Psychological Association.

Klare, M. T. (2001). *Resource wars: The new landscape of global conflict.* New York: Holt.

Klatsky, R. A., & Lederman, S. J. (1992). Stages of manual exploration in haptic object identification. *Perception and Psychophysics, 52,* 661–670.

Klauer, K. C., Musch, J., & Naumer, B. (2000). On belief bias in syllogistic reasoning. *Psychological Review, 107,* 852–884.

Klein, D. F. (1993). False suffocation alarms, spontaneous panics, and related conditions: An integrative hypothesis. *Archives of General Psychiatry, 50,* 306–317.

Klein, R., & Mannuzza, S. (1991). Long-term outcome of hyperactive children: A review. *Journal of the American Academy of Child and Adolescent Psychiatry, 30,* 383–387.

Klein, W. M., & Kunda, Z. (1992). Motivated person perception: Constructing justifications for desired beliefs. *Journal of Experimental Social Psychology, 28,* 135–168.

Kleiner, K. A. (1987). Amplitude and phase spectra as indices of infants' pattern preferences. *Infant Behavior and Development, 10,* 49–59.

Kleinke, C. L. (1986). Gaze and eye contact: A research review. *Psychological Bulletin, 100,* 78–100.

Kleinke, C. L., Peterson, T. R., & Rutledge, T. R. (1998). Effects of self-generated facial expressions on mood. *Journal of Personality and Social Psychology, 74,* 272–279.

Kleinmuntz, B., & Szucko, J. J. (1984). Lie detection in ancient and modern times. *American Psychologist, 39,* 766–776.

Kleitman, N. (1963). *Sleep and wakefulness.* Chicago: University of Chicago Press.

Klerman, G. L., & Weissman, M. M. (1989). Increasing rates of depression. *Journal of the American Medical Association, 261,* 2229–2235.

Kline, P. (1991). *Intelligence: The psychometric view.* New York: Routledge, Chapman & Hall.

Kling, K. C., Hyde, J. S., Showers, C. J., & Buswell, B. N. (1999). Gender differences in self-esteem: A meta-analysis. *Psychological Bulletin, 125,* 470–500.

Klivington, K. A. (Ed.). (1989). *The science of mind.* Cambridge, MA: MIT Press.

Kluegel, J. R. (1990). Trends in whites' explanations of the black-white gap in socioeconomic status, 1977–1989. *American Sociological Review, 55,* 512–525.

Kluft, R. P. (1996). Dissociative identity disorder. In L. K. Michelson & W. J. Ray (Eds.), *Handbook of dissociation: Theoretical, empirical, and clinical perspectives* (pp. 337–366). New York: Plenum.

Knapp, R. R. (1976). *Handbook for the Personal Orientation Inventory.* San Diego: Edits Publishers.

Knight, G. P., Fabes, R. A., & Higgins, D. A. (1996). Concerns about drawing causal inferences from meta-analyses: An example in the study of gender differences in aggression. *Psychological Bulletin, 119,* 410–421.

Knoblich, G., & Ohlsson, S. (1999). Constraint relaxation and chunk decomposition in insight problem solving. *Journal of Experimental Psychology: Learning, Memory, and Cognition, 25,* 1534–1556.

Knoedler, A. J., Hellwig, K. A., & Neath, I. (1999). The shift from recency to primacy with increasing delay. *Journal of Experimental Psychology: Learning, Memory, and Cognition, 25,* 474–487.

Kobasa, S. C. (1979). Stressful life events, personality, and health: An inquiry into hardiness. *Journal of Personality and Social Psychology, 37,* 1–11.

Koch, S. (Ed.). (1959). *Psychology: A study of a science* (Vol. 2). New York: McGraw-Hill.

Koch, S. (1993). "Psychology" or "the psychological studies"? *American Psychologist, 48,* 902–904.

Kodis, M., Moran, D. T., Houy, D., & Berliner, D. C. (1998). *Love scents: How your natural pheromones influence your relationships, your moods, and who you love.* New York: E. P. Dutton.

Koffka, K. (1935). *Principles of gestalt psychology.* New York: Harcourt, Brace & World.

Kohlberg, L. (1969). Stage and sequence: The cognitive-developmental approach to socialization. In D. A. Goslin (Ed.), *Handbook of socialization theory and research.* Chicago: Rand McNally.

Kohlberg, L. (1981). *Essays on moral development: Vol. 1. The philosophy of moral development.* New York: Harper & Row.

Kohlberg, L. (1984). *Essays on moral development: Vol. 2. The psychology of moral development.* New York: Harper & Row.

Kohler, W. (1925). *The mentality of apes.* London: Pelican.

Kohler, W. (1947). *Gestalt psychology.* New York: Liveright.

Kohn, A. (1993). *Punished by rewards.* Boston: Houghton Mifflin.

Kohn, P. M., Lafreniere, K., & Gurevich, M. (1990). The inventory of college students' recent life experiences: A decontaminated hassles scale for a special population. *Journal of Behavioral Medicine, 13,* 619–630.

Kohn, P. M., Lafreniere, K., & Gurevich, M. (1991). Hassles, health, and personality. *Journal of Personality and Social Psychology, 61,* 478–482.

Kolata, G. (2002, May 21). Runner's high? Endorphins? Fiction, some scientists say. *The New York Times, Science Times,* pp. 1, 6.

Kolb, B., & Whishaw, I. Q. (1990). *Fundamentals of human neuropsychology* (3rd ed.). New York: W. H. Freeman.

Kolb, B., & Whishaw, I. Q. (1998). Brain plasticity and behavior. *Annual Review of Psychology, 49,* 43–64.

Konishi, M. (1993). Listening with two ears. *Scientific American, 268,* 66–73.

Konrad, A. M., Ritchie, J. E., Lieb, P., & Corrigall, E. (2000). Sex differences and similarities in job attribute preferences: A meta-analysis. *Psychological Bulletin, 126,* 593–641.

Koocher, G. P., & Keith-Spiegel, P. (1998). *Ethics in psychology: Professional standards and cases* (2nd ed.). New York: Oxford University Press.

Kopelman, P. G., & Stock, M. J. (Eds.). (1998). *Clinical obesity.* Boston: Blackwell Science.

Kopta, S. M., Lueger, R. J., Saunders, S. M., & Howard, K. I. (1999). Individual psychotherapy outcome and process research: Challenges leading to greater turmoil or a positive transition? *Annual Review of Psychology, 50,* 441–469.

Korchmaros, J. D., & Kenney, D. A. (2001). Emotional closeness as a mediator of the effect of genetic relatedness on altruism. *Psychological Science, 12,* 262–265.

Koriat, A., Goldsmith, M., & Pansky, A. (2000). Toward a psychology of memory accuracy. *Annual Review of Psychology, 51,* 481–537.

Korn, J. H., Davis, R., & Davis, S. F. (1991). Historians' and chairpersons' judgments of eminence among psychologists. *American Psychologist, 46,* 789–792.

Kosonen, P., & Winne, P. (1995). Effects of teaching statistical laws of reasoning about everyday problems. *Journal of Educational Psychology, 87,* 33–46.

Kosslyn, S. M. (1980). *Image and mind.* Cambridge, MA: Harvard University Press.

Kosslyn, S. M. (1994). *Image and brain: The resolution of the imagery debate.* Cambridge, MA: MIT Press.

Kosslyn, S. M., Leone-Pascual, A., Felician, O., Camposano, S., Keenan, J. P., Thompson, W. L., Ganis, G., Sukel, K. E., & Alpert, N. M. (1999). The role of Area 17 in visual imagery: Convergent evidence from PET and rTMS. *Science, 284,* 167–170.

Kotovsky, K., Hayes, J. R., & Simon, H. A. (1985). Why are some problems hard? Evidence from Tower of Hanoi. *Cognitive Psychology, 17,* 248–294.

Kotre, J. (1995). *White gloves: How we create ourselves through memory*. New York: Free Press.

Kotre, J., & Hall, E. (1990). *Seasons of life*. Boston: Little, Brown.

Koutsaal, W., Schacter, D. L., Johnson, M. K., & Gallucio, L. (1999). Facilitation and impairment of event memory produced by photographic review. *Memory & Cognition, 27,* 478–493.

Kovecses, Z. (1990). *Emotion concepts*. New York: Springer-Verlag.

Kovera, M. B. (2002). The effects of general pretrial publicity on juror decisions: An examination of moderators and mediating mechanisms. *Law and Human Behavior, 26,* 43–72.

Kowalski, R. M. (1993). Inferring sexual interest from behavioral cues: Effects of gender and sexually relevant attitudes. *Sex Roles, 29,* 13–36.

Kozhevnikov, M., & Hegarty, M. (2001). Impetus beliefs as default heuristics: Dissociation between explicit and implicit knowledge about motion. *Psychonomic Bulletin and Review, 8,* 439–453.

Kraepelin, E. (1883). *Textbook of psychiatry*. New York: Macmillan. (Reprinted in 1923.)

Kramer, P. D. (1993). *Listening to Prozac*. New York: Viking.

Krampe, R. T., & Ericsson, K. A. (1996). Maintaining excellence: Deliberate practice and elite performance in young and older pianists. *Journal of Experimental Psychology: General, 125,* 331–359.

Krantz, D. S., & McCeney, M. K. (2002). Effects of psychological and social factors on organic disease: A critical assessment of research on coronary heart disease. *Annual Review of Psychology, 53,* 341–369.

Krasne, F. B., & Glanzman, D. L. (1995). What we can learn from invertebrate learning. *Annual Review of Psychology, 46,* 585–624.

Krebs, D. L., Denton, K. L., Vermeulen, S. C., Carpendale, J. I., & Bush, A. (1991). Structural flexibility in moral judgment. *Journal of Personality and Social Psychology, 61,* 1012–1023.

Kreitler, S., Weissler, K., Krietler, H., & Brunner, D. (1991). The relation of smoking to psychological and physiological risk factors for coronary heart disease. *Personality and Individual Differences, 12,* 487–495.

Kripke, D. F., Garfinkel, L., Wingard, D. L., Klauber, M. R., & Marler, M. R. (2002). Mortality associated with sleep duration and insomnia. *Archives of General Psychiatry, 59,* 131–136.

Kristof, N. D. (1993, July 21). Peasants of China discover new way to weed out girls. *The New York Times,* pp. A1, A6.

Krosnick, J. A. (1999). Survey research. *Annual Review of Psychology, 50,* 537–567.

Krug, E. G., Kresnow, M., Peddicord, J. P., Dahlberg, L. L., Powell, K. E., Crosby, A. E., & Annest, J. L. (1998). Suicide after natural disasters. *The New England Journal of Medicine, 338,* 373–378.

Kruger, J. & Dunning, D. (1999). Unskilled and unaware of it: How difficulties in recognizing one's own incompetence lead to inflated self-assessments. *Journal of Personality and Social Psychology, 77,* 1121–1134.

Kruger, L. (Ed.). (1996). *Pain and touch*. San Diego: Academic Press.

Krumhansl, C. L. (1991). Music psychology: Tonal structures in perception and memory. *Annual Review of Psychology, 42,* 277–303.

Kryter, K. D. (1994). *The handbook of hearing and the effects of noise*. San Diego: Academic Press.

Kubany, E. S., Leisen, M. B., Kaplan, A. S., Watson, S. B., Haynes, S. N., Owens, J. A., & Burns, K. (2000). Development and preliminary validation of a brief broad-spectrum measure of trauma exposure: The Traumatic Life Events Questionnaire. *Psychological Assessment, 12,* 210–224.

Kübler-Ross, E. (1969). *On death and dying*. New York: Macmillan.

Kubzansky, L. D., Sparrow, D., Vokonas, P., & Kawachi, I. (2001). Is the glass half empty or half full? A prospective study of optimism and coronary heart disease in the Normative Aging Study. *Psychosomatic Medicine, 63,* 910–916.

Küebli, J., & Fivush, R. (1992). Gender differences in parent-child conversations about past emotions. *Sex Roles, 27,* 683–698.

Kuffler, S. W. (1953). Discharge patterns and functional organization of mammalian retina. *Journal of Neurophysiology, 16,* 37–68.

Kuhn, D. (1991). *The skills of argument*. Cambridge, England: Cambridge University Press.

Kulik, J. A., Bangert-Drowns, R. L., & Kulik, C. (1984). Effectiveness of coaching for aptitude tests. *Psychological Bulletin, 95,* 179–188.

Kulik, J. A., & Mahler, H. I. M. (1989). Stress and affiliation in a hospital setting: Preoperative roommate preferences. *Personality and Social Psychology Bulletin, 15,* 183–193.

Kulik, J. A., Mahler, H. I. M., & Earnest, A. (1994). Social comparison and affiliation under threat: Going beyond the affiliate-choice paradigm. *Journal of Personality and Social Psychology, 66,* 301–309.

Kulik, J. A., Mahler, H. I. M., & Moore, P. J. (1996). Social comparison and affiliation under threat: Effects of recovery from major surgery. *Journal of Personality and Social Psychology, 71,* 967–979.

Kunda, Z. (1987). Motivated inference: Self-serving generation and evaluation of causal theories. *Journal of Personality and Social Psychology, 53,* 636–647.

Kunda, Z. (1990). Motivated reasoning. *Psychological Bulletin, 108,* 480–498.

Kuntz-Wilson, W., & Zajonc, R. B. (1980). Affective discrimination of stimuli that cannot be recognized. *Science, 207,* 557–558.

Kurasaki, K. S., Okazaki, S., & Sue, S. (Eds.). (2002). *Asian American mental health: Assessment, theories, and methods*. New York: Kluwer.

Kurdek, L. A. (1991). Sexuality in homosexual and heterosexual couples. In K. McKinney & S. Sprecher (Eds.), *Sexuality in close relationships* (pp. 177–191). Hillsdale, NJ: Erlbaum.

Kurtines, W. M., & Gewirtz, J. L. (Eds.). (1984). *Morality, moral behavior, and moral development*. New York: Wiley.

Kutchins, H., & Kirk, S. A. (1997). *Making us crazy: DSM, the psychiatric bible and the creation of mental disorders*. New York: Free Press.

LaBerge, S. P. (1992). *Physiological studies of lucid dreaming*. Hillsdale, NJ: Erlbaum.

Ladd, G. W. (1999). Peer relationships and social competence during early and middle childhood. *Annual Review of Psychology, 50,* 333–359.

LaFrance, M., & Banaji, M. (1992). Toward a reconsideration of the gender-emotion relationship. *Review of Personality and Social Psychology, 14,* 178–201.

LaFromboise, T., Coleman, H., & Gerton, J. (1993). Psychological impact of biculturalism: Evidence and theory. *Psychological Bulletin, 114,* 395–412.

Laird, J. D. (1974). Self-attribution of emotion: The effects of expressive behavior on the quality of emotional experience. *Journal of Personality and Social Psychology, 33,* 475–486.

Lal, S. K. L., & Craig, A. (2002). Driver fatigue: Electroenchephalography and psychological assessment. *Psychophysiology, 39,* 313–321.

Lalumiere, M., & Quinsey, V. (1998). Pavlovian conditioning of sexual interests in human males. *Archives of Sexual Behavior, 27,* 241–252.

Lam, R. W. (Ed.). (1998). *Seasonal affective disorder and beyond: Light treatment for SAD and non-SAD conditions*. Washington, DC: American Psychiatric Association.

Lamb, M. (1986). *The father's role: Applied perspectives*. New York: Wiley.

Lamb, M. (1987). Predictive implications of individual differences in attachment. *Journal of Consulting and Clinical Psychology, 55,* 817–824.

Lamb, M., Sternberg, K. J., & Prodromidis, M. (1992). Nonmaternal care and the security of the infant-mother attachment: A reanalysis of the data. *Infant Behavior and Development, 15,* 71–83.

Lambert, M. J., & Bergin, A. E. (1994). The effectiveness of psychotherapy. In A. Bergin & S. Garfield (Eds.), *Handbook of psychotherapy and behavior change* (4th ed., pp. 143–189). New York: Wiley.

Lampinen, J. M., Copeland, S. M., & Neuschatz, J. S. (2001). Recollections of things schematic: Room schemas revisited. *Journal of Experimental Psychology: Learning, Memory, & Cognition, 27,* 1211–1222.

Land, M. F., & Fernald, R. D. (1992). The evolution of eyes. *Annual Review of Neuroscience, 15,* 1–29.

Lang, F. R., & Carstensen, L. L. (2002). Time counts: Future time perspective, goals, and social relationships. *Psychology & Aging, 17,* 125–139.

Lang, P. J. (1995). The emotion probe: Studies of motivation and attention. *American Psychologist, 50,* 372–385.

Langer, E. J. (1975). The illusion of control. *Journal of Personality and Social Psychology, 32,* 311–328.

Langevin, B., Sukkar, F., Leger, P., Guez, A., & Robert, D. (1992). Sleep apnea syndromes (SAS) of specific etiology: Review and incidence from a sleep laboratory. *Sleep, 15,* S25–S32.

Langley, G. (Ed.). (1989). *Animal experimentation: The consensus changes*. New York: Chapman & Hall.

Langlois, J. H., Kalakanis, L., Rubenstein, A. J., Larson, A., Hallam, M., & Smoot, M. (2000). Maxims or myths of beauty? A meta-analytic and theoretical review. *Psychological Bulletin, 126,* 390–423.

Langlois, J. H., Ritter, J. M., Roggman, L. A., & Vaughn, L. S. (1991). Facial diversity and infant preferences for attractive faces. *Developmental Psychology, 27,* 79–84.

Langlois, J. H., & Roggman, L. A. (1990). Attractive faces are only average. *Psychological Science, 1,* 115–121.

Langlois, J. H., Roggman, L. A., & Musselman, L. (1994). What is average and what is not average about attractive faces? *Psychological Science, 5,* 214–220.

Lansing, A. K. (1959). General biology of senescence. In J. E. Birren (Ed.), *Handbook of aging and the individual*. Chicago: University of Chicago Press.

LaPiere, R. T. (1934). Attitudes vs. action. *Social Forces, 13,* 230–237.

*Larry P. v. Wilson Riles,* 495 F. Supp. 926 (N. D. Cal. 1979).

Larsen, K. S. (1990). The Asch conformity experiment: Replication and transhistorical comparisons. *Journal of Social Behavior and Personality, 5,* 163–168.

Larsen, R. J., & Diener, E. (1992). Promises and problems with the circumplex model of emotion. *Review of Personality and Social Psychology, 13,* 25–59.

Larsen, R. J., & Kasimatis, M. (1990). Individual differences in entrainment of mood to the weekly calendar. *Journal of Personality and Social Psychology, 58,* 164–171.

Larson, R. W., Richards, M. H., Moneta, G., Holmbeck, G., & Duckett, E. (1996). Changes in adolescents' daily interactions with their families from ages 10 to 18: Disengagement and transformation. *Developmental Psychology, 32,* 744–754.

Larson, R., & Richards, M. H. (1994). *Divergent realities: The emotional lives of mothers, fathers, and adolescents*. New York: Basic Books.

Lashley, K. S. (1950). In search of the engram. In *Society for Experimental Biology, Symposium 4,* 454–482.

Latané, B. (1981). The psychology of social impact. *American Psychologist, 36,* 343–356.

Latané, B., & Darley, J. M. (1970). *The unresponsive bystander: Why doesn't he help?* New York: Appleton-Century-Crofts.

Latané, B., & Nida, S. (1981). Ten years of research on group size and helping. *Psychological Bulletin, 89,* 308–324.

Latané, B., & Werner, C. (1978). Regulation of social contact in laboratory rats: Time, not distance. *Journal of Personality and Social Psychology, 36,* 1128–1137.

Latané, B., Williams, K., & Harkins, S. (1979). Many hands make light the work: The causes and consequences of social loafing. *Journal of Personality and Social Psychology, 37,* 822–832.

Lattal, K. A. (1992). B. F. Skinner and psychology: Introduction to the special issue. *American Psychologist, 47,* 1269–1272.

Lattal, K. A., & Perone, M. (Eds.). (1998). *Handbook of research methods in human operant behavior*. New York: Plenum.

Laumann, E. O., & Michael, R. T. (Eds.). (2001). *Sex, love, and health in America: Private choices and public policies*. Chicago: University of Chicago Press.

Laumann, E. O., Gagnon, J. H., Michael, R. T., & Michaels, S. (1994). *The social organization of sexuality*. Chicago: University of Chicago Press.

Lavie, P. (2001). Sleep-wake as a biological rhythm. *Annual Review of Psychology, 52,* 277–303.

Lavine, H., & Snyder, M. (1996). Cognitive processing and the functional matching effect in persuasion: The mediating role of subjective perceptions of message quality. *Journal of Experimental Social Psychology, 32,* 580–604.

Lazarus, A. A. (1996). Some reflections after 40 years of trying to be an effective psychotherapist. *Psychotherapy, 33,* 142–145.

Lazarus, R. S. (1984). On the primacy of cognition. *American Psychologist, 39,* 124–129.

Lazarus, R. S. (1991). Cognition and motivation in emotion. *American Psychologist, 46,* 352–367.

Lazarus, R. S. (1993). From psychological stress to the emotions: A history of changing outlooks. *Annual Review of Psychology, 44,* 1–21.

Lazarus, R. S., & Folkman, S. (1984). *Stress, appraisal, and coping.* New York: Springer.

Lazarus, R. S., & Lazarus, B. N. (1994). *Passion and reason: Making sense of our emotions.* New York: Oxford University Press.

Leahey, T. H. (1992). The mythical revolutions of American psychology. *American Psychologist, 47,* 308–318.

Leary, D. E. (1992). William James and the art of human understanding. *American Psychologist, 47,* 152–160.

Leary, M. R. (Ed.). (2001). *Interpersonal rejection.* New York: Oxford University Press.

Leary, M. R., & Kowalski, R. M. (1995). *Social anxiety.* New York: Guilford Press.

Lebow, J. (1982). Consumer satisfaction with mental health treatment. *Psychological Bulletin, 91,* 244–259.

Lecanuet, J., Fifer, W. P., Krasnegor, N. A., & Smotherman, W. P. (Eds.). (1995). *Fetal development: A psychobiological perspective.* Mahwah, NJ: Erlbaum.

Lecci, L., Karoly, P., Ruehlman, L. S., & Lanyon, R. I. (1996). Goal-relevant dimensions of hypochondriacal tendencies and their relation to symptom manifestation and psychological distress. *Journal of Abnormal Psychology, 105,* 42–52.

LeDoux, J. (2002). *Synaptic self: How our brains become who we are.* New York: Viking.

LeDoux, J. E. (1993). Emotional networks in the brain. In M. Lewis & J. M. Haviland (Eds.), *Handbook of emotions* (pp. 109–118). New York: Guilford Press.

LeDoux, J. E. (1996). *The emotional brain: The mysterious underpinnings of emotional life.* New York: Simon & Schuster.

LeDoux, J. E., Wilson, D. H., & Gazzaniga, M. S. (1977). A divided mind: Observation on the conscious properties of the separated hemispheres. *Annals of Neurology, 2,* 417–421.

Lee, L. (2000, February 7). Tricks of E*Trade. *Business Week.*

Lee, V. E., Brooks-Gunn, J., Schnur, E., & Liaw, F. R. (1990). Are Head Start effects sustained? A longitudinal follow-up of comparison of disadvantaged children attending Head Start, no preschool, and other preschool programs. *Child Development, 61,* 495–507.

Lee, Y. T., Jussim, L. J., & McCauley, C. R. (1995). *Stereotype accuracy: Toward appreciating group differences.* Washington, DC: American Psychological Association.

Lefcourt, H. M. (1982). *Locus of control: Current trends in theory and research.* Hillsdale, NJ: Erlbaum.

Lefebvre, P. P., Malgrange, B., Staecker, H., Moonen, G., & Van De Water, T. R. (1993). Retinoic acid stimulates regeneration of mammalian hair cells. *Science, 260,* 692–695.

Lehman, D. R., & Nisbett, R. E. (1990). A longitudinal study of the effects of undergraduate training on reasoning. *Developmental Psychology, 26,* 952–960.

Lehman, H. C. (1953). *Age and achievement.* Princeton, NJ: Princeton University Press.

Lehmann, A. C., & Ericsson, K. A. (1999). Research on expert performance and deliberate practice: Some implications for the education of amateur musicians and music students. *Psychomusicology, 16,* 40–58.

Leibowitz, H. W., Brislin, R., Perlmutter, L., & Hennessy, R. (1969). Ponzo perspective illusion as a manifestation of space perception. *Science, 166,* 1174–1176.

Leichtman, M. D., & Ceci, S. J. (1995). The effects of stereotypes and suggestions on preschoolers' reports. *Developmental Psychology, 31,* 568–578.

Leigh, B. C., & Stacy, A. W. (1993). Alcohol outcome expectancies: Scale construction and predictive utility in higher-order confirmatory models. *Psychological Assessment, 5,* 216–229.

Leigh, B. C., Temple, M. T., & Trocki, K. F. (1993). The sexual behavior of U.S. adults: Results from a national survey. *American Journal of Public Health, 83,* 1400–1408.

Leiker, M., & Hailey, B. J. (1988). A link between hostility and disease: Poor health habits? *Behavioral Medicine, 3,* 129–133.

Leinbach, M. D., & Fagot, B. I. (1993). Categorical habituation to male and female faces: Gender schematic processes in infancy. *Infant Behavior and Development, 16,* 317–332.

Lemann, N. (1999). *The big test: The secret history of the American meritocracy.* New York: Farrar, Straus & Giroux.

Lemonick, M. D. (2000, October 30). Teens before their time. *Time Magazine.*

Lenneberg, E. H. (1967). *Biological foundations of language.* New York: Wiley.

Lennie, P. (2000). Color vision. In E. R. Kandel, J. H. Schwartz, & T. M. Jessell (Eds.), *Principles of neural science* (4th ed., pp. 572–589). New York: McGraw-Hill.

Lennon, R. T. (1985). Group tests of intelligence. In B. Wolman (Ed.), *Handbook of intelligence: Theories, measurement, and applications* (pp. 825–845). New York: Wiley.

Lenzenweger, M. F., & Dworkin, R. H. (Eds.). (1998). *Origins and development of schizophrenia.* Washington, DC: American Psychological Association.

Leon, M. (1992). The neurobiology of filial learning. *Annual Review of Psychology, 43,* 377–398.

Lepper, M. R., & Greene, D. (Eds.). (1978). *The hidden costs of reward.* Hillsdale, NJ: Erlbaum.

Lepper, M. R., Greene, D., & Nisbett, R. E. (1973). Undermining children's intrinsic interest with extrinsic reward: A test of the "overjustification" hypothesis. *Journal of Personality and Social Psychology, 28,* 129–137.

Lessard, N., Pare, M., Lepre, F., & Lassonde, M. (1998). Early-blind human subjects localize sound sources better than sighted subjects. *Nature, 395,* 278–280.

Leung, K. (1988). Some determinants of conflict avoidance. *Journal of Cross-Cultural Psychology, 19,* 125–136.

Levanen, S., Jousmaki, V., & Hari, R. (1998). Vibration-induced auditory-cortex activation in a congenitally deaf adult. *Current Biology, 8,* 869–872.

LeVay, S. (1991). A difference in hypothalamic structure between heterosexual and homosexual men. *Science, 253,* 1034–1037.

LeVay, S. (1993). *The sexual brain.* Cambridge, MA: MIT Press.

LeVay, S. (1997). *Queer science: The use and abuse of research on homosexuality.* Cambridge, MA: MIT Press.

LeVay, S., & Mamer, D. H. (1994). Evidence for a biological influence in male homosexuality. *Scientific American, 270*(5), 44–49.

Levenson, R. W. (1992). Autonomic nervous system differences among emotions. *Psychological Science, 3,* 23–27.

Levenson, R. W., Carstensen, L. L., & Gottman, J. M. (1993). Long-term marriage: Age, gender, and satisfaction. *Psychology and Aging, 8,* 301–313.

Levenson, R. W., Ekman, P., Heider, K., & Friesen, W. V. (1992). Emotion and autonomic nervous system activity in the Minangkabau of West Sumatra. *Journal of Personality and Social Psychology, 62,* 972–988.

Leventhal, H. (1970). Findings and theory in the study of fear communications. In L. Berkowitz (Ed.), *Advances in experimental social psychology* (Vol. 5). New York: Academic Press.

Levin, I. P., Schnittjer, S. K., & Thee, S. L. (1988). Information framing effects in social and personal decisions. *Journal of Experimental Social Psychology, 24,* 520–529.

Levine, J. D., Gordon, N. C., & Fields, H. L. (1978). The mechanism of placebo analgesia. *Lancet, 2,* 654–657.

Levine, J. M. (1989). Reaction to opinion deviance in small groups. In P. B. Paulus (Ed.), *Psychology of group influence* (2nd ed., pp. 187–231). Hillsdale, NJ: Erlbaum.

Levine, R. (1997). *A geography of time: The temporal misadventures of a social psychologist, or how every culture keeps time just a little bit differently.* New York: Basic Books.

Levine, R., & Norenzayan, A. (1999). The pace of life in 31 countries. *Journal of Cross-Cultural Psychology, 30,* 178–205.

Levine, R. A., & Campbell, D. T. (1972). *Ethnocentrism: Theories of conflict, ethnic attitudes, and group behavior.* New York: Wiley.

Levine, R. B. (1993). Is love a luxury? *American Demographics, 15*(2), 27–28.

Levine, R. V. (1990). The pace of life. *American Scientist, 78,* 450–459.

Levine, S. C., Huttenlocher, J., Taylor, A., & Langrock, A. (1999). Early sex differences in spatial skill. *Developmental Psychology, 35,* 940–949.

Levinson, D. J. (1996). *The seasons of a woman's life.* New York: Knopf.

Levinson, D. J., Darrow, C. N., Klein, E. B., Levinson, M. H., McKee, B. (1978). *The seasons of a man's life.* New York: Knopf.

Levy, B. R., Slade, M. D., Kunkel, S. R., & Kasl, S. V. (2002). Longevity increased by positive self-perceptions of aging. *Journal of Personality and Social Psychology, 83,* 261–270.

Levy, D. A. (1997). *Tools of critical thinking: Metathoughts for psychology.* Boston: Allyn & Bacon.

Levy, G. D. (1989). Relations among aspects of children's social environments, gender schematization, gender role knowledge, and flexibility. *Sex Roles, 21,* 803–823.

Levy, J., Heller, W., Banich, M., & Burton, L. (1983). Asymmetry of perception in free viewing of chimeric faces. *Brain and Cognition, 2,* 404–419.

Levy, J., Trevarthen, C., & Sperry, R. W. (1972). Perception of bilateral chimeric figures following hemispheric disconnection. *Brain, 95,* 61–78.

Lewinsohn, P. M. (1974). A behavioral approach to depression. In R. Friedman & M. Katz (Eds.), *The psychology of depression: Contemporary theory and research.* Washington, DC: Winston-Wiley.

Lewinsohn, P. M., Duncan, E. M., Stanton, A. K., & Hautzinger, M. (1986). Age at first onset for nonbipolar depression. *Journal of Abnormal Psychology, 95,* 378–383.

Lewinsohn, P. M., Rohde, P., & Seeley, J. R. (1994). Psychosocial risk factors for future adolescent suicide attempts. *Journal of Consulting and Clinical Psychology, 62,* 297–305.

Lewis, M., & Bendersky, M. (Eds.). (1995). *Mothers, babies, and cocaine: The role of toxins in development.* Mahwah, NJ: Erlbaum.

Lewis, M. D., Koroshegyi, C., Douglas, L., & Kampe, K. (1997). Age-specific associations between emotional responses to separation and cognitive performance in infancy. *Developmental Psychology, 33,* 32–42.

Lewis, P., & Boylan, P. (1979). Fetal breathing: A review. *American Journal of Obstetrics and Gynecology, 134,* 587–598.

Lewontin, R. (1970). Race and intelligence. *Bulletin of the Atomic Scientists, 26,* 2–8.

Liben, L. S., et al. (2002). The effects of sex steroids on spatial performance: A review and an experimental clinical investigation. *Developmental Psychology, 38,* 236–253.

Lichstein, K. L., & Morin, C. M. (Eds.). (2000). *Treatment of late life insomnia.* Thousand Oaks, CA: Sage.

Lichtman, S. W., et al. (1992). Discrepancy between self-reported and actual caloric intake and exercise in obese subjects. *New England Journal of Medicine, 327,* 1893–1898.

Lickey, M. E., & Gordon, B. (1991). *Medicine and mental illness.* New York: W. H. Freeman.

Lickona, T. (1976). Research on Piaget's theory of moral development. In T. Lickona (Ed.), *Moral development and behavior.* New York: Holt, Rinehart & Winston.

Lieberman, J. D., & Arndt, J. (2000). Understanding the limits of limiting instructions. *Psychology, Public Policy, & Law, 6,* 677–711.

Lifton, R. J. (1986). *The Nazi doctors.* New York: Basic Books.

Light, L. L. (1991). Memory and aging: Four hypotheses in search of data. *Annual Review of Psychology, 42,* 333–376.

Lightfoot, C. (1999). *The culture of adolescent risk-taking.* New York: Guilford.

Lilienfeld, S. O. (2002). When worlds collide: Social science, politics, and the Rind et al. (1998) child sexual abuse meta-analysis. *American Psychologist, 57,* 176–188.

Lilienfeld, S. O., Lynn, S. J., Kirsch, I., Chaves, J. F., Sarbin, T. R., Ganaway, G. K., & Powell, R. A. (1999). Dissociative identity disorder and the sociocognitive model: Recalling the lessons of the past. *Psychological Bulletin, 125,* 507–523.

Lin, E. L., & Murphy, G. L. (2001). Thematic relations in adults' concepts. *Journal of Experimental Psychology: General, 130,* 3–28.

Linden, E. (1993, March 22). Can animals think? *Time,* pp. 52–61.

Linden, E. (1999). *The parrot's lament.* New York: Dutton.

Lindsay, P. H., & Norman, D. A. (1977). *Human information processing.* New York: Academic Press.

Lindsay, R. C. L., Wells, G. L., & O'Conner, F. J. (1989). Mock-juror belief of accurate and inaccurate eyewitnesses: A replication and extension. *Law and Human Behavior, 13,* 333–339.

Lindsley, O. (1992). Precision teaching: Discoveries and effects. *Journal of Applied Behavior Analysis, 25,* 51–57.

Lindvall, O., et al. (1992). Transplantation of fetal dopamine neurons in Parkinson's disease: One year clinical and neurophysiological observations in two patients with putiminal implants. *Annals of Neurology, 31,* 155–165.

Linet, M. G., Stewart, W. F., Celentano, D. D., Ziegler, D., & Sprecher, M. (1989). An epidemiologic study of headache among adolescents and young adults. *Journal of the American Medical Association, 261,* 2211–2216.

Linn, M. C., & Petersen, A. (1985). Emergence and characterization of sex differences in spatial ability: A meta-analysis. *Child Development, 56,* 1479–1498.

Linn, R. L. (1982). Ability testing: Individual differences, prediction, and differential prediction. In A. K. Wigdor & W. R. Garner (Eds.), *Ability testing: Uses, consequences, and controversies (Part II).* Washington, DC: National Academy Press.

Linton, M. (1982). Transformations of memory in everyday life. In U. Neisser (Ed.), *Memory observed: Remembering in natural contexts* (pp. 77–91). San Francisco: W. H. Freeman.

Linville, P. W., Fischer, G. W., & Fischhoff, B. (1992). Perceived risk and decision-making involving AIDS. In J. B. Pryor & G. D. Reeder (Eds.), *The social psychology of HIV infection.* Hillsdale, NJ: Erlbaum.

Linville, P. W., & Jones, E. E. (1980). Polarized appraisals of out-group members. *Journal of Personality and Social Psychology, 38,* 689–703.

Linz, D., Donnerstein, E., & Penrod, S. (1988). Effects of long-term exposure to violent and sexually degrading depictions of women. *Journal of Personality and Social Psychology, 55,* 758–768.

Lipsey, M. W., &Wilson, D. B. (1993). The efficacy of psychological, educational, and behavioral treatment: Confirmation from metaanalysis. *American Psychologist, 48,* 1181–1209.

Lipsitt, L. (1971, December). Babies: They're a lot smarter than they look. *Psychology Today,* p. 23.

Lipton, R. B., Stewart, W. F., Diamond, S., Diamond, M. L., & Reed, M. (2001). Prevalence and Burden of Migraine in the United States: Data from the American Migraine Study II. *Headache, 41,* 646–657.

Liu, E. (1998). *The accidental Asian: Notes of a native speaker.* New York: Random House.

Liu, S. S. (1971). Differential conditioning and stimulus generalization of the rabbit's nictitating membrane response. *Journal of Comparative and Physiological Psychology, 77,* 136–142.

Livesley, W. J. (Ed.). (2001). *Handbook of personality disorders: Theory, research, and treatment.* New York: Guilford.

Livingstone, M. (2002). *Vision and art: The biology of seeing.* New York: Harry N. Abrams.

Livingstone, M., & Hubel, D. (1988). Segregation of form, color, movement, and depth: Anatomy, physiology, and perception. *Science, 240,* 740–749.

Lockard, J. S., & Paulhus, D. L. (1988). *Self-deception: An adaptive mechanism?* Upper Saddle River, NJ: Prentice-Hall.

Locke, E. A., & Latham, G. P. (1990). *A theory of goal-setting and task performance.* Englewood Cliffs, NJ: Prentice-Hall.

Loeber, R., & Hay, D. (1997). Key issues in the development of aggression and violence from childhood to early adulthood. *Annual Review of Psychology, 48,* 371–410.

Loehlin, J. C. (1992). *Genes and environment in personality development.* Newbury Park, CA: Sage Publications.

Loehlin, J. C., Willerman, L., & Horn, J. M. (1987). Personality resemblance in adoptive families: A 10-year follow-up. *Journal of Personality and Social Psychology, 53,* 961–969.

Loftus, E. F. (1979). *Eyewitness testimony.* Cambridge, MA: Harvard University Press.

Loftus, E. F. (1993a). The reality of repressed memories. *American Psychologist, 48,* 518–537.

Loftus, E. F. (1993b). Desperately seeking memories of the first few years of childhood: The reality of early memories. *Journal of Experimental Psychology: General, 122,* 274–277.

Loftus, E. F. (1996). *Eyewitness testimony* (reprint ed.). Cambridge, MA: Harvard University Press.

Loftus, E. F. (1997). Creating false memories. *Scientific American, 277*(3), 70–75.

Loftus, E. F., Donders, K., Hoffman, H. G., & Schooler, J. W. (1989). Creating new memories that are quickly accessed and confidently held. *Memory and Cognition, 17,* 607–616.

Loftus, E. F., & Ketcham, K. (1994). *The myth of repressed memory: False memories and allegations of sexual abuse.* New York: St. Martin's Press.

Loftus, E. F., & Klinger, M. R. (1992). Is the unconscious smart or dumb? *American Psychologist, 47,* 761–765.

Loftus, E. F., & Loftus, G. R. (1980). On the permanence of stored information in the human brain. *American Psychologist, 35,* 409–420.

Loftus, E. F., Loftus, G. R., & Messo, J. (1987). Some facts about "weapon focus." *Law and Human Behavior, 11,* 55–62.

Loftus, E. F., Miller, D. G., & Burns, H. J. (1978). Semantic integration of verbal information into visual memory. *Journal of Experimental Psychology: Human Learning and Memory, 4,* 19–31.

Loftus, E. F., & Palmer, J. C. (1974). Reconstruction of automobile destruction: An example of the interaction between language and memory. *Journal of Verbal Learning and Verbal Behavior, 13,* 585–589.

Logothetis, N. K., & Schall, J. D. (1989). Neuronal correlates of subjective visual perception. *Science, 245,* 761–763.

Logue, A. W. (1991). *The psychology of eating and drinking: An introduction.* New York: W. H. Freeman.

Lopez, A., & Carrillo, E. (Eds.). (2001). *The Latino psychiatric patient: Assessment and treatment.* Washington, DC: American Psychiatric Press.

Lopez, S. R., & Guarnaccia, P. J. (2000). Cultural psychopathology: Uncovering the social world of mental illness. *Annual Review of Psychology, 51,* 571–598.

Lorenz, K. (1937). Imprinting. *The Auk, 54,* 245–273.

Lorenz, K. (1966). *On aggression.* New York: Harcourt, Brace & World.

Louie, T. A. (1999). Decision makers' hindsight bias after receiving favorable and unfavorable feedback. *Journal of Applied Psychology, 84,* 29–41.

Lourenco, O., & Machado, A. (1996). In defense of Piaget's theory: A reply to 10 common criticisms. *Psychological Review, 103,* 143–164.

Lovaas, O. I. (1987). Behavioral treatment and normal educational and intellectual functioning in young autistic children. *Journal of Consulting and Clinical Psychology, 55,* 3–9.

Low, P. W., Jeffries, J. C., & Bonnie, R. C. (2000). *The trial of John W. Hinckley, Jr.: A case study in the insanity defense* (2nd ed.). New York: Foundation Press.

Lu, Z.-L., Williamson, S. J., & Kaufman, L. (1992). Behavioral lifetime of human auditory sensory memory predicted by physiological measures. *Science, 258,* 1668–1670.

Lubinski, D., Webb, R. M., Morelock, M. J., & Benbow, C. P. (2001). Top 1 in 10,000: A 10-year follow-up of the profoundly gifted. *Journal of Applied Psychology, 86,* 718–729.

Luborsky, L. (1984). *Principles of psychoanalytic psychotherapy.* New York: Basic Books.

Luborsky, L., & Crits-Christoph, P. (1998). *Understanding transference: The Core Conflictual Relationship Theme method.* Washington, DC: American Psychological Association.

Lucas, R. E., & Diener, E. (2001). Understanding extraverts' enjoyment of social situations: The importance of pleasantness. *Journal of Personality and Social Psychology, 81,* 343–356.

Lucy, J. A. (1992). *Language diversity and thought: A reformulation of the linguistic relativity hypothesis.* New York: Cambridge University Press.

Ludwig, A. M. (1995). *The price of greatness: Resolving the creativity and madness controversy.* New York: Guilford Press.

Lundy, B. L., et al. (1999). Prenatal depression effects on neonates. *Infant Behavior and Development, 22,* 119–129.

Luria, A. R. (1968). *The mind of a mnemonist.* New York: Basic Books.

Luthans, F., Paul, R., & Baker, D. (1981). An experimental analysis of the impact of contingent reinforcement on salespersons' performance behavior. *Journal of Applied Psychology, 66,* 314–323.

Lutz, W. (1996). *The new doublespeak: Why no one knows what anyone's saying anymore.* New York: HarperCollins.

Lydiard, R. B., Brawman-Mintzer, O., & Ballenger, J. C. (1996). Recent developments in the psychopharmacology of anxiety disorders. *Journal of Consulting and Clinical Psychology, 64,* 660–668.

Lykken, D. (2000). *Happiness: The nature and nurture of joy and contentment.* New York: St. Martin's Press.

Lykken, D. T. (1981). *A tremor in the blood: Uses and abuses of the lie detector.* New York: McGraw-Hill.

Lykken, D. T. (1995). *The antisocial personalities.* Mahwah, NJ: Erlbaum.

Lykken, D. T. (1999). *Happiness: What studies on twins show us about nature, nurture, and the happiness set point.* New York: Golden Books.

Lykken, D. T., Bouchard, T. J., McGue, M., & Tellegen, A. (1992). Emergenesis: Genetic traits that may not run in families. *American Psychologist, 47,* 1565–1577.

Lykken, D. T., & Tellegen, A. (1996). Happiness is a stochastic phenomenon. *Psychological Science, 7,* 186–189.

Lymburner, J. A., & Roesch, R. (1999). The insanity defense: Five years of research (1993–1997). *International Journal of Law and Psychiatry, 22,* 213–240.

Lynn, S. J., Rhue, J. W., & Weekes, J. R. (1990). Hypnotic involuntariness: A social cognitive analysis. *Psychological Review, 97,* 169–184.

Lyons, L. C., & Woods, P. J. (1991). The efficacy of rational-emotive therapy: A quantitative review of outcome research. *Clinical Psychology Review, 11,* 357–369.

Lytton, H., Romney, D. M. (1991). Parents' differential socialization of boys and girls: A meta-analysis. *Psychological Bulletin, 109,* 267–296.

Lyubomirsky, S., & Ross, L. (1997). Hedonic consequences of social comparison: A contrast of happy and unhappy people. *Journal of Personality and Social Psychology, 73,* 1141–1157.

Lyznicki, J. M., Doege, T. C., Davis, R. M., & Williams, M. A. (1998). Sleepiness, driving, and motor vehicle crashes. *Journal of the American Medical Association, 279,* 1908–1913.

Maas, J. B. (1998). *Power sleep: How to prepare your mind for peak performance.* New York: Random House.

Maccoby, E. E. (1998). *The two sexes: Growing up apart, coming together.* New York: Belknap.

Maccoby, E. E., & Jacklin, C. N. (1974). *The psychology of sex differences.* Palo Alto, CA: Stanford University Press.

Maccoby, E. E., & Jacklin, C. N. (1987). Gender segregation in childhood. In H. W. Reese (Ed.), *Advances in child development and behavior* (Vol. 20, pp. 239–287).

MacCoun, R. J. (1993). Drugs and the law: A psychological analysis of drug prohibition. *Psychological Bulletin, 113,* 497–512.

MacDonald, T. K., MacDonald, G., Zanna, M. P., & Fong, G. T. (2000). Alcohol, sexual arousal, and intentions to use condoms in young men: Applying alcohol myopia theory to risky sexual behavior. *Health Psychology, 19,* 290–298.

MacGregor, J. N., Ormerod, T. C., & Chronicle, E. P. (2001). Information processing and insight: A process model of performance on the nine-dot and related problems. *Journal of Experimental Psychology: Learning, Memory, & Cognition, 27,* 176–201.

Macionis, J. J. (2001). *Sociology* (8th ed.). Upper Saddle River, NJ: Prentice-Hall.

Mack, A., & Joy, J. (2001). *Marijuana as medicine? The science beyond the controversy.* New York: National Academy Press.

Mackavey, W. R., Malley, J. E., & Stewart, A. J. (1991). Remembering autobiographically consequential experiences: Content analysis of psychologists' accounts of their lives. *Psychology and Aging, 6,* 50–59.

Mackie, D. M., & Worth, L. T. (1989). Processing deficits and the mediation of positive affect in persuasion. *Journal of Personality and Social Psychology, 57,* 27–40.

Mackie, D. M., Worth, L. T., & Asuncion, A. G. (1990). Processing of persuasive in-group messages. *Journal of Personality and Social Psychology, 58,* 812–822.

MacKintosh, N. J. (Ed.). (1995). *Cyril Burt: Fraud or Framed?* New York: Oxford University Press.

MacLeod, C. M. (1991). Half a century of research on the Stroop effect: An integrative review. *Psychological Bulletin, 109,* 163–203.

MacLeod-Morgan, C., & Lack, L. (1982). Hemispheric specificity: A physiological concomitant of hypnotizability. *Psychophysiology, 19,* 687–690.

MacMillan, M. (2000). *An odd kind of fame: Stories of Phineas Gage.* Cambridge, MA: MIT Press.

MacQueen, G., Marshall, J., Perdue, M., Siegal, S., & Bienenstock, J. (1989). Pavlovian conditioning of rat mast cells to secrete rat mast cell protease 11. *Science, 234,* 83–85.

Macrae, C. N., & Bodenhausen, G. V. (2000). Social cognition: Thinking categorically about others. *Annual Review of Psychology, 51,* 93–120.

Macrae, C. N., Bodenhausen, G. V., & Calvini, G. (1999). Contexts of cryptomnesia: May the source be with you. *Social Cognition, 17,* 273–297.

MacWhinney, B. (1998). Models of the emergence of language. *Annual Review of Psychology, 49,* 199–227.

Madden, K. S., Boehm, G. W., Lee, S. C., Grota, L. J., Cohen, N., & Ader, R. (2001). One-trial conditioning of the antibody response to hen egg lysozyme in rats. *Journal of Neuroimmunology, 113,* 236–239.

Maddi, S. R., Bartone, P. T., & Puccetti, M. C. (1987). Stressful events are indeed a factor in physical illness: Reply to Schroeder and Costa (1984). *Journal of Personality and Social Psychology, 52,* 833–843.

Maddux, J. E. (1991). Self-efficacy. In C. R. Snyder & D. R. Forsyth (Eds.), *Handbook of social and clinical psychology: The health perspective* (pp. 57–78). New York: Pergamon Press.

Madigan, S., & O'Hara, R. (1992). Short-term memory at the turn of the century: Mary Whiten Calkins's memory research. *American Psychologist, 47,* 170–174.

Madrazo, I., Drucker-Colin, R., Diaz, V., Martinez-Mata, J., Torres, C., & Becerril, J. J. (1987). Open microsurgical autograft of adrenal medulla to the right caudate nucleus in two patients with intractable Parkinson's disease. *New England Journal of Medicine, 316,* 831–834.

Magee, W. J., Eaton, W. W., Wittchen, H. U., McGonagle, K. A., & Kessler, R. C. (1996). Agoraphobia, simple phobia, and social phobia in the National Comorbidity Survey. *Archives of General Psychiatry, 53,* 159–168.

Magnusson, D., & Endler, N. S. (Eds.). (1977). *Personality at the crossroads: Current issues in interactional psychology.* Hillsdale, NJ: Erlbaum.

Mahoney, M. J. (1991). *Human change processes.* New York: Basic Books.

Mahowald, M. W., & Schenck, C. H. (1989). Narcolepsy. In G. Adelman (Ed.), *Neuroscience year: Supplement 1 to the Encyclopedia of Neuroscience.* Boston: Birkhauser.

Maj, M., Veltro, F., Pirozzi, R., Lobrace, S., & Magliano, L. (1992). Pattern of recurrence of illness after recovery from an episode of major depression: A prospective study. *Journal of Personality and Social Psychology, 62,* 795–800.

Major, B., Cozzarelli, C., Sciacchitano, A. M., Cooper, M. L., Testa, M., & Mueller, P. M. (1990). Perceived social support, self-efficacy, and adjustment to abortion. *Journal of Personality and Social Psychology, 59,* 452–463.

Major, B., McFartin, D. B., & Gagnon, D. (1984). Overworked and underpaid: On the nature of gender differences in personal entitlement. *Journal of Personality and Social Psychology, 47,* 1399–1412.

Majors, R. (1991). Nonverbal behaviors and communication styles among African Americans. In R. Jones (Ed.), *Black psychology* (pp. 269–294). Berkeley, CA: Cobb & Henry.

Malamuth, N. M., & Check, J. V. P. (1981). The effects of mass media exposure on acceptance of violence against women: A field experiment. *Journal of Research in Personality,* 15, 436–446.

Malinoski, P. T., & Lynn, S. J. (1999). The plasticity of early memory reports: Social pressure, hypnotizability, compliance, and interrogative suggestibility. *International Journal of Clinical and Experimental Hypnosis, 47.*

Malpass, R. S., & Devine, P. G. (1981). Eyewitness identification: Lineup instructions and the absence of the offender. *Journal of Applied Psychology, 66,* 482–489.

Maltsberger, J. T., & Goldblatt, M. J. (Eds.). (1996). *Essential papers on suicide.* New York: New York University Press.

Mandel, D. R., Jusczyk, P. W., & Pisoni, D. B. (1995). Infants' recognition of the sound patterns of their own names. *Psychological Science, 6,* 314–317.

Mandler, G. (1980). Recognizing: The judgment of previous occurrence. *Psychological Review, 87,* 252–271.

Mann, J. M. (1992). AIDS—the second decade: A global perspective. *Journal of Infectious Diseases, 165,* 245–250.

Manning, C. A., Stone, W. S., Korol, D. L., & Gold, P. E. (1998). Glucose enhancement of 24-h memory retrieval in healthy elderly humans. *Behavioural Brain Research, 93,* 71–76.

Maquet, P., Faymonville, M. E., Degueldre, C., Delfiore, G., Franck, G., Luxen, A., & Lamy, M. (1999). Functional neuroanatomy of hypnotic state. *Biological Psychiatry, 45,* 327–333.

Marcel, A. J. (1983). Conscious and unconscious perception: Experiments on visual masking and word recognition. *Cognitive Psychology, 15,* 197–237.

Marcus-Newhall, A., Pedersen, W. C., Carlson, M., & Miller, N. (2000). Displaced aggression is alive and well: A meta-analytic review. *Journal of Personality and Social Psychology, 78,* 670–689.

Maren, S. (2001). Neurobiology of Pavlovian fear conditioning. *Annual Review of Neuroscience, 24,* 897–931.

Marian, V., & Neisser, U. (2000). Language-dependent recall of autobiographical memories. *Journal of Experimental Psychology: General, 129,* 361–368.

Maris, R. W., Berman, A. L., & Silverman, M. M. (2001). *Comprehensive textbook of suicidology.* New York: Guilford.

Mark, V. H., & Ervin, F. R. (1970). *Violence and the brain.* New York: Harper & Row.

Markey, P. M. (2000). Bystander intervention in computer-mediated communication. *Computers in Human Behavior, 16,* 183–188.

Markman, A. B. (1999). *Knowledge representation.* Mahwah, NJ: Erlbaum.

Markman, A. B., & Gentner, D. (2001). Thinking. *Annual Review of Psychology, 52,* 223–247.

Marks, D. F. (1986). Investigating the paranormal. *Nature, 320,* 119–124.

Marks, G. A., Shaffrey, J. P., Oksenberg, A., Speciale, S. G., & Roffwarg, H. P. (1995). A functional role for the REM sleep in brain maturation. *Behavioural Brain Research, 69,* 1–11.

Marks, I. M. (1987). *Fears, phobias, and rituals: Panic, anxiety, and their disorders.* New York: Oxford University Press.

Markus, H. (1977). Self-schemata and processing information about the self. *Journal of Personality and Social Psychology, 35,* 63–78.

Markus, H., & Kitayama, S. (1991). Culture and the self: Implications for cognition, emotion, and motivation. *Psychological Review, 98,* 224–253.

Markus, H., & Nurius, P. (1986). Possible selves. *American Psychologist,* 41, 954–969.

Marsh, H. W., & Parker, J. W. (1984). Determinants of student self-concept: Is it better to be a relatively large fish in a small pond even if you don't learn to swim as well? *Journal of Personality and Social Psychology, 47,* 213–231.

Marsh, R. L., & Bower, G. H. (1993). Eliciting cryptomnesia: Unconscious plagiarism in a puzzle task. *Journal of Experimental Psychology: Learning, Memory, and Cognition, 19,* 673–688.

Marsh, R. L., Landau, J. D., & Hicks, J. L. (1997). Contributions of inadequate source monitoring to unconscious plagiarism during idea generation. *Journal of Experimental Psychology: Learning, Memory, and Cognition, 23,* 886–897.

Marshall, D. A., & Moulton, D. G. (1981). Olfactory sensitivity to xionone in humans and dogs. *Chemical Senses, 6,* 53–61.

Marshall, G. N. (1991). A multidimensional analysis of internal health locus of control belief: Separating the wheat from the chaff? *Journal of Personality and Social Psychology, 61,* 483–491.

Marti, M. W., & Wissler, R. L. (2000). Be careful what you ask for: The effect of anchors in personal-injury damages awards. *Journal of Experimental Psychology: Applied, 6,* 91–103.

Martin, C. L. (1987). A ratio measure of sex stereotyping. *Journal of Personality and Social Psychology, 52,* 489–499.

Martin, C. L., & Fabes, R. A. (2001). The stability and consequences of young children's same-sex peer interactions. *Developmental Psychology, 37,* 431–446.

Martin, C. L., Wood, C. H., & Little, J. K. (1990). The development of gender stereotype components. *Child Development, 61,* 1891–1904.

Martin, G., & Pear, J. (1998). *Behavior modification—What it is and how to do it* (6th ed.). Upper Saddle River, NJ: Prentice-Hall.

Martin, J. H., Brost, J. C. M., & Hilal, S. (1991). Imaging the living brain. In E. R. Kandel, J. H. Schwartz, & T. M. Jessell (Eds.), *Principles of neural science* (3rd ed., pp. 309–324). New York: Elsevier.

Martin, L. (1986). "Eskimo words for snow": A case study in the genesis and decay of an anthropological example. *American Anthropologist, 88,* 418–423.

Martin, P. (1998). *The healing mind.* New York: St. Martin's Press.

Martino, G., & Marks, L. E. (2001). Synesthesia: Strong and weak. *Current Directions in Psychological Science, 10,* 61–65.

Maser, J. D. (1985). List of phobias. In A. H. Tuma & J. D. Maser (Eds.), *Anxiety and the anxiety disorders.* Hillsdale, NJ: Erlbaum.

Maslach, C. (1982). *Burnout: The cost of caring.* Englewood Cliffs, NJ: Prentice-Hall.

Maslach, C., Schaufeli, W. B., & Leiter, M. P. (2001). Job burnout. *Annual Review of Psychology, 52,* 397–422.

Maslow, A. (1954). *Motivation and personality.* New York: Harper.

Maslow, A. (1968). *Toward a psychology of being.* New York: Van Nostrand.

Masson, J. M., & McCarthy, S. (1995). *When elephants weep: The emotional lives of animals.* New York: Delta.

Master, M. S. (1998). The gender difference on the mental rotations test is not due to performance factors. *Memory and Cognition, 26,* 444–448.

Masters, W. H., & Johnson, V. E. (1966). *Human sexual response.* Boston: Little, Brown.

Matarazzo, J. D. (1992). Psychological testing and assessment in the 21st century. *American Psychologist, 47,* 1007–1018.

Matsumoto, D., & Ekman, P. (1989). Japanese-American cultural differences in intensity ratings of facial expressions of emotion. *Motivation and Emotion, 13,* 143–157.

Matthews, G., Zeidner, M., & Roberts, R. D. (2003). *Emotional intelligence: Science & myth.* Cambridge: MIT Press.

Matthews, K. A. (1988). CHD and Type A behavior: Update on and alternative to the Booth-Kewley and Friedman quantitative review. *Psychological Bulletin, 104,* 373–380.

Matthews, K. A. (1992). Myths and realities of the menopause. *Psychosomatic Medicine, 54,* 1–9.

Maurer, D., & Maurer, C. (1988). *The world of the new born.* New York: Basic Books.

Mauro, R., Sato, K., & Tucker, J. (1992). The role of appraisal in human emotions: A cross-cultural study. *Journal of Personality and Social Psychology, 62,* 301–317.

May, C. P., & Hasher, L. (1998). Synchrony effects in inhibitory control over thought and action. *Journal of Experimental Psychology: Human Perception and Performance, 24,* 363–379.

Mayberg, H. S., Silva, J. A., Brannan, S. K., Tekell, J. L., Mahurin, R. K., McGinnis, S., & Jerabek, P. A. (2002). The functional neuroanatomy of the placebo effect. *American Journal of Psychiatry, 159,* 728–737.

Mayer, J. D., Salovey, P., Caruso, D. R., & Sitarenios, G. (2001). Emotional intelligence as a standard intelligence. *Emotion, 1,* 232–242.

Mazur, A., Booth, A., & Dabbs, J. M., Jr. (1992). Testosterone and chess competition. *Social Psychology Quarterly, 55,* 70–77.

Mazur, J. E. (1998). Choice and self-control. In K. A. Lattal & M. Perone (Eds.), *Handbook of research methods in human operant behavior* (pp. 131–161). New York: Plenum.

McAdams, D. P. (1989). *Intimacy: The need to be close.* New York: Doubleday.

McAdams, D. P., & Constantian, C. A. (1983). Intimacy and affiliation motives in daily living: An experience sampling analysis. *Journal of Personality and Social Psychology, 45,* 851–861.

McAdams, D. P., & de St. Aubin, E. (Eds.). (1998). *Generativity and adult development: How and why we care for the next generation.* Washington, DC: American Psychological Association.

McAdams, D. P., Jackson, R. J., & Kirshnit, C. (1984). Looking, laughing, and smiling in dyads as a function of intimacy motivation and reciprocity. *Journal of Personality, 52,* 261–273.

McArthur, L. A. (1972). The how and what of why: Some determinants and consequences of causal attribution. *Journal of Personality and Social Psychology, 22,* 171–193.

McBurnett, K., Lahey, B. B., Rathouz, P. J., & Loeber, R. (2000). Low salivary cortisol and persistent aggression in boys referred for disruptive behavior. *Archives of General Psychiatry, 57,* 38–43.

McCall, M., & Belmont, H. J. (1996). Credit card insignia and restaurant tipping: Evidence for an associative link. *Journal of Applied Psychology, 81,* 609–613.

McCall, R. B., & Carriger, M. S. (1995). A meta-analysis of infant habituation and recognition memory performance as predictors of later IQ. *Child Development, 64,* 57–79.

McCann, I. L., & Holmes, D. S. (1984). Influence of aerobic exercise on depression. *Journal of Personality and Social Psychology, 46,* 1142–1147.

McCartney, K., Harris, M. J., & Bernieri, F. (1990). Growing up and growing apart: A developmental meta-analysis of twin studies. *Psychological Bulletin, 107,* 226–237.

McCauley, C. (1989). The nature of social influence in groupthink: Compliance and internalization. *Journal of Personality and Social Psychology, 57,* 250–260.

McClelland, D. C. (1985). *Human motivation.* Glenview, IL: Scott, Foresman.

McClelland, D. C. (1998). Identifying competencies with behavioral-event interviews. *Psychological Science, 9,* 331–339.

McClelland, D. C., Atkinson, J. W., Clark, R. A., & Lowell, E. (1953). *The achievement motive.* New York: Appleton-Century-Crofts.

McClelland, D. C., & Koestner, R. (1992). The achievement motive. In C. P. Smith, J. W. Atkinson, D. C. McClelland, & J. Veroff (Eds.), *Motivation and personality: Handbook of thematic content analysis* (pp. 143–152). New York: Cambridge University Press.

McClelland, D. C., Koestner, R., & Weinberger, J. (1989). How do self-attributed and implicit motives differ? *Psychological Review, 96,* 690–702.

McCloskey, M., & Kuhl, D. (1983). Naive physics: The curvilinear impetus principle and its role in interactions with moving objects. *Journal of Experimental Psychology: Learning, Memory, and Cognition, 9,* 146–156.

McCloskey, M., Washburn, A., & Felch, L. (1983). Intuitive physics: The straight-down belief and its origin. *Journal of Experimental Psychology: Learning, Memory, and Cognition, 9,* 636–649.

McCloskey, M., Wible, C. G., & Cohen, N. J. (1988). Is there a special flashbulb-memory mechanism? *Journal of Experimental Psychology: General, 117,* 171–181.

McCloskey, M., & Zaragoza, M. (1985). Misleading postevent information and memory for events: Arguments and evidence against memory impairment hypotheses. *Journal of Experimental Psychology, 114,* 3–18.

McConkey, K. M., & Sheehan, P. W. (1995). *Hypnosis, memory, and behavior in criminal investigation.* New York: Guilford Press.

McConnell, A. R., & Fazio, R. H. (1996). Women and men as people: Effects of gender-marked language. *Personality and Social Psychology Bulletin, 22,* 1004–1013.

McCormick, D. A., & Thompson, R. F. (1984). Cerebellum: Essential involvement in the classically conditioned eyelid response. *Science, 223,* 296–299.

McCrae, R. R. (2001). Trait psychology and culture: Exploring intercultural comparisons. *Journal of Personality, 69,* 819–846.

McCrae, R. R., & Costa, P. T., Jr. (1990). *Personality in adulthood.* New York: Guilford Press.

McCrae, R. R., & Costa, P. T., Jr. (1997). Personality trait structure as a human universal. *American Psychologist, 52,* 509–516.

McCrae, R. R., Costa, P. T., et al. (1999). Age differences in personality across the adult life span: Parallels in five cultures. *Developmental Psychology, 35,* 466–477.

McCrea, M., Kelly, J. P., Kluge, J., Ackley, B., & Randolph, C. (1997). Standardized assessment of concussion in football players. *Neurology, 48,* 586–588.

McCullough, M. E., Hoyt, W. T., Larson, D. B., Koenig, H. G., & Thoresen, C. (2000). Religious involvement and mortality: A meta-analytic review. *Health Psychology, 19,* 211–222.

McDonald, J. W. (1999, September). Repairing the damaged spinal cord. *Scientific American,* 65–73.

McDonald, J. W., Becker, D., Sadowsky, C. L., Jane, J. A., Conturo, T. E., & Schultz, L. M. (2002). Late recovery following spinal cord injury: Case report and review of the literature. *Journal of Neurosurgery: Spine, 97,* 252–265.

McFall, R. M., & Treat, T. A. (1999). Quantifying the information value of clinical assessments with signal detection theory. *Annual Review of Psychology, 50,* 215–241.

McGaugh, J. L. (1990). Significance and remembrance: The role of neuromodulatory systems. *Psychological Science, 1,* 15–25.

McGaugh J. L., & Roozendaal B. (2002). Role of adrenal stress hormones in forming lasting memories in the brain. *Current Opinions in Neurobiology, 12,* 205–210.

McGhie, A., & Chapman, J. (1961). Disorders of attention and perception in early schizophrenia. *British Journal of Medical Psychology, 34,* 102–116.

McGinnis, A. L. (1987). *The power of optimism.* San Francisco: Harper & Row.

McGlashan, T. H., & Fenton, W. S. (1991). Classical subtypes for schizophrenia: Literature review for DSM-IV. *Schizophrenia Bulletin, 17,* 609–623.

McGlashan, T. H., & Fenton, W. S. (1992). The positive-negative distinction in schizophrenia: Review of natural history validators. *Archives of General Psychiatry, 49,* 63–72.

McGlone, J. (1980). Sex differences in human brain asymmetry: A critical survey. *The Behavioral and Brain Sciences, 3,* 215–263.

McGlynn, S. M., & Kaszniak, A. W. (1991). When metacognition fails: Impaired awareness of deficit in Alzheimer's disease. *Journal of Cognitive Neuroscience, 3,* 183–189.

McGue, M., Bacon, S., & Lykken, D. T. (1993). Personality stability and change in early adulthood: A behavioral genetic analysis. *Developmental Psychology, 29,* 96–109.

McGue, M., & Lykken, D. T. (1992). Genetic influence on risk of divorce. *Psychological Science, 3,* 368–373.

McGuffin, P., Katz, R., Watkins, S., & Rutherford, J. (1996). A hospital-based twin register of the heritability of DSM-IV unipolar depression. *Archives of General Psychiatry, 53,* 129–136.

McGuire, A. M. (1994). Helping behaviors in the natural environment: Dimensions and correlates of helping. *Personality and Social Psychology Bulletin, 20,* 45–56.

McIntosh, D. N. (1996). Facial feedback hypothesis: Evidence, implications, and directions. *Motivation and Emotion, 20,* 121–147.

McKenna, K. Y. A., & Bargh, J. A. (1998). Coming out in the age of the Internet: "Demarginalization" through virtual group participation. *Journal of Personality and Social Psychology, 75,* 681–694.

McKinlay, J. B., McKinlay, S. M., & Brambilla, D. J. (1987a). Health status and utilization behavior associated with menopause. *American Journal of Epidemiology, 125,* 110–121.

McKinlay, J. B., McKinlay, S. M., & Brambilla, D. J. (1987b). The relative contributions of endocrine changes and social circumstances to depression in middle-aged women. *Journal of Health and Social Behavior, 28,* 345–363.

McMullin, R. E. (2000). *The new handbook of cognitive therapy techniques.* New York: W. W. Norton.

McNally, R. J. (1987). Preparedness and phobias: A review. *Psychological Bulletin, 101,* 283–303.

McNally, R. J. (1990). Psychological approaches to panic disorder: A review. *Psychological Bulletin, 108,* 403–419.

McNally, R. J. (1994). *Panic disorder: A critical analysis.* New York: Guilford Press.

McNamara, T. P. (1992). Priming and the constraints it places on theories of memory and retrieval. *Psychological Review, 99,* 650–662.

McNamara, T. P. (1994). Theories of priming: II. Types of primes. *Journal of Experimental Psychology: Learning, Memory, and Cognition, 20,* 507–520.

McNatt, D. B. (2000). Ancient Pygmalion joins contemporary management: A meta-analysis of the result. *Journal of Applied Psychology, 85,* 314–322.

McNeal, E. T., & Cimbolic, P. (1986). Antidepressants and biochemical theories of depression. *Psychological Bulletin, 99,* 361–374.

McNeill, D. (1970). *The acquisition of language: The study of developmental psycholinguistics.* New York: Harper & Row.

McPherson, M., Smith-Lovin, L., & Cook, J. M. (2001). Birds of a feather: Homophily in social networks. *Annual Review of Sociology, 27,* 415–444.

McRae, K., & Boisvert, S. (1998). Automatic semantic similarity priming. *Journal of Experimental Psychology: Learning, Memory, and Cognition, 24,* 558–572.

McReynolds, P. (1997). *Lightner Witmer: His life and times.* Washington, DC: American Psychological Association.

McSweeney, F. K., & Swindell, S. (1999). General-process theories of motivation revisited: The role of habituation. *Psychological Bulletin, 125,* 437–457.

McWhorter, K. T. (1988). *Study and thinking skills in college.* Glenview, IL: Scott, Foresman.

Mead, M. (1928). *Coming of age in Samoa.* New York: Morrow.

Mealey, L., Bridgstock, R., & Townsend, G. C. (1999). Symmetry and perceived facial attractiveness: A monozygotic co-twin comparison. *Journal of Personality and Social Psychology, 76,* 151–158.

Medina, J. J. (1996). *The clock of ages: Why we age–how we age–winding back the clock.* New York: Cambridge University Press.

Mednick, S. A. (1962). The associative basis of the creative process. *Psychological Review, 69,* 220–232.

Medvec, V. H., Madey, S. F., & Gilovich, T. (1995). When less is more: Counterfactual thinking and satisfaction among Olympic medalists. *Journal of Personality and Social Psychology, 69,* 603–610.

Medvec, V. H., & Savitsky, K. (1997). When doing better means feeling worse: The effects of categorical cutoff points on counterfactual thinking and satisfaction. *Journal of Personality and Social Psychology, 72,* 1284–1296.

Meehl, P. E. (1962). Schizotaxia, schizotypy, schizophrenia. *American Psychologist, 17,* 827–838.

Meeus, W. H. J., & Raaijmakers, Q. A. W. (1995). Obedience in modern society: The Utrecht studies. *Journal of Social Issues, 51,* 155–175.

Megargee, E. I., Carbonell, J. L., Bohn, M. J., & Sliger, G. L. (2001). *Classifying criminal offenders with the MMPI-2: The Megargee system.* Minneapolis: University of Minnesota Press.

Meichenbaum, D. (1985). *Stress inoculation training.* New York: Pergamon.

Meissner, C. A., & Brigham, J. C. (2001). 30 years of investigating the own-race bias in memory for faces: A meta-analytic review. *Psychology, Public Policy, & Law. 7,* 3–35.

Meltzer, H. Y. (2000). Genetics and etiology of schizophrenia and bipolar disorder. *Biological Psychiatry, 47,* 171–173.

Meltzoff, A. N., & Moore, M. K. (1983). Imitation of facial and manual gestures by human neonates. *Child Development, 54,* 702–709.

Meltzoff, A. N., & Moore, M. K. (1989). Imitation in newborn infants: Exploring the range of gestures imitated and the underlying mechanisms. *Developmental Psychology, 25,* 954–962.

Meltzoff, A. N., & Moore, M. K. (1992). Early imitation within a functional framework: The importance of person identity, movement, and development. *Infant Behavior and Development, 15,* 479–505.

Meltzoff, A. N., & Moore, M. K. (1998). Object representation, identity, and the paradox of early permanence: Steps toward a new framework. *Infant Behavior & Development, 21,* 201–235.

Melzack, R., & Wall, P. (1965). Pain mechanisms: A new theory. *Science, 150,* 971–979.

Melzack, R., & Wall, P. D. (2001). *The challenge of pain* (2nd updated ed.). London: Penguin.

Merikle, P., & Skanes, H. E. (1992). Subliminal self-help audiotapes: A search for placebo effects. *Journal of Applied Psychology, 77,* 772–776.

Merikle, P. M., Smilek, D., & Eastwood, J. D. (2001). Perception without awareness: Perspectives from cognitive psychology. *Cognition, 79,* 115–134.

Merzenich, M., Kass, J. H., Wall, J., Nelson, R. J., Sur, M., & Felleman, D. (1983). Topographic reorganization of somatosensory cortical areas 3b and 1 in adult monkeys following restricted deafferentiation. *Neuroscience, 8,* 33–55.

Mesquita, B., & Frijda, N. H. (1992). Cultural variations in emotions: A review. *Psychological Bulletin, 112,* 179–204.

Messier, C., Desrochers, A., & Gagnon, M. (1999). Effect of glucose, glucose regulation, and word imagery value on human memory. *Behavioral Neuroscience, 113,* 431–438.

Messinger, D. S., Fogel, A., & Dickson, K. L. (1999). What's in a smile? *Developmental Psychology, 35,* 701–708.

Meston, C. M., & Frohlich, P. F. (2000). The neurobiology of sexual function. *Archives of General Psychiatry, 57,* 1012–1030.

Metalsky, G. I., Joiner, T. E., Hardin, T. S., & Abramson, L. Y. (1993). Depressive reactions to failure in a naturalistic setting: A test of the hopelessness and self-esteem theories of depression. *Journal of Abnormal Psychology, 102,* 101–109.

Metcalfe, J., Funnell, M., & Gazzaniga, M. S. (1995). Right-hemisphere memory superiority: Studies of a split-brain patient. *Psychological Science, 6,* 157–164.

Metcalfe, J., & Mischel, W. (1999). A hot/cool system analysis of delay of gratification: Dynamics of willpower. *Psychological Review, 106,* 3–19.

Metcalfe, J., & Weibe, D. (1987). Intuition in insight and non-insight problem solving. *Memory and Cognition, 15,* 238–246.

Meyer, D. E., & Schvaneveldt, R. W. (1971). Facilitation in recognizing pairs of words: Evidence of a dependence between retrieval operations. *Journal of Experimental Psychology, 90,* 227–234.

Meyer, G. E., & Hilterbrand, K. (1984). Does it pay to be "Bashful"? The seven dwarfs and long-term memory. *American Journal of Psychology, 97,* 47–55.

Meyer, G. J., & Archer, R. P. (2001). The hard science of Rorschach research: What do we know and where do we go? *Psychological Assessment, 13,* 486–502.

Meyer, M. (1998, June 22). Truth and consequences. *Newsweek,* 83–84.

Meyer, V. (1966). Modification of expectations in cases with obsessional rituals. *Behaviour Research and Therapy, 4,* 273–280.

Mezzich, J. E., Kleinman, A., Fabrega, H., & Parron, D. L. (Eds.). (1996). *Culture and psychiatric diagnosis: A DSM-IV perspective.* Washington, DC: American Psychiatric Press.

Micale, M. S. (1995). *Approaching hysteria: Disease and its interpretations.* Princeton, NJ: Princeton University Press.

Michelson, L. K., & Ray, W. J. (Eds.). (1996). *Handbook of dissociation: Theoretical, empirical, and clinical perspectives.* New York: Plenum.

Middlebrooks, J. C., & Green, D. M. (1991). Sound localization by human listeners. *Annual Review of Psychology, 42,* 135–159.

Miele, F. (2002). *Intelligence, race, and genetics: Conversations with Arthur R. Jensen.* New York: Westview Press.

Miles, D. R., & Carey, G. (1997). Genetic and environmental architecture of human aggression. *Journal of Personality and Social Psychology, 72,* 207–217.

Milgram, S. (1963). Behavioral study of obedience. *Journal of Abnormal and Social Psychology, 67,* 371–378.

Milgram, S. (1965). Some conditions of obedience and disobedience to authority. *Human Relations, 18,* 57–76.

Milgram, S. (1974). *Obedience to authority: An experimental view.* New York: Harper & Row.

Milgram, S., Bickman, L., & Berkowitz, L. (1969). Note on the drawing power of crowds of different size. *Journal of Personality and Social Psychology, 13,* 79–82.

Millar, S., & Al-Attar, Z. (2002). The Muller-Lyer illusion in touch and vision: Implications for multisensory processes. *Perception and Psychophysics, 64,* 353–365.

Miller, A. G., Gordon, A. K., & Buddie, A. M. (1999). Accounting for evil and cruelty: Is to explain to condone? *Personality and Social Psychology Review, 3,* 254–268.

Miller, G. (1991). *The science of words.* New York: Freeman.

Miller, G. A. (1956). The magical number seven plus or minus two: Some limits on our capacity for processing information. *Psychological Review, 63,* 81–97.

Miller, G. E., & Cohen, S. (2001). Psychological interventions and the immune system: A meta-analytic review and critique. *Health Psychology, 20,* 47–63.

Miller, I. J., & Reedy, F. E. (1990). Variations in human taste bud density and taste intensity perception. *Physiology and Behavior, 47,* 1213–1219.

Miller, J. G. (1984). Culture and the development of everyday social explanation. *Journal of Personality and Social Psychology, 46,* 961–978.

Miller, J. G., & Bersoff, D. M. (1992). Culture and moral judgment: How are conflicts between justice and interpersonal responsibilities resolved? *Journal of Personality and Social Psychology, 62,* 541–554.

Miller, M., & Klaidman, D. (2002, August 4). The hunt for the anthrax killer. *Newsweek.*

Miller, N. E. (1969). Learning of visceral and glandular responses. *Science, 163,* 434–445.

Miller, N. E. (1985). The value of behavioral research on animals. *American Psychologist, 40,* 423–440.

Miller, N. S., & Gold, M. S. (1994). LSD and Ecstasy: Pharmacology, phenomenology, and treatment. *Psychiatric Annals, 24,* 131–133.

Miller, R. R., Barnet, R. C., & Grahame, N. J. (1995). Assessment of the Rescorla-Wagner model. *Psychological Bulletin, 117,* 363–386.

Miller, T. Q., Smith, T. W., Turner, C. W., Guijarro, M. L., & Hallet, A. J. (1996). A meta-analytic review of research on hostility and physical health. *Psychological Bulletin, 119,* 322–348.

Miller, T. Q., Turner, C. W., Tindale, R. S., Posavac, E. J., & Dugon, B. L. (1991). Reasons for the trend toward null findings in research on Type A behavior. *Psychological Bulletin, 110,* 469–485.

Miller, W. I. (1997). *The anatomy of disgust.* Cambridge, MA: Harvard University Press.

Miller-Jones, D. (1989). Culture and testing. *American Psychologist, 44,* 360–366.

Millon, T. (1995). *Disorders of personality: DSM-IV and beyond* (2nd ed.). New York: Wiley Interscience.

Millon, T. (Ed.). (2001). *Disorders of personality: DSM-IV and beyond* (2nd ed.). New York: Wiley.

Millon, T., Simonsen, E., Birket-Smith, M., & Davis, R. (1998). *Psychopathy: Antisocial, criminal, and violent behavior.* New York: Guilford.

Mills, H. L., Agras, W. S., Barlow, D. H., & Mills, J. R. (1973). Compulsive rituals treated by response prevention. *Archives of General Psychiatry, 28,* 524–529.

Milner, B., Corkin, S., & Teuber, H. L. (1968). Further analysis of the hippocampal amnesic syndrome: 14-year follow-up study of H. M. *Neuropsychologica, 6,* 215–234.

Milton, J., & Wiseman, R. (1999). Does Psi exist? Lack of replication of an anomalous process of information transfer. *Psychological Bulletin, 125,* 387–391.

Mimeault, V., & Morin, C. M. (1999). Self-help treatment for insomnia: Bibliotherapy with and without professional guidance. *Journal of Consulting and Clinical Psychology, 67,* 511–519.

Mineka, S., & Cook, M. (1993). Mechanisms involved in the observational conditioning of fear. *Journal of Experimental Psychology: General, 122,* 23–38.

Mineka, S., Mystkowski, J. L., Hladek, D., & Rodriguez, B. I. (1999). The effects of changing contexts on return of fear following exposure therapy for spider fear. *Journal of Consulting and Clinical Psychology, 67,* 599–604.

Minuchin, S. (1974). *Families and family therapy.* Cambridge, MA: Harvard University Press.

Mischel, W. (1968). *Personality and assessment.* New York: Wiley.

Mischel, W. (1973). Toward a cognitive social-learning reconceptualization of personality. *Psychological Review, 80,* 252–283.

Mischel, W., & Shoda, Y. (1995). A cognitive-affective system theory of personality: Reconceptualizing situations, dispositions, dynamics, and invariance in personality structure. *Psychological Review, 102,* 246–268.

Mischel, W., Shoda, Y., & Rodriguez, M. L. (1989). Delay of gratification in children. *Science, 244,* 933–938.

Mita, T. H., Dermer, M., & Knight, J. (1977). Reversed facial images and the mere-exposure hypothesis. *Journal of Personality and Social Psychology, 35,* 597–601.

Mitchell, P. (1976). *Act of love: The killing of George Zygmanik.* New York: Knopf.

Mitchell, S. H. (1999). Measures of impulsivity in cigarette smokers and non-smokers. *Psychopharmacology, 146,* 455–464.

Mitchell, T. R. (1974). Expectancy models of job satisfaction, occupational preference, and effort: A theoretical, methodological, and empirical appraisal. *Psychological Bulletin, 81,* 1096–1112.

Mitler, M. M., Carskadon, M. A., Czeisler, C. A., Dement, W. C., Dinges, D. F., & Graeber, R. C. (1988). Catastrophes, sleep, and public policy: A consensus report. *Sleep, 11,* 100–109.

Mitler, M. M., Miller, J. C., Lipsitz, J. J., Walsh, J. K., & Wylie, C. D. (1997). The sleep of long-haul truck drivers. *New England Journal of Medicine, 337,* 755–761.

Mittler, P. (1971). *The study of twins.* Harmondsworth, England: Penguin.

Mix, K. S., Huttenlocher, J., & Levine, S. C. (2002). Multiple cues for quantification in infancy: Is number one of them? *Psychological Bulletin, 128,* 278–294.

Miyake, A., & Shah, P. (Eds.). (1999). *Models of working memory: Mechanisms of active maintenance and executive control.* New York: Cambridge University Press.

Moffitt, T. E. (1993). Adolescence-limited and life-course persistent antisocial behavior: A developmental taxonomy. *Psychological Review, 100,* 674–701.

Moghaddam, F. M., Taylor, D. M., & Wright, S. C. (1993). *Social psychology in cross-cultural perspective.* New York: W. H. Freeman.

Mohr, C. D., Armeli, S., Tennen, H., Carney, M. A., Affleck, G., & Hromi, A. (2001). Daily interpersonal experiences, context, and alcohol consumption: Crying in your beer and toasting good times. *Journal of Personality and Social Psychology, 80,* 489–500.

Moir, A., & Jessel, D. (1989). *Brain sex: The real difference between men and women.* New York: Dell.

Mokdad, A. H., Serdula, M. K., Dietz, W. H., Bowman, B. A., Marks, J. S., & Koplan, J. P. (1999). The spread of the obesity epidemic in the United States, 1991–1998. *Journal of the American Medical Association, 282,* 1519–1522.

Mondloch, C. J., Lewis, T. L., Budreau, D. R., Maurer, D., Dannemiller, J. L., Stephens, B. R., & Kleiner-Gathercoal, K. A. (1999). Face perception during early infancy. *Psychological Science, 10,* 419–422.

Mondschein, E. R., Adolph, K. E., & Tamis-LeMonda, C. S. (2000). Gender bias in mothers' expectations about infant crawling. *Journal of Experimental Child Psychology, 77,* 304–316.

Moneta, G. B., & Csikszentmihalyi, M. (1996). The effect of perceived challenges and skills on the quality of subjective experience. *Journal of Personality, 64,* 275–310.

Mongeluzi, D. L., Rosellini, R. A., Caldarone, B. J., Stock, H. S., & Abrahamson, G. C. (1996). Pavlovian aversive conditioning using carbon dioxide as the unconditioned stimulus. *Journal of Experimental Psychology: Animal Behavior Processes, 22,* 244–257.

Monk, T. H. (1987). Coping with the stress of jet-lag. *Work & Stress, 1,* 163–166.

Monk, T. H. (1988). Coping with the stress of shift work. *Work & Stress, 2,* 169–172.

Montepare, J. M., & Lachman, M. E. (1989). "You're only as old as you feel": Self perceptions of age, fears of aging, and life satisfaction from adolescence to old age. *Psychology and Aging, 4,* 73–78.

Montepare, J. M., & McArthur, L. Z. (1988). Impressions of people created by age-related qualities of their gait. *Journal of Personality and Social Psychology, 55,* 547–556.

Montgomery, G. H., DuHamel, K. N., & Redd, W. H. (2000). A meta-analysis of hypnotically induced analgesia: How effective is hypnosis? *The International Journal of Clinical and Experimental Hypnosis, 48,* 138–153.

Moore, A. B., & Murphy, C. (1999). A demonstration of classical conditioning of the human eyeblink to an olfactory stimulus. *Physiology and Behavior, 66,* 689–693.

Moore, T. E. (1982). Subliminal advertising: What you see is what you get. *Journal of Marketing, 46,* 38–47.

Moran, G., & Cutler, B. L. (1991). The prejudicial impact of pretrial publicity. *Journal of Applied Social Psychology, 21,* 345–367.

Morawetz, D. (1989). Behavioral self-help treatment for insomnia: A controlled evaluation. *Behavior Therapy, 20,* 365–379.

Moray, N. (1959). Attention in dichotic listening: Affective cues and the influence of instructions. *Quarterly Journal of Experimental Psychology, 11,* 56–60.

Morelli, G. A., Rogoff, B., Oppenheim, D., & Goldsmith, D. (1992). Cultural variation in infants' sleeping arrangements: Questions of independence. *Developmental Psychology, 28,* 604–613.

Morgan, D. R. (1996). *Sleep secrets for shiftworkers and people with off-beat schedules.* New York: Whole Person Associates.

Mori, D., Chaiken, S., & Pliner, P. (1987). Eating lightly and the self-presentation of femininity. *Journal of Personality and Social Psychology, 53,* 693–702.

Morin, C. M. (1996). *Relief from insomnia: Getting the sleep of your dreams.* New York: Doubleday.

Morin, C. M., Hauri, P. J., Espie, C. A., Spielman, A., Buysee, D. J., et al. (1999). Nonpharmacologic treatment of insomnia: An American Academy of Sleep Medicine review. *Sleep, 22,* 1134–1156.

Morris, M. W., & Nisbett, R. E. (1993). Tools of the trade: Deductive schemas taught in psychology and philosophy. In R. E. Nisbett (Ed.), *Rules for reasoning* (pp. 228–256). Hillsdale, NJ: Erlbaum.

Morrison, D. C. (1988). Marine mammals join the navy. *Science, 242,* 1503–1504.

Morrongiello, B. A., & Dawber, T. (2000). Mothers' responses to sons and daughters engaging in injury-risk behaviors on a playground: Implications for sex differences in injury rates. *Journal of Experimental Child Psychology, 76,* 89–103.

Mortimer, J. T., & Larson, R. W. (Eds.). (2002). *The changing adolescent experience: Societal trends and the transition to adulthood.* New York: Cambridge University Press.

Morton, J., & Johnson, M. H. (1991). CONSPEC and CONLERN: A two-process theory of infant face recognition. *Psychological Review, 98,* 164–181.

Moscovici, S. (1985). Social influence and conformity. In G. Lindzey & E. Aronson (Eds.), *The handbook of social psychology* (3rd ed., pp. 347–412). New York: Random House.

Moscovici, S., Lage, E., & Naffrechoux, M. (1969). Influence of a consistent minority on the responses of a majority in a color perception task. *Sociometry, 32,* 365–380.

Moskowitz, D. S. (1982). Coherence and cross-situational generality in personality: A new analysis of old problems. *Journal of Personality and Social Psychology, 43,* 754–768.

Moulton, J., Robinson, G. M., & Elias, C. (1978). Sex bias in language use: "Neutral pronouns that aren't." *American Psychologist, 33,* 1032–1036.

Mounts, N. S., & Steinberg, L. (1995). An ecological analysis of peer influence on adolescent grade point average and drug use. *Developmental Psychology, 31,* 915–922.

Moutoussis, K., & Zeki, S. (2002). Responses of spectrally selective cells in macaque area V2 to wavelengths and colors. *Journal of Neurophysiology, 87,* 2104–2112.

Moynihan, J. A., & Ader, R. (1996). Psychoneuroimmunology: Animal models of disease. *Psychosomatic Medicine, 58,* 546–558.

Mozell, M. M., Smith, B., Smith, P., Sullivan, R., & Swender, P. (1969). Nasal chemoreception in flavor identification. *Archives of Otolaryngology, 90,* 367–373.

Mueller, C. M., & Dweck, C. S. (1998). Praise for intelligence can undermine children's motivation and performance. *Journal of Personality and Social Psychology, 75,* 33–52.

Mullen, B. (1986). Atrocity as a function of lynch mob composition: A self-attention perspective. *Personality and Social Psychology Bulletin, 12,* 187–197.

Muller, R. A., Rothermel, R. D., Behen, M. E., Muzic, O., Chakraborty, P. K., & Chugani, H. T. (1999). Language organization in patients with early and late left-hemisphere lesion: A PET study. *Neuropsychologia, 37,* 545–557.

Mulligan, R., Van Der Linden, M., & Juillera, A. C. (Eds.). (2003). *The clinical management of early Alzheimer's disease: A handbook.* Mahwah, NJ: Erlbaum.

Mullington, J., & Broughton, R. (1993). Scheduled naps in the management of daytime sleepiness in narcolepsy-cataplexy. *Sleep, 16,* 444–456.

Murdock, G. P., & Provost, C. (1973). Factors in the division of labor by sex: A cross-cultural analysis. *Ethnology, 12,* 203–225.

Murray, H. A. (1938). *Explorations in personality.* New York: Oxford University Press.

Murray, H. A. (1943). *Thematic Apperception Test: Pictures and manual.* Cambridge, MA: Harvard University Press.

Murray, S. L., Holmes, J. G., & Griffin, D. W. (1996). The benefits of positive illusions: Idealization and the construction of satisfaction in close relationships. *Journal of Personality and Social Psychology, 70,* 79–98.

Murtagh, D. R. R., & Greenwood, K. M. (1995). Identifying effective psychological treatments for insomnia: A meta-analysis. *Journal of Consulting and Clinical Psychology, 63,* 79–89.

Must, A., Spadano, J., Coakley, E. H., Field, A. E., Colditz, G., & Dietz, W. H. (1999). The disease burden associated with overweight and obesity. *Journal of the American Medical Association, 282,* 1523–1529.

Mydans, S. (1990, January). For jurors, facts could not be sifted from fantasies. *The New York Times,* p. A18.

Myers, D. G. (1993). *The pursuit of happiness.* New York: Avon.

Myers, D. G., & Diener, E. (1995). Who is happy? *Psychological Science, 6,* 10–19.

Myers, M. G., Stewart, D. G., & Brown, S. A. (1998). Progression from conduct disorder to antisocial personality disorder following treatment for adolescent substance abuse. *American Journal of Psychiatry, 155,* 479–485.

Myerson, J., Rank, M. R., Raines, F. Q., & Schintzler, M. A. (1998). Race and general cognitive ability: The myth of diminishing returns to education. *Psychological Science, 9,* 139–142.

Nadel, L., & Jacobs, W. J. (1998). Traumatic memory is special. *Current Directions in Psychological Science, 7,* 154–157.

Nadler, G., & Hibino, S. (1998). *Breakthrough thinking: The seven principles of creative problem solving.* Roseville, CA: Prima Publishing.

Nadon, R., Hoyt, I. P., Register, P. A., & Kihlstrom, J. F. (1991). Absorption and hypnotizability: Context effects reexamined. *Journal of Personality and Social Psychology, 60,* 144–153.

Nantais, K. M., & Schellenberg, E. G. (1999). The Mozart effect: An artifact of preference. *Psychological Science, 10,* 370–373.

Narrow, W. E., Rae, D. S., Robins, L. N., & Regier, D. A. (2002). Revised prevalence estimates of mental disorders in the United States: Using a clinical significance criterion to reconcile 2 surveys' estimates. *Archives of General Psychiatry, 59,* 115–123.

Narvaez, D., Getz, I. Rest, J. R., & Thoma, S. J. (1999). Individual moral judgment and cultural ideologies. *Developmental Psychology, 35,* 478–488.

Nathan, P. E., & Gorman, J. M. (Eds.). (1998). *A guide to treatments that work.* New York: Oxford University Press.

Nathan, P. E., & Langenbucher, J. W. (1999). Psychopathology: Description and classification. *Annual Review of Psychology, 50,* 79–107.

Nathans, J. (1989). The genes for color vision. *Scientific American, 260,* 42–49.

Nathans, J., Piantanida, T. P., Eddy, R. L., Shows, T. B., & Hogness, D. S. (1986). Molecular genetics of inherited variation in human color vision. *Science, 232,* 203–210.

National Center for Health Statistics. (1999). *Teen birth rate down in all states.* Hyattsville, MD: Public Health Service.

National Institute of Mental Health's Genetics Workgroup. (1999). Report of the National Institute of Mental Health's Genetics Workgroup. *Biological Psychiatry, 45,* 559–602.

National Institute on Drug Abuse. (2002). *Monitoring the future survey shows decrease in use of marijuana, club drugs, cigarettes and tobacco.* Washington, DC: U.S. Department of Health and Human Services. Retrieved from the World Wide Web: www.drugabuse.gov/DrugPages/MTF.html

National Law Journal. (1990, September 10). Rock group not liable for deaths, p. 33.

National Sleep Foundation. (2002, April 2). *2002 "Sleep in America" poll.*

*National Television Violence Study, Vol. 2.* (1998). Thousand Oaks, CA: Sage.

Neath, I., & Crowder, R. G. (1996). Distinctiveness and very short-term serial position effects. *Memory, 4,* 225–242.

Nebes, R. D. (1990). The commissurotomized brain: Introduction. In R. D. Nebes & S. Corkin (Eds.), *Handbook of neuropsychology* (Vol. 4). Amsterdam, Netherlands: Elsevier.

Neiberg, P., Marks, J. S., McLaren, N. M., & Remongton, P. (1985). The fetal tobacco syndrome. *Journal of the American Medical Association, 253,* 2998–2999.

Neill, S. R. (1982). Preschool design and child behavior. *Journal of Child Psychology and Psychiatry, 23,* 309–318.

Neisser, U. (1967). *Cognitive psychology.* New York: Appleton-Century-Crofts.

Neisser, U. (1981). John Dean's memory: A case study. *Cognition, 9,* 1–22.

Neisser, U. (Ed.). (1982). *Memory observed.* San Francisco: W. H. Freeman.

Neisser, U. (Ed.). (1998). *The rising curve: Long-term gains in IQ and related measures.* Washington, DC: American Psychological Association.

Neisser, U., & Becklen, R. (1975). Selective looking: Attending to visually specified events. *Cognitive Psychology, 7,* 480–494.

Neisser, U., et al. (1996). Intelligence: Knowns and unknowns. *American Psychologist, 51,* 77–101.

Nelson, C. A. (1995). The ontogeny of human memory: A cognitive neuroscience perspective. *Developmental Psychology, 31,* 723–738.

Nelson, C. A. (1999). Neural plasticity and human development. *Current Directions in Psychological Science, 8,* 42–45.

Nelson, K. (1973). Structure and strategy in learning to talk. *Monographs of the Society for Research in Child Development, 38*(Whole No. 149).

Nelson, R. J. (Ed.). (2001). *The somatosensory system: Deciphering the brain's own body image.* Boca Raton, FL: CRC Press.

Nelson, T. E., Acker, M., & Manis, M. (1996). Irrepressible stereotypes. *Journal of Experimental Social Psychology, 32,* 13–38.

Nemeroff, C. B. (1989). Clinical significance of psychoneuroendocrinology in psychiatry: Focus on the thyroid and adrenal. *Journal of Clinical Psychiatry, 50,* 13–20.

Nersessian, E., & Kopff, R. G., Jr. (Eds.). (1996). *Textbook of psychoanalysis.* Washington, DC: American Psychiatric Press.

Nesse, R. M. (2000). Is depression an adaptation? *Archives of General Psychiatry, 57,* 14–20.

Neugarten, B. L. (1979). Time, age, and the life cycle. *American Journal of Psychiatry, 136,* 887–894.

Neumann, R., & Strack, F. (2000). "Mood contagion": The automatic transfer of mood between persons. *Journal of Personality and Social Psychology, 79,* 211–223.

Nevid, J. S., Lavi, B., & Primavera, L. H. (1987). Principal components analysis of therapeutic orientations of doctoral programs in clinical psychology. *Journal of Clinical Psychology, 43,* 723–729.

Nevin, J. A. (1988). Behavioral momentum and the partial reinforcement effect. *Psychological Bulletin, 103,* 44–56.

Newby-Clark, I. R., McGregor, I., & Zanna, M. P. (2002). Thinking and caring about cognitive consistency: When and for whom does attitudinal ambivalence feel uncomfortable? *Journal of Personality and Social Psychology, 82,* 157–166.

Newcomb, A. F., & Bagwell, C. L. (1995). Children's friendship relations: A meta-analytic review. *Psychological Bulletin, 117,* 306–347.

Newcomb, A. F., Bukowski, W. M., & Pattee, L. (1993). Children's peer relations: A meta-analytic review of popular, rejected, neglected, controversial, and average sociometric status. *Psychological Bulletin, 113,* 99–128.

Newcombe, F., & Ratcliff, G. (1990). Disorders of visuospatial analysis. In H. Goodglass & A. R. Damasio (Eds.), *Handbook of neuropsychology* (Vol. 2). Amsterdam, Netherlands: Elsevier.

Newcombe, N., & Fox, N. A. (1994). Infantile amnesia: Through a glass darkly. *Child Development, 65*, 31–40.

Newcombe, N. S., & Baenninger, M. (1989). Biological change and cognitive ability in adolescence. In G. Adams, R. Montemayor, & T. Gullotta (Eds.), *Biology of adolescent behavior and development* (pp. 168–191). Newbury Park, CA: Sage.

Newell, A., Shaw, J. G., & Simon, H. A. (1958). Elements of a theory of human problem solving. *Psychological Review, 65*, 151–166.

Newell, A., & Simon, H. (1972). *Human problem solving.* Englewood Cliffs, NJ: Prentice-Hall.

Newman, A. W., & Thompson, J. W. (1999). Constitutional rights and hypnotically elicited testimony. *Journal of the American Academy of Psychiatry and the Law, 27*, 149–154.

Newman, C. (2000, January). The enigma of beauty. *National Geographic,* pp. 94–121.

Newmann, J. P. (1989). Aging and depression. *Psychology and Aging, 4*, 150–165.

Nezlek, J. B., Imbrie, M., & Shean, G. D. (1994). Depression and everyday social interaction. *Journal of Personality and Social Psychology, 67*, 1101–1111.

Ng, S. H. (1990). Androcentric coding of *man* and *his* in memory by language users. *Journal of Experimental Social Psychology, 26*, 455–464.

Nickerson, R. S. (1998). Confirmation bias: A ubiquitous phenomenon in many guises. *Review of General Psychology, 2*, 175–220.

Nickerson, R. S., & Adams, M. J. (1979). Long-term memory for a common object. *Cognitive Psychology, 11*, 287–307.

Niedermeyer, E., & Da Silva, Lopes, F. (Eds.). (1999). *Electroencephalography: Basic principles, clinical applications, and related fields* (4th ed.). Baltimore: Lippincott, Williams, & Wilkins.

Nigg, J. T. (2001). Is ADHD a disinhibitory disorder? *Psychological Bulletin, 127*, 571–598.

Nijhawan, R. (1991). Three-dimensional Müller-Lyer illusion. *Perception and Psychophysics, 49*, 333–341.

Nikles, C., Brecht, D., Klinger, E., & Bursell, A. (1998). The effects of current concern- and nonconcern-related waking suggestions and nocturnal dream content. *Journal of Personality and Social Psychology, 75*, 242–255.

Nimmons, D. (1994, March). Sex and the brain. *Discover,* pp. 64–71.

Nisbett, R. E., & Cohen, D. (1996). *Culture of honor: The psychology of violence in the South.* New York: Westview.

Nisbett, R. E., Fong, G. T., Lehman, D. R., & Cheng, P. W. (1987). Teaching reasoning. *Science, 238*, 625–631.

Nisbett, R. E., & Ross, L. (1980). *Human inference: Strategies and shortcomings of social judgment.* Englewood Cliffs, NJ: Prentice-Hall.

Nisbett, R. E., & Wilson, T. D. (1977). Telling more than we can know: Verbal reports on mental processes. *Psychological Review, 84*, 231–259.

Noble, J., & McConkey, K. M. (1995). Hypnotic sex change: Creating and challenging a delusion in the laboratory. *Journal of Abnormal Psychology, 104*, 69–74.

Nolen-Hoeksema, S. (1990). *Sex differences in depression.* Palo Alto, CA: Stanford University Press.

Nolen-Hoeksema, S., & Girgus, J. S. (1994). The emergence of gender differences in depression during adolescence. *Psychological Bulletin, 115*, 424–443.

Nolen-Hoeksema, S., Morrow, J., & Fredrickson, N. (1993). Response styles and the duration of episodes of depressed mood. *Journal of Abnormal Psychology, 102*, 20–28.

Norcross, J. C. (1991). Prescriptive matching in psychotherapy: An introduction. *Psychotherapy, 28*, 439–443.

Norcross, J. C., Hedges, M., & Prochaska, J. O. (2002). The face of 2010: A Delphi poll on the future of psychotherapy. *Professional Psychology: Research and Practice, 33*, 316–322.

Norenzayan, A., & Nisbett, R. E. (2000). Culture and causal cognition. *Current Directions in Psychological Science, 9*, 132–135.

Norton, G. R., Cox, B., & Malan, J. (1992). Nonclinical panickers: A critical review. *Clinical Psychology Review, 12*, 121–139.

Norton, K. I., Olds, T. S., Olive, S., & Dank, S. (1996). Ken and Barbie at life size. *Sex Roles, 34*, 287–294.

Nosek, B. A., Banaji, M. R., & Greenwald, A. G. (2002). Harvesting implicit attitudes and stereotype data from the Implicit Association Test Web site. *Group Dynamics, 6*, 101–115.

Nunez, P. L. (2003). *Electric fields of the brain: Neurophysics of EEG* (2nd ed.). New York: Oxford University Press.

Oakes, J. (1986). *Keeping track: How schools structure inequality.* New Haven, CT: Yale University Press.

Oakhill, J. V., Johnson-Laird, P. N. & Garnham, A. (1989). Believability and syllogistic reasoning. *Cognition, 31*, 117–140.

O'Connell, A. N., & Russo, N. F. (Eds.). (1990). *Women in psychology: A bio-bibliographic sourcebook.* Westport, CT: Greenwood Press.

O'Connor, S. C., & Rosenblood, L. K. (1996). Affiliation motivation in everyday experience: A theoretical comparison. *Journal of Personality and Social Psychology, 70*, 513–522.

O'Craven, K. M., & Kanwisher, N. (2000). Mental imagery of faces and places activates corresponding stimulus-specific brain regions. *Journal of Cognitive Neuroscience, 12*, 1013–1023.

Oesterman, K., Bjoerkqvist, K., Lagerspetz, K. M. J., Kaukiainen, A., Landau, S. F., Fraczek, A., & Caprara, G. V. (1998). Cross-cultural evidence of female indirect aggression. *Aggressive Behavior, 24*, 1–8.

Offer, D. (1987). In defense of adolescents. *Journal of the American Medical Association, 257*, 3407–3408.

Offer, D., Kaiz, M., Howard, K. I., & Bennett, E. S. (1998). Emotional variables in adolescence, and their stability and contribution to the mental health of adult men: Implications for early intervention strategies. *Journal of Youth and Adolescence, 27*, 675–690.

Offer, D., Ostrov, E., & Howard, I. (1981). *The adolescent: A psychological self-portrait.* New York: Basic Books.

Offer, D., & Schonert-Reichl, K. A. (1992). Debunking the myths of adolescence: Findings from recent research. *Journal of the American Academy of Child and Adolescent Psychiatry, 31*, 1003–1013.

Ogbu, J. U. (1978). *Minority education and caste: The American system in cross-cultural perspective.* New York: Academic Press.

Ogilvy, D. (1985). *Ogilvy on advertising.* New York: Vintage Books.

Ohman, A. (1986). Face the beast and fear the face: Animal and social fears as prototypes for evolutionary analyses of emotion. *Psychophysiology, 23*, 123–145.

Ohman, A., & Mineka, S. (2001). Fears, phobias, and preparedness: Toward an evolved module of fear and fear learning. *Psychological Review, 108*, 483–522.

Ohman, A., & Soares, J. J. F. (1998). Emotional conditioning to masked stimuli: Expectancies for aversive outcomes following nonrecognized fear-relevant stimuli. *Journal of Experimental Psychology: General, 127*, 69–82.

Oishi, S., Diener, E. F., Lucas, R. E., & Suh, E. M. (1999). Cross-cultural variations in predictors of life satisfaction: Perspectives from needs and values. *Personality and Social Psychology Bulletin, 25*, 980–990.

Okagaki, L., & Frensch, P. A. (1994). Effects of video game playing on measures of spatial performance: Gender effects in late adolescence. *Journal of Applied Developmental Psychology, 15*, 33–58.

Olds, J., & Milner, P. M. (1954). Positive reinforcement produced by electrical stimulation of septal area and other regions of the rat brain. *Journal of Comparative and Physiological Psychology, 47*, 419–427.

O'Leary, A. (1990). Stress, emotion, and human immune function. *Psychological Bulletin, 108*, 363–382.

Oleson, J., Tfelt-Hansen, P., & Welch, K. M. A. (Eds.). (2000). *The headaches* (2nd ed.). Baltimore: Lippincott, Williams & Wilkins.

Olfson, M., Marcus, S. C., Druss, B., Elinson, L., Tanielian, T., & Pincus, H. A. (2002). National trends in the outpatient treatment of depression. *Journal of the American Medical Association, 287*, 203–209.

Oliver, G., & Wardle, J. (1999). Perceived effects of stress on food choice. *Physiology & Behavior, 66*, 511–515.

Oliver, M. B., & Hyde, J. S. (1993). Gender differences in sexuality: A meta-analysis. *Psychological Bulletin, 114*, 29–51.

Olness, K. (1993). Hypnosis: The power of attention. In D. Goleman & J. Gurin (Eds.), *Mind body medicine* (pp. 277–290). Yonkers, NY: Consumer Reports Books.

Olson, J. M. (1988). Misattribution, preparatory information, and speech anxiety. *Journal of Personality and Social Psychology, 54*, 758–767.

Olson, J. M., Vernon, P. A., Harris, J. A., & Jang, K. L. (2001). The heritability of attitudes: A study of twins. *Journal of Personality and Social Psychology, 80*, 845–860.

Olzak, S., & Nagel, J. (1986). *Competitive ethnic relations.* New York: Academic Press.

Ones, D. S., Viswesvaran, C., & Reiss, A. D. (1996). Role of social desirability in personality testing for personnel selection: The red herring. *Journal of Applied Psychology, 81*, 660–679.

Ones, D. S., Viswesvaran, C., & Schmidt, F. L. (1993). Comprehensive meta-analysis of integrity test validities: Findings and implications for personnel selection and theories of job performance. *Journal of Applied Psychology, 78*, 679–703.

Oren, D. (1995). *How to beat jet lag.* New York: Henry Holt.

Orne, M. T., & Evans, F. J. (1965). Social control in the psychological experiment: Antisocial behavior and hypnosis. *Journal of Personality and Social Psychology, 1*, 189–200.

Orne, M. T., Dinges, D. F., & Orne, E. C. (1984). The differential diagnosis of multiple personality in the forensic court. *International Journal of Clinical and Experimental Hypnosis, 32*, 118–169.

Ornstein, R. E. (1978). The split and whole brain. *Human Nature, 1*, 76–83.

Ornstein, R., & Sobel, D. (1987). *The healing brain.* New York: Simon & Schuster.

Ost, L.-G. (1989). One-session treatment for specific phobias. *Behavioral Research and Therapy, 27*, 1–7.

Ost, L.-G. (1992). Blood and injection phobia: Background and cognitive, physiological, and behavioral variables. *Journal of Abnormal Psychology, 101*, 68–74.

Ost, L.-G., Salkovskis, P. M., & Helistrom, K. (1991). One-session therapist-directed exposure vs. self-exposure in the treatment of spider phobia. *Behavior Therapy, 22*, 407–422.

Ostrom, T. M., & Sedikides, C. (1992). Out-group homogeneity effects in natural and minimal groups. *Psychological Bulletin, 112*, 536–552.

Overman, W. H., Bachevalier, J., Schuhmann, E., & Ryan, P. (1996). Cognitive gender differences in very young children parallel biologically based cognitive gender differences in monkeys. *Behavioral Neuroscience, 110*, 673–684.

Oyserman, D., Coon, H. M., & Kemmelmeier, M. (2002). Rethinking individualism and collectivism: Evaluation of theoretical assumptions and meta-analyses. *Psychological Bulletin, 128*, 3–72.

*P.A.S.E. v. Hannon,* 506 F. Supp. 931 (N. D. Ill. 1980).

Pace-Schott, E. F., Solms, M., Blagrove, M., & Harnad, S. (Eds.). (2002). *Sleep and dreaming: Scientific advances and reconsiderations.* New York: Cambridge University Press.

Packard, V. (1957). *The hidden persuaders.* New York: Pocket Books.

Paffenbarger, R. S., Jr., Hyde, R. T., Wing, A. L., & Hsieh, C. (1986). Physical activity, all-cause mortality, and longevity of college alumni. *New England Journal of Medicine, 314*, 605–613.

Paivio, A. (1969). Mental imagery in associative learning and memory. *Psychological Review, 76*, 241–263.

Paivio, A. (1986). *Mental representations: A dual coding approach.* New York: Oxford University Press.

Palfai, T., & Jankiewicz, H. (1991). *Drugs and human behavior.* Dubuque, IA: William C. Brown.

Palmer, S. E. (1999). *Vision science: Photons to phenomenology.* Cambridge, MA: MIT Press.

Palmore, E. B. (1982). Predictors of the longevity difference: A 25-year follow-up. *The Gerontologist, 22*, 513–518.

Panskepp, J. (1986). The anatomy of emotions. In R. Plutchik & H. Kellerman (Eds.), *Emotion: Theory, research, and experience-Biological foundations of emotion* (Vol. 3, pp. 91–124). San Diego: Academic Press.

Panskepp, J. (1992). A critical role for "affective neuroscience" in resolving what is basic about basic emotions. *Psychological Review, 99*, 554–560.

Parducci, A. (1995). *Happiness, pleasure, and judgment: The contextual theory and its applications.* Mahwah, NJ: Erlbaum.

Parke, R. D. (1981). *Fathers.* Cambridge, MA: Harvard University Press.

Parker, J. G., & Asher, S. R. (1987). Peer relations and later adjustment: Are low-accepted children "at risk"? *Psychological Bulletin, 102,* 357–389.

Parker, K., Hanson, R., & Hinsley, J. (1988). MMPI, Rorschach, and WAIS: A meta-analytic comparison of reliability, stability, and validity. *Psychological Bulletin, 103,* 367–373.

Parks, R. W., Zee, R. F., & Wilson, R. S. (Eds.) (1993). *Neuropsychology of Alzheimer's disease and other dementias.* New York: Oxford University Press.

Parmelee, A. H., Jr., & Sigman, M. D. (1983). Perinatal brain development and behavior. In P. H. Mussen (Ed.), *Handbook of child psychology: Vol. 2. Infancy and developmental psychobiology.* New York: Wiley.

Parsons, L. M., & Fox, P. T. (1998). The neural basis of implicit movements used in recognizing hand shape. *Cognitive-Neuropsychology, 15,* 583–615.

Pascalis, O., de Schonen, S., Morton, J., DeRuelle, C., & Fabre-Grenet, M. (1995). Mother's face recognition by neonates: A replication and an extension. *Infant Behavior and Development, 18,* 79–85.

Pascual-Leone, A., Camarota, A., Wassermann, E. M., et al. (1993). Modulation of motor cortical outputs to the reading hand of Braille readers. *Annals of Neurology, 34,* 33–37.

Pashler, H., Johnston, J. C., & Ruthruff, E. (2001). Attention and performance. *Annual Review of Psychology, 52,* 629–651.

Pashler, H. E. (1998). *The psychology of attention.* Cambridge, MA: MIT Press.

Passman, R. H. (1987). Attachments to inanimate objects: Are children who have security blankets insecure? *Journal of Consulting and Clinical Psychology, 55,* 825–830.

Patel, K. A., & Schlundt, D. G. (2001). Impact of moods and social context on eating behavior. *Appetite, 36,* 111–118.

Patrick, C. J., Bradley, M. M., & Lang, P. J. (1993). Emotion in the criminal psychopath: Startle reflex modulation. *Journal of Abnormal Psychology, 102,* 82–92.

Patrick, C. J., & Iacono, W. G. (1991). Validity of the control question polygraph test: The problem of sampling bias. *Journal of Applied Psychology, 76,* 229–238.

Patterson, F., & Linden, E. (1981). *The education of Koko.* New York: Holt, Rinehart & Winston.

Patterson, M. L. (1983). *Nonverbal behavior: A functional perspective.* New York: Springer-Verlag.

Paulesu, E., Harrison, J., Baron-Cohen, S., et al. (1995). The physiology of coloured hearing: A PET activation study of colour-word synesthesia. *Brain, 118,* 661–676.

Paulos, J. A. (1988). *Innumeracy: Mathematical illiteracy and its consequences.* New York: Hill and Wang.

Paunonen, S. V., & Ashton, M. C. (2001). Big five factors and facets and the prediction of behavior. *Journal of Personality and Social Psychology, 81,* 524–539.

Paunonen, S. V., Jackson, D. N., Trzebinski, J., & Fosterling, F. (1992). Personality structure across cultures: A multimethod evaluation. *Journal of Personality and Social Psychology, 62,* 447–456.

Pavlov, I. (1927). *Conditioned reflexes.* Oxford, England: Oxford University Press.

Pavot, W., & Diener, E. (1993). Review of the Satisfaction with Life Scale. *Psychological Assessment, 5,* 164–172.

Payne, D. G., Elie, C. J., Blackwell, J. M., & Neuschatz, J. S. (1996). Memory illusions: Recalling, recognizing, and recollecting events that never occurred. *Journal of Memory and Language, 35,* 261–285.

Peake, P. K., Hebl, M., & Mischel, W. (2002). Strategic attention deployment for delay of gratification in working and waiting situations. *Developmental Psychology, 38,* 313–326.

Pearce, J. M. (1987). A model for stimulus generalization in Pavlovian conditioning. *Psychological Review, 94,* 61–73.

Pearce, J. M., & Bouton, M. E. (2001). Theories of associative learning in animals. *Annual Review of Psychology, 52,* 111–139.

Pease, B., & Pease, A. (2001). *Why men don't listen and women can't read maps: How we're different and what to do about it.* New York: Broadway Books.

Pederson, D. R., & Moran, G. (1996). Expressions of the attachment relationship outside the strange situation. *Child Development, 67,* 915–927.

Pedone, R., Hummel, J. E., & Holyoak, K. J. (2001). The use of diagrams in analogical problem solving. *Memory and Cognition, 29,* 214–221.

Pelham, B. W. (1995). Self-investment and self-esteem: Evidence for a Jamesian model of self-worth. *Journal of Personality and Social Psychology, 69,* 1141–1150.

Pelham, B. W., & Swann, W. B., Jr. (1989). From self-conceptions to self-worth: The sources and structure of self-esteem. *Journal of Personality and Social Psychology, 57,* 672–680.

Pelham, W. E., Carlson, C. L., Sams, S. E., Vallano, G., et al. (1993). Separate and combined effects of methylphenidate and behavior modification on boys with attention deficit hyperactivity disorder in the classroom. *Journal of Consulting and Clinical Psychology, 61,* 506–515.

Penfield, W., & Perot, P. (1963). The brain's record of auditory and visual experience. *Brain, 86,* 595–696.

Penfield, W., & Roberts, L. (1959). *Speech and brain mechanisms.* Princeton, NJ: Princeton University Press.

Pennebaker, J. W. (1990). *Opening up: The healing power of confiding in others.* New York: Morrow.

Pennebaker, J. W. (1997). *Opening up: The healing power of expressing emotions.* New York: Guilford.

Pennebaker, J. W. (1997). Writing about emotional experiences as a therapeutic process. *Psychological Science, 8,* 162–166.

Penrod, S. D., & Cutler, B. L. (1995). *Mistaken identification: The eyewitness, psychology, and the law.* New York: Cambridge University Press.

Peplau, L. A., Garnets, L. D., Spalding, L. R., Conley, T. D., & Veniegas, R. C. (1998). A critique of Bem's "Exotic becomes erotic" theory of sexual orientation. *Psychological Review, 105,* 387–394.

Pepperberg, I. M. (2000). *The Alex studies: Cognitive and communicative abilities of grey parrots.* Cambridge, MA: Harvard University Press.

Pepperberg, I. M. (2002). Cognitive and communicative abilities of Grey parrots. *Current Directions in Psychological Science, 11,* 83–87.

Perdue, C. W., Dovidio, J. F., Gurtman, M. B., & Tyler, R. B. (1990). Us and them: Social categorization and the process of intergroup bias. *Journal of Personality and Social Psychology, 59,* 475–486.

Perlow, M. J., Freed, W. J., Hoffer, B. J., Seiger, A., Olson, L., & Wyatt, R. J. (1979). Brain grafts reduce motor abnormalities produced by destruction of nigrostriatal dopamine system. *Science, 204,* 643–646.

Perls, F. S. (1969). *Gestalt therapy verbatim.* Lafayette, CA: Real People Press.

Perls, F. S., Heffertine, R. F., & Goodman, P. (1951). *Gestalt therapy.* New York: Julian Press.

Persky, V. W., Kempthorne-Rawson, J., & Shekelle, R. B. (1987). Personality and risk of cancer: 20-year follow-up of the Western Electric Study. *Psychosomatic Medicine, 49,* 435–449.

Pert, C. B., & Snyder, S. H. (1973). Opiate receptor: Demonstration in nervous tissue. *Science, 179,* 1011–1014.

Perugini, E. M., Kirsch, I., Allen, S. T., Coldwell, E., Meredith, J. M., Montgomery, G. H., & Sheehan, J. (1998). Surreptitious observations of responses to hypnotically suggested hallucinations: A test of the compliance hypothesis. *International Journal of Clinical and Experimental Hypnosis, 46,* 191–203.

Peskind, E. R. (1998). Pharmacologic approaches to cognitive deficits in Alzheimer's disease. *Journal of Clinical Psychiatry, 59,* 22–27.

Petersen, A. C. (1984). The early adolescence study: An overview. *Journal of Early Adolescence, 4,* 103–106.

Petersen, A. C. (1985). Pubertal development as a cause of disturbance: Myths, realities, and unanswered questions. *Genetic, Social, and General Psychology Monographs, 111,* 205–232.

Petersen, A. C. (1988). Adolescent development. *Annual Review of Psychology, 39,* 583–607.

Peterson, A. C., Compas, B. E., Brooks-Gunn, J., Stemmler, M., Ey, S., & Grant, K. E. (1993). Depression in adolescence. *American Psychologist, 48,* 155–168.

Peterson, B. E., & Stewart, A. J. (1996). Antecedents and contexts of generativity motivation at midlife. *Psychology and Aging, 11,* 21–33.

Peterson, C. (2000). The future of optimism. *American Psychologist, 55,* 44–55.

Peterson, C., Seligman, M. E. P., & Vaillant, G. E. (1988). Pessimistic explanatory style is a risk factor for physical illness: A thirty-five-year longitudinal study. *Journal of Personality and Social Psychology, 55,* 23–27.

Peterson, C., Seligman, M. E. P., Yurko, K. H., Martin, L. R., & Friedman, H. S. (1998). Catastrophizing and untimely death. *Psychological Science, 9,* 127–130.

Peterson, L. R., & Peterson, M. J. (1959). Short-term retention of individual verbal items. *Journal of Experimental Psychology, 58,* 193–198.

Peterson, S. E., & Fiez, J. A. (1993). The processing of single words studied with positron emission tomography. *Annual Review of Neuroscience, 16,* 509–530.

Peterson, S. E., Fox, P. T., Mintun, M. A., Posner, J. I., & Raichle, M. E. (1989). Studies of the processing of single words using averaged positron emission tomographic measurements of cerebral blood flow change. *Journal of Cognitive Neuroscience, 1,* 153–170.

Petrie, K. J., Booth, R. J., & Pennebaker, J. W. (1998). The immunological effects of thought suppression. *Journal of Personality and Social Psychology, 75,* 1264–1272.

Pettigrew, T. F., & Tropp, L. R. (2000). Does intergroup contact reduce prejudice: Recent meta-analytic findings. In S. Oskamp (Ed.), *Reducing prejudice and discrimination: The Claremont Symposium on Applied Social Psychology* (pp. 93–114). Mahwah, NJ: Erlbaum.

Petty, R. E., & Cacioppo, J. T. (1986). *Communication and persuasion: Central and peripheral routes to attitude change.* New York: Springer-Verlag.

Petty, R. E., & Cacioppo, J. T. (1990). Involvement and persuasion: Tradition versus integration. *Psychological Bulletin, 107,* 367–374.

Petty, R. E., & Wegener, D. T. (1999). The Elaboration Likelihood Model: Current status and controversies. In S. Chaiken & Y. Trope (Eds.), *Dual process theories in social psychology* (pp. 41–72). New York: Guilford.

Petty, R. E., Wegener, D. T., & Fabrigar, L. R. (1997). Attitudes and attitude change. *Annual Review of Psychology, 48,* 609–647.

Pezdek, K., & Banks, W. P. (Eds.). (1996). *The recovered memory/false memory debate.* San Diego: Academic Press.

Pezdek, K., Whetstone, T., Reynolds, K., Askari, N., & Dougherty, T. (1989). Memory for real-world scenes: The role of consistency with schema expectation. *Journal of Experimental Psychology: Learning, Memory, and Cognition, 15,* 587–595.

Phares, E. J. (1976). *Locus of control in personality.* Morristown, NJ: General Learning Press.

Phelps, M. E., & Mazziotta, J. C. (1985). Positron-emission tomography: Human brain function and biochemistry. *Science, 228,* 799–809.

Phillips, A. P., & Dipboye, R. L. (1989). Correlational tests of predictions from a process model of the interview. *Journal of Applied Psychology, 74,* 41–52.

Phillips, D. P., & Feldman, K. A. (1973). A dip in deaths before ceremonial occasions: Some new relationships between social integration and mortality. *American Sociological Review, 38,* 678–696.

Phillips, D. P., Van Voorhees, C. A., & Ruth, T. E. (1992). The birth day: Lifeline or deadline? *Psychosomatic Medicine, 54,* 532–542.

Phillips, K. A. (1998). *The broken mirror: Understanding and treating body dysmorphic disorder.* New York: Oxford University Press.

Phillips, R. B., Sharma, R., Premachandra, B. R., Vaughn, A. J., & Reyes-Lee, M. (1996). Intrauterine exposure to cocaine: Effect on neurobehavior of neonates. *Infant Behavior and Development, 19,* 71–81.

Phinney, J. (2000). Ethnic identity. In A. Kazdin (Ed.), *Encyclopedia of psychology* (Vol. 3, pp. 255–259). Washington, DC: American Psychological Association.

Phinney, J. S. (1996). When we talk about American ethnic groups, what do we mean? *American Psychologist, 51,* 918–927.

Piaget, J. (1932). *The moral judgment of the child.* New York: Harcourt, Brace & World.

Piaget, J. (1936). *The origins of intelligence in children.* New York: International University Press. (Reprinted in 1952.)

Piaget, J. (1976). *The grasp of consciousness: Action and concept in the young child.* Cambridge, MA: Harvard University Press.

Piaget, J., & Inhelder, B. (1969). *The psychology of the child.* New York: Basic Books.

Piccione, C., Hilgard, E. R., & Zimbardo, P. G. (1989). On the degree of stability of measured hypnotizability over a 25-year period. *Journal of Personality and Social Psychology, 56,* 289–295.

Piccirillo, J. F., Duntley, S., & Schotland, H. (2000). Obstructive sleep apnea. *Journal of the American Medical Association, 284,* 1492–1494.

Pickel, K. L. (1999). The influence of context on the “weapon focus” effect. *Law and Human Behavior, 23,* 299–311.

Pijl, S., & Schwarz, D. W. F. (1995). Melody recognition and musical interval perception by deaf subjects stimulated with electrical pulse trains through single cochlear implant electrodes. *Journal of the Acoustical Society of America, 98,* 886–895.

Piliavin, J. A., Dovidio, J. F., Gaertner, S. S., & Clark, R. D., III (1981). *Emergency intervention.* New York: Academic Press.

Pillemer, D. B., Picariello, M. L., Law, A. B., & Reichman, J. S. (1996). Memories of college: The importance of educational episodes. In D. C. Rubin (Ed.), *Remembering our past: Studies in autobiographical memory* (pp. 318–337). New York: Cambridge University Press.

Pillemer, D. B., Picariello, M. L., & Pruett, J. C. (1994). Very long-term memories of a salient preschool event. *Applied Cognitive Psychology, 8,* 95–106.

Pinel, J. P., Assanand, S., Lehman, D. R. (2000). Hunger, eating, and ill health. *American Psychologist, 55,* 1105–1116.

Pinker, S. (1994). *The language instinct: How the mind creates language.* New York: HarperCollins.

Pinker, S. (1999). *Words and rules: The ingredients of language.* New York: Basic Books.

Pinker, S. (2002). *The blank slate: The modern denial of human nature.* New York: Viking Press.

Pinnell, C. M., & Covino, N. M. (2000). Empirical findings on the use of hypnosis in medicine: A critical review. *International Journal of Clinical and Experimental Hypnosis, 48,* 170–194.

Platt, J. J. (2000). *Cocaine addiction: Theory, research, and treatment.* Cambridge, MA: Harvard University Press.

Pliner, P., & Chaiken, S. (1990). Eating, social motives, and self-presentation in men and women. *Journal of Experimental Social Psychology, 26,* 240–254.

Pliner, P., Pelchat, M., & Grabski, M. (1993). Reduction of neophobia in humans by exposure to novel foods. *Appetite, 20,* 111–123.

Plomin, R. (1988). The nature and nurture of cognitive abilities. In R. J. Sternberg (Ed.), *Advances in the psychology of human intelligence* (Vol. 4, pp. 1–33). Hillsdale, NJ: Erlbaum.

Plomin, R., Crabbe, J. C. (2000). DNA. *Psychological Bulletin, 125,* 806–828.

Plomin, R., DeFries, J. C., Craig, I. W., & McGuffin, P. (Eds.). (2002). *Behavioral genetics in the postgenomic era.* Washington, DC: American Psychological Association.

Plomin, R., DeFries, J. C., McClearn, G. E., & McGuffin, P. (2000). *Behavioral genetics* (4th ed.). San Francisco: W. H. Freeman.

Plomin, R., et al. (1993). Genetic change and continuity from fourteen to twenty months: The MacArthur longitudinal twin study. *Child Development, 64,* 1354–1376.

Plomin, R., & McGuffin, P. (2003). Psychopathology in the postgenomic era. *Annual Review of Psychology, 54,* 205–228.

Plomin, R., Reiss, D., Hetherington, E. M., & Howe, G. W. (1994). Nature and nurture: Genetic contributions to measures of the family environment. *Developmental Psychology, 30,* 32–43.

Plotkin, H. (1998). *Evolution in mind: An introduction to evolutionary psychology.* Cambridge, MA: Harvard University Press.

Plous, S. (1996). Attitudes toward the use of animals in psychological research and education: Results from a national survey of psychology majors. *Psychological Science, 7,* 352–358.

Plous, S. (1998). Signs of change within the animal rights movement: Results from a follow-up survey of activists. *Journal of Comparative Psychology, 112,* 48–54.

Plutchik, R. (1980). *Emotion: A psychoevolutionary synthesis.* New York: Harper & Row.

Poincuré, H. (1929). *The foundations of science.* New York: Science House.

Poizner, H., Klima, E. S., & Bellugi, U. (1990). *What the hands reveal about the brain.* Cambridge, MA: MIT Press.

Polidoro, M. (1999). It’s all in the mind: On the mechanisms of deception in psychic fraud. In S. Della Sala (Ed.), *Mind myths: Exploring popular assumptions about the mind and brain* (pp. 220–230). Chicester, England: Wiley.

Poling, A., Schlinger, H. D., Jr., Starin, S., & Blakely, E. (1990). *Psychology: A behavioral overview.* New York: Plenum.

Polivy, J., & Herman, C. P. (2002). Causes of eating disorders. *Annual Review of Psychology, 53,* 187–213.

Poole, D., & Lindsay, D. S. (2001). Children’s eyewitness reports after exposure to misinformation from parents. *Journal of Experimental Psychology: Applied, 7,* 27–50.

Poole, D. A., & White, L. T. (1991). Effects of question repetition on the eyewitness testimony of children and adults. *Developmental Psychology, 27,* 975–986.

Poole, G. D., & Craig, K. D. (1992). Judgments of genuine, suppressed, and faked facial expressions of pain. *Journal of Personality and Social Psychology, 63,* 797–805.

Pope, H. G. J., Kouri, E. M., & Hudson, J. I. (2000). Effects of supraphysiologic doses of testosterone on mood and aggression in normal men: A randomized controlled trial. *Archives of General Psychiatry, 57,* 133–140.

Popkin, J. (1994, March 14). Tricks of the trade. *U.S. News & World Report,* pp. 48–52.

Porac, C., & Coren, S. (1981). *Lateral preferences and human behavior.* New York: Springer-Verlag.

Porte, H. S., & Hobson, J. A. (1996). Physical motion in dreams: One measure of three theories. *Journal of Abnormal Psychology, 105,* 329–335.

Porter, D., & Neuringer, A. (1984). Music discrimination by pigeons. *Journal of Experimental Psychology: Animal Behavior Processes, 10,* 138–148.

Posavac, H. D., Posavac, S. S., & Posavac, E. J. (1998). Exposure to media images of female attractiveness and concern with body weight among young women. *Sex Roles, 38,* 187–201.

Posner, M. I., & Raichle, M. E. (1997). *Images of mind.* New York: Scientific American Library.

Postle, B. R., & Corkin, S. (1998). Impaired word-stem completion priming but intact perceptual identification priming with novel words: Evidence from the amnesic patient H.M. *Neuropsychologia, 36,* 421–440.

Postmes, T., & Spears, R. (1998). Deindividuation and antinormative behavior: A meta-analysis. *Psychological Bulletin, 123,* 238–259.

Postmes, T., Spears, R., & Cihangir, S. (2001). Quality of decision making and group norms. *Journal of Personality and Social Psychology, 80,* 918–930.

Poulin-Dubois, D. (1995). Object parts and the acquisition of the meaning of names. In K. Nelson & Z. Re’ger (Eds.), *Children’s language* (Vol. 8). Mahwah, NJ: Erlbaum.

Poulson, C. L., et al. (1991). Generalized vocal imitation in infants. *Journal of Experimental Child Psychology, 51,* 267–279.

Powers, D. E., & Rock, D. A. (1999). Effects of coaching on SAT-I. Reasoning test scores. *Journal of Educational Measurement, 36,* 93–118.

Prasher, D., & Luxon, L. (Eds.). (1998). *Protection against noise (Advances in noise research, 2).* Lawrence, KS: Whurr Publishers.

Pratkanis, A. R. (1992). The cargo-cult science of subliminal persuasion. *Skeptical Inquirer, 16,* 260–272.

Pratkanis, A. R., & Aronson, E. (1992). *Age of propaganda: The everyday use and abuse of persuasion.* San Francisco: W. H. Freeman.

Pratkanis, A. R., Eskenazi, J., & Greenwald, A. G. (1994). What you expect is what you believe (but not necessarily what you get): A test of the effectiveness of subliminal self-help audiotapes. *Basic and Applied Social Psychology, 15,* 251–276.

Pratkanis, A. R., & Turner, M. E. (1994). Nine principles of successful affirmative action: Mr. Branch Rickey, Mr. Jackie Robinson, and the integration of baseball. *Nine: A Journal of Baseball History and Social Policy Perspectives, 3,* 36–65.

Pratto, F., & Bargh, J. A. (1991). Stereotyping based on apparently individuating information: Trait and global components of sex stereotypes under attention overload. *Journal of Experimental Social Psychology, 27,* 26–47.

Pratto, F., Liu, J. H., Levin, S., Sidanius, J., Shih, M., Bachrach, H., & Hegarty, P. (2000). Social dominance orientation and the legitimization of inequality across cultures. *Journal of Cross-Cultural Psychology, 31,* 369–409.

Premack, A., & Premack, D. (1983). *The mind of an ape.* New York: Norton.

Premack, D. (1971). Language in chimpanzee? *Science, 172,* 808–822.

Prentice, D. A., & Miller, D. T. (1996). Pluralistic ignorance and the perpetuation of social norms by unwitting actors. *Advances in Experimental Social Psychology, 28,* 161–209.

Prentice-Dunn, S., & Rogers, R. W. (1989). Deindividuation and the self-regulation of behavior. In P. B. Paulus (Ed.), *Psychology of group influence* (2nd ed.). Hillsdale, NJ: Erlbaum.

Pressman, J. (1998). *The last resort: Psychosurgery and the limits of medicine.* New York: Cambridge University Press.

Previde, E. P., & Poli, M. D. (1996). Social learning in the golden hamster (*Mesocricetus auratus*). *Journal of Comparative Psychology, 110,* 203–208.

Price, R. A. (2002). Genetics and common obesities: Background, current status, strategies and future prospects. In T. A. Wadden & A. J. Stunkard (Eds.), *Handbook of obesity treatment* (pp. 73–94). New York: Guilford Press.

Principe, G. F., & Ceci, S. J. (2002). “I saw it with my own ears”: The effects of peer conversations on preschoolers’ reports of nonexperienced events. *Journal of Experimental Child Psychology, 83,* 1–25.

Principe, G. F., Ornstein, P. A., Baker-Ward, L., & Gordon, B. N. (2000). The effects of intervening experiences on children’s memory for a physical examination. *Applied Cognitive Psychology, 14,* 59–80.

Prioleau, L., Murdock, M., & Brody, N. (1983). An analysis of psychotherapy versus placebo studies. *Behavioral and Brain Sciences, 6,* 275–310.

Privette, G. (1983). Peak experience, peak performance, and flow: A comparative analysis of positive human experiences. *Journal of Personality and Social Psychology, 45,* 1361–1368.

Pullum, G. K. (1991). *The great Eskimo vocabulary hoax and other irreverent essays on the study of language.* Chicago: University of Chicago Press.

Putnam, F. W., Guroff, J. J., Silberman, E. K., Barban, L., & Post, R. M. (1986). The clinical phenomenology of multiple personality disorder: 100 recent cases. *Journal of Clinical Psychiatry, 47,* 285–293.

Pylyshyn, Z. (1999). Is vision continuous with cognition? The case for cognitive impenetrability of visual perception. *Behavioral and Brain Sciences, 22,* 341–423.

Pyszczynski, T., & Greenberg, J. (1987). Self-regulatory preservation and the depressive self-focusing style: A self-awareness theory of reactive depression. *Psychological Bulletin, 201,* 122–138.

Pyszczynski, T., Greenberg, J., & Solomon, S. (1999). A dual-process model of defense against conscious and unconscious death-related thoughts: An extension of terror management theory. *Psychological Review, 106,* 835–845.

Pyszczynski, T., Solomon, S., & Greenberg, J. (2002). *In the wake of 9/11: The psychology of terror.* Washington, DC: American Psychological Association.

Quinn, P. C., Burke, S., & Rush, A. (1993). Part-whole perception in early infancy: Evidence for perceptual grouping produced by lightness similarity. *Infant Behavior and Development, 16,* 19–42.

Rabkin, J. G., Wagner, G. J., & Rabkin, R. (2000). A double-blind, placebo-controlled trial of testosterone therapy for HIV-positive men with hypogonadal symptoms. *Archives of General Psychiatry, 57,* 141–147.

Rachlin, H. (1995). Self-control: Beyond commitment. *Behavioral and Brain Sciences, 18,* 109–159.

Rachman, S. J. (1990). *Fear and courage* (2nd ed.). San Francisco: W. H. Freeman.

Rachman, S., & Maser, J. D. (Eds.). (1988). *Panic: Psychological perspectives.* Hillsdale, NJ: Erlbaum.

Radford, J. (1990). *Child prodigies and exceptional early achievers.* New York: Free Press.

Rafaeli, A., & Klimoski, R. J. (1983). Predicting sales success through handwriting analysis: An evaluation of the effects of training and handwriting sample context. *Journal of Applied Psychology, 68,* 212–217.

Raichle, M. E. (1994). Images of the mind: Studies with modern imaging techniques. *Annual Review of Psychology, 45,* 333–356.

Rainville, P., Hofbauer, R. K., Paus, T., Duncan, G. H., Bushnell, M. C., & Price, D. P. (1999). Cerebral mechanisms of hypnotic induction and suggestion. *Journal of Cognitive Neuroscience, 11*, 110–125.

Rajecki, D. W., Bledsoe, S. B., & Rasmussen, J. L. (1991). Successful personal ads: Gender differences and similarities in offers, stipulations, and outcomes. *Basic and Applied Social Psychology, 12*, 457–469.

Raloff, J. (1982). Noise can be hazardous to your health. *Science News, 121*, 377–381.

Ramachandran, V. S., & Blakeslee, S. (1998). *Phantoms in the brain: Probing the mysteries of the human mind.* New York: Morrow.

Ramey, S. L. (1999). Head Start and preschool education: Toward continued improvement. *American Psychologist, 54*, 344–346.

Ramnani, N., & Passingham, R. E. (2001). Changes in the human brain during rhythm learning. *Journal of Cognitive Neuroscience, 13*, 952–966.

Randi, J. (1980). *Flim-Flam: The truth about unicorns, para-psychology, and other delusions.* New York: Lippincott & Crowell.

Rapoport, J. L. (1989). *The boy who couldn't stop washing: The experience and treatment of obsessive-compulsive disorder.* New York: Plume.

Raskin, D. C. (1986). The polygraph in 1986: Scientific, professional, and legal issues surrounding application and acceptance of polygraph evidence. *Utah Law Review, 29*–74.

Raskin, N. J. (1985). Client-centered therapy. In S. Lynn & J. Garske (Eds.), *Contemporary psychotherapies: Models and methods* (pp. 155–190). Columbus, OH: Charles E. Merrill.

Raskin, N. J. (1996). The case of Loretta: A psychiatric inpatient. In B. A. Farber, D. C. Brink, & P. M. Raskin (Eds.), *The psychotherapy of Carl Rogers: Cases and commentary* (pp. 44–56). New York: Guilford Press.

Rasmussen, B. K., Jensen, R., Schroll, M., & Olesen, J. (1991). Epidemiology of headache in a general population—a prevalence study. *Journal of Clinical Epidemiology, 44*, 1147–1157.

Rauscher, F. H., Shaw, G. L., & Ky, K. N. (1993). Music and spatial task performance. *Nature, 365*, 611.

Raven, J. C., Court, J. H., & Raven, J. (1985). *A manual for Raven's progressive matrices and vocabulary scales.* London: H. K. Lewis.

Ray, W. J. (1996). Dissociation in normal populations. In L. K. Michelson & W. J. Ray (Eds.), *Handbook of dissociation: Theoretical, empirical, and clinical perspectives* (pp. 51–68). New York: Plenum.

Raynor, H. A., & Epstein, L. H. (2001). Dietary variety, energy regulation, and obesity. *Psychological Bulletin, 127*, 325–341.

Raz, S., & Raz, N. (1990). Structural brain abnormalities in the major psychoses: A quantitative review of the evidence from computerized imaging. *Psychological Bulletin, 108*, 93–108.

Read, D. J., & Lindsay, D. S. (Eds.). (1997). *Recollections of trauma: Scientific research and clinical practice.* New York: Plenum.

Reber, A. S. (1993). *Implicit learning and tacit knowledge: An essay on the cognitive unconscious.* New York: Oxford University Press.

Reber, A. S. (1996). *The new gambler's bible: How to beat the casinos, the track, your bookie, and your buddies.* New York: Crown Publishers.

Reber, A. S., & Reber, E. (2001). *The Penguin dictionary of psychology* (3rd ed.). London: Penguin.

Rechtschaffen, A., & Bergmann, B. M. (1995). Sleep deprivation in the rat by the disk-over-water method. *Behavioural Brain Research, 69*, 55–63.

Rechtschaffen, A., Bergmann, B. M., Gilliland, M. A., & Bauer, K. (1999). Effects of method, duration, and sleep stage on rebounds from sleep deprivation in the rat. *Sleep, 22*, 11–31.

Rechtschaffen, A., & Siegel, J. (2000). Sleep and dreaming. In E. R. Kandel, J. H. Schwartz, & T. M. Jessel (Eds.), *Principles of neural science* (4th ed., pp. 936–947). New York: McGraw-Hill.

Redelmeier, D. A., & Tibshirani, R. J. (1997). Association between cellular-telephone calls and motor vehicle collisions. *New England Journal of Medicine, 336*, 453–458.

Redish, A. D. (1999). *Beyond the cognitive map: From place cells to episodic memory.* Cambridge, MA: MIT Press.

Reed, C. F., & Krupinski, E. A. (1992). The target in the celestial (moon) illusion. *Journal of Experimental Psychology: Human Perception and Performance, 18*, 247–256.

Reed, G. M., Taylor, S. E., & Kemeny, M. E. (1993). Perceived control and psychological adjustment in gay men with AIDS. *Journal of Applied Social Psychology, 23*, 791–824.

Reed, P., & Richards, A. (1996). The von Restorff effect in rats (*Rattus norvegicus*). *Journal of Comparative Psychology, 110*, 193–198.

Reed, S. B., Kirsch, I., Wickless, C., Moffitt, K. H., & Taren, P. (1996). Reporting biases in hypnosis: Suggestion or compliance? *Journal of Abnormal Psychology, 105*, 142–145.

Reed, T. E., & Jensen, A. R. (1992). Conduction velocity in a brain nerve pathway of normal adults correlates with intelligence level. *Intelligence, 16*, 259–272.

Regan, P. C., & Berscheid, E. (1997). Gender differences in characteristics desired in a potential sexual and marriage partner. *Journal of Psychology & Human Sexuality, 9*, 25–37.

Regier, D. A., et al. (1988). One-month prevalence of mental disorders in the United States: Based on five epidemiologic catchment area sites. *Archives of General Psychiatry, 45*, 977–986.

Regier, D. A., Narrow, W., Rae, D., Manderschied, R., Locke, B., & Goodwin, F. (1993). The de facto U.S. mental and addictive disorders service system: Epidemiologic catchment area prospective 1-year prevalence rates of disorders and services. *Archives of General Psychiatry, 50*, 85–94.

Reifman, A. S., Larrick, R. P., & Fein, S. (1991). Temper and temperature on the diamond: The heat-aggression relationship in major league baseball. *Personality and Social Psychology Bulletin, 17*, 580–585.

Reisenzein, R. (1983). The Schachter theory of emotion: Two decades later. *Psychological Bulletin, 94*, 239–264.

Reisenzein, R. (1994). Pleasure-arousal theory and the intensity of emotions. *Journal of Personality and Social Psychology, 67*, 525–539.

Reiser, M. (1980). *Handbook of investigative hypnosis.* Los Angeles: LEHI.

Remley, A. (1988, October). The great parental value shift: From obedience to independence. *Psychology Today*, pp. 56–59.

Renault, E. M., Signoret, J. L., Debruille, B., Breton, F., & Bolgert, F. (1989). Brain potentials reveal covert facial recognition in prosopagnosia. *Neuropsychologia, 27*, 905–912.

Rendell, L., & Whitehead, H. (2001). Culture in whales and dolphins. *Behavioral and Brain Sciences, 24*, 309–382.

Renfrew, J. W. (1997). *Aggression and its causes: A biosocial approach.* New York: Oxford University Press.

Renzulli, J. S. (1986). The three-ring conception of giftedness: A developmental model for creative productivity. In R. J. Sternberg & J. E. Davidson (Eds.), *Conceptions of giftedness* (pp. 53–92). New York: Cambridge University Press.

Rescorla, R. A. (1968). Probability of shock in the presence and absence of CS in fear conditioning. *Journal of Comparative and Physiological Psychology, 66*, 1–5.

Rescorla, R. A. (1980). *Pavlovian second-order conditioning.* Hillsdale, NJ: Erlbaum.

Rescorla, R. A. (1987). A Pavlovian analysis of goal-directed behavior. *American Psychologist, 42*, 119–129.

Rescorla, R. A. (1988). Pavlovian conditioning: It's not what you think it is. *American Psychologist, 43*, 151–160.

Rescorla, R. A. (1996). Preservation of Pavlovian associations through extinction. *Quarterly Journal of Experimental Psychology, 49B*, 245–258.

Rescorla, R. A. (2001). Retraining of extinguished Pavlovian stimuli. *Journal of Experimental Psychology: Animal Behavior Processes, 27*, 115–124.

Resnick, L. R. (1989). Developing mathematical knowledge. *American Psychologist, 44*, 162–169.

Resnick, R. J. (2000). *The hidden disorder: A clinician's guide to attention deficit hyperactivity disorder in adults.* Washington, DC: American Psychological Association.

Resnick, S. M. (1992). Positron emission tomography in psychiatric illness. *Current Directions in Psychological Science, 1*, 92–98.

Rest, J. R. (1986). *Moral development: Advances in research and theory.* New York: Praeger.

Restak, R. M. (1988). *The mind.* New York: Bantam.

Reuman, D. A. (1989). How social comparison mediates the relation between ability-grouping practices and students' achievement expectancies in mathematics. *Journal of Educational Psychology, 81*, 178–189.

Reuter-Lorenz, P. A., & Miller, A. C. (1998). The cognitive neuroscience of human laterality: Lessons from the bisected brain. *Current Directions in Psychological Science, 7*, 15–20.

Rhee, E., Uleman, J. S., Lee, H. K., & Roman, R. J. (1995). Spontaneous self-descriptions and ethnic identities in individualistic and collectivistic cultures. *Journal of Personality and Social Psychology, 69*, 142–152.

Rhodes, G., Sumich, A., & Byatt, G. (1999). Are average facial configurations attractive only because of their symmetry? *Psychological Science, 10*, 52–58.

Rhodes, G. A., & Zebrowitz, L. A. (Eds.). (2001). *Physical attractiveness: Evolutionary, cognitive, and social perspectives.* Westport, CT: Greenwood Publishing.

Rhodes, S. R. (1983). Age-related differences in work attitudes and behavior: A review and conceptual analysis. *Psychological Bulletin, 93*, 328–367.

Rhue, J. W., Lynn, S. J., & Kirsch, I. (Eds.). (1993). *Handbook of clinical hypnosis.* Washington, DC: American Psychological Association.

Rice, C., Koinis, D., Sullivan, K., Tager-Flusberg, H., & Winner, H. (1997). When 3-year-olds pass the appearance-reality test. *Developmental Psychology, 33*, 54–61.

Rice, F. P. (1998). *The adolescent: Development, relationships, and culture* (9th ed.). Needham Heights, MA: Allyn & Bacon.

Rice, M. L. (1989). Children's language acquisition. *American Psychologist, 44*, 149–156.

Rice, M. L., Huston, A. C., Truglio, R., & Wright, J. (1990). Words from "Sesame Street": Learning vocabulary while viewing. *Developmental Psychology, 26*, 421–428.

Richards, M. H., Crowe, P. A., Larson, R., & Swarr, A. (1998). Developmental patterns and gender differences in the experiences of peer companionship during adolescence. *Child Development, 69*, 154–163.

Richardson, J. T. E., & Zucco, G. M. (1989). Cognition and olfaction: A review. *Psychological Bulletin, 105*, 352–360.

Richardson, T. M., & Benbow, C. P. (1990). Long-term effects of acceleration on the social-emotional adjustment of mathematically precocious youths. *Journal of Educational Psychology, 82*, 464–470.

Rickard, T. C., Romero, S. G., Basso, G., Wharton, C., Flitman, S., & Grafman, J. (2000). The calculating brain: An FMRI study. *Neuropsychologia, 38*, 325–335.

Rief, W., Hiller, W., & Margraf, J. (1998). Cognitive aspects of hypochondriasis and the somatization syndrome. *Journal of Abnormal Psychology, 107*, 587–595.

Rilling, M. (1996). The mystery of vanished citations: James McConnell's forgotten 1960s quest for planarian learning, a biochemical engram, and celebrity. *American Psychologist, 51*, 589–598.

Rilling, M. (2000). John Watson's paradoxical struggle to explain Freud. *American Psychologist, 55*, 301–312.

Rimmele, C. T., Howard, M. O., & Hilfrink, M. L. (1995). Aversion therapies. In R. K. Hester & W. R. Miller (Eds.), *Handbook of alcoholism treatment approaches: Effective alternatives* (2nd ed., pp. 134–147). Boston: Allyn & Bacon.

Rinck, M. (1999). Memory for everyday objects: Where are the digits on numerical keypads? *Applied Cognitive Psychology, 13*, 329–350.

Rind, B., Tromovitch, P. & Bauserman, R. (1998). A meta-analytic examination of assumed properties of child sexual abuse using college samples. *Psychological Bulletin, 124*, 22–53.

Rips, L. J. (1975). Inductive judgments about natural categories. *Journal of Verbal Learning and Verbal Behavior, 14*, 665–681.

Ristau, C. A. (Ed.) (1991). *Cognitive ethology: The minds of other animals.* Hillsdale, NJ: Erlbaum.

Ritter, P. L., & Dornbusch, S. M. (1989, March). *Ethnic variation in family influences on academic achievement.* Paper presented at the American Educational Research Association Meeting, San Francisco.

Rivas-Vazquez, R. A., Johnson, S. L., Rey, G. J., Blais, M. A., & Rivas-Vazquez, A. (2002). Current treatments for bipolar disorder: A review and update for psychologists.

*Professional Psychology: Research & Practice, 33,* 212–223.

Roberts, B. W., & DelVecchio, W. F. (2000). The rank-order consistency of personality traits from childhood to old age: A quantitative review of longitudinal studies. *Psychological Bulletin, 126,* 3–25.

Robins, L. N., & Regier, D. A. (Eds.). (1991). *Psychiatric disorders in America: The epidemiologic catchment area study.* New York: Free Press.

Robins, R. W., & Beer, J. S. (2001). Positive illusions about the self: Short-term benefits and long-term costs. *Journal of Personality and Social Psychology, 80,* 340–352.

Robins, R. W., Gosling, S. D., & Craik, K. H. (1999). An empirical analysis of trends in psychology. *American Psychologist, 54,* 117–128.

Robins, R. W., Trzesniewski, K. H., Tracy, J. L., Gosling, S. D., & Potter, J. (2002). Global self-esteem across the life span. *Psychology and Aging, 17,* 423–434.

Robinson, I., Ziss, K., Ganza, B., Katz, S., & Robinson, E. (1991). Twenty years of the sexual revolution, 1965–1985: An update. *Journal of Marriage and the Family, 53,* 216–220.

Robinson, J. L., Kagan, J., Reznick, J. S., & Corley, R. (1992). The heritability of inhibited and uninhibited behavior: A twin study. *Developmental Psychology, 28,* 1030–1037.

Robinson, N. M., Zigler, E., & Gallagher, J. J. (2000). Two tails of the normal curve: Similarities and differences in the study of mental retardation and giftedness. *American Psychologist, 55.*

Rochat, P. (1989). Object manipulation and exploration in 2- to 5-month-old infants. *Developmental Psychology, 25,* 871–884.

Rock, I. (1997). *Indirect perception.* Cambridge, MA: MIT Press.

Rock, I., & Palmer, S. (1990). The legacy of Gestalt psychology. *Scientific American,* 84–90.

Rodgers, J. E. (1992). *Psychosurgery: Damaging the brain to save the mind.* New York: HarperCollins.

Rodgers, J. L. (1996). Sexual transitions in adolescence. In J. A. Graber, J. Brooks-Gunn, & A. C. Petersen, (Eds.), *Transitions through adolescence: Interpersonal domains and context* (pp. 85–110). Mahwah, NJ: Erlbaum.

Rodgers, J. L., Cleveland, H. H., van den Oord, E., & Rowe, D. C. (2000). Resolving the debate over birth order, family size, and intelligence. *American Psychologist, 55,* 599–612.

Rodgers, N. (1998). *Incredible optical illusions.* New York: Barnes & Noble Books.

Rodin, J. (1986). Aging and health: Effects of the sense of control. *Science, 233,* 1271–1276.

Roediger, H. L., III. (1990). Implicit memory: Retention without remembering. *American Psychologist, 45,* 1043–1056.

Roediger, H. L., III, & McDermott, K. B. (1995). Creating false memories: Remembering words not presented in lists. *Journal of Experimental Psychology: Learning, Memory, and Cognition, 21,* 803–814.

Roediger, H. L., Meade, M. L., & Bergman, E. T. (2001). Social contagion of memory. *Psychonomic Bulletin & Review, 8,* 365–371.

Roediger, H. L., Watson, J. M., McDermott, K. B., & Gallo, D. A. (2001). Factors that determine false recall: A multiple regression analysis. *Psychonomic Bulletin & Review, 8,* 385–407.

Roese, N. J. (1997). Counterfactual thinking. *Psychological Bulletin, 121,* 133–148.

Roese, N. J., & Olson, J. M. (Eds.). (1995). *What might have been: The social psychology of counterfactual thinking.* Mahwah, NJ: Erlbaum.

Roethlisberger, F. J., & Dickson, W. J. (1939). *Management and the worker.* Cambridge, MA: Harvard University Press.

Roffwarg, H. P., Muzio, J. N., & Dement, W. C. (1966). Ontogenetic development of the human sleep-dream cycle. *Science, 152,* 604–619.

Rogers, C. R. (1942). *Counseling and psychotherapy: New concepts in practice.* Boston: Houghton Mifflin.

Rogers, C. R. (1951). *Client-centered therapy.* Boston: Houghton Mifflin.

Rogers, C. R. (1961). *On becoming a person.* Boston: Houghton Mifflin.

Rogers, C. R. (1963). Actualizing tendency in relation to "motives" and to consciousness. In M. Jones (Ed.), *Nebraska symposium on motivation.* Lincoln: University of Nebraska Press.

Rogers, C. R. (1970). *Carl Rogers on encounter groups.* New York: Harper & Row.

Rogers, C. R. (1974). In retrospect: Forty-six years. *American Psychologist, 29,* 115–123.

Rogers, P. (1993, February 15). How many gays are there? *Newsweek,* p. 46.

Rogers, R. (Ed.). (1997). *Clinical assessment of malingering and deception* (2nd ed.). New York: Guilford Press.

Rogers, R. W. (1983). Cognitive and psychological processes in fear appeals and attitude change: A revised theory of protection motivation. In J. Cacioppo & R. Petty (Eds.), *Social psychophysiology: A sourcebook* (pp. 153–176). New York: Guilford Press.

Rogers, T. B., Kuiper, N. A., & Kirker, W. S. (1977). Self-reference and the encoding of personal information. *Journal of Personality and Social Psychology, 35,* 677–688.

Rogoff, B. (2002). *The cultural nature of human development.* New York: Oxford University Press.

Rogoff, B., & Morelli, G. (1989). Perspectives on children's development from cultural psychology. *American Psychologist, 44,* 343–348.

Rolls, E. T. (1999). *The brain and emotion.* New York: Oxford University Press.

Rolls, E. T. (2000). Memory systems in the brain. *Annual Review of Psychology, 51,* 599–630.

Romney, A. K., Brewer, D. D., & Batchelder, W. H. (1993). Predicting clustering from semantic structure. *Psychological Science, 4,* 28–34.

Roper Reports. (1989, May).

Rorschach, H. (1921). *Psychodiagnostik.* Bern, Switzerland: Bircher.

Rosch, E. (1973). On the internal structure of perceptual and semantic categories. In T. E. Moore (Ed.), *Cognitive development and the acquisition of language.* New York: Academic Press.

Rosch, E. (1975). Cognitive representations of semantic categories. *Journal of Experimental Psychology: General, 104,* 192–223.

Rosen, R. C., & Ashton, A. K. (1993). Psychosexual drugs: Empirical status of the "new aphrodisiacs." *Archives of Sexual Behavior, 22,* 521–543.

Rosenberg, N. A., Pritchard, J. K., Weber, J. L., Cann, H. M., Kidd, K. K., Zhivotovsky, L. A., & Feldman, M. W. (2002). Genetic structure of human populations. *Science, 298,* 2381–2385.

Rosenfeld, D. S., & Elhajjar, A. J. (1998). Sleepsex: A variant of sleepwalking. *Archives of Sexual Behavior, 27,* 269–278.

Rosenfield, P., Lambert, N. M., & Black, A. (1985). Desk arrangement effects on pupil classroom behavior. *Journal of Educational Psychology, 77,* 101–108.

Rosenfield, R. L., et al. (2000). Current age of onset of puberty. *Pediatrics, 106,* 622–623.

Rosenhan, D. L. (1973). On being sane in insane places. *Science, 179,* 250–258.

Rosenman, R. H., Brand, R. J., Jenkins, C. D., Friedman, M., Strau, R., & Wurm, M. (1975). Coronary heart disease in the Western Collaborative Group Study: Final follow-up experience of 8 Qw years. *Journal of the American Medical Association, 233,* 872–877.

Rosenthal, N. E. (1998). *Winter blues: Seasonal affective disorder: What it is and how to overcome it.* New York: Guilford Press.

Rosenthal, N. E., & Blehard, M. C. (Eds.). (1999). *Seasonal affective disorders and phototherapy.* New York: Guilford Press.

Rosenthal, R. (1985). From unconscious experimenter bias to teacher expectancy effects. In J. B. Dusek, V. C. Hall, & W. J. Meyer (Eds.), *Teacher expectancies.* Hillsdale, NJ: Erlbaum.

Rosenthal, R., & DiMatteo, M. R. (2001). Meta-analysis: Recent developments in quantitative methods for literature reviews. *Annual Review of Psychology, 52,* 59–82.

Rosenthal, R., & Jacobson, L. (1968). *Pygmalion in the classroom: Teacher expectation and pupils' intellectual development.* New York: Holt, Rinehart & Winston.

Rosenzweig, M. R. (1984). Experience, memory, and the brain. *American Psychologist, 39,* 365–376.

Rosenzweig, M. R. (1996). Aspects of the search for neural mechanisms of memory. *Annual Review of Psychology, 47,* 1–32.

Rosnow, R. L., Rotheram-Borus, M. J., Ceci, S. J., Blanck, P. D., & Koocher, G. P. (1993). The institutional review board as a mirror of scientific and ethical standards. *American Psychologist, 48,* 821–826.

Ross, C. A. (1994). *The Osiris complex: Case studies in multiple personality disorder.* Toronto: University of Toronto Press.

Ross, C. A. (1997). *Dissociative identity disorder.* New York: Wiley.

Ross, C. A., Joshi, S., & Currie, R. (1990). Dissociative experiences in the general population. *American Journal of Psychiatry, 147,* 1547–1552.

Ross, D. F., Ceci, S. J., Dunning, D., & Toglia, M. P. (1994). Unconscious transference and mistaken identity: When a witness misidentifies a familiar but innocent person. *Journal of Applied Psychology, 79,* 918–930.

Ross, L. (1977). The intuitive psychologist and his shortcomings: Distortions in the attribution process. In L. Berkowitz (Ed.), *Advances in experimental social psychology* (Vol. 10). New York: Academic Press.

Ross, L., Amabile, T. M., & Steinmetz, J. L. (1977). Social roles, social control, and biases in social-perception processes. *Journal of Personality and Social Psychology, 35,* 485–494.

Ross, M. (1989). The relation of implicit theories to the construction of personal histories. *Psychological Review, 96,* 341–357.

Ross, M., & Sicoly, F. (1979). Egocentric biases in availability and attribution. *Journal of Personality and Social Psychology, 37,* 322–336.

Ross, R. T., & LoLordo, V. M. (1987). Evaluation of the relation between Pavlovian occasion setting and instrumental discriminative stimuli. *Journal of Experimental Psychology: Animal Behavior Processes, 13,* 3–16.

Roth, D. A., Herman, C. P., Polivy, J., & Pliner, P. (2001). Self-presentational conflict in social eating situations: A normative perspective. *Appetite, 36,* 165–171.

Roth, T., Roehrs, T., & Zorick, F. (1987). Sleep disorders. In G. Adelman (Ed.), *Encyclopedia of neuroscience.* Boston: Birkhauser.

Rothbaum, B. O., Hodges, L., Anderson, P. L., Price, L., & Smith, S. (2002). Twelve-month follow-up of virtual reality and standard exposure therapies for the fear of flying. *Journal of Consulting and Clinical Psychology, 70,* 428–432.

Rothbaum, B. O., Hodges, L. F., Kooper, R., Opdyke, D., Williford, J. S., & North, M. (1995). Effectiveness of computer-generated (virtual reality) graded exposure in the treatment of acrophobia. *American Journal of Psychiatry, 152,* 626–628.

Rotter, J. B. (1954). *Social learning and clinical psychology.* Englewood Cliffs, NJ: Prentice-Hall.

Rotter, J. B. (1966). Generalized expectancies for internal versus external control of reinforcement. *Psychological Monographs, 80* (Whole No. 609).

Rotter, J. B. (1990). Internal versus external control of reinforcement: A case history of a variable. *American Psychologist, 45,* 489–493.

Rotter, J. B., Chance, J. E., & Phares, E. J. (Eds.). (1972). *Applications of a social learning theory of personality.* New York: Holt, Rinehart & Winston.

Rousseau, D. L. (1992). Case studies in pathological science. *American Scientist, 80,* 54–63.

Rovee-Collier, C. (1988). The joy of kicking: Memories, motives, and mobiles. In P. Solomon, G. Goethals, C. Kelley, & B. Stephens (Eds.), *Memory: Interdisciplinary approaches.* New York: Springer-Verlag.

Rovee-Collier, C. (2001). Information pick-up by infants: What is it, and how can we tell? *Journal of Experimental Child Psychology, 78,* 35–49.

Rovee-Collier, C., Hankins, E., & Bhatt, R. (1992). Textons, visual pop-out effects, and object recognition in infancy. *Journal of Experimental Psychology: General, 121,* 435–445.

Rowe, D. C. (1994). *The limits of family influence: Genes, experience, and behavior.* New York: Guilford Press.

Rozee, P. D., & Van Boemel, G. V. (1989). The psychological effects of war trauma and abuse on older Cambodian refugee women. *Women and Therapy, 8,* 23–50.

Rozin, P., Dow, S., Moscovitch, M., & Rajaram, S. (1998). What causes humans to begin and end a meal?: A role for memory for what has been eaten, as evidenced by a study of multiple meal eating in amnesic patients. *Psychological Science, 9,* 392–396.

Rozin, P., & Fallon, A. E. (1987). A perspective on disgust. *Psychological Review, 94,* 23–41.

Rubenstein, A. J., Kalakanis, L., & Langlois, J. H. (1999). Infant preferences for attractive faces: A cognitive explanation. *Developmental Psychology, 35,* 848–855.

Rubin, D. C. (Ed.). (1996). *Remembering our past: Studies in autobiographical memory.* New York: Cambridge University Press.

Rubin, D. C., Hinton, S., & Wenzel, A. (1999). The precise time course of retention. *Journal of Experimental Psychology: Learning, Memory, and Cognition, 25,* 1161–1176.

Rubin, D. C., & Kozin, M. (1986). Vivid memories. *Cognition, 16,* 81–95.

Rubin, D. C., & Wenzel, A. E. (1996). One hundred years of forgetting: A quantitative description of retention. *Psychological Review, 103,* 734–760.

Rubin, J. Z., Provenzano, F. J., & Luria, Z. (1974). The eye of the beholder: Parents' views on sex of newborns. *American Journal of Orthopsychiatry, 44,* 512–519.

Ruderman, A. J., & Besbeas, M. (1992). Psychological characteristics of dieters and bulimics. *Journal of Abnormal Psychology, 101,* 383–390.

Rudgley, R. (1999). *The encyclopedia of psychoactive substances.* New York: St. Martin's Press.

Rule, B. G., Taylor, B. R., & Dobbs, A. R. (1987). Priming effects of heat on aggressive thoughts. *Social Cognition, 5,* 131–143.

Rumbaugh, D. M. (1977). *Language learning by a chimpanzee: The Lana project.* New York: Academic Press.

Rumelhart, D. E., & McClelland, J. L. (1986). On learning the past tenses of English verbs. In J. L. McClelland & D. E. Rumelhart (Eds.), *Parallel distributed processing: Explorations in the microstructure of cognition: Vol. 2. Psychological and biological models* (pp. 216–271). Cambridge, MA: MIT Press.

Rumelhart, D. E., McClelland, J. L., & the PDP Research Group. (1986). *Parallel distributed processing: Vol. 1. Foundations.* Cambridge, MA: MIT Press.

Runco, M. A., & Pritzker, S. R. (Eds.) (1999). *Encyclopedia of Creativity* (Vols. 1 & 2). San Diego: Academic Press.

Rushton, J. P. (1989). Genetic similarity, human altruism, and group selection. *Behavioral and Brain Sciences, 12,* 503–559.

Rushton, J. P., & Ankney, C. D. (1996). Brain size and cognitive ability: Correlations with age, sex, social class, and race. *Psychonomic Bulletin & Review, 3,* 21–36.

Russell, J. A. (1980). A circumplex model of affect. *Journal of Personality and Social Psychology, 39,* 1161–1178.

Russell, J. A. (1991). Culture and the categorization of emotions. *Psychological Bulletin, 110,* 426–450.

Russell, J. A. (1994). Is there universal recognition of emotion from facial expression? A review of cross-cultural studies. *Psychological Bulletin, 115,* 102–141.

Russell, J. A. (1995). Facial expressions of emotion: What lies beyond minimal universality? *Psychological Bulletin, 118,* 379–391.

Russell, J. A., & Barrett, L. F. (1999). Core affect, prototypical emotional episodes, and other things called emotion: Dissecting the elephant. *Journal of Personality and Social Psychology, 76,* 805–819.

Russell, J. A., & Carroll, J. M. (1999). On the bipolarity of positive and negative affect. *Psychological Bulletin, 125,* 3–30.

Russell, M. J. (1976). Human olfactory communication. *Nature (London), 260,* 520–522.

Russell, R. L., & Orlinsky, D. E. (1996). Psychotherapy research in historical perspective: Implications for mental health care policy. *Archives of General Psychiatry, 53,* 708–715.

Rust, J., Golombok, S., Hines, M., Johnston, K., & Golding, J. (2000). The role of brothers and sisters in the gender development of preschool children. *Journal of Experimental Child Psychology, 77,* 292–303.

Ruvolo, A., & Markus, H. (1992). Possible selves and performance: The power of self-relevant imagery. *Social Cognition, 9,* 95–124.

Ryan, R. M., & Deci, E. L. (2000). Self-determination theory and the facilitation of intrinsic motivation, social development, and well-being. *American Psychologist, 55,* 68–78.

Ryan, R. M., & Deci, E. L. (2001). On happiness and human potentials: A review of research on hedonic and eudaimonic well-being. *Annual Review of Psychology, 52,* 41–66.

Ryckman, R. M., Robbins, M. A., Kazcor, L. M., & Gold, J. A. (1989). Male and female raters' stereotyping of male and female physiques. *Personality and Social Psychology Bulletin, 15,* 244–251.

Ryder, A. G., Alden, L. E. & Paulhus, D. (2000). Is acculturation unidimensional or bidimensional? A head-to-head comparison in the prediction of personality, self-identity, and adjustment. *Journal of Personality and Social Psychology, 79,* 49–65.

Ryff, C. D. (1989). In the eye of the beholder: Views of psychological well-being among middle-aged and older adults. *Psychology and Aging, 4,* 195–210.

Saal, F. E., Johnson, C. B., & Weber, N. (1989). Friendly or sexy? It may depend on whom you ask. *Psychology of Women Quarterly, 13,* 263–276.

Sacco, W. P., & Dunn, V. K. (1990). Effect of actor depression on observer attributions: Existence and impact of negative attributions toward the depressed. *Journal of Personality and Social Psychology, 59,* 517–524.

Sachs, J. (1967). Recognition memory for syntactic and semantic aspects of connected discourse. *Perception and Psychophysics, 2,* 437–442.

Sacks, O. (1983). *Awakenings.* New York: Dutton.

Sacks, O. (1985). *The man who mistook his wife for a hat and other clinical tales.* New York: Summit Books.

Sacks, O. (1995). *An anthropologist on Mars: Seven paradoxical tales.* New York: Knopf.

Sacks, O. (1998). *The island of the colorblind.* New York: Vintage Books.

Sadato, N., Pascual-Leone, A., Grafman, J., Ibanez, V., Deiber, M. P., Dold, G., & Hallett, M. (1999). Left-hemisphere dominance for motion processing in deaf signers. *Psychological Science, 10,* 256–262.

Salgado, J. F. (1997). The five factor model of personality and job performance in the European community. *Journal of Applied Psychology, 82,* 30–43.

Salk, L. (1962). Mothers' heartbeat as an imprinting stimulus. *Transactions of the New York Academy of Sciences, 24,* 753–763.

Salovey, P., Rothman, A. J., & Rodin, J. (1998). Health behavior. In D. Gilbert, S. Fiske, & G. Lindzey (Eds.), *Handbook of social psychology* (4th ed.). New York: McGraw-Hill.

Salthouse, T. A. (1992). Why do adult age differences increase with task complexity? *Developmental Psychology, 28,* 905–918.

Salthouse, T. A. (1996). The processing-speed theory of adult age differences in cognition. *Psychological Review, 103,* 403–428.

Salthouse, T. A., Berish, D. E., & Miles, J. D. (2002). The role of cognitive stimulation on the relations between age and cognitive functioning. *Psychology & Aging, 17,* 548–557.

Sampson, E. E. (2000). Reinterpreting individualism and collectivism: Their religious roots and monologic versus dialogic person–other relationship. *American Psychologist, 55,* 1425–1432.

Sams, M., Hari, R., Rif, J., & Knuutila, J. (1993). The human auditory memory trace persists about 10 sec: Neuromagnetic evidence. *Journal of Cognitive Neuroscience, 5,* 363–370.

Sanchez, J. I., & Fernandez, D. M. (1993). Acculturative stress among Hispanics: A bidimensional model of ethnic identification. *Journal of Applied Social Psychology, 23,* 654–668.

Sanders, S. A., & Reinisch, J. M. (1999). Would you say you "had sex" if . . . ? *Journal of the American Medical Association, 281,* 275–277.

Sanderson, D. W. (1993). *Smileys.* Sebastopol, CA: O'Reilly.

Sanderson, W. C., DiNardo, P. A., Rapee, R. M., & Barlow, D. H. (1990). Syndrome comorbidity in patients diagnosed with a DSM-III-R anxiety disorder. *Journal of Abnormal Psychology, 99,* 308–312.

Sandstrom, M. J., & Coie, J. D. (1999). A developmental perspective on peer rejection: Mechanisms of stability and change. *Child Development, 70,* 955–966.

Sanna, L. J., Turley-Ames, K. J., & Meier, S. (1999). Mood, self-esteem, and simulated alternatives: Thought-provoking affective influences on counterfactual direction. *Journal of Personality and Social Psychology, 76,* 543–558.

Sansavini, A., Bertoncini, J., & Giovanelli, G. (1997). Newborns discriminate the rhythm of multisyllabic stressed words. *Developmental Psychology, 33,* 3–11.

Saper, C. B., Iverson, S., & Frackowiak, R. (2000). Integration of sensory and motor function: The association areas of the cerebral cortex and the cognitive capabilities of the brain. In E. R. Kandel, J. H. Schwartz, & T. M. Jessell (Eds.), *Principles of neural science* (4th ed., pp. 349–380). New York: McGraw-Hill.

Sapir, E. (1941). *Language, culture, and personality: Essays in honor of Edward Sapir* (L. Sapir, Ed.). Menasha, WI: Sapir Memorial Publication Fund.

Sapolsky, R. M. (1994). *Why zebras don't get ulcers: A guide to stress, diseases, and coping.* New York: W. H. Freeman.

Sarbin, T. R. (1992). Accounting for "dissociative" actions without invoking mentalistic constructs. *Consciousness and Cognition, 1,* 54–58.

Sarter, M., Bernston, G. G., & Cacioppo, J. T. (1996). Brain imaging and cognitive neuroscience: Toward strong inference in attributing function to structure. *American Psychologist, 51,* 13–21.

Sary, G., Vogels, R., & Orban, G. A. (1993). Cue-invariant shape selectivity of macaque inferior temporal neurons. *Science, 260,* 995–997.

Savage-Rumbaugh, S., Murphy, J., Sevcik, R. A., Brakke, K. E., Williams, S. L., & Rumbaugh, D. M. (1993). Language comprehension in ape and child. *Monographs of the Society for Research in Child Development, 58*(3–4, Serial No. 233).

Savage-Rumbaugh, S., Shanker, S. G., & Taylor, T. J. (1998). *Apes, language, and the human mind.* New York: Oxford University Press.

Sawyer, T. F. (2000). Francis Cecil Sumner: His views and influence on African American higher education. *History of Psychology, 3,* 122–141.

Saxe, L., Dougherty, D., & Cross, T. (1985). The validity of polygraph testing: Scientific analysis and public controversy. *American Psychologist, 38,* 355–366.

Scarr, S. (1998). American child care today. *American Psychologist, 53,* 95–108.

Scarr, S., & McCartney, K. (1983). How people make their own environments: A theory of genotype-environment effects. *Child Development, 54,* 424–435.

Scarr, S., & Weinberg, R. A. (1976). I.Q. test performance of black children adopted by white families. *American Psychologist, 31,* 726–739.

Scarr, S., & Weinberg, R. A. (1983). The Minnesota adoption studies: Genetic differences and malleability. *Child Development, 54,* 260–267.

Schaal, B., Marlier, L., & Soussignan, R. (1998). Olfactory function in the human fetus: Evidence from selective neonatal responsiveness to the odor of amniotic fluid. *Behavioral Neuroscience, 112,* 1438–1449.

Schab, F. R. (1990). Odors and the remembrance of things past. *Journal of Experimental Psychology: Learning, Memory, and Cognition, 16,* 648–655.

Schab, F. R., & Crowder, R. G. (Eds.). (1995). *Memory for odors.* Mahwah, NJ: Erlbaum.

Schachter, S. (1959). *The psychology of affiliation.* Palo Alto, CA: Stanford University Press.

Schachter, S. (1964). The interaction of cognitive and physiological determinants of emotional state. In L. Berkowitz (Ed.), *Advances in experimental social psychology* (Vol. 1, pp. 49–80). New York: Academic Press.

Schachter, S., & Gross, L. (1968). Manipulated time and eating behavior. *Journal of Personality and Social Psychology, 10,* 98–106.

Schachter, S., & Singer, J. E. (1962). Cognitive, social, and physiological determinants of emotional state. *Psychological Review, 69,* 379–399.

Schacter, D. L. (1986). Amnesia and crime: How much do we really know? *American Psychologist, 41,* 286–295.

Schacter, D. L. (1992). Understanding implicit memory: A cognitive neuroscience approach. *American Psychologist, 47,* 559–569.

Schacter, D. L. (1996). *Searching for memory.* New York: Basic Books.

Schacter, D. L. (1999). The seven sins of memory: Insights from psychology and cognitive neuroscience. *American Psychologist, 54,* 182–203.

Schacter, D. L. (2001). *The seven sins of memory: How the mind forgets and remembers.* Boston: Houghton Mifflin.

Schaie, K. W. (Ed.). (1983). *Longitudinal studies of adult psychological development.* New York: Guilford Press.

Schaie, K. W. (1989). Perceptual speed in adulthood: Cross-sectional and longitudinal studies. *Psychology and Aging, 4,* 443–453.

Schaie, K. W. (1996). *Intellectual development in adulthood: The Seattle Longitudinal Study.* New York: Cambridge University Press.

Schaie, K. W., & Willis, S. L. (1993). Age difference patterns of psychometric intelligence in adulthood: Generalizability within and across ability domains. *Psychology and Aging, 8,* 44–55.

Schaller, M., & Cialdini, R. B. (1988). The economics of empathic helping: Support for a mood management motive. *Journal of Experimental Social Psychology, 24,* 163–181.

Schanberg, S. M., & Field, T. M. (1987). Sensory deprivation stress and supplemental stimulation in the rat pup and preterm human neonate. *Child Development, 58,* 1431–1447.

Schatzberg, A. F., & Nemeroff, C. B. (Eds.). (1998). *The American Psychiatric Press textbook of psychopharmacology* (2nd ed.). Washington, DC: American Psychiatric Press.

Schedlowski, M., & Tewes, U. (Eds.). (1999). *Psychoneuroimmunology: An interdisciplinary introduction.* New York: Plenum.

Scheibel, A. B. (1995). Structural and functional changes in the aging brain. In J. E. Birren & K. W. Schaie (Eds.), *Handbook of the psychology of aging* (4th ed., pp. 78–128). San Diego: Academic Press.

Scheier, M. F., & Carver, C. S. (1985). Optimism, coping, and health: Assessment and implications of generalized outcome expectancies. *Health Psychology, 4,* 219–247.

Scheier, M. F., & Carver, C. S. (1992). Effects of optimism on psychological and physical well-being: Theoretical overview and empirical update. *Cognitive Therapy and Research, 16,* 201–228.

Schenck, C. H. (1993). REM sleep behavior disorder. In M. A. Carskadon (Ed.), *Encyclopedia of sleep and dreaming* (pp. 499–505). New York: Macmillan.

Scherer, K. R., & Wallbott, H. G. (1994). Evidence for universality and cultural variation of differential emotion response patterning. *Journal of Personality and Social Psychology, 66,* 310–328.

Schiff, W. (1980). *Perception: An applied approach.* Boston: Houghton Mifflin.

Schiffman, S. S., Graham, B. G., Sattely-Miller, E. A., & Warwick, Z. S. (1998). Orosensory perception of dietary fat. *Current Directions in Psychological Science, 7,* 137–143.

Schiller, F. (1992). *Paul Broca.* New York: Oxford University Press.

Schimel, J., Arndt, J., Pyszczynski, T., & Greenberg, J. (2001). Being accepted for who we are: Evidence that social validation of the intrinsic self reduces general defensiveness. *Journal of Personality and Social Psychology, 80,* 35–52.

Schlaug, G., Jancke, L., Huang, Y., & Steinmetz, H. (1995). In vivo evidence of structural brain asymmetry in musicians. *Science, 267,* 699–671.

Schlenker, B. R., Weigold, M. F., & Hallam, J. R. (1990). Self-serving attributions in social context: Effects of self-esteem and social pressure. *Journal of Personality and Social Psychology, 58,* 855–863.

Schmidt, H. G., Peeck, V. H., Paas, F., & van Breukelen, G. (2000). Remembering the street names of one's childhood neighbourhood: A study of very long-term retention. *Memory, 8,* 37–49.

Schmidt, N. B., & Trakowski, J. H. (1997). Body vigilance in panic disorder: Evaluating attention to bodily perturbations. *Journal of Consulting and Clinical Psychology, 65,* 214–220.

Schmidt, S. R. (1991). Can we have a distinctive theory of memory? *Memory and Cognition, 19,* 523–542.

Schmidt, S. R. (2002). Outstanding memories: The positive and negative effects of nudes on memory. *Journal of Experimental Psychology: Learning, Memory, and Cognition, 28,* 353–361.

Schnapf, J. L., Kraft, T. W., & Baylor, D. A. (1987). Spectral sensitivity of human cone photoreceptors. *Nature, 325,* 439–441.

Schneider, A., & Domhoff, G. W. (2002). *The quantitative study of dreams.* Retrieved from the World Wide Web: http://www. dreamresearch.net/

Schneider, B. H., Atkinson, L., & Tardif, C. (2001). Child-parent attachment and children's peer relations: A quantitative review. *Developmental Psychology, 37,* 86–100.

Schneider, D. J., & Shiffrin, R. M. (1977). Controlled and automatic human information processing: I. Detection, search, and attention. *Psychological Review, 84,* 1–66.

Schneider, D. M., & Watkins, M. J. (1996). Response conformity in recognition testing. *Psychonomic Bulletin & Review, 3,* 481–485.

Schneider, E. C., Zaslavsky, A. M., & Epstein, A. M. (2002). Racial disparities in the quality of care for enrollees in Medicare managed care. *Journal of the American Medical Association, 2001,* 1288–1294.

Schneider, P. (2000, February 13). Saving Konrad Latte. *The New York Times Magazine,* pp. 52–57, 72–73, 90, 95.

Schneider, P., Scherg, M., Dosch, H. G., Specht, H. J., Gutschalk, A., & Rupp, A. (2002). Morphology of Heschl's gyrus reflects enhanced activation in the auditory cortex of musicians. *Nature Neuroscience, 5,* 688–694.

Schneider, S. G., Taylor, S. E., Hammen, C., Kemeny, M. E., & Dudley, J. (1991). Factors influencing suicide intent in gay and bisexual suicide ideators: Differing models for men with and without human immunodeficiency virus. *Journal of Personality and Social Psychology, 61,* 776–788.

Schneider, S. L. (2001). In search of realistic optimism: Meaning, knowledge, and warm fuzziness. *American Psychologist, 56,* 250–263.

Schneiderman, N., Antoni, M. H., Saab, P. G., & Ironson, G. (2001). Health psychology: Psychosocial and biobehavioral aspects of chronic disease management. *Annual Review of Psychology, 52,* 555–580.

Schofield, J. W. (1982). *Black and white in school: Trust, tension, or tolerance?* New York: Praeger.

Schooler, J. W., & Engstler-Schooler, T. Y. (1990). Verbal overshadowing of visual memories: Some things are better left unsaid. *Cognitive Psychology, 17,* 36–71.

Schooler, J. W., Ohlsson, S., & Brooks, K. (1993). Thoughts beyond words: When language overshadows insight. *Journal of Experimental Psychology: General, 122,* 166–183.

Schou, M. (1997). Forty years of lithium treatment. *Archives of General Psychiatry, 54,* 9–13.

Schrauf, R. W., & Rubin, D. C. (2001). Effects of voluntary immigration on the distribution of autobiographical memory over the lifespan. *Applied Cognitive Psychology, 29,* S75–S88.

Schroeder, D. A., Dovidio, J. F., Sibicky, M. A., Matthews, L. L., & Allen, J. L. (1995). *The psychology of helping and altruism: Problems and puzzles.* New York: McGraw-Hill.

Schulman, K. A., et al. (1999). The effect of race and sex on physicians' recommendations for cardiac catheterization. The New England Journal of Medicine, 340, 618–626.

Schulz, R., Musa, D., Staszewski, J., & Siegler, R. S. (1994). The relationship between age and major league baseball performance: Implications for development. *Psychology and Aging, 9,* 274–286.

Schuman, H., Steeh, C., Bobo, L., & Krysan, M. (Eds.). (1997). *Racial attitudes in America: Trends and interpretations.* Cambridge, MA: Harvard University Press.

Schuster M. A., Stein, B. D., Jaycox, L. H., Collins, R. L., Marshall, G. N., Elliott, M. N., Zhou, A. J., Kanouse, D. E., Morrison, J. L., & Berry, S. H. (2001). A national survey of stress reactions after the September 11, 2001, terrorist attacks. *The New England Journal of Medicine, 345,* 1507–1512.

Schwartz, A., & Schwartz, R. M. (1993). *Depression–Theories and treatments: Psychological, biological, and social perspectives.* New York: Columbia University Press.

Schwartz, B., & Reisberg, D. (1991). *Learning and memory.* New York: Norton.

Schwartz, B. L. (2002). *Tip-of-the-tongue states: Phenomenology, mechanism, and lexical retrieval.* Mahwah, NJ: Erlbaum.

Schwartz, D. L., & Black, T. (1999). Inferences through imagined actions: Knowing by simulated doing. *Journal of Experimental Psychology: Learning, Memory, and Cognition, 25,* 116–136.

Schwartz, J. M. (1996). *Brain lock.* New York: HarperCollins.

Schwartz, J. M., Stoessel, P. W., Baxter, L. R., Martin, K. M., & Phelps, M. E. (1996). Systematic changes in cerebral glucose metabolic rate after successful behavior modification treatment of obsessive-compulsive disorder. *Archives of General Psychiatry, 53,* 109–113.

Schwartz, M. S., et al. (1999). *Biofeedback: A practitioner's guide* (2nd ed.). New York: Guilford Press.

Schwartz, P. J., Brown, C., Wehr, T. A., & Rosenthal, N. E. (1996). Winter seasonal affective disorder: A follow-up study of the first 59 patients of the National Institute of Mental Health seasonal studies program. *American Journal of Psychiatry, 153,* 1028–1036.

Schwarz, J. R. (1981). *The Hillside strangler: A murderer's mind.* New York: New American Library.

Schwarz, N. (1999). Self-reports: How the questions shape the answers. *American Psychologist, 54,* 93–105.

Schwarz, N., Bless, H., & Bohner, G. (1991). Mood and persuasion: Affective states influence the processing of persuasive communications. *Advances in Experimental Social Psychology, 24,* 161–199.

Scoboria, A., Mazzoni, G., Kirsch, I., & Milling, L. S. (2002). Immediate and persisting effects of misleading questions and hypnosis on memory reports. *Journal of Experimental Psychology: Applied, 8,* 26–32.

Scott, L., & O'Hara, M. W. (1993). Self-discrepancies in clinically anxious and depressed university students. *Journal of Abnormal Psychology, 102,* 282–287.

Scoville, W. B., & Milner, B. (1957). Loss of recent memory after bilateral hippocampal lesions. *Journal of Neurology, Neurosurgery, and Psychiatry, 20,* 11–21.

Scullin, M. H., & Ceci, S. J. (2001). A suggestibility scale for children. *Personality and Individual Differences, 30,* 843–856.

Seamon, J. G., Luo, C. R., & Gallo, D. A. (1998). Creating false memories of words with or without recognition of list items: Evidence for nonconscious processes. *Psychological Science, 9,* 20–26.

Searle, J. R. (1992). *The rediscovery of the mind.* Cambridge, MA: MIT Press.

Sebel, P. S., Bonke, B., Winograd, E. (1993). *Memory and awareness in anesthesia.* Englewood Cliffs, NJ: Prentice-Hall.

Sedikides, C., & Ostrom, T. M. (Eds.). (1993). Perceptions of group variability. *Social Cognition, 11*(1).

Seeman, P., Guan, H.-C., & Van Tol, H. H. M. (1993). Dopamine D4 receptors elevated in schizophrenia. *Nature, 365,* 441–445.

Segal, N. L. (2000). Virtual twins: New findings on within-family environmental influences on intelligence. *Journal of Educational Psychology, 92,* 442–448.

Segall, M. H., Campbell, D. T., & Herskovitz, M. J. (1966). *The influence of culture on visual perception.* Indianapolis, IN: Bobbs-Merrill.

Segerberg, O. (1982). *Living to be 100: 1200 who did and how they did it.* New York: Scribner.

Segestrom, S. C., Taylor, S. E., Kemeny, M. E., & Fahey, J. L. (1998). Optimism is associated with mood, coping, and immune change in response to stress. *Journal of Personality and Social Psychology, 74,* 1646–1655.

Segrin, C., & Abramson, L. Y. (1994). Negative reactions to depressive behaviors: A communications theories analysis. *Journal of Abnormal Psychology, 103,* 655–668.

Seligman, M. E. P. (1971). Phobias and preparedness. *Behavior Therapy, 2,* 307–320.

Seligman, M. E. P. (1975). *Helplessness: On depression, development, and death.* San Francisco: W. H. Freeman.

Seligman, M. E. P. (1991). *Learned optimism.* New York: Knopf.

Seligman, M. E. P. (1995). The effectiveness of psychotherapy: The Consumer Reports Study. *American Psychologist, 50,* 965–974.

Seligman, M. E. P. (1996). Science as an ally of practice. *American Psychologist, 51,* 1072–1079.

Selye, H. (1936). A syndrome produced by diverse nocuous agents. *Nature, 138,* 32.

Selye, H. (1976). *The stress of life.* New York: McGraw-Hill.

Semb, G. B., Ellis, J. A., & Araujo, J. (1993). Long-term memory for knowledge learned in school. *Journal of Educational Psychology, 85,* 305–316.

Sepple, C. P., & Read, N. W. (1989). Gastrointestinal correlates of the development of hunger in man. *Appetite, 13,* 183–191.

Sergent, J. (1983). The role of the input in visual hemispheric asymmetries. *Psychological Bulletin, 93,* 481–512.

Sergent, J. (1990). Furtive incursions into bicameral minds. *Brain, 113,* 537–568.

Seymour, T. L., Seifert, C. M., Shafto, M. G., & Mosmann, A. L. (2000). Using response time measures to assess "guilty knowledge." *Journal of Applied Psychology, 85,* 30–47.

Shadish, W. R., et al. (1997). Evidence that therapy works in clinically representative conditions. *Journal of Consulting and Clinical Psychology, 65,* 355–365.

Shafir, E., & LeBoeuf, R. A. (2002). Rationality. *Annual Review of Psychology, 53,* 491–517.

Shanahan, M. J. (2000). Pathways to adulthood in changing societies: Variability and mechanisms in life course perspective. *Annual Review of Sociology, 26,* 667–692.

Shapiro, D., & Shapiro, D. (1982). Meta-analysis of comparative therapy outcome studies: A replication and refinement. *Psychological Bulletin, 92,* 581–604.

Shapiro, J. P. (1997, January 13). Euthanasia's home. *U.S. News & World Report,* pp. 22–27.

Sharon, T., & Wynn, K. (1998). Individuation of actions from continuous motion. *Psychological Science, 9,* 357–362.

Shaver, P. R., & Clark, C. L. (1996). Forms of adult romantic attachment and their cognitive and emotional underpinnings. In G. G. Noam & K. W. Fischer (Eds.), *Development and vulnerability in close relationships* (pp. 29–58). Mahwah, NJ: Erlbaum.

Shea, D. L., Lubinski, D., & Benbow, C. P. (2001). Importance of assessing spatial ability in intellectually talented young adolescents: A 20-year longitudinal study. *Journal of Educational Psychology, 93,* 604–614.

Shearn, D., Bergman, E., Hill, D., Abel, A., & Hinds, L. (1990). Facial coloration and temperature responses in blushing. *Psychophysiology, 27,* 687–693.

Sheehan, P. W., Statham, D., & Jamieson, G. A. (1991). Pseudomemory effects and their relationship to level of susceptibility to hypnosis and state instruction. *Journal of Personality and Social Psychology, 60,* 130–137.

Sheldon, K. M., Elliot, A. J., Kim, Y., & Kasser, T. (2001). What is satisfying about satisfying events?: Testing 10 candidate psychological needs. *Journal of Personality and Social Psychology, 80,* 325–339.

Sheldon, W. H. (1954). *Atlas of man: A guide for somatotyping the adult male of all ages.* New York: Harper & Row.

Shelton, R. C., & Weinberger, D. R. (1986). X-ray computerized tomography studies in schizophrenia: Review and synthesis. In H. A. Nasrallah & D. R. Weinberger (Eds.), *The neurology of schizophrenia.* Amsterdam, Netherlands: Elsevier.

Shepard, R. N. (1990). *Mind sights.* New York: W. H. Freeman.

Shepard, R. N., & Cooper, L. A. (1982). *Mental images and their transformations.* Cambridge, MA: MIT Press.

Shepard, R. N., & Metzler, J. (1971). Mental rotation of three-dimensional objects. *Science, 171,* 701–703.

Sheppard, J. A. (1993). Productivity loss in performance groups: A motivation analysis. *Psychological Bulletin, 113,* 67–81.

Shepperd, J. A. (1993). Student derogation of the Scholastic Aptitude Test: Biases in perceptions and presentations of college board scores. *Basic and Applied Social Psychology, 14,* 455–473.

Sherif, M. (1936). *The psychology of social norms.* New York: Harper.

Sherman, P. (1977). Nepotism and the evolution of alarm calls. *Science, 197,* 1246–1253.

Sherrod, D. (1989). The influence of gender on same-sex friendships. In C. Hendrick (Ed.), *Review of personality and social psychology* (Vol. 10, pp. 164–186). Newbury Park, CA: Sage.

Sherry, D. F. (1992). Memory, the hippocampus, and natural selection: Studies of food-storing birds. In L. Squire & N. Butters (Eds.), *Neuropsychology of memory* (2nd ed., pp. 521–532). New York: Guilford Press.

Shidlo, A., & Schroeder, M. (2002). Changing sexual orientation: A consumers' report. *Professional Psychology: Research and Practice, 33,* 249–259.

Shih, M., Pittinsky, T. L., & Ambady, N. (1999). Stereotype susceptibility: Identity salience and shifts in quantitative performance. *Psychological Science, 10,* 80–83.

Shimamura, A. P., Berry, J. M., Mangels, J. A., Rusting, C. L., & Jurica, P. J. (1995). Memory and cognitive abilities in university professors: Evidence for successful aging. *Psychological Science, 6,* 271–277.

Shinohara, T., et al. (2002). Neurotrophic factor intervention restores auditory function in deafened animals. *Proceedings of the National Academy of Sciences, 99,* 1657–1660.

Shiraev, E., & Levy, D. (2001). *Introduction to cross-cultural psychology: Critical thinking and contemporary applications.* Boston: Allyn & Bacon.

Shneidman, E. (Ed.). (1984). *Death: Current perspectives.* Palo Alto, CA: Mayfield.

Shneidman, E. (1989). The Indian summer of life: A preliminary study of septuagenarians. *American Psychologist, 44,* 684–694.

Shneidman, E. S. (1996). *The suicidal mind.* New York: Oxford University Press.

Shostrom, E. (1965). An inventory for the measurement of self-actualization. *Educational and Psychological Measurement, 24,* 207–218.

Shuell, T. J. (1996). Teaching and learning in a classroom context. In D. C. Berliner & R. C. Calfee (Eds.), *Handbook of educational psychology* (pp. 726–764). New York: Macmillan.

Shulgin, A. T. (1986). The background and chemistry of MDMA. *Journal of Psychoactive Drugs, 18,* 291–303.

Shulman, D., & Stroumsa, G. G. (Eds.). (1999). *Dream cultures: Explorations in the comparative history of dreaming.* New York: Oxford University Press.

Shum, M. S. (1998). The role of temporal landmarks in autobiographical memory processes. *Psychological Bulletin, 124,* 423–442.

Sidanius, J., Levin, S., Liu, J., & Pratto, F. (2000). Social dominance orientation, anti-egalitarianism, and the political psychology of gender: An extension and cross-cultural replication. *European Journal of Social Psychology, 30,* 41–67.

Sidey, H. (1993, August 9). The flood: A broken heartland. *Time,* p. 28.

Siegel, J. M. (2001). The REM sleep-memory consolidation hypothesis. *Science, 294,* 1058–1063.

Siegel, J. M., et al. (1991). Neuronal activity in narcolepsy: Identification of cataplexy-related cells in the medial medulla. *Science, 252,* 1315–1318.

Siegel, R. K. (1989). *Intoxication: Life in pursuit of artificial paradise.* New York: Dutton.

Siegler, I. C. (1994). Hostility and risk: Demographic and lifestyle variables. In A. W. Siegman & T. W. Smith (Eds.), *Anger, hostility, and the heart* (pp. 199–214). Mahwah, NJ: Erlbaum.

Siegler, R. S. (1996). *Emerging minds: The process of change in children's thinking.* New York: Oxford University Press.

Siegler, R. S. (1998). *Children's thinking* (3rd ed.). Upper Saddle River, NJ: Prentice-Hall.

Siegler, R. S., & Ellis, S. (1996). Piaget on childhood. *Psychological Science, 7,* 211–215.

Siegman, A. W., & Smith, T. W. (Eds.). (1994). *Anger, hostility, and the heart.* Mahwah, NJ: Erlbaum.

Sigelman, L., & Welch, S. (1991). *Black Americans' views of racial inequality: The dream deferred.* New York: Cambridge University Press.

Silbersweig, D. A., Stern, E., Cahill, C., et al. (1995). A functional neuroanatomy of hallucinations in schizophrenia. *Nature, 378,* 176–179.

Silveira, J. (1971). *Incubation: The effect of interruption timing and length on problem solution and quality of problem processing.* Unpublished doctoral dissertation. University of Oregon, Eugene.

Silver, E., Cirincione, C., & Steadman, H. J. (1994). Demythologizing inaccurate perceptions of the insanity defense. *Law and Human Behavior, 18,* 63–70.

Silverberg, S. B., & Steinberg, L. (1990). Psychological well-being of parents with early adolescent children. *Developmental Psychology, 26,* 658–666.

Silverman, K., Evans, S. M., Strain, E. C., & Griffiths, R. R. (1992). Withdrawal syndrome after the double-blind cessation of caffeine consumption. *New England Journal of Medicine, 327,* 1109–1114.

Silverstein, B., Perdue, L., & Kelly, E. (1986). The role of the mass media in promoting a thin standard of bodily attractiveness for women. *Sex Roles, 14,* 519–532.

Simmons, J. V. (1981). *Project sea hunt: A report on prototype development and tests.* Technical Report 746, Naval Ocean Systems Center, San Diego.

Simmons, R. (2002). *Odd girl out: The hidden culture of aggression in girls.* New York: Harcourt.

Simon, H. A. (1975). The functional equivalence of problem solving skills. *Cognitive Psychology, 7,* 268–288.

Simon, H. A. (1989). The scientist as a problem solver. In D. Kiahr and K. Kotovsky (Eds.), *Complex information processing: The impact of Herbert Simon.* Hillsdale, NJ: Erlbaum.

Simon, H. A., & Chase, W. G. (1973). Skill in chess. *American Scientist, 61,* 394–403.

Simon, H. B. (1991). Exercise and human immune function. In R. Ader, D. E. Felton, & N. Cohen (Eds.), *Psychoneuroimmunology* (2nd ed., pp. 869–895). New York: Academic Press.

Simon, R. C., & Hughes, C. C. (1986). *The culture-bound syndromes: Folk illnesses of psychiatric and anthropological interest.* Boston: D. Reidel.

Simons, D. J. (Ed.). (2000). Change blindness and visual memory: A special issue. *Visual Cognition.*

Simons, D. J., & Levin, D. T. (1998). Failure to detect changes to people during a real-world interaction. *Psychonomic Bulletin & Review, 4,* 644–649.

Simonton, D. K. (2002). *Great psychologists and their time: Scientific insights into psychology's history.* Washington, DC: American Psychological Association.

Simpson, J. A. (1987). The dissolution of romantic relationships: Factors involved in relationship stability and emotional distress. *Journal of Personality and Social Psychology, 53,* 683–692.

Simpson, J. A., & Kenrick, D. T. (Eds.). (1997). *Evolutionary social psychology.* Mahwah, NJ: Erlbaum.

Sinden, J. D., Hodges, H., & Gray, J. A. (1995). Neural transplantation and recovery of cognitive function. *Behavioral and Brain Sciences, 18,* 10–35.

Singelis, T. M. (1994). The measurement of independent and interdependent self-construals. *Personality and Social Psychology Bulletin, 20,* 580–591.

Singer, J. L. (Ed.). (1990). *Repression and dissociation: Implications for personality theory, psychopathology, and health.* Chicago: University of Chicago Press.

Singer, L. T., Arendt, R., Fagan, J., Minnes, S., Salvator, A., Bolek, T., & Becker, M. (1999). Neonatal information processing in cocaine-exposed and nonexposed infants. *Infant Behavior and Development, 22,* 1–15.

Siwolop, S. (2000, July 10). Nooses, symbols of race hatred, at center of workplace lawsuits. *New York Times,* pp. A1, A16.

Skinner, B. F. (1938). *The behavior of organisms.* New York: Appleton-Century-Crofts.

Skinner, B. F. (1948). "Superstition" in the pigeon. *Journal of Experimental Psychology, 38,* 168–172.

Skinner, B. F. (1948). *Walden two.* New York: Macmillan.

Skinner, B. F. (1956). A case history in scientific method. *American Psychologist, 11,* 221–233.

Skinner, B. F. (1957). *Verbal behavior.* New York: Appleton-Century-Crofts.

Skinner, B. F. (1971). *Beyond freedom and dignity.* New York: Knopf.

Skinner, B. F. (1988). *The school of the future.* Paper presented at the annual meeting of the American Psychological Association, Atlanta, GA.

Skinner, B. F. (1990). Can psychology be a science of mind? *American Psychologist, 45,* 1206–1210.

Skinner, E. A. (1996). A guide to constructs of control. *Journal of Personality and Social Psychology, 71,* 549–570.

Sklar, L. S., & Anisman, H. (1981). Stress and cancer. *Psychological Bulletin, 89,* 369–406.

Skoog, G., & Skoog, I. (1999). A 40-year follow-up of patients with obsessive-compulsive disorder. *Archives of General Psychiatry, 56,* 121–127.

Sladek, J. R., & Shoulson, I. (1988). Neural transplantation: A call for patience rather than patients. *Science, 240,* 1386–1388.

Slater, A., Mattock, A., & Brown, E. (1990). Size constancy at birth: Newborn infants' responses to retinal and real size. *Journal of Experimental Child Psychology, 49,* 314–322.

Slavin, R. E. (1995). *Cooperative learning* (2nd ed.). Upper Saddle River, NJ: Prentice-Hall.

Sloan, R., Bagiella, E., & Powell, T. (1999). Religion, spirituality, and medicine. *The Lancet, 353,* 664–667.

Slobin, D. I. (1966). Grammatical transformations and sentence comprehension in childhood and adulthood. *Journal of Verbal Learning and Verbal Behavior, 5,* 219–227.

Slovic, P. (2000). *The perception of risk.* London: Earthscan.

Slovic, P., Fischoff, B., & Lichtenstein, S. (1982). Facts versus fears: Understanding perceived risk. In D. Kahneman, P. Slovic, & A. Tversky (Eds.), *Judgment under uncertainty: Heuristics and biases* (pp. 463–489). New York: Cambridge University Press.

Smetana, J. G. (1988). Concepts of self and social convention: Adolescents' and parents' reasoning about hypothetical and actual family conflicts. In M. R. Gunnar &

W. A. Collins (Eds.), *Development during the transition to adolescence: Minnesota symposia on child psychology* (Vol. 21, pp. 79–122). Hillsdale, NJ: Erlbaum.

Smilek, D., Dixon, M. J., Cudahy, C., & Merikle, P. M. (2002). Concept driven color experiences in digit-color synesthesia. *Brain and Cognition, 48,* 570–573.

Smith, C. A., & Ellsworth, P. C. (1985). Patterns of cognitive appraisal in emotion. *Journal of Personality and Social Psychology, 48,* 813–838.

Smith, C. S., Reilly, C., & Midkiff, K. (1989). Evaluation of three circadian rhythm questionnaires with suggestions for an improved measure of morningness. *Journal of Applied Psychology, 74,* 728–738.

Smith, D. (1982). Trends in counseling and psychotherapy. *American Psychologist, 37,* 802–809.

Smith, D. (2002). *Report from Ground Zero: The story of the rescue efforts at the World Trade Center.* New York: Viking.

Smith, D. (2002, June). Where are recent grads getting jobs? *Monitor on Psychology, 33,* pp. 28–29.

Smith, D. E., Thompson, J. K., Raczynski, J. M., & Hilner, J. E. (1999). Body image among men and women in a biracial cohort: The CARDIA study. *International Journal of Eating Disorders, 25,* 71–82.

Smith, D. M., Neuberg, S. L., Judice, T. N., & Biesanz, J. C. (1997). Target complicity in the confirmation and disconfirmation of erroneous perceiver expectations: Immediate and longer term implications. *Journal of Personality and Social Psychology, 73,* 974–991.

Smith, E. E., Shoben, E. J., & Ripps, L. J. (1974). Structure and processes in semantic memory: A featural model for semantic decisions. *Psychological Review, 81,* 214–241.

Smith, M. C. (1983). Hypnotic memory enhancement of witnesses: Does it work? *Psychological Bulletin, 94,* 387–407.

Smith, M. L., Glass, G. V., & Miller, T. I. (1980). *The benefits of psychotherapy.* Baltimore: Johns Hopkins University Press.

Smith, R. F., Mattran, K. M., Kurkjian, M. F., & Kurtz, S. L. (1989). Alterations in offspring behavior induced by chronic prenatal cocaine dosing. *Neurotoxicology and Teratology, 11,* 35–38.

Smith, R. W., & Kounios, J. (1996). Sudden insight: All-or-none processing revealed by speed-accuracy decomposition. *Journal of Experimental Psychology: Learning, Memory, and Cognition, 22,* 1443–1462.

Smith, S. M., McIntosh, W. D., & Bazzani, D. G. (1999). Are the beautiful good in Hollywood? An investigation of the beauty-and-goodness stereotype on film. *Basic and Applied Social Psychology, 21,* 69–80.

Smotherman, W. P., & Robinson, S. R. (1996). The development of behavior before birth. *Developmental Psychology, 32,* 425–434.

Smyth, J., & Lepore, S. J. (2002). *The writing cure: How expressive writing promotes health and emotional well-being.* Washington, DC: American Psychological Association.

Smyth, J. M. (1998). Written emotional expression: Effect sizes, outcome types, and moderating variables. *Journal of Consulting and Clinical Psychology, 66,* 174–184.

Snarey, J. R. (1985). Cross-cultural universality of social-moral development: A critical review of Kohlbergian research. *Psychological Bulletin, 97,* 202–233.

Sno, H. N., & Linszen, D. H. (1990). The déjà vu experience: Remembrance of things past? *American Journal of Psychiatry, 147,* 1587–1595.

Snodgrass, S. E. (1985). Women's intuition: The effect of subordinate roles on interpersonal sensitivity. *Journal of Personality and Social Psychology, 49,* 146–155.

Snodgrass, S. E., Hecht, M. A., & Ploutz-Snyder, R. (1998). Interpersonal sensitivity: Expressivity or perceptivity? *Journal of Personality and Social Psychology, 74,* 238–249.

Snyder, M. (1987). *Public appearances/private realities: The psychology of self-monitoring.* New York: W. H. Freeman.

Snyder, M., & DeBono, K. (1985). Appeals to image and claims about quality: Understanding the psychology of advertising. *Journal of Personality and Social Psychology, 49,* 586–597.

Snyder, M., & Ickes, W. (1985). Personality and social behavior. In G. Lindzey & E. Aronson (Eds.), *Handbook of social psychology* (3rd ed., Vol. II, pp. 883–948). Reading, MA: Addison-Wesley.

Snyder, M., & Stukas, A. A. (1999). Interpersonal processes: The interplay of cognitive, motivational, and behavioral activities in social interaction. *Annual Review of Psychology, 50,* 273–303.

Snyder, M., Tanke, E. D., & Berscheid, E. (1977). Social perception and interpersonal behavior: On the self-fulfilling nature of social stereotypes. *Journal of Personality and Social Psychology, 35,* 656–666.

Snyder, S. H. (1992). Nitric oxide: First in a new class of neurotransmitters? *Science, 257,* 494–496.

Snyder, S. H. (1996). *Drugs and the brain* (2nd ed.). New York: Scientific American Library.

Snyderman, M., & Rothman, S. (1987). Survey of expert opinion on intelligence and aptitude testing. *American Psychologist, 42,* 137–144.

Sokolov, E. M. (1963). Higher nervous functions: The orienting reflex. *Annual Review of Physiology, 25,* 545–580.

Solanto, M. V., Arnsten, A. F. T., & Castellanos, F. X. (2001). *Stimulant drugs and ADHD: Basic and clinical neuroscience.* New York: Oxford University Press.

Solms, M. (1997). *The neuropsychology of dreams: A clinico-anatomical study.* Mahwah, NJ: Erlbaum.

Solomon, A. (2001). *The noonday demon: An atlas of depression.* New York: Scribner.

Solomon, P. R., Adams, F., Silver, A., Zimmer, J., & DeVeaux, R. (2002). Ginkgo for memory enhancement: A randomized controlled trial. *Journal of the American Medical Association, 288,* 835–840.

Solomon, R. L. (1980). The opponent-process theory of motivation. *American Psychologist, 35,* 691–712.

Sommer, R. (1967). Classroom ecology. *Journal of Applied Behavioral Science, 3,* 489–503.

Sompayrac, L. (1999). *How the immune system works.* Malden, MA: Blackwell Science.

Spangler, W. D. (1992). Validity of questionnaire and TAT measures of need for achievement: Two meta-analyses. *Psychological Bulletin, 112,* 140–154.

Spangler, W. D., & House, R. J. (1991). Presidential effectiveness and the leadership motive profile. *Journal of Personality and Social Psychology, 60,* 439–455.

Spanos, N. P. (1986). Hypnotic behavior: A social-psychological interpretation of amnesia, analgesia, and "trance-logic." *Behavioral and Brain Sciences, 9,* 449–467.

Spanos, N. P. (1996). *Multiple identities and false memories: A sociocognitive perspective.* Washington, DC: American Psychological Association.

Spanos, N. P., & Katsanis, J. (1989). Effects of instructional set of nonvolition during hypnotic and nonhypnotic analgesia. *Journal of Personality and Social Psychology, 56,* 182–188.

Spearman, C. (1904). General intelligence objectively determined and measured. *American Journal of Psychology, 15,* 201–293.

Spelke, E. S., Breinlinger, K., Macomber, J., & Jacobson, K. (1992). Origins of knowledge. *Psychological Review, 99,* 605–632.

Spencer, S. J., Steele, C. M., & Quinn, D. M. (1999). Stereotype threat and women's math performance. *Journal of Experimental Social Psychology, 35,* 4–28.

Sperling, G. (1960). The information available in brief visual presentations. *Psychological Monographs, 74*(Whole No. 11), 1–29.

Sperry, R. W. (1966). Brain bisection and consciousness. In J. Eccles (Ed.), *Brain and conscious experience.* New York: Springer-Verlag.

Sperry, R. W. (1968). Hemisphere deconnection and unity in conscious awareness. *American Psychologist, 23,* 723–733.

Sperry, R. W. (1982). Some effects of disconnecting the cerebral hemispheres. *Science, 217,* 1223–1226, 1250.

Sperry, R. W. (1993). The impact and promise of the cognitive revolution. *American Psychologist, 48,* 878–885.

Spiegel, D. (1993). Social support: How friends, family, and groups can help. In D. Goleman & J. Gurin (Eds.), *Mind, body, medicine: How to use your mind for better health* (pp. 331–350). Yonkers, NY: Consumer Reports Books.

Spiro, A., III., Schnurr, P. P., & Aldwin, C. M. (1994). Combat-related posttraumatic stress disorder symptoms in older men. *Psychology and Aging, 9,* 17–26.

Spitz, H. H. (1999). Beleaguered Pygmalion: A history of the controversy over claims that teacher expectancy raises intelligence. *Intelligence, 27,* 199–234.

Spitzer, R. L., Gibbon, M., Skodol, A. E., Williams J. B. W., & First, M. B. (2001). *DSM-IV-TR casebook: A learning companion to the Diagnostic and Statistical Manual of Mental Disorders, Fourth Edition, Text Revision.* Washington, DC: American Psychiatric Press.

Spock, B. J. (1945). *The common sense book of child and baby care.* New York: Duell, Sloan, & Pearce.

Sporer, S. L., Malpass, R. S., & Koehnken, G. (Eds.). (1996). *Psychological issues in eyewitness identification.* Mahwah, NJ: Erlbaum.

Sporer, S. L., Penrod, S. D., Read, J. D., & Cutler, B. L. (1995). Choosing, confidence, and accuracy: A meta-analysis of the confidence-accuracy relation in eyewitness identification studies. *Psychological Bulletin, 118,* 315–327.

Spradley, B. W., Spradley, J. P., & McCurdy, D. W. (Eds.). (2000). *Conformity and conflict: Readings in cultural anthropology* (10th ed.). Needham Heights, MA: Allyn & Bacon.

Sprecher, S., Sullivan, Q., & Hatfield, E. (1994). Mate selection preferences: Gender differences examined in a national sample. *Journal of Personality and Social Psychology, 66,* 1074–1080.

Springer, S. P., & Deutsch, G. (1998). *Left brain right brain: Perspectives from cognitive neuroscience* (5th ed.). New York: W. H. Freeman.

Squier, L. H., & Domhoff, G. W. (1998). The presentation of dreaming and dreams in introductory psychology textbooks: A critical examination with suggestions for textbook authors and course instructors. *Dreaming, 8,* 149–168.

Squire, L. R. (1992). Memory and the hippocampus: A synthesis from findings with rats, monkeys, and humans. *Psychological Review, 99,* 195–231.

Squire, L. R., & Schacter, D. L. (Eds.). (2002). *Neuropsychology of memory* (3rd ed.). New York: Guilford.

Squire, L. R., & Zola-Morgan, S. (1991). The medial temporal lobe memory system. *Science, 253,* 1380–1386.

Staats, A. W., & Staats, C. K. (1958). Attitudes established by classical conditioning. *Journal of Abnormal and Social Psychology, 57,* 37–40.

Stadler, M. A., & Frensch, P. A. (Eds.). (1998). *Handbook of implicit learning.* Thousand Oaks, CA: Sage Publications.

Stadler, M. A., Roediger, H. L., & McDermott, K. B. (1999). Norms for word lists that create false memories. *Memory & Cognition, 27,* 494–500.

Stangor, C., & Lange, J. E. (1994). Mental representations of social groups: Advances in understanding stereotypes and stereotyping. *Advances in Experimental Social Psychology, 26,* 357–416.

Stangor, C., Sullivan, L. A., & Ford, T. E. (1991). Affective and cognitive determinants of prejudice. *Social Cognition, 9,* 359–380.

Stanley, J. C., & Benbow, C. P. (1986). Youths who reason exceptionally well mathematically. In R. J. Sternberg & J. E. Davidson (Eds.), *Conceptions of giftedness* (pp. 361–387). New York: Cambridge University Press.

Stanovich, K. E., & West, R. F. (1998). Individual differences in rational thought. *Journal of Experimental Psychology: General, 127,* 161–188.

Stanovich, K. E., West, R. F., & Harrison, M. R. (1995). Knowledge growth and maintenance across the life span: The role of print exposure. *Developmental Psychology, 31,* 811–826.

Stapp, J., Tucker, A. M., & VandenBos, G. R. (1983). Census of psychological personnel. *American Psychologist, 40,* 1317–1351.

Stark, E. (1984, October). To sleep, perchance to dream. *Psychology Today,* 16.

Stark, E. (1986, October). Young, innocent, and pregnant. *Psychology Today,* 28–35.

Staszewski, J. J. (1988). Skilled memory and expert mental calculation. In M. T. H. Chi, R. Blaser, & M. J. Farr (Eds.), *The nature of expertise* (pp. 71–128). Hillsdale, NJ: Erlbaum.

Stattin, H., & Magnusson, D. (1990). *Pubertal maturation in female development.* Hillsdale, NJ: Erlbaum.

Staub, E. (1996). Cultural-societal roots of violence: The examples of genocidal violence and of contemporary youth violence in the United States. *American Psychologist, 51,* 117–132.

Steblay, N. M. (1992). A meta-analytic review of the weapon-focus effect. *Law and Human Behavior, 16,* 413–424.

Steblay, N. M. (1997). Social influence in eyewitness recall: A meta-analytic review of lineup instruction effects. *Law and Human Behavior, 21,* 283–298.

Steele, C. M. (1988). The psychology of self-affirmation: Sustaining the integrity of the self. *Advances in Experimental Social Psychology, 21,* 261–302.

Steele, C. M. (1997). A threat in the air: How stereotypes shape the intellectual identities and performance of women and African Americans. *American Psychologist,* in press.

Steele, C. M., & Aronson, J. (1995). Stereotype threat and the intellectual test performance of African Americans. *Journal of Personality and Social Psychology, 69,* 797–811.

Steele, C. M., & Josephs, R. A. (1990). Alcohol myopia: Its prized and dangerous effects. *American Psychologist, 45,* 921–933.

Steele, C. M., Spencer, S. J., & Aronson, J. (2002). Contending with group image: The psychology of stereotype and social identity. *Advances in Experimental Social Psychology, 34,* 384–406.

Steele, K. M., Bass, K. E., & Crook, M. D. (1999). The mystery of the Mozart effect: Failure to replicate. *Psychological Science, 10,* 366–369.

Steele, S. (1990). *The content of our character.* New York: St. Martin's Press.

Steenbergh, T. A., Meyers, A. W., May, R. K., & Whelan, J. P. (2002). Development and validation of the Gamblers' Beliefs Questionnaire. *Psychology of Addictive Behaviors, 16,* 143–149.

Stein, B. E., & Meredith, M. A. (1993). *The merging of the senses.* Cambridge, MA: MIT Press.

Stein, D. G., & Glasier, M. M. (1995). Some practical and theoretical issues concerning fetal brain tissue grafts as therapy for brain dysfunctions. *Behavioral and Brain Sciences, 18,* 36–45.

Stein, G. L., Kimiecik, J. C., Daniels, J., & Jackson, S. A. (1995). Psychological antecedents of flow in recreational sport. *Personality and Social Psychology Bulletin, 21,* 125–135.

Stein, J. H., & Reiser, L. W. (1994). A study of white middle-class adolescent boys' responses to "semenarche" (the first ejaculation). *Journal of Youth and Adolescence, 23,* 373–384.

Stein, M. B., Walker, J. R., & Forde, D. R. (1996). Public-speaking fears in a community sample. *Archives of General Psychiatry, 53,* 169–174.

Steinberg, L. (1987, September). Bound to bicker. *Psychology Today,* pp. 36–39.

Steinberg, L. (1989). Pubertal maturation and parent-adolescent distance: An evolutionary perspective. In G. Adams, R. Montemayor, & T. Gullotta (Eds.), *Biology of adolescent behavior and development.* Newbury Park, CA: Sage.

Steinberg, L., & Morris, A. S. (2001). Adolescent development. *Annual Review of Psychology, 52,* 83–110.

Steiner, J. (1979). Human facial expressions in response to taste and smell stimulation. In H. Reese & L. P. Lipsitt (Eds.), *Advances in child development and behavior* (Vol. 13, pp. 257–295). New York: Academic Press.

Stellar, E. (1954). The physiology of motivation. *Psychological Review, 61,* 5–22.

Stellar, E. (1992). Real eating and the measurement of real physiological and behavioral variables. *Appetite, 19,* 78–79.

Stelmack, R. M. (1990). Biological bases of extraversion: Psychophysiological evidence. *Journal of Personality, 58,* 293–311.

Stephan, W. G. (1986). The effects of school desegregation: An evaluation 30 years after Brown. In M. J. Saks & L. Saxe (Eds.), *Advances in applied social psychology* (Vol. 3, pp. 181–206). Hillsdale, NJ: Erlbaum.

Stephan, W. G., Ybarra, O., & Bachman, G. (1999). Prejudice toward immigrants. *Journal of Applied Social Psychology, 29,* 2221–2237.

Stephenson, M. (2000). Development and validation of the Stephenson Multigroup Acculturation Scale (SMAS). *Psychological Assessment, 12,* 77–88.

Stepper, S., & Strack, F. (1993). Proprioceptive determinants of emotional and nonemotional feelings. *Journal of Personality and Social Psychology, 64,* 211–220.

Stern, K., & McClintock, M. K. (1998). Regulation of ovulation by human pheromones. *Nature, 392,* 177–179.

Sternbach, R. A. (1964). The effects of instructional sets of autonomic responsivity. *Psychophysiology, 1,* 67–72.

Sternberg, R. J. (1980). Sketch of a componential subtheory of human intelligence. *Behavioral and Brain Sciences, 3,* 573–584.

Sternberg, R. J. (1985). *Beyond IQ.* Cambridge, MA: Cambridge University Press.

Sternberg, R. J. (1988). *The triarchic mind: A new theory of human intelligence.* New York: Viking.

Sternberg, R. J. (Ed.). (1988). *The nature of creativity: Contemporary psychological perspectives.* New York: Cambridge University Press.

Sternberg, R. J. (Ed.). (1990). *Wisdom: Its nature, origins, and development.* New York: Cambridge University Press.

Sternberg, R. J. (1997). *Successful intelligence.* New York: Plume.

Sternberg, R. J. (1998). A balance theory of wisdom. *Review of General Psychology, 2,* 347–365.

Sternberg, R. J. (Ed.). (1999). *Handbook of creativity.* New York: Cambridge University Press.

Sternberg, R. J. (Ed.). (2000). *Handbook of intelligence.* New York: Cambridge University Press.

Sternberg, R. J. (2001). What is the common thread of creativity? Its dialectical relation to intelligence and wisdom. *American Psychologist, 56,* 360–362.

Sternberg, R. J., Conway, B. E., Ketron, J. L., & Bernstein, M. (1981). People's conceptions of intelligence. *Journal of Personality and Social Psychology, 41,* 37–55.

Sternberg, R. J., & Davidson, J. E. (1999). Insight. In M. A. Runco & S. R. Pritzker (Eds.), *Encyclopedia of Creativity* (Vol. 2). San Diego: Academic Press.

Sternberg, R. J., Forsythe, G. B., Hedlund, J., Horvath, J. A., Wagner, R. K., Williams, W. M., Snook, S. A., & Grigorenko, E. L. (2000). *Practical intelligence in everyday life.* New York: Cambridge University Press.

Sternberg, R. J., Lautrey, J., & Lubart, T. I. (Eds.). (2003). *Models of human intelligence: International perspectives.* Washington, DC: American Psychological Association.

Sternberg, R. J., & Lubart, T. I. (1991). An investment theory of creativity and its development. *Human Development, 34,* 1–31.

Sternberg, R. J., & Okagaki, L. (1989). Continuity and discontinuity in intellectual development are not a matter of "either-or." *Human Development, 32,* 158–166.

Stevens, J. C., Foulke, E., & Patterson, M. Q. (1996). Tactile acuity, aging, and Braille reading in long-term blindness. *Journal of Experimental Psychology: Applied, 2,* 91–106.

Stevenson, H. W., Chen, C., & Lee, S. Y. (1993). Mathematics achievement in Chinese, Japanese, and American children: Ten years later. *Science, 259,* 53–58.

Stevenson, H. W., Lee, S., Chen, C., Stigler, J., Fan, L., & Ge, F. (1990). Mathematics achievement of children in China and the United States. *Child Development, 61,* 1053–1066.

Stewart, A. J., & Ostrove, J. M. (1998). Women's personality in middle age: Gender, history, and midcourse corrections. *American Psychologist, 53,* 1185–1194.

Stewart, A. J., Sokol, M., Healy, J. M., & Chester, N. L. (1986). Longitudinal studies of psychological consequences of life changes in children and adults. *Journal of Personality and Social Psychology, 50,* 143–151.

Stewart, A. J., & Vandewater, E. A. (1999). "If I had to do it over again . . .": Midlife review, midcourse corrections, and women's well-being in midlife. *Journal of Personality and Social Psychology, 76,* 270–283.

Stice, E., Presnell, K., & Bearman, S. K. (2001). Relation of early menarche to depression, eating disorders, substance abuse, and comorbid psychopathology among adolescent girls. *Developmental Psychology, 37,* 608–619.

Stigler, J., Shweder, R. A., & Herdt, G. (Eds.). (1990). *Cultural psychology: Essays on comparative human development.* New York: Cambridge University Press.

Stiles, W. B., Agnew-Davies, R., Hardy, G. E., Barkham, M., & Shapiro, D. A. (1998). Relations of the alliance with psychotherapy outcome: Findings in the second Sheffield Psychotherapy Project. *Journal of Consulting and Clinical Psychology, 66,* 791–802.

Stiles, W. B., Shapiro, D. A., & Elliott, R. (1986). Are all psychotherapies equivalent? *American Psychologist, 41,* 165–180.

Stine, G. J. (2002). *AIDS update 2002.* Upper Saddle River, NJ: Prentice-Hall.

Stobin, D. I. (1966). Grammatical transformations and sentence comprehension in childhood and adulthood. *Journal of Verbal Learning and Verbal Behavior, 5,* 219–227.

Stone, A. A., Neale, J. M., Cox, D. S., Napoli, A., Valdimarsdottir, H., & Kennedy-Moore, E. (1994). Daily events are associated with a secretory immune response to an oral antigen in men. *Health Psychology, 13,* 440–446.

Stone, J., Lynch, C. I., Sjomeling, M., & Darley, J. M. (1999). Stereotype threat effects on black and white athletic performance. *Journal of Personality and Social Psychology, 77,* 1213–1227.

Stone, J., Wiegand, A. W., Cooper, J., & Aronson, E. (1997). When exemplification fails: Hypocrisy and the motive for self-integrity. *Journal of Personality and Social Psychology, 72,* 54–65.

Stone, M. H. (1997). *Healing the mind: A history of psychiatry from antiquity to present.* New York: Norton.

Stoolmiller, M. (1999). Implications for the restricted range of family environments for estimates of heritability and nonshared environment in behavior-genetic adoption studies. *Psychological Bulletin, 125,* 392–409.

Strahan, E. J., Spencer, S. J., & Zanna, M. P. (2002). Subliminal priming and persuasion: Striking while the iron is hot. *Journal of Experimental Social Psychology,* in press.

Straneva, P. A., Maixner, W., Light, K. C., Pedersen, C. A., Costello, N. L., & Girdler, S. S. (2002). Menstrual cycle, beta-endorphins, and pain sensitivity in premenstrual dysphoric disorder. *Health Psychology, 21,* 358–367.

Straube, E. R., & Oades, R. D. (1992). *Schizophrenia: Empirical research and findings.* San Diego: Academic Press.

Strauman, T. J. (1989). Self-discrepancies in clinical depression and social phobia: Cognitive structures that underlie emotional disorders? *Journal of Abnormal Psychology, 98,* 5–14.

Strauman, T. J. (1996). Stability within the self: A longitudinal study of the structural implications of self-discrepancy theory. *Journal of Personality and Social Psychology, 71,* 1142–1153.

Strauman, T. J., Lemieux, A. M., & Coe, C. L. (1993). Self-discrepancy and natural killer cell activity: Immunological consequences of negative self-evaluation. *Journal of Personality and Social Psychology, 64,* 1042–1052.

Straus, M. A., & Donnelly, D. A. (2000). *Beating the devil out of them: Corporal punishment in American children* (2nd ed.). Somerset, NJ: Transaction Publishers.

Strauss, D. H., Spitzer, R. L., Muskin, P. R. (1990). Maladaptive denial of physical illness: A proposal for DSM-IV. *American Journal of Psychiatry, 147,* 1168–1172.

Strawbridge, W. J., Shema, S. J., Cohen, R. D., & Kaplan, G. A. (2001). Religious attendance increases survival by improving and maintaining good health behaviors, mental health, and social relationships. *Annals of Behavioral Medicine, 23,* 68–74.

Streissguth, A. P., Barr, H. M., Bookstein, F. L., & Sampson, P. D. (1993). *The enduring effects of prenatal alcohol exposure on child development: Birth through 7 years.* Ann Arbor: University of Michigan Press.

Streissguth, A. P., Barr, H. M., Bookstein, F. L., Sampson, P. D., & Olson, H. C. (1999). The long-term neurocognitive consequences of prenatal alcohol exposure: A 14-year study. *Psychological Science, 10,* 186–190.

Streissguth, A. P., Barr, H. M., Sampson, P. D., Darby, B. L., & Martin, C. (1989). IQ at age 4 in relation to maternal alcohol use and smoking during pregnancy. *Developmental Psychology, 25,* 3–11.

Streri, A., & Pecheux, M. G. (1986). Tactual habituation and discrimination of form in infancy: A comparison with vision. *Child Development, 57,* 100–104.

Strichartz, A. F., & Burton, R. V. (1990). Lies and truth: A study of the development of the concept. *Child Development, 61,* 211–220.

Strickland, B. R. (1989). Internal-external control expectancies: From contingency to creativity. *American Psychologist, 44,* 1–12.

Striegel-Moore, R., & Smolak, L. (Eds.). (2001). *Eating disorders: Innovative directions in research and practice.* Washington, DC: American Psychological Association.

Stroop, J. R. (1935). Studies of interference in serial verbal reactions. *Journal of Experimental Psychology, 18,* 643–662.

Strube, M. J., & Werner, C. (1985). Relinquishment of control and the Type A behavior pattern. *Journal of Personality and Social Psychology, 48,* 688–701.

Struckman-Johnson, C. J., Gilliland, R. G., Struckman-Johnson, D. L., & North, T. C. (1990). The effects of fear of AIDS and gender on responses to fear-arousing condom advertisements. *Journal of Applied Social Psychology, 20,* 1396–1410.

Strupp, H. H. (1989). Psychotherapy: Can the practitioner learn from the researcher? *American Psychologist, 44,* 717–724.

Strupp, H. H. (1996). The tripartite model and the Consumer Reports study. *American Psychologist, 51,* 1017–1024.

Stumpf, H., & Stanley, J. C. (1996). Gender-related differences on the college board's advanced placement and achievement tests, 1982–1992. *Journal of Educational Psychology, 88,* 353–364.

Stumpf, H., & Stanley, J. C. (1998). Stability and change in gender-related differences on the college board advanced placement achievement tests. *Current Directions in Psychological Science, 7,* 192–196.

Stunkard, A. J., Harris, J. R., Pedersen, N. L., & McClearn, G. E. (1990). The body-mass index of twins who have been reared apart. *New England Journal of Medicine, 332,* 1483–1487.

Subrahmanyan, K., & Greenfield, P. M. (1994). Effects of video game practice on spatial skills in girls and boys. *Journal of Applied Developmental Psychology, 15,* 13–32.

Sue, D. W., & Sue, D. (1999). *Counseling the culturally different: Theory and practice* (3rd ed.). New York: Wiley.

Sue, D. W., & Sue, D. (2002). *Counseling the culturally diverse: Theory and practice* (4th ed.). New York: Wiley.

Sue, S., & Okazaki, S. (1990). Asian-American educational achievements: A phenomenon in search of an explanation. *American Psychologist, 45,* 913–920.

Suh, E., Diener, E., & Fujita, F. (1996). Events and subjective well-being: Only recent events matter. *Journal of Personality and Social Psychology, 70,* 1091–1102.

Sullivan, C. E., Issa, F. G., Berthon-Jones, M., & Eves, L. (1981). Reversal of obstructive sleep apnea by continuous positive airway pressure applied through the nares. *Lancet,* 862–865.

Sullivan, R. M., Taborsky-Barbar, S., Mendoza, R., Itino, A., Leon, M., et al. (1991). Olfactory classical conditioning in neonates. *Pediatrics, 87,* 511–518.

Sundstrom, E. (1986). *Work places.* New York: Cambridge University Press.

Suomi, S. J. (1991). Uptight and laid-back monkeys: Individual differences in the response to social challenges. In S. Branch, W. Hall, & J. E. Dooling (Eds.), *Plasticity of development.* Cambridge, MA: MIT Press.

Suro, R., & Fletcher, M. A. (1999, November 23). 75 percent of military's minorities see racism. *Washington Post,* p. A01.

Sussman, N., & Rosenfeld, H. (1982). Influence of culture, language, and sex on interpersonal distance. *Journal of Personality and Social Psychology, 42,* 66–74.

Suzuki, K. (1991). Moon illusion simulated in complete darkness: Planetarium experiment reexamined. *Perception and Psychophysics, 49,* 349–354.

Suzuki, K. (1998). The role of binocular viewing in a spacing illusion arising in a darkened surround. *Perception, 27,* 355–361.

Swaab, D. F., Chung, W. C. J., Kruijver, F. P. M., Hofman, M. A., & Ishunina, T. A. (2001). Structural and functional sex differences in the human hypothalamus. *Hormones and Behavior, 40,* 93–98.

Swann, W. B., Jr., & Ely, R. J. (1984). A battle of wills: Self-verification versus behavioral confirmation. *Journal of Personality and Social Psychology, 46,* 1287–1302.

Swann, W. B., Langlois, J. H., & Gilbert, L. (Eds.). (1999). *Sexism and stereotypes in modern society: The gender science of Janet Taylor Spence.* Washington, DC: American Psychological Association.

Swayze, V. W. (1995). Frontal leukotomy and related psychosurgical procedures in the era before antipsychotics (1935–1954): A historical overview. *American Journal of Psychiatry, 152,* 505–515.

Swets, J. A. (1996). *Signal detection theory and ROC analysis in psychology and diagnostics.* Mahwah, NJ: Erlbaum.

Swets, J. A., & Bjork, R. A. (1990). Enhancing human performance: An evaluation of "new age" techniques considered by the U.S. Army. *Psychological Science, 1,* 85–96.

Swim, J. K. (1994). Perceived versus meta-analytic effect sizes: An assessment of the accuracy of gender stereotypes. *Journal of Personality and Social Psychology, 66,* 21–36.

Swim, J. K., Borgida, E., Maruyama, G., & Myers, D. G. (1989). Joan McKay versus John McKay: Do gender stereotypes bias evaluations? *Psychological Bulletin, 105,* 409–429.

Symons, C. S., & Johnson, B. T. (1997). The self-reference effect in memory: A meta-analysis. *Psychological Bulletin, 121,* 371–394.

Szasz, T. (1961). *The myth of mental illness.* New York: Harper & Row.

Szasz, T. (1987). *Insanity: The idea and its consequences.* New York: Wiley.

Szymczyk, J. (1995, August 14). Animals, vegetables, and minerals. *Newsweek,* p. 10.

Tajfel, H. (Ed.). (1982). *Social identity and intergroup relations.* London: Cambridge University Press.

Tajfel, H., Billig, M. G., Bundy, R. P., & Flament, C. (1971). Social categorization and intergroup behavior. *European Journal of Social Psychology, 1,* 149–178.

Takeuchi, A. H., & Hulse, S. H. (1993). Absolute pitch. *Psychological Bulletin, 113,* 345–361.

Talwar, S. K., Xu, S., Hawley, E. S., Weiss, S. A., Moxon, K. A., & Chapin, J. K. (2002). Behavioural neuroscience: Rat navigation guided by remote control. *Nature, 417,* 37–38.

Tang, S., & Hall, V. C. (1995). The overjustification effect: A meta-analysis. *Applied Cognitive Psychology, 9,* 365–404.

Tang, Y. P., Shimizu, E., Dube, G. R., Rampon, C., Kerchner, G. A., Zhuo, M., Liu, G., & Tsien, J. Z. (1999). Genetic enhancement of learning and memory in mice. *Nature, 401,* 63–69.

Tangney, J. P., Miller, R. S., Flicker, L., & Barlow, D. H. (1996). Are shame, guilt, and embarrassment distinct emotions? *Journal of Personality and Social Psychology, 70,* 1256–1269.

Tannen, D. (1990). *You just don't understand: Women and men in conversation.* New York: Morrow.

Tartter, V. C. (1986). *Language processes.* New York: Holt, Rinehart & Winston.

Tassinary, L. G., & Cacioppo, J. T. (1992). Unobservable facial actions and emotion. *Psychological Science, 3,* 28–33.

Tavris, C. (1992). *The mismeasure of woman.* New York: Simon & Schuster.

Taylor, D. M., & Moghaddam, F. M. (1994). *Theories of intergroup relations* (2nd ed.). Westport, CT: Praeger.

Taylor, H. (2002). *The obesity epidemic is getting even worse.* Harris Interactive, The Harris Poll #11, March 6.

Taylor, S. E. (1986). *Health psychology.* New York: Random House.

Taylor, S. E. (1989). *Positive illusions: Creative self-deception and the healthy mind.* New York: Basic Books.

Taylor, S. E. (1990). Health psychology: The science and the field. *American Psychologist, 45,* 40–50.

Taylor, S. E. (1998). *Health psychology* (4th ed.). New York: McGraw-Hill.

Taylor, S. E. (2002). *Health psychology* (5th ed.). New York: McGraw-Hill.

Taylor, S. E. (2002). *The tending instinct: Women, men, and the biology of nurturing.* New York: Times Books.

Taylor, S. E., & Armor, D. A. (1996). Positive illusions and coping with adversity. *Journal of Personality, 64,* 873–898.

Taylor, S. E., & Brown, J. D. (1988). Illusion and well-being: A social psychological perspective on mental health. *Psychological Bulletin, 103,* 193–210.

Taylor, S. E., & Brown, J. D. (1994). Positive illusions and well-being revisited: Separating fact from fiction. *Psychological Bulletin, 116,* 21–27.

Taylor, S. E., Falke, R. L., Shoptaw, S. J., & Lichtman, R. R. (1986). Social support, social groups, and the cancer patient. *Journal of Consulting and Clinical Psychology, 54,* 608–615.

Taylor, S. E., Kemeny, M. E., Reed, G. M., Bower, J. E., & Gruenewald, T. L. (2000). Psychological resources, positive illusions, and health. *American Psychologist, 55,* 99–109.

Taylor, S. P., & Leonard, K. E. (1983). Alcohol and human physical aggression. In R. G. Geen & E. I. Donnerstein (Eds.), *Aggression; Theoretical and empirical reviews* (Vol. 2, pp. 77–101). New York: Academic Press.

Taylor, S. E., Repetti, R. L., & Seeman, T. (1997). Health psychology: What is an unhealthy environment and how does it get under the skin? *Annual Review of Psychology, 48,* 411–447.

Technical Working Group for Eyewitness Evidence. (1999). *Eyewitness evidence: A guide for law enforcement.* Washington, DC: U.S. Department of Justice, Office of Justice Programs.

Tedeschi, J. T., Schlenker, B. R., & Bonoma, T. V. (1971). Cognitive dissonance: Private ratiocination or public spectacle? *American Psychologist, 26,* 685–695.

Teitelbaum, P., & Epstein, A. N. (1962). The lateral hypothalamic syndrome: Recovery of feeding and drinking after lateral hypothalamic lesions. *Psychological Review, 69,* 74–90.

Tellegen, A., Lykken, D. T., Bouchard, T. J., Jr., Wilcox, K. J., & Rich, S. (1988). Personality similarity in twins reared apart and together. *Journal of Personality and Social Psychology, 54,* 1031–1039.

Teng, E., & Squire, L. R. (1999). Memory for places learned long ago is intact after hippocampal damage. *Nature, 400,* 675–677.

Tenpenny, P. L., Keriazakos, M. S., Lew-Gavin, S., & Phelan, T. P. (1998). In search of inadvertent plagiarism. *American Journal of Psychology, 111,* 529–559.

Terkel, S. (1992). *Race: How blacks and whites think and feel about the American obsession.* New York: New Press.

Terman, L. M. (1916). *The measurement of intelligence.* Boston: Houghton Mifflin.

Terrace, H. S. (1985). In the beginning was the "name." *American Psychologist, 40,* 1011–1028.

Terrace, H. S. (1986). *Nim: A chimpanzee who learned sign language.* New York: Columbia University Press.

Terrace, H. S., Petitto, L. A., Sanders, R. J., & Bever, T. G. (1979). Can an ape create a sentence? *Science, 206,* 891–902.

Terry, R. D., Katzman, R., Sisodia, S. S., & Bick, K. L. (Eds.). (1999). *Alzheimer's disease.* Philadelphia, PA: Lippincott Williams & Wilkins.

Tesser, A. (1993). The importance of heritability in psychological research: The case of attitudes. *Psychological Review, 100,* 129–142.

Tetlock, P. E. (1998). Social psychology and world politics. In D. Gilbert, S. Fiske, & G. Lindzey (Eds.), *The handbook of social psychology* (4th ed., Vol. 2, pp. 868–912). New York: McGraw-Hill.

Thal, L. J. (1992). Cholinomimetic therapy in Alzheimer's disease. In L. Squire & N. Butters (Eds.), *Neuropsychology of memory* (2nd ed., pp. 277–284). New York: Guilford Press.

Thapar, A., & Greene, R. L. (1993). Evidence against a short-term store account of long-term recency effects. *Memory and Cognition, 21,* 329–337.

Thase, M. E., & Kupfer, D. J. (1996). Recent developments in the pharmacotherapy of mood disorders. *Journal of Consulting and Clinical Psychology, 64,* 646–659.

Thatcher, R. W., Walker, R. A., & Giudice, S. (1986). Human cerebral hemispheres develop at different rates and different ages. *Science, 236,* 1110–1113.

Theeuwes, J., Kramer, A. F., Hahn, S., & Irwin, D. E. (1998). Our eyes do not always go where we want them to go: Capture of the eyes by new objects. *Psychological Science, 9,* 379–385.

Thessing, V. C., Anch, A. M., Muelbach, M. J., Schweitzer, P. K., & Walsh, J. K. (1994). Two- and 4-hour bright-light exposure differentially affect sleepiness and performance the subsequent night. *Sleep, 17,* 140–145.

Thoma S. J., & Rest, J. R. (1999). The relationship between moral decision making and patterns of consolidation and transition in moral judgment development. *Developmental Psychology, 35,* 323–334.

Thoman, E. B., Ingersoll, E. W., & Acebo, C. (1991). Premature infants seek rhythmic stimulation, and the experience facilitates neurobehavioral development. *Journal of Developmental and Behavioral Pediatrics, 12,* 11–18.

Thomas, A. K., & Loftus, E. F. (2002). Creating bizarre false memories through imagination. *Memory & Cognition, 30,* 423–431.

Thomas-Anterion, C., Koenig, O., Navez, M., & Laurent, B. (1999). Midazolam effects on implicit and explicit memory processes in healthy subjects. *Psychopharmacology, 145,* 139–143.

Thompson, C. P., Herrmann, D. J., Read, J. D., Bruce, D., Payne, D. G., & Toglia, M. P. (Eds.). (1998).

*Eyewitness memory: Theoretical and applied perspectives.* Mahwah, NJ: Erlbaum.

Thompson, C. P., Herrmann, D. J., Read, J. D., Bruce, D., Payne, D. G., & Toglia, M. P. (Eds.). (1998). *Autobiographical memory: Theoretical and applied perspectives.* Mahwah, NJ: Erlbaum.

Thompson, J. G. (1988). *The psychobiology of emotions.* New York: Plenum.

Thompson, J. K. (Ed.). (1996). *Body image, eating disorders, and obesity.* Washington, DC: American Psychological Association.

Thompson, J. K., & Gray, J. J. (1995). Development and validation of a new body image assessment scale. *Journal of Personality Assessment, 64,* 258–269.

Thompson, J. K., Heinberg, L. J., Altabe, M., & Tantleff-Dunn, S. (1999). *Exacting beauty: Theory, assessment, and treatment of body image disturbance.* Washington, DC: American Psychological Association.

Thompson, J. K., & Smolak, L. (Eds.). (2001). *Body image, eating disorders, and obesity in youth: Assessment, prevention, and treatment.* Washington, DC: American Psychological Association.

Thompson, P. M., Vidal, C., Giedd, J. N., Gochman, P., Blumenthal, J., Nicolson, R., Toga, A. W., & Rapoport, J. L. (2001). Mapping adolescent brain change reveals dynamic wave of accelerated gray matter loss in very early-onset schizophrenia. *Proceedings of the National Academy of Sciences, 98,* 11650–11655.

Thompson, S. C., Sobolew-Shubin, A., Galbraith, M., Schwankovsky, L., & Cruzen, D. (1993). Maintaining perceptions of control: Finding perceived control in low-control circumstances. *Journal of Personality and Social Psychology, 64,* 293–304.

Thompson, W. F., Schellenberg, E. G., & Husain, G. (2001). Arousal, mood, and the Mozart effect. *Psychological Science, 12,* 248–251.

Thorndike, E. L. (1898). Animal intelligence: An experimental study of the associative processes in animals. *Psychological Monographs, 2*(Whole No. 8).

Thorndike, E. L. (1911). *Animal intelligence: Experimental studies.* New York: Macmillan.

Thorndike, E. L., et al. (1921). Intelligence and its measurement: A symposium. *Journal of Educational Psychology, 12,* 123–247.

Thorndike, R. L., Hagen, E. P., & Sattler, J. M. (1986). *Technical manual for the Stanford-Binet Intelligence Scale:* 4th ed. Chicago: Riverside.

Thorne, B. (1986). Girls and boys together . . . but mostly apart: Gender arrangements in elementary schools. In W. W. Hartup & Z. Rubin (Eds.), *Relationships and development* (pp. 167–184). Hillsdale, NJ: Erlbaum.

Throckmorton, W. (2002). Initial empirical and clinical findings concerning the change process for ex-gays. *Professional Psychology: Research and Practice, 33,* 242–248.

Thurstone, L. L. (1938). *Primary mental abilities.* Chicago: University of Chicago Press.

*Time.* (1994, June 27), p. 26.

Times Books. (2000). *Times atlas of the world: Tenth comprehensive edition.* New York: Times Books.

Tinbergen, N. (1951). *The study of instinct.* New York: Oxford University Press.

Tobias, S. (1989, September). Tracked to fail. *Psychology Today,* pp. 54–60.

Todrank, J., Byrnes, D., Wrzesniewski, A., & Rozin, P. (1995). Odors can change preferences for people in photographs: A cross-modal evaluative conditioning study with olfactory USs and visual CSs. *Learning and Motivation, 26,* 116–140.

Tolman, E. C. (1948). Cognitive maps in rats and men. *Psychological Review, 55,* 189–208.

Tolman, E. C., & Honzik, C. H. (1930). Introduction and removal of reward and maze performance in rats. *University of California Publications in Psychology, 4,* 257–275.

Tomarken, A. J., Davidson, R. J., Wheeler, R. E., & Doss, R. C. (1992). Individual differences in anterior brain asymmetry and fundamental dimensions of emotion. *Journal of Personality and Social Psychology, 62,* 676–687.

Tomblin, J. B., Spencer, L., Flock, S., Tyler, R., & Gantz, B. (1999). A comparison of language achievement in children with cochlear implants and children using hearing aids. *Journal of Speech, Language, and Hearing Research, 42,* 497–511.

Top, T. J. (1991). Sex bias in the evaluation of performance in the scientific, artistic, and literary professions: A review. *Sex Roles, 24,* 73–106.

Torrey, E. F. (1988). *Surviving schizophrenia: A family manual.* New York: Harper & Row.

Totterdell, P., Spelten, E., Smith, L., Barton, J., & Folkard, S. (1995). Recovery from work shifts: How long does it take? *Journal of Applied Psychology, 80,* 43–57.

Toufexis, A. (1989, June 12). Our violent kids. *Time,* pp. 52–58.

Toufexis, A. (1991, August 15). Now hear this—if you can. *Time,* pp. 33–34.

Toufexis, A. (1993, May 24). Sex has many accents. *Time,* p. 66.

Tourangeau, R., Rips, L. J., & Rasinski, K. A. (2000). *The psychology of survey response.* New York: Cambridge University Press.

Trafimow, D., Silverman, E. S., Fan, R. M. T., & Law, J. S. F. (1997). The effects of language and priming on the relative accessibility of the private self and collective self. *Journal of Cross-Cultural Psychology, 28,* 107–123.

Trafimow, D., Triandis, H. C., & Goto, S. G. (1991). Some tests of the distinction between the private and collective self. *Journal of Personality and Social Psychology, 60,* 649–655.

Trainor, L. J., & Heinmiller, B. M. (1998). The development of evaluative responses to music: Infants prefer to listen to consonance over dissonance. *Infant Behavior and Development, 21,* 77–88.

Trainor, L. J., & Zacharias, C. A. (1998). Infants prefer higher-pitched singing. *Infant Behavior & Development, 21,* 799–806.

Tranel, D., & Damasio, A. R. (1985). Knowledge without awareness: An autonomic index of facial recognition by prosopagnosics. *Science, 228,* 1453–1454.

Travis, J. (1994). Glia: The brain's other cells. *Science, 266,* 970–972.

Treisman, A., Viera, A., & Hayes, A. (1992). Automaticity and preattentive processes. *American Journal of Psychology, 105,* 341–362.

Triandis, H. C. (1994). *Culture and social behavior.* New York: McGraw-Hill.

Triandis, H. C. (1995). *Individualism and collectivism.* Boulder, CO: Westview Press.

Triandis, H. C., Chen, X. P., & Chan, D. K. (1998). Scenarios for the measurement of collectivism and individualism. *Journal of Cross-Cultural Psychology, 29,* 275–289.

Triplett, N. (1898). The dynamogenic factors in pacemaking and competition. *American Journal of Psychology, 9,* 507–533.

Trivers, R. L. (1971). The evolution of reciprocal altruism. *Quarterly Review of Biology, 46,* 35–57.

Trotter, R. J. (1986, August). Three heads are better than one. *Psychology Today,* pp. 56–62.

Tseng, W. (2001). *Handbook of cultural psychiatry.* San Diego: Academic Press.

Tsuang, M. T., & Faraone, S. V. (1990). *The genetics of mood disorders.* Baltimore, MD: Johns Hopkins University Press.

Tuerlinckx, F., De Boeck, P., & Lens, W. (2002). Measuring needs with the Thematic Apperception Test: A psychometric study. *Journal of Personality and Social Psychology, 82,* 448–461.

Tulving, E. (1983). *Elements of episodic memory.* Oxford: Clarendon Press.

Tulving, E. (1985). How many memory systems are there? *American Psychologist, 40,* 385–398.

Tulving, E. (2002). Episodic memory: From mind to brain. *Annual Review of Psychology, 53,* 1–25.

Tulving, E., & Schacter, D. L. (1990). Priming and human memory systems. *Science, 247,* 301–306.

Tune, L. E., & Sunderland, T. (1998). Non-cholinergic therapies: Treatment tools for the psychiatrist. *Journal of Clinical Psychiatry, 59,* 31–35.

Turiel, E. (1983). *The development of social knowledge: Morality and convention.* New York: Cambridge University Press.

Turk, C. L., Heimberg, R. G., & Hope, D. A. (2001). Social anxiety disorder. In D. H. Barlow (Ed.), *Anxiety and its disorders: The nature and treatment of anxiety and panic* (2nd ed., pp. 114–153). New York: Guilford.

Turk, D. C., & Gatchel, R. J. (Eds.). (2002). *Psychological approaches to pain management* (2nd ed.). New York: Guilford Press.

Turkheimer, E. (1999). Heritability and biological explanation. *Psychological Review, 105,* 782–791.

Turkkan, J. S. (1989). Classical conditioning: The new hegemony. *Behavioral and Brain Sciences, 12,* 121–179.

Turnbull, C. M. (1961). *The forest people: A study of the Pygmies of the Congo.* New York: Clarion.

Turner, B. (Ed.). (2002). *The statesman's yearbook 2002: The politics, cultures and economies of the world.* New York: Palgrave.

Turner, J. C. (1987). *Rediscovering the social group: A self-categorization theory.* Oxford, England: Basil Blackwell.

Turner, J. C., Oakes, P. J., Haslam, S. A., & McGarty, C. (1994). Self and collective: Cognition and social context. *Personality and Social Psychology Bulletin, 20,* 454–463.

Tversky, A., & Kahneman, D. (1971). Belief in the law of small numbers. *Psychological Bulletin, 76,* 105–110.

Tversky, A., & Kahneman, D. (1973). Availability: A heuristic for judging frequency and probability. *Cognitive Psychology, 5,* 207–232.

Tversky, A., & Kahneman, D. (1981). The framing of decisions and the psychology of choice. *Science, 211,* 453–458.

Tversky, B., & Tuchin, M. (1989). A reconciliation of the evidence on eyewitness testimony: Comments on McCloskey and Zaragoza. *Journal of Experimental Psychology, 118,* 86–91.

Twain, M. (1876). *The adventures of Tom Sawyer.* Hartford: American Publishing Company.

Twenge, J. M., Baumeister, R. F., Tice, D. M., & Stucke, T. S. (2001). If you can't join them, beat them: Effects of social exclusion on aggressive behavior. *Journal of Personality and Social Psychology, 81,* 1058–1069.

Twenge, J. M., & Crocker, J. (2002). Race and self-esteem: Meta-analyses comparing Whites, Blacks, Hispanics, Asians, and American Indians. *Psychological Bulletin, 128,* 371–408.

Tyler, R. S., Lowder, M. W., Parkinson, A. J. (1995). Performance of adult Ineraid and Nucleus cochlear implant patients after 3.5 years of use. *Audiology, 34,* 135–144.

Tyron, R. C. (1940). Genetic differences in maze learning in rats. *Yearbook of the National Society for Studies in Education, 39,* 111–119.

U.S. Bureau of the Census. (1991). *World Population Profile.*

U.S. Census Bureau (October, 2000). *Who's minding the kids?: Child care arrangements.* Washington, DC: U.S. Census Bureau.

U.S. Department of Education. (1990). *America's challenge: Accelerating academic achievement (1990).* Princeton, NJ: Educational Testing Service.

U.S. Department of Education. (1993). *Adult literacy in America (1993).* Princeton, NJ: Educational Testing Service.

Uba, L. (1994). *Asian Americans: Personality patterns, identity, and mental health.* New York: Guilford Press.

Uchino, B. N., Cacioppo, J. T., & Kiecolt-Glaser, J. K. (1996). The relationship between social support and physiological processes: A review with emphasis on underlying mechanisms and implications for health. *Psychological Bulletin, 119,* 488–531.

Underwood, B. J. (1957). Interference and forgetting. *Psychological Review, 64,* 49–60.

*United States v. Scheffer,* 188 S.Ct. 1261 (1998).

Usher, J. A., & Neisser, U. (1993). Childhood amnesia and the beginnings of memory for four early life events. *Journal of Experimental Psychology: General, 122,* 155–165.

Uttal, W. R. (2001). *The new phrenology: The limits of localizing cognitive processes in the brain.* Cambridge, MA: MIT Press.

Vaillant, G. E. (1977). *Adaptation to life.* Boston: Little, Brown.

Valenstein, E. S. (1986). *Great and desperate cures: The rise and decline of psychosurgery and other radical treatments for mental illness.* New York: Basic Books.

Valenza, E., Simion, F., Cassia, V. M., & Umilta, C. (1996). Face preference at birth. *Journal of Experimental Psychology: Human Perception and Performance, 22,* 892–903.

Vallar, G. (1998). Spatial hemineglect in humans. *Trends in Cognitive Science, 2,* 87–97.

Vallee, B. L. (1998, June). Alcohol in the Western world. *Scientific American,* 80–85.

Van Biema, D. (1997, January 13). Is there a right to die? *Time*, 60–61.

Van de Castle, R. L. (1994). *Our dreaming mind*. New York: Ballantine Books.

Van Giffen, K., & Haith, M. M. (1984). Infant visual response to gestalt geometric forms. *Infant Behavior and Development, 7*, 335–346.

van Goozen, S. H. M., et al. (1995). Gender differences in behaviour: Activating effects of cross-sex hormones. *Psychoneuroendocrinology, 20*, 343–363.

Van IJzendoorn, M. H., & Kroonenberg, P. M. (1988). Cross-cultural patterns of attachment: A meta-analysis of the Strange Situation. *Child Development, 59*, 147–156.

Van Loocke, P. (1999). *The nature of concepts: Evolution, structure and representation*. New York: Routledge.

Vauclair, J. (1996). *Animal cognition: An introduction to modern comparative psychology*. Cambridge, MA: Harvard University Press.

Vauclair, J., Fagot, J., & Hopkins, W. D. (1993). Rotation of mental images in baboons when the visual input is directed to the left cerebral hemisphere. *Psychological Science, 4*, 99–103.

Veenhoven, R. (2000). *World database of happiness*. Retrieved from the World Wide Web: http://www.eur.nl/fsw/research/happiness/

Venter, J. C., et al. (2001). The sequence of the human genome. *Science, 291*, 1304–1351.

Verma, A., Hirsch, D. J., Glatt, C. E., Ronnett, G. V., & Snyder, S. H. (1993). Carbon monoxide: A putative neural messenger. *Science, 259*, 381–384.

Vernon, P. A. (1987). *Speed of information-processing and intelligence*. Norwood, NJ: Ablex.

Vernon, P. A. (Ed.). (1993). *Biological approaches to the study of human intelligence*. Norwood, NJ: Ablex.

Vicente, K. J., & Wang, J. H. (1998). An ecological theory of expertise effects in memory recall. *Psychological Review, 105*, 33–57.

Villemure, C., & Bushnell, M. C. (2002). Cognitive modulation of pain: How do attention and emotion influence pain processing? *Pain, 95*, 195–199.

Vimal, R. L. P., Pokorny, J., & Smith, V. C. (1987). Appearance of steadily viewed lights. *Vision Research, 27*, 1309–1318.

Visintainer, M., Volpicelli, J., & Seligman, M. (1982). Tumor rejection in rats after inescapable or escapable shock. *Science, 216*, 437–439.

Vittengl, J. R., & Holt, C. S. (2000). Getting acquainted: The relationship of self-disclosure and social attraction to positive affect. *Journal of Social and Personal Relationships, 17*, 53–66.

Vogel, D. A., Lake, M. A., Evans, S., & Karraker, K. H. (1991). Children's and adults' sex-stereotyped perceptions of infants. *Sex Roles, 24*, 605–616.

Vogel, S. (1999). *The skinny on fat: Our obsession with weight control*. New York: W. H. Freeman.

von Frisch, K. (1974). Decoding the language of the bee. *Science, 185*, 663–668.

von Hippel, W., Sekaquaptewa, D., & Vargas, P. (1995). On the role of encoding processes in stereotype maintenance. *Advances in Experimental Social Psychology, 27*, 177–254.

Von Hippel, W., Silver, L. A., & Lynch, M. E. (2000). Stereotyping against your will: The role of inhibitory ability in stereotyping and prejudice among the elderly. *Personality and Social Psychology Bulletin, 26*, 523–532.

Vosniadou, S., & Brewer, W. F. (1992). Mental models of the earth: A study of conceptual change in childhood. *Cognitive Psychology, 24*, 535–585.

Vroom, V. H. (1964). *Work and motivation*. New York: Wiley.

Vroon, P. A., Vincent, P., & Van Amerongen, A. (1997). *Smell: The secret seducer*. New York: Farrar Straus & Giroux.

Wadden, T. A., Brownell, K. D., & Foster, G. D. (2002). Obesity: Responding to the global epidemic. *Journal of Consulting and Clinical Psychology, 70*, 510–525.

Wadden, T. A., & Stunkard, A. J. (Eds.). (2002). *Handbook of obesity treatment*. New York: Guilford Press.

Wade, M. G., & Whiting, H. T. A. (Eds.). (1986). *Motor development in children: Aspects of coordination and control*. Dordrecht, Netherlands: Martinus Nijhoff.

Wade, N. (1990). *Visual allusions: Pictures of perception*. Hillsdale, NJ: Erlbaum.

Wade, N. J. (1998). *A natural history of vision*. Cambridge, MA: MIT Press.

Wagenaar, W. A. (1988). *Paradoxes of gambling behavior*. Hillsdale, NJ: Erlbaum.

Wagner, H. L., MacDonald, C. J., & Manstead, A. S. R. (1986). Communication of individual emotions by spontaneous facial expressions. *Journal of Personality and Social Psychology, 50*, 737–743.

Wagstaff, G. F. (1981). *Hypnosis, compliance, and belief*. New York: St. Martin's Press.

Wahlsten, D. (1999). Single-gene influences on brain and behavior. *Annual Review of Psychology, 50*, 599–624.

Wald, G. (1964). The receptors of human color vision. *Science, 145*, 1007–1017.

Walk, R. D. (1981). *Perceptual development*. Monterey, CA: Brooks/Cole.

Walker, E., & Lewine, R. J. (1990). Prediction of adult-onset schizophrenia from childhood home movies of the patients. *American Journal of Psychiatry, 147*, 1052–1056.

Walker, E. E., & Diforio, D. (1997). Schizophrenia: A neural diathesis-stress model. *Psychological Review, 104*, 667–685.

Walker, L. J. (1984). Sex differences in the development of moral reasoning. A critical review. *Child Development, 55*, 677–691.

Walker, L. J. (1989). A longitudinal study of moral reasoning. *Child Development, 60*, 157–166.

Wallace, A. (1986). *The prodigy: A biography of William James Sidis, the world's greatest child prodigy*. London: Macmillan.

Wallace, W. P. (1965). Review of the historical, empirical, and theoretical status of the von Restorff phenomenon. *Psychological Bulletin, 63*, 410–424.

Wallis, C. (1995, March 6). How to live to be 120. *Time*, p. 85.

Walther, E. (2002). Guilty by mere association: Evaluative conditioning and the spreading attitude effect. *Journal of Personality and Social Psychology, 82*, 919–934.

Walton, G. E., Bower, N. J. A., & Bower, T. G. R. (1992). Recognition of familiar faces by newborns. *Infant Behavior and Development, 15*, 265–269.

Wampold, B. E., Mondin, G. W., Moody, M., Stich, F., Benson, K., & Ahn, H. (1997). A meta-analysis of outcome studies comparing bona fide psychotherapies: Empirically, "All must have prizes." *Psychological Bulletin, 122*, 203–215.

Wang, X., et al. (2002). Maternal cigarette smoking, metabolic gene polymorphism, and infant birth weight. *Journal of the American Medical Association, 287*, 195–202.

Wang, Y. (2002). Is obesity associated with early sexual maturation? A comparison of the association in American boys versus girls. *Pediatrics, 110*, 903–910.

Warchol, M. E., Lambert, P. R., Goldstein, B. J., Forge, A., & Corwin, J. T. (1993). Regenerative proliferation in inner ear sensory epithelia from adult guinea pigs and humans. *Science, 259*, 1619–1622.

Warga, C. (1988, September). Profile: Albert Ellis. *Psychology Today*, pp. 55–58.

Wark, G. R., & Krebs, D. L. (1996). Gender and dilemma differences in real-life moral judgment. *Developmental Psychology, 32*, 220–230.

Warr, P. (1992). Age and occupational well-being. *Psychology and Aging, 7*, 37–45.

Warrington, E. K., & Weiskrantz, L. (1970). Amnesic syndrome: Consolidation or retrieval? *Nature, 228*, 629–630.

Wason, P. C. (1960). On the failure to eliminate hypotheses in a conceptual task. *Quarterly Journal of Experimental Psychology, 12*, 129–140.

Watanabe, S., Sakamoto, J., & Wakita, M. (1995). Pigeons' discrimination of painting by Monet and Picasso. *Journal of the Experimental Analysis of Behavior, 63*, 165–174.

Watkins, L. R., & Mayer, D. J. (1982). Organization of endogenous opiate and nonopiate pain control systems. *Science, 216*, 1185–1192.

Watkins, M. J., & Peynircioglu, Z. F. (1984). Determining perceived meaning during impression formation: Another look at the meaning change hypothesis. *Journal of Personality and Social Psychology, 46*, 1005–1016.

Watson, D., & Pennebaker, J. W. (1989). Health complaints, stress, and distress: Exploring the central role of negative affectivity. *Psychological Review, 96*, 234–254.

Watson, D., & Tharp, R. G. (2001). *Self-directed behavior: Self-modification for personal adjustment* (8th ed.). Belmont, CA: Wadsworth.

Watson, D., Wiese, D., Vaidya, J., & Tellegen, A. (1999). The two general activation systems of affect: Structural findings, evolutionary considerations, and psychobiological evidence. *Journal of Personality and Social Psychology, 76*, 820–838.

Watson, D. L. (2003). *Self-directed behavior: Self-modification for personal adjustment* (8th ed.). Belmont, CA: Wadsworth.

Watson, J. B. (1913). Psychology as the behaviorist views it. *Psychological Review, 20*, 158–177.

Watson, J. B. (1925). *Behaviorism*. New York: Norton.

Watson, J. B. (1927). The myth of the unconscious. *Harper's, 155*, 502–508.

Watson, J. B., & Rayner, R. (1920). Conditioned emotional reactions. *Journal of Experimental Psychology, 3*, 1–14.

Watson, J. D. & Crick, F. H. C. (1953). Molecular structure of nucleic acids. A structure for deoxyribose nucleic acids. *Nature, 171*, 737–738.

Watson, R. I., & Evans, R. B. (1991). *The great psychologists: A history of psychological thought*. New York: HarperCollins.

Webb, W. B. (1992). *Sleep the gentle tyrant* (2nd ed.). Boston, MA: Anker.

Weber, E. H. (1834). *De pulen, resorptione, auditu et tactu: Annotationes anatomicae et physiologicae*. Leipzig, Germany: Kohler.

Webster, D. M., Richter, L., & Kruglanski, A. W. (1996). On leaping to conclusions when feeling tired: Mental fatigue effects on impressional primacy. *Journal of Experimental Social Psychology, 32*, 181–195.

Webster, R. A., Brown, D., Dickenson, A., Stanford, C., Gibb, A., & Farrant, M. (2001). *Neurotransmitters, drugs and brain function*. New York: Oxford University Press.

Wechsler, D. (1939). *The measurement of adult intelligence*. Baltimore: Williams & Wilkins.

Wechsler, D. (1972). "Hold" and "don't hold" test. In S. M. Chown (Ed.), *Human aging*. New York: Penguin.

Wechsler, D. (1981). *Manual for the Wechsler Adult Intelligence Scale-Revised*. New York: Psychological Corporation.

Wegner, D. M. (1989). *White bears and other unwanted thoughts: Suppression, obsession, and the psychology of mental control*. New York: Viking.

Wegner, D. M. (1994). Ironic processes of mental control. *Psychological Review, 101*, 34–52.

Wegner, D. M. (1997). When the antidote is the poison: Ironic mental control processes. *Psychological Science, 8*, 148–153.

Wegner, D. M., Ansfield, M., & Pilloff, D. (1998). The putt and the pendulum: Ironic effects of the mental control of action. *Psychological Science, 9*, 196–199.

Wegner, D. M., & Zanakos, S. (1994). Chronic thought suppression. *Journal of Personality, 62*, 615–640.

Wehrle, T., Kaiser, S., Schmidt, S., & Scherer, K. R. (2000). Studying the dynamics of emotional expression using synthesized facial muscle movements. *Journal of Personality and Social Psychology, 78*, 105–119.

Weil, A., & Rosen, W. (1993). *From chocolate to morphine: Everyday mind-altering drugs*. Boston: Houghton Mifflin.

Weil, A. T. (1974, July). Parapsychology: Andrew Weil's search for the true Geller: Part II. The letdown. *Psychology Today*, pp. 74–78, 82.

Weinberg, R. A. (1989). Intelligence and IQ: Landmark issues and great debates. *American Psychologist, 44*, 98–104.

Weinberg, R. A., Scarr, S., & Waldman, I. D. (1992). The Minnesota transracial adoption study: The follow-up of IQ test performance at adolescence. *Intelligence, 16*, 117–135.

Weiner, B. (1985). An attributional theory of achievement motivation and emotion. *Psychological Review, 92*, 548–573.

Weiner, B. (1989). *Human motivation*. Mahwah, NJ: Erlbaum.

Weiner, J. (1994). *The beak of the finch: A story of evolution in our time*. New York: Knopf.

Weingardt, K. R., Loftus, E. F., & Lindsay, D. S. (1995). Misinformation revisited: New evidence on the suggestibility of memory. *Memory and Cognition, 23*, 72–82.

Weingarten, G. (1998). *The hypochondriac's guide to life. And death*. New York: Simon & Schuster.

Weingartner, H., Grafman, J., Boutelle, W., Kaye, W., & Martin, P. R. (1983). Forms of memory failure. *Science, 221,* 380–382.

Weinstein, N. D. (1980). Unrealistic optimism about future life events. *Journal of Personality and Social Psychology, 39,* 806–820.

Weinstein, S. (1968). Intensive and extensive aspects of tactile sensitivity as a function of body part, sex, and laterality. In D. R. Kenshalo (Ed.), *The skin senses* (pp. 195–218). Springfield, IL: Thomas.

Weisberg, R. W. (1986). *Creativity: Genius and other myths*. New York: W. H. Freeman.

Weisberg, R. W. (1992). Metacognition and insight during problem solving: Comment on Metcalfe. *Journal of Experimental Psychology: Learning, Memory, and Cognition, 18,* 426–431.

Weiss, D. E. (1991). *The great divide*. New York: Simon & Schuster.

Weiss, G., & Hechtman, L. (1993). *Hyperactive children grown up*. New York: Guilford Press.

Weissberg, M. (1993). Multiple personality disorder and iatrogenesis: The cautionary tale of Anna O. International *Journal of Clinical and Experimental Hypnosis, 41,* 15–34.

Weissman, D. H., & Banich, M. T. (2000). The cerebral hemispheres cooperate to perform complex but not simple tasks. *Neuropsychology, 14,* 41–59.

Weisz, J. R., Suwanlert, S., Chaiyasit, W., Weiss, B., Achenbach, T. M., & Eastman, K. L. (1993). Behavioral and emotional problems among Thai and American adolescents: Parent reports for ages 12–16. *Journal of Abnormal Psychology, 102,* 395–403.

Wells, G. L. (1993). What do we know about eyewitness identification? *American Psychologist, 48,* 553–571.

Wells, G. L., & Bradfield, A. L. (1999). Distortions in eyewitness recollections: Can the postidentification-feedback effect be moderated? *Psychological Science, 10,* 138–144.

Wells, G. L., Lindsay, R. C. L., & Ferguson, T. J. (1979). Accuracy, confidence, and juror perceptions in eyewitness identification. *Journal of Applied Psychology, 64,* 440–448.

Wells, G. L., Malpass, R. S., Lindsay, R. C. L., Fisher, R. P., Turtle, J. W., & Fulero, S. M. (2000). From the lab to the police station: A successful application of eyewitness research. *American Psychologist, 55,* 581–598.

Wells, G. L., & Murray, D. M. (1984). Eyewitness confidence. In G. Wells & E. Loftus (Eds.), *Eyewitness testimony: Psychological perspectives* (pp. 155–170). New York: Cambridge University Press.

Wenzlaff, R. M., & Wegner, D. M. (2000). Thought suppression. *Annual Review of Psychology, 51,* 59–91.

Wernicke, C. (1874). *Das aphasische symptomenkomplex*. Breslau, Poland: Cohn und Weigart.

West, P. D. B., & Evans, E. F. (1990). Early detection of hearing damage in young listeners resulting from exposure to amplified music. *British Journal of Audiology, 24,* 89–103.

Westen, D. (1998). The scientific legacy of Sigmund Freud: Toward a psychodynamically informed psychological science. *Psychological Bulletin, 124,* 333–371.

Wheeler, L., & Kim, Y. (1997). What is beautiful is culturally good: The physical attractiveness stereotype has different content in collectivist cultures. *Personality and Social Psychology Bulletin, 23,* 795–800.

Wheeler, L., & Miyake, K. (1992). Social comparison in everyday life. *Journal of Personality and Social Psychology, 62,* 760–773.

Wheeler, M. A. (1995). Improvement in recall over time without repeated testing: Spontaneous recovery revisited. *Journal of Experimental Psychology: Learning, Memory, and Cognition, 21,* 173–184.

Whitbourne, S. K. (2002). *The aging individual: Physical and psychological perspectives* (2nd ed.). New York: Springer.

White, G. L., Fishbein, S., & Rutstein, J. (1981). Passionate love and misattribution of arousal. *Journal of Personality and Social Psychology, 41,* 52–62.

White, L., & Edwards, J. N. (1990). Emptying the nest and parental well-being: An analysis of national panel data. *American Sociological Review, 55,* 235–242.

White, R. W. (1975). *Lives in progress* (3rd ed.). New York: Holt, Rinehart & Winston.

Whiten, A., Goodall, J., McGrew, W. C., Nishida, T., Reynolds, V., Sugiyama, Y., Tutin, C., Wrangham, R. W., & Boesch, C. (1999). Culture in chimpanzees. *Nature, 399,* 682–685.

Whiting, B. B., & Edwards, C. P. (1988). *Children of different worlds*. Cambridge, MA: Harvard University Press.

Whitley, B. E., Jr. (1999). Right-wing authoritarianism, social dominance orientation, and prejudice. *Journal of Personality and Social Psychology, 77,* 126–134.

Whitney, P. (1986). Processing category terms in context: Instantiations as inferences. *Memory and Cognition, 14,* 39–48.

Whorf, B. L. (1956). Science and linguistics. In J. B. Carroll (Ed.), *Language, thought, and reality: Selected writings of Benjamin Lee Whorf* (pp. 207–219). Cambridge, MA: MIT Press.

Wichmann, F. A., Sharpe, L. T., & Gegenfurtner, K. R. (2002). The contributions of color to recognition memory for natural scenes. *Journal of Experimental Psychology: Learning, Memory, & Cognition, 28,* 509–520.

Wickens, T. D. (2001). *Elementary signal detection theory*. New York: Oxford University Press.

Wicklund, R. A. (1975). Objective self-awareness. In L. Berkowitz (Ed.), *Advances in experimental social psychology* (Vol. 8, pp. 233–275). New York: Academic Press.

Wiedenfeld, S. A., O'Leary, A., Bandura, A., Brown, S., Levine, S., & Raska, K. (1990). Impact of perceived self-efficacy in coping with stressors on coping with the immune system. *Journal of Personality and Social Psychology, 59,* 1082–1094.

Wiens, A. N., & Menustik, C. E. (1983). Treatment outcome and patient characteristics in an aversion therapy program for alcoholism. *American Psychologist, 38,* 1089–1096.

Wiggins, J. S. (Ed.). (1996). *The five-factor model of personality: Theoretical perspectives*. New York: Guilford Press.

Wilder, D. A. (1986). Social categorization: Implications for creation and reduction of intergroup bias. In L. Berkowitz (Ed.), *Advances in experimental social psychology* (Vol. 19, pp. 291–355). New York: Academic Press.

Wilder, D. A., & Shapiro, P. (1991). Facilitation of outgroup stereotypes by enhanced ingroup identity. *Journal of Experimental Social Psychology, 27,* 431–452.

Wilkinson, G. S. (1990). Food sharing in vampire bats. *Scientific American, 2622,* 76–82.

Williams, G. C., Grow, V. M., Freedman, Z. R., & Ryan, R. M. (1996). Motivational predictors of weight loss and weight-loss maintenance. *Journal of Personality and Social Psychology, 70,* 115–176.

Williams, J. E., & Best, D. L. (1982). *Measuring sex stereotypes: A thirty-nation study*. Beverly Hills, CA: Sage.

Williams, J. E., & Best, D. L. (1990). *Sex and psyche: Gender and self viewed cross-culturally*. Newbury Park, CA: Sage.

Williams, J. M. G., Mathews, A., & MacLeod, C. (1996). The emotional Stroop task and psychopathology. *Psychological Bulletin, 120,* 3–24.

Williams, K. D., Cheung, C. K. T., & Choi, W. (2000). Cyberostracism: Effects of being ignored over the internet. *Journal of Personality and Social Psychology, 79,* 748–762.

Williams, K. D., Govan, C. L., Croker, V., Tynan, D., Cruickshank, M., & Lam, A. (2002). Investigations into differences between social- and cyberostracism. *Group Dynamics: Theory, Research, and Practice, 6,* 65–77.

Williams, R. (1993). *Anger kills*. New York: Times Books.

Williams, W. M., Blythe, T., White, N., Li, J., Gardner, H., & Sternberg, R. J. (2002). Practical intelligence for school: Developing metacognitive sources of achievement in adolescence. *Developmental Review, 22,* 162–210.

Williams, W. M., & Ceci, S. J. (1998). *Escaping the advice trap*. New York: Andrews McMeel.

Willis, S. L. (1990). Introduction to the special section on cognitive training in later adulthood. *Developmental Psychology, 26,* 875–878.

Willis, S. L., & Reid, J. D. (Eds.). (1999). *Life in the middle: Psychological and social development in middle age*. San Diego: Academic Press.

Wills, T. A. (Ed.). (1990). Social support in social and clinical psychology. *Journal of Social and Clinical Psychology, 9*. (Special Issue)

Wilson, G. T., Rossiter, E., Kleinfield, E. I., & Lindholm, L. (1986). Cognitive-behavioral treatment of bulimia nervosa: A controlled evaluation. *Behavior Research and Therapy, 24,* 277–288.

Wilson, J. D., George, F. W., & Griffin, J. E. (1981). The hormonal control of sexual development. *Science, 211,* 1278–1284.

Wilson, T. D., Houston, C. E., Brekke, N., & Etling, K. M. (1996). A new look at anchoring effects: Basic anchoring and its antecedents. *Journal of Experimental Psychology: General, 125,* 387–402.

Wilson, T. D., Wheatley, T., Meyers, J. M., Gilbert, D. T., & Axsom, D. (2000). Focalism: A source of durability bias in affective forecasting. *Journal of Personality and Social Psychology, 78,* 821–836.

Windschitl, P. D. (1996). Memory for faces: Evidence of retrieval-based impairment. *Journal of Experimental Psychology: Learning, Memory, and Cognition, 22,* 1101–1122.

Winger, G., Hofmann, F. G., & Woods, J. H. (1992). *A handbook on drug and alcohol abuse* (3rd. ed.). New York: Oxford University Press.

Winner, E. (2000). The origins and ends of giftedness. *American Psychologist, 55,* 159–169.

Winograd, E., & Neisser, U. (Eds.). (1992). *Affect and accuracy in recall: Studies of 'flashbulb' memories*. New York: Cambridge University Press.

Winokur, G., Coryell, W., Keller, M., Endicott, J., & Akiskall, H. S. (1993). A prospective follow-up of patients with bipolar and primary unipolar affective disorder. *Archives of General Psychiatry, 50,* 457–465.

Winter, D. G. (1973). *The power motive*. New York: Free Press.

Winter, D. G. (1993). Power, affiliation, and war: Three tests of a motivational model. *Journal of Personality and Social Psychology, 65,* 532–545.

Winter, D. G. (1998). A motivational analysis of the Clinton first term and the 1996 presidential campaign. *Leadership Quarterly, 9,* 367–376.

Wise, R. A. (1996). Addictive drugs and brain stimulation reward. *Annual Review of Neuroscience, 19,* 319–340.

Wiseman, R. (1997). *Deception and self-deception: Investigating psychics*. New York: Prometheus Books.

Witelson, S. F., Kigar, D. L., & Harvey, T. (1999). The exceptional brain of Albert Einstein. *Lancet, 353,* 2149–2153.

Witteman, P. A. (1990, April 30). Vietnam: 15 years later. *Time,* pp. 19–21.

Wittig, R. (1993). Continuous positive airway pressure. In M. A. Carskadon (Ed.), *Encyclopedia of sleep and dreaming* (pp. 139–141). New York: Macmillan.

Wolpe, J. (1958). *Psychotherapy by reciprocal inhibition*. Palo Alto, CA: Stanford University Press.

Wolpe, J. (1982). *The practice of behavior therapy* (3rd ed.). New York: Pergamon.

Wong, D. F., et al. (1986). Positron emission tomography reveals elevated D-2 dopamine receptors in drug-naive schizophrenics. *Science, 234,* 1558–1563.

Wood, J. M., Garb, H. N., Lilienfeld, S. O., & Nezworski, M. T. (2002). Clinical assessment. *Annual Review of Psychology, 53,* 519–543.

Wood, N. L., & Cowan, N. (1995). The cocktail party phenomenon revisited: Attention and memory in the classic selective learning procedure of Cherry (1953). *Journal of Experimental Psychology: General, 124,* 243–262.

Wood, W. (2000). Attitude change: Persuasion and social influence. *Annual Review of Psychology, 51,* 539–570.

Wood, W., & Eagly, A. H. (2002). A cross-cultural analysis of the behavior of women and men: Implications for the origins of sex differences. *Psychological Bulletin, 128,* 699–727.

Wood, W., Lundgren, S., Ouellette, J. A., Busceme, S., & Blackstone, T. (1994). Minority influence: A meta-analytic review of social influence processes. *Psychological Bulletin, 115,* 323–345.

Wood, W., Pool, G. J., Leck, K., & Purvis, D. (1996). Self-definition, defensive processing, and influence: The normative impact of majority and minority groups. *Journal of Personality and Social Psychology, 71,* 1181–1193.

Wood, W., Wong, F. Y., & Chachere, J. G. (1991). Effects of media violence on viewers' aggression in unconstrained social interaction. *Psychological Bulletin, 109,* 371–383.

Woodhead, M. (1988). When psychology informs public policy: The case of early childhood intervention. *American Psychologist, 43,* 443–454.

Woods, S. C., Schwartz, M. W., Baskin, D. G., & Seeley, R. J. (2000). Food intake and the regulation of body weight. *Annual Review of Psychology, 51,* 255–277.

Woodward, A. L., Markman, E. M., & Fitzsimmons, C. M. (1994). Rapid word-learning in 13- and 18-month-olds. *Developmental Psychology, 30,* 553–566.

Woodward, S. A., McManis, M. H., Kagan, J., Deldin, P., Snidman, N., Lewis, M., & Kahn, V. (2001). Infant temperament and the brainstem auditory evoked response in later childhood. *Developmental Psychology, 37,* 533–538.

Woody, E. Z., & Sadler, P. (1998). On reintegrating dissociated theories: Comment on Kirsch and Lynn (1998). *Psychological Bulletin, 123,* 192–197.

Wright, J. W. (Ed.). (1993). *The universal almanac.* Kansas City, MO: Andrews & McMeel.

Wright, K. P., & Czeisler, C. A. (2002). Absence of circadian phase resetting in response to bright light behind the knees. *Science, 297,* 571.

Wright, L., von Bussman, K., Friedman, A., Khoury, M., & Owens, F. (1990). Exaggerated social control and its relationship to the Type A behavior pattern. *Journal of Research in Personality, 24,* 258–269.

Wust, S., Kasten, E., & Sabel, B. A. (2002). Blindsight after optic nerve injury indicates functionality of spared fibers. *Journal of Cognitive Neuroscience, 14,* 243–253.

Wynn, K. (1992). Addition and subtraction by human infants. *Nature, 358,* 749–750.

Wynn, K. (1996). Infants' individuation and enumeration of actions. *Psychological Science, 7,* 164–169.

Wynn, K., Bloom, P., & Chiang, W.-C. (2002). Enumeration of collections by 5-month-old infants. *Cognition, 83,* B55–B62.

Wyrwicka, W., & Dobrzecka, C. (1960). Relationship between feeding and satiation centers of the hypothalamus. *Science, 132,* 805–806.

Yalom, I. D. (1989). *Love's executioner and other tales of psychotherapy.* New York: HarperCollins.

Yanovski, J. A., Yanovski, S. Z., Sovik, K. N., Nguyen, T. T., O'Neil, P. M., & Sebring, N. G. (2000). A prospective study of holiday weight gain. *The New England Journal of Medicine, 342,* 861–867.

Yau, J., & Smetana, J. G. (1996). Adolescent-parent conflict among Chinese adolescents in Hong Kong. *Child Development, 67,* 1262–1275.

Yost, W. A. (2000). *Fundamentals of hearing: An introduction* (4th ed.). New York: Academic Press.

Young, A. W., & De Haan, E. H. F. (1992). Face recognition and awareness after brain injury. In A. D. Milner & M. D. Rugg (Eds.), *The neuropsychology of consciousness.* London: Academic Press.

Young, K. T. (1990). American conceptions of infant development from 1955 to 1984: What the experts are telling parents. *Child Development, 61,* 17–28.

Young, T. (1802). On the theory of light and colors. *Philosophical Transactions of the Royal Society of London, 92,* 12–48.

Yousem, D. M., et al. (1999). Gender effects on odor-stimulated functional magnetic resonance imaging. *Brain Research, 818,* 480–487.

Yudofsky, S. C., & Hales, R. E. (Eds.). (2002). *American Psychiatric Press textbook of neuropsychiatry and clinical neurosciences.* Washington, DC: American Psychiatric Press.

Zacks, J., Rypma, B., Gabriela, J. D. E., Tversky, B., & Glover, G. H. (1999). Imagined transformations of bodies: An fMRI investigation. *Neuropsychologia, 37,* 1029–1040.

Zacks, J. M., Ollinger, J. M., Sheridan, M. A., & Tversky, B. (2001). A parametric study of mental spatial transformations of bodies. *NeuroImage, 16,* 857–872.

Zadra, A., & Donderi, D. C. (2000). Nightmares and bad dreams: Their prevalence and relationship to well-being. *Journal of Abnormal Psychology, 109,* 273–281.

Zahn-Waxler, C., Radke-Yarrow, M., Wagner, E., & Chapman, M. (1992). Development of concern for others. *Developmental Psychology, 28,* 126–136.

Zahorik, P. (2002). Assessing auditory distance perception using virtual acoustics. *Journal of the Acoustical Society of America, 111,* 1832–1846.

Zajonc, R. B. (1965). Social facilitation. *Science, 149,* 269–274.

Zajonc, R. B. (1968). Attitudinal effects of mere exposure. *Journal of Personality and Social Psychology Monograph, 9*(2, part 2), 1–27.

Zajonc, R. B. (1976). Family configuration and intelligence. *Science, 192,* 227–236.

Zajonc, R. B. (1984). On the primacy of affect. *American Psychologist, 39,* 117–123.

Zajonc, R. B. (1986). The decline and rise of Scholastic Aptitude Scores: A prediction derived from the confluence model. *American Psychologist, 41,* 862–867.

Zajonc, R. B. (1993). Brain temperature and subjective emotional experience. In M. Lewis & J. M. Haviland (Eds.), *Handbook of emotions* (pp. 209–220). New York: Guilford Press.

Zajonc, R. B. (2001). Mere exposure: A gateway to the subliminal. *Current Directions in Psychological Science, 10,* 224–228.

Zajonc, R. B., & Mullally, P. R. (1997). Birth order: Reconciling conflicting effects. *American Psychologist, 52,* 685–699.

Zajonc, R. B., Murphy, S. T., & Inglehart, M. (1989). Feeling and facial efference: Implications of the vascular theory of emotion. *Psychological Review, 96,* 395–416.

Zebrowitz, L. A. (1997). *Reading faces: Window to the soul?* Boulder, CO: Westview Press.

Zeki, S. (1992). The visual image in mind and brain. *Scientific American, 267,* 68–76.

Zentall, S. S., & Zentall, T. R. (1983). Optimal stimulation: A model of disordered activity and performance in normal and deviant children. *Psychological Bulletin, 94,* 446–471.

Zentall, T. R., Sutton, J. E., & Sherburne, L. M. (1996). True imitative learning in pigeons. *Psychological Science, 7,* 343–346.

Zentner, M., & Kagan, J. (1998). Infants' perception of consonance and dissonance in music. *Infant Behavior and Development, 21,* 483–492.

Zigler, E. (1987). Formal schooling for 4-year-olds? No. *American Psychologist, 42,* 254–260.

Zigler, E., & Muenchow, S. (1992). *Head Start: The inside story of America's most successful educational experiment.* New York: Basic Books.

Zillman, D. (1983). Transfer of excitation in emotional behavior. In J. Cacioppo & R. Petty (Eds.), *Social psychophysiology: A sourcebook* (pp. 215–240). New York: Guilford Press.

Zillman, D., & Bryant, J. (Eds.). (1989). *Pornography: Research advances and policy considerations.* Hillsdale, NJ: Erlbaum.

Zimbardo, P. G. (1970). The human choice: Individuation, reason, and order versus deindividuation, impulse, and chaos. In W. J. Arnold & D. Levine (Eds.), *Nebraska symposium on motivation: 1969* (Vol. 17, pp. 237–307). Lincoln: University of Nebraska Press.

Zimbardo, P. G. (1985, June). Laugh where we must, be candid where we can. *Psychology Today,* pp. 43–47.

Zimmerberg, B., & Gray, M. S. (1992). The effects of cocaine on maternal behaviors in the rat. *Physiology and Behavior, 52,* 379–384.

Zinbarg, R. E., Barlow, D. H., Brown, T. A., & Hertz, R. M. (1992). Cognitive-behavioral approaches to the nature and treatment of anxiety disorders. *Annual Review of Psychology, 43,* 235–267.

Zola-Morgan, S. (1995). Localization of brain function: The legacy of Franz Gall (1758–1828). *Annual Review of Neuroscience, 18,* 359–383.

Zoroya, G. (1999, November 18). Passengers behaving badly. *USA Today (Travel Guide).*

Zuckerman, M. (1990). The psychophysiology of sensation seeking. *Journal of Personality, 58,* 313–345.

Zuckerman, M. (1994). *Behavioral expressions and biosocial bases of sensation seeking.* New York: Cambridge University Press.

Zuckerman, M. (2003). *Psychobiology of personality.* New York: Cambridge University Press.

Zuwerink, J. R., & Devine, P. G. (1996). Attitude importance and resistance to persuasion: It's not just the thought that counts. *Journal of Personality and Social Psychology, 70,* 931–944.

# CREDITS

The publishers acknowledge the copyright owners for permission to reprint the following copyrighted materials.

## PHOTO CREDITS

*Chapter 1:* **p. 2:** Nick Daly: Getty Images Inc.—Stone Allstock; **p. 6 (top):** CORBIS; **p. 6 (bottom):** Brown Brothers; **p. 7:** Historical Pictures/StockMontage, Inc./Historical Pictures Collection; **p. 10 (left):** Annie Griffiths Belt; **p. 10 (right):** Will & Deni McIntyre/Photo Researchers, Inc.; **p. 11:** Yoav Levy/Phototake NYC; **p. 13 (left):** AFP Photo/CORBIS; **p. 13 (right):** Anthony Butera/SuperStock, Inc.; **p. 16 (left):** Archives of the History of American Psychology—The University of Akron; **p. 16 (right):** Partridge/Wellesley College Archives; **p. 17 (left):** Clark University Archives; **p. 17 (right):** UPI/CORBIS; **p. 22:** Joe McNally: Corbis/Sygma; **p. 23:** Louvre, Dept. des Antiquites Gracques/Romaines, Paris, France. © Photograph by Erich Lessing/Art Resource, NY; **p. 25:** BIOS/M. Gunther: Peter Arnold, Inc.; **p. 32 (top):** Brad Bower/Mercury Pictures; **p. 32 (bottom):** Paul S. Conklin; **p. 35:** Georg Gerster/Photo Researchers, Inc.

*Chapter 2:* **p. 40:** © 1994 Kay Chernush; **p. 42:** from: Damasio H, Grabowski T, Frank R, Galaburda AM, Damasio AR: "The Return of Phineas Gage: Clues about the brain from a famous patient." "Science," 264:1102–1105, 1994. Department of Neurology and Image Analysis Facility, University of Iowa.: from: Damasio H, Grabowski T, Frank R, Galaburda AM, Damasio AR: "The Return of Phineas Gage: Clues about the brain from a famous patient." "Science," 264:1102–1105, 1994. Department of Neurology and Image Analysis Facility, University of Iowa; **p. 43 (left):** Warren Anatomical Museum, Countway Library of Medicine, Harvard Medical School; **p. 43 (right):** Amy Flynn; **p. 49:** CNRI/SciencePhoto Library/Photo Researchers, Inc; **p. 51:** CNRI/Science Photo Library/Photo Researchers, Inc; **p. 52:** Brooks/Brown/Photo Researchers, Inc; **p. 55 (bottom):** © 1994 Kay Chernush; **p. 55 (top):** Drs. John Mazziota and Michael E. Phelps, UCLA School of Medicine: Drs. John Mazziota and Michael E. Phelps, UCLA School of Medicine; **p. 64 (left):** AP/Wide World Photos; **p. 64 (right):** Copyright 2002, USA TODAY. Reprinted with permission; **p. 64 (center):** AP/Wide World Photos; **p. 68:** Joseph Mehling/Raunder Special Collections Library/Dartmouth College Library; **p. 70:** Marcus E. Raichle, M.D.: Courtesy Marcus E. Raichle, M.D., Washington University; Medical Center, from research based on S.E. Petersen et al., Positron emission tomographic; studies of the cortical anatomy of single-word processing. Nature 331:585–589 (1988); **p. 75 (bottom):** Sachs/Corbis/Sygma; **p. 75 (top):** Bob Strong/SIPA Press; **p. 76:** Getty Images, Inc.

*Chapter 3:* **p. 82:** Photo Lennart Nilsson/Albert Bonniers Forlag; **p. 88:** Bob Krist/Getty Images Inc.—Stone Allstock; **p. 92:** Omikron/Photo Researchers, Inc.; **p. 93:** Cary Sol Wolinsky/Trillium Studios; **p. 97 (left):** Ishihara, "Test for Color Deficiency". Courtesy Kanehara & Co., Ltd. Offered Exclusively in The USA by Graham-Field, Inc., Bay Shore, New York; **p. 97 (right):** Hart-Davis/Science Photo Library/Photo Researchers, Inc.; **p. 99:** Lennart Nilsson/Bonnier Alba AB, BEHOLD MAN, pp. 206–207; **p. 102:** Pine Street Medical Education & Research Group; **p. 103:** Institut Pasteur/CNRI/Phototake NYC; **p. 105:** Omikron/Photo Researchers, Inc.; **p. 107:** Terry Vine/Getty Images Inc.—Stone Allstock; **p. 110:** Christopher Little; **p. 113 (bottom):** Getty Images, Inc.; **p. 115:** Copyright The Exploratorium, www.exploratorium.edu; **p. 116:** Chantra Pramkaew; **p. 117:** James King-Holmes/W Industries/Science Photo Library/Photo Researchers, Inc.; **p. 118 a:** Topham/The Image Works; **p. 118b:** Werner Krutein/Photovault/Getty Images, Inc.—Liaison; **p. 118c:** M. Granitsas/The Image Works; **p. 118d:** M. Everton/The Image Works; **p. 119:** Cornell University Photography; **p. 121:** Petyer Pearson/Getty Images Inc.—Stone Allstock; **p. 122 (bottom left):** Michael J. Howell/Stock Boston; **p. 122 (bottom right):** David Olsen/Getty Images Inc.—Stone Allstock; **p. 122 (top):** Michael Dwyer/Stock Boston; **p. 123 & 124 (top):** Dick Ruhl; **p. 125 (bottom):** James Randi Educational Foundation

*Chapter 4:* **p. 130:** Ralph A. Clevenger/CORBIS; **p. 135:** Getty Images, Inc.; **p. 136 (bottom):** Paul S. Conklin; **p. 142 (top):** ABC News/ABC Photo Archives; **p. 143:** Arnulf Husmo/Getty Images Inc.—Stone Allstock; **p. 152:** Copyright © 2003 by Graham Gordon Ramsay. All rights reserved; **p. 155:** Carlos H. Schenck, M.D., Minnesota Regional Sleep Disorders Center; **p. 158:** The Granger Collection; **p. 160:** Earl & Nazima Kowall/CORBIS; **p. 165 (bottom):** CORBIS;

**p. 165 (top center):** Jed Share/Getty Images Inc.—Stone Allstock; **p. 165 (top left):** Cary Wolinsky/Getty Images Inc.—Stone Allstock; **p. 165 (top right):** Jean-Claude Coutausse; **p. 169:** The Granger Collection; **p. 171 (top):** D. Boone/CORBIS

*Chapter 5:* **p. 176:** Don Mason/CORBIS; **p. 178:** Wolfgang Kaehler/Getty Images, Inc.—Liaison; **p. 181 (top):** The Granger Collection; **p. 188:** Archives of the History of American Psychology—The University of Akron; **p. 189:** REUTERS/Peter Morgan/CORBIS; **p. 190:** Eye of Science/Photo Researchers, Inc.; **p. 193 (top):** Yoav Levy/Phototake NYC; **p. 194:** Copyright © 2002 ABC Photography Archives; **p. 195:** Jan Kopec/Getty Images Inc.—Stone Allstock; **p. 197:** Ellen Shub; **p. 198 (top):** Photo courtesy of Mishawaka Police Department/Getty Images; **p. 200:** Sanjiv Talwar, SUNY Downstate; **p. 201:** Culver Pictures, Inc.; **p. 202:** Charles Gupton/Stock Boston; **p. 207:** John Markham/Bruce Coleman Inc.

*Chapter 6:* **p. 212:** Getty Images, Inc.; **p. 215:** CORBIS; **p. 216:** "Color of Memory," watercolor, collage by Richard E. Schaffer. Photo courtesy of Daniel L. Schacter Collection; **p. 219:** Getty Images, Inc.; **p. 220:** Enrico Ferorelli; **p. 228 (left):** Tim Davis/Photo Researchers, Inc.; **p. 228 (right):** Kathleen Campbell/Getty Images, Inc.—Liaison; **p. 232:** Gregory K. Scott/Photo Researchers, Inc.; **p. 234:** © Disney Enterprises, Inc.; **p. 235:** Christopher Morris/Black Star; **p. 239:** Alex Wong/Getty Images, Inc.; **p. 244:** Copyright © 2002 ABC Photography Archives; **p. 246 (bottom):** W.F. Brewer and J.C. Treyens (1981). Role of schemata in memory for places. "Cognitive Psychology, Volume 11", 207–230. Picture pg. 11. Copyright © 1981 by Academic Press, reproduced by permission of the publisher; **p. 246 (top):** From Intraub, H., and Richardson, M. (1989). Wide-angle memories of close-up scenes. "Journal of Experimental Psychology: Learning Memory and Cognition, 15", 179–187; **p. 247:** Loftus EF, Miller DG, Burns HJ, (1978). Semantic integration of verbal information into a visual memory. "Journal of Experimental Psychology"; Human Learning and Memory, 4, 19–31; **p. 248:** Dr. Elizabeth Loftus; **p. 250 (left):** Chuck Burton/AP/Wide World Photos; **p. 250 (right):** HO/Burlington Police Department/AP/Wide World Photos; **p. 253:** Spencer Platt/Getty Images, Inc.—Liaison

*Chapter 7:* **p. 259:** Ryan McVay/Getty Images, Inc.; **p. 262 (bottom left):** Dan McCoy/Rainbow; **p. 262 (top left):** Frank Siteman/Stock Boston; **p. 262 (top right):** M. Antman/The Image Works; **p. 267:** AP/Wide World Photos; **p. 275:** Daniel Kahneman; **p. 277:** John Chiasson; **p. 278:** AP/Wide World Photos; **p. 282 (left):** Gary Brettnacher/Getty Images Inc.—Stone Allstock; **p. 282 (right):** Kenneth H. Thomas/Photo Researchers, Inc.; **p. 283:** Owen Franken/Stock Boston; **p. 289 (top):** Michael Goldman/Time Life Pictures/Getty Images; **p. 290:** Michael Nichols/Magnum Photos, Inc.; **p. 294:** James Balog/Getty Images Inc.—Stone Allstock; **p. 300:** Christopher Brown/Stock Boston, Inc.

*Chapter 8:* **p. 306:** U.S. Dept. of Energy Human Genome Program; **p. 309 (center):** Wolfgang Kaehler/CORBIS; **p. 309 (left):** Kent, Breck P/Animals Animals/Earth Scenes; **p. 309 (right):** Eric and David Hosking/CORBIS; **p. 310 top:** Peter R. Grant, Princeton University; **p. 311:** AP/Wide World Photos; **p. 313:** Reuters/Michael Dalder/CORBIS; **p. 315:** Bill Ballenberg/Time Life Pictures/Getty Images; **p. 317:** Michael Nichols/Magnum Photos, Inc.; **p. 318 (left):** Roslin Institute/Carolina Biological Supply Company/Phototake; **p. 318 (right):** AP/Wide World Photos; **p. 320:** Robert Plomin; **p. 322:** Sandra Scarr; **p. 323:** Archives of the History of American Psychology—The University of Akron; **p. 327 (bottom):** Zigy Kaluzny/Getty Images Inc.—Stone Allstock; **p. 332:** Jim Bourg/REUTERS/CORBIS; **p. 333:** Gregory Dimijian/Photo Researchers, Inc.

*Chapter 9:* **p. 338:** Karen Kasmauski/NGS Image Collection 1997/11 30-1; **p. 343:** Photo Lennart Nilsson/Bonnier Alba AB, A CHILD IS BORN, Dell Publishing Company; **p. 347:** Carolyn Rovee-Collier; **p. 347:** © 2002 Rutgers/Nick Romanenko/Dr. Carolyn Rovee-Collier; **p. 349 (bottom):** Joe McNally/Corbis/Sygma; **p. 352:** Judith Behling Ford; **p. 354:** Doug Goodman/Photo Researchers, Inc.; **p. 357:** Mandal Ranjir/Photo Researchers, Inc.; **p. 359:** Nina Leen/Life Magazine © TimePix; **p. 360:** Bob Kaussner/Cornell University Photography/Stephen J. Ceci; **p. 362:** Martin Rogers/Stock Boston; **p. 366 (left):** Stephen Trimble; **p. 366 (right):** Miro Vintoniv/Stock Boston; **p. 376:** AP/Wide World Photos; **p. 377:** Figaro Magazine/Getty Images, Inc.—Liaison

*Chapter 10:* **p. 390:** Jose Luis Pelaez, Inc./CORBIS; **p. 393 (left):** Sony Pictures Television; **p. 393 (right):** Rick Smolan/Stock Boston; **p. 394:** Pearson, K. (1914–1930). "The life, letters and labours of Francis Galton" (Vols. 1–3), Cambridge: Cambridge University Press; **p. 395:** Photograph of the Stanford-Binet, Fifth Edition materials reproduced from page 22 of The Riverside Publishing Company 2003 Clinical and Special Needs Catalog with permission of the publisher. Copyright © 2003 by The Riverside Publishing Company. All rights reserved; **p. 396:** Bob Daemmrich/The Image Works; **p. 404 (bottom left):** CORBIS; **p. 404 (top center):** Irene Shulgin/Penguin Putnam, Inc.; **p. 404 (top left):** Philip Schermeister/NGS Image Collection; **p. 404 (top right):** Andy Hayt/Time Inc. Magazines/Sports Illustrated; **p. 405:** Courtesy of Max Tegmark and Per Bergland; **p. 406 (bottom):** Michael Cohen/Corbis/Sygma; **p. 406 (top):** David Strick/Corbis/Outline; **p. 407:** Howard Gardner; **p. 409:** AP/Wide World Photos; **p. 411:** Robert Sternberg; **p. 417:** © Archivo Iconografico, S.A./CORBIS; **p. 420:** Patrick Harbron/Corbis/Outline; **p. 422:** Arthur Tilley/Getty Images Inc.—Stone Allstock; **p. 425:** Claude Steele, Stanford University

*Chapter 11:* **p. 432:** Getty Images, Inc.; **p. 436 (left):** Iwago Photographic; **p. 436 (right):** Addison Geary/Stock Boston; **p. 445:** Gilles Mingasson/Getty Images, Inc.—Liaison; **p. 447 (bottom):** Joel Sartore/National Geographic Image Collection; **p. 448:** Jodi Cobb/NGS Image Collection; **p. 449:** Dr. Stephen Beckerman; **p. 450:** David M. Buss; **p. 455 (bottom):** Denis Paquin/AP/Wide World Photos; **p. 457:** David Bundy/AP/Wide World Photos

*Chapter 12:* **p. 464:** Getty Images, Inc.; **p. 469:** Joe McNally/Corbis/Sygma; **p. 470:** AP/Wide World Photos; **p. 472 (left):** Corbis/Sygma; **p. 472 (right):** AFP Photo/Mike Theiler/CORBIS; **p. 475 (bottom center):** Richard Pan; **p. 475 (bottom left):** Costa Manos/Magnum Photos, Inc.; **p. 475 (bottom right):** Lynn McLaren/Index Stock Imagery, Inc.; **p. 475 (top center):** Alan Weiner/Getty Images, Inc.—Liaison; **p. 475 (top left):** Guido Alberto Rossi; **p. 475 (top right):** David Cooper/Getty Images, Inc.—Liaison; **p. 476:** Jim McHugh/Corbis/Outline; **p. 477:** REUTERS/Jerry Lampen/CORBIS; **p. 478:** Paul Ekman, Ph.D., Professor of Psychology; **p. 486 (center):** Varin-Visage/Jacana/Photo Researchers, Inc.; **p. 486 (left):** Joel Sartore/NGS Collection; **p. 486 (right):** Roland Seitre/Peter Arnold, Inc.; **p. 488 (left):** AP/Wide World Photos; **p. 488 (right):** AP/Wide World Photos; **p. 492:** Tony Garcia/Getty Images Inc.—Stone Allstock

*Chapter 13:* **p. 498:** Chuck Savage/CORBIS; **p. 501 (bottom right):** REUTERS/Kai Pfaffenbach/Getty Images, Inc.—Liaison; **p. 501 (top center):** AP/Wide World Photos; **p. 501 (top left):** AP/Wide World Photos; **p. 501 (top lright):** AP/Wide World Photos; **p. 509:** Robert Rosenthal; **p. 512:** Match.com; **p. 513 (bottom right):** Mark Mainz/Getty Images, Inc.—Liaison; **p. 513 (top left):** Gerard Pile/Getty Images Inc.—Stone Allstock; **p. 513 (top right):** George Steinmetz Photography; **p. 513 (bottom left):** Anthony Cassidy /Getty Images Inc.—Stone Allstock; **p. 516:** Bob Krist/Bob Krist Photography; **p. 520:** AP/Wide World Photos; **p. 521:** Copyright 1965 by Stanley Milgram. From the film OBEDIENCE, distributed by Penn State Media Sales; **p. 522 (top):** REUTERS/George Martell/CORBIS; **p. 523:** Pepsi-Cola North America; **p. 528 (left):** Paul Sutton/Duomo/CORBIS; **p. 528 (right):** Chris Trotman/Duomo/CORBIS; **p. 537:** © 1999, The Washington Post. Reprinted with permission. Photo by Carol Guzy; **p. 541:** John M. Darley

*Chapter 14:* **p. 546:** Lester Lefkowitz/CORBIS; **p. 549:** Corbis/Stock Market; **p. 550:** Mark Downey/Lucid Images; **p. 551 (bottom):** Reuters/Pablo Sanchez/Getty Images, Inc.—Liaison; **p. 552 (left):** Nathan Benn/CORBIS; **p. 552 (right):** EyeWire Collection/Getty Images/EyeWire, Inc.; **p. 554 :** Peter Menzel/Material World; **p. 555:** John Launois/Black Star; **p. 557:** Hazel Rose Markus; **p. 559:** Stuart Franklin/Magnum Photos, Inc.; **p. 560 (center):** Bob Daemmrich/Bob Daemmrich Photography, Inc.; **p. 560 (left):** Charles Lenars/Corbis/Stock Market; **p. 560 (right):** AP/Wide World Photos; **p. 565:** Rob Nelson/Black Star; **p. 566:** Paul Bronstein/Getty Images, Inc.—Liaison; **p. 569 (bottom):** AP/Wide World Photos; **p. 569 (top):** CORBIS; **p. 572:** Carol Iwasaki/Time Life Pictures/Getty Images; **p. 573:** AP/Wide World Photos

*Chapter 15:* **p. 578:** Gail Mooney/CORBIS; **p. 581:** Ann Purcell/Photo Researchers, Inc.; **p. 582:** Photo by Max Halberstatt, Mary Evans Picture Library. Freud Copyrights courtesy of W.E. Freud; **p. 585 (bottom):** Ian O'Leary/Getty Images Inc.—Stone Allstock; **p. 585 (center):** Margaret Miller/Photo Researchers, Inc.; **p. 585 (top left):** Elizabeth Crews Photography; **p. 585 (top right):** Peter Poulides/Getty Images Inc.—Stone Allstock; **p. 588 (bottom):** Getty Images Inc.—Hulton Archive Photos; **p. 588 (top):** Yousuf Karsh/Woodfin Camp & Associates; **p. 589:** Yoav Levy/Phototake NYC; **p. 590:** Reprinted by permission of the publishers from Henry A. Murray, THEMATICAPPERCEPTION TEST, Cambridge, Mass.: Harvard University Press, Copyright © 1943 by the President and Fellows of Harvard College, © 1971 by Henry A. Murray; **p. 595:** Schmid/Langsfeld/Getty Images Inc.—Image Bank; **p. 603:** Bruce McClelland/AP/Wide World Photos; **p. 610:** Bob Sacha/Bob Sacha Photography; **p. 611:** Lynsey Addario/AP/Wide World Photos; **p. 612:** Bobby Model/NGS Collection; **p. 613:** Jerome Kagan

*Chapter 16:* **p. 620:** David de Lossy, Ghislain & Marie/Getty Images Inc.—Image Bank; **p. 624:** Joe McNally/Matrix International, Inc.; **p. 629:** Jose

Azel/Aurora & Quanta Productions Inc.; **p. 630:** Photofest; **p. 631:** Edvard Munch, "The Scream." Oslo, National Gallery. Scala/Art Resource, NY. © 1998 Artists Rights Society (ARS), New York/ADAGP, Paris; **p. 634 (left):** Thomas Broening Photography; **p. 634 (right):** Eric Freeland/Matrix International, Inc.; **p. 635 (top):** Mark Downey/Lucid Images; **p. 641:** David Longstreath/AP/Wide World Photos; **p. 643:** Gregory Hoblit/Corbis/Sygma; **p. 645:** Gogh, Vincent van. "Wheatfield with Crows," 1890. Van Gogh Museum, Amsterdam, The Netherlands. Art Resource, NY; **p. 647:** Rob Nelson/Black Star; **p. 649 (bottom):** Royce Carlton, Inc.; **p. 649 (top):** Drs. Lewis Baxter and Michael Phelps, UCLA School of Medicine; **p. 653 (left):** Sandra Milne; **p. 653 (right):** Anonymous; **p. 654:** Dreamworks/Universal/Eli Reed/Picture Desk, Inc./Kobal Collection; **p. 655:** Nancy Andreason; **p. 656:** Grunnitus/Photo Researchers, Inc.; **p. 660:** AP/Wide World Photos

*Chapter 17:* **p. 668:** Getty Images, Inc.; **p. 671 (center):** Engraving from Rush, B. Observations on the tranquillizer. Phila. Med. Mus. n.s. 1:plate opps. p. 169, 1810. Courtesy National Library of Medicine; **p. 671 (left):** Stock Montage, Inc./Historical Pictures Collection; **p. 671 (right):** Culver Pictures, Inc.; **p. 673 (bottom):** Corbis/Sygma; **p. 673 (top):** Mary Evans/Sigmund Freud copyrights. Mary Evans Picture Library; **p. 678:** AP/Wide World Photos; **p. 681:** Charles Vandermast, Delft University of Technology; **p. 683:** Lester Sloan/Woodfin Camp & Associates; **p. 689:** Aaron T. Beck, M.D.; **p. 693:** Hank Morgan/Science Source/Photo Researchers, Inc.; **p. 696:** Dashow/Anthro-Photo File; **p. 701 (bottom):** Paul S. Howell/Getty Images, Inc.—Liaison; **p. 703:** Laurent/Laeticia/Photo Researchers, Inc.; **p. 704:** W & D McIntyre/Photo Researchers, Inc.; **p. 707:** Copyright © 2002 by the American Psychological Association. Reprinted with permission

*Chapter 18:* **p. 710:** Don Mason/Corbis/Stock Market; **p. 713 (bottom):** FujiFotos/The Image Works; **p. 713 (top):** WebMD Corporation; **p. 718:** Bob Daemmrich Photography, Inc.; **p. 722 (bottom):** David Leeson/The Image Works; **p. 722 (top):** Pat Carter/AP/Wide World Photos; **p. 724:** Kees Van den Berg/Photo Researchers, Inc.; **p. 726:** Shelley Taylor, University California Los Angeles; **p. 730 (center):** Dr. Gilla Kaplan/The Rockefeller Univ.; **p. 730 (left):** Robert Becker, Ph. D./Custom Medical Stock Photo, Inc.; **p. 730 (right):** Copyright Boehringer Ingelheim International GmbH, THE INCREDIBLE MACHINE, p. 170. Photo by Lennart Nilsson/Bonnier Alba AB; **p. 731:** NASA Headquarters; **p. 732:** Janice Kielcolt-Glaser; **p. 735:** Tom Walker/Stock Boston

## TEXT CREDITS

**Page 56,** *Figure 2.11:* Alan Gevins, SAM Technology, Inc., San Francisco, CA.

**Page 69,** *Figure 2.23:* "Perception of Bilateral Chimeric Figures Following Hemisphere Disconnection" by J. Levy, C. Trevarther and R.W. Sperry from BRAIN, 95, 61–78. © 1972 Oxford University Press. Used with permission of Oxford University Press, England.

**Page 148,** *Figure 4.12:* From *The 2002 "Sleep in America" Poll,* National Sleep Foundation, 2002. Reprinted with permission, http://www.sleepfoundation.org.

**Page 225,** *Figure 6.10:* From "Where Do We Stand?" by R.G. Crowder in MEMORY & COGNITION, 21, (1993), pp. 142–145. Copyright © 1993. Reprinted by permission of The Psychonomic Society.

**Page 236,** *Figure 6.15:* From "Language-Dependent Recall of Autobiographical Memories" by V. Marian and U. Neisser, *Journal of Experimental Psychology: General,* 129, (2000), pp. 361–368. Copyright © 2002 by the American Psychological Assn. Adapted with permission.

**Page 241,** *Table 6.2:* Table from HUMAN MEMORY by Alan Baddeley. Copyright © 1990 by Alan Baddeley. Reprinted by permission of Allyn and Bacon, a Pearson Education Company.

**Page 264,** *Figure 7.3:* Figure from p. 1031, "Imagined Transformations of Bodies: An MRI Investigation" by J. Zacks, et al., *Neuropsychologia,* 37, (1999), pp. 1029–1040. Copyright © 1999 by Elsevier. Reprinted with permission of Elsevier.

**Page 265,** *Figure 7.4:* Figure from "Rotation of Mental Images of Baboons When Visual Input is Directed to the Left Cerebral Hemisphere" by J. Vauclair, J. Fagot, W. D. Hopkins, *Psychological Science,* 4, 100, (1993). Copyright © 1993. Reprinted with permission of Blackwell Publishers.

**Page 319,** *Figure 8.7:* Figure from "The Heritability of Attitudes: A Study of Twins" by J.M. Olson, P.A. Vernon, J.A. Harris & K.L. Jang, *Journal of Personality & Social Psychology,* 80, (2001), pp. 845–860. Copyright © 2001 by the American Psychological Assn. Adapted with permission.

**Page 379,** *Figure 9.21:* Graph, "Projected Alzheimer's Patients in the U.S., in Millions" from *Newsweek,* January 31, 2000. Copyright © 2000 by Newsweek, Inc. All rights reserved. Reprinted with permission.